The Weather Almanac 1995

The Weather Almanac 1995

by Jack Williams

VINTAGE BOOKS
A DIVISION OF RANDOM HOUSE, INC.
NEW YORK

Contents

Foreword

A portrait of the USA's weather by the numbers

For the last 13 years, the USA TODAY Weather Page has become the source for the national outlook on the day's weather.

Newspaper readers naturally think of calling USA TODAY with their weather questions, such as "Will it be cold in April in Paris?", "Did last week's cold snap set a record?" and "I'm thinking of retiring to Florida's Gulf Coast. Am I likely to get hit by a hurricane?"

The USA TODAY Weather Almanac aims to answer these questions and many more. Using statistics primarily from the National Climatic Data Center in Asheville, N.C., but also from other U.S. government agencies and private firms, we've come up with a new way to look at the weather and climate.

The Data Center in Asheville is a treasure house of climate data. The information is based on weather observations at stations across the country going back to the nation's earliest days, from weather balloons, from satellites and, in recent years, from commercial airplanes. The data is compiled by meteorologists primarily for meteorologists.

Even if a casual user, interested in finding out the climate at a vacation spot, knew how to obtain data directly from the center, he or she could be overwhelmed by the complexity of the collection.

For the *Almanac* we have combed through many sources of climate data to give readers accurate, understandable answers to weather questions.

This book is a portrait of the nation's weather and climate, not a predictor. While you will find the coldest, hottest, wettest, driest, sunniest and cloudiest places in the country, we don't attempt a crystal ball look at future day-to-day weather — although we will tell you about the latest seasonal forecasts coming soon from the National Weather Service.

Travelers should find this *Almanac* especially useful. From average temperatures at stations along the Appalachian Trail and Pacific Crest Trail to detailed data on 200 U.S. and 50 foreign cities, this is a complete guide to weather and climate.

The USA TODAY Weather Book, now in its 10th printing, explains why weather happens. *The USA TODAY Weather Almanac* tells where and when and how much.

We hope this *Almanac* answers your weather questions. Please let us know what your other questions are, and we'll try to answer them in future editions of the *Almanac*.

Suggestions for future editions should be sent to:

Jack Williams, Weather Editor
USA TODAY
1000 Wilson Blvd.
Arlington, Va. 22229

The Weather Almanac 1995

What is happening to our weather?

Since 1992 the United States has experienced its costliest hurricane, the winter storm of the century, the worst flooding in the history of the Mississippi and Missouri river valleys, one of our coldest winters, record-breaking heat and the beginning of a drought in the West.

What's making the weather change? Is our weather becoming wilder? The second question is easier to answer — at least for now.

The weather is not becoming wilder. This book is the proof of that. The charts, graphs, and histories here show that the USA has long lived with floods, hurricanes, tornadoes, dust storms, blinding winter storms and droughts. Nothing we have experienced so far in the 1990s signals that a long-term change is underway.

Usually the worst weather is spread over decades. Sometimes, however, the worst weather is distilled into a few years — the 1930s were such a time — often followed by a long calm.

Perhaps it is because we have come out of a calm, the relatively quiet 1970s and early '80s, that the weather in the '90s seems so foreboding. Also, during those calmer times, we forget the lessons of harsh weather.

In known hurricane alleys, we replace old-fashioned beach shacks with million-dollar homes. And, after a flood, people often rebuild on flood plains with the hope that floods like those of the past won't happen in the future. When the inevitable storm comes and destroys again, the monetary damage seems astronomical.

Many farmers and others in the West think of "wet" years as being normal and normal years are considered "dry." Past weather records and other kinds of less direct evidence show that what people may consider a "drought" has occurred many times in the past, sometimes lasting scores of years. It may be the normal weather.

When a hurricane hits an area that hasn't been hit in 20 or 30 years, or a flood exceeds those of the past few years, or drought grips an area that has been unusually wet for a few years, people start saying, "The weather must be getting worse." But is it the weather or our ignorance of it?

Recent weather events

Weather gave people a lot to talk about during 1993 and 1994. Here are some of the bigger events:

• **Rain:** Beginning in the fall of 1992, heavy precipitation fell on California and other parts of the West into the spring of 1993, ending a six-year drought.

• **Snow:** The "Storm of the Century" spread snow from Alabama to Maine and broke low pressure records up and down the East Coast on March 12 – 15, 1993.

• **Floods:** During the summer of 1993, the worst flooding in history hit the upper Mississippi and lower Missouri river valleys. Unusually wet weather from March until September left water covering more than 12 million acres at the peak of the flooding during the summer, destroying more than 40,000 buildings and doing more than $20 billion in property damage.

• **Heat:** While the Midwest was being drenched, heat and drought dominated the South from eastern Texas to the Atlantic. July 1993 was the first precipitation-free month in Dallas-Fort Worth, Texas, in 90 years.

• **Fires:** In late October and early November 1993, hot, dry "Santa Ana" winds whipped up fires that destroyed more than 1,000 homes in Southern California. Fires were especially fierce because the drought-ending precipitation earlier in the year had caused thick brush to grow on hillsides, which the dry winds turned into tinder.

• **Cold:** After a mild early December in the U.S., the Midwest and East turned bitterly cold just before Christmas 1993. From then into February 1994 the cold was unrelenting, breaking several all-time temperature and snowfall records.

• **Drought:** As 1993 ended, drought began returning to California and other parts of the West. From fall 1993 through spring 1994, California's "wet" season produced only 65 percent of the normal precipitation.

• **Heat:** The spring of 1994 turned out to be the eighth warmest on record for the U.S. with warmer-than-normal temperatures for 86.5 percent of the country. It was also the seventh driest spring in 100 years of recordkeeping.

• **More heat:** Summer 1994 was the ninth warmest on record and the warmest since 1988, with the West and Northeast being the hottest. The Southwest had its hottest and driest summer ever. Despite a cool August, the Northeast had its 12th hottest summer on record

• **Storm:** Tropical Storm Alberto came ashore from the Gulf of Mexico in west Florida on June 30, 1994, doing virtually no damage. But it stalled over Georgia, dumping more than 20 inches of rain on some places. The resulting flooding forced at least 30,000 people from their homes.

• **More drought:** During summer 1994, drought from the Rockies westward grew worse and by the end of August, 26.9 percent of the nation was in severe or extreme drought. The core of the drought was in the Northwest, Great Basin, and the Colorado and Rio Grande river basins Small areas of the East were dry.

Forecasters go out on a limb about 1995

Scientists are cautious about making claims for weather forecasts.

Forecasts for day-to-day weather are not possible for more than a week ahead. When it comes to predicting the coming month or season, forecasters stick to giving odds for above normal or below normal temperatures and precipitation.

Until May 1994, the National Weather Service made public only 30-day and 90-day predictions from its Climate Analysis Center, which produces the 30-day forecasts at the middle and end of each month. The 90-day predictions are issued at the end of each month.

In May, the Center issued an "experimental" forecast giving the odds for warmer or colder, drier or wetter weather in different parts of the U.S. from January through March 1995.

Beginning in early 1995, the Center will begin issuing regular seasonal forecasts as much as six months before the season begins. These forecasts will be expressed as odds of a particular kind of weather happening.

Usually, the odds are 40 percent that temperature and precipitation for a season will average near normal, 30 percent for above normal, and 30 per-

cent below. The new forecasts will show how these odds are expected to shift.

From January through March 1995, the odds are as high as 50 percent that eastern New York and most of New England will be colder than normal. The odds of normal temperatures stay at 40 percent, but the odds of warmer than normal readings drop to 10 percent.

Around the western Great Lakes, the odds favor normal temperatures between January and March 1995 going as high as 60 percent, making the odds for colder or warmer weather 20 percent each. But for large areas of the country forecasters say the odds will stay at 40 percent for normal, 30 percent for above normal and 30 percent for below normal temperatures and precipitation.

These forecasts are based in part on computer models that link the atmosphere and oceans because ocean patterns can affect the weather several months ahead. Forecasters also examine the patterns of ground temperatures and winds about 10,000 feet above the ground when making the forecast. In some cases, these patterns can be related to what's likely several months ahead. The maps on the next page show where the odds are going to be different from the usual.

The forecasts don't give temperatures or precipitation amounts. They are limted to giving odds for shifts away from normals.

This type of forecast won't predict which days will have thunderstorms six months ahead of time, but it can help some businesses make decisions that are based on odds.

For example, the higher odds for a cold winter in the Northeast mean that a fuel oil company would be taking less risk if it stocked up on extra oil ahead of time.

This new kind of forecast won't deliver the kind of detail a skier would need to decide whether to take a Vermont ski vacation in early February. Even if the forecast does turn out to be right on and Vermont is colder than normal from January through March, the first two weeks of February could be warm enough to turn snow to slush. When the season's average is computed, however, cold weather at other times could more than make up for a couple of warm weeks.

No scientist expects anytime soon to be able to make the kind of detailed forecast a family needs to plan its winter ski vacation before the leaves begin turning in the fall.

The Climate Analysis Center will supply the new forecasts to news media, as it does the 30-day

Experimental forecasts for January through March 1995

These maps show how odds for cold, warm, wet, dry or even normal weather should shift for January through March 1995. The large, unshaded areas on both maps show where no deviation from climatology is expected. In these areas, the odds are 40% for normal, 30% for above normal, and 30% for below normal. Shadings on the maps show areas with different odds from these.

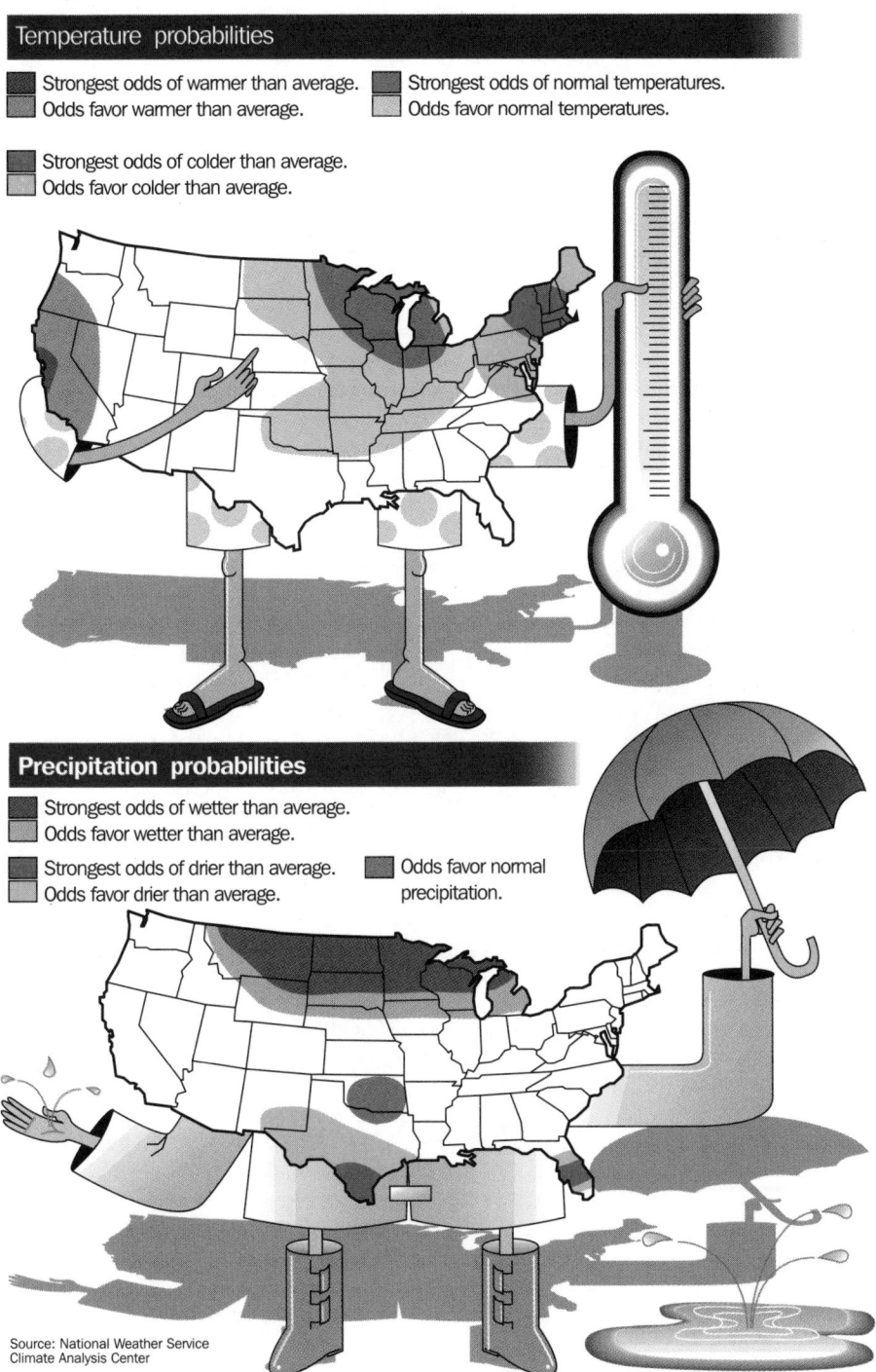

Temperature probabilities

- Strongest odds of warmer than average.
- Odds favor warmer than average.
- Strongest odds of normal temperatures.
- Odds favor normal temperatures.

- Strongest odds of colder than average.
- Odds favor colder than average.

Precipitation probabilities

- Strongest odds of wetter than average.
- Odds favor wetter than average.

- Strongest odds of drier than average.
- Odds favor drier than average.
- Odds favor normal precipitation.

Source: National Weather Service
Climate Analysis Center

and 90-day forecasts. Some television weathercasters, newspapers and magazines might use them.

Weather flashbacks

Even before it ended, people were calling the March 12 – 15, 1993, eastern blizzard "The Storm of the Century."

Compared with the Blizzard of 1888, which hit on the same March dates, the 1993 storm covered more territory. The 1888 storm is remembered because it paralyzed the USA's biggest cities from Washington to New England. The 1993 storm paralyzed transportation along the East Coast, closing every major airport in the East from Atlanta northward, a first.

More than half of the USA's population lives in the 26 states the storm hit. Winds were in the hurricane range near the East Coast and on mountaintops from the Gulf of Mexico to New England. But the real measure of a storm's strength is in the air pressure reading — the lower the pressure, the stronger the storm.

The Blizzard of '93 set air pressure records — as low as in a Category 3 hurricane — at White Plains, N.Y., Philadelphia, New York's Kennedy Airport and Dover, Del. At least nine other places from the Carolinas to New England set pressure records in the Category 2 hurricane range.

Snowfall amounts were impressive, not only in places like Syracuse, N.Y., which are used to snow, but also in the South. The 17 inches of snow that fell on Birmingham, Ala., is more than the city would expect in a normal decade.

The National Weather Service estimated that the storm's melting snow would release as much water as 40 days flow of the Mississippi River at its mouth. There was fear of East Coast flooding. But the snow melted slowly and caused only minor flooding in central and western New York and in New England.

The National Climatic Data Center estimated that the storm killed 270 people and that another 48 were reported missing at sea. The toll includes deaths indirectly caused by the storm, such as people who had heart attacks while shoveling snow.

The storm began March 12 as an intense low pressure area over the Gulf of Mexico. That day the storm killed three in Havana and left Cuba's largest city without power. That evening a tornado spawned by the storm left 5,000 people homeless in Reynosa, Mexico, near the Texas border. The storm's center crossed Florida on March 12. Winds and waves kicked up by the growing storm equaled those of many hurricanes. For instance, a 12-foot storm surge smashed Taylor County, Fla., killing seven people. At least 15 tornadoes hit parts of Florida, killing 44.

On March 13 and 14 the storm moved up the East Coast into Canada, pulling in bitter cold air from the North-Central states.

While the worst of the storm battered the USA, it also affected Canada, Cuba and Mexico. A 131 mph wind gust hit Grand Etang, Nova Scotia, on March 14 and temperatures fell 45 degrees in 18 hours in parts of New Brunswick.

The Blizzard of 1888 is remembered because it brought normal life to a halt in the most advanced

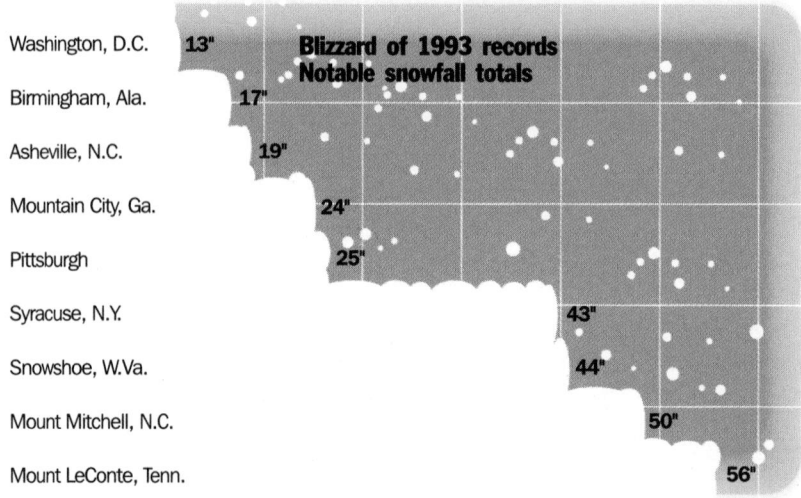

Washington, D.C.	13"
Blizzard of 1993 records	
Notable snowfall totals	
Birmingham, Ala.	17"
Asheville, N.C.	19"
Mountain City, Ga.	24"
Pittsburgh	25"
Syracuse, N.Y.	43"
Snowshoe, W.Va.	44"
Mount Mitchell, N.C.	50"
Mount LeConte, Tenn.	56"

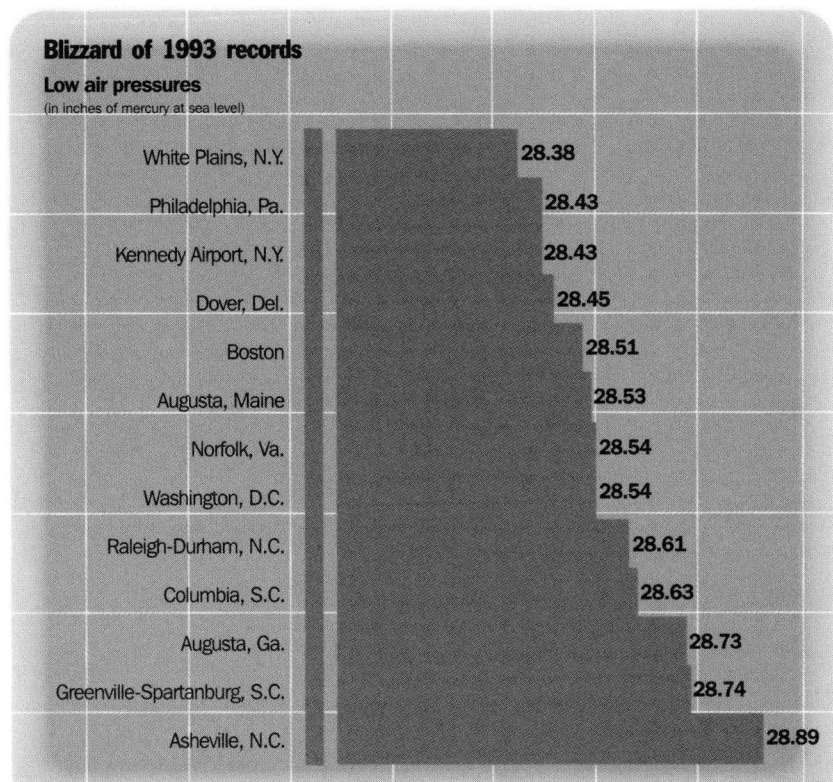

Blizzard of 1993 records

Low air pressures
(in inches of mercury at sea level)

White Plains, N.Y.	28.38
Philadelphia, Pa.	28.43
Kennedy Airport, N.Y.	28.43
Dover, Del.	28.45
Boston	28.51
Augusta, Maine	28.53
Norfolk, Va.	28.54
Washington, D.C.	28.54
Raleigh-Durham, N.C.	28.61
Columbia, S.C.	28.63
Augusta, Ga.	28.73
Greenville-Spartanburg, S.C.	28.74
Asheville, N.C.	28.89

cities of the time. The Blizzard of 1993 also demonstrated that weather still rules the most advanced forms of transportation.

The storm closed highways, including interstates, even in places such as New England and central New York where heavy snow is common. And beginning March 13, travelers were in even worse shape across the South where snowplows are rare. Snowy, icy roads stranded thousands in the Georgia, North Carolina and Virginia mountains.

On the 13th and 14th, passenger trains were shut down on the routes between Washington and Florida and between Washington and Chicago.

But air travel was hardest hit.

With major airports from Atlanta to Boston closed for hours at a time, there was a domino effect. Travelers in Honolulu and Europe, including people who weren't trying to go anywhere near the East Coast, were affected. Around a quarter of the USA's normal air traffic never left the ground on the 13th and 14th.

For example, United Flight 575 was scheduled to go from Boston to Washington to Orange County, Calif., and finally San Francisco on Saturday, March 13. But the Boeing 757 never left the East Coast and people planning to fly from Orange County to San Francisco, along with those planning to fly to California, ended up waiting at airports — for two or three days in some cases. That day alone, New York City's three major airports canceled 1,600 flights, a total of 273,000 seats.

While the storm showed that transportation technology is no match for nature's worst, it also demonstrated the promise of the latest weather forecasting technology.

On March 7, five days before the storm hit, supercomputers in both the USA and Europe that prepare generalized, global forecasts were pointing to a major weekend storm along the USA's East Coast. By Wednesday, March 10, as both the European and American forecasts continued to agree on the general picture of the storm, National Weather Service and other forecasters began issuing storm warnings.

While the forecasts didn't catch all the details, especially snow as far south as the Florida Panhandle, the big picture was on the mark and the warnings surely saved lives. They also helped businesses, such as the airlines, get ready for the storm.

The storm, like the Blizzard of 1888, is a reminder that some of the worst blizzards hit in March, when there's still plenty of cold air available and when warm air is beginning to move northward. Great storms get their strength from the clash of warm and cold air.

The Great Flood of 1993

The flood that washed down the upper Mississippi and lower Missouri rivers during the summer of 1993 was easily the flood of the century. Its destruction and duration surpassed all U.S. floods since at least the mid-1800s.

It affected large parts of nine states, more than 15 percent of the contiguous U.S. With damages totaling at least $20 billion, it was the costliest flood in U.S. history and, along with Hurricane Andrew in 1992, one of the nation's most expensive natural disasters.

The flood destroyed or damaged more than 50,000 homes and covered more than 16,000 square miles of farmland. More than 75 small towns were completely flooded. Some of these towns are in the process of moving to new locations to escape future floods.

Most floods last days to weeks; this one lasted for months. Most Midwest floods happen in the spring; this happened in summer.

Normally, upper Mississippi River flooding is rare in summer because most of the region's rain comes from hit-or-miss thunderstorms. Also, during the long summer days, large amounts of water evaporate or go into the air via "evapotranspiration" as growing plants take up water and release it into the air as water vapor.

From time to time, a thunderstorm might dump several inches of rain on an area, causing a flash flood. But during normal summers such storms are too widespread for flash floods to add up to major river flooding.

A highly unusual weather pattern during much of June and July 1993 changed all of this.

This pattern had other effects. Alaska was warmer than normal, the Pacific Northwest and northern Plains states were cool and wet, and the Southeast was hot and dry.

Normally in the summer, the jet stream — the high altitude river of wind that steers storms — flows over Canada. But in June and July 1993, it was flowing over the Northwest and northern Plains. This jet stream position brought cool air to the northwestern quarter of the country.

At the same time, winds around a strong high pressure area off the Atlantic Coast — a "Bermuda High" — were pushing warm, humid air from as far away as the Caribbean Sea northward toward the upper Mississippi Valley.

The humid air flowed over the heavier cool air covering the Midwest. As the air rose it cooled and the humidity condensed into clouds and rain. Winds bringing the humid air north were unusually strong, which ensured a good supply of moisture to feed rainstorms.

The results:

• **Nearly continuous rainfall.** Many places in the nine-state area had rain on 16 to 22 days in July, compared to an average of eight or nine days. Measurable rain fell somewhere in the upper Mississippi Basin every day between late June and late July. Such rain is typical of spring, but not summer.

• **Rain over great areas.** Many days in June and July saw areas of rain 100 to 200 miles wide and 400 to 600 miles long across the region. Many of these storms dumped one to two inches of rain over from 5,000 to 15,000 square miles. Midwestern summers normally bring a few large rain clusters, but 1993 had at least 40 of them.

• **Huge rainstorms over rivers.** Several days in June and July saw these large rain areas lined up along the major rivers. In late June they tended to line up along the Mississippi River from central Minnesota into northern Illinois and in July, along the Mississippi from Quincy, Ill., to southern Wisconsin. By mid-July several rain areas lined up along the Missouri River across the state of Missouri. Large amounts of water fell directly into the big rivers.

• **Concentrated blasts of rain in smaller areas.** These rainstorms covered 1,000 to 5,000 square miles and brought up to 12 inches of rain in 24 hours. From May through August, meteorologists counted at least 175 of these rain blasts in the nine flooded states.

• **Little evaporation.** From June to August, around half of the days were cloudy, compared to 20 percent normally in the summer. This cloudiness combined with cooler temperatures — sometimes 5°F below average — and high humidity to reduce the amount of water that evaporated or that plants put into the air with evapotranspiration. The result was more water to flow into the rivers.

A hard flood to predict

The flood's magnitude made forecasting difficult. Flood forecasts are based on the amount of water in a river and its tributaries, how much snow melts or rain falls, and how wet the ground is, which determines how much water runs off. Forecasters' computer models include how much water is flowing down a river and how deep it should be. These statistics determine where and when flooding will begin.

But major floods change the shape and size of rivers, making it harder to determine what's going to happen. The Great Flood of 1993 did all that. It also obliterated the distinction between river and land in many places.

Levee breaks were the forecasters' biggest hurdle. When a levee breaks, some of the water rushes through the breech, lowering flood levels downstream. But when the low-lying land behind the levee is filled, most of the water resumes flowing downstream. Sometimes during the summer of 1993 water left the main channel at breaks, flowed downstream on the normally dry sides of the levees and re-entered the main channel through other breaks downstream.

Knowing the effects of levee breaks beforehand is virtually impossible because until a levee gives way, there's no way of knowing where the hole will be, how much water will flow through, or exactly where it will go.

For instance, at the peak of the flood, forecasters estimated that about half of the 4 million gallons of water a second flowing down the Mississippi near Hannibal, Mo., was outside the main channel, behind levees.

Narrow places in rivers, such as where the Mississippi flows between the levees and flood walls protecting St. Louis, caused the water to back up, causing higher floods upstream.

The Great Flood of 1993 timeline

Fall 1992: The upper Midwest is unusually wet.

December 1992: Minor flooding begins in parts of the upper Mississippi Valley.

Winter 1992 – 93: Normal to above normal snowfall in the upper Midwest.

March 1993: Spring flooding begins in the upper Midwest as snow rapidly melts and heavy rain falls.

April through June: An average of 16.13 inches of rain falls on the upper Mississippi Valley, the wettest such period since records began in 1895. Normal for the period is 11.04 inches.

May 8: Record flooding on Split Rock Creek at Corson, S.D., and on the Rock River at Luverne, Minn.

May 22 – 24: Heavy thunderstorms bring 3 to 7 inches of rain to Sioux Falls, S.D., causing major urban and residential flooding in the city.

Late May: Big Sioux and Vermillion rivers in South Dakota go above flood stage, stay there through mid-June.

June 8: Flood water pouring into the Gulf of Mexico increases sea-surface temperatures around the Mississippi Delta and Atchafalaya Bay — the Atchafalaya River carries some of the Mississippi's water to the Gulf. Water temperatures are as much as 5.4°F above normal into mid-September when water is warmed by the sun as it flows down the Mississippi.

June 11: First federal disaster declaration of the flood is issued for several counties in Minnesota. By August, all of Iowa and large parts of Illinois, Kansas, Minnesota, Missouri, Nebraska, North Dakota, South Dakota and Wisconsin are federal disaster areas.

June 13: Four inches of rain falls in one hour on Lenox, Iowa.

June 19 – 21: Heavy rain falls on southwestern Wisconsin, southern Minnesota, southeastern South Dakota and most of Iowa, starting serious flooding on the upper Mississippi and many of its tributaries.

June 20: Levee on the Black River breaks, flooding about 100 homes in Black River Falls, Wis. This is the first of the estimated 1,269 levee or floodwall failures during the flood.

June 22: Measurable rain falls somewhere in Iowa every day through July 25.

June 23: Ten inches of rain falls in four hours near Armstrong, Iowa. Eleven inches of rain falls during the afternoon in Hamms Park, Minn., including 9 inches in two hours.

June 25 – 27: Heavy rain falls on Iowa, Missouri and southern Illinois just as water from previous weekend's rain farther north is flowing through the region. Flood waters rise even farther.

June 30: Seven inches of rain falls in four hours in Dickinson and Emmet counties, Iowa.

Late June: No river traffic moves on the 585 miles of the Mississippi from St. Paul, Minn., to Cairo, Ill., and on 535 miles of the Missouri River from Sioux City, Iowa, to its confluence with the Mississippi until early August, stranding more than 5,000 loaded barges.

July 3: Five inches of rain falls in two hours in McCook County, S.D.

July 9: Eleven inches of rain falls overnight in Scranton, Iowa. Water covers much of downtown Davenport, Iowa.

July 10: Seven inches of rain falls in one hour in Adrian, Minn.

July 11 – 22: Flood water closes the Des Moines, Iowa, water treatment plant, leaving 250,000 people without water.

July 16 – 20: All bridges across the Mississippi River between Burlington, Iowa, and St. Louis — 212 miles — are closed.

July 17: Two inches of rain falls in 12 minutes in Montgomery County, Iowa, and 12 inches falls in three hours near Baraboo, Wis.

July 21: Flood stage of 46.9 feet in St. Louis breaks record of 43.2 feet established April 28, 1973.

July 26: Rising water stops all rail traffic through Kansas City.

July 27: Army Corps of Engineers fears flood crests on both the Missouri and Kansas rivers will arrive in Kansas City at the same time, which would push water over the city's flood walls and levees. But the crests arrive about six hours apart and water stays just below the tops of the levees.

July 28: Flood waters dislodge hundreds of burial vaults and caskets from a Hardin, Mo., cemetery.

July: Worth County, Mo., has 30.3 inches of rain during the month, 90 percent of its normal annual precipitation.

July and August: Almost half of St. Charles County, Mo., at the confluence of the Missouri and Mississippi rivers, is under water for weeks.

Aug. 1: Flood stage of 49.58 feet in St. Louis breaks record set 11 days before. A Burger King restaurant moored along the waterfront breaks loose and slams into the Interstate 55-70 bridge on the Mississippi.

Aug. 3 – 4: Workers deliberately break a 400-foot hole and then a 1,000-foot hole in a levee near Prairie du Rocher, Ill., to slow water heading toward the historic town from a Mississippi River levee break upstream. The gamble saves the town.

Aug. 7: Main flood crest reaches the Ohio River's confluence with the Mississippi at Cairo, Ill. No serious flooding occurs to the south because the Mississippi becomes wider and deeper.

Aug. 12: 832,000 cubic feet of water per second flows past Tarbert Landing, Miss. The average for August is 280,000 cubic feet per second.

Aug. 14: Main crest is hardly noticed, except for unusual amount of debris in the water, as it passes New Orleans. The river rises to 12.5 feet. Flood stage is 17 feet.

Aug. 29: Heavy rain in the Des Moines, Iowa, area forces thousands of people to again flee homes they had just returned to after evacuating in July.

Sept. 1: Hannibal, Louisiana and Clarksville, Mo., have experienced 153 consecutive days of flooding.

Sept. 9 – 13: Water as much as 13 percent less salty than normal is measured off the Florida Keys as flood water flows out of the Gulf of Mexico.

Sept. 22: Low salinity water is found in the Atlantic Ocean 25 miles off Cape Lookout, N.C., as the Gulf Stream carries flood water northward.

Winter 1993 – 94 and Spring 1994: Saturated soil across the upper Midwest and high streams along with deep snow in many areas lead to fears of new, major floods. But spring brings warm days and many freezing nights that slow the melting of snow, allowing rivers to carry away water without flooding. The timing and amount of rain from spring showers and thunderstorms work to minimize flooding — the opposite of the previous year. The region escapes with only small-scale flooding.

Measuring the Flood of '93

One measure of the magnitude of the Great Flood of 1993 is the number of records it broke over a nine-state area. The places listed here are only a sample of the communities that suffered from the flood. Hundreds of other locations had serious flooding, but didn't quite break their old records. And there is no way of knowing of many places that had the highest water levels ever, but no flood gauge to measure it.

Most of figures are based on arbitrary local flood gauges. This means that a flood listed as 20 feet in one city could be more serious than one listed as 40 feet in another. A few places, those with figures above 100 feet, use the elevation above mean sea level for river level readings. Flood stage is the river height at which flooding begins.

Location	Flood stage in feet	Old record in feet	Date of record	New record in feet	Date of record
Upper Mississippi River Basin					
Mississippi River					
Quad Cities, Iowa, Ill.	15	22.5	4/28/65	22.6	7/09/93
Muscatine, Iowa	16	24.8	4/29/65	25.6	7/09/93
Keithsburg, Ill.	13	20.4	4/27/65	24.2	7/09/93
Burlington, Iowa	15	21.5	4/25/73	25.1	7/10/93
Keokuk, Iowa	16	23.4	4/24/73	27.2	7/10/93
Gregory Landing, Mo.	15	24.6	4/24/73	26.4	7/07/93
Quincy, Ill.	17	28.9	4/23/73	32.2	7/13/93
Hannibal, Mo.	16	28.6	4/25/73	31.8	7/16/93
Louisiana, Mo.	15	27.0	4/24/73	28.4	7/28/93
Clarksville, Mo.	25	36.4	4/24/73	37.7	7/29/93
Winfield, Mo.	26	36.8	4/27/73	39.6	8/01/93

Location	Flood stage in feet	Old record in feet	Date of record	New record in feet	Date of record
Grafton, Ill.	18	33.1	4/28/73	38.2	8/01/93
Melvin Price, Ill.	21	36.7	4/28/73	42.7	8/01/93
St. Louis, Mo.	30	43.2	4/28/73	49.58	8/01/93
Chester, Ill.	27	43.3	4/30/73	49.7	8/07/93
Illinois River					
Hardin, Ill.	425	438.2	4/29/73	442.3	8/03/93
Rock River					
Joslin, Ill.	12	17.8	3/22/79	18.4	3/26/93
Spoon River					
Seville, Ill.	22	31.8	6/24/74	33.1	7/26/93
Squaw Creek					
Ames, Iowa	7	16.0	6/17/90	18.5	7/09/93
South Skunk River					
Oskaloosa, Iowa	15	23.1	6/23/90	25.2	7/15/93
Squaw Creek, Iowa	9	13.9	5/20/44	14.2	7/09/93
Cedar River					
Conesville, Iowa	12	16.9	6/18/90	17.2	4/06/93
English River					
Kalona, Iowa	14	21.5	9/21/65	22.6	7/06/93
Iowa River					
Marshalltown, Iowa	13	20.5	6/18/90	20.6	7/09/93
Marengo, Iowa	14	19.8	7/12/69	20.3	7/19/93
Lone Tree, Iowa	15	20.3	9/22/65	22.9	7/07/93
Wapello, Iowa	20	28.9	6/19/90	29.5	7/07/93
East Fork Des Moines River					
Algona, Iowa	14	22.0	8/23/79	22.65	4/01/93
Raccoon River					
Van Meter, Iowa	13	22.7	7/01/86	25.8	7/10/93
Des Moines SW 18, Iowa	12	19.8	6/13/47	26.7	7/11/93
North Raccoon River					
Perry, Iowa	13	22.7	3/20/79	23.0	7/10/93
Des Moines River					
Des Moines 2nd Ave., Iowa	23	30.2	6/24/54	31.7	7/11/93
Des Moines SE 14th, Iowa	23	29.8	4/11/65	34.3	7/11/93
Ottumwa, Iowa	10	21.0	6/07/47	22.1	7/12/93
Keosauqua, Iowa	25	29.4	4/11/65	32.7	7/13/93
St. Francisville, Mo.	18	30.2	3/14/79	32.0	7/15/93
Baraboo River					
Baraboo, Wis.	16	20.7	9/20/92	22.8	7/18/93
Black River					
Galesville, Wis.	12	15.5	9/23/80	16.6	6/21/93
Pecatonica River					
Blanchardville, Wis.	19	21.5	2/28/48	22.0	7/06/93
Little Minnesota River					
Peever, S.D.	11	13.4	3/25/43	13.6	7/27/93
Minnesota River					
Mankato, Minn.	19	29.1	4/15/65	30.1	6/21/93
Redwood River					
Marshall, Minn.	14	15.6	4/19/69	17.0	5/09/93
Meramec River					
Arnold, Mo.	24	43.9	12/06/82	45.3	8/01/93
Missouri Basin **Pipestem Creek**					
Pipestem, N.D.	1,496.3	1,468.35	5/10/79	1,472	8/4/93
James River					
Mitchell, S.D.	14	18.3	4/11/69	19.1	7/04/93
Weeping Water Creek					
Union, Neb.	25	29.8	5/09/58	31.2	7/23/93
Wood River					
Grand Island, Neb.	4.8	6.0	6/16/67	6.4	7/22/93
Salt Creek River					
Greenwood, Neb.	20	26.5	6/13/84	26.5	7/24/93
Ashland, Neb.	16	22.0	6/13/84	23.0	7/23/93
West Nishnabotna River					
Hancock, Iowa	14	22.1	9/13/72	23.53	7/10/93
Nishnabotna River					
Hamburg, Iowa	16	28.1	5/27/87	30.52	7/25/93
Rock River					
Rock Rapids, Iowa	6	10.2	4/08/69	12.5	5/09/93
Nodaway River					
Graham, Mo.	NA	20.4	6/15/84	26.1	7/23/93

Location	Flood stage in feet	Old record in feet	Date of record	New record in feet	Date of record
Hundred and Two River					
Bedford, Iowa	21	23.5	7/14/86	23.79	7/05/93
Maryville, Mo.	14	19.3	10/12/73	20.3	7/06/93
Platte River					
Sharps Station, Mo.	23	34.6	6/10/84	36.4	7/26/93
Agency, Mo.	20	35.1	7/20/65	36.0	7/25/93
South Fork Solomon River					
Osborne, Kan.	14	27.7	7/13/51	28.5	7/21/93
Waconda, Kan.	1,488.3	1,471.3	4/27/87	1,487	7/28/93
Saline River					
Russell, Kan.	18	19.7	9/01/64	25.4	7/21/93
Wilson, Kan.	1,554	1,528.1	4/26/93	1,547.9	8/01/93
Lincoln, Kan.	30	34.7	5/19/58	37.8	7/22/93
Tescott, Kan.	25	30.1	7/13/51	30.8	7/23/93
Big Creek River					
Munjor, Kan.	18	NA	NA	26.2	7/21/93
Smoky Hill River					
Abilene, Kan.	27	NA	NA	32.1	7/22/93
Enterprise, Kan.	26	34.0	7/13/51	34.2	7/23/93
Junction City, Kan.	22	NA	NA	29.6	7/22/93
Delaware River					
Perry Reservoir, Kan.	920.6	917.07	10/19/73	920.9	7/25/93
Big Blue River					
Blue Rapids, Kan.	26	53.1	10/18/73	63.3	7/23/93
Tuttle Creek, Kan.	1,136	1,127.9	10/18/73	1,137.76	7/22/93
Fancy Creek					
Randolph, Kan.	11	26.5	10/18/73	36.3	7/22/93
Black Vermillion					
Frankfort, Kan.	19	30.1	10/11/73	32.2	7/22/93
Republican River					
Milford, Kan.	1,176.2	1,170.03	10/17/73	1,181.85	7/25/93
Grand River					
Pattonsburg, Mo.	25	34.3	6/01/47	37.6	7/24/93
Chillicothe, Mo.	24	34.7	5/01/91	38.5	7/09/93
Sumner, Mo.	26	39.5	6/07/47	42.6	7/10/93
Brunswick, Mo.	16	26.1	7/17/51	31.7	7/13/93
Chariton River					
Rathbun, Iowa	926	924.46	7/22/82	927.2	7/28/93
Missouri River					
Plattsmouth, Neb.	26	34.66	6/14/84	35.7	7/25/93
Brownville, Neb.	32	41.2	6/15/84	44.3	7/24/93
St. Joseph, Mo.	17	26.8	4/22/52	32.69	7/26/93
Kansas City, Mo.	32	46.2	7/14/51	48.9	7/28/93
Napoleon, Mo.	17	26.8	7/15/51	27.76	7/27/93
Lexington, Mo.	22	33.3	7/15/51	33.4	7/08/93
Waverly, Mo.	20	29.2	6/23/84	31.2	7/28/93
Miami, Mo.	18	29.0	7/16/51	32.4	7/29/93
Glasgow, Mo.	25	36.7	7/18/51	39.6	7/29/93
Boonville, Mo.	21	32.8	7/17/51	37.1	7/29/93
Jefferson City, Mo.	23	34.2	7/18/51	38.6	7/30/93
Gasconade, Mo.	22	38.7	10/05/86	39.6	7/31/93
Hermann, Mo.	21	35.8	10/05/56	36.3	7/31/93
St. Charles, Mo.	25	37.5	10/07/86	39.5	8/01/93
Red River of the North Basin					
Buffalo River					
Hawley, Minn.	7	9.8	7/01/75	10.9	7/18/93
Two Rivers					
Hallock, Minn.	802	807.5	6/27/85	808.1	8/15/93

Source: National Oceanic and Atmospheric Administration, *Natural Disaster Survey Report: The Great Flood of 1993*

Meanwhile, Southeast swelters, dries out

While the upper Mississippi Valley was suffering through the Great Flood of 1993, hot, dry weather dominated the Southeast.

During June and July, as the rain was falling on the Midwest, much of the Southeast had half of its normal rain and temperatures from 3°F to 6°F above normal.

For the Southeast as a whole, July was the second driest on record and the states of Alabama, Georgia, North Carolina, South Carolina, Tennessee, and Virginia had their hottest July since records began in 1895.

Here are some highlights of the summer of 1993 in the Southeast compiled by Neal Lott of the National Climatic Data Center:

• South Carolina lost 95% of its corn crop, 70% of its soybean crop, and 50% of its wheat crop.

• Asheville, N.C., had 25 days in July above 90°F, breaking the record of 18 days.

• Greenville-Spartanburg, S.C., Chattanooga, Tenn., and Atlanta were above 90°F every day during July.

• Columbia, S.C., had 17 consecutive days above 100°F in July.

• The state of Florida had its hottest summer

— July through August — on record with an average of 82.3°F for the three months.

• Chattanooga, Tenn., with an average of 82°F, had its hottest summer on record.

Then came the hurricane

As Hurricane Emily's winds began battering North Carolina's Outer Banks early on Aug. 31, 1993, hurricane forecasters wrestled with their classic dilemma: When to issue the warnings and how big an area should be covered?

If Emily turned back out to sea, hurricane winds and storm surge would endanger only the Outer Banks and maybe the coast as far north as Delaware Bay.

If Emily continued along the coast, it could rake crowded beach towns along the New Jersey, New York and New England coasts.

But a hurricane warning covering areas north of Delaware Bay would prompt evacuations that would cost millions to businesses and cities. Also, forecasters always worry about false alarms because they make residents less likely to heed the next warning.

Robert Sheets, director of the National Hurricane Center, decided not to extend warnings north of Delaware Bay.

It was a good call. Emily turned back out over the Atlantic with only one side of its eye brushing Cape Hatteras with 115 mph winds.

Not only were evacuations avoided in New Jersey and most of New York, the forecast for Emily's seaward turn led the Navy to limit costly hurricane preparations in the Norfolk, Va., area and prompted Ocean City, Md., officials to ask visitors to leave, but not to order evacuations.

Sheets says a new computer model developed by the National Oceanic and Atmospheric Administration's Geophysical Fluid Dynamics Laboratory in Princeton, N.J., was key to the decision. Forecasters were confident in the model, thanks to tests with data from past hurricanes.

In July 1994, forecasters at the Hawaiian Hurricane Center in Honolulu relied on the same model to forecast that Hurricane Emilia, with 150 mph winds, would pass south of the islands. It did.

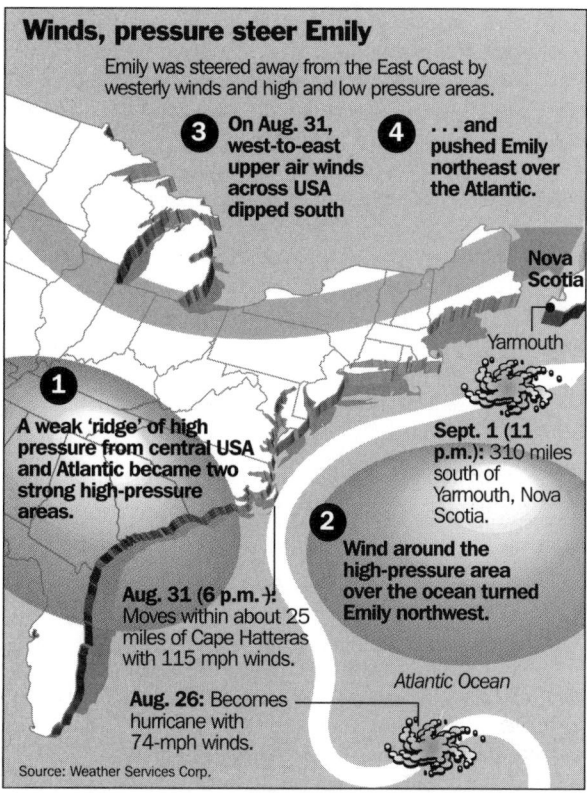

Winds, pressure steer Emily

Emily was steered away from the East Coast by westerly winds and high and low pressure areas.

3 On Aug. 31, west-to-east upper air winds across USA dipped south

4 ...and pushed Emily northeast over the Atlantic.

Nova Scotia

Yarmouth

1 A weak 'ridge' of high pressure from central USA and Atlantic became two strong high-pressure areas.

Sept. 1 (11 p.m.): 310 miles south of Yarmouth, Nova Scotia.

2 Wind around the high-pressure area over the ocean turned Emily northwest.

Aug. 31 (6 p.m.): Moves within about 25 miles of Cape Hatteras with 115 mph winds.

Atlantic Ocean

Aug. 26: Becomes hurricane with 74-mph winds.

Source: Weather Services Corp.

These successes followed near right-on forecasts for Hurricanes Hugo in 1989 and Andrew in 1992, based on older models and other techniques.

Still, hurricane forecasters live with the fear of not warning some areas in time for all in danger to evacuate. They'll continue to warn areas that end up not being hit. While hurricane forecasts are getting better, no one expects any sudden big improvement ending the need for evacuations that turn out, after the fact, to be unnecessary.

New satellites, radars and computer models are helping, but they aren't going to give forecasters all the answers about what hurricanes are likely to do.

Faster and more powerful computers handle more calculations, which improves forecasting models by calculating the weather in finer detail. But no matter how good the computer and how detailed the model, the quality of the forecast ultimately depends on how much good data the computer has to start with. Forecasters are often tripped up by hurricanes, which originate over oceans where collecting data is hard.

The big need is for more data about the upper air winds that steer storms.

The new generation of weather satellites will

help because they'll supply more upper atmosphere temperature readings. Temperatures are used to calculate air pressures at various altitudes. Pressure patterns, in turn, determine the speed and direction of winds that steer storms.

Even the most up-to-date satellites, however, give relatively crude upper air temperature measurements. Hurricane forecasters need a way to carry thermometers, barometers and other instruments into the area about 1,000 miles around a hurricane and as high as 40,000 feet over the ocean.

By 1996, they should have it.

In 1994, the U.S. Congress appropriated $43 million for the National Atmospheric and Oceanic Administration to purchase and equip a "midsize" jet for hurricane measurements and research. The airplane will be the kind of business jet used for trans-Atlantic flights and will be able to make the measurements that the new models need to live up to their potential.

The Aug. 31, 1993, Emily forecast showed the potential. At least four older, turboprop airplanes made measurements around the storm, supplying data for the new model. When the new airplane is available, it will be able to do what four planes did in Emily, plus fly to higher altitudes.

While the older planes can't fly high or far enough to take all the measurements new computer models need, they are perfect for the rough work of probing hurricane eyes.

Measurements taken as these airplanes bounce in the turbulence around hurricane eyes are helping scientists better understand exactly what's going on there. A particularly tough question they're trying to answer is why hurricanes go through cycles of growing stronger and then weaker as their eyes shrink and expand.

Understanding why hurricanes pulsate in strength will help forecasters do a better job of saying how strong storms will be when they hit.

Alternatives to evacuation

Knowing storm surge is the big killer in hurricanes, many South Florida residents who live inland stayed in their homes to ride out Hurricane Andrew in 1992. People on the coast went to high ground.

This had two results: Of the 15 deaths in Florida, only two were drownings and both victims were washed off boats, not caught in the 14-foot storm surge that hit Biscayne Bay. But many of those who decided to tough it out in their homes were left in

fear for their lives when 100 mph plus winds ripped away parts of their houses, as they huddled in terror inside.

Next time many of the inlanders will try to evacuate, too. If that happens, it is estimated that the traffic jam would last three days. So the evacuation order would have to be issued three days before a hurricane comes.

Let's see how things would have worked out if large numbers of people had planned to flee Andrew. Andrew first began battering Dade County with 40 mph winds and heavy rain around 1 a.m. Monday, Aug. 24. By that time, wind and rain were making driving difficult and debris was flying through the air.

A successful evacuation of the entire Miami metro area would have needed to start no later than 1 a.m. Aug. 21. But nighttime evacuations are dangerous. Noon on Aug. 20 would have been the time to start evacuating.

What was Andrew doing around noon on Aug. 20?

It was a tropical storm about 900 miles east of Miami that seemed to be coming back to life after nearly dying the day before. In fact, by 8 p.m. on Aug. 20, Andrew was still so disorganized that an Air Force plane scouting the storm was unable to find an eye.

No forecasting tool available then or likely to be available this century could have shown that Andrew would grow over the next three days into the third strongest storm to hit the USA this century.

Dangers in Florida

Areas in danger of storm surge flooding should be evacuated. But anyone living outside the surge zone in large metropolitan areas such as Dade County, Fla., should be prepared to ride out a hurricane's winds, unless they're in a mobile home or a poorly constructed building.

Andrew could have been worse.

"Florida was spared from an even larger disaster," a National Oceanic and Atmospheric Administration team that studied Andrew says in its report. "Andrew was a compact, fast-moving, relatively dry storm. Had it been larger, slower or carried more rain, its consequences would have been even more devastating."

The team noted that "a track just 10 miles to the north would have devastated downtown Miami with more loss of life and tens of billions of more in property damage." And if such a track had been followed into Louisiana, Andrew would have hit New Orleans, not the sparsely settled coastal area it did hit.

1993 Atlantic, Caribbean, Gulf of Mexico storms

Eight tropical storms formed in the Atlantic Basin during 1993 and four became hurricanes. Not only was this below the 50-year annual average of 10 storms and six hurricanes, but the hurricanes had generally short lives. The last storm died on Sept. 21, which was the earliest end to the actual season since 1930.

Here are the storms:

• **Tropical Storm Arlene, June 18 – 21:** Heavy rain caused local flooding from southeastern Mexico through coastal Texas into western Louisiana and Arkansas. Strongest winds: 40 mph. Six people killed. $20 million damage in USA.

• **Tropical Storm Bret, Aug. 4 – 11:** Extensive mudslides and flooding followed heavy rain near Caracas, Venezuela, killing 184 people.

• **Tropical Storm Cindy, Aug. 14 – 16:** Cindy formed near Martinique and dissipated three days later over Hispaniola after killing two people in Martinique and two in the Dominican Republic with floods and mudslides.

• **Hurricane Emily, Aug. 21 – Sept. 6:** The season's first hurricane formed about 600 miles northeast of the Leeward Islands and became a hurricane on Aug. 26. It struck the Outer Banks of North Carolina on Aug. 31 as a Category 3 hurricane, then turned back toward sea. Three people were killed, two in North Carolina and one in Virginia.

• **Tropical Storm Dennis, Aug. 23 – 28:** This storm had no effect on land.

• **Hurricane Floyd, Sept. 7 – 10:** Floyd reached tropical storm strength and was named on Sept. 7 in the Atlantic east of the Bahamas. It passed between the U.S. and Bermuda as a tropical storm. But on Sept. 9, it became a hurricane northeast of Bermuda and raced eastward. The following day, Floyd lost its eye and other characteristics of a hurricane but began developing into a major "extra-tropical" storm as it moved east on Sept. 11. The storm lashed southern England and Brittany in France with winds of 70 to 80 mph and gusts to 100 mph. Its rain helped make September and October unusually wet in parts of southern Europe.

• **Hurricane Gert, Sept. 14 – 21:** As a tropical storm, it brought heavy rain, flash flooding and mudslides to the southwestern Caribbean. It struck

near Tampico, Mexico, as a hurricane with 100 mph winds, killing 76 people.

• **Hurricane Harvey, Sept. 18 – 21:** This storm had no effect on land.

Eastern Pacific tropical storms, hurricanes

Fourteen tropical storms formed in the eastern Pacific during 1993 and 10 of these grew into hurricanes. Only five of the storms hit land, all on Mexico's West Coast.

Here are the storms that hit land:

• **Tropical Storm Beatriz, June 18 – 20:** The storm brought heavy rain to southern Mexico. Six people died.

• **Hurricane Calvin, July 4 – 9:** Even though it lasted only five days, Calvin forced the evacuation of 42,000 people and left at least 1,600 homeless in 11 states as it brushed Mexico's Pacific Coast. The death toll was 34. It hit near Manzanillo as a Category 2 hurricane and sent 15-foot waves into some streets in Acapulco.

• **Hurricane Hilary, Aug. 17 – 27:** Hilary had weakened to a 65 mph tropical storm when it hit the southern part of Mexico's Baja Peninsula. It brought heavy rain to the Mexican state of Colima and to Arizona in the U.S.

• **Tropical Storm Irwin, Aug. 21 – 22:** Irwin brushed Mexico's coast with 65 mph winds during the two days it lasted before being absorbed by the much-larger Hurricane Hilary.

• **Hurricane Lidia, Sept. 8 – 14:** Lidia's winds reached 150 mph over the ocean but weakened to 100 mph when it hit near Culiacan, where it killed at least two people and did extensive damage.

1994 tropical storms and hurricanes

• **Tropical Storm Alberto, June 30:** This storm formed in the Gulf of Mexico and came ashore at Destin, Fla., with winds estimated at 65 mph. Then it stalled over Georgia dumping drenching rain that caused some of the worst flooding in the history of Georgia, Alabama and western Florida. At least 20 people were killed and damage estimates were more than $500,000.

• **Hurricane Emilia, July 16 – 22, and Hurricane Gilma, July 22 – 27:** These formed off the Mexican Coast and moved west to pass south of Hawaii. Both had winds up to 150 mph and were threats to Hawaii. Tropical Storm Fabio followed Emilia briefly, but it never developed into a serious storm. Forecasters suspect that Emilia stirred up the ocean water, bringing up cool water from below. Fabio never had the good supply of the warm water that hurricanes need to grow.

Weathermakers

What causes the weather to swing from calm to stormy, from dry to wet?

Everything. Earth is a great weather machine. It's as simple as the sun warming some places more than others and as complicated as the chaos theory. Day to day, week to week, and month to month weather is the result of the interaction of millions of factors, including many that aren't well understood.

Scientists describe weather's usual ups and downs as "normal climate variability." They also talk of climate "forcing," events that can push the climate in one direction or the other. An increase in the amount of carbon dioxide and other gases in the atmosphere could cause the Earth's average temperature to warm up. It would still mean cold winters, hot summers, droughts and floods, but hot summers could become more common, and patterns of floods, drought, and even bitter cold winters could change. But separating normal climate variability from effects of a warmer Earth would be difficult.

Some argue that recent cold winters and the Mississippi floods are the result of global warming. But the general opinion of climate scientists is that these events fall well within normal variability and they aren't "proof" that the Earth's climate is changing.

However, these scientists agree that two events have had an effect on the weather: the eruption of Mount Pinatubo in 1991 in the Philippines and the unusually long lasting El Nino that began in 1991. Because they occurred so close together, it's hard to sort out what each did to the weather.

Gases shot out of Mount Pinatubo and into the stratosphere blocked sunlight and cooled the Earth slightly.

El Nino refers to changes in wind and ocean temperature in the tropical Pacific that affect weather around the world.

Mount Pinatubo

When the Mount Pinatubo volcano in the Philippines erupted in June 1991 — after 611 years of inactivity — it began a long-term global climate experiment that scientists never could have created.

For scientists, it was a golden opportunity to study in detail how volcanoes affect the Earth's climate and to look for links to day-to-day weather

patterns. They knew it would slightly cool the Earth. What else would it do?

Scientists estimated that Pinatubo shot 22 million tons of sulfur dioxide gas into the stratosphere, too high to be washed out by rain. While most of the material that shot as high as 100,000 feet into the air fell back to Earth on the Philippines, tons of sulfur dioxide gas stayed in the stratosphere to mix with water and turn into tiny drops of sulfuric acid that created a thin veil over most of the planet. Scientists call such tiny drops an "aerosol."

Pinatubo's most noticeable effects were benign, sometimes even beautiful. The aerosols created a slight haze that was noticeable in the normally clear Rocky Mountains, where the sky wasn't quite as deep a blue as normal during 1992 and into 1993. The haze also fogged astronomers' view of the sky.

On the good side, the haze, like that from other volcanoes, added color to sunrises and sunsets around the world by creating more vivid red, orange and purple shades in the sky.

But there was more to Pinatubo's effects than beautiful sunsets.

Because of Pinatubo's tropical location, stratospheric winds pushed material in three directions: west as would be expected, but also north and south as upper air made its way from the equator toward the poles.

For the first few months after the eruption, most of Pinatubo's material remained in a belt from about 30 degrees north latitude to 20 degrees south latitude. By early 1992, however, it had spread over most of the globe.

The droplets of sulfuric acid were just the right size to reflect sunlight and solar heat away from the Earth.

Measurements from NASA's Earth Radiation Budget satellites showed that during 1992, when large amounts of sulfuric acid from Pinatubo were in the stratosphere, about 4.7 percent more solar energy than normal was reflected away from the Earth. Other satellite measurements showed that the lower atmosphere of the Earth cooled an average of about 1°F. This stopped a slight warming trend of the late 1980s and early 1990s.

The satellite measurements, compiled by John Christy of the University of Alabama in Huntsville, showed that the Earth turned slightly cooler than average in the fall of 1991 and didn't warm back up to average-and-above readings until the fall of 1993, after the Pinatubo aerosol had disappeared.

Exactly what this cooling meant to the weather is impossible to pin down.

The summer of 1992 was unusually cool from the Rockies into the Northeast in the United States and was the coldest summer on record in Michigan. Was Pinatubo responsible?

Kevin Trenberth of the National Center for Atmospheric Research says no one has been able to find a direct link between Pinatubo's general global cooling and particular weather patterns such as the cool summer of 1992 and the cold 1992-93 winter in parts of the United States.

Still, Pinatubo might have affected the weather during 1992 and into early 1993.

"It's possible that Pinatubo kicked the atmosphere into a different mode of behavior," Trenberth says. "Subtle changes in sea temperatures or land-sea temperature contrasts could have changed the wave patterns" of upper air winds.

El Nino

"El Nino" is a complex set of ocean and atmospheric changes that move warm water from the western part of the tropical Pacific east across the International Date Line and eventually to the coast of South America. It happens every three to seven years and lasts for varying lengths of time.

Scientists call it El Nino-Southern Oscillation (ENSO). El Nino is Spanish for child, in this case "Christ Child," and was named for the warming of the water off Peru around Christmas every few years. Southern Oscillation refers to changes in air pressure around Australia and Tahiti. Usually the pressure around Australia is lower than around Tahiti and winds blow from east to west along the equator. During an El Nino, Australia's air pressure rises while Tahiti's drops and winds blow more from the west along the equator.

Effects of these shifts are felt around the world because changes in the locations of the Pacific's warmest water change the location of the heaviest thunderstorms, which pump air up and affect the jet streams that move storms.

El Nino years normally see fewer strong hurricanes in the Atlantic and Caribbean. But, as Hurricane Andrew showed in the El Nino year of 1992, an El Nino isn't a sure hurricane killer.

Also, El Nino years are normally wet in the U.S. Southeast and bring warm winters to the Northwest. Places even farther away from the tropical Pacific than the U.S., such as southern Africa, are affected. In July 1994, climatologists announced that they had found a strong link between El Nino, rainfall and the size of the corn crop in Zimbabwe. Such links had already been established between El Nino and rainfall in Australia and Peru.

El Nino also affects California's weather, but in different ways. Some El Nino years are wet, some are dry.

David Rodenhuis, head of the National Weather Service's Climate Analysis Center, says the latest El Nino, which began late in 1991, "could have been a factor in ending the severe drought that had plagued California since 1986" with the heavy precipitation of the 1992-93 wet season. He says it also probably helped establish the wet conditions that left the Mississippi Valley vulnerable to flooding in 1993 Mississippi Valley floods. Precipitation across the upper Midwest was heavier than usual during the fall of 1992, through the winter and into the spring of 1993. When the heavy rain of June 1993 began, the ground was saturated with water and streams filled.

The atmosphere goes about its everyday busi-

Pinatubo's rampage starts with minor explosions

Pinatubo's 1991 rampage began with two minor explosive eruptions on June 9 and 11, followed by nine "major" explosive eruptions from June 12 into June 15, then two, nearly continuous "cataclysmic" eruptions on June 15 and 16 before quieting down with another minor eruption on June 17.

The volcano hurled debris up to 20,000 feet in the minor explosions, up to 80,000 feet in the major ones and up to 100,000 feet in its cataclysmic eruptions.

Molten rock at 1,500°F came racing down the mountain at 60 mph, filling streams with ash that

washed down over the next several weeks as mud. It clogged other streams, causing floods. Smoke and ash darkened the sky in Manila 55 miles away and ash rained down over hundreds of square miles in the Philippines.

Pinatubo killed 343 people and forced 200,000 from their homes. Buildings collapsed under the weight of a concrete-like substance made when falling ash and sand mixed with the torrential rain that came at the same time. Mud flowed down the mountain for weeks, covering roads and forcing entire villages to flee.

ness of making weather with its complex interplay of temperatures, winds, air pressures, condensation and evaporation. But from time to time something like an El Nino or a Pinatubo comes along to push things in one direction or another. The exact results of such pushes are hard to untangle from all of the other things the weather is doing.

So we can't say that El Nino caused the big floods nor that Pinatubo caused the record lows in the winter of '92–'93. Simple explanations of "wild" weather are attractive. In the 1950s, some blamed unusual weather on atmospheric tests of nuclear bombs. But any explanation that gives only one cause is bound to be too simple to be correct.

Weather forecasts are getting better

While global climate is important, most people care more about what their local weather will be doing over the next few hours or days. Here, big improvements are occurring.

"People are more likely to say, 'That was a nasty storm we had, thanks for the accurate warning,' " says Skip Ely, head of the Dallas-Fort Worth National Weather Service Office. "I'm getting more of these calls than the other kind now. There's a lot of satisfaction in that."

With the old equipment, especially the 1957-model weather radar that's being replaced, "a lot of times people would ask why we hadn't warned them of a storm," Ely says. "I'd have to tell them, 'well, our radar doesn't see tornadoes.' "

The better forecasting is a result of improvements in the way data is collected and analysed:

• New Next Generation Radars (NEXRAD) will be watching most of the U.S. except some mountain valleys as well as several overseas military bases by spring 1996. The new radars use the Doppler effect to show winds.

• A new generation weather satellite was launched in April 1994 and went into full operation in the fall of 1994. A twin will join it in 1995, giving U.S. forecasters views from the world's most advanced weather satellites of not only the entire country, but far out into the Atlantic and Pacific oceans, breeding grounds of storms.

• In May 1994, the National Weather Service's National Meteorological Center began using a new supercomputer, which has five times the computing power of the computer it replaced. The old computer is being used to run experimental versions of the computer models used for forecasts.

The new computer will help the National Weather Service improve the generalized computer forecasts that are the basis of all local forecasts. Eventually, it will also make detailed, regional forecasts for all parts of the U.S.

• During the 1990s, the Weather Service is adding automated systems for collecting ground-level temperature, air pressure, humidity, wind, precipitation and other data. When the decade began, reports came in each hour from about 800 stations around the U.S. By the end of the decade, the automated stations will bring this total to around 1,700.

People "in regions with the new radars are already seeing improved short range forecasts," says Charles Hosler Jr., head of a National Research Council committee that's keeping tabs on National Weather Service modernization.

A study of six of the first weather offices to use the new radars shows that they cut the share of tornadoes that hit without warning from 33 percent to 13 percent. Just as important, the new radars are best at spotting the strong tornadoes that account for most deaths.

Offices with the new radars are also issuing fewer severe thunderstorm and tornado warnings that turn out to be false alarms. The Norman, Okla., Weather Service office, the first to use the new radar, reduced its false alarm rate from around 80 percent of all warnings in the early 1980s to less than 18 percent in 1992.

Also people served by the new radars "should expect the areas warned to be smaller and the warnings to be for shorter durations. Warnings will be more specific," Hosler says.

Forecasters using the computer will be able to combine different kinds of data to get a better three-dimensional picture of what's going on.

Along with the new equipment, the National Weather Service is setting up 115 new forecast offices and reducing the staff at many older offices.

In addition to improving tornado and severe thunderstorm forecasts, the new radars are giving better pictures of winter storms and more accurate measurements of rainfall.

Forecasters have relied on gauges that measure stream levels and the amount of rain that has fallen to predict flash floods. Often, however, the downpours that start flash floods fall on places without instruments to measure stream levels or rainfall.

The new radars keep track of how much rain is falling on various parts of the area they cover. Forecasters can get an accurate picture of whether enough rain has fallen to cause flooding.

As cities across the country start using the new

equipment, meteorologists are seeing small weather details that older radars and other instruments didn't show. For instance, new radars in the Mid-Atlantic states are detecting what appear to be "mini supercells," smaller versions of the large, well-organized, long-lasting thunderstorms that cause the strongest tornadoes on the Great Plains.

Such discoveries are one reason why the new offices have science officers who will focus on local research. Previously, forecasters seldom worked with researchers. Local research is needed because different places have different forecasting problems.

While the new radars are improving forecasts of events likely to happen in an hour or two, other new technology will bring better longer range forecasts — for 24, 36 or 48 hours ahead.

Getting the word out

The best forecast is of no use if people don't receive it. On March 27, 1994, the Birmingham, Ala., National Weather Service office used its new radar to issue a tornado warning a few minutes before a twister smashed into the Goshen United Methodist Church in Piedmont, Ala., during Palm Sunday services, killing 20 people. But the warning didn't reach the church, which is in a rural area without warning sirens.

After the Palm Sunday disaster, Vice President Al Gore announced an effort by the Weather Service, the Federal Emergency Management Agency and the U.S. Department of Agriculture to expand the current NOAA Weather Radio network to include at least 95 percent of all Americans.

About 75 percent of all Americans can receive broadcasts from 350 stations that broadcast only weather information. The broadcasts include special tones that will sound an alarm when a warning is about to be broadcast. Some weather radios have alarms that will sound even when the radio is turned off.

Better warnings of tornadoes, flash floods, and blizzards along with improved hurricane forecasts will save lives. Better warnings should also help the economy, Hosler says. "There are tens of millions of individual decisions made every day in this country based on weather. The more informed the decisions are, the more productive the society will be."

As forecasts improve, and people realize they are improved, "people will have more confidence to act on them," Hosler says. "The forecasts will be more useful to people in many ways, whether they're planning to paint a barn, pave a road, or go shopping."

But the experts have a caution. In 1993 Robert Ryan, then president of the American Meteorological Society, told a congressional hearing: "The more our skill, utilizing all the power of the modernized National Weather Service, improves, the more the public will expect. Our future challenge ... may be as much educating the public as to our scientific limitations, as it is detailing our present accomplishments."

Major weather experiments in 1995

Standing in an Oklahoma wheat field, a scientist aims a portable Doppler radar at a tornado less than a mile away.

Sitting in a cramped weather office in Maryland, a researcher tries to coax a picture of the global climate in the year 2050 from a super computer.

These are just two ways researchers are trying to understand more about how the atmosphere works, and then, if possible, apply this knowledge to improving weather and long-range climate forecasts.

Some researchers focus on weather: the storms, rain, snow, and winds that affect day-to-day activities. Others are more concerned with climate, the years-long averages of the weather that determine things such as what parts of the world are desert, what parts are productive farmland.

1. Tornadoes: During the Great Plains tornado season in the spring of 1995, any thunderstorm that's a candidate to produce tornadoes is likely to be pounced on by 50 to 60 researchers in 15 cars, vans and trucks as a four-engine research airplane and a single-engine airplane examine the storm from above.

Those on the ground will launch weather balloons in and around the storm and take extensive measurements of winds, temperatures and air pressures around and in the storm.

The field researchers will be working closely with scientists who are improving computer models of storms and the atmosphere around them. Computer simulations give the field researchers new ideas of what to look for. Reports from storms help the computer wizards improve their models.

This is a search for what puts the twist in tornadoes.

Scientists have been "chasing" severe storms on the Plains for years, but never before on the scale of this experiment called VORTEX (Verification of the Origins of Rotation in Tornadoes EXperiment). It began in 1994.

In the words of Morris Weisman of the National Center for Atmospheric Research, the crowd of researchers converging on storms "is a phenomenon in search of a phenomenon."

Scientists are trying to discover why air rising into some thunderstorms takes on the whirling motion of a tornado while air rising into other thunderstorms doesn't.

Some people think a tornado's motion comes from the Earth's rotation. But scientists have known for a couple of decades that the Earth's rotation does not cause tornadoes, although it is responsible for the circular winds in large storms such as hurricanes.

Researchers have many theories and forecasters have found that particular patterns of upper altitude winds around thunderstorms make tornadoes more likely. Doppler radars spot swirling winds high in thunderstorms, maybe six or so miles across, that can lead to tornadoes. But not all such "mesocyclones" spawn tornadoes.

If scientists can find out what puts the twist in a twister, warnings can come sooner and lives can be saved.

2. Warnings: As National Weather Service offices acquire new technology for keeping up with the weather, including animated color displays on video screens, most of them continue to send information about dangerous weather to emergency management officials as text bulletins.

A map on a video screen showing a storm's exact location, how much rain is falling and pinpointing each lightning bolt that hits the ground gives an immediate picture of what's going on. A few sentences describing the same thing don't have the same impact. The reader has to relate the words to a map, and often the text doesn't do a good job of describing a storm's or a flood's location.

In Boulder, Colo., the NOAA's Forecast Systems Laboratory is working on The Dissemination Project. Its goal is to present the same information available to meteorologists to emergency officials in Boulder and Denver in easily understandable forms. The project also is looking for better ways for local officials to get data, such as reports from

New weather radar will cover the USA

This listing shows when the National Weather Service's new weather radars went into operation or are scheduled to go into operation. The system is a joint effort of the Weather Service, the Defense Department and the Federal Aviation Administration.

Radar data are also being made available to television stations and other private users. When a new unit goes into operation, television weathercasters in the area often begin broadcasting images from the new radar.

Locations listed are the metropolitan area served by the radar. Radars on military bases serve the area around the base. Each radar's Doppler capability extends about 140 miles in all directions from the antenna. Beyond that, the radars detect weather as far as 250 miles from the antenna.

Alabama		**Arizona**		March AFB	April 1995	**Florida**	
Birmingham	May 1994	Flagstaff	Sept. 1995	Los Angeles	March 1994	Eglin AFB	Aug. 1992
Maxwell AFB	Feb. 1994	Tucson	Jan. 1995	Sacramento	Feb. 1994	Jacksonville	Feb. 1995
Ft. Rucker	Nov. 1993	Phoenix	March 1993	San Diego	Feb. 1996	Key West	Feb. 1996
Mobile	Aug. 1994	Yuma	May 1995	San Francisco Bay		Melbourne	July 1992
				Area	April 1994	Miami	April 1993
Alaska		**Arkansas**		Vandenberg AFB	May 1993	Tallahassee	Jan. 1995
Anchorage	Nov. 1993	North Little Rock	March 1993			Tampa	March 1994
Bethel	Dec. 1995			**Colorado**			
Fairbanks	Oct. 1993	**California**		Denver	May 1993	**Georgia**	
King Salmon	Oct. 1995	Beale AFB	Feb. 1995	Grand Junction	Oct. 1995	Atlanta	July 1994
Middleton Island	NA	Edwards AFB	April 1995	Pueblo	Dec. 1994	Moody AFB	June 1995
Nome	Jan. 1996	Eureka	Dec. 1994			Robins AFB	Jan. 1994
Sitka	Aug. 1995	Hanford (San Joaquin		**Delaware**			
		Valley)	March 1995	Dover AFB	Jan. 1993		

Guam

Andersen AFB	Feb. 1993

Hawaii

Kamuela	April 1995
Molokai	Jan. 1994
South Hawaii	NA
South Kauai	Sept. 1994

Idaho

Boise	Nov. 1993
Pocatello-Idaho Falls	June 1995

Illinois

Chicago	June 1993
Lincoln	May 1995

Indiana

Indianapolis	Aug. 1993

Iowa

Des Moines	Dec. 1993
Quad Cities (Davenport)	Jan. 1995

Kansas

Dodge City	Nov. 1992
Goodland	Nov. 1992
Topeka	June 1993
Wichita	Oct. 1992

Kentucky

Ft. Campbell	Feb. 1994
Louisville	Sept. 1993
Paducah	Jan. 1995

Louisiana

Ft. Polk	May 1994
Lake Charles	May 1994
Shreveport	May 1995
New Orleans – Baton Rouge	April 1994

Maine

Houlton	Aug. 1995
Portland	Dec. 1993

Massachusetts

Boston	Nov. 1993

NA = Not Available

Michigan

Detroit	June 1993
Grand Rapids	July 1995
Marquette	July 1995
Gaylord	Nov. 1995

Minnesota

Duluth	July 1995
Minneapolis-St. Paul	Sept. 1994

Mississippi

Columbus AFB	April 1994
Jackson	March 1993

Missouri

Kansas City	Dec. 1992
Springfield	Jan. 1995
St. Louis	Nov. 1992

Montana

Billings	Nov. 1995
Glasgow	Dec. 1995
Great Falls	Sept. 1994
Missoula	Oct. 1994

Nebraska

Grand Island	June 1993
North Platte	June 1995
Omaha	June 1994

Nevada

Elko	Oct. 1995
Las Vegas	Feb. 1995
Reno	Oct. 1994

New Mexico

Albuquerque	July 1994
Cannon AFB	May 1994
Holloman AFB	June 1994

New York

Albany	Nov. 1993
Binghamton	Sept. 1993
New York	Sept. 1993
Buffalo	Sept. 1995
Griffiss AFB	Dec. 1992

North Carolina

Morehead City	Dec. 1993
Raleigh-Durham	March 1994
Wilmington	Oct. 1994

North Dakota

Bismarck	Nov. 1994
Fargo, Grand Forks	Dec. 1995
Minot AFB	Aug. 1994

Ohio

Cincinnati	July 1994
Cleveland	Aug. 1993

Oklahoma

Altus AFB	Sept. 1992
Oklahoma City	Aug. 1992
Tulsa	April 1993
Vance AFB	Dec. 1993

Oregon

Medford	Sept. 1995
Pendleton	June 1995
Portland	Dec. 1994

Pennsylvania

Philadelphia	Oct. 1993
Pittsburgh	Aug. 1993
State College	Oct. 1993

Puerto Rico

San Juan	March 1995

South Carolina

Charleston	NA
Columbia	Jan. 1994
Greenville – Spartanburg	March 1995

South Dakota

Aberdeen	Nov. 1994
Rapid City	Nov. 1995
Sioux Falls	Dec. 1993

Tennessee

Knoxville	Sept. 1994
Memphis	Oct. 1993
Nashville	Oct. 1994

Texas

Amarillo	Feb. 1993
Austin – San Antonio	June 1994
Brownsville	March 1995
Dyess AFB	Oct. 1993
El Paso	Feb. 1996

Dallas-Ft. Worth	Jan. 1994
Fort Hood	April 1993
Houston	June 1992
Laughlin AFB	March 1994
Lubbock	March 1994
Midland-Odessa	April 1995
San Angelo	Feb. 1996

Utah

Cedar City	Oct. 1995
Salt Lake City	Oct. 1994

Vermont

Burlington	Jan. 1996

Virginia

Norfolk	July 1994
Roanoke	Nov. 1994
Washington, D.C.	June 1992

Washington

Seattle	March 1994
Spokane	Oct. 1995

West Virginia

Charleston	Aug. 1994

Wisconsin

Green Bay	Oct. 1994
La Crosse	Sept. 1994
Milwaukee	Oct. 1993

Wyoming

Cheyenne	June 1994
Riverton	Aug. 1995

Azores

Lajes Air Base	July 1996

Bahamas

Georgetown	NA

British West Indies

Grand Turk	NA

Japan

Kadena	April 1996

Korea

Camp Humphreys	Jan. 1996
Kunsan Air Base	March 1996

Details behind the giant geostationary weather satellites

Some facts about the new geostationary weather satellites that began to be launched in April 1994:

• When the satellites leave earth in a rocket's nose cone, they are folded into a 80x85x93-inch box. In space, they unfold to an 88-foot span, the height of a nine-story building.

• Each GOES has more than a mile of wire connecting 105 electronic "black boxes."

• More than 3,000 screws hold each GOES and its components together.

• 2,662 solar cells generate 1,164 watts of electric power, about a tenth the amount supplied to an average house.

• About 60,000 separately identifiable parts are in each satellite's sounder and imager alone. The sounder measures upper air temperatures. The imager is the "camera."

• Each spacecraft weighs 2,161 pounds and carries another 2,384 pounds of fuel for the tiny rockets that keep the satellite in the correct orbit and pointing in the right direction for more than five years.

Source: National Oceanic and Atmospheric Administration

snowplow drivers about accumulations on highways, to forecasters.

3. Short-range forecasts: The U.S. Weather Research Program, which began in early 1994, is continuing work on improving short-range forecasts of severe weather, especially heavy precipitation and floods.

Experimental Forecasting Facilities at Norman, Okla., Denver and Boulder, Colo., and Kansas City, Mo., should speed up the transfer of new knowledge and technology to forecasters.

The National Severe Storms Laboratory in Norman, Okla., is setting up a NEXRAD research and development center to learn more about the potential of Doppler radar. Researchers also are improving computer models used for both short-range and long-range forecasts, including those for hurricanes. A major focus is on developing new models for making local forecasts in different parts of the country.

4. Climate: Much of the climate research in the U.S., especially larger projects, is part of the United States Global Change Research Program. This program began in 1990 with the Global Change Research Act, which was aimed at understanding changes in the global environment that "may alter the capacity of the Earth to sustain life." So far its focus has been:

• Gathering climate data from land, ocean and space systems.

• Making the data accessible.

• Supporting research on physical, biological and chemical processes that influence the global system.

• Developing computer models for predicting global change.

• Analyzing the impact of global change.

• Developing ways to assess policies for responding to global change.

In his proposed budget for the 1995 federal fiscal year, which runs from Oct. 1, 1994 through Sept. 30, 1995, President Clinton proposed spending $1.8 billion on the Global Change Research Program, an increase of around $3 million over the previous year.

The biggest share of this, $1.2 billion, would go to NASA for satellite observations and related research.

Amounts for other agencies are:

• Agriculture Department, $58.4 million

• Commerce Department, $84 million

• Defense Department, $6.4 million

• Energy Department, $126.1 million

• Health and Human Services Department, $25.5 million

• Interior Department, $31 million

• Environmental Protection Agency, $31.8 million

• National Science Foundation, $207.5 million

• Smithsonian Institution, $7.3 million

• Tennessee Valley Authority, $1 million

Probably the best way to get an idea of what's involved in Global Change Research is to glance at some of the programs for which each agency is responsible.

Agriculture Department efforts focus on the relationship between the atmosphere and farmland, forests and range land and how climate change could affect production of food and fiber.

Commerce Department funds go to NOAA, which studies both the atmosphere and the oceans. Its projects include studies of atmospheric chemistry, the workings of climate, experimental climatic prediction, global climate observations,

Focusing on better weather forecasting

The first in a new series of geostationary weather satellites called **GOES NEXT** was launched April 15, 1994, and went into operation in October 1994. It and a similar satellite to be launched in 1995 will help forecasters do a better job of tracking dangerous weather.

IMAGE CHANGE: Top part of photo shows image of Hurricane Andrew from the old GOES satellite. Bottom simulates transmission by new GOES.

New GOES

Sounder: Measures temperature, humidity at 19 levels of atmosphere

Imager: Takes regular and infrared photos

Length: 88.3 feet
Weight: 4,640 pounds

Advantages
Speed: Can send more images, improving tracking of dangerous storms.
Sharper photos: More detailed pictures of clouds that could develop into dangerous thunderstorms or hurricanes.
Night photos: Improved infrared images will end virtual night-blindness of present system.
Emergency: Satellite can pick up, relay emergency radio signals from downed aircraft, ships, and even hikers in trouble.
Fires: Sensors can spot forest fires before smoke plumes rise.

Orbiting at 22,238 miles, the GOES will remain above one spot on the Earth.

Western coverage area   Eastern coverage area

Coverage
Satellite will replace a borrowed European satellite watching most of the USA and Atlantic. Second satellite in spring 1995 will replace an aging U.S. satellite watching the western USA and Pacific. Can focus on an area as small as 600 by 600 miles, when needed.

Sources: National Oceanic and Atmospheric Administration, NASA

studies of past climates, climate variability, and clouds, energy and water.

Defense Department projects deal with both defense needs and global change program objectives. They include studies of the Arctic and ocean weather and climate.

The Energy Department's largest program is measuring the amount of solar energy reaching the Earth and heat energy leaving the Earth and how clouds and other factors affect it. Other projects study ways to reduce greenhouse gas emissions. The department also supports basic research on how carbon gets into the air and where it goes when it leaves the air.

The Health and Human Services Department is studying the human health effects of chemicals that are replacing the chlorofluorocarbons that have been banned because of their effects on ozone, and the effects on humans of ultraviolet radiation.

Interior Department programs include studies of past climates and the interactions of ecological systems with climate. The systems being studied include arid and semiarid regions, cold regions, coastal lands, and the ocean. The Department's U.S. Geological Survey, National Biological Survey, Fish and Wildlife Service, and Bureau of Reclamation are involved.

Environmental Protection Agency projects include developing computer models to predict the effects of global change at the regional level. It also examines the relative risk of potential global change in various kinds of areas such as forests. Other studies are trying to determine the amounts of various gases that come from human activity and from nature.

NASA's share includes about $740 million for the international Earth Observing System, which is a series of satellites, and the ground equipment needed to collect the data they send back. NASA programs also include global change experiments on the space shuttle and several satellites. NASA also conducts research aimed at relating data from satellites to what's happening near the ground.

The National Science Foundation supports a wide range of studies at the National Center for Atmospheric Research, several universities and other organizations. Its largest projects focus on the Arctic, chemistry of the lower atmosphere, human dimensions of climate change, how the oceans take up, give off and move heat, interactions between tropical oceans and the atmosphere, and global ocean currents.

The Smithsonian Institution has several rela-tively small studies of ecosystem response to environmental change, ranging from the tropics to Chesapeake Bay.

Tennessee Valley Authority is concerned with regional effects of climate change.

The big questions about climate eventually come down to relatively small changes in lots of different places. Are temperatures and precipitation increasing, decreasing or staying the same?

Ordinary weather instruments, such as thermometers and rain gauges, supply the answers. But how good are the answers? That's the concern of 75 to 100 climate experts coming to Asheville, N.C., in January 1995.

Tom Karl, senior scientist at the National Climatic Data Center in Asheville, explains that when researchers began an international effort in the late 1980s to understand climate change, they realized "we don't have an observation system globally to document the types of changes that are important."

To understand the climate, you need trustworthy, long-term records. But because measuring techniques change as better technology comes along, the records can't always be trusted.

For instance, the records of rainfall in a particular place might show a 10 percent increase during the 1990s compared to the 1970s. This might not sound like much, but if it's true it could be a sign of climate change. But did the rainfall really increase or did improved rain gauges catch more of the rain that falls?

"You'd be surprised how difficult it is to document changes" in observations, Karl says.

One answer the climate experts urge is keeping old observing systems in operation near new ones for a period of time. This would produce figures showing how much difference the observing technology makes. Scientists would then know whether apparent changes are real.

Climate researchers also want to obtain more data from areas with few weather observations, such as over the oceans. Satellites can supply a lot of information, but on-the-spot measurements are needed to calibrate the satellites.

5. El Nino: The Tropical Ocean and Global Atmosphere (TOGA) program will be winding up in 1995 after solving many of the mysteries of the changes in Tropical Pacific Ocean water temperatures and winds that affect the weather around the globe. This international effort was planned to last long enough to capture more than one El Nino cycle with a network of ocean and air observatons.

In one part, from November 1992 through February 1993, more than 1,000 scientists and technicians from 21 nations conducted a concentrated study of the western Pacific "warm pool." This is an area of the Pacific Ocean northeast of Australia that's larger than the United States. It has the Earth's warmest ocean temperatures, consistently above 82°F with large areas near 90°F. On satellite photos that use colors to show ocean temperatures, the region looks like an earthly version of Jupiter's Great Red Spot.

During an El Nino, warm water from this region spreads east across the Pacific to the South American coast. This shifts patterns of wind and precipitation around the globe and can raise the Earth's average temperature as much as a half-degree Fahrenheit.

The first conference to talk about the data collected was held in Toulouse, France in August 1994.

One discovery was that a significant amount of the heavy rain over the warm pool comes from shallow clouds, not the large thunderstorms scientists had thought were responsible for most rain. Researchers also found clues to what drives warm water eastward during an El Nino.

These findings and others will be used to improve computer models of the oceans and atmosphere. But the data will take years to analyze fully.

6. Research aircraft: Thanks to the end of the Cold War, two new aircraft are joining the atmosphere research fleet.

The National Center for Atmospheric Research is getting a Navy EC-130Q and an Air Force WB-57F spy plane.

As many as 16 researchers will be able to fly on the EC-130Q on flights as high as 30,000 feet. The plane's first project was a study of storms over the Beaufort Sea in the Arctic north of Canada and Alaska during the fall of 1994.

The WB-57F, expected to be in operation by the summer of 1995, will be the first research aircraft able to carry a scientist, not just a pilot, to 60,000 feet or more.

Questions to be studied by the WB-57F include chemical reactions in the stratosphere, including destruction of ozone, the movement of water vapor and ozone between the high and low parts of the atmosphere, and the nature of high-altitude clouds.

Greenhouse update

A potential "greenhouse" warming of the Earth will remain a key research topic over the next several years. Scientists are refining climate measurements and improving the computer models that try to mimic the workings of the oceans and atmosphere. But they aren't likely any time soon to give a final, "no-doubts-remain" answer to whether global warming is a danger that demands costly responses.

Key facts about the "greenhouse effect" that no scientist disputes include:

• Some gases, such as water vapor, carbon dioxide and methane, allow most solar heat to pass through the atmosphere to warm the Earth. But they block some infrared "heat" energy from leaving the Earth. The effect is to make the Earth warmer than it would otherwise be, which is why they're called "greenhouse" gases.

• Without the "greenhouse" effect, the Earth's average surface temperature would be around 0°F, instead of the 59°F it actually is. The current temperature balances energy arriving at the Earth and energy leaving.

• Human activities, such as burning coal and oil, have been adding carbon dioxide and other greenhouse gases to the atmosphere since the 19th century. Also, more greenhouse gases seem sure to be added to the atmosphere as the global economy grows and nations such as China become more industrialized.

The big question is: Are greenhouse gases likely to throw the global climate out of whack, turning fertile farmland into deserts and causing rising oceans to eat valuable land along the coasts?

Policymakers want to know how much danger the Earth faces. If the danger is high, measures might be called for that would reduce greenhouse gas emissions. Some of these measures might be economically painful ones.

Computer models are the only way to gain any idea of what should happen over the next several decades. Improving such models is a major climate research goal. To do it scientists need to learn more about the detailed workings of the climate, including how the atmosphere, the oceans and living things interact.

Because people have been adding carbon dioxide to the air for more than 100 years, figuring out what the greenhouse effect could do might seem like merely a matter of seeing what it has done so far to the climate.

But climate isn't that simple.

While the lack of reliable, long-term records makes an exact answer impossible, climate scien-

Taking the Earth's temperature

The graphs on the next page show how the Earth's average temperature changed month by month from January 1990 into mid-1994.

Both graphs show how temperatures have gone up and down compared to averages.

The Global Satellite Temperatures are worldwide averages of the lower part of the atmosphere as measured from satellites.

The Global Land-Based Temperatures are from thermometers at ground level only over land.

Differences in what's being measured explain why the graphs look so different.

Since the satellite temperatures include readings from over the oceans, where temperatures are slower to change, they don't bounce up and down as much. Also, air near the ground cools off and warms up faster than air in the lower several thousand feet of the atmosphere, which the satellites measure.

The land-based temperatures would be more representative of those that directly affect people.

Global cooling caused by the eruption of Mount Pinatubo in June 1991 shows up clearly in the satellite graph. Temperatures went below average in October 1991 and stayed there until December 1993. Land temperatures were below normal only for four months in 1992.

tists generally agree that the Earth's average temperature is now between a half-degree and a degree Fahrenheit warmer than 100 years ago.

But while greenhouse gases increased at fairly steady rates over this time, the Earth warmed between the years 1900 and 1940, then cooled until around 1975 and has been warming since.

Tom Karl, senior scientist at the National Climatic Data Center, notes that the details are even more complicated. He says the temperature since the mid-1980s is averaging close to the temperature of the 1930s, but with two key differences:

• The second half of the years, July through December, remain as cold now as during the 1960s.

• The first half of the years have been warmer than any other time in the 20th century.

Karl and others also have found that most of the warming over land has been at night while daytime temperatures have changed little. An increase in clouds is responsible. During the day, clouds block some solar heat, which is why cloudy days are cooler than clear days. At night, however, clouds block infrared radiation from leaving the Earth, keeping the warmth in like a blanket. Cloudy nights are warmer than clear nights.

Why clouds are increasing isn't known, but pollutants that help water vapor condense into cloud droplets could be part of the reason.

Even though the Earth is a little warmer than 100 years ago, scientists can't blame the greenhouse effect because the warming is within the normal ups and downs that could happen without greenhouse gases pushing temperatures upward.

As Karl points out: The key problem is separating natural warming from warming caused by human activities.

Some climate computer models say that the warming so far this century should be greater than it has been. Why hasn't the Earth warmed more?

Some of the possible reasons are:

• Pollution, especially sulfur particles, could be blocking enough sunlight to offset greenhouse warming.

• Oceans could be storing more heat than most theories allow.

• The climate might be in a natural cooling phase, offsetting some of the greenhouse warming.

• Natural "thermostats" could limit the Earth's heating. One idea is that as oceans warm, thicker clouds would form, blocking more sunlight and keeping temperatures from rising further.

Climate models that take the effects of sulfur into account and that have more details of ocean currents come close to creating the current conditions. Karl says enough sulfur is in the air over the eastern U.S., and parts of China and Europe to easily offset a greenhouse warming. Heat stored in the oceans and changes in ocean currents could account for the 1940 to 1975 cooling.

John Firor, director of the Advanced Study Program at the National Center for Atmospheric Research, notes that computer models are getting better. In general, the models did a good job of predicting the effects of the Mount Pinatubo volcanic eruption, which cooled the globe slightly. Computer models are also doing a pretty good job of predicting El Ninos, the global weather shifts

Average global temperatures by month

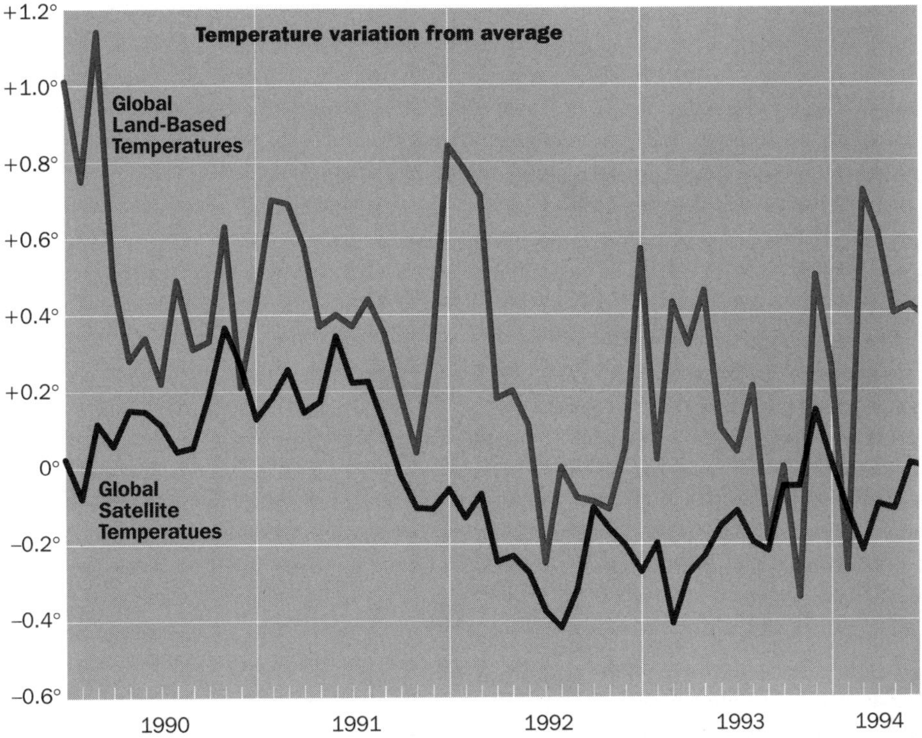
+1.2°
+1.0°
+0.8°
+0.6°
+0.4°
+0.2°
0°
–0.2°
–0.4°
–0.6°
Temperature variation from average
Global
Land-Based
Temperatures
Global
Satellite
Temperatues
1990
1991
1992
1993
1994

Average U.S. yearly temperatures by season

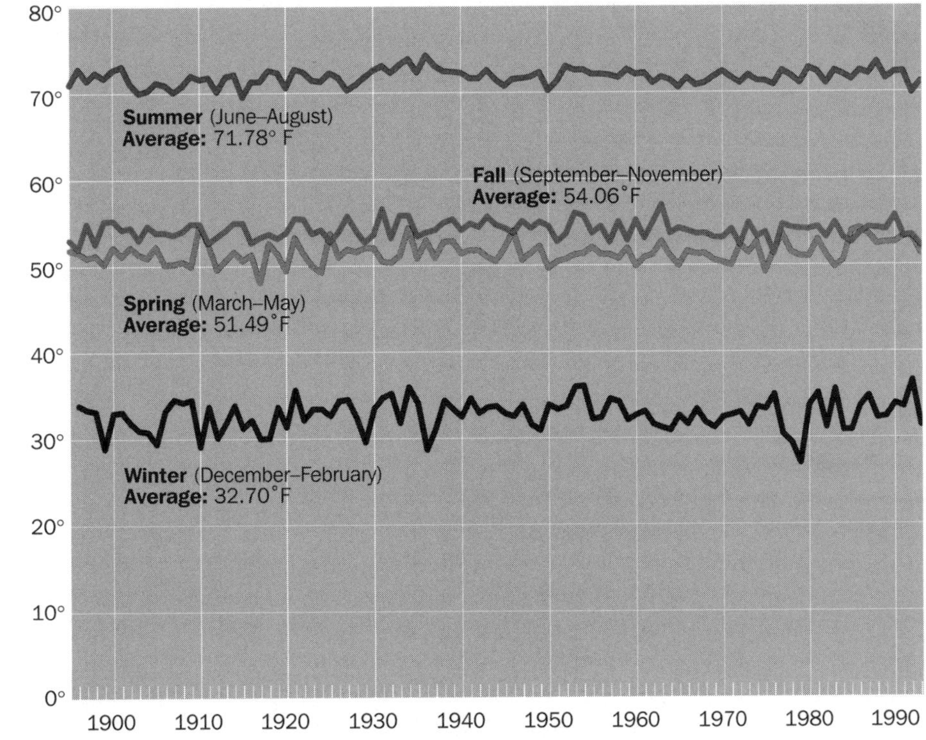
80°
70°
60°
50°
40°
30°
20°
10°
0°
Summer (June–August)
Average: 71.78° F
Fall (September–November)
Average: 54.06°F
Spring (March–May)
Average: 51.49°F
Winter (December–February)
Average: 32.70°F
1900
1910
1920
1930
1940
1950
1960
1970
1980
1990

caused by changes in the tropical Pacific.

Firor says changes in the strength and directions of ocean currents caused by a warmer climate could not only delay a general warm-up, but also result in some surprises. Some models indicate, for instance, that a general warming of the globe could actually cool Europe and other places around the North Atlantic for a few decades as the Gulf Stream becomes weaker.

Climate models agree that a greenhouse warming would bring not only cooling to some regions, but also more rain to some, more frequent droughts to others.

This leads to speculation that the weather's ups and downs of the last few years are caused by global warming. Some have blamed greenhouse gases for Hurricane Andrew, the 1993 Mississippi floods and other events. But there's no real evidence that global warming was involved. In fact, Hurricane Andrew hit in August 1992, the Earth's coldest month in a year that was cooler than any since the 1970s because of the Mount Pinatubo volcanic eruption in 1991.

Over the last few years, various scientific findings have been publicized as either proof or refutation of the idea that greenhouse gases are warming the climate. Reports of these findings could leave "the impression that science changes its mind each six months," Firor says. Instead, what's really happening, is "every year we learn a little bit by thinking very hard" about climate. "Science progresses very slowly." In climate science, "changes have been minor, even since 1988 when all the fuss about global warming was front page news."

This means that policymakers will have to continue making decisions about the balance between economics and the danger of greenhouse warming without firm predictions from scientists.

2 A weather guide for vacations

How to plan your vacation around the weather

A sure way to ruin a vacation is to encounter weather that's not expected.

Sometimes it can't be avoided. A place that's normally dry in July could have 20 days of rain. Cold waves can plunge southern Florida, Texas or California into winter weather. Snow might decide to pass up a favorite ski area for weeks.

But year in and year out, there are general weather patterns that travelers should be aware of. For example, some people could be uncomfortably chilly on a summer trip to the Grand Canyon if they aren't aware that temperatures normally fall into the 40s during the summer in northern Arizona. Over the years, hundreds of Caribbean vacationers have had September trips turned into horror stories when hurricanes strike.

In addition to knowing what temperatures to expect, when the worst weather is likely, and which months are wet or dry, visitors also should be concerned with a destination's elevation. People who have always lived near sea level may be amazed at how quickly walking or bicycling has them puffing when they visit places such as Colorado's Rocky Mountains National Park, where the bottoms of the mountains are at elevations above 6,000 feet.

This chapter, along with the U.S. and world listings for individual cities in the back of this book, should help you avoid unpleasant weather surprises while traveling.

Water temperature

When you hear that water temperature at the beach is 85°F, you might think that's great for swimming. But most people find 85-degree water uncomfortably warm for swimming. Generally, swimming is best when the water is from 70°F to 80°F.

Since water takes longer than air to heat and cool, average values are a good guide to what to expect. Ocean temperatures sometimes vary from the normals, however. Winds and storms can change day-to-day temperatures by 10 degrees. An unusually cold winter can leave the ocean cooler

than usual and slower to warm up. From time to time, ocean currents or prolonged, unusual winds can cool or warm the water.

Listings on the following pages are a general guide to what to expect. They show, for example, that the surf at Miami Beach normally stays above 70°F all year, while the water at Eastport, Maine, stays in the 40s and 50s or colder all year.

Comfortable water temperatures vary from person to person. But here is a general guide to what temperatures mean:

• Below 60°F: Dangerous for swimming.

• 60°F to 70°F: Uncomfortable to most swimmers.

• 70°F to 80°F: Generally comfortable, but temperatures at the lower end are comfortable only for short dips to many people.

• Above 80°F: Uncomfortably warm for vigorous swimming.

Warning: Even in summer, prolonged immersion in water colder than 70°F can produce hypothermia, a subnormal body temperature that can be deadly. Also, physicians have recently learned that divers, even in tropical water, can develop hypothermia slowly without symptoms such as shivering, if they don't rest and warm up between dives.

Winds for sailors

You can tell sailors from Buffalo, N.Y. Look under the decks of their boats. They have extra reinforcement, big blocks of wood, under every deck fitting. It blows on Lake Erie in sailing season and the boats have to be up to it.

On the Chesapeake Bay and Long Island Sound, high summer is the worst time to sail. Best to have some kind of sunshade and a good engine. Winds here blow strongest in spring and fall.

But in San Francisco, especially in summer, strong winds pipe up on the Bay almost every day. Places like San Francisco Bay and Barnegat Bay in New Jersey have strong summer sea breezes because hot air rises from the land bringing in the

East Coast water temperatures (°F)

Locations	Jan.	Feb.	Mar.	April 1	April 2	May 1	May 2	June 1	June 2	July 1	July 2	Aug. 1	Aug. 2	Sept. 1	Sept. 2	Oct. 1	Oct. 2	Nov.	Dec.
Eastport, Me.	40	37	38	39	41	43	44	46	46	50	51	51	51	52	51	50	49	49	45
Bar Harbor, Me.	38	36	38	42	45	47	51	54	56	58	60	63	60	58	57	55	53	52	44
Portland, Me.	34	33	37	39	41	47	51	54	57	60	61	62	61	59	58	54	50	47	39
Portsmouth Harbor, Me.	40	35	37	41	45	48	52	54	56	60	60	63	60	60	57	53	51	48	41
Boston Harbor, Mass.	40	36	41	45	49	54	58	61	63	66	67	68	68	66	63	58	56	51	42
Woods Hole, Mass.	34	35	37	44	47	54	56	61	65	70	72	72	71	69	66	62	56	50	41
Newport, R.I.	37	36	37	44	48	52	57	61	63	68	69	71	69	67	66	61	59	52	44
New London, Conn.	37	37	40	47	51	54	59	62	66	68	72	72	71	70	67	62	57	52	42
Bridgeport, Conn.	39	37	40	46	50	55	61	65	69	72	73	77	75	74	71	67	60	55	45
Willets Point, N.Y.	35	34	39	45	49	54	59	63	66	70	71	73	73	72	69	64	59	54	42
The Battery, N.Y.	38	36	41	45	49	54	60	64	67	70	73	74	73	72	68	63	58	53	43
Montauk, N.Y.	36	35	38	42	46	50	54	59	62	67	70	70	70	69	66	62	57	56	43
Sandy Hook, N.J.	37	36	40	44	48	52	58	60	63	67	71	72	72	70	66	61	57	51	43
Atlantic City, N.J.	37	35	42	46	50	54	58	62	64	69	70	72	73	72	67	63	58	53	44
Cape May, N.J.	37	37	42	48	51	56	62	67	69	71	74	74	73	73	70	63	58	52	42
Philadelphia, Pa.	36	36	44	49	54	61	70	71	75	78	80	79	76	77	71	64	57	52	41
Lewes, Del.	37	36	41	49	53	58	62	66	69	71	74	76	75	73	70	65	58	52	44
Ocean City, Md.	37	34	42	48	51	53	58	60	65	68	69	71	71	71	69	65	59	53	44
Cape Charles, Va.	36	39	46	51	56	60	66	70	69	76	77	78	77	76	74	66	61	54	44
Solomons, Md.	37	37	43	50	55	61	66	72	75	79	81	82	84	79	73	66	61	57	45
Washington, D.C.	37	37	46	54	61	64	71	74	79	80	83	83	81	78	72	64	58	52	41
Annapolis, Md.	36	35	42	50	54	58	63	69	74	76	78	78	77	75	71	66	60	53	45
Baltimore, Md.	40	37	43	51	57	61	67	70	75	77	78	79	79	77	72	66	61	54	43
Cape Hatteras, N.C.	49	46	52	58	60	68	68	72	75	76	79	80	80	78	75	72	68	58	55
Myrtle Beach, S.C.	48	50	55	62	66	70	75	77	80	81	83	83	82	81	79	72	67	61	53
Charleston, S.C.	50	50	57	64	68	71	75	79	80	82	84	84	83	82	79	73	68	63	54
Savannah Beach, Ga.	51	52	59	65	69	72	76	79	82	84	86	85	84	83	80	75	70	64	54
Fernandina Beach, Fla.	55	55	62	68	72	75	78	81	81	83	84	84	84	83	81	76	72	66	58
Jacksonville Beach, Fla.	57	56	61	68	71	74	77	80	81	83	84	83	83	83	82	78	72	67	60
Daytona Beach, Fla.	61	59	65	70	73	75	78	79	80	80	80	80	81	83	82	79	76	71	65
Stuart Beach, Fla.	67	66	70	71	74	75	78	79	79	79	79	80	80	81	80	79	77	75	70
Miami Beach, Fla.	71	73	75	78	78	80	81	84	85	86	86	86	84	84	83	83	79	76	73
Key West, Fla.	69	70	75	79	79	82	83	86	86	87	87	87	87	86	86	83	80	76	72
San Juan, Puerto Rico	77	78	78	79	80	80	81	81	82	81	81	83	83	83	83	83	82	81	80
Bermuda	64	63	64	66	67	72	76	78	79	82	84	83	82	80	79	77	74	70	65

1 - first half of the month   2 - second half of the month

West Coast water temperatures (°F)

Locations	Jan.	Feb.	Mar.	April 1	April 2	May 1	May 2	June 1	June 2	July 1	July 2	Aug. 1	Aug. 2	Sept. 1	Sept. 2	Oct. 1	Oct. 2	Nov.	Dec.
Scripps Pier, Calif.	58	57	58	59	60	61	63	64	65	66	67	68	68	66	66	65	63	61	59
Oceanside, Calif.	57	57	58	59	60	61	62	63	65	66	67	69	69	67	66	65	63	61	59
San Clemente, Calif.	57	57	58	58	59	60	61	63	63	64	66	68	67	66	66	65	63	61	58
Avalon, Calif.	58	57	58	58	59	60	62	62	64	66	67	69	70	69	68	68	66	63	60
Dana Point, Calif.	57	57	59	60	62	62	63	65	67	67	68	68	68	67	66	65	64	61	58
Balboa, Calif.	57	57	58	59	59	60	62	63	64	65	66	67	67	65	65	65	63	61	59
Newport Beach, Calif.	58	60	60	60	61	63	64	66	66	69	69	70	69	69	68	68	65	64	61
Los Angeles	58	58	60	60	60	61	61	62	64	65	67	68	68	67	66	66	66	64	60
Santa Monica, Calif.	57	57	58	58	59	60	61	63	65	66	67	68	68	67	66	65	63	61	59
Zuma Beach, Calif.	57	57	57	57	57	57	58	59	60	61	63	66	66	65	64	64	62	61	58
Point Mugu, Calif.	57	57	56	55	54	55	56	58	58	59	60	62	61	61	62	62	60	60	59
Anacapa Island, Calif.	56	56	56	56	57	58	59	60	61	63	64	65	65	65	64	64	63	61	59
Port Hueneme, Calif.	56	56	56	56	56	57	57	58	60	60	62	62	62	62	62	62	61	60	58
Ventura, Calif.	55	57	58	59	59	60	61	62	64	64	65	67	67	66	65	65	62	60	56
Santa Barbara, Calif.	56	57	57	58	58	59	60	61	62	63	63	64	65	64	64	64	62	60	57
Gaviota, Calif.	57	57	56	56	57	57	58	58	60	62	63	64	64	64	63	62	62	61	58
Avila Beach, Calif.	55	56	55	54	54	55	55	56	57	58	60	60	60	60	60	59	59	57	55
Morro Bay, Calif.	54	54	54	53	54	54	55	56	57	57	58	58	58	58	58	57	57	56	55
S. Point Lobos, Calif.	53	53	52	52	51	51	51	52	53	53	54	54	55	55	56	55	55	55	53
Pacific Grove, Calif.	53	54	54	54	55	55	55	56	57	57	57	57	57	58	58	57	56	55	55
Santa Cruz, Calif.	53	54	54	54	54	55	55	56	57	58	59	59	60	60	59	59	59	56	54
Alameda, Calif.	51	54	56	57	60	62	63	64	65	66	66	66	66	66	65	64	61	58	53
Fort Point, Calif.	53	53	54	54	55	55	55	56	58	58	58	59	60	60	60	59	58	56	55
Bodega Bay, Calif.	52	52	52	51	50	50	50	51	51	51	53	53	54	54	55	55	54	54	53
Medocino, Calif.	52	52	50	50	50	50	50	51	51	51	51	52	52	53	53	54	53	53	53
Crescent City, Calif.	50	51	51	51	52	53	54	54	56	57	58	59	59	58	56	54	54	53	51
Port Orford, Ore.	50	50	50	50	50	50	51	51	51	51	51	51	53	53	53	52	52	52	51
Charleston, Ore.	50	50	51	51	52	52	53	54	55	55	55	55	55	55	55	53	53	53	50
Newport, Ore.	49	50	50	50	50	51	53	55	55	55	55	55	55	55	56	54	53	53	52
Seaside, Ore.	49	49	50	51	51	53	55	57	58	58	58	58	58	58	57	55	54	53	51
Astoria, Ore.	42	42	46	48	52	56	58	60	62	64	67	68	67	67	64	61	57	52	45
Umatilla Lightship, Wa.	48	47	47	48	49	50	51	53	54	54	55	55	55	56	56	54	53	52	50
Neah Bay, Wa.	45	46	47	48	49	50	51	52	53	53	53	53	53	53	52	52	51	49	47
Port Townsend, Wa.	44	44	46	47	48	49	50	51	52	53	54	54	54	54	53	52	51	50	46
Seattle, Wa.	47	46	46	48	49	50	51	53	54	55	56	56	56	56	55	54	53	51	49

Source: National Oceanic and Atmospheric Administration   1 - first half of the month   2 - second half of the month

Gulf of Mexico water temperatures (°F)

Locations	Jan.	Feb.	Mar.	April	May	June	July	Aug.	Sept.	Oct.	Nov.	Dec.
Key West, Fla.	71	72	75	78	82	85	87	87	86	82	76	72
Naples, Fla.	66	66	71	77	82	86	87	87	86	81	73	68
St. Petersburg, Fla.	62	64	68	74	80	84	86	86	84	78	70	64
Cedar Key, Fla.	58	60	66	73	80	84	86	86	83	76	66	60
Pensacola, Fla.	56	58	63	71	78	84	85	86	82	74	65	58
Dauphin Island, Ala.	51	53	60	70	75	82	84	84	80	72	62	56
Grand Isle, La.	61	61	64	70	77	83	85	85	83	77	70	65
Eugene Island, La.	51	53	60	68	76	83	85	85	82	74	63	55
Galveston, Texas	54	55	61	71	78	83	86	86	83	75	67	59
Galveston Channel, Texas	56	58	62	71	78	84	86	87	83	76	66	59
Freeport, Texas	53	56	62	71	77	82	84	85	82	75	66	59
Port Mansfield, Texas	58	61	66	75	79	83	85	85	83	76	69	62
South Padre Island, Texas	58	60	64	70	77	79	79	80	83	78	71	64
Ciudad Madero, Mexico	67	68	71	77	81	83	84	84	82	80	76	71
Tuxpan, Mexico	68	70	72	78	82	83	83	84	82	80	76	72
Veracruz, Mexico	72	73	74	78	81	83	84	85	84	82	78	74
Alvarado, Mexico	72	73	75	78	81	82	80	82	80	78	76	74
Coatzacoalcos, Mexico	73	75	78	82	84	84	81	82	81	78	76	74
Carmen, Mexico	77	77	78	80	82	84	84	84	84	83	80	78
Progreso, Mexico	76	76	78	79	81	82	82	82	82	82	80	77
Buoy 42003	75	76	77	78	80	83	85	85	84	82	81	79
Buoy 42001	73	71	70	74	78	82	84	85	84	81	77	75
Buoy 42002	71	69	70	73	77	82	85	86	84	82	78	74

cold air from the ocean. The Chesapeake and Long Island Sound don't have such strong ocean sea breezes because large intervening land masses block the strong ocean winds. In summer these places often get a local sea breeze with flukey winds — one day may bring a great afternoon of sailing, the next, a dying breeze that seems to come from every direction at once.

Tables on the next two pages give wind speeds along the U.S. coasts.

Weather guide for hikers

Thousands of people hike every year on the Appalachian Trail from Georgia to Maine and on the Pacific Crest Trail from the Mexican border across California, Oregon and Washington to the Canadian border.

Harsh winter weather is the norm for both trails, which means late spring, summer and early fall are the most popular hiking seasons.

The climate information about the Appalachian and Pacific Crest trails on the following pages is from points near the trails where weather observations have been taken for enough years to establish average temperatures and precipitation. Observation locations are not on the trails themselves, and are usually at lower elevations than most points on the trails.

Maps and guide books available through the Appalachian Trail Conference and the Pacific Crest Trail Association give elevations for various parts of the trails. As a rule of thumb, the temperature

East Coast wind speeds (mph)

U.S. coastal station	Jan.	Feb.	Mar.	April	May	June	July	Aug.	Sept.	Oct.	Nov.	Dec.
Eastport, Maine	14	13	13	11	10	8	8	7	9	11	12	13
Brunswick, Maine	9	9	10	10	9	7	7	7	7	7	8	9
Portland, Maine	9	10	10	10	9	8	8	8	8	9	9	9
Boston	14	14	14	14	12	11	11	11	12	12	13	14
Nantucket, Mass.	15	15	15	15	13	12	11	11	12	13	13	14
Block Island, R.I.	20	20	19	17	15	14	13	12	14	17	19	20
Bridgeport, Conn.	13	14	14	13	12	10	10	10	11	12	13	13
Suffolk County, L.I., N.Y.	11	11	11	11	9	9	8	8	9	9	9	10
J.F.K. International Airport, N.Y.	13	14	14	13	12	11	10	10	11	11	12	13
Lakehurst, N.J.	10	11	11	10	9	8	7	7	7	7	8	9
Atlantic City, N.J.	12	12	13	12	11	10	9	9	9	10	11	12
Wallops Island, Va.	11	13	13	12	12	10	9	9	10	10	11	12
Norfolk, Va.	12	12	13	12	10	10	9	9	10	11	12	11
Cape Hatteras, N.C.	13	13	13	13	12	11	11	10	11	12	12	12
Wilmington, N.C.	10	11	11	11	10	9	8	8	8	9	9	9
Myrtle Beach, S.C.	7	8	8	8	7	7	7	7	7	6	6	6
Charleston, S.C.	9	10	10	10	9	9	8	8	8	8	8	9
Savannah, Ga.	9	10	10	9	8	8	7	7	8	8	8	8
Brunswick, Ga.	7	7	7	7	7	6	6	5	6	6	6	6
Jacksonville, Fla.	9	10	10	9	9	9	8	8	9	9	9	8
Daytona Beach, Fla.	9	10	10	10	9	9	8	8	9	10	9	9
Cape Kennedy, Fla.	10	11	11	11	10	8	7	7	9	9	9	9
West Palm Beach, Fla.	10	10	11	11	10	8	8	7	9	10	10	10
Miami Beach, Fla.	12	12	13	13	12	11	11	11	12	14	13	12
Key West, Fla.	12	12	13	13	11	10	10	9	10	11	12	12

Data extracted from Local Climatological Data publications (EDS), Station Climatic Summaries (U.S. Navy), and Climatic Briefs (USAF). Prepared by the National Climatic Center, Asheville, N.C.

decreases about 3.5°F for each 1,000 feet of elevation gained. Also, rain and snow are likely to be heavier at higher elevations.

Snow can remain on higher elevations long after spring has come to the valleys, especially along the New England portions of the Appalachian Trail and along much of the Pacific Crest Trail.

In addition to generally being cooler, wetter and windier than lower elevations, long portions of both trails are wilderness areas. Help can be far away.

Hypothermia, a lowering of the body's core temperature, is the biggest danger of outdoor activities. Hypothermia can be fatal.

Frigid temperatures aren't needed for hypothermia. A combination of weather in the 50s and rain that leaves a hiker soaked can lead to fatal hypothermia. Wind can chill a cold, wet victim even faster.

Hikers, even in the arid West, should be prepared for chilly winds and rain in the summer.

The first defense is to stay dry. Wet clothing has little insulating value and some materials are worse than others. Cotton is the quickest to become

Average Gulf of Mexico wind speeds (mph)

	J	F	M	A	M	J	J	A	S	O	N	D
Tampa, Fla.	9	9	9	9	9	8	7	7	8	9	8	8
Pensacola, Fla.	9	9	10	9	9	8	7	7	8	8	8	9
Mobile, Ala.	10	11	11	10	9	8	7	7	8	8	9	10
Lake Charles, La.	10	10	11	10	9	8	7	6	7	8	9	10
Galveston, Texas	12	12	12	12	12	11	10	9	10	10	11	11
Corpus Christi, Texas	12	13	14	14	13	12	12	11	10	10	12	12
Brownsville, Texas	11	12	13	14	13	12	11	10	9	9	11	11

Average Pacific Coast wind speeds (mph)

	J	F	M	A	M	J	J	A	S	O	N	D
San Diego, Calif.	6	7	8	8	8	8	7	7	7	7	6	6
Los Angeles, Calif.	7	7	8	9	8	8	8	8	7	7	7	7
Santa Barbara, Calif.	5	6	7	8	7	7	6	6	6	6	5	5
San Francisco, Calif.	7	9	11	12	13	14	14	13	11	9	8	7
Eureka, Calif.	7	7	8	8	8	7	7	6	6	6	6	6
Astoria, Ore.	9	9	9	9	9	9	9	8	8	8	9	9
Quillayute, Wash.	7	7	7	6	6	6	6	5	5	6	6	7
Puget Sound												
Seattle, Wash.	10	10	10	10	9	9	8	8	8	9	9	10
Hawaii												
Hilo	8	8	8	8	7	7	7	7	7	7	7	7
Honolulu	10	10	11	12	12	13	13	13	11	11	11	10
Kahului	11	11	12	13	13	15	16	15	13	12	12	11
Lihue	11	12	13	13	13	13	14	13	12	11	12	12

Average Great Lakes Coasts wind speeds

	J	F	M	A	M	J	J	A	S	O	N	D
Lake Ontario												
Rochester, N.Y.	12	11	11	11	9	9	8	8	8	9	10	11
Toronto, Canada	13	12	13	13	10	9	8	7	8	9	12	13
Lake Erie												
Buffalo, N.Y.	14	14	13	13	11	11	10	10	10	11	13	13
Cleveland, Ohio	12	12	12	12	10	9	9	8	9	10	12	12
Toledo, Ohio	11	11	11	11	10	8	7	7	8	9	10	11
Lake Huron												
Alpena, Mich.	9	8	9	9	8	8	7	7	7	8	9	9
Lake Michigan												
Muskegon, Mich.	13	12	12	12	10	9	9	9	9	11	12	12
Chicago, Ill.	12	12	12	12	11	9	8	8	9	10	11	11
Milwaukee, Wis.	13	12	13	13	12	10	10	10	10	11	13	12
Green Bay, Wis.	11	11	11	11	10	9	8	8	9	10	11	11
Lake Superior												
S.Ste. Marie, Mich.	10	9	10	10	10	9	8	8	9	9	10	10
Duluth, Minn.	12	11	12	13	12	11	9	9	10	11	12	11

soaked and lose its ability to insulate against cold. This means blue jeans are not appropriate hiking clothes. Wool is much better than cotton, but some of the synthetic fabrics can be the best.

Both the Appalachian Trail Conference and Pacific Crest Trail Association can supply information about safely using the trails, which includes recommendations about clothing and equipment.

How to contact them:

Pacific Crest Trail Association
1350 Castle Rock Road
Walnut Creek, Calif. 94598

Appalachian Trail Conference
P.O. 807
Harpers Ferry, W.Va. 25425

The Pacific Crest Trail

There is no single weather pattern on the Pacific Crest Trail. It traverses some of the highest mountains in the United States where snow can occur any month of the year. It also crosses deserts where temperatures can be in the 120°F range.

Parts of the trail can receive more than 400 inches of snow a year and more than 100 inches of precipitation — melted snow and rain.

In general, summer is the best time to hike the higher elevations of the trail, but water can be hard to find. Anyone planning to hike on the trail should contact the Pacific Crest Trail Association for information — especially about where to find water and what kind of special precautions hikers should take on different sections of the trail.

Outdoors recreation areas

The United States offers a variety of recreational areas unmatched by any other nation.

Hawaii, Puerto Rico and the Virgin Islands are tropical. Beaches in Florida and along the Gulf Coast are nearly tropical. The Southwest offers deserts and California has a climate much like that around the Mediterranean Sea.

Northern Alaska is in the Arctic. Other parts of Alaska and the higher elevations of the West have frigid winters and summers that can see snow any month of the year.

Travelers from Europe and the Eastern U.S. can be unprepared for the sudden changes the weather

Appalachian Trail climate April – October

All temperatures in degrees Fahrenheit. All precipitation in inches

Location and elevation	Temperatures Average highs and lows							Precipitation Wettest Driest (in.)		
	A	M	J	J	A	S	O			
1 Greenville, Maine 1,060 feet	48° 26°	62° 37°	72° 47°	77° 52°	74° 50°	67° 42°	55° 34°	July 4.02	April 3.20	
2 Mt. Washington, N.H. 6,252 feet	31° 17°	36° 23°	51° 39°	53° 42°	54° 43°	44° 34°	30° 16°	Aug. 7.19	April 5.46	
3 Barre-Montpelier, Vt. 1,122 feet	51° 31°	64° 41°	74° 51°	78° 55°	76° 52°	68° 44°	58° 36°	Aug. 3.22	Sept. 2.66	
4 Somerset, Vt. 2,080 feet	48° 27°	61° 38°	70° 47°	75° 51°	73° 49°	66° 42°	56° 33°	Sept. 4.92	Oct. 4.00	
5 Pittsfield, Mass. 1,170 feet	53° 33°	66° 43°	75° 52°	79° 56°	78° 55°	69° 47°	59° 37°	July 4.89	Oct. 3.25	
6 Bear Mountain, N.Y. 1,300 feet	55° 38°	66° 48°	75° 57°	79° 63°	77° 61°	70° 54°	61° 44°	July 5.66	Oct. 3.41	
7 Pocono, Pa. 1,915 feet	58° 33°	67° 43°	76° 51°	80° 56°	77° 54°	70° 47°	60° 38°	Aug. 5.25	Oct. 4.32	
8 Harrisburg, Pa. 338 feet	64° 42°	75° 52°	83° 61°	87° 65°	85° 63°	78° 56°	67° 45°	May 3.76	Oct. 2.57	
9 Hagerstown, Md. 560 feet	63° 40°	74° 50°	82° 59°	86° 63°	84° 61°	78° 54°	67° 43°	May 3.62	Oct. 2.49	
10 Big Meadows, Va. 3,535 feet	59° 37°	67° 46°	74° 54°	76° 57°	75° 56°	69° 50°	60° 41°	Aug. 5.47	April 3.63	
11 Peaks of Otter, Va. 2,605 feet	64° 43°	72° 52°	77° 58°	81° 63°	79° 62°	73° 56°	63° 46°	Aug. 5.50	April 3.51	
12 Burkes Garden, Va. 3,300 feet	62° 38°	70° 45°	76° 52°	79° 56°	78° 55°	73° 48°	64° 38°	July 4.78	Oct. 2.39	
13 Banner Elk, N.C. 3,710 feet	61° 36°	69° 44°	75° 52°	77° 55°	77° 54°	73° 48°	64° 38°	July 5.47	Oct. 3.34	
14 Gatlinburg, Tenn. 1,454 feet	71° 42°	79° 50°	86° 58°	88° 59°	87° 60°	83° 55°	73° 43°	July 6.37	Oct. 3.03	
15 Blairsville, Ga. 1,917 feet	70° 41°	77° 49°	83° 57°	85° 61°	85° 60°	80° 54°	71° 42°	July 5.11	Oct. 3.09	

can undergo in the West. Travelers from the West can be unprepared for the combination of heat and humidity that arrives during Eastern summers.

The descriptions of the climates of recreation areas on the following pages are a general guide to what kind of weather to expect.

For anyone planning to stay close to roads and lodges, these guides should help ensure that a visit isn't ruined by completely unexpected weather. And they should help in decisions about the best times of the year to visit.

Anyone planning to venture off paved roads on long hikes, horseback trips or river journeys should consult rangers, outfitters, guides or others who know the area and its weather.

Since many recreation areas are far from regular National Weather Service offices, less data is available than for cities. Most of the information in the listings here is based on data, often from volunteer weather observers, collected by the National Climatic Data Center. In some cases, complete data is not available and only average temperatures and precipitation are given.

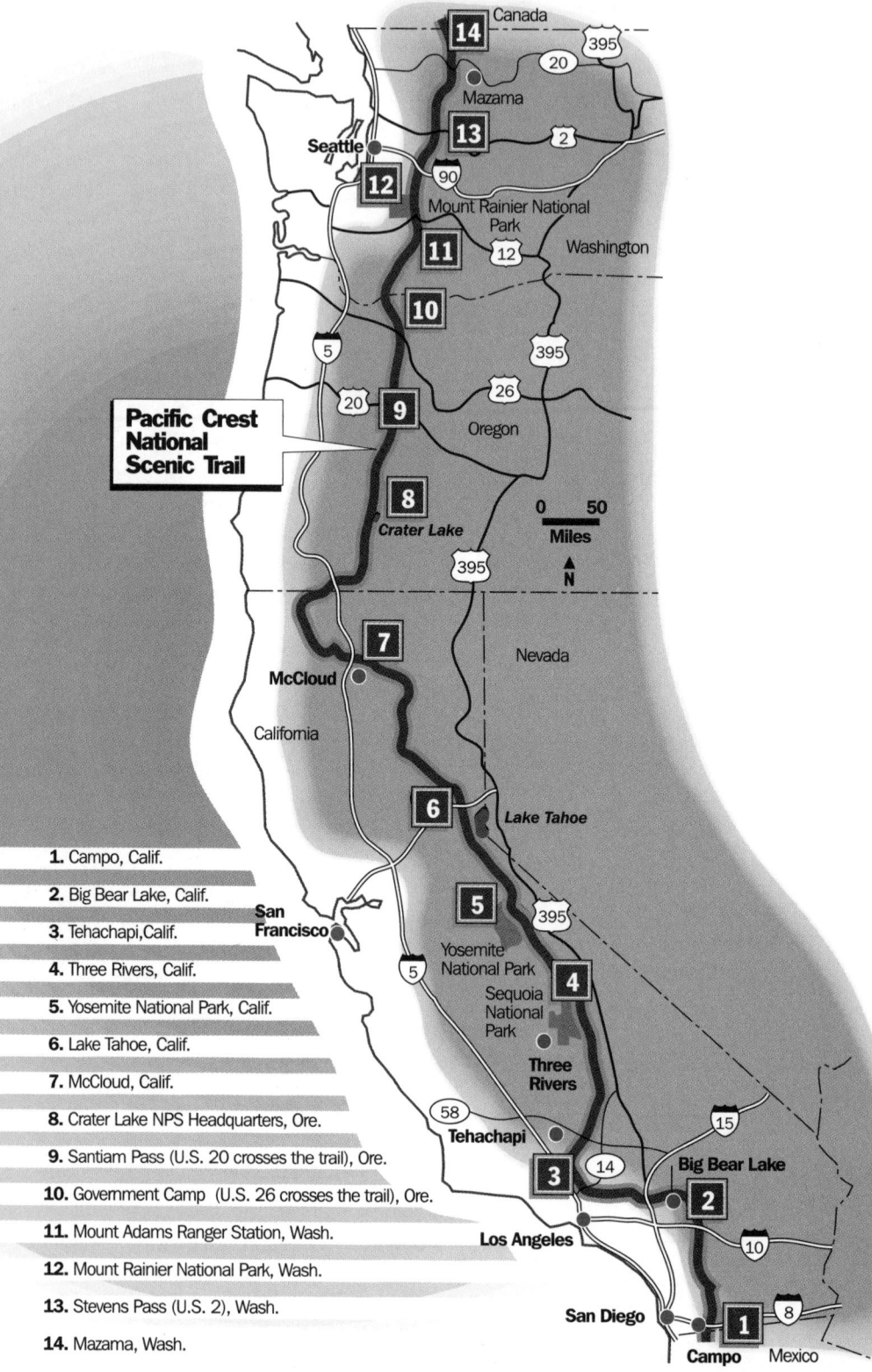

Pacific Crest
National
Scenic Trail

0   50
Miles

N

1. Campo, Calif.
2. Big Bear Lake, Calif.
3. Tehachapi,Calif.
4. Three Rivers, Calif.
5. Yosemite National Park, Calif.
6. Lake Tahoe, Calif.
7. McCloud, Calif.
8. Crater Lake NPS Headquarters, Ore.
9. Santiam Pass (U.S. 20 crosses the trail), Ore.
10. Government Camp (U.S. 26 crosses the trail), Ore.
11. Mount Adams Ranger Station, Wash.
12. Mount Rainier National Park, Wash.
13. Stevens Pass (U.S. 2), Wash.
14. Mazama, Wash.

Pacific Crest Trail Climate

All temperatures in degrees Fahrenheit. All precipitation in inches.

1. Campo, Calif.
Latitude: 32° 38' N
Longitude: 116° 28' W
Elevation: 2,630 ft.

	Avg. high	Avg. low	Avg. precip.
Jan.	62	34	2.5
Feb.	64	34	2.32
March	65	35	2.56
April	71	36	1.08
May	77	40	0.27
June	86	45	0.07
July	94	52	0.32
Aug.	93	53	0.56
Sept.	88	49	0.44
Oct.	79	42	0.62
Nov.	69	36	1.74
Dec.	62	33	2.27

2. Big Bear Lake, Calif.
Latitude 34° 15' N
Longitude: 116° 53'
Elevation: 6,790 ft.

	high	low	precip.
Jan.	47	19	4.01
Feb.	49	21	3.75
March	50	23	3.53
April	57	28	1.53
May	66	34	0.5
June	75	40	0.12
July	80	47	0.82
Aug.	79	46	0.99
Sept.	73	40	0.62
Oct.	65	31	0.6
Nov.	54	25	2.54
Dec.	48	20	3.48

3. Tehachapi, Calif.
Latitude: 35° 8' N
Longitude: 118° 27' W
Elevation: 4,017 ft.

	high	low	precip.
Jan.	53	31	1.6
Feb.	55	32	1.62
March	57	34	1.98
April	63	37	0.87
May	71	44	0.41
June	80	52	0.11
July	87	58	0.09
Aug.	86	56	0.39
Sept.	80	50	0.34
Oct.	71	41	0.4
Nov.	59	35	1.48
Dec.	52	31	1.57

4. Three Rivers, Calif.
Latitude: 36° 28' N
Longitude: 118° 52' W
Elevation: 1,140 ft.

	Avg. high	Avg. low	Avg. precip.
Jan.	59	34	4.76
Feb.	64	38	4.11
March	68	41	4.32
April	75	44	2.35
May	84	51	0.7
June	93	58	0.27
July	100	64	0.04
Aug.	98	63	0.1
Sept.	92	57	0.75
Oct.	82	49	1.05
Nov.	67	40	3.28
Dec.	58	35	3.65

5. Yosemite National Park
(See Yosemite National Park in Recreation section)

6. Lake Tahoe, Calif.
(See the Lake Tahoe Region in Recreation section)

7. McCloud, Calif.
Latitude: 41° 15'N
Longitude: 122° 8'W
Elevation: 3,280 ft.

	high	low	precip.
Jan.	47	23	8.49
Feb.	50	26	7.07
March	53	28	7.13
April	60	31	3.33
May	70	37	1.95
June	79	44	0.77
July	87	48	0.23
Aug.	86	46	0.48
Sept.	80	40	1.1
Oct.	69	34	3.28
Nov.	53	29	7.57
Dec.	47	24	7.83

8. Crater Lake, Ore.
(See listing under "Oregon Cascades" in the Recreation section)

9. Santiam Pass, Ore.
Latitude: 44° 25'N
Longitude: 121° 52'W
Elevation: 4,748 ft.

	Avg. high	Avg. low	Avg. precip.
Jan.	33	20	12.22
Feb.	36	22	9.06
March	40	24	8.24
April	45	26	5.31
May	52	31	3.55
June	63	37	2.91
July	72	43	1.12
Aug.	71	43	1.65
Sept.	62	38	3.2
Oct.	52	32	5.55
Nov.	39	25	11.5
Dec.	34	21	12.98

10. Government Camp, Ore.
(See the listing under Oregon Cascades in the Recreation section)

11. Mount Adams, Wash. Ranger Station
Latitude: 46° 0' N
Longitude: 121° 32'W
Elevation: 1,960 ft.

	high	low	precip.
Jan.	37	23	8.05
Feb.	43	27	5.93
March	50	29	4.65
April	58	33	2.06
May	67	38	1.28
June	75	45	0.99
July	83	48	0.36
Aug.	82	47	0.84
Sept.	74	41	1.4
Oct.	62	34	2.97
Nov.	45	30	7.21
Dec.	37	25	8.07

12. Mount Rainier National Park, Wash.
(see Mount Rainier National Park listing in Recreation section.)

13. Stevens Pass, Wash.
Latitude: 47° 44'N
Longitude: 121° 5'W
Elevation: 4,070 ft.

	Avg. high	Avg. low	Avg. precip.
Jan.	29	19	13.69
Feb.	32	22	9.19
March	36	23	7.56
April	41	27	4.98
May	49	33	3.55
June	57	40	2.86
July	65	45	1.43
Aug.	66	46	1.99
Sept.	58	40	3.43
Oct.	47	33	6.49
Nov.	34	25	12.16
Dec.	29	20	13.69

14. Mazama, Wash.
Latitude: 48° 37' N
Longitude: 120° 27' W
Elevation: 2,170 ft.

	high	low	precip.
Jan.	28	12	4.23
Feb.	37	16	2.47
March	46	24	1.71
April	57	30	1.08
May	66	39	0.99
June	75	46	0.84
July	82	50	0.69
Aug.	82	50	0.85
Sept.	72	40	1.01
Oct.	57	30	1.63
Nov.	38	23	3.25
Dec.	28	13	4.44

Terms used in ski reports

Most ski areas offer snow condition reports by phone, radio or TV. Generally they use standard terms to describe conditions. "Primary" conditions are true for at least 70 percent of the ski area. "Secondary" conditions are for at least 20 percent of the area.

Sno Country Reports, a national snow condition reporting service in Woodstock, Vt., uses these definitions in its ski reports:

Corn snow: Usually found in the spring, corn snow is characterized by large, loose granules during the day, which freeze together at night.

Frozen granular: A hard surface of old snow formed by granules freezing together after rain or warm temperatures. It is different from icy conditions. Unlike ice, frozen granular is opaque and will support a ski pole stuck into the surface.

Hard packed: Natural or machine-made snow that is very firmly packed. It has never melted and recrystallized, but is tightly compressed by grooming and wind. You can plant a pole in hard-packed snow, but not as easily as in packed powder.

Unlike frozen granular snow, hard-packed snow is generally white.

Icy: Not to be confused with frozen granular, ice is a hard, glazed surface created by freezing rain, ground water seeping up into the snow and freezing, or by the rapid freezing of snow that is saturated with water. Ice is usually translucent and will not support a ski pole.

Loose granular: The surface left after powder or packed powder thaws, then refreezes and recrystallizes. The same surface can result from an accumulation of sleet or from machine grooming of frozen or icy snow.

Machine groomed: Loose granular snow that is repeatedly groomed by power tillers so that the texture is between that of loose granular and packed powder. Some of the snow is granular and some is so pulverized that the crystals are like fine powdered sugar.

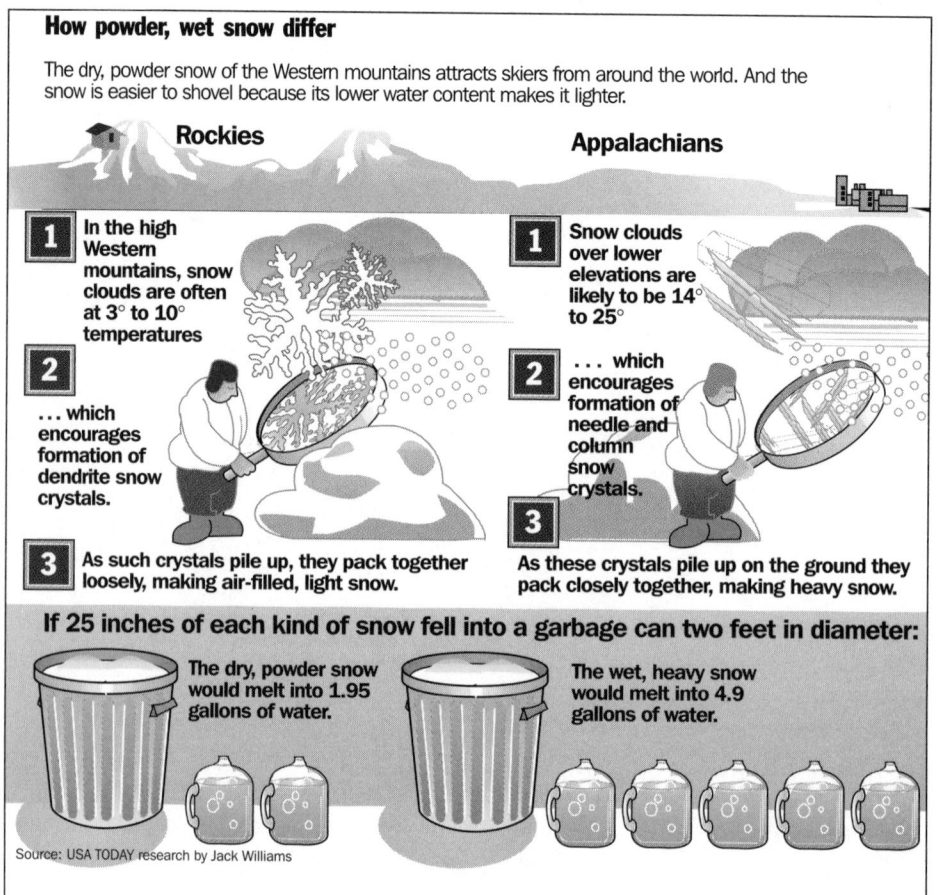

How powder, wet snow differ

The dry, powder snow of the Western mountains attracts skiers from around the world. And the snow is easier to shovel because its lower water content makes it lighter.

Rockies

1 In the high Western mountains, snow clouds are often at 3° to 10° temperatures

2 ... which encourages formation of dendrite snow crystals.

3 As such crystals pile up, they pack together loosely, making air-filled, light snow.

Appalachians

1 Snow clouds over lower elevations are likely to be 14° to 25°

2 ... which encourages formation of needle and column snow crystals.

3 As these crystals pile up on the ground they pack closely together, making heavy snow.

If 25 inches of each kind of snow fell into a garbage can two feet in diameter:

The dry, powder snow would melt into 1.95 gallons of water.

The wet, heavy snow would melt into 4.9 gallons of water.

Source: USA TODAY research by Jack Williams

Packed powder: Powder snow, either natural or machine-made, that is packed down by skiers or grooming machines. The snow is no longer fluffy, but it is not so compacted that it is hard.

Powder: New, loose, fluffy, dry snow that is not compacted. It's usually from fresh, natural snowfall.

Spring conditions: Used only after March 1 when no single term can describe at least 70 percent of the surface open to skiing. Bare spots are likely.

Wet granular: Loose or frozen granular snow that became wet from rain or melting in high temperatures.

Wet packed: Natural or machine-made snow that was previously packed and then became wet, usually from rain.

Wet snow: Powder snow that was moistened by rain or by partial thawing or snow that was moist as it fell.

Windblown snow: Wind can blow either powder or granular snow into drifts in some places, leaving a firmly packed base of snow.

National parks and recreation areas, state by state

Alaska

While northern Alaska is above the Arctic Circle, the state is hardly the "frozen North." Alaska has a variety of weather, as shown in the *Almanac's* city listings for Anchorage, Barrow, Fairbanks, Juneau, Nome and St. Paul Island. Here is information on the Alaska Highway, the main route to the state from the lower 48 states, and on three Alaskan regions of special interest to travelers.

The Alaska Highway: Driving the Alaska Highway all the way north is a dream of many travelers longing for a little adventure. Those planning this trip should have information about highway conditions and a vehicle in good shape. The climate tables here show why summer is the best time. Built during World War II, the "highway" was unpaved until recently. Over the past few years it finally was paved, but don't expect interstate-quality highway. The freezing and thawing of the ground under the road create "frost heaves," or ridges and valleys that can make for a rough ride.

Anchorage to Valdez, Alaska: Prince William Sound with its wooded islands and the glacier-filled Chugach Mountains are the dominant features in this area. They can be explored by car on an inland highway and by ferry and cruise ship.

Dawson Creek, British Columbia, Canada

(On Alaska Highway)
Lat. 55° 44'N, Lon. 120° 11'W, Elev. 2,146 ft.

	Record high temp.	Avg. high temp.	Avg. low temp.	Record low temp.	Avg. precip. (inches)
Jan.	52	19	0	-55	1.19
Feb.	60	22	2	-53	1.43
March	57	32	12	-45	1.15
April	71	49	27	-37	0.79
May	86	61	35	10	1.39
June	89	68	43	28	2.52
July	94	74	48	30	1.24
Aug.	93	72	46	29	1.33
Sept.	88	61	38	14	1.12
Oct.	80	50	30	-13	1.39
Nov.	66	34	16	-43	1.45
Dec.	52	25	7	-48	1.33

(Snowfall measurements not available for Dawson Creek)

Whitehorse, Yukon, Canada

(On Alaska Highway)
Lat. 60° 43'N, Lon. 135° 04'W, Elev. 2,303 ft.

	Record high temp.	Avg. high temp.	Avg. low temp.	Record low temp.	Avg. precip. (inches)	Avg. snow (inches)
Jan.	47	13	-3	-62	20.64	6.4
Feb.	50	16	-2	-59	0.47	4.7
March	51	31	12	-37	0.6	6.0
April	69	41	22	-15	0.41	3.9
May	86	57	34	11	0.57	0.8
June	89	66	43	27	1	0
July	91	67	45	29	1.63	0
Aug.	86	64	43	17	1.53	0.1
Sept.	80	55	37	14	1.34	0.9
Oct.	66	41	28	-12	0.71	3.9
Nov.	51	21	8	-43	0.98	9.1
Dec.	47	11	-4	-54	0.75	7.4

The area is divided into three climatic zones:

• Prince William Sound has a marine climate characterized by heavy precipitation, relatively warm winters and cool summers.

• The northern slopes of the Chugach Mountains have a continental climate with light precipitation, cold winters and mild summers.

• The transition zone between the two is sometimes marine, sometimes continental and sometimes neither. This is a narrow zone that travelers might not notice as different from areas on either side.

Prince George, British Columbia, Canada

(On route from West Coast to connect with Alaska Highway)
Lat. 53° 53'N, Lon. 122° 41'W, Elev. 2,268 ft.

	Record high temp.	Avg. high temp.	Avg. low temp.	Record low temp.	Avg. precip. (inches)	Avg. snow (inches)
Jan.	49	23	3	-58	1.81	16.2
Feb.	55	31	6	-49	1.21	10.1
March	64	42	18	-36	1.44	8.1
April	74	54	27	-14	0.84	0.6
May	86	64	34	17	1.34	0
June	93	70	42	27	2.06	0
July	94	75	44	29	1.63	0
Aug.	92	74	43	25	1.94	0
Sept.	81	65	36	10	2.00	0.2
Oct.	76	52	30	-14	1.99	1.7
Nov.	61	38	21	-43	1.87	10
Dec.	53	25	8	-50	1.85	15.8

Valdez, Alaska

Lat. 61° 8'N, Lon. 146° 21'W, Elev. 23 ft.

	Avg. high temp.	Avg. low temp.	Avg. precip. (inches)	Avg. snow (inches)	Wet days
Jan.	25	11	5.79	56	12
Feb.	29	14	4.88	47	11
March	34	18	3.70	37	11
April	43	26	2.96	13	11
May	52	34	3.48	2	14
June	59	42	2.61	0	13
July	60	45	4.72	T	16
Aug.	60	43	6.48	0	19
Sept.	54	38	8.39	0.1	19
Oct.	43	31	7.95	8	18
Nov.	32	20	6.27	31	13
Dec.	26	13	5.15	50	13

T = Trace

Glennallen, Alaska

(In Chugach Mountains)
Lat. 62° 7'N, Lon. 145° 32'W, Elev. 1,456 ft.

	Avg. high temp.	Avg. low temp.	Avg. precip. (inches)	Avg. snow (inches)	Wet days
Jan.	-2.7	-27.8	.29	5.8	4
Feb.	18.5	-8.4	.77	6.9	5
March	32.4	0.4	.23	2.9	3
April	43.4	16.7	.11	1.6	2
May	56.4	28.1	.60	0.3	7
June	67.5	39.6	1.44	0	10
July	69.3	42.2	1.51	0	10
Aug.	64.7	36.6	1.17	0	9
Sept.	54.6	25.8	1.02	1.5	7
Oct.	35.4	11.9	0.57	6.6	5
Nov.	16.9	-3.6	0.57	9.9	7
Dec.	3.3	-20.1	.63	5.5	7

As in any mountainous terrain, winds are variable in direction and speed. This is critical on Prince William Sound, especially on the Valdez Arm where several valleys funnel wind with dramatic changes in speed. Winds here can gust to 100 mph in winter, 60 mph in summer.

Denali National Park, Mount McKinley, Alaska: Because of its severe winters, most visitors come to Denali National Park from June into early September.

Mount McKinley, at 20,320 feet, is the highest mountain in North America and dominates the park and surrounding area. As with any large mountain, weather changes can be extreme. At any time of the year hurricane-force winds, snow and bitter cold are possible.

The park's terrain also includes lowlands and stream valleys with a variety of plants and animals. In this part of Alaska annual snowfall varies from less than 60 inches to more than 100 inches.

Throughout the summer, four-day rainy periods are likely an average of once a month; four straight days of dry weather are likely twice a month.

Weather observations are taken at McKinley Park, elevation 2,070 feet, which is the park entrance from the Anchorage-Fairbanks highway. Observations are also taken at Minchumina, northwest of the park about 50 miles from Kantishna in the park's center at an elevation of 684 feet. No observations are available elsewhere in the park..

Southeast Alaska: This part of the state is one of the most scenic areas of the world, with a combination of sea, inland waterways, hundreds of small islands and mountainous, heavily wooded mainland.

The roads are short and local. All travel between towns is by air or water. The best way to see the region is from one of the state-run ferries or by cruise ship. These serve various ports in Alaska, Seattle and Prince Rupert, British Columbia. It's possible to drive to Prince Rupert from the U.S. and take the ferry to Alaska.

Relatively warm ocean water gives this part of Alaska a milder, but also wetter, climate than other parts of the state. Proper rain gear is important.

When using the climate charts here, or the one for Juneau in the cities section of the *Almanac*, be aware that precipitation can vary widely.. Some

McKinley Park, Alaska
Lat. 63° 43'N, Lon. 148° 58'W, Elev. 2,070 ft.

	Avg. high temp.	Avg. low temp.	Avg. precip. (inches)
Jan.	10	-8	0.7
Feb.	14	-6	0.51
March	26	1	0.57
April	38	15	0.38
May	53	29	0.8
June	64	39	2.47
July	67	42	3.19
Aug.	62	39	2.41
Sept.	51	30	1.57
Oct.	32	13	1.06
Nov.	17	-1	0.94
Dec.	12	-6	0.9

Glacier Bay, Alaska
Lat. 58° 27'N, Lon. 135° 53'W, Elev. 50 ft.

	Record high	Avg. high	Avg. low	Record low	Avg. precip. (inches)
		temperatures			
Jan.	41	26	16	-4	3.93
Feb.	45	34	26	-4	4.85
March	48	37	28	7	3.77
April	59	45	33	19	3.52
May	65	53	38	29	3.95
June	76	61	44	37	1.5
July	72	62	48	42	5.55
Aug.	75	60	47	39	7.7
Sept.	60	54	44	31	11.88
Oct.	58	46	37	27	8.93
Nov.	53	37	30	9	10.51
Dec.	45	32	29	5	5.11

Minchumina, Alaska
Lat. 63° 53'N, Lon. 152° 18'W, Elev. 684 ft.

	Record high	Avg. high	Avg. low	Record low	Avg. precip.	Avg. snow	Wet days
		temperatures			(in inches)		
Jan.	47	1	-14	-62	0.67	10.2	2
Feb.	38	6	-10	-62	0.55	8.4	2
March	51	20	-1	-44	0.44	7.6	1
April	67	37	16	-23	0.24	2.7	1
May	84	55	35	-8	0.74	0.4	2
June	89	67	47	31	1.51	0	3
July	88	69	50	38	2.2	0	4
Aug.	83	62	46	28	2.85	0	5
Sept.	74	50	36	14	1.37	1.1	3
Oct.	58	31	19	-15	0.61	6.4	2
Nov.	44	11	-2	-46	0.56	8.5	2
Dec.	38	-1	-14	-59	0.48	7.9	2

Ketchikan, Alaska
Lat. 55° 21'N, Lon. 131° 39'W, Elev. 80 ft.

	Record high	Avg. high	Avg. low	Record low	Avg. precip. (inches)
		temperatures			
Jan.	62	40	30	-8	13.90
Feb.	63	42	31	2	11.24
March	69	45	33	3	12.29
April	73	51	36	12	12.12
May	93	58	43	25	8.63
June	96	62	48	28	7.23
July	92	65	51	36	8.13
Aug.	88	66	52	34	10.65
Sept.	80	61	48	28	14.08
Oct.	72	53	42	21	22.26
Nov.	65	46	36	10	17.84
Dec.	62	41	32	-1	15.64

mountains will receive heavy rain or snow, while also shielding nearby areas. Temperatures also can vary widely between nearby areas.

Arizona

Grand Canyon National Park, Arizona: Most visitors go to the Grand Canyon for the view. And since people first arrived at the canyon, fog, rain and winter storms sometimes have clouded the otherworldly view. Now, however, air pollution hampers the view more often than natural limitations.

In summer, prevailing winds bring sulfur oxides and other pollutants from urban or industrial areas of southern California, Arizona and New Mexico, forming a regionwide haze that dims the canyon's distinctive colors and textures. In winter, the air comes from less-populated areas to the north much of the time.

Air quality still is better than many other areas, though, and many visitors may wonder what all the fuss is about. At least half the time during the year, the visual range at the Grand Canyon rim is 107 miles. This means a black object can be seen from that distance. In the eastern U.S., Europe and much of Asia, a visual range of 30 miles would be considered an extraordinarily clear day.

Those concerned with Grand Canyon visibility point out that people come expecting unusually clear air and sharp views of the canyon. They con-

Prince Rupert, British Columbia, Canada

Lat. 54° 17'N, Lon. 130° 27'W, Elev. 111 ft.

	Record high	Avg. high	Avg. low	Record low	Avg. precip.	Avg. snow	Wet days
		temperatures			(in inches)		
Jan.	64	39	30	-3	9.76	12.4	14
Feb.	66	42	31	2	7.57	7	13
March	68	45	33	15	8.43	8.6	17
April	74	50	37	22	6.67	3.3	14
May	84	55	41	29	5.30	0	12
June	90	60	46	34	4.05	0	8
July	87	62	49	33	4.76	0	9
Aug.	86	64	51	39	5.15	0	9
Sept.	79	60	47	30	7.72	0	14
Oct.	71	53	42	22	12.22	0.1	21
Nov.	68	46	37	14	12.25	1.9	21
Dec.	66	40	32	1	11.28	7.3	NA

NA = Not Available

Grand Canyon Airport, Arizona

(About 10 miles from the South Rim visitor's center)

Lat. 35° 57'N, Lon. 112° 8'W, Elev. 6,611 ft.

	Record high	Avg. high	Avg. low	Record low	Avg. precip.	Avg. snow	Wet days
		temperatures			(in inches)		
Jan.	68	41	18	-22	1.46	15.8	4
Feb.	65	45	21	-17	1.63	12.6	4
March	74	51	25	-7	1.35	9.7	4
April	81	60	32	9	0.87	3.2	3
May	89	70	39	10	0.65	1.6	2
June	98	81	46	26	0.39	T	1
July	98	84	54	35	1.94	T	4
Aug.	96	81	53	35	2.32	T	5
Sept.	93	76	47	22	1.6	T	3
Oct.	82	65	36	13	1.18	0.9	3
Nov.	78	52	27	-1	0.91	5.3	2
Dec.	70	43	20	-14	1.69	12.5	4

T = Trace

Other areas in Grand Canyon park

	North Rim			Inner Gorge		
	Avg. high temperatures	Avg. low	Avg. precip. (in.)	Avg. high temperatures	Avg. low	Avg. precip. (in.)
Jan.	37	16	3.17	56	36	0.68
Feb.	39	18	3.22	62	42	0.75
March	44	21	2.63	71	48	0.79
April	53	29	1.73	82	56	0.47
May	62	34	1.17	92	63	0.36
June	73	40	0.86	101	72	0.3
July	77	46	1.93	106	78	0.84
Aug.	75	45	2.85	103	75	1.4
Sept.	69	39	1.99	97	69	0.97
Oct.	59	31	1.38	84	58	0.65
Nov.	46	24	1.48	68	46	0.43
Dec.	40	20	2.83	57	37	0.87

sider that clarity as much worthy of preservation as the plants and wildlife of the park.

Fall, winter and spring are the best times to view the Grand Canyon. In winter, cold fronts — the leading edges of masses of clear, cold air — arrive every few days to scour out hazy air in the canyon. Visitors who stay from a few days to a week in winter are almost sure to be there when a cleansing cold front pushes through.

The first day or two after the arrival of a cold front before pollution builds up again offer the best views. Then, over a few days, heavier cold air drains into the canyon, creating an "inversion" with warm air atop cold air. Inversions trap air in the canyon, allowing pollution from nearby sources, including coal-powered generating plants, to build up. The power plant nearest the park has been required to reduce its emissions and winter haze should diminish in the future.

Unlike the winter haze, which comes from a few sources, the summer haze comes from millions of sources — including all of the cars in the Los Angeles area — and no immediate reduction is likely.

Bad weather can help create some of the most photogenic views of the canyon. Sometimes clouds form within the canyon, creating scenes of white clouds and colored rocks for those on the rim. Falling snow and rain often evaporate as they fall into the dry air in the canyon. Snow or rain that evaporates before reaching the ground is called "virga." It can add drama to canyon photos.

The main visitor's center is on the Canyon's South Rim. Facilities are also available at the North Rim. Trails lead to the bottom of the canyon.

The tables here give average monthly weather conditions at the South Rim, as well as average temperatures and precipitation at the North Rim and in the Inner Gorge.

Each area has its own climate. Elevations at the South Rim range from around 6,000 to 7,000 feet. The North Rim is at about 8,000 feet, which makes it cooler and wetter. At the South Rim, snow usually melts between storms. But it tends to stay on the ground all winter at the North.

The floor of the canyon is at about 2,400 feet, and is a completely different climate zone from either rim. Descending into the canyon is like traveling south and west in terms of plant and animal life. The bottom is much like the deserts of south-western Arizona and southeastern California in temperature, precipitation and plant and animal life.

As you might expect in this desert environment, at the bottom afternoon high temperatures are warmer than on the rims. But overnight lows are higher as well. In most climates warm lows, such as July's average of 78°F, tend to indicate high humidity, which slows nighttime cooling and causes higher overnight temperatures. But the canyon is dry. Overnight warmth comes from heat radiated by the canyon's massive rock walls.

Those soaked while rafting down the Colorado River through the canyon dry off quickly in the warm, dry breezes blowing along the bottom of the Grand Canyon.

Arkansas

Hot Springs National Park, Arkansas: The relatively mild southern climate plus the hot springs (normal temperature of 143°F) are attractions here.

Bitter cold air sometimes reaches the region in winter, but cold weather seldom lasts long. Summers tend to be hot and humid — the temperature exceeds 90°F an average of 90 days a year. About a third of the annual precipitation falls from March through May. Summer rain comes mostly from showers or thunderstorms that are brief, but can be downpours.

California

Death Valley, California: Death Valley is famous as the hottest place in the U.S. and one of the hottest in the world.

It is near California's eastern border with Nevada and is lower than sea level.

It easily meets the definition of a desert: a place where the annual evaporation is higher than the precipitation. All the water that falls evaporates; if more fell, it would evaporate, too.

Global climate patterns help make Death Valley a desert. It's on the northern edge of the area where air that rises in the tropics sinks. Air that sinks is warmed and clouds and precipitation are suppressed. On a regional scale, storms moving eastward from the Pacific Ocean lose their moisture over the four mountain ranges between the ocean and Death Valley.

An elevation below sea level also warms the area. As air flows downward it compresses and heats up.

Hot Springs (Arkansas) National Park						
Lat. 34° 31'N, Lon. 93° 3'W, Elev. 680 ft.						
	Record high	Avg. high	Avg. low	Record low	Avg. precip.	Avg. snow
		temperatures			(in inches)	
Jan.	81	54	35	-2	5.3	1.7
Feb.	85	58	37	1	4.8	0.6
March	92	66	43	7	5.2	0.3
April	94	76	52	26	5.9	T
May	103	83	59	36	6.1	0
June	112	91	68	50	4.3	0
July	111	95	71	54	4.2	0
Aug.	115	95	71	52	3.2	0
Sept.	109	89	64	35	3.8	0
Oct.	99	78	54	28	3.5	0
Nov.	89	67	42	15	4.6	0.1
Dec.	80	55	36	9	4.6	0.8
T = Trace						

Death Valley's record high of 134°F was set on July 10, 1913, when a strong, hot wind blew from Nevada's desert and warmed even more as it descended. That remained the world record high temperature until 1922, when a weather station in the Sahara Desert at Azizia, Libya, recorded 136°F, a record that still stands.

As it happens, 1913 also saw the coldest reading ever at Death Valley, 15°F in January. And 1913 was a wet year with 4.54 inches of rain.

In 1984 flash floods closed park roads for several weeks. That year's total was 4.04 inches.

The best time to visit is from November through February, months when temperatures above 100°F have never been reported.

Those who visit in the summer need to be extremely careful. On July 15, 1972, the official temperature recorded in an instrument shelter about five feet above the ground was 128°F. But the temperature on the ground was recorded at 201°F.

Some Death Valley records:
• **Most rain in a year:** 4.60 inches in 1941.
• **Least rain in a year:** 0 in 1929 and 1953.
• **Most consecutive days above 100°F:** 134 in 1974.

Lake Tahoe region, California and Nevada: Interstate highways, Amtrak trains and local airports make the Lake Tahoe region easily accessible to the heavily populated parts of California and the rest of the world, even during the winter.

Lake Tahoe straddles the California-Nevada border. The region's ski areas and other recreation-

| Death Valley, California | | | | | |
| Lat. 36° 28'N, Lon. 116° 52'W, Elev. 194 ft. below sea level | | | | | |
	Record high	Avg. high temperatures	Avg. low	Record low	Avg. precip. (inches)
Jan.	87	65	39	15	0.2
Feb.	91	73	46	27	0.33
March	101	81	54	30	0.18
April	111	88	62	35	0.11
May	120	100	72	42	0.05
June	125	110	81	49	0.01
July	134	116	88	52	0.11
Aug.	126	113	86	65	0.06
Sept.	120	106	81	41	0.1
Oct.	113	91	62	32	0.11
Nov.	97	75	48	24	0.19
Dec.	86	66	40	19	0.19

| South Lake Tahoe, California | | | | | | | |
| Lat. 38° 53'N, Lon. 119° 59'W, Elev. 6,263 ft. | | | | | | | |
	Record high	Avg. high temperatures	Avg. low	Record low	Avg. precip. (inches)	Avg. snow	Wet days
Jan	60	37	17	-15	6.09	58.2	10
Feb.	58	39	18	-12	5.43	45.3	9
March	64	43	22	-5	3.86	35.3	7
April	74	50	26	1	2.15	16.7	5
May	88	59	32	12	1.21	4	3
June	92	69	37	22	0.56	0.3	2
July	93	79	43	26	0.26	0	1
Aug.	94	78	42	28	0.17	0	1
Sept.	87	70	38	21	0.48	0.3	2
Oct.	80	58	31	11	1.61	2.8	3
Nov.	66	47	25	1	3.1	14.1	5
Dec.	58	40	20	-10	5.35	36.4	9

al sites are in both states. The lake is surrounded by the peaks of the Sierra Nevada range.

Interstate 80, running from San Francisco and Sacramento, crosses the mountains in Donner Pass, about 10 miles north of the lake, and descends to Reno, Nev.

In 1869, the first railroad to cross the United States used the Donner Pass route. Today, Amtrak's California Zephyr crosses the pass on its Chicago to San Francisco route. Donner Pass is one reason why many feel the Zephyr follows America's most scenic passenger train route.

A party of settlers led by George and Jacob Donner gave their name to the pass when heavy snow trapped them during the 1846–47 winter. The story of starvation, death — and eventually cannibalism — became part of the folklore of America's westward expansion. Only 45 of 79 men, women and children survived.

Today, even with the best snow-clearing equipment, snow still sometimes closes the highway and railroad routes across Donner Pass, as well as U.S. Route 50, which crosses the mountains on the south side of Lake Tahoe.

This heavy snow also makes the Lake Tahoe Basin one of America's premier ski regions. Like other places in the western mountains, most of the year's precipitation falls as winter snow and fall and spring rain. Enough precipitation falls during the wet season to support thick forests. Summers are generally dry, but thunderstorms do occur.

Most of the moisture from Pacific Ocean winds falls as rain or snow on the western sides of the mountains. The countryside changes from thick forest to desert scrub during the descent from Donner Pass to Reno.

Palm Springs: Palm Springs is in the Coachella Valley desert east of Los Angeles.

The climate is typical of deserts with little precipitation, mild winters and hot summers. The temperature falls below 32°F only about 10 days a year, but rises above 90 °F an average of 181 days.

Normal high temperatures are above 100 °F in June, July, August and September and have been above 100°F in every month except November, December and January.

Making up for the heat, at least somewhat, is the low relative humidity during the hot part of the year. In July, for example, afternoon relative humidities are usually around 20 to 25 percent.

Normal precipitation is only 5.47 inches a year.

On the average, the sky is reported as "clear" 241 days a year, as "partly cloudy" on 84 days and "cloudy" on only 40 days.

Palm Springs is at the foot of the massive Mount San Jacinto, which rises to 10,831 feet above sea level.

An average of more than 90 inches of snow a year falls on the summit of Mount San Jacinto and average temperatures there are 20 to 30 degrees colder than in the city.

Yosemite National Park: As in all mountain regions, the weather in Yosemite National Park can change quickly and depends to a large extent on elevation.

Pacific Ocean storms bring the region most of its precipitation. Since such storms hit from November through March, approximately 75 percent of the park's precipitation falls from late fall through early spring.

Much more snow falls on the higher elevations, which forces the closing of the park's high country roads during the winter, and cuts park access from the east.

From early November until late May, snow closes the Tioga Road (Highway 120 East), Glacier Point Road, and Tuolumne Grove Road. Glacier Point Road is plowed to the Badger Pass Ski Area. Travelers driving to Yosemite during late fall, winter and early spring should carry tire chains, which are sometimes mandatory on park roads.

Winters in Yosemite are relatively mild since Pacific storms bring in mild air.

Snow begins accumulating on the higher peaks as early as September, but not in the valley until after Nov. 1. Snow in the valley rarely is more than two feet deep, although as much as five feet have been on the ground. Yosemite's famous waterfalls are at their fullest in spring when snow is melting. May and June are the best times for viewing the falls. Mule deer migrate up the slopes as the snow melts. Black oaks in Yosemite Valley begin to leaf out in April, the dogwoods bloom in early- to mid-May and western azalea bushes bloom in late May and early June.

Summer is warm and dry with less than 5 percent of the year's precipitation. Daytime temperatures in the valley sometimes climb above 100°F but nights are generally cool. Even in midsummer, temperatures in Tuolumne Meadows, at an elevation of 8,600 feet, are usually in the 70s during the days and 30s at night.

Sudden thunderstorms sometimes bring dramatically changing clouds, intense but brief downpours, lighting, hail, and gusty winds. Lightning is a danger for hikers, especially on mountaintops. Anyone planning a hike far from shelter should check before leaving to see if thunderstorms are expected.

Since melting snow feeds the waterfalls, some are mere trickles or even completely dry in August.

During the fall, nights turn cooler, but days remain warm through October. September and October typically bring clear, brilliant days as the leaves of dogwood, cottonwood, maple and willow trees take on their fall colors. Autumn color peaks in late October and early November.

Colorado

Rocky Mountain National Park: Along Trail Ridge Road, the scenery is sublime. The road's high

Palm Springs, California						
Lat. 33° 49'N, Lon. 116° 30'W, Elev. 448 ft.						
	Record high	Avg. high	Avg. low	Record low	Avg. precip. (inches)	Wet days
		temperatures				
Jan.	98	69	40	18	1.03	3
Feb.	105	73	44	24	1.19	3
March	105	79	47	29	0.59	2
April	110	86	52	35	0.21	*
May	118	94	58	38	0.05	0
June	121	102	64	48	0.01	*
July	122	108	73	54	0.17	*
Aug.	121	106	71	52	0.22	*
Sept.	121	102	66	46	0.22	1
Oct.	110	91	57	30	0.28	1
Nov.	98	79	48	26	0.33	1
Dec.	93	70	42	23	1.17	3
* Less than 1 but more than 0						

Yosemite National Park, California						
Lat. 37° 45'N, Lon. 119° 35'W, Elev. 3,970 ft.						
	Record high	Avg. high	Avg. low	Record low	Avg. precip. (inches)	Avg. snow	Wet days
		temperatures					
Jan.	69	47	26	7	6.63	16.1	8
Feb.	79	55	29	10	5.02	12.5	6
Mar.	89	59	31	10	4.95	16.2	7
Apr.	89	66	35	20	3.46	9.3	6
May	91	73	42	26	1.49	0.4	4
June	102	82	48	30	0.65	0	2
July	104	90	53	38	0.37	0	1
Aug.	104	90	52	32	0.28	0	1
Sept.	102	85	47	28	0.08	0	1
Oct.	98	74	39	21	1.3	0	2
Nov.	86	58	31	16	4.07	3.5	6
Dec.	65	46	26	-1	6.89	14.7	7

point is the Continental Divide with massive mountains in all directions. Streams running down the eastern slopes of the mountains flow ultimately into the Mississippi River and then the Gulf of Mexico. Water running down western slopes flows toward the Colorado River and the Gulf of California.

As the highway ascends, the vegetation becomes more stunted, like that of the Far North. At around 11,500 feet the low, wind-blasted spruce or fir trees — many more than 1,000 years old — give way to open meadows. This is a region of alpine tundra similar to the arctic tundra of the Far North.

Both alpine and arctic tundra regions are too

Estes Park, Colorado

(Eastern entrance to Rocky Mountain National Park)

Lat. 40° 23'N, Lon. 105° 31'W, Elev. 7,497 ft.

	Record high	Avg. high	Avg. low	Record low	Avg. precip. (inches)	Avg. snow
		temperatures				
Jan.	61	38	17	-38	0.42	6.5
Feb.	62	41	18	-39	0.39	5
March	65	44	20	-22	0.78	9.5
April	77	53	26	-19	1.34	6
May	81	62	34	9	2.13	1
June	92	73	41	24	1.64	0.1
July	90	79	46	33	2.12	0
Aug.	89	76	44	29	1.97	0
Sept.	85	70	37	3	1.21	0.7
Oct.	85	60	30	-9	0.76	2.3
Nov.	73	47	22	-18	0.54	5.5
Dec.	64	40	18	-30	0.52	7.2

Granby, Colorado

(About 5 miles from Rocky Mountain National Park's southwest entrance)

Lat. 40° 6'N, Lon. 105° 56'W, Elev. 8,210 ft.

	Record high	Avg. high	Avg. low	Record low	Avg. precip. (inches)
		temperatures			
Jan.	49	28	1	-37	1.17
Feb.	53	31	1	-41	0.82
March	56	37	9	-21	1.2
April	67	47	20	-9	1.07
May	76	59	29	15	1.34
June	88	69	36	22	1.2
July	86	75	41	28	1.52
Aug.	82	73	40	26	1.72
Sept.	80	68	33	14	1.11
Oct.	71	56	24	5	0.75
Nov.	58	40	14	-20	0.88
Dec.	47	30	5	-30	1.43

(Snowfall records not available)

cold for trees. The highest elevations in Rocky Mountain National Park have only about 40 frost-free days a year and snow can fall anytime. Temperatures stay below freezing about five months each year. About a third of the park is tundra.

The tundra's cold temperatures, combined with strong winds, thin air, intense sunlight and limited water, account for its unique plant life. Plants cope by developing extensive root systems — only about 10 percent of most plants are above ground. These plants have waxy or hairy leaves to resist wind and hold water.

The elevation at the park's entrance on the edge of the town of Estes Park is about 7,800 feet. Each 1,000 feet gained as the highway climbs is like traveling 600 miles north in terms of climate and vegetation.

Because of snow and high winds, Trail Ridge Road is closed more than half of the year. It has closed as early as the second week of October and stayed open as late as the first week of November. The National Park Service tries to reopen the highway for Memorial Day weekend; sometimes it opens a week or two earlier.

Winds up to 170 mph have been recorded on Trail Ridge Road in the winter and as high as 201 mph on Long's Peak. While summer winds aren't as bad, visitors should inquire about conditions before starting across the park.

Lingering snow also affects hiking. On Long's Peak, for example, winter conditions last from about October until July and "technical" mountain-climbing skills and equipment are required.

Normally the last snow melts on at least one route to the top in mid-July and hikers can reach the peak from then until well into September.

Here is a month-by-month look at the weather in Rocky Mountain National Park:

January is the coldest month. At Bear Lake, elevation 9,400 feet, 25 inches of snow normally is on the ground.

February brings gusty winds and an average snowfall of 10.6 inches. Skiing and snowshoeing are possible.

March is wetter than January and February, with most of the precipitation falling as snow.

April is often a wet month with one or two inches of precipitation. It falls mostly as rain on the lower elevations and as snow higher. Trails are still snow covered.

May finds lower elevations generally snow-free, but snow can occur. Less than an inch of precipitation is usual as the pattern of afternoon showers begins and lasts through the summer.

June normally brings an inch or more of rain. Snow remains on Long's Peak and other high elevations.

July is the warmest month. An inch or more of rain usually falls, often from thunderstorms. High country travelers need to be careful of lightning.

August is the wettest month with an average of 2 inches of rain. Late in the month cold air can begin arriving.

September usually brings a mix of rain and snow. Trail Ridge Road may close temporarily.

Aspen, Colorado

Lat. 39° 11'N, Lon. 106° 50'W, Elev. 7,928 ft.

	Record high	Avg. high	Avg. low	Record low	Avg. precip.	Avg. snow	Wet days
			temperatures			(inches)	
Jan.	58	34	8	-33	1.96	25.4	6
Feb.	60	37	10	-30	1.61	21.2	5
March	70	43	16	-14	1.9	21.9	5
April	73	53	24	-1	1.69	12.8	5
May	80	63	33	14	1.52	3.3	4
June	93	74	39	23	1.21	0.6	3
July	91	80	45	31	1.46	0	5
Aug.	92	77	44	27	1.85	0	6
Sept.	89	70	37	15	1.56	2.0	4
Oct.	78	60	28	3	1.54	7.4	4
Nov.	66	44	17	-19	1.55	18.7	5
Dec.	59	35	9	-21	1.82	23.3	5

Crested Butte, Colorado

Lat. 38° 52'N, Lon. 106° 58'W, Elev. 8,855 ft.

	Record high	Avg. high	Avg. low	Record low	Avg. precip.	Avg. snow	Wet days
			temperatures			(inches)	
Jan.	48	28	-1	-43	3.15	47.5	8
Feb.	52	31	1	-40	2.31	34.7	7
March	55	37	8	-25	2.63	36.2	7
April	64	47	19	-11	1.89	19.1	6
May	80	60	29	-1	1.39	4.5	4
June	90	71	34	22	1.29	0.2	4
July	88	77	40	23	1.91	0	6
Aug.	87	74	39	25	2.11	0	7
Sept.	85	67	32	10	1.90	1.3	5
Oct.	76	57	24	-3	1.64	8.9	5
Nov.	63	41	11	-26	1.9	26.3	6
Dec.	50	30	1	-34	3.11	40.9	8

October brings an inch or more of precipitation to the mountains, mostly falling on the west side.

November precipitation usually falls as snow, which is usually light. Skiing is generally poor.

December usually brings little snow. Winds are often gusty and skiing is poor.

The Rockies, including Rocky Mountain National Park, are the key tourist attraction in Colorado. The resorts in the charts here are open for skiing and summer entertainment.

Idaho

Sun Valley: Like other parts of the West far from the Pacific Ocean, Sun Valley is dry, with only a little over 17 inches of precipitation a year. Most of that falls as dry, powdery snow from November through March. Even during the winter "wet season" more than a tenth of an inch of precipitation falls on average on only one day out of five.

As in other dry areas, the sky in this region of south-central Idaho is clear much more than it's cloudy. Clear skies allow the sun to warm the ground and the air near it during the day. But clear skies also allow the ground's heat to radiate away at night. This is why the average range between high and low temperatures is more than 30 degrees.

Maine

Acadia National Park: Coastal mountains as high as 1,500 feet, numerous bays and rocky Atlantic beaches are among the attractions of Acadia National Park.

The park's location on Mount Desert Island on Maine's seacoast accounts for its cool, generally wet

Steamboat Springs, Colorado

Lat. 40° 30'N, Lon. 106° 50'W, Elev. 6,770 ft.

	Record high	Avg. high	Avg. low	Record low	Avg. precip.	Avg. snow	Wet days
			temperatures			(inches)	
Jan.	51	29	2	-50	2.86	39.3	9
Feb.	55	34	5	-44	2.16	29.4	7
March	61	41	12	-31	2.07	23.6	7
April	74	53	24	-10	2.18	14.1	6
May	87	65	31	12	1.98	2.8	6
June	94	75	35	22	1.44	0.3	4
July	96	83	41	25	1.39	0	4
Aug.	95	80	40	24	1.57	0	4
Sept.	91	72	32	12	1.54	1.3	4
Oct.	81	61	24	-4	1.65	6.0	4
Nov.	68	43	14	-28	1.89	20.9	5
Dec.	58	31	4	-36	2.57	33.3	8

climate. The park is open all year, but its visitor's center is open only from May 1 to Oct. 31. Parts of the park's scenic loop road are closed in winter.

Massachusetts

Cape Cod, Nantucket and **Martha's Vineyard** are all seaside areas. Cape Cod juts east into the Atlantic and then curves north. The Cape Cod National Seashore includes the east-facing Atlantic beaches. Provincetown is on the northern tip of Cape Cod, at the northern end of the National Seashore.

Martha's Vineyard is an island south of Falmouth, on the western end of Cape Cod. Nantucket is also an island in the Atlantic, about 25

Sun Valley, Idaho
Lat. 43° 42'N, Lon. 114° 21'W, Elev. 5.980 ft.

	Record high	Avg. high	Avg. low	Record low	Avg. precip.	Avg. snow	Wet days
		temperatures			(inches)		
Jan.	50	31	1	-38	2.63	35.8	6
Feb.	53	36	4	-35	1.57	19	4
March	61	40	9	-28	1.15	13.5	4
April	75	52	22	-1	1.04	4.3	3
May	86	64	29	14	1.57	1.4	5
June	90	71	35	17	1.8	0	5
July	96	83	38	21	0.71	0	2
Aug.	96	82	37	20	0.84	0	2
Sept.	93	72	30	11	0.81	0.4	3
Oct.	85	61	23	0	0.9	2.3	3
Nov.	68	44	14	-25	1.59	12.1	4
Dec.	55	32	4	-37	2.76	33	7

Bar Harbor, Maine
(Acadia National Park)
Lat. 44° 26'N, Lon. 68° 21'W, Elev. 84 ft.

	Record high	Avg. high	Avg. low	Record low	Avg. precip.	Avg. snow	Wet days
		temperatures			(inches)		
Jan.	63	33	14	-20	4.7	17.3	8
Feb.	57	32	15	-21	3.94	19.3	7
March	78	41	23	-9	4.68	12.1	7
April	83	52	32	11	3.73	4.4	7
May	92	63	42	22	3.6	0.1	7
June	97	71	50	32	3.25	0	6
July	96	77	56	36	3.3	0	6
Aug.	98	75	55	36	3.23	0	6
Sept.	96	69	50	27	3.86	0	6
Oct.	89	58	40	20	4.36	0.1	7
Nov.	70	47	31	-3	4.91	3.8	8
Dec.	66	36	19	-21	4.45	10	8

Martha's Vineyard, Massachusetts
Lat. 41° 23'N, Lon. 70° 36'W, Elev. 68 ft.

	Record high	Avg. high	Avg. low	Record low	Avg. precip.	Avg. snow	Wet days
		temperatures			(inches)		
Jan.	59	38	24	-7	4.83	8.9	9
Feb.	59	39	25	-9	4.21	7.5	7
March	65	43	29	3	4.66	10.7	9
April	79	54	39	19	4.47	1.5	8
May	83	63	47	31	3.43	0	7
June	97	73	57	41	1.96	0	5
July	94	79	63	50	3.28	0	5
Aug.	93	77	62	51	5.35	0	6
Sept.	89	71	56	36	3.62	0	5
Oct.	82	62	47	29	3.62	0	6
Nov.	74	53	38	15	4.57	0.3	8
Dec.	65	42	27	-2	4.95	7.3	8

miles south of Chatham on Cape Cod.

Stockbridge, Massachusetts: Stockbridge is in the Berkshire Hills of western Massachusetts, west of the main ridge of the hills. These protect the area from the worst effects of "nor'easter" storms along the Atlantic Coast, about 100 miles to the east.

Summers generally bring comfortable temperatures; winters can be cold. Snowfall varies widely from the average of 66.6 inches a year. Some winters can bring half of that, others more than 100 inches.

Michigan

Isle Royale National Park: Isle Royale National Park is an island in Lake Superior that is actually closer to the Canadian and Minnesota shores than to Michigan. The park is about 70 miles north of Houghton on Michigan's Upper Peninsula (not to be confused with Houghton Lake in lower Michigan), but the park headquarters is in Houghton. The nearest U.S. city, however, is Grand Portage, Minn., about 22 miles from the park. And the park is about 30 miles south of Thunder Bay, Ontario, Canada.

The only access is by boat or by airplane capable of landing on water. No cars are allowed in the park, so the only way to get around is by foot or boat. The park usually is open from mid-April to the end of October.

Tables on the next page give weather information for May through October for the park and for the whole year for Thunder Bay, the closest point with year-round weather observations. Thunder Bay's weather is typical of the Lake Superior shore

of northeastern Minnesota.

Montana

Glacier National Park: Glacier National Park straddles the Rocky Mountains in northwestern Montana. This rugged park includes about 50 glaciers and many lakes and streams fed by the heavy snow that can fall on the peaks any month of the year.

In the mountains the west slopes and high areas receive the most snow and winter is the wettest season. The east side of the park receives much less snow and here thunderstorms make May and June the wettest months. This is because the most

Nantucket, Massachusetts

Lat. 41° 16'N, Lon. 70° 3'W, Elev. 48 ft.

	Record high	Avg. high	Avg. low	Record low	Avg. precip.	Avg. snow	Wet days
		temperatures			(inches)		
Jan.	57	40	27	5	4.35	6.2	8
Feb.	56	39	26	0	4.21	9.7	8
March	62	42	30	7	4.66	8.6	7
April	73	51	38	20	4.01	1.1	7
May	77	59	46	30	3.44	0	7
June	88	68	54	39	1.85	0	4
July	90	75	62	50	2.73	0	5
Aug.	95	74	61	49	4.25	0	7
Sept.	84	69	56	35	3.25	0	5
Oct.	77	62	48	29	3.07	0	5
Nov.	69	53	40	20	4.33	0.2	7
Dec.	58	43	30	3	4.01	6	8

Provincetown, Massachusetts

Lat. 42° 04'N, Lon. 70° 13'W, Elev. 8 ft.

	Record high	Avg. high	Avg. low	Record low	Avg. precip.	Avg. snow	Wet days
		temperatures			(inches)		
Jan.	60	38	25	0	3.89	12.6	7
Feb.	60	37	23	-3	3.43	10.1	7
March	76	43	29	0	3.72	7.9	7
April	83	52	37	16	3.53	0.7	7
May	90	63	46	26	2.94	0	6
June	94	72	55	37	2.74	0	5
July	104	78	62	45	2.69	0	5
Aug.	96	77	61	42	3.18	0	6
Sept.	93	71	55	32	3.32	0	5
Oct.	82	61	46	26	3.43	0	6
Nov.	77	51	37	14	3.17	1.5	5
Dec.	68	41	29	-6	3.62	6.6	7

Stockbridge, Massachusetts

Lat. 42° 17'N, Lon. 73° 18'W, Elev. 870 ft.

	Record high	Avg. high	Avg. low	Record low	Avg. precip.	Avg. snow	Wet days
		temperatures			(inches)		
Jan.	65	32	13	-29	3.26	18.3	7
Feb.	63	34	14	-28	2.63	16.3	6
March	82	42	23	-17	3.26	12.4	8
April	89	56	33	10	3.74	3.8	8
May	92	68	43	24	3.61	0.2	8
June	91	75	52	30	3.99	0	8
July	97	79	56	37	4.46	0	8
Aug.	95	76	55	32	3.81	0	7
Sept.	91	70	47	22	4.1	0	7
Oct.	87	61	37	12	2.93	T	6
Nov.	79	48	29	-8	3.82	4.8	7
Dec.	63	35	18	-18	3.22	10.8	7

T = Trace

Isle Royale National Park, Michigan

Lat. 48° 6'N, Lon. 88° 33'W, Elev. 610 ft.

	Record high	Avg. high	Avg. low	Record low	Avg. precip.	Avg. snow	Wet days
		temperatures			(inches)		
May	79	54	36	19	2.54	0.7	5
June	87	62	43	32	3.08	0	6
July	89	68	50	37	2.54	0	6
Aug.	86	69	54	34	3.23	0	7
Sept.	82	60	47	29	3.45	0.2	7
Oct.	72	52	39	12	2.12	0.5	5

Thunder Bay, Ontario, Canada

Lat. 48° 22'N, Lon. 89° 19'W, Elev. 653 ft.

	Record high	Avg. high	Avg. low	Record low	Avg. precip.	Avg. snow	Wet days
		temperatures			(inches)		
Jan.	48	17	-4	-42	0.91	8.9	3
Feb.	52	20	-2	-40	0.76	7.1	2
March	73	31	10	-34	0.95	8	3
April	83	44	26	-10	1.49	3.8	5
May	91	56	37	16	2.11	0.5	6
June	97	67	47	27	2.81	0	6
July	104	74	52	35	3.56	0	7
Aug.	96	71	49	31	2.78	0	6
Sept.	89	62	44	17	3.37	0	7
Oct.	83	50	34	4	2.45	1.2	6
Nov.	69	34	19	-22	1.52	5.9	4
Dec.	54	22	5	-38	0.95	7.5	3

humid air comes from the Pacific Ocean to the west and much of the air's moisture is deposited as snow on the west sides and summits of the mountains.

Up to 10 feet of snow accumulate on most of the park's mountains each winter. By May 1, the snow usually has melted at the lower elevations, such as around the shore of Lake McDonald, but snow may last into August on some of the higher trails.

As in other western mountains, temperatures and precipitation depend on elevation. The higher areas are colder and wetter.

Chinook winds, which warm up as they blow down the east sides of the mountains, can gust to 100 mph. These winds keep the east slopes warmer than the west side of the park in winter.

Starr School, Montana

Lat. 48° 36'N, Lon. 113° 6'W, Elev. 4,650 ft.

(Near Browning, Mont., on east side of Glacier National Park)

	Record high	Avg. high	Avg. low	Record low	Avg. precip.	Avg. snow	Wet days
		temperatures				(inches)	
Jan.	66	29	8	-56	0.69	8.4	2
Feb.	68	31	10	-46	0.65	8.3	2
March	72	38	16	-38	0.82	10.3	2
April	91	51	27	-14	1.01	7.7	3
May	93	62	35	1	2	3.5	5
June	98	68	41	21	2.93	0.6	6
July	99	78	46	24	1.51	0	3
Aug.	98	76	44	23	1.33	0.1	3
Sept.	94	65	37	0	1.58	3.3	3
Oct.	83	55	30	-17	0.86	5.4	2
Nov.	72	40	20	-39	0.83	7.9	2
Dec.	69	33	13	-47	0.7	9.2	2

Summit, Montana

Lat. 48° 19'N, Lon. 113° 21'W, Elev. 5,213 ft.

(Marias Pass, where U.S. Route 2 crosses Continental Divide)

	Record high	Avg. high	Avg. low	Record low	Avg. precip.	Avg. snow	Wet days
		temperatures				(inches)	
Jan.	47	24	7	-55	4.26	48	11
Feb.	56	27	9	-53	3.54	40.4	10
March	62	34	14	-42	3.08	39.3	11
April	75	45	23	-30	2.78	25.8	8
May	81	56	31	0	2.86	7.9	8
June	90	62	37	15	3.7	1.4	9
July	93	74	40	25	1.24	T	4
Aug.	94	72	39	19	1.52	T	4
Sept.	91	62	34	6	2.52	4.6	7
Oct.	82	49	29	-30	3.1	11	8
Nov.	61	34	18	-42	3.96	37	10
Dec.	57	29	14	-38	4.31	40.9	12

T = Trace

New Hampshire

White Mountains: The White Mountains of New Hampshire are both summer and winter recreation areas with resorts, hiking trails and ski areas. Mount Washington is the highest peak in New England and is one of the rare mountain peaks with a long record of weather observations.

Weather at Pinkham Notch is more typical of what vacationers can expect to encounter. Mount Washington's weather statistics on the next page offer warnings to those who hike on the higher trails in the Presidential Range. The peak can be reached by a cog railroad, a road and hiking trails.

In addition to possible freezing weather and snow any month of the year, dangerous winds can rake the tops of Mount Washington and other peaks in the Presidential Range. Winds faster than 180 mph are not uncommon and the station's highest measured wind, 231 mph in May 1934, is still a world record.

New Mexico

Carlsbad Caverns: Carlsbad Caverns National Park is in the southeastern part of New Mexico in the foothills of the Guadalupe Mountains. The town of Carlsbad is in the Pecos River Valley at 1,315 feet. The park's elevation is around 4,000 feet.

It is in a semiarid region with mild winters and warm summers. Summer showers account for much of the region's sparse precipitation. Clear skies and dry air cause a wide range in daily temperatures.

West Glacier, Montana

Lat. 48° 30'N, Lon. 113° 59'W, Elev. 3,154 ft.

(Western entrace to Glacier National Park)

	Record high	Avg. high	Avg. low	Record low	Avg. precip.	Avg. snow	Wet days
		temperatures				(inches)	
Jan.	52	28	14	-37	3.13	36.4	10
Feb.	58	33	16	-40	2.42	26.5	7
March	64	41	21	-30	1.81	16.2	6
April	80	54	29	-8	1.87	4.3	6
May	91	65	37	13	2.36	0.4	7
June	92	70	44	24	3.02	T	8
July	101	81	47	34	1.27	T	4
Aug.	95	79	46	31	1.33	0	3
Sept.	88	67	39	16	1.89	T	5
Oct.	79	54	33	-9	2.64	2.3	7
Nov.	67	38	24	-29	3.06	15.8	8
Dec.	57	32	20	-22	3.26	31.4	10

T = Trace

The park's centerpiece is one of the world's largest caves with a series of enormous rooms that are as deep as 829 feet below the surface. Like other large caves, temperatures and humidity remain nearly the same all year. Except near the entrance, the temperature in the caverns is a nearly constant 56°F, while the relative humidity is 90 percent.

Outside most days are clear or partly cloudy and only about 15 percent are overcast. Snowfall averages only seven inches a year, but more than 38 inches fell in 1931. Snow seldom stays on the ground long.

Pinkham Notch, New Hampshire

Lat. 44° 16'N, Lon. 71° 15'W, Elev. 2,069 ft.

	Record high	Avg. high	Avg. low	Record low	Avg. precip. (inches)	Avg. snow	Wet days
Jan.	55	26	6	-31	3.96	31.4	8
Feb.	58	28	7	-28	4.75	38.2	8
March	68	35	16	-13	4.76	34.2	9
April	82	47	28	-4	4.19	16	9
May	89	61	38	17	4.4	2.1	9
June	90	69	48	29	4.76	0	10
July	91	73	53	32	4.81	0	8
Aug.	89	71	51	33	4.53	0	8
Sept.	89	64	44	23	4.4	0	7
Oct.	82	55	34	3	5.08	2.20	7
Nov.	69	40	24	-1	6.52	14.60	10
Dec.	61	29	11	-19	5.61	35.50	9

Mount Washington, New Hampshire

Lat. 44° 16'N, Lon. 71° 18'W, Elev. 6,262 ft.

	Record high	Avg. high	Avg. low	Record low	Avg. precip. (inches)	Avg. snow	Wet days
Jan.	44	13	-3	-47	7.32	40.1	19
Feb.	43	13	-3	-46	8.01	40.7	18
March	52	19	5	-38	8.19	42.5	19
April	60	29	16	-20	7.03	31.5	18
May	66	41	28	-2	6.46	10.5	17
June	71	51	38	8	7.06	1.1	16
July	71	54	43	25	6.9	T	17
Aug.	72	53	42	20	7.60	0.2	16
Sept.	67	46	35	9	7.15	1.9	15
Oct.	59	37	25	-5	6.73	11.8	15
Nov.	52	27	14	-20	8.54	31.9	19
Dec.	45	17	1	-46	8.94	42.8	20

T = Trace

Taos: The city of Taos is at the foot of the San-gre de Cristo mountains, which rise nearly 12,000 feet above sea level. Even though this part of northern New Mexico has a semiarid climate, more than 300 inches of snow a year falls on the higher mountains, which makes for good skiing. For every inch of snow that falls in the valley, where the city is located, 10 inches may fall on the surrounding mountains.

In the valley the daily temperature rarely stays below freezing more than 10 days a winter. But winter nights are frigid, with an average low of 10°F in January. Freezing nights can be expected from mid-October until late April. Summers are generally sunny and mild.

Carlsbad Caverns, New Mexico

Lat. 32° 11'N, Lon. 104° 27'W, Elev. 4,435 ft.

	Record high	Avg. high	Avg. low	Record low	Avg. precip. (inches)	Avg. snow
Jan.	81	57	34	0	0.5	2.4
Feb.	84	61	36	-10	0.4	1.1
March	90	67	41	10	0.5	0.7
April	96	76	49	21	0.8	T
May	103	84	57	31	1.5	T
June	108	92	65	48	1.6	0
July	106	91	67	50	2	0
Aug.	105	90	66	50	1.9	0
Sept.	100	85	61	33	2.6	0
Oct.	92	76	53	31	1.7	T
Nov.	88	66	42	16	0.4	1.1
Dec.	88	59	36	3	0.6	2.0

T = Trace

New York

Adirondack Mountains: The Adirondack Mountains in northeastern New York include the largest wilderness areas in the East. An extensive network of hiking trails laces the "High Peaks" region with 42 mountains higher than 4,000 feet. The region's numerous wilderness lakes and rivers can be explored by canoe.

In winter, several ski areas and other winter hiking sites attract visitors. Lake Placid is a Winter Olympics training site.

North Carolina

North Carolina's mountains are the highest in the eastern United States. The region became a major summer resort early this century, offering a cool escape from hotter parts of the Southeast in the days before air conditioning. The region is still a summer resort, but now several ski areas also make it a winter destination. Many of the ski areas are near Banner Elk, which is northeast of Asheville, the region's major city.

Beaches along North Carolina's Atlantic Coast are the state's other major recreation area. Listings for Cape Hatteras and Wilmington in the *Almanac's* cities section give climate data for the state's beach resorts.

Oregon

Oregon Cascades, including Crater Lake National Park: The Cascade Mountain Range runs from Canada across Washington and Oregon into northern California. Since the Pacific Ocean is only

Taos, New Mexico

Lat. 36° 25'N, Lon. 105° 37'W, Elev. 6,965 ft.

	Record high	Avg. high	Avg. low	Record low	Avg. precip.	Avg. snow	Wet days
		temperatures				(inches)	
Jan.	62	40	10	-24	0.83	9.1	3
Feb.	73	45	15	-27	0.72	6.2	2
March	72	53	22	-11	0.79	6.4	3
April	80	64	29	0	0.92	2.9	3
May	91	73	37	20	1.21	1.7	3
June	97	83	44	28	0.75	0	2
July	98	87	50	36	1.58	0	5
Aug.	99	85	50	38	1.77	0	5
Sept.	94	79	42	22	1.11	0.1	3
Oct.	84	67	32	11	1.13	0.1	3
Nov.	83	52	18	-16	0.71	3.2	2
Dec.	63	43	12	-17	0.57	4.7	2

Lake Placid, New York

Lat. 44° 17'N, Lon. 73° 59'W, Elev. 1,880 ft.

	Record high	Avg. high	Avg. low	Record low	Avg. precip.	Avg. snow	Wet days
		temperatures				(inches)	
Jan.	54	24	2	-36	2.57	27.6	9
Feb.	59	28	4	-30	2.62	27.4	8
March	69	36	14	-14	2.72	23.9	8
April	82	50	28	-2	2.92	8.5	9
May	90	63	38	19	3.23	1.1	9
June	93	73	48	22	3.31	0	8
July	97	77	52	35	3.76	0	9
Aug.	93	74	50	30	4.21	0	9
Sept.	90	67	43	19	3.36	0	7
Oct.	87	56	34	15	2.73	1.8	7
Nov.	67	42	24	-11	3.33	14.1	10
Dec.	60	29	9	-26	3.05	28.7	10

about 100 miles west of the mountains, ocean storms bring in large amounts of humid air that condenses into rain or snow as it rises over the mountains.

Since air from over the ocean is warmer on average than the cold air from northern Canada that comes into the Rockies, temperatures in the Cascades are warmer on the average than at similar elevations and latitudes in the Rockies. Even at relatively high elevations, temperatures in the Cascades drop below zero only a few times each winter.

Mount Hood, at elevation 11,235 feet, is the highest point in Oregon.

Winters are cold, but not extremely so, with abundant snow.

The Pacific storms, which bring most of the moisture, become infrequent in late spring and summer. These seasons are usually sunny with moderate temperatures and only brief, infrequent showers.

Summer thunderstorms occur about one day out of four. Hikers and mountain climbers need to beware of lightning and try to avoid being on peaks when thunderstorms arrive.

South Carolina

Hilton Head, a coastal island between Charleston, S.C., and Savannah, Ga., is a major resort. It and other islands are also major retirement areas.

Beaufort, a pre-Civil War town, is about 10 miles inland. The Marine Corps Air Station, which has the most complete record of weather observations in the area, is about 12 miles from the ocean.

Banner Elk, North Carolina

Lat. 36° 10'N, Lon. 81° 52'W, Elev. 3,750 ft.

	Record high	Avg. high	Avg. low	Record low	Avg. precip.	Avg. snow	Wet days
		temperatures				(inches)	
Jan.	67	42	21	-17	3.89	11.3	8
Feb.	73	44	22	-11	3.92	11.4	8
March	76	51	29	-3	5.06	9.3	9
April	82	61	38	12	4.36	1.5	8
May	82	68	45	23	4.35	0	9
June	87	74	51	27	4.38	0	9
July	88	76	55	36	4.81	0	10
Aug.	87	76	55	36	4.56	0	8
Sept.	89	71	49	29	4.2	0	7
Oct.	82	62	38	8	3.55	0.4	6
Nov.	74	52	30	-4	3.63	4.1	7
Dec.	74	45	24	-18	3.55	7.9	7

In general, sea breezes lower summer temperatures for places closer to the ocean. But average temperatures at Beaufort and Hilton Head are usually within a degree of each other.

While average snowfall is zero, snow occasionally falls. In February 1973, 6.4 inches of snow fell on Beaufort.

Myrtle Beach and Grand Strand: The Grand Strand beaches along South Carolina's northern coast, centered on Myrtle Beach, have been a Southeast summer resort for decades. In recent years, the area has become a year-round resort, attracting golfers to its many courses.

Government Camp, Oregon

(In the Cascades)
Lat. 45° 18'N, Lon. 121° 45'W, Elev. 3,980 ft.

	Record high	Avg. high	Avg. low	Record low	Avg. precip.	Avg. snow	Wet days
		temperatures			(inches)		
Jan.	62	36	24	-8	13.14	62.2	18
Feb.	69	39	25	-6	10.04	50.8	15
March	67	40	25	4	10.07	58.9	16
April	72	46	29	13	7.24	28.3	12
May	81	53	34	18	5.20	7.7	11
June	92	59	40	23	4.03	0.8	8
July	99	69	45	29	.72	0	2
Aug.	98	68	45	32	1.62	0	4
Sept.	92	67	42	25	3.38	0	7
Oct.	82	55	36	22	7.92	6.7	11
Nov.	68	43	29	-4	9.98	24.3	14
Dec.	65	38	26	-14	12.34	49.4	17

Crater Lake, Oregon

(National Park headquarters)
Lat. 42° 54'N, Lon. 122° 8'W, Elev. 6,475 ft.

	Record high	Avg. high	Avg. low	Record low	Avg. precip.	Avg. snow	Wet days
		temperatures			(inches)		
Jan.	64	35	18	-21	10.85	109.1	16
Feb.	66	35	18	-18	8.68	96.7	13
March	67	38	19	-6	8.22	90.9	13
April	71	45	24	-3	4.34	43.3	9
May	80	52	29	5	3.31	23.3	7
June	96	60	35	11	2.54	3.3	5
July	100	70	42	18	0.63	0	2
Aug.	94	70	41	16	.56	0.1	2
Sept.	86	63	37	16	2.05	2.1	4
Oct.	81	52	31	22	6.42	21.2	8
Nov.	75	42	25	-7	7.95	54.6	11
Dec.	67	35	20	-18	11.69	96.4	15

Hilton Head Island area, South Carolina

(Beaufort Marine Corps Air Station, South Carolina)
Lat. 32° 29'N, Lon. 80° 43'W, Elev. 38 ft.

	Record high	Avg. high	Avg. low	Record low	Avg. precip.	Avg. snow	Wet days
		temperatures			(inches)		
Jan.	83	58	38	5	3.6	0	10
Feb.	85	61	41	16	3.4	0	9
March	91	68	48	21	4.0	0	9
April	94	76	55	32	2.8	0	7
May	97	83	64	41	3.7	0	8
June	106	88	70	51	5.6	0	10
July	106	90	74	62	6.2	0	13
Aug.	102	89	73	57	7.5	0	12
Sept.	98	85	69	45	4.9	0	9
Oct.	94	77	58	31	2.7	0	6
Nov.	88	69	48	19	2.1	0	7
Dec.	82	61	41	11	3.1	0.3	8

Myrtle Beach, South Carolina

Lat. 33° 41'N, Lon. 78° 56'W, Elev. 33 ft.

	Record high	Avg. high	Avg. low	Record low	Avg. precip.	Avg. snow	Wet days
		temperatures			(inches)		
Jan.	82	56	37	7	3.69	0.1	10
Feb.	84	58	39	9	3.38	0.3	9
March	88	64	45	19	4.53	0.3	10
April	93	72	53	28	2.77	0	7
May	98	79	62	36	3.69	0	9
June	104	85	69	48	4.93	0	9
July	103	87	73	54	6.10	0	12
Aug.	104	87	72	54	5.86	0	11
Sept.	99	83	67	42	5.69	0	9
Oct.	96	75	55	25	3.30	0	6
Nov.	85	67	45	16	2.87	0	7
Dec.	84	58	38	9	3.33	0.3	9

Tennessee

Great Smoky Mountains National Park: The park, which straddles the Tennessee-North Carolina border, is open all year with some activities curtailed in winter.

Humid air from the Gulf of Mexico gives the Smoky Mountains more than 56 inches of precipitation a year, mostly rain. This helps support a thick, temperate-zone forest with more than 1,500 types of flowering plants.

The park is between Asheville, N.C., and Knoxville, Tenn., and the data on those two cities in the *Almanac's* cities section can supply additional information. Gatlinburg, Tenn., is the nearest place with regular weather observations.

Texas

Big Bend National Park: Big Bend National Park includes lush vegetation along the Rio Grande River flood plain, the Chihauhauan Desert and the Chisos Mountains.

Horseback riding and hiking are available and the National Park Service offers guided walks. As the climate tables on the next page show, the weather is likely to change with elevation.

Weather observations for the park are taken at Chisos Basin and Panther Junction.

Gatlinburg, Tennessee
Lat. 35° 41'N, Lon. 83° 32'W, Elev. 1,454 ft.

	Record high	Avg. high	Avg. low	Record low	Avg. precip.	Avg. snow	Wet days
		temperatures			(inches)		
Jan.	78	48	25	-10	4.8	4.5	8
Feb.	84	52	26	-13	4.34	3.8	8
March	86	61	33	-6	5.81	1.5	9
April	92	72	42	19	4.88	0	8
May	94	78	49	29	4.81	0	9
June	100	84	57	33	5.6	0	9
July	105	86	61	43	6.05	0	10
Aug.	98	86	60	43	5.08	0	8
Sept.	101	81	54	32	3.93	0	7
Oct.	93	71	42	15	3.13	0	5
Nov.	85	60	32	3	4.12	0.5	7
Dec.	79	52	27	-12	4.38	1.9	8

Chisos Basin, Texas
Lat. 29° 16'N, Lon. 103° 18'W, Elev. 5,300 ft.

	Avg. high temp.	Avg. low temp.	Avg. precip. (in.)
Jan.	57	35	0.61
Feb.	61	38	0.58
March	68	44	0.37
April	76	52	0.6
May	82	58	1.63
June	86	63	2.27
July	85	64	3.14
Aug.	83	62	3.62
Sept.	79	59	3.29
Oct.	73	51	1.89
Nov.	65	43	0.58
Dec.	59	38	0.58

Panther Junction, Texas
Lat. 29° 19'N, Lon. 103° 13'W, Elev. 3,740 ft.

	Avg. high temp.	Avg. low temp.	Avg. precip. (in.)
Jan.	61	35	0.46
Feb.	66	38	0.47
March	74	45	0.33
April	83	54	0.53
May	89	60	1.43
June	93	66	1.9
July	93	68	1.95
Aug.	91	67	2.2
Sept.	86	62	2.17
Oct.	79	53	1.55
Nov.	70	44	0.51
Dec.	63	37	0.5

Utah

Bryce Canyon and Zion National Park: Bryce Canyon and Zion National Park are in the southwestern corner of Utah. Bryce Canyon is known for the intricate shapes and brilliant colors created as water and wind have eroded the rock. The park is open all year. Some side roads are closed to cars in the winter, but open to cross-country skiing.

Zion National Park offers spectacular cliffs and canyons and wilderness areas. It includes the world's largest natural arch, Kolob Arch, which has a span of 310 feet. Zion is open all year.

Both parks are east of St. George, Utah, on Interstate 15.

Wasatch Mountains: The Wasatch Range runs north-south to the east of Salt Lake City, along Interstate 15, and the Great Salt Lake.

Several canyons stretch from the lake into the mountains. Melting snow creates streams that run down the canyons and feed the lake. Since the canyons open to the west, they catch the moisture that is left in Pacific storms after they have crossed California's Sierras or the Northwest's Cascades. Cold wind blowing over the warmer water of the

Zion National Park, Utah
Lat. 37° 13'N, Lon. 112° 59'W, Elev. 4,050 ft.

	Avg. high temp.	Avg. low temp.	Avg. precip. (in.)
Jan.	52	29	1.59
Feb.	57	33	1.6
March	63	37	2.05
April	72	43	1.15
May	82	52	0.84
June	94	61	0.48
July	99	69	1.25
Aug.	96	67	1.79
Sept.	89	60	1
Oct.	78	49	0.92
Nov.	62	37	1.46
Dec.	53	30	1.28

Bryce Canyon Airport, Utah
Lat. 37° 42'N, Lon. 112° 9'W, Elev. 7,589 ft.

	Record high	Avg. high	Avg. low	Record low	Avg. precip.	Avg. snow
		temperatures			(inches)	
Jan.	58	36	4	-29	0.69	14.5
Feb.	61	39	8	-22	0.48	10.6
March	65	44	15	-20	0.72	12.4
April	74	54	23	3	0.64	4.4
May	82	63	29	4	0.66	1.8
June	92	75	36	18	0.36	0
July	90	80	44	29	1.04	0
Aug.	92	77	43	27	1.41	0
Sept.	87	72	35	18	1.13	0.1
Oct.	76	61	26	2	0.95	2.5
Nov.	65	46	14	-16	0.63	5.9
Dec.	61	39	8	-25	0.8	8.8

Great Salt Lake picks up some moisture, which adds to the snow falling on the mountains.

Snow amounts can vary widely by location and elevation, but the listings on the next page for Brighton (southeast of Salt Lake City) give a good idea of the climate of the Wasatch Mountains.

Vermont

The hills and Green Mountains of Vermont offer hiking, camping and skiing. Autumn leaves offer a colorful landscape for scenic drives.

Averages given here for the Barre-Montpelier area in north-central Vermont are a good indication of what to expect, especially with allowance for

St. George, Utah

Lat. 37° 5'N, Lon. 113° 35'W, Elev. 2,936 ft.

	Record high	Avg. high	Avg. low	Record low	Avg. precip. (inches)
		temperatures			
Jan.	72	53	24	-11	0.98
Feb.	81	59	29	1	1.04
March	89	67	35	12	0.88
April	98	76	42	18	0.5
May	108	85	49	25	0.41
June	116	96	57	35	0.19
July	115	101	65	41	0.76
Aug.	113	99	63	43	0.80
Sept.	108	93	53	25	0.62
Oct.	99	80	41	20	0.71
Nov.	86	65	30	4	0.52
Dec.	75	54	24	-4	0.84

Brighton, Utah

Lat. 40° 36'N, Lon. 111° 35'W, Elev. 8,740 ft.

	Record high	Avg. high	Avg. low	Record low	Avg. precip. (inches)	Avg. snow	Wet days
		temperatures					
Jan.	53	31	8	-34	5.46	69.4	11
Feb.	56	33	8	-30	4.68	63.2	10
March	59	37	11	-21	5.13	70.1	11
April	65	44	19	-6	4.76	51.2	10
May	74	54	29	0	2.72	15.8	6
June	83	64	36	18	2.10	1.7	5
July	85	73	44	23	1.40	0	4
Aug.	85	71	42	24	1.96	0.2	5
Sept.	80	63	34	6	1.99	2.4	4
Oct.	70	52	26	-2	3.04	21.2	6
Nov.	61	39	15	-20	4.44	49.8	8
Dec.	64	32	8	-23	5.44	66.3	11

Barre-Montpelier, Vermont

Lat. 44° 12'N, Lon. 72° 33'W, Elev. 1,157 ft.

	Record high	Avg. high	Avg. low	Record low	Avg. precip. (inches)	Avg. snow	Wet days
		temperatures					
Jan.	66	27	8	-33	2.61	23.3	6
Feb.	58	30	9	-26	2.82	25.2	6
March	77	37	18	-18	2.58	16.4	6
April	83	52	31	2	2.6	4.8	6
May	88	64	41	21	2.99	0	6
June	92	74	51	29	2.97	0	6
July	96	79	55	31	2.92	0	6
Aug.	93	76	52	31	3.37	0	6
Sept.	91	68	45	20	3.11	0	5
Oct.	84	58	36	15	3.06	0.6	5
Nov.	76	44	27	-7	3.06	6.7	5
Dec.	61	30	13	-23	2.6	16.8	6

Big Meadows, Virginia

(Shenandoah National Park)

Lat. 38° 31'N, Lon. 78° 26'W, Elev. 3,535 ft.

	Record high	Avg. high	Avg. low	Record low	Avg. precip. (inches)	Avg. snow	Wet days
		temperatures					
Jan.	74	37	19	-11	3.09	11.2	6
Feb.	65	38	20	-14	3.31	10.7	6
March	74	45	26	0	4.34	10.9	8
April	82	57	37	9	3.81	2.3	8
May	85	66	46	18	4.44	0	8
June	87	72	54	31	4.35	0	8
July	90	76	58	41	3.89	0	7
Aug.	89	74	57	35	5.31	0	8
Sept.	90	68	51	28	4.78	0	6
Oct.	84	59	41	14	5.08	0.3	5
Nov.	77	48	31	-1	4.10	4.8	6
Dec.	67	39	22	-7	3.46	7.9	6

cooler temperatures and higher precipitation at higher elevations.

Virginia

Shenandoah National Park, Virginia: The Skyline Drive, which winds along the highlands of the Blue Ridge Mountains, is one of the major attractions of the Shenandoah National Park.

The park is in the highest and most scenic part of the northern Blue Ridge Mountains of Virginia, which reach their highest elevation — 4,049 feet — at Hawksbill Mountain.

Both cool, relatively dry air from the northwest and warm, humid air from the Gulf of Mexico and Atlantic Ocean reach the Blue Ridge Mountains.

The mountains help shape the climate with temperatures dropping around 3.5°F for each 1,000 feet of elevation gained. Heavy vegetation in the mountains also has a cooling effect during summer.

Precipitation is fairly evenly distributed through the year. Occasionally the remnants of a hurricane will bring extremely heavy rain to the mountains.

Washington

Mount Rainier National Park: The ice-covered, 14,410-foot Mount Rainier volcano dominates the landscape of the park, east of the Seattle-Tacoma metropolitan area. Lower elevations of the park — up to about 3,500 feet — are thick, lowland forests filling the valleys along the streams flowing away from the volcano. An intermediate zone, with different species of trees, lies between the dense lower forests and the alpine meadows that begin at about 5,000 feet.

Scenic attractions include not only the mountain, streams and forests, but also the variety of clouds that can form over the top of Mount Rainier and in waves of wind flowing over the mountain. These wind waves create lens-shaped "lenticular" clouds that sometimes look like hovering flying saucers.

In general, fall, winter and spring are wet. Summer, especially in July and August, is relatively dry. During late summer, fog and low clouds often form at night in the lower valleys between the ocean and the mountain. Usually they disappear by noon. The tops are often less than 2,500 feet above sea level, which means that many areas popular with visitors are above the clouds in the sunlight while lower elevations are gloomy.

Differences in temperature and precipitation between the Longmire Ranger Station, at 2,762 feet, and the Paradise Ranger Station nearly 2,800 feet higher, illustrate how elevation affects climate.

Olympic National Park: Washington's Olympic Peninsula includes some of the few wilderness beaches left in the United States and one of the rare rain forests in a temperate, rather than tropical, climate.

The Pacific Ocean to the west, Strait of Juan de Fuca to the north, and Puget Sound to the east supply plenty of humid air to produce snow and rain, especially when the humid air flows over the Olympic Mountains. Compared to 14,410-foot Mount Rainier only about 100 miles to the southeast, Mount Olympus at 7,965 feet seems like a pygmy. But, Olympus is 1,281 feet higher than North Carolina's Mount Mitchell, the highest point east of the Mississippi River.

Most storms and humid winds come from the Pacific and drop more than 200 inches of rain a year on higher areas of the Olympic Mountains.

A glance at the climate data for Quillayute and Port Angeles shows how the mountains catch much of the moisture coming from the Pacific. The Quillayute weather station is only about eight miles from the west-facing shore, near the town of Forks. Port Angeles is on the Strait of Juan de Fuca, but sheltered by the mountains from Pacific moisture. Result: 103 inches of precipitation, mostly rain, in Quillayute; 25 inches a year in Port Angeles.

Pacific air also evens out temperatures. Neither Quillayute nor Port Angeles has recorded temperatures below zero or above 100°F.

Quillayute is also notable as the wettest, cloudiest, most humid, and rainiest U.S. location for which regular weather observations are available. Here are the figures:

Annual average precipitation: 104.50 inches.

Annual average, cloudy days: 240 (tie with Astoria, Ore.).

Annual relative humidity: 83 percent.

Annual average, days with rain: 210.

Wyoming

Grand Teton National Park: The Grand Teton peaks rise as much as 7,000 feet above the Snake River Valley, or 13,000 feet above sea level, north of

---

Longmire Ranger Station, Washington

Lat. 46° 45'N, Lon. 121° 49'W, Elev. 2,762 ft.

	Record high	Avg. high	Avg. low	Record low	Avg. precip.	Avg. snow	Wet days
		temperatures			(inches)		
Jan.	60	36	24	-9	10.84	48.4	16
Feb.	64	40	26	-8	8.89	37.6	14
March	73	44	28	-1	8.11	32.2	15
April	83	53	32	12	4.94	9	11
May	95	62	37	21	3.96	0.7	10
June	95	66	43	28	3.62	T	9
July	105	75	47	35	1.35	0	3
Aug.	100	74	47	33	1.58	0	4
Sept.	97	68	43	28	3.89	T	7
Oct.	88	57	38	17	8.59	1.4	12
Nov.	72	45	31	-3	11.54	14.4	15
Dec.	60	39	28	-1	13.69	34	18

T = Trace

Paradise Ranger Station, Washington

Lat. 46° 47'N, Lon. 121° 44'W, Elev. 5,550 ft.

	Record high	Avg. high	Avg. low	Record low	Avg. precip.	Avg. snow	Wet days
		temperatures			(inches)		
Jan.	62	33	21	-14	14.48	117.6	19
Feb.	62	35	22	-12	10.62	88.7	15
March	65	37	22	-2	10.4	98.6	17
April	70	44	27	2	6.73	54.1	12
May	88	50	32	14	4.42	21.3	10
June	86	56	37	13	4.7	4.3	10
July	87	64	44	20	1.69	0.3	4
Aug.	92	63	43	24	2.62	T	5
Sept.	89	57	39	18	6.94	5.2	9
Oct.	79	48	33	2	12	22	12
Nov.	78	41	27	-11	14.54	64.9	15
Dec.	62	34	22	-20	16.65	105.1	19

T = Trace

Quillayute, Washington

Lat. 47° 57'N, Lon. 124° 33'W, Elev. 179 ft.

	Record high	Avg. high	Avg. low	Record low	Avg. precip. (inches)	Avg. snow	Wet days
Jan.	65	46	34	7	13.8	6	23
Feb.	72	49	35	11	12.3	3	19
March	71	52	35	19	11.6	2	21
April	83	55	37	24	7.4	T	19
May	92	60	42	29	5.6	T	17
June	96	64	47	33	3.2	0	14
July	97	68	49	38	2.6	0	11
Aug.	99	69	50	36	2.3	0	10
Sept.	97	67	46	28	5.1	T	12
Oct.	83	59	41	24	10.4	T	18
Nov.	69	51	37	5	14.1	1	22
Dec.	64	46	34	7	15.1	3	23

T = Trace

Port Angeles, Washington

Lat. 48° 8'N, Lon. 123° 24'W, Elev. 13 ft.

	Record high	Avg. high	Avg. low	Record low	Avg. precip. (inches)	Avg. snow	Wet days
Jan.	60	42	34	11	3.72	6.1	10
Feb.	60	45	36	22	4.03	1.3	8
March	55	47	38	26	2.08	0.7	6
April	65	53	41	36	0.81	0	3
May	70	57	46	38	1.1	0	2
June	80	61	49	43	0.55	0	2
July	80	62	51	46	0.59	0	2
Aug.	80	62	51	45	0.83	0	3
Sept.	79	61	49	42	0.78	0	3
Oct.	65	54	45	38	2.34	0	7
Nov.	66	49	41	34	3.77	0.2	11
Dec.	61	45	38	24	3.97	1.5	11

Jackson, Wyoming

Lat. 43° 28'N, Lon. 110° 46'W, Elev. 6,244 ft.

	Record high	Avg. high	Avg. low	Record low	Avg. precip. (inches)	Avg. snow	Wet days
Jan.	55	27	5	-50	1.63	23.3	5
Feb.	56	32	8	-44	1.04	12.2	3
March	64	39	14	-32	1.05	12.5	3
April	75	51	24	-5	1.08	6.8	3
May	83	63	31	12	1.72	1.3	5
June	92	72	37	19	1.72	0.2	5
July	94	82	40	24	0.84	0	3
Aug.	94	79	38	18	1.15	0	4
Sept.	93	71	31	14	1.16	0.3	3
Oct.	84	59	23	2	1.09	2.2	3
Nov.	64	39	16	-27	1.14	9.2	3
Dec.	51	28	7	-49	1.65	18.6	5

Jackson.

During the summer, the area attracts vacationers who want to hike in the mountains, camp or just enjoy the scenery. In winter, the region is a major destination for skiing, both cross-country and alpine.

Jackson Hole is a valley about 50 miles long and 10 to 40 miles wide, with the Teton Ridge on the west side. Jackson is the biggest town in the valley.

The Grand Targhee Ski Resort is on the west side of the Teton Mountains, about 12 miles from Driggs, Idaho.

Yellowstone National Park: Visitors to Yellowstone National Park should be ready for cool, even wintry weather, especially at higher elevations.

An example: Those who work in the park traditionally celebrate "Christmas in August" each Aug. 25. The tradition began on Aug. 25, 1939 when workers at the Old Faithful Inn were snowbound. In recent years, snow briefly closed roads in the park on July 4, 1993 and June 14, 1994.

As with other mountain areas in the western U.S., temperature and precipitation can vary widely in the park. The climate table here is based on data collected at park headquarters in Mammoth Hot Springs, which at an elevation of 6,241 feet, is one of the lowest places in the park. Most of the valleys in the park are at elevations of 7,000 to 8,000 feet with peaks rising above 11,000.

During summer, average afternoon temperatures are in the 70s with occasional 80s or even 90s, but a high of 100°F has never been recorded. The cold water of Lake Yellowstone keeps places along its shore several degrees cooler than other low elevations.

Summer nights are cool and visitors should be prepared for readings as low as the 30s or 40s near dawn, although 50s are more common.

Pleasant weather normally continues into September with temperatures only a few degrees cooler than August. Many regular visitors think September is the best month, with mostly comfortable temperatures and fall just beginning.

Mammoth Hot Springs has less snow and rain than the higher elevations around it because the flow of humid air over the mountains encourages the humidity to condense into rain or snow clouds there and leave Mammoth Hot Springs dry.

Some Yellowstone records:

Hottest ever: 98°F on June 23, 1936 at the Lamar Ranger Station.

Coldest in summer: 9°F on Aug. 25, 1910 at the Canyon Station.

Coldest ever: -66°F on Feb. 9, 1933 near the West Yellowstone Station.

Mammoth Hot Springs, Wyoming

Lat. 44° 58'N, Lon. 110° 42'W, Elev. 6,241 ft.

	Record high	Avg. high	Avg. low	Record low	Avg. precip. (inches)	Avg. snow
Jan.	50	29	9	-41	1.35	17.5
Feb.	55	34	13	-40	0.91	11.7
March	63	38	15	-25	1.15	14.3
April	77	50	25	-8	1.25	6.6
May	89	61	33	6	1.99	1.8
June	92	68	40	20	2.47	0.1
July	96	80	45	25	1.18	0
Aug.	95	78	44	23	1.34	0.1
Sept.	92	67	37	0	1.34	1.5
Oct.	82	56	29	-20	1.12	4
Nov.	68	39	20	-27	1.26	10.4
Dec.	58	31	13	-34	1.23	15

3 **A weather guide for business travel**

Airport weather, day lengths, metric conversions

Weather delay.

The plane is late. The train is sidetracked. The road is closed. It often means being stranded in an airport or station, a truck stop or a service area. Sometimes it means being stuck at home as a planned trip unravels. For business travelers weather delays cost money.

The weather is going to happen regardless of a traveler's plans. But the smart traveler will keep up on what the weather is doing and change with it.

This chapter includes NOAA weather radio stations for the United States and times and frequencies of Voice of America broadcasts, which include weather information around the world. Also, a special airport weather guide shows the most likely times for weather delays at 19 U.S. airports and nine others around the world.

Tables for the length of day in this chapter answer questions such as, how much daylight travelers are likely to have in different parts of the world each month. These tables include not only the time from sunrise to sunset, but also the length of morning and evening twilight.

Global travelers often need to know how the time at their destination compares with the time at home. This chapter's time zone information and rules for figuring out differences between zones will help travelers who want to make sure their call home doesn't arrive in the middle of the night.

Out of the holding pattern

Before 1981, airplanes flying into bad weather or other delays circled near their destination until they could land. Today, when air-traffic controllers know delays are likely, they hold up takeoffs. Weather is the major cause of flight delays. And it's not just winter weather that's the culprit. While January had the most delays at U.S. airports in the first half of 1994, June, with its thunderstorms, accounted for more weather-related delays than either February or March.

Weather-related delays by month in '94

	Delays	Pct. delayed by weather
January	20,925	77%
February	12,412	73%
March	12,063	74%
April	16,104	78%
May	11,407	68%
June	18,998	78%

Weather delays at major U.S. airports

Airport	Number of flights delayed		
	1991	**1992**	**1993**
Hartsfield Atlanta Intl.	11,605	15,015	9,817
Boston Logan Intl.	9,933	12,125	14,180
Chicago O'Hare Intl.	26,503	25,260	28,273
Dallas-Fort Worth Intl.	17,416	16,353	18,996
Denver Stapleton Intl.	12,046	11,886	18,259
Newark Intl.	15,019	18,069	19,559
John F. Kennedy Intl.	8,107	8,679	8,131
LaGuardia	8,187	6,515	5,893
Philadelphia Intl.	NA	6,050	NA
Lambert-St. Louis	11,220	NA	7,318
San Francisco Intl.	21,992	11,081	8,300

NA – Not Available

Source: Federal Aviation Administration

How to use the airport guide

Imagine you are taking a flight to Chicago's O'Hare International Airport. You can schedule your time to arrive in the morning, the afternoon or at night. Is there a time when odds are best for good landing weather? Yes. Tables here show how often weather that could delay flights occurs at different times of the day each month for 28 major airports.

Figures are based on regular weather observations over several years. Because the listings are averages, actual weather will vary, but the tables are an indication of the times when weather is most likely or least likely to delay flights.

Today's airplanes can take off and land safely in bad weather, but poor visibility, thunderstorms, freezing rain, or snow still can cause delays. Length of delays depends not only on weather, but also on the airport layout and the number of aircraft taking off and landing.

All of the listings show the average percent of time the listed conditions occur:

Times listed are local standard time. They should be taken as general indications of what to expect in the morning, around midday and in the early evening.

"Poor visibility" is the percent of time the "ceiling" is less than 200 feet above the ground and the visibility is less than three-quarters of a mile. Ceiling is the distance from the ground to the bottom of the lowest layer of clouds covering more than half the sky. Visibility is the distance at which someone can make out objects when fog, rain or snow obstruct vision. While there are exceptions, a 200 foot ceiling or three-quarters of a mile visibility is likely to slow operations.

"T'storm" refers to thunderstorms near the airport. Pilots generally avoid flying through or too near thunderstorms.

"Freezing precip." refers to freezing rain or drizzle, which can cause delays as aircraft are de-iced before taking off.

"Snow" is listed because it can cause delays while runways are plowed, and sometimes requires planes to be de-iced.

You can use these charts in various ways.

Assume you're planning to fly from New York's Kennedy Airport to Los Angeles International Airport in June and you're trying to decide whether to leave in the morning or around noon. A glance at the chart shows a 4% chance of low ceiling or visibility at 7 a.m., none at 1 p.m. But the odds for thunderstorms near the airport in June increase from 0.2% at 7 a.m. to 0.5% at 1 p.m. Chances of weather delays leaving Kennedy are slim at both times, but a delay is just a little bit more possible in the morning. That could be an excuse not to get up at dawn to leave.

How about on the Los Angeles end? If you arrive around midday or in the evening, chances of weather problems are almost zero.

For the same trip, assume you can get a lower fare by changing planes either at Chicago O'Hare or Dallas-Fort Worth.

Thunderstorms are the big weather concern during the summer in the U.S. Let's see where you're least likely to be delayed by thunderstorms.

At O'Hare, thunderstorm odds range from 0.5% at 6 a.m. to only 0.3% at noon to 2.2% at 6 p.m. At Dallas-Fort Worth, thunderstorms are

more likely than at O'Hare, ranging from 3% at 6 a.m. to 1.4% at noon to 2.2% at 6 p.m. Discovering that thunderstorms are more likely at 6 a.m. than at noon or 6 p.m. is a surprise to most people who associate thunderstorms with afternoons.

But in the central U.S., thunderstorms are more likely to occur overnight. In Dallas, for instance, the peak thunderstorm time is 3 a.m.

If you're flying to Miami in June, however, a morning arrival is the best bet with thunderstorm odds of 1.3% at 7 a.m., going up to 9.3% at 1 p.m. and down to 5% at 7 p.m.

The good news from these charts is how relatively small the odds are for weather delays at most places.

But small odds aren't a guarantee.

In Atlanta, for instance, the odds for snow in March range from 0.2% to 0.6%. But the Hartsfield Atlanta International Airport, along with every other Eastern airport north to Boston, was closed by the "Storm of the Century" in March 1993.

The lesson: Use these charts for general planning or as a rough guide of what to expect. But before taking off on a long air journey, check the weather forecasts for your area, any airports where you'll be changing planes, and your destination.

Index to airports

Anchorage, Alaska
Lat. 61° 10' N Lon. 150° 1' W
Airport code: ANC

Anchorage International Airport, which averages about 230 flights a day, is the gateway to Alaska for most visitors. It is also a hub for several cargo and air express companies. Low ceilings and visibility are most likely in the mornings during the winter. Snow is more than 10 percent likely from November into April. Thunderstorms, which can cause major delays in the eastern, southern and central U.S., are virtually unknown here. Odds of a summer thunderstorm are less than 1 in 100.

| | | Average % of time these conditions occur | | | |
Month	Time of day	Poor visibility	T'storm	Freezing precip.	Snow
Jan.	6 a.m.	7	0	0.9	14.8
	Noon	4	0	0.3	13.0
	6 p.m.	4	0	1.1	11.7
Feb.	6 a.m.	6	0	0.7	15.4
	Noon	2	0	0.6	14.7
	6 p.m.	1	0	0.4	13.6
March	6 a.m.	1	0	0	11.1
	Noon	1	0	0	10.7
	6 p.m.	1	0	0	9.6
April	6 a.m.	1	0	0.2	10.3
	Noon	*	0	0	6.8
	6 p.m.	1	0	0	6.7
May	6 a.m.	*	0	0	0.3
	Noon	*	0	0	0.3
	6 p.m.	0	0	0	0.3
June	6 a.m.	*	0	0	0
	Noon	0	0	0	0
	6 p.m.	0	0	0	0
July	6 a.m.	*	0	0	0
	Noon	0	0	0	0
	6 p.m.	0	0	0	0
Aug.	6 a.m.	1	0	0	0
	Noon	0	0	0	0
	6 p.m.	*	0.1	0	0
Sept.	6 a.m.	3	0.1	0	0.3
	Noon	0	0.1	0	0.2
	6 p.m.	*	0.1	0	0.2
Oct.	6 a.m.	2	0	0.1	8.0
	Noon	1	0	0.3	7.8
	6 p.m.	1	0	0.3	6.9
Nov.	6 a.m.	4	0	0.8	11.9
	Noon	3	0	0.4	11.8
	6 p.m.	2	0	0.7	10.4
Dec	6 a.m.	5	0	0.8	17.1
	Noon	6	0	0.3	16.8
	6 p.m.	3	0	0.9	16.7

* Less than 0.5 percent

Atlanta, Georgia
Lat. 33° 39' N Lon. 84° 26' W
Airport code: ATL

Hartsfield Atlanta International Airport is a major hub for Delta Air Lines. The airport has about 1,800 takeoffs and landings during an average day. Low ceilings and visibility are most likely to cause delays in the morning from December through March; January mornings are the most likely for delays. Like other parts of the eastern U.S., thunderstorms can be a problem in the late afternoons from June into September. Freezing rain and snow are most likely in January.

| | | Average % of time these conditions occur | | | |
Month	Time of day	Poor visibility	T'storm	Freezing precip.	Snow
Jan.	7 a.m.	8	0.1	1.0	1.2
	1 p.m.	4	0.2	0.6	1.1
	7 p.m.	3	0.1	0.6	0.8
Feb.	7 a.m.	6	0.5	0.6	0.8
	1 p.m.	2	0.2	0.1	1.1
	7 p.m.	3	0.7	0.3	0.2
March	7 a.m.	6	0.6	0.4	0.6
	1 p.m.	1	0.4	0.2	0.5
	7 p.m.	1	1.1	0.2	0.2
April	7 a.m.	2	0.7	0	0
	1 p.m.	*	0.9	0	0
	7 p.m.	*	1.3	0	0.1
May	7 a.m.	3	0.5	0	0
	1 p.m.	*	1.1	0	0
	7 p.m.	*	2.5	0	0
June	7 a.m.	2	0.2	0	0
	1 p.m.	0	2.1	0	0
	7 p.m.	*	4.0	0	0
July	7 a.m.	3	0.2	0	0
	1 p.m.	*	2.5	0	0
	7 p.m.	0	4.4	0	0
Aug.	7 a.m.	4	0.1	0	0
	1 p.m.	*	2.1	0	0
	7 p.m.	0	4.1	0	0
Sept.	7 a.m.	4	0.1	0	0
	1 p.m.	*	0.6	0	0
	7 p.m.	*	1.5	0	0
Oct.	7 a.m.	5	0	0	0
	1 p.m.	*	0.1	0	0
	7 p.m.	*	0.1	0	0
Nov.	7 a.m.	5	0.2	0	0.1
	1 p.m.	1	0.1	0	0.3
	7 p.m.	2	0.3	0	0.1
Dec.	7 a.m.	7	0	0.7	0.6
	1 p.m.	3	0.1	0.3	0.6
	7 p.m.	3	0.1	0.4	0.1

* Less than 0.5 percent

Boston, Massachusetts

Lat. 42° 22' N Lon. 71° 2' W
Airport code: BOS

Logan International Airport isn't a major airline hub, but passengers heading for smaller New England cities often change to commuter flights here. On an average day, 1,200 to 1,400 aircraft arrive or depart. The airport's location on a peninsula means fog is likely 15 to 20 percent of the time in the morning and evening. But visibility drops below three-quarters of a mile no more than 3 percent of the year. Snow and ice can cause winter delays. In summer, thunderstorms are uncommon.

Month	Time of day	Poor visibility	T'storm	Freezing precip.	Snow
Jan.	7 a.m.	2	0	1.3	10.6
	1 p.m.	3	0	0.4	10.5
	7 p.m.	2	0.1	0.8	9.4
Feb.	7 a.m.	3	0	0.8	10.8
	1 p.m.	2	0.1	0.5	10.7
	7 p.m.	2	0	0.3	8.8
March	7 a.m.	3	0.1	0.3	6.9
	1 p.m.	2	0.2	0.4	6.2
	7 p.m.	1	0.1	0.4	5.9
April	7 a.m.	3	0	0	1.7
	1 p.m.	1	0.1	0	0.9
	7 p.m.	1	0.3	0	0.8
May	7 a.m.	3	0.1	0	0
	1 p.m.	1	0.4	0	0.1
	7 p.m.	2	0.7	0	0.1
June	7 a.m.	2	0.4	0	0
	1 p.m.	1	0.6	0	0
	7 p.m.	1	1.2	0	0
July	7 a.m.	2	0.2	0	0
	1 p.m.	*	0.5	0	0
	7 p.m.	1	1.4	0	0
Aug.	7 a.m.	2	0.4	0	0
	1 p.m.	*	0.3	0	0
	7 p.m.	1	1.1	0	0
Sept.	7 a.m.	3	0.2	0	0
	1 p.m.	1	0.6	0	0
	7 p.m.	1	0.4	0	0
Oct.	7 a.m.	3	0	0	0.1
	1 p.m.	1	0	0	0.2
	7 p.m.	1	0.1	0	0.1
Nov.	7 a.m.	2	0	0.1	1.7
	1 p.m.	1	0	0.1	1.5
	7 p.m.	1	0.1	0.1	1.7
Dec.	7 a.m.	2	0	0.8	7.6
	1 p.m.	1	0.1	0.4	7.2
	7 p.m.	1	0	0.2	7.6

* Less than 0.5 percent

Chicago, Illinois

Lat. 41° 59' N Lon. 87° 54' W
Airport code: ORD

With more than 2,300 flights a day, Chicago O'Hare International is the world's busiest airport 51 weeks of the year. (During the annual Experimental Aircraft Association air show in late July, the Oshkosh, Wis., airport displaces O'Hare.) Both American Airlines and United Airlines use O'Hare as a major hub. From November into March, snow is likely 10 to 15 percent of the time, but low ceilings and visibility occur less than 2 percent of the year. Thunderstorms are relatively uncommon.

Month	Time of day	Poor visibility	T'storm	Freezing precip.	Snow
Jan.	6 a.m.	2	0	1.2	16.8
	Noon	3	0	0.9	14.5
	6 p.m.	1	0.1	1.2	14.4
Feb.	6 a.m.	3	0	1.1	15.0
	Noon	2	0	0.2	13.4
	6 p.m.	2	0.1	0.4	14.8
March	6 a.m.	3	0.2	1.0	9.2
	Noon	1	0.1	0.4	8.7
	6 p.m.	2	0.2	0.7	0.8
April	6 a.m.	2	0.2	0	2.2
	Noon	1	0.5	0	1.9
	6 p.m.	1	0.7	0	2.1
May	6 a.m.	2	0.8	0	0.4
	Noon	*	0.1	0	0.1
	6 p.m.	*	1.0	0	0
June	6 a.m.	1	0.5	0	0
	Noon	*	0.3	0	0
	6 p.m.	0	2.2	0	0
July	6 a.m.	1	1.2	0	0
	Noon	0	0.2	0	0
	6 p.m.	0	1	0	0
Aug.	6 a.m.	2	1.5	0	0
	Noon	0	0.5	0	0
	6 p.m.	0	1.1	0	0
Sept.	6 a.m.	2	0.7	0	0
	Noon	0	0.3	0	0
	6 p.m.	*	1.1	0	0
Oct.	6 a.m.	2	0.1	0	0.7
	Noon	0	0	0	0.4
	6 p.m.	0	0.4	0	0.3
Nov.	6 a.m.	2	0	0	5.5
	Noon	1	0.1	0	4.9
	6 p.m.	*	0.5	0	5.1
Dec.	6 a.m.	2	0	1.0	14.3
	Noon	3	0	0.3	13.0
	6 p.m.	1	0.1	0.9	11.2

* Less than 0.5 percent

Dallas-Fort Worth, Texas

Lat. 32° 54' N Lon. 97° 2' W
Airport code: DFW

Dallas-Fort Worth International Airport is a major hub for American Airlines and a secondary hub for Delta Air Lines. About 2,300 flights each day go to 210 worldwide destinations. Delays here can affect flights across the U.S. and even overseas. Thunderstorms from April into September, especially in the afternoon or early evening, are most likely to cause delays. In mornings from November through February, poor visibility or low clouds can cause delays up to 4 percent of the time.

| | | Average % of time these conditions occur | | | |
| | Time | Poor | | Freezing | |
Month	of day	visibility	T'storm	precip.	Snow
Jan.	6 a.m.	4	0.3	1.7	1.1
	Noon	1	0	1.2	1.4
	6 p.m.	1	0.2	0.8	1.0
Feb.	6 a.m.	3	0.9	1.0	1.4
	Noon	*	0.1	0.3	1.4
	6 p.m.	1	0	0.4	1.1
March	6 a.m.	2	1.1	0.1	0.3
	Noon	*	0.2	0.1	0.4
	6 p.m.	*	0.7	0.1	0.1
April	6 a.m.	1	1.7	0	0
	Noon	0	1.3	0	0
	6 p.m.	*	2.2	0	0
May	6 a.m.	1	2.9	0	0
	Noon	0	2.3	0	0
	6 p.m.	*	3.0	0	0
June	6 a.m.	*	3.0	0	0
	Noon	0	1.4	0	0
	6 p.m.	0	2.2	0	0
July	6 a.m.	*	1.1	0	0
	Noon	0	0.7	0	0
	6 p.m.	0	1.4	0	0
Aug.	6 a.m.	*	0.9	0	0
	Noon	0	1.0	0	0
	6 p.m.	*	2.3	0	0
Sept.	6 a.m.	*	0.8	0	0
	Noon	*	0.8	0	0
	6 p.m.	*	1.2	0	0
Oct.	6 a.m.	1	1.3	0	0
	Noon	*	0.7	0	0
	6 p.m.	*	0.7	0	0
Nov.	6 a.m.	3	0.8	0	0.2
	Noon	*	0.4	0	0.2
	6 p.m.	*	0.4	0.1	0
Dec.	6 a.m.	3	0.2	0.7	0.5
	Noon	1	0.3	0.2	0.4
	6 p.m.	1	0.3	0.2	0.4

* Less than 0.5 percent

Denver, Colorado

Lat. 39° 46' N Lon. 104° 52' W
Airport code: DEN

Stapleton International Airport is a hub for both United Airlines and Continental Airlines with about 1,400 flights each day. The new Denver International Airport is to replace Stapleton in 1995. Weather at the two airports is similar. Problems include snow from winter into April and summer afternoon thunderstorms. Denver's location near major research labs in Boulder means many aviation weather studies are conducted there. Denver is often the first place to use new technology.

| | | Average % of time these conditions occur | | | |
| | Time | Poor | | Freezing | |
Month	of day	visibility	T'storm	precip.	Snow
Jan.	8 a.m.	2	0	0	10.2
	2 p.m.	1	0	0	8.3
	8 p.m.	1	0	0.1	10.4
Feb.	8 a.m.	2	0	0.7	11.4
	2 p.m.	1	0	0.2	8.8
	8 p.m.	1	0	0.3	11.4
March	8 a.m.	3	0	0.5	12.7
	2 p.m.	1	0	0	9.5
	8 p.m.	1	0.2	0.2	13.6
April	8 a.m.	2	0	0.1	7.1
	2 p.m.	1	0.5	0.1	5.0
	8 p.m.	*	0.2	0.1	6.9
May	8 a.m.	1	0.1	0	1.6
	2 p.m.	*	3.4	0	1.2
	8 p.m.	*	2.1	0	1.5
June	8 a.m.	0	0.2	0	0
	2 p.m.	0	5.3	0	0
	8 p.m.	0	3.7	0	0.1
July	8 a.m.	*	0.2	0	0
	2 p.m.	*	4.9	0	0
	8 p.m.	0	4.0	0	0
Aug.	8 a.m.	*	0	0	0
	2 p.m.	*	3.1	0	0
	8 p.m.	0	2.0	0	0
Sept.	8 a.m.	1	0	0	0.8
	2 p.m.	*	1.3	0	0.5
	8 p.m.	*	1.2	0	0.7
Oct.	8 a.m.	1	0	0.2	3.2
	2 p.m.	*	0.3	0	2.4
	8 p.m.	1	0.3	0.1	3.4
Nov.	8 a.m.	2	0	0.1	8.5
	2 p.m.	1	0	0.1	6.4
	8 p.m.	1	0	0.2	9.0
Dec.	8 a.m.	2	0	0.7	8.9
	2 p.m.	1	0	0.2	7.1
	8 p.m.	1	0	0.5	9.7

* Less than 0.5 percent

Kansas City, Missouri

Lat. 39° 19' N Lon. 94° 43' W

Airport code: MCI

The Kansas City International Airport, on the Missouri side of the Kansas-Missouri border, averages about 534 takeoffs and landings a day. Low ceilings and visibility occur from 2 to 5 percent of the time all year. Snow or freezing rain occurs 5 percent or more of the time from December through February and can be a problem in November and March. Summer thunderstorms are more common late at night, especially around 3 a.m., often easing up around dawn. They still can delay flights.

Month	Time of day	Poor visibility	T'storm	Freezing precip.	Snow
Jan.	6 a.m.	3	0.2	0.9	7.9
	Noon	3	0	0.4	7.2
	6 p.m.	3	0	0.7	7.3
Feb.	6 a.m.	5	0.2	1.0	6.9
	Noon	3	0	1.0	7.7
	6 p.m.	2	0.2	0.6	8.5
March	6 a.m.	4	0	0.5	4.3
	Noon	1	0.4	0.5	2.7
	6 p.m.	1	0.4	0.4	2.5
April	6 a.m.	2	1.5	0	1.5
	Noon	*	0.6	0	0.7
	6 p.m.	*	1.1	0	0.9
May	6 a.m.	2	3.2	0	0
	Noon	0	2.0	0	0
	6 p.m.	*	2.3	0	0
June	6 a.m.	1	4.4	0	0
	Noon	0	0.9	0	0
	6 p.m.	*	2.0	0	0
July	6 a.m.	2	2.7	0	0
	Noon	*	0.9	0	0
	6 p.m.	0	1.3	0	0
Aug.	6 a.m.	4	3.4	0	0
	Noon	0	0.7	0	0
	6 p.m.	0	2.2	0	0
Sept.	6 a.m.	4	2.6	0	0
	Noon	*	1.1	0	0
	6 p.m.	*	1.3	0	0
Oct.	6 a.m.	3	1.5	0	0
	Noon	*	0.5	0	0.2
	6 p.m.	*	0.5	0	0
Nov.	6 a.m.	3	0	0.4	2.3
	Noon	2	0.2	0.5	2.5
	6 p.m.	1	0	0.4	2.3
Dec.	6 a.m.	4	0.2	1.2	5.6
	Noon	3	0.2	1.7	6.3
	6 p.m.	3	0.2	1.7	4.9

* Less than 0.5 percent

Los Angeles, California

Lat. 33° 56' N Lon. 118° 23' W

Airport code: LAX

Even though it's not a hub, Los Angeles International is the world's third busiest airport with around 1,900 flights a day. Its Southern California location means snow is not a problem and thunderstorms are rare. But smoke or haze — smog — restrict visibility from 25 to 67 percent of time. The airport's location on the coast means fog is a problem, especially in the mornings in fall and winter when visibility is low as often as 9 percent of the time.

Month	Time of day	Poor visibility	T'storm	Freezing precip.	Snow
Jan.	7 a.m.	6	0	0	0
	1 p.m.	1	0	0	0
	7 p.m.	2	0.1	0	0
Feb.	7 a.m.	6	0.1	0	0
	1 p.m.	1	0	0	0
	7 p.m.	2	0.2	0	0
March	7 a.m.	6	0.1	0	0
	1 p.m.	*	0	0	0
	7 p.m.	1	0	0	0
April	7 a.m.	4	0	0	0
	1 p.m.	0	0.1	0	0
	7 p.m.	1	0	0	0
May	7 a.m.	1	0	0	0
	1 p.m.	0	0	0	0
	7 p.m.	*	0	0	0
June	7 a.m.	1	0	0	0
	1 p.m.	0	0	0	0
	7 p.m.	*	0	0	0
July	7 a.m.	2	0.1	0	0
	1 p.m.	0	0.1	0	0
	7 p.m.	1	0	0	0
Aug.	7 a.m.	3	0.1	0	0
	1 p.m.	0	0	0	0
	7 p.m.	1	0.1	0	0
Sept.	7 a.m.	7	0	0	0
	1 p.m.	0	0.2	0	0
	7 p.m.	1	0.5	0	0
Oct.	7 a.m.	9	0	0	0
	1 p.m.	*	0.1	0	0
	7 p.m.	1	0	0	0
Nov.	7 a.m.	8	0	0	0
	1 p.m.	1	0.1	0	0
	7 p.m.	2	0.2	0	0
Dec.	7 a.m.	8	0.1	0	0
	1 p.m.	1	0.1	0	0
	7 p.m.	3	0.1	0	0

* Less than 0.5 percent

Miami, Florida

Lat. 28° 48' N Lon. 80° 18' W
Airport code: MIA

Miami International, which is a hub for American Airlines and Iberia Airlines, has about 1,500 takeoffs and landings a day. Its south Florida location means that weather delays are rare. January mornings have the highest odds of low ceilings and visibility, mostly from fog, which is most common in December and January. Thunderstorms occur all year. Chances of thunderstorms are highest around midday from June through September.

Month	Time of day	Poor visibility	T'storm	Freezing precip.	Snow
		Average % of time these conditions occur			
Jan.	7 a.m.	3	0.2	0	0
	1 p.m.	0	0.4	0	0
	7 p.m.	0	0.1	0	0
Feb.	7 a.m.	2	0.3	0	0
	1 p.m.	*	0.2	0	0
	7 p.m.	0	0.2	0	0
March	7 a.m.	2	0.2	0	0
	1 p.m.	0	0.8	0	0
	7 p.m.	0	0.5	0	0
April	7 a.m.	1	0.2	0	0
	1 p.m.	0	1.2	0	0
	7 p.m.	0	1.2	0	0
May	7 a.m.	1	1.9	0	0
	1 p.m.	*	4.3	0	0
	7 p.m.	*	2.6	0	0
June	7 a.m.	*	1.3	0	0
	1 p.m.	*	9.3	0	0
	7 p.m.	*	5.0	0	0
July	7 a.m.	*	1.6	0	0
	1 p.m.	*	10.5	0	0
	7 p.m.	*	3.6	0	0
Aug.	7 a.m.	*	2.0	0	0
	1 p.m.	*	9.8	0	0
	7 p.m.	*	4.5	0	0
Sept.	7 a.m.	*	1.0	0	0
	1 p.m.	*	6.9	0	0
	7 p.m.	*	4.4	0	0
Oct.	7 a.m.	1	0.5	0	0
	1 p.m.	*	2.0	0	0
	7 p.m.	0	1.7	0	0
Nov.	7 a.m.	1	0.2	0	0
	1 p.m.	*	0.4	0	0
	7 p.m.	0	0.2	0	0
Dec.	7 a.m.	2	0.1	0	0
	1 p.m.	0	0.4	0	0
	7 p.m.	0	0.2	0	0

* Less than 0.5 percent

Nashville, Tennessee

Lat. 36° 7' N Lon. 86° 41' W
Airport code: BNA

Metropolitan Nashville Airport is a hub for American Airlines and averages about 600 takeoffs and landings a day. Early morning fog is common, occurring more than 15 percent of the time. The odds of visibility being less than three-quarters of a mile are highest from August through October. Thunderstorms are the most common late in the day in June, July and August. Snow is most common in the mornings in January and February, but does occur from November to April.

Month	Time of day	Poor visibility	T'storm	Freezing precip.	Snow
		Average % of time these conditions occur			
Jan.	6 a.m.	3	0.5	1.1	6.1
	Noon	1	0.2	0.5	4.4
	6 p.m.	1	0.3	0.7	3.8
Feb.	6 a.m.	3	0.4	0.3	5.1
	Noon	1	0.2	0.2	3.9
	6 p.m.	1	0.6	0.2	3.0
March	6 a.m.	2	1.1	0	2.3
	Noon	*	0.7	0.1	2.0
	6 p.m.	*	1.3	0	1.2
April	6 a.m.	1	0.9	0	0.1
	Noon	0	0.3	0	0
	6 p.m.	*	1.7	0	0
May	6 a.m.	2	1.4	0	0
	Noon	*	1.7	0	0
	6 p.m.	0	2.0	0	0
June	6 a.m.	2	1.1	0	0
	Noon	*	2.2	0	0
	6 p.m.	*	3.7	0	0
July	6 a.m.	2	1.0	0	0
	Noon	*	3.4	0	0
	6 p.m.	*	4.8	0	0
Aug.	6 a.m.	4	1.0	0	0
	Noon	*	2.0	0	0
	6 p.m.	*	4.1	0	0
Sept.	6 a.m.	5	0.5	0	0
	Noon	0	0.7	0	0
	6 p.m.	0	1.0	0	0
Oct.	6 a.m.	5	0.4	0	0
	Noon	0	0.2	0	0
	6 p.m.	0	0.6	0	0
Nov.	6 a.m.	3	0.4	0.2	0.9
	Noon	*	0.4	0.1	0.9
	6 p.m.	*	0.3	0	0.8
Dec.	6 a.m.	2	0.1	0.3	3.1
	Noon	1	0	0.2	2.3
	6 p.m.	*	0.3	0.2	1.9

* Less than 0.5 percent

Newark, New Jersey

Lat. 40° 42' N Lon. 74° 10' W
Airport code: EWR

Newark International is one of the three major airports serving New York City. Though it is across the Hudson River from New York, it's by far the busiest of the three with about 1,200 flights a day. Its location, in a metropolitan area on the shore of Newark Bay less than nine miles from the Atlantic Ocean, means visibility is often restricted by fog and haze, especially in the mornings. Snow falls most often in January and February. In summer, thunderstorms cause few delays.

Month	Time of day	Poor visibility	T'storm	Freezing precip.	Snow
		Average % of time these conditions occur			
Jan.	7 a.m.	3	0	0.8	6.6
	1 p.m.	3	0.1	0.8	5.8
	7 p.m.	2	0	0.7	5.0
Feb.	7 a.m.	3	0.1	0.7	6.7
	1 p.m.	2	0.3	0.5	5.9
	7 p.m.	2	0.1	0.4	5.5
March	7 a.m.	2	0.2	0.2	4.5
	1 p.m.	1	0.3	0.1	4.1
	7 p.m.	1	0.3	0.3	3.3
April	7 a.m.	2	0.1	0	1.0
	1 p.m.	1	0.2	0	0.5
	7 p.m.	*	0.4	0	0.1
May	7 a.m.	2	0	0	0
	1 p.m.	*	0.5	0	0
	7 p.m.	1	1.5	0	0
June	7 a.m.	2	0.2	0	0
	1 p.m.	0	0.6	0	0
	7 p.m.	0	1.2	0	0
July	7 a.m.	1	0.4	0	0
	1 p.m.	*	0.8	0	0
	7 p.m.	0	1.8	0	0
Aug.	7 a.m.	1	0.2	0	0
	1 p.m.	*	0.8	0	0
	7 p.m.	0	1.6	0	0
Sept.	7 a.m.	2	0	0	0
	1 p.m.	*	0.2	0	0
	7 p.m.	0	0.6	0	0
Oct.	7 a.m.	4	0	0	0.1
	1 p.m.	*	0.2	0	0.1
	7 p.m.	*	0.2	0	0.1
Nov.	7 a.m.	2	0.1	0	0.6
	1 p.m.	*	0.3	0	1.2
	7 p.m.	1	0.2	0.1	0.6
Dec.	7 a.m.	2	0	0.2	4.1
	1 p.m.	2	0.1	0.6	3.6
	7 p.m.	1	0	0.5	4.0

New York (J.F.K. International), New York

Lat. 40° 39' N Lon. 73° 47' W
Airport code: JFK

John F. Kennedy International Airport is the major East Coast departure and arrival airport for overseas flights. Each day about 900 flights depart or land. International flights make 3 p.m. to 9 p.m. the busiest time of the day. This works out well since weather-related delays are most likely in the morning when fog comes from nearby Jamaica Bay. Snow is most likely to delay flights from December into March. Thunderstorms are most likely in late afternoon or early evening in June and July.

Month	Time of day	Poor visibility	T'storm	Freezing precip.	Snow
		Average % of time these conditions occur			
Jan.	7 a.m.	4	0	0.2	5.1
	1 p.m.	2	0.1	0.2	4.8
	7 p.m.	3	0.1	0.3	3.3
Feb.	7 a.m.	3	0	0.3	5.8
	1 p.m.	3	0.2	0.3	4.5
	7 p.m.	2	0.1	0.3	4.7
March	7 a.m.	4	0.2	0.2	4.1
	1 p.m.	2	0	0	3.1
	7 p.m.	2	0	0	3.2
April	7 a.m.	4	0	0	1.0
	1 p.m.	2	0.2	0	0.6
	7 p.m.	2	0.5	0	0.2
May	7 a.m.	4	0.2	0	0
	1 p.m.	1	0.2	0	0
	7 p.m.	3	0.9	0	0
June	7 a.m.	4	0.2	0	0
	1 p.m.	0	0.5	0	0
	7 p.m.	1	1.6	0	0
July	7 a.m.	2	0.3	0	0
	1 p.m.	*	0.7	0	0
	7 p.m.	1	1.7	0	0
Aug.	7 a.m.	2	0.4	0	0
	1 p.m.	0	0.7	0	0
	7 p.m.	1	1.4	0	0
Sept.	7 a.m.	1	0.2	0	0
	1 p.m.	*	0	0	0
	7 p.m.	*	0.9	0	0
Oct.	7 a.m.	3	0	0	0
	1 p.m.	*	0.1	0	0
	7 p.m.	1	0.2	0	0.1
Nov.	7 a.m.	3	0	0	0.5
	1 p.m.	1	0.2	0	0.9
	7 p.m.	1	0.2	0	0.5
Dec.	7 a.m.	3	0	0.3	3.2
	1 p.m.	2	0.1	0.1	2.6
	7 p.m.	1	0.1	0.3	2.0

* Less than 0.5 percent

* Less than 0.5 percent

New York (LaGuardia Airport), New York

Lat. 40° 46' N Lon. 73° 54' W

Airport code: LGA

LaGuardia Airport is on the north side of Long Island. About 915 flights a day take off or land with peak hours being from 6 a.m.to 9 a.m., 2 p.m. to 3 p.m. and 4 p.m. to 7 p.m. Its urban location near water means that either fog or haze often limits visibility. Delays from low ceilings or limited visibility are most likely in the mornings. Snow or freezing precipitation are most likely from December into March. Thunderstorms, relatively uncommon, are most likely late in the day from May through June.

Philadelphia, Pennsylvania

Lat. 39° 53' N Lon. 75° 14' W

Airport code: PHL

Philadelphia International Airport has about 1,400 flights take off or land each day. Haze or smog are common and fog occurs often in the mornings year round. Snow occurs more than 5 percent of the time in January and February. As with other places in the East, thunderstorms are most common on summer afternoons.

		Average % of time these conditions occur						Average % of time these conditions occur			
Month	Time of day	Poor visibility	T'storm	Freezing precip.	Snow	Month	Time of day	Poor visibility	T'storm	Freezing precip.	Snow
Jan.	7 a.m.	2	0	0.9	6.2	Jan.	7 a.m.	4	0	1.4	5.5
	1 p.m.	2	0	0.8	5.6		1 p.m.	3	0	0.6	4.7
	7 p.m.	1	0.1	0.6	4.5		7 p.m.	2	0	0.6	5.2
Feb.	7 a.m.	3	0.1	0.6	6.4	Feb.	7 a.m.	4	0	0.7	5.2
	1 p.m.	2	0	0.6	5.3		1 p.m.	3	0	0.1	4.5
	7 p.m.	2	0	0.3	6.2		7 p.m.	2	0	0.8	5.2
March	7 a.m.	3	0	0.2	4.9	March	7 a.m.	3	0	0.3	3.4
	1 p.m.	1	0.2	0.1	4.3		1 p.m.	1	0	0	3.1
	7 p.m.	1	0.1	0.2	3.5		7 p.m.	1	0.2	0.1	2.3
April	7 a.m.	2	0.1	0	1.0	April	7 a.m.	2	0.1	0	0.8
	1 p.m.	*	0.2	0	0.4		1 p.m.	*	0.1	0	0.3
	7 p.m.	1	0.5	0	0.2		7 p.m.	*	1.1	0	0.3
May	7 a.m.	3	0.1	0	0	May	7 a.m.	3	0.1	0	0
	1 p.m.	*	0.5	0	0		1 p.m.	0	0.4	0	0
	7 p.m.	1	1.4	0	0		7 p.m.	0	1.5	0	0
June	7 a.m.	3	0.2	0	0	June	7 a.m.	2	0.1	0	0
	1 p.m.	*	0.6	0	0		1 p.m.	0	0.5	0	0
	7 p.m.	*	1.1	0	0		7 p.m.	*	2.4	0	0
July	7 a.m.	1	0.5	0	0	July	7 a.m.	1	0.6	0	0
	1 p.m.	0	0.4	0	0		1 p.m.	*	0.8	0	0
	7 p.m.	*	2.0	0	0		7 p.m.	*	2.8	0	0
Aug.	7 a.m.	1	0.2	0	0	Aug.	7 a.m.	2	0.2	0	0
	1 p.m.	0	0.7	0	0		1 p.m.	*	0.6	0	0
	7 p.m.	0	1.0	0	0		7 p.m.	0	2.4	0	0
Sept.	7 a.m.	1	0.2	0	0	Sept.	7 a.m.	5	0.1	0	0
	1 p.m.	0	0.1	0	0		1 p.m.	*	0.3	0	0
	7 p.m.	*	0.8	0	0		7 p.m.	*	1.0	0	0
Oct.	7 a.m.	1	0	0	0.1	Oct.	7 a.m.	8	0.1	0	0
	1 p.m.	*	0.1	0	0.2		1 p.m.	*	0.2	0	0.1
	7 p.m.	*	0.2	0	0		7 p.m.	*	0.1	0	0.1
Nov.	7 a.m.	2	0.1	0.1	0.3	Nov.	7 a.m.	5	0	0	0.6
	1 p.m.	1	0.1	0	1.3		1 p.m.	1	0.1	0	0.7
	7 p.m.	*	0.1	0	0.7		7 p.m.	1	0.2	0	0.8
Dec.	7 a.m.	2	0	0.3	3.2	Dec.	7 a.m.	4	0.1	0.7	2.7
	1 p.m.	1	0.1	0.2	2.9		1 p.m.	3	0	0.2	3.2
	7 p.m.	1	0.1	0.2	3.5		7 p.m.	2	0.1	0.5	2.5

* Less than 0.5 percent

* Less than 0.5 percent

Raleigh–Durham, North Carolina

Lat. 35° 52' N Lon. 78° 47' W

Airport code: RDU

Raleigh–Durham International Airport is an American Airlines hub with about 560 takeoffs and landings each day. Late-day summer thunderstorms are most likely to cause delays. On average, June and July afternoons are worst. A humid climate means morning fog is common with August and September being the months when poor visibility is most likely to delay flights. Snow, most common in January, is not likely to delay flights.

Month	Time of day	Average % of time these conditions occur Poor visibility	T'storm	Freezing precip.	Snow
Jan.	7 a.m.	5	0.1	0.8	2.2
	1 p.m.	2	0	0.6	2.1
	7 p.m.	2	0.3	0.8	1.6
Feb.	7 a.m.	5	0.1	0.8	1.8
	1 p.m.	1	0.2	0.3	1.6
	7 p.m.	2	0.2	0.4	1.5
March	7 a.m.	5	0.3	0.6	0.9
	1 p.m.	1	0.2	0.1	1.0
	7 p.m.	1	0.5	0.1	0.8
April	7 a.m.	2	0.3	0	0
	1 p.m.	*	0.6	0	0.1
	7 p.m.	*	2.1	0	0
May	7 a.m.	4	0.6	0	0
	1 p.m.	*	0.8	0	0
	7 p.m.	*	4.0	0	0
June	7 a.m.	3	0.6	0	0
	1 p.m.	*	2.3	0	0
	7 p.m.	0	5.2	0	0
July	7 a.m.	2	0.5	0	0
	1 p.m.	*	2.2	0	0
	7 p.m.	*	6.5	0	0
Aug.	7 a.m.	7	0.3	0	0
	1 p.m.	*	2.2	0	0
	7 p.m.	*	4.6	0	0
Sept.	7 a.m.	9	0.3	0	0
	1 p.m.	0	0.4	0	0
	7 p.m.	*	1.6	0	0
Oct.	7 a.m.	8	0.2	0	0
	1 p.m.	*	0.2	0	0
	7 p.m.	1	0.4	0	0
Nov.	7 a.m.	6	0.2	0	0.1
	1 p.m.	*	0	0	0.2
	7 p.m.	1	0.2	0	0.5
Dec.	7 a.m.	6	0	0.8	0.7
	1 p.m.	1	0	0.2	1.1
	7 p.m.	2	0	0.6	0.5

* Less than 0.5 percent

St. Louis, Missouri

Lat. 38° 45' N Lon. 90° 22' W

Airport code: STL

Lambert – St. Louis International is a Trans World Airlines hub with about 1,100 takeoffs and landings each day. Since St. Louis is in the central U.S., snow and freezing rain are common in the winter, with snow falling more than 6 percent of the time in January and February. Thunderstorms, while not common, are most likely later during the day in summer but do occur overnight and in the early morning. Morning fog is common all year, but seldom causes delays.

Month	Time of day	Average % of time these conditions occur Poor visibility	T'storm	Freezing precip.	Snow
Jan	6 a.m.	2	0.1	2.7	6.9
	Noon	2	0.2	1.3	7.6
	6 p.m.	2	0.1	1.3	6.3
Feb.	6 a.m.	3	0.1	0.8	7.3
	Noon	1	0.1	0.5	7.3
	6 p.m.	1	0.2	0.8	6.5
March	6 a.m.	2	0.6	0.3	5.1
	Noon	1	0.3	0.3	3.8
	6 p.m.	1	0.6	0.3	3.8
April	6 a.m.	1	0.9	0	0.7
	Noon	*	0.9	0	0.7
	6 p.m.	*	1.9	0	0.5
May	6 a.m.	1	1.5	0	0
	Noon	0	0.7	0	0
	6 p.m.	*	2.2	0	0
June	6 a.m.	*	1.7	0	0
	Noon	0	0.9	0	0
	6 p.m.	*	2.6	0	0
July	6 a.m.	1	2.1	0	0
	Noon	0	0.8	0	0
	6 p.m.	*	2.3	0	0
Aug.	6 a.m.	1	1.2	0	0
	Noon	*	0.4	0	0
	6 p.m.	0	2.0	0	0
Sept.	6 a.m.	2	0.7	0	0
	Noon	0	0.4	0	0
	6 p.m.	*	1.7	0	0
Oct.	6 a.m.	2	0.6	0	0
	Noon	*	0.4	0	0
	6 p.m.	*	1.3	0	0.1
Nov.	6 a.m.	2	0.4	0.2	2.0
	Noon	*	0.1	0	2.3
	6 p.m.	*	0.4	0.1	2.2
Dec.	6 a.m.	2	0.2	1.1	5.0
	Noon	1	0	0.9	5.7
	6 p.m.	2	0.1	1.3	5.6

* Less than 0.5 percent

San Francisco, California

Lat. 37° 37' N Lon. 122° 23' W

Airport code: SFO

San Francisco International has about 1,250 takeoffs and landings each day. United Air Lines accounts for about one-third of the flights even though the airport is not a hub. The airport is on San Francisco Bay and morning fog is common, especially from September through February. Low ceilings or visibility are most likely to delay morning flights from December through February. Snow or freezing precipitation are rare. Thunderstorms, while rare, can occur about any time of the year.

Month	Time of day	Poor visibility	T'storm	Freezing precip.	Snow
Jan.	7 a.m.	6	0.2	0	0.1
	1 p.m.	1	0.1	0	0
	7 p.m.	*	0	0	0
Feb.	7 a.m.	5	0	0	0.1
	1 p.m.	1	0.1	0	0
	7 p.m.	*	0.2	0	0
March	7 a.m.	1	0.1	0	0
	1 p.m.	*	0.5	0	0
	7 p.m.	0	0.1	0	0
April	7 a.m.	*	0	0	0
	1 p.m.	0	0.2	0	0
	7 p.m.	0	0.1	0	0
May	7 a.m.	0	0.2	0	0
	1 p.m.	0	0	0	0
	7 p.m.	0	0	0	0
June	7 a.m.	0	0.1	0	0
	1 p.m.	0	0	0	0
	7 p.m.	0	0	0	0
July	7 a.m.	*	0	0	0
	1 p.m.	0	0	0	0
	7 p.m.	0	0.1	0	0
Aug.	7 a.m.	*	0.1	0	0
	1 p.m.	0	0	0	0
	7 p.m.	0	0	0	0
Sept.	7 a.m.	*	0	0	0
	1 p.m.	0	0	0	0
	7 p.m.	0	0	0	0
Oct.	7 a.m.	3	0	0	0
	1 p.m.	*	0	0	0
	7 p.m.	0	0	0	0
Nov.	7 a.m.	3	0.1	0	0
	1 p.m.	*	0.1	0	0
	7 p.m.	*	0	0	0
Dec.	7 a.m.	5	0	0	0
	1 p.m.	1	0.2	0	0
	7 p.m.	1	0	0	0

* Less than 0.5 percent

Seattle, Washington

Lat. 47° 27' N Lon. 122° 18' W

Airport code: SEA

Seattle-Tacoma International Airport is a hub for Alaska Airlines and averages about 1,000 takeoffs and landings a day. The airport's Pacific Northwest location means the airport rarely has thunderstorms. Snow can fall as much as 6.5 percent of the time in January. Fog, especially in September and October, can be the most troublesome. It can cause poor visibility 13 percent of the time on September mornings and 17 percent of the time on October mornings.

Month	Time of day	Poor visibility	T'storm	Freezing precip.	Snow
Jan.	7 a.m.	8	0.2	0.4	6.5
	1 p.m.	4	0.2	0.1	4.7
	7 p.m.	3	0	0.2	5.0
Feb.	7 a.m.	6	0	0	2.5
	1 p.m.	1	0.3	0	1.9
	7 p.m.	*	0.1	0.2	2.1
March	7 a.m.	4	0	0	2.1
	1 p.m.	*	0	0	0.9
	7 p.m.	*	0.1	0	1.7
April	7 a.m.	3	0	0	0.2
	1 p.m.	0	0.1	0	0.1
	7 p.m.	0	0.1	0	0.1
May	7 a.m.	1	0	0	0
	1 p.m.	0	0.2	0	0
	7 p.m.	0	0	0	0
June	7 a.m.	2	0	0	0
	1 p.m.	0	0	0	0
	7 p.m.	0	0.1	0	0
July	7 a.m.	4	0	0	0
	1 p.m.	0	0	0	0
	7 p.m.	*	0.1	0	0
Aug.	7 a.m.	7	0	0	0
	1 p.m.	*	0.2	0	0
	7 p.m.	0	0.1	0	0
Sept.	7 a.m.	13	0	0	0
	1 p.m.	*	0.2	0	0
	7 p.m.	*	0.2	0	0
Oct.	7 a.m.	17	0.1	0	0.1
	1 p.m.	1	0	0	0
	7 p.m.	1	0.1	0	0
Nov.	7 a.m.	9	0	0	1.2
	1 p.m.	2	0.2	0	0.5
	7 p.m.	3	0.2	0	1.1
Dec.	7 a.m.	7	0.2	0.1	3.6
	1 p.m.	4	0	0.1	2.9
	7 p.m.	4	0.2	0	2.4

* Less than 0.5 percent

Washington (National Airport), D.C.

Lat. 38° 51' N Lon. 77° 2' W
Airport code: DCA

Washington National Airport is on the Potomac River only about two miles from the heart of Washington, D.C. An average of 850 flights take off and land each day. Because it is in the Mid-Atlantic region, operations are sometimes delayed by snow in the winter, as in the North, and by late-day summer thunderstorms, as in the Southeast. Snow is most likely in January and February, but some of the region's biggest snowstorms have been in March.

| | Average % of time these conditions occur | | | |
Month	Time of day	Poor visibility	T'storm	Freezing precip.	Snow
Jan.	7 a.m.	2	0	1.1	4.0
	1 p.m.	2	0.2	0.7	4.1
	7 p.m.	1	0	0.9	4.0
Feb.	7 a.m.	2	0	0.6	3.5
	1 p.m.	1	0	0.4	3.6
	7 p.m.	1	0.1	0.4	3.5
March	7 a.m.	2	0	0.1	2.6
	1 p.m.	*	0.1	0.1	1.9
	7 p.m.	*	0.5	0.2	2.0
April	7 a.m.	1	0.2	0	0.2
	1 p.m.	0	0.2	0	0.1
	7 p.m.	0	0.6	0	0.1
May	7 a.m.	1	0.1	0	0
	1 p.m.	0	0.5	0	0
	7 p.m.	*	2.5	0	0
June	7 a.m.	*	0	0	0
	1 p.m.	0	0.3	0	0
	7 p.m.	*	2.5	0	0
July	7 a.m.	*	0.1	0	0
	1 p.m.	*	0.7	0	0
	7 p.m.	*	3.3	0	0
Aug.	7 a.m.	1	0.1	0	0
	1 p.m.	0	0.5	0	0
	7 p.m.	0	2.5	0	0
Sept.	7 a.m.	1	0	0	0
	1 p.m.	0	0.3	0	0
	7 p.m.	0	0.9	0	0
Oct.	7 a.m.	4	0.1	0	0.1
	1 p.m.	0	0.1	0	0
	7 p.m.	*	0.3	0	0
Nov.	7 a.m.	3	0.1	0	0.7
	1 p.m.	*	0.1	0	0.8
	7 p.m.	*	0.2	0	0.5
Dec.	7 a.m.	3	0.1	0.5	2.8
	1 p.m.	1	0	0.3	2.8
	7 p.m.	1	0.1	0.6	2.1

* Less than 0.5 percent

Amsterdam, Netherlands

Lat. 52° 18' N Lon. 4° 46' E
Airport code: AMS

Western Europe is known for its cloudy flying weather. Some kind of obstruction to visibility is common each month at Amsterdam Airport Schiphol. Fall, winter and early spring, with their long nights and low sun angle, are worst. In the mornings from September into March, low ceilings or visibility are reported at least 6 percent of the time. Snow is most likely from December through February. Thunderstorms are fairly rare, but most likely later in the day in summer.

| | Average % of time these conditions occur | | | |
Month	Time of day	Poor visibility	T'storm	Freezing precip.	Snow
Jan.	7 a.m.	7	0.2	1.0	4.4
	1 p.m.	5	0.2	0.2	7.2
	7 p.m.	5	1.0	0.2	3.4
Feb.	7 a.m.	8	0	0.2	4.6
	1 p.m.	4	0.2	0.2	4.4
	7 p.m.	3	0.4	0	2.7
March	7 a.m.	7	0.2	0	2.7
	1 p.m.	1	0	0	1.1
	7 p.m.	1	0.8	0	1.3
April	7 a.m.	4	0.6	0	1.0
	1 p.m.	0	0.4	0	1.0
	7 p.m.	0	1.2	0	0.2
May	7 a.m.	2	0.6	0	0.2
	1 p.m.	0	0.6	0	0.2
	7 p.m.	*	1.1	0	0
June	7 a.m.	2	0.8	0	0
	1 p.m.	0	0.4	0	0
	7 p.m.	0	1.6	0	0
July	7 a.m.	3	1.2	0	0
	1 p.m.	0	0.4	0	0
	7 p.m.	0	1.5	0	0
Aug.	7 a.m.	5	0.4	0	0
	1 p.m.	0	0	0	0
	7 p.m.	0	1.0	0	0
Sept.	7 a.m.	9	0.6	0	0
	1 p.m.	*	0.2	0	0
	7 p.m.	*	1.6	0	0
Oct.	7 a.m.	9	1.1	0	0
	1 p.m.	1	0.6	0	0
	7 p.m.	1	1.3	0	0
Nov.	7 a.m.	7	0.4	0.2	2.0
	1 p.m.	3	0.4	0	1.8
	7 p.m.	3	1.2	0	1.4
Dec.	7 a.m.	6	0.8	0.9	3.4
	1 p.m.	3	0.4	0	3.0
	7 p.m.	3	0.9	0.8	2.1

* Less than 0.5 percent

Hong Kong

Lat. 22° 20' N Lon. 114° 11' E

Airport code: HKG

Since Hong Kong is in the tropics, snow, sleet, or freezing rain never cause airport delays. But Hong Kong, like other tropical places, has plenty of rain. At the Hong Kong International Airport, rain is reported at least 15 percent of the time from March through October. But these abundant rain showers rarely cause extremely low ceilings or poor visibility. Thunderstorms are relatively uncommon.

London (Heathrow), England

Lat. 51° 29' N Lon. 0° 27' W

Airport code: LHR

London is famous for its fog. But it's not fog alone that causes the low ceilings and visibility that can cause morning delays at least 6 percent of the time from October through February. Rain, drizzle, smoke and haze combine with fog to slow things down. Snow can also be a problem from time to time, especially from December into March. Summer days usually offer fewer problems. Thunderstorms are reported more than 2 percent of the time only in May and June later in the day.

Month	Time of day	Poor visibility	T'storm	Freezing precip.	Snow
Jan.	6 a.m.	0	0	0	0
	Noon	0	0	0	0
	6 p.m.	0	0	0	0
Feb.	6 a.m.	*	0.5	0	0
	Noon	0	0	0	0
	6 p.m.	0	0	0	0
March	6 a.m.	1	0.8	0	0
	Noon	0	1.7	0	0
	6 p.m.	*	0.6	0	0
April	6 a.m.	1	1.3	0	0
	Noon	*	1.8	0	0
	6 p.m.	*	1.3	0	0
May	6 a.m.	0	1.8	0	0
	Noon	0	1.4	0	0
	6 p.m.	0	0.9	0	0
June	6 a.m.	0	1.4	0	0
	Noon	0	0.7	0	0
	6 p.m.	0	0.9	0	0
July	6 a.m.	*	1.8	0	0
	Noon	0	2.2	0	0
	6 p.m.	0	1.1	0	0
Aug.	6 a.m.	0	2.7	0	0
	Noon	0	2.7	0	0
	6 p.m.	0	1.3	0	0
Sept.	6 a.m.	0	0.9	0	0
	Noon	0	1.2	0	0
	6 p.m.	0	0.9	0	0
Oct.	6 a.m.	0	0.2	0	0
	Noon	*	0	0	0
	6 p.m.	0	0	0	0
Nov.	6 a.m.	0	0	0	0
	Noon	0	0	0	0
	6 p.m.	0	0	0	0
Dec.	6 a.m.	0	0	0	0
	Noon	0	0	0	0
	6 p.m.	0	0	0	0

Average % of time these conditions occur

Month	Time of day	Poor visibility	T'storm	Freezing precip.	Snow
Jan.	6 a.m.	6	0	0.2	3.4
	Noon	2	0.2	0	4.2
	6 p.m.	2	0	0	2.2
Feb.	6 a.m.	6	0	0.4	6.0
	Noon	2	0	0.2	5.8
	6 p.m.	*	0.2	0	3.8
March	6 a.m.	3	0	0	2.6
	Noon	0	0.6	0	2.0
	6 p.m.	0	0.6	0	1.6
April	6 a.m.	3	0	0	0.2
	Noon	0	0.6	0	0
	6 p.m.	*	0.6	0	1.0
May	6 a.m.	1	0.4	0	0
	Noon	0	0.6	0	0
	6 p.m.	0	2.0	0	0
June	6 a.m.	1	0.4	0	0
	Noon	0	1.5	0	0
	6 p.m.	0	2.3	0	0
July	6 a.m.	1	0.4	0	0
	Noon	0	0.2	0	0
	6 p.m.	0	1.0	0	0
Aug.	6 a.m.	3	0.4	0	0
	Noon	0	0.4	0	0
	6 p.m.	0	1.2	0	0
Sept.	6 a.m.	4	0.2	0	0
	Noon	0	0.4	0	0
	6 p.m.	0	0.2	0	0
Oct.	6 a.m.	8	0	0	0
	Noon	1	0	0	0
	6 p.m.	*	0.4	0	0
Nov.	6 a.m.	7	0	0	0.2
	Noon	4	0.4	0	0
	6 p.m.	2	0.4	0	0.2
Dec.	6 a.m.	6	0.2	0	1.8
	Noon	2	0	0	2.4
	6 p.m.	2	0.2	0	1.8

Average % of time these conditions occur

* Less than 0.5 percent

* Less than 0.5 percent

Mexico City, Mexico

Lat. 19° 26' N Lon. 99° 5' W
Airport code: MEX

Although Mexico City is located in the tropics, its high elevation — Benito Juarez International Airport is 7,328 feet above sea level — makes it comparatively cool. Freezing rain or snow are never reported. Fog is most likely on November and December mornings. Few airports have afternoon thunderstorms as often as Mexico City. Late-day thunderstorms are reported 12 to 14 percent of the time from June through August, and at least 6 percent of the time in May, September and October.

Month	Average % of time these conditions occur Time of day	Poor visibility	T'storm	Freezing precip.	Snow
Jan.	6 a.m.	3	0	0	0
	Noon	2	0.2	0	0
	6 p.m.	3	0.2	0	0
Feb.	6 a.m.	1	0.2	0	0
	Noon	1	0	0	0
	6 p.m.	3	1.5	0	0
March	6 a.m.	0	0	0	0
	Noon	1	0	0	0
	6 p.m.	1	3.1	0	0
April	6 a.m.	2	0	0	0
	Noon	1	0.4	0	0
	6 p.m.	1	4.9	0	0
May	6 a.m.	2	0	0	0
	Noon	1	0.2	0	0
	6 p.m.	1	9.8	0	0
June	6 a.m.	1	0.6	0	0
	Noon	2	0	0	0
	6 p.m.	1	12.0	0	0
July	6 a.m.	1	0	0	0
	Noon	2	0	0	0
	6 p.m.	1	14.9	0	0
Aug.	6 a.m.	2	0	0	0
	Noon	2	0.2	0	0
	6 p.m.	1	14.1	0	0
Sept.	6 a.m.	1	0	0	0
	Noon	2	0	0	0
	6 p.m.	1	8.1	0	0
Oct.	6 a.m.	3	0	0	0
	Noon	3	0.2	0	0
	6 p.m.	1	6.3	0	0
Nov.	6 a.m.	5	0	0	0
	Noon	2	0	0	0
	6 p.m.	1	0.6	0	0
Dec.	6 a.m.	5	0	0	0
	Noon	3	0	0	0
	6 p.m.	1	1.0	0	0

* Less than 0.5 percent

Paris, France

Lat. 48° 44' N Lon. 2° 24' E
Airport code: ORY

Paris can be gloomy from fall into winter. Morning flights at Orly Airport in the morning are mostly likey to be delayed by low ceilings or poor visibility from October through February. On October mornings, for example, rain or drizzle is reported 13 percent of the time and fog 22 percent of the time. Heavy snow seldom falls, but when it does it can cause delays. Most likely times are from November into March. Thunderstorms are most likely late in the day from May into September.

Month	Average % of time these conditions occur Time of day	Poor visibility	T'storm	Freezing precip.	Snow
Jan.	7 a.m.	9	0	0.4	2.5
	1 p.m.	4	0	0.2	4.2
	7 p.m.	3	0.2	0.4	3.3
Feb.	7 a.m.	6	0	0.2	4.5
	1 p.m.	3	0	0	5.7
	7 p.m.	1	0.2	0	3.0
March	7 a.m.	2	0	0	1.5
	1 p.m.	*	0	0	0.8
	7 p.m.	*	0.4	0	1.3
April	7 a.m.	2	0.2	0	0.2
	1 p.m.	0	0	0	0.4
	7 p.m.	*	1.2	0	0.4
May	7 a.m.	2	0	0	0
	1 p.m.	0	0.2	0	0
	7 p.m.	0	2.5	0	0
June	7 a.m.	1	1.0	0	0
	1 p.m.	0	0.6	0	0
	7 p.m.	*	2.3	0	0
July	7 a.m.	*	0.6	0	0
	1 p.m.	0	0.6	0	0
	7 p.m.	0	2.3	0	0
Aug.	7 a.m.	2	0.2	0	0
	1 p.m.	*	0.6	0	0
	7 p.m.	0	3.0	0	0
Sept.	7 a.m.	5	0.4	0	0
	1 p.m.	0	0.8	0	0
	7 p.m.	0	1.0	0	0
Oct.	7 a.m.	10	0.4	0	0
	1 p.m.	1	0	0	0
	7 p.m.	1	0.6	0	0
Nov.	7 a.m.	10	0	0	1.0
	1 p.m.	5	0	0	1.4
	7 p.m.	3	0	0	1.2
Dec.	7 a.m.	9	0	0.2	1.3
	1 p.m.	7	0	0.2	1.1
	7 p.m.	5	0.2	0.2	1.0

* Less than 0.5 percent

Rio de Janeiro, Brazil

Lat. 22° 49' N Lon. 43° 15' W

Airport code: RIO

Freezing rain and snow are never a concern at Rio de Janeiro International Airport. Poor visibility is most likely in the mornings in May, June and July when fog and rain occur. This is winter in the Southern Hemisphere, even though winter and summer differ little in the tropics. Thunderstorms are most likely late in the day during December, January and February.

Month	Time of day	Average % of time these conditions occur Poor visibility	T'storm	Freezing precip.	Snow
Jan.	6 a.m.	1	0	0	0
	Noon	*	0.4	0	0
	6 p.m.	*	10.0	0	0
Feb.	6 a.m.	0	0	0	0
	Noon	0	1.1	0	0
	6 p.m.	*	9.4	0	0
March	6 a.m.	1	0.4	0	0
	Noon	0	0	0	0
	6 p.m.	*	6.1	0	0
April	6 a.m.	1	0.2	0	0
	Noon	0	0.6	0	0
	6 p.m.	*	2.1	0	0
May	6 a.m.	3	0	0	0
	Noon	*	0.2	0	0
	6 p.m.	0	0.6	0	0
June	6 a.m.	5	0.2	0	0
	Noon	*	0	0	0
	6 p.m.	*	0.4	0	0
July	6 a.m.	5	0	0	0
	Noon	*	0.2	0	0
	6 p.m.	0	0.4	0	0
Aug.	6 a.m.	2	0.2	0	0
	Noon	0	0.2	0	0
	6 p.m.	*	0.2	0	0
Sept.	6 a.m.	1	0.6	0	0
	Noon	*	0.4	0	0
	6 p.m.	0	0.4	0	0
Oct.	6 a.m.	*	0.4	0	0
	Noon	0	0.2	0	0
	6 p.m.	*	1.6	0	0
Nov.	6 a.m.	*	0	0	0
	Noon	0	0	0	0
	6 p.m.	*	3.1	0	0
Dec.	6 a.m.	0	0	0	0
	Noon	0	0.8	0	0
	6 p.m.	0	7.7	0	0

* Less than 0.5 percent

Rome, Italy

Lat. 41° 48' N Lon. 12° 14' E

Airport code: FCO

Even though Rome's Aeroporti di Roma is a few miles farther north than Boston, its climate is more like northern California's. Rome is on the Tyrrhenian Sea, an arm of the warm Mediterranean Sea. Snow occurs rarely. Airport delays are most likely to be caused by poor visibility or low ceilings from fog or rain in the mornings during March, April, May and October. Thunderstorms are most common any time of the day in June, and from September through November.

Month	Time of day	Average % of time these conditions occur Poor visibility	T'storm	Freezing precip.	Snow
Jan.	7 a.m.	3	1.4	0	0.4
	1 p.m.	*	1.1	0	0.4
	7 p.m.	*	1.3	0	0
Feb.	7 a.m.	3	0.6	0	0.4
	1 p.m.	*	0.8	0	0.2
	7 p.m.	*	1.4	0	0
March	7 a.m.	5	1.4	0	0
	1 p.m.	*	0.5	0	0
	7 p.m.	0	1.8	0	0.2
April	7 a.m.	5	1.1	0	0
	1 p.m.	*	0.4	0	0
	7 p.m.	*	0.7	0	0
May	7 a.m.	4	1.1	0	0
	1 p.m.	0	0.9	0	0
	7 p.m.	0	0	0	0
June	7 a.m.	2	0.6	0	0
	1 p.m.	0	0.6	0	0
	7 p.m.	*	1.7	0	0
July	7 a.m.	3	0.4	0	0
	1 p.m.	0	0.2	0	0
	7 p.m.	0	0.7	0	0
Aug.	7 a.m.	2	1.4	0	0
	1 p.m.	0	0.5	0	0
	7 p.m.	0	0.7	0	0
Sept.	7 a.m.	2	2.2	0	0
	1 p.m.	0	0.7	0	0
	7 p.m.	0	2.2	0	0
Oct.	7 a.m.	6	2.9	0	0
	1 p.m.	*	2.0	0	0
	7 p.m.	*	2.3	0	0
Nov.	7 a.m.	2	2.2	0	0
	1 p.m.	0	1.7	0	0
	7 p.m.	0	1.9	0	0
Dec.	7 a.m.	2	0.4	0	0.2
	1 p.m.	*	1.1	0	0
	7 p.m.	2	1.3	0	0

* Less than 0.5 percent

Sydney, Australia

Lat. 33° 75' N Lon. 151° 22' E

Airport code: SYD

Sydney Kingsford Smith Airport is far enough south to have some snow from time to time but it's rare. Furthermore, poor visibility and thunderstorms also are rare. Mornings in May offer the greatest chance of low visibility, only 3 percent of the time. In May, rain is reported 13 percent of the time in the morning and fog 6.8 percent. Thunderstorms are most likely on spring days in November and summer days in December.

Month	Average Time of day	% of time these conditions occur Poor visibility	T'storm	Freezing precip.	Snow
Jan.	6 a.m.	*	0.2	0	0
	Noon	0	0.2	0	0
	3 p.m.[1]	*	1.1	0	0
Feb.	6 a.m.	*	0.2	0	0
	Noon	0	0	0	0
	3 p.m.[1]	0	0	0	0
March	6 a.m.	*	0	0	0
	Noon	*	0.2	0	0
	3 p.m.[1]	*	0.2	0	0
April	6 a.m.	1	0.2	0	0
	Noon	*	0	0	0
	3 p.m.[1]	0	0.2	0	0
May	6 a.m.	3	0.2	0	0
	Noon	*	0.2	0	0
	3 p.m.[1]	1	0.2	0	0.2
June	6 a.m.	1	0.2	0	0.2
	Noon	*	0	0	0
	3 p.m.[1]	0	0	0	0
July	6 a.m.	1	0	0	0
	Noon	0	0	0	0
	3 p.m.[1]	*	0	0	0
Aug.	6 a.m.	*	0.2	0	0.2
	Noon	*	0.2	0	0
	3 p.m.[1]	*	0.4	0	0
Sept.	6 a.m.	*	0.2	0	0
	Noon	0	0	0	0
	3 p.m.[1]	*	0.6	0	0
Oct.	6 a.m.	1	0	0	0
	Noon	*	0.4	0	0
	3 p.m.[1]	*	0.6	0	0
Nov.	6 a.m.	1	0.4	0	0
	Noon	0	0.6	0	0
	6 p.m.	0	1.2	0	0
Dec.	6 a.m.	0	0.4	0	0
	Noon	0	0.6	0	0
	6 p.m.	0	1.8	0	0

* Less than 0.5 percent   [1] 6 p.m. reports missing for these months

Tokyo (Narita), Japan

Lat. 35° 33' N Lon. 139° 47' E

Airport code: NRT

Weather can be expected to delay few flights to New Tokyo International in Narita. Poor visibility is reported 2 percent of the time or less all year. Snow does fall, but rarely. It's most likely in the morning and at midday in February and has occurred from December into April. Thunderstorms are reported every month of the year except January and February, but never more than 1.7 percent of the time. July and August are the most likely months for rare thunderstorms to occur.

Month	Average Time of day	% of time these conditions occur Poor visibility	T'storm	Freezing precip.	Snow
Jan.	6 a.m.	*	0	0	1.5
	Noon	*	0	0	1.7
	6 p.m.	*	0	0	1.5
Feb.	6 a.m.	1	0	0	3.8
	Noon	*	0	0	4.4
	6 p.m.	1	0	0	2.9
March	6 a.m.	1	0.2	0	1.3
	Noon	1	0	0	1.5
	6 p.m.	*	0.4	0	1.3
April	6 a.m.	2	0	0	0.2
	Noon	1	0.4	0	0
	6 p.m.	*	0	0	0
May	6 a.m.	*	0.2	0	0
	Noon	0	0	0	0
	6 p.m.	0	0.6	0	0
June	6 a.m.	2	0.2	0	0
	Noon	*	0.2	0	0
	6 p.m.	0	0.4	0	0
July	6 a.m.	2	0.4	0	0
	Noon	*	0.8	0	0
	6 p.m.	*	1.7	0	0
Aug.	6 a.m.	1	0.4	0	0
	Noon	0	0.6	0	0
	6 p.m.	0	1.6	0	0
Sept.	6 a.m.	*	0.4	0	0
	Noon	0	0.4	0	0
	6 p.m.	0	0.2	0	0
Oct.	6 a.m.	*	0.2	0	0
	Noon	*	0.2	0	0
	6 p.m.	*	0	0	0
Nov.	6 a.m.	1	0.2	0	0
	Noon	0	0.2	0	0
	6 p.m.	*	0	0	0
Dec.	6 a.m.	*	0.2	0	0.4
	Noon	0	0	0	0.4
	6 p.m.	0	0	0	0.2

* Less than 0.5 percent

Weather radio

Even with the best technology and forecasting techniques, warnings of tornadoes, severe thunderstorms and flash floods often give people only a few minutes to flee or prepare.

Getting warnings in time can be a lifesaver. The best way to make sure of receiving weather warnings is to have a weather radio that picks up broadcasts from NOAA weather radio stations. Twenty-four hours a day the National Weather Service broadcasts over 390 NOAA weather radio stations. There are regional forecasts and specialized ones for boaters, farmers and travelers.

Weather offices break in on these routine forecasts to announce watches and warnings of dangerous weather. Some weather radios with a tone-alert automatically sound an alarm when a watch or warning is issued.

Today 70 to 75 percent of the people in the U.S. can receive weather radio broadcasts at their homes or workplaces. The Weather Service, the U.S. Department of Agriculture and the Federal Emergency Management Agency are working through private funding and civic groups to add new broadcast stations that will bring weather radio to 95 percent of the population. About 250 new stations would be needed. The expansion will also make tone-alert weather radios available to schools, nursing homes, and other places where dangerous weather can threaten large numbers of people.

The Weather Service is also working with emergency management organizations and the U.S. Geological Survey to make weather radio an "all hazards" radio that would broadcast information about emergencies such as toxic spills and earthquakes.

In Florida, the Weather Service is working with the state to make post-disaster information, such as where to obtain help, available over weather radio. Such information would have helped victims of Hurricane Andrew in Dade County, Fla., in 1992. Eventually this service will be extended to other states.

Here is the list of NOAA weather radio sites and frequencies:

Location	Frequency
Alaska	
Anchorage	162.550
Cordova	162.550
Craig	162.400
Fairbanks	162.550
Haines	162.400
Homer	162.400
Juneau	162.550
Ketchikan	162.550
Kodiak	162.550
Nome	162.550
Petersburg	162.550
Seward	162.550
Sitka	162.550
Valdez	162.550
Wrangell	162.400
Yakutat	162.400
Alabama	
Anniston	162.475
Birmingham	162.550
Demopolis/Linden	162.475
Dozier	162.550
Florence	162.475
Huntsville	162.400
Louisville	162.475
Mobile	162.550
Montgomery	162.400
Tuscaloosa	162.400
Arkansas	
Fayetteville	162.475
Fort Smith	162.550
Gurdon	162.475
Jonesboro	162.550
Little Rock	162.550
Mountain View	162.400
Star City	162.400
Texarkana	162.550
Arizona	
Flagstaff	162.400
Phoenix	162.550
Porter Mountain	162.400
Tucson	162.400
Yuma	162.550
California	
Bakersfield	162.550
Coachella	162.400
Eureka	162.400
Fresno	162.400
Lindsay	162.550
Los Angeles	162.550
Monterey	162.550
Pt. Arena/Ukiah	162.550
Redding	162.550
Sacramento	162.400
San Diego	162.400
San Francisco	162.400
San Luis Obispo	162.550
Santa Barbara	162.400
Colorado	
Alamosa	162.475
Colorado Springs	162.475
Denver	162.550
Fort Collins	162.450
Grand Junction	162.550
Greeley	162.400
Mead/Longmount	162.475
Pueblo	162.400
Sterling	162.400
Connecticut	
Hartford	162.475
Meriden	162.400
New London	162.550
Delaware	
Lewes	162.550
Florida	
Belle Glade	162.400
Daytona Beach	162.400
Fort Myers	162.475
Gainesville	162.475
Inverness	162.400
Jacksonville	162.550
Key West	162.400
Melbourne	162.550
Miami	162.550
Orlando	162.475
Panama City	162.550
Pensacola	162.400
Sebring	162.500
Tallahassee	162.400
Tampa	162.550
W. Palm Beach	162.475
Georgia	
Athens	162.400
Atlanta	162.550
Augusta	162.550
Baxley	162.525
Chatsworth	162.400
Columbus	162.400
Macon	162.475
Pelham	162.550
Savannah	162.400
Valdosta	162.500
Waycross	162.475
Waynesboro	162.425
Hawaii	
Hawaii	162.550
Kauai (Kokee)	162.400
Maui	162.400
Oahu (Mt. Kaala)	162.550

Iowa

Cedar Rapids	162.475
Des Moines	162.550
Dubuque	162.400
Sioux City	162.475
Waterloo	162.550

Idaho

Boise	162.550
Lewiston	162.550
Pocatello	162.550
Twin Falls	162.400

Illinois

Champaign	162.550
Chicago	162.550
Marion	162.425
Peoria	162.475
Rock Island/ Moline	162.550
Rockford	162.475
Springfield	162.400
Bloomington	162.400

Indiana

Evansville	162.550
Fort Wayne	162.550
Indianapolis	162.550
Marion	162.450
Monticello	162.475
South Bend	162.400
Terre Haute	162.400

Kansas

Chanute	162.400
Colby/Goodland	162.475
Concordia	162.550
Dodge City	162.475
Ellsworth	162.400
Topeka	162.475
Wichita	162.550

Kentucky

Ashland	162.550
Bowling Green	162.400
Covington	162.550
Elizabethtown	162.550
Hazard	162.475
Lexington	162.400
Louisville	162.475
Mayfield	162.475
Paintsville	162.525
Pikeville	162.400

Somerset	162.550

Louisiana

Alexandria	162.475
Baton Rouge	162.400
Buras	162.400
Lafayette	162.550
Lake Charles	162.400
Monroe	162.550
Morgan City	162.475
New Orleans	162.550
Shreveport	162.400

Massachusetts

Boston	162.475
Camp Edwards	162.550
Hyannis	162.550
Worcester	162.550

Maryland

Baltimore	162.400
Hagerstown	162.475
Salisbury	162.475

Maine

Caribou	162.525
Dresden	162.475
Ellsworth	162.400
Falmouth	162.550

Michigan

Alpena	162.550
Detroit	162.550
Flint	162.475
Grand Rapids	162.550
Hesperia	162.475
Houghton	162.400
Marquette	162.550
Onondaga	162.400
Oshtemo	162.475
Sault Ste Marie	162.550
Traverse City	162.400

Minnesota

Bemidji	162.425
Detroit Lakes	162.400
Duluth	162.550
International Falls	162.550
Mankato	162.400
Mpls/St. Paul	162.550
Rochester	162.475
St. Cloud	162.475
Thief River Falls	162.550

Wilmer	162.475

Missouri

Camdenton	162.550
Columbia	162.400
Hannibal	162.475
Hermitage	162.450
Joplin	162.550
Kansas City	162.550
Sikeston	162.400
Springfield	162.400
St. Joseph	162.400
St. Louis	162.550

Mississippi

Ackerman	162.475
Booneville	162.550
Bude	162.550
Columbia	162.400
Gulfport	162.400
Hattiesburg	162.475
Inverness	162.550
Jackson	162.400
Meridian	162.550
Oxford	162.400

Montana

Billings	162.550
Butte	162.550
Glasgow	162.400
Great Falls	162.550
Harve/ Squaw Butte	162.400
Helena	162.400
Kalispell	162.550
Miles City	162.400
Missoula	162.400

Nebraska

Bassette	162.475
Grand Island	162.400
Holdrege	162.475
Lincoln	162.475
Merriman	162.400
Norfolk	162.550
North Platte	162.550
Omaha	162.400
Scottsbluff	162.550

New Hampshire

Concord	162.400

New Jersey

Atlantic City	162.400

New Mexico

Albuquerque	162.400
Carlsbad	162.475
Clovis	162.475
Des Moines	162.550
Farmington	162.475
Hobbs/Maljamar	162.400
Las Cruces	162.400
Ruidoso	162.550
Santa Fe	162.550

Nevada

Boulder City	162.550
Elko	162.550
Ely/Cave Mountain	162.400
Las Vegas	162.550
Reno	162.550
Winnemucca	162.400

New York

Albany	162.550
Binghamton	162.475
Buffalo	162.550
Elmira	162.400
Kingston	162.475
New York City	162.550
Riverhead	162.475
Rochester	162.400
Stamford	162.400
Syracuse	162.550
Watertown	162.475

North Carolina

Asheville	162.400
Cape Hatteras	162.475
Charlotte	162.475
Fayetteville	162.475
New Bern	162.400
Raleigh/Durham	162.550
Rocky Mount	162.475
Wilmington	162.550
Winston Salem	162.400

North Dakota

Bismarck	162.475
Dickinson	162.400
Fargo	162.475
Jamestown	162.550
Minot	162.400
Petersburg	162.400

Williston	162.550

Ohio

Akron	162.400
Bridgeport	162.525
Caldwell	162.475
Cleveland	162.550
Columbus	162.550
Dayton	162.475
Lima	162.400
Sandusky	162.400
Toledo	162.550

Oklahoma

Clinton	162.475
Enid	162.475
Lawton	162.550
McAlester	162.475
Oklahoma City	162.400
Ponca City	162.450
Tulsa	162.550

Oregon

Astoria	162.400
Brookings	162.550
Coos Bay	162.400
Eugene	162.400
Klamath Falls	162.550
Medford	162.400
Newport	162.550
Pendleton	162.400
Portland/Estacada	162.550
Roseburg	162.550
Salem	162.475

Pacific Islands

Agana	162.400
Saipan	162.550

Pennsylvania

Allentown	162.400
Clearfield	162.550
Erie	162.400
Harrisburg	162.550
Johnstown	162.400
Philadelphia	162.475
Pittsburgh	162.550
State College	162.475
Towanda	162.550
Wellsboro	162.475
Wilkes-Barre	162.550
Williamsport	162.400

Puerto Rico

Maricao	162.550
San Juan	162.400

Rhode Island

Providence	162.400

South Carolina

Beaufort	162.475
Charleston	162.550
Columbia	162.400
Conway	162.400
Cross	162.475
Florence	162.550
Greenville	162.550
Myrtle Beach	162.400
Sumter	162.475

South Dakota

Aberdeen	162.475
Huron	162.550
Pierre	162.400
Rapid City	162.550
Sioux Falls	162.400

Tennessee

Bristol	162.550
Chattanooga	162.550
Cookeville	162.400
Jackson	162.550
Knoxville	162.475
Memphis	162.475
Nashville	162.550
Shelbyville	162.475
Waverly	162.400

Texas

Abilene	162.400
Amarillo	162.550
Austin	162.400
Beaumont	162.475
Big Spring	162.475
Brownsville	162.550
Bryan	162.550
Corpus Christi	162.550
Dallas	162.400
Del Rio	162.400
El Paso	162.475
Fort Worth	162.550
Galveston	162.550
Houston	162.400
Laredo	162.400
Lubbock	162.400

Lufkin	162.550
Odessa/Midland	162.400
Paris	162.550
Pharr	162.400
San Angelo	162.550
San Antonio	162.550
Sherman	162.475
Tyler	162.475
Victoria	162.400
Waco	162.475
Wichita Falls	162.475

Utah

Logan	162.400
Milford/Cedar City	162.400
Navajo Mountain	162.550
Salt Lake City	162.550
Vernal	162.400

Vermont

Burlington	162.400
Marlboro	162.425
Windsor	162.475

Virginia

Heathsville	162.400
Lynchburg	162.550
Norfolk	162.550
Richmond	162.475
Roanoke	162.475
Manassas	162.550

Virgin Islands

St. Thomas	162.475

Washington

Neah Bay	162.550
Olympia	162.475
Seattle	162.550
Spokane	162.400
Wenatchee	162.475
Yakima	162.550

West Virginia

Beckley	162.550
Charleston	162.400
Clarksburg	162.550
Gilbert	162.475
Hinton	162.425
Moorefield	162.400
Spencer	162.500
Sutton	162.450

Wisconsin

Adams	162.400
Green Bay	162.550
La Crosse	162.550
Madison	162.550
Menomonie	162.400
Milwaukee	162.400
Park Falls	162.500
Sister Bay	162.425
Wausau	162.475

Wyoming

Casper Mountain	162.550
Cheyenne	162.475
Lander	162.475
Sheridan	162.475

Weather hot line

USA TODAY's WeatherTrak provides weather information for 450 U.S. cities and 250 overseas locations. Calls to 1-900-370-USAT (8728) are billed at 95¢ a minute. Calls to 1-800-USA-TODAY (872-8632) are charged 95¢ a minute on a major credit card. Forecasts are for four days plus a 10-day outlook.

Callers select U.S. cities by using the telephone area code; foreign cities by entering the first three letters of that city's name.

From overseas, callers can access USA TODAY's WeatherTrak by calling AT&T's USADirect Access Number for the country they are in from a touch-tone telephone. Then, dial 800-872-8632. An AT&T-acceptable calling card and a major credit card are needed.

Tuning in overseas

Voice of America has English-language broadcasts with weather reports that U.S. tourists can pick up overseas. Here are the times and frequencies where weather reports can be heard:

Day	Show	Time	Frequencies (kHz)
East Asia, Southeast Asia, Pacific			
Sun.-Sat.	Newsline	19:10	9525, 11870, 15180 (mainly to Pacific)
Mon.	VOA Pacific	21:10	11870, 15185, 17735 (mainly to Pacific)
Mon.-Sat.	Newsline	22:10	7215, 9705, 9770, 11760, 15185, 15290, 15305,17735, 17820
Mon.-Fri.	Newsline	23:10	7215, 9705, 9770, 11760, 15185, 15290, 15305,17735, 17820
Mon.-Fri.	Newsline	10:10	5985, 11720, 15425 (mainly to Pacific)
Mon.-Fri.	Newsline	12:10	1143[1], 6110, 9645, 9760, 11715, 11805, 15160, 15425
Mon.-Fri.	Asia Report	14:10	1143, 6110, 7215[2], 9645, 9760, 15160, 15425
Sat.	Newsline	00:10	1575, 7215, 9770, 11760, 15185, 15290, 17735, 17820
South Asia			
Mon.-Fri.	Newsline	01:10	7115, 7205, 9635, 11705, 11725, 15170, 15250,17740, 21550
Mon.-Fri.	Newsline	02:10	7115, 7205, 9635, 11705, 11725, 15170, 15250,17740, 21550
Mon.-Fri.	Asia Report	14:10	6110, 7125, 7215, 9645, 9760, 15255, 15395
Mon.-Sat.	Newsline	15:10	1575[2], 6110, 7125, 7215, 9645, 9700, 9760, 15255, 15395
Mon.-Sat.	Newsline	17:10	6110, 7125, 7215, 9645, 9700, 15395
Middle East, North Africa, Europe			
Sun.-Sat.	Newsline	19:10	3980, 6040, 9760, 9770, 15205
Mon.-Fri.	Newsline	04:10	792, 3980[2], 5995, 6010, 6040, 7170, 7200, 11965, 15205
Mon.-Fri.	Newsline	06:10	792, 1197, 1260, 3980, 5995, 6040, 6060, 6140, 7170, 7325, 11805, 11965
Mon.-Sat.	Newsline	15:10	1197, 1260, 1548, 9700, 15205, 15255
Mon.-Sat.	Newsline	17:10	6040, 9700, 9760, 15205, 15255
Africa			
Sun.-Fri.	Newsline	19:10	909, 7415, 11920, 12040, 13710, 15410, 15445, 15580, 17800
Mon.-Fri.	Newsline	04:10	909, 1530[1], 7265, 7280, 7340[1], 7405, 9575, 9885[1]
Mon.-Sat.	Newsline	17:10	909[1], 1530[1], 11920, 12040, 13710, 15410, 15445, 17895
Caribbean, Latin America			
Mon.-Fri.	Newsline	10:10	930, 7405, 9590, 11915, 15120
Mon.-Fri.	Newsline	12:10	930
Mon.-Sat.	Newsline	17:10	930
Mon.-Fri.	Report to Caribbean	00:10	930, 6130, 9455, 11695

Note: All times are Universal Time (UTC), also known as Greenwich Mean Time (GMT). Program schedule subject to change.

1 VOA English is broadcast on this frequency during first half of this hour program only.

2 VOA English is broadcast on this frequency during second half of this hour program only.

Length of the day

Travelers often want to know how much daylight they'll have in different parts of the world. The tables on the following pages give the number of hours and minutes from sunrise to sunset and the length of morning and evening twilight for each 10 degrees of latitude from 80° north southward across the equator to 80° south.

To find the period of daylight, start with the latitude, found by city in Chapter 6, then read across the day length charts:

Day lengths are given for the first day of each month as well as June 21 and Dec. 22, which are the dates for the spring and winter solstices in 1995.

The year's longest days in the Northern Hemisphere and the shortest in the Southern Hemisphere are around the time of the June solstice. The year's longest days in the Southern Hemisphere and shortest in the Northern Hemisphere are around the time of the December solstice.

Sunrise and **sunset** are when someone at sea level would see the uppermost edge of the sun on the horizon. The length of days will be shorter in valleys than on level places at the same latitude.

Morning twilight times are for "morning civil

twilight," which is the time from when the sun is six degrees below the horizon until sunrise.

Evening twilight is "evening civil twilight" from sunset until the sun is six degrees below the horizon. On clear days, civil twilight is generally the time before sunrise and after sunset when outdoor activities are possible without lights. Automatic street lights usually turn off at the beginning of morning civil twilight and come on at the end of evening civil twilight.

There are two additional twilight times that are not on the charts here. **Nautical twilight** is the period when the sun is from 6 degrees to 12 degrees below the horizon. At the end, it's impossible to distinguish the horizon at sea. **Astronomical twilight** is when the sun is between 12° and 18° below the horizon. At the end of astronomical twilight, the sun's last light is gone from the sky.

White nights in the far North and far South occur during the summer when evening twilight fades into morning twilight and the sky never becomes dark. On the charts here it is listed as **Twilight lasts all night.** In common use, "twilight" often refers to the time before sunset when the sun is low in the sky as well as the actual twilight. During the summer in far northern or far southern latitudes, twilight in this sense lasts much longer than the actual twilight times given in these tables because the sun is low in the sky for long periods after sunrise or before sunset.

Date	Morning twilight	Sunrise to sunset	Evening twilight

Latitude 80° N

Date	Morning twilight	Sunrise to sunset	Evening twilight
Jan. 1	No twilight; sun never rises		
Feb. 1	No twilight; sun never rises		
March 1	2 hr., 15 min.	6 hr., 18 min.	2 hr., 16 min.
April 1	*	16 hr., 15 min.	*
May 1		No sunset	
June 1		No sunset	
June 21		No sunset	
July 1		No sunset	
Aug. 1		No sunset	
Sept. 1	*	20 hr., 52 min.	*
Oct. 1	2 hr., 01 min.	10 hr., 16 min.	2 hr., 00 min.
Nov. 1	Twilight lasts 4 hr., 31 min.; sun never rises		
Dec. 1	No twilight; sun never rises		
Dec. 22	No twilight; sun never rises		

* Twilight lasts all night

Latitude 70° N

Date	Morning twilight	Sunrise to sunset	Evening twilight
Jan. 1	Twilight lasts 4 hr., 27 min.; sun never rises		
Feb. 1	1 hr., 26 min.	4 hr., 52 min.	1 hr., 27 min.
March 1	1 hr., 03 min.	9 hr., 27 min.	1 hr., 02 min.
April 1	1 hr., 06 min.	13 hr., 59 min.	1 hr., 06 min.
May 1	*	18 hr., 51 min.	*
June 1		No sunset	
June 21		No sunset	
July 1		No sunset	
Aug. 1	*	21 hr., 21 min.	*
Sept. 1	1 hr., 17 min.	15 hr., 32 min.	1 hr., 14 min.
Oct. 1	1 hr., 00 min.	11 hr., 11 min.	1 hr., 01 min.
Nov. 1	1 hr., 14 min.	6 hr., 30 min.	1 hr., 14 min.
Dec. 1	Twilight lasts 5 hr., 19 min.; sun never rises		
Dec. 22	Twilight lasts 4 hr., 07 min.; sun never rises		

Latitude 60° N

Date	Morning twilight	Sunrise to sunset	Evening twilight
Jan. 1	57 min.	6 hr., 02 min.	56 min.
Feb. 1	47 min.	7 hr., 58 min.	47 min.
March 1	42 min.	10 hr., 26 min.	42 min.
April 1	43 min.	13 hr., 16 min.	43 min.
May 1	52 min.	15 hr., 58 min.	53 min.
June 1	1 hr., 22 min.	18 hr., 17 min.	1 hr., 24 min.
June 21	1 hr., 47 min.	18 hr., 52 min.	1 hr., 46 min.
July 1	1 hr., 40 min.	18 hr., 43 min.	1 hr., 39 min.
Aug. 1	1 hr., 01 min.	16 hr., 53 min.	1 hr., 00 min.
Sept. 1	46 min.	14 hr., 11 min.	45 min.
Oct. 1	41 min.	11 hr., 30 min.	41 min.
Nov. 1	45 min.	8 hr., 44 min.	45 min.
Dec. 1	54 min.	6 hr., 29 min.	54 min.
Dec. 22	58 min.	5 hr., 53 min.	57 min.

Latitude 50° N

Date	Morning twilight	Sunrise to sunset	Evening twilight
Jan. 1	39 min.	8 hr., 09 min.	39 min.
Feb. 1	35 min.	9 hr., 19 min.	35 min.
March 1	33 min.	10 hr., 56 min.	33 min.
April 1	33 min.	12 hr., 53 min.	33 min.
May 1	36 min.	14 hr., 41min.	37 min.
June 1	42 min.	16 hr., 04 min.	43 min.
June 21	45 min.	16 hr., 22 min.	45 min.
July 1	45 min.	16 hr., 18 min.	44 min.
Aug. 1	38 min.	15 hr., 15 min.	39 min.
Sept. 1	34 min.	13 hr., 31 min.	34 min.
Oct. 1	32 min.	11 hr., 41 min.	32 min.
Nov. 1	34 min.	9 hr., 49 min.	34 min.
Dec. 1	37 min.	8 hr., 25 min.	38 min.
Dec. 22	38 min.	8 hr., 05 min.	38 min.

Latitude 40° N

Date	Morning twilight	Sunrise to sunset	Evening twilight
Jan. 1	31 min.	9 hr., 23 min.	31 min.
Feb. 1	29 min.	10 hr., 10 min.	28 min.
March 1	27 min.	11 hr., 17 min.	27 min.
April 1	27 min.	12 hr., 39 min.	27 min.

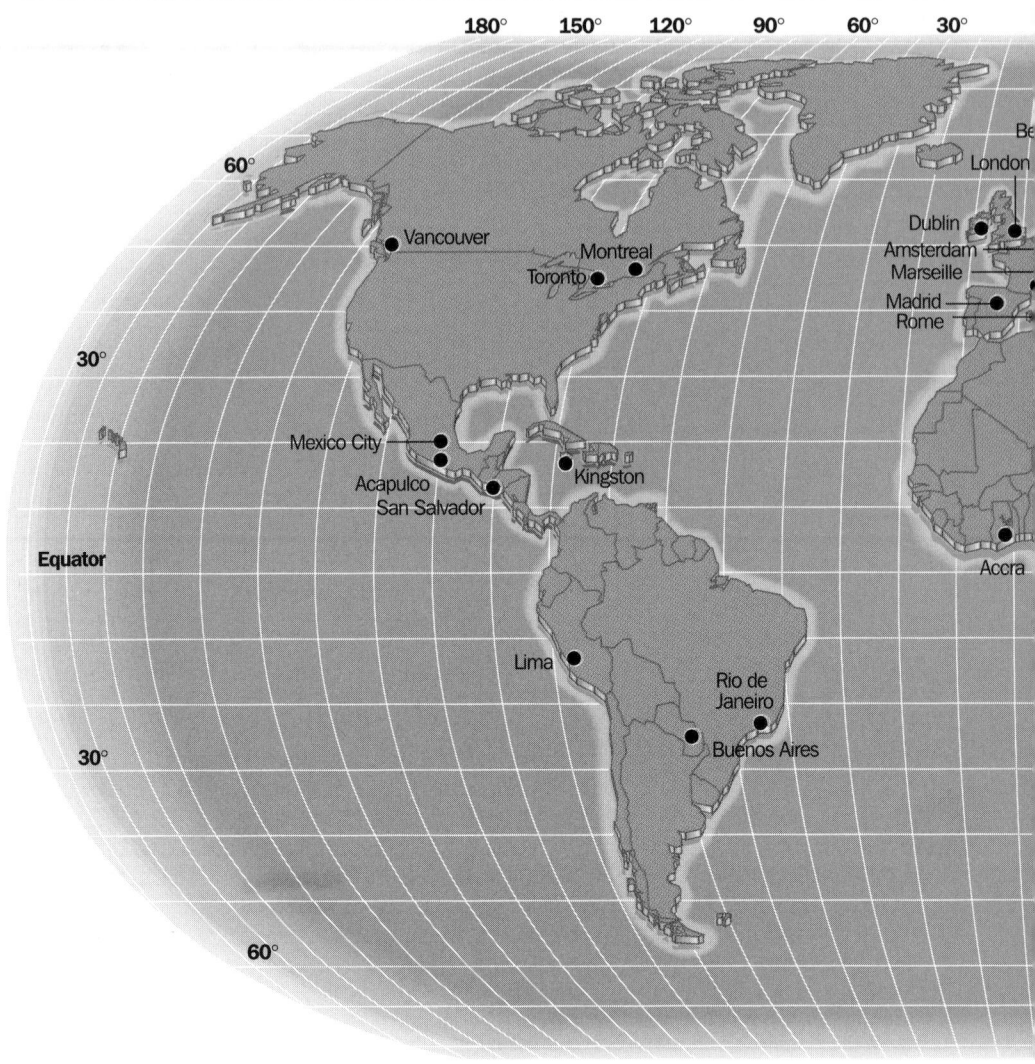

Date	Morning twilight	Sunrise to sunset	Evening twilight	Latitude 30° N		
				Jan. 1	26 min.	10 hr., 15 min.	26 min.
May 1	29 min.	13 hr., 53 min.	29 min.	Feb. 1	25 min.	10 hr., 46 min.	25 min.
June 1	33 min.	14 hr., 48 min.	33 min.	March 1	24 min.	11 hr., 32 min.	24 min.
June 21	33 min.	15 hr., 01 min.	33 min.	April 1	24 min.	12 hr., 28 min.	24 min.
July 1	33 min.	14 hr., 58 min.	32 min.	May 1	26 min.	13 hr., 19 min.	25 min.
Aug. 1	31 min.	14 hr., 16 min.	31 min.	June 1	27 min.	13 hr., 56 min.	27 min.
Sept. 1	28 min.	13 hr., 05 min.	28 min.	June 21	27 min.	14 hr., 05 min.	28 min.
Oct. 1	27 min.	11 hr., 47 min.	27 min.	July 1	27 min.	14 hr., 03 min.	28 min.
Nov. 1	28 min.	10 hr., 30 min.	28 min.	Aug. 1	26 min.	13 hr., 35 min.	26 min.
Dec. 1	30 min.	9 hr., 33 min.	30 min.	Sept. 1	25 min.	12 hr., 46 min.	25 min.
Dec. 22	31 min.	9 hr., 19 min.	31 min.	Oct. 1	24 min.	11 hr., 53 min.	24 min.
				Nov. 1	24 min.	11 hr., 00 min.	25 min.
				Dec. 1	26 min.	10 hr., 22 min.	26 min.
				Dec. 22	26 min.	10 hr., 13 min.	26 min.

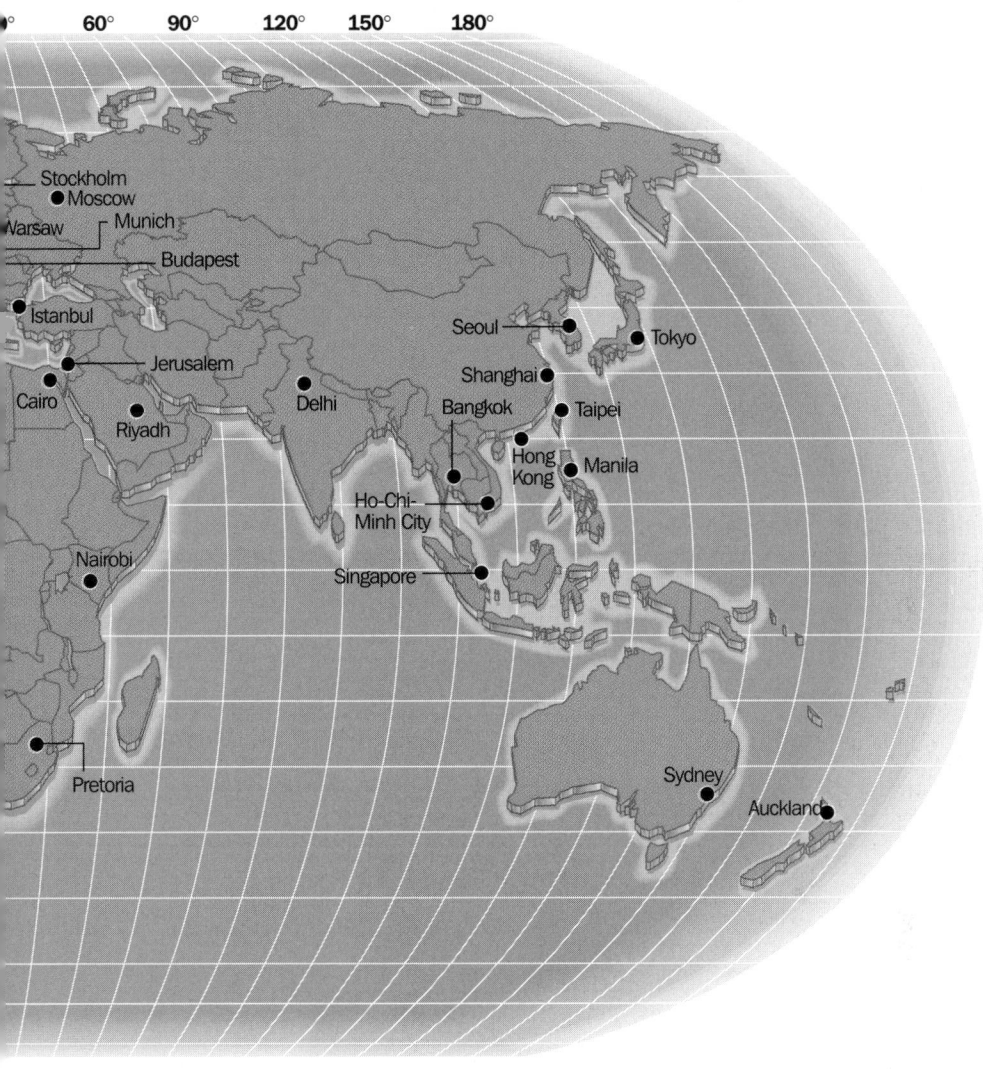

| 0° | 60° | 90° | 120° | 150° | 180° |

Latitude 20° N

Jan. 1	24 min.	10 hr., 57 min.	24 min.
Feb. 1	23 min.	11 hr., 16 min.	23 min.
March 1	22 min.	11 hr., 45 min.	22 min.
April 1	22 min.	12 hr., 20 min.	22 min.
May 1	23 min.	12 hr., 52 min.	23 min.
June 1	24 min.	13 hr., 16 min.	24 min.
June 21	24 min.	13 hr., 21 min.	25 min.
July 1	25 min.	13 hr., 19 min.	25 min.
Aug. 1	23 min.	13 hr., 02 min.	24 min.
Sept. 1	22 min.	12 hr., 32 min.	22 min.
Oct. 1	22 min.	11 hr., 58 min.	22 min.
Nov. 1	22 min.	11 hr., 25 min.	22 min.
Dec. 1	23 min.	11 hr., 01 min.	24 min.
Dec. 22	24 min.	10 hr., 55 min.	24 min.

Latitude 10° N

Jan. 1	23 min.	11 hr., 33 min.	23 min.
Feb. 1	22 min.	11 hr., 42 min.	22 min.
March 1	22 min.	11 hr., 55 min.	22 min.
April 1	21 min.	12 hr., 13 min.	21 min.
May 1	22 min.	12 hr., 29 min.	21 min.
June 1	23 min.	12 hr., 40 min.	23 min.
June 21	23 min.	12hr., 43 min.	23 min.
July 1	23 min.	12 hr., 42 min.	23 min.
Aug. 1	23 min.	12 hr., 33 min.	22 min.
Sept. 1	21 min.	12 hr., 18 min.	22 min.
Oct. 1	21 min.	12 hr., 02 min.	21 min.
Nov. 1	21 min.	11 hr., 47 min.	21 min.
Dec. 1	22 min.	11 hr., 35 min.	23 min.
Dec. 22	23 min.	11 hr., 33 min.	23 min.

Date	Morning twilight	Sunrise to sunset	Evening twilight
Equator			
Jan. 1	23 min.	12 hr., 07 min.	23 min.
Feb. 1	22 min.	12 hr., 07 min.	22 min.
March 1	21 min.	12 hr., 07 min.	21 min.
April 1	21 min.	12 hr., 06 min.	21 min.
May 1	22 min.	12 hr., 07 min.	21 min.
June 1	22 min.	12 hr., 07 min.	23 min.
June 21	23 min.	12 hr., 07 min.	23 min.
July 1	22 min.	12 hr., 07 min.	23 min.
Aug. 1	22 min.	12 hr., 07 min.	22 min.
Sept. 1	21 min.	12 hr., 06 min.	21 min.
Oct. 1	21 min.	12 hr., 06 min.	21 min.
Nov. 1	21 min.	12 hr., 07 min.	21 min.
Dec. 1	22 min.	12 hr., 08 min.	22 min.
Dec. 22	23 min.	12 hr., 08 min.	22 min.
Latitude 10° S			
Jan. 1	23 min.	12 hr., 42 min.	23 min.
Feb. 1	22 min.	12 hr., 33 min.	22 min.
March 1	22 min.	12 hr., 17 min.	21 min.
April 1	21 min.	12 hr., 00 min.	21 min.
May 1	21 min.	11 hr., 46 min.	21 min.
June 1	22 min.	11 hr., 35 min.	23 min.
June 21	22 min.	11 hr., 38 min.	23 min.
July 1	22 min.	11 hr., 33 min.	23 min.
Aug. 1	22 min.	11 hr., 41 min.	22 min.
Sept. 1	21 min.	11 hr., 55 min.	21 min.
Oct. 1	21 min.	12 hr., 11 min.	21 min.
Nov. 1	22 min.	12 hr., 28 min.	21 min.
Dec. 1	23 min.	12 hr., 40 min.	23 min.
Dec. 22	23 min.	12 hr., 43 min.	23 min.
Latitude 20° S			
Jan. 1	25 min.	13 hr., 19 min.	24 min.
Feb. 1	23 min.	12 hr., 59 min.	23 min.
March 1	23 min.	12 hr., 29 min.	22 min.
April 1	22 min.	11 hr., 54 min.	22 min.
May 1	23 min.	11 hr., 22 min.	23 min.
June 1	24 min.	11 hr., 00 min.	23 min.
June 21	24 min.	10 hr., 55 min.	24 min.
July 1	24 min.	10 hr., 54 min.	24 min.
Aug. 1	23 min.	11 hr., 13 min.	23 min.
Sept. 1	22 min.	11 hr., 42 min.	23 min.
Oct. 1	22 min.	12 hr., 16 min.	22 min.
Nov. 1	23 min.	12 hr., 50 min.	23 min.
Dec. 1	25 min.	13 hr., 14 min.	25 min.
Dec. 22	25 min.	13 hr., 21 min.	24 min.
Latitude 30° S			
Jan. 1	27 min.	14 hr., 03 min.	27 min.
Feb. 1	26 min.	13 hr., 31 min.	25 min.
March 1	25 min.	12 hr., 43 min.	24 min.
April 1	24 min.	11 hr., 47 min.	24 min.
May 1	25 min.	10 hr., 56 min.	25 min.
June 1	26 min.	10 hr., 21 min.	26 min.
June 21	26 min.	10 hr., 13 min.	26 min.
July 1	27 min.	10 hr., 14 min.	26 min.
Aug. 1	25 min.	10 hr., 41 min.	25 min.
Sept. 1	24 min.	11 hr., 29 min.	24 min.
Oct. 1	24 min.	12 hr., 22 min.	24 min.
Nov. 1	25 min.	13 hr., 16 min.	25 min.
Dec. 1	27 min.	13 hr., 56 min.	27 min.
Dec. 22	28 min.	14 hr., 05 min.	27 min.
Latitude 40° S			
Jan. 1	33 min.	14 hr., 57 min.	33 min.
Feb. 1	30 min.	14 hr., 10 min.	30 min.
March 1	28 min.	13 hr., 00 min.	28 min.
April 1	27 min.	11 hr., 39 min.	27 min.
May 1	28 min.	10 hr., 25 min.	29 min.
June 1	30 min.	9 hr., 31 min.	30 min.
June 21	31 min.	9 hr., 19 min.	31 min.
July 1	31 min.	9 hr., 22 min.	30 min.
Aug. 1	29 min.	10 hr., 03 min.	29 min.
Sept. 1	27 min.	11 hr., 12 min.	28 min.
Oct. 1	27 min.	12 hr., 30 min.	27 min.
Nov. 1	29 min.	13 hr., 48 min.	29 min.
Dec. 1	32 min.	14 hr., 47 min.	32 min.
Dec. 22	33 min.	15 hr., 01 min.	33 min.
Latitude 50° S			
Jan. 1	44 min.	16 hr., 17 min.	44 min.
Feb. 1	38 min.	15 hr., 04 min.	38 min.
March 1	34 min.	13 hr., 24 min.	33 min.
April 1	32 min.	11 hr., 27 min.	33 min.
May 1	34 min.	9 hr., 42 min.	34 min.
June 1	38 min.	8 hr., 22 min.	37 min.
June 21	39 min.	8 hr., 04 min.	38 min.
July 1	39 min.	8 hr., 08 min.	38 min.
Aug. 1	35 min.	9 hr., 09 min.	35 min.
Sept. 1	33 min.	10 hr., 49 min.	33 min.
Oct. 1	32 min.	12 hr., 40 min.	33 min.
Nov. 1	36 min.	14 hr., 34 min.	36 min.
Dec. 1	42 min.	16 hr., 00 min.	43 min.
Dec. 22	45 min.	16 hr., 23 min.	44 min.
Latitude 60° S			
Jan. 1	1 hr., 37 min.	18 hr., 42 min.	1 hr., 36 min.
Feb. 1	58 min.	16 hr., 35 min.	58 min.
March 1	45 min.	14 hr., 01 min.	45 min.
April 1	42 min.	11 hr., 11 min.	41 min.
May 1	46 min.	8 hr., 34 min.	45 min.
June 1	55 min.	6 hr., 23 min.	55 min.
June 21	58 min.	5 hr., 52 min.	58 min.

Date	Morning twilight	Sunrise to sunset	Evening twilight
July 1	57 min.	6 hr., 00 min.	57 min.
Aug. 1	49 min.	7 hr., 41 min.	49 min.
Sept. 1	42 min.	10 hr., 16 min.	42 min.
Oct. 1	42 min.	12 hr., 57 min.	42 min.
Nov. 1	51 min.	15 hr., 47 min.	52 min.
Dec. 1	1 hr., 20 min.	18 hr., 11 min.	1 hr., 21 min.
Dec. 22	1 hr., 47 min.	18 hr., 53 min.	1 hr., 46 min.

Latitude 70° S

Date	Morning twilight	Sunrise to sunset	Evening twilight
Jan. 1		No sunset	
Feb. 1	*	20 hr., 25 min.	*
March 1	1 hr., 14 min.	15 hr., 14 min.	1 hr., 13 min.
April 1	1 hr., 01 min.	10 hr., 40 min.	1 hr., 01 min.
May 1	1 hr., 16 min.	6 hr., 09 min.	1 hr., 16 min.
June 1	Twilight lasts 5 hr., 09 min.; sun never rises		
June 21	Twilight lasts 4 hr., 07 min.; sun never rises		
July 1	Twilight lasts 4 hr., 22 min.; sun never rises		
Aug. 1	1 hr., 33 min.	4 hr., 13 min.	1 hr., 34 min.
Sept. 1	1 hr., 03 min.	9 hr., 10 min.	1 hr., 03 min.
Oct. 1	1 hr., 04 min.	13 hr., 28 min.	1 hr., 05 min.
Nov. 1	*	18 hr., 27 min.	*
Dec. 1		No sunset	
Dec. 22		No sunset	

Latitude 80° S

Date	Morning twilight	Sunrise to sunset	Evening twilight
Jan. 1		No sunset	
Feb. 1		No sunset	
March 1	*	19 hr., 43 min.	*
April 1	2 hr., 02 min.	9 hr., 11 min.	2 hr., 00 min.
May 1	Twilight lasts 3 hr., 28 min.; sun never rises		
June 1	No twilight; sun never rises		
June 21	No twilight; sun never rises		
July 1	No twilight; sun never rises		
Aug. 1	No twilight; sun never rises		
Sept. 1	2 hr., 21 min.	5 hr., 33 min.	2 hr., 22 min.
Oct. 1	2 hr., 45 min.	15 hr., 04 min.	2 hr., 57 min.
Nov. 1		No sunset	
Dec. 1		No sunset	
Dec. 22		No sunset	

* Twilight lasts all night

Time zones and time differences

Before the mid-1800s, every city had its own time. Clocks were set at noon when the sun was at its highest point in the sky. This meant that clocks in places only a few miles apart would differ by a few minutes. Then came the railroads. It was pretty hard to keep on schedule if every station had its own time. Some standard had to be set. Today's time zones grew out of the need to have the same time over wide areas.

Today the system of time zones is global.

Where do time zones come from? Start with the Earth's 360 degrees of longitude.

Divide that by 24 hours in the day and you get zones that are 15 degrees across from east to west. But the zones aren't exactly 15 degrees wide because political boundaries were taken into account when they were set up. Some time zones are much wider than 15 degrees.

In most cases, the time changes by an hour as you move from zone to zone. But some places use half-hour changes. And a few zones are 45 minutes or 15 minutes different from the adjoining zones, depending on whether you're heading east or west.

Universal Time, which used to be called Greenwich Mean Time, is the standard time along the 0° longitude line, which runs through Greenwich, England, near London. Countries around the world that send out radio time signals coordinate their signals so everyone is giving the same time. This worldwide standard time is abbreviated UTC, for Universal Time, Coordinated. Each of the time zones around the world is given a letter. UTC is also known as Zulu time, the international phonetic for the letter "Z." Here are other global time terms: 24-hour clock, also known as military time, continues counting up after noon instead of using a.m. and p.m. In the afternoon, 1 p.m. becomes 13:00, 2 p.m. becomes 14:00, 3:30 p.m. is 15:30, and so on. Just add 12 hours to any p.m. time. In the morning, use four digits. 8 a.m. becomes 08:00 while 10 a.m. is 10:00.

The International Date Line

The north-south line on or near the 180-degree longitude line where those traveling from east to west gain a day and those traveling west to east lose a day. The line jogs between Alaska and Siberia to keep Russia on the west side and all of the U.S. on the east. It also jogs away from the 180-degree line in the South Pacific to keep parts of island groups together.

Figuring time difference around the world

In the tables on the following pages, each nation is listed in the left-hand column. When a nation has more than one time zone, each zone is listed in this column. In some cases, major cities also are listed in this column.

The middle column lists the hours ahead or behind UTC for each nation or time zone.

The right-hand column gives the dates when

Daylight Savings Time is in effect. For example, New York City, which is in the U.S. eastern zone, is four hours behind UTC from April 3 to October 29 when the USA is on Daylight Time. The rest of the year it is five hours behind the UTC.

To avoid confusion when using the tables, remember that the sun moves from east to west across the Earth. When the sun is rising over the middle of the U.S., it has come from the east, from Europe. At dawn in Iowa, the sun has been up a few hours in Europe and has yet to come up in Hawaii.

An easy way to figure the differences is to imagine traveling from the place where you know the time to the other place. Are you going east or west? If you are going west, subtract the time difference from the time you know. Going east, add the differences.

How to figure time differences from Tucson to Timbuktu

The easiest differences to figure out are those when both places are either ahead or behind UTC.

If it's 1 p.m. in December in New York City. What time is it in Los Angeles?

New York: 5 hours behind UTC in December.

Los Angeles: 8 hours behind UTC in December.

Difference: 3 hours.

Direction traveled: west. Subtract 3 hours from New York time.

1 p.m. is 13:00 in 24-hour time.

13:00 minus 3:00 is 10:00, or 10 a.m. in Los Angeles.

If it's 1 p.m. in Switzerland in June. What time is it in Japan?

Switzerland: 2 hours ahead of UTC in June.

Japan: 9 hours ahead of UTC all year.

Difference: 7 hours.

Direction traveled: east. Add 7 hours to Swiss time.

1 p.m. is 13:00 in 24 hour time.

13:00 plus 7:00 is 20:00, or 8 p.m. in Japan.

1. What happens if you end up with a negative number?

Add 24 hours to the starting time. If it's 1 a.m. in New York on December 2, what time is it in Los Angeles?

New York City: 1 a.m., or 01:00 on Dec. 2. What time in Los Angeles?

Difference: 3 hours.

Add 24:00 to 01:00 to make it 25:00.

Subtract 3:00 hours from 25:00.

It's 22:00, or 10 p.m., on Dec. 1 in Los Angeles.

2. What happens if the answer is more than 24:00?

Subtract 24 from the answer. When you do this, the place to the east will be one day ahead. If it is 11 p.m. in Switzerland, what time is it in Japan?.

Switzerland, 11 p.m., or 23:00, on June 1. What time is it in Japan?

Difference: 7 hours.

Add 7 hours to the Swiss time.

23:00 plus 7:00 is 30:00.

30:00 minus 24:00 is 06:00, or 6 a.m. on June 2 in Japan.

3. How do you figure the difference between a place that's ahead of UTC and one that's behind?

Make the imaginary trip to the UTC zone, even if it would be the long way around the world on a real trip. The rule for adding the difference when going east and subtracting the difference when going west still applies.

If it's 2 p.m. in Chicago in January. What time is it in France?

Chicago to UTC time: 6 hours to the east.

UTC time to France: 1 hour to the east.

Direction traveled: East. Add 7 hours to Chicago time.

2 p.m. is 14:00 in 24-hour time.

14:00 plus 7:00 is 21:00, or 9 p.m. in France.

If it's 2 p.m. in Paris in January. What time is it in Chicago?

Paris to UTC, 1 hour to the west.

UTC to Chicago, 6 hours to the west.

Direction traveled: West. Subtract 7 hours from French time, 14:00 minus 7:00 is 07:00, or 7 a.m. in Chicago.

Country	Time hours ahead (+) or behind (-) UTC	Savings Time Dates
Afghanistan	+4.5	
Albania	+1	
	+2	March 27 – Sept. 24
Algeria	+1	
America Samoa	-11	
Andorra	+1	
	+2	March 27 – Sept. 24
Angola	+1	
Argentina	-3	
Armenia	+3	
	+4	March 27 – Sept. 24
Aruba	-4	
Australia		
New South Wales	+10	
Victoria	+11	Oct. 30 – March 4
Northern Territory	+9.5	
Queensland	+10	
South Australia	+9.5	
	+10.5	Oct. 30 – March 4
Tasmania	+10	
	+11	Oct. 2 – March 25
Western Australia	+8	
Austria	+1	
	+2	March 27 – Sept. 24
Azerbajian	+4	
Azores	See Portugal	
Bahamas,	-5	
(Excluding Turks and Caicos Islands)	-4	April 3 – Oct. 29
Bahrain	+3	
Bangladesh	+6	
Barbados	-4	
Belarus	+2	
	+3	March 27 – Sept. 24
Belgium	+1	
	+2	March 27 – Sept. 24
Belize	-6	
Benin	+1	
Bermuda	-4	
	-3	April 3 – Oct. 29
Bhutan	+6	
Bolivia	-4	
Bosnia Hercegovina	+1	
	+2	March 27 – Sept. 24
Botswana	+2	

Brazil		
East	-3	
(Brasilia, Rio, Sao Paulo)	-2	Oct. 23 – Jan. 28
West	-4	
	-3	Oct. 23 – Jan. 28
Territory of Acre	-5	
Fernando De Noronha	-2	
British Virgin Islands	-4	
Brunei (Darussalam)	+8	
Bulgaria	+2	
	+3	March 27 – Sept. 24
Burkina Faso	on UTC	
Burma	See Myanmar	
Burundi	+2	
Cambodia	+7	
Republic of Cameroon	+1	
Canada		
Newfoundland	-3.5	
(St. John's)	-2.5	April 3 – Oct. 29
Atlantic	-4	
(Halifax)	-3	April 3 – Oct. 29
Eastern	-5	
(Toronto, Montreal, Ottawa)	-4	April 3 – Oct. 29
Central	-6	
(Regina, Winnipeg)	-5	April 3 – Oct. 29
Mountain	-7	
(Calgary, Edmonton)	-6	April 3 – Oct. 29
Pacific	-8	
(Vancouver, Dawson)	-7	April 3 – Oct. 29
Cape Verde	-1	
Cayman Islands	-5	
Central African Rep.	+1	
Ceylon	See Sri Lanka	
Chad	+1	
Chile		
Continental	-4	
	-3	Oct. 9 – March 11
Easter Island	-6	
	-5	Oct. 9 – March 11
China, People's Rep.	+8	

Country	Time hours ahead (+) or behind (-) UTC	Savings Time Dates
Cocos (Keeling) Is.	+6.5	
Colombia	-5	
Comoros	See Mayotte	
Congo	+1	
Cook Islands	-10	
Costa Rica	-6	
Cote D'Ivoire	on UTC	
Croatia	+1	
	+2	March 27 – Sept. 24
Cuba	-5	
	-4	April 3 – Oct. 9
Cyprus	+2	
	+3	March 27 – Sept. 24
Czech Republic	+1	
	+2	March 27 – Sept. 24
Denmark	+1	
	+2	March 27 – Sept. 24
Djibouti	+3	
Dominican Republic	-4	
Ecuador		
Continental	-5	
Galapagos Islands	-6	
Egypt	+2	
	+3	May 1 – Sept. 30
El Salvador	-6	
England	See United Kingdom	
Equitorial Guinea	+1	
Eritrea	+3	
Estonia	+2	
	+3	March 27 – Sept.24
Ethiopia	+3	
Falkland Islands	-4	
	-3	Sept. 12, 1993 – April 17
Faroe Island	on UTC	
	+1	March 27 – Sept. 24
Fiji	+12	
Finland	+2	
	+3	March 27 – Sept. 24
France	+1	
	+2	March 27 – Sept. 24
French Guiana	-3	
French Polynesia		
Gambier Island	-9	
Marquesas Islands	-9.5	
Society Island, Tahiti,		
Tubuai Island,		
Tuamotu Island	-10	
Gabon	+1	
Gambia	on UTC	
Georgia	+3	
	+4	March 27 – Sept. 24
Germany	+1	
	+2	March 27 – Sept. 24
Ghana	on UTC	
Gibraltar	+1	
	+2	March 27 – Sept. 24
Greece	+2	
	+3	March 27 – Sept. 24
Greenland	-3	
(Angmagssalik)	-2	March 27 – Sept. 24
(Scoresbysund)	-1	
	on UTC	March 27 – Sept. 24
(Thule)	-4	
	-3	March 27 – Sept. 24
Guadeloupe	-4	
(St. Barthelemy, Northern St. Martin)		
Guam	+10	
Guatemala	-6	
Guinea	on UTC	
Guinea - Bissau	on UTC	
Guyana	-4	
Haiti	-5	
	-4	April 3 – Oct. 29
Honduras	-6	
	-5	May 8 – NA
Hong Kong	+8	
Hungary	+1	
	+2	March 27 – Sept. 24
Iceland	on UTC	
India (Andaman Is.)	+5.5	
Indonesia		
Central	+8	
(Kalimantan, Sulawesi)		
East (Irian, Barat)	+9	
West	+7	
(Sumatra, Java, Bali, Jakarta)		
Iran	+3.5	
	+4.5	March 21 – Sept. 22
Iraq	+3	
	+4	April 1 – Sept. 30
Ireland, Republic of	on UTC	
	+1	March 27 – Oct. 22
Israel	+2	
	+3	April 1 – Aug. 28
Italy	+1	
	+2	March 27 – Sept. 24
Jamaica	-5	
Japan	+9	
Johnston Island	-10	

Country	Time hours ahead (+) or behind (-) UTC	Savings Time dates
Jordan	+2	
	+3	April 1 – Sept. 15
Kampuchea	See Cambodia	
Kazakhastan	+6	
	+7	March 27 – Sept. 24
Kenya	+3	
Kiribati	+12	

Kiribati and its islands straddle the International Dateline.

Canton, Enderbury Islands	-11	
Christmas Islands	-10	
Korea, Dem. Republic	+9	
Korea, Republic of	+9	
Kuwait	+3	
Kyrgyzstan	+5	
	+6	March 27 – Sept. 24
Laos	+7	
Latvia	+2	
	+3	March 27 – Sept. 24
Lebanon	+2	
	+3	March 27 – Sept. 24
Leeward Islands	-4	
(Antigua, Dominica, Nevis, Montserrat, St. Kitts, St. Christopher, Anguilla)		
Lesotho	+2	
Liberia	on UTC	
Libyan Arab Jamihiriya	+2	
Lithuania	+2	
	+3	March 27 – Sept. 24
Luxembourg	+1	
	+2	March 27 – Sept. 24
Macedonia	+1	
	+2	March 27 – Sept. 24
Madagascar	+3	
Madeira	See Portugal	
Malawi	+2	
Malaysia	+8	
Maldives	+5	
Mali	on UTC	
Malta	+1	
	+2	March 27 – Sept. 24
Martinique	-4	
Mauritania	on UTC	
Mauritius	+4	
Mayotte	+3	
Mexico	-6	
Southern Baja California Northern Pacific states	-7	
Northern Baja	-8	
	-7	April 3 – Oct. 29
Midway Island	-11	
Moldova	+2	
	+3	March 27 – Sept. 24
Monaco	+1	
	+2	March 27 – Sept. 24
Mongolia	+8	
(Ulan Bator)	+9	March 27 – Sept. 24
Morocco	on UTC	
Mozambique	+2	
Myanmar (Formerly Burma)	+6.5	
Namibia	+1	
	+2	Sept. 4 – April 1
Nauru	+12	
Nepal	+5.75	
Netherlands	+1	
	+2	March 27 – Sept. 24
Netherlands Antilles	-4	
New Caledonia	+11	
New Hebrides	See Vanuatu	
New Zealand	+12	
(Excluding Chatham Island)	+13	Oct. 2 – March 18
Chatham Island	+12.75	
	+13.75	Oct. 2 – March 18
Nicaragua	-6	
Niger	+1	
Nigeria	+1	
Niue Island	-11	
Norfolk Island	+11.5	
Northern Ireland	See United Kingdom	
Norway	+1	
	+2	March 27 – Sept. 24
Oman	+4	

Pacific Island Trust

The Pacific Island Trust islands straddle the International Dateline.

Caroline Island	+11	
Kusaie, Pingelap, Marshall Islands	+12	
Kwajalein	-12	
Mariana Islands (Excluding Guam)	+10	
Palau Island	+9	
Ponape	+11	
Pakistan	+5	

Country	Time hours ahead (+) or behind (-) UTC	Savings Time dates
Panama	-5	
Papua New Guinea	+10	
(Including Bougainville Island)		
Paraguay	-4	
	-3	Oct. 2 – Feb. 25
Peru	-5	
Philippines	+8	
Poland	+1	
	+2	March 27 – Sept. 24
Portugal	+1	
	+2	March 27 – Sept. 24
Azores	-1	
	on UTC	March 27 – Sept. 24
Madeira	on UTC	
	+1	March 27 – Sept. 24
Puerto Rico	-4	
Qatar	+3	
Reunion	+4	
Romania	+2	
	+3	March 27 – Sept. 24
Russian Federation		
Zone 1	+2	
(Kaliningrad)	+3	March 27 – Sept. 24
Zone 2	+3	
(Moscow, St. Petersburg,		
Murmarsk, Astrahan,		
Volrograd)	+4	March 27 – Sept. 24
Zone 3	+4	
(Samara, Izhevsk)	+5	March 27 – Sept. 24
Zone 4	+5	
(Chelyabinsk, Ekatrinburg, Perm,		
Nizhnevartovsk)	+6	March 27 – Sept. 24
Zone 5	+6	
(Novosibirsk,	+7	March 27 – Sept. 24
Omsk)		
Zone 6	+7	
(Krasnojarsk, Kyzyl,		
Norilsk)	+8	March 27 – Sept. 24
Zone 7	+8	
(Irkutsk, Ulan-Ude,		
Bratsk)	+9	March 27 – Sept. 24
Zone 8	+9	
(Chita, Yakatsk)	+10	March 27 – Sept. 24
Zone 9	+10	
(Khabarovsk,		
Vladivostok)	+11	March 27 – Sept. 24
Zone 10	+11	
(Magadan)	+12	March 27 – Sept. 24
Zone 11	+12	
(Petropavlovsk-		
Kamchatsky)	+13	March 24 – Sept. 24
Rwanda	+2	
St. Maarten	See Netherlands Antilles	
St. Pierre and Miquelon	-3	
	-2	April 3 – Oct. 29
St. Vincent and the Grenadines	-4	
Samoa	-11	
San Marino	+1	
	+2	March 27 – Sept. 24
Sao Tome Island and Principe Island	on UTC	
Saudi Arabia	+3	
Scotland	See United Kingdom	
Senegal	on UTC	
Seychelles	+4	
Sierra Leone	on UTC	
Singapore	+8	
Slovakia	+1	
	+2	March 27 – Sept. 24
Slovenia	+1	
	+2	March 27 – Sept. 24
Solomon Islands excluding Bougainville Island	+11	
Somalia	+3	
South Africa	+2	
Spain	+1	
	+2	March 27 – Sept. 24
Canary Islands	on UTC	
	+1	March 27 – Sept. 24
Sri Lanka	+5.5	
St. Helena	on UTC	
Sudan	+2	
Suriname	-3	
Swaziland	+2	
Sweden	+1	
	+2	March 27 – Sept. 24
Switzerland	+1	
	+2	March 27 – Sept. 24
Syria	+2	
	+3	April 1 – Sept. 30
Taiwan	+8	
Tajikstan	+5	
Tanzania	+3	
Thailand	+7	
Togo	on UTC	
Tonga	+13	
Trinidad and Tobago	-4	
Tunisia	+1	

Country	Time hours ahead (+) or behind (-) UTC	Savings Time dates
Turkey	+2	
	+3	March 27 – Sept. 24
Turkmenistan	+5	
Turks and Caicos	-5	
Islands	-4	April 3 – Oct. 29
Tuvalu	+12	
Uganda	+3	
Ukraine	+2	
	+3	March 27 – Sept. 24
United Arab Emirates	+4	
United Kingdom	on UTC	
including Channel Islands, Scotland, Northern Ireland, Wales		
	+1	March 27 – Oct. 22

United States

Eastern	-5	
	-4	April 3 – Oct. 29
Central	-6	
	-5	April 3 – Oct. 29
Mountain	-7	
	-6	April 3 – Oct. 29
Pacific	-8	
	-7	April 3 – Oct. 29
Alaska	-9	
	-8	April 3 – Oct. 29
Aleutian Islands	-10	
west of 169.30° Longitude West		
	-9	April 3 – Oct. 29
Arizona	-7	
Hawaii	-10	
Indiana (east)	-5	
Uruguay	-3	
USSR	See Russian Federation	
Uzbekistan	+5	
Vanuatu	+11	
Venezuela	-4	
Vietnam	+7	

Virgin Islands	-4	
Wake Islands	+12	
Wales	See United Kingdom	
Wallis and Futuna Is.	+12	
Windward Islands	-4	
Yemen, Rep. of	+3	
Yugoslavia	+1	
	+2	March 27 – Sept. 2

Source: *OAG Desktop Flight Guide, Worldwide Edition, Aug. 1994* © Official Airline Guides

How to convert to metric

Travelers to and from the United States have to adjust to hearing weather forecasts in different units. While most of the world measures temperatures in Celsius degrees, wind speeds (and highway speed limits) in kilometers per hour, and rain in millimeters, the United States uses Fahrenheit degrees, miles per hour and inches.

Temperature conversions

(All numbers rounded to nearest whole number)

Fahrenheit	Celsius	Notes
-40°	-40°	Only point at which the two scales are the same
32°	0°	Water freezes
212°	100°	Water boils at sea level

For exact temperature conversions:

Fahrenheit to Celsius:

°F minus 32. Multiply the answer by five and divide by nine.

Example: 212° F to Celsius:

1. 212 - 32 = 180
2. 180 x 5 = 900
3. 900 divided by 9 = 100°C

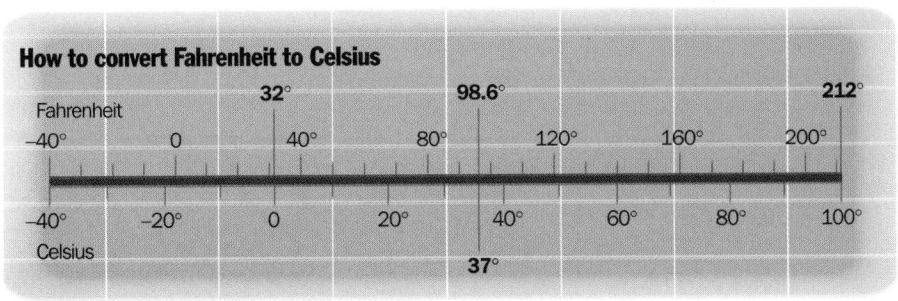

How to convert Fahrenheit to Celsius

Celsius to Fahrenheit:

Multiply °C by 9, divide the answer by 5 and then add 32.

Example: 100°C to Fahrenheit:
1. 100 x 9 = 900
2. 900 divided by 5 = 180
3. 180 plus 32 = 212°C

How to convert distances and speeds

This chart works for converting both distances in miles to kilometers or kilometers to miles, and for converting speeds in miles per hour (MPH) to kilometers per hour (KPH) or KPH to MPH.

(All numbers rounded to nearest whole number)

Miles (mph)	Kilometers (kph)	Notes on speeds
10	16	Gentle breeze
12	20	
25	40	
31	50	
35	56	Common speed limit in U.S. towns
40	64	
43	70	
55	88	Common speed limit on rural U.S. highways
60	97	
62	100	
75	120	Hurricane force wind
100	161	
124	200	

For exact numbers

Kilometers to miles:
Multiply kilometers by 0.6214
Miles to kilometers:
Multiply miles by 1.609

Knots and miles per hour

Knots, which are nautical miles per hour, are used for wind speeds in aviation and marine weather reports and also aircraft, boat and ship speeds. A nautical mile is 6,076 feet, compared to 5,280 feet for a statute, or ordinary, mile.

To convert nautical miles to statute miles and knots to mph:
Multiply by 1.151
To convert statute miles to nautical miles or mph to knots:
Multiply by 0.869
Note: The speed is knots; it is never "knots per hour."

Converting rainfall, snowfall measurements

In the metric system, precipitation is measured in millimeters. The table below also lists measurements in centimeters, since snow depths are sometimes measured in centimeters.

(Inches rounded to the nearest hundredth inch. Millimeters and centimeters rounded to nearest whole number.)

Inches	Millimeters	Centimeters
0.04	1	
0.39	10	1
0.79	20	2
1.00	25	
1.18	30	3
1.57	40	4
1.97	50	5
2.00	51	
3.00	76	
3.94	100	10
4.00	102	
5.00	127	
6.00	152	
7.87	200	20
11.81	300	30
12.00	305	
15.75	400	40
19.68	500	50
24.00	610	
36.00	914	
39.37	1,000	100 (1 meter)

For exact measurements

To convert inches to millimeters:
Multiply inches by 25.4
To convert millimeters to inches:
Multiply millimeters by 0.03937
To convert inches to centimeters:
Multiply inches by 2.54
To convert centimeters to inches:
Multiply centimeters by 0.3937

4 Natural hazards

Nature unleashes its terrible fury

Hurricanes, tornadoes, floods, earthquakes, thunderstorms, snowstorms and droughts.

The USA has them all.

The statistics and stories in this chapter tell the what, when and where of natural disasters. That historical information paints a picture of the event, but it should serve two other purposes: first, as a guide to knowing when storms are likely to occur and second, as a primer of what to do if caught in a storm, earthquake, flood or other disaster.

Consider:

• Most flood victims die in their cars, trying to drive through high waters.

• Hurricane deaths most often come from the storm surge that precedes or arrives with the high winds.

• The most dangerous place to be in a tornado is a mobile home.

Such simple facts can save lives.

Knowing the likely regions and seasons for various storms, understanding the levels of warning from the National Weather Service or being able to survive for a long period in a car stuck in a snowstorm offers protection from the hazards of weather and natural disasters.

The best protection is to avoid being in the way of predicted disaster. Every time a hurricane moves toward the coast, there are people who will not evacuate — some surfing in the high waves, some wanting to simply experience the storm firsthand. After early signs of a volcano eruption, some people refuse to leave their nearby houses. During snow emergencies, some people insist on driving to work or continuing with a vacation trip. They are putting themselves, and rescuers, in jeopardy.

Neil Frank, former director of the National Hurricane Center, said it best in *The USA TODAY Weather Book:* "If human beings would learn to live in harmony with the forces of nature, we could minimize our problems. Building a house on an earthquake fault line in California is not very wise. Likewise, we should limit development along river valleys subject to flooding or on small, sandy coastal islands exposed to devastating hurricanes. But we have decided not to do that in this country, so we are extremely vulnerable to storms.

"To live in harmony with nature, we must understand atmospheric forces. We need to understand storms ... . Then we can adjust to them and keep out of harm's way."

In most cases, the weather isn't becoming any worse. But more people are building more expensive homes, apartment buildings, hotels, motels and businesses in areas hit by killer weather.

Of the billion dollar weather disasters since 1980, only the Great Flood of 1993 on the Mississippi and Missouri rivers, and perhaps the March 1993 "Storm of the Century," were worse than similar weather events earlier in this century.

None of the hurricanes was as strong as the unnamed storm that hit the Florida Keys in 1935. None of the droughts was as severe as the 1936 Great Plains dust bowl drought. But drought and heat waves account for two of the three most expensive disasters because their economic cost was so high. Their estimated death tolls are also high, but heat waves aren't perceived as major killers because most deaths aren't directly caused by the heat. Except for a relatively small number of obvious heat exhaustion victims, heat wave deaths are caused indirectly by the weather.

Billion dollar weather disasters

Here are the major weather disasters in the U.S. since 1980 with damage estimates greater than $1 billion. All figures, in 1990 dollars, are the estimated total cost, including damage and costs to the economy.

$40 billion Drought and heat wave, summer 1988, Central and Eastern USA.

$25 billion Hurricane Andrew, August 1992, Florida and Louisiana.

$20 billion Drought and heat wave, June – September 1980, Central and Eastern USA.

$12 billion The Great Flood of 1993, June and July, 1993, Midwest.

$7.1 billion Hurricane Hugo, September 1989, North and South Carolina.

$6 billion "Storm of the Century," March 13 - 14, 1993, East.

$2 billion Hurricane Alicia, August 1983, Texas.

$1.8 billion Hurricane Iniki, September 1992, Hawaiian island of Kauai.

$1.5 billion Hurricane Bob, August 1991, North Carolina coast, Long Island and New England.

$1.5 billion Hurricane Juan, October – November 1985, Louisiana and Southeast USA.

$1.3 billion Hurricane Elena, August – September 1985, Florida to Louisiana.

When weather causes deaths

In adding up the number of people killed by weather, the National Weather Service attempts to count only deaths that are a direct result of the weather.

This is why the list at right shows that heat killed 41 people in 1988, but some other "weather deaths" lists show 5,000 to 10,000 deaths from heat that summer.

The 41 people on this Weather Service list died of heat stroke or heat exhaustion. The much larger figures are estimates of the number who died because heat stress was at least partly responsible for their deaths.

In a similar way, the Weather Service lists of winter storm or cold weather deaths do not include those who died of heart attacks while shoveling snow, but the Weather Service list does include those who died of hypothermia.

Aviation deaths, for which weather might have been at least partly responsible, are not included. Traffic deaths are included for fog, ice storms, and dust storms, but not for snowstorms or blizzards.

Hurricane deaths include people killed directly by wind or flooding, but not deaths from accidents during the cleanup, or from fires caused by using open flame when electrical power is not available.

Lightning deaths include people hit by lightning, but not those killed in fires started by lightning.

Hurricanes

Hurricanes can be called Earth's most awesome storms. They are huge, more than 100 miles wide, stirring up more than a million cubic miles of atmosphere every second. While other natural disasters, such as earthquakes, tornadoes and lightning strikes, come with little warning, hurricanes give forecasters many days to track possible courses. We watch them form via satellite photos. We give them names. We rank them by power and damage and death tolls.

Building along the coast has increased the damage totals. Better forecasting and evacuation planning has cut the death toll.

The National Hurricane Center bases its records of hurricane intensity on the lowest barometric pressure recorded in the storm, not on measured wind speeds. Barometric pressure is a more exact

Weather-related deaths

Thunderstorm related	'93	'92	'91	'90	'89	'88
Lightning	39	41	73	74	67	68
Tornado	30	39	39	53	50	32
Winds	19	13	32	39	30	18
Hail	1	0	0	0	0	0
Extreme temperature						
Cold	16	14	13	13	121	17
Heat	11	8	36	32	6	41
Floods						
Flash floods	46	55	45	109	62	30
River floods	36	7	16	33	23	1
Oceans						
Coastal storm	0	0	4	3	19	16
Tropical cyclones						
Hurricane, tropical storm	1	27	13	0	38	9
Winter						
Snow or blizzard	54	43	37	35	56	48
Ice storm	7	16	8	13	7	7
Avalanches	1	5	0	0	1	0
Others						
Dust storm	0	3	17	2	6	4
Rain	1	2	9	6	3	5
Fog	5	14	17	17	0	0
High winds	38	15	32	32	12	22
Waterspout	1	0	0	0	0	0
Mudslides	2	2	0	0	0	0
Total	308	304	391	461	501	318

measurement than wind speed, which can vary widely even in the eye of a storm. But, the lower the pressure, the faster the winds. Storm surge, which often kills more people and does more damage than wind, is also related to barometric pressure.

In addition to wind and storm surge, hurricanes often bring extremely heavy rain. But precise rainfall measurements are impossible in hurricanes because large amounts of wind-blown rain don't fall into rain gauges. Rainfall amounts do not depend on a storm's strength. Some tropical storms have brought heavier rain than many hurricanes.

Since the 1970s, the National Hurricane Center has classified hurricanes on the one to five "Saffir-Simpson" scale developed by Herbert Saffir, a consulting engineer who specializes in wind damage to buildings, and Robert Simpson, a retired director of the National Hurricane Center.

Storms in categories 3, 4 and 5 are considered "major" hurricanes and account for the biggest share of the damage.

Strictly speaking, the scale applies only to Atlantic Basin storms — those that form in the Atlantic Ocean, Caribbean Sea or Gulf of Mexico. But the categories are often used for storms elsewhere.

Saffir–Simpson hurricane scale

Category damage	Barometric pressure in inches	Winds in mph	Storm surge in feet
1 Minimal	More than 28.94	74–95	4–5
2 Moderate	28.50–28.91	96–110	6–8
3 Extensive	27.91–28.47	111–130	9–12
4 Extreme	27.17–27.88	131–155	13–18
5 Catastrophic	Less than 27.17	155+	18+

Definitions of hurricane terms

Eye: The center of a tropical cyclone where winds are nearly calm. As a storm grows, the eye becomes better developed. Often, on satellite photos, the eye is seen as a clear area in the middle of a storm, but sometimes it is covered by clouds over a storm's top.

Eye wall: The wall of clouds, usually extending 40,000 feet or higher, around a hurricane's eye, which contains the storm's fastest winds.

Hurricane: A tropical cyclone with winds of 74 mph or more.

National Hurricane Center: The U.S. National Weather Service office located in Coral Gables, Fla., has responsibility for forecasting tropical storms and hurricanes in the Atlantic Ocean, Caribbean Sea, Gulf of Mexico and the Pacific Ocean east of the International Date Line.

Spiral band: A line of thunderstorms that spirals into a hurricane's eye wall.

Storm surge: The rise in sea level caused by a storm. It is caused by a combination of low atmospheric pressure in the storm's center and by water pushed by wind. The height depends on the strength of the storm and the nature of the ocean floor offshore. When the surge pushes into bays or rivers, it can pile up water higher than on open beaches. Over the years, storm surge in hurricanes has been a bigger killer than wind.

Tropical cyclone: A low pressure weather system in which the central core is warmer than the surrounding atmosphere. Such systems form only in the tropics but can move north or south into temperate zones. Storms called hurricanes or typhoons elsewhere are called tropical cyclones in the Indian Ocean and around the Coral Sea off northeastern Australia.

Tropical depression: A tropical cyclone with maximum sustained winds near the surface of less than 39 mph.

Tropical storm: A tropical cyclone with 39 to 74 mph winds.

Typhoon: A hurricane in the North Pacific west of the International Date Line.

Biggest killers in hurricane history

No hurricane has killed more than 1,000 people in the United States since 1928, but at least seven storms are estimated to have killed more than 2,000 people each on Caribbean islands or in Central America since then.

And since 1775 at least 18 Atlantic Ocean, Caribbean Sea or Gulf of Mexico hurricanes are estimated to have killed at least 2,000 people.

The figures on the next page were compiled by Edward N. Rappeport and Jose Fernandez-Portagas for the National Hurricane Center in their 1994 study, "The Deadliest Atlantic Tropical Cyclones 1492-1994." Old records are incomplete and in many cases the estimates vary widely.

Rappeport and Fernandez-Portagas are interested in hearing from anyone with good information on past storms. They can be reached at the National Hurricane Center in Coral Gables, Fla.

10 strongest U.S. hurricanes since 1900

1. Unnamed Storm, Sept. 2, 1935: The Labor Day storm that slammed the Florida Keys in 1935 was the most intense U.S. storm of this century and one of only two Category 5 storms to hit the United States. Its lowest barometric pressure, 26.35, measured on Long Key on Sept. 2, 1935, is the lowest sea level pressure ever measured in the United States. Winds were estimated at nearly 200 mph. In 1935, the only route along the Keys to Key West was the Florida East Coast Railroad. Approximately 700 men, mostly World War I veterans, were building a highway down to the Keys. As winds began picking up along the Keys, a rescue train was sent south from Homestead, but the storm's wind and surge knocked over 10 cars of the 11-car rescue train, killing most aboard. The official death toll is 408, but some accounts say twice that many might have died. After the storm, the railroad was abandoned, but work on the highway to Key West continued.

This storm still gives forecasters nightmares. About 36 hours before its hurricane-force winds hit the Keys, it was a tropical storm — winds less than 74 mph — south of Andros Island in the Bahamas. More than 36 hours is needed to evacuate the Keys even today, and people are not likely to begin evacuating for a storm that was as weak as the Labor Day hurricane 36 hours before it hit.

2. Hurricane Camille, Aug. 17, 1969: This intense storm that slammed into the Gulf Coast was the second Category 5 storm to hit the United States this century. Camille became a hurricane on Aug. 15 south of Cuba and began intensifying that evening when it moved into the Gulf of Mexico. On the morning of Aug. 17, when Camille was about 250 miles south of Mobile, Ala., an Air Force reconnaissance plane measured a barometric pressure of 26.61 and winds of more than 200 mph. Camille came ashore Aug. 17 with a central pressure of 26.84 and a storm surge that pushed water 24.6 feet above its normal level in the Pass Christian-Long Beach area of Mississippi. The surge and winds killed 143 people along the coast. Camille weakened to a tropical depression with winds less than 39 mph as it moved across Mississippi. It continued across western Tennessee, central Kentucky and into southern Virginia. Over the Appalachians,

Killer hurricanes

Hurricanes believed to have killed at least 2,000 people, listed by death toll:

Location	Name	Date	Estimated deaths
Barbados, Martinique, St. Eustatius	None	Oct. 10-16, 1780	Up to 22,000
Galveston, Texas	None	Sept. 8, 1900	Up to 12,000[1]
Honduras	Fifi	Sept. 14-19, 1974	Up to 10,000
Dominican Republic	None	Sept. 1-6, 1930	2,000-8,000
Haiti	Flora	Oct. 3, 1963	7,186-8,000
South of Newfoundland in Atlantic	None	Sept. 9, 1775	4,000
Puerto Rico	None	Aug. 8, 1899	3,000-3,369
Guadeloupe, Puerto Rico, Turks Island, Florida	None	Sept. 12-16, 1928	3,354-3,366
Cuba, Cayman Islands, Jamaica	None	Nov.4-10, 1932	2,500-3,107
El Salvador, Honduras	None	June 4-8, 1934	2,000-3,006
Western Cuba	None	June 21-22, 1791	3,000
Barbados	None	Aug. 10-11, 1831	1,477-2,500
Haiti, Honduras, offshore Jamaica	None	Oct. 19-25, 1935	1,000-2,150
Dominica, Dominican Republic, USA	David	Aug. 29-Sept. 1, 1979	2,063-2,068[2]
South Carolina, Georgia	None	Aug. 27-28, 1893	1,000-2,500
Eastern Gulf of Mexico	None	Oct. 17-21, 1780	2,000
Cuba	None	Oct. 7-8, 1870	1,000-2,000
Louisiana	None	Oct. 1-2, 1893	1,800-2,000

[1] Official estimate is more than 6,000. [2] Less than 25 in USA. Source: National Hurricane Center

it produced torrential rain that killed 113 people in flash floods and landslides.

3. Hurricane Andrew, Aug. 24, 1992: Andrew hit Dade County, Fla., with 145 mph winds on Aug. 24, 1992, and hit the Louisiana Coast two days later. It was by far the costliest U.S. hurricane. But with only 23 deaths directly attributed to it, Andrew did not make the list of deadliest U.S. hurricanes. As Andrew neared the Florida Coast, forecasters feared it could grow into a Category 5 storm over warm, Gulf Stream water. But it remained a Category 4 storm as it hit. Even though Andrew pushed a 16.9-foot storm surge ashore from Biscayne Bay south of downtown Miami, its 145 mph winds accounted for most of the damage.

4. Unnamed storm, Sept. 9 – 10 and 14, 1919: This storm reached its strongest intensity, barometric pressure 27.37, near the Dry Tortugas, 65 miles west of Key West, Fla. Little damage was reported in the Keys, but the storm sank at least 10 ships, killing an estimated 500 people, before hitting land near Corpus Christi, Texas, on Sept. 14, and killing 287 more. A 16-foot storm surge swept over the beaches and low-lying parts of Corpus Christi, destroying almost all the wooden buildings there. Port Aransas, on Mustang Island about 25 miles north of Corpus Christi, was virtually demolished.

5. Unnamed storm, Sept. 16, 1928: The second deadliest U.S. hurricane came ashore near Palm Beach, Fla., but caused most of its 1,836 deaths around Lake Okeechobee. Waves on the lake breached a dike along the southern shore, flooding farm settlements. Some victims climbed trees to escape the flood water only to be killed by the bites of poisonous snakes, which had also fled to the trees. Today's higher dikes around Lake Okeechobee and wide canals running to the Atlantic and Gulf of Mexico were built in response to this storm.

6. Hurricane Donna, Sept. 3 – 13, 1960: Long-lived Donna is the only storm on record to hit Florida, the mid-Atlantic states and New England with hurricane force winds. In Florida's Central Keys, winds were estimated at 140 mph with gusts to 180 mph. After crossing the Keys into the Gulf of Mexico, Donna went inland near Naples, Fla., crossed the state and moved back over the Atlantic near Daytona Beach. The storm's center stayed just offshore as it skirted the Atlantic coast until going ashore between Wilmington and Morehead City, N.C. Instead of heading inland, Donna moved parallel to the shore and crossed the Outer Banks.

Hurricanes, 1900 – 1993

Number of hurricanes by category that have hit the USA from 1900 – 1993. (Only direct hits, a storm whose eye crossed land, are counted.) Major storms are considered those in categories 3, 4 and 5.

Area	Number of storms by category					Major storms	Total
	1	2	3	4	5		
South Texas	3	4	5	1	0	6	13
Central Texas	2	2	1	1	0	2	6
North Texas	7	3	3	4	0	7	17
Louisiana	8	5	8	3	1	12	25
Mississippi	1	1	5	0	1	6	8
Alabama	4	1	5	0	0	5	10
N.W. Florida	9	7	6	0	0	6	22
S.W. Florida	6	3	6	2	1	9	18
S.E. Florida	4	10	7	4	0	11	25
N.E. Florida	1	7	0	0	0	0	8
Georgia	1	4	0	0	0	0	5
South Carolina	6	4	2	2	0	4	14
North Carolina	10	3	8	1	0	9	22
Virginia	2	1	1	0	0	1	4
Maryland	0	1	0	0	0	0	1
Delaware	0	0	0	0	0	0	0
New Jersey	1	0	0	0	0	0	1
New York	3	1	5	0	0	5	9
Connecticut	2	3	3	0	0	3	8
Rhode Island	0	2	3	0	0	3	5
Massachusetts	2	2	2	0	0	2	6
New Hampshire	1	1	0	0	0	0	2
Maine	5	0	0	0	0	0	5
USA total	**57**	**35**	**44**	**15**	**2**	**61**	**153**

(Storms that affected more than one state are counted for each state. For example, the Category 5 Hurricane Camille in 1969 is counted with both Louisiana and Mississippi but only counted once for the USA total.)

After shooting across eastern Long Island, it hit land for the last time in Connecticut and died over Maine and eastern Canada. Despite its long course and extensive damage ($1.8 billion in 1990 dollars), Donna's death toll of 50 was remarkably low.

7. Unnamed storm, Sept. 8, 1900: With a death toll of at least 6,000, this hurricane that hit Galveston, Texas, is by far the nation's worst natural disaster. But in intensity, it is tied with three other storms as the seventh strongest since 1900. The storm hit Galveston with 120 mph winds, but the 8 to 15 feet of storm surge that washed over low-lying Galveston Island caused most of the deaths.

At the turn of the century, coastal locations had

little warning of approaching storms. On the morning of Sept. 8, rising winds and water and a falling barometer alarmed Isaac Cline, head of the Galveston Weather Bureau. He rode a horse along the beach front, urging people to flee. But most took shelter on higher parts of the island, which had been safe in previous storms. This time, however, water from the Gulf of Mexico washed completely across the island. Afterward Galveston built a 17-foot-high, three-mile-long sea wall, which has protected the central part of the city from hurricane surges since then.

8. Unnamed storm, Sept. 20, 1909: This storm, which came ashore about 50 miles west of New Orleans, killed approximately 350 people when it pushed Gulf of Mexico water over most of the Louisiana Coast. The storm's eye came ashore near Houma, destroying homes, warehouses and sugar mills as well as hundreds of fishing and pleasure boats. East of New Orleans, the storm destroyed almost all the piers and shore-side buildings from Gulfport, Miss., to the Louisiana line. The storm also destroyed many state records in the capitol building in Baton Rouge.

9. Unnamed storm, Sept. 29, 1915: The storm hit land almost due south of New Orleans on Sept. 29, 1915, and lost little strength as it crossed the marshes south of the city. As with all hurricanes, the storm surge and winds were strongest on the right side. The surge pushed water into Lake Pontchartrain, which opens to the Gulf east of New Orleans. The surge and wind destroyed about 90 percent of the buildings around the lake. Winds

faster than 60 mph raked New Orleans for more than seven hours. The storm's central pressure of 27.49 made it a Category 4 when it hit. The barometer dropped to 28.11 in the city, Category 3. The storm surge reached 16 feet in places east of New Orleans and large ships were left on land as water rose 10 to 15 feet above the normal high tide. The death toll was 275.

10. Hurricane Carla, Sept. 11, 1961: An estimated half-million people in Texas began evacuating on Sept. 9 as Carla's winds enveloped the entire Gulf of Mexico. The evacuation, the largest ever in the United States up to that time, helped hold the death toll to 46, even though Carla did $408 million in damage ($1.9 billion in 1990 dollars).

As Carla neared shore on Sept. 10, winds were estimated at 150 mph and a reconnaissance aircraft measured its pressure at 27.59. When Carla hit the morning of Sept. 11 near Port Lavaca, between Corpus Christi and Galveston, pressure was 27.49. It pushed a 10-foot surge over the barrier beaches along the shore, but the water rose as much as 18 feet in the narrow bays behind the barrier beaches. Storm surges were 10 to 15 feet high along the beaches all the way to Galveston, 120 miles northeast of the eye's landfall. Water squeezed into the narrow end of Galveston Bay pushed the tide 16 feet above normal when it reached the head of the bay. In addition to the wind and storm surge, Carla's torrential rain added to the damage.

Andrew's victims

Considering the storm's strength and the number of people affected, Hurricane Andrew's death toll was low. In Florida, 15 deaths were attributed directly to the storm and another 29 indirectly. In Louisiana, eight deaths were directly attributed to the hurricane, nine indirectly.

Direct fatalities are those caused by the effects of the storm's winds and flooding. Indirect fatalities are caused by electrocution, cleanup accidents, fires and other incidents after the storm, but listed by medical examiners as being caused by the storm. Some unofficial counts of indirect fatalities included causes such as auto accidents at intersections where Andrew had blown down traffic lights or stop signs.

Here are causes listed in official reports of the circumstances of the direct deaths in Florida and Louisiana from Hurricane Andrew.

Florida
- Tree fell on camper. Male, 47.
- Roof beam in home fell. Female, 12.

Tropical storms vs. hurricanes

Total number in the Atlantic, Caribbean Sea and Gulf of Mexico by month from 1886 through 1993:

Month formed	Tropical storms	Hurricanes
Jan. – April	4	1
May	14	3
June	57	23
July	68	35
August	221	152
September	311	196
October	188	96
November	42	22
December	6	3

• Home's roof caved in. Male, 25.

• Truck trailer being used as shelter rolled over and collapsed. Male, 47, and male, 32. Eleven others survived.

• Washed off anchored boat. Male, 32.

• Trailer collapsed and rolled over. Male, 62.

• Ceiling collapsed. Male, 67.

• Refused evacuation, was buried under debris when trailer collapsed. Female, 80.

• Residence destroyed. Male, 46.

• Left home when it began to collapse, killed by flying debris outside. Male, 49.

• Townhouse collapsed. Female, 67.

• Roof collapsed. Male, 54.

• On board a boat, hit by flying object and fell overboard. Male, 37.

• Washed overboard from boat. Male, 56.

Louisiana

• Commercial fishing boat sunk in the Gulf of Mexico. Six males, ages 30 to 44.

• Hurricane-related tornado struck home. Male, 63, and female, 2.

When Atlantic hurricanes hit

Major hurricanes, those in categories 3, 4 and 5 that do the most damage, are most likely to hit in September. Since 1900, 35 of the 61 major hurricanes to hit the U.S. have hit in September. August is the second most likely month with 14 major hurricanes. October has had 7. July, 3. June, 2.

But four of the most devastating hurricanes did not hit in September: Andrew in August 1992, Audrey in June 1957, Camille in August 1969, and Hazel in October 1954.

In Texas and Louisiana, August and September are almost equally bad for major hurricanes. Texas has had seven in August and six in September. Louisiana has had four in August, five in September.

Five of October's seven major hurricanes have hit Florida.

Pacific hurricanes

While the strongest hurricanes to hit the U.S. come from the Atlantic Ocean or Gulf of Mexico, the eastern and central Pacific Ocean also produces hurricanes that affect the West Coast and Hawaii.

Along Mexico's Pacific Coast, hurricanes and tropical storms can bring heavy rain with flash floods and mudslides or dangerous winds. Hurricanes from the Caribbean Sea and the Gulf of Mexico regularly hit Mexico's East Coast.

While a hurricane-strength storm has never

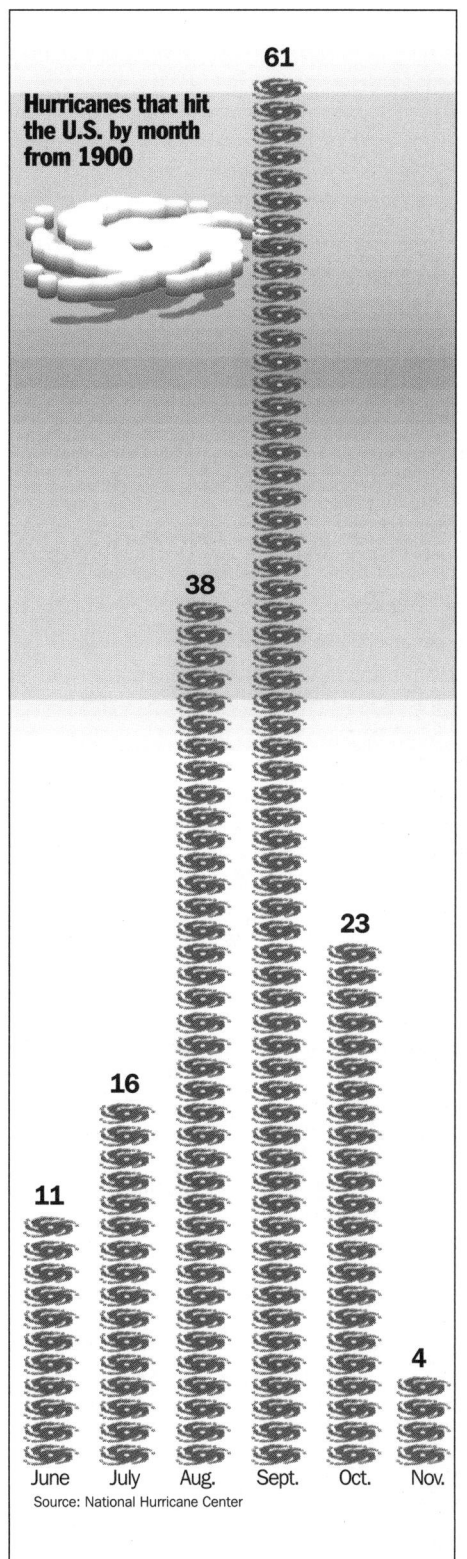

Hurricanes that hit the U.S. by month from 1900

61

38

23

16

11

4

June July Aug. Sept. Oct. Nov.

Source: National Hurricane Center

been known to hit the California Coast, at least one tropical storm and several tropical depressions — weakened from hurricane or tropical storm strength — have. Most of the damage to California, Arizona or other parts of the Southwest has been from drenching rain. Some of these storms have sent flooding rain into the central Mississippi Valley.

Hurricanes are very rare in Hawaii and usually are relatively weak by the time they arrive. But, as Hurricane Iniki showed in 1992, these storms can threaten lives and do millions or even billions of dollars in damage.

Until weather satellites began "seeing" Eastern Pacific hurricanes in the 1970s, meteorologists had underestimated how many occur because many

storms never come near land and fewer ships sail the eastern Pacific than the Atlantic, Caribbean and Gulf of Mexico.

Here are some notable Pacific hurricanes, tropical storms, and tropical depressions. Since information about many of these storms is incomplete, they are listed in chronological order without any ranking for strength, deaths or damage.

Unnamed storm, Aug. 18, 1906: This storm, strength unknown, came up the Gulf of California, giving Needles, Calif., 5.66 inches of rain, twice its annual average.

Unnamed storm, Sept. 25, 1939: Winds were about 50 mph when this tropical storm hit Southern California, killing at least 45 people, sinking

Deadliest hurricanes to hit the U.S. since 1900

Rank	Deaths	Year	Name	Category	Areas hit
1	6,000 plus	1900	Unnamed	4	Galveston, Texas
2	1,836	1928	Unnamed	4	Lake Okeechobee, Fla.
3	600-900	1919	Unnamed	4	Florida Keys[1]
4	600	1938	Unnamed	3	New England
5	408	1935	Unnamed	5	Florida Keys
6	390	1957	Audrey	4	Southwest Louisiana, Texas
7	390	1944	Unnamed	3	Northeast[1]
8	350	1909	Unnamed	4	Grand Isle, La.
9	275	1915	Unnamed	4	New Orleans, La.
10	275	1915	Unnamed	4	Galveston, Texas
11	256	1969	Camille	5	Mississippi, Louisiana, Virginia
12	243	1926	Unnamed	4	Miami, Fla.
13	184	1955	Diane	1	Northeast
14	164	1906	Unnamed	2	Southeast Florida
15	134	1906	Unnamed	3	Pensacola, Fla., Alabama, Mississippi
16	122	1972	Agnes	1	Northeast
17	95	1954	Hazel	4	South Carolina, North Carolina
18	75	1965	Betsy	3	Southeast Florida, Louisiana
19	60	1954	Carol	3	Northeast
20	51	1947	Unnamed	4	Florida, Louisiana, Mississippi
21	50	1960	Donna	4	Florida and East Coast
22	50	1940	Unnamed	2	Georgia, the Carolinas
23	46	1961	Carla	4	Texas
24	41	1909	Unnamed	3	Texas
25	40	1932	Unnamed	4	Freeport, Texas
26	40	1933	Unnamed	3	Southern Texas
27	38	1964	Hilda	3	Louisiana
28	34	1918	Unnamed	3	Southwest Louisiana
29	30	1910	Unnamed	3	Southwest Florida
30	25	1955	Connie	3	North Carolina
31	25	1926	Unnamed	3	Louisiana

Source: National Hurricane Center   [1]Most victims were on ships at sea

boats, damaging structures along the shore and bringing heavy rain. Researchers at Mount Wilson, north of Los Angeles, measured 10.6 inches of rain.

Hurricane Hiki, Aug. 12 – 16, 1950: While reconnaissance aircraft found 90 mph winds as the storm approached Hawaii, the storm passed by the islands and the strongest winds in Hawaii were gusts to 68 mph on Kauai. These winds blew the roofs off several houses and one person was killed by a downed power line. The greatest property damage came from flooding of the Waimea River on Kauai, which forced the evacuation of more than 200 residents. The Kanalohuluhulu Ranger Station of Kauai recorded more than 52 inches of rain from the storm.

Unnamed storm, Oct. 21, 1957: Hurricane force winds hit Mazatlan, Mexico, doing extensive damage to buildings, sinking 20 boats and pushing another 20 up on the shore. Winds were measured at 130 mph in Mazatlan before the anemometer blew away. Eight people were killed when the city's jail blew down.

Hurricane Dot, Aug. 1 – 8, 1959: Aircraft measured winds greater than 100 mph when Dot was still over the ocean, but weakened to an estimated 60 mph as Dot passed over the Hawaiian island of Kauai. Even these relatively weak winds destroyed an estimated $5.5 million to $6 million worth of sugar cane on Kauai. The storm also damaged hundreds of buildings and blew down several hundred trees on macadamia nut farms. No deaths were reported.

Hurricane Katrina, Aug. 31 to Sept. 2, 1967: Storm surge and winds partially destroyed San Felipe, Mexico, leaving 2,500 people homeless. It also sank 60 vessels. Up to 1,500 were left homeless by damage in Mulege, Mexico.

Tropical Depression Norma, Oct. 5, 1970: Even though the storm's winds had weakened to 30 mph by the time it hit the U.S., Norma's rain

Costliest hurricanes to hit the U.S. since 1900

(All figures are in 1990 dollars)

Rank	Cost	Year	Name	Category	Areas most damage done
1	$25 billion	1992	Andrew	4	Dade County, Fla., Louisiana
2	$7.1 billion	1989	Hugo	4	South Carolina
3	$6.5 billion	1965	Betsy	3	South Florida, Louisiana
4	$6.4 billion	1972	Agnes	1	Northeast
5	$5.2 billion	1969	Camille	5	Mississippi, Alabama, Louisiana
6	$4.2 billion	1955	Diane	1	Northeast
7	$3.6 billion	1938	Unnamed	3	New England
8	$3.5 billion	1979	Frederic	3	Alabama, Mississippi
9	$2.4 billion	1983	Alicia	3	Northeastern Texas
10	$2.4 billion	1954	Carol	3	Northeast
11	$1.9 billion	1961	Carla	4	Texas
12	$1.8 billion	1960	Donna	4	Florida and East Coast
13	$1.8 billion	1992	Iniki	NA[1]	Kauai, Hawaii
14	$1.7 billion	1985	Juan	1	Louisiana
15	$1.6 billion	1970	Celia	3	Southern Texas
16	$1.5 billion	1991	Bob	2	North Carolina, Northeast
17	$1.4 billion	1954	Hazel	4	South Carolina, North Carolina
18	$1.4 billion	1985	Elena	3	Florida, Alabama, Mississippi
19	$1.3 billion	1926	Unnamed	4	Miami, Fla.
20	$1.2 billion	1915	Unnamed	4	Galveston, Texas
21	$1.2 billion	1964	Dora	2	Northeast Florida
22	$1.1 billion	1975	Eloise	3	Northwest Florida
23	$1.0 billion	1985	Gloria	3	Northeast
24	$925 million	1944	Unnamed	3	Northeast
25	$844 million	1967	Beulah	3	Southern Texas

[1] No official category given
Source: National Hurricane Center

caused an estimated $1 million in damage and 22 deaths in Arizona.

Hurricane Bridget, June 17, 1971: The hurricane's eye passed 30 miles offshore from Acapulco, Mexico, bringing gusts of more than 100 mph to the city and harbor, sinking 10 boats, including the flagship of the admiral of the Mexican Navy. It was Acapulco's worst storm in 25 years. Estimated death toll: 40.

Tropical Depression Hyacinth, Sept. 6, 1972: This was the first tropical cyclone to hit California since 1939. No deaths or serious damage reported with winds of less than 30 mph.

Hurricane Olivia, Oct. 25, 1975: Winds greater than 100 mph killed 30 people, left an estimated 30,00 homeless, and forced 50,000 to evacuate Mazatlan, Mexico.

Tropical Storm Kathleen, Sept. 10, 1976: After hitting Mexico's Baja Peninsula, the storm brought 50 mph winds to the Imperial and Lower Colorado valleys in California and Arizona. It brought up to 3.5 inches of rain to the deserts and 14.5 inches to mountains in the Southwest U.S. A five-foot-high, half-mile-wide wall of flood water destroyed the town of Ocotillo, Calif., killing two people. It caused heavy flooding in Las Vegas and rain spread north into Idaho and Montana. The losses in 1976 dollars were estimated at $333 million ($756 million in 1990 dollars).

Hurricane Liza, Oct. 1, 1976: Heavy rain and winds up to 130 mph collapsed a dam on the Cajoncito River in Mexico killing at least 630 people when a wall of water rushed into La Paz. The earthen dam was only four years old.

Hurricane Doreen, Aug. 16 – 18, 1977: After hitting the southern part of Mexico's Baja Peninsula, the storm weakened as it moved into southeastern California, but more than seven inches of rain caused floods that killed five people, destroyed 325 houses and caused heavy damage to agriculture in

Most intense hurricanes to hit the U.S. since 1900

The lowest recorded barometric pressure is used to rank hurricane intensity because it is a more reliable measurement than wind speed, but is directly related to wind speed and storm surge height.

Rank	Pressure	Year	Name	Category	Areas hit
1	26.35	1935	Unnamed	5	Florida Keys
2	26.84	1969	Camille	5	Mississippi, Louisiana, Alabama
3	27.23	1992	Andrew	4	Dade County, Fla., Louisiana
4	27.37	1919	Unnamed	4	Florida Keys, Southern Texas
5	27.43	1928	Unnamed	4	Lake Okeechobee, Fla.
6	27.46	1960	Donna	4	Florida and East Coast
7	27.49	1900	Unnamed	4	Galveston, Texas
7 (tie)	27.49	1909	Unnamed	4	Grand Isle, La.
7 (tie)	27.49	1915	Unnamed	4	New Orleans, La.
7 (tie)	27.49	1961	Carla	4	Texas
11	27.58	1989	Hugo	4	South Carolina
12	27.61	1926	Unnamed	4	Miami, Fla.
13	27.70	1954	Hazel	4	The Carolinas
14	27.76	1947	Unnamed	4	Florida, Louisiana, Mississippi
15	27.79	1932	Unnamed	4	Northeastern Texas
16	27.82	1985	Gloria	3[1]	Northeast
17	27.91	1957	Audrey	4[2]	Louisiana, Northeast Texas
17 (tie)	27.91	1915	Unnamed	4[2]	Galveston, Texas
17 (tie)	27.91	1970	Celia	3	Southern Texas
17 (tie)	27.91	1980	Allen	3[3]	Southern Texas
21	27.94	1938	Unnamed	3	New England
21 (tie)	27.94	1979	Frederic	3	Florida, Alabama, Mississippi
23	27.97	1944	Unnamed	3	Northeast
23 (tie)	27.97	1906	Unnamed	3	The Carolinas

[1]Pressure was in Category 4 range, but winds and tides did not justify that ranking. [2]Classified as Category 4 because of extreme tides. [3]Reached Category 5 intensity in the Caribbean and Gulf of Mexico, but weakened to Category 3 before hitting the U.S.
Source: National Hurricane Center

San Diego and Imperial counties California.

Tropical Depression Norman, Sept. 6, 1978: Winds were less than 30 mph when the storm came ashore in the Los Angeles area, but heavy rain destroyed 95 percent of California's raisin crop, which was drying outdoors during a normally very dry time of the year. Damage was $1 billion in 1990 dollars.

Hurricane Norma, Oct. 12, 1981: After hitting land near Mazatlan, Mexico, with little damage reported, this storm quickly weakened to a tropical depression and moved across Mexico into the Red River Valley between Texas and Oklahoma, where up to 26 inches of rain, severe flooding and 13 tornadoes killed seven people.

Hurricane Paul, Sept. 19 – 30, 1982: This first hit El Salvador and Guatemala as a tropical storm with heavy rain that sent water and mudslides into villages, killing more than 1,000 people and leaving 33,000 homeless. It moved back over the Pacific

and grew into a 100 mph hurricane that killed eight people when it hit near Los Mochis, Mexico.

Hurricane Iwa, Nov. 19 – 24, 1982: When Iwa hit Kauai, Hawaii, its winds were about 80 mph, but it was moving forward at almost 30 mph, making the winds on its right side over 100 mph. Iwa caused one death and severe property damage on Kauai.

Hurricane Tico, Oct. 19, 1983: Winds hit more than 125 mph when this storm hit Mazatlan, Mexico, sank nine small ships, flooded parts of the city and left more than 25,000 homeless. As the storm weakened, it caused heavy flooding farther inland in Mexico and in a narrow band from western Texas into eastern Missouri. It brought 17 inches of rain to Chickasha, Okla.

Tropical Storm Roslyn, Oct. 22, 1986: This storm caused flood and wind damage near Mazatlan, Mexico, then moved into Texas, Oklahoma and Kansas as a depression that brought Oklahoma

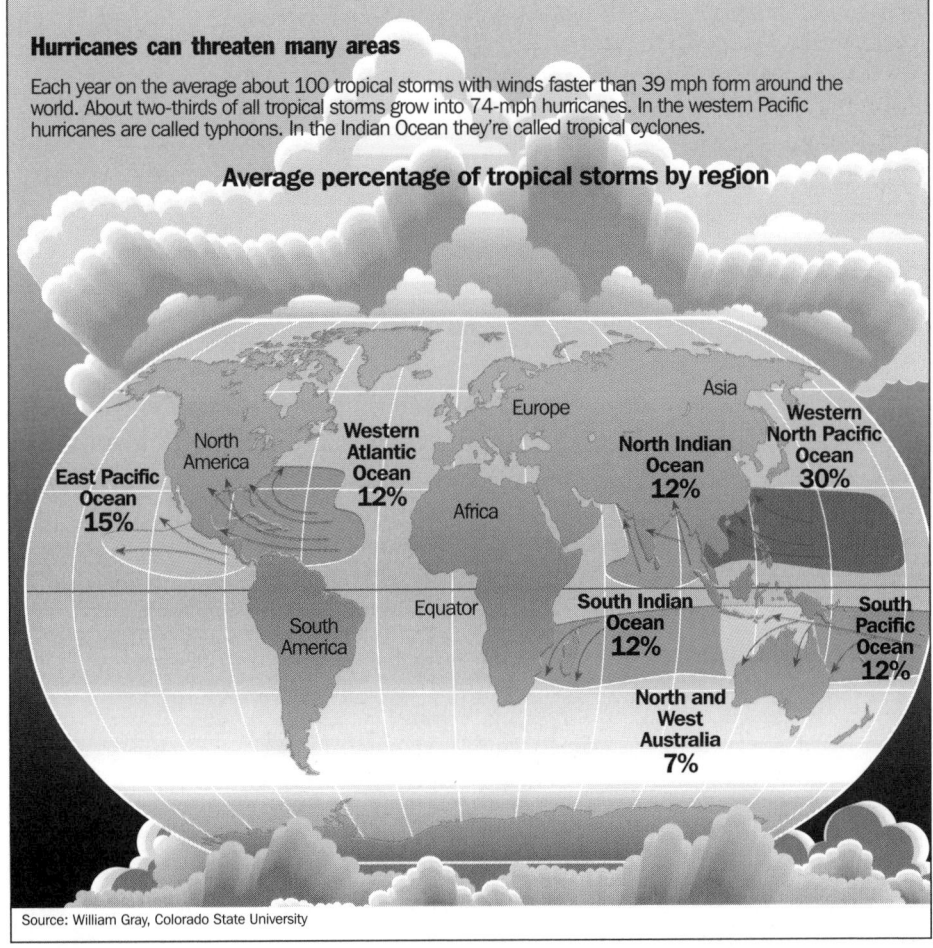

Hurricanes can threaten many areas

Each year on the average about 100 tropical storms with winds faster than 39 mph form around the world. About two-thirds of all tropical storms grow into 74-mph hurricanes. In the western Pacific hurricanes are called typhoons. In the Indian Ocean they're called tropical cyclones.

Average percentage of tropical storms by region

East Pacific Ocean **15%**

Western Atlantic Ocean **12%**

North Indian Ocean **12%**

Western North Pacific Ocean **30%**

South Indian Ocean **12%**

South Pacific Ocean **12%**

North and West Australia **7%**

Source: William Gray, Colorado State University

Name cycle for Atlantic Basin storms

1995	1996	1997	1998	1999	2000
Allison	Arthur	Ana	Alex	Arlene	Alberto
Barry	Bertha	Bill	Bonnie	Bret	Beryl
Chantal	Cesar	Claudette	Charley	Cindy	Chris
Dean	Diana	Danny	Danielle	Dennis	Debby
Erin	Edouard	Erika	Earl	Emily	Ernesto
Felix	Fran	Fabian	Frances	Floyd	Florence
Gabrielle	Gustav	Grace	Georges	Gert	Gordon
Humberto	Hortense	Henri	Hermine	Harvey	Helene
Iris	Isidore	Isabel	Ivan	Irene	Isaac
Jerry	Josephine	Juan	Jeanne	Jose	Joyce
Karen	Klaus	Kata	Karl	Katrina	Keith
Luis	Lili	Larry	Lisa	Lenny	Leslie
Marilyn	Marco	Mindy	Mitch	Maria	Michael
Noel	Nana	Nicholas	Nicole	Nate	Nadine
Opal	Omar	Odette	Otto	Ophelia	Oscar
Pablo	Paloma	Peter	Paula	Philippe	Patty
Roxanne	Rene	Rose	Richard	Rita	Rafael
Sebastien	Sally	Sam	Shary	Stan	Sandy
Tanya	Teddy	Teresa	Tomas	Tammy	Tony
Van	Vicky	Victor	Virginie	Vince	Valerie
Wendy	Wilfred	Wanda	Walter	Wilma	Willi

Hurricane names that have been retired

Once an Atlantic Basin hurricane has caused great damage, its name is retired from the six-year cycle. These names have been retired:

Alicia, 1993	Frederic, 1979
Allen, 1980	Gilbert, 1988
Andrew, 1992	Gloria, 1985
Bob, 1991	Hugo, 1989
David, 1979	Joan, 1988
Elena, 1985	

some of its worst 20th century flooding.

Hurricane Iniki, Sept. 11, 1992: Like the other damaging storms of this century, Iniki hit Hawaii's northwestern island, Kauai, leaving five people dead, more than 10,000 homes destroyed or damaged, most hotels unusable, and agriculture devastated. In 1990 dollars, Iniki's $1.8 billion damage would rank 13th on the costliest list, behind a dozen much stronger East and Gulf Coast hurricanes. In addition, damage to tourist hotels continued to hurt the island's economy for more than a year.

Naming hurricanes

Tropical storms and hurricanes are given names to avoid confusion when more than one storm is being followed at the same time. A storm is named when it reaches tropical storm strength.

Separate sets of hurricane names are used in the central Pacific, eastern Pacific, and the Atlantic Basin, which includes the Caribbean Sea and Gulf of Mexico.

The central Pacific is the area from the International Date Line east to 140 degrees west longitude, about 1,200 miles east of Hawaii. In the central Pacific, Hawaiian names are used for storms.

Name cycle for eastern Pacific storms

1995	1996	1997	1998	1999	2000
Adolph	Alma	Andres	Agatha	Adrian	Aletta
Barbara	Boris	Blanca	Blas	Beatriz	Bud
Cosme	Cristina	Carlos	Celia	Calvin	Carlotta
Dalila	Douglas	Dolores	Darby	Dora	Daniel
Erick	Elida	Enrique	Estelle	Eugene	Emilia
Flossie	Fausto	Felicia	Frank	Fernanda	Fabio
Gil	Genevieve	Guillermo	Georgette	Greg	Gilma
Henriette	Hernan	Hilda	Howard	Hilary	Hector
Ismael	Iselle	Ignacio	Isis	Irwin	Ileana
Juliette	Julio	Jimena	Javier	Jova	John
Kiko	Kenna	Kevin	Kay	Kenneth	Kristy
Lorena	Lowell	Linda	Lester	Lidia	Lane
Manuel	Marie	Marty	Madeline	Max	Miriam
Narda	Norbert	Nora	Newton	Norma	Norman
Octave	Odile	Olaf	Orlene	Otis	Olivia
Priscilla	Polo	Pauline	Paine	Pilar	Paul
Raymond	Rachel	Rick	Roslyn	Ramon	Rosa
Sonia	Simon	Sandra	Seymour	Selma	Sergio
Tico	Trudy	Terry	Tina	Todd	Tara
Velma	Vance	Vivian	Virgil	Veronica	Vicente
Wallis	Winnie	Waldo	Winifred	Wiley	Willa
Xina	Xavier	Xina	Xavier	Xina	Xavier
York	Yolanda	York	Yolanda	York	Yolanda
Zelda	Zeke	Zelda	Zeke	Zelda	Zeke

Names for central Pacific tropical cyclones 1995 and beyond

Li	Ele	Peni	Loke	Ema	Peke
Mele	Huko	Ulia	Malia	Hana	Uleki
Nona	Ioke	Wali	Niala	Io	Wila
Oliwa	Kika	Ana	Oko	Keli	Aka
Paka	Lana	Ela	Pali	Lala	Ekeka
Upana	Maka	Halola	Ulika	Moke	Hali
Wene	Neki	Iune	Walaka	Nele	Iolona
Alika	Oleka	Kimo	Akoni	Oka	Keoni

In the eastern Pacific, from 140 degrees east to North and Central America, six lists of English and Spanish names are used. Each list is for a particular year. After the year is over, the same list is used six years later with names of any notable storms retired. No "Q" or "U" names are used since names beginning with these letters are rare. Since some seasons see more than 24 tropical storms in the eastern Pacific, the Greek alphabet is used after the "Z" name. When an eastern Pacific storm crosses 140 degrees into the central Pacific it keeps the same name.

Atlantic Basin names follow the same system as in the eastern Pacific. Because more Atlantic storms do major damage, names are more likely to be retired. For instance, 1992's "Andrew" will be replaced with "Alex" when the list is used again in 1998.

Self-defense

Hurricane winds probably aren't as strong as those in a large tornado, but a hurricane more than makes up with size and duration. A mile-wide tornado is huge, while a 100-mile-wide hurricane is small. Few tornadoes last even an hour. Hurricanes easily can last a week or more.

Even the biggest tornado will devastate only a part of a city or county. Those who are not hit can quickly rally to help victims. But a major hurricane can turn an entire community into wreckage. Victims must not only survive the storm itself, but also may have to live without electrical power, safe drinking water, and operating service stations and grocery stores for days.

At least hurricanes don't hit without warning. The National Hurricane Center and local emergency management agencies work to give people plenty of time to evacuate in daylight before gale winds begin to make driving difficult. Still, anyone who lives in an area that could be hit by a hurricane should prepare well ahead of time.

The U.S. East Coast from Maine to Florida and the entire Gulf of Mexico Coast are in the hurricane danger area. Some parts of the coast get few hurricanes, but preparations made for hurricanes can help save lives and property during ordinary storms, which can do more serious damage to some coastal areas than hurricanes.

Anyone in an area likely to be flooded by storm surge, and anyone in a mobile home or a house or apartment that might not stand up to strong winds, should plan to evacuate.

But evacuation isn't the answer for everyone, especially in south Florida. Those in well-built homes well inland from areas of potential storm surge are probably better off staying put.

Hurricane warnings can't be given in time to allow everyone in south Florida to evacuate. If too many people try to leave at once, many would be caught in traffic jams when hurricane force winds begin.

In hurricane winds, a sturdy home, office building or other shelter is a much safer place than a car.

Those who plan to stay should make sure their houses are as strong as possible and can make a "last-resort" shelter by strengthening the walls and ceiling of an interior, bottom-floor closet or bathroom.

Before moving to a coastal area: Learn about the area's hurricane and winter storm history. How bad have past storms been? Is evacuation from the area you're thinking of considered a problem?

National Weather Service offices or emergency management agencies in the area you plan to move to should be able to help.

• Don't believe stories about "a reef offshore" or "weather patterns" protecting particular parts of the coast from hurricanes.

• Find out whether the area has building codes that are enforced.

• Make sure a home you're thinking of buying meets building code standards.

Before the start of hurricane season: Put an up-to-date list of furnishings — with photos — in a safe-deposit box or another place away from a hurricane danger.

• Copy important financial and other records, such as insurance policies, and make sure the copies or originals are in a safe place. Some people like to have such documents and family photos in one place, ready to be put in a "grab and run" bag if evacuation is necessary.

• Cut dead trees or branches that could be blown into houses by high winds.

• Arrange some method of quickly covering windows and glass doors when a hurricane threatens. This may be with shutters or pieces of half-inch thick plywood. The plywood should be cut to size, and any needed frames made and any holes needed for installation drilled long before a storm threatens.

• Stock up on emergency supplies of drinking water, food that doesn't need refrigeration and cooking, medications, flashlights, batteries, a weather radio and a battery-powered radio or TV.

• If evacuation is likely in case of a storm, learn the best route and decide where you will go.

When a hurricane watch is issued: Check to make sure needed emergency supplies are on hand.

• Bring in lawn furniture, trash cans and other objects that could become missiles in high winds.

• If you live on a barrier island or other place with limited evacuation routes, avoid the rush. Consider leaving before the official order is given.

• Keep up with news of the storm and be ready to evacuate with little notice.

• Make sure all materials and tools needed to cover windows and glass doors are handy. If evacuation seems likely, cover windows and doors.

When a hurricane warning is issued: If evacuation is ordered or suggested, finish boarding up doors and windows and other protective measures and turn off the power.

• Make sure emergency supplies and irreplaceable photos and documents are in the car before leaving.

• If evacuation isn't required, finish covering windows and glass doors and make sure objects that could be blown around are inside.

• When the wind begins blowing, stay away from windows, even those that are covered. If wind seems to be damaging the house, retreat into a small, interior room such as a bathroom or closet.

Thunderstorms

Compared to a hurricane or winter storm, any thunderstorm is small. A typical thunderstorm is about 15 miles across and lasts only 30 minutes. Even the largest, longest-lasting thunderstorm isn't likely to be more than 25 miles across and will last only a few hours.

But what thunderstorms lack in size, they can make up in violence. Even the smallest thunderstorm is dangerous because it produces lightning, which is the second leading cause of weather deaths in the U.S. behind floods. In fact, many of the flash floods that cause most flood deaths come from thunderstorms.

The National Weather Service estimates that 100,000 thunderstorms occur in the United States each year.

Of these, about 10,000 are classified as severe with hail at least ¾-inch in diameter, winds faster than 58 mph or with tornadoes.

Thunderstorms can occur any time of the year. "Thunder snow" is reported fairly regularly in the north in the winter. But spring and summer are the usual times for thunderstorms.

Along the Gulf Coast and in the southeastern and western states, most thunderstorms occur during the afternoon. But on the Great Plains, thunderstorms often occur in the late afternoon and at night. There are four dangers of thunderstorms: lightning, downbursts, hail and tornadoes.

Lightning

A lightning bolt is a giant, 100-million volt or more, electrical spark within a cloud, from one cloud to another or from a cloud to the ground. A lightning bolt heats a narrow channel of air to more than 50,000°F, hotter than the surface of the sun.

Obviously, this much electrical energy and heat is dangerous. Anyone who is outdoors is at the greatest danger from lightning. The most dangerous places are under or near tall trees, in or near the water, or in an open field. The safest place to be is inside a building, but there also are dangers inside.

Lightning can hit electrical or telephone wires and people have been killed by lightning while talking on the telephone. It's safer to stay away from electrical appliances when lightning is nearby.

Rain doesn't have to be falling for lightning to hit. In fact, the cloud that produces the lightning may not be overhead.

Rubber-sole shoes or a car's rubber tires do not provide enough insulation to protect a person from lightning. But being in a car is safer than being outside because the metal body will carry the lightning to the ground.

To play it safe in a car during a lightning storm, don't touch any metal parts of the car and roll up the windows.

If someone is hit by lightning, first aid should begin immediately. A person hit by lightning does not retain an electrical charge and is safe to touch. But someone who comes in contact with a live wire shouldn't be touched until the power is shut off or the wire is no longer touching the victim.

Downbursts

Thunderstorms normally produce gusty winds, which can be dangerous. The strongest come from "downbursts," which is air that comes down from the storm in a concentrated blast and spreads out when it hits the ground. Speeds faster than 100 mph have been recorded.

The best protection is the same as from a thunderstorm's lightning: Stay inside away from windows.

Hail

Balls of ice that fall from thunderstorms are called "hail." Most hailstones are smaller than a quarter, but they can be as big as baseballs and fall at speeds around 100 mph. Such hailstones are another reason to be inside during a thunderstorm.

Sometimes a burst of hail falls minutes or seconds before a tornado hits. It could be a warning to rush into a small room, such as a bathroom, or get under a table.

Tornadoes

Tornadoes can produce winds faster than 200 mph, the greatest found on the Earth's surface. The strongest tornadoes can rip apart even well-built houses, but these tornadoes are rare.

Weaker tornadoes, which are much more common, are dangerous to mobile homes and cars as well as to people caught outdoors.

Scientists are still trying to determine just how

fast the winds in a tornado can blow, but they are sure that 200 mph winds occur, and there's a chance that higher speeds are possible. Tornado winds can cause extraordinary destruction.

The good news is that tornadoes are small as storms go. A tornado a mile wide would be extremely large. In addition, the fastest tornadoes, the ones that cause the most deaths, account for only two percent of all tornadoes. And Doppler weather radars, now being installed around the United States, are proving to be good at spotting early signs of large tornadoes.

Tornadoes are atmospheric vortexes, spinning air, that come in a variety of sizes. In fact, tornadoes and other relatively small vortexes such as waterspouts are like a family. Each resembles the others in many ways — in all cases, the swirling air is going up — but there are individual traits:

Dust devils are vortexes that are not attached to a cloud. They are caused when rising, warm air begins to swirl. Dust devils are most common on deserts and their winds seem usually to be less than 60 mph. The vortex is likely to be only a few yards across. No dust devil deaths have been reported in the U.S.

Gustnadoes are short-lived vortexes (few last more than five minutes) that form in the wind flowing outward from a thunderstorm, much like the vortexes that form in water rushing down a mountain stream. They last only a few minutes and are generally weak.

Waterspouts, unlike tornadoes, come from cumulus congestus clouds over water, not from thunderstorms like larger tornadoes. Often, cumulus congestus clouds will grow into thunderstorms. But, waterspouts can form before the cloud becomes a thunderstorm. Such waterspouts can have winds around 100 mph and can be several yards across. Sometimes, the term "waterspout" is used loosely for any tornado over water. In the U.S., waterspouts are most common in the Florida Keys.

Landspout refers to vortexes similar to waterspouts in that they come from cumulus congestus clouds, not from thunderstorms, but they form over land. Because they come from clouds that aren't as well organized as thunderstorms, they, like waterspouts, tend to be weaker than many thunderstorm tornadoes. Some scientists don't like the term "landspout," but no one has come up with a better one.

The strongest and longest-lasting thunderstorms come from thunderstorms known as super-

cells. Such thunderstorms have highly organized wind patterns that enable them to last longer than other kinds of thunderstorms. A supercell tornado can be a mile wide and carve a path of destruction 200 miles long.

A funnel or funnel cloud is a vortex that isn't touching the ground or water. When it touches, it becomes a tornado or waterspout.

Tornadoes can hit just about anywhere, but they are most common in the U.S. east of the Rockies, especially on the Plains and in the Southeast.

The most tornado-prone region is between the Rockies and the Appalachians. Within those bounds, odds of a tornado striking are lower in northern Michigan and Wisconsin, most of Minnesota, North Dakota and Montana. It's the southern section between the Rockies and the Appalachians that is most at risk for tornadoes.

Don't believe stories that lakes or hills protect particular areas from tornadoes. In many cases tornadoes have traveled up and down hills, destroying houses in a valley.

Exactly how likely a tornado is to hit any particular place is hard to determine. While climatologists use 30-year records of temperatures and precipitation to establish "normals," that doesn't seem to work for tornadoes.

For example, Illinois ranked fifth in the number of tornadoes from 1970 to 1979, but 15th from 1980 to 1989. Yet, there is no climatic change that can explain why tornadoes came in the '70s and not the '80s.

Probably the best bet is to assume that if a killer tornado has ever hit a place, one could hit there again. And if more than one has hit, the odds are higher, and people who live there should learn as much as possible about tornadoes and be ready to act when they threaten.

Major U.S. tornado outbreaks

The six biggest U.S. tornado outbreaks:

Super Outbreak, April 3 – 4, 1973: The country's largest known outbreak included at least 148 storms, among them some of the strongest ever recorded. Tornadoes hit the area from just east of the Mississippi to the Appalachians and from Mississippi, Alabama and Georgia north to the Great Lakes. Tornadoes killed 315 and did $600 million in damage ($1.7 billion, 1990 dollars).

1884 Enigma Outbreak, Feb. 19, 1884: At least 60 tornadoes swept east from Mississippi, western Tennessee and Kentucky across Alabama, Georgia and the Carolinas. Death estimates ranged

Where biggest tornadoes hit

Tornadoes, including those with winds above 110 mph that cause more than 95% of all tornado deaths, can hit virtually any part of the nation. But, they are rare from the Rockies westward. Killer tornadoes target mainly the middle of the USA.

Average number of tornadoes with winds above 110 mph per 10,000 square miles[1]

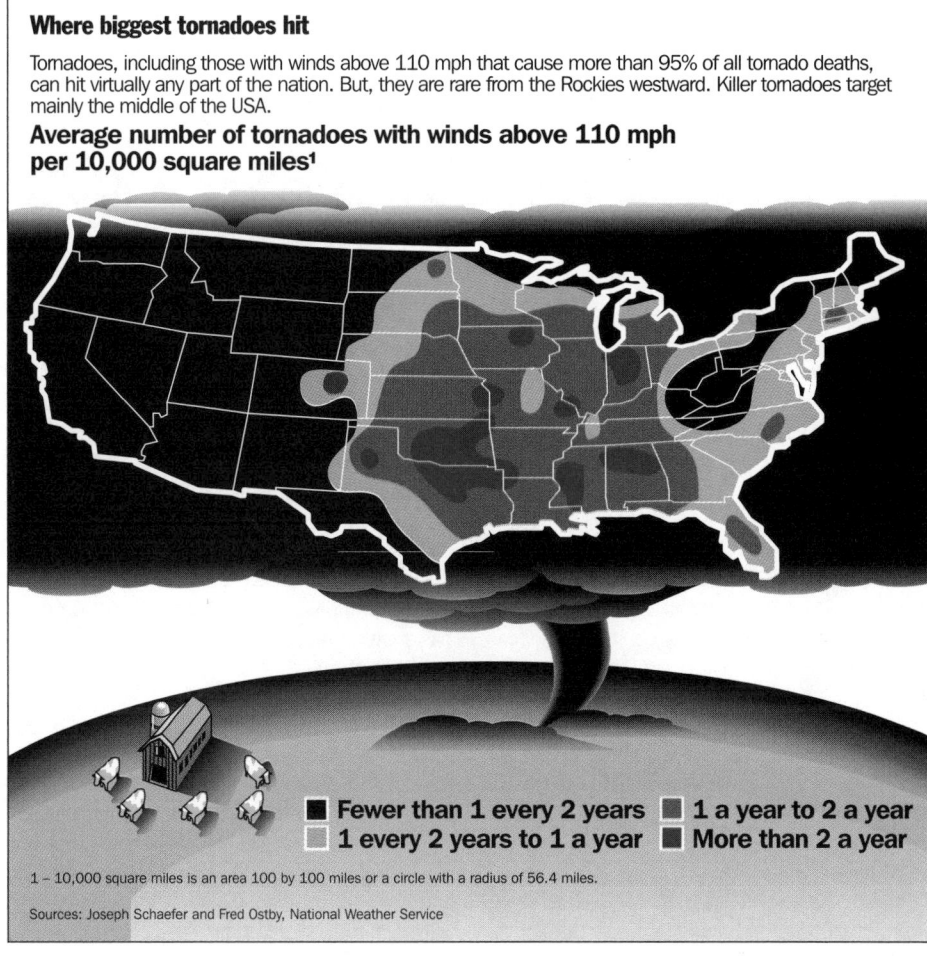

- ■ **Fewer than 1 every 2 years**
- □ **1 every 2 years to 1 a year**
- ▨ **1 a year to 2 a year**
- ■ **More than 2 a year**

1 ~ 10,000 square miles is an area 100 by 100 miles or a circle with a radius of 56.4 miles.

Sources: Joseph Schaefer and Fred Ostby, National Weather Service

from 182 to 1,200. Lack of reliable information about the number killed gives the outbreak its name.

Palm Sunday Outbreak, April 11 – 12, 1965: From 1 p.m. on the 11th until 1 a.m. on the 12th, 51 tornadoes hit Iowa, Wisconsin, Illinois, Michigan, Indiana, and Ohio, killing 256 people and doing $200 million in damage ($820 million, 1990 dollars).

Tri-State Outbreak, March 18, 1925: Only seven tornadoes were reported in Missouri, Illinois, Indiana, Kentucky, Tennessee and Alabama, but the death toll of 740 makes it the deadliest outbreak in U.S. history. The name comes from the outbreak's worst tornado, which traveled 219 miles from Ellington, Mo., across the southern tip of Illinois to Petersburg, Ind. Two worst hit towns: Murphysboro, Ill., with 234 killed, and West Frankfort, Ill., with 127 killed.

Tupelo – Gainesville Outbreak, April 5 – 6,

1936: At least 17 tornadoes swept from northern Mississippi across Tennessee, northern Alabama, and northern Georgia into South Carolina, killing 446 people. This outbreak began at 8 p.m. and ended at 9 a.m. One of the first tornadoes hit Tupelo, Miss., killing 216; one of the last hit Gainesville, Ga., killing 203.

St. Louis Outbreak, May 27, 1896. At least 18 tornadoes hit eastern Missouri and southeastern Illinois, killing 306 people. Of these, 255 were killed in St. Louis.

Recent major outbreaks

Carolinas Outbreak, March 28, 1984: A supercell and smaller thunderstorms spawned 22 tornadoes in the afternoon and evening across South and North Carolina, killing 57 people and doing $200 million in damage ($249 million, 1990 dollars).

Pennsylvania – Ohio Outbreak, May 31,

1985: At least 41 tornadoes, including 27 in Ohio and Pennsylvania and the rest in Ontario, Canada, killed 75 people in the U.S. and did $450 million in damage ($540 million, 1990 dollars).

Plains Outbreak, April 26 – 17, 1991: A total of 54 tornadoes hit from Texas north across Oklahoma, Kansas and Nebraska into Missouri and Iowa, killing 21 people, including 15 in or near mobile homes. The damage was more than $277 million.

November Outbreak, Nov. 21 – 23, 1992: This unusually strong outbreak for November included 94 tornadoes in an area from Houston, Texas, to Raleigh, N.C., and from the Gulf Coast to the Ohio Valley. It killed 26 people.

The Palm Sunday Outbreak, March 27 – 28, 1994: Tornadoes began in the morning in Alabama. One hit the Goshen United Methodist Church in Piedmont during Palm Sunday services, killing 20. During the day and into the next morning, the tornadoes and other damaging thunderstorm winds swept from Alabama, across northern Georgia and into the Carolinas with a total death toll of 44.

Self-defense

In general, the safety rules for all thunderstorms apply to those that spawn tornadoes. But tornadoes present additional dangers.

Weather statistics show that those most at risk from tornadoes are people in cars, the elderly, the very young, people who are physically or mentally impaired, people in mobile homes, and people who may not understand warnings because of a language barrier.

Anyone who lives in tornado-prone parts of the U.S. should have one of the special NOAA weather radios with a warning alarm tone and battery backup. Weather radios pick up only broadcasts by National Weather Service offices and are handy for keeping up with the weather at all times.

Weather radios with a warning alarm tone automatically turn on when the weather office broadcasts a special warning signal.

Sometimes tornadoes develop too quickly for warnings. This is why it's a good idea to stay alert when a tornado watch is posted or the clouds look menacing.

Some signs of a possible tornado are:
• Dark, often greenish sky.
• "Wall cloud" hanging from the bottom of a larger cloud.
• Large hail.

• A loud roar, often described as sounding like a freight train.

Sometimes a tornado will look like a funnel cloud that isn't touching the ground. But look for signs of debris being kicked up below the funnel. That shows that it is reaching the ground, and the bottom part just isn't visible. Sometimes, especially in the East, rain, other clouds, haze, trees or hills will hide a tornado.

What to do before a storm: Develop a tornado plan for your home, work place or school.

• Know the county or parish you're in and have a map that will help you to follow reports of storm movement.

• Have a weather radio with a tone alert.

• Follow weather reports to know when severe thunderstorms are possible and when tornado watches, which mean conditions are right for tornadoes, are issued.

What to do when a storm threatens: In a home or building, move to a safe area such as a basement or to an inside room such as a bathroom or closet.

• Stay away from windows.

• Don't try to outrun a tornado in a car. Instead leave the car and find shelter, even if only in a ditch or under a bridge.

• Get out of a mobile home. Find safe shelter.

For schools, the Weather Service recommends:

• Planning what to do if severe weather strikes, and holding frequent drills.

• Selecting tornado shelter areas in the school with the help of an engineer or architect. Basements are best. For schools without basements, interior rooms and hallways on the lowest floor without windows are best.

• Having someone responsible for monitoring NOAA weather radio.

• Installing a backup alarm that will work if power fails.

• Making special provisions for disabled students and those in portable classrooms.

• Keeping children at school beyond regular hours if severe weather threatens. Children are safer in a school building than in a bus or car. Students should not be sent home early if the weather is threatening.

• Postponing lunch or assemblies in large rooms if severe weather is expected.

Floods

Unlike hurricanes, which can be ranked based

on their intensity, floods are difficult to classify.

Compared to other disasters that bring great social and economic disruption, floods have relatively low death rates. However, the number killed by a flash flood that affects only a 20-mile stream can equal the deaths from a flood that affects several states.

Any attempt to classify floods by the amount of water involved would rank relatively minor Mississippi River floods above important floods on smaller rivers. Estimates of the economic costs are unreliable, especially those of many years ago. The floods described here are extreme events that were overwhelming either in terms of area affected or in severity. Many helped spur reforms that have led to today's system of flood protection and forecasting. Dollar amounts in parentheses are conversions to 1990 dollars.

Johnstown, Pa., May 31, 1889: The deadliest U.S. flood began when a dam at a private club collapsed 14 miles and 450 feet above the city. Water first rushed down a narrow valley, demolishing smaller towns and then pushed into Johnstown, which had a population of about 30,000 people. Witnesses described a 35-foot wall of water filled with debris. The debris piled up against a stone bridge in Johnstown, forming a dam. About 80 of the flood's victims were trapped in the debris pile when it caught fire. The final death toll was 2,209. A second flood hit Johnstown on July 19, 1977, killing 77 people.

Miami River near Dayton, Ohio, March 1913: More than 400 people died when flood waters swept into Dayton and other towns along the Great Miami River. Another 400 were said to have died as a result of exposure. This was the tenth major flood since the valley was settled in 1790 and residents decided it would be the last one. The state legislature approved formation of a valleywide "conservancy district," which spent $17 million ($222 million, 1990 dollars) — no federal aid was available at the time — building reservoirs, levees and channel improvements. In 1937, rain totals in the area were virtually the same as in 1913, but while major floods hit other parts of the Midwest, the Miami Valley was safe. The plan was an early model for widespread flood-control projects.

Mississippi River from Cairo, Ill., to the Gulf of Mexico, March through August, 1927: Most of the Mississippi's feeder rivers, including the Ohio, added record amounts to the Mississippi after a year of extremely wet weather. Flood waters covered about 16.5 million acres in seven states and

246 people died. The flood drove 600,000 people from their homes and damage amounted to $230 million ($1.7 billion, 1990 dollars). Since many levees along the river failed, the flood led to a demand for flood control reservoirs as well as improved levees. Under the Flood Control Act of 1928, which gave the Army Corps of Engineers responsibility for the Mississippi, $325 million ($2.4 billion, 1990 dollars) was spent on reservoirs, levees, and other flood prevention measures. It worked. In 1937, little damage was done as more water flowed down the Mississippi than a decade before.

Santa Clara Valley, Calif., March 12, 1928: The 208-foot-high, 700-foot-long St. Francis Dam across San Francisquito Canyon was only 22 months old when it broke a little before midnight, spilling more than 138,000 acre-feet of water. Four hundred people died, as the flood washed down the Santa Clara River to the Pacific Ocean south of Ventura. Investigators determined that the rock of the canyon walls was not strong enough to support the dam. The disaster helped make California a leader in dam inspection and safe dam construction.

Northeast and Upper Ohio Valley, March 1936: Floods from New England to Virginia and west into the Ohio Valley broke records on several rivers, killed at least 107 people and caused more than $270 million ($2.5 billion, 1990 dollars) in damage. As a result, the U.S. Congress passed the Flood Control Act of 1936 which authorized $310 million ($2.9 billion, 1990 dollars) for flood control. The flood also showed the need for improved flood forecasting and the Weather Bureau established special flood forecasting offices. These were the forerunners of the current River Forecast Centers.

Ohio River Valley, January – February, 1937: The floods of 1936 were followed less than a year later by the largest floods in 175 years of record-keeping. The 1936 floods hit upstream areas, such as Pittsburgh, hardest. The 1937 flood was highest from Cincinnati to Cairo, Ill., where the Ohio enters the Mississippi. Nearly 70 percent of Louisville, Ky., was underwater, forcing 175,000 people from their homes. Many smaller cities were completely underwater. The death toll is unknown, but is estimated as "dozens."

The Northeast and Mid-Atlantic, June 15 – 23, 1972: As hurricanes go, Agnes wasn't much when it hit the Florida Panhandle on June 19 with winds barely in the 74 mph hurricane range. It brought 4 to 8 inches of needed rain to dry parts of the Southeast as it moved from Florida into the Atlantic off the North Carolina Coast. But Agnes went inland over New Jersey and turned from a tropical storm into one of the wettest storms ever in the Northeast and Mid-Atlantic states. The rain caused record or near-record flooding from Virginia to New England and west into the upper Ohio Valley. The James River broke a 1771 flood record in Richmond, Va. Major floods swept down the Potomac, Susquehanna, Schuylkill, Allegheny, and upper Ohio, among other rivers. Many records set during the 1936 flood were broken. More than 100,000 dwellings were damaged or destroyed and 122 people killed. Even though Agnes was not a strong hurricane, the storm's $6.4 billion damage in 1990 dollars makes it the nation's fourth most expensive hurricane.

Big Thompson Canyon, Colo., July 31 – Aug. 1, 1976: Unlike other major floods, widespread, long-lasting rain didn't cause the Big Thompson flood. Instead, thunderstorms stayed over the headwaters of the Big Thompson River and dumped up to a foot of rain in four hours while nearby areas enjoyed sunny skies. By nightfall, this water was running downstream, through the narrow canyon where it formed a wave 20 feet high that killed at least 139 people. The flood destroyed 418 homes, 52 businesses, and most of U.S. Route 34 in the canyon. The lack of warnings prompted changes in flood warnings and preparedness not only in Colorado but elsewhere. It also led to new research on flash flood forecasting.

Upper Mississippi and Lower Missouri basins, March– September, 1993: In both human and economic terms, The Great Flood of 1993 was the most devastating in modern U.S. history. It was a catastrophe for nine states with losses ranging up to $20 billion. More than 50,000 homes were damaged or destroyed and 54,000 people evacuated. The flood killed 50 people. Water level records fell at 49 places on the Missouri River system, at 43 on the upper Mississippi system, and at two on the Red River of the North, which runs into Canada along the border between the Dakotas and Minnesota. The flood was notable for its duration as well as size: Flooding began in March, the first record floods came in May, and some flooding continued in September. The flood opened a debate that is sure to continue for years over how much control humans should try to exercise over rivers.

Flood definitions

Acre-foot: The amount of water needed to cover one acre a foot deep. An acre is roughly the size of a football field. One acre-foot of water is 326,700 gallons.

Backwater: A flood upstream from an obstruction, such as an ice jam or debris.

Crest: The highest water level at a given location during a flood. Normally the crest moves downstream like a very long wave.

Flood plain: The part of a river valley that historically has been inundated by the river during floods.

Flood pool: The space in a reservoir reserved for storing flood water.

Flood stage: The height of a river above which damage begins to occur. Normally this is the level at which a river overflows its banks.

Flood wall: A wall, usually in an urban area, made of concrete or stone, parallel to a river meant to prevent flooding.

Floodway: Land set aside and left clear of development for the passage of flood waters.

Freeboard: The vertical distance between the water surface and the top of a dam, levee or floodwall.

Gauge: A vertical measuring device to determine the height of a river above its bottom or some fixed point.

Levee: An earth or stone structure parallel to a river that protects land from flooding.

Runoff: Water from rain or melting snow that is not absorbed into the ground, but flows along the surface of the ground until it runs into a stream.

Stage: The height of a river as measured by a gauge. Each location has its own zero point, which might not be the current bottom of the river but was the bottom at some time. When rivers are deepened, flood gauges along it are not changed. During droughts, stages along some rivers can be measured in negative values.

Self-defense

• Flood safety begins with knowing the danger. A call to the local National Weather Service office, emergency management agency or Red Cross office is the best way to find out whether a home or workplace is in a flood danger zone.

If floods can threaten either place, be prepared to move to safety when a flood threatens. This includes knowing the best evacuation routes.

As with any weather hazard, a key to safety is

Little floods danger to cars

Floods are the USA's biggest weather killer — about 140 people each year — and about 60% of these victims are caught in cars or trucks. Almost always, the victims are in cars that were driven into water flowing across a road.

1 Water weighs 62.4 pounds per cubic foot.

2 Weight and speed of moving water give it more momentum than many think — for each foot the water rises, it pushes on the car with 500 pounds of force.

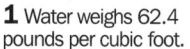

Water moves 6 to 12 mph in floods.

3 Buoyancy is more important. In effect a car weighs 1,500 pounds less for each foot the water rises.

4 Water only two feet deep will carry away most cars.

Source: National Weather Service

learning of threats in time to act. This begins with paying attention to the weather and keeping up with the reports and forecasts in newspapers and on radio and television.

Prepare before floods come: Keep your car's gas tank filled. Floods can cut off electrical power, making gas pumps inoperable for days.

• Store drinking water. Often, regular water service is cut or water reservoirs and treatment plants become contaminated during floods.

• Stock up on food that needs little cooking and no refrigeration.

• Keep first-aid supplies and any necessary medications on hand.

• Keep a NOAA weather radio, a battery-powered portable radio or television, emergency cooking equipment and flashlights in working order.

Evacuation orders or recommendations should be followed. Staying behind to try to save a home, business or car can be deadly.

Since flash floods give little warning, quick action is needed. When a flash flood *watch* is

issued, be alert to signs of flooding and be ready to evacuate on a moment's notice. Those in places of greatest danger should evacuate when a watch is issued.

A flash flood *warning* may mean only seconds to make it to safety. Don't linger for any reason.

Vacationers, especially campers, need to be alert to flood dangers. It's wise not to park or camp along streams or dry stream beds, especially when rain or thunderstorms are expected.

Anyone who's hiking or camping needs to stay alert to the weather. In dry parts of the West, distant thunderstorms can start a deadly flash flood.

Many victims of the 1976 Big Thompson Canyon, Colo., flood died in their cars. Climbing a few yards up the sides of the canyon would have saved them. Today, canyons in Colorado have signs reading: "Climb to Safety! in case of a flash flood." This is life-saving advice in any canyon or low place. Trying to outrun a flood in a car can be deadly.

Motorists should not drive into water covering a road, especially if the water is moving. The water

When the rains won't come

Droughts are almost impossible to measure, with no clear-cut beginning or end, and no exact amount of precipitation to define a drought. Annual precipitation that would be a drought in Georgia would be a wet year in Colorado.

Here are some of the major droughts in U.S. history:

- **1887 to 1896 on the Plains:** This early drought forced thousands of settlers to give up. The population of many counties in Kansas and Nebraska dropped by one-quarter to one-half.
- **1934 to 1941 from the Appalachians to the Rockies:** The great "Dust Bowl" drought included two of the driest years on record in the U.S., 1934 and 1936. As the Plains soil dried out, at times dust blew all of the way to the East Coast. As farming became impossible for many on the Plains, people migrated to California and other parts of the West. The drought helped encourage national soil conservation measures as part of President Franklin Roosevelt's New Deal.
- **1987 to 1989 from the Plains into the East:** This drought was most severe during the extremely hot summer of 1988. The dryness reduced U.S. grain production by 39 percent and cost an estimated $39 billion. Grain surpluses helped keep prices from soaring and the drought did not affect most consumers. This drought also brought major fires to Yellowstone National Park, Wyo.

can hide a washed-out roadway and only a little water is needed to wash a car away. If the car stalls in flood water, leave it immediately and wade to safety. The water could rise and wash the vehicle away, possibly turning it over. Escaping from a worse danger is the only reason to wade in flood water.

Wading in moving water more than ankle deep can be dangerous. Parents should never allow children to play near high water, storm drains or other places where swift-moving water could carry them away.

After a flood: Throw out food that has come in contact with flood water.

- Boil drinking water.
- Pump out wells and have the water tested before drinking it.
- Don't visit flood areas. Sightseers hamper emergency operations.
- Dry and check electrical equipment that's

become wet.

- Use flashlights, not lanterns, torches or candles to examine buildings.
- Report broken utility lines and downed power lines.

Winter storms

All winter storms bring cold, wind, snow and ice. But there is a difference in winter storms from region to region. Some areas have more ice storms. In others, intense winds make visibility nearly impossible. Some regions have heavy, wet snow and others, deep powder. Here is a look at the USA's winter storms:

Alaska: Wind-driven waves from intense storms crossing the Bering Sea cause coastal flooding and can drive large chunks of sea ice inland, destroying buildings. High winds can combine with loose snow to produce blinding blizzards and wind chills down to 90°F below zero.

Temperatures in the -40°F range may last a week or longer. When the weather is this cold, fog made of ice crystals, instead of water droplets, can form. Heavy snow is common inland and along Alaska's southern coast. In mountains, this snow builds glaciers. Accumulations also can collapse the roofs of buildings and cause avalanches.

West Coast to the Rockies: Pacific storms slamming into the coast from California up to Washington can bring heavy rain and snow because the ocean provides an unlimited source of moisture. Rain usually falls on the low elevations along and near the coast, while heavy snow piles up in the mountains.

Anyone taking the two-hour drive from Sacramento to Lake Tahoe would go from the Central Valley, where snow is extremely rare, to the Sierras where snow is normally measured in feet, not inches, and where storm winds often reach 100 mph as they funnel through canyons and flow over ridges.

Snow is common in the higher mountains north of Los Angeles, while no more than a trace has ever been reported in the city.

With the nearby supply of Pacific Ocean moisture, the Cascades in Washington and Oregon and the Sierra Nevada in California have heavier snowfall than any part of the United States outside Alaska. But these mountains don't capture all of winter's moisture. Snowstorms occur in the intermountain region eastward to the Rockies.

Snowfall also is heavy in the Rockies, but it

tends to be drier powder than snow in the mountains of the West Coast states.

The Plains and Midwest: Storms from the Pacific break up as they move across the West Coast mountains and Rockies, but re-form east of the Rockies. Here, they pull in both cold air from Canada and humid air from the Gulf of Mexico to produce heavy snow and sometimes blizzards. Storms that form on the western plains of Colorado tend to move slowly northeast toward the Great Lakes or east to the Appalachians.

Storms that form in Canada's Alberta province tend to move quickly slightly south and east across the Plains and Great Lakes states and into the Northeast as "Alberta Clippers." Snow from these storms is usually lighter because the storms move so quickly.

Heavy "lake effect" snow gives places south and east of the Great Lakes the highest snowfall totals east of the Rockies. Cold air moving across the warmer lakes picks up moisture that falls in bands of heavy snow around the lakes. Travelers on Interstate 90 from Cleveland east along Lake Erie to Buffalo, N.Y., and then to Rochester and Syracuse should expect delays in winter.

The Gulf Coast and Southeast: Winter storms that wouldn't be considered major elsewhere cause serious problems in the South because motorists aren't used to slick roads and public works departments have few, if any, snowplows and road salters. From time to time, air cold enough to bring snow and freezing rain penetrates south well into Florida, the Gulf of Mexico and southern Texas. The snow is often wet and builds up on tree branches until they snap. Power lines come down. Also many homes in this usually warm area are poorly insulated and lack heaters capable of supplying enough warmth. Storms that affect the South often move into the Gulf of Mexico from the Plains, cross Florida and then continue northeast along the Atlantic Coast.

Mid-Atlantic and Northeast: Storms may move in from the west or up the Atlantic Coast. Often, storms from the west weaken or die over the Appalachians. But these storms' upper air portions continue moving eastward to initiate new, or "secondary," storms over the Atlantic. The contrast between warm ocean water, especially off the North Carolina coast, and cold air moving southeast from Canada supplies energy to make storms especially fierce.

Storms that move northeast along the coast or with their centers a few miles offshore are tradi-

tionally called "Nor'easters" because the counter-clockwise flow around these storms' low pressure centers first brings winds from the northeast.

Winds blowing over the ocean create waves and a storm surge that can cause major beach damage along the East Coast.

Since such storms pull in moist air from over the Atlantic, snowfall is often heavy. Usually, rain will fall near the coast while snow falls farther inland. Determining the rain-snow dividing line is a major forecasting challenge.

Because the region is on a dividing line between warm and cold air, sleet and freezing rain is common. Heavy snow and freezing rain can paralyze the heavily-populated cities from Richmond, Va., north to Boston, affecting more people than storms in other regions.

Self-defense

Shoveling heavy snow, pushing a car in cold weather, or just walking in deep snow can lead to physical problems from strained muscles to heart attack. Take it easy in the winter. Sweating could lead to hypothermia.

Hypothermia is a lowered body temperature that can be a danger even in moderate cold if the victim is wet. Warning signs include uncontrollable shivering, memory loss, disorientation, incoherence, slurred speech, drowsiness, and apparent exhaustion.

Immediate medical care is needed, especially if the victim's body temperature is below 95°F.

If medical care is not available, the victim should be slowly warmed. The body core should be warmed before the arms and legs. Warming the arms and legs first can drive cold blood toward the heart, causing heart failure. Do not give the victim alcohol, drugs, coffee, or any hot beverage or food. Warm, but not hot, broth is best.

If caught in a winter storm:

• Find shelter, try to stay dry, and cover exposed parts of the body.

• If shelter isn't available, prepare a lean-to, windbreak or snow cave for protection from the wind.

• Build a fire for heat and to attract attention.

• Do not eat snow; it will lower your body temperature. Melt snow first.

What to do if caught in a car during a winter storm:

• Stay in the car and run the engine about 10 minutes each hour for heat. Before starting the engine, open the window a little for fresh air and make sure the exhaust pipe isn't blocked. If the tailpipe isn't clear, deadly carbon monoxide could seep into the car.

• Attract help by tying a colored cloth to the antenna or door and turn on dome light when running the engine.

• Exercise from time to time by vigorously moving your arms, legs, fingers and toes.

If caught at home or in a building:

• Stay inside. If using a fireplace, wood stove or space heater, be aware of the fire danger and ensure proper ventilation.

• If heat isn't available, close off unneeded rooms, stuff towels or rags in cracks, cover windows at night.

• Eat and drink since food provides energy needed to stay warm. Fluids are needed to avoid dehydration.

Heat

Anyone can tell when it's hot, but knowing when hot weather becomes dangerous is more difficult.

The dangers of heat vary widely among people. In fact, the dangers are not only different among individuals. Studies of death statistics by Laurence Kalkstein of the University of Delaware show that the temperature at which death rates increase varies from city to city. In Dallas, a temperature of 103°F is needed to increase the death rate. In San Francisco, the rate begins going up at 84°F.

The National Weather Service doesn't have an official definition of "heat wave," but local offices do have criteria for deciding when to issue special heat warnings.

Whenever the apparent temperature, which combines heat and humidity, reaches or is forecast to reach 105°F or higher and doesn't fall below 80°F at night for two days, most Weather Service offices begin warning of heat dangers. These alerts normally include safety rules for dealing with the heat. (An apparent temperature chart is in the Appendix.)

High apparent temperatures, or hot temperatures in places where they are rare, prompt more urgent advisories and special weather statements.

Nights that stay hot add to the physical stress of heat for those who don't have air-conditioned houses, or at least air-conditioned bedrooms. When heat and humidity make it hard to sleep, fatigue creates physical stress.

The elderly are especially likely to suffer from heat. As a result of deaths during heat waves in the

1980s, some cities began programs to open air-conditioned shelters.

Cities are especially dangerous during heat waves because the stagnant air that usually accompanies hot weather causes pollutants to build up.

In addition to the elderly, heat waves can be especially dangerous for small children, chronic invalids, people taking certain medications, and those who are overweight or who drink alcohol excessively.

National Weather Service heat death figures include only those whose cause of death was listed as being directly from the heat. But many scientists are convinced that the toll would be much higher if there were some way to determine the role of heat in making other illnesses fatal.

In addition to the dangers of heat itself, hot weather is also usually sunburn weather. By itself, sunburn can be serious and exposure to the sun is now recognized as increasing the danger of skin cancer. In addition, sunburn makes it even harder for the body to get rid of excess heat, increasing the danger of heat disorders. (Sunburn tables are in the Appendix.)

Self-defense

The key health risks of heat are heat cramps and heat exhaustion, and heat stroke.

• **Heat cramps:** Signs are painful spasms, usually in the muscles of the legs and abdomen, and heavy sweating. The victim should get out of the sun and into a cool place if possible. Firm pressure or gentle massage of the cramping muscles should relieve the spasms.

• **Heat exhaustion:** Signs are heavy sweating with weakness. Often the skin is cold, pale and clammy. Body temperature may be normal. Fainting and vomiting are possible. The victim should move out of the sun and lie down — if possible in an air-conditioned room. If there is no air conditioning, fan the victim. Clothing should be loosened and cool, wet cloths applied. If vomiting continues, call a doctor.

• **Heat stroke, sometimes called sun stroke:** Signs include high body temperatures — 106°F or more — hot, dry skin, rapid pulse, possible unconsciousness. Heat stroke is a severe medical emergency. Get medical help quickly. Delay can be fatal. Victim should be moved to a cool area, but not given fluids.

Staying well in a heat wave: Slow down. Even those used to the heat and in good health should stop strenuous activities or wait until the coolest time of the day. Elderly people or others most in danger should stay in the coolest place possible, which might not be their houses.

• Dress for hot weather in lightweight, light-colored clothing that reflects heat and sun. Wear a hat outdoors.

• Drink plenty of water or non-alcoholic drinks, even if you're not thirsty. Those with epilepsy or heart, kidney or liver disease, or those on a fluid restrictive diet, should consult a doctor before drinking more fluids.

• Don't take salt tablets without consulting a doctor. They're no longer routinely recommended.

• Spend as much time as possible in air-conditioned places.

Earthquakes

In many ways earthquakes are nature's most frightening phenomena because they hit without warning and they offer no escape.

An earthquake is the wavelike, sometimes violent movement of the Earth's surface, usually caused by dislocations of the crust.

They usually occur along faults, which are fractures in the Earth's crust between two blocks of the crust. The blocks may move horizontally in relation to each other or one may move up, the other down.

Forces from inside the Earth are pushing the blocks, but the blocks can become locked together. Then, they suddenly break free, releasing energy that is felt as an earthquake.

The epicenter is the spot on the Earth's surface directly above the focus of the quake.

Waves of Earth movement, both with particles of rock or dirt going up and down and moving back and forth, radiate out from the quake's center. They cause the ground shaking that does the damage relatively near the quake. The waves weaken as they travel, but can be detected by instruments thousands of miles away, long after they're much too weak to be felt by humans.

Today earthquakes can't be predicted. The best that scientists can do is give the odds that an earthquake will occur in a particular location by a particular time.

There have been media reports that tell of animals acting strangely before earthquakes. But scientists have been unable to find any reliable way to connect animal behavior to earthquakes.

Researchers have also been unable to find any links between earthquakes and tides and earthquakes and the weather.

Prediction research is focused on measuring tiny movements of the ground and activities deep below the surface with the hope of finding some kind of measurement that can be a reliable indicator that a quake is about to occur.

Measuring earthquakes

Scientists measure earthquakes in terms of magnitude and intensity.

Magnitude is based on seismograph measurements of movements of the Earth. Today's sensitive instruments can detect even relatively small earthquakes around the globe.

The magnitude scale used today is based on one developed in 1935 by Charles F. Richter of the California Institute of Technology.

While an earthquake's damage is related to its magnitude, the distance from the quake and the nature of the soil, among other factors, determine how much damage is actually done. A 6.5 magnitude quake under a city will do more damage than an 8.5 magnitude quake in a remote area.

The mathematical nature of the magnitude scale means that each whole number increase represents a tenfold increase in size of the waves. Each whole number increase also corresponds to the release of about 31 times more energy.

Quakes with a magnitude of about 2.0 or less are called "microearthquakes" and are usually not felt by people. Only nearby instruments record them. When the magnitude reaches about 4.5 or greater, the quake usually can be felt and is recorded by faraway instruments. The magnitude scale has no upper limit, but the largest known earthquakes are in the 8.8 or 8.9 range.

Intensity: The effect of an earthquake on the surface is called its intensity. It is measured in the USA with the Modified Mercalli Intensity Scale. To avoid confusion with magnitude, it is expressed in Roman numerals.

Earthquakes under the ocean or large landslides, either underwater or down seaside mountains into the water, can cause the huge waves known as tsunamis. This Japanese word is much better than a common term, "tidal wave." Such waves have nothing to do with the tide.

When the ocean floor moves, or when a landslide falls into the water, waves are formed, much as when a rock is thrown into a pond.

At sea, a tsunami isn't noticeable. The water rises very little, less than the normal rise and fall of ocean swells. But as the wave nears shore, it begins piling up and can rush onshore as a wall of water.

Tsunamis move incredibly fast with the speed

depending on the depth of the water. In water that's 30,000 feet deep, a tsunami moves at 670 mph. In 3,000 feet of water it will slow down to 212 mph, and in 60 feet of water to 30 mph. But, as a tsunami rushes toward shore, it's impossible to outrun.

A Japanese name is appropriate since more tsunamis hit Japan than any other place. But any site along the Pacific Coast can be hit.

On July 12, 1993, a 7.8 magnitude quake off the west coast of Hokkaido, Japan's northernmost island, generated a major tsunami. In less than five minutes a wave with a top height of 100 feet crashed into Hokkaido, killing 180 people.

In the U.S., Alaska and Hawaii face the greatest tsunami danger.

The National Oceanic and Atmospheric Administration operates the tsunami warning center in Hawaii and can warn of waves from faraway quakes. But sometimes, as in Japan in July 1993, the quake occurs so close to shore that there is no time for warnings. If an earthquake occurs near the ocean, people near the coast should head for higher ground without delay.

Significant earthquakes in U.S. history

The U.S. Geological Survey lists these as the most important U.S. earthquakes based on their magnitude, damage and casualties. No attempt is made here to estimate damage before 1913.

Cape Ann, Mass., Nov. 18, 1775: This quake was centered in the Atlantic 200 miles east of Cape Ann and felt over more than 400,000 square miles from Nova Scotia to the Chesapeake Bay and from Lake George, N.Y., into the Atlantic. Damage was heaviest on Cape Ann and Boston with about 100 chimneys destroyed. No deaths were reported.

New Madrid, Mo., 1811 – 1812: Two quakes on Dec. 16, 1811, one on Jan. 23, 1812, and one on Feb. 7, 1812, were the most violent series in U.S. history. They shook southeast Missouri and northeast Arkansas. Since the area was sparsely settled, damage and casualties were low. But the quakes were felt over all of the U.S. east of the Mississippi River.

Virgin Islands, Nov. 18, 1867: This quake was felt from the Dominican Republic to the Leeward Islands and caused 20-foot sea waves to hit the Virgin Islands and Puerto Rico.

Charleston, S.C., Aug. 31, 1886: Sixty people were killed and most of the buildings in the Charleston area were destroyed or damaged. People in New York, Boston, Milwaukee, Havana, Cuba, and Ontario, Canada felt the quake.

Charleston, Mo., Oct. 31, 1895: This was the strongest shock in the New Madrid seismic zone since the big quakes of 1811 and 1812. It was felt in 23 states and Canada and caused considerable damage. It created a four-acre lake near Charleston.

San Francisco, Calif., April 18, 1906: This quake ruptured a 270-mile segment of the San Andreas Fault from San Benito County north to Humboldt County. In Marin County, the fault slipped 21 feet. More than 700 people were killed.

Significant U.S. earthquakes

Date	Location	Magnitude	Intensity
Nov. 18, 1775	Cape Ann, Mass.	6.0[1]	VIII
Dec. 16, 1811	New Madrid, Mo., seismic zone	8.5[1]	XI
Dec. 16, 1811	New Madrid, Mo., seismic zone	8.0[1]	XI
Jan. 23, 1812	New Madrid, Mo., seismic zone	8.4[1]	XI
Feb. 7, 1812	New Madrid, Mo., seismic zone	8.8[1]	XI
Nov. 18, 1867	Virgin Islands	7.5[1]	VIII
Aug. 31, 1886	Charleston, S.C.	6.6[1]	X
Oct. 31, 1895	Charleston, Mo.	6.2[1]	IX
April 18, 1906	San Francisco, Calif.	8.3[1]	XI
Oct. 11, 1918	Mona Passage, Puerto Rico	7.5[1]	IX
March 10, 1933	Long Beach, Calif.	6.2	VIII
April 13, 1949	Olympia, Wash.	7.1	VIII
Aug. 17, 1959	Hebgen Lake, Mont.	7.3	X
March 27, 1964	Prince William Sound, Alaska	8.4	X
April 29, 1965	Seattle, Wash.	6.5	VIII
Feb. 9, 1971	San Fernando, Calif.	6.6	XI
Oct. 25, 1983	Borah Peak, Idaho	7.0	IX
Oct. 17, 1989	Loma Prieta, Calif.	7.1	IX
June 28, 1992	Landers – Big Bear, Calif.	7.6	NA
Aug. 8, 1993	Guam	8.3	NA
Jan. 17, 1994	Northridge, Calif.	6.7	IX

[1]Magnitude estimated   Source: U.S. Geological Survey   NA = Not Available

Mona Passage, Puerto Rico, Oct. 11, 1918: One of the most violent earthquakes recorded in Puerto Rico created a great killer wave, a tsunami. Death toll was 116 and the damage estimated at $4 million ($34 million, 1990 dollars).

Long Beach, Calif., March 10, 1933: Even though the magnitude was only 6.2, this was one of the most destructive U.S. quakes because it hit a heavily populated area with many poorly constructed buildings, including schools. About 115 people were killed and hundreds more injured. The damage was estimated at $40 million ($398 million, 1990 dollars). As a result of the widespread damage, California began adopting stricter construction codes.

Olympia, Wash., April 13, 1949: The quake caused heavy damage in Washington and Oregon and killed eight people. It was felt eastward to Montana and south to Cape Blanco, Oregon.

Hebgen Lake, Mont., Aug. 17, 1959: This is the strongest earthquake ever recorded in Montana and was felt from Seattle, Wash., to Banff, Canada, from Dickinson, N.D., to Provo, Utah. On Hebgen Lake, it caused huge waves that lasted 12 hours. It also caused a massive landslide that blocked the Madison River canyon, creating a lake. Death toll: 28.

Prince William Sound, Alaska, March 27, 1964: This Good Friday earthquake with its 8.4 magnitude is the 20th century's second strongest. The only stronger one was an 8.6 magnitude quake that hit Chile in 1960. The Alaska earthquake caused extensive landslides and generated tsunamis. It killed 131 people and caused $311 million ($1.3 billion in 1990 dollars) in damage in Anchorage and south-central Alaska.

Seattle, Wash., April 29, 1965: This quake was felt over 130,000 square miles in Washington, Oregon, Idaho, Montana and British Columbia. It killed seven people and caused $12.5 million ($51 million, 1990 dollars) in damage.

San Fernando, Calif., Feb. 9, 1971: Sixty-five people died, scores were injured and $1 billion ($3 billion, 1990 dollars) in damage resulted from this quake. This and the Prince William Sound earthquake prompted the federal government to greatly expand earthquake research.

Borah Peak, Idaho, Oct. 25, 1983: This quake, which was felt over 330,000 square miles, is the largest ever recorded in Idaho. It killed two children in Challis and did $12.5 million ($16 million in 1990 dollars) damage.

Loma Prieta, Calif., Oct. 17, 1989: This was

Intensity of earthquakes

No.	Effects
I	Felt by only a very few people.
II	Felt by only a few persons at rest, especially on the upper floors of buildings.
III	Felt quite noticeably by persons indoors, especially on upper floors. Cars that aren't moving may rock slightly.
IV	Felt indoors by many, outdoors by a few during the day. At night, some people are awakened. Dishes, windows, doors are disturbed. Walls make cracking sounds. Sensation like a heavy truck hitting the building. Cars that aren't moving rock noticeably.
V	Felt by nearly everyone. Many awakened. Some dishes, windows broken. Unstable objects overturned. Pendulum clocks may stop.
VI	Felt by all and many frightened. Some heavy furniture moved. A few instances of fallen plaster. Slight damage.
VII	Damage is negligible in well-designed and well-constructed buildings. Slight to moderate damage in ordinary buildings. Considerable damage in poorly built or badly designed buildings. Some chimneys broken.
VIII	Damage is slight in specially designed structures, but considerable in ordinary, but substantial buildings. Damage is great in poorly built structures. Chimneys, factory stacks, monuments and walls fall. Heavy furniture overturned.
IX	Considerable damage in specially designed buildings and great damage in substantial buildings with partial collapse. Buildings shifted off foundations.
X	Some well-built, wooden buildings destroyed. Most masonry and frame structures destroyed with foundations. Railroad rails bent.
XI	Few, if any, masonry structures remain standing. Bridges destroyed. Railroad rails bent greatly.
XII	Damage total. Lines of sight and level are distorted. Objects are thrown into the air.

Source: U.S.Geological Survey

the strongest earthquake in California since the one that hit San Francisco in 1906. It killed more than 60 people and caused an estimated $6 billion in damage in the greater San Francisco area. Though it was centered in the Santa Cruz Mountains 60 miles south of San Francisco, much of the damage and many of the deaths were in San Francisco and Oakland. It was felt over 400,000 square miles.

Guam, Aug. 8, 1993: Although this was the largest earthquake in four years, it caused no deaths and only 48 injuries in Guam. It triggered landslides, rock slides and a moderate tsunami.

Northridge, Calif., Jan. 17, 1994: This earthquake caused extensive damage to the San Fernando Valley and lighter damage to other parts of the Los Angeles area. Freeway repairs caused traffic delays for months. Death toll was 61 and damage estimates ranged from $15 to $30 billion.

Self-defense

Since earthquakes cannot yet be predicted, staying safe depends on making homes and other buildings as quake-resistant as possible. When a quake strikes, safety could depend on quickly doing the right things. And the danger isn't over when the quake ends.

Actual movement of the ground in a quake rarely causes deaths or injuries. Falling objects and building collapse are the biggest hazards during a quake. Downed power lines and fires often bring danger after the ground stops shaking.

Volcanoes

Volcanoes form where molten rock — rock hot enough to be liquid — forces its way to the Earth's surface. A volcano can be on land or under the sea.

When the molten rock finds its way to the surface, it may flow out slowly or it may explode into the air as dense clouds of lava fragments that fall back around the opening of the volcano. These fragments may flow downhill as ash. Some of the smaller pieces can be carried miles by the wind and the smallest can shoot high into the atmosphere and be carried around the globe by stratospheric winds.

Molten rock below the surface is magma, but after it erupts, it's called lava.

Lava can blast out in a series of explosions such as the Mount St. Helens (Wash.) volcano from 1980 to 1986. Lava also can flow slowly, as the Kilauea Volcano in Hawaii has been doing since 1983.

Things to do before a quake

• Practice the "duck, cover, hold" drill with your family. During a quake you should duck under a strong table or desk, cover your head and face and hold onto the table or desk and be ready to move with it.

• Develop a plan for what to do if a quake occurs and members of the family are separated.

• Store emergency supplies of food, water, flashlights, battery-operated radio, first-aid kit, warm clothes and sturdy shoes.

• Make sure everyone in your family knows where the supplies are and how to use them.

• Move any heavy objects that could fall on your bed.

• Securely attach tall furniture and bookcases to the wall. Add lips to shelves to prevent items from sliding off.

• Put strong latches on cabinet doors.

• In offices, make sure heavy objects are attached to the building structure, not just to a movable wall.

• Fasten gas hot water heaters to wall studs and connect all gas appliances to the gas pipe with a short piece of flexible tubing.

Things to do during a quake

• As mentioned before, duck under a strong table or desk, cover your head and face and hold onto the table or desk and be ready to move with it. Or stand in a doorway and hold onto the frame.

• Do not try to run outdoors.

• If outdoors, try to get away from walls, power poles and other objects that could fall.

• If in a vehicle, stop in the safest place possible, preferably in an open area.

Things to do after a quake

• Quickly check for fires or fire hazards.

• Check utility lines and appliances for damage. If there are any leaks, shut off the main gas valve. Shut off the power if there is damage to electrical wiring

.• Do not use the telephone except for emergency calls.

• Be ready for additional earthquakes. Although such aftershocks are usually smaller than the main quake, they can be strong enough to cause more damage.

Source: U.S. Geological Survey

Around the world, more than 500 volcanoes have erupted at least once during recorded history, and 50 of these are in the USA — in Hawaii, Alaska, Washington, Oregon and California.

Most of the world's active volcanoes are in the "ring of fire" around the Pacific Ocean near the edges of the continents. There are also volcanoes around the Mediterranean Sea.

Scientists are concerned about the potential of an eruption of Mount Rainier, which is only 25 miles from the edge of the Seattle – Tacoma, Wash., metropolitan area. Here more than 100,000 people live on the mudflow deposits that the volcano left over the last 10,000 years.

"A major volcanic eruption or debris flow could kill thousands of residents and cripple the economy of the Pacific Northwest," according to the National Research Council, which conducts studies for the National Academy of Sciences in Washington, D.C. The report was issued in May 1994.

"Despite the potential for such danger," the report says, "Mount Rainier has received little study. Most of the geologic work on Mount Rainier was done more than two decades ago."

The report recommended learning more about the volcano's past to get a better idea of what it's capable of. It also recommended closer monitoring of ground movements, small earthquakes or the emission of gases and liquids that could warn of a potential eruption.

Mount Rainier's dangers are common to all volcanoes:

• Volcanic eruptions that would send lava and ash into the air and flowing down the mountain.

• Glacier outburst floods (jokulhlaups) caused by the sudden melting of the snow and ice on the volcano and by the release of water from lakes now held back by glaciers.

• Lahars, or mudflows, that send volcanic debris mixed with water down the mountain and into nearby valleys.

Wind

One of the most dangerous myths is that your house is going to be destroyed if a tornado hits it — and there's no way to build a house strong enough to stand up to a tornado.

True, if the tornado happens to be one of the rare twisters with winds above 261 mph, even a well-built home will be seriously damaged. But such tornadoes are rare — one hits the U.S. about every two years.

After more than two decades of examining damage from tornadoes, hurricanes and other wind storms, scientists and engineers say there's plenty that can be done to increase the odds a house will escape serious damage.

And, for those rare, extremely strong storms, a small, inside room can be turned into a life-saving emergency shelter.

In its report on Hurricane Andrew, the National Oceanic and Atmospheric Administration said

Notable U.S. volcanic eruptions in the 20th century

Years	Volcano	Impact
1912	Novarupta, Alaska	Largest eruption of the 20th century, but was in a remote area and had little effect.
1914-1917	Lassen Peak, Calif.	Lava and debris flow covered about six square miles.
1980-1986	Mount St. Helens, Wash.	The initial blast on May 18, 1980 blew off the top 1,300 feet of the mountain. It killed 57 people. It destroyed 230 square miles of timber worth several million dollars. Ash fell as far east as North Dakota.
1983 to now	Kilauea, Hawaii	Slowly flowing lava has covered about 30 square miles and 180 dwellings. In 1990, it destroyed the entire community of Kalapana.
1984	Maunaloa, Hawaii	Threatened the city of Hilo.
1986	Augustine Volcano, Alaska	Ash plume disrupted air traffic and ash fell on Anchorage.
1989-1990	Redoubt Volcano, Alaska	Debris flow forced the temporary closing of the Drift River Oil Terminal. A 747 jet lost power in all four engines when it flew into the ash plume. It landed safely.

Source: U.S. Geological Survey

Which roofs do best in windstorms

Studies of tornado and hurricane wind damage since the 1970s show that houses with hip roofs are more likely to survive than houses with gable or flat roofs. No matter what kind of roof a house has, it needs to be firmly attached to the walls and well-built to stand up to wind.

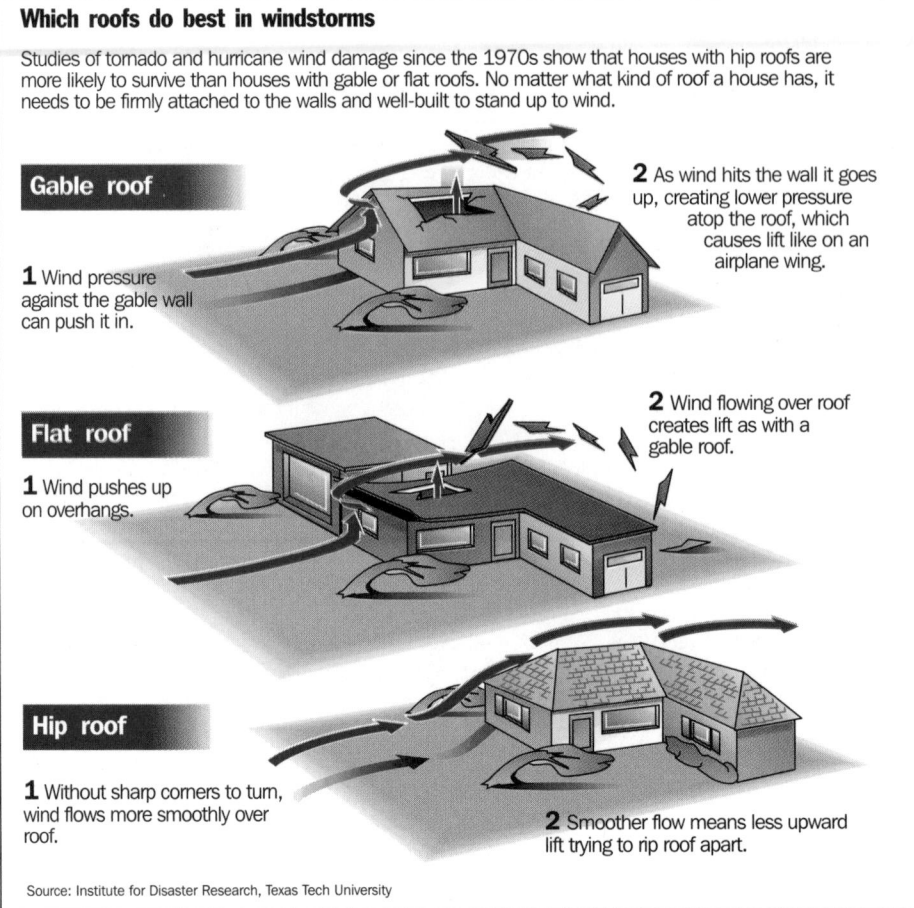

Gable roof

1 Wind pressure against the gable wall can push it in.

2 As wind hits the wall it goes up, creating lower pressure atop the roof, which causes lift like on an airplane wing.

Flat roof

1 Wind pushes up on overhangs.

2 Wind flowing over roof creates lift as with a gable roof.

Hip roof

1 Without sharp corners to turn, wind flows more smoothly over roof.

2 Smoother flow means less upward lift trying to rip roof apart.

Source: Institute for Disaster Research, Texas Tech University

"many residents whose houses began to disintegrate during the storm followed 'tornado safety rules' and went to the interior part of the house away from windows and outside walls." The report urged better education on making such last-resort shelters even safer.

Scientists and engineers at the Institute for Disaster Research at Texas Tech University in Lubbock have developed designs for reinforcing interior closets or bathrooms with plywood in existing houses, or making a shelter area part of the design of new homes. Similar work has been done for schools and other public buildings.

On the tornado-prone Plains and in the Southeast, some schools have been built with libraries or other interior rooms designed to do double duty as tornado shelters.

The key to building, or improving, a house to stand up to strong winds is to have the building firmly attached to the foundation and have the roof strongly attached to the walls.

After tornadoes hit rural areas and some cities, investigators often find that houses merely were sitting on their foundations, not firmly attached to them. When the wind pushed the house just a few feet off the foundation, it often began a chain reaction of damage that wrecked the house and much in it.

Fast winds blowing around a house or other building create areas of lower pressure, which can often begin these chain reactions. Part of a roof is lifted, or part of a corner torn off. This allows wind inside the building to push against the roof and walls.

An open door to an attached garage can allow the wind inside to lift the garage roof, which then tears off part of the roof over the main part of a house.

Large trees can shield a house, but they can also be blown over onto it.

Houses in the middle of a group of houses tend to suffer less wind damage, but can be targets of windblown pieces of other houses that have been torn apart.

Research into wind damage led to an important change in tornado advice. At one time people were told to open a window as a tornado approached. The idea was to equalize the pressure inside the house with the low pressure in the tornado to keep the house from "exploding."

But when engineers looked closely at "exploded" houses, they found that the damage began with the wind lifting the roof, which allowed the walls to fall. The walls generally fall outward — as in an "explosion" — because interior walls keep them from falling inward.

Opening a window wastes time that should be spent taking shelter. Also, if the open window is on the side the wind's coming from, it will allow wind inside to push up on the roof. And with a tornado, there is no way to tell which way the wind will blow.

Normal buildings have enough natural openings to allow air pressure to equalize. Wind, not low pressure, destroys buildings.

What winds can do to houses

Teams from the Institute for Disaster Research at Texas Tech University in Lubbock looked at houses damaged by winds and then developed this list of general guidelines about wind and house damage:

Windspeeds in mph	Types of damage
40 – 75	A few roof shingles blow off; TV antennas bend; lightweight awnings, canopies damaged.
75 – 100	Flying debris breaks windows; large sections of shingles blow off roof corners and eaves; chimneys collapse.
110 – 130	Large sections of gable roofs may tear away, carport roofs lift off; sections of roofs and porches are damaged.
130 – 160	Entire roofs blow away; roofs stay undamaged only if extraordinary anchorage precautions have been taken.
160 – 200	Two-story houses in near collapse; exterior walls on single-story dwellings collapse with only well-supported interior walls standing.
200+	Little remains intact; debris scatters down the path of the tornado.

Source: National Weather Services, "The Tornado: An Engineering-Oriented Perspective"

5 Record-breaking weather

If you think the weather's wild now ...

The last few years have brought more than their share of wild weather. But where do today's weather patterns fit in the big picture?

This chapter shows the benchmarks the 1990s will be measured against. Past weather records here put today's weather in perspective. New records get set, but not that often. Most of the time when it seems extraordinarily hot or cold, wet or dry, a check of the records reveals that it actually has been a lot hotter or colder, wetter or drier in the past.

The 1990s — at least so far — pale in comparison to the 1930s, which had more wild weather than the country has seen before or since. And no single year in U.S. weather history matches 1936.

The bad weather really began the previous year. By spring of 1935, the center of the United States was well into the worst drought since farmers and ranchers moved onto the Great Plains. Terrible dust storms became commonplace.

On April 14, 1935, what came to be known as the "black blizzard" moved from Colorado into Kansas and Oklahoma with 60 mph winds and dust so thick people couldn't see their outstretched hands. This storm, and others like it, stopped traffic and ripped soil from fields only to smother crops with dust in other fields. Homes became gritty from the dust that pushed in through the cracks around windows and doors.

That wasn't the only weather that added to the woes of the Great Depression. The summer of 1935 ended on Sept. 2 with the Labor Day Hurricane, the strongest hurricane to hit the U.S. in this century. It slammed into the Florida Keys with winds up to 200 mph and a low-pressure record that still stands.

While winter brought no end to the drought on the Plains, the West was wet. Eureka, Calif., saw 26 consecutive days with rain. A total of 11.02 inches fell from Dec. 25, 1935 through Jan. 19, 1936.

Other places even closer to the Plains got record precipitation. On Feb. 12, 1936, 22.8 inches of snow fell on Missoula, Mont. The month's total there was 43.5 inches. Both records still stand.

Beyond rain and drought, scores of cities set record winter lows and record summer highs in 1936. In Fargo, N.D., the temperature went below zero on 37 consecutive days, another record that still stands. All-time cold records that still stand were set in Great Falls, Mont., with a -49°F on Feb. 15, 1936, and in Lander, Wyo., with a -40°F on Feb. 8, 1936.

Bismarck, N.D., and Minneapolis, Minn., both set cold records early in 1936 and then saw record highs that summer that still stand. On Jan. 22, 1936, Minneapolis was -34°F. On Feb. 16, Bismarck was -45°F. Bismarck set its all-time high of 114°F on July 6, and Minneapolis its all-time high of 108°F on July 14.

If winter was too cold and summer was too hot, spring was too wet. During March 1936, some of the worst flooding on record struck from Virginia to New England and west into the Ohio Valley, breaking high-water records on several rivers. Floods killed at least 107 people.

On April 5 and 6, 1936, at least 17 tornadoes killed 446 people across the Southeast, including 216 in Tupelo, Miss., and 203 in Gainesville, Ga.

The 8.10 inches of rain that fell in May on Colorado Springs, Colo., at the edge of the Great Plains, must have raised hopes that a break in the drought was coming. But the only lasting effect was a monthly rainfall record for that city that still stands.

The United States was, instead, headed for the hottest summer since recordkeeping began in 1895. The national average temperature of 74.33°F pushed the 73.90°F of 1934 into second place to stay. The nation's third hottest summer is 1988, at 73.47°F. In fact, the nation's average summer temperature has been 73° or warmer only eight times since records began in 1895: in 1901, 1931, 1933, 1934, 1936, 1937, 1952 and 1988.

Fifteen statewide high-temperature records that still stand go back to 1936. This is three times as many records as any decade since 1900. Of the 50 state high-temperature records, 26 were set in the

1930s. And 11 of the low records were set during that same wild decade.

Some of the many still-standing city records set that hot summer include:

City/State	Record	Date
Des Moines, Iowa	110°F	July 25, 1936
Dubuque, Iowa	110°F	July 14, 1936
Fargo, N.D.	114°F	July 6, 1936
Fort Smith, Ark.	113°F	Aug. 10, 1936
Grand Island, Neb.	117°F	July 24, 1936
Kansas City, Mo.	113°F	Aug. 14, 1936
Moline, Ill.	111°F	July 14, 1936
Omaha, Neb.	114°F	July 25, 1936
Topeka, Kan.	114°F	July 24, 1936
Tulsa, Okla.	115°F	Aug. 10, 1936
Waterloo, Iowa	112°F	July 14, 1936
Wichita, Kan.	114°F	Aug. 12, 1936
Williamsport, Pa.	106°F	July 9, 1936

Even Yellowstone National Park set a record high of 98°F at the Lamar Ranger Station on June 23, 1936.

In Minneapolis, an 81.4°F average made July 1936 the hottest month ever. Above 100°F temperatures July 10 through 14, the most ever, helped set that record. Dayton, Ohio, had seven consecutive days above 100°F in July 1936 and 10 days above 100°F for the entire summer.

While the Plains were still looking for rain, the biggest floods in 175 years of record hit the Ohio River Valley in January and February, 1937. But the Dust Bowl drought continued into 1941.

A new way to define the seasons

Two systems are commonly used to define the seasons.

The traditional definition is based on the relationship between Earth and the sun. In the Northern Hemisphere, the seasons begin with the winter solstice (the shortest day of the year) on Dec. 21 or 22, the spring equinox (daylight and night equal) on March 20 or 21, the summer solstice (the longest day of the year) on June 20 or 21, and fall equinox (day and night again equal) on Sept. 22 or 23. The exact dates for these events can vary by a day or two from year to year. They also may differ in a given year for a given location depending on the time zone. (A year-by-year season schedule is in the Appendix.)

The second way to define the seasons, the one used by meteorologists, uses a straight monthly approach. Winter is December through February, spring is March through May, summer is June through August and autumn is September through November.

Both systems of measuring the seasons are arbitrary. Actual seasonal weather characteristics are

Decades with the wildest weather

Statewide weather records are a good measure of extreme weather. Only the worst heat waves, cold snaps, droughts or rainy years are likely to break statewide records for annual precipitation or temperature.

Using this standard, the 1930s saw the most extreme weather in the United States since the keeping of extensive records began in the 19th century. Of the 200 statewide records that still stand, 59 (30 percent) were set in the 1930s.

Statewide records that still stand, by decade:

Maximum annual precipitation		Minimum annual precipitation		Highest one-day temperatures		Lowest one-day temperatures	
Before 1900	11	Before 1900	1	Before 1900	2	Before 1900	5
1900 – 1909	2	1900 – 1909	0	1900 – 1909	2	1900 – 1909	6
1910 – 1919	1	1910 – 1919	1	1910 – 1919	5	1910 – 1919	4
1920 – 1929	0	1920 – 1929	1	1920 – 1929	2	1920 – 1929	3
1930 – 1939	3	1930 – 1939	19	1930 – 1939	26	1930 – 1939	11
1940 – 1949	7	1940 – 1949	5	1940 – 1949	1	1940 – 1949	4
1950 – 1959	10	1950 – 1959	11	1950 – 1959	5	1950 – 1959	3
1960 – 1969	5	1960 – 1969	10	1960 – 1969	1	1960 – 1969	4
1970 – 1979	3	1970 – 1979	1	1970 – 1979	2	1970 – 1979	4
1980 – 1989	6	1980 – 1989	1	1980 – 1989	2	1980 – 1989	6
Since 1990	2	Since 1990	0	Since 1990	2	Since 1990	0

How the decades rank

Decades	Statewide records
1930s	59
1950s	29
1960s	20
1940s	17
1980s	15
1900s	11
1910s	10
1970s	10
1920s	6
Since 1990	4
Before 1900	19*

*Includes 1890s – 9, 1880s – 4, 1870s – 2, 1850s – 2, 1860s – 1, 1840s – 1

determined by the balance between solar energy received by Earth and heat given up to space. So an alternative to these systems is to determine the seasons by using average daily temperatures.

Under this system, the block of days with the coldest fourth of the year's average temperatures is winter and the block with the warmest fourth is summer. The other 50 percent of average temperatures on either side are defined as spring and fall.

This system has the advantage of putting all the normally warmest days in summer and the coldest days in winter. It also gives spring and fall the widest range of temperatures, which is how we normally think of the transition seasons. But this alternative system does not produce seasons of equal length. It does give us seasons, however, that more closely correspond with most people's expectations of seasonal weather.

How the new system works

These listings give an idea of how close the "real" seasons — as defined by average temperature — match those that begin with the solstices and equinoxes.

To see how the temperature approach would work, we looked at 12 cities across the country. For these cities the coldest quarter of the year begins at least three weeks before the winter solstice. And only one city begins its hottest quarter of the year within a week of the summer solstice. That's Los Angeles, which has a climate different from most of the U.S.

The spring equinox works out better. Eight of the 12 cities begin the transition from the cold to the warm season during the week ending with or beginning with the spring equinox.

Fall comes nearest to beginning with the equinox. Nine of the 12 cities here begin the cool down from summer to winter within a week of the fall equinox.

The figures here make it obvious that once the days are longer than the nights (beginning with the spring equinox), North America quickly warms up. Most places reach their warmest quarter by late May or early June.

The opposite happens in the fall. After days begin to be shorter than the nights (beginning with the fall equinox), temperatures fall rapidly. They reach the winter range, the coldest quarter of the year, by late November, three or four weeks before the winter solstice.

Here are temperature-defined seasons for 12 cities:

Boston, Massachusetts

	Daily average	Dates
Coldest time of year	29°	Jan. 20 – Feb. 5
Warmest time of year	74°	July 13 – Aug. 5

Season	Dates	Temperature range	Days
Winter	Nov. 28 – March 22	40° to 29° to 40°	115
Spring	March 23 – May 28	41° to 62°	67
Summer	May 29 – Sept. 22	63° to 74° to 63°	117
Fall	Sept. 23 – Nov. 27	62° to 41°	66

Chicago, Illinois

	Daily average	Dates
Coldest time of year	21°	Jan. 8 – 27
Warmest time of year	74°	July 25 – 30

Season	Dates	Temperature range	Days
Winter	Nov. 28 – March 12	34° to 21° to 34°	105
Spring	March 13 – May 20	35° to 60°	69
Summer	May 21 – Sept. 28	61° to 74° to 61°	131
Fall	Sept. 29 – Nov. 27	60° to 35°	60

Denver, Colorado

	Daily average	Dates
Coldest time of year	29°	Jan. 5 – 22
Warmest time of year	74°	July 15 – Aug. 4

Season	Dates	Temperature range	Days
Winter	Nov. 10 – March 26	40° to 29° to 40°	137
Spring	March 27 – May 31	41° to 62°	66
Summer	June 1 – Sept. 15	63° to 74° to 63°	107
Fall	Sept. 16 – Nov. 9	62° to 41°	55

Los Angeles, California, airport

	Daily average	Dates
Coldest time of year	56°	Dec. 21 – Jan. 31
Warmest time of year	71°	Aug. 16 – 23

Season	Dates	Temperature range	Days
Winter	Nov. 20 – April 26	60° to 56° to 60°	158
Spring	April 27 – June 23	61° to 66°	58
Summer	June 24 – Oct. 15	67° to 71° to 67°	114
Fall	Oct. 16 – Nov. 19	66° to 61°	35

Miami, Florida

	Daily average	Dates
Coldest time of year	67°	Dec. 28 – Feb. 12
Warmest time of year	83°	July 20 – Aug. 25

Season	Dates	Temperature range	Days
Winter	Nov. 24 – March 13	71° to 67° to 71°	110
Spring	March 14 – May 15	72° to 78°	63
Summer	May 16 – Oct. 12	79° to 83° to 79°	150
Fall	Oct. 13 – Nov. 23	78° to 72°	42

St. Louis, Missouri

	Daily average	Dates
Coldest time of year	28°	Jan. 10 – 21
Warmest time of year	79°	July 6 – Aug. 5

Season	Dates	Temperature range	Days
Winter	Nov. 24 – March 12	41° to 28° to 41°	109
Spring	March 13 – May 15	42° to 65°	64
Summer	May 16 – Sept. 27	66° to 79° to 66°	135
Fall	Sept. 28 – Nov. 23	65° to 42°	57

Minneapolis-St. Paul, Minnesota

	Daily average	Dates
Coldest time of year	10°	Jan. 13 – 20
Warmest time of year	74°	July 19 – 27

Season	Dates	Temperature range	Days
Winter	Nov. 29 – March 11	26° to 10° to 26°	103
Spring	March 12 – May 13	27° to 57°	63
Summer	May 14 – Sept. 24	58° to 74° to 58°	134
Fall	Sept. 25 – Nov. 28	57° to 27°	65

San Francisco, California, downtown

	Daily average	Dates
Coldest time of year	48°	Dec. 22 – Jan. 19
Warmest time of year	64°	Aug. 29 – Sept. 27

Season	Dates	Temperature range	Days
Winter	Nov. 26 – Feb. 27	52° to 48° to 52°	94
Spring	Feb. 28 – May 31	53° to 59°	93
Summer	June 1 – Oct. 22	60° to 64° to 60°	144
Fall	Oct. 23 – Nov. 25	59° to 53°	34

New York, New York

	Daily average	Dates
Coldest time of year	31°	Jan. 20 – 27
Warmest time of year	77°	July 15 – Aug. 7

Season	Dates	Temperature range	Days
Winter	Nov. 26 – March 23	43° to 31° to 43°	118
Spring	March 24 – May 24	44° to 64°	62
Summer	May 25 – Sept. 26	65° to 77° to 65°	125
Fall	Sept. 27 – Nov. 25	64° to 44°	60

Seattle, Washington

	Daily average	Dates
Coldest time of year	38°	Jan 10 – 13
Warmest time of year	66°	July 23 – 27

Season	Dates	Temperature range	Days
Winter	Nov. 11 – March 29	45° to 38° to 45°	139
Spring	March 30 – June 5	46° to 58°	68
Summer	June 6 – Sept. 23	59° to 66° to 59°	110
Fall	Sept. 24 – Nov. 10	58° to 46°	48

Phoenix, Arizona

	Daily average	Dates
Coldest time of year	51°	Jan. 5 – 7
Warmest time of year	93°	July 13 – 26

Season	Dates	Temperature range	Days
Winter	Nov. 10 – March 25	62° to 51° to 62°	136
Spring	March 26 – May 30	63° to 81°	66
Summer	May 31 – Sept. 26	82° to 93° to 82°	119
Fall	Sept. 27 – Nov. 9	81° to 61°	44

Washington, D.C.

	Daily average	Dates
Coldest time of year	35°	Jan 7 – Feb. 1
Warmest time of year	80°	July 23 – 25

Season	Dates	Temperature range	Days
Winter	Nov. 22 – March 18	46° to 35° to 46°	117
Spring	March 19 – May 24	47° to 68°	67
Summer	May 25 – Sept. 23	69° to 80° to 69°	122
Fall	Sept. 24 – Nov. 21	68° to 46°	59

10 hottest cities

Average annual temperature in °F

1. Key West, Fla.	77.7
2. Miami, Fla.	75.6
3. West Palm Beach, Fla.	74.6
4. (tie) Fort Myers, Fla.	73.9
Yuma, Ariz.	73.9
6. Brownsville, Texas	73.6
7. (tie) Orlando, Fla.	72.4
Vero Beach, Fla.	72.4
9. Corpus Christi, Texas	72.1
10. Tampa, Fla.	72.0

10 coldest cities

Average annual temperature in °F

1. International Falls, Minn.	36.4
2. Duluth, Minn.	38.2
3. Caribou, Maine	38.9
4. Marquette, Mich.	39.2
5. Sault Ste. Marie, Mich.	39.7
6. Fargo, N.D.	40.5
7. Williston, N.D.	40.8
8. Alamosa, Colo.	41.2
9. Bismarck, N.D.	41.3
10. St. Cloud, Minn.	41.4

10 driest cities

Average annual precip., in inches

1. Yuma, Ariz.	2.65
2. Las Vegas, Nev.	4.19
3. Bishop, Calif.	5.61
4. Bakersfield, Calif.	5.72
5. Phoenix, Ariz.	7.11
6. Alamosa, Colo.	7.13
7. Reno, Nev.	7.49
8. Winslow, Ariz.	7.64
9. El Paso, Tex.	7.82
10. Winnemucca, Nev.	7.87

Record setters

The chart above lists the 10 hottest places in the U.S. based on annual average temperature.

How can Key West and the other Florida locations be hotter than, say, Yuma, Ariz., which regularly has temperatures in the 115°F range, when Key West has never recorded a temperature above 97°F? The nature of averages is the answer — consistency counts.

Monthly average temperatures are used to calculate the yearly average temperature in the 10 hottest cities list. These monthly averages are the average of each month's high and low temperature.

Here's how Key West and Yuma compare:

Key West, Fla.

Coldest month (in °F)			Warmest month		
High	Low	Avg.	High	Low	Avg.
75	65	70	89	79	84

Yuma, Ariz.

Coldest months (in °F)			Warmest month		
High	Low	Avg.	High	Low	Avg.
69	44	56	107	80	94

Why this is the case: Key West is surrounded by ocean water, which varies little in temperature during the year. As a result, Key West has only a 14-degree difference between the averages for January, the coldest month, and July and August, the hottest.

Yuma, which is far from any large body of water, varies by 38 degrees from the December and January averages of 56 to the July average of 94.

To look at it another way: In Key West, the average low temperature during the coldest month and the average high during the hottest month are only 24 degrees apart. But in Yuma, this spread is 63 degrees.

Anyone who visits both places in the summer would say Yuma is by far hotter. But winter visitors would vote Key West the warmer of the two. Yuma's colder winters push the yearly average below not only Key West, but also two other Florida cities near the ocean.

Locations listed here are those with the most extreme weather of all places with regular weather observations and are based on annual averages.

10 wettest cities

Average annual precip., in inches

1. Hilo, Hawaii	128.00
2. Quillayute, Wash.	104.50
3. Astoria, Ore.	69.60
4. Blue Canyon, Calif.	67.87
5. Mobile, Ala.	64.64
6. Tallahassee, Fla.	64.59
7. Pensacola, Fla.	61.16
8. New Orleans, La.	59.74
9. West Palm Beach, Fla.	59.72
10. Miami, Fla.	59.55

10 snowiest cities

Average annual snowfall in inches

1. Blue Canyon, Calif.	240.8
2. Marquette, Mich.	128.6
3. Sault Ste. Marie, Mich.	116.7
4. Syracuse, N.Y.	111.6
5. Caribou, Maine	110.4
6. Mount Shasta, Calif.	104.9
7. Lander, Wyo.	102.5
8. Flagstaff, Ariz.	99.9
9. Sexton Summit, Ore.	97.8
10. Muskegon, Mich.	97.0

10 windiest cities

Avg. annual wind speed in mph

1. Blue Hill, Mass.	15.4
2. Dodge City, Kan.	14.0
3. Amarillo, Texas	13.5
4. Rochester, Minn.	13.1
5. (tie) Casper, Wyo.	12.9
Cheyenne, Wyo.	12.9
7. Great Falls, Mont.	12.7
8. Goodland, Kan.	12.6
9. Boston, Mass.	12.5
10. Lubbock, Texas	12.4

10 sunniest cities

Annual % of possible sunshine

1. Yuma, Ariz.	90
2. (tie) Las Vegas, Nev.,	85
Phoenix, Ariz., Tucson, Ariz.	
5. El Paso, Texas	83
6. (tie) Flagstaff, Ariz.,	79
Fresno, Calif., Reno, Nev.	
9. Sacramento, Calif.	78
10. (tie) Albuquerque, N.M.,	76
Key West, Fla., Pueblo,	
Colo.	

10 cloudiest cities

Number of cloudy days per year

1. Astoria, Ore.	240
(tie) Quillayute, Wash.	240
3. Olympia, Wash.	229
4. Seattle, Wash.	227
5. Portland, Ore.	223
6. Kalispell, Mont.	213
7. Binghamton, N.Y.	212
8. (tie) Beckley, W.Va.	211
Elkins, W.Va.	211
10. Eugene, Ore.	209

10 most humid cities

Average relative humidity, in %

1. Quillayute, Wash.	83.0
2. Olympia, Wash.	78.0
3. Port Arthur, Texas	77.5
4. Lake Charles, La.	77.0
5. Apalachicola, Fla.	76.5
(tie) Gainesville, Fla.	76.5
7. Corpus Christi, Texas	76.0
8. (tie) Eugene, Ore.	75.5
New Orleans, La.	75.5
10. Houston, Texas	75.0

10 least humid cities

Average relative humidity, in %

1. Las Vegas, Nev.	30.5
2. Phoenix, Ariz.	37.0
3. Yuma, Ariz.	38.0
4. Tucson, Ariz.	39.0
5. El Paso, Texas	42.5
6. Albuquerque, N.M.	44.5
7. Winslow, Ariz.	46.0
8. Grand Junction, Colo.	48.0
9. Winnemucca, Nev.	48.5
10. Reno, Nev.	50.5

10 rainiest cities

Number of days per year with rain

1. Hilo, Hawaii	277
2. Quillayute, Wash.	210
3. Astoria, Ore.	191
4. (tie) Elkins, W.Va.	171
Syracuse, N.Y.	171
6. Buffalo, N.Y.	169
7. Marquette, Mich.	168
8. Sault Ste. Marie, Mich.	166
9. Erie, Pa.	165
10. Binghamton, N.Y.	162

10 least rainy cities

Number of days per year with rain

1. Yuma, Ariz.	17
2. Las Vegas, Nev.	26
3. Bishop, Calif.	29
4. Santa Barbara, Calif.	30
5. Long Beach, Calif.	32
6. Los Angeles City, Calif.	35
(tie) Los Angeles Airport	35
8. Phoenix, Ariz.	36
9. Bakersfield, Calif.	37
10. San Diego, Calif.	42

Quick changes in temperature

Fastest warming: Chinook winds, which warm up as they blow down the eastern slopes of the Rockies, Black Hills and other mountains, can bring abrupt changes in temperatures. Amazing rises in temperature:

12-hour warm-up: 83 degrees. From -33° in very early morning to 50° by late afternoon in Granville, N.D., on Feb. 21, 1918.

15-minute warm up: 42 degrees. From -5°F to 37°F in Fort Assiniboine, Mont., on Jan. 19, 1893.

7-minute warm up: 34 degrees. This was part of an 80-degree rise in one day that also saw 30 inches of snow melt in Kipp, Mont., on Dec. 1, 1896 (beginning and ending temperatures not available).

Fastest cooling: Cold air masses often can move in and drop temperatures 40 to 50 degrees in a few hours in the U.S. interior. These changes often are followed on clear nights by additional heat loss. Notable drops in temperature:

24-hour chill: 100 degree drop. From 44°F to -56°F in Browning, Mont., on Jan. 23-24, 1916.

12-hour chill: 84 degree drop. From 63°F at noon to -21°F at midnight in Fairfield, Mont., on Dec. 24, 1924.

2-hour chill: 62 degree drop. From 49°F at 6 a.m. to -13°F at 8 a.m. in Rapid City, S.D., on Jan. 12, 1911.

15-minute chill: 47 degree drop. From 55°F at 7 a.m. to 8°F at 7:15 a.m. in Rapid City, S.D., on Jan. 10, 1911.

Flip-flop: Jan. 22, 1943, was a day to remember in Spearfish, S.D. The temperature first did a two-minute warm-up of 49 degrees from -4°F at 7:30 a.m. to 45°F at 7:32 a.m. It then rose slightly higher to 54°F by 9 a.m. before plunging in a 27-minute chill of 58 degrees to -4°F by 9:27 a.m. The phenomena was likely due to cold and warm air sloshing back and forth on the plains at the base of the mountains. The effect is like what would happen if you quickly poured warm water into a shallow bowl of cold water. The water would slosh back and forth a few times. This is most likely what happened to the cold and warm air.

Record highest temperatures by state

State	Temp. in °F	Date	Station	Elev. (in feet)
Ala.	112	Sept. 5, 1925	Centerville	345
Alaska	100	June 27, 1915	Ft. Yukon	420
Ariz.	128	June 29, 1994	Lake Havasu	780
Ark.	120	Aug. 10, 1936	Ozark	396
Calif.	134	July 10, 1913	Greenland Ranch	-178
Colo.	118	July 11, 1888	Bennett	5,484
Conn.	105	July 21, 1991	Danbury	450
Del.	110	July 21, 1930	Millsboro	20
Fla.	109	June 29, 1931	Monticello	207
Ga.	112	July 24, 1952	Louisville	132
Hawaii	100	April 27, 1931	Pahala	850
Idaho	118	July 28, 1934	Orofino	1,027
Ill.	117	July 14, 1954	E. St. Louis	410
Ind.	116	July 14, 1936	Collegeville	672
Iowa	118	July 20, 1934	Keokuk	614
Kansas	121	July 24, 1936	Alton (near)	1,651
Ky.	114	July 28, 1930	Greensburg	581
La.	114	Aug. 10, 1936	Plain Dealing	268
Maine	105	July 10, 1911	N. Bridgton	450
Md.	109	July 10, 1936	Cumberland	623
			Frederick	325
Mass.	107	Aug. 2, 1975	New Bedford	120
			Chester	640
Mich.	112	July 13, 1936	Mio	963
Minn.	114	July 6, 1936	Moorhead	904
Miss.	115	July 29, 1930	Holly Springs	600
Mo.	118	July 14, 1954	Warsaw	687
			Union	560
Mont.	117	July 5, 1937	Medicine Lake	1,950
Neb.	118	July 24, 1936	Minden	2,169
Nev.	125	June 29, 1994	Laughlin	680
N.H.	106	July 4, 1911	Nashua	125
N.J.	110	July 10, 1936	Runyon	18
N.M.	122	June 27, 1994	Lakewood	3,418
N.Y.	108	July 22, 1926	Troy	35
N.C.	110	Aug. 21, 1983	Fayetteville	213
N.D.	121	July 6, 1936	Steele	1,857
Ohio	113	July 21, 1934	Gallipolis	673
Okla.	120	June 29, 1994	Tipton	1,248
Ore.	119	Aug. 10, 1898	Pendleton	1,074
Pa.	111	July 10, 1936	Phoenixville	100
R.I.	104	Aug. 2, 1975	Providence	51
S.C.	111	June 28, 1954	Camden	170
S.D.	120	July 5, 1936	Gannvalley	1,750
Tenn.	113	Aug. 9, 1930	Perryville	377
Texas	120	Aug. 12, 1936	Seymour	1,291
Utah	117	July 5, 1985	Saint George	2,880
Vt.	105	July 4, 1911	Vernon	310
Va.	110	July 15, 1954	Balcony Falls	725
Wash.	118	Aug. 5, 1961	Ice Harbor Dam	475
W.Va.	112	July 10, 1936	Martinsburg	435
Wis.	114	July 13, 1936	Wisconsin Dells	900
Wyo.	114	July 12, 1900	Basin	3,500

Record lowest temperatures by state

State	Temp. in °F	Date	Station	Elev. (in feet)
Ala.	-27	Jan. 30, 1966	New Market	760
Alaska	-80	Jan. 23, 1971	Prospect Creek	1,100
Ariz.	-40	Jan. 7, 1971	Hawley Lake	8,180
Ark.	-29	Feb. 13, 1905	Pond	1,250
Calif.	-45	Jan. 20, 1937	Boca	5,532
Colo.	-61	Feb. 1, 1985	Maybell	5,920
Conn.	-32	Feb. 16, 1943	Falls Village	585
Del.	-17	Jan. 17, 1893	Millsboro	20
Fla.	-2	Feb. 13, 1899	Tallahassee	193
Ga.	-17	Jan. 27, 1940	No. Floyd County	1,000
Hawaii	12	May 17, 1979	Mauna Kea	13,770
Idaho	-60	Jan. 18, 1943	Island Park Dam	6,285
Ill.	-35	Jan. 22, 1930	Mount Carroll	817
Ind.	-35	Feb. 2, 1951	Greensburg	954
Iowa	-47	Jan. 12, 1912	Washta	1,157
Kansas	-40	Feb. 13, 1905	Lebanon	1,812
Ky.	-34	Jan. 28, 1963	Cynthiana	684
La.	-16	Feb. 13, 1899	Minden	194
Maine	-48	Jan. 19, 1925	Van Buren	510
Md.	-40	Jan. 13, 1912	Oakland	2,461
Mass.	-35	Jan. 12, 1981	Chester	640
Mich.	-51	Feb. 9, 1934	Vanderbilt	785
Minn.	-59	Feb. 16, 1903	Pokegama Dam	1,280
Miss.	-19	Jan. 30, 1966	Corinth	420
Mo.	-40	Feb. 13, 1905	Warsaw	700
Mont.	-70	Jan. 20, 1954	Rogers Pass	5,470
Neb.	-47	Feb. 12, 1899	Camp Clarke	3,700
Nev.	-50	Jan. 8, 1937	San Jacinto	5,200
N.H.	-46	Jan. 28, 1925	Pittsburg	1,575
N.J.	-34	Jan. 5, 1904	River Vale	70
N.M.	-50	Feb. 1, 1951	Gavilan	7,350
N.Y.	-52	Feb. 18, 1979	Old Forge	1,720
N.C.	-34	Jan. 21, 1985	Mt. Mitchell	6,525
N.D.	-60	Feb. 15, 1936	Parshall	1,930
Ohio	-39	Feb. 10, 1899	Milligan	800
Okla.	-27	Jan. 18, 1930	Watts	958
Ore.	-54	Feb. 10, 1933	Seneca	4,700
Pa.	-42	Jan. 5, 1904	Smethport	1,500
R.I.	-23	Jan. 11, 1942	Kingston	100
S.C.	-19	Jan. 21, 1985	Caesars Head	3,100
S.D.	-58	Feb. 17, 1936	McIntosh	2,277
Tenn.	-32	Dec. 30, 1917	Mountain City	2,471
Texas	-23	Feb. 8, 1933	Seminole	3,275
Utah	-69	Feb. 1, 1985	Peter's Sink	8,092
Vt.	-50	Dec. 30, 1933	Bloomfield	915
Va.	-30	Jan. 22, 1985	Mountain Lake	3,870
Wash.	-48	Dec. 30, 1968	Mazama	2,120
			Winthrop	1,765
W.Va.	-37	Dec. 30, 1917	Lewisburg	2,200
Wis.	-54	Jan. 24, 1922	Danbury	908
Wyo.	-63	Feb. 9, 1933	Moran	6,770

Record annual minimum precip. by state

State	Precip. (in.)	Date	Station	Elev. (in feet)
Ala.	22.00	1954	Primose Farm	180
Alaska	1.61	1935	Barrow	31
Ariz.	0.07	1956	Davis Dam	660
Ark.	19.11	1936	Index	300
Calif.	0.00	1929	Death Valley	-282
Colo.	1.69	1939	Buena Vista	7,980
Conn.	23.60	1965	Baltic	140
Del.	21.38	1965	Dover	30
Fla.	21.16	1989	Conch Key	6
Ga.	17.14	1954	Swainsboro	320
Hawaii	0.19	1953	Kawaihae	75
Idaho	2.09	1947	Grand View	2,360
Ill.	16.59	1956	Keithsburg	540
Ind.	18.67	1934	Brooksville	630
Iowa	12.11	1958	Cherokee	1,360
Kansas	4.77	1956	Johnson	3,270
Ky.	14.51	1968	Jeremiah	1,160
La.	26.44	1936	Shreveport	170
Maine	23.06	1930	Machias	30
Md.	17.76	1930	Picardy	1,030
Mass.	21.76	1965	Chatham L.S.	20
Mich.	15.64	1936	Croswell	730
Minn.	7.81	1936	Angus	870
Miss.	25.97	1936	Yazoo City	120
Mo.	16.14	1956	La Belle	770
Mont.	2.97	1960	Belfry	4,040
Neb.	6.30	1931	Hull	4,400
Nev.	Trace	1898	Hot Springs	4,072
N.H.	22.31	1930	Bethlehem	1,440
N.J.	19.85	1965	Canton	20
N.M.	1.00	1910	Hermanas	4,540
N.Y.	17.64	1941	Lewiston	320
N.C.	22.69	1930	Mt. Airy	1,070
N.D.	4.02	1934	Parshall	1,930
Ohio	16.96	1963	Elyria	730
Okla.	6.53	1956	Regnier	4,280
Ore.	3.33	1939	Warm Springs Reservoir	3,330
Pa.	15.71	1965	Breezewood	1,350
R.I.	24.08	1965	Block Island	40
S.C.	20.73	1954	Rock Hill	667
S.D.	2.89	1936	Ludlow	2,850
Tenn.	25.23	1941	Halls	310
Texas	1.64	1956	Presidio	2,580
Utah	1.34	1974	Myton	5,080
Vt.	22.98	1941	Burlington	330
Va.	12.52	1941	Moores Creek Dam	1,950
Wash.	2.61	1930	Wahluke	416
W.Va.	9.50	1930	Upper Tract	1,540
Wis.	12.00	1937	Plum Island	590
Wyo.	1.28	1960	Lysite	5,260

Record annual maximum precip. by state

State	Precip. (in.)	Date	Station	Elev. (in feet)
Ala.	106.57	1853	Mt. Vernon Barracks	49
Alaska	332.29	1976	MacLeod Harbor	40
Ariz.	58.92	1978	Hawley Lake	8,180
Ark.	98.55	1957	Newhope	850
Calif.	153.54	1909	Monumental	2,420
Colo.	92.84	1897	Ruby	10,000
Conn.	78.53	1955	Burlington Dam	460
Del.	72.75	1948	Lewes	10
Fla.	112.43	1966	Wewahitchka	50
Ga.	112.16	1959	Flat Top	3,600
Hawaii	704.83	1982	Kukui	5,788
Idaho	81.05	1933	Roland	4,150
Ill.	74.58	1950	New Burnside	560
Ind.	97.38	1890	Marengo	570
Iowa	74.50	1851	Muscatine	680
Kansas	67.02	1985	Columbus	900
Ky.	79.68	1950	Russelville	590
La.	113.74	1991	New Orleans	6
Maine	75.64	1845	Brunswick	70
Md.	72.59	1948	Salisbury	50
Mass.	72.19	1983	Pembroke	74
Mich.	64.01	1881	Adrian	770
Minn.	51.53	1911	Grand Meadow	1,340
Miss.	104.36	1991	Waveland	8
Mo.	92.77	1957	Portageville	280
Mont.	55.51	1953	Summit	5,210
Neb.	64.52	1869	Omaha	980
Nev.	59.03	1969	Mt. Rose Resort	7,300
N.H.	130.14	1969	Mt. Washington	6,260
N.J.	85.99	1882	Paterson	100
N.M.	62.45	1941	White Tail	7,450
N.Y.	82.06	1903	Wappingers Falls	200
N.C.	129.60	1964	Rosman	2,220
N.D.	37.98	1944	Milnor	2,600
Ohio	70.82	1870	Little Mountain	1,187
Okla.	84.47	1957	Kiamichi Tower	2,350
Ore.	168.88	1937	Valsetz	1,150
Pa.	81.64	1952	Mt. Pocono	1,910
R.I.	70.21	1983	Kingston	100
S.C.	101.65	1961	Caesar's Head	3,120
S.D.	48.42	1946	Deadwood	4,550
Tenn.	114.88	1957	Haw Knob	4,900
Texas	109.38	1873	Clarksville	440
Utah	108.54	1983	Alta	8,700
Vt.	92.88	1983	Mt. Mansfield	3,960
Va.	81.78	1972	Montebello	2,450
Wash.	184.56	1931	Wynoochee Oxbow	670
W.Va.	94.01	1948	Romney	820
Wis.	62.07	1884	Embarrass	808
Wyo.	55.46	1945	Grassy Lake Dam	7,240

Wettest location in each state (inches of precipitation)

City, State	Jan.	Feb.	March	April	May	June	July	Aug.	Sept.	Oct.	Nov.	Dec.	Annual
Robertsdale, Ala.	4.49	4.67	6.78	5.16	4.70	7.03	8.55	7.17	7.61	2.96	3.56	5.02	67.70
Crown King, Ariz.	2.98	2.25	2.62	1.34	0.40	0.46	3.72	5.09	1.92	1.42	1.72	3.60	27.52
Glenwood, Ark.	3.95	4.17	5.45	6.20	7.03	4.27	3.97	3.81	4.48	3.65	4.18	4.28	55.44
Little Port Walter, Ak.	20.65	17.51	16.33	14.33	11.58	8.13	9.06	13.48	24.06	34.32	26.78	24.99	187.89
Gasquet, Calif.	17.73	13.10	11.01	6.34	4.62	1.00	0.44	0.66	1.57	7.46	14.06	16.62	93.61
Rico, Colo.	2.53	1.95	2.50	2.27	1.58	1.28	2.58	2.80	2.44	2.49	1.91	2.52	26.85
Wolcott, Conn.	3.86	3.89	4.90	4.60	4.44	3.48	4.31	4.35	4.28	4.00	5.70	4.96	52.77
Bridgeville, Del.	3.11	2.81	3.92	3.28	3.32	3.72	5.03	4.86	3.46	2.97	3.18	3.41	43.07
De Funiak Springs, Fla.	4.70	4.72	6.81	5.01	4.37	6.36	8.82	7.66	6.78	3.21	3.52	4.96	66.92
Clayton, Ga.	6.08	6.47	7.49	5.99	4.98	5.37	6.60	5.57	4.97	4.61	5.02	6.30	69.45
Papaikou Mauka, Hi.	13.95	17.99	23.44	23.24	19.53	11.96	17.12	21.11	12.83	17.00	19.89	23.95	222.01
Pierce, Idaho	5.53	4.31	4.18	3.80	3.51	3.47	1.03	1.14	2.34	3.65	5.00	5.61	43.57
Anna, Ill.	3.77	3.45	4.89	4.70	5.34	4.39	3.58	4.07	3.61	2.85	3.76	3.69	48.10
La Porte, Ind.	2.83	2.78	3.47	5.01	4.85	5.21	4.83	3.83	4.14	4.29	3.27	3.21	47.72
Dubuque, Iowa	1.73	1.26	2.97	4.15	4.67	5.29	4.31	4.02	4.64	2.83	2.48	1.92	40.27
Garnett, Kansas	1.35	1.34	2.81	4.26	4.83	5.75	4.90	4.38	5.26	3.46	1.71	1.63	41.68
Liberty, Ky.	4.69	4.37	5.22	4.16	4.36	5.06	5.16	3.78	3.37	2.47	3.88	4.27	50.79
Schriever, La.	4.58	5.27	5.50	4.73	5.64	5.89	8.47	6.15	7.63	3.03	4.09	5.58	66.56
Machias, Maine	4.21	4.19	3.68	3.78	4.08	3.36	3.33	3.13	4.01	4.08	5.93	4.94	48.72
Snow Hill, Md.	3.60	3.62	4.69	3.35	3.43	3.85	4.37	5.01	3.82	3.65	3.56	3.69	46.64
Heath, Mass.	3.59	3.47	3.92	4.06	4.57	4.17	4.28	3.70	4.18	3.96	4.74	4.31	48.95
Bergland, Mich.	2.26	1.94	2.26	2.92	3.84	4.48	3.84	4.13	3.96	2.84	3.42	2.66	38.55
Winona, Minn.	1.02	0.82	2.02	2.60	4.15	4.87	3.98	3.72	3.23	2.07	1.72	1.13	31.33
Vancleave, Miss.	5.01	4.44	6.93	5.23	4.35	6.98	8.65	7.85	7.47	3.11	3.94	5.47	69.43
New Madrid, Mo.	4.18	4.22	5.09	4.46	5.43	4.30	3.28	2.96	3.47	2.91	4.20	3.98	48.48
Summit, Mont.	4.81	3.80	3.18	2.93	3.04	3.97	1.28	1.62	2.58	3.21	4.29	4.51	39.22
Falls City, Neb.	1.05	1.11	2.18	3.06	4.93	5.94	3.99	4.40	4.38	2.66	1.43	1.16	36.29
Lamoille, Nev.	1.43	1.53	2.10	2.53	2.37	1.97	0.54	0.67	0.70	1.38	1.74	1.65	18.61
Woodstock, N.H.	2.78	2.89	3.01	3.65	3.86	3.79	4.60	3.67	3.78	3.60	4.61	3.57	43.81
Charlotteburg, N.J.	3.29	3.19	4.22	3.96	4.12	3.74	4.69	4.72	3.82	3.57	4.79	4.26	48.37
Cloudcroft, N.M.	1.65	1.33	1.70	0.73	0.71	1.86	5.97	5.09	2.46	1.39	0.78	1.75	25.42
Highmarket, N.Y.	3.62	3.52	3.61	4.21	4.88	3.98	4.27	4.30	4.90	4.82	5.07	4.38	51.56
Rosman, N.C.	6.37	6.84	8.01	6.35	5.66	6.76	7.84	7.52	6.24	5.78	5.71	7.27	80.35
Wahpeton, N.D.	0.55	0.52	0.80	2.25	2.82	4.27	3.25	2.93	2.02	1.16	0.79	0.65	22.01
Wilmington, Ohio	3.83	3.18	4.55	4.38	4.32	3.73	3.99	3.07	3.05	2.30	3.45	3.14	42.99
Idabel, Okla.	3.41	3.93	4.48	5.71	6.42	3.45	3.57	2.70	4.03	3.56	3.47	3.40	48.13
Valsetz, Ore.	21.10	15.94	14.38	8.03	4.61	2.73	1.07	1.72	4.25	12.09	18.78	21.62	126.32
Tamaqua, Pa.	3.06	2.93	4.00	4.13	4.67	3.55	5.15	4.48	3.97	3.63	4.68	4.06	48.31
Greenville, R.I.	3.36	3.37	4.04	3.87	3.86	3.24	3.46	4.08	3.83	3.70	5.46	4.30	46.57
Caesars Head, S.C.	6.23	6.42	7.69	6.29	5.59	6.55	8.00	6.73	5.85	5.48	5.72	6.62	77.17
Deadwood, S.D.	1.23	1.36	1.95	3.25	4.88	4.90	2.37	1.87	2.06	1.60	1.71	1.20	28.38
Monteagle, Tenn.	6.37	6.18	6.59	5.54	4.31	4.29	5.45	4.23	3.92	3.13	4.72	6.25	60.98
Orange, Texas	4.28	4.94	3.47	4.91	4.85	5.04	6.70	5.43	6.76	3.70	4.24	5.60	59.92
Silver Lake, Utah	5.35	4.80	5.53	4.50	2.87	2.65	1.28	1.95	1.74	3.05	4.75	5.34	43.81
Searsburg Station, Vt.	3.96	3.81	4.24	4.61	4.79	4.03	4.20	4.01	4.25	3.96	5.26	4.86	51.98
Pennington Gap, Va.	4.87	4.76	5.48	3.93	3.69	4.09	5.46	4.09	3.20	2.45	3.71	4.56	50.29
Quinault, Wash.	19.43	16.01	13.46	9.77	5.44	3.86	2.32	3.06	6.06	13.68	18.22	21.64	132.95
Pickens, W.Va.	5.51	5.02	6.25	5.35	5.61	5.87	7.00	5.94	4.58	4.27	4.60	5.47	65.47
Monroe, Wis.	1.39	1.06	2.33	3.38	3.65	4.88	4.00	3.86	3.95	2.77	2.17	1.66	35.10
Moran, Wyo.	2.81	2.10	1.82	1.72	2.03	1.85	0.88	1.30	1.46	1.40	2.32	2.69	22.38

Note: Most locations here are not regular reporting stations and are not on the lists on pages 125 and 126.

Guide to using the city pages

The climate information on U.S. and foreign cities in this almanac gives the clearest picture available of what weather to expect during all seasons of the year. It's impossible to know what the weather will be like even a week in advance, much less a month or two ahead. But climatic information, which is based on averages of day-to-day weather, is a good guide to the most likely weather.

The USA TODAY Weather Almanac's data on 200 U.S. cities and 50 foreign cities is based on the wealth of data available at the National Climatic Data Center in Asheville, N.C. The Center's scientists helped select the data and gave advice on using it. National Weather Service offices across the United States supplied additional information.

How to use each section:

❶ **Monthly averages:** All of the U.S averages in this table are based on records of weather over at least 30 years.

• Average precipitation: Amount of water from rain or the amount of water from melting ice or snow. "T" represents a "trace" or less than 0.01 inch, the smallest amount that can be measured.

• Average snow: Amount of snow that falls each month, not how deep the snow is on average during the month.

To find out if snow is powder or wet, dividing the average snow by the average precipitation shows how many inches of snow melts down to an inch of water. The higher the snow, the more powdery it is.

• Wet days: Average number of days with at least 0.01 inch of rain or melted snow.

• Thunderstorm days: Number of days the local weather office hears thunder or sees lightning.

• Percent sky is cloudy: Amount of time every month when the sky is mostly covered by clouds. It is based on hourly weather observations during the day and night. Where 24-hour observations aren't available, the information was obtained from sunrise to sunset.

• Afternoon relative humidity: Most common measure of how much water vapor is in the air.

• Dew point: Measures humidity. Generally, it feels humid when the dew point is above 60°F. It is uncomfortably hot and sticky when the dew point approaches and passes 70°F.

• Wind speed is the average of sustained winds, not wind gusts. For winter months, average wind speeds can be combined with temperatures to indicate expected wind chill, using the chart in the appendix.

❷ **Annual averages:** These are based on unrounded numbers for each month. They may not equal totals of monthly averages shown because monthly averages are rounded.

• Precipitation: Yearly total of the monthly averages.

• Snow: Yearly total of the monthly averages.

• Heating, cooling degree days: Figures indicate how costly heating and air conditioning should be. The higher the figures, the greater the cost.

• Days with thunderstorms: Total number of days each year with thunderstorms reported.

• Days with fog does not take into account the fog's thickness.

• Days above 90°: Temperature must rise above 90°F at least once.

• Days below 32°: Temperature must fall below 32°F at any time during the 24-hour period of a calendar day.

• Wet days: Total of the wet days in the monthly table.

• Days with snow: Annual number of days with 0.1 inch of snow or more.

• Days with 1.5 inches or more snow: Annual average number of days with snow amounts of 1.5 inches or more.

❸ **Temperatures**: This graph is designed to show information about what kinds of temperatures to expect, not merely the monthly average highs and lows.

Record highs and lows show the worst to be expected. Since monthly records seldom are broken by more than a degree or two, it's safe to assume that temperatures are never likely to be more than a degree or so warmer or colder than the monthly records listed.

❹ **Text**: The descriptions of each city's climate are based on narratives available from the National Climatic Data Center.

• Latitude: The number of degrees and minutes — each degree has 60 minutes — north or south of the equator.

• Longitude: The number of degrees and minutes east or west of the prime meridian, which passes through Greenwich, England, near London. Places from Greenwich westward halfway around the world to 180° longitude are west longitude. This includes all of the United States. Places from Greenwich eastward halfway around the world to 180° are east longitude.

• Elevation: The number of feet above mean sea level of the city's weather station.

The narratives refer to different types of climate:

• Continental climate: A climate typical of places far from any ocean with warm summers and cold winters.

• Maritime climate: A climate typical of places near an ocean, characterized by smaller differences in average summer and winter temperatures than inland.

• Temperate climate: A climate typical of the regions outside of the tropics and the Arctic or Antarctic with distinct winter and summer seasons.

• Tropical climate: A climate typical of the tropics with warm weather all year and no pronounced summer or winter seasons, although there can be wet and dry seasons.

❺ **Weather extremes**: These are the best available from the National Climatic Data Center or local weather offices. In some cases, old records are not complete and only a month and year are available.

❻ **Percent sky is clear**: Amount of time every month when less than one-tenth of the sky is covered by clouds. It is based on hourly weather observations during the day and night. Where 24-hour observations aren't available, the information was obtained during sunrise to sunset.

An important note on records: City records that follow may not agree with listings elsewhere in the *Almanac* because records are sometimes from a different source.

Index to city pages

West Palm Beach	325	**Maine**		**Nevada**		**Oregon**	
		Caribou	166	Elko	192	Astoria	145
Georgia		Portland	279	Ely	194	Eugene	196
Atlanta	146			Las Vegas	240	Medford	250
Augusta	148	**Maryland**		Reno	286	Portland	280
Columbus	179	Baltimore	150				
Savannah	304			**New Hampshire**		**Pennsylvania**	
		Massachusetts		Concord	181	Allentown	140
Hawaii		Boston	159			Erie	195
Hilo	220	Worcester	331	**New Jersey**		Harrisburg	217
Honolulu	221			Atlantic City	147	Philadelphia	274
		Michigan		Newark	262	Pittsburgh	276
Idaho		Alpena	141			Wilkes-Barre-Scranton	327
Boise	158	Detroit	188	**New Mexico**		Williamsport	328
Lewiston	241	Flint	202	Albuquerque	139		
Pocatello	277	Grand Rapids	212	Roswell	292	**Puerto Rico**	
		Houghton Lake	222			San Juan	301
Illinois		Lansing	239	**New York**			
Chicago	173	Marquette	249	Albany	138	**Rhode Island**	
Moline	259	Sault Ste. Marie	303	Binghamton	155	Providence	281
Peoria	273			Buffalo	163		
Rockford	291	**Minnesota**		Islip	229	**South Carolina**	
Springfield	313	Duluth	191	New York	264	Charleston	168
		International Falls	228	Rochester	290	Columbia	178
Indiana		Minneapolis	256	Syracuse	315	Greenville-Spartanburg	216
Evansville	198	Rochester	289				
Fort Wayne	205			**North Carolina**		**South Dakota**	
Indianapolis	227	**Mississippi**		Asheville	144	Huron	226
South Bend	311	Jackson	230	Cape Hatteras	165	Rapid City	284
		Meridian	252	Charlotte	170	Sioux Falls	310
Iowa				Greensboro	215		
Des Moines	187	**Missouri**		Raleigh-Durham	283	**Tennessee**	
Dubuque	190	Columbia	177	Wilmington	330	Bristol	161
Sioux City	309	Kansas City	234			Chattanooga	171
Waterloo	324	St. Louis	294	**North Dakota**		Knoxville	236
		Springfield	314	Bismarck	157	Memphis	251
Kansas				Fargo	200	Nashville	261
Dodge City	189	**Montana**					
Goodland	209	Billings	154	**Ohio**		**Texas**	
Topeka	319	Glasgow	208	Akron	136	Abilene	135
Wichita	326	Great Falls	213	Cincinnati	174	Amarillo	142
		Helena	219	Cleveland	175	Austin	149
Kentucky		Kalispell	233	Columbus	180	Brownsville	162
Lexington	242	Missoula	257	Dayton	184	Corpus Christi	182
Louisville	246			Toledo	318	Dallas-Fort Worth	183
Paducah	271	**Nebraska**		Youngstown	333	El Paso	193
		Grand Island	210			Galveston	207
Louisiana		North Platte	267	**Oklahoma**		Houston	223
Baton Rouge	152	Omaha	269	Oklahoma City	268	Lubbock	247
Lake Charles	237	Scottsbluff	305	Tulsa	321	Midland-Odessa	254
New Orleans	263	Valentine	322			Port Arthur	278
Shreveport	308					San Angelo	297

San Antonio	298	**World cities**		Toyko	357	
		Argentina		**Kenya**		
Utah		Buenos Aires	339	Nairobi	348	
Salt Lake City	296	**Australia**		**Korea**		
		Sydney	356	Seoul	353	
Vermont		**Austria**		**Mexico**		
Burlington	164	Vienna	358	Acalpulco	335	
		Bahamas		Mexico City	346	
Virginia		Nassau	349	**Netherlands**		
Norfolk	266	**Bermuda**		Amsterdam	336	
Richmond	287	Hamilton	341	**New Zealand**		
Roanoke	288	**Brazil**		Auckland	337	
		Rio de Janeiro	351	**Norway**		
Washington		**Canada**		Oslo	349	
Seattle-Tacoma	306	Montreal	347	**Peru**		
Spokane	312	Toronto	357	Lima	344	
Yakima	332	Vancouver	358	**Philippines**		
		China		Manila	345	
West Virginia		Shanghai	354	**Poland**		
Beckley	153	**Czech Republic**		Warsaw	359	
Charleston	169	Prague	350	**Russia**		
Huntington	224	**Egypt**		Moscow	347	
		Cairo	339	St. Petersburg	355	
Wisconsin		**El Salvador**		**Saudi Arabia**		
Green Bay	214	San Salvador	353	Riyadh	352	
Madison	248	**England**		**Singapore**		
Milwaukee	255	London	344	Singapore	354	
		France		**South Africa**		
Wyoming		Marseille	346	Pretoria	351	
Casper	167	Paris	350	**Spain**		
Cheyenne	172	**Germany**		Madrid	345	
Lander	238	Berlin	338	**Sweden**		
Sheridan	307	Munich	348	Stockholm	355	
		Ghana		**Switzerland**		
		Accra	335	Zurich	359	
		Greece		**Taiwan**		
		Athens	336	Taipei	356	
		Hong Kong		**Thailand**		
		Hong Kong	342	Bangkok	337	
		Hungary		**Turkey**		
		Budapest	338	Istanbul	342	
		India		**Vietman**		
		Delhi	340	Ho Chi Minh City	341	
		Ireland				
		Dublin	340			
		Israel				
		Jerusalem	343			
		Italy				
		Rome	352			
		Jamaica				
		Kingston	343			
		Japan				

Abilene, Texas

Lat. 32° 25' N **Lon.** 99° 41' W **Elev.** 1,784 ft.

Abilene is on the boundary between the humid east Texas climate and the semiarid west and north Texas climate. The rainfall pattern is typical of the Great Plains. The large range of high and low temperatures, also characteristic of the Great Plains, extends south to the Abilene area. High daytime temperatures prevail in the summer, but normally are broken by thunderstorms about five times a month. Rapid cooling after sunset results in pleasant nights with low summertime temperatures in the upper 60s and low 70s. Rapid wintertime temperature changes occur when cold, dry arctic air replaces warm, moist tropical air. Drops in temperature of 20 to 30 degrees in one hour are not unusual. However, fair, mild weather is typical.

Weather extremes

Most rain in 24 hours:	6.78 in. May 22 – 23, 1908
Most rain in a month:	15.19 in. August 1914
Most snow in 24 hours:	8.0 in. Jan. 15 – 16, 1919
Most snow in a month:	13.5 in. January 1973

Temperatures

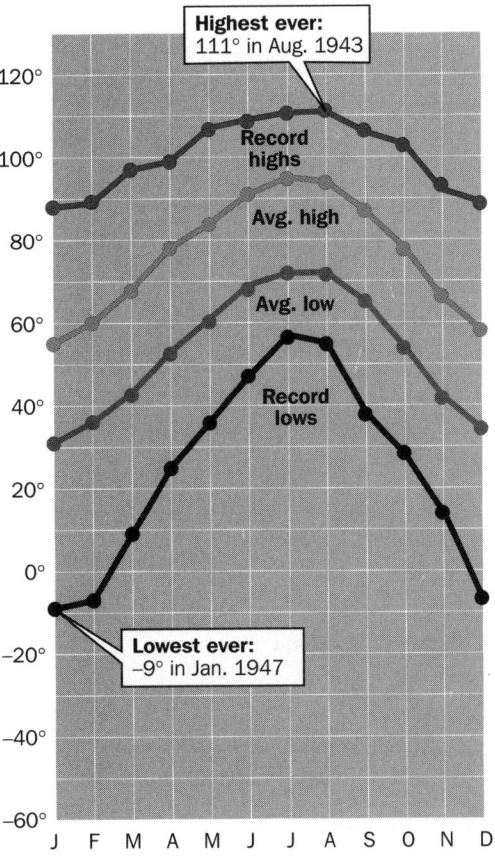

Highest ever: 111° in Aug. 1943
Record highs
Avg. high
Avg. low
Record lows
Lowest ever: −9° in Jan. 1947

Monthly averages

Month	Avg. precip. (in.)	Avg. snow (in.)	Wet days	Thunder-storm days	Pct. sky is cloudy	% p.m. relative humidity	Dew point	Wind speed (mph)
Jan.	0.9	2	5	1	37	44	28	12.7
Feb.	1.1	1	5	1	38	44	32	13.8
March	1.1	1	5	3	34	37	36	15.0
April	2.1	0	6	5	31	38	45	15.0
May	3.4	0	8	8	30	43	56	15.0
June	2.7	0	6	6	20	41	62	15.0
July	2.3	0	5	5	17	38	63	11.5
Aug.	2.4	0	5	5	16	37	62	10.4
Sept.	2.8	0	6	4	22	43	59	11.5
Oct.	2.5	T	6	3	24	43	49	12.7
Nov.	1.3	1	4	1	29	42	38	12.7
Dec.	1.0	1	4	1	34	43	30	12.7

T - Trace of rain or snow   * - Less than 1   NA - Not Available

Annual averages

Precipitation (in inches)	23.6
Snow (in inches)	5
Heating degree days	2,613
Cooling degree days	2,524
Days with thunderstorms	43
Days with fog	49
Days above 90°	102
Days below 32°	52
Wet days	130
Days with snow	6
Days with 1.5 inches or more snow	1

Percent time sky is clear

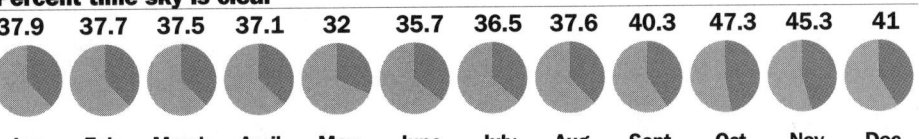

37.9	37.7	37.5	37.1	32	35.7	36.5	37.6	40.3	47.3	45.3	41
Jan.	Feb.	March	April	May	June	July	Aug.	Sept.	Oct.	Nov.	Dec.

Akron, Ohio

Lat. 40° 55' N **Lon.** 81° 26' W **Elev.** 1,208 ft.

Lake Erie has considerable influence on the Akron area, tempering cold air masses during the late fall and winter and contributing to the formation of brief but heavy snow squalls until the lake freezes over. Summers are moderately warm but quite humid, while September, October and sometimes November are usually pleasant although with considerable morning fog. The weather station for Akron is located midway between Akron and Canton. Because of Lake Erie, snowfall is usually much heavier north of the station.

Temperatures

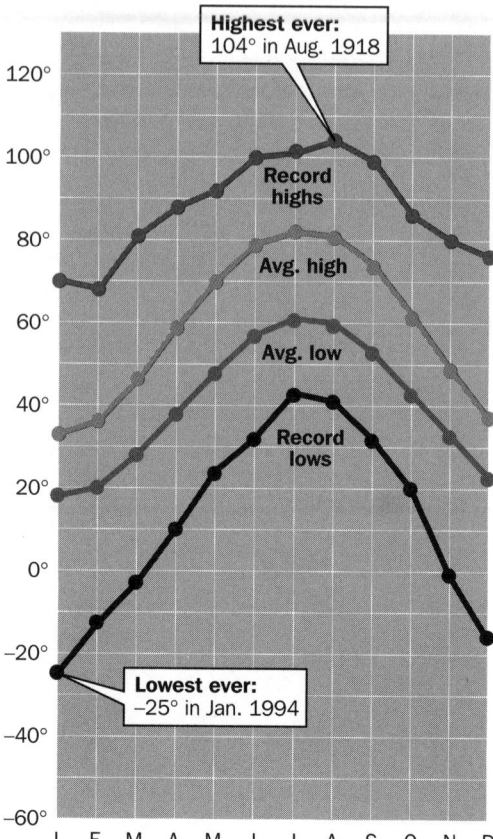

Highest ever: 104° in Aug. 1918

Record highs

Avg. high

Avg. low

Record lows

Lowest ever: −25° in Jan. 1994

Weather extremes

Most rain in 24 hours:	6.30 in.	Sept. 13 – 14, 1979
Most rain in a month:	11.98 in.	September 1926
Most snow in 24 hours:	20.6 in.	April 3 – 4, 1987
Most snow in a month:	37.5 in.	January 1978

Monthly averages

Month	Avg. precip. (in.)	Avg. snow (in.)	Wet days	Thunder-storm days	Pct. sky is cloudy	% p.m. relative humidity	Dew point	Wind speed (mph)
Jan.	2.6	11	16	*	64	68	19	12.7
Feb.	2.3	9	14	*	59	65	20	11.5
March	3.2	9	16	2	56	59	27	12.7
April	3.3	3	14	4	47	53	36	11.5
May	3.7	T	13	6	40	53	47	10.4
June	3.4	0	11	7	32	54	56	9.2
July	4.0	0	11	8	26	54	61	8.1
Aug.	3.2	0	10	6	27	55	60	8.1
Sept.	3.1	0	9	3	32	56	54	8.1
Oct.	2.3	1	10	1	38	56	42	9.2
Nov.	2.8	5	14	1	58	64	33	11.5
Dec.	2.8	10	15	*	66	70	23	11.5

T - Trace of rain or snow   * - Less than 1   NA - Not Available

Annual averages

Precipitation (in inches)	36.7
Snow (in inches)	47
Heating degree days	6,169
Cooling degree days	694
Days with thunderstorms	38
Days with fog	173
Days above 90°	8
Days below 32°	129
Wet days	153
Days with snow	94
Days with 1.5 inches or more snow	19

Percent time sky is clear

Jan.	Feb.	March	April	May	June	July	Aug.	Sept.	Oct.	Nov.	Dec.
12.0	13.6	15.3	18.5	19.7	19.6	22.1	23.2	26.1	26.1	14.1	11.2

Alamosa, Colorado

Lat. 37° 27' N **Lon.** 105° 52' W **Elev.** 7,536 ft.

Alamosa is in south-central Colorado near the center of the San Luis Valley, a broad depression between mountain ranges converging to the north. The valley, the first of a series of basins along the Rio Grande River, is marked by cold winters and moderate summers, light precipitation, and much sunshine. About 80 percent of the annual precipitation occurs from April to October. Winter snows occur as early as September or as late as May. A good snow cover will remain on the ground for several weeks during the coldest months. Agriculture is dependent on irrigation, using water from the surrounding mountains. Summer frequently has high temperatures in the mid-80s and lows in the low 40s. Winds are strong, with occasional blowing dust in spring and early summer.

Temperatures

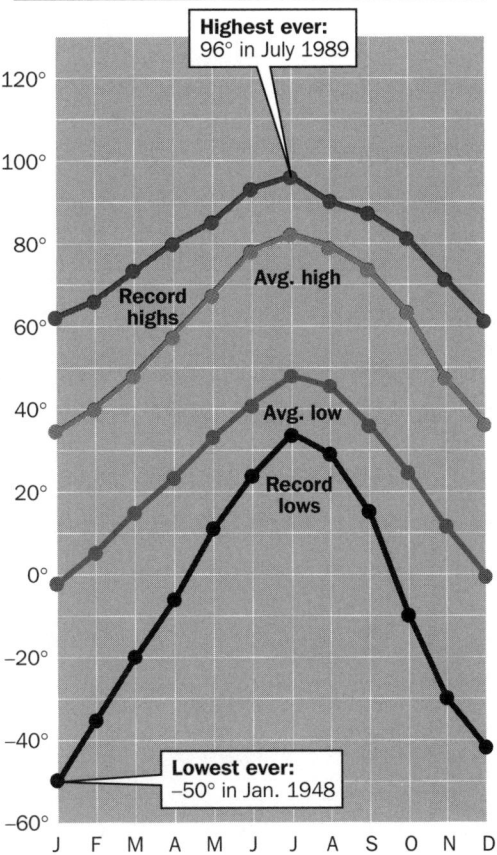

Highest ever: 96° in July 1989

Record highs

Avg. high

Avg. low

Record lows

Lowest ever: −50° in Jan. 1948

Weather extremes

Most rain in 24 hours:	1.82 in. Sept. 30, 1959
Most rain in a month:	5.04 in. August 1993
Most snow in 24 hours:	15.8 in. Dec. 13, 1967
Most snow in a month:	29.2 in. March 1973

Monthly averages

Month	Avg. precip. (in.)	Avg. snow (in.)	Wet days	Thunder-storm days	Pct. sky is cloudy	% p.m. relative humidity	Dew point	Wind speed (mph)
Jan.	0.3	4.5	4	*	26	59	NA	6.3
Feb.	0.3	4.2	4	*	26	50	NA	6.1
March	0.4	6.1	5	*	29	37	NA	10.2
April	0.5	4.4	5	1	26	30	NA	11.9
May	0.7	1.6	6	6	25	28	NA	12.1
June	0.6	T	5	6	13	25	NA	10.2
July	1.2	T	9	12	18	36	NA	8.6
Aug.	1.1	0	10	12	21	38	NA	8.1
Sept.	0.7	0.2	6	5	16	33	NA	7.3
Oct.	0.7	3.2	4	1	20	34	NA	6.9
Nov.	0.4	4.3	4	*	22	48	NA	5.8
Dec.	0.4	5.7	4	0	24	58	NA	5.0

T - Trace of rain or snow   * - Less than 1   NA - Not Available

Annual averages

Precipitation (in inches)	7.3
Snow (in inches)	34.3
Heating degree days	8,717
Cooling degree days	69
Days with thunderstorms	44
Days with fog	17
Days above 90°	1
Days below 32°	227
Wet days	68
Days with snow	NA
Days with 1.0 inches or more snow	12

Percent time sky is clear

Jan.	Feb.	March	April	May	June	July	Aug.	Sept.	Oct.	Nov.	Dec.
41.3	40.4	33.9	32.7	29.4	46.0	28.4	35.2	51.7	53.9	48.0	45.2

Albany, New York

Lat. 42° 45′ N **Lon.** 73° 48′ W **Elev.** 275 ft.

Albany's winters are usually cold and sometimes fairly severe. Maximum temperatures during the colder winters are often below freezing, and nighttime lows are frequently below 10°F. Subzero readings occur about twelve times a year. Snowfall throughout the area is quite variable, and snow flurries are quite frequent during the winter. Most of the rainfall in the summer is from thunderstorms. Tornadoes are quite rare, and hail is not usually of any consequence. The average first occurrence of 32°F in the fall is September 29, and the average last occurrence in the spring is May 7.

Temperatures

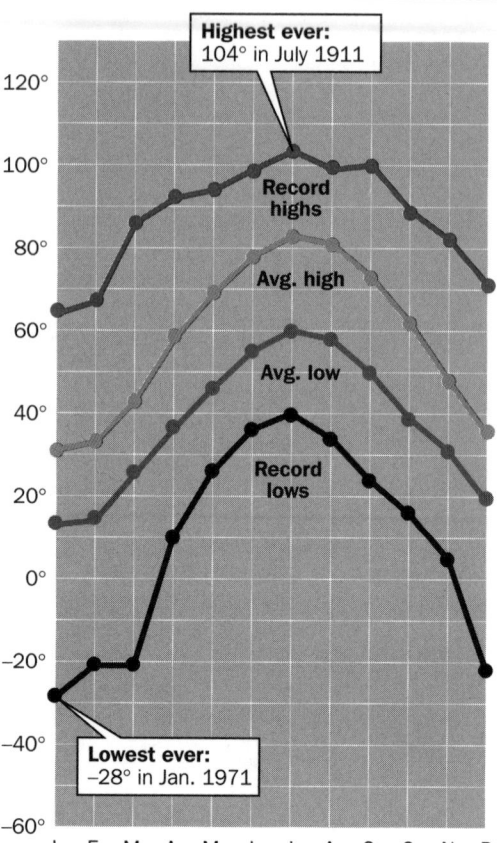

Highest ever: 104° in July 1911

Record highs

Avg. high

Avg. low

Record lows

Lowest ever: −28° in Jan. 1971

Weather extremes

Most rain in 24 hours:	4.75 in. Oct. 8 – 9, 1903
Most rain in a month:	13.48 in. October, 1969
Most snow in 24 hours:	21.9 in. Nov. 24 – 25, 1971
Most snow in a month:	57.5 in. December 1969

Monthly averages

Month	Avg. precip. (in.)	Avg. snow (in.)	Wet days	Thunder-storm days	Pct. sky is cloudy	% p.m. relative humidity	Dew point	Wind speed (mph)
Jan.	2.4	16	12	*	52	64	14	15.0
Feb.	2.3	14	10	*	49	60	15	15.0
March	2.8	11	12	1	48	54	23	15.0
April	2.9	3	12	1	46	49	33	15.0
May	3.6	T	13	3	44	51	45	9.2
June	3.4	0	11	5	37	53	55	9.2
July	3.1	0	10	6	31	53	60	8.1
Aug.	3.3	0	10	5	33	55	59	8.1
Sept.	3.1	0	10	2	35	57	52	8.1
Oct.	2.9	T	9	1	38	56	41	9.2
Nov.	3.1	4	12	*	53	64	31	13.8
Dec.	2.9	14	12	*	55	67	19	13.8

T - Trace of rain or snow   * - Less than 1   NA - Not Available

Annual averages

Precipitation (in inches)	35.8
Snow (in inches)	63
Heating degree days	6,883
Cooling degree days	576
Days with thunderstorms	24
Days with fog	151
Days above 90°	11
Days below 32°	147
Wet days	133
Days with snow	71
Days with 1.5 inches or more snow	24

Percent time sky is clear

Jan.	Feb.	March	April	May	June	July	Aug.	Sept.	Oct.	Nov.	Dec.
16.0	17.9	17.7	16.7	14.3	13.0	13.9	15.7	20.7	22.4	11.8	13.5

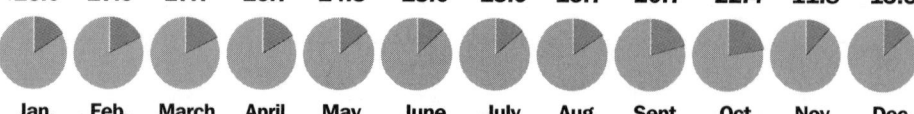

Albuquerque, New Mexico

Lat. 35° 03' N **Lon.** 106° 37' W **Elev.** 5,326 ft.

Albuquerque is situated in the Rio Grande Valley on the mesas and piedmont slopes. The Sandia and Manzano Mountains rise abruptly at the eastern edge of the city with Tijeras Canyon separating the two ranges. West of the city the land gradually rises to the Continental Divide 90 miles away. The climate is arid with abundant sunshine, low humidity, scant precipitation, and a wide yet tolerable seasonal range of temperatures. Nearly half its precipitation comes from summer thunderstorms, which peak in August, then taper off through September. Blowing dust accompanies the occasional strong winds of winter and spring.

Temperatures

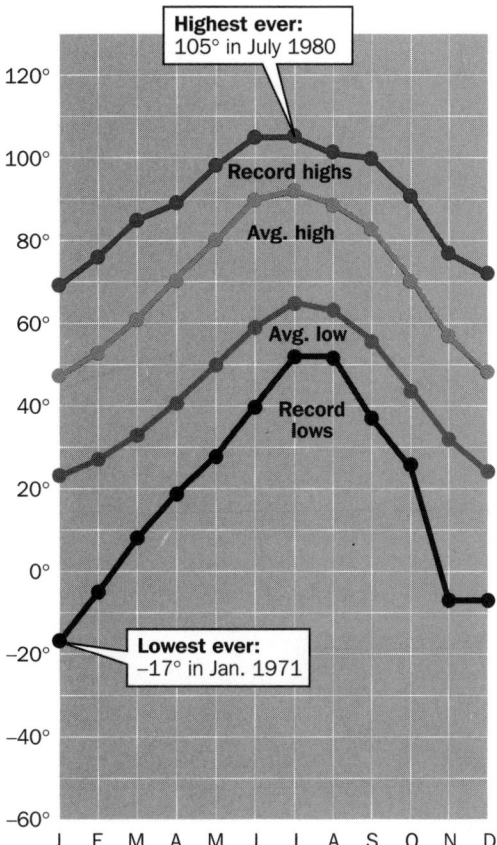

Highest ever: 105° in July 1980

Record highs

Avg. high

Avg. low

Record lows

Lowest ever: −17° in Jan. 1971

Weather extremes

Most rain in 24 hours:	2.26 in. Sept. 27 – 28, 1893
Most rain in a month:	8.15 in. June 1852
Most snow in 24 hours:	14.2 in. Dec. 28 – 29, 1958
Most snow in a month:	14.7 in. December, 1959

Monthly averages

Month	Avg. precip. (in.)	Avg. snow (in.)	Wet days	Thunder-storm days	Pct. sky is cloudy	% p.m. relative humidity	Dew point	Wind speed (mph)
Jan.	0.4	3	4	*	25	41	18	9.2
Feb.	0.4	2	4	*	24	33	19	9.2
March	0.5	2	5	1	23	25	19	9.2
April	0.5	1	3	1	18	19	22	10.4
May	0.5	T	4	4	15	18	28	10.4
June	0.5	0	4	5	10	17	36	10.4
July	1.3	0	9	10	16	27	49	12.7
Aug.	1.5	0	9	10	16	30	50	8.1
Sept.	0.9	T	5	4	13	29	43	8.1
Oct.	0.9	T	4	2	13	30	32	8.1
Nov.	0.4	1	3	1	17	35	23	8.1
Dec.	0.5	3	4	*	22	43	19	9.2

T - Trace of rain or snow   * - Less than 1   NA - Not Available

Annual averages

Precipitation (in inches)	8.3
Snow (in inches)	11
Heating degree days	4,304
Cooling degree days	1,356
Days with thunderstorms	38
Days with fog	14
Days above 90°	66
Days below 32°	114
Wet days	58
Days with snow	18
Days with 1.5 inches or more snow	6

Percent time sky is clear

Jan.	Feb.	March	April	May	June	July	Aug.	Sept.	Oct.	Nov.	Dec.
40.5	37.5	35.6	39.2	38.2	41.8	21.2	24.8	44.3	52.1	47.8	43.9

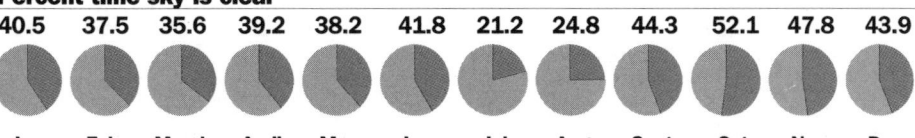

Allentown, Pennsylvania

Lat. 40° 39' N **Lon.** 75° 26' W **Elev.** 388 ft.

Allentown is in the Lehigh River Valley. Twelve miles to the north is Blue Mountain, and the South Mountain fringes the southern edge of the city. Temperatures are usually moderate and precipitation generally ample and dependable with the largest amounts occurring during the summer. Climatological features of the area are slightly modified by the mountain ranges so that at times during the winter there is a temperature difference of 10 to 15 degrees between Allentown and Philadelphia, only 50 miles to the south. Although temperatures during most years are not excessively high, the average humidity in the valley is quite high. Winters in the valley are comparatively mild, although freezing rain is a common problem.

Temperatures

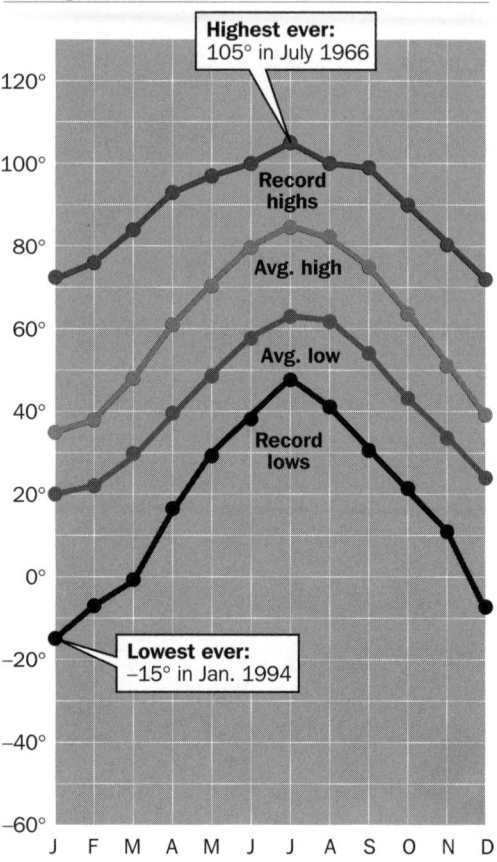

Highest ever: 105° in July 1966

Record highs

Avg. high

Avg. low

Record lows

Lowest ever: −15° in Jan. 1994

Weather extremes

Most rain in 24 hours:	7.85 in. Sept. 26 – 27, 1985
Most rain in a month:	12.10 in. August 1955
Most snow in 24 hours:	25.2 in. Feb. 11 – 12, 1983
Most snow in a month:	43.2 in. January 1925

Monthly averages

Month	Avg. precip. (in.)	Avg. snow (in.)	Wet days	Thunder-storm days	Pct. sky is cloudy	% p.m. relative humidity	Dew point	Wind speed (mph)
Jan.	3.2	9	11	*	46	62	18	13.8
Feb.	3.0	9	10	*	44	57	20	15.0
March	3.5	6	11	1	43	51	26	16.1
April	3.8	1	11	2	41	48	36	10.4
May	4.2	T	12	4	40	52	48	9.2
June	3.6	0	10	6	32	52	57	9.2
July	4.3	0	10	7	29	52	62	8.1
Aug.	4.4	0	10	6	31	55	61	8.1
Sept.	3.9	0	9	3	34	57	55	8.1
Oct.	2.9	T	8	1	33	56	44	9.2
Nov.	3.8	1	10	1	43	60	33	12.7
Dec.	3.6	6	11	*	47	64	23	12.7

T - Trace of rain or snow   * - Less than 1   NA - Not Available

Annual averages

Precipitation (in inches)	44.2
Snow (in inches)	32
Heating degree days	5,740
Cooling degree days	831
Days with thunderstorms	31
Days with fog	187
Days above 90°	15
Days below 32°	123
Wet days	123
Days with snow	38
Days with 1.5 inches or more snow	14

Percent time sky is clear

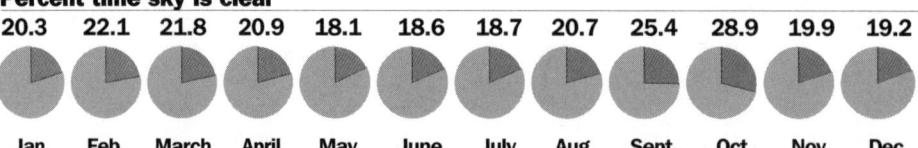

20.3	22.1	21.8	20.9	18.1	18.6	18.7	20.7	25.4	28.9	19.9	19.2
Jan.	Feb.	March	April	May	June	July	Aug.	Sept.	Oct.	Nov.	Dec.

Alpena, Michigan

Lat. 45° 04' N **Lon.** 83° 34' W **Elev.** 689 ft.

Alpena lies on the northwest shore of Thunder Bay, 8 miles from the open waters of Lake Huron. Summer showers moving from the southwest weaken and sometimes dissipate as they approach Alpena. Winter storms often bring east winds. The climate of Alpena is influenced by its location with respect to major storm tracks and the effects of the Great Lakes, which modify most climatic extremes. Precipitation amounts are distributed evenly throughout the year. Summers in Alpena are warm and sunny. Winter months are cloudy and marked by frequent snow flurries. Storms bring heavier snowfall. Freezing temperatures have occurred as late as late June and as early as late August.

Weather extremes

Most rain in 24 hours:	3.02 in. Sept. 10, 1968
Most rain in a month:	8.37 in. June 1969
Most snow in 24 hours:	17.30 in. March 4, 1985
Most snow in a month:	46 in. December 1989

Temperatures

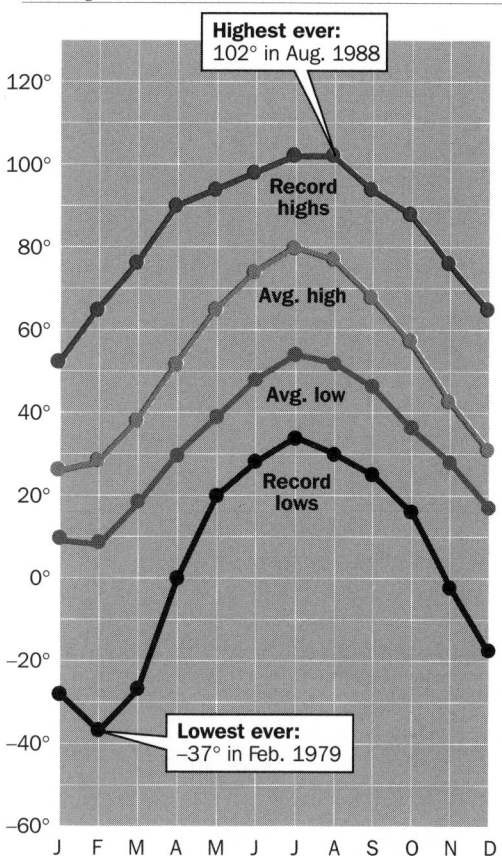

Highest ever: 102° in Aug. 1988

Record highs

Avg. high

Avg. low

Record lows

Lowest ever: −37° in Feb. 1979

Monthly averages

Month	Avg. precip. (in.)	Avg. snow (in.)	Wet days	Thunder-storm days	Pct. sky is cloudy	% p.m. relative humidity	Dew point	Wind speed (mph)
Jan.	1.6	22	14	*	61	67	12	10.4
Feb.	1.3	16	11	*	55	62	12	9.2
March	2.1	14	13	1	50	59	20	10.4
April	2.3	5	12	2	47	53	29	9.2
May	2.8	T	11	4	40	51	40	9.2
June	3.1	0	11	5	34	53	51	9.2
July	2.9	0	10	7	27	53	56	6.9
Aug.	3.3	0	11	6	31	59	56	6.9
Sept.	3.1	T	12	4	40	62	50	8.1
Oct.	2.1	1	13	1	48	61	39	8.1
Nov.	2.2	9	13	*	66	68	29	9.2
Dec.	2.0	21	16	*	69	72	19	8.1

T - Trace of rain or snow   * - Less than 1   NA - Not Available

Annual averages

Precipitation (in inches)	28.8
Snow (in inches)	86
Heating degree days	8,307
Cooling degree days	290
Days with thunderstorms	30
Days with fog	156
Days above 90°	7
Days below 32°	177
Wet days	147
Days with snow	134
Days with 1.5 inches or more snow	38

Percent time sky is clear

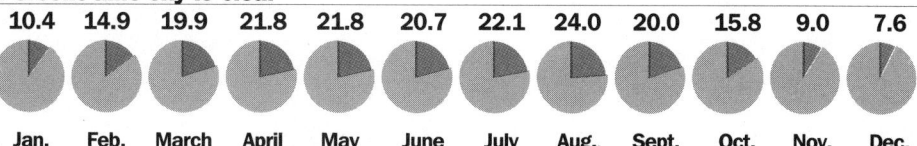

Jan.	Feb.	March	April	May	June	July	Aug.	Sept.	Oct.	Nov.	Dec.
10.4	14.9	19.9	21.8	21.8	20.7	22.1	24.0	20.0	15.8	9.0	7.6

Amarillo, Texas

Lat. 35° 14' N **Lon.** 101° 42' W **Elev.** 3,590 ft.

The Amarillo area is subject to rapid and large temperature changes, especially during the winter when cold fronts from the northern Rocky Mountains and Plains states sweep across the area. Temperature drops of 50 to 60 degrees within a 12-hour period are not uncommon. Temperature drops of 40 degrees have occurred within a few minutes. Low humidity moderates the effect of high summer afternoon temperatures, providing many pleasant evenings and nights. A few thunderstorms with damaging hail, lightning, and wind in a very localized area occur most years, usually in spring and summer. These storms are often accompanied by heavy rain, which produces local flooding. The average first occurrence of 32°F in the fall is October 29 and the average last occurrence in the spring is April 14.

Weather extremes

Most rain in 24 hours:	6.75 in. May 15 – 16, 1951
Most rain in a month:	10.73 in. June 1965
Most snow in 24 hours:	20.6 in. March 25–26, 1934
Most snow in a month:	28.7 in. February 1903

Temperatures

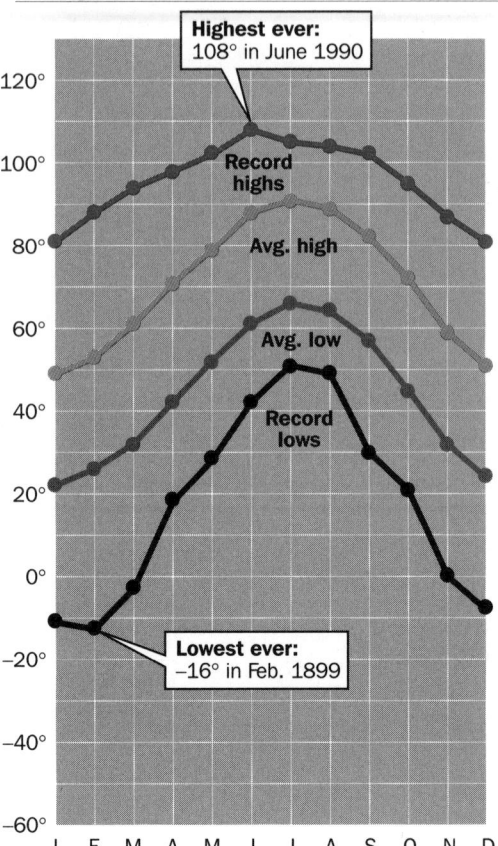

Highest ever: 108° in June 1990

Record highs

Avg. high

Avg. low

Record lows

Lowest ever: −16° in Feb. 1899

Monthly averages

Month	Avg. precip. (in.)	Avg. snow (in.)	Wet days	Thunder-storm days	Pct. sky is cloudy	% p.m. relative humidity	Dew point	Wind speed (mph)
Jan.	0.5	4	4	*	30	41	19	13.8
Feb.	0.6	4	5	1	32	41	22	13.8
March	0.9	3	5	2	30	34	25	16.1
April	1.1	1	5	3	26	31	33	16.1
May	2.8	T	8	8	27	36	45	16.1
June	3.5	0	8	10	19	37	54	15.0
July	2.8	0	8	9	17	36	58	13.8
Aug.	3.1	0	8	9	17	38	58	12.7
Sept.	1.9	T	6	4	22	40	51	13.8
Oct.	1.4	T	5	2	20	36	39	13.8
Nov.	0.6	2	3	1	24	38	28	13.8
Dec.	0.5	2	4	*	27	40	21	13.8

T - Trace of rain or snow   * - Less than 1   NA - Not Available

Annual averages

Precipitation (in inches)	19.8
Snow (in inches)	15
Heating degree days	4,229
Cooling degree days	1,456
Days with thunderstorms	49
Days with fog	68
Days above 90°	66
Days below 32°	111
Wet days	69
Days with snow	23
Days with 1.5 inches or more snow	8

Percent time sky is clear

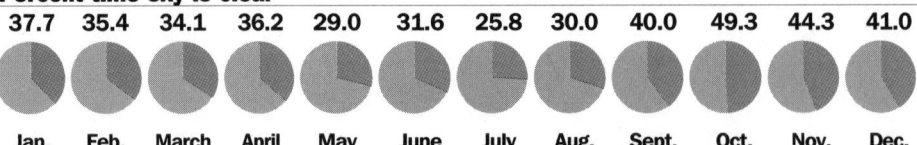

37.7	35.4	34.1	36.2	29.0	31.6	25.8	30.0	40.0	49.3	44.3	41.0
Jan.	Feb.	March	April	May	June	July	Aug.	Sept.	Oct.	Nov.	Dec.

Anchorage, Alaska

Lat. 61° 10' N **Lon.** 150° 01' W **Elev.** 114 ft.

Anchorage is in a broad valley with the Cook Inlet to the west, north, and south and the Chugach Mountains, with elevations from 4,000 to 10,000 feet, lying north-northeast to south-southwest. This range acts as a barrier to warm, moist air from the Gulf of Alaska. The Alaska Mountain Range, which arcs southwest to northeast about 100 miles distant, keeps out cold air from the north side of the range. In the summer, rain increases. About two-thirds of July and August days are cloudy and one-third have rain. Autumn is brief and winter runs from mid-October to early April. In January, very cold days have high temperatures below zero. Most winter precipitation is light or dry snow. Spring days are warm and sunny and precipitation is slight.

Weather extremes

Most rain in 24 hours:	4.12 in. Aug. 25 – 26, 1989
Most rain in a month:	9.77 in. August 1989
Most snow in 24 hours:	22.3 in. Dec. 28 – 29, 1955
Most snow in a month:	48.5 in. February 1955

Temperatures

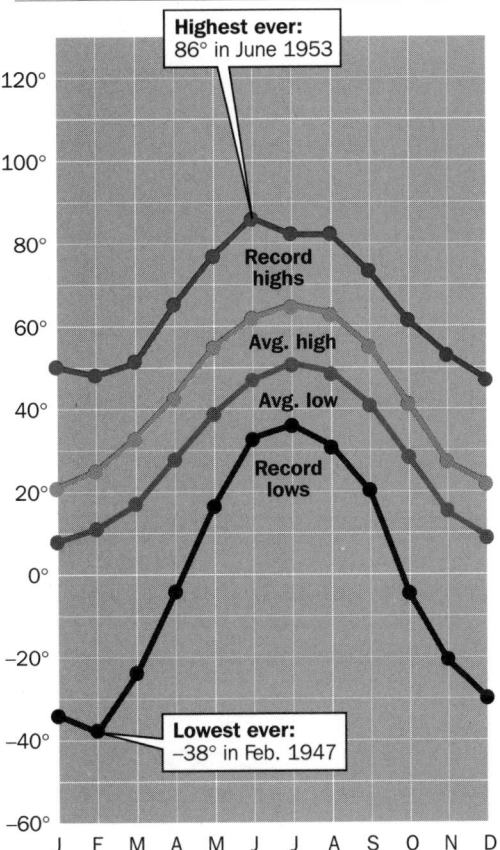

Highest ever: 86° in June 1953

Record highs

Avg. high

Avg. low

Record lows

Lowest ever: −38° in Feb. 1947

Monthly averages

Month	Avg. precip. (in.)	Avg. snow (in.)	Wet days	Thunder-storm days	Pct. sky is cloudy	% p.m. relative humidity	Dew point	Wind speed (mph)
Jan.	0.8	9	8	0	52	72	8	9.2
Feb.	0.8	12	8	0	52	66	10	9.2
March	0.6	9	7	0	48	56	15	8.1
April	0.6	6	7	0	51	54	24	6.9
May	0.7	T	7	*	54	50	34	12.7
June	1.1	0	8	*	56	55	42	12.7
July	1.9	0	12	*	58	62	48	11.5
Aug.	2.4	0	14	*	58	64	48	11.5
Sept.	2.6	T	14	*	59	64	40	10.4
Oct.	1.9	8	11	0	58	66	27	8.1
Nov.	1.1	11	9	0	54	74	15	8.1
Dec.	1.1	15	11	0	56	76	10	8.1

T - Trace of rain or snow   * - Less than 1   NA - Not Available

Annual averages

Precipitation (in inches)	15.8
Snow (in inches)	70
Heating degree days	10,570
Cooling degree days	2
Days with thunderstorms	2
Days with fog	73
Days above 65°	40
Days below 32°	194
Wet days	116
Days with snow	99
Days with 1.5 inches or more snow	32

Percent time sky is clear

Jan.	Feb.	March	April	May	June	July	Aug.	Sept.	Oct.	Nov.	Dec.
20.4	21.5	23.4	16	8.7	5.1	6.4	8.2	10.6	14.9	18	17.3

Asheville, North Carolina
Lat. 35° 26′ N **Lon.** 82° 33′ W **Elev.** 2,140 ft.

Asheville is located on both banks of the French Broad River, near the center of the French Broad Basin. It is flanked by mountain ridges to the east and west whose peaks range from 2,000 to 4,400 feet above the valley floor. Asheville has a temperate but invigorating climate. The temperature can vary considerably from day to day, particularly in summer. The valley's orientation results in a year-round prevailing wind from the northwest. The mountains cause precipitation to be spread unevenly. These conditions cause floods on the French Broad River at roughly 12-year intervals.

Temperatures

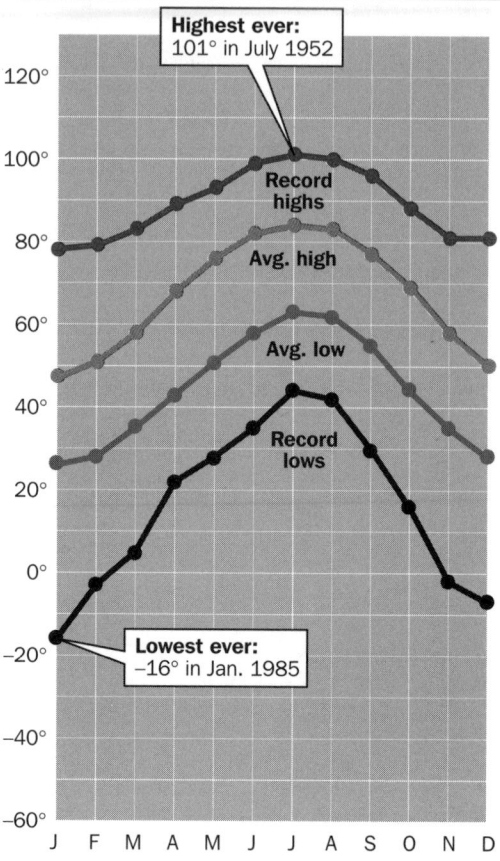

Highest ever: 101° in July 1952

Record highs

Avg. high

Avg. low

Record lows

Lowest ever: −16° in Jan. 1985

Weather extremes

Most rain in 24 hours:	5.13 in. March 11–12, 1968
Most rain in a month:	11.28 in. August 1967
Most snow in 24 hours:	16.5 in. March 13–14, 1993
Most snow in a month:	26 in. February 1969

Monthly averages

Month	Avg. precip. (in.)	Avg. snow (in.)	Wet days	Thunder-storm days	Pct. sky is cloudy	% p.m. relative humidity	Dew point	Wind speed (mph)
Jan.	3.1	4	10	*	42	56	27	13.8
Feb.	3.6	4	10	1	40	53	28	13.8
March	4.6	3	12	2	38	50	34	13.8
April	3.4	1	10	3	32	47	42	12.7
May	4.0	0	11	7	33	56	53	10.4
June	3.8	0	11	8	30	59	61	9.2
July	4.2	0	13	10	30	63	65	8.1
Aug.	4.5	0	12	9	31	64	64	8.1
Sept.	3.6	0	9	3	36	62	58	9.2
Oct.	3.3	T	8	1	30	55	46	10.4
Nov.	3.3	1	9	1	33	54	36	12.7
Dec.	3.4	2	10	*	39	56	29	12.7

T - Trace of rain or snow   * - Less than 1   NA - Not Available

Annual averages

Precipitation (in inches)	44.8
Snow (in inches)	14
Heating degree days	4,253
Cooling degree days	868
Days with thunderstorms	45
Days with fog	209
Days above 90°	11
Days below 32°	99
Wet days	125
Days with snow	9
Days with 1.5 inches or more snow	2

Percent time sky is clear

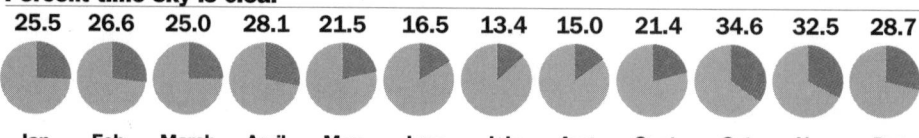

Jan.	Feb.	March	April	May	June	July	Aug.	Sept.	Oct.	Nov.	Dec.
25.5	26.6	25.0	28.1	21.5	16.5	13.4	15.0	21.4	34.6	32.5	28.7

Astoria, Oregon

Lat. 46° 09' N **Lon.** 123° 53' W **Elev.** 8 ft.

When air temperature falls below water temperature in Astoria, fog forms easily or rolls in from the ocean, river, or bay. Even with moderate surface winds, airplanes at an altitude of 800 feet may feel wind and turbulence severe enough to upset a heavy plane. Occasionally in fair weather, wind and wave may produce a breaker — known as the widowmaker — that can swamp a boat. Heavy rains inundate lowlands, and high tides aggravated by gales may push seawater across highways or up beaches. Rain may cause earthslides, mostly in highway cuts.

Temperatures

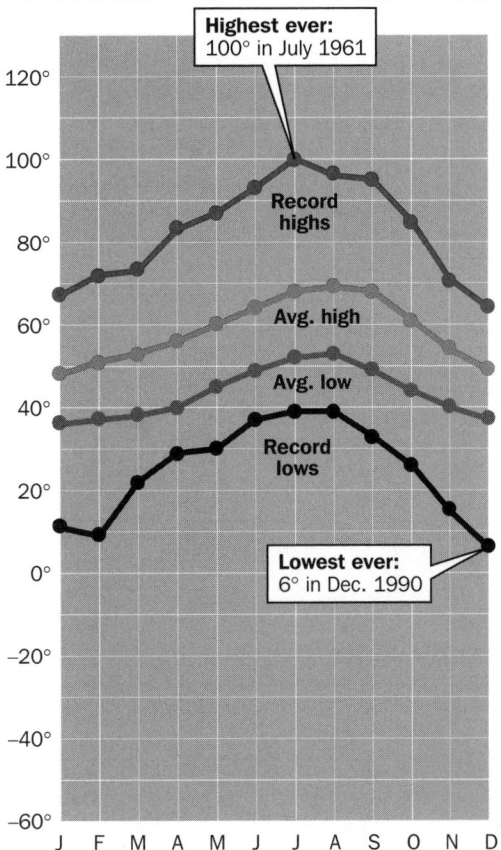

Highest ever:
100° in July 1961

Record highs

Avg. high

Avg. low

Record lows

Lowest ever:
6° in Dec. 1990

Weather extremes

Most rain in 24 hours:	5.14 in. January 8-9, 1990
Most rain in a month:	21.89 in. February 1961
Most snow in 24 hours:	10.8 in. January 12, 1971
Most snow in a month:	26.3 in. January 1969

Monthly averages

Month	Avg. precip. (in.)	Avg. snow (in.)	Wet days	Thunder-storm days	Pct. sky is cloudy	% p.m. relative humidity	Dew point	Wind speed (mph)
Jan.	10.3	2	22	1	66	79	37	8.1
Feb.	7.6	T	19	*	63	75	39	8.1
March	7.2	1	21	*	60	71	39	5.8
April	4.6	T	18	1	56	69	41	10.4
May	3.0	T	15	*	53	70	46	12.7
June	2.6	0	13	*	56	71	50	11.5
July	1.1	0	7	*	51	69	53	11.5
Aug.	1.4	0	8	*	49	71	54	11.5
Sept.	2.9	0	10	1	43	70	52	9.2
Oct.	6.1	T	16	1	51	73	48	5.8
Nov.	10.2	T	21	1	61	78	42	6.9
Dec.	10.6	1	22	1	64	81	38	8.1

T - Trace of rain or snow   * - Less than 1   NA - Not Available

Annual averages

Precipitation (in inches)	67.7
Snow (in inches)	5
Heating degree days	5,090
Cooling degree days	19
Days with thunderstorms	6
Days with fog	186
Days above 65°	99
Days below 32°	38
Wet days	192
Days with snow	8
Days with 1.5 inches or more snow	1

Percent time sky is clear

10.1	10.4	9.9	9.6	9.6	9.7	18.2	17.1	23.0	15.8	10.4	9.2

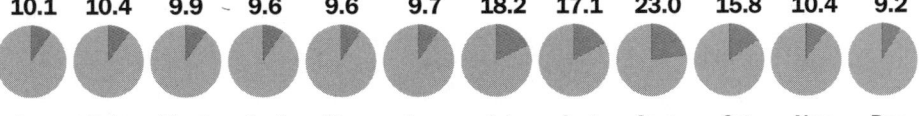

| Jan. | Feb. | March | April | May | June | July | Aug. | Sept. | Oct. | Nov. | Dec. |

Atlanta, Georgia

Lat. 33° 39' N **Lon.** 84° 26' W **Elev.** 1,010 ft.

The Appalachian Mountains, the Gulf of Mexico, and the Atlantic Ocean exert an important influence on the Atlanta climate. Temperatures are moderated throughout the year. Prolonged hot weather is unusual and 100 degree heat is rare. The mountains tend to retard the southward movement of polar air masses, and Atlanta winters are rather mild. Late March is the average date of the last temperature of 32°F in the spring and mid-November is the average date of the first temperature of 32°F in the fall. Maximum thunderstorm activity occurs during July, but severe local thunderstorms occur most frequently in March, April and May, some spawning damaging tornadoes.

Temperatures

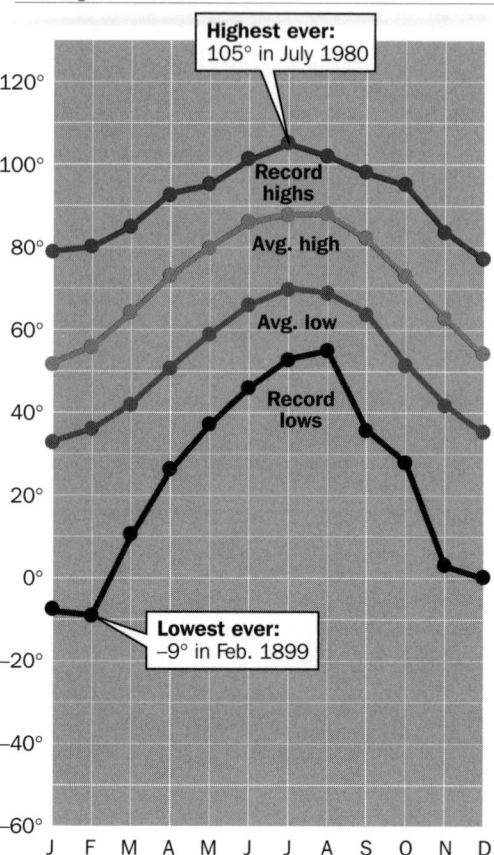

Highest ever: 105° in July 1980

Record highs

Avg. high

Avg. low

Record lows

Lowest ever: −9° in Feb. 1899

Weather extremes

Most rain in 24 hours:	7.36 in. March 29, 1886
Most rain in a month:	17.71 in. July 1994
Most snow in 24 hours:	10.0 in. Jan. 23, 1940
Most snow in a month:	11.6 in. February 1895

Monthly averages

Month	Avg. precip. (in.)	Avg. snow (in.)	Wet days	Thunder-storm days	Pct. sky is cloudy	% p.m. relative humidity	Dew point	Wind speed (mph)
Jan.	4.7	1	12	1	47	56	31	12.7
Feb.	4.6	1	10	2	42	50	32	12.7
March	5.7	T	11	3	41	48	39	12.7
April	4.3	T	9	4	32	45	46	11.5
May	4.0	0	9	6	28	49	56	10.4
June	3.5	0	10	8	26	52	64	9.2
July	5.1	0	12	10	27	57	68	8.1
Aug.	3.6	0	9	8	24	56	67	8.1
Sept.	3.4	0	8	3	29	56	62	10.4
Oct.	2.8	0	7	1	26	51	50	9.2
Nov.	3.8	T	9	1	35	52	41	11.5
Dec.	4.2	T	10	1	43	55	33	11.5

T - Trace of rain or snow   * - Less than 1   NA - Not Available

Annual averages

Precipitation (in inches)	49.8
Snow (in inches)	2
Heating degree days	2,941
Cooling degree days	1,756
Days with thunderstorms	48
Days with fog	148
Days above 90°	38
Days below 32°	49
Wet days	116
Days with snow	4
Days with 1.5 inches or more snow	*

Percent time sky is clear

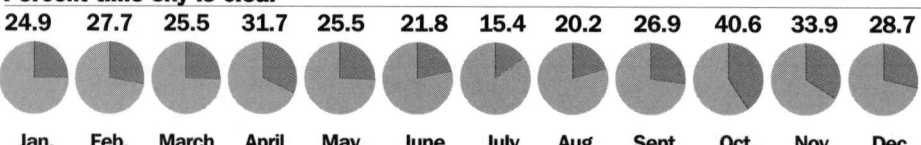

24.9	27.7	25.5	31.7	25.5	21.8	15.4	20.2	26.9	40.6	33.9	28.7
Jan.	Feb.	March	April	May	June	July	Aug.	Sept.	Oct.	Nov.	Dec.

Atlantic City, New Jersey

Lat. 39° 27' N **Lon.** 74° 34' W **Elev.** 138 ft.

Atlantic City is located on Absecon Island on the southeast coast of New Jersey. The surrounding terrain of tidal marshes and beach sand lies slightly above sea level. The climate is moderated by the Atlantic Ocean, making summers cooler and winters milder than elsewhere at the same latitude. Land and sea breezes often prevail. In summer, sea breezes keep Atlantic City cool — often several degrees cooler than places inland. Precipitation is moderate and well distributed throughout the year. Tropical storms or hurricanes occasionally bring excessive rain.

Temperatures

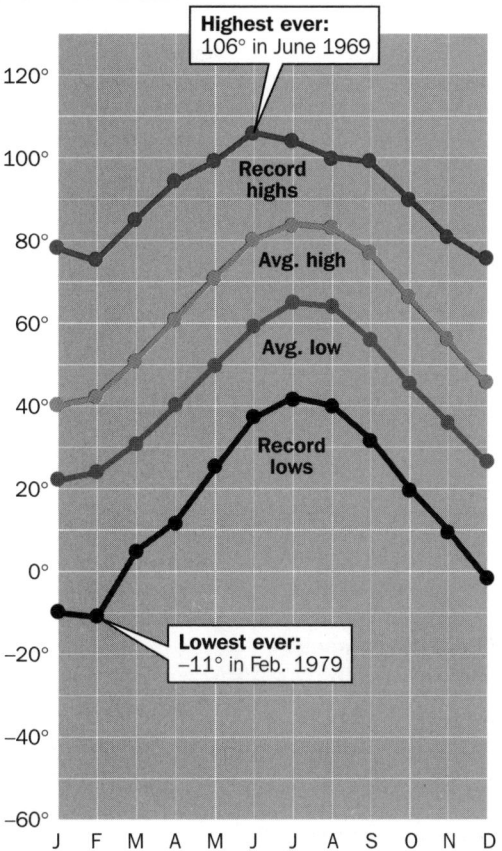

Weather extremes

Most rain in 24 hours:	6.46 in. July 10, 1959
Most rain in a month:	13.09 in. July 1959
Most snow in 24 hours:	17.1 in. Feb. 19, 1979
Most snow in a month:	35.2 in. February 1967

Monthly averages

Month	Avg. precip. (in.)	Avg. snow (in.)	Wet days	Thunder-storm days	Pct. sky is cloudy	% p.m. relative humidity	Dew point	Wind speed (mph)
Jan.	3.4	6	10	*	41	59	22	13.8
Feb.	3.1	6	10	*	42	58	23	13.8
March	3.6	2	10	1	40	55	30	15.0
April	3.5	T	10	2	39	53	38	13.8
May	3.3	T	10	3	38	57	50	11.5
June	2.5	0	9	5	32	58	59	10.4
July	4.4	0	9	6	30	60	65	10.4
Aug.	4.3	0	9	5	29	61	65	9.2
Sept.	2.9	0	8	2	30	61	58	9.2
Oct.	3.0	T	7	1	31	59	47	10.4
Nov.	3.5	1	9	1	36	61	37	12.7
Dec.	3.3	3	10	*	41	61	27	13.8

T - Trace of rain or snow   * - Less than 1   NA - Not Available

Annual averages

Precipitation (in inches)	40.7
Snow (in inches)	18
Heating degree days	4,763
Cooling degree days	964
Days with thunderstorms	26
Days with fog	174
Days above 90°	17
Days below 32°	108
Wet days	111
Days with snow	19
Days with 1.5 inches or more snow	8

Percent time sky is clear

26.8	27.3	26.1	24.7	18.6	18.4	17.1	19.7	25.1	30.7	25.2	25.7

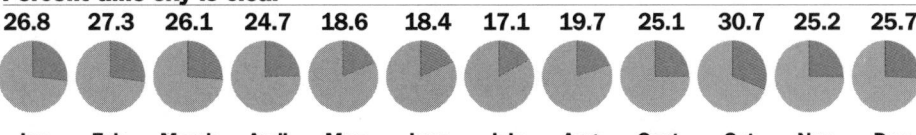

| Jan. | Feb. | March | April | May | June | July | Aug. | Sept. | Oct. | Nov. | Dec. |

Augusta, Georgia

Lat. 33° 22' N **Lon.** 81° 58' W **Elev.** 148 ft.

The boundary between the Piedmont Plateau and the Coastal Plain, known as the Fall Line, crosses the Savannah River basin in a general northeast-southwest direction near Augusta. There are hills to the west and south, swampland to the north, east, and south. The average last occurrence in the spring of temperatures of 32°F is mid-March, and the first in the fall is mid-November. Very low temperatures and measurable snow are both rare. The length of the growing season averages 241 days. Augusta is protected from the flooding of the Savannah River by the Clark Hill and Hartwell dams.

Temperatures

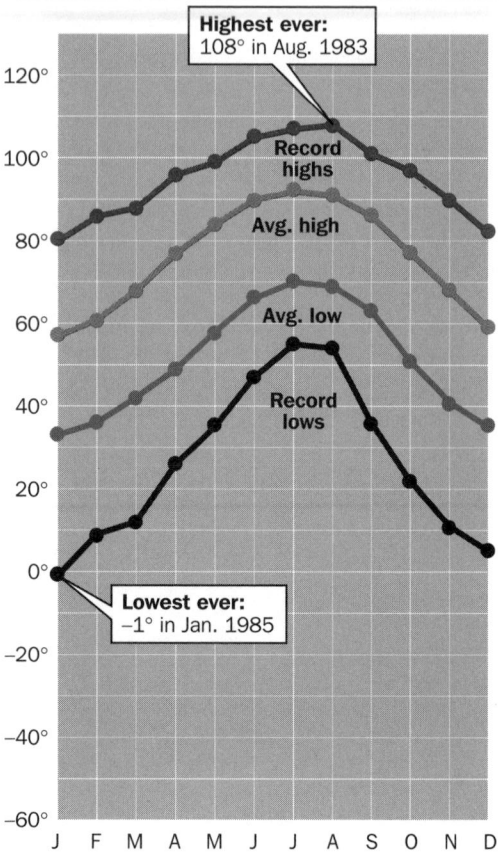

Highest ever: 108° in Aug. 1983

Record highs

Avg. high

Avg. low

Record lows

Lowest ever: −1° in Jan. 1985

Weather extremes

Most rain in 24 hours:	5.9 in. Aug. 29, 1964
Most rain in a month:	14.8 in. October 1990
Most snow in 24 hours:	8.0 in. Feb. 9, 1973
Most snow in a month:	14 in. February 1973

Monthly averages

Month	Avg. precip. (in.)	Avg. snow (in.)	Wet days	Thunder-storm days	Pct. sky is cloudy	% p.m. relative humidity	Dew point	Wind speed (mph)
Jan.	3.8	T	10	1	43	51	34	10.4
Feb.	4.1	1	9	2	40	47	36	11.5
March	4.5	T	10	3	39	45	41	11.5
April	3.3	0	8	4	29	43	49	6.9
May	3.7	0	9	7	28	47	59	6.9
June	3.8	0	9	9	26	51	66	6.9
July	4.4	0	11	13	27	55	70	6.9
Aug.	4.2	0	10	10	25	55	69	5.8
Sept.	3.2	0	8	4	30	54	64	8.1
Oct.	2.6	0	6	1	26	48	53	8.1
Nov.	2.3	T	7	1	31	47	43	9.2
Dec.	3.3	T	9	1	39	51	36	9.2

T - Trace of rain or snow   * - Less than 1   NA - Not Available

Annual averages

Precipitation (in inches)	43.2
Snow (in inches)	1
Heating degree days	2,528
Cooling degree days	2,058
Days with thunderstorms	56
Days with fog	188
Days above 90°	76
Days below 32°	55
Wet days	106
Days with snow	1
Days with 1.5 inches or more snow	*

Percent time sky is clear

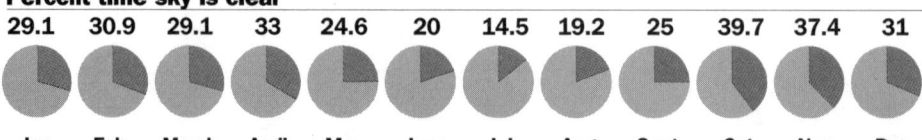

Jan.	Feb.	March	April	May	June	July	Aug.	Sept.	Oct.	Nov.	Dec.
29.1	30.9	29.1	33	24.6	20	14.5	19.2	25	39.7	37.4	31

Austin, Texas

Lat. 30° 18' N **Lon.** 97° 42' W **Elev.** 597 ft.

Austin, capital of Texas, is located on the Colorado River where the stream crosses the Balcones escarpment separating the Texas Hill Country from the Blackland Prairies to the east. Elevations within the city vary from 400 feet to nearly 1,000 feet above sea level. The climate of Austin is humid subtropical with hot summers. Winters are mild. Strong northerly winds accompanied by sharp drops in temperature frequently occur during the winter months, but cold spells seldom last more than two days. Daytime temperatures in summer are hot, but summer nights are usually pleasant. Prevailing winds are southerly. Blowing dust occurs occasionally in spring, but visibility rarely drops substantially, and then only for a few hours.

Temperatures

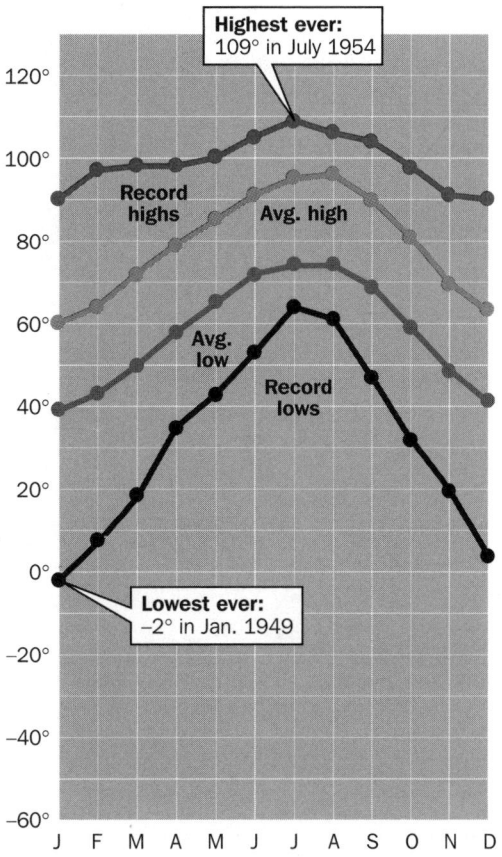

Highest ever: 109° in July 1954

Record highs

Avg. high

Avg. low

Record lows

Lowest ever: –2° in Jan. 1949

Weather extremes

Most rain in 24 hours:	7.22 in. Oct. 28 – 29, 1960
Most rain in a month:	14.96 in. June 1981
Most snow in 24 hours:	7.0 in. Jan. 13 – 14, 1944
Most snow in a month:	7.5 in. January 1985

Monthly averages

Month	Avg. precip. (in.)	Avg. snow (in.)	Wet days	Thunder-storm days	Pct. sky is cloudy	% p.m. relative humidity	Dew point	Wind speed (mph)
Jan.	1.6	1	8	1	45	53	37	9.2
Feb.	2.3	T	8	2	43	51	41	10.4
March	1.8	T	7	3	41	47	46	11.5
April	2.9	0	7	4	42	50	55	11.5
May	4.3	0	9	7	35	53	63	11.5
June	3.5	0	6	5	19	49	68	10.4
July	1.9	0	5	4	12	43	69	9.2
Aug.	1.9	0	5	5	11	42	68	8.1
Sept.	3.3	0	7	4	22	47	65	8.1
Oct.	3.5	0	7	3	25	47	56	8.1
Nov.	2.1	T	7	2	35	49	47	9.2
Dec.	1.9	T	7	1	41	51	40	9.2

T - Trace of rain or snow   * - Less than 1   NA - Not Available

Annual averages

Precipitation (inches)	31.1
Snow (in inches)	1
Heating degree days	1,710
Cooling degree days	3,013
Days with thunderstorms	41
Days with fog	115
Days above 90°	111
Days below 32°	20
Wet days	83
Days with snow	1
Days with 1.5 inches or more snow	*

Percent time sky is clear

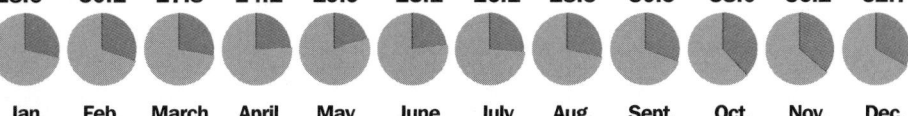

Jan.	Feb.	March	April	May	June	July	Aug.	Sept.	Oct.	Nov.	Dec.
28.6	30.1	27.8	24.1	19.9	23.1	26.1	28.5	30.5	38.0	36.2	32.7

Baltimore, Maryland

Lat. 39°11' N **Lon.** 76°40' W **Elev.** 196 ft.

Baltimore lies in a region about midway between the rigorous climates of the North and the mild climates of the South, and adjacent to the modifying influences of the Chesapeake Bay and Atlantic Ocean to the east and the Appalachian Mountains to the west. Since this region is near the average path of the low pressure systems that move across the country, changes in wind direction are frequent and contribute to the changeable character of the weather. Winter and spring have the highest average wind speed. Destructive velocities are rare and occur mostly during summer thunderstorms. Only rarely have hurricanes in the vicinity caused widespread damage, then primarily through flooding.

Weather extremes

Most rain in 24 hours:	7.82 in.
	Aug. 12 – 13, 1955
Most rain in a month:	18.3 in.
	August 1955
Most snow in 24 hours:	22.8 in.
	Feb. 11, 1983
Most snow in a month:	33.1 in.
	February 1979

Temperatures

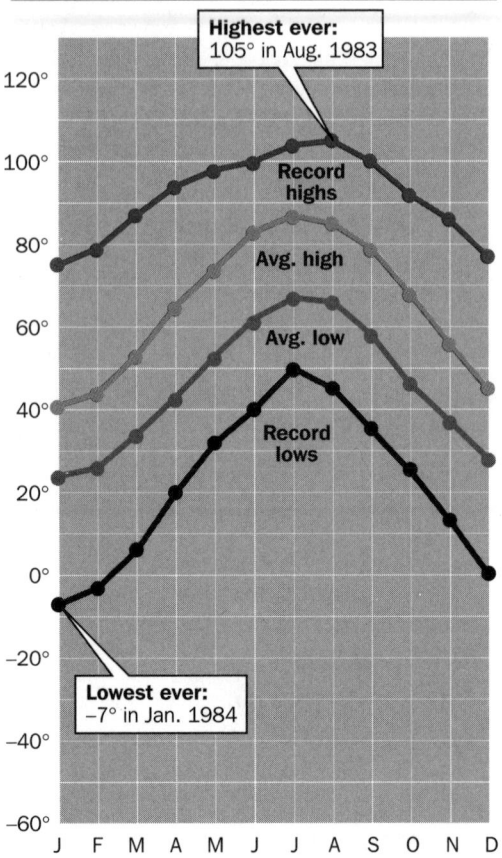

Highest ever: 105° in Aug. 1983

Record highs

Avg. high

Avg. low

Record lows

Lowest ever: –7° in Jan. 1984

Monthly averages

Month	Avg. precip. (in.)	Avg. snow (in.)	Wet days	Thunder-storm days	Pct. sky is cloudy	% p.m. relative humidity	Dew point	Wind speed (mph)
Jan.	2.9	6	10	*	44	56	22	12.7
Feb.	3.0	7	9	*	43	53	23	13.8
March	3.5	4	11	1	41	48	29	13.8
April	3.3	T	11	2	39	47	38	12.7
May	3.7	T	11	4	39	52	51	9.2
June	3.7	0	9	6	29	53	60	8.1
July	3.9	0	9	6	28	53	65	8.1
Aug.	4.2	0	10	5	29	55	64	6.9
Sept.	3.4	0	8	2	31	55	58	6.9
Oct.	3.0	T	7	1	31	54	46	8.1
Nov.	3.2	1	9	*	37	55	35	11.5
Dec.	3.3	4	9	*	43	57	26	12.7

T - Trace of rain or snow   * - Less than 1   NA - Not Available

Annual averages

Precipitation (in inches)	41.2
Snow (in inches)	21
Heating degree days	4,666
Cooling degree days	1,232
Days with thunderstorms	27
Days with fog	146
Days above 90°	31
Days below 32°	97
Wet days	113
Days with snow	23
Days with 1.5 inches or more snow	8

Percent time sky is clear

Jan.	Feb.	March	April	May	June	July	Aug.	Sept.	Oct.	Nov.	Dec.
25.6	26.5	25.6	23.8	20.7	20.8	19.7	22.4	28.0	34.0	27.3	25.4

Barrow, Alaska

Lat. 71° 18′ N **Lon.** 156° 47′ W **Elev.** 31 ft.

Barrow has the Arctic Ocean to the north, east, and west, and level tundra to the south. Thus, there are no natural wind barriers and no downslope drainage areas to aid the flow of cold air to lower levels. Temperatures remain below freezing much of the year. Daily highs above 32°F are reached an average of just 109 days annually. February is generally the coldest month, with May the transitional period from winter to summer. By late July or early August, the Arctic Ocean usually is ice-free for the first time, but by November, Barrow returns to winter and the sun dips below the horizon until January 24. By May 10th the possible sunshine increases to 24 hours per day, and remains visible until August 2. Strong winds have been recorded in all months.

Temperatures

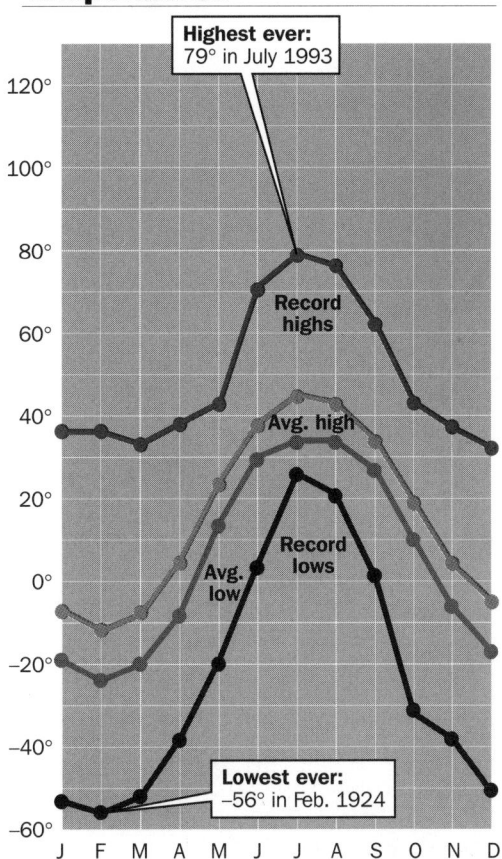

Highest ever: 79° in July 1993

Record highs

Avg. high

Record lows

Avg. low

Lowest ever: −56° in Feb. 1924

Weather extremes

Most rain in 24 hours:	1.38 in. July 21 – 22, 1987
Most rain in a month:	2.81 in. August 1963
Most snow in 24 hours:	15.0 in. Oct. 26, 1926
Most snow in a month:	26.5 in. April 1916

Monthly averages

Month	Avg. precip. (in.)	Avg. snow (in.)	Wet days	Thunder-storm days	Pct. sky is cloudy	% p.m. relative humidity	Dew point	Wind speed (mph)
Jan.	0.2	2	5	*	33	67	-21	12.7
Feb.	0.2	2	5	*	34	65	-25	12.7
March	0.1	2	4	*	29	66	-22	13.8
April	0.2	2	5	0	39	72	-7	13.8
May	0.1	2	5	0	71	83	16	13.8
June	0.3	1	6	*	66	86	31	13.8
July	0.9	T	9	*	60	86	36	13.8
Aug.	1.0	1	12	*	78	88	36	15.0
Sept.	0.6	4	12	0	83	88	28	15.0
Oct.	0.5	6	13	0	71	84	12	16.1
Nov.	0.3	3	7	*	48	76	-7	15.0
Dec.	0.2	2	6	0	39	69	-18	13.8

T - Trace of rain or snow   * - Less than 1   NA - Not Available

Annual averages

Precipitation (in inches)	4.7
Snow (in inches)	28
Heating degree days	20,370
Cooling degree days	0
Days with thunderstorms	1
Days with fog	206
Days above 65°	1
Days below 32°	321
Wet days	89
Days with snow	134
Days with 1.5 inches or more snow	4

Percent time sky is clear

38.1	36.7	41.3	33.3	10.8	6.4	7.7	2.7	1.9	6.7	22.8	34.4

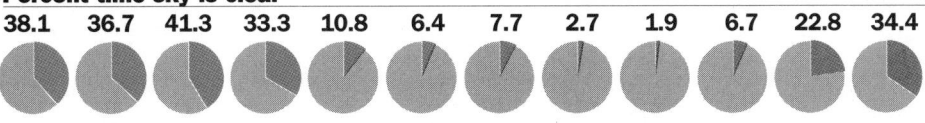

| Jan. | Feb. | March | April | May | June | July | Aug. | Sept. | Oct. | Nov. | Dec. |

Baton Rouge, Louisiana

Lat. 30° 32' N **Lon.** 91° 8' W **Elev.** 64 ft.

Baton Rouge, the capital city, is located on the east side of the Mississippi River some 65 miles inland from the coast. The general climate of Baton Rouge is humid subtropical, but the city is subject to significant polar influences during winter. Prevailing wind flow is from the south during much of the year. This maritime air from the Gulf of Mexico helps to temper summer heat, shorten winter cold spells, and give abundant moisture and rainfall. Winds usually are rather light. High humidity occurs mainly at night.

Temperatures

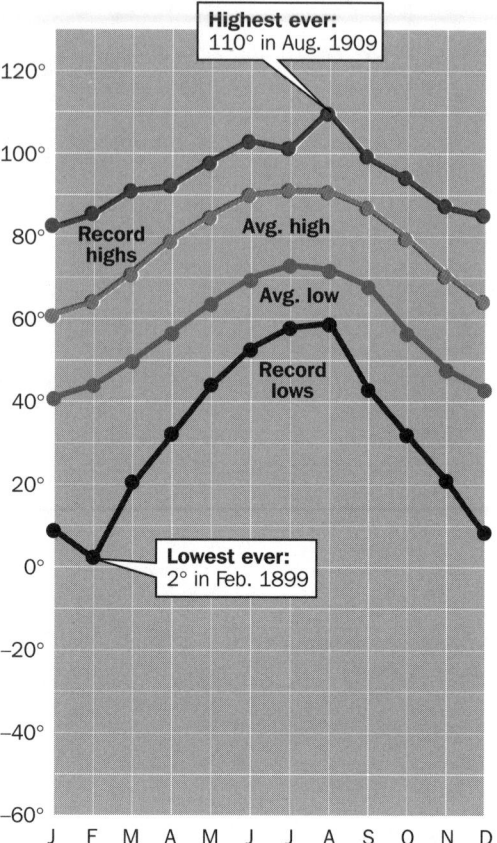

Highest ever: 110° in Aug. 1909

Record highs

Avg. high

Avg. low

Record lows

Lowest ever: 2° in Feb. 1899

Weather extremes

Most rain in 24 hours:	12.08 in. April 15 – 16, 1967
Most rain in a month:	23.73 in. May 1907
Most snow in 24 hours:	12.5 in. Feb. 14 – 15, 1895
Most snow in a month:	12.5 in. February 1895

Monthly averages

Month	Avg. precip. (in.)	Avg. snow (in.)	Wet days	Thunder-storm days	Pct. sky is cloudy	% p.m. relative humidity	Dew point	Wind speed (mph)
Jan.	4.6	T	10	2	48	58	42	10.4
Feb.	5.2	T	9	3	45	55	43	10.4
March	4.7	T	9	4	40	52	49	11.5
April	5.1	0	7	5	33	51	57	10.4
May	4.8	0	8	6	26	53	64	9.2
June	4.1	0	10	10	19	56	70	8.1
July	6.7	0	14	15	23	62	72	6.9
Aug.	5.4	0	12	13	21	61	72	6.9
Sept.	4.3	0	9	7	24	59	68	6.9
Oct.	3.0	0	5	2	23	50	57	8.1
Nov.	4.1	T	7	3	34	53	49	9.2
Dec.	5.4	T	10	2	44	57	44	10.4

T - Trace of rain or snow   * - Less than 1   NA - Not Available

Annual averages

Precipitation (in inches)	57.5
Snow (in inches)	T
Heating degree days	1,644
Cooling degree days	2,689
Days with thunderstorms	72
Days with fog	198
Days above 90°	86
Days below 32°	22
Wet days	110
Days with snow	*
Days with 1.5 inches or more snow	*

Percent time sky is clear

Jan.	Feb.	March	April	May	June	July	Aug.	Sept.	Oct.	Nov.	Dec.
24.6	27	26.2	26.7	25.7	24.4	17.8	23	30	42.9	33.9	28.5

Beckley, West Virginia

Lat. 37° 47' N **Lon.** 81° 07' W **Elev.** 2,504 ft.

The climate of Beckley, located in the Appalachian Mountains, is characterized by sharp temperature contrasts, both seasonal and from day to day. May through September is generally warm, with cool nights. November through March is moderately cold. April and October are months of fairly rapid transition. Cold waves occur on an average of two or three times during the winter, but severe cold spells seldom last more than two or three days. Summer rainfall occurs mostly during thunderstorms or showers. Snowfall occurs chiefly from November through March. The seasonal snowfall is greater than snowfall at places to the west at lower elevations, but considerably less than the totals for places at higher elevations to the east and northeast.

Temperatures

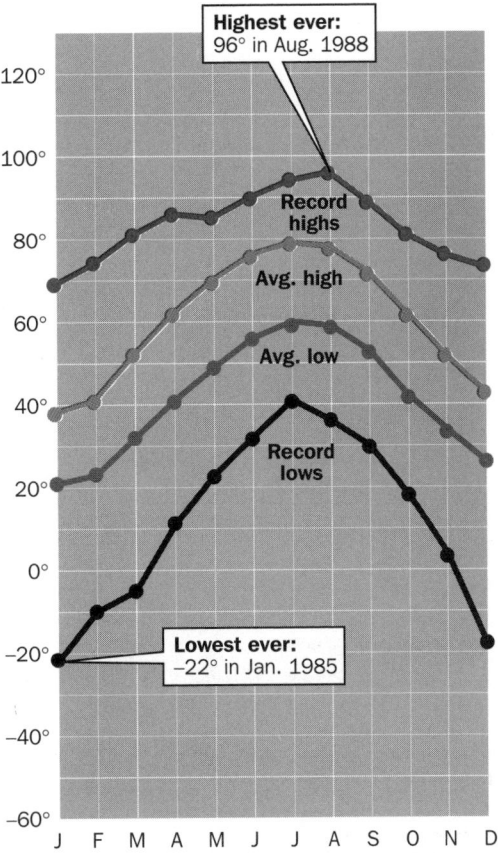

Highest ever: 96° in Aug. 1988

Record highs

Avg. high

Avg. low

Record lows

Lowest ever: −22° in Jan. 1985

Weather extremes

Most rain in 24 hours:	4.3 in. Sept. 29, 1964
Most rain in a month:	9.84 in. March 1935
Most snow in 24 hours:	13.7 in. Dec. 28, 1967
Most snow in a month:	48 in. March 1960

Monthly averages

Month	Avg. precip. (in.)	Avg. snow (in.)	Wet days	Thunder-storm days	Pct. sky is cloudy	% p.m. relative humidity	Dew point	Wind speed (mph)
Jan.	3.0	18	16	*	62	65	21	12.7
Feb.	2.8	16	15	1	59	62	23	12.7
March	3.2	8	15	2	55	54	30	12.7
April	3.5	3	14	4	48	48	36	12.7
May	4.0	T	14	6	45	53	48	10.4
June	3.8	0	12	8	38	59	57	9.2
July	4.6	0	13	10	38	61	62	8.1
Aug.	3.4	0	11	8	36	62	61	8.1
Sept.	3.4	T	11	3	38	63	55	10.4
Oct.	2.8	T	10	1	39	55	42	11.5
Nov.	3.0	4	13	1	51	58	33	11.5
Dec.	3.1	11	15	*	60	65	26	12.7

T - Trace of rain or snow   * - Less than 1   NA - Not Available

Annual averages

Precipitation (in inches)	40.6
Snow (in inches)	61
Heating degree days	5,487
Cooling degree days	517
Days with thunderstorms	44
Days with fog	194
Days above 90°	1
Days below 32°	114
Wet days	159
Days with snow	80
Days with 1.5 inches or more snow	29

Percent time sky is clear

15.4	15.9	17	19.1	17	14.9	14	15.9	21.8	28.8	19.7	14.9
Jan.	Feb.	March	April	May	June	July	Aug.	Sept.	Oct.	Nov.	Dec.

Billings, Montana

Lat. 45° 48' N **Lon.** 108° 32' W **Elev.** 3,567 ft.

Billings is situated in the borderline area between the Great Plains and the Rocky Mountains, and has a climate that takes on some of the characteristics of both regions. The period of least precipitation is November through February. The heaviest snows occur during spring and fall when the temperature and moisture conditions are most favorable. Winter is usually cold, though not extremely so. Spring brings a period of frequent and rapid fluctuations in the weather. The last freezing temperatures in spring usually occur before mid-May though they have occurred as late as late June. Summer is characterized by warm days with abundant sunshine and low humidities. The first freezing temperatures of the fall season occur in late September.

Temperatures

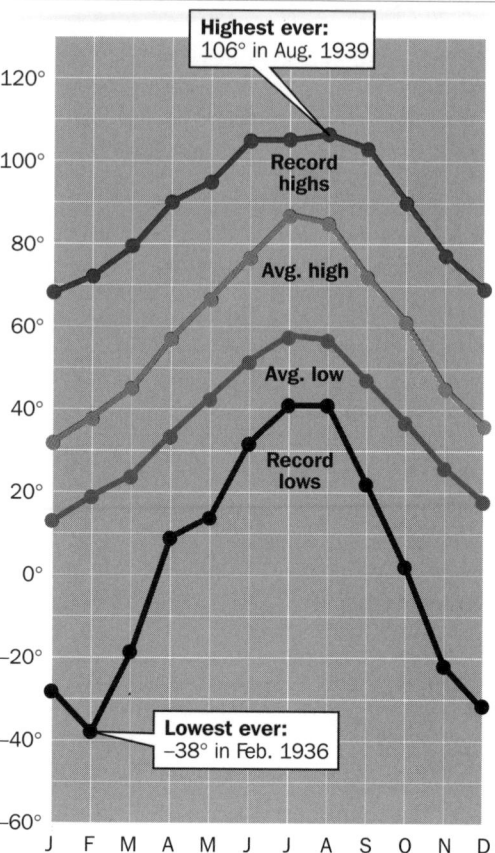

Highest ever: 106° in Aug. 1939

Record highs

Avg. high

Avg. low

Record lows

Lowest ever: −38° in Feb. 1936

Weather extremes

Most rain in 24 hours:	3.19 in.	April 27 – 28, 1978
Most rain in a month:	7.71 in.	May 1981
Most snow in 24 hours:	23.7 in.	April 4, 1955
Most snow in a month:	42.3 in.	April 1955

Monthly averages

Month	Avg. precip. (in.)	Avg. snow (in.)	Wet days	Thunder-storm days	Pct. sky is cloudy	% p.m. relative humidity	Dew point	Wind speed (mph)
Jan.	0.8	10	8	*	46	57	10	15.0
Feb.	0.7	8	8	*	46	53	15	13.8
March	1.1	11	9	*	45	49	20	11.5
April	1.7	9	10	1	43	41	27	10.4
May	2.4	2	12	4	36	42	37	10.4
June	1.9	T	11	7	27	40	45	9.2
July	0.9	0	7	7	15	31	47	9.2
Aug.	1.0	0	7	6	16	30	45	9.2
Sept.	1.3	1	7	2	26	37	38	10.4
Oct.	1.1	4	6	*	31	42	30	11.5
Nov.	0.8	7	6	0	41	53	20	12.7
Dec.	0.8	9	7	*	43	56	13	13.8

T - Trace of rain or snow   * - Less than 1   NA - Not Available

Annual averages

Precipitation (in inches)	14.5
Snow (in inches)	61
Heating degree days	7,045
Cooling degree days	611
Days with thunderstorms	27
Days with fog	48
Days above 90°	29
Days below 32°	150
Wet days	98
Days with snow	82
Days with 1.5 inches or more snow	28

Percent time sky is clear

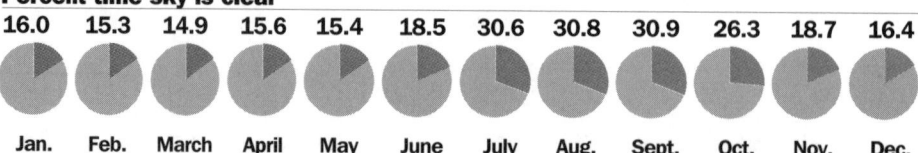

16.0	15.3	14.9	15.6	15.4	18.5	30.6	30.8	30.9	26.3	18.7	16.4
Jan.	Feb.	March	April	May	June	July	Aug.	Sept.	Oct.	Nov.	Dec.

Binghamton, New York

Lat. 42° 13' N **Lon.** 75° 59' W **Elev.** 1,600 ft.

The climate here is representative of the humid area of the northeastern United States. Being adjacent to the so-called St. Lawrence Valley storm track and also subject to cold air masses approaching from the west and north, Binghamton's climate has frequent and rapid changes. Winters are usually cold, but not severe. Highest daytime temperatures average in the high 20s to low 30s. Ordinarily a few subzero readings may be expected in January and February. In the summer, the nights are sufficiently cool to provide favorable sleeping conditions and relief from the heat of the day. Usually the last spring frost occurs during early May and the first frost in autumn during early October.

Temperatures

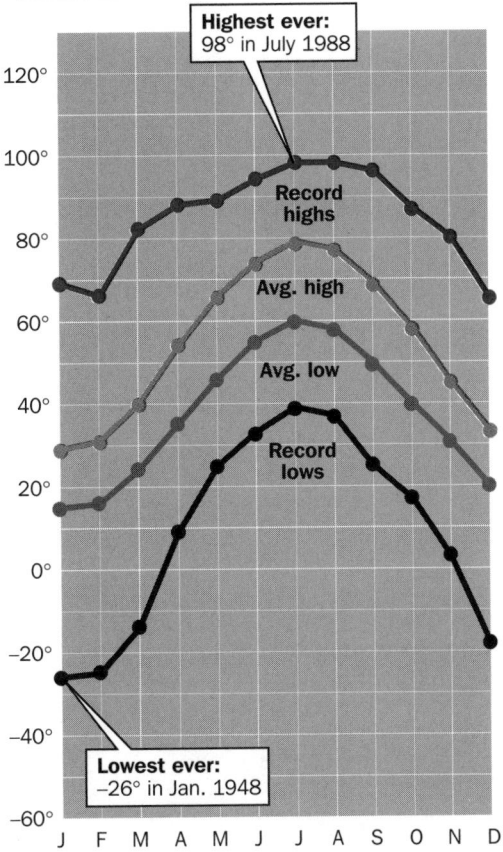

Highest ever: 98° in July 1988

Record highs

Avg. high

Avg. low

Record lows

Lowest ever: −26° in Jan. 1948

Weather extremes

Most rain in 24 hours:	3.88 in. Oct. 15 – 16, 1955
Most rain in a month:	9.66 in. September 1977
Most snow in 24 hours:	23 in. Feb. 3 – 4, 1961
Most snow in a month:	59.6 in. December 1969

Monthly averages

Month	Avg. precip. (in.)	Avg. snow (in.)	Wet days	Thunder-storm days	Pct. sky is cloudy	% p.m. relative humidity	Dew point	Wind speed (mph)
Jan.	2.4	19	16	*	60	69	15	13.8
Feb.	2.4	16	14	*	57	65	16	13.8
March	2.8	13	15	1	56	60	23	13.8
April	3.2	5	14	2	50	54	32	12.7
May	3.4	T	13	4	45	55	44	11.5
June	3.6	0	12	6	37	57	54	9.2
July	3.6	0	11	7	31	57	59	8.1
Aug.	3.4	0	11	5	34	59	58	8.1
Sept.	3.2	T	10	3	38	62	52	9.2
Oct.	2.9	T	11	1	44	60	40	9.2
Nov.	3.1	8	15	*	60	69	31	10.4
Dec.	2.9	18	17	*	65	73	20	13.8

T - Trace of rain or snow   * - Less than 1   NA - Not Available

Annual averages

Precipitation (in inches)	36.9
Snow (in inches)	80
Heating degree days	7,222
Cooling degree days	431
Days with thunderstorms	29
Days with fog	168
Days above 90°	3
Days below 32°	145
Wet days	159
Days with snow	134
Days with 1.5 inches or more snow	33

Percent time sky is clear

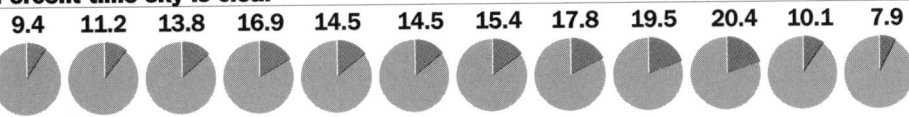

Jan.	Feb.	March	April	May	June	July	Aug.	Sept.	Oct.	Nov.	Dec.
9.4	11.2	13.8	16.9	14.5	14.5	15.4	17.8	19.5	20.4	10.1	7.9

Birmingham, Alabama

Lat. 33° 34' N **Lon.** 86° 45' W **Elev.** 620 ft.

Birmingham is far enough inland to be protected from destructive tropical hurricanes, yet close enough to the coast so that the Gulf has a modifying effect on the climate. Although summers are long and hot, they are not generally excessively hot. In winter just one or two inches of snow can effectively shut down this Sunbelt city because of the hilly terrain and the wetness of the snow. The time of the year with the greatest risk of severe thunderstorms and tornadoes comes in March and April.

Temperatures

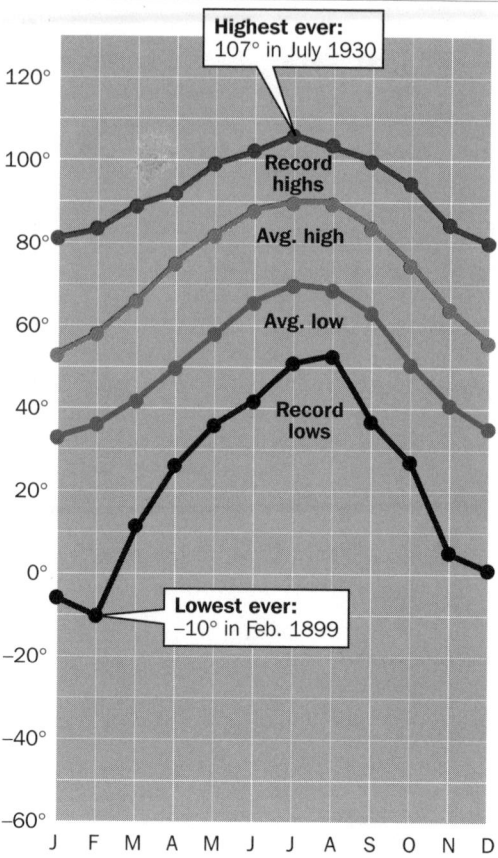

Highest ever: 107° in July 1930

Record highs

Avg. high

Avg. low

Record lows

Lowest ever: −10° in Feb. 1899

Weather extremes

Most rain in 24 hours:	8.84 in. July 6 – 7, 1916
Most rain in a month:	20.12 in. July 1916
Most snow in 24 hours:	13 in. March 12–13, 1993
Most snow in a month:	13 in. March 1993

Monthly averages

Month	Avg. precip. (in.)	Avg. snow (in.)	Wet days	Thunder- storm days	Pct. sky is cloudy	% p.m. relative humidity	Dew point	Wind speed (mph)
Jan.	5.1	1	11	2	48	57	33	9.2
Feb.	4.9	T	10	2	45	52	35	9.2
March	6.1	T	11	4	41	47	41	10.4
April	4.7	T	9	5	32	45	49	10.4
May	4.4	0	10	7	27	50	58	9.2
June	3.7	0	9	8	22	53	65	5.8
July	5.2	0	12	12	23	57	69	5.8
Aug.	3.8	0	10	9	19	55	68	5.8
Sept.	4.0	0	8	4	25	54	63	8.1
Oct.	2.8	0	6	1	24	49	51	5.8
Nov.	4.2	T	9	2	33	51	42	9.2
Dec.	4.9	T	11	1	44	56	36	9.2

T - Trace of rain or snow   * - Less than 1   NA - Not Available

Annual averages

Precipitation (in inches)	53.6
Snow (in inches)	1
Heating degree days	2,790
Cooling degree days	1,934
Days with thunderstorms	57
Days with fog	159
Days above 65°	261
Days below 32°	57
Wet days	116
Days with snow	2
Days with 1.5 inches or more snow	*

Percent time sky is clear

Jan.	Feb.	March	April	May	June	July	Aug.	Sept.	Oct.	Nov.	Dec.
23.6	24.4	24.2	28.7	23.4	21.4	15.7	19.7	27.0	38.8	31.4	26.2

Bismarck, North Dakota

Lat. 46° 46' N **Lon.** 100° 46' W **Elev.** 1,647 ft.

Bismarck is on the east bank of the Missouri River in a shallow basin seven miles wide and 11 miles long. The semiarid climate is typically continental. Temperature ranges are large from summer to winter. Summers are warm, but not usually hot or humid. Winters are long and cold, but have pleasant, mild days. Most summer precipitation is late afternoon or evening thunderstorms, some with damaging winds. Winter runs from late November to late March. Snow, which has been reported every month except July and August, often comes with strong winds and low temperatures, producing storms and blizzards. Some blizzards last two or three days. Over 75 percent of annual precipitation falls from April through September.

Temperatures

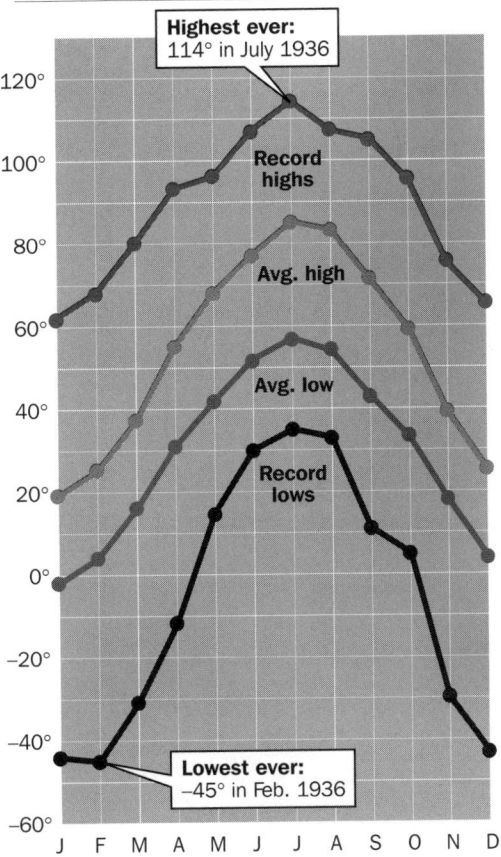

Highest ever: 114° in July 1936

Record highs

Avg. high

Avg. low

Record lows

Lowest ever: –45° in Feb. 1936

Weather extremes

Most rain in 24 hours:	5.27 in. July 15 – 16, 1993
Most rain in a month:	13.75 in. July 1993
Most snow in 24 hours:	15.9 in. Oct. 28 – 29, 1991
Most snow in a month:	31.1 in. March 1975

Monthly averages

Month	Avg. precip. (in.)	Avg. snow (in.)	Wet days	Thunder-storm days	Pct. sky is cloudy	% p.m. relative humidity	Dew point	Wind speed (mph)
Jan.	0.5	8	8	0	45	67	2	13.8
Feb.	0.5	7	7	*	47	66	8	12.7
March	0.8	8	8	*	46	60	18	16.1
April	1.5	4	8	1	43	45	29	16.1
May	2.2	1	10	4	37	43	40	13.8
June	2.8	0	11	9	33	47	51	12.7
July	2.1	0	9	9	20	41	55	12.7
Aug.	1.8	0	8	8	22	39	52	12.7
Sept.	1.3	T	7	3	29	42	43	12.7
Oct.	0.9	1	6	*	35	43	32	12.7
Nov.	0.5	6	6	*	45	57	20	13.8
Dec.	0.5	8	8	0	47	66	8	13.8

T - Trace of rain or snow   * - Less than 1   NA - Not Available

Annual averages

Precipitation (in inches)	15.4
Snow (in inches)	42
Heating degree days	8,932
Cooling degree days	499
Days with thunderstorms	34
Days with fog	59
Days above 90°	23
Days below 32°	186
Wet days	96
Days with snow	82
Days with 1.5 inches or more snow	17

Percent time sky is clear

Jan.	Feb.	March	April	May	June	July	Aug.	Sept.	Oct.	Nov.	Dec.
22.3	21.1	19.4	21.4	18.6	20.2	26.6	29.5	30.3	28.2	21.9	21.4

Boise, Idaho

Lat. 43° 34' N **Lon.** 116° 13' W **Elev.** 2,838 ft.

Boise is situated in the Boise River Valley about 8 miles below the mouth of a mountain canyon. The Boise climate in general may be described as dry and temperate. Although air masses from the Pacific are considerably modified by the time they reach Boise, their influence, particularly in winter, alternates with that of atmospheric developments from other directions. The result is almost a typical upland continental type of climate in summer, while winters are usually tempered by periods of cloudy or stormy and mild weather. Autumns have prolonged periods of near ideal weather, while springtime is noted for changeable weather and varied temperatures. Summer hot periods rarely last longer than a few days.

Temperatures

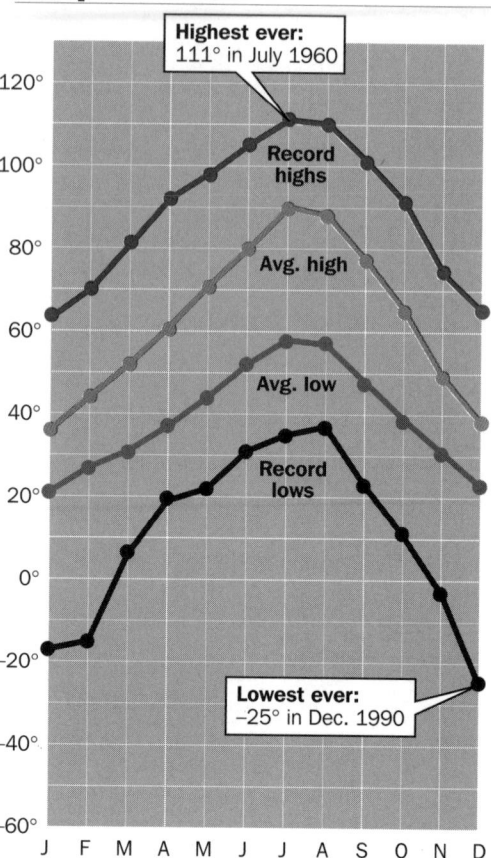

Highest ever: 111° in July 1960

Record highs

Avg. high

Avg. low

Record lows

Lowest ever: −25° in Dec. 1990

Weather extremes

Most rain in 24 hours:	2.24 in. July 11 – 12, 1958
Most rain in a month:	4.23 in. December 1983
Most snow in 24 hours:	17.0 in. Dec. 16 – 17, 1884
Most snow in a month:	25.2 in. February 1949

Monthly averages

Month	Avg. precip. (in.)	Avg. snow (in.)	Wet days	Thunder-storm days	Pct. sky is cloudy	% p.m. relative humidity	Dew point	Wind speed (mph)
Jan.	1.5	7	12	*	62	69	22	10.4
Feb.	1.1	4	10	*	52	59	26	10.4
March	1.3	2	10	1	45	44	27	10.4
April	1.2	1	8	1	39	35	31	12.7
May	1.2	T	8	3	32	33	37	12.7
June	0.8	T	6	3	22	29	42	11.5
July	0.3	0	3	2	9	21	44	10.4
Aug.	0.4	0	3	3	12	23	42	10.4
Sept.	0.7	0	4	1	16	29	38	9.2
Oct.	0.7	T	6	1	27	38	33	9.2
Nov.	1.4	2	10	*	49	58	29	10.4
Dec.	1.4	6	11	*	58	70	23	10.4

T - Trace of rain or snow   * - Less than 1   NA - Not Available

Annual averages

Precipitation (in inches)	11.9
Snow (in inches)	22
Heating degree days	5,832
Cooling degree days	771
Days with thunderstorms	15
Days with fog	51
Days above 90°	44
Days below 32°	124
Wet days	91
Days with snow	45
Days with 1.5 inches or more snow	9

Percent time sky is clear

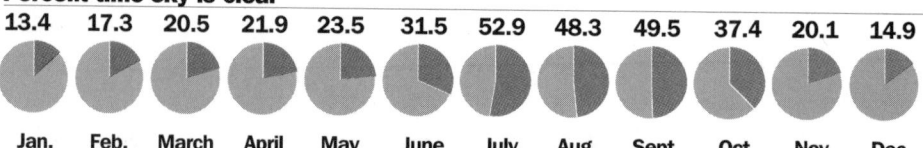

Jan.	Feb.	March	April	May	June	July	Aug.	Sept.	Oct.	Nov.	Dec.
13.4	17.3	20.5	21.9	23.5	31.5	52.9	48.3	49.5	37.4	20.1	14.9

Boston, Massachusetts

Lat. 42° 22' N **Lon.** 71°02' W **Elev.** 15 ft.

Important influences on Boston's climate include its latitude, weather fluctuations from fair to cloudy to stormy, and the ocean's moderating influence on temperature extremes in both winter and summer. Hot summer afternoons are frequently relieved by the sea breeze, which displaces the warm air over the land. In winter, the severity of cold waves is reduced by the relatively warm ocean. Coastal storms, or northeasters, are prolific producers of rain and snow. The main snow season extends from December through March. Heavy fog occurs about two days per month. Although winds of 30 mph or higher may be expected at least one day every month, gales are more common and severe in winter.

Temperatures

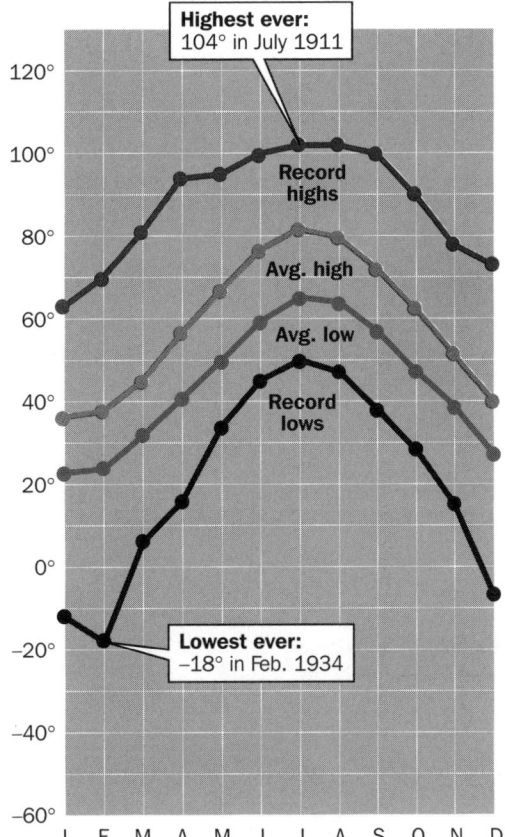

Highest ever: 104° in July 1911

Record highs

Avg. high

Avg. low

Record lows

Lowest ever: −18° in Feb. 1934

Weather extremes

Most rain in 24 hours:	8.40 in. Aug. 18 – 19, 1955
Most rain in a month:	17.09 in. August 1955
Most snow in 24 hours:	23.6 in. Feb. 6 – 7, 1978
Most snow in a month:	41.3 in. February 1969

Monthly averages

Month	Avg. precip. (in.)	Avg. snow (in.)	Wet days	Thunder-storm days	Pct. sky is cloudy	% p.m. relative humidity	Dew point	Wind speed (mph)
Jan.	4.0	12.0	11	*	46	57	NA	13.9
Feb.	3.7	11.2	11	*	44	56	NA	13.8
March	4.1	7.4	12	*	46	56	NA	13.7
April	3.7	0.9	11	1	46	55	NA	13.2
May	3.5	T	12	2	45	59	NA	12.2
June	2.9	0	11	4	39	58	NA	11.5
July	2.7	0	9	4	35	57	NA	11.0
Aug.	3.7	0	10	4	34	59	NA	10.8
Sept.	3.4	0	9	2	35	60	NA	11.3
Oct.	3.4	T	9	*	35	58	NA	12.0
Nov.	4.2	1.3	11	*	45	59	NA	12.9
Dec.	4.5	7.4	12	*	46	58	NA	13.6

T - Trace of rain or snow   * - Less than 1   NA - Not Available

Annual averages

Precipitation (in inches)	43.8
Snow (in inches)	40.2
Heating degree days	5,593
Cooling degree days	699
Days with thunderstorms	19
Days with fog	23
Days above 90°	13
Days below 32°	98
Wet days	126
Days with snow	NA
Days with 1.5 inches or more snow	11

Percent time sky is clear

28.2	28.8	25.8	22.1	18.3	17.7	17.1	21.5	27.9	31.4	24.3	27.2
Jan.	Feb.	March	April	May	June	July	Aug.	Sept.	Oct.	Nov.	Dec.

Bridgeport, Connecticut

Lat. 41° 10' N **Lon.** 73° 8' W **Elev.** 7 ft.

Bridgeport is on Long Island Sound, near the foothills of the Berkshires, 30 miles to the north and northwest. The most pronounced climatic effect is the sea breeze. Mean monthly temperatures during the summer average 3 to 5 degrees lower than those inland because of the sea breeze effect. Temperatures during the fall and winter also are moderated because of proximity of the Sound. Winter snowfall is around 10 inches less than areas a few miles inland. One of the hazards along the low-lying coastal areas is flooding, usually during periods of high tide associated with the approach of slow-moving deepening low pressure systems. They can result in tides 3 to 5 feet higher than normal.

Temperatures

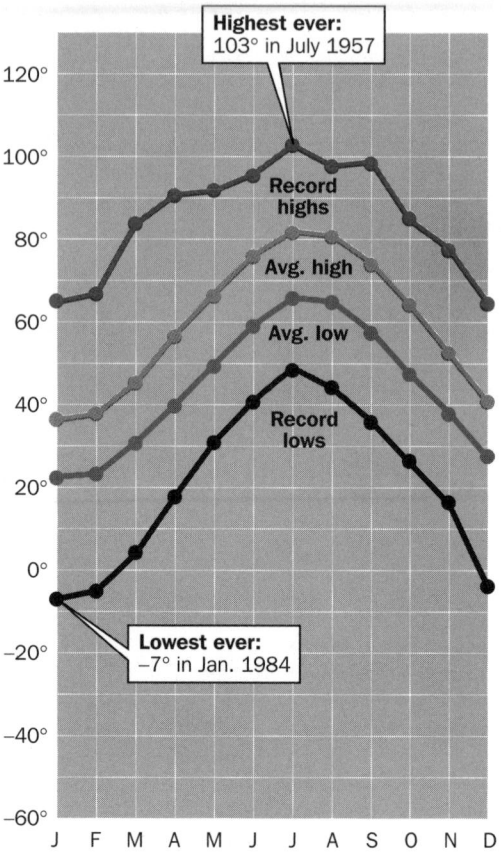

Highest ever: 103° in July 1957

Record highs

Avg. high

Avg. low

Record lows

Lowest ever: −7° in Jan. 1984

Weather extremes

Most rain in 24 hours:	6.89 in. June 18 – 19, 1972
Most rain in a month:	17.70 in. June 1972
Most snow in 24 hours:	16.7 in. Jan. 19 – 20, 1978
Most snow in a month:	47.0 in. February 1934

Monthly averages

Month	Avg. precip. (in.)	Avg. snow (in.)	Wet days	Thunder-storm days	Pct. sky is cloudy	% p.m. relative humidity	Dew point	Wind speed (mph)
Jan.	3.3	7.4	11	*	48	60	NA	13.2
Feb.	3.0	7.2	10	*	48	58	NA	13.6
March	3.9	4.6	11	1	46	56	NA	13.5
April	3.7	0.5	11	2	48	54	NA	13.0
May	3.4	T	11	3	46	60	NA	11.6
June	2.9	0.0	10	4	41	61	NA	10.5
July	3.5	T	9	5	38	61	NA	10.0
Aug.	3.7	T	9	4	37	62	NA	10.1
Sept.	3.3	0.0	9	2	38	61	NA	11.2
Oct.	3.3	T	7	1	39	59	NA	11.9
Nov.	3.8	0.6	10	*	48	61	NA	12.7
Dec.	3.8	4.5	11	*	48	61	NA	13.0

T - Trace of rain or snow   * - Less than 1   NA - Not Available

Annual averages

Precipitation (in inches)	42
Snow (in inches)	25
Heating degree days	5,501
Cooling degree days	746
Days with thunderstorms	22
Days with fog	30
Days above 90°	6
Days below 32°	99
Wet days	118
Days with snow	NA
Days with 1.5 inches or more snow	7

Percent time sky is clear

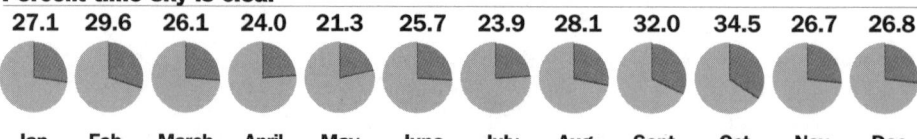

Jan.	Feb.	March	April	May	June	July	Aug.	Sept.	Oct.	Nov.	Dec.
27.1	29.6	26.1	24.0	21.3	25.7	23.9	28.1	32.0	34.5	26.7	26.8

Bristol, Tennessee

Lat. 36° 29' N **Lon.** 82° 24' W **Elev.** 1,525 ft.

Bristol straddles the Tennessee-Virginia border in the upper East Tennessee Valley. With Johnson City and Kingsport, Tenn., it forms a triangle known as the Tri-City area. The terrain features rolling hills with a mountain range to the southeast (with peaks up to 6,000 feet) and a lower range to the northwest. The mountains have considerable influence — precipitation in the higher mountains is almost double that of lower elevations. The wettest period is July, usually from thunderstorms. Snowfall seldom occurs before November and rarely remains on the ground for more than a few days, except in the mountains. The growing season runs to 180 days and usually offers ample sunshine and rainfall.

Temperatures

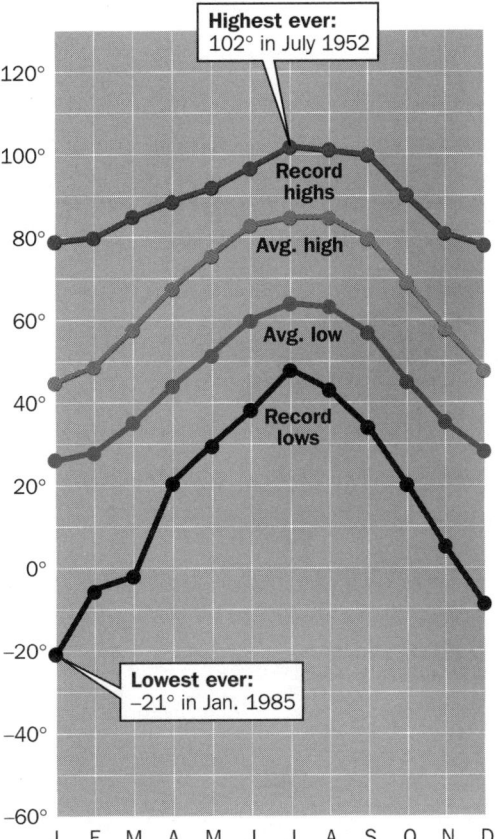

Highest ever: 102° in July 1952

Record highs

Avg. high

Avg. low

Record lows

Lowest ever: −21° in Jan. 1985

Weather extremes

Most rain in 24 hours:	3.65 in. Oct. 16, 1964
Most rain in a month:	9.73 in. July 1949
Most snow in 24 hours:	16.2 in. Nov. 21, 1952
Most snow in a month:	29.9 in. March 1960

Monthly averages

Month	Avg. precip. (in.)	Avg. snow (in.)	Wet days	Thunder-storm days	Pct. sky is cloudy	% p.m. relative humidity	Dew point	Wind speed (mph)
Jan.	3.4	6	14	*	55	59	26	10.4
Feb.	3.5	5	12	1	50	54	28	11.5
March	3.9	2	13	2	47	49	34	11.5
April	3.4	1	11	4	39	46	41	11.5
May	3.8	T	12	7	36	52	53	9.2
June	3.5	0	11	8	29	54	61	8.1
July	4.5	0	12	9	31	57	65	6.9
Aug.	3.4	0	10	7	28	56	64	4.6
Sept.	3.0	0	8	3	30	54	58	4.6
Oct.	2.4	T	8	1	31	50	46	4.6
Nov.	3.0	1	11	*	42	53	36	10.4
Dec.	3.4	3	12	*	50	59	29	10.4

T - Trace of rain or snow   * - Less than 1   NA - Not Available

Annual averages

Precipitation (in inches)	41.3
Snow (in inches)	18
Heating degree days	4,269
Cooling degree days	1,077
Days with thunderstorms	42
Days with fog	169
Days above 90°	17
Days below 32°	96
Wet days	134
Days with snow	26
Days with 1.5 inches or more snow	7

Percent time sky is clear

Jan.	Feb.	March	April	May	June	July	Aug.	Sept.	Oct.	Nov.	Dec.
19	20.9	20.8	23	19.6	17.4	14.6	18	25.1	33.2	25.3	21.3

Brownsville, Texas

Lat. 25° 54' N **Lon.** 97° 26' W **Elev.** 19 ft.

Brownsville, located at the southern tip of Texas, is the largest city of the lower Rio Grande Valley. The Gulf of Mexico, 18 miles east, is the dominant influence on local weather. Prevailing southeast breezes off the Gulf provide a humid but generally mild climate. Winds are frequently strong and gusty in the spring. Sometimes west winds bring hot, dry air from Mexico and temperatures of 100°F or more. Very hot temperatures often are moderated by a cooling sea breeze from the Gulf during the afternoon.

Temperatures

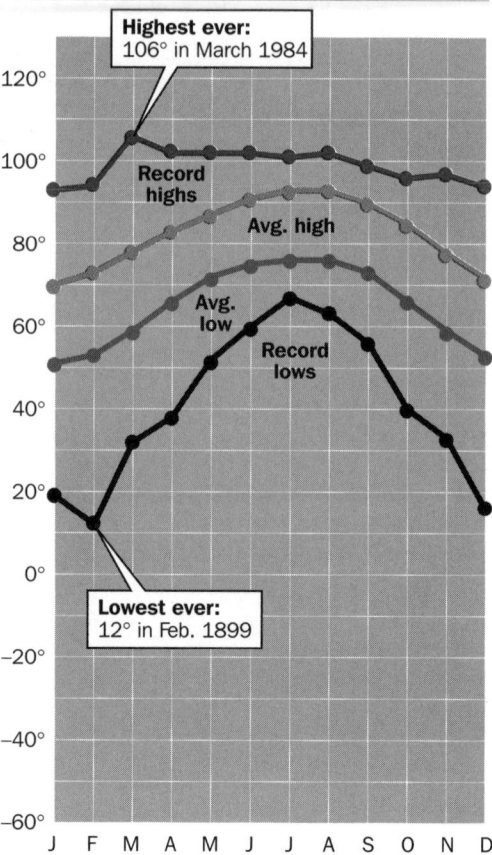

Highest ever: 106° in March 1984

Record highs

Avg. high

Avg. low

Record lows

Lowest ever: 12° in Feb. 1899

Weather extremes

Most rain in 24 hours:	12.09 in. Sept. 20, 1967
Most rain in a month:	30.57 in. September 1886
Most snow in 24 hours:	5 in. mid-March 1895
Most snow in a month:	5 in. March 1895

Monthly averages

Month	Avg. precip. (in.)	Avg. snow (in.)	Wet days	Thunder-storm days	Pct. sky is cloudy	% p.m. relative humidity	Dew point	Wind speed (mph)
Jan.	1.4	T	7	1	47	62	52	12.7
Feb.	1.4	T	6	1	43	60	54	17.3
March	0.6	0	4	1	42	57	59	17.3
April	1.5	0	4	2	40	58	65	17.3
May	2.5	0	5	3	27	60	70	15.0
June	2.8	0	6	3	11	59	73	13.8
July	1.8	0	5	3	9	54	73	12.7
Aug.	2.6	0	7	5	10	55	73	11.5
Sept.	5.6	0	10	5	15	60	72	10.4
Oct.	3.2	0	7	2	17	58	66	10.4
Nov.	1.5	T	5	1	28	59	59	13.8
Dec.	1.1	T	6	*	41	61	54	12.7

T - Trace of rain or snow   * - Less than 1   NA - Not Available

Annual averages

Precipitation (in inches)	25.8
Snow (in inches)	T
Heating degree days	614
Cooling degree days	3,926
Days with thunderstorms	27
Days with fog	112
Days above 90°	116
Days below 32°	2
Wet days	72
Days with snow	0
Days with 1.5 inches or more snow	0

Percent time sky is clear

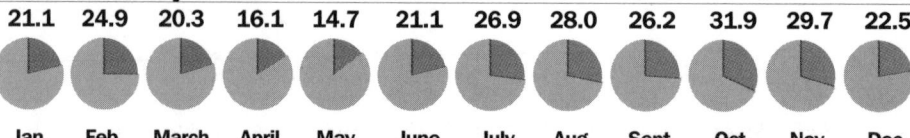

Jan.	Feb.	March	April	May	June	July	Aug.	Sept.	Oct.	Nov.	Dec.
21.1	24.9	20.3	16.1	14.7	21.1	26.9	28.0	26.2	31.9	29.7	22.5

Buffalo, New York

Lat. 42° 56' N **Lon.** 78° 44' W **Elev.** 705 ft.

The main weathermaker for Buffalo is Lake Erie. The lake lies to the southwest of the city. That is also the direction of the prevailing wind. Snow flurries off the lake begin in mid-November or early December. Outbreaks of arctic air in December and throughout the winter months produce locally heavy snowfalls. Temperatures well below zero over Canada and the Midwest are raised 10 to 30 degrees crossing the lake. With heavy winter ice accumulations in the lake, typical spring conditions are delayed until late May or early June. Summer comes suddenly in mid-June. Lake breezes temper the extreme heat of the summer season. There is more summer sunshine here than in any other section of the state.

Temperatures

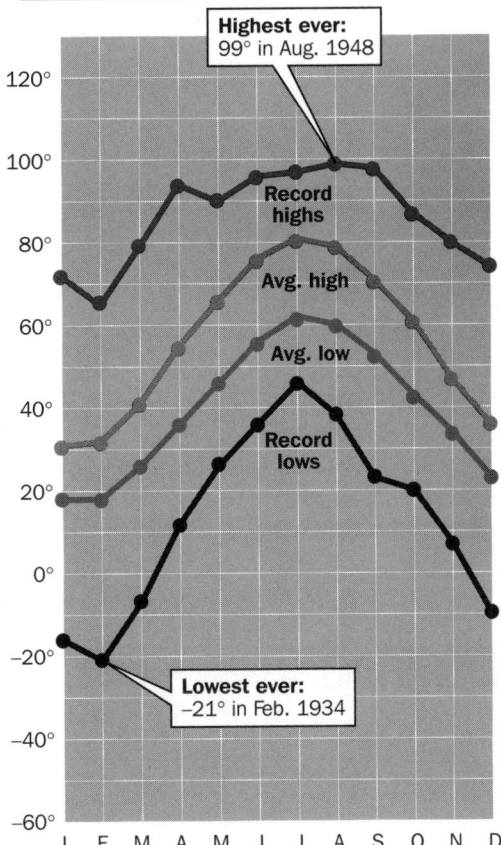

Highest ever: 99° in Aug. 1948

Record highs

Avg. high

Avg. low

Record lows

Lowest ever: −21° in Feb. 1934

Weather extremes

Most rain in 24 hours:	5.01 in. June 22, 1987
Most rain in a month:	10.67 in. August 1977
Most snow in 24 hours:	25.3 in. Jan. 10 – 11, 1982
Most snow in a month:	68.4 in. December 1985

Monthly averages

Month	Avg. precip. (in.)	Avg. snow (in.)	Wet days	Thunderstorm days	Pct. sky is cloudy	% p.m. relative humidity	Dew point	Wind speed (mph)
Jan.	2.9	24	20	*	66	73	18	18.4
Feb.	2.5	18	17	*	60	70	18	17.3
March	2.9	11	16	1	55	65	25	16.1
April	3.0	3	14	2	49	57	34	15.0
May	3.1	T	12	3	42	55	44	13.8
June	3.1	0	10	5	34	55	54	13.8
July	2.9	0	10	6	29	53	59	12.7
Aug.	3.9	0	11	6	31	56	59	12.7
Sept.	3.3	T	11	4	36	59	53	12.7
Oct.	3.0	T	12	2	42	60	42	9.2
Nov.	3.9	11	16	1	62	70	33	15.0
Dec.	3.5	22	20	*	67	74	23	15.0

T - Trace of rain or snow   * - Less than 1   NA - Not Available

Annual averages

Precipitation (in inches)	38.1
Snow (in inches)	90
Heating degree days	6,668
Cooling degree days	573
Days with thunderstorms	30
Days with fog	158
Days above 90°	4
Days below 32°	131
Wet days	169
Days with snow	129
Days with 1.5 inches or more snow	36

Percent time sky is clear

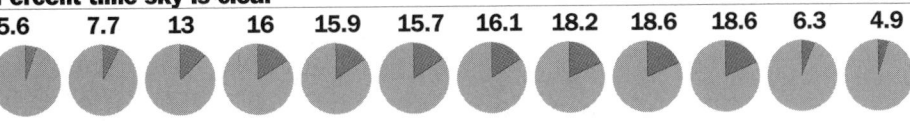

5.6	7.7	13	16	15.9	15.7	16.1	18.2	18.6	18.6	6.3	4.9
Jan.	Feb.	March	April	May	June	July	Aug.	Sept.	Oct.	Nov.	Dec.

Burlington, Vermont

Lat. 44° 28' N **Lon.** 73° 09' W **Elev.** 332 ft.

Burlington, located on the eastern shore of Lake Champlain, is about 35 miles east of the highest peaks of the Adirondacks. Due to its location in the path of the St. Lawrence Valley storm track and the lake effects, the city is one of the cloudiest in the United States. During the winter and prior to the lake freezing, temperatures along the lake shore are often 5 – 10 degrees warmer than at the airport 3 miles inland. Moderate summer heat gives way to a cooler but pleasant fall, usually extending well into October. The heaviest rainfall usually occurs during summer thunderstorms, but excessively heavy rainfall is quite uncommon. During the spring and fall months, fog occasionally forms along the Winooski River to the north and east and may drift over the airport.

Temperatures

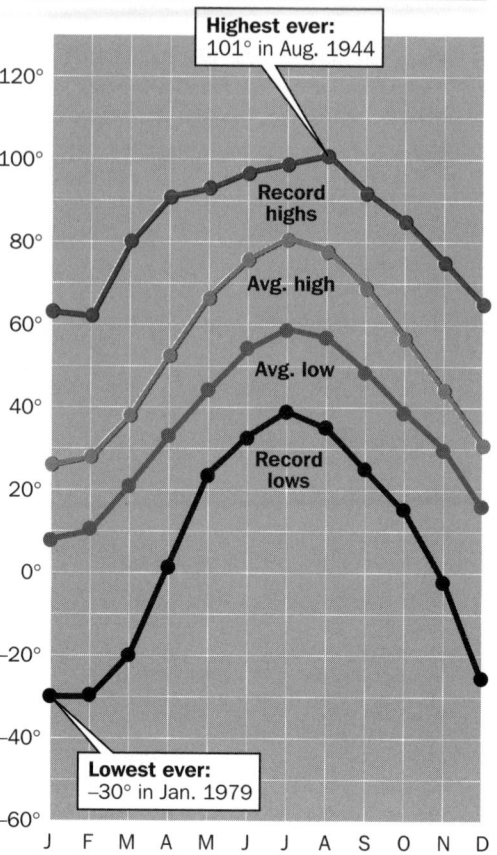

Weather extremes

Most rain in 24 hours:	3.59 in. Aug. 17, 1955
Most rain in a month:	11.54 in. August 1955
Most snow in 24 hours:	22.4 in. March 13–14, 1993
Most snow in a month:	56.7 in. December 1970

Monthly averages

Month	Avg. precip. (in.)	Avg. snow (in.)	Wet days	Thunder- storm days	Pct. sky is cloudy	% p.m. relative humidity	Dew point	Wind speed (mph)
Jan.	1.8	19	14	*	57	65	9	12.7
Feb.	1.8	16	11	0	53	61	11	11.5
March	2.2	13	13	*	51	58	19	11.5
April	2.7	4	12	1	50	52	31	11.5
May	3.0	T	14	2	43	51	43	11.5
June	3.5	0	13	5	37	54	54	10.4
July	3.5	0	12	6	30	53	58	10.4
Aug.	4.0	0	13	5	33	56	57	10.4
Sept.	3.2	T	12	2	38	61	51	11.5
Oct.	2.9	T	12	1	45	61	39	11.5
Nov.	3.1	7	14	*	61	68	29	11.5
Dec.	2.4	19	15	*	63	69	16	12.7

T - Trace of rain or snow   * - Less than 1   NA - Not Available

Annual averages

Precipitation (in inches)	34.1
Snow (in inches)	78
Heating degree days	7,763
Cooling degree days	471
Days with thunderstorms	22
Days with fog	120
Days above 90°	6
Days below 32°	157
Wet days	155
Days with snow	109
Days with 1.5 inches or more snow	32

Percent time sky is clear

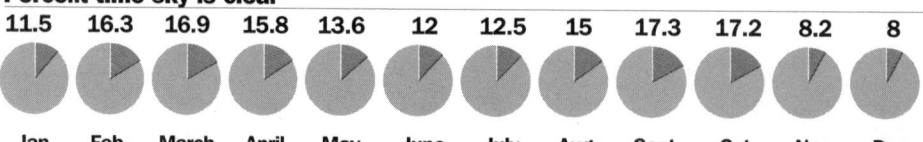

11.5	16.3	16.9	15.8	13.6	12	12.5	15	17.3	17.2	8.2	8
Jan.	Feb.	March	April	May	June	July	Aug.	Sept.	Oct.	Nov.	Dec.

Cape Hatteras, N.C.

Lat. 35° 16' N **Lon.** 75° 33' W **Elev.** 11 ft.

Much of Hatteras Island, the largest and easternmost island in North Carolina, is a National Seashore. It is separated from the mainland by the Pamlico Sound and is part of a chain of islands known as the Outer Banks. The island is 54 miles long and ranges from a few hundred yards wide to a few miles wide. Weather observations have been taken continuously since 1874, all from sites near the famous Cape Hatteras Lighthouse. With its maritime climate, the island is very humid, with cooler summers and warmer winters than the mainland. Storms frequently breed offshore in winter, producing strong winds, heavy rains and tidal flooding. Late summer and fall tracks of tropical cyclones can threaten the island. More than a million tourists visit each year.

Temperatures

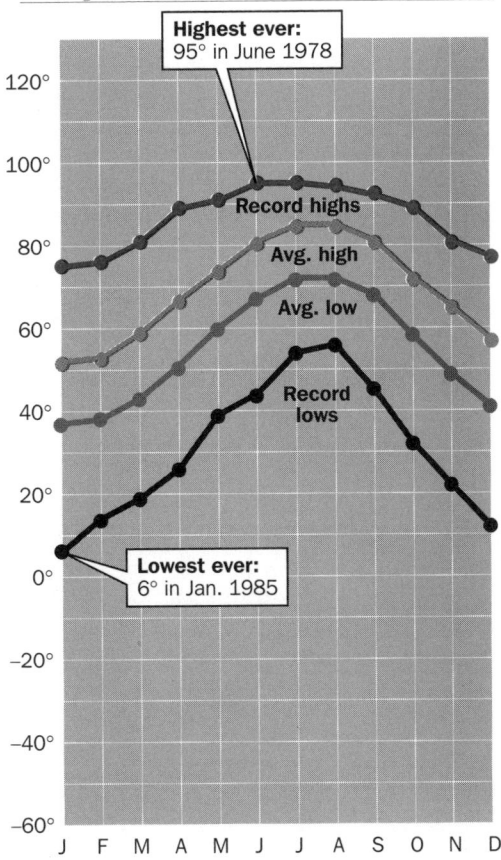

Highest ever: 95° in June 1978

Record highs

Avg. high

Avg. low

Record lows

Lowest ever: 6° in Jan. 1985

Weather extremes

Most rain in 24 hours:	8.11 in. Aug. 27 – 28, 1962
Most rain in a month:	20.0 in. September 1989
Most snow in 24 hours:	8.2 in. Dec. 23, 1989
Most snow in a month:	13.5 in. December 1989

Monthly averages

Month	Avg. precip. (in.)	Avg. snow (in.)	Wet days	Thunder-storm days	Pct. sky is cloudy	% p.m. relative humidity	Dew point	Wind speed (mph)
Jan.	5.2	T	11	1	45	69	37	2.3
Feb.	4.1	1	10	1	46	67	37	3.5
March	4.4	1	11	2	42	65	42	3.5
April	3.5	T	9	3	35	62	50	2.3
May	4.0	0	10	5	37	68	59	2.3
June	4.2	0	9	5	36	70	67	2.3
July	5.0	0	12	9	35	72	72	1.2
Aug.	5.9	0	11	8	33	72	72	2.3
Sept.	5.2	0	9	3	31	70	67	2.3
Oct.	5.0	0	9	2	32	68	57	2.3
Nov.	4.9	T	9	2	34	69	49	3.5
Dec.	4.6	1	10	1	40	69	41	2.3

T - Trace of rain or snow   * - Less than 1   NA - Not Available

Annual averages

Precipitation (in inches)	56.1
Snow (in inches)	2
Heating degree days	2,682
Cooling degree days	1,556
Days with thunderstorms	42
Days with fog	118
Days above 90°	5
Days below 32°	31
Wet days	120
Days with snow	1
Days with 1.5 inches or more snow	*

Percent time sky is clear

Jan.	Feb.	March	April	May	June	July	Aug.	Sept.	Oct.	Nov.	Dec.
30.1	29.2	29.9	33.4	24.8	21.5	17.2	19.3	25.1	31.5	32.4	30.9

Caribou, Maine

Lat. 46° 52' N **Lon.** 68° 1' W **Elev.** 624 ft.

Even though Caribou is located only 150 miles from the Atlantic coast, its climate can be classed as a severe typical continental type. Winters are particularly long and windy, and seasonal snowfalls averaging over 100 inches are not unusual. Temperatures of zero or lower normally occur over 40 times per year. Summers are cool and generally favored with abundant rainfall, which is one of the most important factors in the high yield of the potato and grain crops. Autumn is ideal, with mostly sunny warm days and crisp cool nights predominating. The Caribou area offers sparkling visibility and relatively pollen-free air in the late summer months.

Temperatures

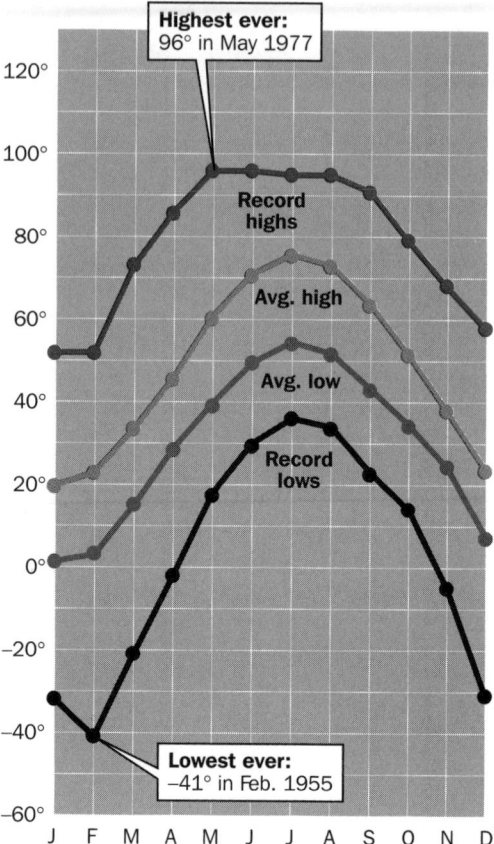

Highest ever: 96° in May 1977

Record highs

Avg. high

Avg. low

Record lows

Lowest ever: −41° in Feb. 1955

Weather extremes

Most rain in 24 hours:	6.89 in. Aug. 17, 1981
Most rain in a month:	12.09 in. August 1981
Most snow in 24 hours:	28.6 in. March 14, 1984
Most snow in a month:	59.9 in. December 1972

Monthly averages

Month	Avg. precip. (in.)	Avg. snow (in.)	Wet days	Thunder-storm days	Pct. sky is cloudy	% p.m. relative humidity	Dew point	Wind speed (mph)
Jan.	2.4	23.7	15	*	55	66	NA	12.4
Feb.	2.1	21.6	12	0	57	63	NA	12.0
March	2.4	19.1	13	*	55	61	NA	12.9
April	2.6	8.4	13	1	60	57	NA	11.7
May	2.9	0.7	13	2	58	52	NA	11.4
June	3.2	T	14	4	56	56	NA	10.4
July	4.0	T	14	7	48	58	NA	9.8
Aug.	4.0	0.0	13	4	49	59	NA	9.3
Sept.	3.5	T	12	1	51	61	NA	10.4
Oct.	3.1	1.7	13	1	59	62	NA	10.9
Nov.	3.2	12.1	14	*	70	71	NA	11.1
Dec.	3.2	23.1	15	0	61	70	NA	11.5

T - Trace of rain or snow   * - Less than 1   NA - Not Available

Annual averages

Precipitation (in inches)	37
Snow (in inches)	110
Heating degree days	9,616
Cooling degree days	147
Days with thunderstorms	20
Days with fog	27
Days above 90°	2
Days below 32°	187
Wet days	161
Days with snow	NA
Days with 1.5 inches or more snow	30

Percent time sky is clear

Jan.	Feb.	March	April	May	June	July	Aug.	Sept.	Oct.	Nov.	Dec.
21.9	21.8	22.3	17.3	13.2	11.0	10.0	14.5	18.0	15.5	9.7	17.7

Casper, Wyoming

Lat. 42° 55′ N **Lon.** 106° 28′ W **Elev.** 5,338 ft.

Casper is located in central Wyoming, in the high North Platte River Valley. The climate of the valley is semiarid. About 70 percent of the annual precipitation occurs as rain during the growing season of late spring and summer. Monthly snowfall amounts are unusually uniform from November through February and then get a bit heavier in March and April. But snowfalls have occurred as early as September and as late as early June. Windy days occur quite frequently during the winter and in the spring. The average first occurrence of 32°F in the fall is September 22 and the average last occurrence in the spring is May 22.

Temperatures

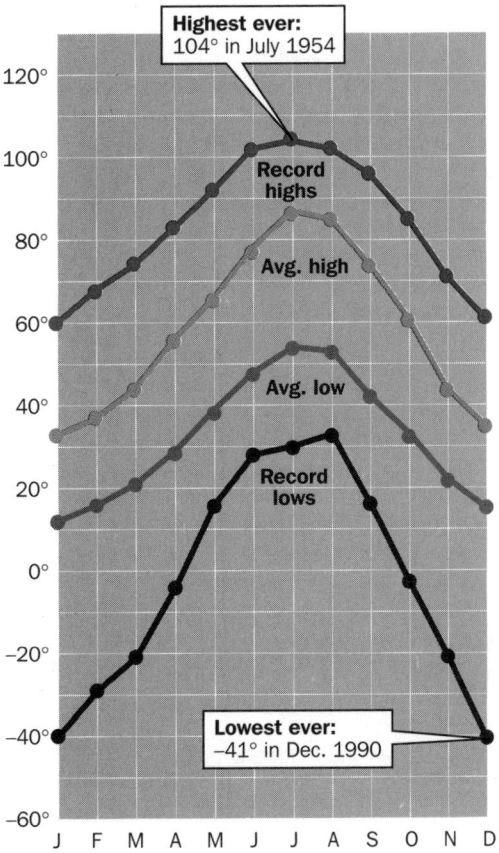

Highest ever: 104° in July 1954

Record highs

Avg. high

Avg. low

Record lows

Lowest ever: −41° in Dec. 1990

Weather extremes

Most rain in 24 hours:	3 in. May 19 – 20, 1978
Most rain in a month:	6.59 in. May 1978
Most snow in 24 hours:	31.1 in. Dec. 23 – 24, 1982
Most snow in a month:	62.8 in. December 1982

Monthly averages

Month	Avg. precip. (in.)	Avg. snow (in.)	Wet days	Thunder-storm days	Pct. sky is cloudy	% p.m. relative humidity	Dew point	Wind speed (mph)
Jan.	0.5	11	7	0	41	60	12	20.7
Feb.	0.6	10	8	*	43	57	15	18.4
March	1.0	14	10	*	45	49	19	17.3
April	1.5	13	10	1	45	41	25	16.1
May	2.0	4	11	6	41	39	34	15.0
June	1.4	T	8	8	27	31	40	12.7
July	1.2	0	8	9	18	25	43	11.5
Aug.	0.6	0	6	7	17	24	41	13.8
Sept.	0.9	1	6	3	24	30	33	15.0
Oct.	0.9	6	7	*	31	39	26	16.1
Nov.	0.7	10	7	*	39	56	19	18.4
Dec.	0.6	11	7	0	39	61	14	19.6

T - Trace of rain or snow   * - Less than 1   NA - Not Available

Annual averages

Precipitation (in inches)	12.0
Snow (in inches)	81
Heating degree days	7,642
Cooling degree days	457
Days with thunderstorms	34
Days with fog	37
Days above 90°	28
Days below 32°	180
Wet days	95
Days with snow	106
Days with 1.5 inches or more snow	33

Percent time sky is clear

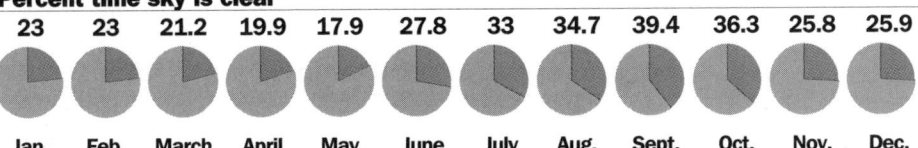

Jan.	Feb.	March	April	May	June	July	Aug.	Sept.	Oct.	Nov.	Dec.
23	23	21.2	19.9	17.9	27.8	33	34.7	39.4	36.3	25.8	25.9

Charleston, South Carolina

Lat. 32° 54' N **Lon.** 80° 2' W **Elev.** 41 ft.

Charleston's climate is temperate, modified considerably by the nearby ocean. Summer is warm and humid. High temperatures are generally several degrees lower along the coast than inland due to the cooling effect of the sea breeze. Summer is the rainiest season with 41 percent of the annual total. The fall season passes through the warm Indian summer period to the pre-winter cold spells that begin late in November. From late September to early November, the weather is mostly sunny and temperature extremes are rare. In late summer and early fall there is a threat of hurricanes. Winter is mild with periods of rain.

Temperatures

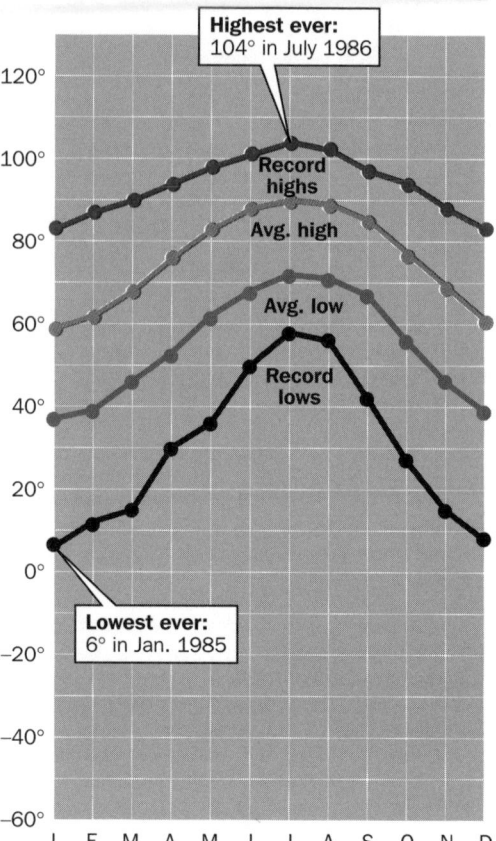

Highest ever: 104° in July 1986

Record highs

Avg. high

Avg. low

Record lows

Lowest ever: 6° in Jan. 1985

Weather extremes

Most rain in 24 hours:	10.10 in. June 10 – 11, 1973
Most rain in a month:	27.24 in. June 1973
Most snow in 24 hours:	6.6 in. Dec. 22 – 23, 1989
Most snow in a month:	8 in. December 1989

Monthly averages

Month	Avg. precip. (in.)	Avg. snow (in.)	Wet days	Thunder-storm days	Pct. sky is cloudy	% p.m. relative humidity	Dew point	Wind speed (mph)
Jan.	3.2	T	10	1	41	55	38	9.2
Feb.	3.2	T	9	1	39	52	39	11.5
March	4.4	T	10	2	37	51	45	11.5
April	2.8	0	7	3	28	51	52	11.5
May	4.1	0	9	7	29	57	61	9.2
June	5.9	0	11	10	27	62	68	8.1
July	7.4	0	13	13	27	66	72	9.2
Aug.	6.7	0	13	12	25	66	72	8.1
Sept.	5.6	0	10	5	28	65	67	9.2
Oct.	2.9	0	6	2	26	57	56	9.2
Nov.	2.4	T	7	1	29	55	47	9.2
Dec.	3.1	T	8	1	36	55	40	9.2

T - Trace of rain or snow   * - Less than 1   NA - Not Available

Annual averages

Precipitation (in inches)	51.8
Snow (in inches)	1
Heating degree days	2,084
Cooling degree days	2,210
Days with thunderstorms	58
Days with fog	160
Days above 90°	52
Days below 32°	34
Wet days	113
Days with snow	1
Days with 1.5 inches or more snow	*

Percent time sky is clear

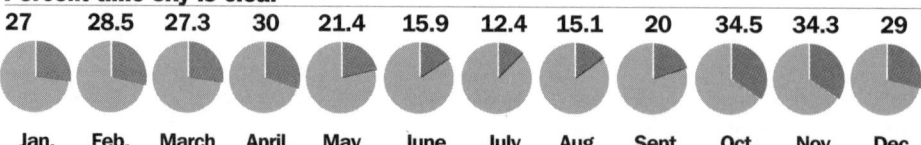

Jan.	Feb.	March	April	May	June	July	Aug.	Sept.	Oct.	Nov.	Dec.
27	28.5	27.3	30	21.4	15.9	12.4	15.1	20	34.5	34.3	29

Charleston, West Virginia

Lat. 38° 22' N **Lon.** 81° 36' W **Elev.** 1,015 ft.

Charleston, at the junction of the Kanawha and Elk rivers in the western foothills of Appalachian Mountains, is the capital of West Virginia. The hilltops are around 1,100 feet above sea level, about 500 feet higher than the valleys. Winters vary greatly from one season to the next, but typically have two or three extended cold spells when temperatures stay below freezing for a few consecutive days. Most snowfalls are 4 inches or less. Generally conditions are much more severe over the nearby mountains. Temperatures warm rapidly in the spring and are accompanied by low daytime humidity. Summer precipitation falls mostly in brief, but sometimes heavy, showers.

Temperatures

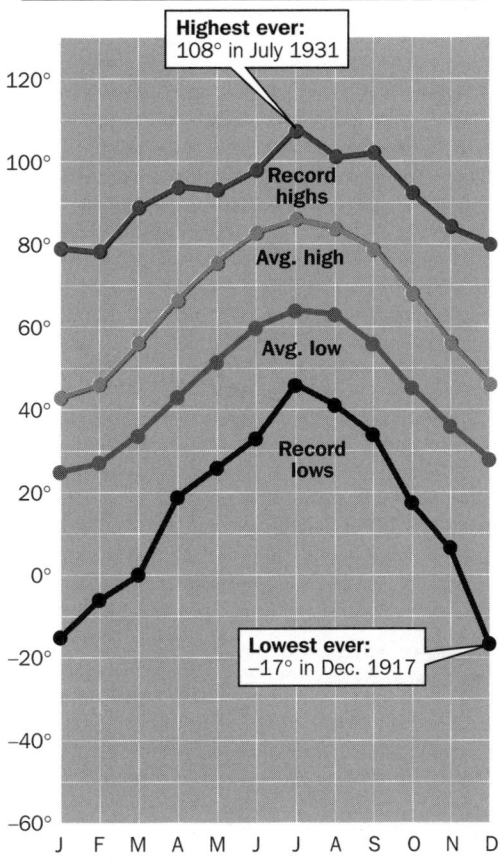

Highest ever: 108° in July 1931

Record highs

Avg. high

Avg. low

Record lows

Lowest ever: −17° in Dec. 1917

Weather extremes

Most rain in 24 hours:	5.60 in. July 19, 1961
Most rain in a month:	13.54 in. July 1961
Most snow in 24 hours:	17.2 in. March 12–13, 1993
Most snow in a month:	39.5 in. January 1978

Monthly averages

Month	Avg. precip. (in.)	Avg. snow (in.)	Wet days	Thunderstorm days	Pct. sky is cloudy	% p.m. relative humidity	Dew point	Wind speed (mph)
Jan.	3.4	10	16	1	61	59	23	11.5
Feb.	3.2	9	14	1	57	55	25	11.5
March	3.8	5	15	2	52	48	31	11.5
April	3.3	1	14	4	45	44	39	11.5
May	3.9	T	13	7	39	49	51	9.2
June	3.6	0	11	8	32	52	60	8.1
July	5.1	0	13	10	34	56	65	8.1
Aug.	4.0	0	11	7	33	56	64	8.1
Sept.	3.1	0	10	3	35	55	58	5.8
Oct.	2.7	T	10	1	38	51	46	8.1
Nov.	3.3	2	12	1	49	53	35	9.2
Dec.	3.3	5	14	*	58	59	27	10.4

T - Trace of rain or snow   * - Less than 1   NA - Not Available

Annual averages

Precipitation (in inches)	42.8
Snow (in inches)	32
Heating degree days	4,697
Cooling degree days	1,007
Days with thunderstorms	45
Days with fog	236
Days above 90°	22
Days below 32°	100
Wet days	153
Days with snow	51
Days with 1.5 inches or more snow	13

Percent time sky is clear

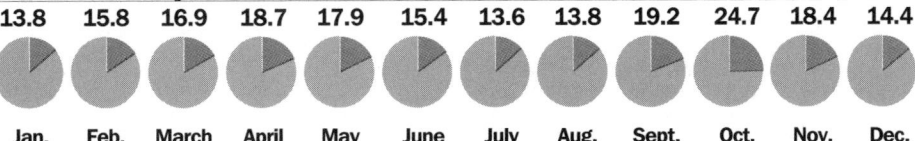

13.8	15.8	16.9	18.7	17.9	15.4	13.6	13.8	19.2	24.7	18.4	14.4
Jan.	Feb.	March	April	May	June	July	Aug.	Sept.	Oct.	Nov.	Dec.

Charlotte, North Carolina

Lat. 35° 13' N **Lon.** 80° 56' W **Elev.** 700 ft.

Charlotte enjoys a moderate climate, characterized by cool winters and quite warm summers. Winter weather is changeable, with occasional cold periods, but extreme cold is rare. Snow is infrequent, and the first snowfall of the season usually comes in late November or December. Summers are long and quite warm, with afternoon temperatures frequently in the low 90s. On the average, the last occurrence in spring with a temperature of 32°F is early April. In the fall, the average first occurrence of 32°F is early November. Rainfall is evenly distributed throughout the year, the driest weather usually coming in the fall. Hurricanes that strike the Carolina coast may produce heavy rain but seldom cause dangerous winds.

Temperatures

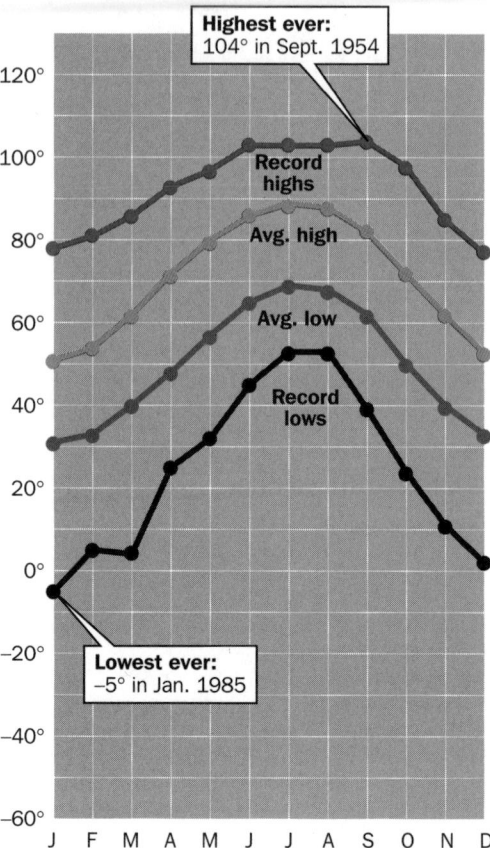

Highest ever: 104° in Sept. 1954

Record highs

Avg. high

Avg. low

Record lows

Lowest ever: −5° in Jan. 1985

Weather extremes

Most rain in 24 hours:	5.91 in. July 1, 1944
Most rain in a month:	14.72 in. October 1990
Most snow in 24 hours:	12.1 in. Jan. 7, 1988
Most snow in a month:	19.3 in. March 1960

Monthly averages

Month	Avg. precip. (in.)	Avg. snow (in.)	Wet days	Thunder-storm days	Pct. sky is cloudy	% p.m. relative humidity	Dew point	Wind speed (mph)
Jan.	3.6	2	10	1	44	53	29	10.4
Feb.	3.8	2	10	1	42	49	30	11.5
March	4.5	1	11	2	40	46	36	11.5
April	3.0	T	9	3	33	43	44	11.5
May	3.7	0	10	6	33	49	55	9.2
June	3.4	0	10	7	29	51	63	8.1
July	3.9	0	11	9	29	54	67	8.1
Aug.	3.9	0	10	7	28	55	67	8.1
Sept.	3.4	0	7	3	31	54	61	8.1
Oct.	3.2	0	7	1	28	50	50	9.2
Nov.	3.1	T	8	1	34	50	39	9.2
Dec.	3.4	1	10	*	41	54	32	9.2

T - Trace of rain or snow   * - Less than 1   NA - Not Available

Annual averages

Precipitation (in inches)	42.8
Snow (in inches)	6
Heating degree days	3,260
Cooling degree days	1,669
Days with thunderstorms	41
Days with fog	162
Days above 90°	44
Days below 32°	65
Wet days	113
Days with snow	5
Days with 1.5 inches or more snow	1

Percent time sky is clear

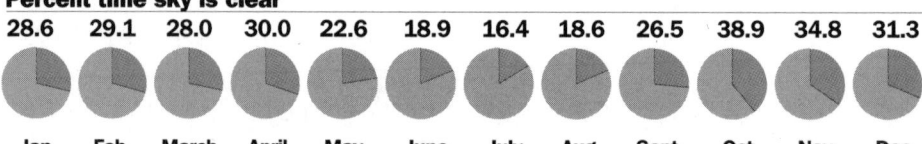

28.6	29.1	28.0	30.0	22.6	18.9	16.4	18.6	26.5	38.9	34.8	31.3
Jan.	Feb.	March	April	May	June	July	Aug.	Sept.	Oct.	Nov.	Dec.

Chattanooga, Tennessee

Lat. 35°02' N **Lon.** 85°12' W **Elev.** 692 ft.

Chattanooga is nestled between the Cumberland Mountains to the west and the Appalachian Mountains to the east. The local topography is complex with a number of minor valleys and ridges. The Tennessee River approaches Chattanooga from the northeast and forms a loop southwest to west to northwest of the city. Most of the city lies on the south side of the river. On the north and southwest, the terrain rises abruptly about 1,200 feet. This complex topography results in marked variations in wind and temperatures within short distances. In winter the Cumberland Mountains retard the flow of cold air from the north and west. In summer most afternoon temperatures are modified by thunderstorms when temperatures can plunge 10 to 15 degrees in minutes.

Temperatures

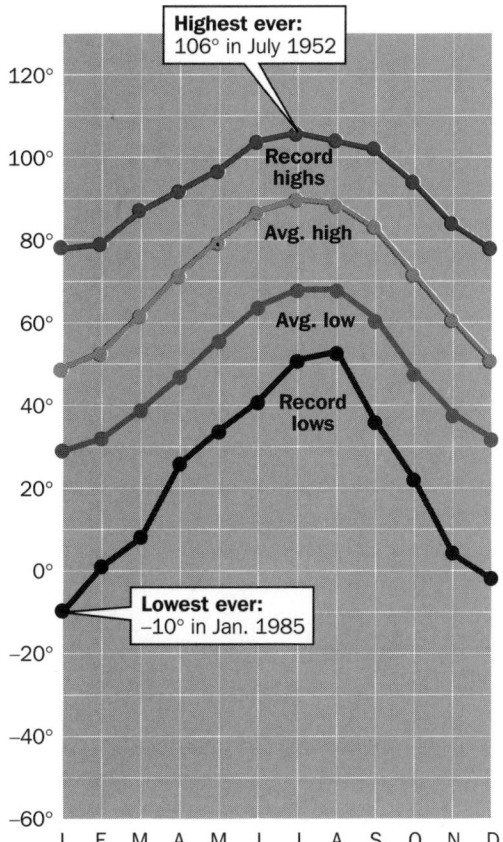

Highest ever: 106° in July 1952

Record highs

Avg. high

Avg. low

Record lows

Lowest ever: −10° in Jan. 1985

Weather extremes

Most rain in 24 hours:	7.61 in.	March 29 – 30, 1886
Most rain in a month:	16.32 in.	March 1980
Most snow in 24 hours:	20 in.	March 12 – 13, 1993
Most snow in a month:	20 in.	March 1993

Monthly averages

Month	Avg. precip. (in.)	Avg. snow (in.)	Wet days	Thunder-storm days	Pct. sky is cloudy	% p.m. relative humidity	Dew point	Wind speed (mph)
Jan.	5.3	2	12	1	53	58	29	8.1
Feb.	5.0	1	10	2	49	53	32	9.2
March	5.9	T	12	4	46	48	38	9.2
April	4.3	T	10	4	36	44	46	9.2
May	4.1	0	10	7	33	50	56	8.1
June	3.6	0	10	9	28	52	64	6.9
July	4.8	0	11	11	27	55	68	5.8
Aug.	3.5	0	10	9	25	55	68	5.8
Sept.	4.2	0	8	4	32	55	62	6.9
Oct.	3.2	T	7	2	30	50	50	6.9
Nov.	4.5	T	9	1	40	52	39	8.1
Dec.	5.1	1	11	1	50	57	32	8.1

T - Trace of rain or snow   * - Less than 1   NA - Not Available

Annual averages

Precipitation (in inches)	53.3
Snow (in inches)	4
Heating degree days	3,583
Cooling degree days	1,578
Days with thunderstorms	55
Days with fog	160
Days above 90°	48
Days below 32°	73
Wet days	120
Days with snow	5
Days with 1.5 inches or more snow	1

Percent time sky is clear

21.4	23.5	22.8	27.1	23.1	20.9	16.9	20.7	25.6	36.4	28.6	24.5

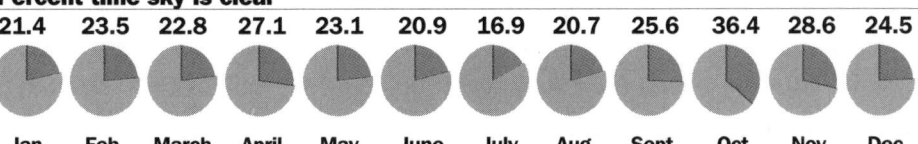

| Jan. | Feb. | March | April | May | June | July | Aug. | Sept. | Oct. | Nov. | Dec. |

Cheyenne, Wyoming

Lat. 41° 09' N **Lon.** 104° 49' W **Elev.** 6,120 ft.

Cheyenne is located on a broad plateau between the North and South Platte rivers in the southeastern corner of Wyoming. The ground level rises rapidly almost 3,000 feet to a ridge of approximately 9,000 feet in elevation about 30 miles west of the city. The ridge, called the Laramie Mountains, helps produce warm, dry winds called chinooks. These winds tend to raise the temperature because the air warms up as it moves down the slope. In the summer, precipitation occurs mainly with thunderstorms. They frequently contain hail that is occasionally large enough to be destructive. Most of the snow falls in late winter and early spring. Heavy snow often falls in May. Relative annual humidity averages near 50 percent.

Temperatures

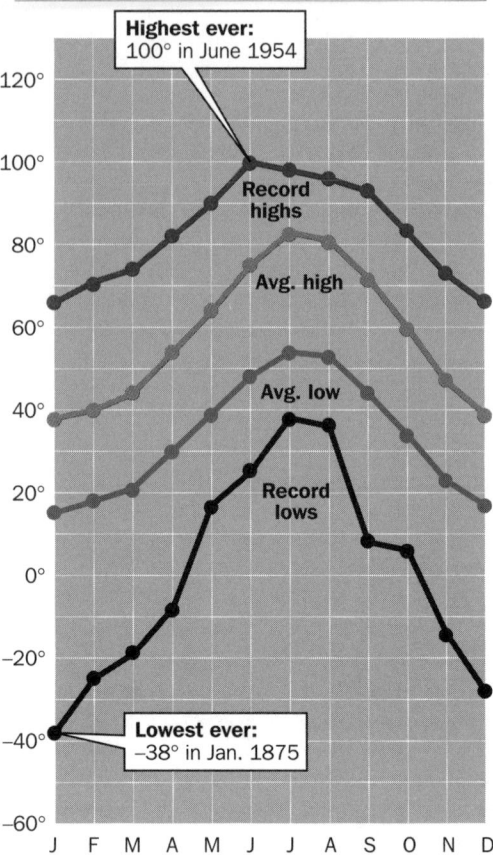

Highest ever: 100° in June 1954
Record highs
Avg. high
Avg. low
Record lows
Lowest ever: −38° in Jan. 1875

Weather extremes

Most rain in 24 hours:	6.06 in. Aug. 1, 1985
Most rain in a month:	7.66 in. April 1900
Most snow in 24 hours:	19.8 in. Nov. 20, 1979
Most snow in a month:	46.5 in. April 1905

Monthly averages

Month	Avg. precip. (in.)	Avg. snow (in.)	Wet days	Thunder-storm days	Pct. sky is cloudy	% p.m. relative humidity	Dew point	Wind speed (mph)
Jan.	0.4	6	5	0	29	51	10	18.4
Feb.	0.4	6	6	*	31	49	13	17.3
March	1.1	12	9	*	36	48	17	17.3
April	1.4	8	9	2	35	43	24	16.1
May	2.5	3	12	8	35	45	34	13.8
June	2.1	T	10	11	23	41	42	12.7
July	2.0	T	11	13	18	39	46	11.5
Aug.	1.6	0	10	11	18	38	45	11.5
Sept.	1.1	1	7	4	21	38	36	12.7
Oct.	0.7	4	5	1	23	41	26	13.8
Nov.	0.6	7	6	*	28	50	17	17.3
Dec.	0.4	6	6	0	28	53	12	18.4

T - Trace of rain or snow   * - Less than 1   NA - Not Available

Annual averages

Precipitation (in inches)	14.4
Snow (in inches)	51
Heating degree days	7,238
Cooling degree days	310
Days with thunderstorms	50
Days with fog	58
Days above 90°	9
Days below 32°	173
Wet days	96
Days with snow	83
Days with 1.5 inches or more snow	19

Percent time sky is clear

27.2	25	21.5	20.5	16.1	24.7	25.3	27.3	36.5	37.4	28.6	28.2

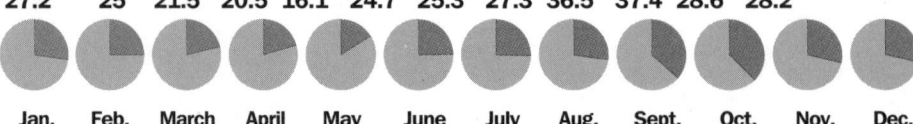

| Jan. | Feb. | March | April | May | June | July | Aug. | Sept. | Oct. | Nov. | Dec. |

Chicago, Illinois

Lat. 41° 59' N **Lon.** 87° 54' W **Elev.** 674 ft.

Since it's near the center of the continent, Chicago sees wide weather variations during the year with bitter winter winds and occasional muggy summer heat waves. The city's location on Lake Michigan does moderate the climate somewhat. During the summer, cool breezes from the lake can lower temperatures near the shore by 10 degrees. During the winter, the lake's water is warmer than the land and helps increase temperatures slightly near the lake. The lake is also responsible for heavy snow that falls near the shore a few times during most winters. This occurs when cold air blows over the lake, picking up additional moisture. The added moisture creates "lake effect" snow that falls within a few miles of shore. While ice often covers harbors and other areas near the shore, Lake Michigan does not freeze over during the winter.

Temperatures

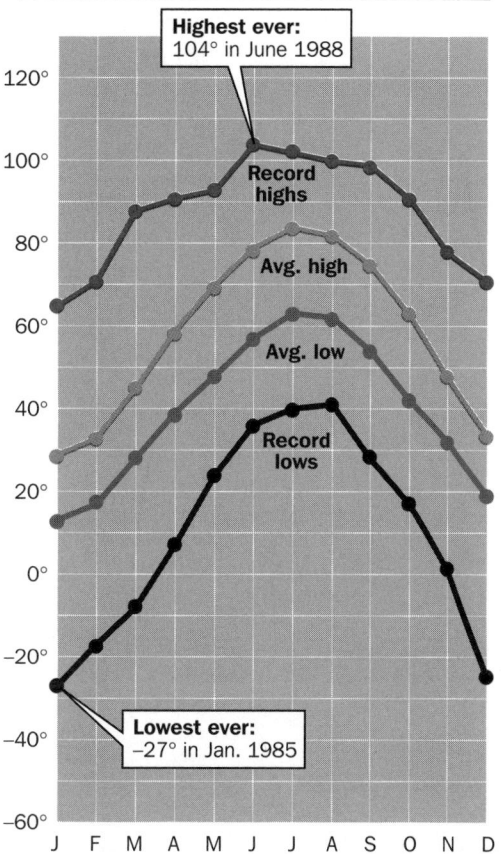

Weather extremes

Most rain in 24 hours:	6.5 in. Aug. 10, 1913
Most rain in a month:	17.1 in. August 1913
Most snow in 24 hours:	15 in. Jan. 5, 1932
Most snow in a month:	34 in. January 1932

Monthly averages

Month	Avg. precip. (in.)	Avg. snow (in.)	Wet days	Thunderstorm days	Pct. sky is cloudy	% p.m. relative humidity	Dew point	Wind speed (mph)
Jan.	1.6	11	11	*	51	65	14	11.5
Feb.	1.4	8	10	*	49	63	18	10.4
March	2.7	7	12	2	51	59	27	11.5
April	3.6	2	12	4	45	53	36	12.7
May	3.3	T	11	5	36	51	46	11.5
June	3.7	0	10	6	29	52	56	10.4
July	3.7	0	10	6	24	54	62	9.2
Aug.	4.1	0	9	6	25	55	61	9.2
Sept.	3.7	0	9	5	30	55	54	9.2
Oct.	2.4	1	9	2	35	53	42	10.4
Nov.	2.8	2	11	1	52	61	31	11.5
Dec.	2.3	9	11	1	55	68	20	11.5

T - Trace of rain or snow   * - Less than 1   NA - Not Available

Annual averages

Precipitation (in inches)	35.4
Snow (in inches)	39
Heating degree days	6,533
Cooling degree days	834
Days with thunderstorms	38
Days with fog	124
Days above 90°	17
Days below 32°	132
Wet days	125
Days with snow	62
Days with 1.5 inches or more snow	17

Percent time sky is clear

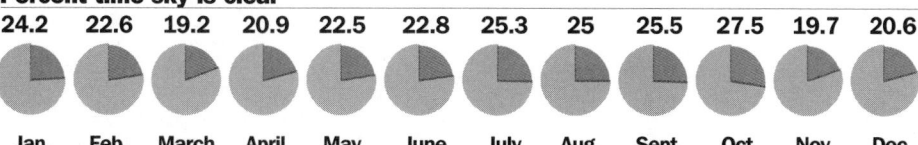

24.2	22.6	19.2	20.9	22.5	22.8	25.3	25	25.5	27.5	19.7	20.6
Jan.	Feb.	March	April	May	June	July	Aug.	Sept.	Oct.	Nov.	Dec.

Cincinnati, Ohio

Lat. 39° 04' N **Lon.** 84° 40' W **Elev.** 869 ft.

Cincinnati sits beside the Ohio River surrounded by rolling hills. The climate is continental with pronounced daily and seasonal temperature changes. In general, winters are moderately cold, with frequent periods of extensive cloudiness. Maximum snowfall usually comes in January. Summers are warm, with temperatures above 90°F fairly common. The temperature will reach 100°F or more in one year out of three. The heaviest precipitation, as well as precipitation of the longest duration, is normally associated with low pressure disturbances moving from southwest to northeast through the Ohio Valley. Last frost usually occurs by mid-April and the first frost usually arrives in the latter part of October.

Temperatures

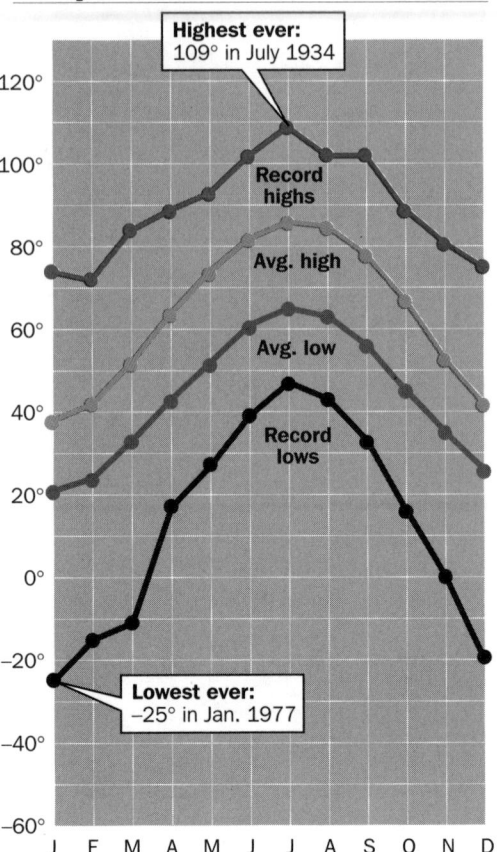

Highest ever: 109° in July 1934

Record highs

Avg. high

Avg. low

Record lows

Lowest ever: −25° in Jan. 1977

Weather extremes

Most rain in 24 hours:	5.21 in.	March 9, 1964
Most rain in a month:	12.18 in.	March 1964
Most snow in 24 hours:	9.8 in.	March 22, 1968
Most snow in a month:	31.5 in.	January 1978

Monthly averages

Month	Avg. precip. (in.)	Avg. snow (in.)	Wet days	Thunderstorm days	Pct. sky is cloudy	% p.m. relative humidity	Dew point	Wind speed (mph)
Jan.	3.2	7	12	1	60	65	21	11.5
Feb.	2.9	5	11	1	56	60	24	11.5
March	3.9	4	13	2	54	55	31	12.7
April	3.5	1	12	4	48	50	40	11.5
May	4.0	T	11	6	41	51	51	9.2
June	3.9	0	10	7	33	53	60	8.1
July	4.2	0	10	7	29	54	64	8.1
Aug.	3.1	0	9	6	27	52	63	8.1
Sept.	2.8	0	8	3	31	52	56	8.1
Oct.	2.8	T	8	1	35	51	44	9.2
Nov.	3.4	2	11	1	52	58	34	11.5
Dec.	3.1	4	12	*	59	65	26	11.5

T - Trace of rain or snow   * - Less than 1   NA - Not Available

Annual averages

Precipitation (in inches)	40.9
Snow (in inches)	23
Heating degree days	5,140
Cooling degree days	1,114
Days with thunderstorms	39
Days with fog	160
Days above 90°	23
Days below 32°	107
Wet days	127
Days with snow	47
Days with 1.5 inches or more snow	9

Percent time sky is clear

Jan.	Feb.	March	April	May	June	July	Aug.	Sept.	Oct.	Nov.	Dec.
17.5	19.3	18	20	21	21.1	21.3	25.2	30	32.6	21.7	17.5

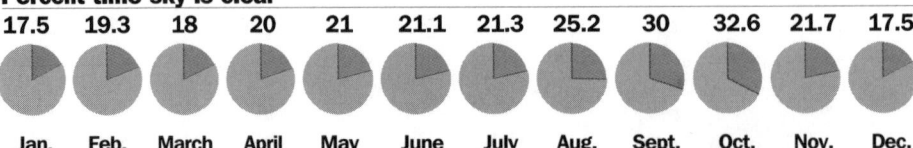

Cleveland, Ohio

Lat. 41° 25' N **Lon.** 81° 52' W **Elev.** 770 ft.

Cleveland is in northeast Ohio, on the shores of Lake Erie. The lake — which borders 31 miles of the city's shoreline — is the major force in Cleveland's weather. The city is largely flat, although it is bisected north-south by the shallow Cuyahoga River Valley. The climate is described as continental, though west to northerly winds blowing off Lake Erie tend to lower daily high temperatures in summer. While those winds slightly raise temperatures in winter, subzero readings are not unknown. Precipitation is normally abundant and well distributed all year. Thunderstorms are most frequent from April through August. Snowfall may fluctuate widely.

Temperatures

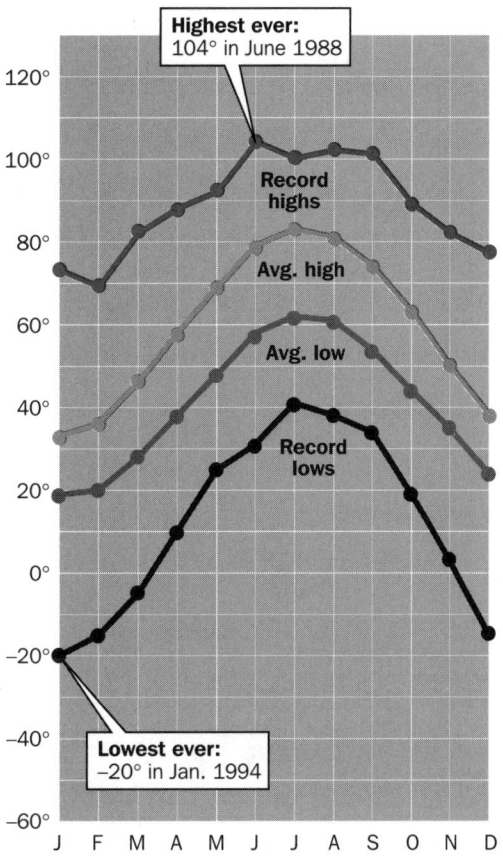

Weather extremes

Most rain in 24 hours:	4.97 in. Sept. 1 – 2, 1901
Most rain in a month:	9.77 in. June 1902
Most snow in 24 hours:	17.4 in. Nov. 10 – 11, 1913
Most snow in a month:	42.8 in. January 1978

Monthly averages

Month	Avg. precip. (in.)	Avg. snow (in.)	Wet days	Thunder-storm days	Pct. sky is cloudy	% p.m. relative humidity	Dew point	Wind speed (mph)
Jan.	2.4	13	17	*	67	70	19	12.7
Feb.	2.3	12	14	*	62	67	21	12.7
March	3.1	10	15	2	58	62	27	12.7
April	3.4	2	15	4	50	56	36	12.7
May	3.5	T	13	5	41	54	47	10.4
June	3.5	0	11	6	34	55	57	10.4
July	3.5	0	10	6	28	55	61	9.2
Aug.	3.4	0	10	5	29	58	61	8.1
Sept.	3.2	0	10	3	34	58	54	9.2
Oct.	2.6	1	11	2	42	58	43	10.4
Nov.	3.2	5	15	1	62	65	33	12.7
Dec.	2.9	12	16	*	69	70	24	12.7

T - Trace of rain or snow   * - Less than 1   NA - Not Available

Annual averages

Precipitation (in inches)	37.1
Snow (in inches)	55
Heating degree days	6,079
Cooling degree days	746
Days with thunderstorms	34
Days with fog	146
Days above 90°	12
Days below 32°	123
Wet days	157
Days with snow	95
Days with 1.5 inches or more snow	24

Percent time sky is clear

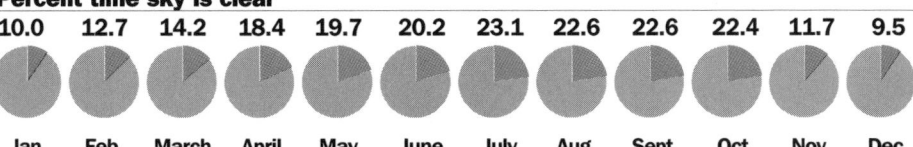

10.0	12.7	14.2	18.4	19.7	20.2	23.1	22.6	22.6	22.4	11.7	9.5
Jan.	Feb.	March	April	May	June	July	Aug.	Sept.	Oct.	Nov.	Dec.

Colorado Springs, Colorado

Lat. 38° 49' N **Lon.** 104° 43' W **Elev.** 6,090 ft.

Colorado Springs is located in relatively flat semiarid country on the eastern slope of the Rocky Mountains. To the west mountains rise abruptly to heights averaging near 11,000 feet. To the east are undulating prairie lands. The land slopes up to the north, reaching an average height of about 8,000 feet at the top of Palmer Lake Divide. A wide range of elevations gives Colorado Springs its weather. Higher elevations to the west and north of the city produce significant differences in temperature and precipitation. Precipitation in higher elevations to the west and north is approximately twice that of lower elevations and the number of rainy days is almost triple. Relative humidity is normally low and winds are moderately high, especially the west-to-east chinook winds that cause rapid rises in winter temperatures.

Temperatures

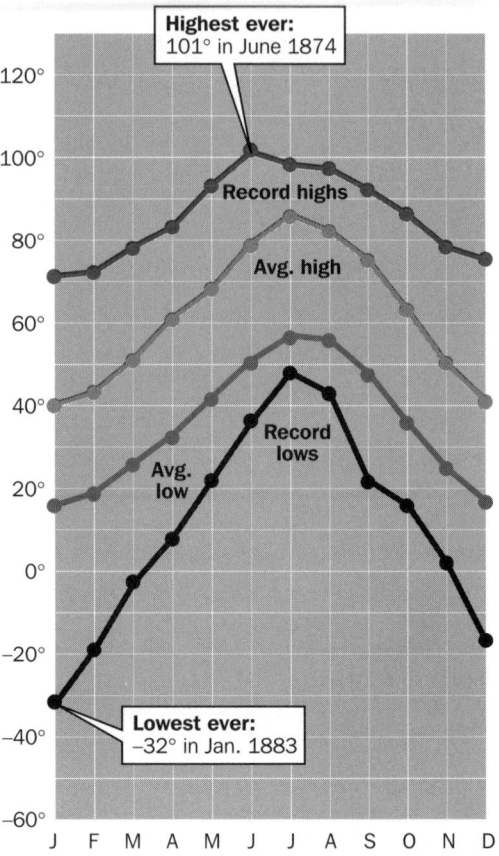

Highest ever: 101° in June 1874

Record highs

Avg. high

Record lows

Avg. low

Lowest ever: −32° in Jan. 1883

Weather extremes

Most rain in 24 hours:	3.73 in. Aug. 1 – 2, 1976
Most rain in a month:	8.10 in. May 1936
Most snow in 24 hours:	18 in. April 1 – 2, 1957
Most snow in a month:	42.7 in. April 1957

Monthly averages

Month	Avg. precip. (in.)	Avg. snow (in.)	Wet days	Thunder-storm days	Pct. sky is cloudy	% p.m. relative humidity	Dew point	Wind speed (mph)
Jan.	0.4	7	6	0	27	46	10	9.2
Feb.	0.5	7	6	0	31	41	12	11.5
March	1.2	12	8	1	35	39	16	13.8
April	1.2	5	8	2	32	35	23	13.8
May	2.7	3	13	7	33	37	33	12.7
June	2.1	0	10	10	22	34	41	11.5
July	2.5	0	11	12	20	39	47	10.4
Aug.	3.6	0	14	13	21	41	47	10.4
Sept.	1.0	T	7	4	21	36	38	10.4
Oct.	0.8	3	5	1	22	36	26	11.5
Nov.	0.5	5	4	0	25	44	17	9.2
Dec.	0.7	10	6	0	26	47	11	9.2

T - Trace of rain or snow   * - Less than 1   NA - Not Available

Annual averages

Precipitation (in inches)	17.2
Snow (in inches)	51
Heating degree days	6,366
Cooling degree days	497
Days with thunderstorms	50
Days with fog	55
Days above 90°	19
Days below 32°	160
Wet days	98
Days with snow	37
Days with 1.5 inches or more snow	8

Percent time sky is clear

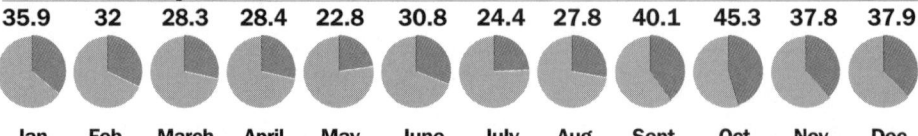

35.9	32	28.3	28.4	22.8	30.8	24.4	27.8	40.1	45.3	37.8	37.9
Jan.	Feb.	March	April	May	June	July	Aug.	Sept.	Oct.	Nov.	Dec.

Columbia, Missouri

Lat. 38° 49' N **Lon.** 92° 13' W **Elev.** 887 ft.

With its interior continental location, Columbia has moderately cold winters and warm, often humid, summers. In winter, periods of cold weather are usually interrupted by at least a few mild days. It is not uncommon to find some winter days with temperatures in the 60s. Some snow falls each winter, but the snow cover rarely persists for more than three weeks. Most of the time snow stays on the ground for less than a week. Temperatures of over 100°F occur in most summers. Late spring and early summer produce the most frequent and largest amounts of rain. Thus, in addition to being warm, these months are often quite humid.

Temperatures

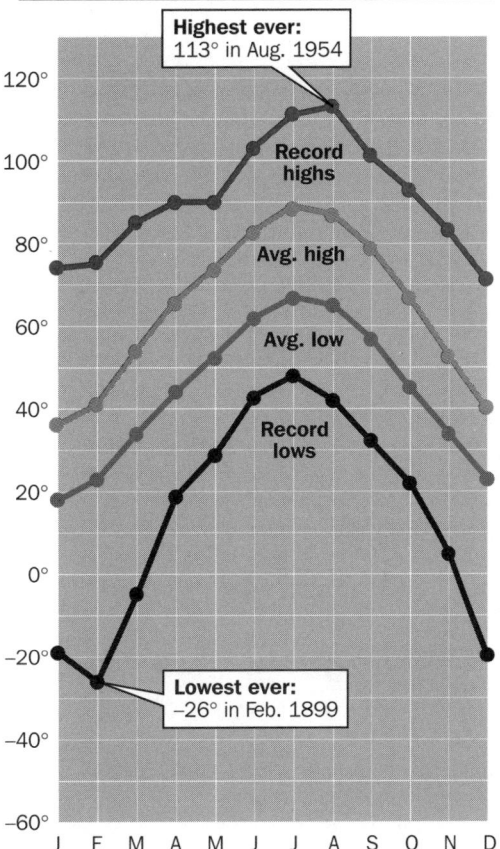

Highest ever: 113° in Aug. 1954

Record highs

Avg. high

Avg. low

Record lows

Lowest ever: −26° in Feb. 1899

Weather extremes

Most rain in 24 hours:	6.61 in.	Sept. 2, 1918
Most rain in a month:	14.86 in.	June 1928
Most snow in 24 hours:	12.8 in.	March 12–13, 1937
Most snow in a month:	24.5 in.	March 1960

Monthly averages

Month	Avg. precip. (in.)	Avg. snow (in.)	Wet days	Thunder-storm days	Pct. sky is cloudy	% p.m. relative humidity	Dew point	Wind speed (mph)
Jan.	1.5	7	7	1	45	60	18	12.7
Feb.	2.0	8	9	1	49	59	23	11.5
March	3.5	4	11	3	48	54	32	12.7
April	3.9	1	11	5	41	51	41	11.5
May	5.1	0	12	8	37	56	53	10.4
June	3.9	0	8	8	29	55	62	9.2
July	3.6	0	8	8	21	51	66	8.1
Aug.	3.7	0	8	7	24	52	64	8.1
Sept.	3.5	0	9	5	29	54	57	9.2
Oct.	3.2	T	9	3	35	53	45	10.4
Nov.	3.3	2	9	2	45	58	34	10.4
Dec.	2.7	5	9	1	51	64	24	12.7

T - Trace of rain or snow   * - Less than 1   NA - Not Available

Annual averages

Precipitation (in inches)	39.9
Snow (in inches)	27
Heating degree days	5,166
Cooling degree days	1,294
Days with thunderstorms	52
Days with fog	123
Days above 90°	37
Days below 32°	108
Wet days	110
Days with snow	36
Days with 1.5 inches or more snow	11

Percent time sky is clear

29.4	26.4	22.9	25.1	22.5	23.0	29.3	29.6	32.3	34.1	28.4	26.4
Jan.	Feb.	March	April	May	June	July	Aug.	Sept.	Oct.	Nov.	Dec.

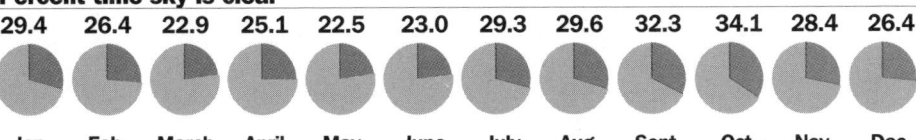

Columbia, South Carolina

Lat. 33° 57' N **Lon.** 81° 07' W **Elev.** 213 ft.

The climate in the Columbia area is relatively temperate. The Appalachian Mountain chain, some 150 miles to the northwest, frequently retards the approach of unseasonable cold weather in the winter. The terrain offers little moderating effect on the summer heat. Long summers are prevalent with warm weather usually lasting from May into September. In summer, the Bermuda High is the greatest single weather factor. This permanent high more or less blocks the entry of cold fronts so that many stall before reaching central South Carolina. More than three days of sustained snow cover is rare. Spring is the most changeable season of the year, varying from an occasional cold snap in March to generally warm and pleasant temperatures in May.

Temperatures

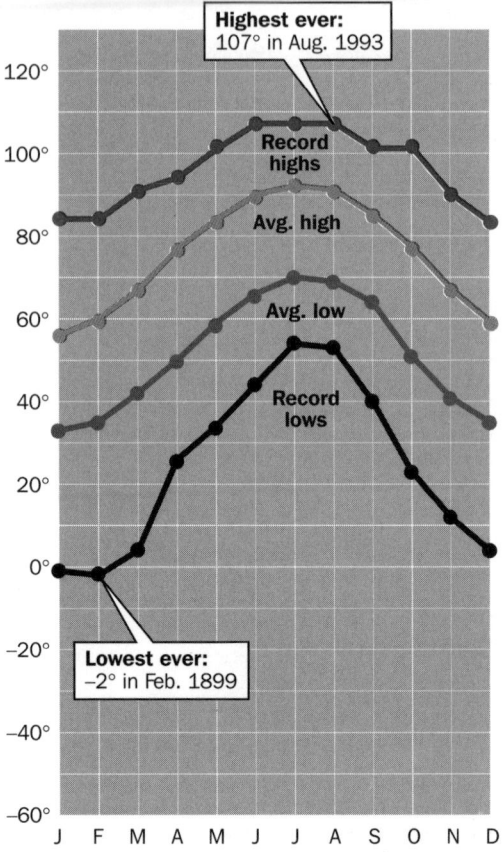

Highest ever: 107° in Aug. 1993
Record highs
Avg. high
Avg. low
Record lows
Lowest ever: -2° in Feb. 1899

Weather extremes

Most rain in 24 hours:	7.66 in. Aug. 16 – 17, 1949
Most rain in a month:	17.46 in. July 1991
Most snow in 24 hours:	15.7 in. Feb. 9 – 10, 1973
Most snow in a month:	16 in. February 1973

Monthly averages

Month	Avg. precip. (in.)	Avg. snow (in.)	Wet days	Thunder-storm days	Pct. sky is cloudy	% p.m. relative humidity	Dew point	Wind speed (mph)
Jan.	4.0	1	10	1	43	51	33	2.3
Feb.	4.0	1	10	1	41	47	35	3.5
March	4.7	T	11	3	39	44	41	2.3
April	3.4	0	8	4	30	41	48	2.3
May	3.6	0	9	6	30	46	58	2.3
June	4.2	0	9	9	27	50	65	2.3
July	5.5	0	12	13	29	54	69	2.3
Aug.	5.9	0	11	10	27	56	69	2.3
Sept.	4.0	0	8	4	31	54	64	2.3
Oct.	2.9	0	6	1	27	49	52	2.3
Nov.	2.7	T	7	1	32	48	43	2.3
Dec.	3.4	T	9	*	39	51	36	2.3

T - Trace of rain or snow   * - Less than 1   NA - Not Available

Annual averages

Precipitation (in inches)	48.3
Snow (in inches)	2
Heating degree days	2,599
Cooling degree days	2,116
Days with thunderstorms	53
Days with fog	168
Days above 90°	77
Days below 32°	58
Wet days	110
Days with snow	1
Days with 1.5 inches or more snow	*

Percent time sky is clear

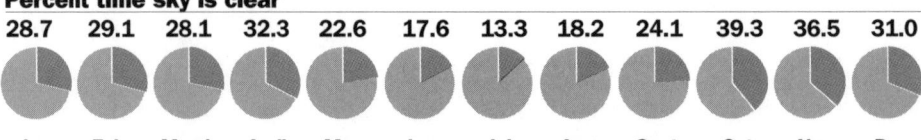

28.7	29.1	28.1	32.3	22.6	17.6	13.3	18.2	24.1	39.3	36.5	31.0
Jan.	Feb.	March	April	May	June	July	Aug.	Sept.	Oct.	Nov.	Dec.

Columbus, Georgia

Lat. 32° 31' N **Lon.** 84° 57' W **Elev.** 449 ft.

The climate of Columbus, located on the Chattahoochee River, is that of the humid southeast, with pronounced maritime effects at some periods, and equally pronounced continental effects at others. Heavy midsummer rainfall is commonly the result of frequent local thunderstorms. Heavy rains occur occasionally in autumn due to Gulf or Caribbean hurricanes moving inland near the Columbus area. Snow is rare, but almost every winter sees a few snowflakes falling in the area and occasionally there is a moderate to heavy snowfall. The coldest month is usually January and the warmest is usually July. The average first occurrence of 32°F in the fall is November 9 and the average last occurrence in the spring is March 21.

Temperatures

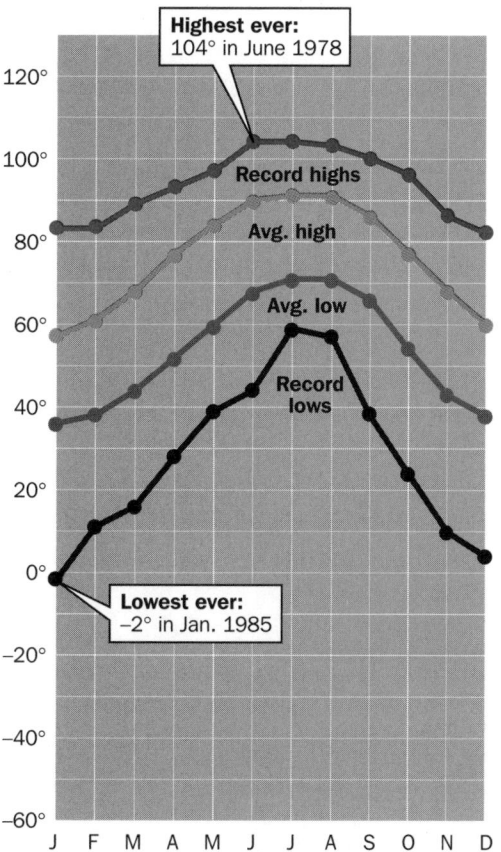

Highest ever: 104° in June 1978
Record highs
Avg. high
Avg. low
Record lows
Lowest ever: -2° in Jan. 1985

Weather extremes

Most rain in 24 hours:	7.22 in.	March 16–17, 1990
Most rain in a month:	13.24 in.	July 1971
Most snow in 24 hours:	14 in.	Feb. 9 – 10, 1973
Most snow in a month:	14 in.	February 1973

Monthly averages

Month	Avg. precip. (in.)	Avg. snow (in.)	Wet days	Thunder-storm days	Pct. sky is cloudy	% p.m. relative humidity	Dew point	Wind speed (mph)
Jan.	4.2	T	10	1	46	54	36	10.4
Feb.	4.7	T	10	2	45	50	38	10.4
March	5.8	T	10	4	40	47	44	10.4
April	4.4	T	8	4	31	43	51	10.4
May	4.1	0	8	7	28	48	60	8.1
June	3.9	0	9	8	25	51	66	8.1
July	5.7	0	13	13	29	58	70	8.1
Aug.	3.8	0	10	9	23	55	70	6.9
Sept.	3.3	0	8	4	29	54	65	9.2
Oct.	2.0	0	5	1	25	48	54	9.2
Nov.	3.4	T	8	1	34	50	45	8.1
Dec.	4.8	T	10	1	42	54	39	9.2

T - Trace of rain or snow   * - Less than 1   NA - Not Available

Annual averages

Precipitation (in inches)	50.2
Snow (in inches)	1
Heating degree days	2,260
Cooling degree days	2,254
Days with thunderstorms	55
Days with fog	178
Days above 90°	77
Days below 32°	43
Wet days	109
Days with snow	*
Days with 1.5 inches or more snow	*

Percent time sky is clear

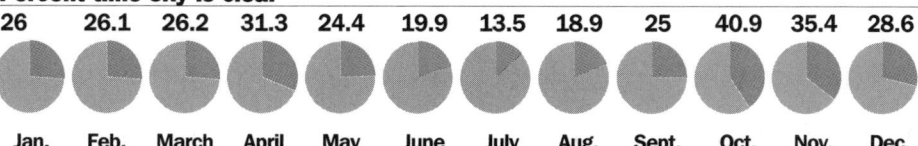

Jan.	Feb.	March	April	May	June	July	Aug.	Sept.	Oct.	Nov.	Dec.
26	26.1	26.2	31.3	24.4	19.9	13.5	18.9	25	40.9	35.4	28.6

Columbus, Ohio

Lat. 40° 00' N **Lon.** 82° 53' W **Elev.** 812 ft.

Columbus is located in an area of change-able weather. Air masses from central and northwest Canada frequently invade this region. Air from the Gulf of Mexico often reaches central Ohio during the summer. There are also occasional weather changes brought about by cool outbreaks from the Hudson Bay region of Canada, especially dur-ing spring. The average occurrence of the last freezing temperature in the spring within the city proper is mid-April, and the first freeze in the fall is very late October, but in the imme-diate surroundings, there is much variation. Records show a high frequency of calm or very low wind speeds during late evening and early morning from June through September.

Temperatures

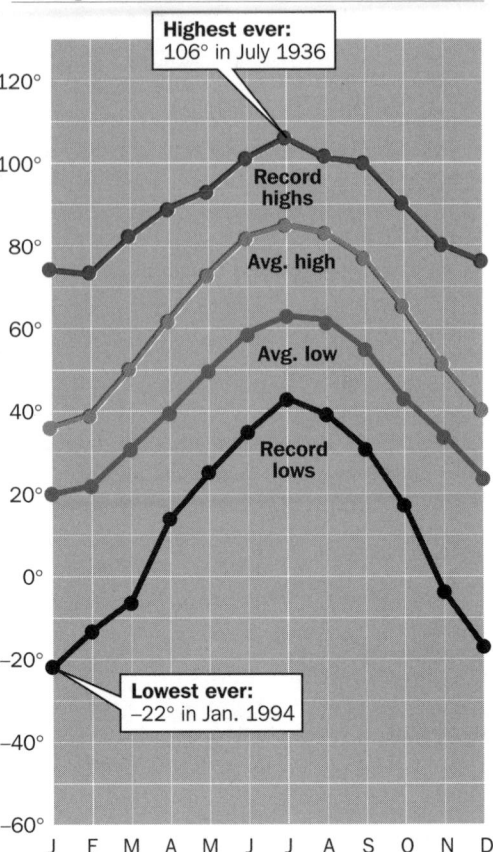

Highest ever: 106° in July 1936

Record highs

Avg. high

Avg. low

Record lows

Lowest ever: −22° in Jan. 1994

Weather extremes

Most rain in 24 hours:	5.16 in. July 12 – 13, 1992
Most rain in a month:	12.36 in. July 1992
Most snow in 24 hours:	12.3 in. April 4, 1987
Most snow in a month:	34.4 in. January 1978

Monthly averages

Month	Avg. precip. (in.)	Avg. snow (in.)	Wet days	Thunder-storm days	Pct. sky is cloudy	% p.m. relative humidity	Dew point	Wind speed (mph)
Jan.	2.8	8	13	*	61	66	20	9.2
Feb.	2.4	6	11	1	56	62	22	9.2
March	3.1	5	14	2	53	55	29	12.7
April	3.3	1	13	4	45	51	38	9.2
May	3.9	T	12	6	38	52	49	9.2
June	4.0	0	11	8	29	53	59	8.1
July	4.3	0	11	8	27	53	63	6.9
Aug.	3.3	0	9	6	26	54	62	6.9
Sept.	2.7	T	8	3	30	53	55	8.1
Oct.	2.1	T	9	1	35	53	43	8.1
Nov.	3.0	2	12	1	53	61	33	9.2
Dec.	2.8	6	13	*	61	68	25	9.2

T - Trace of rain or snow　　* - Less than 1　　NA - Not Available

Annual averages

Precipitation (in inches)	37.9
Snow (in inches)	28
Heating degree days	5,580
Cooling degree days	933
Days with thunderstorms	40
Days with fog	158
Days above 90°	19
Days below 32°	118
Wet days	136
Days with snow	56
Days with 1.5 inches or more snow	11

Percent time sky is clear

14.6	16.3	15.9	18.7	19.7	19.0	20.4	23.0	27.7	30.3	17.7	14.0

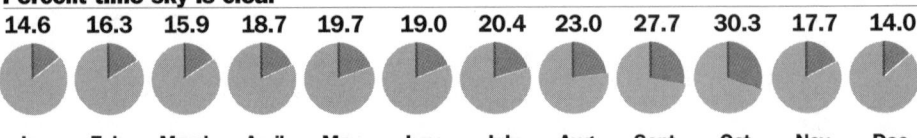

| Jan. | Feb. | March | April | May | June | July | Aug. | Sept. | Oct. | Nov. | Dec. |

Concord, New Hampshire

Lat. 43° 12′ N **Lon.** 71° 30′ W **Elev.** 346 ft.

Concord, the capital of New Hampshire, is situated near the geographical center of New England on the Merrimack River. Northwesterly winds bring cold, dry air during the winter and pleasantly cool, dry air in the summer. Winter breezes are somewhat lighter, and winds are frequently calm during the night and early morning hours. Low temperatures, as a rule, do not interrupt normal out-of-doors activity because winds are calm or light, producing a low wind chill factor. Very hot summer weather is infrequent. The first snowfall of an inch or more is likely to come between mid-November and mid-December. The average first occurrence of 32°F in the fall is Sept. 22 and the average last occurrence in the spring is May 23.

Temperatures

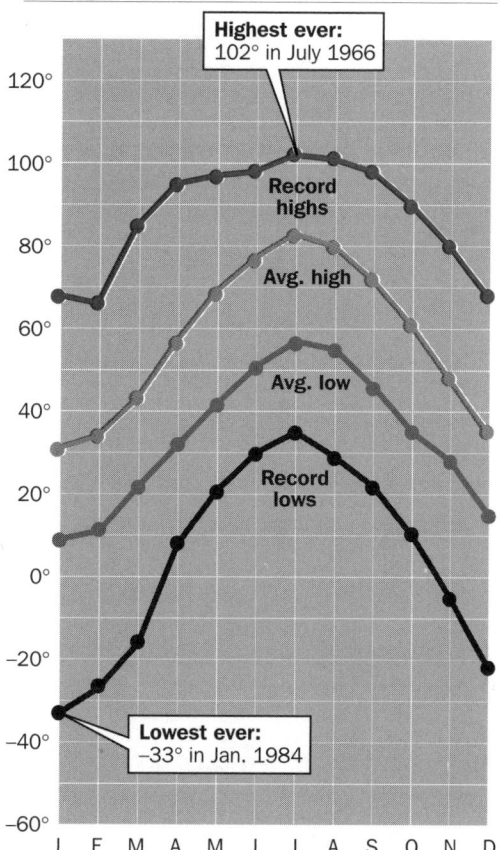

Highest ever: 102° in July 1966

Record highs

Avg. high

Avg. low

Record lows

Lowest ever: −33° in Jan. 1984

Weather extremes

Most rain in 24 hours:	4.47 in.	June 20 – 21, 1944
Most rain in a month:	10.10 in.	June 1944
Most snow in 24 hours:	19 in.	January 1944
Most snow in a month:	49.8 in.	February 1969

Monthly averages

Month	Avg. precip. (in.)	Avg. snow (in.)	Wet days	Thunder-storm days	Pct. sky is cloudy	% p.m. relative humidity	Dew point	Wind speed (mph)
Jan.	2.8	18	11	*	43	59	11	11.5
Feb.	2.5	15	9	*	42	55	13	11.5
March	2.9	11	11	*	44	52	21	11.5
April	3.1	2	11	1	44	46	31	11.5
May	3.2	T	12	2	43	47	42	10.4
June	3.1	0	11	4	37	52	54	9.2
July	3.1	0	10	5	32	51	59	9.2
Aug.	3.3	0	10	4	32	53	58	8.1
Sept.	2.9	0	9	2	37	55	50	9.2
Oct.	3.1	T	9	1	37	53	39	10.4
Nov.	3.8	4	11	*	47	61	29	10.4
Dec.	3.2	14	11	*	45	63	17	10.4

T - Trace of rain or snow   * - Less than 1   NA - Not Available

Annual averages

Precipitation (in inches)	36.9
Snow (in inches)	63
Heating degree days	7,432
Cooling degree days	439
Days with thunderstorms	19
Days with fog	185
Days above 90°	12
Days below 32°	171
Wet days	125
Days with snow	62
Days with 1.5 inches or more snow	26

Percent time sky is clear

28.7	29.5	26.9	23.1	18.9	18.0	18.6	21.5	25.7	29.2	21.3	26.0

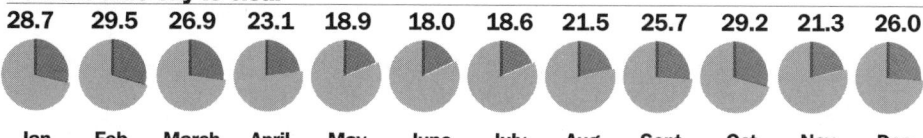

| Jan. | Feb. | March | April | May | June | July | Aug. | Sept. | Oct. | Nov. | Dec. |

Corpus Christi, Texas

Lat. 27° 46' N **Lon.** 97° 30' W **Elev.** 44 ft.

Corpus Christi is on Corpus Christi Bay, an inlet of the Gulf of Mexico. The moderating influence of the water can make temperatures in the city substantially different from inland areas during calm winter mornings and summer afternoons. The Gulf also keeps humidity high throughout the year. Peak rainfall months are May and September; winter is the driest season. The hurricane season from June to November can greatly affect rainfall totals. Chief hurricane months are August and September. Severe tropical storms occur, on average, about one every 10 years. Weaker storms average about one every five.

Temperatures

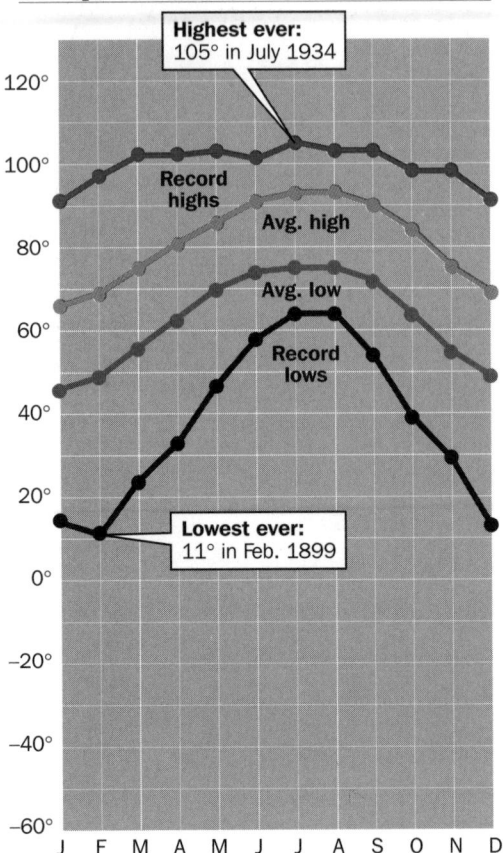

Weather extremes

Most rain in 24 hours:	8.92 in. Aug. 9 – 10, 1980
Most rain in a month:	20.33 in. September 1967
Most snow in 24 hours:	6.0 in. Jan. 29, 1897
Most snow in a month:	6.0 in. January 1897

Monthly averages

Month	Avg. precip. (in.)	Avg. snow (in.)	Wet days	Thunderstorm days	Pct. sky is cloudy	% p.m. relative humidity	Dew point	Wind speed (mph)
Jan.	1.6	T	8	1	49	62	48	15.0
Feb.	1.9	T	7	1	45	59	50	16.1
March	1.0	T	5	1	44	57	55	17.3
April	1.9	0	5	2	43	60	63	15.0
May	3.0	0	6	4	30	64	70	13.8
June	3.0	0	6	3	12	61	73	12.7
July	2.1	0	5	2	8	56	74	12.7
Aug.	3.2	0	6	4	9	56	74	12.7
Sept.	5.4	0	9	5	14	60	71	11.5
Oct.	3.3	0	6	2	17	57	64	10.4
Nov.	1.5	T	6	1	30	58	56	13.8
Dec.	1.3	T	6	1	42	59	50	15.0

T - Trace of rain or snow   * - Less than 1   NA - Not Available

Annual averages

Precipitation (in inches)	29.2
Snow (in inches)	T
Heating degree days	961
Cooling degree days	3,534
Days with thunderstorms	27
Days with fog	108
Days above 90°	106
Days below 32°	7
Wet days	75
Days with snow	*
Days with 1.5 inches or more snow	0

Percent time sky is clear

Jan.	Feb.	March	April	May	June	July	Aug.	Sept.	Oct.	Nov.	Dec.
23.1	26.5	21.5	17.6	14.2	17.6	23.9	23.9	23.7	32.9	31.1	25.8

Dallas-Fort Worth, Texas

Lat. 32° 54' N **Lon.** 97° 02' W **Elev.** 551 ft.

The Dallas-Fort Worth metropolitan area, located in the rolling hills of north central Texas, is near the headwaters of the Trinity River about 250 miles north of the Gulf of Mexico. It has a humid subtropical climate with wide annual temperature and precipitation ranges. Precipitation ranges from less than 20 inches to more than 50. Winters are mild, and periods of extreme cold are short-lived. The highest temperatures of summer are associated with fair skies, westerly winds and low humidities and summer daytime temperatures frequently exceed 100°F. Characteristically, hot spells in summer are broken by thunderstorm activity. Much of the annual precipitation results from these thunderstorms, with occasional heavy rainfall. Snowfall is rare.

Temperatures

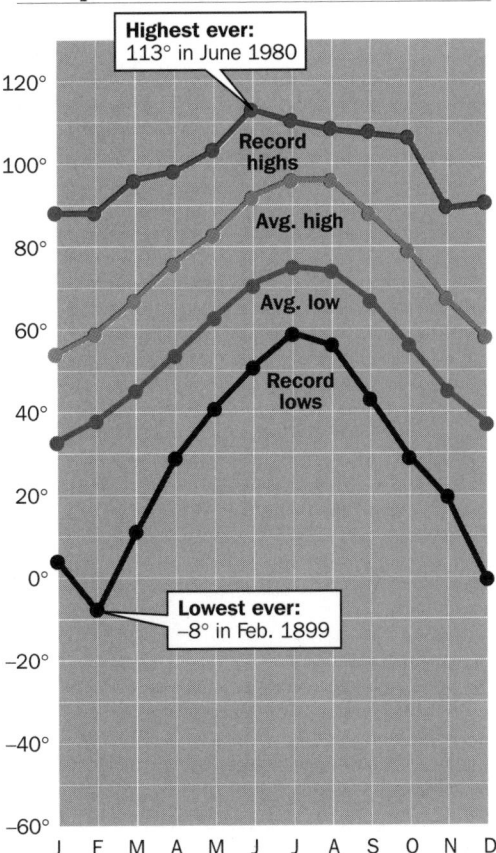

Highest ever: 113° in June 1980

Record highs

Avg. high

Avg. low

Record lows

Lowest ever: -8° in Feb. 1899

Weather extremes

Most rain in 24 hours:	9.57 in. Sept. 4 – 5, 1932
Most rain in a month:	17.64 in. April 1922
Most snow in 24 hours:	12.1 in. Jan. 15 – 16, 1964
Most snow in a month:	13.5 in. February 1978

Monthly averages

Month	Avg. precip. (in.)	Avg. snow (in.)	Wet days	Thunderstorm days	Pct. sky is cloudy	% p.m. relative humidity	Dew point	Wind speed (mph)
Jan.	1.8	1	7	1	42	52	32	12.7
Feb.	2.2	1	7	2	40	51	35	12.7
March	2.6	T	7	4	38	48	42	16.1
April	3.7	0	8	6	37	50	52	15.0
May	4.9	0	9	8	33	53	61	13.8
June	2.8	0	6	6	20	47	66	12.7
July	2.1	0	5	5	13	42	67	10.4
Aug.	1.9	0	5	5	13	41	67	10.4
Sept.	3.0	0	7	4	22	46	63	11.5
Oct.	3.3	0	6	3	25	47	53	11.5
Nov.	2.1	T	6	2	33	49	43	12.7
Dec.	1.7	T	6	1	38	51	35	12.7

T - Trace of rain or snow   * - Less than 1   NA - Not Available

Annual averages

Precipitation (in inches)	32.3
Snow (in inches)	3
Heating degree days	2,414
Cooling degree days	2,730
Days with thunderstorms	47
Days with fog	79
Days above 90°	100
Days below 32°	40
Wet days	79
Days with snow	4
Days with 1.5 inches or more snow	1

Percent time sky is clear

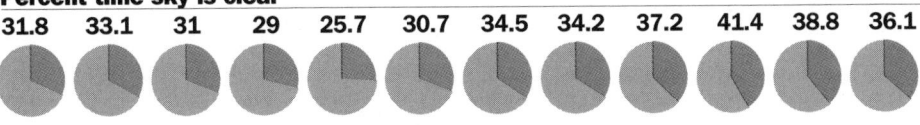

31.8	33.1	31	29	25.7	30.7	34.5	34.2	37.2	41.4	38.8	36.1
Jan.	Feb.	March	April	May	June	July	Aug.	Sept.	Oct.	Nov.	Dec.

Dayton, Ohio

Lat. 39° 54' N **Lon.** 84° 12' W **Elev.** 995 ft.

Dayton is near the center of the Miami River Valley, a nearly flat plain 50 to 200 feet below the adjacent rolling country. Three tributaries — Mad River, Stillwater River and Wolf Creek — converge from the north to join the Miami within the city. Dams built after a disastrous 1913 flood have prevented flooding since. Precipitation is fairly evenly distributed throughout the year and moderate temperatures help make the valley a rich agricultural region. Humidity is relatively high throughout the year. Temperatures of zero or below occur about four years out of five, while temperatures of 100°F or higher occur about one year out of five. Extreme temperatures are usually of short duration. Polar air flowing across the Great Lakes causes much winter cloudiness.

Temperatures

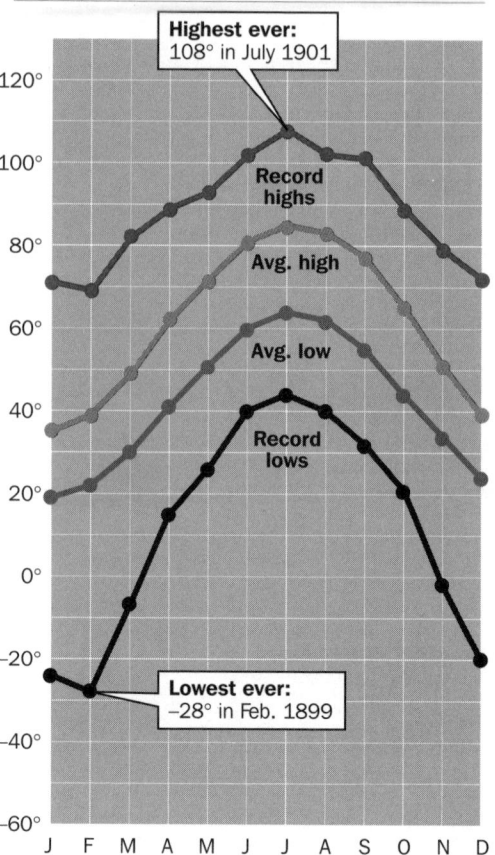

Highest ever: 108° in July 1901

Record highs

Avg. high

Avg. low

Record lows

Lowest ever: −28° in Feb. 1899

Weather extremes

Most rain in 24 hours:	4.56 in. Sept. 12 – 13, 1925
Most rain in a month:	12.41 in. January 1937
Most snow in 24 hours:	12.2 in. Jan. 26, 1978
Most snow in a month:	40.2 in. January 1978

Monthly averages

Month	Avg. precip. (in.)	Avg. snow (in.)	Wet days	Thunder-storm days	Pct. sky is cloudy	% p.m. relative humidity	Dew point	Wind speed (mph)
Jan.	2.7	8	13	*	61	67	20	12.7
Feb.	2.4	6	11	1	57	64	22	12.7
March	3.2	6	13	2	55	59	29	13.8
April	3.4	1	13	4	49	52	38	12.7
May	3.8	T	12	6	42	52	49	11.5
June	3.9	0	10	7	34	51	58	10.4
July	3.6	0	10	7	31	52	62	9.2
Aug.	3.0	0	9	6	29	53	61	9.2
Sept.	2.5	0	8	3	32	52	55	10.4
Oct.	2.3	T	9	1	37	53	43	10.4
Nov.	3.0	2	11	1	55	62	33	12.7
Dec.	2.8	6	12	*	62	69	24	12.7

T - Trace of rain or snow   * - Less than 1   NA - Not Available

Annual averages

Precipitation (in inches)	36.7
Snow (in inches)	29
Heating degree days	5,641
Cooling degree days	981
Days with thunderstorms	38
Days with fog	166
Days above 90°	17
Days below 32°	117
Wet days	131
Days with snow	56
Days with 1.5 inches or more snow	12

Percent time sky is clear

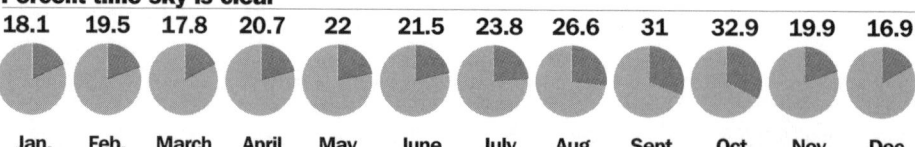

18.1	19.5	17.8	20.7	22	21.5	23.8	26.6	31	32.9	19.9	16.9
Jan.	Feb.	March	April	May	June	July	Aug.	Sept.	Oct.	Nov.	Dec.

Daytona Beach, Florida

Lat. 29° 11' N **Lon.** 81° 3' W **Elev.** 29 ft.

Daytona Beach is on the Atlantic Ocean and the Halifax River. The climate is tempered by land and sea breezes. In the summer, afternoon convective thunderstorms lower the temperature to the comfortable 80s. Occasionally heavy, the storms can produce as much as 2 or 3 inches of rain and may be accompanied by strong gusty winds. The June through mid-October rainy season produces 60 percent of the annual rainfall. Winters are mild due to the ocean and latitude. Long periods of cloudiness and rain are infrequent. Generally, hurricanes in the Atlantic tend to pass well offshore. Gulf of Mexico hurricanes lose much of their intensity while crossing the state. Heavy fog occurs mostly during the winter and early spring.

Temperatures

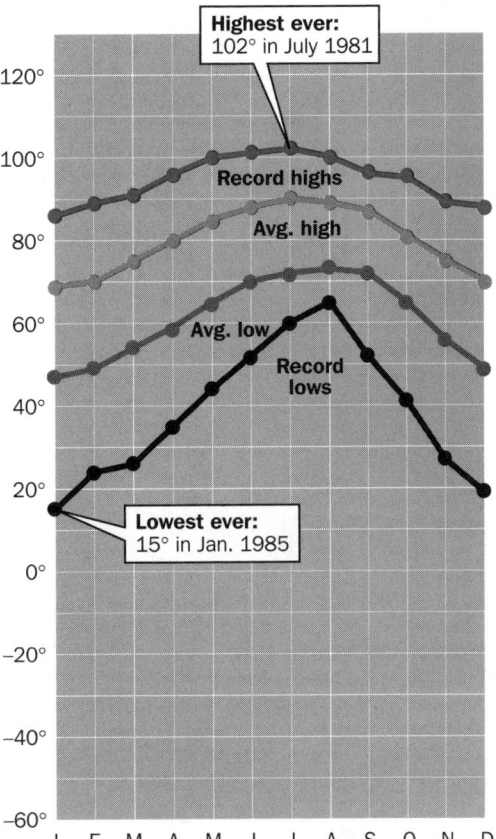

Weather extremes

Most rain in 24 hours:	9.29 in. Oct. 8 – 9, 1953
Most rain in a month:	19.89 in. August 1953
Most snow in 24 hours:	Trace Dec. 23, 1989
Most snow in a month:	Trace December 1989

Monthly averages

Month	Avg. precip. (in.)	Avg. snow (in.)	Wet days	Thunder-storm days	Pct. sky is cloudy	% p.m. relative humidity	Dew point	Wind speed (mph)
Jan.	2.5	T	7	1	30	61	49	9.2
Feb.	3.0	T	8	2	31	58	50	11.5
March	3.2	0	8	3	27	57	54	10.4
April	2.5	0	6	3	21	56	58	12.7
May	3.1	0	8	8	20	61	64	11.5
June	5.7	0	12	13	24	67	70	10.4
July	5.5	0	13	17	21	69	72	10.4
Aug.	6.3	0	13	15	20	71	73	10.4
Sept.	6.7	0	13	8	25	70	71	11.5
Oct.	4.6	0	10	3	23	66	64	11.5
Nov.	2.6	0	7	1	23	63	57	8.1
Dec.	2.4	T	7	1	29	63	51	8.1

T - Trace of rain or snow   * - Less than 1   NA - Not Available

Annual averages

Precipitation (in inches)	48.1
Snow (in inches)	T
Heating degree days	843
Cooling degree days	2,942
Days with thunderstorms	75
Days with fog	124
Days above 90°	54
Days below 32°	6
Wet days	112
Days with snow	0
Days with 1.5 inches or more snow	0

Percent time sky is clear

28.8	29.4	28.3	31.7	26	16.1	15.2	14.9	13.5	22.6	28.9	27.8
Jan.	Feb.	March	April	May	June	July	Aug.	Sept.	Oct.	Nov.	Dec.

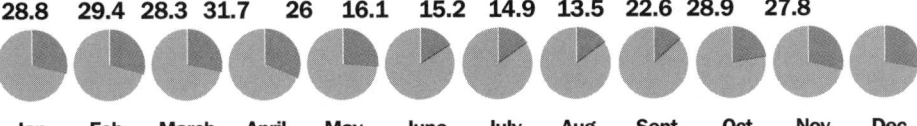

Denver, Colorado

Lat. 39° 46′ N **Lon.** 104° 52′ W **Elev.** 5,286 ft.

Denver's climate is central Rocky Mountain: low relative humidity, light precipitation, and abundant sunshine. In winter, high altitude and mountains make for moderate temperatures. Cold air from the north, intensified by the high altitude, can be abrupt and severe. However, surges of air from the west moderate as they come down the Rockies. These chinook winds often raise temperatures into the 60s, even in midwinter. In summer, mornings usually are clear and sunny, with clouds forming in early afternoon. Severe thunderstorms, with large, damaging hail and heavy rain, occur occasionally. Autumn is the most pleasant season with more sunshine and less severe weather than any other time of the year.

Temperatures

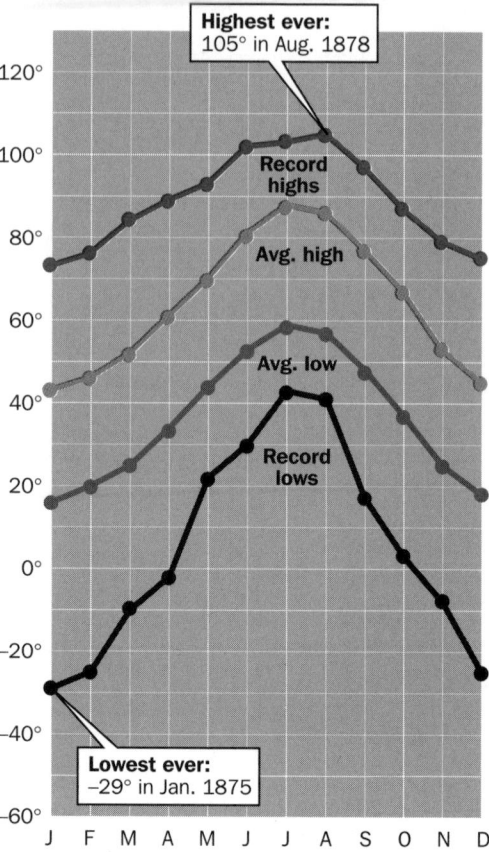

Highest ever: 105° in Aug. 1878

Record highs

Avg. high

Avg. low

Record lows

Lowest ever: −29° in Jan. 1875

Weather extremes

Most rain in 24 hours:	6.53 in.	May 21 – 22, 1876
Most rain in a month:	8.57 in.	May 1876
Most snow in 24 hours:	23.6 in.	Dec. 24, 1982
Most snow in a month:	57.4 in.	December 1913

Monthly averages

Month	Avg. precip. (in.)	Avg. snow (in.)	Wet days	Thunder-storm days	Pct. sky is cloudy	% p.m. relative humidity	Dew point	Wind speed (mph)
Jan.	0.5	8	6	*	26	48	12	9.2
Feb.	0.6	8	6	*	30	44	16	9.2
March	1.3	14	9	*	34	40	19	9.2
April	1.8	9	8	1	31	35	25	10.4
May	2.6	2	11	6	30	38	36	10.4
June	1.7	T	9	10	20	34	43	10.4
July	1.9	0	9	10	16	33	48	9.2
Aug.	1.4	0	9	8	17	34	47	9.2
Sept.	1.1	2	6	3	19	33	39	9.2
Oct.	1.0	4	5	1	21	34	28	8.1
Nov.	0.8	9	5	*	26	46	20	9.2
Dec.	0.6	8	6	0	26	50	14	9.2

T - Trace of rain or snow   * - Less than 1   NA - Not Available

Annual averages

Precipitation (in inches)	15.4
Snow (in inches)	63
Heating degree days	5,937
Cooling degree days	700
Days with thunderstorms	39
Days with fog	53
Days above 90°	33
Days below 32°	155
Wet days	89
Days with snow	75
Days with 1.5 inches or more snow	27

Percent time sky is clear

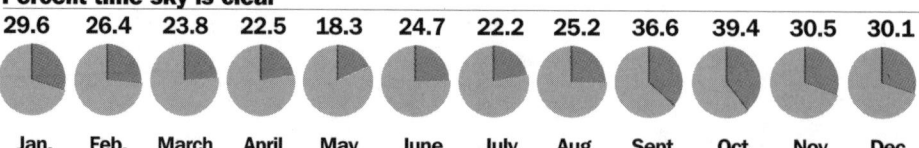

Jan.	Feb.	March	April	May	June	July	Aug.	Sept.	Oct.	Nov.	Dec.
29.6	26.4	23.8	22.5	18.3	24.7	22.2	25.2	36.6	39.4	30.5	30.1

Des Moines, Iowa

Lat. 41° 32' N **Lon.** 93° 39' W **Elev.** 938 ft.

Located in the heart of North America, Des Moines' climate is a contrast in both temperature and precipitation. Winter's cold dry air is interrupted by storms of short duration. Drifting snow may be extensive and impede transportation. Although occasional cold waves follow the storms, bitterly cold days on which the temperatures fail to rise above zero occur on an average of only three days in four years. Late April to mid-October is characterized by prevailing southerly winds and precipitation falling as showers and thunderstorms, occasionally with damaging wind, erosive downpours or hail. The autumn is characteristically sunny with diminishing precipitation, a condition favorable for drying and harvesting crops.

Temperatures

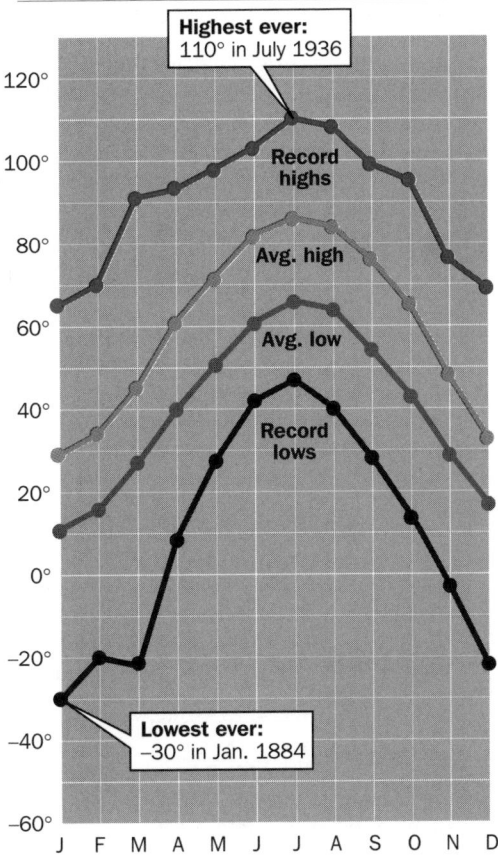

Weather extremes

Most rain in 24 hours:	6.18 in. Aug. 27, 1975
Most rain in a month:	15.79 in. June 1881
Most snow in 24 hours:	17.7 in. Jan. 1, 1942
Most snow in a month:	37.0 in. January 1886

Monthly averages

Month	Avg. precip. (in.)	Avg. snow (in.)	Wet days	Thunderstorm days	Pct. sky is cloudy	% p.m. relative humidity	Dew point	Wind speed (mph)
Jan.	1.1	8	8	*	46	65	12	15.0
Feb.	1.1	7	7	*	46	63	17	15.0
March	2.3	7	10	2	49	57	26	16.1
April	3.1	2	10	4	43	50	37	16.1
May	3.8	T	11	7	38	51	48	11.5
June	4.4	0	10	9	30	52	58	11.5
July	3.5	0	9	8	23	52	64	9.2
Aug.	3.9	0	9	7	25	54	62	9.2
Sept.	3.1	T	9	5	29	52	53	10.4
Oct.	2.4	T	8	3	31	50	41	11.5
Nov.	1.7	3	7	1	45	58	29	15.0
Dec.	1.2	7	8	*	50	66	18	15.0

T - Trace of rain or snow   * - Less than 1   NA - Not Available

Annual averages

Precipitation (in inches)	31.8
Snow (in inches)	33
Heating degree days	6,515
Cooling degree days	1,062
Days with thunderstorms	46
Days with fog	109
Days above 90°	26
Days below 32°	137
Wet days	106
Days with snow	51
Days with 1.5 inches or more snow	17

Percent time sky is clear

26.9	27.2	21.6	24.7	22.1	22.7	28.2	31.1	36.1	35.8	26.7	25.1

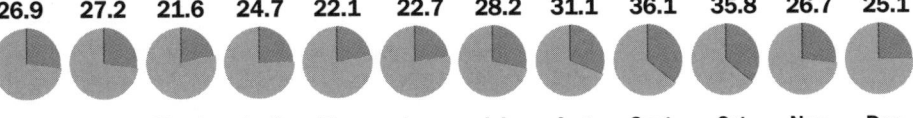

Jan.   Feb.   March   April   May   June   July   Aug.   Sept.   Oct.   Nov.   Dec.

Detroit, Michigan

Lat. 42° 14' N **Lon.** 83° 20' W **Elev.** 633 ft.

Detroit lies between Lake St. Clair and Lake Erie to the east and the Irish Hills to the west. The lakes warm and moisten arctic air during the winter, producing an excess of cloudiness but a moderation of temperatures. The wintertime storm track can bring combinations of rain, snow, freezing rain and sleet, with very heavy snowfall possible. Most summer storms pass to the north of the city, allowing for intervals of warm, humid, sunny skies; occasional thunderstorms are followed by days of mild, dry, and fair weather. On warm days in early summer, lake breezes often lower temperatures by 10 to 15 degrees in the eastern part of the city closest to the water and the northeastern suburbs.

Temperatures

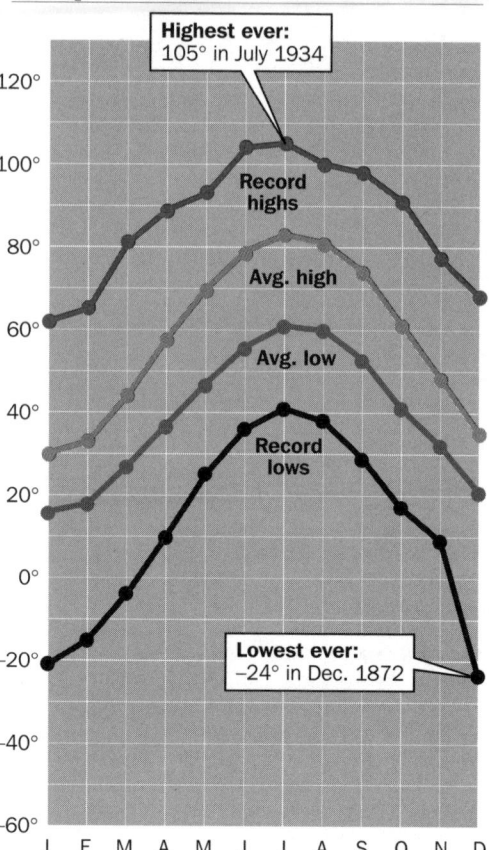

Highest ever: 105° in July 1934

Record highs

Avg. high

Avg. low

Record lows

Lowest ever: −24° in Dec. 1872

Weather extremes

Most rain in 24 hours:	4.75 in. July 31, 1925
Most rain in a month:	8.76 in. July 1878
Most snow in 24 hours:	24.5 in. April 6, 1886
Most snow in a month:	38.5 in. February 1908

Monthly averages

Month	Avg. precip. (in.)	Avg. snow (in.)	Wet days	Thunder-storm days	Pct. sky is cloudy	% p.m. relative humidity	Dew point	Wind speed (mph)
Jan.	1.8	10	13	*	58	67	16	13.8
Feb.	1.8	9	11	*	53	63	18	12.7
March	2.5	7	13	2	51	59	25	13.8
April	3.0	2	13	3	45	53	35	13.8
May	2.9	T	11	4	39	51	46	12.7
June	3.6	0	10	6	30	52	55	10.4
July	3.1	0	9	6	25	52	60	9.2
Aug.	3.4	0	9	5	27	54	60	9.2
Sept.	2.8	0	10	4	33	55	53	10.4
Oct.	2.2	T	10	1	39	55	41	11.5
Nov.	2.6	3	12	1	56	64	32	12.7
Dec.	2.7	11	14	*	63	70	22	12.7

T - Trace of rain or snow   * - Less than 1   NA - Not Available

Annual averages

Precipitation (in inches)	32.4
Snow (in inches)	41
Heating degree days	6,540
Cooling degree days	707
Days with thunderstorms	32
Days with fog	157
Days above 90°	12
Days below 32°	136
Wet days	135
Days with snow	77
Days with 1.5 inches or more snow	17

Percent time sky is clear

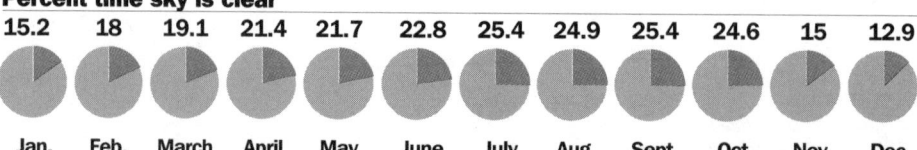

15.2	18	19.1	21.4	21.7	22.8	25.4	24.9	25.4	24.6	15	12.9
Jan.	Feb.	March	April	May	June	July	Aug.	Sept.	Oct.	Nov.	Dec.

Dodge City, Kansas

Lat. 37° 46' N **Lon.** 99° 58' W **Elev.** 2,582 ft.

The climate of Dodge City and southwestern Kansas is classified as semiarid. Dodge City is nearly 300 miles east of the Rocky Mountains, but the weather reflects the influence of the mountains. The Rockies form a barricade against all except high-level moisture from the southwest, west, and northwest. Afternoon and evening thunderstorms during the growing season contribute most of the moisture. They are occasionally accompanied by hail and strong winds, but damage typically is spotty and variable. Winter is the dry season. The duration of snow cover is generally brief due to mild temperatures and an abundance of sunshine. The exception results from the occasional blizzard that spreads across the flat, treeless prairie.

Weather extremes

Most rain in 24 hours:	4.55 in.	Oct. 15 - 16, 1968
Most rain in a month:	12.82 in.	May 1881
Most snow in 24 hours:	14.3 in.	Nov. 24 – 25, 1993
Most snow in a month:	27.7 in.	February 1903

Temperatures

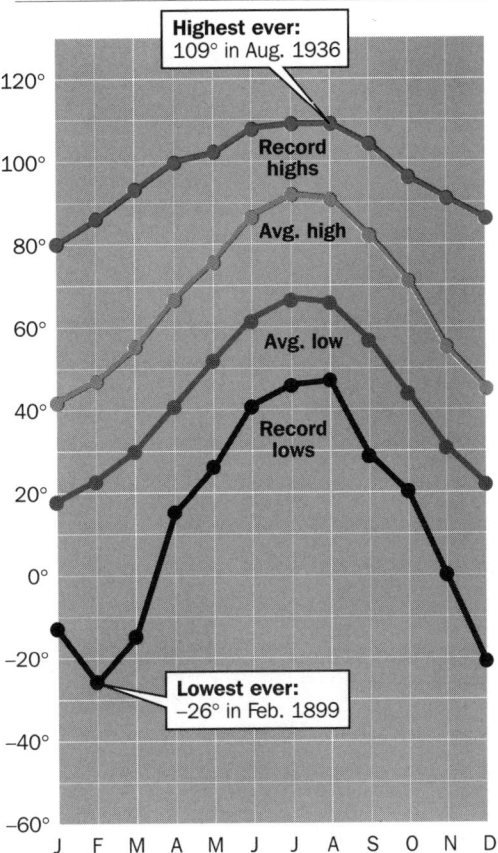

Highest ever: 109° in Aug. 1936

Record highs

Avg. high

Avg. low

Record lows

Lowest ever: –26° in Feb. 1899

Monthly averages

Month	Avg. precip. (in.)	Avg. snow (in.)	Wet days	Thunder-storm days	Pct. sky is cloudy	% p.m. relative humidity	Dew point	Wind speed (mph)
Jan.	0.5	4	5	*	33	50	18	16.1
Feb.	0.6	4	5	*	36	50	22	16.1
March	1.5	5	7	1	37	44	26	17.3
April	1.8	1	7	3	32	39	36	17.3
May	3.2	T	10	8	32	45	49	17.3
June	3.0	0	9	10	23	41	57	16.1
July	3.1	0	9	10	18	38	60	15.0
Aug.	2.5	0	8	9	19	39	59	13.8
Sept.	1.8	T	6	5	23	41	51	16.1
Oct.	1.3	T	5	2	23	39	39	15.0
Nov.	0.7	2	4	1	29	44	28	15.0
Dec.	0.5	3	4	*	31	49	20	16.1

T - Trace of rain or snow   * - Less than 1   NA - Not Available

Annual averages

Precipitation (in inches)	20.7
Snow (in inches)	19
Heating degree days	5,020
Cooling degree days	1,526
Days with thunderstorms	49
Days with fog	79
Days above 90°	65
Days below 32°	125
Wet days	79
Days with snow	30
Days with 1.5 inches or more snow	9

Percent time sky is clear

35	31.7	30.3	29.6	23.6	26.8	27.9	30.2	40.1	44.6	38.8	36.7

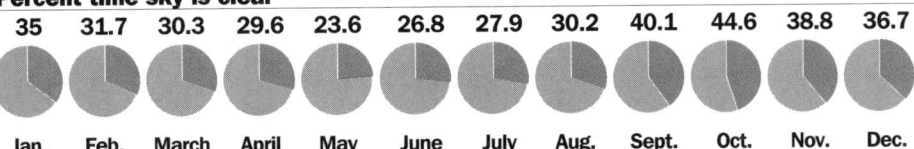

| Jan. | Feb. | March | April | May | June | July | Aug. | Sept. | Oct. | Nov. | Dec. |

Dubuque, Iowa

Lat. 42° 24' N **Lon.** 90° 42' W **Elev.** 1,056 ft.

Dubuque's terrain varies from gently rolling to steep hills and bluffs along the Mississippi River. The principal feature of the climate is variety. The area can be variously covered by mild Pacific air; by cool, dry Canadian air; or by warm, moist air from the Gulf of Mexico. The seasons vary widely from year to year, but all seasons are marked by storms. In winter, rain changes to sleet and snow. In summer, thunderstorms are occasionally accompanied by hail and tornadoes. Thunderstorms have been sufficiently intense to raise the Mississippi River nearly 5 feet overnight. Hot, dry spells occasionally plague the crops and livestock in summer, but there are frequent periods of mild weather in spring and autumn.

Temperatures

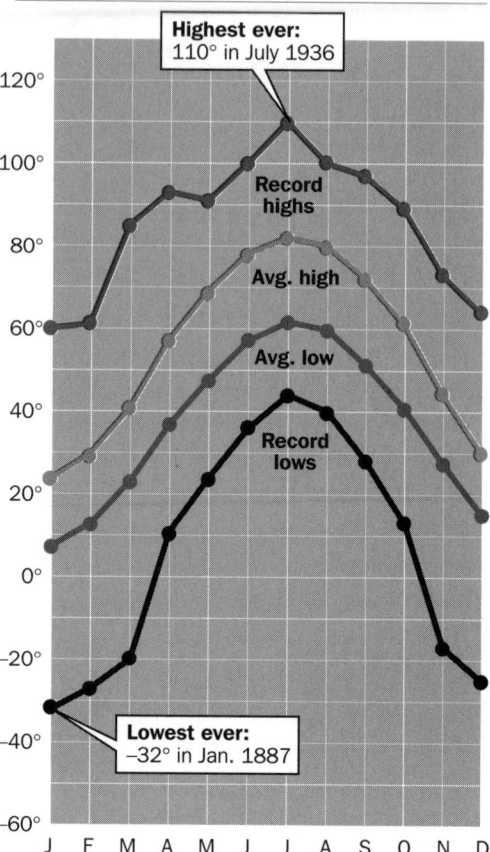

Highest ever: 110° in July 1936

Record highs

Avg. high

Avg. low

Record lows

Lowest ever: −32° in Jan. 1887

Weather extremes

Most rain in 24 hours:	8.85 in. Sept. 14, 1967
Most rain in a month:	15.46 in. September 1965
Most snow in 24 hours:	15.5 in. March 4 – 5, 1959
Most snow in a month:	34.3 in. January 1929

Monthly averages

Month	Avg. precip. (in.)	Avg. snow (in.)	Wet days	Thunder-storm days	Pct. sky is cloudy	% p.m. relative humidity	Dew point	Wind speed (mph)
Jan.	1.4	9.2	9	*	55	68	NA	NA
Feb.	1.3	7.8	8	*	53	66	NA	NA
March	2.9	9.5	11	2	55	62	NA	NA
April	4.2	2.3	12	3	54	56	NA	NA
May	4.4	0.1	11	5	50	57	NA	NA
June	4.2	0.0	10	6	43	59	NA	NA
July	4.3	0.0	10	6	34	60	NA	NA
Aug.	4.5	0.0	9	6	36	61	NA	NA
Sept.	4.1	T	9	4	39	61	NA	NA
Oct.	2.9	0.2	9	3	41	58	NA	NA
Nov.	2.5	3.8	9	1	58	66	NA	NA
Dec.	1.9	10.6	10	*	58	72	NA	NA

T - Trace of rain or snow   * - Less than 1   NA - Not Available

Annual averages

Precipitation (in inches)	39
Snow (in inches)	44
Heating degree days	7,375
Cooling degree days	580
Days with thunderstorms	36
Days with fog	29
Days above 90°	9
Days below 32°	148
Wet days	117
Days with snow	NA
Days with 1.5 inches or more snow	14

Percent time sky is clear

Jan.	Feb.	March	April	May	June	July	Aug.	Sept.	Oct.	Nov.	Dec.
22.9	26.8	19.7	21.0	21.9	21.3	25.8	30.3	35.0	33.2	22.3	21.6

Duluth, Minnesota

Lat. 46° 50' N **Lon.** 92° 11' W **Elev.** 1,428 ft.

Duluth lies at the base of a range of hills that rise abruptly to 600 – 800 feet above Lake Superior. It is known as the Air Conditioned City: East winds automatically cool the city. Even with westerly flow in the summer, the wind abates at night allowing cool lake air to move back into the city. Lake Superior, the largest and coldest of the Great Lakes, makes summer temperatures cooler and winter temperatures warmer. In the summer, warm, moist air flowing over the cold lake results in cool, cloudy weather. During the winter, cold air flowing over the warm open lake produces snow. The "lake effect," however, causes fewer severe storms such as wind, hail, tornadoes, freezing rain and blizzards compared with areas farther from the lake.

Temperatures

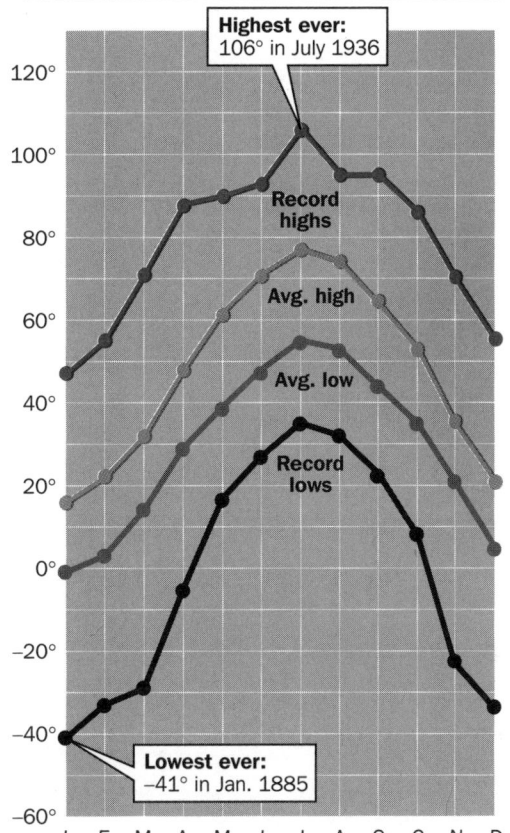

Highest ever: 106° in July 1936

Record highs

Avg. high

Avg. low

Record lows

Lowest ever: –41° in Jan. 1885

Weather extremes

Most rain in 24 hours:	5.79 in. Aug. 22 - 23, 1978
Most rain in a month:	11.52 in. September 1881
Most snow in 24 hours:	25.4 in. December 1950
Most snow in a month:	50.1 in. November 1991

Monthly averages

Month	Avg. precip. (in.)	Avg. snow (in.)	Wet days	Thunderstorm days	Pct. sky is cloudy	% p.m. relative humidity	Dew point	Wind speed (mph)
Jan.	1.2	17	12	*	50	66	1	13.8
Feb.	0.8	11	10	*	49	62	5	12.7
March	1.8	14	11	1	50	61	15	15.0
April	2.3	7	11	2	46	52	26	13.8
May	3.1	1	12	4	42	50	37	12.7
June	4.0	0	12	7	39	56	49	10.4
July	3.9	0	11	8	30	55	55	10.4
Aug.	3.9	0	12	7	33	59	54	9.2
Sept.	3.5	T	12	4	41	60	46	11.5
Oct.	2.4	1	10	1	46	58	34	12.7
Nov.	1.8	11	11	*	60	67	21	13.8
Dec.	1.3	16	12	*	56	70	8	12.7

T - Trace of rain or snow   * - Less than 1   NA - Not Available

Annual averages

Precipitation (in inches)	30.2
Snow (in inches)	79
Heating degree days	9,792
Cooling degree days	203
Days with thunderstorms	34
Days with fog	134
Days above 90°	2
Days below 32°	186
Wet days	136
Days with snow	121
Days with 1.5 inches or more snow	30

Percent time sky is clear

Jan.	Feb.	March	April	May	June	July	Aug.	Sept.	Oct.	Nov.	Dec.
24.6	26.2	22.7	21.2	20.1	16.8	20.3	22.7	21.5	22.1	15.8	20.4

Elko, Nevada

Lat. 40° 50' N **Lon.** 115° 47' W **Elev.** 5,075 ft.

Elko is in the Humbolt River Valley of northeastern Nevada. The Ruby mountain range, with peaks near or above 10,000 feet, dominates the landscape from about 40 miles northeast through 40 miles southeast of Elko. Because of the high elevation and proximity of the mountains, there is a wide range between the average high and average low temperatures. High radiative cooling at night makes cool nights the rule, even in the warmest period of midsummer. Normal precipitation is light, especially during the summer when the precipitation falls mostly as light showers. The precipitation between November and June (rain and snow) is a benefit to farmers and ranchers.

Temperatures

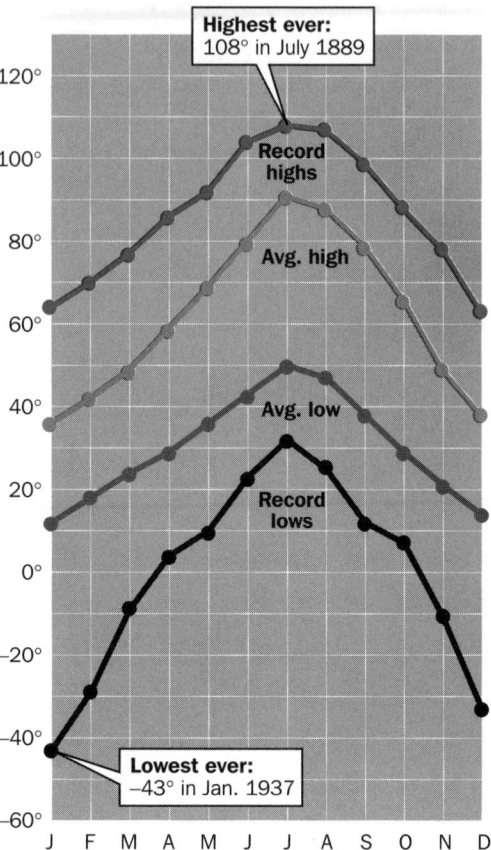

Weather extremes

Most rain in 24 hours:	4.13 in. Aug. 27, 1970
Most rain in a month:	6.00 in. January 1903
Most snow in 24 hours:	16.7 in. January 1951
Most snow in a month:	48.5 in. January 1916

Monthly averages

Month	Avg. precip. (in.)	Avg. snow (in.)	Wet days	Thunderstorm days	Pct. sky is cloudy	% p.m. relative humidity	Dew point	Wind speed (mph)
Jan.	1.1	10	9	*	43	61	16	9.2
Feb.	0.8	6	8	*	40	54	20	9.2
March	0.9	6	9	*	39	43	23	10.4
April	0.8	3	7	1	35	33	25	10.4
May	0.9	1	8	3	28	31	31	9.2
June	0.8	T	6	4	18	25	36	9.2
July	0.3	0	4	5	9	19	37	9.2
Aug.	0.5	0	4	4	10	19	35	9.2
Sept.	0.5	T	4	2	11	22	30	9.2
Oct.	0.6	1	4	*	20	29	25	9.2
Nov.	1.0	4	7	*	35	48	22	9.2
Dec.	1.1	9	9	*	40	61	17	9.2

T - Trace of rain or snow   * - Less than 1   NA - Not Available

Annual averages

Precipitation (in inches)	9.3
Snow (in inches)	40
Heating degree days	7,248
Cooling degree days	406
Days with thunderstorms	19
Days with fog	19
Days above 90°	44
Days below 32°	198
Wet days	79
Days with snow	70
Days with 1.5 inches or more snow	16

Percent time sky is clear

23.3	23	23.6	24.9	26.6	38.5	46.5	47.9	54	46	29.2	25.9
Jan.	Feb.	March	April	May	June	July	Aug.	Sept.	Oct.	Nov.	Dec.

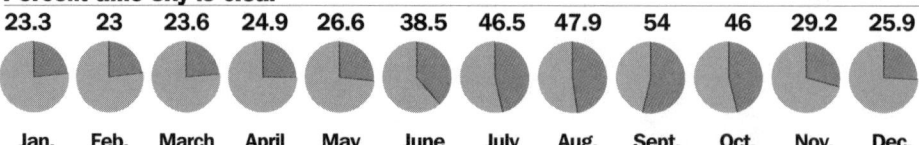

El Paso, Texas

Lat. 31° 48' N **Lon.** 106° 24' W **Elev.** 3,918 ft.

El Paso is on the north bank of the Rio Grande River across from Ciudad Juarez, Mexico. It has an abundance of sunshine, high daytime summer temperatures, very low humidity, and a relatively mild winter. Rainfall is scanty, insufficient for any plant growth except desert vegetation. Irrigation is necessary for crops, gardens, and lawns. Almost half of the precipitation occurs in July through September in brief but often heavy thunderstorms. Summer nights are usually comfortable with temperatures in the 60s. Dust and sandstorms are the most unpleasant climate features, occurring most frequently in March and April. Although wind velocities are not extreme, moderately strong winds raise considerable dust and sand due to dry and loose soil.

Temperatures

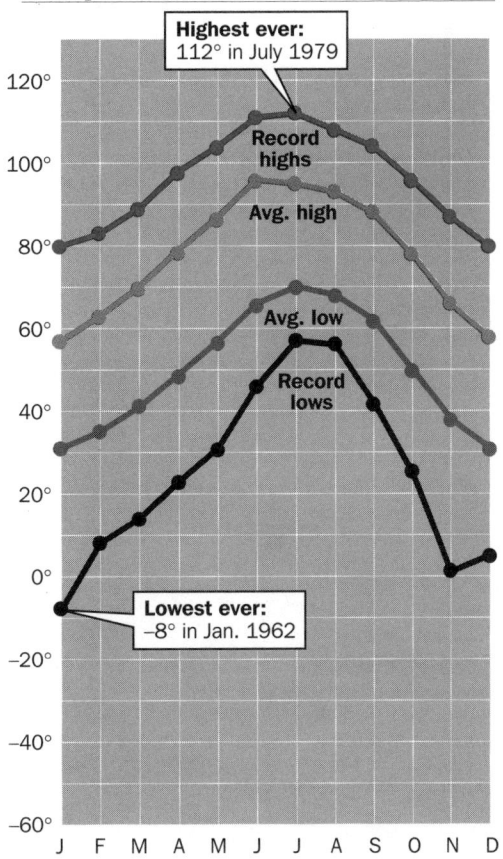

Highest ever: 112° in July 1979

Record highs

Avg. high

Avg. low

Record lows

Lowest ever: −8° in Jan. 1962

Weather extremes

Most rain in 24 hours:	6.50 in.
	July 9, 1881
Most rain in a month:	8.18 in.
	July 1881
Most snow in 24 hours:	16.8 in.
	Dec. 13 – 14, 1987
Most snow in a month:	25.9 in.
	December 1987

Monthly averages

Month	Avg. precip. (in.)	Avg. snow (in.)	Wet days	Thunder-storm days	Pct. sky is cloudy	% p.m. relative humidity	Dew point	Wind speed (mph)
Jan.	0.4	1	4	*	21	34	23	6.9
Feb.	0.4	1	3	*	18	27	23	12.7
March	0.3	T	2	*	17	20	23	15.0
April	0.2	T	2	1	13	17	26	13.8
May	0.3	0	2	3	11	16	32	12.7
June	0.6	0	3	4	9	18	42	8.1
July	1.6	0	8	10	14	29	55	8.1
Aug.	1.5	0	8	10	15	33	56	6.9
Sept.	1.4	0	6	4	15	34	52	6.9
Oct.	0.8	T	4	2	12	31	40	6.9
Nov.	0.3	1	3	*	15	32	29	6.9
Dec.	0.5	2	4	*	20	37	25	6.9

T - Trace of rain or snow   * - Less than 1   NA - Not Available

Annual averages

Precipitation (in inches)	8.5
Snow (in inches)	6
Heating degree days	2,603
Cooling degree days	2,210
Days with thunderstorms	34
Days with fog	9
Days above 90°	105
Days below 32°	61
Wet days	49
Days with snow	6
Days with 1.5 inches or more snow	1

Percent time sky is clear

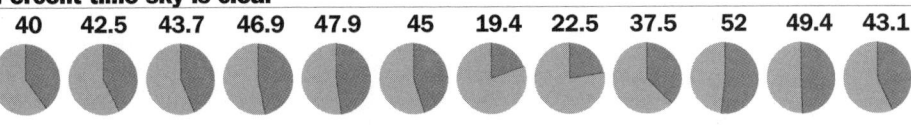

40	42.5	43.7	46.9	47.9	45	19.4	22.5	37.5	52	49.4	43.1
Jan.	Feb.	March	April	May	June	July	Aug.	Sept.	Oct.	Nov.	Dec.

Ely, Nevada

Lat. 39° 17' N **Lon.** 114° 51' W **Elev.** 6,262 ft.

Ely, near the southern rim of the Great Basin, is about 60 miles west of Great Basin National Park. The neighboring terrain consists of alternating mountain ranges and sagebrush covered valleys. Valley floors in this region are near 6,000 feet above sea level. This high elevation produces pleasant summer nights but also reduces the season that is free from freezing temperatures. The mountains of the Egan Range to the west and the Schell Creek Range to the east prevent strong surface winds from these directions. A very pronounced drainage wind sweeps down the valley during the morning hours. More precipitation is noted near the mountains than in the center of the valley.

Temperatures

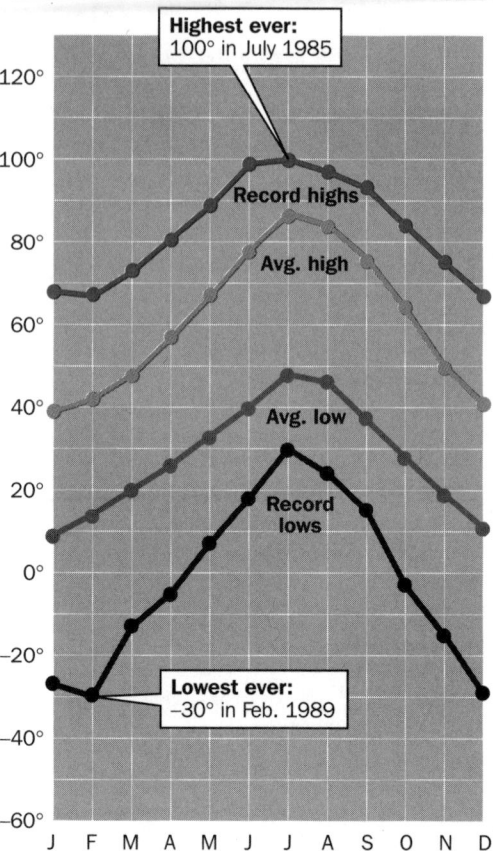

Highest ever: 100° in July 1985

Record highs

Avg. high

Avg. low

Record lows

Lowest ever: −30° in Feb. 1989

Weather extremes

Most rain in 24 hours:	2.87 in.
	Sept. 26 – 27, 1982
Most rain in a month:	4.99 in.
	September 1982
Most snow in 24 hours:	12.7 in.
	Dec. 16 – 17, 1970
Most snow in a month:	24.8 in.
	January 1967

Monthly averages

Month	Avg. precip. (in.)	Avg. snow (in.)	Wet days	Thunder- storm days	Pct. sky is cloudy	% p.m. relative humidity	Dew point	Wind speed (mph)
Jan.	0.7	9	7	*	34	55	13	12.7
Feb.	0.6	7	7	*	34	51	17	12.7
March	0.9	10	8	*	32	43	19	12.7
April	0.9	6	7	1	30	34	21	12.7
May	1.1	3	7	4	24	31	27	11.5
June	0.7	T	5	5	14	23	31	11.5
July	0.7	0	6	8	10	22	35	10.4
Aug.	0.7	0	6	8	10	23	35	11.5
Sept.	0.9	T	4	3	10	24	29	11.5
Oct.	0.7	2	5	1	17	31	24	11.5
Nov.	0.6	5	5	*	28	46	18	11.5
Dec.	0.7	8	6	*	29	55	13	11.5

T - Trace of rain or snow   * - Less than 1   NA - Not Available

Annual averages

Precipitation (in inches)	9.3
Snow (in inches)	51
Heating degree days	7,578
Cooling degree days	202
Days with thunderstorms	30
Days with fog	9
Days above 90°	20
Days below 32°	218
Wet days	73
Days with snow	73
Days with 1.5 inches or more snow	24

Percent time sky is clear

26.5	23.7	24.6	23.8	24.6	35.9	38.4	39.4	49.6	43.1	30.5	30.9

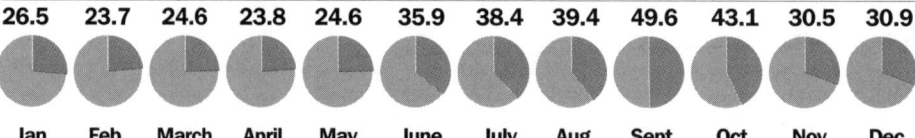

Jan.   Feb.   March   April   May   June   July   Aug.   Sept.   Oct.   Nov.   Dec.

Erie, Pennsylvania

Lat. 42° 05' N **Lon.** 80° 11' W **Elev.** 732 ft.

Erie is located on the southeastern shore of Lake Erie. During the winter, cold air masses moving south out of Canada are moderated by the relatively warm waters of the lake. But the temperature differential between the air and the water also produces an excess of cloudiness and frequent heavy "lake effect" snow. Spring can be quite variable, but it is generally cloudy and cool. Summer heat waves are tempered by cool breezes off the lake, making days above 90°F infrequent. The stabilizing effects of the lake also make summer thunderstorms somewhat less destructive in Erie than areas farther inland. Autumn, often with long dry periods and an abundance of sunshine, is usually the most pleasant season of the year.

Temperatures

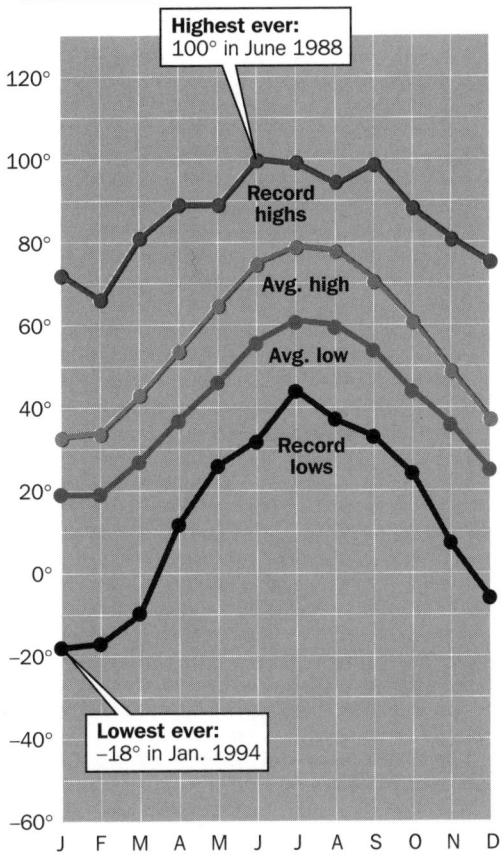

Highest ever: 100° in June 1988

Record highs

Avg. high

Avg. low

Record lows

Lowest ever: −18° in Jan. 1994

Weather extremes

Most rain in 24 hours:	10.42 in.	July 22 – 23, 1947
Most rain in a month:	13.27 in.	July 1946
Most snow in 24 hours:	26.5 in.	Dec. 11 – 12, 1944
Most snow in a month:	66.9 in.	December 1989

Monthly averages

Month	Avg. precip. (in.)	Avg. snow (in.)	Wet days	Thunder-storm days	Pct. sky is cloudy	% p.m. relative humidity	Dew point	Wind speed (mph)
Jan.	2.4	21	19	*	73	74	19	13.8
Feb.	2.3	16	15	*	64	72	20	13.8
March	3.1	10	15	2	57	67	26	13.8
April	3.3	2	14	3	49	60	35	13.8
May	3.6	T	12	4	40	59	45	10.4
June	3.9	0	11	6	32	60	56	9.2
July	3.4	0	9	6	27	61	60	8.1
Aug.	3.8	0	10	7	29	62	60	8.1
Sept.	4.1	0	11	4	35	63	54	9.2
Oct.	3.6	T	13	2	44	64	43	10.4
Nov.	4.0	9	16	1	66	69	33	12.7
Dec.	3.4	22	19	*	77	73	24	15.0

T - Trace of rain or snow   * - Less than 1   NA - Not Available

Annual averages

Precipitation (in inches)	40.9
Snow (in inches)	81
Heating degree days	6,500
Cooling degree days	540
Days with thunderstorms	35
Days with fog	135
Days above 90°	3
Days below 32°	125
Wet days	164
Days with snow	110
Days with 1.5 inches or more snow	34

Percent time sky is clear

Jan.	Feb.	March	April	May	June	July	Aug.	Sept.	Oct.	Nov.	Dec.
7	10.4	15	18.6	19.7	20.8	22.2	22.2	20.1	19.4	8	5.3

Eugene, Oregon

Lat. 44° 7' N **Lon.** 123° 13' W **Elev.** 364 ft.

Eugene, at the upper or southern end of the fertile Willamette Valley, is near the Willamette River — a main source of local fog. To the east is the Cascade Range with elevations of 10,000 feet and to the west are coastal mountains with peaks of 1,500 to 2,500 feet. Low hills to the south nearly close the valley, but to the north the level valley floor broadens rapidly. The Cascades block westward passage of all but the strongest continental air masses while the coastal range blocks coastal fog. Sometimes in summer, when air flows into the valley from the east, dry, hot weather develops, causing an extreme fire hazard. In winter this situation causes clear, sunny days and cool, frosty nights. Abundant moisture and moderate temperatures result in rapid growth of evergreen timber, a major industry here.

Temperatures

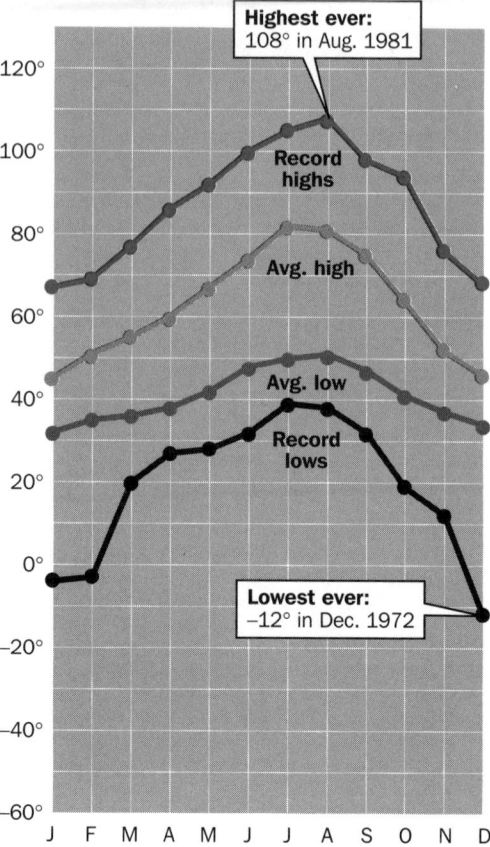

Highest ever: 108° in Aug. 1981

Record highs

Avg. high

Avg. low

Record lows

Lowest ever: −12° in Dec. 1972

Weather extremes

Most rain in 24 hours:	4.75 in. Jan. 15, 1974
Most rain in a month:	20.99 in. December 1964
Most snow in 24 hours:	22.9 in. Jan. 25 – 26, 1969
Most snow in a month:	47.1 in. January 1969

Monthly averages

Month	Avg. precip. (in.)	Avg. snow (in.)	Wet days	Thunder-storm days	Pct. sky is cloudy	% p.m. relative humidity	Dew point	Wind speed (mph)
Jan.	7.8	4	18	*	70	80	35	10.4
Feb.	5.9	1	15	*	64	75	38	10.4
March	5.2	1	16	*	57	66	39	10.4
April	2.8	T	12	*	50	60	40	9.2
May	2.1	T	10	1	41	57	45	9.2
June	1.4	T	6	1	38	52	50	9.2
July	0.3	0	2	*	21	43	51	10.4
Aug.	0.9	T	4	*	25	44	51	10.4
Sept.	1.6	T	6	1	29	49	49	10.4
Oct.	3.7	T	11	*	48	65	45	8.1
Nov.	7.5	T	16	*	67	77	41	10.4
Dec.	8.3	1	19	*	73	82	37	10.4

T - Trace of rain or snow   * - Less than 1   NA - Not Available

Annual averages

Precipitation (in inches)	47.3
Snow (in inches)	7
Heating degree days	4,799
Cooling degree days	261
Days with thunderstorms	4
Days with fog	137
Days above 90°	15
Days below 32°	56
Wet days	137
Days with snow	4
Days with 1.5 inches or more snow	2

Percent time sky is clear

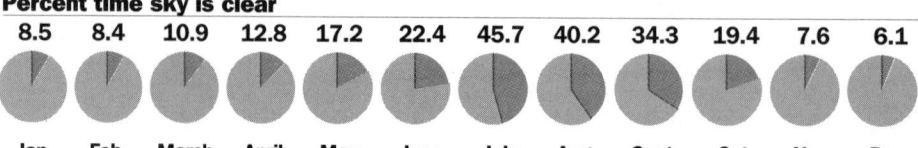

Jan.	Feb.	March	April	May	June	July	Aug.	Sept.	Oct.	Nov.	Dec.
8.5	8.4	10.9	12.8	17.2	22.4	45.7	40.2	34.3	19.4	7.6	6.1

Eureka, California

Lat. 40° 48' N **Lon.** 124° 10' W **Elev.** 60 ft.

There are no hills in Eureka of any consequence; the land slopes upward gently from Humboldt Bay toward the Coast Ranges. Eureka has a completely maritime climate with high humidity prevailing the entire year. There are definite rainy and dry seasons. The rainy season, from October through April, accounts for about 90 percent of the annual precipitation. The dry season from May through September is marked by considerable fog or low cloudiness that clears in the late morning. Sunny weather generally prevails during the dry season afternoons. Temperatures are moderate the entire year. The mild temperatures and lack of intense sunshine are ideal for cultivation of berries and flowers.

Temperatures

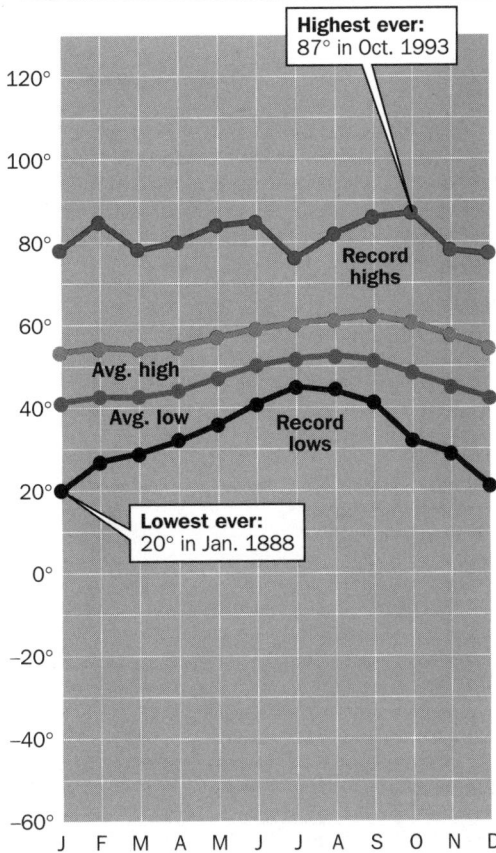

Highest ever:
87° in Oct. 1993

Record highs

Avg. high

Avg. low

Record lows

Lowest ever:
20° in Jan. 1888

Weather extremes

Most rain in 24 hours:	5.83 in. Oct. 28 – 29, 1950
Most rain in a month:	19.49 in. February 1902
Most snow in 24 hours:	3.4 in. Jan. 13, 1907
Most snow in a month:	6.9 in. January 1907

Monthly averages

Month	Avg. precip. (in.)	Avg. snow (in.)	Wet days	Thunder-storm days	Pct. sky is cloudy	% p.m. relative humidity	Dew point	Wind speed (mph)
Jan.	7.0	0.2	16	1	61	NA	NA	6.9
Feb.	5.2	0.1	14	1	61	NA	NA	7.2
March	5.1	T	16	*	57	NA	NA	7.6
April	2.9	T	12	*	52	NA	NA	8.1
May	1.6	0.0	8	*	47	NA	NA	7.9
June	0.6	0.0	5	*	44	NA	NA	7.4
July	0.1	0.0	2	*	44	NA	NA	6.8
Aug.	0.4	0.0	3	*	48	NA	NA	5.8
Sept.	0.9	0.0	5	*	42	NA	NA	5.6
Oct.	2.7	0.0	9	*	47	NA	NA	5.6
Nov.	5.9	T	13	1	57	NA	NA	6.0
Dec.	6.2	T	15	1	58	NA	NA	6.4

T - Trace of rain or snow   * - Less than 1   NA - Not Available

Annual averages

Precipitation (in inches)	39
Snow (in inches)	*
Heating degree days	4,725
Cooling degree days	11
Days with thunderstorms	4
Days with fog	51
Days above 90°	0
Days below 32°	5
Wet days	117
Days with snow	NA
Days with 1.5 inches or more snow	*

Percent time sky is clear

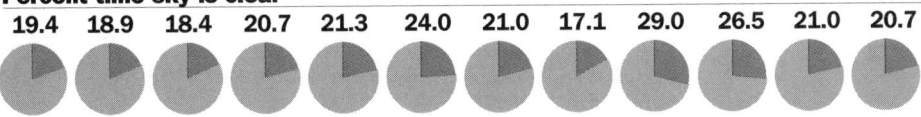

19.4	18.9	18.4	20.7	21.3	24.0	21.0	17.1	29.0	26.5	21.0	20.7
Jan.	Feb.	March	April	May	June	July	Aug.	Sept.	Oct.	Nov.	Dec.

Evansville, Indiana

Lat. 38° 03′ N **Lon.** 87° 32′ W **Elev.** 380 ft.

Evansville is on the Ohio River and lies in the path of moisture-bearing low pressure from the western Gulf of Mexico region. There is considerable variation in temperature and precipitation by year, depending on the frequency of storm and frontal passages. Much of the precipitation results from these storm systems, especially in the cooler part of the year. In summer and early autumn, changes are less severe and periods of polar air invasions are less prolonged. Severe storms are rather infrequent but thunderstorms cause some wind damage each year. Hail often occurs with the stronger thunderstorms. Evansville is in "tornado alley" with the most frequent occurrences coming in early spring and late fall.

Temperatures

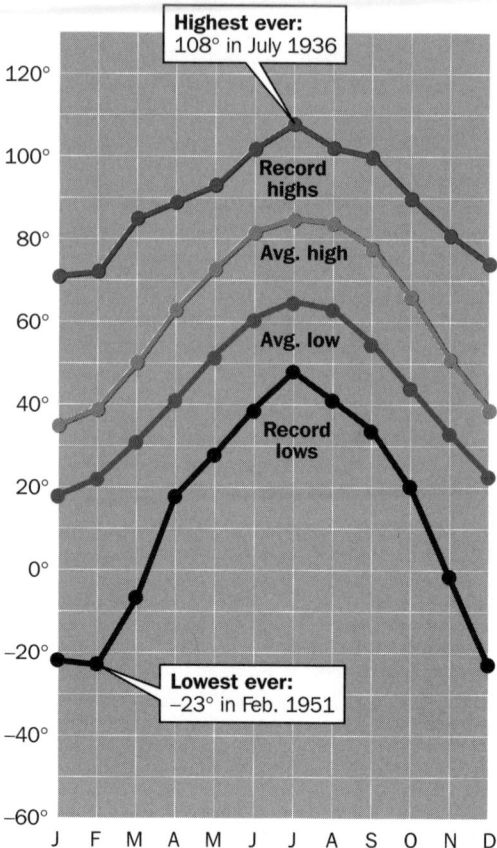

Highest ever: 108° in July 1936

Record highs

Avg. high

Avg. low

Record lows

Lowest ever: −23° in Feb. 1951

Weather extremes

Most rain in 24 hours:	6.94 in. Oct. 5 – 6, 1910
Most rain in a month:	14.78 in. January 1937
Most snow in 24 hours:	20.0 in. Jan. 14 – 15, 1918
Most snow in a month:	41.0 in. January 1918

Monthly averages

Month	Avg. precip. (in.)	Avg. snow (in.)	Wet days	Thunder-storm days	Pct. sky is cloudy	% p.m. relative humidity	Dew point	Wind speed (mph)
Jan.	2.8	7	12	1	57	68	20	11.5
Feb.	2.5	6	10	1	54	64	23	12.7
March	3.6	4	13	3	54	59	30	13.8
April	3.6	1	12	4	46	53	40	12.7
May	4.0	T	12	6	39	53	51	10.4
June	3.9	0	10	7	31	53	60	9.2
July	4.3	0	10	8	27	56	65	8.1
Aug.	3.4	0	9	6	26	56	63	8.1
Sept.	2.9	0	8	4	30	53	56	9.2
Oct.	2.6	T	8	2	34	53	44	10.4
Nov.	3.3	2	10	1	52	63	34	11.5
Dec.	3.3	5	13	*	58	70	25	11.5

T - Trace of rain or snow   * - Less than 1   NA - Not Available

Annual averages

Precipitation (in inches)	40.2
Snow (in inches)	25
Heating degree days	4,729
Cooling degree days	1,378
Days with thunderstorms	43
Days with fog	163
Days above 90°	19
Days below 32°	119
Wet days	127
Days with snow	46
Days with 1.5 inches or more snow	10

Percent time sky is clear

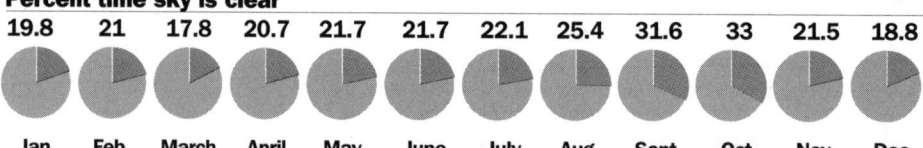

Jan.	Feb.	March	April	May	June	July	Aug.	Sept.	Oct.	Nov.	Dec.
19.8	21	17.8	20.7	21.7	21.7	22.1	25.4	31.6	33	21.5	18.8

Fairbanks, Alaska

Lat. 64° 49′ N **Lon.** 147° 52′ W **Elev.** 436 ft.

Rolling hills reaching elevations of up to 2,000 feet rise above Fairbanks, which lies in the Tanana Valley. During the winter, low lying areas nearby, such as the community of North Pole, are sometimes 15 degrees colder than the city. The sun is above the horizon up to 21 hours during June and July, while temperatures range from the lower 30s to the mid 90s. From November to early March, daylight ranges from 10 to less than 4 hours per day. Winter temperatures range from about 65 below zero to 45 above, reflecting either frigid arctic air or mild chinook winds off the Alaska Range, 80 miles south of Fairbanks. Snow cover is persistent from October through April, and ice fog makes visibility quite low. Rivers are normally frozen from early October until April.

Temperatures

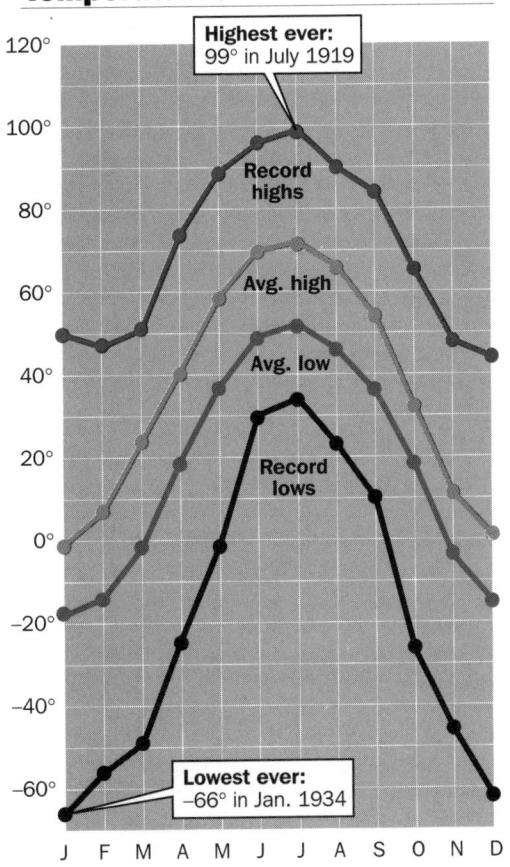

Highest ever: 99° in July 1919
Record highs
Avg. high
Avg. low
Record lows
Lowest ever: −66° in Jan. 1934

Weather extremes

Most rain in 24 hours:	3.42 in. Aug. 12, 1967
Most rain in a month:	6.2 in. August 1967
Most snow in 24 hours:	20.1 in. Feb. 11 – 12, 1966
Most snow in a month:	65.6 in. January 1937

Monthly averages

Month	Avg. precip. (in.)	Avg. snow (in.)	Wet days	Thunder- storm days	Pct. sky is cloudy	% p.m. relative humidity	Dew point	Wind speed (mph)
Jan.	0.5	10	8	*	42	69	-14	4.6
Feb.	0.4	9	7	*	39	64	-11	5.8
March	0.3	6	6	0	35	54	1	6.9
April	0.3	3	5	*	40	46	17	8.1
May	0.6	1	7	*	39	39	31	8.1
June	1.4	0	11	3	43	44	44	10.4
July	2.0	0	13	3	46	51	50	9.2
Aug.	1.9	T	12	1	51	55	47	9.2
Sept.	1.0	1	9	*	54	57	36	5.8
Oct.	0.8	11	11	*	59	69	19	6.9
Nov.	0.7	13	10	*	47	73	-2	5.8
Dec.	0.8	14	9	*	46	72	-13	5.8

T - Trace of rain or snow   * - Less than 1   NA - Not Available

Annual averages

Precipitation (in inches)	10.8
Snow (in inches)	67
Heating degree days	13,880
Cooling degree days	60
Days with thunderstorms	7
Days with fog	78
Days above 90°	79
Days below 32°	225
Wet days	108
Days with snow	127
Days with 1.5 inches or more snow	28

Percent time sky is clear

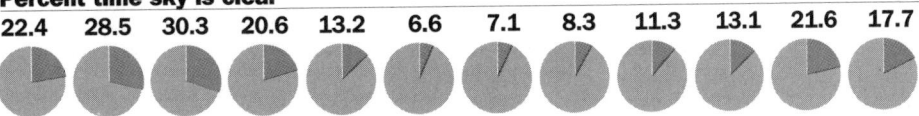

22.4	28.5	30.3	20.6	13.2	6.6	7.1	8.3	11.3	13.1	21.6	17.7
Jan.	Feb.	March	April	May	June	July	Aug.	Sept.	Oct.	Nov.	Dec.

Fargo, North Dakota

Lat. 46° 54' N **Lon.** 96° 48' W **Elev.** 900 ft.

Fargo is in the Red River Valley. In recent years, spring floods due to melting snow have been common. North winds blowing up the valley occasionally cause fog. Summers are generally comfortable with very few hot, humid days. Nights are mostly cool. The winter months are cold and dry with temperatures above freezing an average of only six days each month and nighttime lows below zero about half of the time. The growing season (April to September) gets 75 percent of the precipitation, often accompanied by electrical storms with heavy rainfall. Heavy snowfall is the exception in winter. But the flat terrain and wind can lead to the legendary Dakota blizzards. Strong winds with even light snow cause much drifting and blowing, reducing visibility to near zero several times each winter.

Temperatures

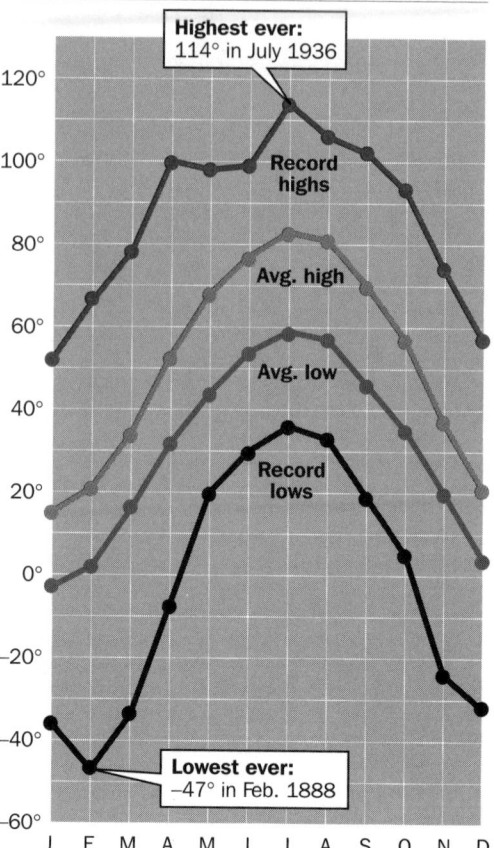

Highest ever: 114° in July 1936

Record highs

Avg. high

Avg. low

Record lows

Lowest ever: −47° in Feb. 1888

Weather extremes

Most rain in 24 hours:	5.17 in. July 3 – 4, 1886
Most rain in a month:	9.58 in. August 1900
Most snow in 24 hours:	19.4 in. Jan. 6 – 7, 1989
Most snow in a month:	31.5 in. January 1989

Monthly averages

Month	Avg. precip. (in.)	Avg. snow (in.)	Wet days	Thunder-storm days	Pct. sky is cloudy	% p.m. relative humidity	Dew point	Wind speed (mph)
Jan.	0.6	9	8	0	45	70	0	16.1
Feb.	0.4	6	7	*	45	71	6	13.8
March	0.9	7	8	*	46	68	18	15.0
April	1.7	3	8	1	42	52	30	16.1
May	2.3	T	10	4	36	45	40	15.0
June	3.0	0	10	7	31	50	53	13.8
July	3.1	0	10	8	20	49	59	13.8
Aug.	2.4	0	9	7	23	47	56	13.8
Sept.	1.8	T	8	3	31	50	46	13.8
Oct.	1.5	1	7	1	36	51	35	15.0
Nov.	0.8	5	6	*	51	65	21	15.0
Dec.	0.6	7	8	*	49	72	7	12.7

T - Trace of rain or snow   * - Less than 1   NA - Not Available

Annual averages

Precipitation (in inches)	19.3
Snow (in inches)	38
Heating degree days	9,175
Cooling degree days	547
Days with thunderstorms	31
Days with fog	77
Days above 90°	15
Days below 32°	180
Wet days	99
Days with snow	75
Days with 1.5 inches or more snow	16

Percent time sky is clear

24.1	23.5	20.2	21.5	19.4	18.2	24.1	26.2	27.7	26.7	19.9	21.7

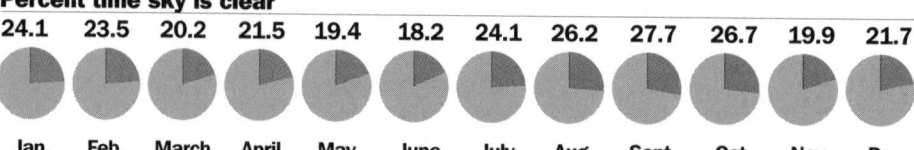

| Jan. | Feb. | March | April | May | June | July | Aug. | Sept. | Oct. | Nov. | Dec. |

Flagstaff, Arizona

Lat. 35° 8' N **Lon.** 111° 40' W **Elev.** 7,006 ft.

Flagstaff is on a volcanic plateau at the base of the highest mountains in Arizona, with cold winters and mild, pleasantly cool summers. Humidity is moderate and there is considerable temperature change from day to night. The daily range of temperature is especially high from October to March, as a result of extensive snow cover and clear skies. The average first occurrence of 32°F in fall is Sept. 21 and the average last occurrence in the spring is June 13. Winter minimums frequently reach zero or below, while summer maximums are often above 80°F. Several months have little or no precipitation. Winter snowfalls can exceed 100 inches in one month and over 200 inches a season. However, accumulations vary widely by year.

Temperatures

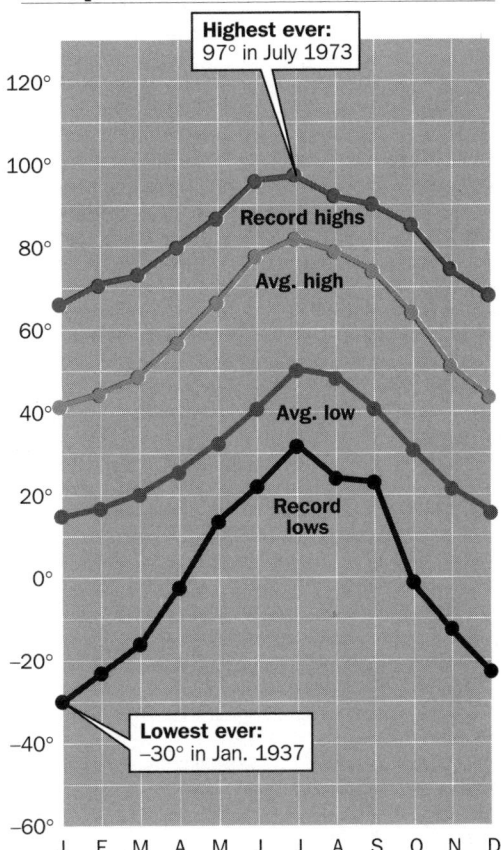

Highest ever: 97° in July 1973

Record highs

Avg. high

Avg. low

Record lows

Lowest ever: −30° in Jan. 1937

Weather extremes

Most rain in 24 hours:	3.93 in. Feb. 19, 1993
Most rain in a month:	10.05 in. February 1993
Most snow in 24 hours:	31.0 in. Dec. 30, 1915
Most snow in a month:	104.8 in. January 1949

Monthly averages

Month	Avg. precip. (in.)	Avg. snow (in.)	Wet days	Thunderstorm days	Pct. sky is cloudy	% p.m. relative humidity	Dew point	Wind speed (mph)
Jan.	2.1	19.9	7	0	39	50	NA	6.8
Feb.	2.0	17.9	7	*	40	45	NA	6.8
March	2.1	22.5	9	1	37	41	NA	7.3
April	1.4	9.7	6	1	29	31	NA	7.7
May	0.8	1.8	4	3	21	27	NA	7.4
June	0.6	T	3	4	13	21	NA	7.0
July	2.5	T	12	17	29	38	NA	5.5
Aug.	2.6	T	11	16	26	43	NA	5.2
Sept.	1.5	0.1	6	7	16	36	NA	5.8
Oct.	1.5	2.1	5	2	22	36	NA	5.9
Nov.	1.7	9.9	5	1	27	43	NA	6.9
Dec.	2.3	16.0	7	*	35	52	NA	6.8

T - Trace of rain or snow   * - Less than 1   NA - Not Available

Annual averages

Precipitation (in inches)	21
Snow (in inches)	100
Heating degree days	7,254
Cooling degree days	127
Days with thunderstorms	51
Days with fog	11
Days above 90°	3
Days below 32°	209
Wet days	82
Days with snow	N/A
Days with 1.5 inches or more snow	22

Percent time sky is clear

Jan.	Feb.	March	April	May	June	July	Aug.	Sept.	Oct.	Nov.	Dec.
40.3	39.3	37.4	42.0	49.4	61.3	28.7	31.9	51.7	55.5	51.3	44.5

Flint, Michigan

Lat. 42° 58' N **Lon.** 83° 45' W **Elev.** 766 ft.

Flint, in the Flint River Valley, is heavily influenced by the Great Lakes. Lake Huron is 65 miles east, Saginaw Bay is 40 miles north and Lake Michigan 120 miles west. The terrain is generally level with a slight rise to hills southeast of the city. Extreme heat is rare and cold waves are less severe than might be expected. Lake Michigan tempers northwest cold waves, though winter snow showers can occur with northwest wind. The "lake effect" also delays warming in spring and prolongs warmth into autumn. Late spring is wettest; winter is driest. Most snow occurs as frequent flurries. Winter is cloudy and humid, while summer has abundant sunshine and moderate humidity. Violent thunderstorms and squall lines occasionally hit the area and infrequent tornadoes have caused major damage.

Temperatures

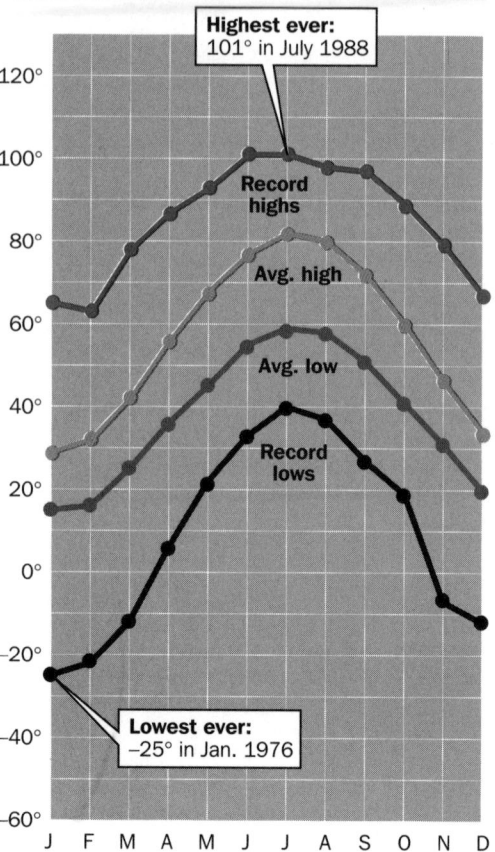

Highest ever: 101° in July 1988

Record highs

Avg. high

Avg. low

Record lows

Lowest ever: −25° in Jan. 1976

Weather extremes

Most rain in 24 hours:	6.04 in. Sep. 10, 1950
Most rain in a month:	11.04 in. August 1975
Most snow in 24 hours:	19.8 in. Jan. 26 – 27, 1967
Most snow in a month:	28.5 in. January 1976

Monthly averages

Month	Avg. precip. (in.)	Avg. snow (in.)	Wet days	Thunderstorm days	Pct. sky is cloudy	% p.m. relative humidity	Dew point	Wind speed (mph)
Jan.	1.6	12	13	*	63	70	16	11.5
Feb.	1.5	10	11	*	57	66	17	12.7
March	2.1	8	13	1	54	60	24	13.8
April	3.0	2	13	3	49	53	34	12.7
May	2.8	T	10	4	41	51	45	11.5
June	3.2	0	10	6	34	53	55	9.2
July	2.9	0	9	6	28	52	59	9.2
Aug.	3.5	0	9	6	30	55	59	8.1
Sept.	3.2	T	10	4	35	57	52	8.1
Oct.	2.2	T	9	2	42	57	41	10.4
Nov.	2.5	4	12	1	61	66	31	11.5
Dec.	2.0	10	14	*	66	72	22	12.7

T - Trace of rain or snow   * - Less than 1   NA - Not Available

Annual averages

Precipitation (in inches)	30.5
Snow (in inches)	47
Heating degree days	6,972
Cooling degree days	560
Days with thunderstorms	33
Days with fog	143
Days above 90°	8
Days below 32°	143
Wet days	133
Days with snow	91
Days with 1.5 inches or more snow	19

Percent time sky is clear

13.5	17.1	18.8	22.3	21.7	21.6	24.1	26.3	26.1	25.6	14.2	12.9

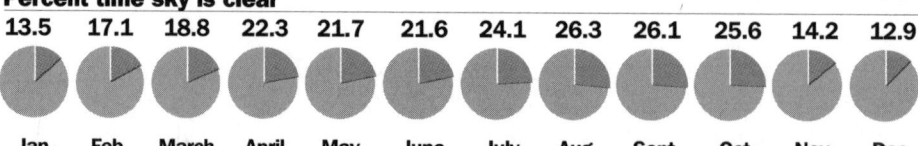

| Jan. | Feb. | March | April | May | June | July | Aug. | Sept. | Oct. | Nov. | Dec. |

Fort Myers, Florida

Lat. 26° 35' N **Lon.** 81° 52' W **Elev.** 15 ft.

Located about 15 miles from the Gulf of Mexico, Fort Myers has a climate characterized as subtropical, with temperature extremes of both summer and winter tempered by the marine influence of the Gulf. Winters are mild, with many bright, warm days and moderately cool nights. Most rain during the summer occurs as thunderstorms in late afternoon or early evening, bringing welcome cooling on summer days. These showers seldom last long, even though they yield large amounts of rain. Winds approximating 100 mph have been experienced with the passage of hurricanes during fall. Heavy fog is rather infrequent, occurring mostly in winter during the early mornings. There is seldom a day without sunshine at some time.

Temperatures

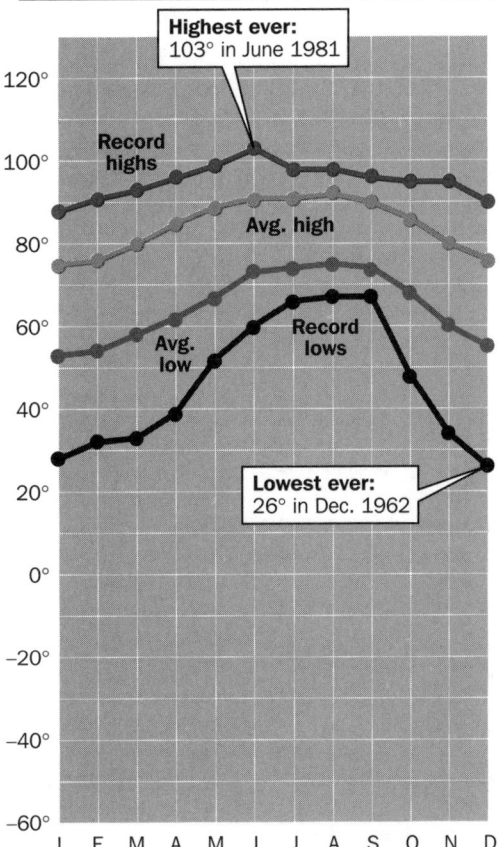

Weather extremes

Most rain in 24 hours:	7.75 in. May 18, 1989
Most rain in a month:	20.10 in. June 1974
Most snow in 24 hours:	none
Most snow in a month:	none

Monthly averages

Month	Avg. precip. (in.)	Avg. snow (in.)	Wet days	Thunderstorm days	Pct. sky is cloudy	% p.m. relative humidity	Dew point	Wind speed (mph)
Jan.	1.7	0	5	1	17	55	55	8.1
Feb.	2.1	0	6	1	18	54	55	9.2
March	2.7	0	5	2	15	52	58	9.2
April	1.3	0	4	2	11	50	61	9.2
May	3.7	0	7	6	11	53	66	8.1
June	9.0	0	15	16	15	64	72	6.9
July	8.5	0	18	22	16	68	73	6.9
Aug.	9.0	0	18	21	13	67	74	6.9
Sept.	8.3	0	15	13	16	66	73	8.1
Oct.	3.5	0	7	3	13	60	67	9.2
Nov.	1.5	0	4	1	13	57	61	8.1
Dec.	1.5	0	4	1	15	57	56	8.1

T - Trace of rain or snow   * - Less than 1   NA - Not Available

Annual averages

Precipitation (in inches)	52.8
Snow (in inches)	0
Heating degree days	337
Cooling degree days	3,833
Days with thunderstorms	89
Days with fog	105
Days above 90°	114
Days below 32°	19
Wet days	108
Days with snow	0
Days with 1.5 inches or more snow	0

Percent time sky is clear

Jan.	Feb.	March	April	May	June	July	Aug.	Sept.	Oct.	Nov.	Dec.
33.3	32.8	31.4	34.5	28.1	17.7	14.1	14.9	17	29.4	32.7	34.3

Fort Smith, Arkansas

Lat. 35° 20' N **Lon.** 94° 22' W **Elev.** 449 ft.

Fort Smith is on the Arkansas River at its confluence with the Poteau River. To the north are the Boston Mountains and to the south are the Ouachita Mountains. The terrain in the city consists of low broken hills separated by creek and river bottom land, which has a definite influence on the weather. Temperature extremes of cold and heat and high humidity do occur. In summer there is an average of 10 days when the temperature rises to 100°F or higher. The average first occurrence of 32°F in the fall is October 30 and the average last occurrence in the spring is April 3.

Temperatures

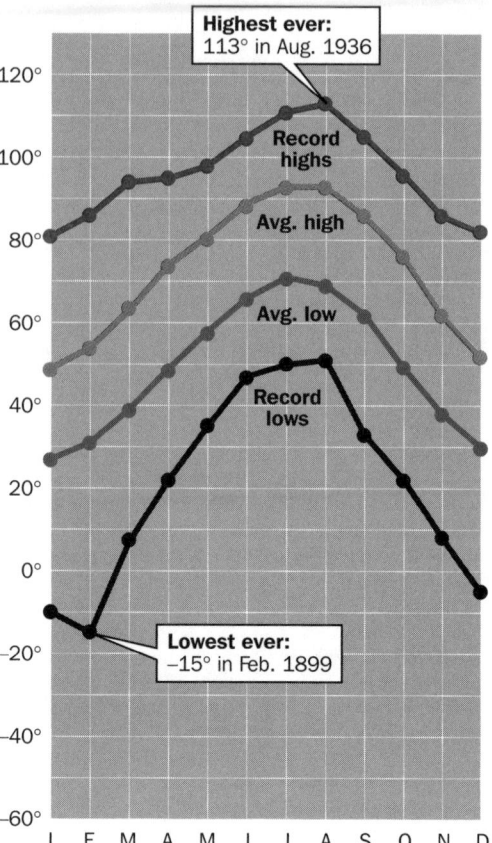

Highest ever: 113° in Aug. 1936

Record highs

Avg. high

Avg. low

Record lows

Lowest ever: −15° in Feb. 1899

Weather extremes

Most rain in 24 hours:	8.58 in. June 9 – 10, 1945
Most rain in a month:	15.02 in. June 1945
Most snow in 24 hours:	17.5 in. Feb. 18 – 19, 1921
Most snow in a month:	18.3 in. February 1921

Monthly averages

Month	Avg. precip. (in.)	Avg. snow (in.)	Wet days	Thunder-storm days	Pct. sky is cloudy	% p.m. relative humidity	Dew point	Wind speed (mph)
Jan.	2.3	3	7	1	46	54	27	8.1
Feb.	2.9	2	8	2	45	51	31	8.1
March	3.8	1	9	5	44	47	37	8.1
April	4.0	T	10	7	40	45	47	8.1
May	5.3	0	10	8	37	51	58	6.9
June	3.5	0	8	8	26	51	66	5.8
July	3.3	0	8	8	21	49	69	6.9
Aug.	2.9	0	7	7	20	47	67	6.9
Sept.	3.2	0	8	4	27	48	61	6.9
Oct.	3.5	0	7	3	30	45	50	6.9
Nov.	3.6	1	7	2	38	48	38	6.9
Dec.	2.9	1	7	2	43	53	31	8.1

T - Trace of rain or snow   * - Less than 1   NA - Not Available

Annual averages

Precipitation (in inches)	41.0
Snow (in inches)	7
Heating degree days	3,428
Cooling degree days	2,020
Days with thunderstorms	57
Days with fog	93
Days above 90°	77
Days below 32°	77
Wet days	96
Days with snow	10
Days with 1.5 inches or more snow	4

Percent time sky is clear

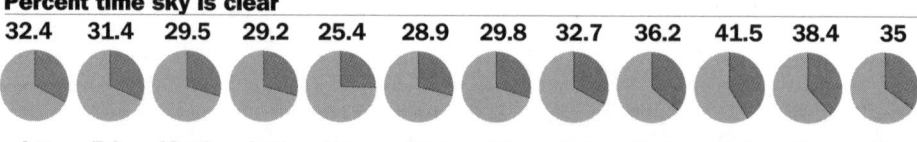

Jan.	Feb.	March	April	May	June	July	Aug.	Sept.	Oct.	Nov.	Dec.
32.4	31.4	29.5	29.2	25.4	28.9	29.8	32.7	36.2	41.5	38.4	35

Fort Wayne, Indiana

Lat. 41° 0' N **Lon.** 85° 12' W **Elev.** 797 ft.

Fort Wayne's climate is influenced by the Great Lakes and is typical of midwestern cities at the same latitude. It is located at the junction of the St. Marys, St. Joseph, and Maumee rivers in northeastern Indiana and the terrain is level south and east of the city. Temperature differences between daily highs and lows average about 20 degrees. In late spring and early summer, rain is more frequent — severe flooding has occurred in the area. Snow usually covers the ground for about 30 days during the winter, but heavy snowstorms are infrequent. There is considerable cloudiness during the winter.

Temperatures

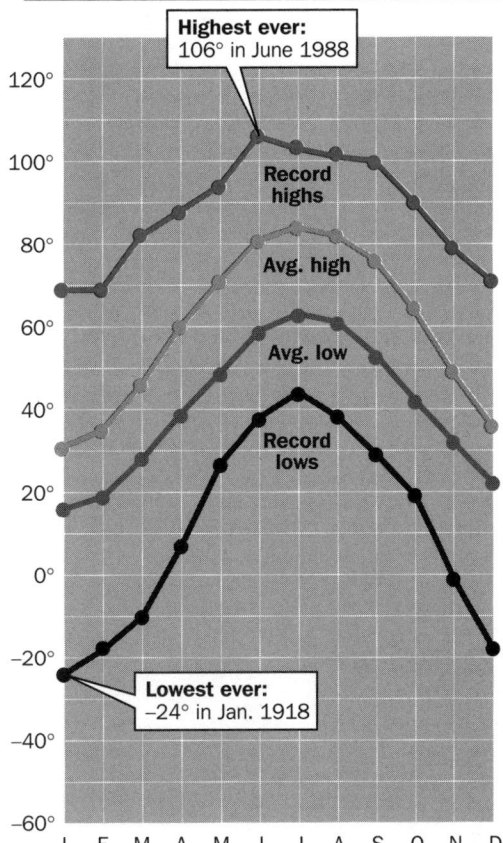

Weather extremes

Most rain in 24 hours:	4.93 in. August 1, 1926
Most rain in a month:	11.0 in. July 1986
Most snow in 24 hours:	13.6 in. March 9, 1964
Most snow in a month:	29.5 in. January 1982

Monthly averages

Month	Avg. precip. (in.)	Avg. snow (in.)	Wet days	Thunder-storm days	Pct. sky is cloudy	% p.m. relative humidity	Dew point	Wind speed (mph)
Jan.	2.3	8	12	*	57	71	18	13.8
Feb.	2.1	8	11	1	52	68	20	13.8
March	2.9	5	13	2	51	62	28	13.8
April	3.4	2	13	4	45	54	38	13.8
May	3.6	T	11	5	36	52	48	12.7
June	3.8	0	10	7	29	52	57	11.5
July	3.6	0	10	7	24	53	62	9.2
Aug.	3.4	0	9	6	25	55	61	9.2
Sept.	2.6	0	9	4	30	53	54	10.4
Oct.	2.7	T	9	2	35	55	43	11.5
Nov.	2.8	3	11	1	53	67	33	12.7
Dec.	2.7	7	13	*	59	74	23	12.7

T - Trace of rain or snow   * - Less than 1   NA - Not Available

Annual averages

Precipitation (in inches)	35.9
Snow (in inches)	33
Heating degree days	6,219
Cooling degree days	850
Days with thunderstorms	39
Days with fog	157
Days above 90°	16
Days below 32°	131
Wet days	131
Days with snow	63
Days with 1.5 inches or more snow	15

Percent time sky is clear

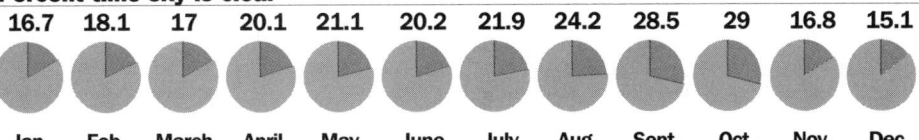

16.7	18.1	17	20.1	21.1	20.2	21.9	24.2	28.5	29	16.8	15.1
Jan.	Feb.	March	April	May	June	July	Aug.	Sept.	Oct.	Nov.	Dec.

Fresno, California

Lat. 36° 46' N **Lon.** 119° 43' W **Elev.** 100 ft.

Fresno is located toward the eastern edge of the San Joaquin Valley. About 15 miles east the terrain slopes upward with the foothills of the Sierra Nevada, which then rise to more than 14,000 feet. About 45 miles to the west lie the Coast Range foothills. The climate is dry and mild in winter, very hot in summer. Even in the warmest months evenings and nights are generally comfortable due to northwest winds, which increase in the evenings, and the normally large temperature variation of about 35 degrees between highs and lows. Fog can be a winter travel hazard. The growing season is 291 days. Nearly nine-tenths of the annual precipitation falls between November and April. Any summer rainfall generally is very light. Snow is rare.

Temperatures

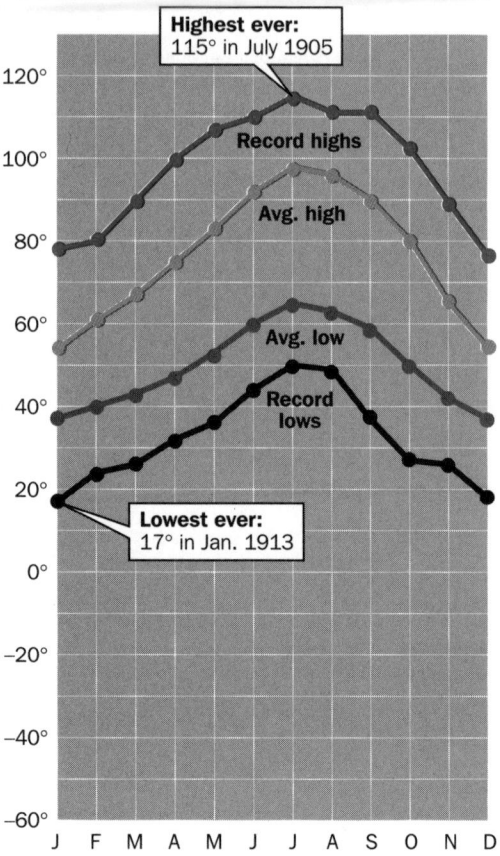

Highest ever: 115° in July 1905

Record highs

Avg. high

Avg. low

Record lows

Lowest ever: 17° in Jan. 1913

Weather extremes

Most rain in 24 hours:	2.86 in. Nov. 16 – 17, 1900
Most rain in a month:	8.56 in. January 1969
Most snow in 24 hours:	2.5 in. Jan. 12, 1930
Most snow in a month:	2.5 in. January 1930

Monthly averages

Month	Avg. precip. (in.)	Avg. snow (in.)	Wet days	Thunder- storm days	Pct. sky is cloudy	% p.m. relative humidity	Dew point	Wind speed (mph)
Jan.	2.0	T	8	*	53	67	40	6.9
Feb.	1.8	T	7	*	38	56	42	8.1
March	1.8	T	7	1	29	45	43	9.2
April	1.1	0	4	1	21	35	44	9.2
May	0.3	0	2	1	13	27	45	9.2
June	0.1	0	1	*	6	23	49	9.2
July	T	0	*	*	3	21	52	9.2
Aug.	T	0	*	*	3	24	54	8.1
Sept.	0.2	0	1	1	6	28	52	8.1
Oct.	0.4	0	2	1	12	34	47	8.1
Nov.	1.3	T	5	*	31	53	43	4.6
Dec.	1.5	T	T	*	51	68	39	6.9

T - Trace of rain or snow   * - Less than 1   NA - Not Available

Annual averages

Precipitation (in inches)	10.6
Snow (in inches)	T
Heating degree days	2,513
Cooling degree days	1,874
Days with thunderstorms	5
Days with fog	96
Days above 90°	105
Days below 32°	26
Wet days	44
Days with snow	*
Days with 1.5 inches or more snow	*

Percent time sky is clear

20.7	31.1	36.6	44	56.4	70.7	78.4	76.8	73.7	63.7	39.3	23.3

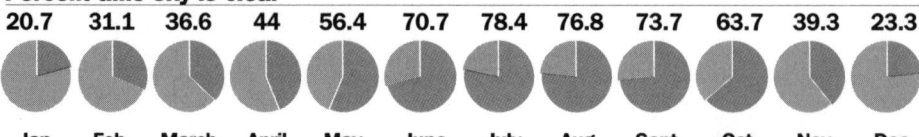

| Jan. | Feb. | March | April | May | June | July | Aug. | Sept. | Oct. | Nov. | Dec. |

Galveston, Texas

Lat. 29° 18' N **Lon.** 94° 48' W **Elev.** 7 ft.

Since it is located on Galveston Island off the southeast coast of Texas — bounded on the southeast by the Gulf of Mexico and on the northwest by Galveston Bay — Galveston's climate is predominantly marine. High humidities prevail throughout the year. Cold fronts which do reach Galveston are seldom severe and temperatures below 32°F are rare, thanks to the coastal location and relatively low latitude. Winter precipitation comes mainly from frontal activity and from low stratus clouds, which produce slow, steady rains. Summer rainfall varies greatly on different parts of the island, as most of it is from local thunderstorm activity.

Temperatures

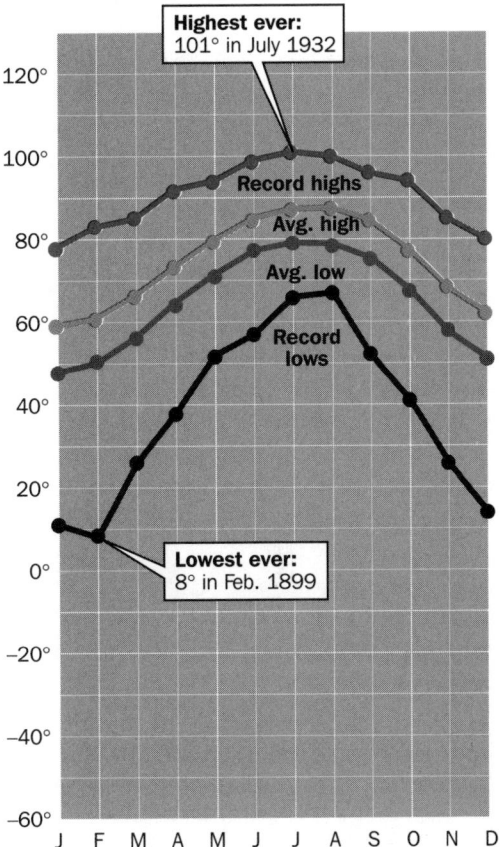

Highest ever: 101° in July 1932

Record highs
Avg. high
Avg. low
Record lows

Lowest ever: 8° in Feb. 1899

J F M A M J J A S O N D

Weather extremes

Most rain in 24 hours:	14.35 in. July 13 – 14, 1900
Most rain in a month:	26.01 in. September 1885
Most snow in 24 hours:	15.4 in. Feb. 14 – 15, 1895
Most snow in a month:	15.4 in. February 1895

Monthly averages

Month	Avg. precip. (in.)	Avg. snow (in.)	Wet days	Thunder-storm days	Pct. sky is cloudy	% p.m. relative humidity	Dew point	Wind speed (mph)
Jan.	3.0	T	10	NA	16	77	NA	11.6
Feb.	2.3	0.2	9	NA	15	74	NA	11.8
March	2.1	T	8	2	15	74	NA	11.9
April	2.6	T	6	2	15	75	NA	12.1
May	3.3	T	6	4	13	73	NA	11.5
June	3.5	0.0	7	5	8	70	NA	10.7
July	3.8	0.0	9	4	9	70	NA	9.8
Aug.	4.4	0.0	9	1	9	69	NA	9.4
Sept.	5.8	0.0	9	7	10	68	NA	10.1
Oct.	2.6	0.0	6	2	9	65	NA	10.3
Nov.	3.2	0.0	8	3	12	72	NA	11.2
Dec.	3.6	T	10	2	16	76	NA	11.3

T - Trace of rain or snow   * - Less than 1   NA - Not Available

Annual averages

Precipitation (in inches)	40
Snow (in inches)	*
Heating degree days	1,253
Cooling degree days	2,967
Days with thunderstorms	NA
Days with fog	NA
Days above 90°	12
Days below 32°	4
Wet days	96
Days with snow	NA
Days with 1.5 inches or more snow	*

Percent time sky is clear

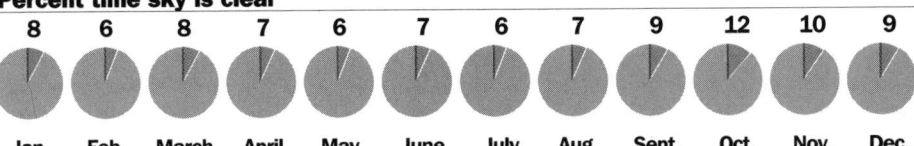

8	6	8	7	6	7	6	7	9	12	10	9
Jan.	Feb.	March	April	May	June	July	Aug.	Sept.	Oct.	Nov.	Dec.

Glasgow, Montana

Lat. 48° 13' N **Lon.** 106° 37' W **Elev.** 2,284 ft.

Founded as a railroad shop town in the valley of the Milk River, Glasgow is about 20 miles upstream from where the Milk joins the Missouri River. Glasgow's climate is continental with a large annual range in temperature. Seventy-eight percent of the precipitation falls from April through September. Glasgow is well protected in winter from most strong winds and blizzard conditions by the hills to the north. Snow seldom accumulates. Winters are quite cold, but mild winter weather occasionally occurs when warm, dry chinook winds coming down from higher country to the west reach as far east as Glasgow. Summers are warm and sunny but clouds and showers can occur late in the day. Hot days are usually accompanied by low relative humidity.

Temperatures

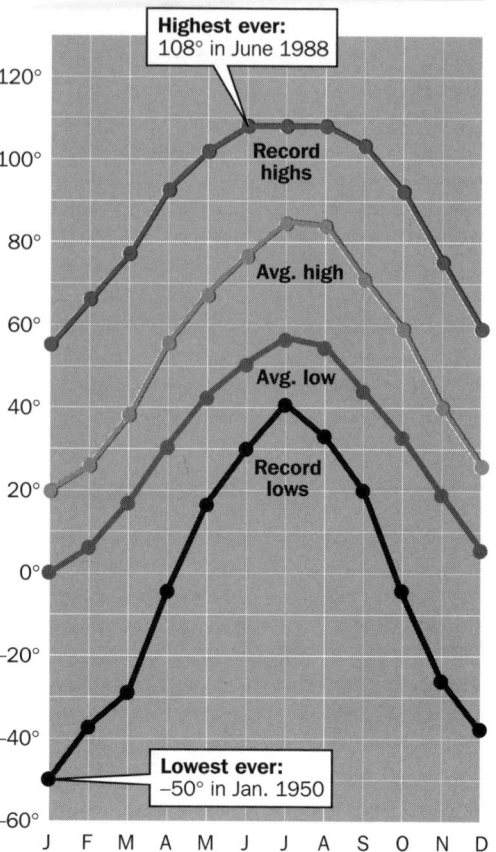

Highest ever: 108° in June 1988
Record highs
Avg. high
Avg. low
Record lows
Lowest ever: −50° in Jan. 1950

Weather extremes

Most rain in 24 hours:	4.99 in. Aug. 2 – 3, 1985
Most rain in a month:	5.74 in. August 1985
Most snow in 24 hours:	10.9 in. March 21–22, 1987
Most snow in a month:	24.2 in. January 1971

Monthly averages

Month	Avg. precip. (in.)	Avg. snow (in.)	Wet days	Thunder-storm days	Pct. sky is cloudy	% p.m. relative humidity	Dew point	Wind speed (mph)
Jan.	0.4	7	9	0	47	73	4	12.7
Feb.	0.4	5	7	0	44	72	10	12.7
March	0.4	4	7	*	43	59	20	12.7
April	0.8	3	7	1	39	41	27	12.7
May	1.8	1	10	4	36	39	37	12.7
June	2.3	T	10	7	27	38	46	12.7
July	1.6	0	8	8	16	32	49	11.5
Aug.	1.4	0	7	6	19	31	46	12.7
Sept.	0.9	T	6	2	27	37	38	12.7
Oct.	0.5	1	5	*	32	45	30	11.5
Nov.	0.3	3	6	*	43	64	19	11.5
Dec.	0.4	6	8	0	45	74	9	12.7

T - Trace of rain or snow   * - Less than 1   NA - Not Available

Annual averages

Precipitation (in inches)	11.3
Snow (in inches)	31
Heating degree days	8,668
Cooling degree days	522
Days with thunderstorms	28
Days with fog	45
Days above 90°	25
Days below 32°	179
Wet days	90
Days with snow	77
Days with 1.5 inches or more snow	12

Percent time sky is clear

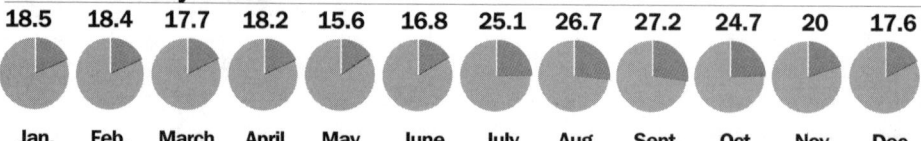

Jan.	Feb.	March	April	May	June	July	Aug.	Sept.	Oct.	Nov.	Dec.
18.5	18.4	17.7	18.2	15.6	16.8	25.1	26.7	27.2	24.7	20	17.6

Goodland, Kansas

Lat. 39° 22' N **Lon.** 101° 42' W **Elev.** 3,650 ft.

Goodland is on an intermediate plain with few native trees, conditions favorable for up-slope fog, low clouds, and drizzle with east winds. General storms provide the main source of precipitation during the spring, while thunderstorms help during the summer. Inadequate spring moisture often results in a summer drought. Winds during thunderstorms have been recorded with gusts up to 80 mph. Snow, an important factor in the production of winter wheat here, may cover the ground one third of the time from November through March. Winters are often modified by persistent chinook winds but polar outbreaks have been known to drop the temperature 70 degrees in a 24-hour period. Low humidity during the summer makes most nights comfortable.

Temperatures

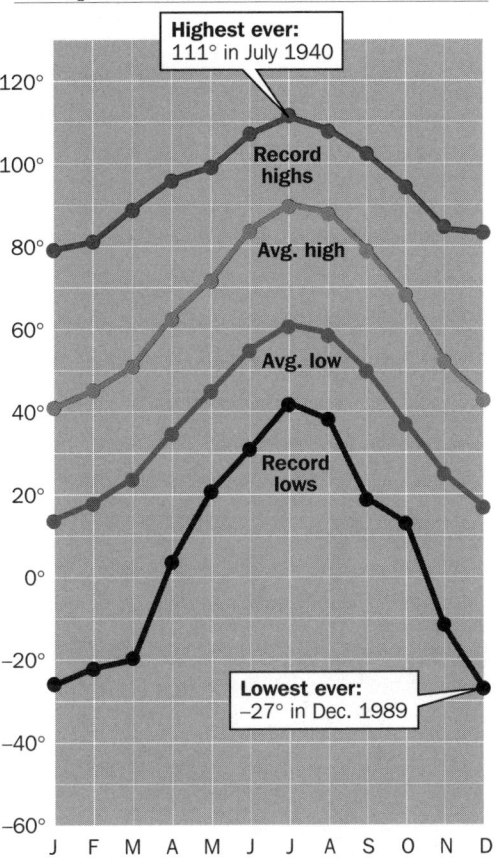

Highest ever: 111° in July 1940

Record highs

Avg. high

Avg. low

Record lows

Lowest ever: −27° in Dec. 1989

Weather extremes

Most rain in 24 hours:	4.15 in. June 28, 1989
Most rain in a month:	10.10 in. June 1985
Most snow in 24 hours:	17.9 in. Feb. 27, 1939
Most snow in a month:	32.0 in. March 1912

Monthly averages

Month	Avg. precip. (in.)	Avg. snow (in.)	Wet days	Thunderstorm days	Pct. sky is cloudy	% p.m. relative humidity	Dew point	Wind speed (mph)
Jan.	0.4	7	5	*	31	60	15	10.4
Feb.	0.4	5	5	*	34	55	19	16.1
March	1.1	10	7	1	38	50	23	18.4
April	1.3	4	7	2	33	41	32	16.1
May	3.2	1	10	8	34	47	44	15.0
June	3.1	0	9	10	22	40	52	13.8
July	2.7	0	9	11	18	38	56	13.8
Aug.	1.9	0	8	9	19	40	55	12.7
Sept.	1.4	T	6	4	23	39	45	13.8
Oct.	0.8	2	4	1	23	43	34	12.7
Nov.	0.6	5	4	*	29	57	24	16.1
Dec.	0.4	6	4	*	30	60	17	10.4

T - Trace of rain or snow   * - Less than 1   NA - Not Available

Annual averages

Precipitation (in inches)	17.3
Snow (in inches)	39
Heating degree days	6,019
Cooling degree days	963
Days with thunderstorms	46
Days with fog	79
Days above 90°	52
Days below 32°	159
Wet days	78
Days with snow	50
Days with 1.5 inches or more snow	17

Percent time sky is clear

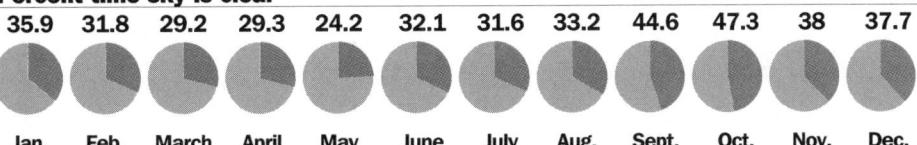

35.9	31.8	29.2	29.3	24.2	32.1	31.6	33.2	44.6	47.3	38	37.7
Jan.	Feb.	March	April	May	June	July	Aug.	Sept.	Oct.	Nov.	Dec.

Grand Island, Nebraska

Lat. 40° 58′ N **Lon.** 98° 19′ W **Elev.** 1,841 ft.

Grand Island is in the shallow Platte River Valley where the terrain slopes upward from the Missouri River Valley in eastern Nebraska to the Rocky Mountains of Colorado and Wyoming. Wintertime outbreaks of cold, dry, arctic air from Canada are common, usually accompanied by strong, biting winds. Temperatures vary from mild to bitterly cold. Summers are usually hot and dry with temperatures reaching 100°F or more. Late spring and early summer are the peak seasons for severe thunderstorms with frequent hail and occasional tornados. The east-west upslope produces periods of fog and low stratus clouds when the prevailing winds are from the east. When they are from the west, the west-east downslope can produce warm, dry chinook winds.

Temperatures

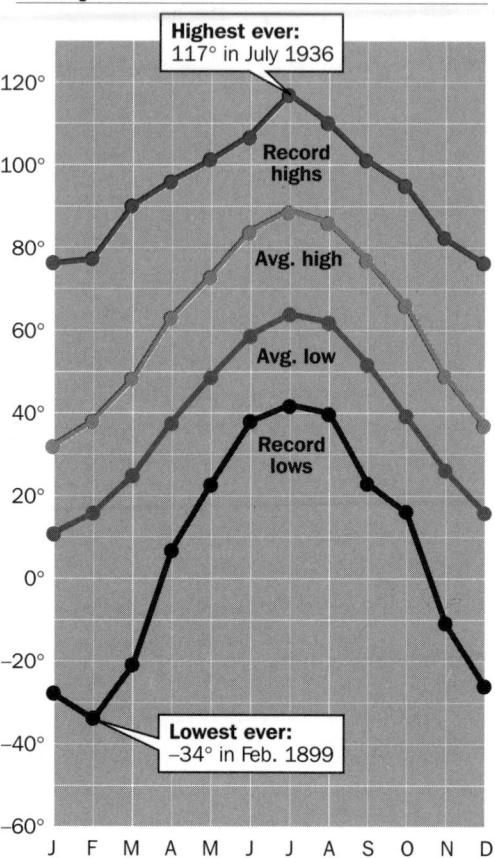

Highest ever: 117° in July 1936

Record highs

Avg. high

Avg. low

Record lows

Lowest ever: −34° in Feb. 1899

Weather extremes

Most rain in 24 hours:	5.88 in. Sept. 1 – 2, 1977	
Most rain in a month:	13.96 in. June 1967	
Most snow in 24 hours:	15.0 in. Feb. 17 – 18, 1984	
Most snow in a month:	31.0 in. February 1915	

Monthly averages

Month	Avg. precip. (in.)	Avg. snow (in.)	Wet days	Thunder-storm days	Pct. sky is cloudy	% p.m. relative humidity	Dew point	Wind speed (mph)
Jan.	0.5	6	5	*	40	58	13	16.1
Feb.	0.8	6	6	*	44	58	18	16.1
March	1.8	7	8	1	46	52	25	17.3
April	2.5	2	9	4	41	44	35	15.0
May	3.9	T	11	7	40	48	47	15.0
June	3.8	0	10	10	29	46	57	13.8
July	2.9	0	9	9	22	46	62	12.7
Aug.	2.7	0	8	8	24	47	60	12.7
Sept.	2.5	T	7	5	28	45	50	12.7
Oct.	1.2	T	5	2	29	42	38	12.7
Nov.	0.9	4	5	*	38	49	26	11.5
Dec.	0.6	7	5	*	40	57	17	16.1

T - Trace of rain or snow   * - Less than 1   NA - Not Available

Annual averages

Precipitation (in inches)	24.2
Snow (in inches)	31
Heating degree days	6,401
Cooling degree days	1,075
Days with thunderstorms	46
Days with fog	86
Days above 90°	40
Days below 32°	149
Wet days	88
Days with snow	44
Days with 1.5 inches or more snow	11

Percent time sky is clear

34.5	30.6	28.2	29.3	25.9	29.2	34.9	36.3	43.4	43.9	34.8	34.8

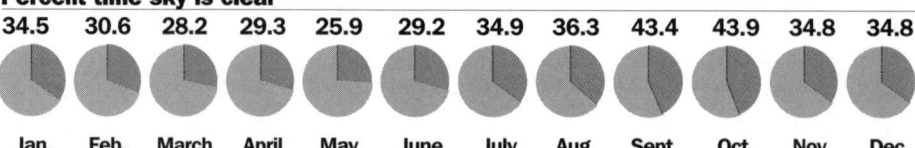

| Jan. | Feb. | March | April | May | June | July | Aug. | Sept. | Oct. | Nov. | Dec. |

Grand Junction, Colorado

Lat. 39° 06' N **Lon.** 108° 33' W **Elev.** 4,849 ft.

Grand Junction is at the meeting of the Colorado and Gunnison rivers, in a valley on the west slope of the Rockies. The climate is marked by wide seasonal variations typical of interior locations at this latitude. Mountains reaching heights of 9,000 to over 12,000 feet surround Grand Junction and provide protection from spring and fall frosts. Summer rains occur chiefly as scattered light showers, which develop over the mountains. Winter snows are frequent, but are mostly light and quick to melt. Spells of cold winter weather are prolonged when cold air is trapped in the valley, but winds are usually very light during the coldest weather. Changes in winter are normally gradual, and cold waves are rare. Sunny days predominate in all seasons.

Temperatures

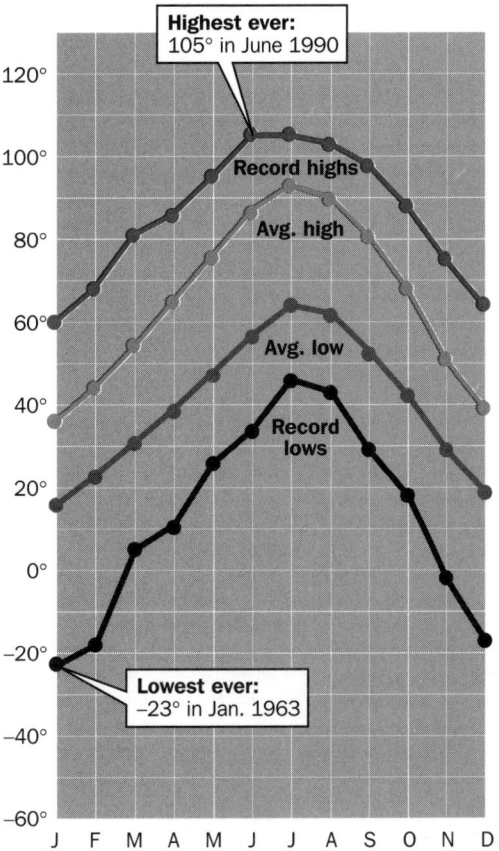

Highest ever: 105° in June 1990

Record highs

Avg. high

Avg. low

Record lows

Lowest ever: -23° in Jan. 1963

Weather extremes

Most rain in 24 hours:	1.57 in.	June 23 – 24, 1969
Most rain in a month:	3.48 in.	August 1957
Most snow in 24 hours:	9.1 in.	Jan. 26 – 27, 1957
Most snow in a month:	33.7 in.	January 1957

Monthly averages

Month	Avg. precip. (in.)	Avg. snow (in.)	Wet days	Thunder-storm days	Pct. sky is cloudy	% p.m. relative humidity	Dew point	Wind speed (mph)
Jan.	0.6	7	7	*	37	62	16	6.9
Feb.	0.5	4	6	*	33	49	20	8.1
March	0.9	4	8	1	33	36	22	9.2
April	0.7	1	6	2	27	26	24	9.2
May	0.8	T	6	5	21	24	30	10.4
June	0.4	0	4	5	12	18	34	10.4
July	0.6	0	5	8	11	21	43	10.4
Aug.	0.9	0	6	8	13	24	43	9.2
Sept.	0.8	T	6	5	12	25	36	10.4
Oct.	0.9	1	5	2	19	32	29	9.2
Nov.	0.7	3	5	*	28	47	24	8.1
Dec.	0.6	5	6	*	33	59	18	8.1

T - Trace of rain or snow   * - Less than 1   NA - Not Available

Annual averages

Precipitation (in inches)	8.5
Snow (in inches)	26
Heating degree days	5,590
Cooling degree days	1,204
Days with thunderstorms	36
Days with fog	26
Days above 90°	62
Days below 32°	134
Wet days	70
Days with snow	45
Days with 1.5 inches or more snow	12

Percent time sky is clear

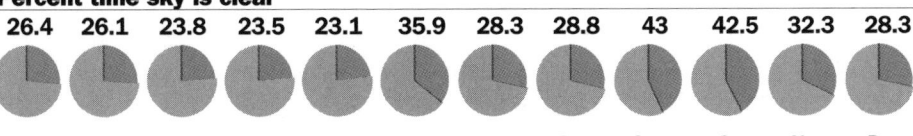

26.4	26.1	23.8	23.5	23.1	35.9	28.3	28.8	43	42.5	32.3	28.3
Jan.	Feb.	March	April	May	June	July	Aug.	Sept.	Oct.	Nov.	Dec.

Grand Rapids, Michigan

Lat. 42° 53' N **Lon.** 85° 31' W **Elev.** 707 ft.

Located in the Grand River Valley, Grand Rapids is under the climatic influence of Lake Michigan, nearby to the west. In spring, the cooling effect of the lake helps retard the growth of vegetation until the danger of frost has passed. In the fall, the warming effect retards frost until most crops have matured. These effects promote growth of a variety of fruit trees and berries. In winter, there is cloudiness and frequent snow flurries with strong west winds. Snowfalls can be heavy. While summer days are pleasantly warm and most nights comfortable, about three weeks of hot, humid weather occur. Precipitation is ample, although short droughts can occur. Floods on the Grand River, which flows through the city, generally are limited to the low flood plain.

Weather extremes

Most rain in 24 hours:	5.48 in. May 10 – 11, 1981
Most rain in a month:	13.22 in. June 1892
Most snow in 24 hours:	16.1 in. Jan. 26, 1978
Most snow in a month:	54.0 in. December 1951

Temperatures

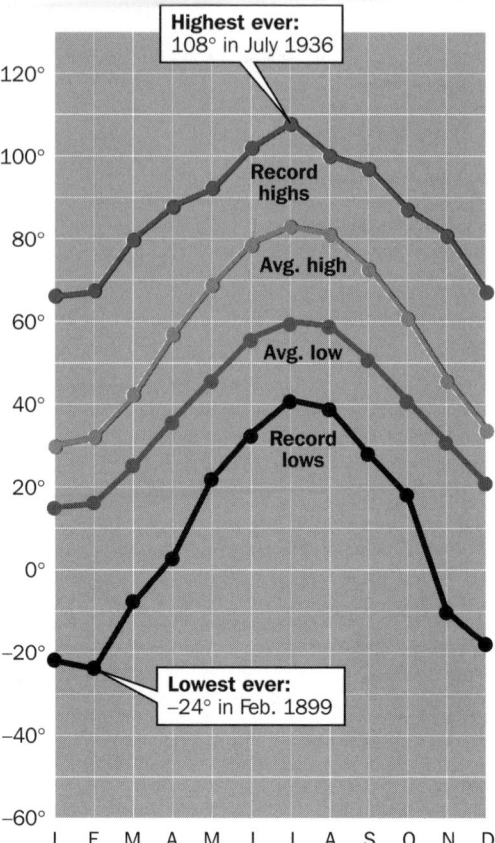

Highest ever: 108° in July 1936

Record highs

Avg. high

Avg. low

Record lows

Lowest ever: −24° in Feb. 1899

Monthly averages

Month	Avg. precip. (in.)	Avg. snow (in.)	Wet days	Thunderstorm days	Pct. sky is cloudy	% p.m. relative humidity	Dew point	Wind speed (mph)
Jan.	1.9	21	16	*	69	71	16	13.8
Feb.	1.6	12	12	*	59	66	17	12.7
March	2.6	11	13	2	54	61	25	12.7
April	3.5	3	13	4	49	54	34	12.7
May	3.0	T	11	4	42	50	45	11.5
June	3.5	0	10	6	36	52	55	10.4
July	3.2	0	9	6	28	52	60	10.4
Aug.	3.2	0	9	5	31	55	59	9.2
Sept.	3.7	T	10	4	39	58	53	8.1
Oct.	2.7	1	10	2	45	60	41	9.2
Nov.	3.1	8	13	1	66	68	32	12.7
Dec.	2.7	18	16	*	73	74	22	11.5

T - Trace of rain or snow   * - Less than 1   NA - Not Available

Annual averages

Precipitation (in inches)	34.7
Snow (in inches)	73
Heating degree days	6,852
Cooling degree days	636
Days with thunderstorms	34
Days with fog	137
Days above 90°	11
Days below 32°	146
Wet days	142
Days with snow	113
Days with 1.5 inches or more snow	34

Percent time sky is clear

Jan.	Feb.	March	April	May	June	July	Aug.	Sept.	Oct.	Nov.	Dec.
9.4	14.5	17.5	23.4	21.6	21.4	24	25.5	23.3	20.8	12	8.2

Great Falls, Montana

Lat. 47° 29' N **Lon.** 111° 22' W **Elev.** 3,663 ft.

Great Falls is along the main stem of the Missouri River at its confluence with the Sun River. Topography plays an important part in the climate of Great Falls. The Continental Divide to the west, and Big Belt and Little Belt ranges to the south contribute in winter to the frequent warm, dry chinook winds. Frost occurs frequently in October and April, but the winters between are not as cold as expected because of the chinooks. Subzero weather is usually terminated by southwest chinook winds, which can raise temperatures 40 degrees or more in 24 hours. Summer is quite pleasant, with cool nights and warm and sunny days. Average annual precipitation would normally classify the area as semiarid, but 70 percent of the annual total falls during the growing season.

Temperatures

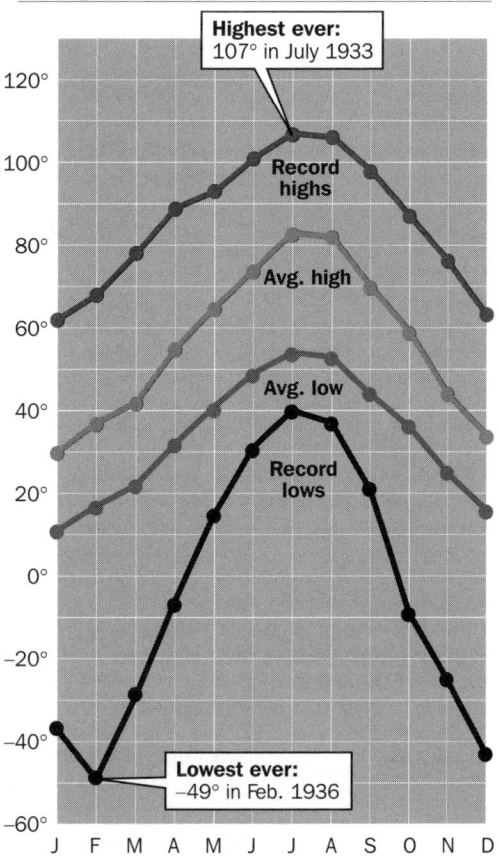

Weather extremes

Most rain in 24 hours:	3.42 in. May 24 – 25, 1980
Most rain in a month:	8.13 in. May 1953
Most snow in 24 hours:	16.8 in. April 20, 1973
Most snow in a month:	35.4 in. April 1967

Monthly averages

Month	Avg. precip. (in.)	Avg. snow (in.)	Wet days	Thunder-storm days	Pct. sky is cloudy	% p.m. relative humidity	Dew point	Wind speed (mph)
Jan.	0.9	11	10	*	47	61	9	19.6
Feb.	0.7	8	8	*	46	56	14	18.4
March	1.1	11	10	*	46	50	18	16.1
April	1.3	9	9	1	44	41	25	15.0
May	2.6	2	12	3	40	40	34	12.7
June	2.5	T	11	7	32	39	42	12.7
July	1.3	0	7	7	17	29	44	11.5
Aug.	1.5	0	8	6	21	30	42	11.5
Sept.	1.1	2	7	1	29	36	36	12.7
Oct.	0.8	4	6	*	33	43	29	16.1
Nov.	0.7	7	7	*	42	54	20	18.4
Dec.	0.8	9	8	*	44	60	13	19.6

T - Trace of rain or snow   * - Less than 1   NA - Not Available

Annual averages

Precipitation (in inches)	15.2
Snow (in inches)	63
Heating degree days	7,605
Cooling degree days	390
Days with thunderstorms	25
Days with fog	45
Days above 90°	18
Days below 32°	155
Wet days	103
Days with snow	97
Days with 1.5 inches or more snow	28

Percent time sky is clear

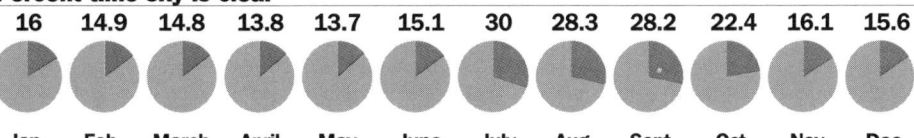

16	14.9	14.8	13.8	13.7	15.1	30	28.3	28.2	22.4	16.1	15.6
Jan.	Feb.	March	April	May	June	July	Aug.	Sept.	Oct.	Nov.	Dec.

Green Bay, Wisconsin

Lat. 44° 29' N Lon. 88° 08' W Elev. 682 ft.

Green Bay, at the mouth of the Fox River — one of the largest rivers flowing northward in the United States — has a continental climate modified by the bay and by lakes Michigan and Superior. There are few occurrences of 90°F heat in summer and few subzero temperatures in winter. The lake effects and the limited hours of sunshine caused by cloudiness result in a narrow range of temperatures. Three-fifths of the annual precipitation is in the growing season, usually during thunderstorms. During the winter, snowfall is less than in nearby communities, where the ground is slightly higher; but snowstorms are still the principal winter hazard. High winds, excessive precipitation, and electrical storms cause occasional damage.

Temperatures

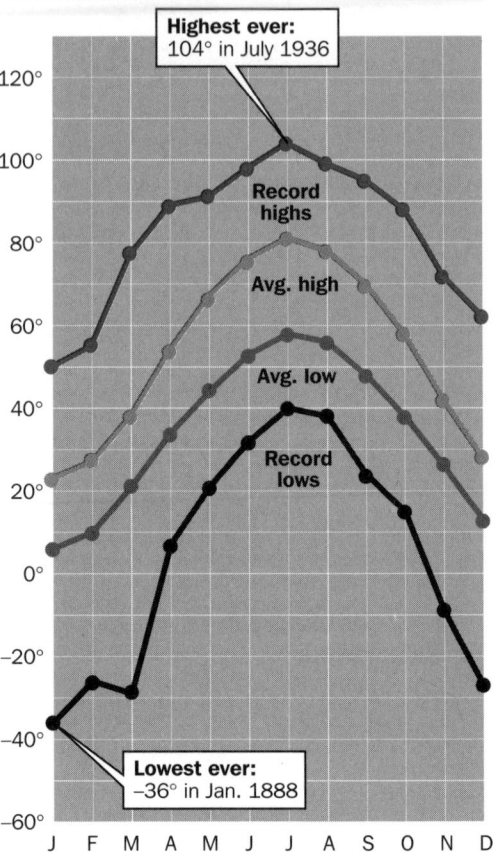

Highest ever: 104° in July 1936

Record highs

Avg. high

Avg. low

Record lows

Lowest ever: −36° in Jan. 1888

Weather extremes

Most rain in 24 hours:	4.90 in. June 22, 1990
Most rain in a month:	10.29 in. June 1990
Most snow in 24 hours:	22 in. January 1889
Most snow in a month:	32.5 in. January 1889

Monthly averages

Month	Avg. precip. (in.)	Avg. snow (in.)	Wet days	Thunder-storm days	Pct. sky is cloudy	% p.m. relative humidity	Dew point	Wind speed (mph)
Jan.	1.1	11	10	*	51	68	8	11.5
Feb.	1.1	8	8	*	48	65	12	10.4
March	1.9	9	11	1	48	63	21	12.7
April	2.6	2	11	2	47	54	32	12.7
May	2.9	T	11	4	38	52	43	11.5
June	3.2	0	10	7	32	55	54	10.4
July	3.3	0	10	6	27	55	60	10.4
Aug.	3.3	0	10	6	31	58	59	9.2
Sept.	3.2	T	10	4	36	59	51	10.4
Oct.	2.2	T	9	2	42	59	40	11.5
Nov.	2.0	5	9	1	55	67	27	11.5
Dec.	1.4	11	11	*	56	71	15	10.4

T - Trace of rain or snow   * - Less than 1   NA - Not Available

Annual averages

Precipitation (in inches)	28.3
Snow (in inches)	46
Heating degree days	8,067
Cooling degree days	451
Days with thunderstorms	33
Days with fog	124
Days above 90°	7
Days below 32°	163
Wet days	120
Days with snow	79
Days with 1.5 inches or more snow	19

Percent time sky is clear

25.7	26.3	23.5	22.2	22.3	23.3	24.5	25.5	25.8	24.7	18.7	21.4

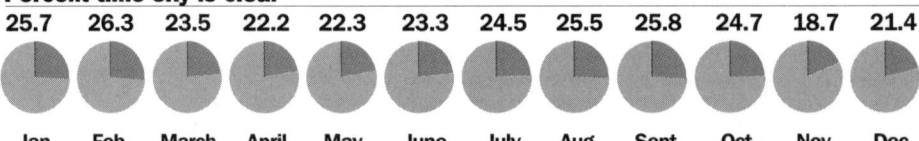

| Jan. | Feb. | March | April | May | June | July | Aug. | Sept. | Oct. | Nov. | Dec. |

Greensboro, North Carolina

Lat. 36° 05' N **Lon.** 79° 57' W **Elev.** 886 ft.

Greensboro, in the northern Piedmont section of North Carolina, is near the headwaters of the Haw and Deep rivers, both branches of the Cape Fear River system. The Blue Ridge Mountains form a northeast-southwest barrier with heights occasionally exceeding 3,000 feet, and modify winter temperatures and rainfall. Summer temperatures vary with the cloudiness and shower activity, but are generally mild. When moist winds blowing from the east or south meet cold air moving out of the north or northwest, snow, sleet, or glaze may occur. The frequency and amount of summer rain varies by year and place. Hail is reported each year, but winds of destructive force are rare.

Temperatures

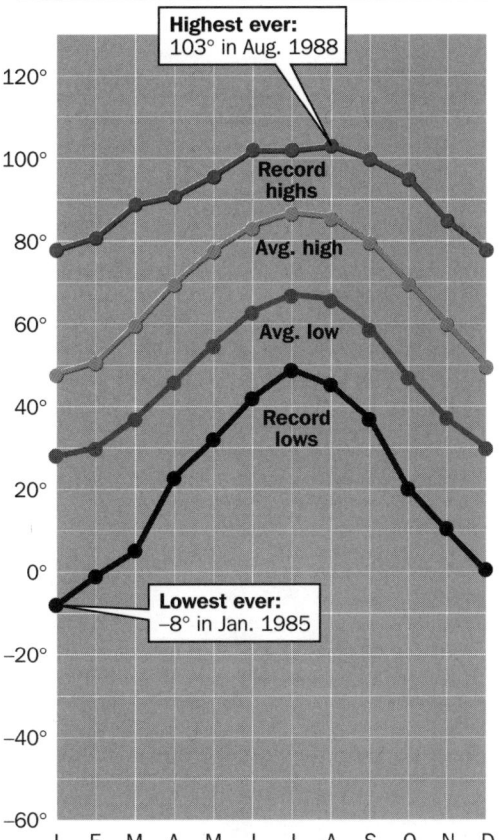

Highest ever: 103° in Aug. 1988

Record highs

Avg. high

Avg. low

Record lows

Lowest ever: –8° in Jan. 1985

Weather extremes

Most rain in 24 hours:	7.49 in. Sept. 24 – 25, 1947
Most rain in a month:	13.26 in. September 1947
Most snow in 24 hours:	14.3 in. Dec. 17, 1930
Most snow in a month:	22.9 in. January 1966

Monthly averages

Month	Avg. precip. (in.)	Avg. snow (in.)	Wet days	Thunder- storm days	Pct. sky is cloudy	% p.m. relative humidity	Dew point	Wind speed (mph)
Jan.	3.2	4	10	*	44	53	27	9.2
Feb.	3.4	3	10	1	42	50	28	9.2
March	3.7	2	11	2	40	47	34	9.2
April	3.1	T	9	4	35	44	43	9.2
May	3.7	0	10	6	35	51	54	8.1
June	3.8	0	10	7	30	54	63	6.9
July	4.5	0	12	10	30	57	67	6.9
Aug.	4.2	0	10	8	29	58	66	6.9
Sept.	3.4	0	7	3	32	56	60	9.2
Oct.	3.4	0	7	1	30	51	48	9.2
Nov.	2.9	T	8	1	35	51	37	8.1
Dec.	3.3	1	9	*	40	54	29	8.1

T - Trace of rain or snow   * - Less than 1   NA - Not Available

Annual averages

Precipitation (in inches)	42.5
Snow (in inches)	10
Heating degree days	3,835
Cooling degree days	1,378
Days with thunderstorms	43
Days with fog	168
Days above 90°	32
Days below 32°	85
Wet days	113
Days with snow	10
Days with 1.5 inches or more snow	4

Percent time sky is clear

Jan.	Feb.	March	April	May	June	July	Aug.	Sept.	Oct.	Nov.	Dec.
27.2	27.8	27.2	27.9	20.7	18.6	16.5	18.3	26.6	37.6	32.7	29.7

Greenville-Spartanburg, S.C.

Lat. 34° 54' N **Lon.** 82° 13' W **Elev.** 973 ft.

Greenville-Spartanburg is located on the eastern slope of the Appalachian Mountains. The mountains usually protect the area from the full force of cold air masses moving southeast from central Canada in winter. The relatively high elevation of the area causes cool nights, especially during the summer. Winters are pleasant, with usually two freezing rainstorms each winter and two or three small snowstorms. Temperatures seldom remain below freezing during an entire day in a normal year. Rainfall in this area is usually abundant and spread quite evenly throughout the year. Droughts have been experienced, but rarely last very long. Destructive winds occur occasionally, while tornadoes are infrequent.

Temperatures

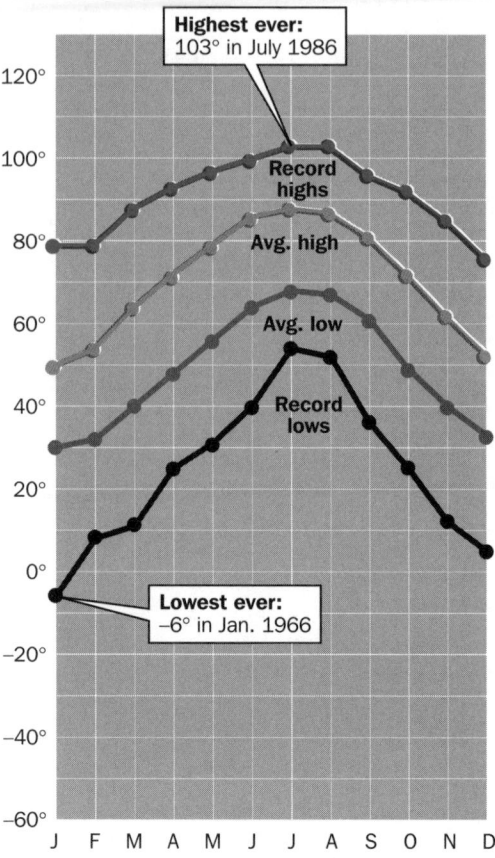

Highest ever: 103° in July 1986
Record highs
Avg. high
Avg. low
Record lows
Lowest ever: −6° in Jan. 1966

Weather extremes

Most rain in 24 hours:	6.21 in. Sept. 13 – 14, 1973
Most rain in a month:	13.57 in. July 1984
Most snow in 24 hours:	12.0 in. Jan. 7, 1988
Most snow in a month:	12.3 in. February 1979

Monthly averages

Month	Avg. precip. (in.)	Avg. snow (in.)	Wet days	Thunderstorm days	Pct. sky is cloudy	% p.m. relative humidity	Dew point	Wind speed (mph)
Jan.	4.0	3	11	1	42	51	28	2.3
Feb.	4.2	2	9	1	39	47	29	2.3
March	5.4	1	11	3	37	45	37	2.3
April	3.7	T	9	3	31	43	44	2.3
May	4.5	0	11	6	32	51	55	2.3
June	4.5	0	10	7	29	53	63	2.3
July	4.7	0	12	10	30	58	67	2.3
Aug.	3.8	0	10	7	28	58	67	2.3
Sept.	4.1	0	9	3	32	57	61	1.2
Oct.	4.1	0	7	1	28	50	49	1.2
Nov.	3.6	T	9	1	35	51	39	2.3
Dec.	3.9	1	10	1	41	53	32	2.3

T - Trace of rain or snow   * - Less than 1   NA - Not Available

Annual averages

Precipitation (in inches)	50.6
Snow (in inches)	6
Heating degree days	3,270
Cooling degree days	1,540
Days with thunderstorms	44
Days with fog	151
Days above 90°	35
Days below 32°	66
Wet days	118
Days with snow	5
Days with 1.5 inches or more snow	2

Percent time sky is clear

Jan.	Feb.	March	April	May	June	July	Aug.	Sept.	Oct.	Nov.	Dec.
31.7	32.4	29.9	32.9	24	20.5	15.3	18.9	25.2	40.6	36.2	32.4

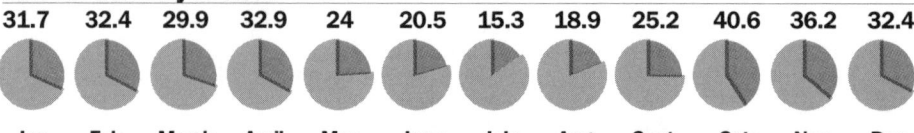

Harrisburg, Pennsylvania

Lat. 40° 13' N **Lon.** 76° 51' W **Elev.** 338 ft.

Harrisburg, the capital of Pennsylvania, is situated on the east bank of the Susquehanna River. Harrisburg is in the Great Valley formed by the foothills of the Appalachian chain and it is nestled in a saucerlike area south of Blue Mountain, which serves as a barrier to severe winter weather experienced 50 to 100 miles to the north and west. Although the severity of winter is lessened, the city lies too far inland to derive full benefits of the coastal climate. The city is favorably located to receive precipitation produced when warm, maritime air from the Atlantic Ocean is forced upslope to cross the Blue Ridge Mountains. Tropical hurricanes rarely reach Harrisburg with destructive winds, but they have produced rainfalls in excess of 15 inches.

Temperatures

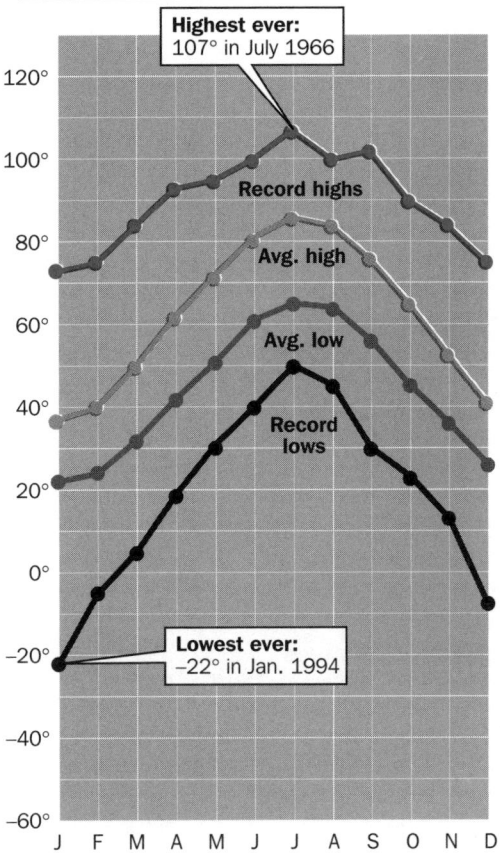

Highest ever: 107° in July 1966

Record highs

Avg. high

Avg. low

Record lows

Lowest ever: −22° in Jan. 1994

Weather extremes

Most rain in 24 hours:	12.55 in. June 21 – 22, 1972
Most rain in a month:	18.55 in. June 1972
Most snow in 24 hours:	25.0 in. Feb. 11 – 12, 1983
Most snow in a month:	34.2 in. January 1994

Monthly averages

Month	Avg. precip. (in.)	Avg. snow (in.)	Wet days	Thunder-storm days	Pct. sky is cloudy	% p.m. relative humidity	Dew point	Wind speed (mph)
Jan.	2.8	10	11	*	49	56	18	12.7
Feb.	2.8	10	10	*	47	54	20	13.8
March	3.3	6	11	1	45	49	26	13.8
April	3.2	1	12	2	44	47	36	12.7
May	4.1	T	13	5	43	51	48	8.1
June	3.6	0	11	6	34	52	58	8.1
July	3.5	0	10	7	32	52	63	6.9
Aug.	3.3	0	10	5	32	54	62	6.9
Sept.	3.3	0	9	3	35	56	56	6.9
Oct.	2.8	T	8	1	36	53	44	8.1
Nov.	3.3	2	10	1	45	56	33	12.7
Dec.	3.2	7	10	*	50	58	23	12.7

T - Trace of rain or snow   * - Less than 1   NA - Not Available

Annual averages

Precipitation (in inches)	39.1
Snow (in inches)	35
Heating degree days	5,335
Cooling degree days	1,006
Days with thunderstorms	31
Days with fog	152
Days above 90°	21
Days below 32°	106
Wet days	125
Days with snow	40
Days with 1.5 inches or more snow	13

Percent time sky is clear

Jan.	Feb.	March	April	May	June	July	Aug.	Sept.	Oct.	Nov.	Dec.
21.3	23.5	23.4	22.7	20.5	20.6	21.1	22.8	27.6	31	21.8	19.9

Hartford, Connecticut

Lat. 41° 56' N **Lon.** 72° 41' W **Elev.** 160 ft.

Rapid weather changes occur here when storms move north along the mid-Atlantic coast. These frequently produce strong, persistent northeast winds known locally as coastals or northeasters. Summer thunderstorms develop in the Berkshire Mountains to the west and northwest, and move over the Connecticut Valley. In winter, rain often falls through cold air trapped in the valley, creating extremely hazardous ice conditions. On clear nights in late summer and early fall, cool air draining into the valley meets moisture from the Connecticut River and produces ground fog.

Temperatures

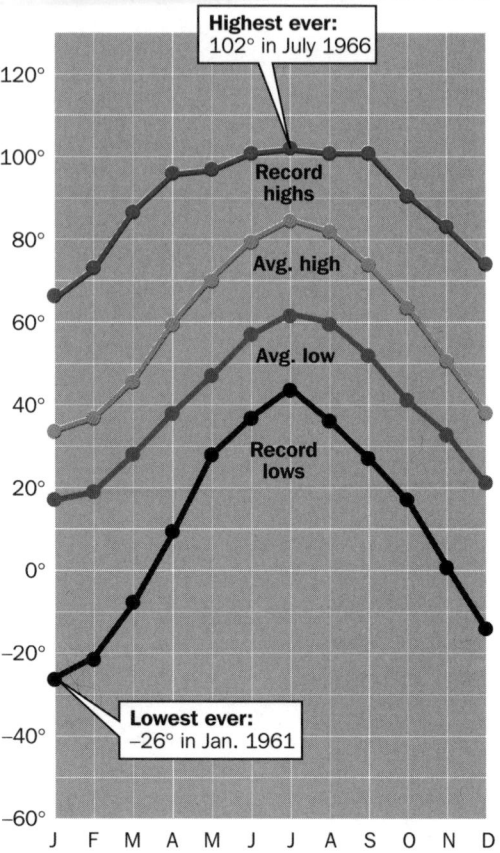

Highest ever: 102° in July 1966

Record highs

Avg. high

Avg. low

Record lows

Lowest ever: −26° in Jan. 1961

J F M A M J J A S O N D

Weather extremes

Most rain in 24 hours:	12.12 in. Aug. 18 – 19, 1955
Most rain in a month:	21.87 in. August 1955
Most snow in 24 hours:	21 in. Feb. 11 – 12, 1983
Most snow in a month:	45.3 in. December 1945

Monthly averages

Month	Avg. precip. (in.)	Avg. snow (in.)	Wet days	Thunderstorm days	Pct. sky is cloudy	% p.m. relative humidity	Dew point	Wind speed (mph)
Jan.	3.4	12	11	*	44	58	15	11.5
Feb.	3.2	11	10	*	43	55	17	12.7
March	3.8	9	11	1	44	50	24	12.7
April	3.9	1	11	1	43	46	33	10.4
May	3.8	T	12	2	41	48	45	9.2
June	3.6	0	11	4	36	52	56	9.2
July	3.2	0	10	5	32	52	61	8.1
Aug.	3.9	0	10	4	33	54	60	8.1
Sept.	3.7	0	9	2	35	55	53	8.1
Oct.	3.6	T	8	1	35	53	42	8.1
Nov.	4.1	2	11	*	44	58	32	8.1
Dec.	3.9	10	12	*	46	61	20	8.1

T - Trace of rain or snow * - Less than 1 NA - Not Available

Annual averages

Precipitation (in inches)	44.0
Snow (in inches)	46
Heating degree days	6,169
Cooling degree days	757
Days with thunderstorms	20
Days with fog	165
Days above 90°	18
Days below 32°	135
Wet days	126
Days with snow	50
Days with 1.5 inches or more snow	17

Percent time sky is clear

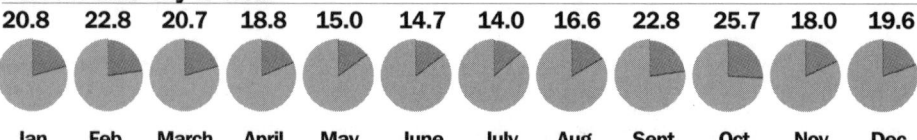

Jan.	Feb.	March	April	May	June	July	Aug.	Sept.	Oct.	Nov.	Dec.
20.8	22.8	20.7	18.8	15.0	14.7	14.0	16.6	22.8	25.7	18.0	19.6

Helena, Montana

Lat. 46° 36' N **Lon.** 112° 0' W **Elev.** 3,893 ft.

Helena is on the south side of an intermountain valley bounded on the west and south by the main chain of the Continental Divide. The climate is continental, modified by Pacific Ocean air masses, cool air draining into the valley and mountains shielding the valley in all directions. Following extreme cold, when maritime air has returned to warm most of eastern Montana, cold air may be trapped in the valley for several days in an inversion. Winter temperatures may drop below zero. Summer temperatures are moderate — highs under 90°F — with a marked drop at night. Most of the precipitation falls from April through August as frequent showers or thunderstorms. Snow can be expected from September through May. Strong winds can occur at any time.

Temperatures

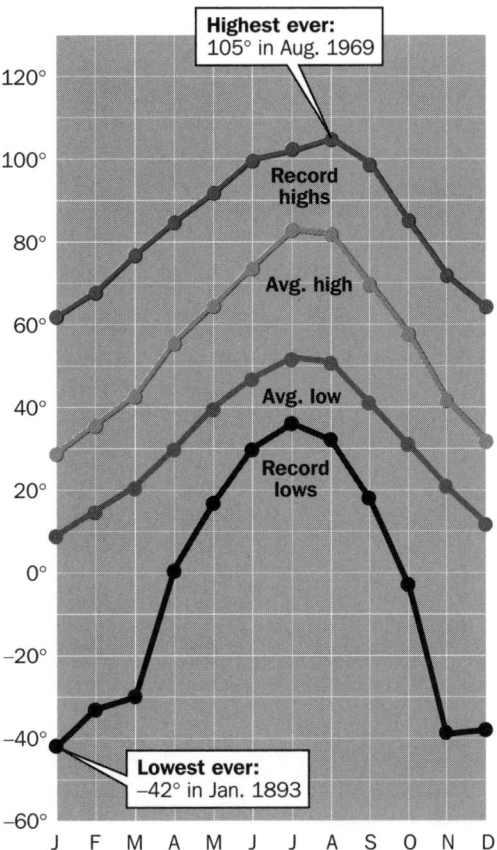

Highest ever: 105° in Aug. 1969

Record highs

Avg. high

Avg. low

Record lows

Lowest ever: −42° in Jan. 1893

Weather extremes

Most rain in 24 hours:	2.31 in. May 21, 1981
Most rain in a month:	6.09 in. May 1981
Most snow in 24 hours:	21.50 in. Nov. 11 - 12, 1959
Most snow in a month:	46.4 in. December 1880

Monthly averages

Month	Avg. precip. (in.)	Avg. snow (in.)	Wet days	Thunderstorm days	Pct. sky is cloudy	% p.m. relative humidity	Dew point	Wind speed (mph)
Jan.	0.6	9	8	*	51	63	9	10.4
Feb.	0.4	6	7	*	47	56	15	11.5
March	0.7	8	9	*	46	48	19	11.5
April	0.9	6	8	1	45	39	26	11.5
May	1.8	2	11	4	41	39	34	11.5
June	1.9	T	11	7	32	39	41	11.5
July	1.1	T	7	8	16	30	44	10.4
Aug.	1.2	0	8	8	20	30	43	9.2
Sept.	1.0	2	7	2	28	36	36	10.4
Oct.	0.6	2	6	*	34	43	29	10.4
Nov.	0.5	6	7	*	44	58	20	10.4
Dec.	0.6	9	8	*	49	66	13	10.4

T - Trace of rain or snow   * - Less than 1   NA - Not Available

Annual averages

Precipitation (in inches)	11.3
Snow (in inches)	49
Heating degree days	8,025
Cooling degree days	287
Days with thunderstorms	30
Days with fog	18
Days above 90°	17
Days below 32°	182
Wet days	97
Days with snow	83
Days with 1.5 inches or more snow	19

Percent time sky is clear

Jan.	Feb.	March	April	May	June	July	Aug.	Sept.	Oct.	Nov.	Dec.
14.7	14.5	14.6	15.3	16.1	19.1	37.4	34.4	33.6	25.9	16.1	13.6

Hilo, Hawaii

Lat. 19° 43' N **Lon.** 155° 4' W **Elev.** 36 ft.

Hilo is near the midpoint of the eastern shore of the big island of Hawaii. Mauna Loa and Mauna Kea, on the southern half of the island, are active volcanoes and, at 13,653 feet and 13,796 feet respectively, dominate the topography. The moderating effect of the ocean gives Hilo a very narrow range of annual average temperatures. Within Hilo, average rainfall varies from about 130 inches a year near the shore to as much as 200 inches up-slope. The wettest part of the island lies about 6 miles upslope from the city limits. Relative humidity is moderate due to the prevailing winds. The trade winds prevail throughout the year and profoundly influence the climate. Except for heavy rain, really severe weather seldom occurs.

Temperatures

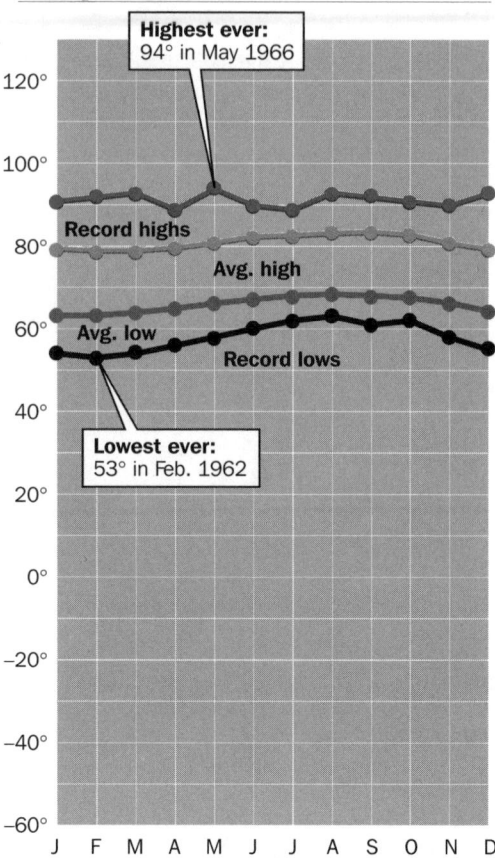

Highest ever: 94° in May 1966

Record highs

Avg. high

Avg. low

Record lows

Lowest ever: 53° in Feb. 1962

Weather extremes

Most rain in 24 hours:	22.3 in. Feb. 19-20, 1979
Most rain in a month:	66.96 in. March 1992
Most snow in 24 hours:	None
Most snow in a month:	None

Monthly averages

Month	Avg. precip. (in.)	Avg. snow (in.)	Wet days	Thunder-storm days	Pct. sky is cloudy	% p.m. relative humidity	Dew point	Wind speed (mph)
Jan.	9.4	0	17	1	43	66	NA	7.5
Feb.	13.5	0	17	1	45	66	NA	7.7
March	13.6	0	23	2	59	67	NA	7.7
April	13.1	0	25	1	68	69	NA	7.5
May	9.4	0	25	1	62	68	NA	7.4
June	6.1	0	24	*	58	65	NA	7.1
July	8.7	0	27	*	58	68	NA	6.9
Aug.	10.0	0	27	*	55	69	NA	6.8
Sept.	6.6	0	24	1	50	68	NA	6.8
Oct.	10.0	0	24	1	53	69	NA	6.7
Nov.	14.9	0	23	1	54	71	NA	6.8
Dec.	12.9	0	21	1	48	69	NA	7.2

T - Trace of rain or snow   * - Less than 1   NA - Not Available

Annual averages

Precipitation (in inches)	128
Snow (in inches)	0
Heating degree days	0
Cooling degree days	3,134
Days with thunderstorms	10
Days with fog	0
Days above 90°	1
Days below 32°	0
Wet days	277
Days with snow	0
Days with 1.5 inches or more snow	0

Percent time sky is clear

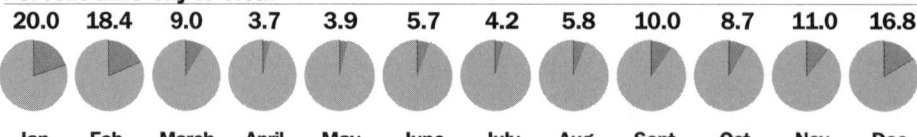

| 20.0 | 18.4 | 9.0 | 3.7 | 3.9 | 5.7 | 4.2 | 5.8 | 10.0 | 8.7 | 11.0 | 16.8 |
| Jan. | Feb. | March | April | May | June | July | Aug. | Sept. | Oct. | Nov. | Dec. |

Honolulu, Hawaii

Lat. 21° 20' N **Lon.** 157° 55' W **Elev.** 7 ft.

Honolulu is on Oahu, the third largest Hawaiian Island. A number of Honolulu's residential areas lie along the southern coastal plain. Heavy mountain rainfall sustains extensive irrigation of cane fields and provides Honolulu's water supply. Daytime showers, usually light, often occur while the sun shines, referred to locally as liquid sunshine. The moderate temperature range results from the tempering effect of the ocean. Trade winds make even the warmest months comfortable. But when the trades diminish or give way to south winds, the humidity becomes oppressive. Intense rains from October to April sometimes cause flash flooding.

Temperatures

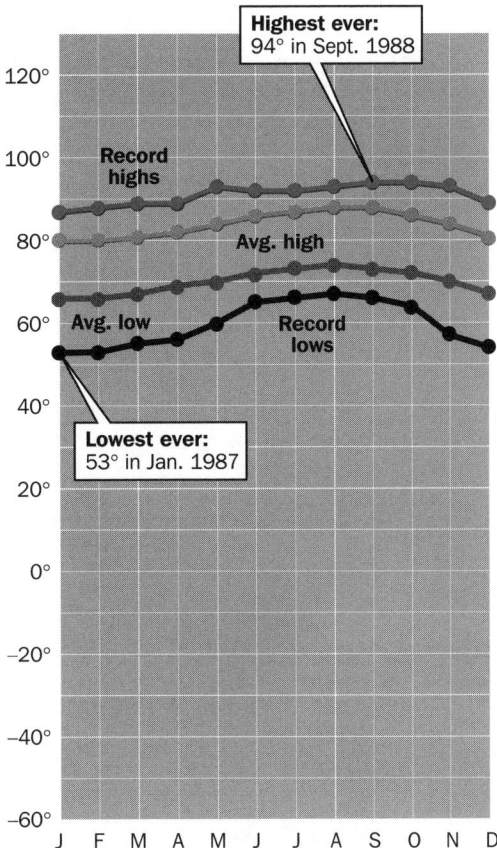

Highest ever: 94° in Sept. 1988

Record highs

Avg. high

Avg. low

Record lows

Lowest ever: 53° in Jan. 1987

Weather extremes

Most rain in 24 hours:	17.07 in. March 5, 1958
Most rain in a month:	20.79 in. March 1951
Most snow in 24 hours:	none
Most snow in a month:	none

Monthly averages

Month	Avg. precip. (in.)	Avg. snow (in.)	Wet days	Thunder-storm days	Pct. sky is cloudy	% p.m. relative humidity	Dew point	Wind speed (mph)
Jan.	3.7	0	10	1	19	66	63	12.7
Feb.	2.5	0	9	1	18	64	62	12.7
March	2.8	0	9	1	20	62	62	13.8
April	1.4	0	9	1	20	61	63	13.8
May	1.0	0	7	*	17	60	64	13.8
June	0.4	0	6	*	11	58	65	13.8
July	0.5	0	7	*	8	58	66	13.8
Aug.	0.6	0	6	*	9	58	67	13.8
Sept.	0.7	0	7	*	8	60	67	12.7
Oct.	2.0	0	9	1	14	63	67	12.7
Nov.	2.8	0	9	1	18	66	65	12.7
Dec.	3.7	0	10	2	19	66	63	12.7

T - Trace of rain or snow   * - Less than 1   NA - Not Available

Annual averages

Precipitation (in inches)	22.4
Snow (in inches)	0
Heating degree days	0
Cooling degree days	4,389
Days with thunderstorms	7
Days with fog	*
Days above 90°	23
Days below 32°	0
Wet days	98
Days with snow	0
Days with 1.5 inches or more snow	0

Percent time sky is clear

11.8	11.1	7.9	4.7	4.7	4.0	3.4	4.1	6.7	7.1	6.8	10.3
Jan.	Feb.	March	April	May	June	July	Aug.	Sept.	Oct.	Nov.	Dec.

Houghton Lake, Michigan

Lat. 44° 22′ N **Lon.** 84° 41′ W **Elev.** 1,149 ft.

Houghton Lake is the largest inland lake in Michigan. Temperatures vary more extremely than near the shores of either Lake Michigan or Lake Huron, reaching the 100°F mark about one summer out of ten, and falling below zero an average of 22 times in the winter. Precipitation is a little heavier during the summer, with the heaviest as summertime thunderstorms. Heavy snows, averaging over 100 inches a season, fall within a 30-60 mile radius to the north and west. Seasonal totals have ranged from 24 inches to over 124 inches. Measurable amounts of snow have occurred in nine of the 12 months. Moisture and warmth picked up by the west and northwest winds, while crossing Lake Michigan, increase cloudiness in the late fall.

Temperatures

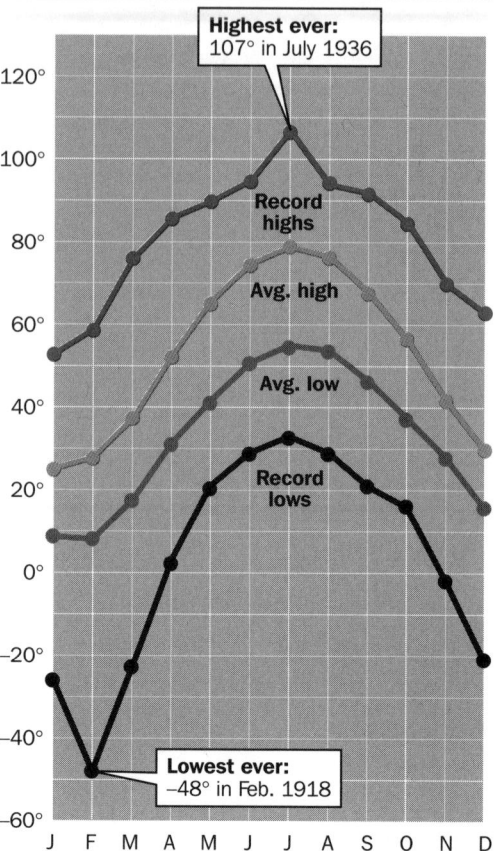

Highest ever: 107° in July 1936

Record highs

Avg. high

Avg. low

Record lows

Lowest ever: −48° in Feb. 1918

Weather extremes

Most rain in 24 hours:	3.83 in. July 10 – 11, 1984
Most rain in a month:	9.49 in. September 1986
Most snow in 24 hours:	15.4 in. Jan. 26, 1978
Most snow in a month:	38.0 in. January 1982

Monthly averages

Month	Avg. precip. (in.)	Avg. snow (in.)	Wet days	Thunder-storm days	Pct. sky is cloudy	% p.m. relative humidity	Dew point	Wind speed (mph)
Jan.	1.5	19.3	15	*	70	72	NA	10.1
Feb.	1.3	12.9	11	*	62	68	NA	9.2
March	1.9	11.6	12	1	58	63	NA	9.3
April	2.6	4.1	12	2	55	55	NA	9.8
May	2.6	0.3	10	4	46	50	NA	9.0
June	3.1	0.0	10	5	40	55	NA	8.0
July	2.9	T	9	6	32	55	NA	7.6
Aug.	3.0	0.0	10	6	38	60	NA	7.2
Sept.	2.8	T	12	4	48	63	NA	8.0
Oct.	2.3	0.8	12	2	58	65	NA	9.1
Nov.	2.3	9.8	14	1	75	74	NA	9.9
Dec.	1.9	17.0	15	*	74	77	NA	9.6

T - Trace of rain or snow   * - Less than 1   NA - Not Available

Annual averages

Precipitation (in inches)	28
Snow (in inches)	76
Heating degree days	8,298
Cooling degree days	293
Days with thunderstorms	31
Days with fog	28
Days above 90°	3
Days below 32°	171
Wet days	142
Days with snow	NA
Days with 1.5 inches or more snow	24

Percent time sky is clear

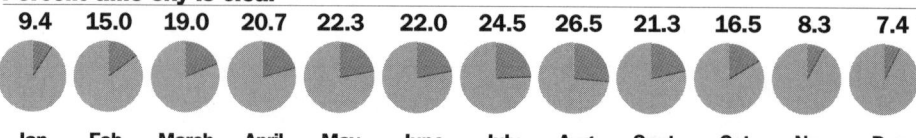

9.4	15.0	19.0	20.7	22.3	22.0	24.5	26.5	21.3	16.5	8.3	7.4
Jan.	Feb.	March	April	May	June	July	Aug.	Sept.	Oct.	Nov.	Dec.

Houston, Texas

Lat. 29° 58' N **Lon.** 95° 21' W **Elev.** 96 ft.

Houston has a mostly marine climate due to proximity to Galveston Bay and the Gulf of Mexico. All that water combined with a terrain that has numerous small streams and bayous create conditions favorable for fog — heavy fog averages 16 days a year; light fog occurs about 62 days. Winds off the Gulf moderate temperatures, resulting in mild winters, and generate abundant rainfall and high humidity. Polar air penetrates the area frequently enough to provide variability in the weather. Destructive windstorms are mostly infrequent, but both thunder squalls and tropical storms have passed through the area.

Temperatures

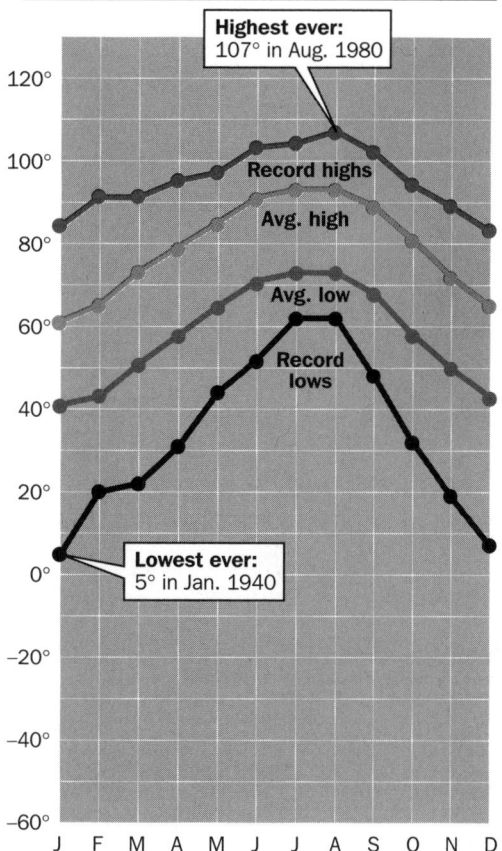

Highest ever: 107° in Aug. 1980

Record highs

Avg. high

Avg. low

Record lows

Lowest ever: 5° in Jan. 1940

Weather extremes

Most rain in 24 hours:	15.65 in. Aug. 27 – 28, 1945
Most rain in a month:	16.28 in. June 1989
Most snow in 24 hours:	4.4 in. Feb. 12, 1960
Most snow in a month:	20.0 in. February 1895

Monthly averages

Month	Avg. precip. (in.)	Avg. snow (in.)	Wet days	Thunderstorm days	Pct. sky is cloudy	% p.m. relative humidity	Dew point	Wind speed (mph)
Jan.	3.3	T	10	2	51	58	42	9.2
Feb.	2.7	T	8	2	46	55	44	9.2
March	3.3	0	9	4	47	54	51	11.5
April	3.3	0	7	3	40	54	58	11.5
May	5.6	0	8	7	31	57	65	10.4
June	4.9	0	8	7	17	56	70	10.4
July	3.7	0	9	10	15	55	72	8.1
Aug.	3.7	0	9	10	13	55	72	9.2
Sept.	4.8	0	9	8	19	57	69	6.9
Oct.	4.7	0	7	4	23	53	60	9.2
Nov.	3.7	T	8	3	35	55	52	8.1
Dec.	3.3	T	9	2	45	57	45	9.2

T - Trace of rain or snow   * - Less than 1   NA - Not Available

Annual averages

Precipitation (in inches)	46.9
Snow (in inches)	T
Heating degree days	1,568
Cooling degree days	2,876
Days with thunderstorms	62
Days with fog	193
Days above 90°	96
Days below 32°	21
Wet days	101
Days with snow	*
Days with 1.5 inches or more snow	*

Percent time sky is clear

Jan.	Feb.	March	April	May	June	July	Aug.	Sept.	Oct.	Nov.	Dec.
21.3	25.3	22.9	21.7	17.6	20.5	17.2	17.7	24.9	32.4	29.1	24.4

Huntington, West Virginia

Lat. 38° 22' N **Lon.** 82° 33' W **Elev.** 827 ft.

Huntington is located near the confluence of the Ohio and Big Sandy rivers. Summer is moderately warm and humid — more so in the valley locations than at the airport, which is higher and generally cooler. Winter is moderately cold, with an occasional severe cold wave lasting a few days. The heaviest rainfall is in July and August, mostly thunderstorms, and flash floods are common. Winter rainfall frequently lasts from two to four days, causing frequent general flooding of area streams. Snow seldom remains on the ground more than two days in the valleys. However, at higher elevations surrounding the airport, roads are frequently blocked for several days during winter.

Temperatures

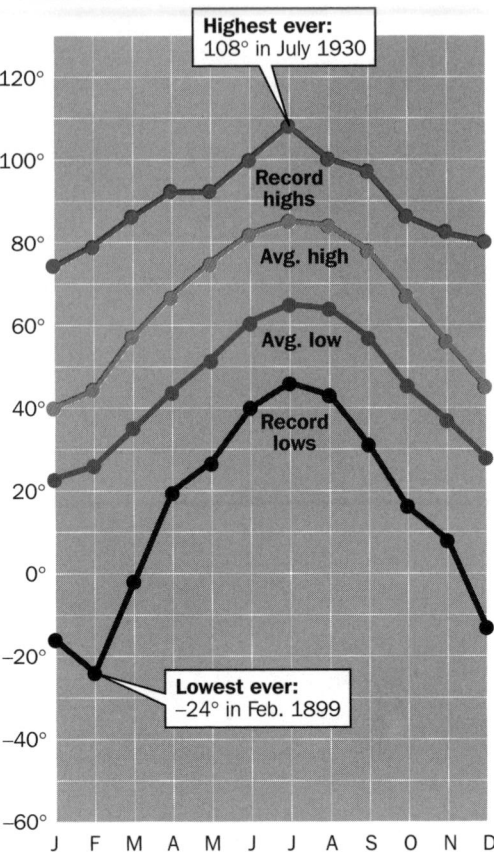

Highest ever: 108° in July 1930

Record highs

Avg. high

Avg. low

Record lows

Lowest ever: −24° in Feb. 1899

Weather extremes

Most rain in 24 hours:	4.27 in. July 1 – 2, 1962
Most rain in a month:	12.07 in. January 1937
Most snow in 24 hours:	21.1 in. March 13, 1993
Most snow in a month:	30.3 in. January 1978

Monthly averages

Month	Avg. precip. (in.)	Avg. snow (in.)	Wet days	Thunder- storm days	Pct. sky is cloudy	% p.m. relative humidity	Dew point	Wind speed (mph)
Jan.	2.8	9	14	*	60	60	22	11.5
Feb.	2.9	7	13	1	58	56	24	10.4
March	3.6	4	14	3	53	49	32	10.4
April	3.4	1	13	4	47	45	39	10.4
May	4.3	T	13	6	43	51	51	6.9
June	3.3	0	11	7	36	55	61	6.9
July	4.6	0	12	9	37	58	65	6.9
Aug.	3.9	0	10	7	36	58	65	6.9
Sept.	3.0	0	9	3	39	57	58	6.9
Oct.	2.8	T	9	1	38	51	45	4.6
Nov.	3.3	1	11	1	52	56	36	8.1
Dec.	3.4	4	13	*	60	62	27	8.1

T - Trace of rain or snow   * - Less than 1   NA - Not Available

Annual averages

Precipitation (in inches)	41.4
Snow (in inches)	26
Heating degree days	4,631
Cooling degree days	1,114
Days with thunderstorms	42
Days with fog	197
Days above 90°	19
Days below 32°	97
Wet days	142
Days with snow	43
Days with 1.5 inches or more snow	11

Percent time sky is clear

Jan.	Feb.	March	April	May	June	July	Aug.	Sept.	Oct.	Nov.	Dec.
16.2	16.1	16.4	18.9	18	16.6	15.1	15.4	21.1	26.9	18.8	14.4

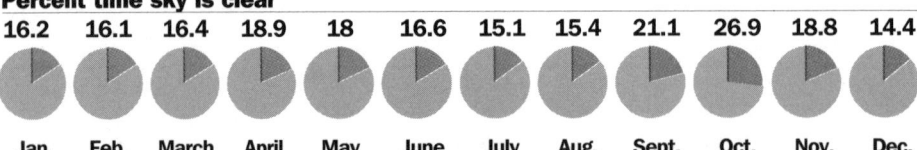

Huntsville, Alabama

Lat. 34° 39' N **Lon.** 86° 46' W **Elev.** 624 ft.

Huntsville is almost surrounded by the foothills of the Appalachian Mountains. The broad, fertile Tennessee River Valley extends to the west. Summers are warm and humid, but frequent thunderstorms provide relief from the heat. Winters are cool, but can vary by year. In winter, the contrast between cold air from the continent and mild air from the Gulf of Mexico produces much low cloudiness and rain. Snow can be expected each winter. The transition from winter to spring has the greatest variety of weather. Spring thunderstorms are more likely to involve severe weather conditions than those in other seasons. The fall is usually dry and pleasant. The average last occurrence of 32°F is late March; the average first freeze is late October.

Temperatures

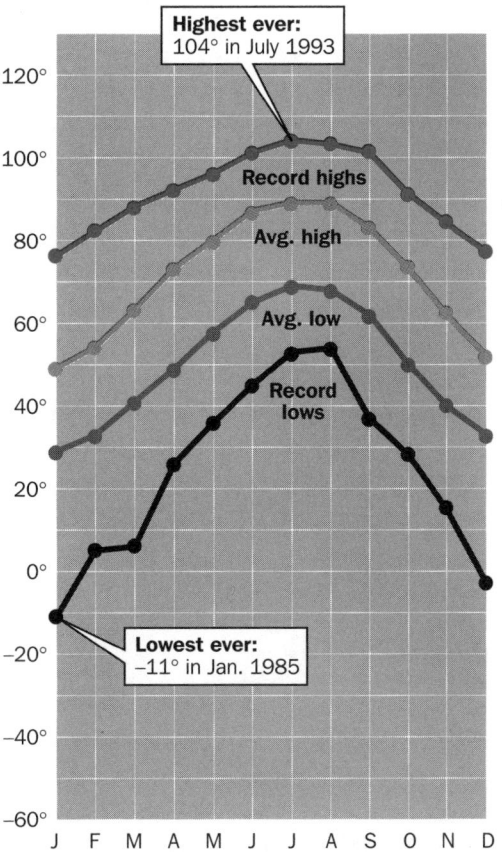

Highest ever: 104° in July 1993

Record highs

Avg. high

Avg. low

Record lows

Lowest ever: −11° in Jan. 1985

Weather extremes

Most rain in 24 hours:	10.22 in. Dec. 21 – 22, 1990
Most rain in a month:	18.68 in. December 1990
Most snow in 24 hours:	17.1 in. Dec. 31, 1963 – Jan. 1, 1964
Most snow in a month:	21.7 in. December 1963

Monthly averages

Month	Avg. precip. (in.)	Avg. snow (in.)	Wet days	Thunder-storm days	Pct. sky is cloudy	% p.m. relative humidity	Dew point	Wind speed (mph)
Jan.	5.2	2	11	1	50	59	30	10.4
Feb.	4.8	1	10	2	49	54	32	10.4
March	6.6	T	11	4	45	51	39	10.4
April	4.8	T	10	5	36	46	47	10.4
May	5.0	0	10	7	32	50	57	8.1
June	4.1	0	9	8	25	52	64	8.1
July	4.8	0	11	10	25	55	69	6.9
Aug.	3.5	0	9	8	22	55	68	6.9
Sept.	4.1	0	8	4	30	55	62	8.1
Oct.	3.3	T	7	2	28	49	50	9.2
Nov.	4.7	T	10	2	39	54	41	9.2
Dec.	5.6	1	11	1	48	58	33	10.4

T - Trace of rain or snow   * - Less than 1   NA - Not Available

Annual averages

Precipitation (in inches)	56.4
Snow (in inches)	4
Heating degree days	3,287
Cooling degree days	1,764
Days with thunderstorms	54
Days with fog	148
Days above 90°	50
Days below 32°	67
Wet days	117
Days with snow	8
Days with 1.5 inches or more snow	1

Percent time sky is clear

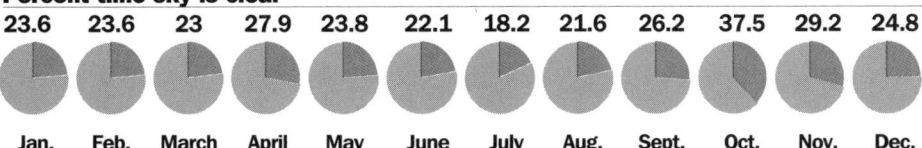

Jan.	Feb.	March	April	May	June	July	Aug.	Sept.	Oct.	Nov.	Dec.
23.6	23.6	23	27.9	23.8	22.1	18.2	21.6	26.2	37.5	29.2	24.8

Huron, South Dakota

Lat. 44° 23' N **Lon.** 98° 13' W **Elev.** 1,282 ft.

Located on the west bank of the James River at about the middle of the river valley, Huron has a continental climate with frequent daily temperature fluctuations and distinct seasons. Winter is usually cold and dry with storms of short duration. Precipitation is mainly in the form of snow, which has varied from under 9 inches to over 75 inches. Spring is characterized by increases in both precipitation and temperature, with moisture increasing by three to four times winter levels. Some of this precipitation falls as snow in the early spring. Summers are hot, but not extreme. Summer nights are normally cool and comfortable. Summertime precipitation is mainly in the form of showers and thunderstorms.

Temperatures

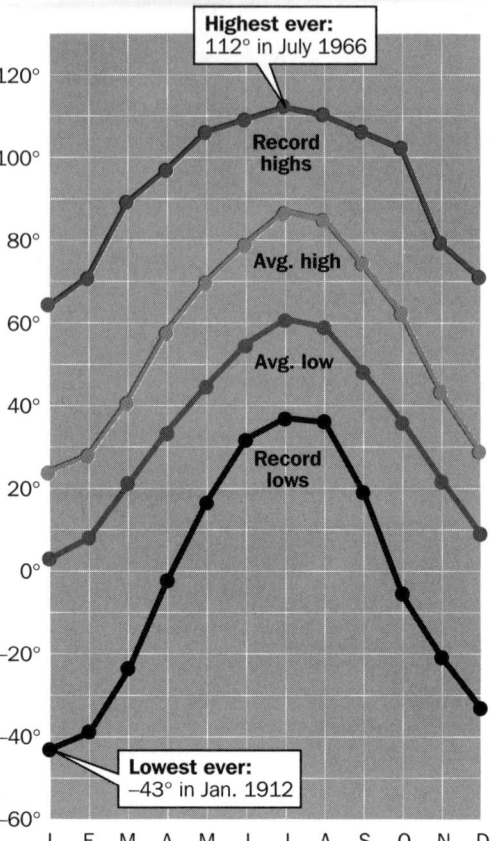

Highest ever: 112° in July 1966

Record highs

Avg. high

Avg. low

Record lows

Lowest ever: −43° in Jan. 1912

Weather extremes

Most rain in 24 hours:	5.48 in. June 18 – 19, 1967
Most rain in a month:	11.56 in. June 1914
Most snow in 24 hours:	18.3 in. March 3, 1985
Most snow in a month:	39.9 in. February 1962

Monthly averages

Month	Avg. precip. (in.)	Avg. snow (in.)	Wet days	Thunder-storm days	Pct. sky is cloudy	% p.m. relative humidity	Dew point	Wind speed (mph)
Jan.	0.5	7	6	*	44	66	6	13.8
Feb.	0.6	7	6	*	47	67	12	13.8
March	1.2	8	8	*	49	62	22	15.0
April	1.9	3	9	2	43	49	33	16.1
May	2.7	T	10	5	37	48	45	15.0
June	3.4	0	11	9	31	51	56	13.8
July	2.5	0	9	9	20	45	60	13.8
Aug.	2.2	0	9	8	21	45	58	13.8
Sept.	1.7	T	7	4	27	45	48	13.8
Oct.	1.3	1	6	1	32	46	36	13.8
Nov.	0.7	4	5	*	44	58	23	15.0
Dec.	0.5	6	6	*	46	66	12	12.7

T - Trace of rain or snow   * - Less than 1   NA - Not Available

Annual averages

Precipitation (in inches)	19.2
Snow (in inches)	35
Heating degree days	8,103
Cooling degree days	738
Days with thunderstorms	38
Days with fog	60
Days above 90°	29
Days below 32°	170
Wet days	92
Days with snow	64
Days with 1.5 inches or more snow	13

Percent time sky is clear

24.4	23.2	19.8	21.5	21.5	22.4	27.9	30.5	34.3	32.4	24	23.1
Jan.	Feb.	March	April	May	June	July	Aug.	Sept.	Oct.	Nov.	Dec.

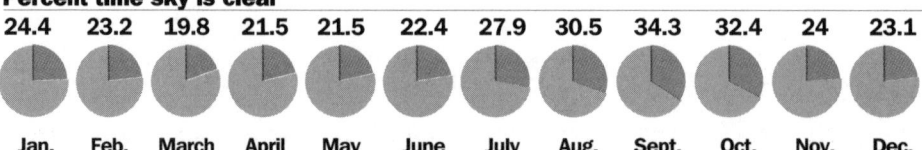

Indianapolis, Indiana

Lat. 39° 44' N **Lon.** 86° 16' W **Elev.** 792 ft.

Indianapolis is in the central part of the state on level or slightly rolling terrain. The greater part of the city lies east of the White River, which flows in a north to south direction. Indianapolis has a temperate climate with very warm summers and no dry season. Very cold temperatures may be produced by the invasion of continental polar air in the winter. The arrival of maritime tropical air from the Gulf of Mexico in the summer brings warm temperatures and moderate humidity. Rainfall in the spring and summer is produced mostly by showers and thunderstorms. Snowfalls of 3 inches or more occur an average of two or three times in the winter.

Temperatures

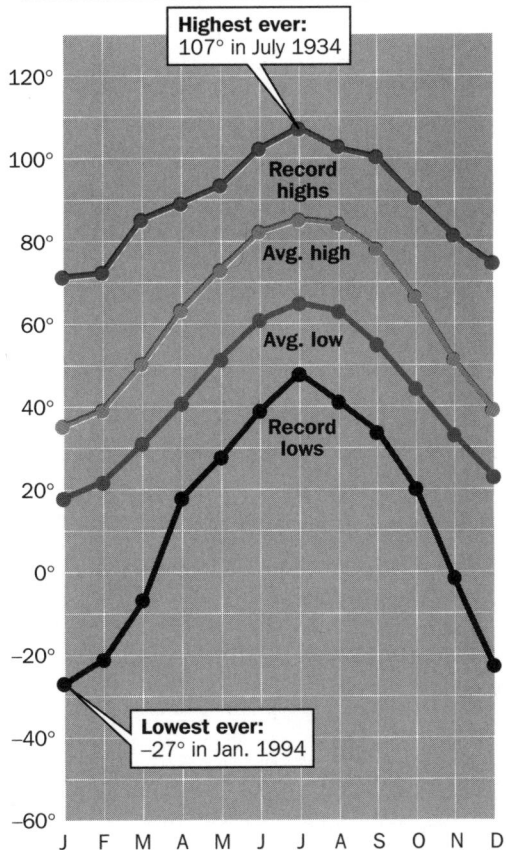

Highest ever: 107° in July 1934

Record highs

Avg. high

Avg. low

Record lows

Lowest ever: –27° in Jan. 1994

Weather extremes

Most rain in 24 hours:	6.80 in. Sept. 3 – 4, 1895
Most rain in a month:	13.12 in. July 1875
Most snow in 24 hours:	12.5 in. Feb. 24 – 25, 1965
Most snow in a month:	30.6 in. January 1978

Monthly averages

Month	Avg. precip. (in.)	Avg. snow (in.)	Wet days	Thunder- storm days	Pct. sky is cloudy	% p.m. relative humidity	Dew point	Wind speed (mph)
Jan.	2.8	7	12	1	57	68	20	11.5
Feb.	2.5	6	10	1	54	64	23	12.7
March	3.6	4	13	3	54	59	30	13.8
April	3.6	1	12	4	46	53	40	12.7
May	4.0	T	12	6	39	53	51	10.4
June	3.9	0	10	7	31	53	60	9.2
July	4.3	0	10	8	27	56	65	8.1
Aug.	3.4	0	9	6	26	56	63	8.1
Sept.	2.9	0	8	4	30	53	56	9.2
Oct.	2.6	T	8	2	34	53	44	10.4
Nov.	3.3	2	10	1	52	63	34	11.5
Dec.	3.3	5	13	*	58	70	25	11.5

T - Trace of rain or snow   * - Less than 1   NA - Not Available

Annual averages

Precipitation (in inches)	40.2
Snow (in inches)	25
Heating degree days	5,561
Cooling degree days	1,043
Days with thunderstorms	43
Days with fog	163
Days above 90°	19
Days below 32°	119
Wet days	127
Days with snow	46
Days with 1.5 inches or more snow	10

Percent time sky is clear

Jan.	Feb.	March	April	May	June	July	Aug.	Sept.	Oct.	Nov.	Dec.
19.8	21	17.8	20.7	21.7	21.7	22.1	25.4	31.6	33	21.5	18.8

International Falls, Minn.

Lat. 48° 34′ N **Lon.** 93° 23′ W **Elev.** 1,179 ft.

On the Canadian border, International Falls receives continental polar air most of the year. From June to August, when areas to the north and northwest have been warmed by long days of sunshine, there are periods of mild weather. Small lakes supply the moisture for the late afternoon and evening showers and store heat that tempers cold air during the fall. From December through February, temperatures fall below zero on most days. In winter, frost penetrates into the ground to depths of 36 to 60 inches. The transition to summer is rapid after the spring thaw. Spring lasts only about a month, and freezing can continue through most of June.

Temperatures

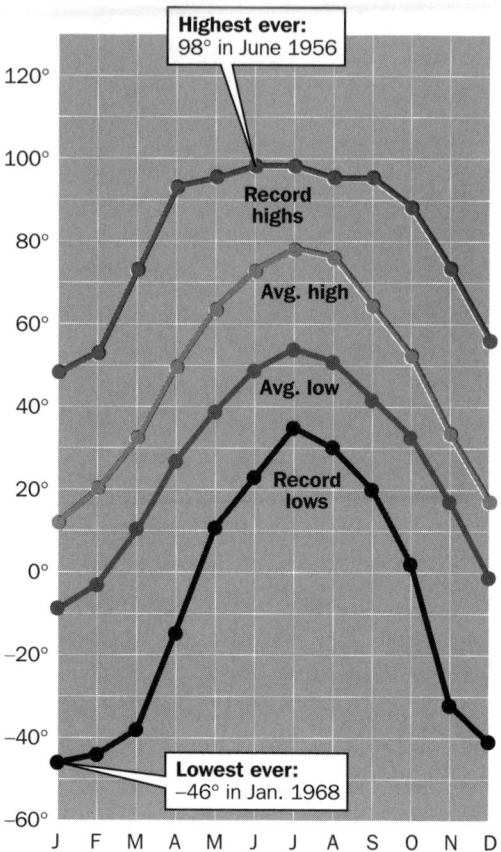

Highest ever: 98° in June 1956

Record highs

Avg. high

Avg. low

Record lows

Lowest ever: −46° in Jan. 1968

Weather extremes

Most rain in 24 hours:	4.86 in. July 2 – 3, 1966
Most rain in a month:	11.26 in. August 1942
Most snow in 24 hours:	17.7 in. Jan. 10 – 11, 1975
Most snow in a month:	43.9 in. December 1992

Monthly averages

Month	Avg. precip. (in.)	Avg. snow (in.)	Wet days	Thunder-storm days	Pct. sky is cloudy	% p.m. relative humidity	Dew point	Wind speed (mph)
Jan.	0.8	13	12	*	51	64	-4	10.4
Feb.	0.6	9	9	0	46	60	0	10.4
March	1.1	10	10	*	47	57	12	11.5
April	1.5	6	9	1	45	49	25	11.5
May	2.5	1	11	4	42	46	37	10.4
June	3.9	T	13	7	39	53	50	9.2
July	3.9	0	12	9	29	53	56	8.1
Aug.	3.0	0	11	7	31	55	54	8.1
Sept.	3.0	T	11	4	42	58	45	9.2
Oct.	1.9	2	10	1	50	58	34	9.2
Nov.	1.3	12	11	*	63	69	19	11.5
Dec.	0.9	12	12	*	56	71	3	10.4

T - Trace of rain or snow   * - Less than 1   NA - Not Available

Annual averages

Precipitation (in inches)	24.4
Snow (in inches)	64
Heating degree days	10,363
Cooling degree days	235
Days with thunderstorms	33
Days with fog	84
Days above 90°	4
Days below 32°	198
Wet days	131
Days with snow	122
Days with 1.5 inches or more snow	26

Percent time sky is clear

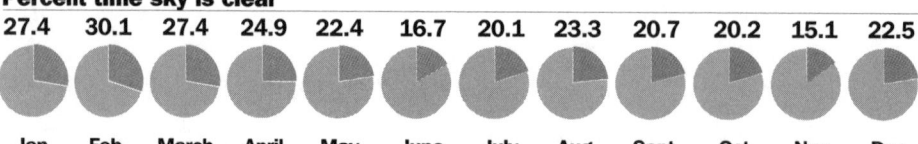

27.4	30.1	27.4	24.9	22.4	16.7	20.1	23.3	20.7	20.2	15.1	22.5
Jan.	Feb.	March	April	May	June	July	Aug.	Sept.	Oct.	Nov.	Dec.

Islip, New York

Lat. 40° 47' N **Lon.** 73° 6' W **Elev.** 84 ft.

Islip is located at about the midpoint of Long Island's southern coast, facing the Atlantic Ocean. It is protected from flooding during high tides by Fire Island, about three miles offshore. Most air masses affecting Islip are continental, but the ocean has a strong, moderating influence. A sea breeze helps alleviate summer afternoon heat. Winter is relatively mild. Almost all snow falls between December and March. Coastal low pressure systems — Northeasters — are the main source. There are usually extended periods of winter when the ground is bare of snow. It is uncommon for the eye of a tropical storm to pass directly over Long Island, but such storms moving along the Atlantic Coast can produce heavy rain and strong winds in late summer or fall.

Weather extremes

Most rain in 24 hours:	6.92 in. Aug. 23 – 24, 1990
Most rain in a month:	13.78 in. August 1990
Most snow in 24 hours:	9.2 in. Dec. 13, 1988
Most snow in a month:	13.5 in. January 1985

Temperatures

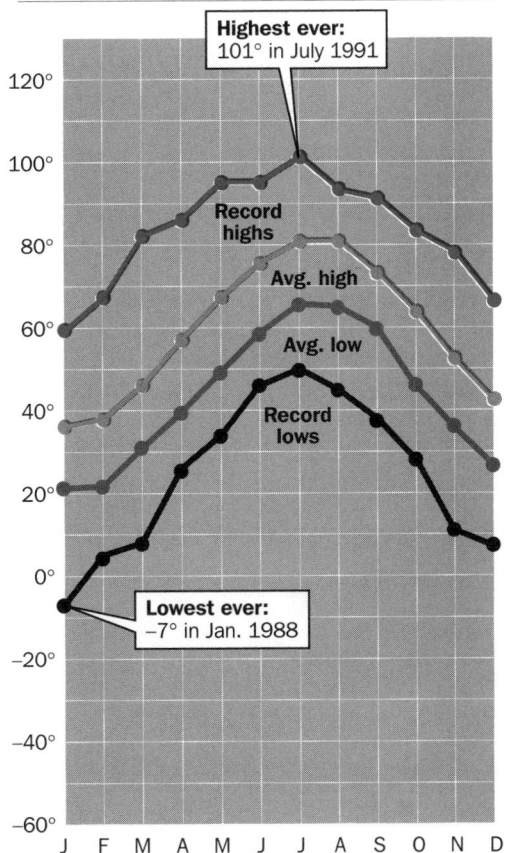

Highest ever: 101° in July 1991

Record highs

Avg. high

Avg. low

Record lows

Lowest ever: −7° in Jan. 1988

Monthly averages

Month	Avg. precip. (in.)	Avg. snow (in.)	Wet days	Thunder-storm days	Pct. sky is cloudy	% p.m. relative humidity	Dew point	Wind speed (mph)
Jan.	3.69	6.6	10	*	NA	61	NA	9.4
Feb.	3.48	4.1	9	*	NA	60	NA	9.9
March	4.10	3.9	10	1	NA	55	NA	10.6
April	4.23	0.3	12	2	NA	55	NA	9.8
May	3.94	T	10	3	NA	57	NA	8.8
June	3.82	0.0	10	6	NA	57	NA	8.5
July	3.46	0.0	10	6	NA	61	NA	7.5
Aug.	4.04	0.0	8	4	NA	61	NA	7.3
Sept.	3.48	0.0	8	2	NA	61	NA	7.8
Oct.	3.55	0.0	8	1	NA	59	NA	8.6
Nov.	4.23	1.0	11	1	NA	61	NA	9.7
Dec.	4.05	3.7	10	*	NA	59	NA	9.6

T - Trace of rain or snow   * - Less than 1   NA - Not Available

Annual averages

Precipitation (in inches)	46
Snow (in inches)	20
Heating degree days	NA
Cooling degree days	NA
Days with thunderstorms	26
Days with fog	40
Days above 90°	6
Days below 32°	98
Wet days	117
Days with snow	NA
Days with 1.5 inches or more snow	7

Percent time sky is clear

Data not available

Jackson, Mississippi

Lat. 32° 19′ N **Lon.** 90° 5′ W **Elev.** 330 ft.

Jackson is located on the west bank of the Pearl River, about 45 miles east of the Mississippi River and 150 miles north of the Gulf of Mexico. The nearby terrain is gently rolling. The climate is humid most of the year, with short, mild winters and long, warm summers. The Gulf of Mexico has a moderating effect on both. Cold spells are frequent but short. In summer, temperatures pass 90°F about two-thirds of the days. Snowfall averages less than two inches per season, while rainfall is abundant and fairly well-distributed throughout the year. In spite of the normally abundant rainfall, fairly serious droughts occasionally occur during the summer or fall. Thunderstorms occur in each month, although they are most frequent in summer.

Temperatures

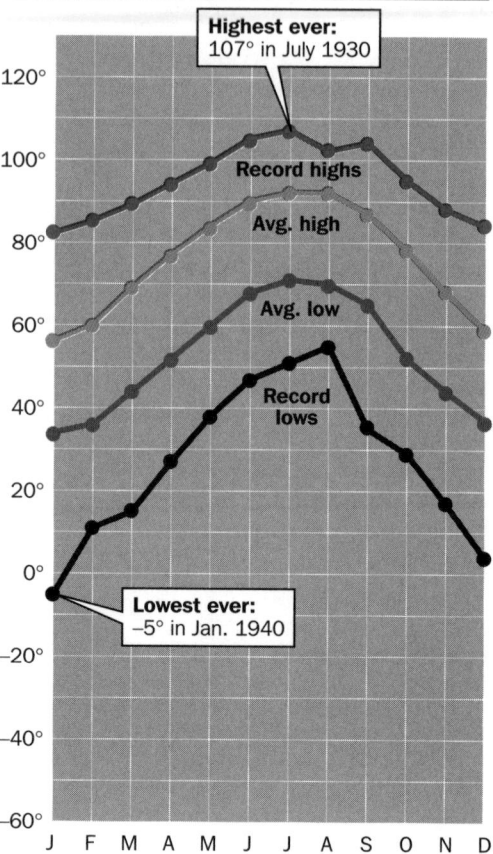

Highest ever: 107° in July 1930

Record highs

Avg. high

Avg. low

Record lows

Lowest ever: −5° in Jan. 1940

Weather extremes

Most rain in 24 hours:	8.42 in. April 11 – 12, 1979
Most rain in a month:	17.70 in. December 1982
Most snow in 24 hours:	11.7 in. Jan. 28, 1904
Most snow in a month:	11.7 in. January 1904

Monthly averages

Month	Avg. precip. (in.)	Avg. snow (in.)	Wet days	Thunder-storm days	Pct. sky is cloudy	% p.m. relative humidity	Dew point	Wind speed (mph)
Jan.	5.1	1	11	2	49	59	36	10.4
Feb.	4.7	T	9	3	44	54	38	10.4
March	5.8	T	10	6	41	51	46	10.4
April	5.7	T	8	6	33	50	54	10.4
May	5.4	0	9	7	30	53	62	8.1
June	3.0	0	8	8	20	52	68	8.1
July	4.5	0	10	12	22	56	71	6.9
Aug.	3.8	0	9	11	20	56	71	6.9
Sept.	3.6	0	8	5	26	55	66	8.1
Oct.	3.3	0	6	2	25	49	54	8.1
Nov.	4.7	T	8	3	36	52	47	9.2
Dec.	5.8	T	10	3	45	58	40	10.4

T - Trace of rain or snow   * - Less than 1   NA - Not Available

Annual averages

Precipitation (in inches)	55.4
Snow (in inches)	1
Heating degree days	2,394
Cooling degree days	2,314
Days with thunderstorms	68
Days with fog	195
Days above 90°	84
Days below 32°	50
Wet days	106
Days with snow	1
Days with 1.5 inches or more snow	*

Percent time sky is clear

Jan.	Feb.	March	April	May	June	July	Aug.	Sept.	Oct.	Nov.	Dec.
26	27.7	26.9	28.8	25.6	26.5	18.9	24.2	29.6	42.9	33.9	28.5

Jacksonville, Florida

Lat. 30° 30′ N **Lon.** 81° 42′ W **Elev.** 26 ft.

Jacksonville extends from the Atlantic Ocean to 40 miles inland. The downtown is on the St. Johns River. Winds blow off the ocean about 40 percent of the time, modifying both summer heat and winter cold. Summers are long, warm and relatively humid. Winters are mild due to latitude and the ocean. Climatic features can vary across the city based on distance from the ocean. June through August are the hottest months; December through February are the coolest. Summertime night temperatures rarely drop below 80°F. Local thundershowers occur during the summer an average of one day in two. Although in the hurricane belt, the storms at this latitude tend to move parallel to the coast, keeping well out to sea.

Weather extremes

Most rain in 24 hours:	10.17 in. Sept. 5 – 6, 1950
Most rain in a month:	19.36 in. September 1949
Most snow in 24 hours:	1.5 in. Feb. 13, 1958
Most snow in a month:	1.5 in. February 1958

Temperatures

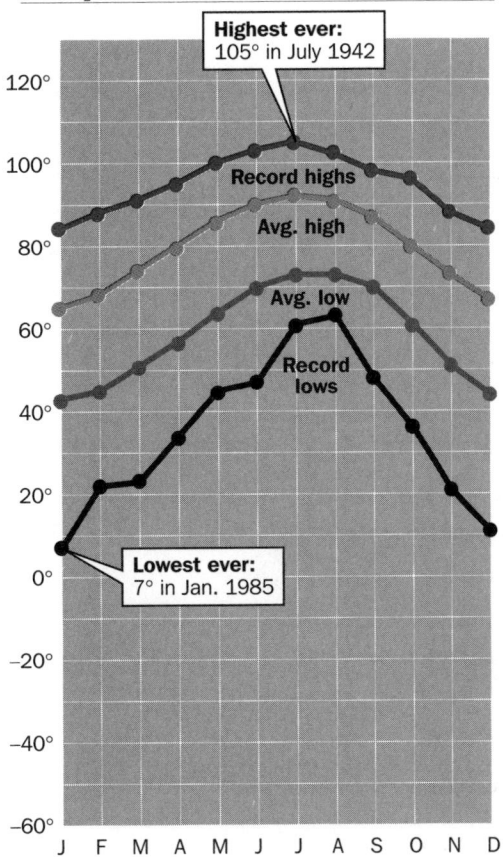

Highest ever: 105° in July 1942
Record highs
Avg. high
Avg. low
Record lows
Lowest ever: 7° in Jan. 1985

Monthly averages

Month	Avg. precip. (in.)	Avg. snow (in.)	Wet days	Thunder-storm days	Pct. sky is cloudy	% p.m. relative humidity	Dew point	Wind speed (mph)
Jan.	3.0	T	8	1	35	56	44	9.2
Feb.	3.7	T	8	2	34	53	46	10.4
March	3.8	T	8	3	31	50	50	10.4
April	3.0	0	6	3	23	49	56	9.2
May	3.6	0	8	6	22	54	63	10.4
June	5.3	0	12	11	23	61	70	8.1
July	6.2	0	14	15	22	64	72	6.9
Aug.	7.4	0	14	13	22	65	72	6.9
Sept.	7.8	0	13	7	27	66	70	11.5
Oct.	3.7	0	9	2	26	62	62	11.5
Nov.	2.0	0	6	1	27	58	53	8.1
Dec.	2.6	T	8	1	34	58	47	8.1

T - Trace of rain or snow   * - Less than 1   NA - Not Available

Annual averages

Precipitation (in inches)	52.0
Snow (in inches)	0
Heating degree days	1,303
Cooling degree days	2,812
Days with thunderstorms	65
Days with fog	175
Days above 90°	83
Days below 32°	16
Wet days	114
Days with snow	*
Days with 1.5 inches or more snow	*

Percent time sky is clear

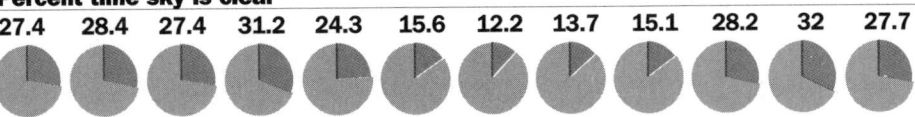

Jan.	Feb.	March	April	May	June	July	Aug.	Sept.	Oct.	Nov.	Dec.
27.4	28.4	27.4	31.2	24.3	15.6	12.2	13.7	15.1	28.2	32	27.7

Juneau, Alaska

Lat. 58° 22' N **Lon.** 134° 35' W **Elev.** 12 ft.

Maritime influences and storms crossing the Gulf of Alaska give Juneau abundant precipitation, little sunshine and relatively moderate temperatures, with limited daily and seasonal variation. Brief periods of severe cold can be brought by Canadian air flowing through nearby mountain passes, sometimes with strong winds. Rugged terrain produces wide local variations. Juneau's airport, on flatland by the Mendenhall River, has a 146-day growing season; downtown, eight miles away on a slope, averages 181 days. Airport yearly precipitation is 53 inches vs. 93 inches downtown. Ice due to thawing and freezing of snow or freezing precipitation is a winter problem.

Temperatures

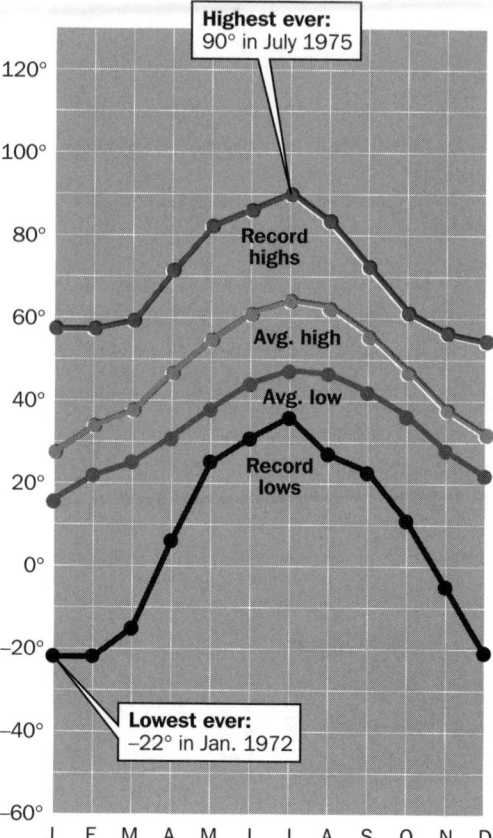

Highest ever: 90° in July 1975

Record highs

Avg. high

Avg. low

Record lows

Lowest ever: −22° in Jan. 1972

Weather extremes

Most rain in 24 hours:	4.66 in. Oct. 10, 1946
Most rain in a month:	15.25 in. October 1974
Most snow in 24 hours:	31.0 in. March 21, 1948
Most snow in a month:	86.3 in. February 1965

Monthly averages

Month	Avg. precip. (in.)	Avg. snow (in.)	Wet days	Thunder-storm days	Pct. sky is cloudy	% p.m. relative humidity	Dew point	Wind speed (mph)
Jan.	3.7	25.8	18	*	74	77	NA	8.3
Feb.	3.7	18.6	17	0	76	75	NA	8.5
March	3.3	15.2	18	0	76	68	NA	8.5
April	2.9	3.6	17	0	75	63	NA	8.7
May	3.4	T	17	0	75	63	NA	8.3
June	3.0	T	15	*	75	65	NA	7.7
July	4.1	0.0	17	*	76	70	NA	7.5
Aug.	5.0	0.0	18	*	73	74	NA	7.5
Sept.	6.4	T	20	*	80	78	NA	8.0
Oct.	7.7	1.1	24	0	86	79	NA	9.5
Nov.	5.2	12.0	20	*	82	81	NA	8.5
Dec.	4.7	22.8	21	0	83	83	NA	9.0

T - Trace of rain or snow   * - Less than 1   NA - Not Available

Annual averages

Precipitation (in inches)	53
Snow (in inches)	99
Heating degree days	9,105
Cooling degree days	0
Days with thunderstorms	*
Days with fog	21
Days above 90°	19
Days below 32°	141
Wet days	222
Days with snow	NA
Days with 1.5 inches or more snow	27

Percent time sky is clear

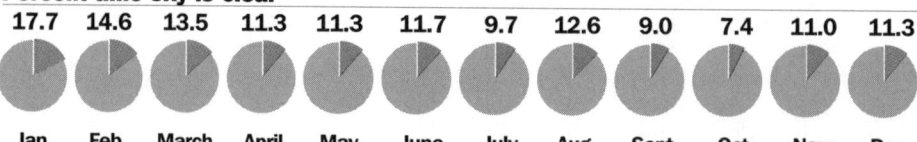

17.7	14.6	13.5	11.3	11.3	11.7	9.7	12.6	9.0	7.4	11.0	11.3
Jan.	Feb.	March	April	May	June	July	Aug.	Sept.	Oct.	Nov.	Dec.

Kalispell, Montana

Lat. 48° 18' N **Lon.** 114° 16' W **Elev.** 2,965 ft.

The Flathead Valley climate is influenced by high mountains to the north and east, which form a barrier to many winter cold waves from Alberta that move into areas east of the Rockies. The mountains rise abruptly 4,500 feet above the valley floor. Mountain snows and spring rains assure an adequate water supply. The valley contains Flathead Lake, many smaller lakes, three rivers, and numerous streams. Until freezing in late winter, this water limits temperature extremes, more so in the southern valley because Flathead Lake seldom freezes over entirely. There is more precipitation on the east side of the valley due to air rising over the mountains.

Temperatures

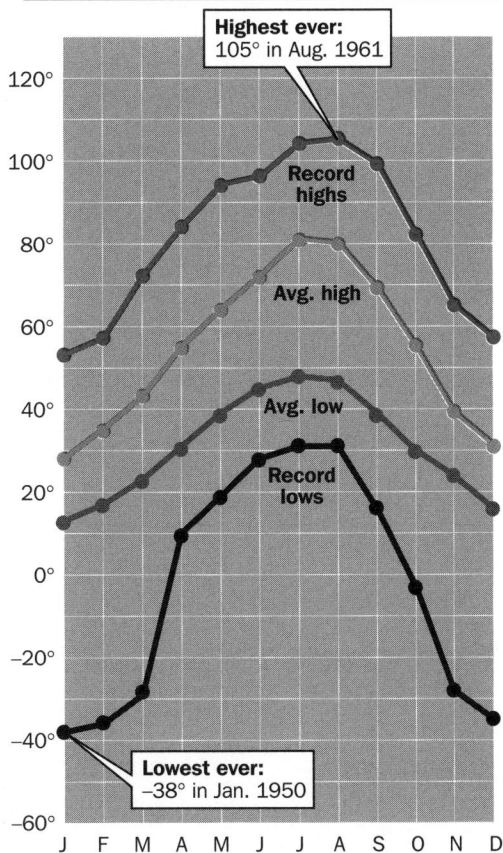

Highest ever:
105° in Aug. 1961

Record highs

Avg. high

Avg. low

Record lows

Lowest ever:
−38° in Jan. 1950

Weather extremes

Most rain in 24 hours:	2.71 in. June 19, 1982
Most rain in a month:	6.02 in. July 1993
Most snow in 24 hours:	15.4 in. Dec. 21 – 22, 1951
Most snow in a month:	52.1 in. December 1990

Monthly averages

Month	Avg. precip. (in.)	Avg. snow (in.)	Wet days	Thunder-storm days	Pct. sky is cloudy	% p.m. relative humidity	Dew point	Wind speed (mph)
Jan.	1.5	18	15	0	72	73	15	9.2
Feb.	1.1	11	12	*	63	67	19	8.1
March	1.0	7	12	*	54	55	23	9.2
April	1.1	3	10	1	47	43	28	9.2
May	1.9	1	11	3	42	43	37	9.2
June	2.2	T	12	5	36	45	44	9.2
July	1.2	0	7	6	19	36	47	8.1
Aug.	1.4	0	8	5	22	36	46	8.1
Sept.	1.2	T	8	2	30	42	39	8.1
Oct.	1.0	1	9	1	44	54	32	8.1
Nov.	1.3	8	13	0	67	72	25	8.1
Dec.	1.6	17	16	*	75	79	19	9.2

T - Trace of rain or snow   * - Less than 1   NA - Not Available

Annual averages

Precipitation (in inches)	16.6
Snow (in inches)	65
Heating degree days	8,202
Cooling degree days	155
Days with thunderstorms	23
Days with fog	75
Days above 90°	12
Days below 32°	186
Wet days	133
Days with snow	114
Days with 1.5 inches or more snow	29

Percent time sky is clear

6.9	9.7	12.2	14.4	14.7	16.5	35.3	33.1	30.5	20.4	7.4	5.4
Jan.	Feb.	March	April	May	June	July	Aug.	Sept.	Oct.	Nov.	Dec.

Kansas City, Missouri

Lat. 39° 19' N **Lon.** 94° 43' W **Elev.** 973 ft.

Kansas City is near the geographical center of the U.S., in gently rolling terrain and has a modified continental climate. There are no obstructions to the free sweep of air from all directions. Moist air from the Gulf of Mexico or dry air from southwest determine whether wet or dry conditions prevail. There is often conflict between the warm, moist Gulf air and the cold, polar continental air. Early spring brings a period of frequent and rapid fluctuations. Summer is characterized by warm days and mild nights, with moderate humidities. Fall is normally mild and usually includes a period of mild, sunny days, and cool nights. Winters are not severely cold. January is the coldest month. Snowfall over 10 inches is rare. About 75 percent of annual moisture falls in the growing season.

Temperatures

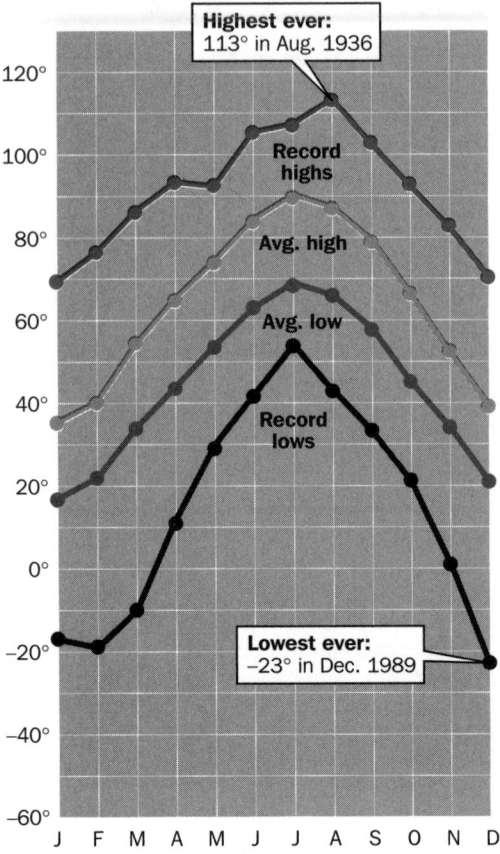

Highest ever: 113° in Aug. 1936

Record highs

Avg. high

Avg. low

Record lows

Lowest ever: −23° in Dec. 1989

Weather extremes

Most rain in 24 hours:	8.82 in. Sept. 12, 1977
Most rain in a month:	16.17 in. September 1914
Most snow in 24 hours:	25.0 in. March 23–24, 1912
Most snow in a month:	40.2 in. March 1912

Monthly averages

Month	Avg. precip. (in.)	Avg. snow (in.)	Wet days	Thunder- storm days	Pct. sky is cloudy	% p.m. relative humidity	Dew point	Wind speed (mph)
Jan.	1.1	6	7	*	37	58	17	13.8
Feb.	1.2	5	7	*	44	59	21	12.7
March	2.8	3	10	3	44	54	32	15.0
April	3.0	1	10	5	38	50	41	15.0
May	5.5	0	11	9	33	54	52	13.8
June	4.1	0	10	9	24	54	62	12.7
July	3.8	0	7	7	16	51	66	11.5
Aug.	4.1	0	9	8	21	53	64	11.5
Sept.	4.9	0	8	5	25	53	57	12.7
Oct.	3.6	T	8	3	29	51	44	12.7
Nov.	2.1	1	8	1	41	57	33	13.8
Dec.	1.6	5	8	1	42	60	21	12.7

T - Trace of rain or snow   * - Less than 1   NA - Not Available

Annual averages

Precipitation (in inches)	38.1
Snow (in inches)	21
Heating degree days	5,326
Cooling degree days	1,388
Days with thunderstorms	51
Days with fog	124
Days above 90°	39
Days below 32°	110
Wet days	103
Days with snow	34
Days with 1.5 inches or more snow	9

Percent time sky is clear

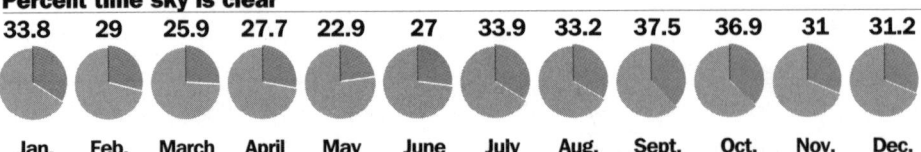

33.8	29	25.9	27.7	22.9	27	33.9	33.2	37.5	36.9	31	31.2
Jan.	Feb.	March	April	May	June	July	Aug.	Sept.	Oct.	Nov.	Dec.

Key West, Florida

Lat. 24° 33′ N **Lon.** 81° 45′ W **Elev.** 4 ft.

Key West is near the end of the Florida Keys, a chain of islands in a southwest arc from the southeast coast of Florida. Because of proximity to the Gulf Stream and the tempering effects of the Gulf of Mexico, Key West has a notably mild, tropical-maritime climate. Average temperatures during the winter are only about 14 degrees lower than in the summer. Prevailing east trade winds and sea breezes suppress the usual summertime heating. December through April has abundant sunshine. June through October is the wet season. Humidity remains relatively high during the entire year.

Temperatures

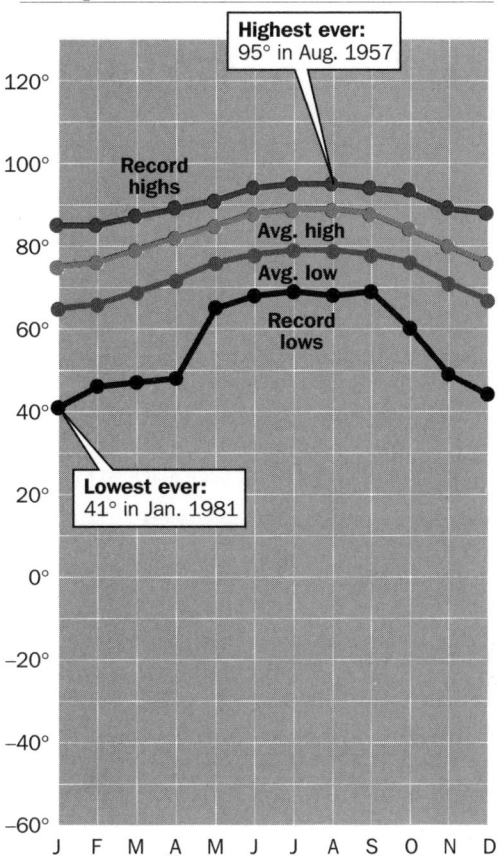

Highest ever:
95° in Aug. 1957

Record highs

Avg. high

Avg. low

Record lows

Lowest ever:
41° in Jan. 1981

Weather extremes

Most rain in 24 hours:	23.28 in. Nov. 11, 1980
Most rain in a month:	27.67 in. November 1980
Most snow in 24 hours:	none
Most snow in a month:	none

Monthly averages

Month	Avg. precip. (in.)	Avg. snow (in.)	Wet days	Thunder-storm days	Pct. sky is cloudy	% p.m. relative humidity	Dew point	Wind speed (mph)
Jan.	2.1	0	6	1	16	69	61	11.5
Feb.	1.6	0	6	1	15	67	61	11.5
March	1.7	0	5	2	13	66	64	13.8
April	1.9	0	4	2	10	63	66	13.8
May	3.3	0	8	4	14	65	70	12.7
June	4.7	0	11	10	19	68	73	10.4
July	3.8	0	12	13	15	66	74	11.5
Aug.	5.2	0	15	15	14	67	75	11.5
Sept.	6.3	0	15	11	17	69	74	11.5
Oct.	4.5	0	11	4	16	69	71	12.7
Nov.	2.7	0	7	1	14	70	67	12.7
Dec.	2.0	0	7	1	15	70	63	11.5

T - Trace of rain or snow   * - Less than 1   NA - Not Available

Annual averages

Precipitation (in inches)	39.9
Snow (in inches)	0
Heating degree days	68
Cooling degree days	4,820
Days with thunderstorms	65
Days with fog	9
Days above 90°	45
Days below 32°	0
Wet days	107
Days with snow	0
Days with 1.5 inches or more snow	0

Percent time sky is clear

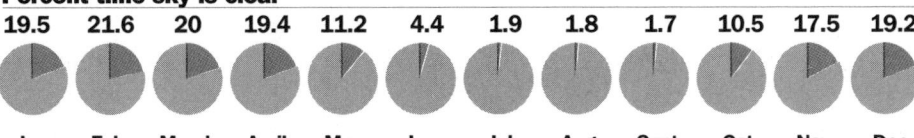

Jan.	Feb.	March	April	May	June	July	Aug.	Sept.	Oct.	Nov.	Dec.
19.5	21.6	20	19.4	11.2	4.4	1.9	1.8	1.7	10.5	17.5	19.2

Knoxville, Tennessee

Lat. 35° 48' N **Lon.** 84° 00' W **Elev.** 949 ft.

Knoxville is located in a broad valley between the Cumberland Mountains, which lie northwest of the city, and the Great Smoky Mountains, which lie southeast. These two ranges exercise a marked influence upon the climate of the valley. The Cumberland Mountains serve to weaken the force of cold winter air and modify the hot summer winds common to the Plains. They also tend to lift warm, moist air from the Gulf of Mexico, thereby generating thunderstorms that cool the valley in summer. July is usually the warmest month and January the coldest. Precipitation is greatest in winter and lowest in fall. Winds tend to be southwest by day and northeast at night.

Temperatures

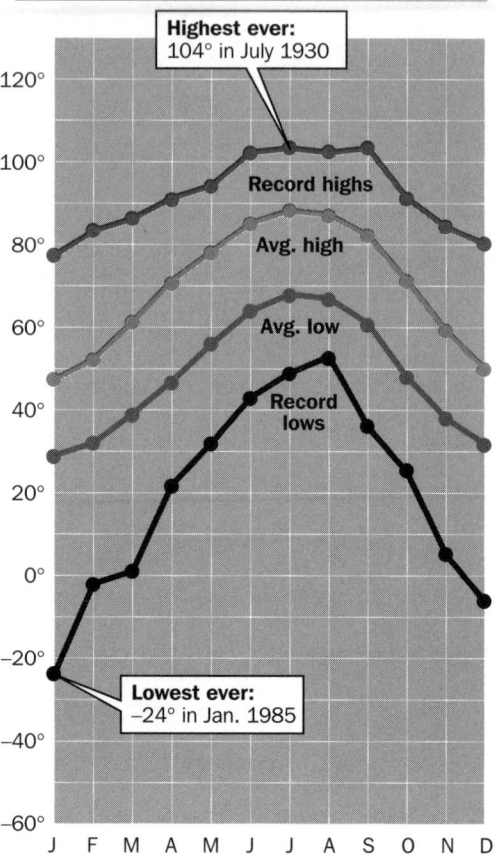

Highest ever: 104° in July 1930
Record highs
Avg. high
Avg. low
Record lows
Lowest ever: −24° in Jan. 1985

Weather extremes

Most rain in 24 hours:	6.14 in. July 16, 1917
Most rain in a month:	17.32 in. April 1874
Most snow in 24 hours:	18.2 in. Nov. 21 – 22, 1952
Most snow in a month:	25.7 in. February 1895

Monthly averages

Month	Avg. precip. (in.)	Avg. snow (in.)	Wet days	Thunder-storm days	Pct. sky is cloudy	% p.m. relative humidity	Dew point	Wind speed (mph)
Jan.	4.5	5	12	1	54	60	29	8.1
Feb.	4.3	4	11	1	50	54	31	8.1
March	5.0	2	12	3	47	50	37	12.7
April	3.6	1	11	4	39	46	45	11.5
May	3.9	0	11	7	34	52	55	10.4
June	3.8	0	10	8	28	54	63	9.2
July	4.5	0	11	10	28	56	67	8.1
Aug.	3.1	0	10	7	26	55	67	6.9
Sept.	2.9	0	8	3	30	54	61	6.9
Oct.	2.8	T	8	1	30	51	49	6.9
Nov.	3.8	1	10	1	41	54	39	6.9
Dec.	4.5	2	11	1	50	59	32	6.9

T - Trace of rain or snow   * - Less than 1   NA - Not Available

Annual averages

Precipitation (in inches)	46.7
Snow (in inches)	13
Heating degree days	3,646
Cooling degree days	1,510
Days with thunderstorms	47
Days with fog	172
Days above 90°	33
Days below 32°	73
Wet days	125
Days with snow	14
Days with 1.5 inches or more snow	5

Percent time sky is clear

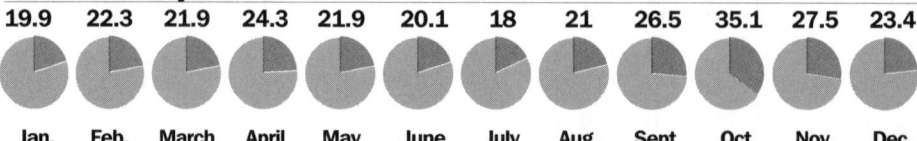

Jan.	Feb.	March	April	May	June	July	Aug.	Sept.	Oct.	Nov.	Dec.
19.9	22.3	21.9	24.3	21.9	20.1	18	21	26.5	35.1	27.5	23.4

Lake Charles, Louisiana

Lat. 30° 7' N **Lon.** 93° 13' W **Elev.** 9 ft.

Lake Charles is located on the east side of the lake of the same name. The Calcasieu River enters and exits Lake Charles on its way to the Gulf of Mexico. The terrain is a flat coastal plain. Extensive marshes begin some 10 to 15 miles south and extend to the coast. Lake Charles' climate is humid subtropical with a strong maritime character. The climate is influenced by the amount of water in the area and proximity of the Gulf of Mexico. A flow of air from the Gulf tempers extremes of summer heat, shortens winter cold spells, and provides abundant rain. Amounts are substantial in all seasons, although dry spells of two or three weeks duration are not uncommon. Winters are mild, with temperatures below 20°F occurring on average only one year in five.

Temperatures

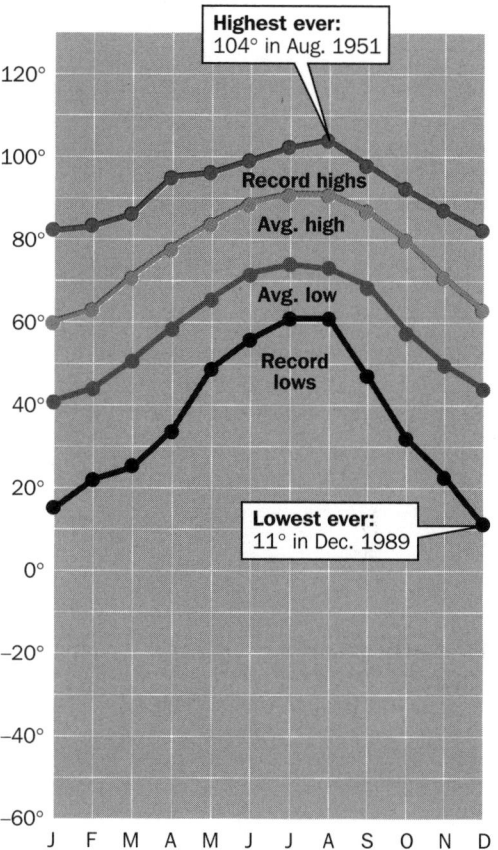

Highest ever: 104° in Aug. 1951

Record highs

Avg. high

Avg. low

Record lows

Lowest ever: 11° in Dec. 1989

Weather extremes

Most rain in 24 hours:	16.9 in. May 15 – 16, 1980
Most rain in a month:	25.33 in. June 1989
Most snow in 24 hours:	5.0 in. Feb. 12 – 13, 1960
Most snow in a month:	5.0 in. February 1960

Monthly averages

Month	Avg. precip. (in.)	Avg. snow (in.)	Wet days	Thunder-storm days	Pct. sky is cloudy	% p.m. relative humidity	Dew point	Wind speed (mph)
Jan.	4.5	T	9	3	51	63	43	11.5
Feb.	3.4	T	8	3	45	59	45	11.5
March	3.3	T	8	4	44	59	52	11.5
April	3.3	0	6	4	37	58	59	11.5
May	5.7	0	8	7	28	59	66	11.5
June	5.4	0	8	9	16	61	71	9.2
July	5.1	0	11	14	19	63	74	8.1
Aug.	5.4	0	11	14	17	62	73	6.9
Sept.	5.8	0	9	9	21	60	69	6.9
Oct.	4.0	0	6	3	21	52	59	8.1
Nov.	4.3	T	8	3	32	57	52	10.4
Dec.	5.0	T	9	3	45	62	46	11.5

T - Trace of rain or snow   * - Less than 1   NA - Not Available

Annual averages

Precipitation (in inches)	55.3
Snow (in inches)	T
Heating degree days	1,579
Cooling degree days	2,715
Days with thunderstorms	76
Days with fog	197
Days above 90°	72
Days below 32°	15
Wet days	101
Days with snow	*
Days with 1.5 inches or more snow	*

Percent time sky is clear

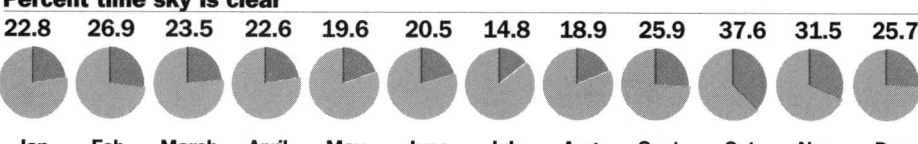

Jan.	Feb.	March	April	May	June	July	Aug.	Sept.	Oct.	Nov.	Dec.
22.8	26.9	23.5	22.6	19.6	20.5	14.8	18.9	25.9	37.6	31.5	25.7

Lander, Wyoming

Lat. 42° 49' N **Lon.** 108° 44' W **Elev.** 5,370 ft.

Lander, located in the central Wyoming valley of the Popo Agie River, lies at the foot of the Wind River Range. Because Lander is in a pocket, winds from all directions except northeast are downslope and produce warm, dry winds called chinooks. Due to light winds, steep temperature inversions are the rule during winter nights and early mornings. Temperatures in the valley can be 15 degrees lower than surrounding areas on calm, clear nights when there is a snow cover; for several days each winter, temperatures are 20 to 30 degrees lower. Mountains block moisture from the Pacific, creating a semiarid climate. More than a third of the annual precipitation occurs in April and May. Summer moisture is light and very erratic.

Temperatures

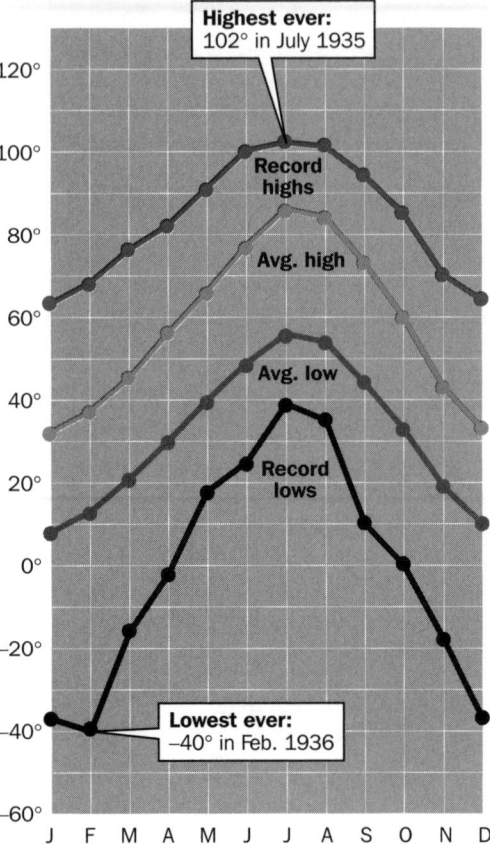

Highest ever: 102° in July 1935

Record highs

Avg. high

Avg. low

Record lows

Lowest ever: −40° in Feb. 1936

Weather extremes

Most rain in 24 hours:	3.48 in. June 11, 1947
Most rain in a month:	6.88 in. June 1947
Most snow in 24 hours:	23.1 in. Nov. 15 – 16, 1958
Most snow in a month:	66.0 in. April 1973

Monthly averages

Month	Avg. precip. (in.)	Avg. snow (in.)	Wet days	Thunderstorm days	Pct. sky is cloudy	% p.m. relative humidity	Dew point	Wind speed (mph)
Jan.	0.5	9	4	0	25	59	8	9.2
Feb.	0.6	12	5	0	29	54	12	9.2
March	1.1	18	7	*	30	46	17	9.2
April	2.1	21	8	1	33	40	24	10.4
May	2.5	7	9	4	30	37	32	10.4
June	1.4	1	6	7	19	31	39	10.4
July	0.8	0	6	10	13	27	42	10.4
Aug.	0.5	0	5	7	12	27	40	10.4
Sept.	1.1	3	5	3	18	33	34	10.4
Oct.	1.1	9	5	*	21	41	27	9.2
Nov.	0.8	14	5	*	26	56	17	8.1
Dec.	0.5	11	5	0	24	62	10	8.1

T - Trace of rain or snow   * - Less than 1   NA - Not Available

Annual averages

Precipitation (in inches)	13.0
Snow (in inches)	105
Heating degree days	7,801
Cooling degree days	456
Days with thunderstorms	32
Days with fog	13
Days above 90°	21
Days below 32°	185
Wet days	70
Days with snow	80
Days with 1.5 inches or more snow	41

Percent time sky is clear

25.2	24.6	21.9	20	18.1	27.3	32.7	33	38.9	35.9	26.4	28.4

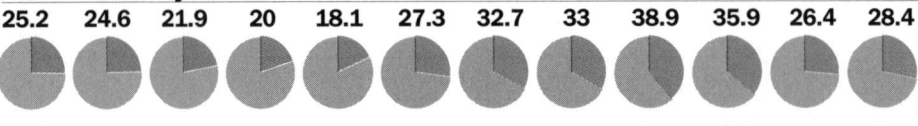

| Jan. | Feb. | March | April | May | June | July | Aug. | Sept. | Oct. | Nov. | Dec. |

Lansing, Michigan

Lat. 42° 46' N **Lon.** 84° 36' W **Elev.** 841 ft.

The climate at Lansing alternates between continental and semimarine, depending on meteorological conditions. In the absence of strong wind, the weather becomes continental — hot in the summer and severely cold in the winter. A strong wind from the Great Lakes, however, can transform Lansing's weather into semimarine. The Great Lakes are less responsive to temperature changes, and, thus, prolong summer warmth in the fall and winter cold in the spring. Clouds prevail during winter, but sunshine is abundant in summer. Similarly, relative humidity remains high during the winter, but is only moderate in summer. Tornadoes are less frequent than in states farther south, but destructive thunder and wind storms are not uncommon.

Weather extremes

Most rain in 24 hours:	5.01 in.
	June 11 – 12, 1986
Most rain in a month:	10.21 in.
	June 1986
Most snow in 24 hours:	20.4 in.
	Jan. 26 – 27, 1967
Most snow in a month:	34.0 in.
	January 1978

Temperatures

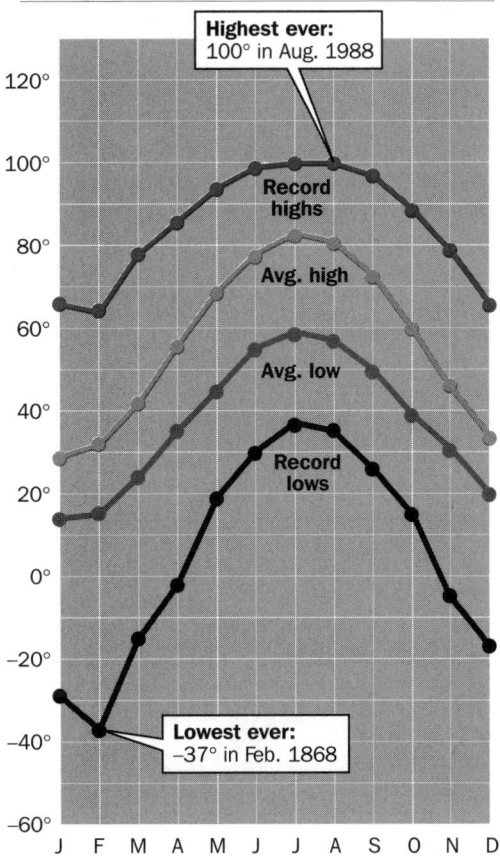

Highest ever: 100° in Aug. 1988

Record highs

Avg. high

Avg. low

Record lows

Lowest ever: -37° in Feb. 1868

120° 100° 80° 60° 40° 20° 0° -20° -40° -60°

J F M A M J J A S O N D

Monthly averages

Month	Avg. precip. (in.)	Avg. snow (in.)	Wet days	Thunder-storm days	Pct. sky is cloudy	% p.m. relative humidity	Dew point	Wind speed (mph)
Jan.	1.7	12	15	*	62	72	17	13.8
Feb.	1.6	10	12	*	56	68	17	13.8
March	2.3	8	14	1	53	62	25	13.8
April	2.8	3	12	3	47	54	35	13.8
May	2.7	T	11	4	38	52	45	12.7
June	3.6	0	11	6	31	53	56	11.5
July	2.6	0	10	6	25	53	60	10.4
Aug.	3.1	0	9	6	28	55	60	9.2
Sept.	3.2	T	10	4	34	58	53	10.4
Oct.	2.1	T	10	1	41	59	41	11.5
Nov.	2.6	5	13	1	60	68	32	11.5
Dec.	2.3	12	15	*	66	74	22	12.7

T - Trace of rain or snow   * - Less than 1   NA - Not Available

Annual averages

Precipitation (in inches)	30.6
Snow (in inches)	51
Heating degree days	7,022
Cooling degree days	598
Days with thunderstorms	32
Days with fog	153
Days above 90°	11
Days below 32°	149
Wet days	142
Days with snow	93
Days with 1.5 inches or more snow	23

Percent time sky is clear

12	16	18.1	21.8	20.9	21.3	24.5	25.8	25.2	24.6	14	11.6
Jan.	Feb.	March	April	May	June	July	Aug.	Sept.	Oct.	Nov.	Dec.

Las Vegas, Nevada

Lat. 36° 5' N **Lon.** 115° 10' W **Elev.** 2,162 ft.

Las Vegas is near the center of a broad desert valley almost surrounded by mountains rising 2,000 to 10,000 feet above the valley floor. Since mountains encircle the valley, drainage winds are usually downslope toward the center, or lowest portion of the valley. This also affects minimum temperatures, which in lower portions of the valley can be from 15 to 25 degrees colder than at McCarran Airport. Spring and fall are considered most ideal, although rather sharp temperature changes can occur. The Sierra Nevada Mountains of California and the Spring Mountains immediately west of the Vegas Valley act as barriers to moisture from the Pacific Ocean.

Temperatures

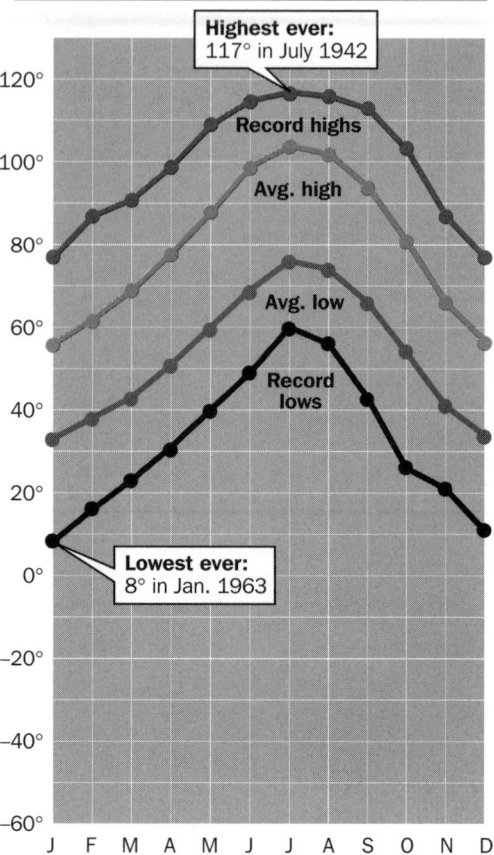

Weather extremes

Most rain in 24 hours:	2.59 in. Aug. 21, 1957
Most rain in a month:	4.80 in. March 1992
Most snow in 24 hours:	9.0 in. Jan. 4 – 5, 1974
Most snow in a month:	16.7 in. January 1949

Monthly averages

Month	Avg. precip. (in.)	Avg. snow (in.)	Wet days	Thunder-storm days	Pct. sky is cloudy	% p.m. relative humidity	Dew point	Wind speed (mph)
Jan.	0.5	1	3	*	24	32	22	8.1
Feb.	0.4	T	3	*	22	25	23	8.1
March	0.4	T	3	*	20	20	22	13.8
April	0.2	T	2	*	15	15	23	15.0
May	0.2	0	1	1	11	13	27	15.0
June	0.1	0	1	1	5	10	29	15.0
July	0.4	0	3	4	8	14	40	12.7
Aug.	0.5	0	3	4	7	16	42	12.7
Sept.	0.3	0	2	2	6	16	35	12.7
Oct.	0.2	0	2	1	9	18	29	8.1
Nov.	0.4	T	2	*	16	26	25	8.1
Dec.	0.3	T	2	*	20	31	22	8.1

T - Trace of rain or snow   * - Less than 1   NA - Not Available

Annual averages

Precipitation (in inches)	4.0
Snow (in inches)	1
Heating degree days	2,420
Cooling degree days	3,081
Days with thunderstorms	13
Days with fog	4
Days above 90°	134
Days below 32°	37
Wet days	27
Days with snow	1
Days with 1.5 inches or more snow	*

Percent time sky is clear

41.2	40.3	41.1	47.2	49.3	64.4	52.2	55.5	65.5	59.5	49	45.4

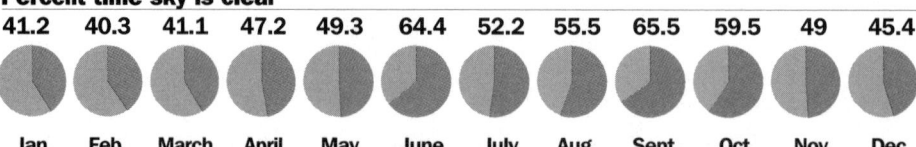

| Jan. | Feb. | March | April | May | June | July | Aug. | Sept. | Oct. | Nov. | Dec. |

Lewiston, Idaho

Lat. 46° 23' N **Lon.** 117° 01' W **Elev.** 1,413 ft.

Lewiston is in a narrow valley at the confluence of the Snake and Clearwater rivers. Elevations to the south rise gradually from the old downtown's 845 feet to the airport on a more or less flat bench at 1,413 feet. To the north, a range of hills rises abruptly to about 2,000 feet above the valley floor. On the prairies surrounding the valley, winter temperatures are much lower than in the valley and precipitation is almost double. Lewiston's precipitation amounts to about 13 inches annually. Temperatures range from more than 115°F to less than -20°F. Summers typically are hot and dry with stretches of 100°F days. Considerable cooling after sunset makes the nights very comfortable. Winds are light, usually prevailing from the east.

Temperatures

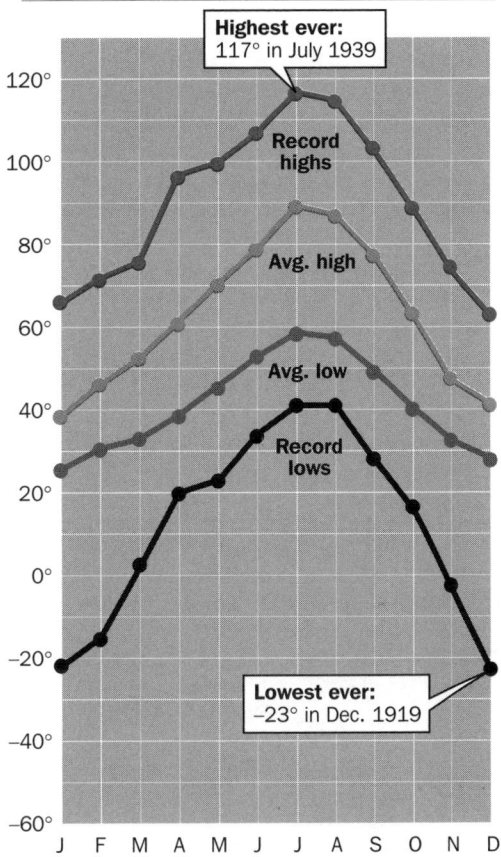

Highest ever: 117° in July 1939
Record highs
Avg. high
Avg. low
Record lows
Lowest ever: −23° in Dec. 1919

Weather extremes

Most rain in 24 hours:	1.73 in. Sept. 14, 1955
Most rain in a month:	4.80 in. May 1948
Most snow in 24 hours:	12.8 in. Jan. 2 – 3, 1966
Most snow in a month:	27.2 in. February 1916

Monthly averages

Month	Avg. precip. (in.)	Avg. snow (in.)	Wet days	Thunder- storm days	Pct. sky is cloudy	% p.m. relative humidity	Dew point	Wind speed (mph)
Jan.	1.4	6.0	11	0	77	70	NA	NA
Feb.	0.9	2.4	9	*	75	61	NA	NA
March	1.0	1.4	11	*	66	49	NA	NA
April	1.1	0.1	10	1	63	42	NA	NA
May	1.4	T	10	3	52	39	NA	NA
June	1.4	0.0	9	4	44	35	NA	NA
July	0.5	T	5	4	18	24	NA	NA
Aug.	0.8	0.0	5	3	23	25	NA	NA
Sept.	0.8	0.0	5	1	31	32	NA	NA
Oct.	1.0	0.1	8	*	48	49	NA	NA
Nov.	1.2	1.7	11	*	72	69	NA	NA
Dec.	1.3	4.3	11	0	78	73	NA	NA

T - Trace of rain or snow   * - Less than 1   NA - Not Available

Annual averages

Precipitation (in inches)	13
Snow (in inches)	16
Heating degree days	5,429
Cooling degree days	742
Days with thunderstorms	16
Days with fog	21
Days above 90°	40
Days below 32°	89
Wet days	102
Days with snow	NA
Days with 1.5 inches or more snow	5

Percent time sky is clear

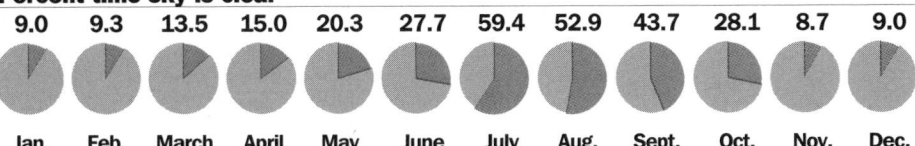

| 9.0 | 9.3 | 13.5 | 15.0 | 20.3 | 27.7 | 59.4 | 52.9 | 43.7 | 28.1 | 8.7 | 9.0 |
| Jan. | Feb. | March | April | May | June | July | Aug. | Sept. | Oct. | Nov. | Dec. |

Lexington, Kentucky

Lat. 38° 02' N **Lon.** 84° 36' W **Elev.** 966 ft.

Lexington is in the heart of the famed Kentucky Blue Grass region, on a gently rolling plateau noted for its beauty and fertility. The soil's high phosphorus content makes it valuable for growing pasture grasses for cattle and horses. The climate is temperate, suited to a varied plant and animal life. And it's decidedly continental, subject to sudden, large changes in temperature in spells of short duration. Precipitation is evenly distributed throughout the year. Snowfall is variable and the ground does not retain snow cover more than a few days at a time. September and October are the most pleasant months of the year, with the least precipitation, the greatest number of clear days and generally comfortable temperatures.

Temperatures

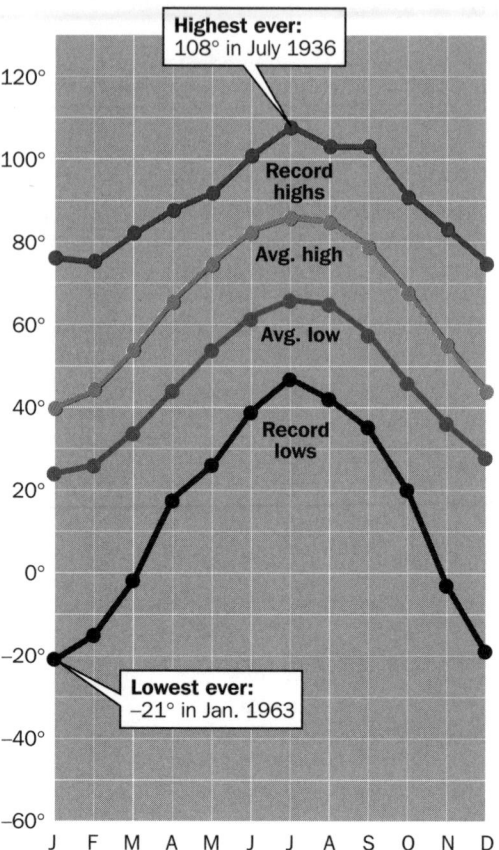

Highest ever: 108° in July 1936

Record highs

Avg. high

Avg. low

Record lows

Lowest ever: −21° in Jan. 1963

Weather extremes

Most rain in 24 hours:	8.04 in. Aug. 2, 1932
Most rain in a month:	16.65 in. January 1950
Most snow in 24 hours:	13.5 in. Jan. 26, 1943
Most snow in a month:	21.9 in. January 1978

Monthly averages

Month	Avg. precip. (in.)	Avg. snow (in.)	Wet days	Thunder-storm days	Pct. sky is cloudy	% p.m. relative humidity	Dew point	Wind speed (mph)
Jan.	3.6	6	12	1	58	67	24	11.5
Feb.	3.4	5	11	1	54	61	26	11.5
March	4.4	3	13	3	50	55	33	11.5
April	3.9	T	12	4	42	51	41	11.5
May	4.3	T	12	6	35	54	52	9.2
June	4.0	0	10	8	27	54	61	8.1
July	4.8	0	11	9	24	56	65	6.9
Aug.	3.7	0	9	7	23	55	64	6.9
Sept.	3.0	0	8	3	27	54	57	8.1
Oct.	2.4	T	8	1	32	53	45	9.2
Nov.	3.5	1	11	1	46	60	35	11.5
Dec.	3.9	3	12	*	55	66	28	11.5

T - Trace of rain or snow   * - Less than 1   NA - Not Available

Annual averages

Precipitation (in inches)	45.1
Snow (in inches)	17
Heating degree days	4,718
Cooling degree days	1,210
Days with thunderstorms	44
Days with fog	152
Days above 90°	22
Days below 32°	96
Wet days	129
Days with snow	32
Days with 1.5 inches or more snow	6

Percent time sky is clear

Jan.	Feb.	March	April	May	June	July	Aug.	Sept.	Oct.	Nov.	Dec.
18.9	20.9	19.6	21.4	21.8	21	22.1	26.5	31	35.9	24.9	19.7

Little Rock, Arkansas

Lat. 34° 44' N **Lon.** 92° 14' W **Elev.** 257 ft.

Little Rock is on the Arkansas River between the Ouachita Mountains to the west and the flat lowlands comprising the Mississippi River Valley to the east. The modified continental climate includes exposure to all types of North American air masses. However, proximity to the Gulf of Mexico marks summer with prolonged warm and humid weather. The growing season averages 233 days. Winters are mild, but polar outbreaks are not uncommon. Precipitation is well-distributed throughout the year. Ice storms, although infrequent, are at times severe. Warm-front weather in winter and early spring, with shallow cold air from the north flowing under warm moist Gulf air, results in excellent conditions for freezing precipitation.

Weather extremes

Most rain in 24 hours:	8.81 in. April 9, 1913
Most rain in a month:	18.04 in. January 1937
Most snow in 24 hours:	11.3 in. Jan. 5, 1960
Most snow in a month:	19.4 in. January 1918

Temperatures

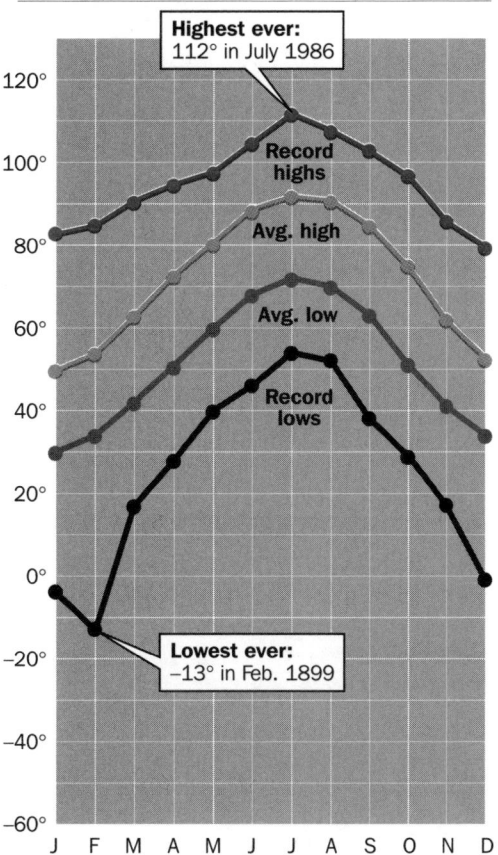

Highest ever: 112° in July 1986

Record highs

Avg. high

Avg. low

Record lows

Lowest ever: −13° in Feb. 1899

Monthly averages

Month	Avg. precip. (in.)	Avg. snow (in.)	Wet days	Thunder-storm days	Pct. sky is cloudy	% p.m. relative humidity	Dew point	Wind speed (mph)
Jan.	4.1	3	10	2	45	57	30	8.1
Feb.	4.2	2	9	2	43	54	33	10.4
March	4.9	1	10	5	41	50	40	9.2
April	5.2	T	10	6	35	50	49	9.2
May	5.4	0	10	7	30	53	59	9.2
June	3.6	0	8	8	20	52	66	8.1
July	3.5	0	9	9	19	54	70	8.1
Aug.	3.2	0	7	7	16	52	69	8.1
Sept.	3.8	0	7	4	23	52	63	8.1
Oct.	3.5	0	7	2	25	48	51	6.9
Nov.	4.8	T	8	3	35	52	41	8.1
Dec.	4.5	1	9	2	43	57	33	8.1

T - Trace of rain or snow   * - Less than 1   NA - Not Available

Annual averages

Precipitation (in inches)	50.7
Snow (in inches)	5
Heating degree days	3,095
Cooling degree days	2,107
Days with thunderstorms	57
Days with fog	142
Days above 90°	73
Days below 32°	57
Wet days	104
Days with snow	6
Days with 1.5 inches or more snow	2

Percent time sky is clear

Jan.	Feb.	March	April	May	June	July	Aug.	Sept.	Oct.	Nov.	Dec.
28.3	29.7	27.3	27.7	24.7	27.6	25.6	29.6	33.6	40.6	35.6	31.5

Los Angeles Airport, Calif.

(International Airport — typical of L.A. coastal areas)
Lat. 33° 56′ N **Lon.** 118° 23′ W **Elev.** 100 ft.

Marine air, the buffering effect of coastal mountains and Pacific Ocean storms in late fall, winter, and early spring make for mild temperatures all year along the coast. Differences occur over short distances on the coastal plain due to topography and decreased marine effect. Farther inland, temperature range is less, rainfall less and humidity higher. Nights are cool, rarely below 40°F, and up to 10 years have passed with no readings below 32°F at the airport. Night and morning low clouds often give way to sunny afternoons in spring and summer. From fall through spring, inland Santa Ana winds with extremely dry air occasionally reach the coast. Heavy fog occurs about one night or morning in four during winter.

Weather extremes

Most rain in 24 hours:	6.19 in. Jan. 25 – 26, 1956
Most rain in a month:	11.07 in. February 1962
Most snow in 24 hours:	Trace Rare occasions
Most snow in a month:	Trace Rare occasions

Temperatures

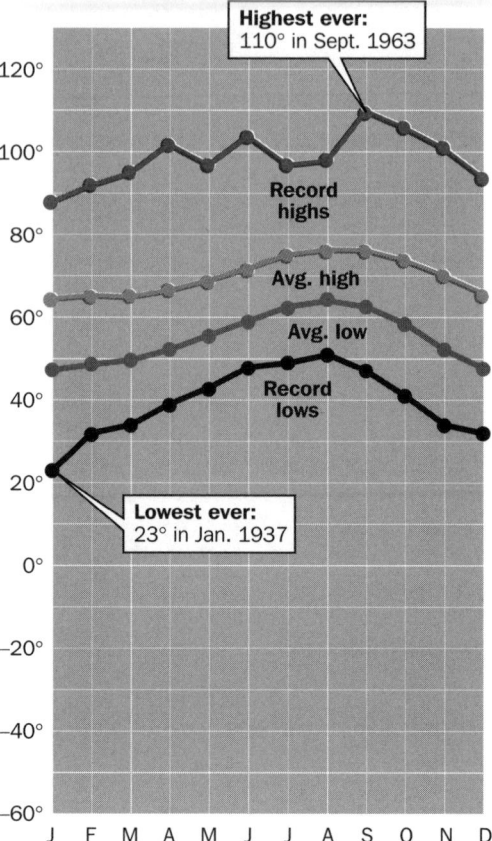

Highest ever: 110° in Sept. 1963

Record highs

Avg. high

Avg. low

Record lows

Lowest ever: 23° in Jan. 1937

Monthly averages

Month	Avg. precip. (in.)	Avg. snow (in.)	Wet days	Thunder- storm days	Pct. sky is cloudy	% p.m. relative humidity	Dew point	Wind speed (mph)
Jan.	2.6	T	6	*	29	60	41	9.2
Feb.	2.3	0	5	*	32	62	44	9.2
March	1.8	0	6	1	30	64	46	10.4
April	0.8	0	3	*	30	64	49	10.4
May	0.1	0	1	*	36	66	52	10.4
June	T	0	*	*	38	67	56	10.4
July	T	0	*	*	28	67	60	9.2
Aug.	0.1	0	*	*	28	68	61	9.2
Sept.	0.2	0	1	*	30	67	59	9.2
Oct.	0.3	0	2	*	30	66	54	9.2
Nov.	1.5	0	4	*	26	61	46	9.2
Dec.	1.5	0	5	*	27	60	41	5.8

T - Trace of rain or snow　　* - Less than 1　　NA - Not Available

Annual averages

Precipitation (in inches)	11.3
Snow (in inches)	T
Heating degree days	1,595
Cooling degree days	728
Days with thunderstorms	1
Days with fog	100
Days above 90°	5
Days below 32°	*
Wet days	33
Days with snow	0
Days with 1.5 inches or more snow	0

Percent time sky is clear

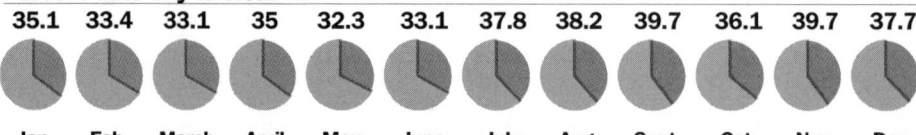

Jan.	Feb.	March	April	May	June	July	Aug.	Sept.	Oct.	Nov.	Dec.
35.1	33.4	33.1	35	32.3	33.1	37.8	38.2	39.7	36.1	39.7	37.7

Los Angeles Civic Center

(typical of inland L.A. areas)
Lat. 34° 3' N **Lon.** 118° 14' W **Elev.** 270 ft.

Los Angeles is pleasant and mild. The Pacific Ocean is the primary moderating influence, and the coastal mountain ranges buffer against extremes of heat and cold. There are pronounced climatic differences over fairly short distances with temperatures more extreme and the humidity lower as one goes inland or up foothill slopes. Even when temperatures are high, humidity is below normal. In fall, winter, and early spring, Santa Ana winds may reach 35 to 50 mph in north and east sections of the city, with higher speeds in outlying areas, although they rarely reach the coast. During spring and summer, low clouds at night and in early morning are common along the coast, but form later and clear earlier near the foothills.

Temperatures

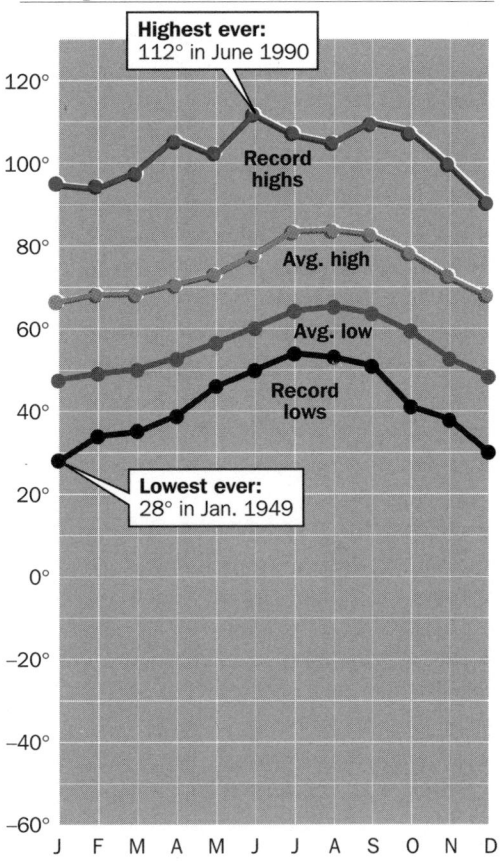

Highest ever: 112° in June 1990
Record highs
Avg. high
Avg. low
Record lows
Lowest ever: 28° in Jan. 1949

J F M A M J J A S O N D

Weather extremes

Most rain in 24 hours:	7.36 in. Dec. 31, 1933 – Jan. 1, 1934
Most rain in a month:	14.94 in. January 1969
Most snow in 24 hours:	3.00 in. Jan. 19-20, 1949
Most snow in a month:	3.00 in. January 1949

Monthly averages

Month	Avg. precip. (in.)	Avg. snow (in.)	Wet days	Thunder- storm days	Pct. sky is cloudy	% p.m. relative humidity	Dew point	Wind speed (mph)
Jan.	3.7	T	6	1	27	50	NA	6.8
Feb.	3.0	T	5	1	32	52	NA	6.9
March	2.4	0	6	1	28	52	NA	7.0
April	1.2	0	4	1	27	54	NA	6.6
May	0.2	0	1	*	25	55	NA	6.3
June	0.0	0	1	*	20	56	NA	5.7
July	0.0	0	0	*	4	53	NA	5.4
Aug.	0.1	0	1	*	4	55	NA	5.3
Sept.	0.3	0	1	*	11	54	NA	5.3
Oct.	0.2	0	2	*	18	56	NA	5.7
Nov.	1.9	0	3	1	20	49	NA	6.4
Dec.	2.0	T	5	1	26	50	NA	6.6

T - Trace of rain or snow   * - Less than 1   NA - Not Available

Annual averages

Precipitation (in inches)	15
Snow (in inches)	T
Heating degree days	1,204
Cooling degree days	1,339
Days with thunderstorms	6
Days with fog	17
Days above 90°	22
Days below 32°	*
Wet days	35
Days with snow	NA
Days with 1.5 inches or more snow	0

Percent time sky is clear

46.1	44.3	41.6	40.0	36.8	45.3	67.4	72.3	61.3	51.9	55.0	48.4
Jan.	Feb.	March	April	May	June	July	Aug.	Sept.	Oct.	Nov.	Dec.

Louisville, Kentucky

Lat. 38° 11′ N **Lon.** 85° 44′ W **Elev.** 477 ft.

Louisville is on the south bank of the Ohio River. A range of low hills five miles northwest presents a partial barrier to arctic blasts in winter — snow is frequently seen on these hills when there is no snow in the city. The climate of Louisville, while continental, is variable because of the usual paths of high and low pressure systems and the occasional influx of warm, moist air from the Gulf of Mexico. As a whole, winters are moderate and summers quite warm. Thunderstorms are common during spring and summer. Fall is usually the driest season. Relative humidity remains high throughout the summer.

Weather extremes

Most rain in 24 hours:	6.97 in. March 9, 1964
Most rain in a month:	19.17 in. January 1937
Most snow in 24 hours:	15.9 in. Jan. 16 – 17, 1994
Most snow in a month:	28.4 in. January 1978

Temperatures

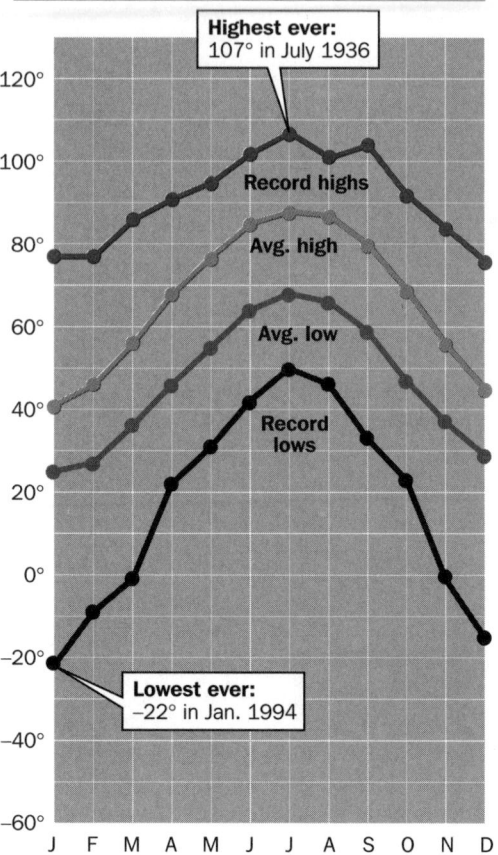

Highest ever: 107° in July 1936

Record highs

Avg. high

Avg. low

Record lows

Lowest ever: −22° in Jan. 1994

J F M A M J J A S O N D

Monthly averages

Month	Avg. precip. (in.)	Avg. snow (in.)	Wet days	Thunder-storm days	Pct. sky is cloudy	% p.m. relative humidity	Dew point	Wind speed (mph)
Jan.	3.4	5	11	1	56	62	24	10.4
Feb.	3.5	4	11	1	52	58	26	12.7
March	4.5	3	13	3	49	52	33	10.4
April	4.0	T	12	4	41	49	42	10.4
May	4.5	T	12	7	35	52	53	8.1
June	3.7	0	10	7	27	53	62	8.1
July	4.2	0	11	8	25	55	66	6.9
Aug.	3.2	0	8	7	22	53	65	6.9
Sept.	3.0	0	8	3	27	53	58	6.9
Oct.	2.6	T	8	2	31	51	47	8.1
Nov.	3.7	1	10	1	45	57	36	9.2
Dec.	3.6	2	11	1	53	62	28	9.2

T - Trace of rain or snow   * - Less than 1   NA - Not Available

Annual averages

Precipitation (in inches)	43.9
Snow (in inches)	17
Heating degree days	4,435
Cooling degree days	1,423
Days with thunderstorms	45
Days with fog	142
Days above 90°	35
Days below 32°	90
Wet days	125
Days with snow	28
Days with 1.5 inches or more snow	7

Percent time sky is clear

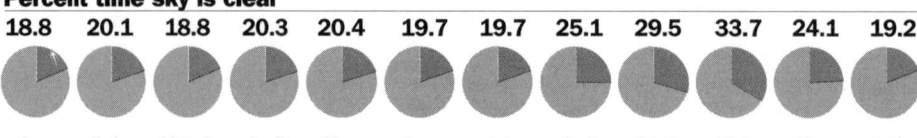

Jan.	Feb.	March	April	May	June	July	Aug.	Sept.	Oct.	Nov.	Dec.
18.8	20.1	18.8	20.3	20.4	19.7	19.7	25.1	29.5	33.7	24.1	19.2

Lubbock, Texas

Lat. 33° 39' N **Lon.** 101° 49' W **Elev.** 3,254 ft.

Lubbock is in a transition area between the desert conditions to the west and humid climates to the east and southeast. The greatest monthly rainfall occurs from May through September when warm, moist tropical air from the Gulf of Mexico may bring afternoon and evening thunderstorms with hail. Snow may occur from late October until April with light accumulation that seldom remains on the ground for more than two or three days. In late winter and spring, winds in excess of 25 mph occasionally occur for periods of 12 hours or more. Spring winds often bring widespread dust for several hours. Summer heat is not considered oppressive; dry air from the west and a usually gentle wind sometimes lower temperatures into the 60s.

Temperatures

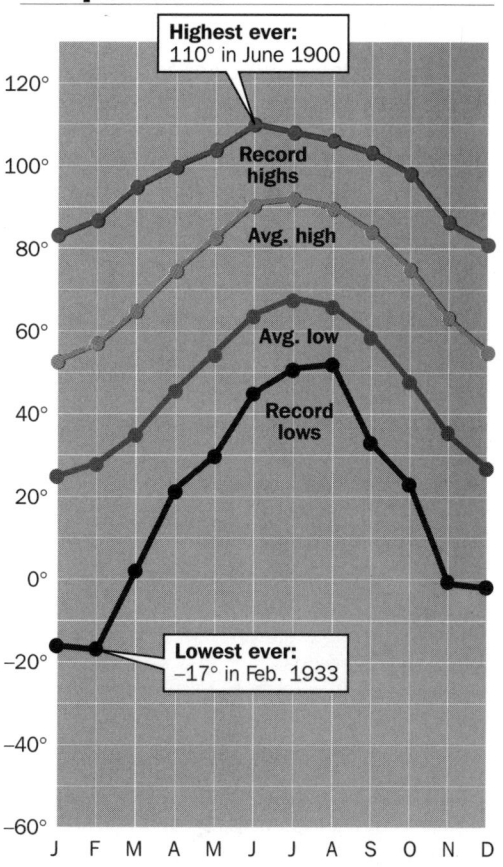

Highest ever: 110° in June 1900

Record highs

Avg. high

Avg. low

Record lows

Lowest ever: −17° in Feb. 1933

Weather extremes

Most rain in 24 hours:	5.83 in. Oct. 18 – 19, 1983
Most rain in a month:	13.93 in. September 1936
Most snow in 24 hours:	16.3 in. Jan. 20 – 21, 1983
Most snow in a month:	25.3 in. January 1983

Monthly averages

Month	Avg. precip. (in.)	Avg. snow (in.)	Wet days	Thunder-storm days	Pct. sky is cloudy	% p.m. relative humidity	Dew point	Wind speed (mph)
Jan.	0.5	2	4	*	30	40	21	11.5
Feb.	0.6	3	4	*	30	39	24	12.7
March	0.8	2	4	2	28	32	29	13.8
April	1.0	T	4	4	24	29	36	15.0
May	2.6	0	7	8	24	33	47	15.0
June	2.8	0	7	9	18	36	57	13.8
July	2.3	0	7	8	15	38	60	12.7
Aug.	2.1	0	7	7	17	42	60	11.5
Sept.	2.3	0	6	5	25	46	56	11.5
Oct.	2.0	T	5	3	21	39	44	11.5
Nov.	0.6	1	3	1	25	38	32	11.5
Dec.	0.5	2	4	*	29	41	24	12.7

T - Trace of rain or snow   * - Less than 1   NA - Not Available

Annual averages

Precipitation (in inches)	18.1
Snow (in inches)	10
Heating degree days	3,488
Cooling degree days	1,760
Days with thunderstorms	47
Days with fog	57
Days above 90°	80
Days below 32°	93
Wet days	62
Days with snow	15
Days with 1.5 inches or more snow	3

Percent time sky is clear

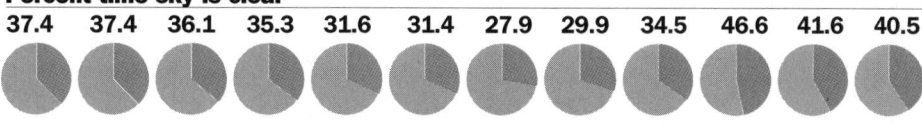

Jan.	Feb.	March	April	May	June	July	Aug.	Sept.	Oct.	Nov.	Dec.
37.4	37.4	36.1	35.3	31.6	31.4	27.9	29.9	34.5	46.6	41.6	40.5

Madison, Wisconsin

Lat. 43° 8' N **Lon.** 89° 20' W **Elev.** 858 ft.

Madison is between Lake Mendota and Lake Monona. The lakes are normally frozen from mid-December to early April. The climate is continental, with large annual temperature ranges and frequent short-term changes. The city is in the path of frequent storms during fall, winter and spring. Outbreaks of arctic air affect the area in winter. Summers have little extreme heat or high humidity. There are no dry and wet seasons, but about 60 percent of the annual precipitation falls from May through September. Precipitation in the cold season is lighter, but lasts longer. The ground is covered with an inch or more of snow 60 percent of the time from December 10 to near February 25.

Temperatures

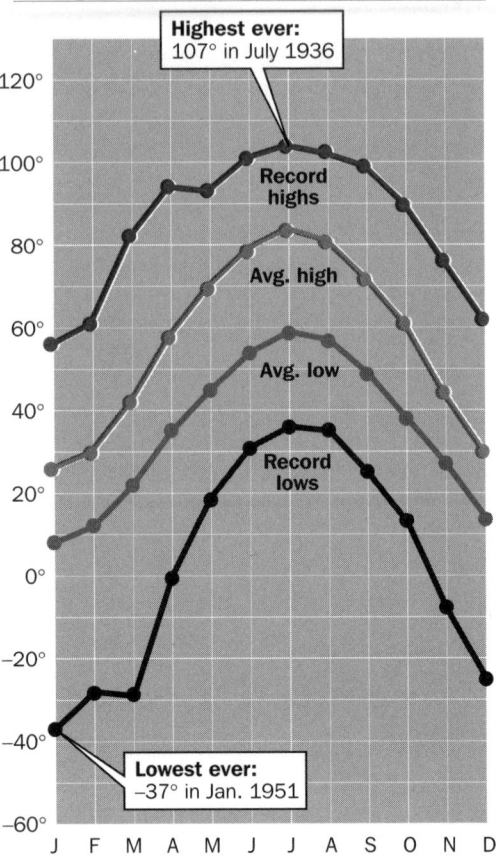

Highest ever: 107° in July 1936

Record highs

Avg. high

Avg. low

Record lows

Lowest ever: −37° in Jan. 1951

Weather extremes

Most rain in 24 hours:	4.96 in. Aug. 8, 1906
Most rain in a month:	10.69 in. September 1915
Most snow in 24 hours:	17.3 in. Dec. 3, 1990
Most snow in a month:	37 in. February 1994

Monthly averages

Month	Avg. precip. (in.)	Avg. snow (in.)	Wet days	Thunder-storm days	Pct. sky is cloudy	% p.m. relative humidity	Dew point	Wind speed (mph)
Jan.	1.1	10	10	*	52	66	10	11.5
Feb.	1.1	7	8	*	50	63	14	11.5
March	2.1	9	11	2	52	59	23	12.7
April	2.9	2	11	4	49	50	34	11.5
May	3.2	T	11	5	42	50	45	10.4
June	3.8	0	11	7	35	51	55	9.2
July	3.9	0	9	7	29	53	61	9.2
Aug.	3.9	0	9	7	31	55	59	9.2
Sept.	3.0	T	9	5	34	55	51	10.4
Oct.	2.3	T	9	2	39	54	40	10.4
Nov.	2.0	4	10	1	54	64	28	10.4
Dec.	1.7	11	10	*	56	69	17	11.5

T - Trace of rain or snow   * - Less than 1   NA - Not Available

Annual averages

Precipitation (in inches)	31.1
Snow (in inches)	42
Heating degree days	7,513
Cooling degree days	603
Days with thunderstorms	40
Days with fog	140
Days above 90°	14
Days below 32°	161
Wet days	118
Days with snow	74
Days with 1.5 inches or more snow	18

Percent time sky is clear

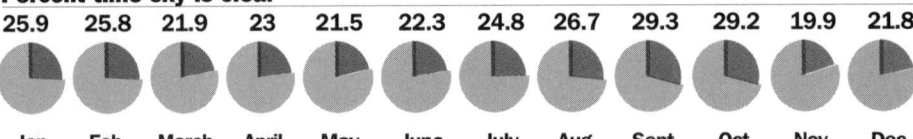

Jan.	Feb.	March	April	May	June	July	Aug.	Sept.	Oct.	Nov.	Dec.
25.9	25.8	21.9	23	21.5	22.3	24.8	26.7	29.3	29.2	19.9	21.8

Marquette, Michigan

Lat. 46° 32' N **Lon.** 87° 33' W **Elev.** 1,415 ft.

Marquette is on the southern shore of Lake Superior in Michigan's Upper Peninsula. The climate is influenced considerably by the lake, the deepest and coldest of the Great Lakes. This cool expanse of water makes long periods of sweltering summer heat a rarity. In winter, cold outbreaks are tempered by the lake if it is unfrozen. However, winds blowing across these relatively warmer waters pick up moisture and cause cloudy weather throughout the winter, as well as frequent periods of light snow. Lake-formed snow showers and squalls are intensified by upslope winds from the north. In nine out of ten winter seasons, 100 inches or more of snow will fall. Extended periods of drought are extremely rare.

Temperatures

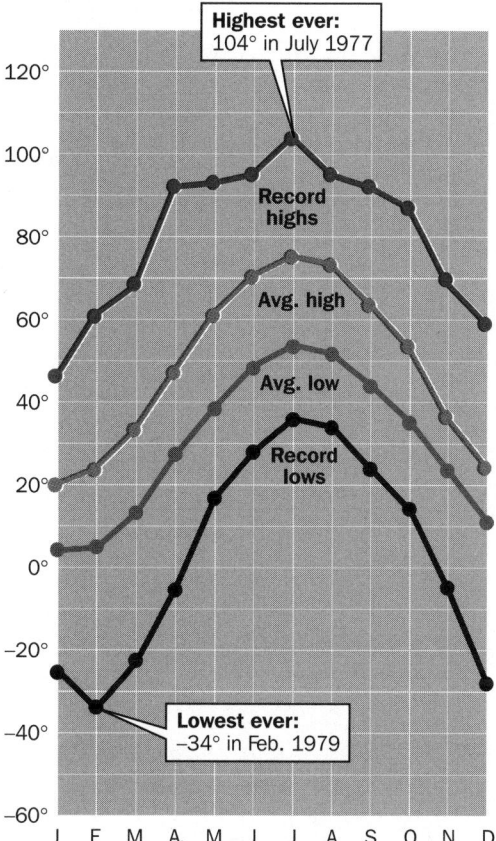

Highest ever: 104° in July 1977

Record highs

Avg. high

Avg. low

Record lows

Lowest ever: -34° in Feb. 1979

Weather extremes

Most rain in 24 hours:	3.66 in. Oct. 4 – 5, 1985
Most rain in a month:	8.59 in. August 1988
Most snow in 24 hours:	25.8 in. Dec. 1 – 2, 1985
Most snow in a month:	82.6 in. December 1981

Monthly averages

Month	Avg. precip. (in.)	Avg. snow (in.)	Wet days	Thunder-storm days	Pct. sky is cloudy	% p.m. relative humidity	Dew point	Wind speed (mph)
Jan.	2.0	26.8	18	0.0	NA	NA	NA	NA
Feb.	1.9	23.0	13	0.1	NA	NA	NA	NA
March	2.8	21.2	15	0.5	NA	NA	NA	NA
April	3.6	8.7	13	1.2	NA	NA	NA	NA
May	4.0	1.4	10	3.3	NA	NA	NA	NA
June	3.9	T	12	5.7	NA	NA	NA	NA
July	3.2	0.0	11	6.3	NA	NA	NA	NA
Aug.	3.3	T	13	5.5	NA	NA	NA	NA
Sep.	3.9	0.2	15	4.3	NA	NA	NA	NA
Oct.	3.3	3.9	16	1.5	NA	NA	NA	NA
Nov.	2.9	16.6	16	0.1	NA	NA	NA	NA
Dec.	2.4	26.8	18	0.0	NA	NA	NA	NA

T - Trace of rain or snow   * - Less than 1   NA - Not Available

Annual averages

Precipitation (in inches)	37.1
Snow (in inches)	129
Heating degree days	9,520
Cooling degree days	148
Days with thunderstorms	28
Days with fog	28
Days above 90°	3
Days below 32°	197
Wet days	168
Days with snow	NA
Days with 1.5 inches or more snow	47

Percent time sky is clear

Data not available.

Medford, Oregon

Lat. 42° 23' N **Lon.** 122° 53' W **Elev.** 1,300 ft.

Marine air makes late fall, winter, and early spring in Medford damp, cloudy, and cool. Late spring, summer, and early fall are warm, dry, and sunny. Most of the annual rainfall comes in winter, but the rain shadow from the Siskiyou Mountains and coastal range results in a relatively light annual total. Snowfall is heavy in the mountains during the winter, providing excellent skiing. Summer heat is accompanied by low humidity, and hot days give way to cool nights as cool air drains down the slopes into the valley. Valley winds are usually very light, prevailing from the north or northwest much of the year. Fog, never lasting more than three days, often fills the lower portion of the valley during winter and early spring.

Temperatures

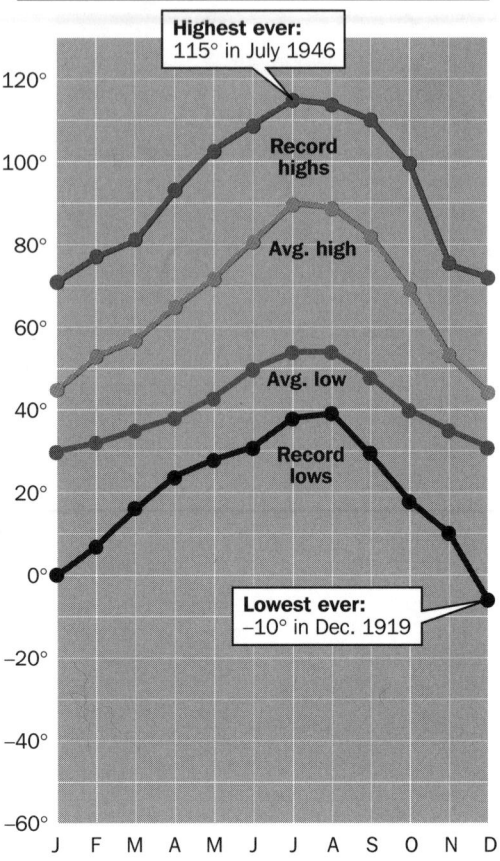

Highest ever: 115° in July 1946
Record highs
Avg. high
Avg. low
Record lows
Lowest ever: −10° in Dec. 1919

Weather extremes

Most rain in 24 hours:	3.75 in. Dec. 21 – 22, 1964
Most rain in a month:	12.72 in. December 1964
Most snow in 24 hours:	11 in. Dec. 11, 1919
Most snow in a month:	22.6 in. January 1930

Monthly averages

Month	Avg. precip. (in.)	Avg. snow (in.)	Wet days	Thunder-storm days	Pct. sky is cloudy	% p.m. relative humidity	Dew point	Wind speed (mph)
Jan.	3.0	3	13	0	67	71	32	4.6
Feb.	2.2	1	11	*	55	58	34	5.8
March	1.8	1	12	*	52	50	35	6.9
April	1.0	T	9	1	44	43	38	8.1
May	1.1	T	8	1	36	39	42	8.1
June	0.7	0	5	2	25	34	46	8.1
July	0.3	0	2	1	9	26	49	9.2
Aug.	0.4	0	3	1	13	27	49	8.1
Sept.	0.8	0	4	1	18	31	45	8.1
Oct.	1.7	T	7	*	35	45	42	5.8
Nov.	2.9	1	13	*	63	67	37	5.8
Dec.	3.4	2	14	*	72	77	33	4.6

T - Trace of rain or snow   * - Less than 1   NA - Not Available

Annual averages

Precipitation (in inches)	19.4
Snow (in inches)	8
Heating degree days	4,649
Cooling degree days	676
Days with thunderstorms	7
Days with fog	100
Days above 90°	52
Days below 32°	86
Wet days	101
Days with snow	13
Days with 1.5 inches or more snow	3

Percent time sky is clear

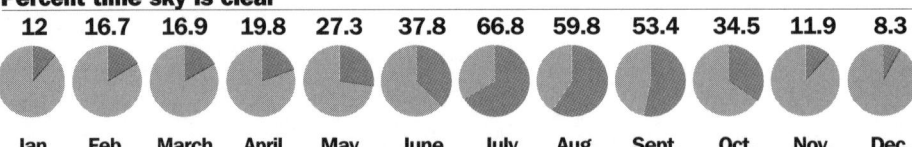

Jan.	Feb.	March	April	May	June	July	Aug.	Sept.	Oct.	Nov.	Dec.
12	16.7	16.9	19.8	27.3	37.8	66.8	59.8	53.4	34.5	11.9	8.3

Memphis, Tennessee

Lat. 35° 3' N **Lon.** 90° 00' W **Elev.** 258 ft.

Memphis is located on the Mississippi River, in the far southwest corner of the state near the Mississippi state border. Its topography varies from a level alluvial area to slightly rolling terrain. Although not in the normal paths of storms coming from the Gulf of Mexico or western Canada, Memphis can be affected by both and has relatively frequent changes in weather. Extremely high or low temperatures, however, are relatively rare. Freezing temperatures occur between November and March. The growing season is about 230 days and sunshine averages slightly over 70 percent of the possible amount during that period. Relative humidity averages about 70 percent for the year.

Temperatures

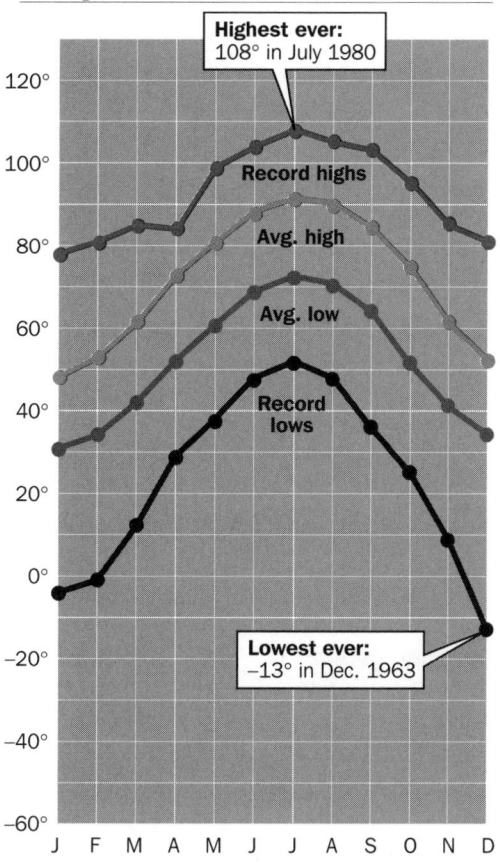

Highest ever: 108° in July 1980

Record highs

Avg. high

Avg. low

Record lows

Lowest ever: −13° in Dec. 1963

Weather extremes

Most rain in 24 hours:	10.48 in. Nov. 20 – 21, 1934
Most rain in a month:	18.16 in. June 1877
Most snow in 24 hours:	18.0 in. March 16–17, 1892
Most snow in a month:	18.5 in. March 1892

Monthly averages

Month	Avg. precip. (in.)	Avg. snow (in.)	Wet days	Thunder- storm days	Pct. sky is cloudy	% p.m. relative humidity	Dew point	Wind speed (mph)
Jan.	4.6	2	10	2	56	63	NA	10.0
Feb.	4.3	1	10	3	52	60	NA	10.1
March	5.4	1	11	5	54	56	NA	10.8
April	5.8	T	10	6	47	53	NA	10.3
May	5.1	T	9	7	42	55	NA	8.8
June	3.6	0	8	7	30	56	NA	7.9
July	4.0	0	9	8	29	57	NA	7.5
Aug.	3.7	0	8	6	25	57	NA	6.9
Sept.	3.6	0	7	3	34	56	NA	7.5
Oct.	2.4	T	6	2	30	51	NA	7.7
Nov.	4.2	T	9	2	45	56	NA	9.1
Dec.	4.9	1	10	2	53	61	NA	9.7

T - Trace of rain or snow   * - Less than 1   NA - Not Available

Annual averages

Precipitation (in inches)	51.6
Snow (in inches)	5
Heating degree days	3,207
Cooling degree days	2,067
Days with thunderstorms	53
Days with fog	10
Days above 90°	66
Days below 32°	56
Wet days	106
Days with snow	NA
Days with 1.5 inches or more snow	2

Percent time sky is clear

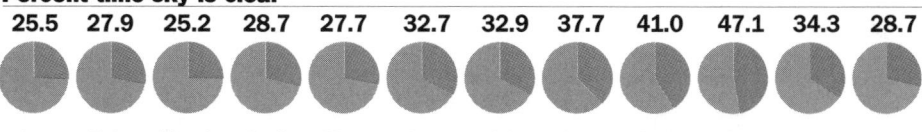

25.5	27.9	25.2	28.7	27.7	32.7	32.9	37.7	41.0	47.1	34.3	28.7
Jan.	Feb.	March	April	May	June	July	Aug.	Sept.	Oct.	Nov.	Dec.

Meridian, Mississippi

Lat. 32° 20' N **Lon.** 88° 45' W **Elev.** 294 ft.

Mild winters and warm summers characterize Meridian, although the hills around Meridian leave it in a valley, where cold air drainage lowers temperatures as much as 10 degrees below surrounding areas. January is usually coldest. Summer temperatures are consistently warm. The widespread rains of winter reach a maximum in March and the driest period is late September and October. Summer thunderstorms occur on one in three days during July and August. Humidities of greater than 90 percent occur nightly every month except for short periods during the autumn and winter when cool continental air is flowing from the north. March is the windiest month, although spring and summer thunderstorms produce high winds.

Temperatures

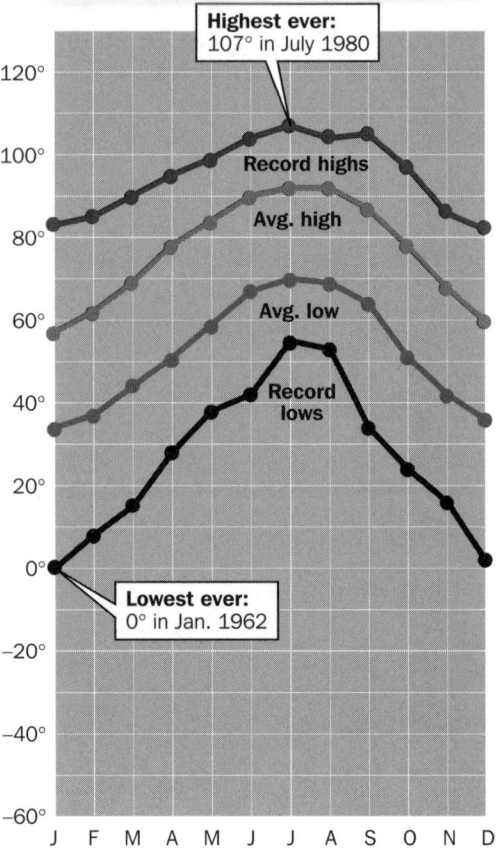

Highest ever: 107° in July 1980

Record highs

Avg. high

Avg. low

Record lows

Lowest ever: 0° in Jan. 1962

Weather extremes

Most rain in 24 hours:	9.23 in. Feb. 15 – 16, 1990
Most rain in a month:	16.82 in. April 1964
Most snow in 24 hours:	15 in. Dec. 31, 1963–Jan. 1, 1964
Most snow in a month:	17.6 in. December 1963

Monthly averages

Month	Avg. precip. (in.)	Avg. snow (in.)	Wet days	Thunder-storm days	Pct. sky is cloudy	% p.m. relative humidity	Dew point	Wind speed (mph)
Jan.	5.0	T	11	2	55	60	NA	7.0
Feb.	4.6	T	9	3	51	56	NA	7.5
March	6.7	T	10	5	49	52	NA	7.9
April	5.4	T	9	6	42	51	NA	7.1
May	4.2	T	9	7	38	55	NA	5.9
June	3.5	0	8	7	31	54	NA	5.1
July	5.3	T	11	12	32	58	NA	4.8
Aug.	3.4	0	9	9	28	57	NA	4.6
Sept.	3.6	0	8	4	36	57	NA	5.3
Oct.	2.6	0	5	2	30	51	NA	5.1
Nov.	3.5	T	8	2	42	54	NA	6.2
Dec.	5.7	T	10	2	50	59	NA	6.9

T - Trace of rain or snow   * - Less than 1   NA - Not Available

Annual averages

Precipitation (in inches)	53.3
Snow (in inches)	1
Heating degree days	2,479
Cooling degree days	2,158
Days with thunderstorms	58
Days with fog	27
Days above 90°	79
Days below 32°	52
Wet days	106
Days with snow	NA
Days with 1.5 inches or more snow	*

Percent time sky is clear

23.9	26.8	27.1	30.7	27.7	27.7	18.4	30	34.7	46.5	34.3	28.4

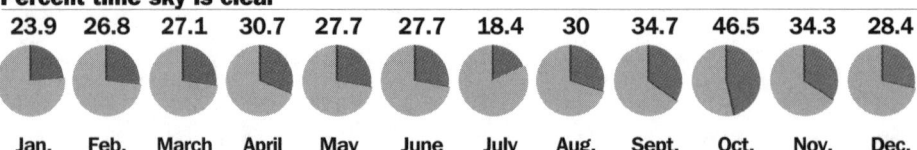

| Jan. | Feb. | March | April | May | June | July | Aug. | Sept. | Oct. | Nov. | Dec. |

Miami, Florida

Lat. 25° 48' N **Lon.** 80° 18' W **Elev.** 12 ft.

Miami sits on Biscayne Bay, an arm of the Atlantic. The bay is protected from open water to the east by the island of Miami Beach, a mile wide and about 10 miles long. The climate is subtropical marine, featuring long, warm summers with abundant rainfall and mild, dry winters. Winds are from the east or southeast about half the time. Hurricanes are a danger, mostly in September and October. The strong marine influence is shown in the narrow daily range of temperature and climate features differing from just a few miles inland: It has one-fourth of the daily highs over 90°F as inland areas. And its lows can be 15 degrees warmer than inland, especially in winter.

Temperatures

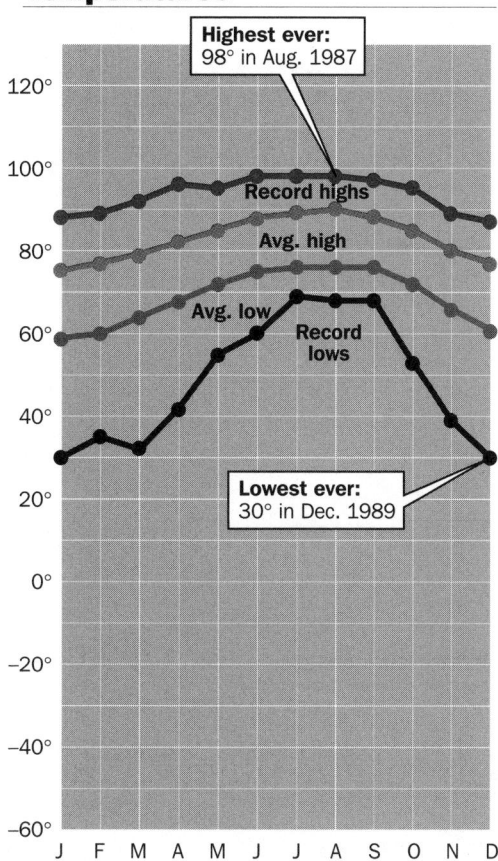

Highest ever: 98° in Aug. 1987

Record highs

Avg. high

Avg. low

Record lows

Lowest ever: 30° in Dec. 1989

Weather extremes

Most rain in 24 hours:	16.21 in. April 24 – 25, 1979
Most rain in a month:	24.4 in. September 1960
Most snow in 24 hours:	none
Most snow in a month:	none

Monthly averages

Month	Avg. precip. (in.)	Avg. snow (in.)	Wet days	Thunder-storm days	Pct. sky is cloudy	% p.m. relative humidity	Dew point	Wind speed (mph)
Jan.	1.9	0	6	1	16	59	57	9.2
Feb.	2.0	0	6	1	16	57	58	11.5
March	2.3	0	6	2	14	57	60	11.5
April	3.0	0	6	3	11	57	63	11.5
May	6.2	0	10	7	15	62	68	10.4
June	8.7	0	15	12	19	68	72	10.4
July	6.1	0	16	15	13	66	73	9.2
Aug.	7.5	0	17	16	12	67	74	9.2
Sept.	8.2	0	17	11	17	69	73	10.4
Oct.	6.6	0	14	4	16	65	69	11.5
Nov.	2.7	0	8	1	14	63	64	12.7
Dec.	1.8	0	7	1	15	60	59	9.2

T - Trace of rain or snow   * - Less than 1   NA - Not Available

Annual averages

Precipitation (in inches)	57.1
Snow (in inches)	0
Heating degree days	175
Cooling degree days	4,234
Days with thunderstorms	74
Days with fog	39
Days above 90°	55
Days below 32°	*
Wet days	128
Days with snow	0
Days with 1.5 inches or more snow	0

Percent time sky is clear

21.1	20.9	18.8	18.7	12.6	7	5.2	4.7	4	11.8	16.4	20

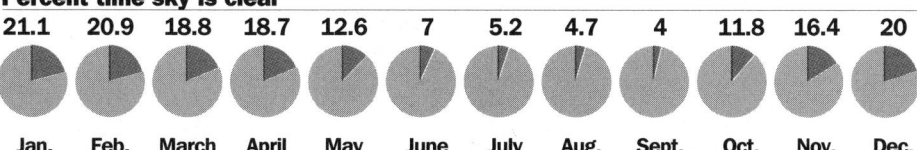

| Jan. | Feb. | March | April | May | June | July | Aug. | Sept. | Oct. | Nov. | Dec. |

Midland-Odessa, Texas

Lat. 31° 57' N **Lon.** 102° 11' W **Elev.** 2,857 ft.

The Midland-Odessa climate is typical of a semiarid region. Most precipitation comes as very violent spring and early summer thunderstorms. These can bring excessive rainfall over limited areas and sometimes hail. Due to the flat countryside, flooding occurs, but is short. Tornadoes are occasionally sighted. In late winter and early spring, blowing dust occurs frequently. Summer afternoon temperatures are frequently above 90°F, but very low humidities help make them relatively comfortable. The climate is generally quite pleasant overall, with disagreeable weather concentrated in late winter and spring.

Temperatures

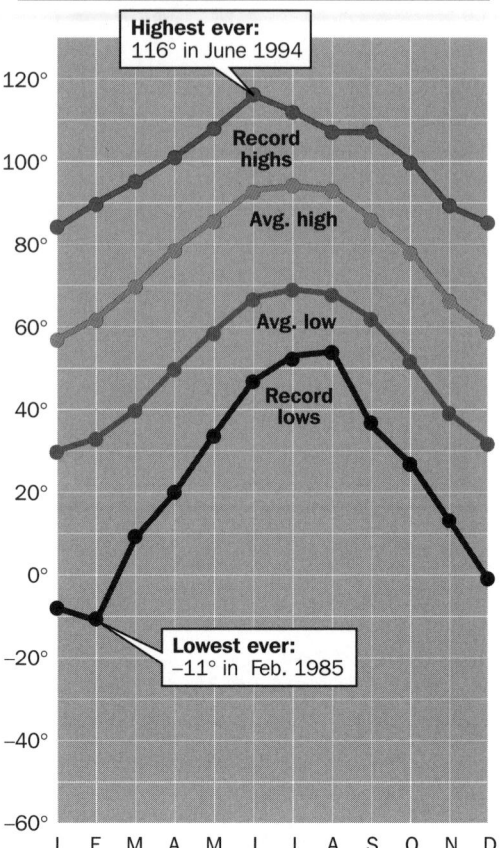

Highest ever: 116° in June 1994

Record highs

Avg. high

Avg. low

Record lows

Lowest ever: −11° in Feb. 1985

Weather extremes

Most rain in 24 hours:	5.99 in.	July 21 – 22, 1961
Most rain in a month:	9.7 in.	September 1980
Most snow in 24 hours:	6.8 in.	Jan. 23 – 24, 1974
Most snow in a month:	9 in.	January 1985

Monthly averages

Month	Avg. precip. (in.)	Avg. snow (in.)	Wet days	Thunder-storm days	Pct. sky is cloudy	% p.m. relative humidity	Dew point	Wind speed (mph)
Jan.	0.5	2	4	*	32	38	25	9.2
Feb.	0.6	1	4	*	30	35	28	10.4
March	0.5	T	3	1	26	27	30	12.7
April	0.8	T	3	3	25	27	38	12.7
May	2.1	0	6	7	23	30	48	13.8
June	1.5	0	5	6	16	32	57	12.7
July	1.8	0	5	6	14	34	59	11.5
Aug.	1.6	0	6	6	14	34	59	10.4
Sept.	2.2	0	6	4	21	39	56	10.4
Oct.	1.8	T	5	3	21	38	47	11.5
Nov.	0.6	1	3	1	24	35	34	10.4
Dec.	0.5	1	3	*	28	36	27	10.4

T - Trace of rain or snow   * - Less than 1   NA - Not Available

Annual averages

Precipitation (in inches)	14.3
Snow (in inches)	4
Heating degree days	2,681
Cooling degree days	2,212
Days with thunderstorms	37
Days with fog	47
Days above 90°	103
Days below 32°	63
Wet days	53
Days with snow	6
Days with 1.5 inches or more snow	1

Percent time sky is clear

Jan.	Feb.	March	April	May	June	July	Aug.	Sept.	Oct.	Nov.	Dec.
38.6	39.6	40.2	39.3	36.6	37.6	33.6	34.5	41.4	49.8	47.8	43.4

Milwaukee, Wisconsin

Lat. 42° 57' N **Lon.** 87° 54' W **Elev.** 672 ft.

Milwaukee possesses a continental climate characterized by a wide range of temperatures between summer and winter. The Great Lakes, especially Lake Michigan, significantly affect the local climate. Initially frigid air masses are often tempered by traveling over the lakes during the winter, while in summer the lakes serve as a cooling influence. Repeated incursions of arctic air masses from over the lakes will result in several days of bitterly cold weather during the winter, and severe winter storms sometimes produce in excess of 10 inches of snow. In summer, high temperatures and humidity occasionally develop. Winter rain and snow are usually of long duration and low intensity, but warm-season precipitation falls mostly as intense showers.

Temperatures

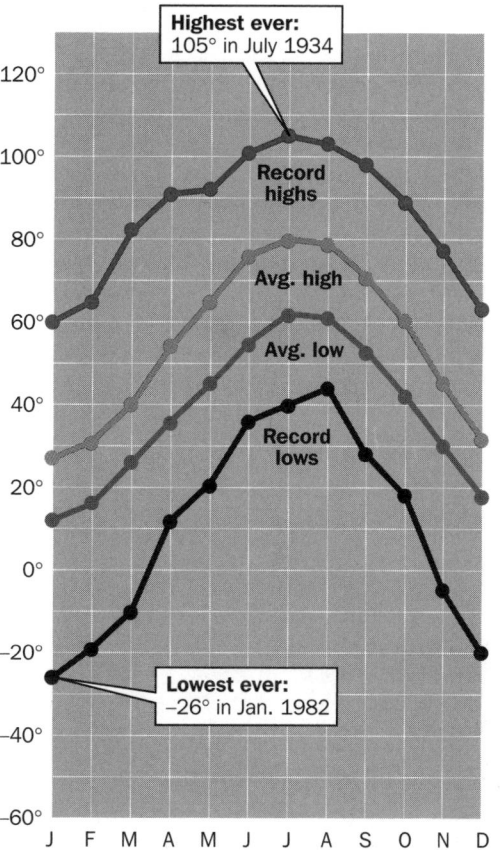

Highest ever: 105° in July 1934

Record highs

Avg. high

Avg. low

Record lows

Lowest ever: −26° in Jan. 1982

Weather extremes

Most rain in 24 hours:	6.84 in. Aug. 6, 1986
Most rain in a month:	10.02 in. June 1917
Most snow in 24 hours:	20.3 in. Feb. 4 – 5, 1924
Most snow in a month:	52.6 in. January 1918

Monthly averages

Month	Avg. precip. (in.)	Avg. snow (in.)	Wet days	Thunder-storm days	Pct. sky is cloudy	% p.m. relative humidity	Dew point	Wind speed (mph)
Jan.	1.6	13	11	*	53	68	13	12.7
Feb.	1.4	10	10	*	52	66	16	12.7
March	2.6	9	12	2	52	64	24	12.7
April	3.3	2	12	4	49	58	34	13.8
May	2.9	T	11	4	40	58	44	12.7
June	3.4	0	11	6	33	58	54	11.5
July	3.6	0	10	6	28	59	61	10.4
Aug.	3.4	0	9	6	29	62	61	10.4
Sept.	2.9	0	9	4	33	61	53	11.5
Oct.	2.3	T	9	2	39	61	42	11.5
Nov.	2.3	3	10	1	54	66	30	12.7
Dec.	2.2	11	12	*	58	70	19	12.7

T - Trace of rain or snow   * - Less than 1   NA - Not Available

Annual averages

Precipitation (in inches)	32.0
Snow (in inches)	49
Heating degree days	7,207
Cooling degree days	589
Days with thunderstorms	35
Days with fog	133
Days above 90°	10
Days below 32°	141
Wet days	126
Days with snow	75
Days with 1.5 inches or more snow	20

Percent time sky is clear

24.9	24.4	21.1	23.1	24.3	24.7	27.6	28.9	29.8	29.2	19.8	21.2
Jan.	Feb.	March	April	May	June	July	Aug.	Sept.	Oct.	Nov.	Dec.

Minneapolis–St. Paul, Minn.

Lat. 44° 53' N **Lon.** 93° 13' W **Elev.** 834 ft.

The Twin Cities of Minneapolis and St. Paul are at the confluence of the Mississippi and Minnesota rivers. The gently rolling terrain has numerous lakes. The largest, at 15,000 acres, is Lake Minnetonka, about 15 miles west. The climate is predominantly continental. Seasonal temperature variations are quite large. The Twin Cities are at the northern edge of the influx of Gulf of Mexico moisture. Severe storms such as blizzards, freezing rain, tornadoes, wind and hail occur. Winter recreation is excellent because of the abundant dry snow, averaging a depth of about 8 inches from Christmas to early March. Floods occur along the rivers due to spring snow melt, excessive rainfall, or both. Flood stage at St. Paul can be expected about once every eight years.

Temperatures

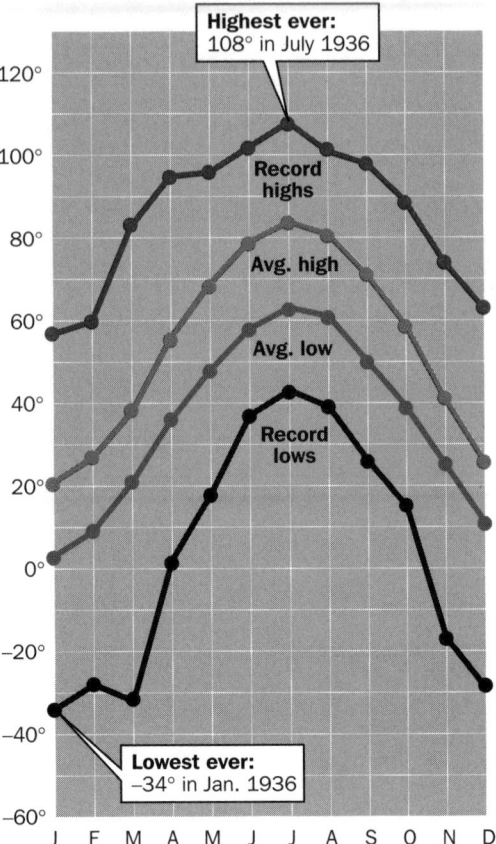

Highest ever:
108° in July 1936

Record highs

Avg. high

Avg. low

Record lows

Lowest ever:
–34° in Jan. 1936

Weather extremes

Most rain in 24 hours:	10.00 in. July 23 – 24, 1987
Most rain in a month:	17.80 in. July 1987
Most snow in 24 hours:	21.0 in. Oct. 31–Nov. 1,1981
Most snow in a month:	46.9 in. November 1991

Monthly averages

Month	Avg. precip. (in.)	Avg. snow (in.)	Wet days	Thunder-storm days	Pct. sky is cloudy	% p.m. relative humidity	Dew point	Wind speed (mph)
Jan.	0.8	11	9	*	46	64	5	13.8
Feb.	0.8	9	7	*	44	62	10	13.8
March	1.9	12	10	1	49	58	20	13.8
April	2.2	3	10	3	46	48	32	13.8
May	3.1	T	11	5	39	47	43	11.5
June	4.0	0	11	7	33	50	55	10.4
July	3.8	0	10	7	24	50	60	10.4
Aug.	3.6	0	10	7	28	52	59	10.4
Sept.	2.5	T	9	4	33	53	50	11.5
Oct.	1.9	T	8	2	38	52	38	12.7
Nov.	1.4	7	8	1	52	62	25	13.8
Dec.	1.0	10	10	*	54	68	12	12.7

T - Trace of rain or snow   * - Less than 1   NA - Not Available

Annual averages

Precipitation (in inches)	27.1
Snow (in inches)	52
Heating degree days	7,936
Cooling degree days	736
Days with thunderstorms	37
Days with fog	96
Days above 90°	16
Days below 32°	156
Wet days	113
Days with snow	80
Days with 1.5 inches or more snow	21

Percent time sky is clear

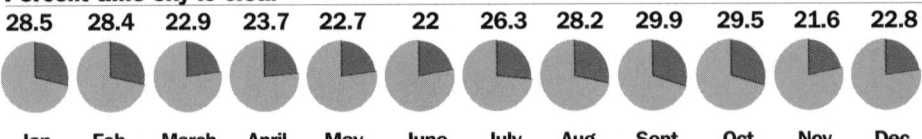

28.5	28.4	22.9	23.7	22.7	22	26.3	28.2	29.9	29.5	21.6	22.8
Jan.	Feb.	March	April	May	June	July	Aug.	Sept.	Oct.	Nov.	Dec.

Missoula, Montana

Lat. 46° 55' N **Lon.** 114° 5' W **Elev.** 3,190 ft.

Missoula is in the heart of the Montana Rocky Mountains, in the extreme north Bitterroot River Valley. It is just east of the confluence of the Bitterroot and Clark Fork rivers. The Bitterroot Range affects Missoula's climate since air passing over the range loses its moisture. The spring is cool, with almost daily showers during May and June. Summer is dry with moderate temperatures and cool nights. In the winter, the Continental Divide to the east shields Missoula from many of the cold waves sweeping down from Canada over eastern Montana. However, Missoula experiences "Hell Gate Blizzards" when cold air is funneled to the city through Hell Gate, the mouth of the Clark Fork River canyon at Missoula. Prolonged cold spells may occur.

Temperatures

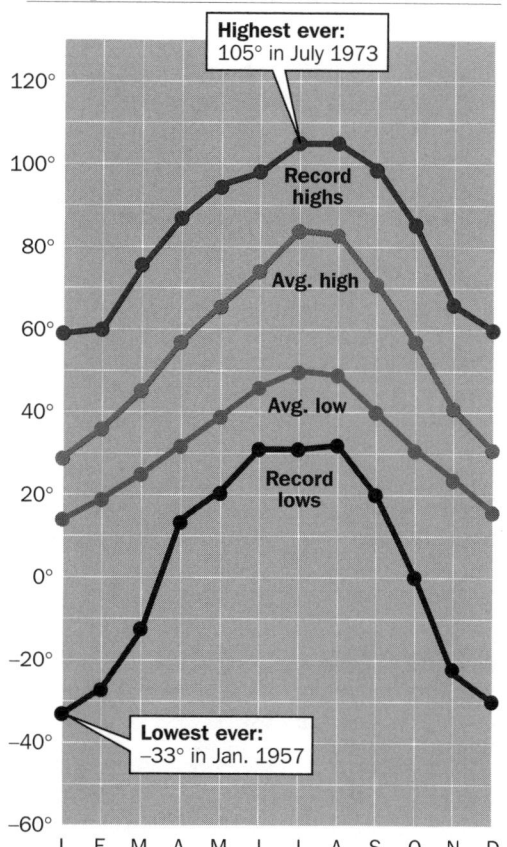

Highest ever: 105° in July 1973

Record highs

Avg. high

Avg. low

Record lows

Lowest ever: −33° in Jan. 1957

Weather extremes

Most rain in 24 hours:	2.23 in. Nov. 5, 1927
Most rain in a month:	7.38 in. May 1980
Most snow in 24 hours:	22.8 in. Feb. 12, 1936
Most snow in a month:	43.5 in. February 1936

Monthly averages

Month	Avg. precip. (in.)	Avg. snow (in.)	Wet days	Thunder-storm days	Pct. sky is cloudy	% p.m. relative humidity	Dew point	Wind speed (mph)
Jan.	1.2	13	14	*	67	76	16	9.2
Feb.	0.8	8	11	*	61	67	21	6.9
March	0.9	6	12	*	54	52	24	8.1
April	1.0	2	10	1	48	41	29	9.2
May	1.8	1	12	3	43	42	37	9.2
June	1.8	T	11	5	35	42	44	9.2
July	0.9	0	7	6	16	30	45	9.2
Aug.	1.0	0	8	6	21	31	44	9.2
Sept.	1.1	T	7	2	30	38	39	8.1
Oct.	0.8	1	8	*	42	50	33	8.1
Nov.	0.9	6	11	*	61	71	26	6.9
Dec.	1.1	11	13	0	68	79	19	8.1

T - Trace of rain or snow   * - Less than 1   NA - Not Available

Annual averages

Precipitation (in inches)	13.4
Snow (in inches)	48
Heating degree days	7,779
Cooling degree days	259
Days with thunderstorms	23
Days with fog	68
Days above 90°	21
Days below 32°	183
Wet days	124
Days with snow	100
Days with 1.5 inches or more snow	19

Percent time sky is clear

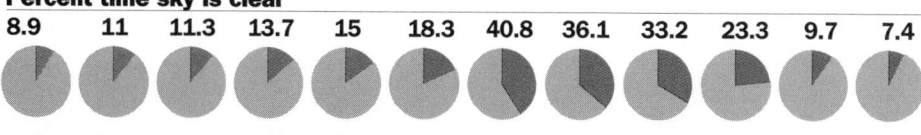

Jan.	Feb.	March	April	May	June	July	Aug.	Sept.	Oct.	Nov.	Dec.
8.9	11	11.3	13.7	15	18.3	40.8	36.1	33.2	23.3	9.7	7.4

Mobile, Alabama

Lat. 30° 41′ N **Lon.** 88° 15′ W **Elev.** 211 ft.

Mobile, at the head of Mobile Bay and 30 miles from the Gulf of Mexico, is considerably affected by the Gulf. Summers are consistently warm, reaching the high 80s or low 90s before noon, but temperatures are checked by sea breezes. Winters are usually mild except for occasional cold air lasting about three days. January is the coldest month of the year. The average first occurrence of 32°F in the fall is November 26 and the average last occurrence in the spring is February 27. Yearly rainfall is among the US's highest, but it usually falls as showers. Long periods of continuous rain are rare. Although there may be a thunderstorm every other day in July and August, they're usually not violent and seldom produce hail. The area is subject to hurricanes.

Temperatures

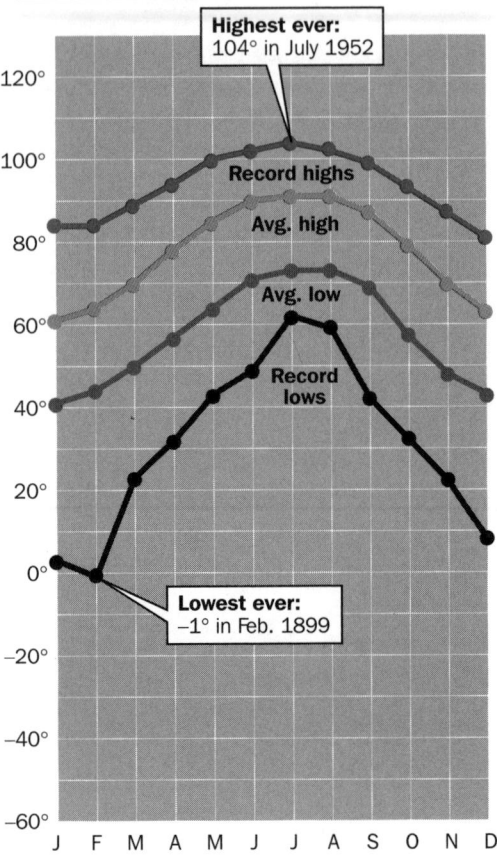

Highest ever: 104° in July 1952

Record highs

Avg. high

Avg. low

Record lows

Lowest ever: −1° in Feb. 1899

Weather extremes

Most rain in 24 hours:	13.36 in. April 13, 1955
Most rain in a month:	26.67 in. June 1900
Most snow in 24 hours:	6.0 in. Feb. 14 – 15, 1895
Most snow in a month:	6.0 in. February 1895

Monthly averages

Month	Avg. precip. (in.)	Avg. snow (in.)	Wet days	Thunder- storm days	Pct. sky is cloudy	% p.m. relative humidity	Dew point	Wind speed (mph)
Jan.	4.5	T	11	2	46	58	41	12.7
Feb.	5.3	T	10	2	42	55	43	12.7
March	6.7	T	10	5	40	53	48	11.5
April	5.2	T	7	5	30	52	56	11.5
May	5.4	0	8	7	23	53	63	10.4
June	5.4	0	11	12	18	57	69	9.2
July	7.7	0	16	18	21	63	72	8.1
Aug.	7.0	0	14	15	18	63	72	8.1
Sept.	6.4	0	10	7	23	59	68	8.1
Oct.	2.8	0	6	2	21	51	57	8.1
Nov.	3.9	T	8	2	30	54	49	11.5
Dec.	5.4	T	10	2	43	58	43	12.7

T - Trace of rain or snow   * - Less than 1   NA - Not Available

Annual averages

Precipitation (in inches)	65.6
Snow (in inches)	T
Heating degree days	1,657
Cooling degree days	2,627
Days with thunderstorms	79
Days with fog	150
Days above 90°	76
Days below 32°	86
Wet days	121
Days with snow	*
Days with 1.5 inches or more snow	*

Percent time sky is clear

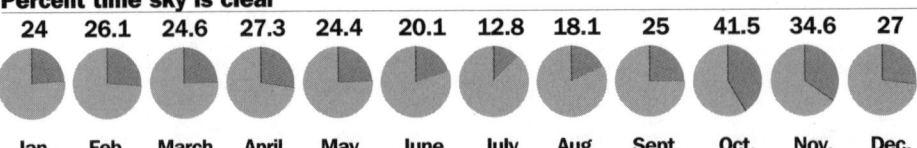

24	26.1	24.6	27.3	24.4	20.1	12.8	18.1	25	41.5	34.6	27
Jan.	Feb.	March	April	May	June	July	Aug.	Sept.	Oct.	Nov.	Dec.

Moline, Illinois

Lat. 41° 27' N **Lon.** 90° 30' W **Elev.** 582 ft.

Moline, located in the heart of the Corn Belt, is close to the Mississippi River. The area has a temperate continental climate, with a wide temperature range throughout the year. There are some intensely hot, unusually humid periods in summer and severely cold periods in winter. Freezing has occurred as late as late May and as early as late September. Precipitation is usually well distributed throughout the year, with the greatest amounts falling during the growing season. Damaging droughts are rare. Substantial weather changes frequently occur at three- or four-day intervals as a result of proximity to some of the most important storm tracks.

Temperatures

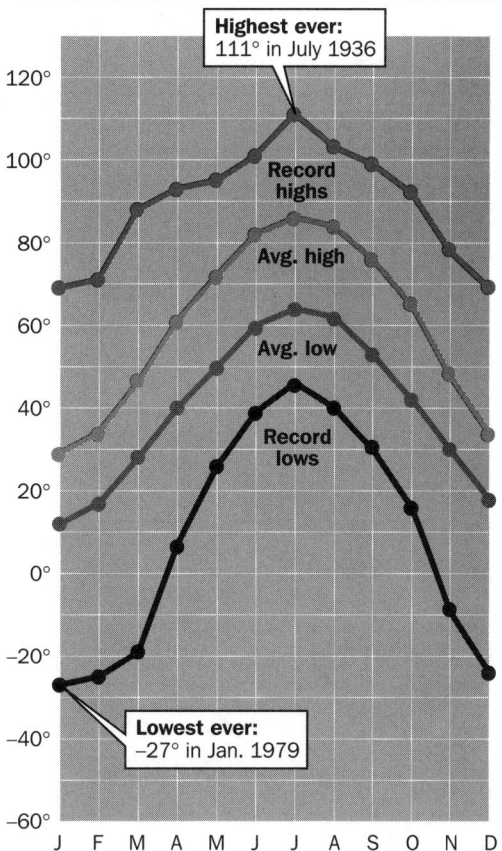

Highest ever: 111° in July 1936

Record highs

Avg. high

Avg. low

Record lows

Lowest ever: −27° in Jan. 1979

Weather extremes

Most rain in 24 hours:	6.29 in. Sept. 12 – 13, 1961
Most rain in a month:	15.23 in. August 1987
Most snow in 24 hours:	16.4 in. Jan. 3, 1971
Most snow in a month:	26.7 in. January 1979

Monthly averages

Month	Avg. precip. (in.)	Avg. snow (in.)	Wet days	Thunder-storm days	Pct. sky is cloudy	% p.m. relative humidity	Dew point	Wind speed (mph)
Jan.	1.5	8	9	*	49	65	13	15.0
Feb.	1.4	7	8	*	47	62	17	13.8
March	2.9	6	11	2	50	57	26	15.0
April	3.8	1	11	5	44	50	37	15.0
May	4.1	T	12	7	36	49	48	12.7
June	4.4	0	10	8	29	50	58	11.5
July	4.5	0	10	8	24	53	64	9.2
Aug.	4.0	0	9	7	26	54	63	9.2
Sept.	3.5	0	8	5	29	52	54	10.4
Oct.	2.7	T	8	2	33	49	42	11.5
Nov.	2.2	3	8	1	48	59	30	15.0
Dec.	2.0	8	9	1	53	67	19	13.8

T - Trace of rain or snow   * - Less than 1   NA - Not Available

Annual averages

Precipitation (in inches)	37.1
Snow (in inches)	33
Heating degree days	6,481
Cooling degree days	970
Days with thunderstorms	46
Days with fog	144
Days above 90°	23
Days below 32°	135
Wet days	113
Days with snow	54
Days with 1.5 inches or more snow	15

Percent time sky is clear

Jan.	Feb.	March	April	May	June	July	Aug.	Sept.	Oct.	Nov.	Dec.
27.5	28.9	22.9	25	24.8	24.4	27.9	30.1	35.2	36	26	25.6

Montgomery, Alabama
Lat. 32° 18' N **Lon.** 86° 24' W **Elev.** 221 ft.

Montgomery has no local topographic features influencing weather and climate. From June through September, temperature and humidity show little daily change, but from December through February there are frequent shifts between mild, moist air from the Gulf of Mexico and dry, cool continental air. From late June through early August, there are apt to be considerable differences in daily rainfall in different parts of the area. In late August and September, summer conditions persist, but local thunderstorms become less frequent. All types and intensities of rain may occur at any time from December through early April making floods frequent during this period. During the spring, late summer and early autumn, droughts sometimes occur.

Temperatures

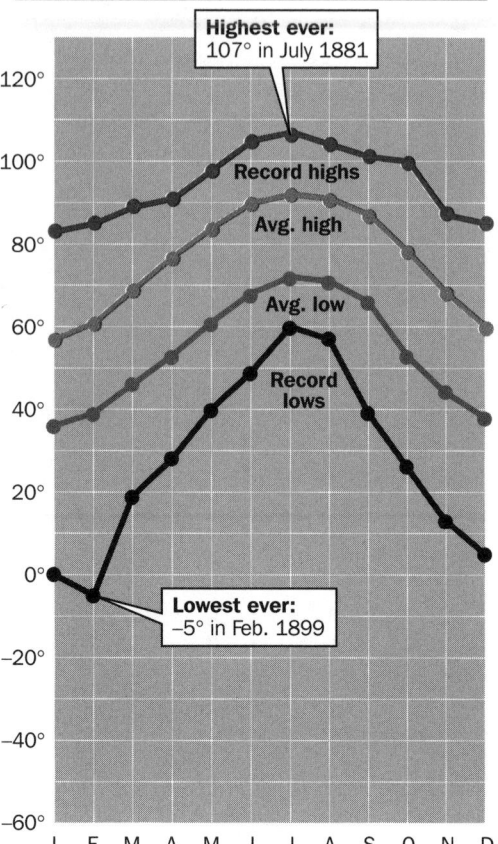

Highest ever: 107° in July 1881
Record highs
Avg. high
Avg. low
Record lows
Lowest ever: −5° in Feb. 1899

Weather extremes

Most rain in 24 hours:	9.70 in. Jan. 13, 1892
Most rain in a month:	20.10 in. November 1948
Most snow in 24 hours:	3.8 in. March 13, 1993
Most snow in a month:	11.0 in. December 1886

Monthly averages

Month	Avg. precip. (in.)	Avg. snow (in.)	Wet days	Thunder- storm days	Pct. sky is cloudy	% p.m. relative humidity	Dew point	Wind speed (mph)
Jan.	4.3	T	10	2	46	54	36	10.4
Feb.	5.0	T	9	2	43	51	38	10.4
March	6.1	T	10	5	40	48	44	10.4
April	4.5	T	8	5	30	46	52	9.2
May	3.9	0	8	6	26	50	61	6.9
June	3.8	0	9	9	22	52	67	6.9
July	5.1	0	12	12	24	57	71	6.9
Aug.	3.4	0	9	9	20	55	70	5.8
Sept.	4.5	0	8	4	27	53	65	8.1
Oct.	2.4	0	6	1	24	47	54	6.9
Nov.	3.9	T	8	2	33	49	45	9.2
Dec.	4.9	T	10	2	43	54	39	9.2

T - Trace of rain or snow   * - Less than 1   NA - Not Available

Annual averages

Precipitation (in inches)	51.8
Snow (in inches)	T
Heating degree days	2,198
Cooling degree days	2,334
Days with thunderstorms	59
Days with fog	164
Days above 90°	81
Days below 32°	38
Wet days	107
Days with snow	*
Days with 1.5 inches or more snow	*

Percent time sky is clear

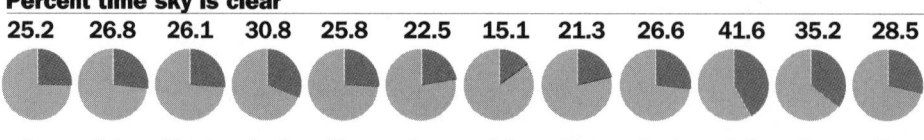

Jan.	Feb.	March	April	May	June	July	Aug.	Sept.	Oct.	Nov.	Dec.
25.2	26.8	26.1	30.8	25.8	22.5	15.1	21.3	26.6	41.6	35.2	28.5

Nashville, Tennessee

Lat. 36° 7' N **Lon.** 86° 41' W **Elev.** 580 ft.

Nashville temperatures are moderate, with great extremes of either heat or cold rarely occurring, yet there are frequent and ample changes to give variety. The average first occurrence of 32°F in the fall is October 29 and the average last occurrence in the spring is April 5. The average relative humidity here is moderate compared with the general conditions east of the Mississippi River and south of the Ohio. Nashville is not in the most frequented path of general storms that cross the country. However, it is in the zone of moderate frequency of thunderstorms. The thunderstorm season usually begins in the later part of March and continues through September.

Temperatures

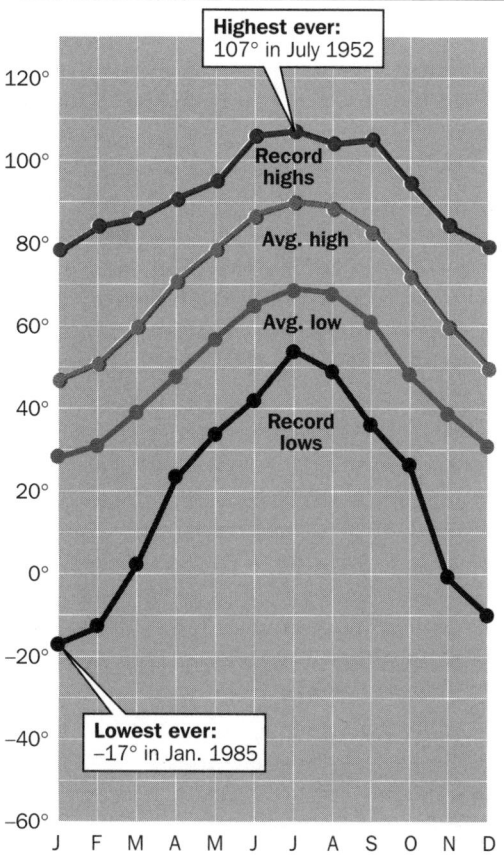

Highest ever: 107° in July 1952
Record highs
Avg. high
Avg. low
Record lows
Lowest ever: −17° in Jan. 1985

Weather extremes

Most rain in 24 hours:	6.68 in. Sep. 13 – 14, 1979
Most rain in a month:	14.75 in. January 1937
Most snow in 24 hours:	17.0 in. March 17, 1892
Most snow in a month:	21.5 in. March 1892

Monthly averages

Month	Avg. precip. (in.)	Avg. snow (in.)	Wet days	Thunder-storm days	Pct. sky is cloudy	% p.m. relative humidity	Dew point	Wind speed (mph)
Jan.	4.4	4	11	1	54	61	28	10.4
Feb.	4.2	3	11	2	51	57	31	10.4
March	5.0	1	12	4	47	51	37	10.4
April	4.1	T	11	5	38	48	46	10.4
May	4.6	0	11	7	32	52	56	8.1
June	3.7	0	9	8	24	52	64	6.9
July	3.8	0	10	10	23	54	68	6.9
Aug.	3.3	0	8	8	21	53	67	6.9
Sept.	3.2	0	8	4	27	52	61	6.9
Oct.	2.6	T	7	2	29	49	49	8.1
Nov.	3.9	1	10	2	42	55	39	9.2
Dec.	4.6	1	11	1	50	59	32	9.2

T - Trace of rain or snow   * - Less than 1   NA - Not Available

Annual averages

Precipitation (in inches)	47.4
Snow (in inches)	11
Heating degree days	3,691
Cooling degree days	1,718
Days with thunderstorms	54
Days with fog	149
Days above 90°	51
Days below 32°	76
Wet days	119
Days with snow	14
Days with 1.5 inches or more snow	4

Percent time sky is clear

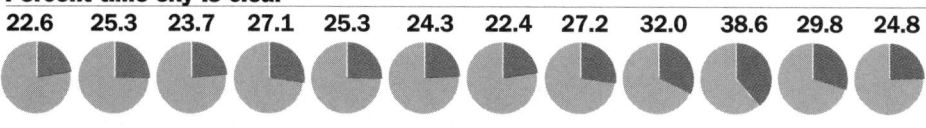

22.6	25.3	23.7	27.1	25.3	24.3	22.4	27.2	32.0	38.6	29.8	24.8
Jan.	Feb.	March	April	May	June	July	Aug.	Sept.	Oct.	Nov.	Dec.

Newark, New Jersey

Lat. 40° 42' N **Lon.** 74° 10' W **Elev.** 7 ft.

Newark is flat and rather marshy. Ridges rise from 200 to 600 feet, at 5 to 7 miles north and northeast. All winds from that direction are downslope and produce a drying effect. Periods of very hot weather are often associated with a west-southwestly air flow. Temperature falls of 5 to 15 degrees, depending on the season, are not uncommon when the wind shifts back from southwesterly to southeasterly. Showers, typical of the fall and winter, generally last for a period of two days and commonly produce a few inches of precipitation. Storms producing 4 inches or more of snow occur from two to five times a winter; but snowstorms and the duration of snow cover increase dramatically within a few miles west.

Temperatures

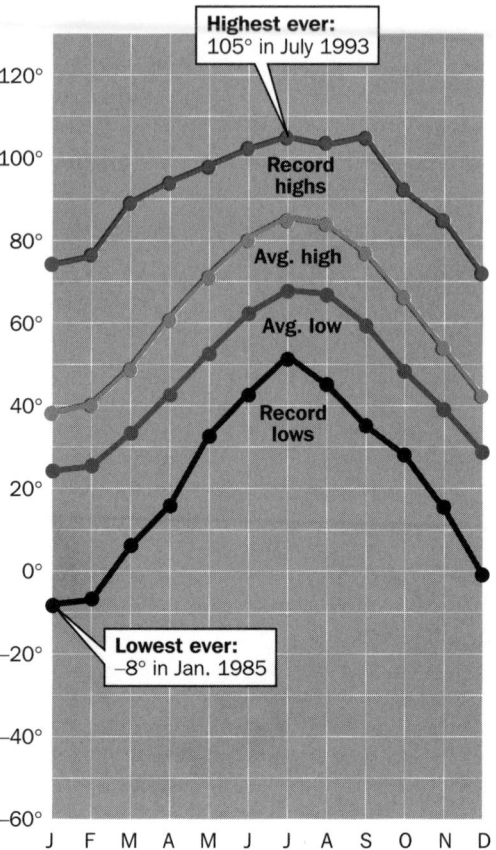

Highest ever: 105° in July 1993

Record highs

Avg. high

Avg. low

Record lows

Lowest ever: −8° in Jan. 1985

Weather extremes

Most rain in 24 hours:	15.0 in. Aug. 5, 1843
Most rain in a month:	22.48 in. August 1843
Most snow in 24 hours:	26.0 in. Dec. 26 – 27, 1947
Most snow in a month:	33.4 in. February 1994

Monthly averages

Month	Avg. precip. (in.)	Avg. snow (in.)	Wet days	Thunder-storm days	Pct. sky is cloudy	% p.m. relative humidity	Dew point	Wind speed (mph)
Jan.	3.1	7.6	11	*	50	58	NA	11.2
Feb.	3.1	7.8	10	*	48	54	NA	11.5
March	4.2	4.6	11	1	46	50	NA	11.9
April	3.6	T	11	2	46	48	NA	11.2
May	3.6	T	12	4	45	51	NA	10.0
June	2.9	0	10	5	41	51	NA	9.5
July	3.9	0	10	6	40	52	NA	8.9
Aug.	4.3	0	10	5	38	53	NA	8.7
Sept.	3.7	0	8	2	38	55	NA	9.0
Oct.	3.1	T	8	1	38	53	NA	9.4
Nov.	3.6	0.5	10	*	47	56	NA	10.2
Dec.	3.4	5.5	11	*	49	59	NA	10.8

T - Trace of rain or snow   * - Less than 1   NA - Not Available

Annual averages

Precipitation (in inches)	42.3
Snow (in inches)	27
Heating degree days	4,972
Cooling degree days	1,091
Days with thunderstorms	26
Days with fog	150
Days above 90°	23
Days below 32°	86
Wet days	122
Days with snow	NA
Days with 1.5 inches or more snow	7

Percent time sky is clear

Jan.	Feb.	March	April	May	June	July	Aug.	Sept.	Oct.	Nov.	Dec.
25.2	26.1	25.8	24.3	20.3	22.7	21.0	25.2	32.0	34.8	25.0	25.5

New Orleans, Louisiana

Lat. 29° 59' N **Lon.** 90° 15' W **Elev.** 4 ft.

The New Orleans area is virtually surrounded by water — rivers, lakes, bayous and marshy delta land. And with elevations ranging within a few feet above or below sea level, a massive levee system is needed to protect against flooding. Storm runoff must be pumped into surrounding lakes and bayous. The climate is humid, with the water and proximity to the Gulf of Mexico moderating temperatures and the ranges between extremes. Almost daily afternoon thunderstorms in summer keep temperatures from rising much above 90°F. In winter the area alternates between warm tropical air flows and cold continental air masses, but cold spells seldom last more than three to four days. Hurricanes have caused serious damage to the area.

Temperatures

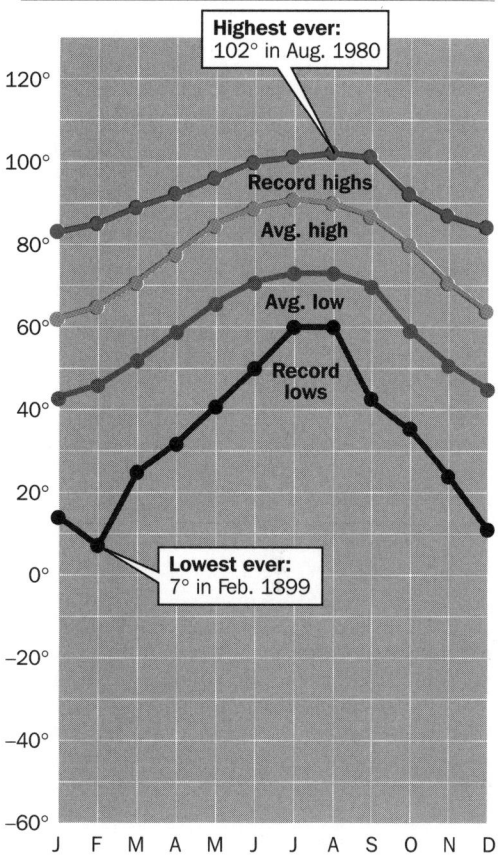

Weather extremes

Most rain in 24 hours:	14.01 in. April 15 – 16, 1927
Most rain in a month:	25.11 in. October 1937
Most snow in 24 hours:	8.2 in. Feb. 14 – 15, 1895
Most snow in a month:	8.2 in. February 1895

Monthly averages

Month	Avg. precip. (in.)	Avg. snow (in.)	Wet days	Thunder-storm days	Pct. sky is cloudy	% p.m. relative humidity	Dew point	Wind speed (mph)
Jan.	4.7	T	10	2	45	62	45	11.5
Feb.	5.6	T	9	3	41	59	46	11.5
March	5.2	T	9	4	39	57	52	11.5
April	4.7	0	7	4	29	57	59	11.5
May	4.4	0	8	6	23	58	65	10.4
June	5.4	0	10	9	18	61	71	9.2
July	6.4	0	15	15	22	66	73	6.9
Aug.	5.9	0	13	13	19	65	73	8.1
Sept.	5.5	0	10	7	23	63	70	9.2
Oct.	2.8	0	6	2	20	56	60	9.2
Nov.	4.4	0	7	2	30	59	52	8.1
Dec.	5.5	T	10	2	42	62	47	9.2

T - Trace of rain or snow   * - Less than 1   NA - Not Available

Annual averages

Precipitation (in inches)	60.6
Snow (in inches)	T
Heating degree days	1,432
Cooling degree days	2,769
Days with thunderstorms	69
Days with fog	175
Days above 90°	70
Days below 32°	13
Wet days	114
Days with snow	*
Days with 1.5 inches or more snow	*

Percent time sky is clear

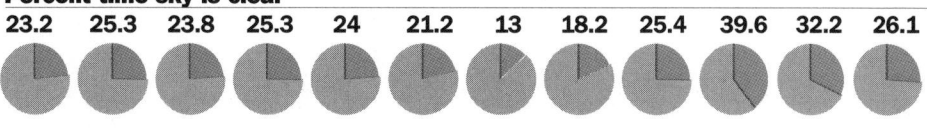

23.2	25.3	23.8	25.3	24	21.2	13	18.2	25.4	39.6	32.2	26.1
Jan.	Feb.	March	April	May	June	July	Aug.	Sept.	Oct.	Nov.	Dec.

New York, New York

Lat. 40° 46' N **Lon.** 73° 54' W **Elev.** 11 ft.

New York City is on the Atlantic coastal plain at the mouth of the Hudson River. All but one of the five boroughs or districts of the city are on islands. The area is in the path of most storm and frontal systems moving across the continent. Weather conditions thus often approach from the west, bringing hotter summers and colder winters than would be expected in a coastal area. Although continental influence dominates, oceanic influence brings breezes to moderate summer heat. The relatively warm ocean delays the advent of winter snows, while its lag in warming keeps spring relatively cool. Precipitation is moderate. Most rainfall from May through October comes from thunderstorms. For the other months daylong rain or snow is more common.

Temperatures

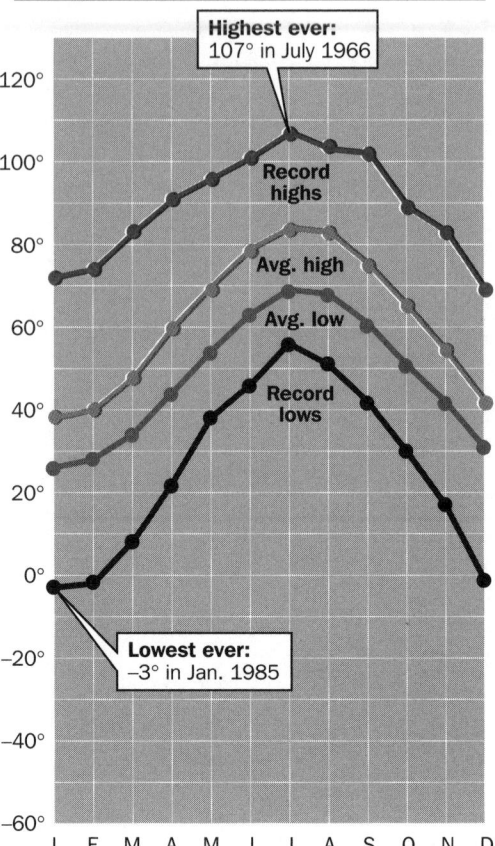

Highest ever: 107° in July 1966
Record highs
Avg. high
Avg. low
Record lows
Lowest ever: −3° in Jan. 1985

Weather extremes

Most rain in 24 hours:	6.40 in. Aug. 12, 1955
Most rain in a month:	16.05 in. August 1955
Most snow in 24 hours:	17.00 in. Feb. 11, 1983
Most snow in a month:	26.8 in. December 1947

Monthly averages

Month	Avg. precip. (in.)	Avg. snow (in.)	Wet days	Thunder- storm days	Pct. sky is cloudy	% p.m. relative humidity	Dew point	Wind speed (mph)
Jan.	3.2	7	11	*	41	57	20	16.1
Feb.	3.0	8	10	*	41	55	21	17.3
March	3.8	4	11	1	39	52	27	17.3
April	3.8	1	11	2	38	51	36	16.1
May	3.8	T	12	3	36	53	47	11.5
June	3.3	0	10	4	30	54	57	11.5
July	4.0	0	9	5	27	54	62	11.5
Aug.	4.2	0	9	5	27	56	62	11.5
Sept.	3.3	0	8	2	30	56	56	10.4
Oct.	3.2	T	8	1	29	56	45	12.7
Nov.	3.8	1	10	1	37	57	35	15.0
Dec.	3.6	4	11	*	41	59	25	16.1

T - Trace of rain or snow   * - Less than 1   NA - Not Available

Annual averages

Precipitation (in inches)	43.1
Snow (in inches)	24
Heating degree days	4,821
Cooling degree days	1,134
Days with thunderstorms	24
Days with fog	107
Days above 90°	15
Days below 32°	73
Wet days	120
Days with snow	28
Days with 1.5 inches or more snow	10

Percent time sky is clear

22.7	23.4	22.9	21.5	17	16.5	16	18.5	23.5	27.7	21.4	21.1

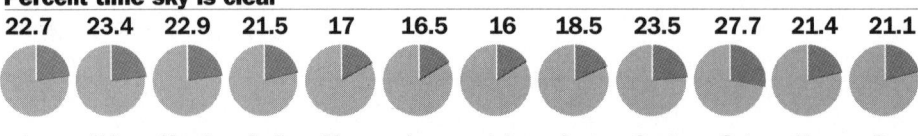

| Jan. | Feb. | March | April | May | June | July | Aug. | Sept. | Oct. | Nov. | Dec. |

Nome, Alaska

Lat. 64° 30' N **Lon.** 165° 26' W **Elev.** 13 ft.

Nome is located on coastal flats with a series of foothills four to eight miles north and the Kigluaik Mountains, which reach a height of 5,000 feet, at about 30 miles north. The flats are swampy in summer, but permanently frozen below 2 to 3 feet. The Norton Sound moderates June to November storms into cloudiness and rain, with nearly continuous cloud cover during July and August. The Sound freezes in November causing an abrupt change to a continental climate, with lows moving south of Nome, resulting in strong easterly to northerly winds and frequent blizzards. Snow starts in September; it begins to accumulate in November. Snow cover normally disappears by mid-June. Depths have exceeded 70 inches. Severe windstorms occur and blowing snow severely hinders transportation.

Temperatures

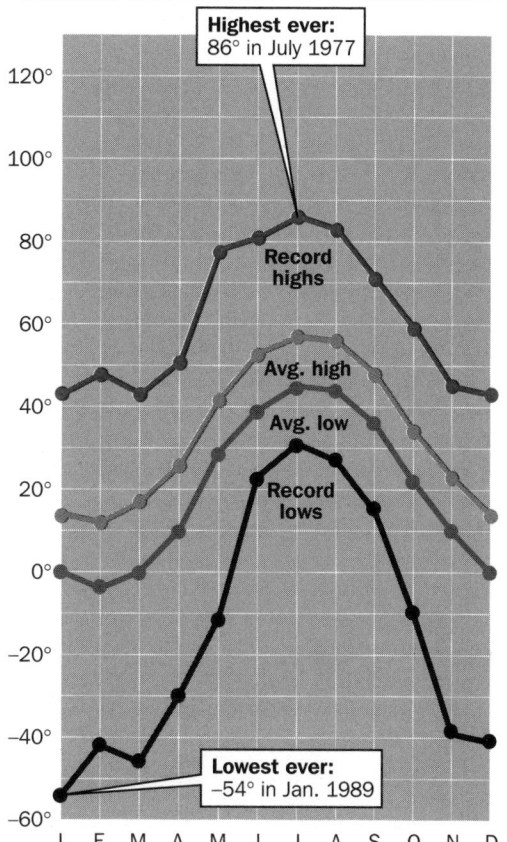

Weather extremes

Most rain in 24 hours:	2.38 in. Aug. 8 – 9, 1956
Most rain in a month:	8.43 in. July 1920
Most snow in 24 hours:	14.0 in. Feb. 14, 1920
Most snow in a month:	43.2 in. January 1937

Monthly averages

Month	Avg. precip. (in.)	Avg. snow (in.)	Wet days	Thunderstorm days	Pct. sky is cloudy	% p.m. relative humidity	Dew point	Wind speed (mph)
Jan.	0.9	9	11	*	45	75	0	16.1
Feb.	0.6	6	8	0	40	71	-1	16.1
March	0.6	7	9	0	41	70	1	13.8
April	0.7	7	9	0	46	75	13	13.8
May	0.6	2	8	*	51	73	29	12.7
June	1.1	T	9	*	47	74	39	12.7
July	2.3	0	13	*	60	80	46	11.5
Aug.	3.3	T	16	*	65	79	45	12.7
Sept.	2.5	T	14	0	56	74	36	10.4
Oct.	1.3	5	10	0	48	73	22	9.2
Nov.	1.0	11	12	0	51	76	10	15.0
Dec.	0.8	9	10	0	46	74	0	16.1

T - Trace of rain or snow   * - Less than 1   NA - Not Available

Annual averages

Precipitation (in inches)	15.7
Snow (in inches)	56
Heating degree days	14,022
Cooling degree days	3
Days with thunderstorms	1
Days with fog	119
Days above 90°	12
Days below 32°	239
Wet days	129
Days with snow	143
Days with 1.5 inches or more snow	21

Percent time sky is clear

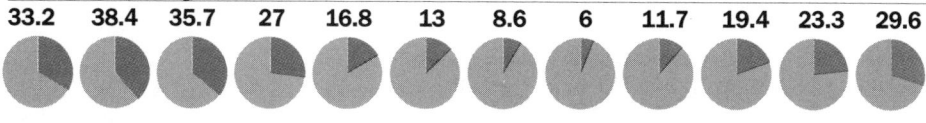

33.2	38.4	35.7	27	16.8	13	8.6	6	11.7	19.4	23.3	29.6
Jan.	Feb.	March	April	May	June	July	Aug.	Sept.	Oct.	Nov.	Dec.

Norfolk, Virginia

Lat. 36° 54' N **Lon.** 76° 12' W **Elev.** 22 ft.

Norfolk is west of the Atlantic Coast and almost surrounded by the Chesapeake Bay. The climate is generally marine. Its location is south of the principal track of storms coming from higher latitudes and north of the usual tracks of hurricanes and other tropical storms. Winters are usually mild, while autumn and spring usually are pleasant. Summers, though warm and long, frequently are tempered by cooling associated with northeast winds off the Atlantic. Temperatures of 100°F or higher occur infrequently. Extreme cold waves seldom penetrate the area; temperatures of zero or below are almost nonexistent. Most of the snowfall in Norfolk is light and generally melts within 24 hours. Some winters pass without a measurable amount of snowfall.

Temperatures

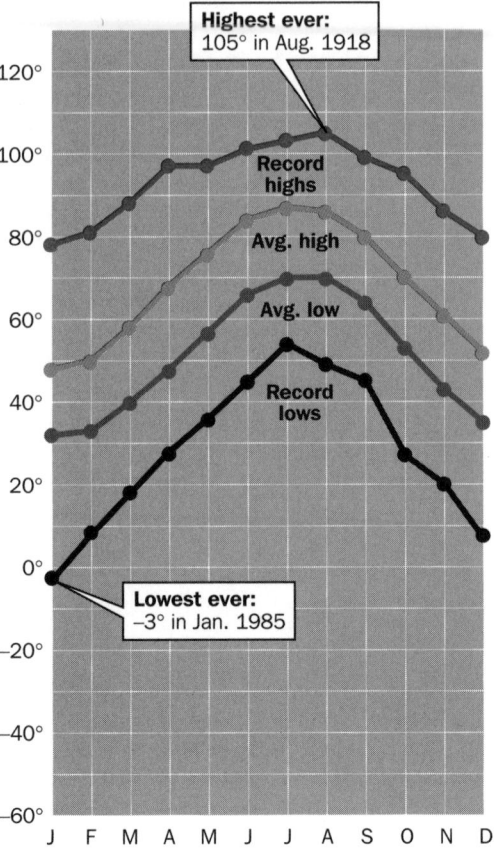

Highest ever: 105° in Aug. 1918

Record highs

Avg. high

Avg. low

Record lows

Lowest ever: -3° in Jan. 1985

Weather extremes

Most rain in 24 hours:	11.40 in., Aug. 31 – Sept. 1, 1964
Most rain in a month:	15.61 in. August 1942
Most snow in 24 hours:	17.7 in. Dec. 27, 1892
Most snow in a month:	24.4 in. February 1989

Monthly averages

Month	Avg. precip. (in.)	Avg. snow (in.)	Wet days	Thunder-storm days	Pct. sky is cloudy	% p.m. relative humidity	Dew point	Wind speed (mph)
Jan.	3.6	3	10	*	44	59	29	12.7
Feb.	3.4	3	10	1	44	57	30	13.8
March	3.7	1	11	2	41	54	36	13.8
April	3.1	T	10	3	36	51	44	13.8
May	3.8	0	10	5	36	56	55	11.5
June	3.6	0	9	6	29	57	63	11.5
July	5.1	0	11	8	28	60	68	10.4
Aug.	5.4	0	11	7	28	63	68	9.2
Sept.	4.0	0	8	3	29	62	63	12.7
Oct.	3.3	0	8	1	32	61	52	12.7
Nov.	3.0	T	8	1	33	58	42	10.4
Dec.	3.2	1	9	*	39	59	33	11.5

T - Trace of rain or snow   * - Less than 1   NA - Not Available

Annual averages

Precipitation (in inches)	45.0
Snow (in inches)	8
Heating degree days	3,425
Cooling degree days	1,586
Days with thunderstorms	37
Days with fog	157
Days above 90°	32
Days below 32°	54
Wet days	115
Days with snow	9
Days with 1.5 inches or more snow	4

Percent time sky is clear

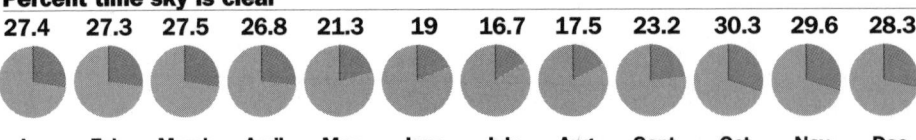

Jan.	Feb.	March	April	May	June	July	Aug.	Sept.	Oct.	Nov.	Dec.
27.4	27.3	27.5	26.8	21.3	19	16.7	17.5	23.2	30.3	29.6	28.3

North Platte, Nebraska

Lat. 41° 8′ N **Lon.** 100° 41′ W **Elev.** 2,775 ft.

North Platte experiences frequent, rapid changes in weather. During the winter, most North Pacific lows cross the country north of North Platte, bringing little snowfall, and only a moderate drop in temperature. Only a major outbreak of Canadian air sends the temperature to zero or below, and rarely for more than two mornings. If the cold outbreak meets an intense low from the mid-Rockies, there is severe cold and snow. Summer and fall bring frequent changes from hot to cool weather; nights almost always cool rapidly to lows in the 60s or below. Most summer and fall rain comes as thunderstorms, so amounts are variable. The average first occurrence of 32°F in the fall is September 24 and the average last occurrence in the spring is May 11.

Temperatures

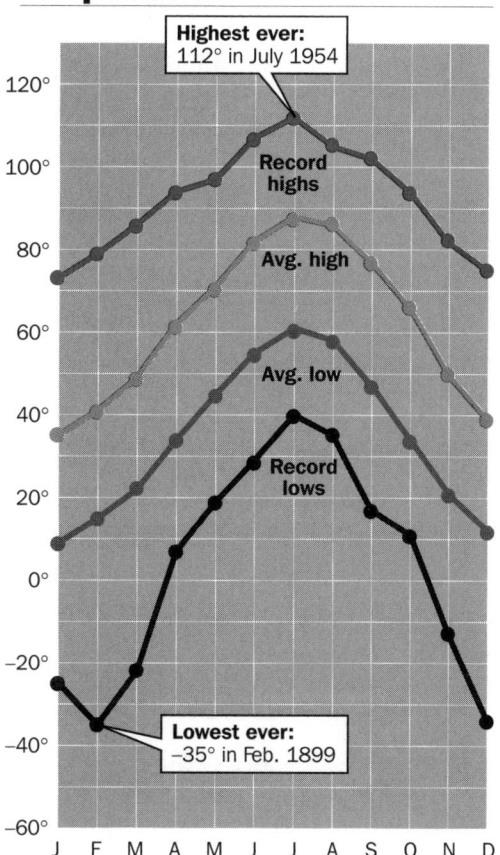

Weather extremes

Most rain in 24 hours:	6.32 in. Sept. 1 – 2, 1942
Most rain in a month:	10.47 in. June 1951
Most snow in 24 hours:	15.1 in. March 27–28, 1980
Most snow in a month:	27.8 in. March 1912

Monthly averages

Month	Avg. precip. (in.)	Avg. snow (in.)	Wet days	Thunder-storm days	Pct. sky is cloudy	% p.m. relative humidity	Dew point	Wind speed (mph)
Jan.	0.4	5	5	*	36	53	12	10.4
Feb.	0.5	5	5	*	39	51	17	10.4
March	1.2	7	7	1	42	47	23	16.1
April	1.8	3	8	3	37	41	32	16.1
May	3.5	T	11	7	37	46	44	13.8
June	3.4	T	10	10	26	45	54	12.7
July	3.0	0	10	11	19	43	59	11.5
Aug.	2.0	0	8	9	21	43	58	11.5
Sept.	1.5	T	7	4	25	40	47	11.5
Oct.	1.0	1	5	1	25	37	35	10.4
Nov.	0.6	4	5	*	33	44	23	10.4
Dec.	0.4	5	4	0	34	51	15	10.4

T - Trace of rain or snow   * - Less than 1   NA - Not Available

Annual averages

Precipitation (in inches)	19.5
Snow (in inches)	31
Heating degree days	6,783
Cooling degree days	804
Days with thunderstorms	46
Days with fog	77
Days above 90°	37
Days below 32°	175
Wet days	85
Days with snow	49
Days with 1.5 inches or more snow	11

Percent time sky is clear

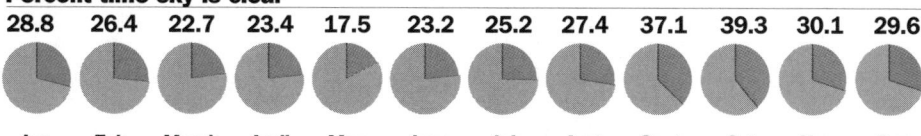

28.8	26.4	22.7	23.4	17.5	23.2	25.2	27.4	37.1	39.3	30.1	29.6
Jan.	Feb.	March	April	May	June	July	Aug.	Sept.	Oct.	Nov.	Dec.

Oklahoma City, Oklahoma

Lat. 35° 24' N **Lon.** 97° 36' W **Elev.** 1,280 ft.

Oklahoma City sits on the North Canadian River, an often nearly-dry stream, amid rolling hills. The nearest mountains are the Arbuckles, a 1,250-foot range 80 miles south. The climate is mainly continental, with pronounced daily and seasonal temperature changes and considerable variation in precipitation. Winters are comparatively mild and short. Summers are hot, although extreme heat is mitigated by low humidity. Temperatures of 100°F or more occur an average of 10 days, but have occurred as many as 50. Approximately one winter in three has temperatures below zero. Thunderstorms occur mainly in spring and early summer, sometimes with hail and strong winds. Annual snowfall averages about 10 inches, but there are occasional periods of freezing rain and sleet.

Temperatures

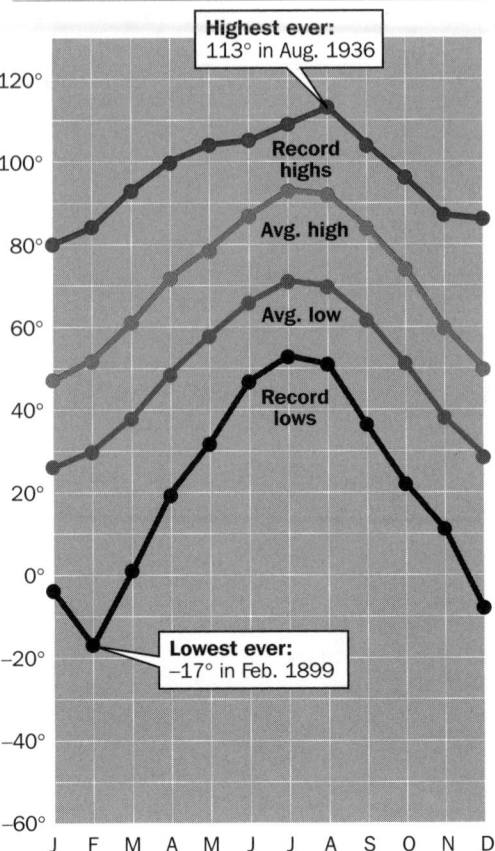

Highest ever: 113° in Aug. 1936
Record highs
Avg. high
Avg. low
Record lows
Lowest ever: −17° in Feb. 1899

Weather extremes

Most rain in 24 hours:	8.95 in. Oct. 19 – 20, 1983
Most rain in a month:	14.66 in. June 1989
Most snow in 24 hours:	11.3 in. March 19, 1924
Most snow in a month:	20.7 in. March 1924

Monthly averages

Month	Avg. precip. (in.)	Avg. snow (in.)	Wet days	Thunder-storm days	Pct. sky is cloudy	% p.m. relative humidity	Dew point	Wind speed (mph)
Jan.	1.2	3	5	1	39	53	25	15.0
Feb.	1.5	3	6	1	40	52	29	16.1
March	2.5	2	7	3	39	47	35	15.0
April	2.8	T	7	5	36	46	45	16.1
May	5.6	0	10	9	35	52	56	13.8
June	4.4	0	8	9	24	51	64	12.7
July	2.8	0	7	6	17	46	66	10.4
Aug.	2.5	0	7	6	17	44	65	10.4
Sept.	3.5	0	7	5	24	47	59	11.5
Oct.	3.1	T	6	3	26	46	48	12.7
Nov.	1.6	1	5	1	32	48	36	13.8
Dec.	1.3	2	5	1	37	52	28	13.8

T - Trace of rain or snow   * - Less than 1   NA - Not Available

Annual averages

Precipitation (in inches)	32.8
Snow (in inches)	10
Heating degree days	3,690
Cooling degree days	1,963
Days with thunderstorms	50
Days with fog	89
Days above 90°	70
Days below 32°	79
Wet days	80
Days with snow	15
Days with 1.5 inches or more snow	4

Percent time sky is clear

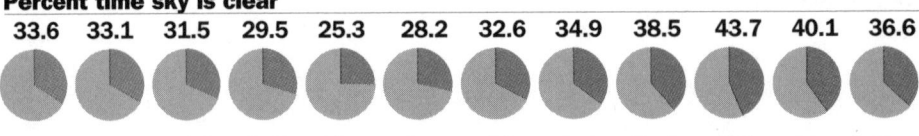

| 33.6 | 33.1 | 31.5 | 29.5 | 25.3 | 28.2 | 32.6 | 34.9 | 38.5 | 43.7 | 40.1 | 36.6 |
| Jan. | Feb. | March | April | May | June | July | Aug. | Sept. | Oct. | Nov. | Dec. |

Omaha, Nebraska

Lat. 41° 18' N **Lon.** 95° 54' W **Elev.** 980 ft.

Omaha is among rolling hills on the west bank of the Missouri River. The climate is typically continental, with warm summers and cold, dry winters. It is situated between two distinct climatic zones, the humid east and the dry west. Fluctuations between these two zones can produce weather characteristic of either zone, or combinations of both. Omaha is also affected by most low pressure systems that cross the country, causing periodic and rapid changes. Most precipitation falls during sharp showers or thunderstorms, generally during the growing season from April to September. Although winters are relatively cold, precipitation is light, with only 10 percent of the annual precipitation falling during winter. Sunshine is fairly abundant.

Temperatures

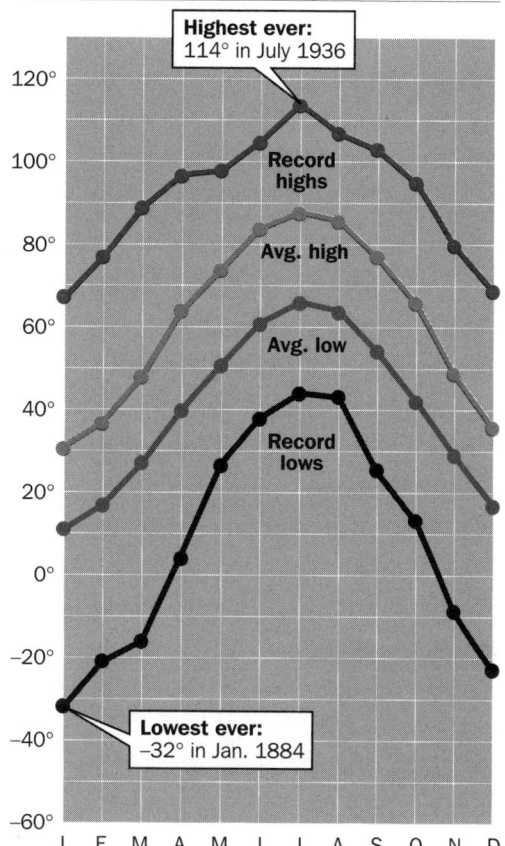

Highest ever: 114° in July 1936

Record highs

Avg. high

Avg. low

Record lows

Lowest ever: −32° in Jan. 1884

Weather extremes

Most rain in 24 hours:	7.03 in. Aug. 26 – 27, 1903
Most rain in a month:	13.75 in. September 1965
Most snow in 24 hours:	18.3 in. Feb. 11, 1965
Most snow in a month:	29.2 in. March 1912

Monthly averages

Month	Avg. precip. (in.)	Avg. snow (in.)	Wet days	Thunder-storm days	Pct. sky is cloudy	% p.m. relative humidity	Dew point	Wind speed (mph)
Jan.	0.8	7	6	*	39	61	13	15.0
Feb.	0.9	6	6	*	42	59	18	13.8
March	1.9	7	9	1	44	54	26	15.0
April	2.7	1	9	4	39	45	37	11.5
May	4.4	T	11	7	35	49	49	11.5
June	3.9	0	10	9	26	49	59	10.4
July	3.6	0	9	8	21	51	65	9.2
Aug.	3.8	0	9	8	22	53	63	9.2
Sept.	3.4	T	8	5	26	51	54	10.4
Oct.	2.1	T	7	2	27	47	41	10.4
Nov.	1.4	3	6	1	38	54	29	9.2
Dec.	0.9	6	7	*	42	61	18	9.2

T - Trace of rain or snow   * - Less than 1   NA - Not Available

Annual averages

Precipitation (in inches)	29.8
Snow (in inches)	29
Heating degree days	6,219
Cooling degree days	1,177
Days with thunderstorms	45
Days with fog	121
Days above 90°	36
Days below 32°	139
Wet days	97
Days with snow	43
Days with 1.5 inches or more snow	14

Percent time sky is clear

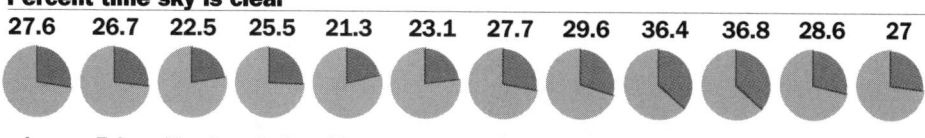

Jan.	Feb.	March	April	May	June	July	Aug.	Sept.	Oct.	Nov.	Dec.
27.6	26.7	22.5	25.5	21.3	23.1	27.7	29.6	36.4	36.8	28.6	27

Orlando, Florida

Lat. 28° 26' N **Lon.** 81° 20' W **Elev.** 91 ft.

Orlando is in central Florida, surrounded by many lakes. Relative humidity is high year-round, with values near 90 percent at night and 40 to 50 percent in the afternoon. The rainy season begins in June and can extend as late as October when tropical storms are near. Scattered afternoon thunderstorms are an almost daily occurrence in this season. There is usually a breeze. Winter rainfall is light. While winter temperatures may occasionally drop to near freezing at night, they rise rapidly during the day. This, coupled with brilliant sunshine, makes most winter afternoons quite pleasant. Hurricanes are not a great threat, since to reach Orlando they must pass over a substantial stretch of land and consequently lose much of their punch.

Temperatures

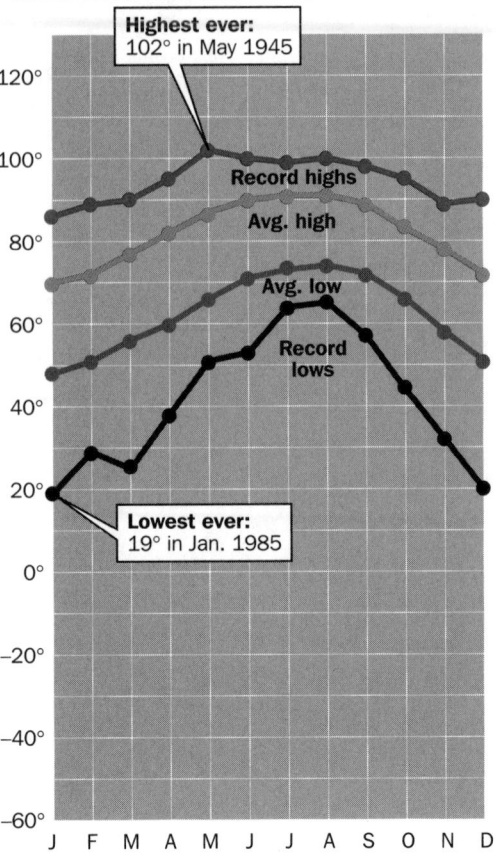

Highest ever: 102° in May 1945

Record highs

Avg. high

Avg. low

Record lows

Lowest ever: 19° in Jan. 1985

Weather extremes

Most rain in 24 hours:	8.43 in. Sept. 16, 1945
Most rain in a month:	18.28 in. June 1968
Most snow in 24 hours:	Trace January 1977
Most snow in a month:	Trace January 1977

Monthly averages

Month	Avg. precip. (in.)	Avg. snow (in.)	Wet days	Thunderstorm days	Pct. sky is cloudy	% p.m. relative humidity	Dew point	Wind speed (mph)
Jan.	2.3	T	7	1	28	53	49	8.1
Feb.	2.8	0	7	2	28	51	50	9.2
March	3.4	0	7	3	25	49	55	10.4
April	2.0	0	5	3	18	47	58	8.1
May	3.2	0	9	8	19	51	64	8.1
June	7.0	0	14	14	23	61	70	8.1
July	7.2	0	16	18	21	65	72	6.9
Aug.	5.8	0	16	17	20	66	73	6.9
Sept.	5.8	0	14	10	22	66	71	6.9
Oct.	2.7	0	8	2	19	59	64	8.1
Nov.	3.5	0	6	1	21	56	58	8.1
Dec.	2.0	0	6	1	26	55	52	8.1

T - Trace of rain or snow   * - Less than 1   NA - Not Available

Annual averages

Precipitation (in inches)	47.7
Snow (in inches)	T
Heating degree days	652
Cooling degree days	3,327
Days with thunderstorms	80
Days with fog	148
Days above 90°	90
Days below 32°	3
Wet days	115
Days with snow	0
Days with 1.5 inches or more snow	0

Percent time sky is clear

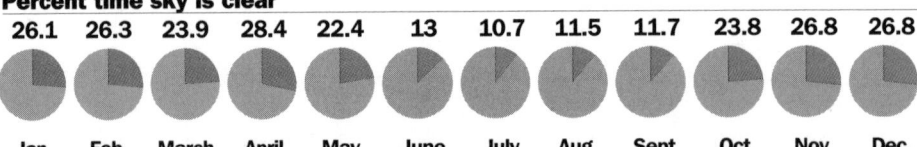

26.1	26.3	23.9	28.4	22.4	13	10.7	11.5	11.7	23.8	26.8	26.8
Jan.	Feb.	March	April	May	June	July	Aug.	Sept.	Oct.	Nov.	Dec.

Paducah, Kentucky

Lat. 37° 04′ N **Lon.** 88° 46′ W **Elev.** 394 ft.

Paducah lies in an area of bottom land and rolling hills on the Ohio River just west of its confluence with the Tennessee and Cumberland rivers, and about 20 miles west of the large recreational area which includes Kentucky and Barkley lakes. The climate is temperate, with moderately cold winters and warm, humid summers. All seasons are marked by variable weather that comes from passing fronts and associated with centers of high and low pressure. This variability is least in late spring and summer, somewhat greater in fall and greatest in winter and early spring. Precipitation is evenly distributed through the year; thunderstorms are most frequent in spring and summer, but can occur any time. Snowfall varies widely by year; some winters have very little.

Weather extremes

Most rain in 24 hours:	7.53 in. Sept. 4 – 5, 1985
Most rain in a month:	13.33 in. February 1989
Most snow in 24 hours:	7.9 in. Feb. 15, 1993
Most snow in a month:	16.8 in. January 1985

Temperatures

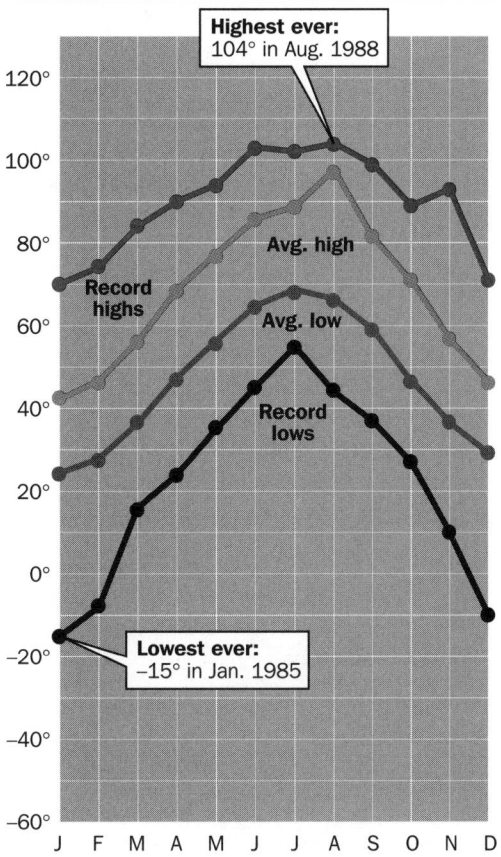

Highest ever: 104° in Aug. 1988

Avg. high

Record highs

Avg. low

Record lows

Lowest ever: −15° in Jan. 1985

Monthly averages

Month	Avg. precip. (in.)	Avg. snow (in.)	Wet days	Thunder-storm days	Pct. sky is cloudy	% p.m. relative humidity	Dew point	Wind speed (mph)
Jan.	3.7	3.0	8	1	57	65	NA	9.3
Feb.	3.4	3.6	10	2	55	64	NA	9.4
March	5.0	0.5	10	4	52	57	NA	10.1
April	4.6	T	11	6	44	51	NA	8.9
May	4.7	0.0	11	8	48	56	NA	7.6
June	4.5	T	8	9	36	55	NA	6.7
July	3.7	T	9	9	31	58	NA	6.5
Aug.	3.2	0.0	7	8	27	58	NA	5.6
Sept.	3.5	0.0	7	5	37	57	NA	6.4
Oct.	2.6	T	8	4	39	54	NA	7.3
Nov.	5.0	T	10	3	57	60	NA	9.4
Dec.	4.2	2.5	10	1	55	64	NA	9.2

T - Trace of rain or snow   * - Less than 1   NA - Not Available

Annual averages

Precipitation (in inches)	47
Snow (in inches)	10
Heating degree days	4,283
Cooling degree days	1,491
Days with thunderstorms	60
Days with fog	21
Days above 90°	51
Days below 32°	85
Wet days	109
Days with snow	NA
Days with 1.5 inches or more snow	3

Percent time sky is clear

Jan.	Feb.	March	April	May	June	July	Aug.	Sept.	Oct.	Nov.	Dec.
22.3	21.4	22.3	30.3	23.9	25.3	34.2	35.2	36.3	36.5	29.7	25.2

Pensacola, Florida

Lat. 30° 28' N **Lon.** 87° 12' W **Elev.** 112 ft.

Pensacola is on a somewhat hilly, sandy slope bordering Pensacola Bay, a deep water bay several miles wide. The bay is separated from the Gulf of Mexico by a long, narrow island that forms a natural breakwater. The Gulf moderates the climate by tempering cold north wind in winter and causing cooling sea breezes on most summer days. The average summer temperature is around 80°F; the winter average is in the mid-50s. Rainfall is usually well distributed through the year, but much of the summer rainfall comes in the form of heavy, daytime thunderstorms. Snow occurs in about 30 percent of the winters. Hurricanes, some seriously destructive, have occurred here from early July to mid-October.

Temperatures

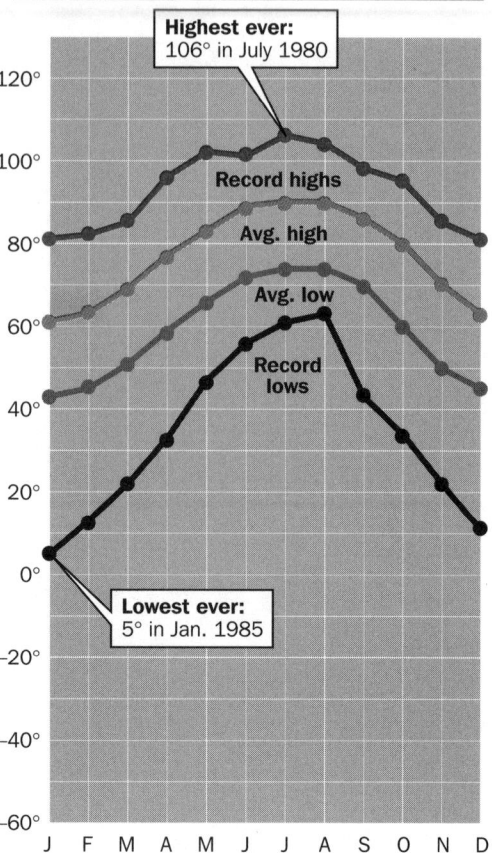

Weather extremes

Most rain in 24 hours:	11.10 in. March 3, 1979
Most rain in a month:	20.36 in. July 1979
Most snow in 24 hours:	2.30 in. March 6, 1954
Most snow in a month:	2.50 in. January 1977

Monthly averages

Month	Avg. precip. (in.)	Avg. snow (in.)	Wet days	Thunderstorm days	Pct. sky is cloudy	% p.m. relative humidity	Dew point	Wind speed (mph)
Jan.	4.2	T	9	1	39	70	51	10.4
Feb.	5.1	T	9	3	37	63	50	11.5
March	5.7	T	9	4	39	60	51	12.7
April	4.1	0	7	4	28	60	56	11.5
May	4.4	0	7	5	23	60	65	10.4
June	6.3	0	10	10	19	61	71	6.9
July	7.4	0	14	15	22	66	73	8.1
Aug.	6.9	0	12	14	15	65	73	6.9
Sept.	5.8	0	9	6	25	65	69	10.4
Oct.	3.8	0	5	2	13	58	59	9.2
Nov.	3.4	0	7	2	20	60	47	10.4
Dec.	4.4	T	10	2	40	68	46	11.5

T - Trace of rain or snow   * - Less than 1   NA - Not Available

Annual averages

Precipitation (in inches)	61.4
Snow (in inches)	T
Heating degree days	1,571
Cooling degree days	2,680
Days with thunderstorms	68
Days with fog	178
Days above 90°	61
Days below 32°	15
Wet days	108
Days with snow	*
Days with 1.5 inches or more snow	*

Percent time sky is clear

24.2	27.9	26.5	30.2	27.3	21	12.2	22.4	28.6	47.1	48.7	27.1

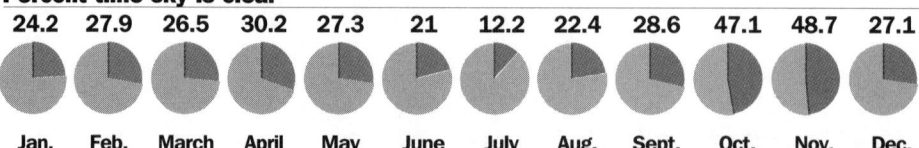

| Jan. | Feb. | March | April | May | June | July | Aug. | Sept. | Oct. | Nov. | Dec. |

Peoria, Illinois

Lat. 40° 40' N **Lon.** 89° 41' W **Elev.** 650 ft.

The climate of this area is typically continental as shown by its changeable weather and the wide range of temperature extremes. June and September are usually the most pleasant months of the year, but during October or the first of November, Indian summer brings an extended period of warm, dry weather. Precipitation is normally heaviest during the growing season and lowest during midwinter. The earliest snowfalls have been in September and the latest in May. Heavy snowfalls have rarely exceeded 20 inches. The average first occurrence of 32°F in the fall is Oct. 20 and the average last occurrence in the spring is April 24.

Temperatures

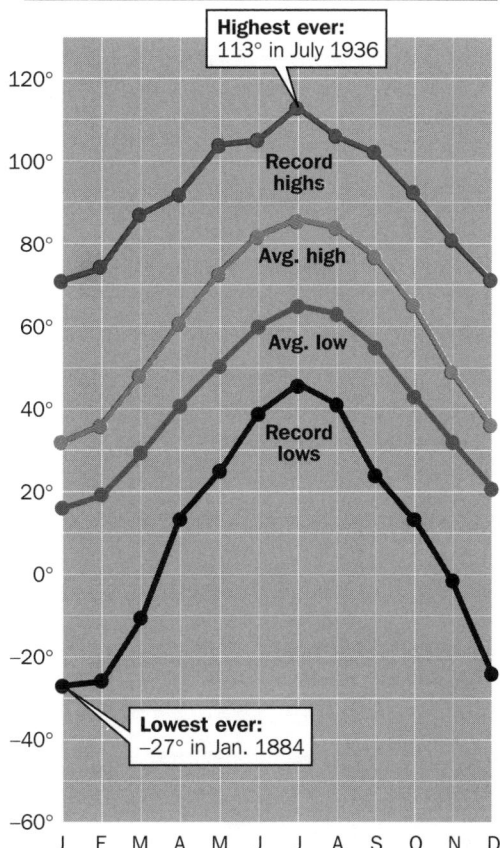

Highest ever: 113° in July 1936

Record highs

Avg. high

Avg. low

Record lows

Lowest ever: –27° in Jan. 1884

Weather extremes

Most rain in 24 hours:	5.52 in. May 18, 1927
Most rain in a month:	13.09 in. September 1961
Most snow in 24 hours:	18.0 in. Feb. 27 – 28, 1900
Most snow in a month:	24.7 in. January 1979

Monthly averages

Month	Avg. precip. (in.)	Avg. snow (in.)	Wet days	Thunder-storm days	Pct. sky is cloudy	% p.m. relative humidity	Dew point	Wind speed (mph)
Jan.	1.8	6	9	1	51	66	16	11.5
Feb.	1.6	5	8	1	50	64	20	11.5
March	2.8	4	11	3	53	58	28	12.7
April	3.8	1	12	5	46	52	38	11.5
May	4.0	T	12	7	39	51	49	10.4
June	4.0	0	10	9	30	52	59	10.4
July	3.7	0	9	8	26	55	64	9.2
Aug.	3.0	0	9	7	27	55	63	8.1
Sept.	3.6	T	9	5	31	52	55	9.2
Oct.	2.6	T	8	2	34	52	43	10.4
Nov.	2.4	2	9	1	49	61	32	11.5
Dec.	2.0	5	9	1	55	69	21	11.5

T - Trace of rain or snow   * - Less than 1   NA - Not Available

Annual averages

Precipitation (in inches)	35.3
Snow (in inches)	24
Heating degree days	5,870
Cooling degree days	1,162
Days with thunderstorms	50
Days with fog	103
Days above 90°	27
Days below 32°	127
Wet days	115
Days with snow	43
Days with 1.5 inches or more snow	9

Percent time sky is clear

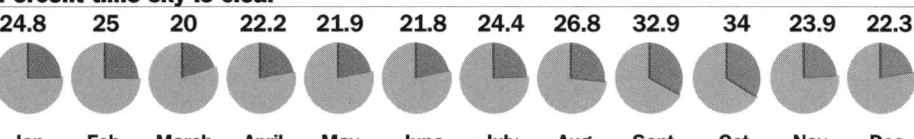

24.8	25	20	22.2	21.9	21.8	24.4	26.8	32.9	34	23.9	22.3
Jan.	Feb.	March	April	May	June	July	Aug.	Sept.	Oct.	Nov.	Dec.

Philadelphia, Pennsylvania

Lat. 39° 53' N **Lon.** 75° 14' W **Elev.** 10 ft.

The Appalachian Mountains to the west and Atlantic Ocean to the east have a moderating effect on climate. Periods of extreme temperatures are seldom long-lasting. On occasion, the area is engulfed with maritime air during summer and high humidity adds to the discomfort of seasonably warm temperatures. Although precipitation is fairly evenly distributed throughout the year, maximum amounts occur during the late summer mostly as local thunderstorms. Snowfall is often greater in the higher northern suburbs than the central and southern parts of the city. Often precipitation will change from snow to rain within the city. Flood stages in the Schuylkill River normally occur twice a year. Flooding rarely occurs on the Delaware River.

Temperatures

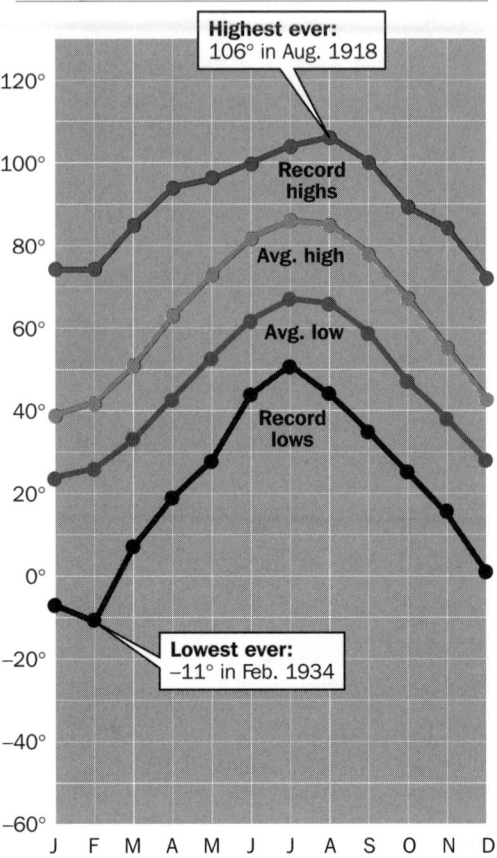

Highest ever: 106° in Aug. 1918

Record highs

Avg. high

Avg. low

Record lows

Lowest ever: −11° in Feb. 1934

Weather extremes

Most rain in 24 hours:	5.89 in. Aug. 3 – 4, 1898
Most rain in a month:	12.10 in. August 1911
Most snow in 24 hours:	21.3 in. Feb. 11 – 12, 1983
Most snow in a month:	31.5 in. February 1899

Monthly averages

Month	Avg. precip. (in.)	Avg. snow (in.)	Wet days	Thunder-storm days	Pct. sky is cloudy	% p.m. relative humidity	Dew point	Wind speed (mph)
Jan.	3.2	7	11	*	45	60	22	12.7
Feb.	2.8	7	10	*	43	55	22	13.8
March	3.7	4	11	1	42	51	29	13.8
April	3.5	T	11	2	41	48	38	10.4
May	3.7	T	11	4	41	51	50	10.4
June	3.6	0	10	5	33	52	59	9.2
July	4.1	0	9	6	32	54	65	9.2
Aug.	4.0	0	9	5	31	55	64	8.1
Sept.	3.3	0	8	2	33	55	57	9.2
Oct.	2.7	T	7	1	32	54	46	8.1
Nov.	3.4	1	10	1	39	57	36	11.5
Dec.	3.3	4	10	*	44	60	26	12.7

T - Trace of rain or snow   * - Less than 1   NA - Not Available

Annual averages

Precipitation (in inches)	41.4
Snow (in inches)	22
Heating degree days	4,872
Cooling degree days	1,173
Days with thunderstorms	27
Days with fog	163
Days above 90°	23
Days below 32°	94
Wet days	117
Days with snow	27
Days with 1.5 inches or more snow	10

Percent time sky is clear

23.1	24.9	24.1	21.8	17	17.7	16.6	19.2	24.9	30.1	23.6	23.1
Jan.	Feb.	March	April	May	June	July	Aug.	Sept.	Oct.	Nov.	Dec.

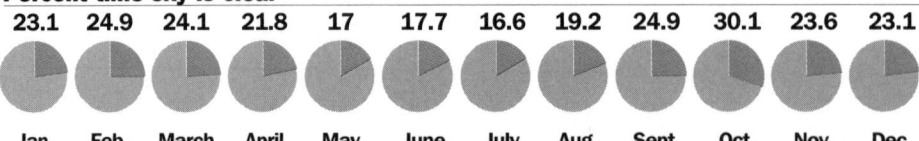

Phoenix, Arizona

Lat. 33° 26' N **Lon.** 112° 1' W **Elev.** 1,110 ft.

Phoenix is in the Salt River Valley in the Sonoran Desert. The valley is oval shaped and flat except for scattered precipitous mountains rising a few hundred feet to as much as 1,500 feet above the valley floor. More distant mountains to the south, west and east rise to between 2,500 and 5,000 feet. The valley supports large agricultural acreage, along with one of the largest urban populations in the U.S. The water supply for this community is from reservoirs, a large underground water table and an aqueduct. Temperatures range from very hot in summer to mild in winter and the climate is very dry. The valley is characterized by light winds; strong thunderstorm winds can occur, mostly in summer.

Temperatures

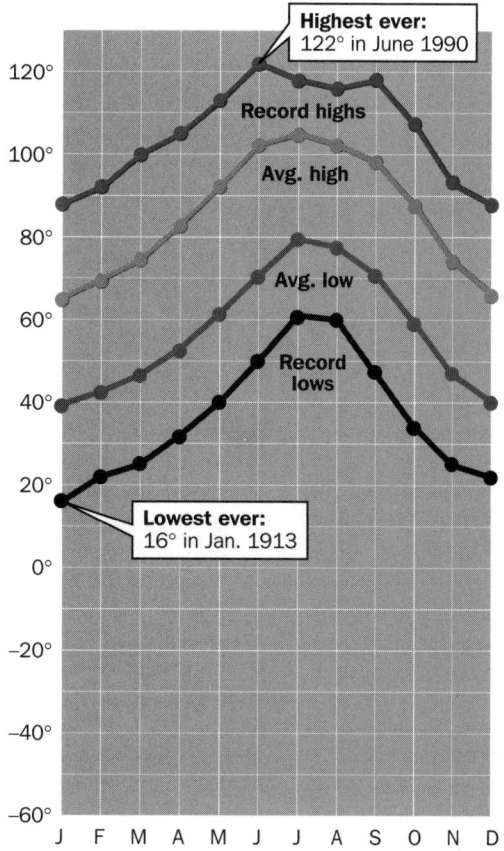

Highest ever: 122° in June 1990

Record highs

Avg. high

Avg. low

Record lows

Lowest ever: 16° in Jan. 1913

Weather extremes

Most rain in 24 hours:	4.98 in.	July 1-2, 1911
Most rain in a month:	6.47 in.	July 1911
Most snow in 24 hours:	1.0 in.	Jan. 20, 1937
Most snow in a month:	1.0 in.	January 1937

Monthly averages

Month	Avg. precip. (in.)	Avg. snow (in.)	Wet days	Thunder-storm days	Pct. sky is cloudy	% p.m. relative humidity	Dew point	Wind speed (mph)
Jan.	0.7	T	4	*	24	34	33	5.8
Feb.	0.6	T	4	*	23	28	33	6.9
March	0.8	0	4	1	21	24	33	6.9
April	0.3	0	2	1	14	17	33	6.9
May	0.1	0	1	1	8	14	35	6.9
June	0.1	0	1	1	5	12	40	9.2
July	0.8	0	4	6	15	21	57	8.1
Aug.	1.0	0	5	7	13	24	59	6.9
Sept.	0.7	0	3	4	8	23	52	6.9
Oct.	0.6	0	3	1	9	24	44	6.9
Nov.	0.6	0	2	1	15	28	36	5.8
Dec.	0.9	T	4	*	22	34	33	6.9

T - Trace of rain or snow   * - Less than 1   NA - Not Available

Annual averages

Precipitation (in inches)	7.3
Snow (in inches)	T
Heating degree days	1,442
Cooling degree days	3,746
Days with thunderstorms	23
Days with fog	6
Days above 90°	167
Days below 32°	10
Wet days	37
Days with snow	*
Days with 1.5 inches or more snow	0

Percent time sky is clear

44.7	44.9	45.3	53.5	60.2	67.4	33.6	41.1	59.6	60.2	55.3	48

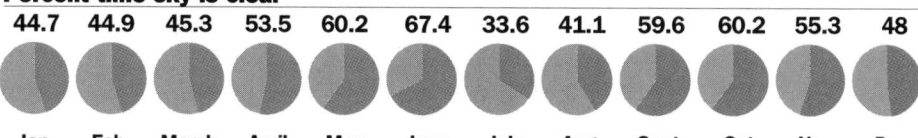

| Jan. | Feb. | March | April | May | June | July | Aug. | Sept. | Oct. | Nov. | Dec. |

Pittsburgh, Pennsylvania

Lat. 40° 30′ N **Lon.** 80° 13′ W **Elev.** 1,150 ft.

Situated in the Allegheny Mountain foot-hills and at the confluence of the Allegheny and Monongahela rivers, Pittsburgh has a humid continental climate modified only slightly by its nearness to the Atlantic seaboard and the Great Lakes. Air from the Gulf of Mexico, which brings warm humid weather during the summer, occasionally reaches as far as Pittsburgh in winter and produces thawing. Induced by the many hills, cold air drainage leads to frequent early morning fog, which can be quite persistent in the river valleys in colder months. Heavier rainfall and steeper topography cause the Monongahela River to flood more frequently than the Allegheny.

Temperatures

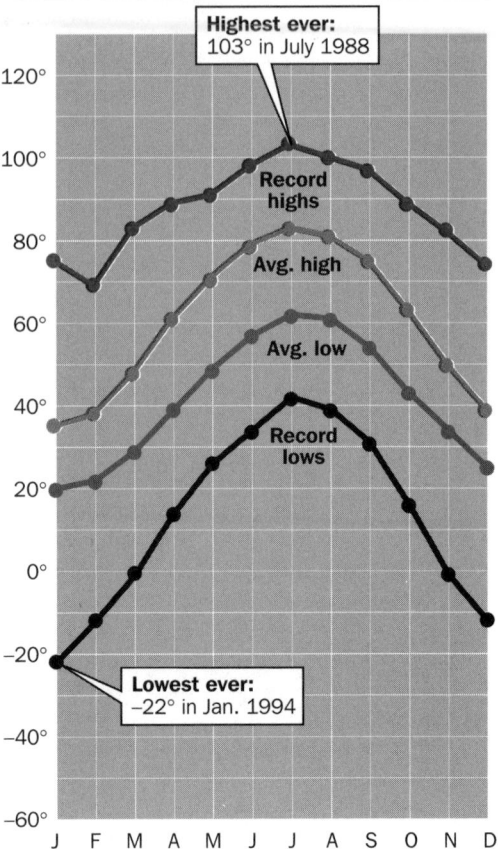

Highest ever: 103° in July 1988

Record highs

Avg. high

Avg. low

Record lows

Lowest ever: −22° in Jan. 1994

Weather extremes

Most rain in 24 hours:	3.57 in. Aug. 21, 1888
Most rain in a month:	11.05 in. November 1985
Most snow in 24 hours:	23.3 in. March 13, 1993
Most snow in a month:	40.2 in. January 1978

Monthly averages

Month	Avg. precip. (in.)	Avg. snow (in.)	Wet days	Thunder-storm days	Pct. sky is cloudy	% p.m. relative humidity	Dew point	Wind speed (mph)
Jan.	2.8	11	17	*	62	64	18	13.8
Feb.	2.4	9	14	*	58	60	20	12.7
March	3.4	8	16	2	54	54	26	13.8
April	3.3	2	14	3	47	49	35	13.8
May	3.6	T	13	5	41	50	46	11.5
June	3.9	0	12	7	33	51	55	10.4
July	3.8	0	11	7	30	53	60	9.2
Aug.	3.2	0	9	6	31	54	60	9.2
Sept.	2.8	0	9	3	33	55	53	10.4
Oct.	2.4	T	10	1	38	53	41	11.5
Nov.	2.7	4	13	1	55	60	32	12.7
Dec.	2.8	8	16	*	65	66	23	13.8

T - Trace of rain or snow   * - Less than 1   NA - Not Available

Annual averages

Precipitation (in inches)	37.1
Snow (in inches)	43
Heating degree days	5,828
Cooling degree days	739
Days with thunderstorms	35
Days with fog	178
Days above 90°	8
Days below 32°	121
Wet days	154
Days with snow	82
Days with 1.5 inches or more snow	17

Percent time sky is clear

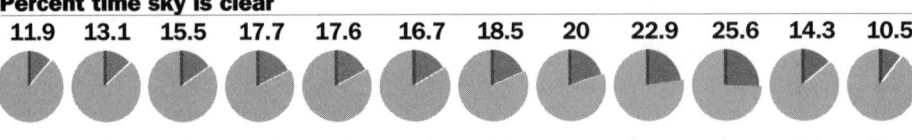

Jan.	Feb.	March	April	May	June	July	Aug.	Sept.	Oct.	Nov.	Dec.
11.9	13.1	15.5	17.7	17.6	16.7	18.5	20	22.9	25.6	14.3	10.5

Pocatello, Idaho

Lat. 42° 55' N **Lon.** 112° 36' W **Elev.** 4,454 ft.

Pocatello is located in the Snake River Valley, at the mouth of Portneuf Canyon, with a desert extending to the west and the crests of the Continental Divide to the east. The main feature of the climate is its variety. In winter, frequent periods of persistent southwest wind result in a mildness that matches the winters of the north Pacific Coast. Spring months are the wettest and windiest. Winds of 20 to 30 mph for days at a time are common. During the summer, afternoon temperatures may run into the 90s, but nights are usually cool. Precipitation is often accompanied by thunderstorms. Exceptionally fine weather predominates during the autumn. Agriculture, which is extensive in the Snake River Valley, depends upon irrigation for all crops because rainfall during the growing season is insufficient.

Temperatures

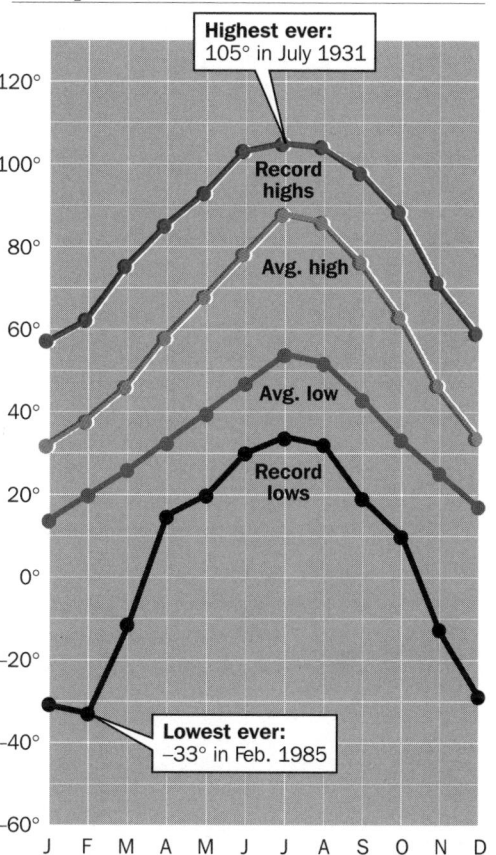

Highest ever: 105° in July 1931

Record highs

Avg. high

Avg. low

Record lows

Lowest ever: -33° in Feb. 1985

Weather extremes

Most rain in 24 hours:	2.60 in. Sept. 29 – 30, 1926
Most rain in a month:	4.34 in. March 1907
Most snow in 24 hours:	14.6 in. March 23, 1916
Most snow in a month:	33.7 in. December 1983

Monthly averages

Month	Avg. precip. (in.)	Avg. snow (in.)	Wet days	Thunder-storm days	Pct. sky is cloudy	% p.m. relative humidity	Dew point	Wind speed (mph)
Jan.	1.1	10	12	*	59	71	16	12.7
Feb.	0.9	6	10	*	50	63	21	12.7
March	1.1	6	10	*	44	51	24	12.7
April	1.1	4	8	1	38	38	27	12.7
May	1.3	1	9	4	32	35	34	12.7
June	1.0	T	7	5	21	31	40	11.5
July	0.5	0	4	6	11	23	43	10.4
Aug.	0.6	0	4	5	11	22	40	10.4
Sept.	0.7	T	5	3	16	27	35	11.5
Oct.	0.9	2	5	*	25	37	29	11.5
Nov.	1.1	5	9	*	47	59	25	12.7
Dec.	1.0	9	11	*	55	72	19	12.7

T - Trace of rain or snow   * - Less than 1   NA - Not Available

Annual averages

Precipitation (in inches)	11.3
Snow (in inches)	43
Heating degree days	7,079
Cooling degree days	449
Days with thunderstorms	24
Days with fog	47
Days above 90°	33
Days below 32°	166
Wet days	94
Days with snow	84
Days with 1.5 inches or more snow	17

Percent time sky is clear

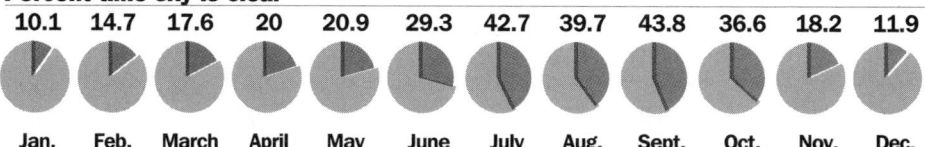

Jan.	Feb.	March	April	May	June	July	Aug.	Sept.	Oct.	Nov.	Dec.
10.1	14.7	17.6	20	20.9	29.3	42.7	39.7	43.8	36.6	18.2	11.9

Port Arthur, Texas

Lat. 29° 57' N **Lon.** 94° 01' W **Elev.** 16 ft.

Port Arthur is on the coastal plain on Sabine Lake off the Gulf of Mexico. It has a tropical and temperate climate with abundant rainfall and moderate temperatures. Sea breezes limit extreme heat; freezing temperature occur briefly fewer than six times a year. High humidity results from even distribution of high rainfall and prevailing south winds off the Gulf. Cloudy, rainy weather is most common in winter. Even a trace of sleet or snow falls in only half the winters. Summer rain is heavy, but brief. Slow-moving systems in spring and fall often bring three to five days of rain. Funnel clouds and water spouts are common near the coast. Fog is most frequent in midwinter, but usually dissipates before noon.

Temperatures

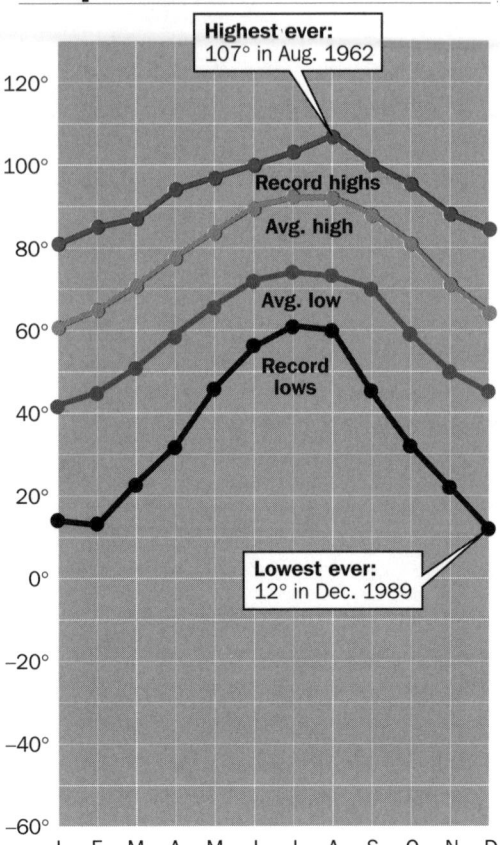

Highest ever: 107° in Aug. 1962

Record highs

Avg. high

Avg. low

Record lows

Lowest ever: 12° in Dec. 1989

Weather extremes

Most rain in 24 hours:	17.16 in. Sept. 5 – 6, 1980
Most rain in a month:	21.96 in. September 1980
Most snow in 24 hours:	4.4 in. Feb. 12 – 13, 1960
Most snow in a month:	4.4 in. February 1960

Monthly averages

Month	Avg. precip. (in.)	Avg. snow (in.)	Wet days	Thunder-storm days	Pct. sky is cloudy	% p.m. relative humidity	Dew point	Wind speed (mph)
Jan.	4.4	T	10	2	50	64	45	11.5
Feb.	4.0	T	9	3	47	61	47	11.5
March	3.2	T	8	4	44	59	52	12.7
April	3.6	0	7	4	39	61	60	13.8
May	5.1	0	7	6	27	62	67	11.5
June	5.1	0	8	8	15	62	72	10.4
July	5.5	0	12	14	17	64	74	8.1
Aug.	5.3	0	11	12	16	62	74	8.1
Sept.	5.8	0	10	7	20	61	70	9.2
Oct.	4.1	0	6	3	21	55	60	9.2
Nov.	4.3	T	8	3	33	59	52	10.4
Dec.	5.0	T	10	3	45	63	47	11.5

T - Trace of rain or snow　　* - Less than 1　　NA - Not Available

Annual averages

Precipitation (in inches)	55.3
Snow (in inches)	T
Heating degree days	1,468
Cooling degree days	2,861
Days with thunderstorms	69
Days with fog	167
Days above 90°	83
Days below 32°	15
Wet days	106
Days with snow	*
Days with 1.5 inches or more snow	*

Percent time sky is clear

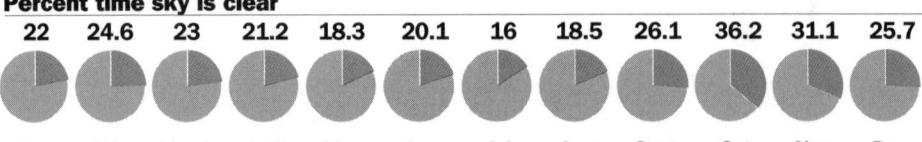

Jan.	Feb.	March	April	May	June	July	Aug.	Sept.	Oct.	Nov.	Dec.
22	24.6	23	21.2	18.3	20.1	16	18.5	26.1	36.2	31.1	25.7

Portland, Maine

Lat. 43° 39' N **Lon.** 70° 19' W **Elev.** 57 ft.

Portland has pleasant summers and falls, cold winters with frequent thaws. The White Mountains, to the northwest, keep considerable snow from reaching the Portland area and also moderate the temperature. Very few summer nights are too warm and humid for comfortable sleeping. Autumn has the greatest number of sunny days. Winters are quite severe, beginning late but extending far into the normal springtime. Temperatures well below zero are recorded frequently. Winds are generally light with the highest velocities confined mostly to March and November. Mid-May is the average occurrence of the last freeze in spring, and the average first freeze in fall is late September.

Temperatures

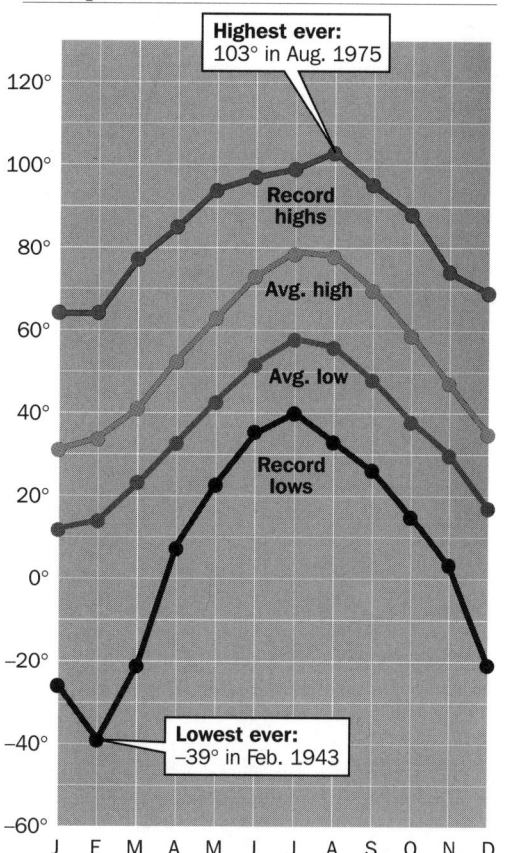

Weather extremes

Most rain in 24 hours:	7.83 in. Aug. 18 – 19, 1991
Most rain in a month:	15.22 in. August 1991
Most snow in 24 hours:	24.4 in. Jan. 17 – 18, 1979
Most snow in a month:	62.4 in. January 1979

Monthly averages

Month	Avg. precip. (in.)	Avg. snow (in.)	Wet days	Thunder-storm days	Pct. sky is cloudy	% p.m. relative humidity	Dew point	Wind speed (mph)
Jan.	3.7	20	11	*	45	62	13	9.2
Feb.	3.4	17	10	*	43	60	14	9.2
March	3.8	13	11	*	46	60	22	10.4
April	3.9	3	12	*	47	58	32	11.5
May	3.7	T	12	2	46	61	43	11.5
June	3.2	0	11	4	41	63	53	10.4
July	2.9	0	10	4	36	62	59	10.4
Aug.	2.7	0	9	4	35	63	58	10.4
Sept.	3.2	T	9	1	36	64	51	10.4
Oct.	3.7	T	10	1	38	64	40	9.2
Nov.	5.0	3	12	*	48	67	31	9.2
Dec.	4.3	15	12	*	45	65	18	9.2

T - Trace of rain or snow   * - Less than 1   NA - Not Available

Annual averages

Precipitation (in inches)	43.5
Snow (in inches)	71
Heating degree days	7,383
Cooling degree days	328
Days with thunderstorms	16
Days with fog	170
Days above 90°	5
Days below 32°	156
Wet days	129
Days with snow	63
Days with 1.5 inches or more snow	29

Percent time sky is clear

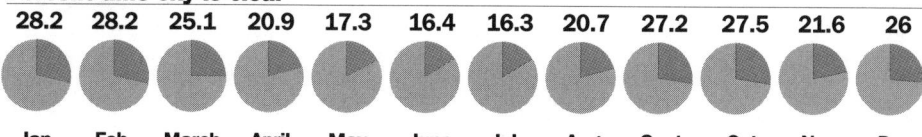

28.2	28.2	25.1	20.9	17.3	16.4	16.3	20.7	27.2	27.5	21.6	26
Jan.	Feb.	March	April	May	June	July	Aug.	Sept.	Oct.	Nov.	Dec.

Portland, Oregon

Lat. 45° 36' N **Lon.** 122° 36' W **Elev.** 21 ft.

Portland is on the Columbia River about 65 miles from the Pacific Ocean and midway between a low coastal range to the west and the towering Cascades to the east. The coast range provides limited shielding from the Pacific; the Cascades form a barrier to continental air. Their steep slope also lifts moist west winds, creating rainfall. Portland has a definite winter rainfall climate — 88 percent of annual rain falls from October through May. Marine air moderates the climate. Winter is mild, cloudy and rainy; only about five days see measurable snow. Summer is mild with little precipitation. Fall and early winter can be foggy. Extremes of summer heat and winter cold can result from occasional outbreaks of continental high pressure from east of the Cascades in a strong flow down the Columbia River Gorge.

Weather extremes

Most rain in 24 hours:	2.62 in.	November 15, 1973
Most rain in a month:	12.83 in.	January 1953
Most snow in 24 hours:	10.6 in.	Jan. 20, 1950
Most snow in a month:	41.4 in.	January 1950

Temperatures

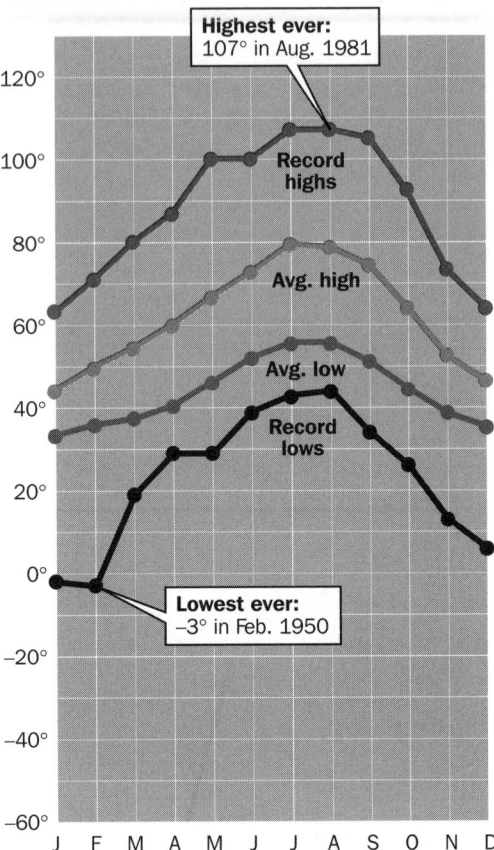

Highest ever: 107° in Aug. 1981

Record highs

Avg. high

Avg. low

Record lows

Lowest ever: -3° in Feb. 1950

Monthly averages

Month	Avg. precip. (in.)	Avg. snow (in.)	Wet days	Thunder-storm days	Pct. sky is cloudy	% p.m. relative humidity	Dew point	Wind speed (mph)
Jan.	6.2	3	18	*	68	82	NA	9.9
Feb.	3.9	1	16	*	63	80	NA	9.1
March	3.6	T	17	1	58	73	NA	8.2
April	2.3	T	14	1	52	69	NA	7.4
May	2.1	T	12	1	47	66	NA	7.1
June	1.5	T	9	1	43	65	NA	7.2
July	0.5	0	4	1	27	62	NA	7.6
Aug.	1.1	T	5	1	31	64	NA	7.1
Sept.	1.6	T	8	1	33	67	NA	6.5
Oct.	3.1	T	12	*	48	78	NA	6.5
Nov.	5.2	T	18	*	64	82	NA	8.6
Dec.	6.4	1	19	*	70	84	NA	9.5

T - Trace of rain or snow   * - Less than 1   NA - Not Available

Annual averages

Precipitation (in inches)	37.4
Snow (in inches)	7
Heating degree days	4,691
Cooling degree days	332
Days with thunderstorms	7
Days with fog	33
Days above 90°	11
Days below 32°	42
Wet days	151
Days with snow	NA
Days with 1.5 inches or more snow	2

Percent time sky is clear

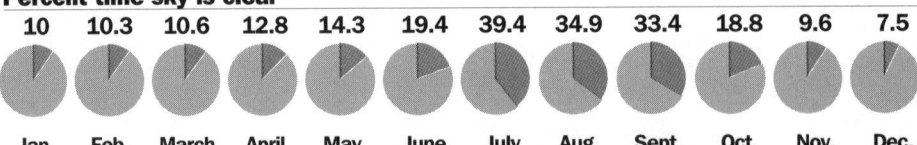

10	10.3	10.6	12.8	14.3	19.4	39.4	34.9	33.4	18.8	9.6	7.5
Jan.	Feb.	March	April	May	June	July	Aug.	Sept.	Oct.	Nov.	Dec.

Providence, Rhode Island

Lat. 41° 44' N **Lon.** 71° 26' W **Elev.** 51 ft.

Providence's proximity to Narragansett Bay and the Atlantic Ocean determines its climate. In winter, the closeness to the ocean considerably modifies temperatures and changes many major snowstorms into rain. In summer, refreshing sea breezes cool days that would otherwise be uncomfortably warm. At other times winds may blow sea fog in over land. Severe coastal storms, primarily in the fall, bring destructive winds. Measurable precipitation occurs on about one day out of three. Thunderstorms are responsible for much of the rainfall from May through August. They sometimes include heavy downpours with extremely gusty winds, but since their duration is relatively short, damage ordinarily is light.

Temperatures

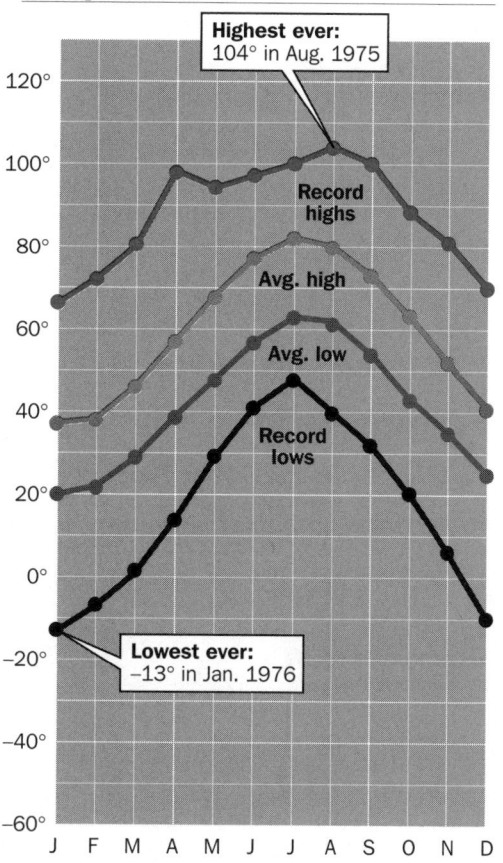

Highest ever: 104° in Aug. 1975

Record highs

Avg. high

Avg. low

Record lows

Lowest ever: −13° in Jan. 1976

Weather extremes

Most rain in 24 hours:	6.71 in. Aug. 3 – 4, 1979
Most rain in a month:	12.74 in. April 1983
Most snow in 24 hours:	27.6 in. Feb. 6 – 7, 1978
Most snow in a month:	31.9 in. January 1948

Monthly averages

Month	Avg. precip. (in.)	Avg. snow (in.)	Wet days	Thunder-storm days	Pct. sky is cloudy	% p.m. relative humidity	Dew point	Wind speed (mph)
Jan.	3.9	10	11	*	43	58	17	12.7
Feb.	3.6	10	10	*	43	56	18	13.8
March	4.1	7	12	1	44	54	25	13.8
April	4.2	1	11	1	44	51	34	12.7
May	3.7	T	12	3	42	55	45	10.4
June	2.9	0	11	4	37	58	56	9.2
July	3.2	0	9	4	34	58	62	10.4
Aug.	3.9	0	9	4	34	60	61	9.2
Sept.	3.4	0	8	2	35	59	54	10.4
Oct.	3.6	T	8	1	34	58	43	10.4
Nov.	4.4	1	11	1	43	60	34	11.5
Dec.	4.2	7	12	*	44	60	22	12.7

T - Trace of rain or snow   * - Less than 1   NA - Not Available

Annual averages

Precipitation (in inches)	45.3
Snow (in inches)	36
Heating degree days	5,846
Cooling degree days	682
Days with thunderstorms	21
Days with fog	167
Days above 90°	10
Days below 32°	117
Wet days	124
Days with snow	42
Days with 1.5 inches or more snow	15

Percent time sky is clear

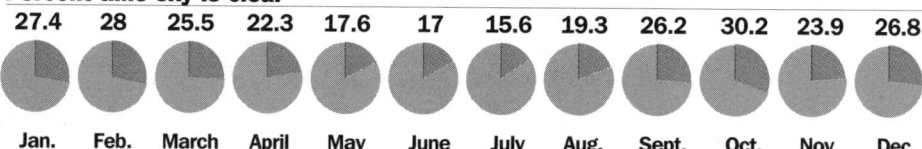

Jan.	Feb.	March	April	May	June	July	Aug.	Sept.	Oct.	Nov.	Dec.
27.4	28	25.5	22.3	17.6	17	15.6	19.3	26.2	30.2	23.9	26.8

Pueblo, Colorado

Lat. 38° 17′ N **Lon.** 104° 30′ W **Elev.** 4,726 ft.

Pueblo is at the junction of the Arkansas and Fountain rivers, with mountains to the west. The surrounding area consists of rolling plains and is generally treeless. Large daily temperature variations are a hallmark of Pueblo's semiarid climate. Thanks to the low relative humidity, the heat is not oppressive in the summer. Summer nights are cool since mountain breezes prevail from shortly after sunset to about noon the following day. Summer rains usually occur in the form of afternoon thunderstorms. Winter is comparatively mild due to the abundant sunshine and the protection afforded by the nearby mountains. Cold spells are generally broken after a few days by warm chinook winds.

Temperatures

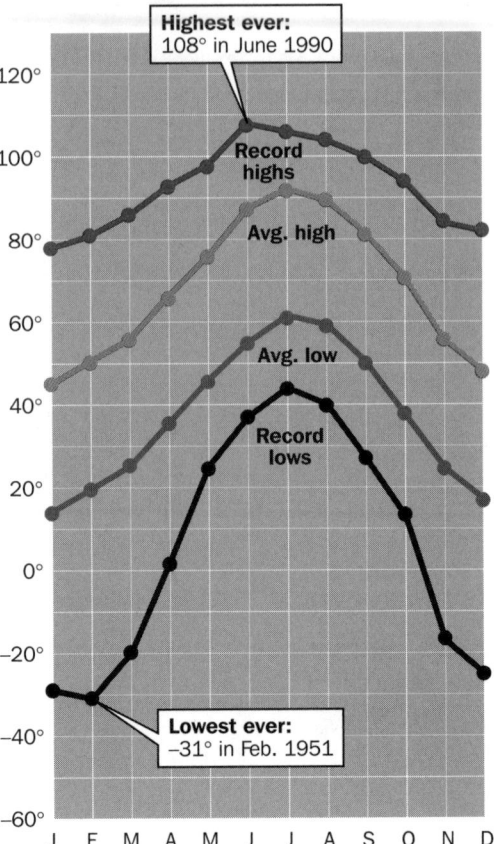

Highest ever: 108° in June 1990
Record highs
Avg. high
Avg. low
Record lows
Lowest ever: −31° in Feb. 1951

Weather extremes

Most rain in 24 hours:	3.77 in. Oct. 7 – 8, 1957
Most rain in a month:	8.13 in. April 1900
Most snow in 24 hours:	16.8 in. April 29 – 30, 1990
Most snow in a month:	29.3 in. November 1946

Monthly averages

Month	Avg. precip. (in.)	Avg. snow (in.)	Wet days	Thunderstorm days	Pct. sky is cloudy	% p.m. relative humidity	Dew point	Wind speed (mph)
Jan.	0.3	5.9	4.4	*	34	52	NA	8.0
Feb.	0.3	4.3	4.3	0	38	46	NA	8.6
March	0.7	6.9	6.2	*	38	42	NA	9.8
April	1.0	3.5	5.9	2	37	35	NA	10.5
May	1.5	0.7	8.2	6	35	37	NA	9.8
June	1.2	T	7.1	8	23	34	NA	9.4
July	1.8	T	9.5	12	17	36	NA	8.7
Aug.	1.8	T	8.7	9	22	39	NA	8.0
Sept.	0.8	0.5	4.9	3	21	38	NA	8.0
Oct.	0.8	1.3	3.6	1	25	37	NA	7.5
Nov.	0.5	4.6	0.7	*	30	46	NA	7.5
Dec.	0.3	5.3	3.8	0	32	52	NA	7.9

T - Trace of rain or snow   * - Less than 1   NA - Not Available

Annual averages

Precipitation (in inches)	10.9
Snow (in inches)	33
Heating degree days	5,465
Cooling degree days	1,042
Days with thunderstorms	41
Days with fog	9
Days above 90°	65
Days below 32°	157
Wet days	70
Days with snow	NA
Days with 1.5 inches or more snow	10

Percent time sky is clear

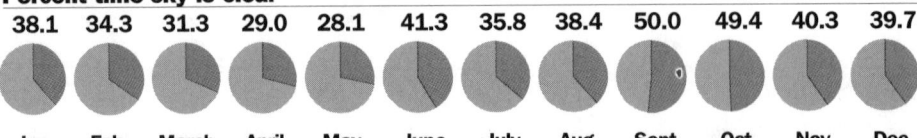

Jan.	Feb.	March	April	May	June	July	Aug.	Sept.	Oct.	Nov.	Dec.
38.1	34.3	31.3	29.0	28.1	41.3	35.8	38.4	50.0	49.4	40.3	39.7

Raleigh-Durham, N.C.

Lat. 35° 52' N **Lon.** 78° 47' W **Elev.** 376 ft.

Centrally located between the mountains on the west and the coast on the south and east, the Raleigh-Durham area enjoys a favorable climate. The mountains form a partial barrier to cold air masses moving eastward from the interior of the nation so that in the heart of winter the temperature rarely falls below 20 °F. Tropical air brings warm temperatures and rather high humidity to the area in summer. However, early morning temperatures almost always drop into the lower 70s. Rainfall is well distributed throughout the year. Most summer rain is produced by thunderstorms, which may occasionally be accompanied by strong winds, intense rains, and hail. Although snow and sleet occur each year, excessive accumulations of snow are rare.

Temperatures

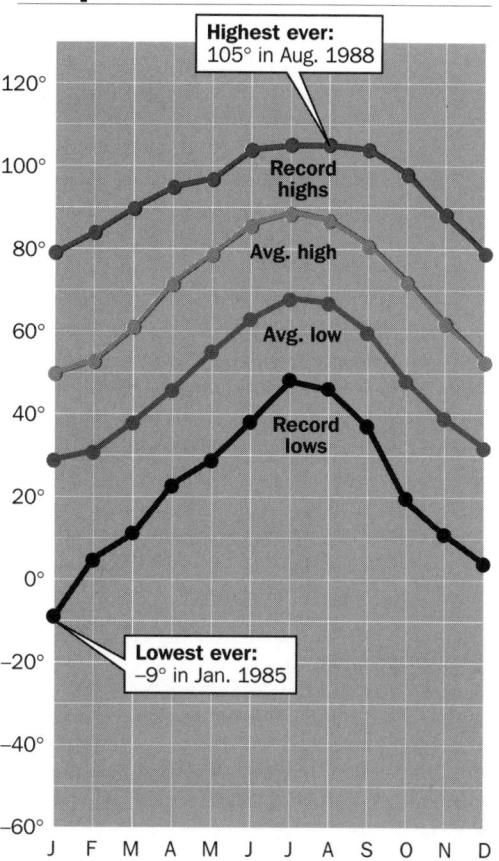

Highest ever: 105° in Aug. 1988

Record highs

Avg. high

Avg. low

Record lows

Lowest ever: −9° in Jan. 1985

Weather extremes

Most rain in 24 hours:	6.66 in. Sept. 30-Oct. 1, 1929
Most rain in a month:	13.63 in. August 1908
Most snow in 24 hours:	17.8 in. March 2, 1927
Most snow in a month:	20.0 in. January 1893

Monthly averages

Month	Avg. precip. (in.)	Avg. snow (in.)	Wet days	Thunder-storm days	Pct. sky is cloudy	% p.m. relative humidity	Dew point	Wind speed (mph)
Jan.	3.4	2	10	*	44	53	28	9.2
Feb.	3.6	3	10	1	42	49	29	10.4
March	3.6	1	10	2	39	46	35	10.4
April	2.9	T	9	3	33	43	44	10.4
May	3.9	0	10	6	33	51	56	9.2
June	3.6	0	9	7	28	54	64	8.1
July	4.4	0	11	10	29	57	68	8.1
Aug.	4.4	0	10	8	29	59	67	6.9
Sept.	3.2	0	7	3	31	57	61	8.1
Oct.	2.9	0	7	1	30	53	50	9.2
Nov.	3.0	T	8	1	33	51	39	9.2
Dec.	3.1	1	9	*	38	53	31	9.2

T - Trace of rain or snow   * - Less than 1   NA - Not Available

Annual averages

Precipitation (in inches)	42.0
Snow (in inches)	8
Heating degree days	3,502
Cooling degree days	1,523
Days with thunderstorms	42
Days with fog	181
Days above 90°	39
Days below 32°	77
Wet days	110
Days with snow	2
Days with 1.5 inches or more snow	2

Percent time sky is clear

Jan.	Feb.	March	April	May	June	July	Aug.	Sept.	Oct.	Nov.	Dec.
29.2	29.4	29.2	29.9	21.7	20.6	16.8	17.8	26.4	37.6	34.6	31.8

Rapid City, South Dakota

Lat. 44° 3' N **Lon.** 103° 4' W **Elev.** 3,162 ft.

Rapid City, not far from the geographical center of North America, experiences the large temperature ranges, both daily and seasonal, that are typical of semiarid continental climates. The Black Hills, immediately to the west, exert a pronounced influence on the climate. Due to the hills' protection and other factors, winter temperatures are among the warmest in South Dakota. Snowfall is normally light, with the greatest monthly average occurring in March. Wide variations in temperatures are usual in the spring. Summer days are normally warm with cool, comfortable nights. Nearly all summer precipitation occurs as thunderstorms.

Temperatures

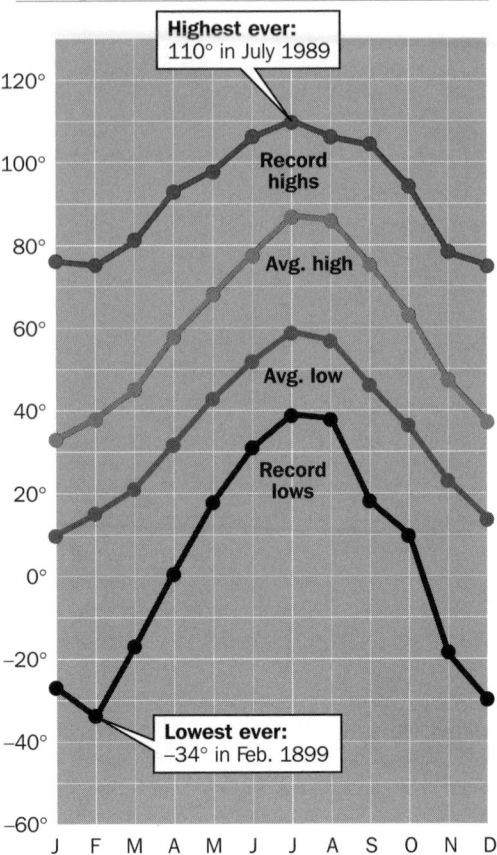

Highest ever: 110° in July 1989

Record highs

Avg. high

Avg. low

Record lows

Lowest ever: –34° in Feb. 1899

Weather extremes

Most rain in 24 hours:	4.01 in. June 14 – 15, 1963
Most rain in a month:	7.35 in. May 1946
Most snow in 24 hours:	16.3 in. Jan. 27, 1944
Most snow in a month:	33.6 in. November 1985

Monthly averages

Month	Avg. precip. (in.)	Avg. snow (in.)	Wet days	Thunder-storm days	Pct. sky is cloudy	% p.m. relative humidity	Dew point	Wind speed (mph)
Jan.	0.4	5	6	0	38	63	11	18.4
Feb.	0.5	7	7	0	40	61	15	18.4
March	1.0	9	9	*	41	54	21	20.7
April	1.8	7	9	1	39	45	28	19.6
May	2.7	1	12	6	36	47	40	17.3
June	3.0	T	12	10	27	48	50	15.0
July	1.9	0	9	11	16	40	53	13.8
Aug.	1.6	0	8	9	16	36	50	13.8
Sept.	1.2	T	7	3	22	38	40	16.1
Oct.	0.9	2	5	*	26	45	30	17.3
Nov.	0.6	5	6	*	35	59	21	17.3
Dec.	0.4	5	6	*	36	64	14	18.4

T - Trace of rain or snow   * - Less than 1   NA - Not Available

Annual averages

Precipitation (in inches)	16.1
Snow (in inches)	40
Heating degree days	7,186
Cooling degree days	668
Days with thunderstorms	40
Days with fog	40
Days above 90°	32
Days below 32°	169
Wet days	96
Days with snow	73
Days with 1.5 inches or more snow	16

Percent time sky is clear

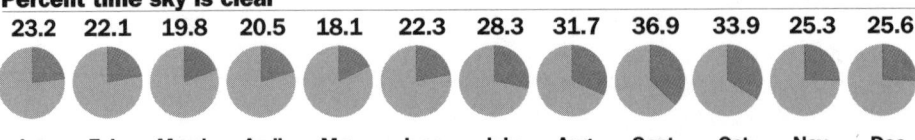

23.2	22.1	19.8	20.5	18.1	22.3	28.3	31.7	36.9	33.9	25.3	25.6
Jan.	Feb.	March	April	May	June	July	Aug.	Sept.	Oct.	Nov.	Dec.

Redding, California

Lat. 40° 30' N **Lon.** 122° 18' W **Elev.** 502 ft.

Redding is in low hills at the north end of the Sacramento Valley. Mountains rise on three sides, dominated by Mount Lassen at 10,457 feet and Mount Shasta at 14,200 feet. The Trinity Mountains reach 7,000 feet just 12 miles west and northwest; the same elevations in the Cascades are 30 miles north and east. Summers are warm and dry, winters cool and wet. The Pacific Ocean is only 100 miles west, but the mountain barrier gives Redding a more continental climate, with a 37 degree temperature difference in the coldest and warmest months. The terrain also causes moisture-bearing southerly winds to bring rain. Annual precipitation averages one-third more than areas 30 miles south. October through May receive 95 percent of the yearly precipitation. Note: Data for only six years were available to calculate these averages.

Temperatures

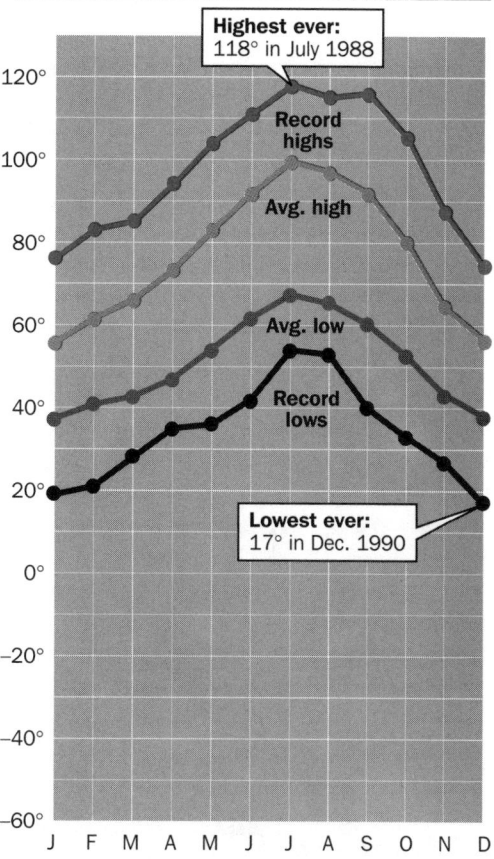

Highest ever: 118° in July 1988
Record highs
Avg. high
Avg. low
Record lows
Lowest ever: 17° in Dec. 1990

Weather extremes

Most rain in 24 hours:	7.30 in. Dec. 22, 1964
Most rain in a month:	28.84 in. January 1970
Most snow in 24 hours:	23 in. Jan. 1, 1889
Most snow in a month:	29 in. January 1950

Monthly averages

Month	Avg. precip. (in.)	Avg. snow (in.)	Wet days	Thunder-storm days	Pct. sky is cloudy	% p.m. relative humidity	Dew point	Wind speed (mph)
Jan.	8.5	0.5	11	0	54	74	NA	6.1
Feb.	6.2	0.2	8	*	44	62	NA	7.1
March	5.0	0.3	13	1	51	62	NA	8.0
April	2.8	T	6	1	43	50	NA	7.4
May	1.3	0.3	6	2	30	41	NA	8.1
June	0.8	T	4	2	16	37	NA	8.2
July	0.2	0	1	1	4	32	NA	7.2
Aug.	0.5	0	1	1	7	32	NA	6.7
Sept.	1.1	0	3	1	13	35	NA	6.6
Oct.	2.0	0	4	1	19	43	NA	6.6
Nov.	5.6	T	7	*	35	63	NA	6.3
Dec.	7.0	2.5	9	*	47	72	NA	7.0

T - Trace of rain or snow   * - Less than 1   NA - Not Available

Annual averages

Precipitation (in inches)	41.0
Snow (in inches)	3.8
Heating degree days	2,544
Cooling degree days	2,139
Days with thunderstorms	11.2
Days with fog	15.5
Days above 90°	104.7
Days below 32°	40.5
Wet days	72.5
Days with snow	NA
Days with 1.5 inches or more snow	1.3

Percent time sky is clear

Jan.	Feb.	March	April	May	June	July	Aug.	Sept.	Oct.	Nov.	Dec.
26.8	32.1	26.8	26.0	41.9	56.7	81.3	74.2	73.3	58.4	39.7	37.7

Reno, Nevada

Lat. 39° 30′ N **Lon.** 119° 47′ W **Elev.** 4,404 ft.

Reno is located at 4,400 feet above sea level, at the western edge of Truckee Meadows in a semiarid plateau. It lies in the lee of the Sierra Nevada range, which rises to 11,000 feet. Daily temperatures generally are mild, but with a drop from high to low often exceeding 45 degrees. While afternoons may exceed 90°F, a light wrap is often needed after sunset. Nights with lows above 60°F are rare. Afternoons in winter are moderate. There is an average of 25 inches of snow a year, but it seldom remains on the ground for more than three or four days at a time. Summer rain comes mainly as afternoon thunderstorms. Humidity is very low during summer, and moderately low during the winter. Sunshine is abundant throughout the year.

Temperatures

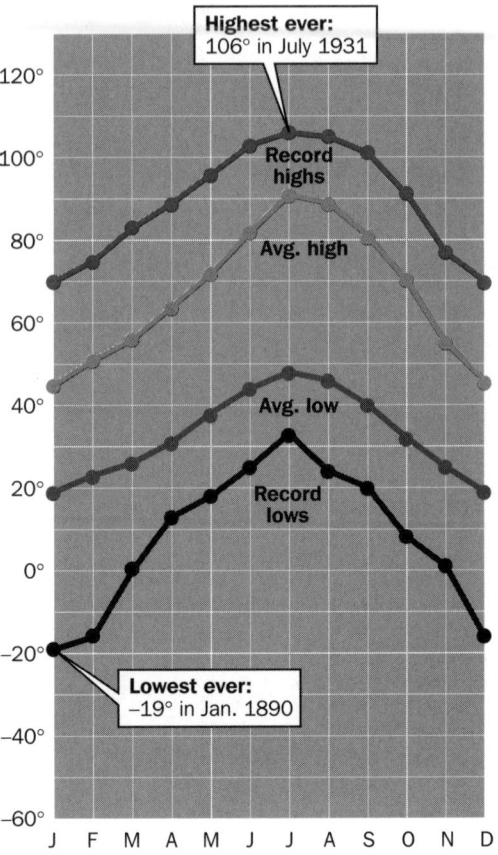

Highest ever: 106° in July 1931

Record highs

Avg. high

Avg. low

Record lows

Lowest ever: −19° in Jan. 1890

Weather extremes

Most rain in 24 hours:	2.37 in. Jan. 20 – 21, 1903
Most rain in a month:	6.76 in. January 1916
Most snow in 24 hours:	18 in. Feb. 16, 1990
Most snow in a month:	65.7 in. January 1916

Monthly averages

Month	Avg. precip. (in.)	Avg. snow (in.)	Wet days	Thunder-storm days	Pct. sky is cloudy	% p.m. relative humidity	Dew point	Wind speed (mph)
Jan.	1.0	6	6	0	39	51	21	9.2
Feb.	0.9	5	6	*	35	42	23	10.4
March	0.7	4	6	*	33	33	23	12.7
April	0.5	1	4	*	28	27	26	12.7
May	0.7	1	4	2	23	26	32	13.8
June	0.4	T	3	3	14	22	36	13.8
July	0.3	0	2	4	7	19	40	13.8
Aug.	0.2	0	2	3	7	19	39	12.7
Sept.	0.3	T	3	1	9	22	35	11.5
Oct.	0.4	T	3	1	16	27	30	6.9
Nov.	0.8	2	5	0	30	41	25	9.2
Dec.	1.0	4	6	0	34	51	21	9.2

T - Trace of rain or snow　　* - Less than 1　　　NA - Not Available

Annual averages

Precipitation (in inches)	7.3
Snow (in inches)	25
Heating degree days	5,878
Cooling degree days	366
Days with thunderstorms	14
Days with fog	15
Days above 90°	50
Days below 32°	180
Wet days	50
Days with snow	35
Days with 1.5 inches or more snow	10

Percent time sky is clear

Jan.	Feb.	March	April	May	June	July	Aug.	Sept.	Oct.	Nov.	Dec.
24.5	26.1	26.1	29.2	33.6	45.9	60.8	59.2	60.1	48.9	31.6	28.5

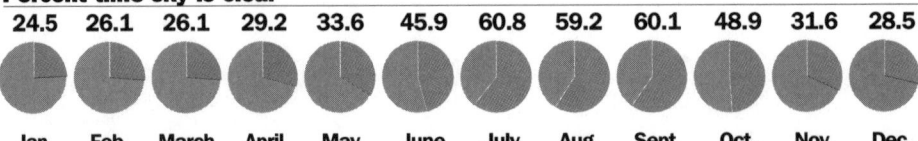

Richmond, Virginia

Lat. 37° 30′ N **Lon.** 77° 20′ W **Elev.** 164 ft.

Richmond straddles the James River, where the Piedmont Plateau gives way to the coastal plain. The Blue Ridge Mountains lie 90 miles west and the Chesapeake Bay 60 miles east. The climate is modified continental. Summers are warm and humid; winters are generally mild. The mountains are a partial barrier to cold, continental air in winter. The bay and Atlantic Ocean contribute to the humid summers and mild winters. Winter lows are normally in the 20s; zero is rare. Precipitation is fairly evenly distributed, but dry spells can occur, especially in fall when long periods of pleasant, mild weather are most common. Snow usually remains on the ground only one or two days. Freezing rain is not uncommon. Hurricanes passing nearby have produced record rainfalls.

Temperatures

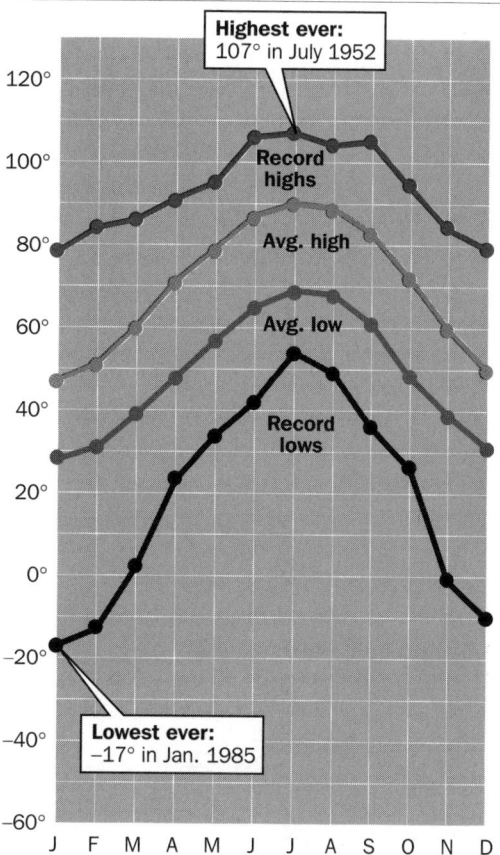

Highest ever: 107° in July 1952

Record highs

Avg. high

Avg. low

Record lows

Lowest ever: −17° in Jan. 1985

Weather extremes

Most rain in 24 hours:	8.79 in. Aug. 12, 1955
Most rain in a month:	18.87 in. July 1945
Most snow in 24 hours:	21.6 in. Jan. 23 – 24, 1940
Most snow in a month:	28.5 in. January 1940

Monthly averages

Month	Avg. precip. (in.)	Avg. snow (in.)	Wet days	Thunder-storm days	Pct. sky is cloudy	% p.m. relative humidity	Dew point	Wind speed (mph)
Jan.	3.3	5	10	*	44	54	26	8.1
Feb.	3.0	4	10	*	43	51	27	9.2
March	3.5	2	11	2	40	46	33	10.4
April	3.1	T	10	3	36	43	42	9.2
May	3.7	0	11	6	36	51	54	8.1
June	3.7	0	10	8	29	53	63	6.9
July	5.2	0	11	10	29	56	68	8.1
Aug.	4.9	0	10	8	29	58	67	6.9
Sept.	3.3	0	8	4	31	57	61	8.1
Oct.	3.1	T	7	1	32	53	49	8.1
Nov.	2.9	1	8	1	34	51	38	8.1
Dec.	3.1	2	9	*	40	55	30	8.1

T - Trace of rain or snow   * - Less than 1   NA - Not Available

Annual averages

Precipitation (in inches)	43
Snow (in inches)	13
Heating degree days	3,691
Cooling degree days	1,718
Days with thunderstorms	43
Days with fog	138
Days above 90°	41
Days below 32°	79
Wet days	115
Days with snow	6
Days with 1.5 inches or more snow	2

Percent time sky is clear

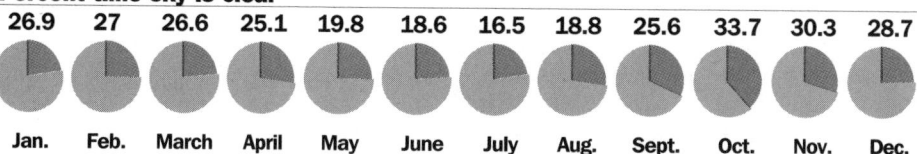

Jan.	Feb.	March	April	May	June	July	Aug.	Sept.	Oct.	Nov.	Dec.
26.9	27	26.6	25.1	19.8	18.6	16.5	18.8	25.6	33.7	30.3	28.7

Roanoke, Virginia

Lat. 37° 19' N **Lon.** 79° 58' W **Elev.** 1,149 ft.

The climate of Roanoke is relatively mild. The city is nestled among mountains that interrupt the Great Valley, which extends from northern Virginia southwestward into east Tennessee. This location offers a natural barrier to the winter cold as it moves southward. It is also far enough inland that hurricanes lose much of their destructive force before reaching Roanoke. Several creeks and small streams from nearby mountainous areas empty into the Roanoke River. Flood damage has been widespread on occasion. Rainfall is well apportioned throughout the year. Snow usually falls each winter, ranging from only a trace to more than 60 inches.

Temperatures

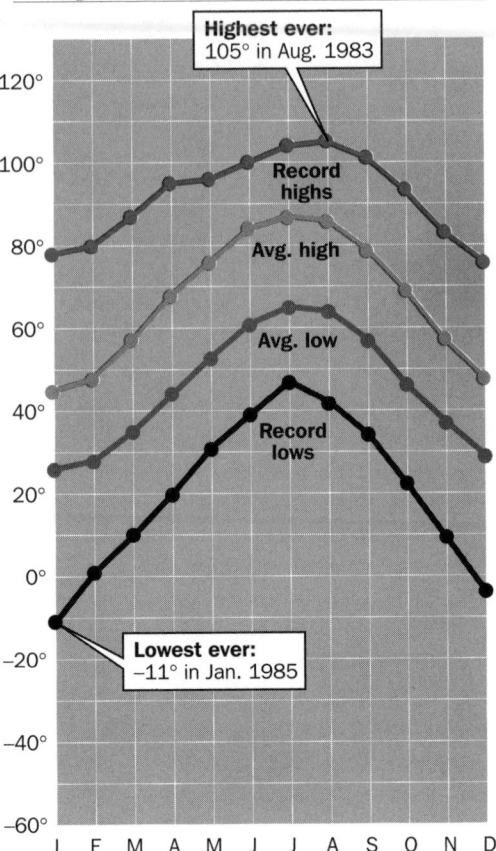

Highest ever: 105° in Aug. 1983

Record highs

Avg. high

Avg. low

Record lows

Lowest ever: −11° in Jan. 1985

Weather extremes

Most rain in 24 hours:	6.63 in. Nov. 4, 1985
Most rain in a month:	16.71 in. August 1940
Most snow in 24 hours:	18.6 in. Feb. 11 – 12, 1983
Most snow in a month:	41.2 in. January 1966

Monthly averages

Month	Avg. precip. (in.)	Avg. snow (in.)	Wet days	Thunderstorm days	Pct. sky is cloudy	% p.m. relative humidity	Dew point	Wind speed (mph)
Jan.	2.7	7	10	*	42	51	22	15.0
Feb.	3.2	8	10	*	40	48	24	15.0
March	3.5	4	11	1	39	45	30	13.8
April	3.3	T	10	3	34	43	39	13.8
May	4.0	T	12	6	35	50	51	9.2
June	3.3	0	10	6	28	52	60	8.1
July	3.7	0	12	8	28	54	64	8.1
Aug.	4.2	0	11	7	27	54	63	6.9
Sept.	3.4	0	8	3	32	54	57	8.1
Oct.	3.5	T	8	1	30	50	45	10.4
Nov.	2.9	2	9	*	34	50	34	12.7
Dec.	3.0	4	9	*	38	52	26	12.7

T - Trace of rain or snow   * - Less than 1   NA - Not Available

Annual averages

Precipitation (in inches)	40.9
Snow (in inches)	24
Heating degree days	4,277
Cooling degree days	1,179
Days with thunderstorms	35
Days with fog	122
Days above 90°	31
Days below 32°	90
Wet days	120
Days with snow	21
Days with 1.5 inches or more snow	9

Percent time sky is clear

24.7	24.5	23.9	26.4	21.5	20.2	19	21	27.2	35.3	28.2	25.1

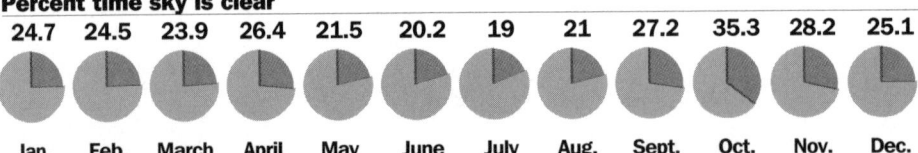

| Jan. | Feb. | March | April | May | June | July | Aug. | Sept. | Oct. | Nov. | Dec. |

Rochester, Minnesota

Lat. 43° 55' N **Lon.** 92° 30' W **Elev.** 1,297 ft.

Rochester is in the Zumbro River valley; the south branch of the Zumbro flows through the city. A succession of high and low pressure systems over Rochester produce a changeable weather pattern. The climate is continental with four definite seasons — winters are cold, summers pleasant. The season-to-season temperature variation is quite large. Rochester lies near the northern edge of the influx of moisture from the Gulf of Mexico. Severe storms such as blizzards, freezing rain, tornadoes, wind, and hail do occur. The snow season usually begins in November. Rolling terrain and the thunderstorm probability make the south branch of the Zumbro and its tributaries susceptible to flash flooding.

Temperatures

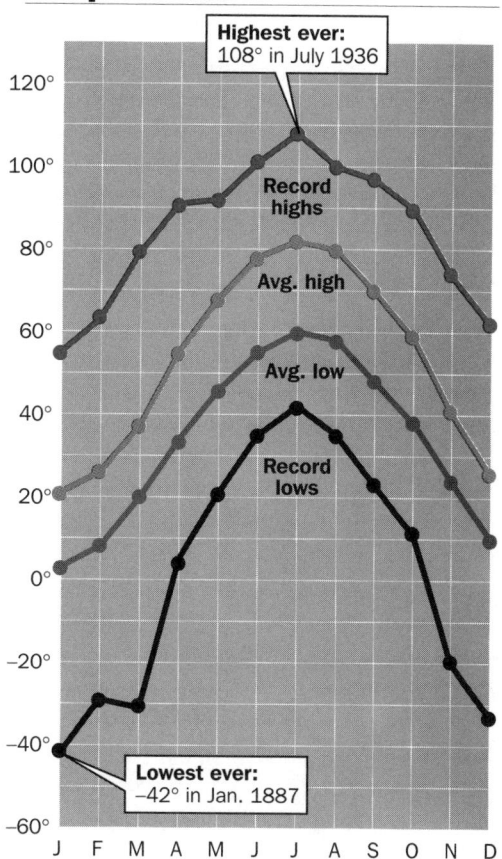

Highest ever: 108° in July 1936

Record highs

Avg. high

Avg. low

Record lows

Lowest ever: −42° in Jan. 1887

Weather extremes

Most rain in 24 hours:	7.47 in. July 11, 1981
Most rain in a month:	12.33 in. July 1978
Most snow in 24 hours:	15.4 in. Jan. 22, 1982
Most snow in a month:	35.1 in. March 1951

Monthly averages

Month	Avg. precip. (in.)	Avg. snow (in.)	Wet days	Thunder-storm days	Pct. sky is cloudy	% p.m. relative humidity	Dew point	Wind speed (mph)
Jan.	0.8	9	8	*	48	71	6	15.0
Feb.	0.8	8	7	*	46	68	11	15.0
March	1.8	10	10	1	51	65	21	15.0
April	2.6	4	11	3	47	54	33	15.0
May	3.4	T	11	6	40	52	45	13.8
June	4.1	0	11	8	33	53	55	11.5
July	4.1	0	10	8	26	55	60	11.5
Aug.	3.8	0	10	7	29	56	59	11.5
Sept.	3.1	T	10	5	34	56	50	12.7
Oct.	2.1	1	8	2	38	54	38	13.8
Nov.	1.5	5	8	1	53	65	25	15.0
Dec.	1.0	10	9	*	54	74	13	15.0

T - Trace of rain or snow   * - Less than 1   NA - Not Available

Annual averages

Precipitation (in inches)	29.0
Snow (in inches)	46
Heating degree days	8,179
Cooling degree days	557
Days with thunderstorms	41
Days with fog	120
Days above 90°	10
Days below 32°	165
Wet days	113
Days with snow	80
Days with 1.5 inches or more snow	20

Percent time sky is clear

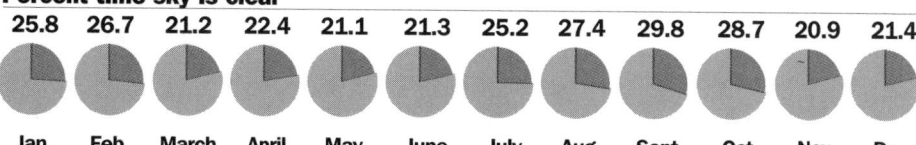

25.8	26.7	21.2	22.4	21.1	21.3	25.2	27.4	29.8	28.7	20.9	21.4
Jan.	Feb.	March	April	May	June	July	Aug.	Sept.	Oct.	Nov.	Dec.

Rochester, New York

Lat. 43° 7' N **Lon.** 77° 40' W   **Elev.** 547 ft.

Rochester is at the mouth of the Genesee River at about the midpoint of the south shore of Lake Ontario. The lake plays a major role in the weather, keeping summer temperatures from rising much above the low- to mid-90s, and in the winter, preventing temperatures from falling below -15°F most of the time. The lake effect plays a major role in winter snowfall distribution. Snowfalls of one to two feet or more in 24 hours are common near the lake. The lake rarely freezes over because of its depth. The area is also prone to other heavy snowstorms and blizzards because of its proximity to the paths of low pressure systems coming up the East Coast. Hail occurs occasionally; heavy fog is rare. The year's first frost usually occurs in late September and the last frost typically occurs in mid-May.

Temperatures

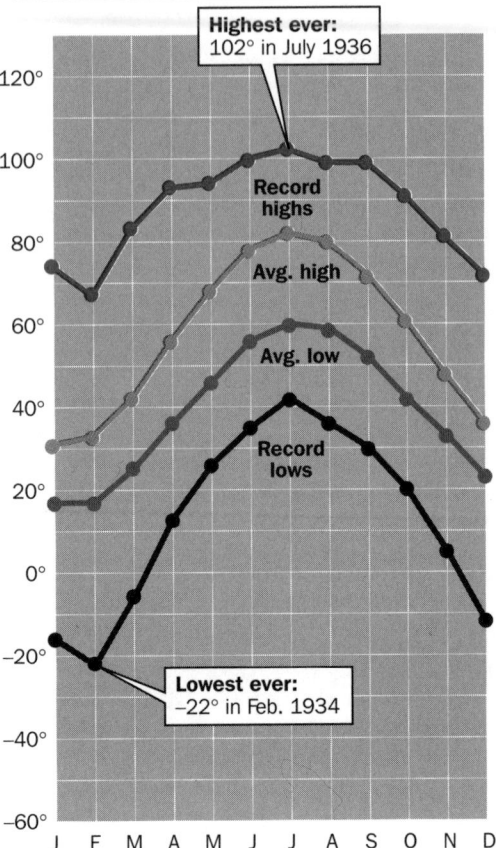

Highest ever: 102° in July 1936

Record highs

Avg. high

Avg. low

Record lows

Lowest ever: -22° in Feb. 1934

Weather extremes

Most rain in 24 hours:	3.85 in. May 16 – 17, 1974
Most rain in a month:	9.70 in. July 1947
Most snow in 24 hours:	22.8 in. Feb. 6 – 7, 1978
Most snow in a month:	64.8 in. February 1958

Monthly averages

Month	Avg. precip. (in.)	Avg. snow (in.)	Wet days	Thunderstorm days	Pct. sky is cloudy	% p.m. relative humidity	Dew point	Wind speed (mph)
Jan.	2.2	24	17	*	65	71	17	16.1
Feb.	2.3	23	15	*	60	69	18	15.0
March	2.5	14	14	1	54	63	25	15.0
April	2.6	4	13	2	47	56	35	13.8
May	2.7	T	12	3	40	53	45	12.7
June	2.8	0	10	5	32	53	55	11.5
July	2.6	0	10	6	26	52	60	8.1
Aug.	3.3	0	10	6	30	55	59	8.1
Sept.	2.8	T	11	3	35	59	53	8.1
Oct.	2.5	T	12	1	44	61	42	11.5
Nov.	2.8	7	15	*	62	69	33	13.8
Dec.	2.6	20	18	*	68	74	23	13.8

T - Trace of rain or snow   * - Less than 1   NA - Not Available

Annual averages

Precipitation (in inches)	31.8
Snow (in inches)	92
Heating degree days	6,680
Cooling degree days	609
Days with thunderstorms	27
Days with fog	123
Days above 90°	11
Days below 32°	135
Wet days	157
Days with snow	128
Days with 1.5 inches or more snow	39

Percent time sky is clear

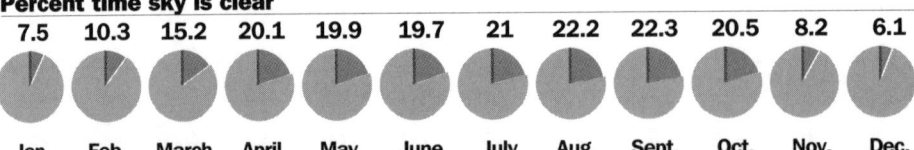

7.5	10.3	15.2	20.1	19.9	19.7	21	22.2	22.3	20.5	8.2	6.1
Jan.	Feb.	March	April	May	June	July	Aug.	Sept.	Oct.	Nov.	Dec.

Rockford, Illinois

Lat. 42° 12' N **Lon.** 89° 6' W **Elev.** 724 ft.

Rockford's climate is characterized by hot summers and cold winters. The influence of Lake Michigan, about 60 miles away, is felt as far west as Rockford when northeasterly winds blow across the lake. In winter they generate more cloudiness and somewhat higher temperatures in Rockford than in areas west of the city toward the Mississippi River. Winters remain cold, however, and snow cover usually is continuous from late December through February. In the summer, the lake exerts a cooling effect. Though summers are hot, seldom does oppressive heat prevail for extended periods. About 34 percent of the precipitation occurs in the three summer months of June to August and 64 percent in six months from April to September. But no month averages less than 4 percent of the total.

Temperatures

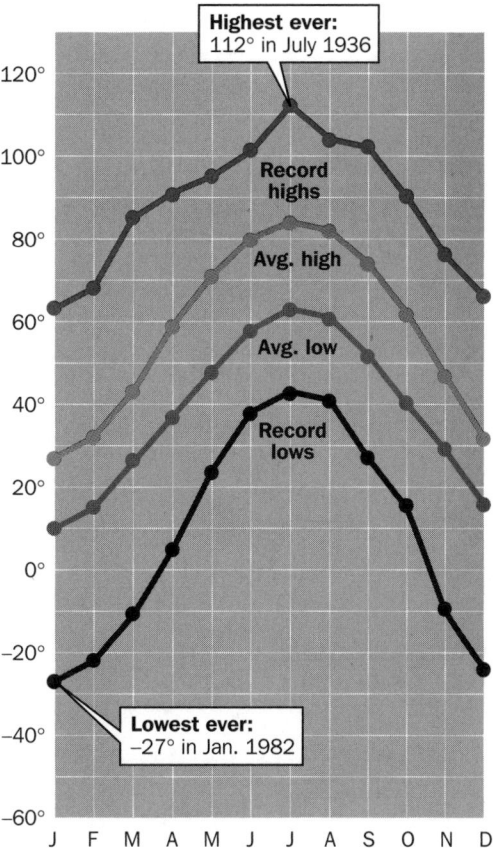

Highest ever: 112° in July 1936

Record highs

Avg. high

Avg. low

Record lows

Lowest ever: −27° in Jan. 1982

Weather extremes

Most rain in 24 hours:	8.41 in. July 17 – 18, 1952
Most rain in a month:	11.81 in. July 1952
Most snow in 24 hours:	16.3 in. Jan. 6 – 7, 1918
Most snow in a month:	36.1 in. January 1918

Monthly averages

Month	Avg. precip. (in.)	Avg. snow (in.)	Wet days	Thunder-storm days	Pct. sky is cloudy	% p.m. relative humidity	Dew point	Wind speed (mph)
Jan.	1.4	9	9	*	51	68	12	12.7
Feb.	1.2	7	8	*	50	64	17	12.7
March	2.6	7	11	2	52	60	26	12.7
April	3.9	2	12	4	48	51	36	12.7
May	3.8	T	11	6	39	50	47	10.4
June	4.6	0	10	8	32	51	57	9.2
July	4.5	0	10	8	27	53	62	8.1
Aug.	4.1	0	9	6	28	56	61	8.1
Sept.	3.8	0	9	5	33	53	53	9.2
Oct.	3.1	T	9	3	38	53	41	9.2
Nov.	2.6	3	9	1	52	62	30	10.4
Dec.	2.0	10	10	*	56	70	19	12.7

T - Trace of rain or snow   * - Less than 1   NA - Not Available

Annual averages

Precipitation (in inches)	37.4
Snow (in inches)	37
Heating degree days	6,903
Cooling degree days	797
Days with thunderstorms	43
Days with fog	142
Days above 90°	15
Days below 32°	145
Wet days	117
Days with snow	61
Days with 1.5 inches or more snow	17

Percent time sky is clear

Jan.	Feb.	March	April	May	June	July	Aug.	Sept.	Oct.	Nov.	Dec.
25.5	25.9	21.1	22.2	22.4	21.8	26.5	27	30.2	30.4	22.6	21.9

Roswell, New Mexico

Lat. 33° 18' N **Lon.** 104° 32' W **Elev.** 3,669 ft.

Roswell is located on the Rio Hondo in the Pecos Plains. The Rocky Mountains are just to the west. In winter, air warms as it comes down the mountains, keeping winter temperatures relatively moderate. Summer features frequent showers and thunderstorms, which account for over half the annual precipitation. Rainfall tapers off in the fall with a decline in storm activity, leaving low wind movement and mostly clear skies, and frosty nights alternate with warm days. Subzero cold spells are of short duration and winter is the season of least precipitation. Rain is most erratic in spring.

Temperatures

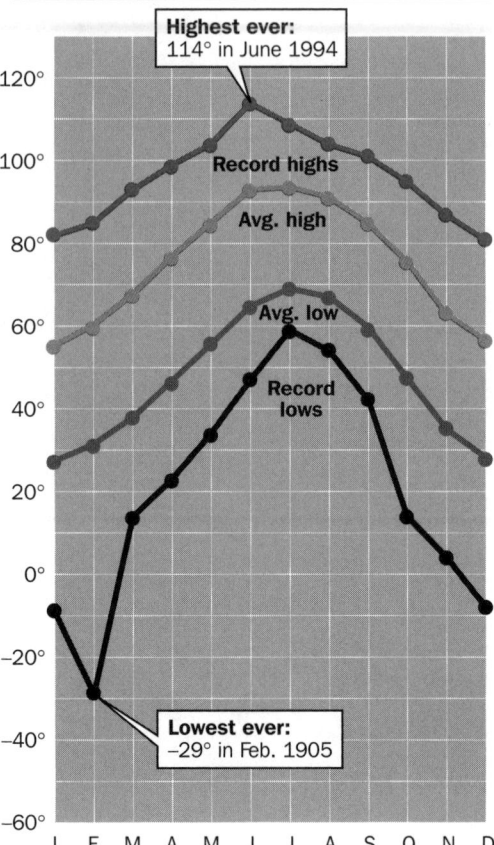

Highest ever: 114° in June 1994

Record highs

Avg. high

Avg. low

Record lows

Lowest ever: −29° in Feb. 1905

Weather extremes

Most rain in 24 hours:	5.65 in. Nov. 1, 1901
Most rain in a month:	9.56 in. August 1916
Most snow in 24 hours:	16.5 in. Feb. 4 – 5, 1988
Most snow in a month:	23.3 in. February 1905

Monthly averages

Month	Avg. precip. (in.)	Avg. snow (in.)	Wet days	Thunder-storm days	Pct. sky is cloudy	% p.m. relative humidity	Dew point	Wind speed (mph)
Jan.	0.4	2	3	*	25	39	21	9.2
Feb.	0.4	3	3	*	24	33	23	9.2
March	0.3	1	2	1	20	24	24	10.4
April	0.5	T	2	2	18	22	29	11.5
May	1.1	T	4	5	15	24	38	11.5
June	1.4	0	4	6	12	25	49	11.5
July	1.6	0	7	8	13	31	56	10.4
Aug.	2.1	0	7	8	13	35	57	9.2
Sept.	1.8	0	6	4	18	37	51	9.2
Oct.	1.2	T	4	2	16	35	40	9.2
Nov.	0.4	1	2	1	18	37	28	9.2
Dec.	0.4	2	3	*	21	41	22	9.2

T - Trace of rain or snow　　* - Less than 1　　NA - Not Available

Annual averages

Precipitation (in inches)	11.6
Snow (in inches)	10
Heating degree days	3,126
Cooling degree days	1,863
Days with thunderstorms	37
Days with fog	40
Days above 90°	91
Days below 32°	87
Wet days	47
Days with snow	12
Days with 1.5 inches or more snow	5

Percent time sky is clear

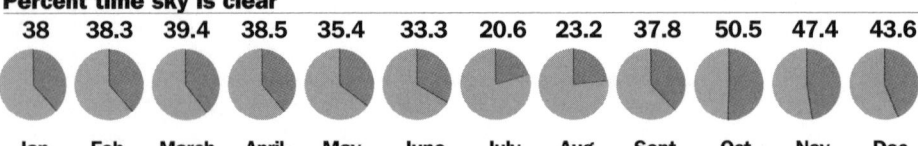

38	38.3	39.4	38.5	35.4	33.3	20.6	23.2	37.8	50.5	47.4	43.6
Jan.	Feb.	March	April	May	June	July	Aug.	Sept.	Oct.	Nov.	Dec.

Sacramento, California

Lat. 38° 31' N **Lon.** 121° 30' W **Elev.** 18 ft.

Sacramento is in the northern end of California's interior valley which runs from Red Bluff in the north to the Tehachapi Mountains above Los Angeles. Weather is mild with abundant sunshine. Mountains to the north, west and east moderate winter storms, although heavy snowfall and torrential rains frequently fall on the western Sierra Nevada slopes and may produce flooding along the Sacramento River. Summers are dry with warm to hot afternoons and mostly mild nights, but the low humidity should be considered when comparing temperatures here with those of cities in more humid regions. The rainy season is November through March. Heavy fog occurs in midwinter; moderate fogs may come anytime during the wet, cold season.

Temperatures

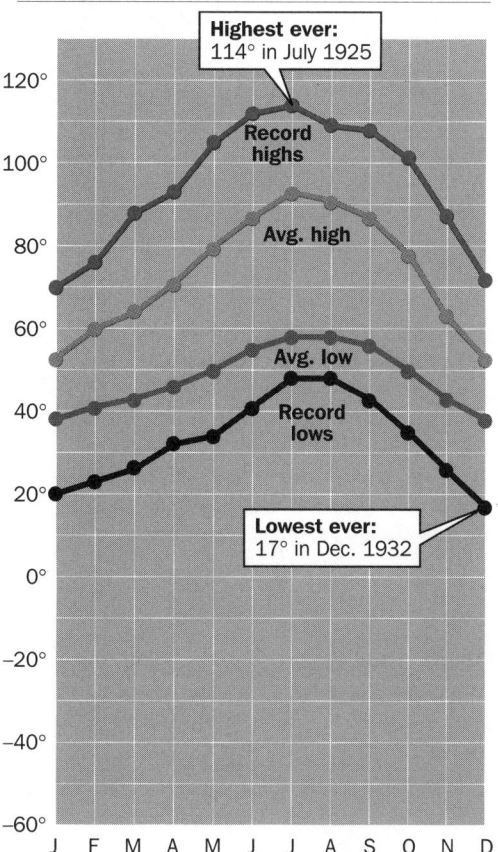

Highest ever: 114° in July 1925

Record highs

Avg. high

Avg. low

Record lows

Lowest ever: 17° in Dec. 1932

Weather extremes

Most rain in 24 hours:	7.24 in. April 20 – 21, 1880
Most rain in a month:	15.04 in. January 1862
Most snow in 24 hours:	3.5 in. Jan. 4 – 5, 1888
Most snow in a month:	4.0 in. January 1888

Monthly averages

Month	Avg. precip. (in.)	Avg. snow (in.)	Wet days	Thunder-storm days	Pct. sky is cloudy	% p.m. relative humidity	Dew point	Wind speed (mph)
Jan.	3.6	T	10	*	52	70	39	9.2
Feb.	2.8	T	8	*	37	59	41	9.2
March	2.4	T	9	1	29	51	42	10.4
April	1.3	T	5	1	21	43	44	10.4
May	0.4	0	3	*	12	36	47	11.5
June	0.1	0	1	*	6	31	50	12.7
July	T	0	*	*	2	28	53	10.4
Aug.	0.1	0	*	*	3	29	53	10.4
Sept.	0.3	0	2	*	6	31	51	10.4
Oct.	1.0	0	3	*	13	39	47	10.4
Nov.	2.4	0	7	*	32	57	43	9.2
Dec.	2.8	T	9	*	50	70	39	9.2

T - Trace of rain or snow   * - Less than 1   NA - Not Available

Annual averages

Precipitation (in inches)	17.3
Snow (in inches)	T
Heating degree days	2,698
Cooling degree days	1,200
Days with thunderstorms	2
Days with fog	95
Days above 90°	73
Days below 32°	21
Wet days	57
Days with snow	*
Days with 1.5 inches or more snow	*

Percent time sky is clear

22	28.7	35.1	40.5	50.3	62.2	78.4	74.8	71.1	56.1	34.2	23.1
Jan.	Feb.	March	April	May	June	July	Aug.	Sept.	Oct.	Nov.	Dec.

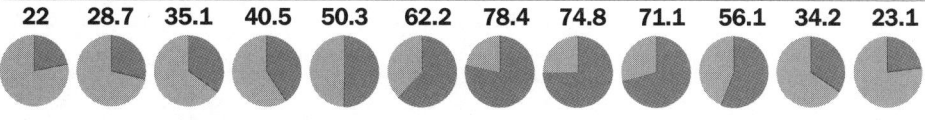

St. Louis, Missouri

Lat. 38° 45' N **Lon.** 90° 22' W **Elev.** 535 ft.

St. Louis is just below the confluence of the Missouri and Mississippi rivers, which gives it a modified continental climate. Warm, moist air from the Gulf of Mexico, and cold Canadian air alternately invade the area and the conflict produces a variety of weather conditions, none of which is likely to persist. Winters are seldom severe, with zero or below an average of two or three days. Snowfall of an inch or more comes on five to 10 days in most years. No more than five days over 100°F are expected per summer. It is not unusual to have one- to two-week dry periods during the growing season. Thunderstorms occur on 40 to 50 days per year — a few severe, with hail and damaging winds. Tornadoes have produced extensive damage and loss of life.

Temperatures

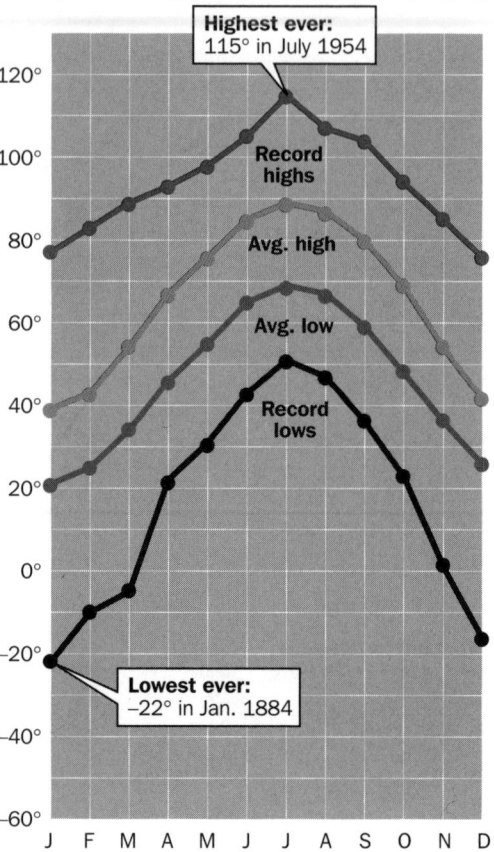

Highest ever: 115° in July 1954

Record highs

Avg. high

Avg. low

Record lows

Lowest ever: −22° in Jan. 1884

Weather extremes

Most rain in 24 hours:	8.78 in. Aug. 15 – 16, 1946
Most rain in a month:	14.78 in. August 1946
Most snow in 24 hours:	20.4 in. March 30–31, 1890
Most snow in a month:	28.8 in. March 1912

Monthly averages

Month	Avg. precip. (in.)	Avg. snow (in.)	Wet days	Thunder- storm days	Pct. sky is cloudy	% p.m. relative humidity	Dew point	Wind speed (mph)
Jan.	1.9	6	8	1	47	62	21	12.7
Feb.	2.2	4	8	1	47	59	25	12.7
March	3.4	4	11	3	46	54	33	13.8
April	3.4	T	11	5	41	49	42	13.8
May	3.8	0	11	7	34	51	53	10.4
June	4.0	0	10	7	27	51	62	10.4
July	3.8	0	8	7	21	51	66	9.2
Aug.	2.9	0	8	6	21	52	65	8.1
Sept.	2.9	0	8	4	25	50	58	9.2
Oct.	2.8	T	8	2	29	50	46	10.4
Nov.	3.0	1	9	2	42	56	35	12.7
Dec.	2.6	4	9	1	49	63	26	12.7

T - Trace of rain or snow　　*　- Less than 1　　NA - Not Available

Annual averages

Precipitation (in inches)	36.8
Snow (in inches)	20
Heating degree days	4,822
Cooling degree days	1,529
Days with thunderstorms	46
Days with fog	141
Days above 90°	43
Days below 32°	100
Wet days	109
Days with snow	28
Days with 1.5 inches or more snow	8

Percent time sky is clear

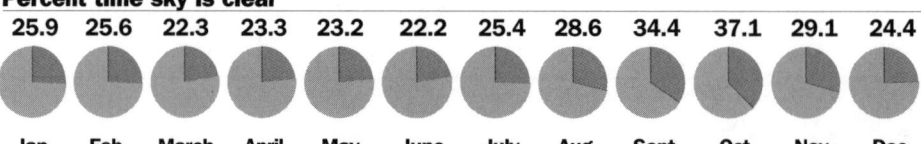

Jan.	Feb.	March	April	May	June	July	Aug.	Sept.	Oct.	Nov.	Dec.
25.9	25.6	22.3	23.3	23.2	22.2	25.4	28.6	34.4	37.1	29.1	24.4

St. Paul Island, Alaska

Lat. 57° 09' N **Lon.** 170° 13' W **Elev.** 22 ft.

St. Paul is one of the Pribilof Islands in the Bering Sea and is the summer home of the Alaskan fur seals. Its maritime climate results in cloudiness, heavy fog, high humidity, and daily temperature ranges of only 7 degrees. Humidity is high from May to late September, and during the summer there is almost continuous low cloudiness and occasional heavy fog. Despite the high humidities, precipitation is meager; August through October is wettest. Temperatures are cool year-round with summer highs only in the 50s. High winds are common. October to April is stormy, often with gale-force winds and blizzard conditions. Prolonged north and northeasterly winds between January and April sometimes cause the ice pack to move south and surround the island.

Temperatures

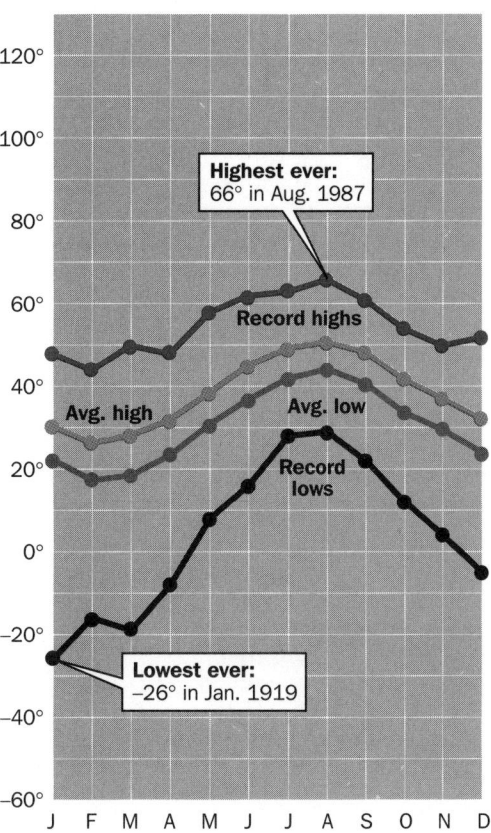

Weather extremes

Most rain in 24 hours:	2.00 in. Aug. 23 – 24, 1984
Most rain in a month:	9.32 in. August 1953
Most snow in 24 hours:	13.8 in. Jan. 30, 1964
Most snow in a month:	55.8 in. February 1964

Monthly averages

Month	Avg. precip. (in.)	Avg. snow (in.)	Wet days	Thunder-storm days	Pct. sky is cloudy	% p.m. relative humidity	Dew point	Wind speed (mph)
Jan.	1.8	11.8	18	0	74	83	NA	20.4
Feb.	1.3	9.5	15	0	70	84	NA	20.9
March	1.3	9.1	16	0	66	83	NA	19.3
April	1.2	5.6	14	0	73	82	NA	18.0
May	1.2	2.1	14	0	84	82	NA	15.6
June	1.2	0.1	13	*	86	84	NA	13.9
July	2.0	0.0	15	0	91	89	NA	12.3
Aug.	3.1	0.0	19	0	89	90	NA	14.1
Sept.	2.5	0.1	20	0	79	84	NA	15.7
Oct.	2.9	2.6	22	0	74	79	NA	18.3
Nov.	2.5	6.6	22	*	75	80	NA	20.7
Dec.	1.8	9.4	20	0	78	84	NA	21.3

T - Trace of rain or snow   * - Less than 1   NA - Not Available

Annual averages

Precipitation (in inches)	22.7
Snow (in inches)	56.9
Heating degree days	11,178
Cooling degree days	0.0
Days with thunderstorms	*
Days with fog	58
Days above 90°	0
Days below 32°	188
Wet days	207
Days with snow	NA
Days with 1.5 inches or more snow	18

Percent time sky is clear

7.4	8.8	10.3	7.0	3.9	4.0	1.9	2.3	2.3	2.3	4.0	4.8

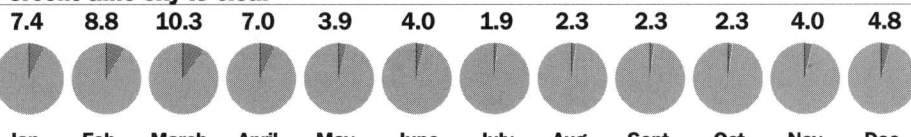

| Jan. | Feb. | March | April | May | June | July | Aug. | Sept. | Oct. | Nov. | Dec. |

Salt Lake City, Utah

Lat. 40° 47' N **Lon.** 111° 57' W **Elev.** 4,222 ft.

Salt Lake City is in a northern Utah valley surrounded by mountains on three sides and by the Great Salt Lake to the northwest, with elevations ranging from near 4,200 to 5,000 feet above sea level. Mountain ranges, including the Wasatch, rise from between 6,000 and 12,000 feet above sea level and help shelter the valley from storms in the winter. But they also help thunderstorms develop in the summer. The Great Salt Lake, which never freezes over, can moderate the temperatures of cold winter winds blowing from the northwest. Summers are hot and dry; winters are cold, but not severe. The average annual snowfall is under 60 inches at the airport but much higher amounts fall in the mountains.

Temperatures

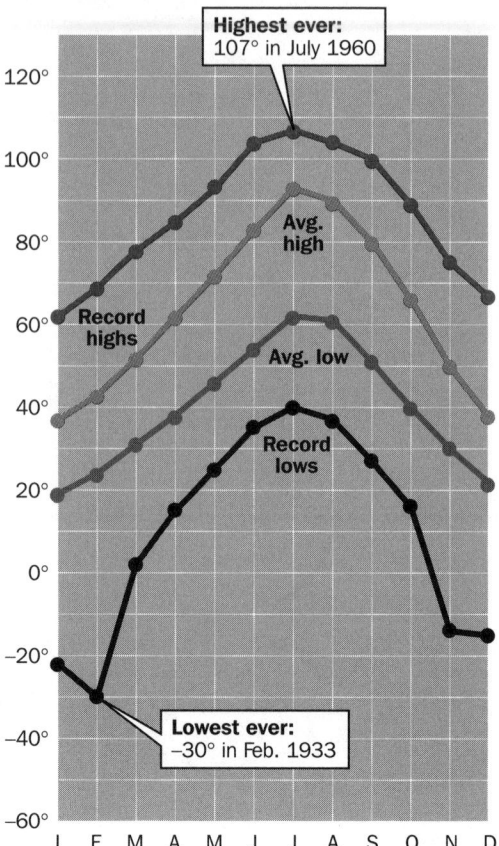

Highest ever: 107° in July 1960

Avg. high

Record highs

Avg. low

Record lows

Lowest ever: −30° in Feb. 1933

Weather extremes

Most rain in 24 hours:	2.41 in. April 22 – 23, 1957
Most rain in a month:	7.04 in. September 1982
Most snow in 24 hours:	18.4 in. Oct. 17 – 18, 1984
Most snow in a month:	50.3 in. January 1993

Monthly averages

Month	Avg. precip. (in.)	Avg. snow (in.)	Wet days	Thunder- storm days	Pct. sky is cloudy	% p.m. relative humidity	Dew point	Wind speed (mph)
Jan.	1.3	13	10	*	55	69	20	10.4
Feb.	1.2	10	8	1	48	59	24	10.4
March	1.8	11	10	2	45	47	27	10.4
April	2.0	6	9	2	40	38	31	10.4
May	1.7	1	9	6	30	33	37	10.4
June	0.9	T	6	6	18	26	41	10.4
July	0.8	0	5	7	12	22	45	10.4
Aug.	0.9	0	5	7	12	23	45	10.4
Sept.	1.1	T	6	4	15	28	40	10.4
Oct.	1.3	2	6	2	24	40	34	9.2
Nov.	1.3	6	8	1	42	59	28	9.2
Dec.	1.4	13	10	*	53	71	22	9.2

T - Trace of rain or snow　　* - Less than 1　　NA - Not Available

Annual averages

Precipitation (in inches)	15.6
Snow (in inches)	63
Heating degree days	5,752
Cooling degree days	1,042
Days with thunderstorms	38
Days with fog	42
Days above 90°	56
Days below 32°	128
Wet days	92
Days with snow	74
Days with 1.5 inches or more snow	27

Percent time sky is clear

Jan.	Feb.	March	April	May	June	July	Aug.	Sept.	Oct.	Nov.	Dec.
12.1	15.1	17.4	20	20.8	33.9	37.3	36.5	43.4	38.5	20.5	13.3

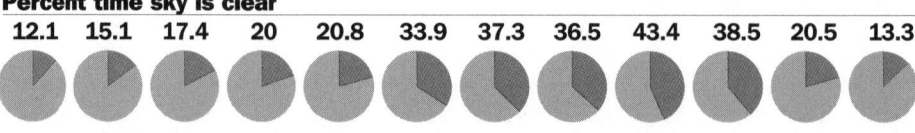

San Angelo, Texas

Lat. 31° 22' N **Lon.** 100° 30' W **Elev.** 1,903 ft.

Warm, dry weather predominates here, although changes may be rapid and frequent with the passage of cold fronts or "northers." Summer brings fair skies, south to southwest winds and dry air. Rapid temperature drops occur after sunset; lows range from the upper 60s to lower 70s. In winter, temperature drops of 20 to 30 degrees are common. Cold polar outbreaks have produced record lows of zero or below. Heavy rainfall occurs from April through October, but in late summer heavy precipitation may occur when tropical disturbances move inland over south Texas. Although high winds may blow for several days, the frequency and intensity of dust storms depend on soil conditions in the Texas Panhandle and in New Mexico.

Temperatures

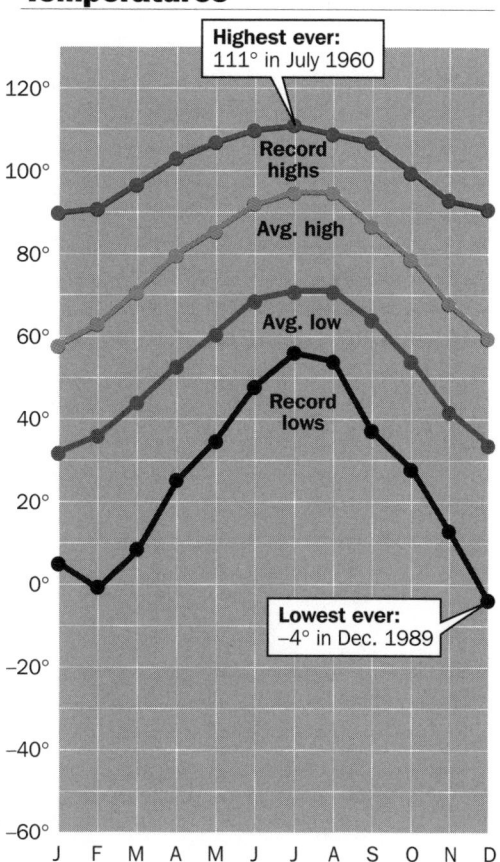

Highest ever: 111° in July 1960

Record highs

Avg. high

Avg. low

Record lows

Lowest ever: −4° in Dec. 1989

Weather extremes

Most rain in 24 hours:	11.75 in. Sept. 15, 1936
Most rain in a month:	27.65 in. September 1936
Most snow in 24 hours:	7.4 in. Jan. 20 – 21, 1978
Most snow in a month:	13.0 in. January 1926

Monthly averages

Month	Avg. precip. (in.)	Avg. snow (in.)	Wet days	Thunder-storm days	Pct. sky is cloudy	% p.m. relative humidity	Dew point	Wind speed (mph)
Jan.	0.8	2	5	*	36	42	29	12.7
Feb.	1.0	1	4	1	34	41	32	12.7
March	0.9	T	4	2	32	35	38	13.8
April	1.7	T	5	5	30	35	46	12.7
May	2.9	0	7	7	29	40	56	12.7
June	2.1	0	5	5	19	40	62	12.7
July	1.3	0	4	4	14	36	62	11.5
Aug.	1.6	0	5	5	16	37	63	10.4
Sept.	3.0	0	6	4	24	46	61	10.4
Oct.	2.3	0	5	3	24	44	52	11.5
Nov.	0.9	1	4	1	29	43	41	11.5
Dec.	0.7	T	4	1	34	43	32	11.5

T - Trace of rain or snow   * - Less than 1   NA - Not Available

Annual averages

Precipitation (in inches)	19.3
Snow (in inches)	3
Heating degree days	2,349
Cooling degree days	2,530
Days with thunderstorms	38
Days with fog	43
Days above 90°	109
Days below 32°	50
Wet days	58
Days with snow	4
Days with 1.5 inches or more snow	1

Percent time sky is clear

37.4	37.9	38	33.6	29.3	32.4	35.1	34	33.5	44.1	43.1	39.7

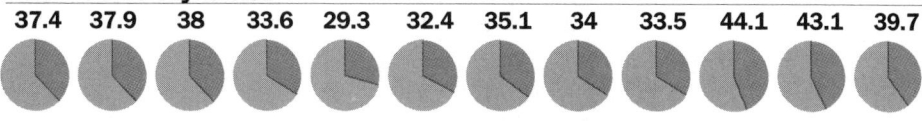

| Jan. | Feb. | March | April | May | June | July | Aug. | Sept. | Oct. | Nov. | Dec. |

San Antonio, Texas

Lat. 29° 32' N **Lon.** 98° 28' W **Elev.** 794 ft.

San Antonio, 140 miles from the Gulf of Mexico, has a modified subtropical climate with temperatures ranging from 50°F in January to the middle 80s in July and August. Due to its proximity to the Gulf, San Antonio sometimes suffers the effects of tropical storms. One of the fastest winds recorded, 74 mph, occurred as a tropical storm moved inland east of the city in August 1942. While summers are hot, extremely high temperatures are rare. Mild weather prevails during much of the winter. While clouds form frequently in the late evening, they usually dissipate around noon, and clear skies prevail during the afternoon.

Temperatures

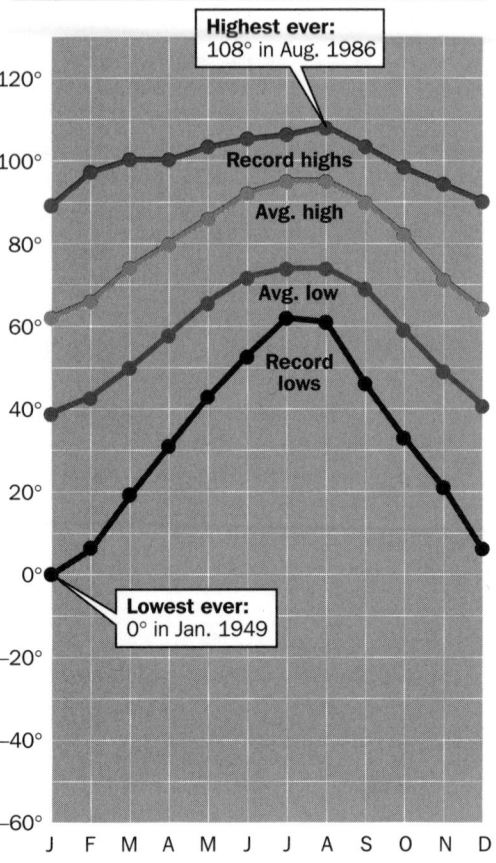

Highest ever: 108° in Aug. 1986

Record highs

Avg. high

Avg. low

Record lows

Lowest ever: 0° in Jan. 1949

Weather extremes

Most rain in 24 hours:	7.28 in. Sept. 26 – 27, 1973
Most rain in a month:	15.78 in. September 1946
Most snow in 24 hours:	13.2 in. Jan. 12, 1985
Most snow in a month:	15.9 in. January 1985

Monthly averages

Month	Avg. precip. (in.)	Avg. snow (in.)	Wet days	Thunder-storm days	Pct. sky is cloudy	% p.m. relative humidity	Dew point	Wind speed (mph)
Jan.	1.5	1	8	1	45	51	38	10.4
Feb.	1.8	T	8	1	44	48	41	11.5
March	1.5	T	7	2	42	45	46	11.5
April	2.6	0	7	4	44	48	55	11.5
May	3.8	0	8	6	38	51	63	11.5
June	3.6	0	6	5	21	48	68	11.5
July	2.0	0	5	3	13	43	69	10.4
Aug.	2.5	0	5	4	13	42	68	10.4
Sept.	3.3	0	7	4	20	47	65	9.2
Oct.	3.2	0	7	3	25	46	57	10.4
Nov.	2.3	T	6	2	35	48	47	10.4
Dec.	1.4	T	7	1	41	49	40	10.4

T - Trace of rain or snow   * - Less than 1   NA - Not Available

Annual averages

Precipitation (in inches)	29.6
Snow (in inches)	1
Heating degree days	1,592
Cooling degree days	3,075
Days with thunderstorms	36
Days with fog	115
Days above 90°	112
Days below 32°	23
Wet days	81
Days with snow	*
Days with 1.5 inches or more snow	*

Percent time sky is clear

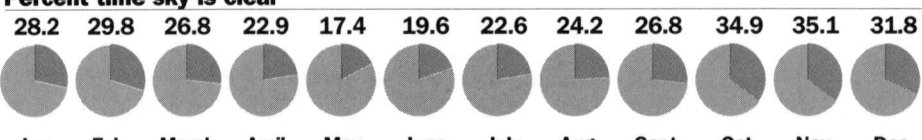

Jan.	Feb.	March	April	May	June	July	Aug.	Sept.	Oct.	Nov.	Dec.
28.2	29.8	26.8	22.9	17.4	19.6	22.6	24.2	26.8	34.9	35.1	31.8

San Diego, California

Lat. 32° 44' N **Lon.** 117° 10' W **Elev.** 13 ft.

San Diego is located on San Diego Bay in the southwest corner of southern California where the prevailing winds and weather are tempered by the Pacific Ocean. Dry easterly winds sometimes blow for several days at a time, bringing temperatures in the 90s and 100s in eastern sections of the city and outlying suburbs. Highest temperatures occur in September and October, but are usually accompanied by very low humidity. A marked feature of the climate is the wide variation in temperature a few miles inland. Spring and summer typically have low marine clouds at night and in early morning, which "burn off" as the day warms. In fall and winter there can be coastal fog. Sunshine is plentiful for a marine location.

Temperatures

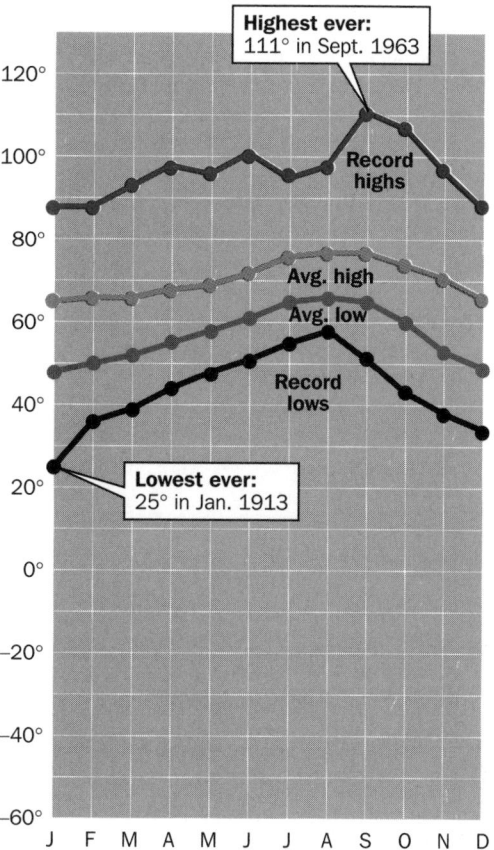

Highest ever: 111° in Sept. 1963

Record highs

Avg. high

Avg. low

Record lows

Lowest ever: 25° in Jan. 1913

Weather extremes

Most rain in 24 hours:	3.23 in. April 5, 1926
Most rain in a month:	9.26 in. December 1921
Most snow in 24 hours:	none
Most snow in a month:	none

Monthly averages

Month	Avg. precip. (in.)	Avg. snow (in.)	Wet days	Thunder-storm days	Pct. sky is cloudy	% p.m. relative humidity	Dew point	Wind speed (mph)
Jan.	1.9	T	7	*	29	57	43	8.1
Feb.	1.4	0	5	*	30	58	45	9.2
March	1.7	0	7	*	32	59	47	10.4
April	0.8	0	4	*	34	59	50	10.4
May	0.2	0	2	*	45	63	53	9.2
June	0.1	0	1	*	49	66	57	9.2
July	T	0	*	*	37	65	61	9.2
Aug.	0.1	0	1	*	35	66	62	9.2
Sept.	0.2	0	1	*	36	65	61	9.2
Oct.	0.4	0	2	*	33	63	55	9.2
Nov.	1.2	T	5	*	25	60	48	9.2
Dec.	1.4	T	5	*	26	58	43	8.1

T - Trace of rain or snow   * - Less than 1   NA - Not Available

Annual averages

Precipitation (in inches)	9.5
Snow (in inches)	T
Heating degree days	1,121
Cooling degree days	824
Days with thunderstorms	5
Days with fog	97
Days above 90°	4
Days below 32°	*
Wet days	40
Days with snow	0
Days with 1.5 inches or more snow	0

Percent time sky is clear

34.7	33	28.4	28.3	22.5	23.6	29.6	31.5	35.9	34.3	40.1	37.9

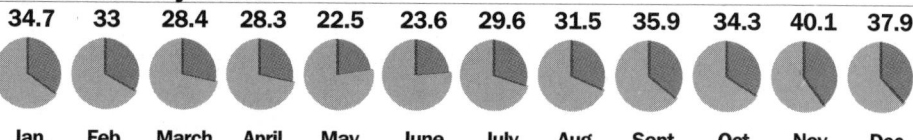

| Jan. | Feb. | March | April | May | June | July | Aug. | Sept. | Oct. | Nov. | Dec. |

San Francisco, California

Lat. 37° 46' N **Lon.** 122° 26' W **Elev.** 75 ft.

San Francisco is on a narrow peninsula between San Francisco Bay and the Pacific Ocean with elevations ranging from sea level to a range of hills nearly 1,000 feet high. The combination of the ocean, the bay and the hills gives the city's 49 square miles more variability in temperatures, cloudiness and fog than many much larger areas. Fog or low clouds moving in from the ocean are blocked by hills from some areas, but come through gaps to others. Summers are cool and the winters are mild, which means warm clothing may be needed in the summer, but also that flowers bloom all year. The city has a June through September dry season with virtually no rain, and a November through March wet season when about 80 percent of the year's precipitation falls.

Temperatures

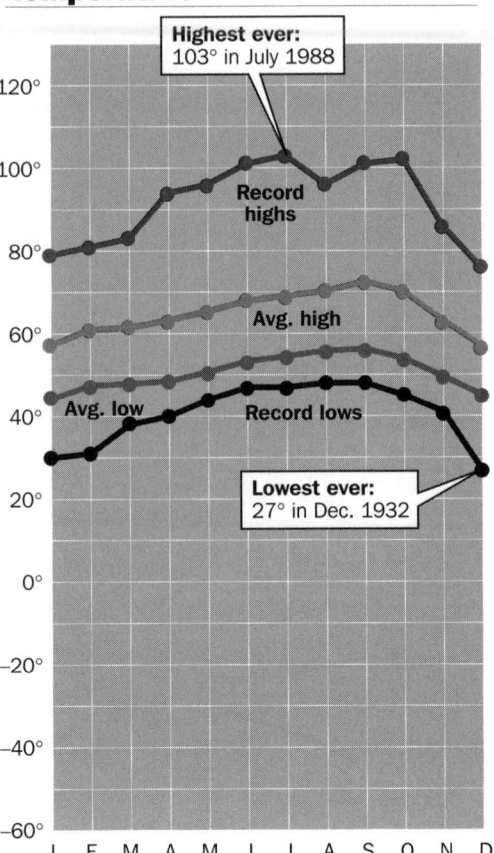

Highest ever: 103° in July 1988

Record highs

Avg. high

Avg. low

Record lows

Lowest ever: 27° in Dec. 1932

Weather extremes

Most rain in 24 hours:	6.16 in. Jan. 4, 1982
Most rain in a month:	11.47 in. December 1952
Most snow in 24 hours:	Trace January 1962
Most snow in a month:	Trace December 1972

Monthly averages

Month	Avg. precip. (in.)	Avg. snow (in.)	Wet days	Thunder-storm days	Pct. sky is cloudy	% p.m. relative humidity	Dew point	Wind speed (mph)
Jan.	4.5	T	11	*	NA	63	NA	6.7
Feb.	2.8	T	10	*	NA	63	NA	7.5
March	2.6	T	11	*	NA	61	NA	8.5
April	1.5	0	6	*	NA	61	NA	9.5
May	0.4	0	3	*	NA	68	NA	10.4
June	0.2	0	1	*	NA	72	NA	10.9
July	0.0	0	1	*	NA	74	NA	11.2
Aug.	0.1	0	1	*	NA	73	NA	10.5
Sept.	0.2	0	2	*	NA	66	NA	9.1
Oct.	1.1	0	4	*	NA	60	NA	7.6
Nov.	2.5	0	8	*	NA	63	NA	6.3
Dec.	3.5	T	10	*	NA	63	NA	6.5

T - Trace of rain or snow   * - Less than 1   NA - Not Available

Annual averages

Precipitation (in inches)	19
Snow (in inches)	T
Heating degree days	2,750
Cooling degree days	109
Days with thunderstorms	2
Days with fog	NA
Days above 90°	2
Days below 32°	*
Wet days	67
Days with snow	NA
Days with 1.5 inches or more snow	*

Percent time sky is clear

Data not available.

San Juan, Puerto Rico

Lat. 18° 26' N **Lon.** 66° 0' W **Elev.** 13 ft.

San Juan is on the north coast of Puerto Rico. The old city lies on the coast, but the metro area extends inland about 12 miles, with varying temperature and rainfall from the coast. Mountain ranges of up to 4,000 feet, 15 to 20 miles from San Juan, influence the rainfall of the area. The climate is tropical maritime, typical of tropical islands. During the day, the wind blows almost constantly off the ocean, while after sunset the wind comes off the land. The variation contributes to a pleasant climate. There is about a 5 – 6 degree difference between temperatures of the warmest and coldest months. Puerto Rico has been hit by hurricanes.

Temperatures

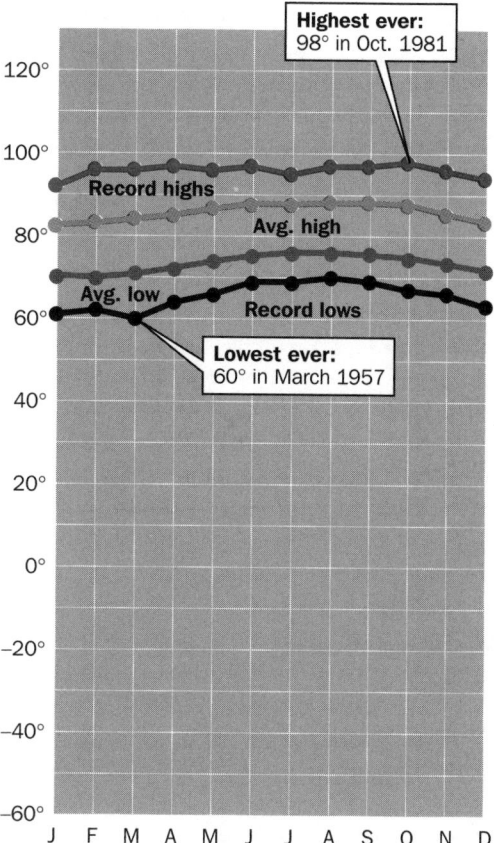

Highest ever: 98° in Oct. 1981

Record highs

Avg. high

Avg. low

Record lows

Lowest ever: 60° in March 1957

Weather extremes

Most rain in 24 hours:	8.84 in. Sep. 18, 1989
Most rain in a month:	16.81 in. December 1981
Most snow in 24 hours:	Trace September 1989
Most snow in a month:	Trace September 1989

Monthly averages

Month	Avg. precip. (in.)	Avg. snow (in.)	Wet days	Thunder-storm days	Pct. sky is cloudy	% p.m. relative humidity	Dew point	Wind speed (mph)
Jan.	3.0	0	17	*	13	64	NA	8.5
Feb.	2.0	0	13	*	16	62	NA	8.8
March	2.3	0	13	*	14	60	NA	9.2
April	3.6	0	13	1	21	62	NA	8.9
May	5.6	0	17	5	38	66	NA	8.4
June	4.7	0	15	5	33	66	NA	8.9
July	4.9	0	19	5	28	67	NA	9.6
Aug.	5.9	0	18	6	27	67	NA	8.8
Sept.	6.0	T	17	8	31	67	NA	7.5
Oct.	5.9	0	17	8	31	66	NA	6.8
Nov.	5.6	0	18	3	23	67	NA	7.5
Dec.	4.5	0	19	1	20	66	NA	8.3

T - Trace of rain or snow   * - Less than 1   NA - Not Available

Annual averages

Precipitation (in inches)	54.0
Snow (in inches)	0
Heating degree days	0
Cooling degree days	5,366
Days with thunderstorms	42
Days with fog	*
Days above 90°	61
Days below 32°	0
Wet days	196
Days with snow	NA
Days with 1.5 inches or more snow	0

Percent time sky is clear

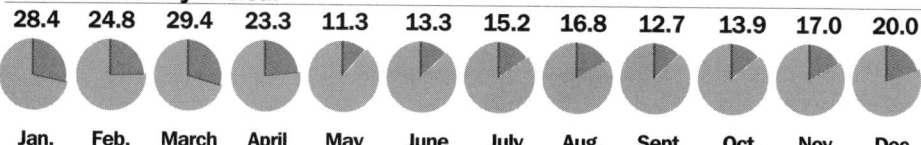

28.4	24.8	29.4	23.3	11.3	13.3	15.2	16.8	12.7	13.9	17.0	20.0
Jan.	Feb.	March	April	May	June	July	Aug.	Sept.	Oct.	Nov.	Dec.

Santa Barbara, California

Lat. 34° 26' N **Lon.** 119° 50' W **Elev.** 9 ft.

Santa Barbara is on south-facing coastline bordering the Santa Barbara Channel, with the Pacific Ocean beyond the Channel Islands. The Santa Ynez mountains reach 3,500 feet within 5 miles of the city and beyond are the San Rafael and Sierra Madre mountains with peaks up to 6,800 feet. Santa Barbara is protected from northwest and occasional strong northerly winds, but is exposed to the southerly winds associated with winter storms. Mild temperatures reign: There is only a 15 degree average difference between winter and summer. Precipitation is light and varies yearly, but intensifies during winter storms. Winds are generally light and sunshine is abundant.

Temperatures

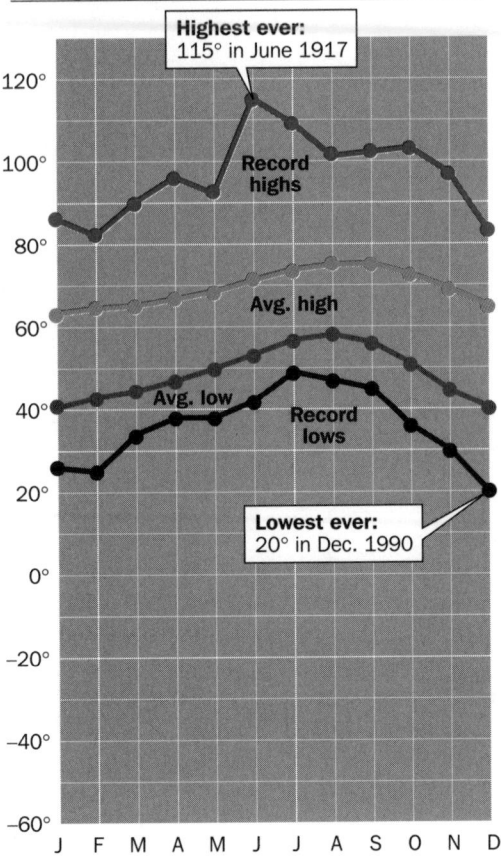

Highest ever: 115° in June 1917

Record highs

Avg. high

Avg. low

Record lows

Lowest ever: 20° in Dec. 1990

Weather extremes

Most rain in 24 hours:	4.47 in. March 18, 1991
Most rain in a month:	11.45 in. March 1991
Most snow in 24 hours:	Trace February 1939
Most snow in a month:	Trace February 1939

Monthly averages

Month	Avg. precip. (in.)	Avg. snow (in.)	Wet days	Thunder-storm days	Pct. sky is cloudy	% p.m. relative humidity	Dew point	Wind speed (mph)
Jan.	3.8	0.0	4	*	NA	55	NA	4.8
Feb.	3.5	0.0	5	*	NA	56	NA	6.3
March	2.4	0.0	6	*	NA	58	NA	6.7
April	1.4	0.0	2	*	NA	58	NA	7.6
May	0.2	0.0	1	*	NA	59	NA	7.1
June	0.0	0.0	0	*	NA	62	NA	6.8
July	0.0	0.0	1	*	NA	64	NA	6.5
Aug.	0.0	0.0	0	*	NA	64	NA	6.1
Sept.	0.3	0.0	1	*	NA	63	NA	5.8
Oct.	0.4	0.0	2	*	NA	62	NA	5.5
Nov.	1.9	0.0	3	*	NA	53	NA	5.3
Dec.	2.3	0.0	5	1	NA	54	NA	5.0

T - Trace of rain or snow　　* - Less than 1　　NA - Not Available

Annual averages

Precipitation (in inches)	16
Snow (in inches)	0
Heating degree days	2,487
Cooling degree days	269
Days with thunderstorms	3
Days with fog	21
Days above 90°	4
Days below 32°	9
Wet days	30
Days with snow	NA
Days with 1.5 inches or more snow	0

Percent time sky is clear

Data not available.

Sault Ste. Marie, Michigan

Lat. 46° 28' N **Lon.** 84° 22' W **Elev.** 724 ft.

Since Sault Ste. Marie lies at the extreme eastern tip of the Upper Peninsula of Michigan, at the intersection of Lake Superior and Lake Huron, its climate is essentially maritime during ice-free periods of the year. Lake ice usually develops in December and reaches peak coverage in February. As ice cover develops, the climate gradually changes to continental polar. Since water in the northern Great Lakes remains relatively cool during the summer and seldom freezes over during the winter, temperatures are moderate most of the year. Heavy fogs from passing cold air masses over the warmer waters of the northern Great Lakes usually occur in August, September, and October. Snow cover normally lasts from November 21 to around April 7.

Weather extremes

Most rain in 24 hours:	5.92 in.	Aug. 3, 1974
Most rain in a month:	9.48 in.	August 1974
Most snow in 24 hours:	15.3 in.	Jan. 5, 1988
Most snow in a month:	71.0 in.	January 1982

Temperatures

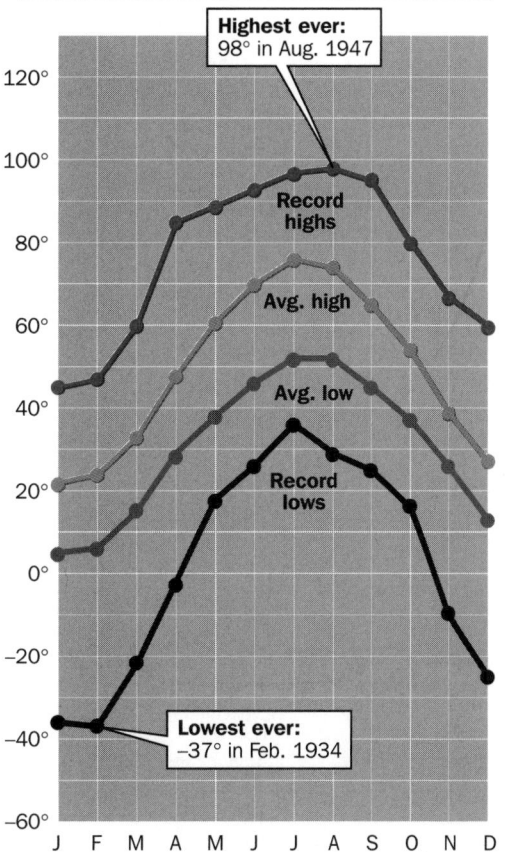

Highest ever: 98° in Aug. 1947

Record highs

Avg. high

Avg. low

Record lows

Lowest ever: −37° in Feb. 1934

J F M A M J J A S O N D

Monthly averages

Month	Avg. precip. (in.)	Avg. snow (in.)	Wet days	Thunderstorm days	Pct. sky is cloudy	% p.m. relative humidity	Dew point	Wind speed (mph)
Jan.	2.3	30	19	*	65	75	8	8.1
Feb.	1.6	20	15	*	57	71	9	11.5
March	2.1	15	13	1	51	67	17	12.7
April	2.4	5	11	1	50	59	29	12.7
May	2.6	1	11	3	43	53	39	11.5
June	3.3	0	12	6	41	60	49	10.4
July	2.8	0	10	6	33	60	56	9.2
Aug.	3.3	0	11	5	37	62	56	10.4
Sept.	3.7	T	13	4	46	67	49	11.5
Oct.	3.0	2	14	2	54	67	39	9.2
Nov.	3.4	15	17	1	70	76	28	9.2
Dec.	2.6	30	20	*	70	78	15	8.1

T - Trace of rain or snow   * - Less than 1   NA - Not Available

Annual averages

Precipitation (in inches)	33.1
Snow (in inches)	119
Heating degree days	9,210
Cooling degree days	156
Days with thunderstorms	29
Days with fog	146
Days above 90°	1
Days below 32°	181
Wet days	166
Days with snow	83
Days with 1.5 inches or more snow	54

Percent time sky is clear

Jan.	Feb.	March	April	May	June	July	Aug.	Sept.	Oct.	Nov.	Dec.
12.3	17	20.8	22	23.2	20.9	23.3	23.2	16.2	14.8	7.7	9.7

Savannah, Georgia

Lat. 32° 08′ N **Lon.** 81° 12′ W **Elev.** 46 ft.

Savannah has a temperate climate. It is surrounded by flat terrain, much of it low and marshy. Snow is rare — the heaviest snowfalls are under 5 inches. Severe tropical storms affect this area about once in 10 years and hurricanes are possible. Sunshine is adequate in all seasons and seldom are there two or more days in succession without it. Sea- and land-breeze effect is usually not felt in Savannah proper, though it is a daily feature on the nearby islands. Dry, continental air masses reach this area in summer mostly by sliding down the Atlantic coast and giving cooler northeast winds. About half the average rainfall occurs in afternoon thunderstorms — some severe — during the storm season of June 15 through September 15.

Temperatures

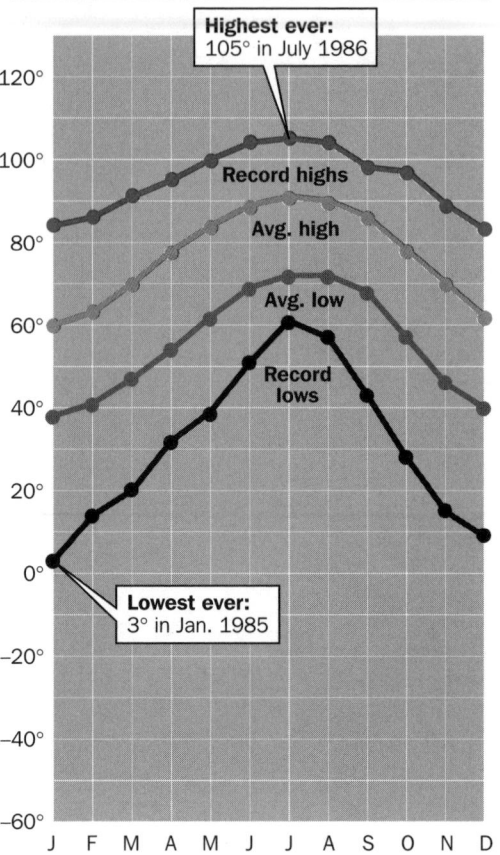

Highest ever: 105° in July 1986

Record highs
Avg. high
Avg. low
Record lows

Lowest ever: 3° in Jan. 1985

J F M A M J J A S O N D

Weather extremes

Most rain in 24 hours:	11.44 in. Sept. 17 – 18, 1928
Most rain in a month:	22.88 in. September 1924
Most snow in 24 hours:	3.6 in. Feb. 8, 1989
Most snow in a month:	3.6 in. February 1989

Monthly averages

Month	Avg. precip. (in.)	Avg. snow (in.)	Wet days	Thunder-storm days	Pct. sky is cloudy	% p.m. relative humidity	Dew point	Wind speed (mph)
Jan.	3.3	T	9	1	40	53	38	11.5
Feb.	3.2	T	9	1	39	50	40	12.7
March	3.8	T	9	3	36	49	46	11.5
April	3.1	0	7	4	28	48	52	9.2
May	4.2	0	9	7	28	52	61	9.2
June	5.5	0	11	10	27	58	68	8.1
July	6.8	0	14	15	26	61	71	6.9
Aug.	7.0	0	13	12	25	63	71	6.9
Sept.	5.0	0	10	6	29	62	68	9.1
Oct.	2.5	0	6	2	26	55	57	9.1
Nov.	2.0	T	6	*	30	52	48	9.1
Dec.	2.8	T	8	1	37	53	40	9.1

T - Trace of rain or snow   * - Less than 1   NA - Not Available

Annual averages

Precipitation (in inches)	49.2
Snow (in inches)	T
Heating degree days	1,881
Cooling degree days	2,421
Days with thunderstorms	62
Days with fog	172
Days above 90°	69
Days below 32°	31
Wet days	111
Days with snow	*
Days with 1.5 inches or more snow	*

Percent time sky is clear

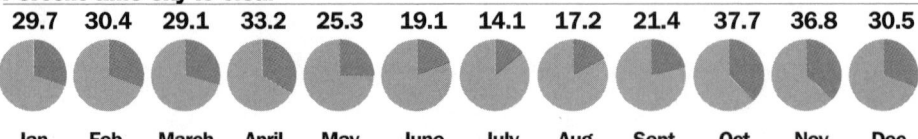

29.7	30.4	29.1	33.2	25.3	19.1	14.1	17.2	21.4	37.7	36.8	30.5
Jan.	Feb.	March	April	May	June	July	Aug.	Sept.	Oct.	Nov.	Dec.

Scottsbluff, Nebraska

Lat. 41° 52' N **Lon.** 103° 36' W **Elev.** 3,945 ft.

Scottsbluff is located in the North Platte River Valley with a range of hills to the north and south. To the south, the hills average 600 to 700 feet above the river. To the north, rolling hills range from 300 to 400 feet. Due to the protection of the higher hills to the south, southerly winds in the valley are rare. West to northwest winds are intensified by the funneling action of the valley and velocities of 30 to 50 mph are common during the winter and early spring. Quite often these winds are warmed as they come down the slopes from the higher elevations to the west and bring rapid warming and melting of the snow. Easterly winds during the winter and early spring cause low cloudiness and precipitation.

Temperatures

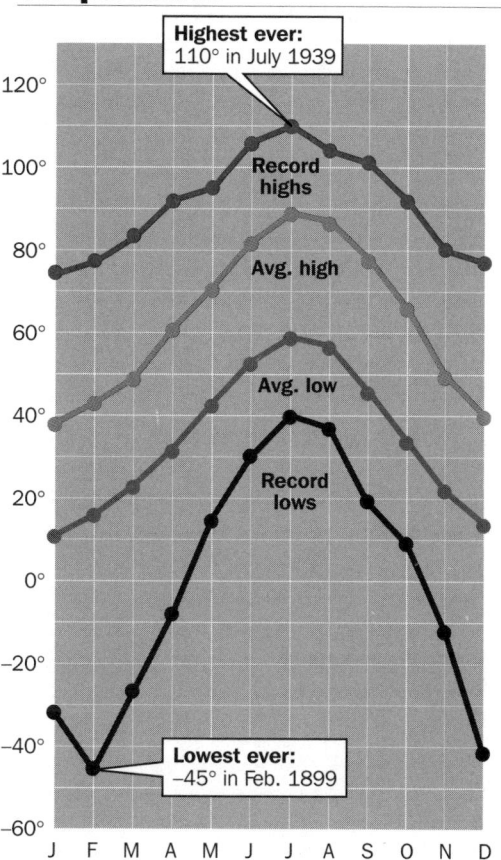

Weather extremes

Most rain in 24 hours:	3.74 in.
	June 6 – 7, 1953
Most rain in a month:	8.33 in.
	June 1957
Most snow in 24 hours:	17.6 in.
	April 25, 1935
Most snow in a month:	29.7 in.
	April 1927

Monthly averages

Month	Avg. precip. (in.)	Avg. snow (in.)	Wet days	Thunder-storm days	Pct. sky is cloudy	% p.m. relative humidity	Dew point	Wind speed (mph)
Jan.	0.4	7	6	0	36	58	13	13.8
Feb.	0.4	5	5	0	37	51	17	12.7
March	1.0	9	8	*	42	46	21	13.8
April	1.5	5	8	2	38	40	29	13.8
May	2.8	1	12	8	37	43	40	11.5
June	2.9	T	11	11	25	40	49	11.5
July	2.0	0	9	11	17	37	54	10.4
Aug.	1.0	0	7	8	18	38	53	10.4
Sept.	1.1	T	7	4	23	38	42	10.4
Oct.	0.8	2	5	1	26	41	31	11.5
Nov.	0.6	5	5	*	34	52	21	12.7
Dec.	0.5	7	5	*	34	59	15	13.8

T - Trace of rain or snow   * - Less than 1   NA - Not Available

Annual averages

Precipitation (in inches)	15.1
Snow (in inches)	42
Heating degree days	6,614
Cooling degree days	759
Days with thunderstorms	45
Days with fog	41
Days above 90°	42
Days below 32°	172
Wet days	88
Days with snow	64
Days with 1.5 inches or more snow	17

Percent time sky is clear

27.6	26.6	22.2	22.8	19.8	27.4	31.5	32.1	41.2	38.9	29.5	28.9
Jan.	Feb.	March	April	May	June	July	Aug.	Sept.	Oct.	Nov.	Dec.

Seattle-Tacoma, Washington

Lat. 47° 27' N **Lon.** 122° 18' W **Elev.** 450 ft.

The mild climate of the Pacific Coast is modified in Seattle by the Cascade Mountains and, to a lesser extent, the Olympic Mountains, which rise sharply from Puget Sound on the west. The Cascades shield the Seattle-Tacoma area from cold, dry continental air during the winter and hot, dry air during the summer. In winter, the prevailing southwesterly winds keep the average daytime temperatures in the 40s and nighttime readings in the 30s, while summer usually finds highs in the 70s with lows in the 50s. Extremes of temperatures are usually of short duration. Over 75 percent of Seattle's precipitation falls during winter and early spring, primarily as rain. Snow is variable and usually melts before accumulating measurable depths.

Temperatures

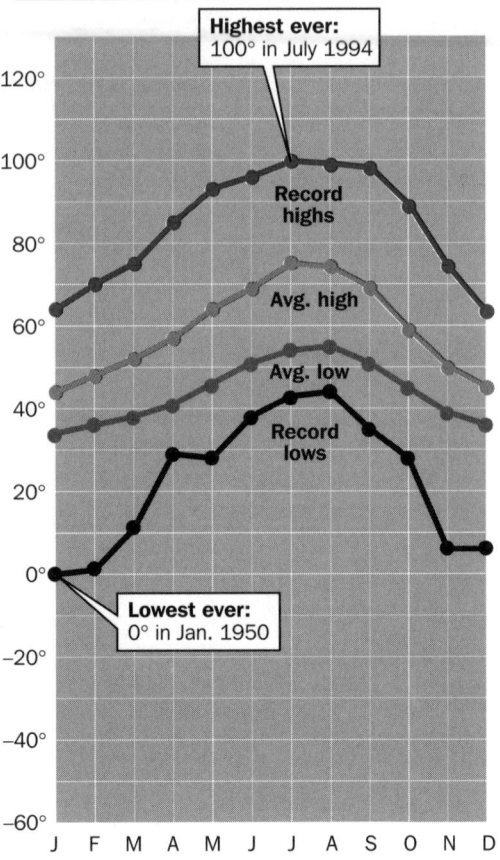

Highest ever: 100° in July 1994

Record highs

Avg. high

Avg. low

Record lows

Lowest ever: 0° in Jan. 1950

Weather extremes

Most rain in 24 hours:	3.74 in. Oct. 5 – 6, 1981
Most rain in a month:	12.91 in. January 1953
Most snow in 24 hours:	21.4 in. Jan. 13 – 14, 1950
Most snow in a month:	57.2 in. January 1950

Monthly averages

Month	Avg. precip. (in.)	Avg. snow (in.)	Wet days	Thunder-storm days	Pct. sky is cloudy	% p.m. relative humidity	Dew point	Wind speed (mph)
Jan.	5.7	5	19	*	69	76	33	13.8
Feb.	4.2	2	16	*	63	69	35	13.8
March	3.7	1	17	1	57	63	36	12.7
April	2.4	T	14	1	52	57	39	11.5
May	1.7	T	11	1	45	54	44	10.4
June	1.4	0	9	1	44	54	48	10.4
July	0.8	0	5	1	32	49	51	9.2
Aug.	1.1	0	7	1	35	51	53	9.2
Sept.	1.9	0	9	1	38	57	50	9.2
Oct.	3.5	T	13	*	51	68	45	10.4
Nov.	5.9	1	18	1	65	76	39	11.5
Dec.	5.9	3	19	*	69	79	35	11.5

T - Trace of rain or snow   * - Less than 1   NA - Not Available

Annual averages

Precipitation (in inches)	38.4
Snow (in inches)	13
Heating degree days	5,003
Cooling degree days	151
Days with thunderstorms	8
Days with fog	161
Days above 90°	3
Days below 32°	38
Wet days	157
Days with snow	14
Days with 1.5 inches or more snow	5

Percent time sky is clear

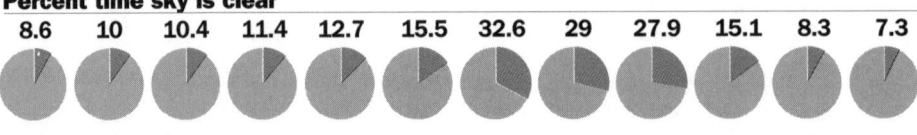

8.6	10	10.4	11.4	12.7	15.5	32.6	29	27.9	15.1	8.3	7.3
Jan.	Feb.	March	April	May	June	July	Aug.	Sept.	Oct.	Nov.	Dec.

Sheridan, Wyoming

Lat. 44° 46' N **Lon.** 106° 58' W **Elev.** 3,964 ft.

Mountains have a marked effect on the climate at Sheridan. To the west lie the Rocky Mountains. Closer and to the southwest and west, the Bighorn Mountains rise abruptly. In winter, the winds generally shift to the west or southwest and increase in velocity. These winds coming down the mountains produce a pronounced warming or chinook, which makes the climate less severe. Wind going up the mountain causes precipitation year-round, but most frequently during the winter and spring. Sheridan often receives much heavier snow or rain than the surrounding country away from the mountains. In the summer, the mountains act as a breeding ground for thunderstorms, which frequently bring afternoon or evening showers to Sheridan.

Weather extremes

Most rain in 24 hours:	4.41 in. July 22 – 23, 1923
Most rain in a month:	9.54 in. June 1944
Most snow in 24 hours:	26.7 in. April 3 – 4, 1955
Most snow in a month:	43.5 in. December 1989

Temperatures

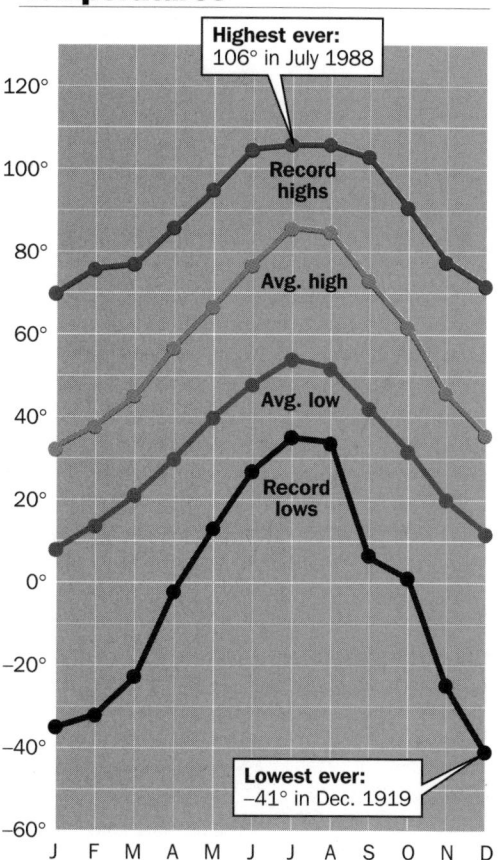

Highest ever: 106° in July 1988

Record highs

Avg. high

Avg. low

Record lows

Lowest ever: −41° in Dec. 1919

Monthly averages

Month	Avg. precip. (in.)	Avg. snow (in.)	Wet days	Thunder- storm days	Pct. sky is cloudy	% p.m. relative humidity	Dew point	Wind speed (mph)
Jan.	0.7	11	9	0	42	64	10	13.8
Feb.	0.7	11	9	*	42	61	16	13.8
March	1.1	13	11	*	42	52	21	15.0
April	1.9	11	11	1	39	44	28	15.0
May	2.3	2	11	4	35	46	38	13.8
June	2.2	T	11	9	24	44	46	12.7
July	1.0	0	7	9	13	33	48	11.5
Aug.	0.9	0	7	7	14	30	45	11.5
Sept.	1.3	2	7	3	23	38	38	12.7
Oct.	1.1	4	7	*	29	45	30	12.7
Nov.	0.8	9	8	*	38	61	21	12.7
Dec.	0.7	11	9	0	39	66	13	12.7

T - Trace of rain or snow   * - Less than 1   NA - Not Available

Annual averages

Precipitation (in inches)	14.7
Snow (in inches)	75
Heating degree days	7,632
Cooling degree days	432
Days with thunderstorms	33
Days with fog	19
Days above 90°	28
Days below 32°	185
Wet days	107
Days with snow	110
Days with 1.5 inches or more snow	34

Percent time sky is clear

17.3	16.8	15.5	16.2	14	19.4	27.9	27.9	30.5	27.3	18.5	18.6

| Jan. | Feb. | March | April | May | June | July | Aug. | Sept. | Oct. | Nov. | Dec. |

Shreveport, Louisiana

Lat. 32° 28′ N **Lon.** 93° 49′ W **Elev.** 254 ft.

Shreveport is in northwestern Louisiana, near Arkansas and Texas, on Red River bottom land and adjacent rolling hills. The climate is transitional between the subtropical humid type of the South and the continental climate of the Midwest. Rainfall is abundant. Winters are normally mild with cold spells of short duration. Temperatures drop below 15°F in about half the winters. The summer months are consistently quite warm and humid. Measurable snow occurs only once every other year on average. More troublesome are ice and sleet storms, which can cause considerable damage. Severe local storms, some including hail and tornadoes, are most frequent during the spring months.

Temperatures

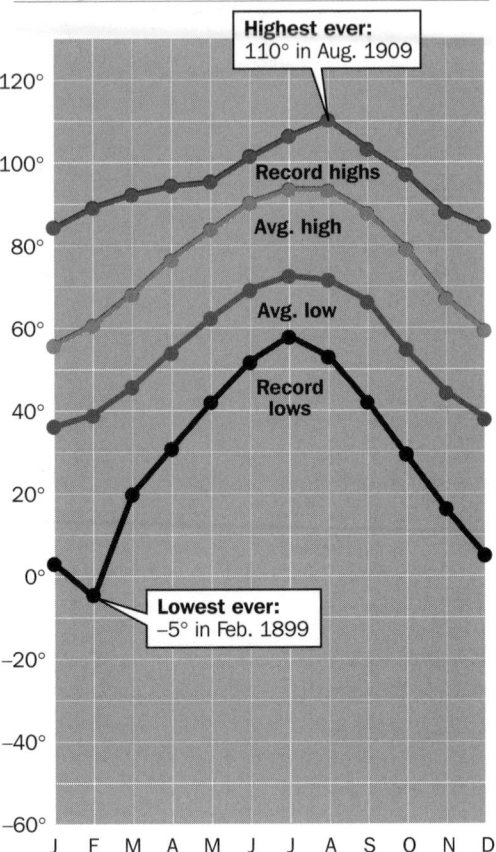

Highest ever: 110° in Aug. 1909

Record highs

Avg. high

Avg. low

Record lows

Lowest ever: −5° in Feb. 1899

Weather extremes

Most rain in 24 hours:	12.44 in. July 24, 1933
Most rain in a month:	25.44 in. July 1933
Most snow in 24 hours:	11.0 in. Dec. 21 – 22, 1929
Most snow in a month:	15.0 in. January 1948

Monthly averages

Month	Avg. precip. (in.)	Avg. snow (in.)	Wet days	Thunder-storm days	Pct. sky is cloudy	% p.m. relative humidity	Dew point	Wind speed (mph)
Jan.	4.0	1	10	2	49	57	36	11.5
Feb.	3.9	1	8	3	45	53	39	11.5
March	3.6	T	9	5	43	50	45	12.7
April	4.1	T	9	6	39	51	54	11.5
May	5.1	0	9	7	32	54	62	10.4
June	4.0	0	8	7	21	54	69	9.2
July	3.6	0	8	8	18	53	71	8.1
Aug.	2.4	0	7	7	17	51	70	8.1
Sept.	3.1	0	7	4	24	52	65	6.9
Oct.	3.6	0	7	3	25	49	55	8.1
Nov.	4.2	T	8	3	35	52	45	10.4
Dec.	4.1	T	9	2	44	56	39	10.4

T - Trace of rain or snow   * - Less than 1   NA - Not Available

Annual averages

Precipitation (in inches)	45.7
Snow (in inches)	2
Heating degree days	2,269
Cooling degree days	2,444
Days with thunderstorms	57
Days with fog	107
Days above 90°	90
Days below 32°	36
Wet days	99
Days with snow	2
Days with 1.5 inches or more snow	*

Percent time sky is clear

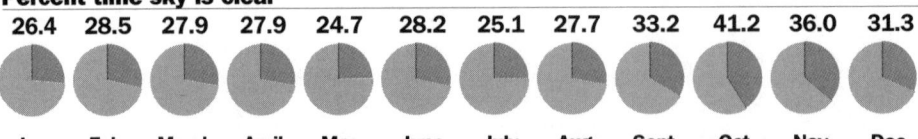

Jan.	Feb.	March	April	May	June	July	Aug.	Sept.	Oct.	Nov.	Dec.
26.4	28.5	27.9	27.9	24.7	28.2	25.1	27.7	33.2	41.2	36.0	31.3

Sioux City, Iowa

Lat. 42° 24′ N **Lon.** 96° 23′ W **Elev.** 1,103 ft.

Sioux City is located along the Missouri River where Iowa borders Nebraska and South Dakota. Located in the midland of a continent and in the northern half of the Great Plains, the climate is largely determined by the movement and interaction of the large-scale weather systems from the north, west and south. Under normal conditions, winters are cold and summers warm, and most of the precipitation comes from April to September. Except for an occasional dry year, the climate is quite favorable for agriculture with corn, the small grains, and grasses producing abundantly. Summers are sunny; most summer rains are associated with showers or thunderstorms. Winds are lightest in the summer months and heaviest in April.

Temperatures

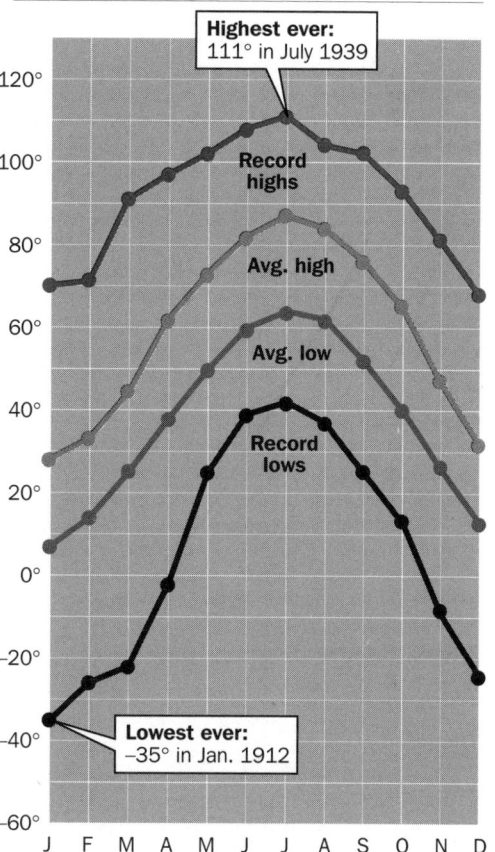

Highest ever: 111° in July 1939
Record highs
Avg. high
Avg. low
Record lows
Lowest ever: −35° in Jan. 1912

Weather extremes

Most rain in 24 hours:	5.5 in.	July 17, 1972
Most rain in a month:	11.78 in.	May 1903
Most snow in 24 hours:	20.0 in.	April 10, 1913
Most snow in a month:	29.1 in.	January 1982

Monthly averages

Month	Avg. precip. (in.)	Avg. snow (in.)	Wet days	Thunder-storm days	Pct. sky is cloudy	% p.m. relative humidity	Dew point	Wind speed (mph)
Jan.	0.6	7	7	*	44	63	10	15.0
Feb.	0.8	6	6	*	46	62	15	15.0
March	1.8	8	9	1	49	58	25	16.1
April	2.3	2	9	4	43	46	35	16.1
May	3.6	T	11	7	39	48	47	11.5
June	3.8	0	10	9	30	50	58	12.7
July	3.4	0	9	8	23	52	63	11.5
Aug.	3.0	0	9	7	25	54	62	9.2
Sept.	2.6	T	8	5	30	50	52	9.2
Oct.	1.8	1	6	2	31	46	39	10.4
Nov.	1.1	4	5	*	43	55	26	16.1
Dec.	0.7	6	7	*	47	64	15	15.0

T - Trace of rain or snow   * - Less than 1   NA - Not Available

Annual averages

Precipitation (in inches)	25.6
Snow (in inches)	32
Heating degree days	6,899
Cooling degree days	977
Days with thunderstorms	43
Days with fog	94
Days above 90°	29
Days below 32°	151
Wet days	96
Days with snow	53
Days with 1.5 inches or more snow	13

Percent time sky is clear

Jan.	Feb.	March	April	May	June	July	Aug.	Sept.	Oct.	Nov.	Dec.
28.4	27.3	22.9	26.1	23.4	25.5	31.1	32.5	38	37.3	28.2	27.5

Sioux Falls, South Dakota

Lat. 43° 34' N **Lon.** 96° 44' W **Elev.** 1,418 ft.

Sioux Falls, in the Big Sioux River Valley of southeast South Dakota, is surrounded by gently rolling terrain. The climate is continental, with frequent weather changes caused by air masses from Canada, the Gulf of Mexico, or the southwest. During the late fall and winter, cold fronts accompanied by strong, gusty winds can drop temperatures by 20 to 30 degrees in a 24-hour period, but severe cold spells last only a few days. Extreme highs are rare in the summer and night temperatures are usually below 70°F. Rainfall is heavier during the spring and summer. One or two very heavy snows usually fall each winter, and eight to 12 inches may fall in 24 hours. Thunderstorms are frequent during the late spring and summer, especially in June and July.

Temperatures

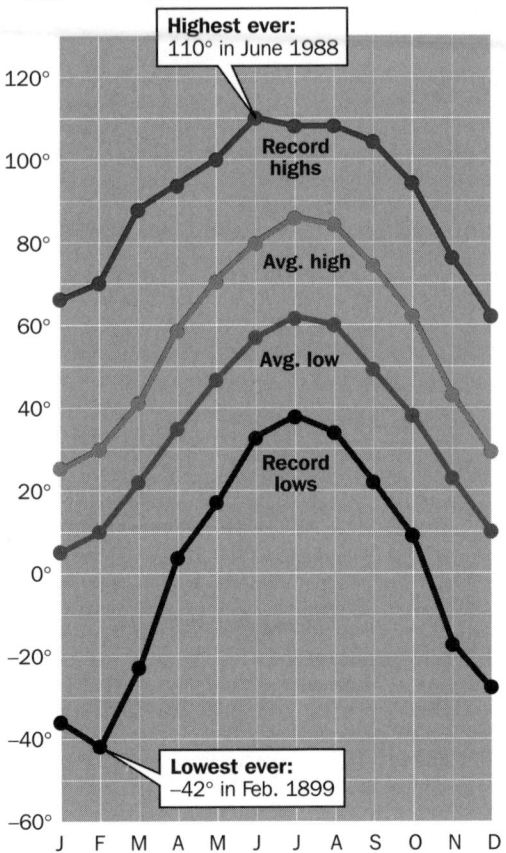

Weather extremes

Most rain in 24 hours:	4.58 in. Aug. 1, 1975
Most rain in a month:	9.42 in. May 1898
Most snow in 24 hours:	26.0 in. Feb. 17 – 18, 1962
Most snow in a month:	48.4 in. February 1962

Monthly averages

Month	Avg. precip. (in.)	Avg. snow (in.)	Wet days	Thunder-storm days	Pct. sky is cloudy	% p.m. relative humidity	Dew point	Wind speed (mph)
Jan.	0.5	6.4	6	*	43	68	NA	11.0
Feb.	0.9	8.0	7	*	46	68	NA	11.1
March	1.6	9.5	9	*	49	63	NA	12.5
April	2.4	2.2	9	3	43	54	NA	13.2
May	3.2	T	11	6	37	53	NA	11.9
June	3.7	T	11	9	30	55	NA	10.7
July	2.7	0	10	9	21	53	NA	9.8
Aug.	3.1	0	9	8	24	55	NA	9.8
Sept.	2.8	T	8	6	29	57	NA	10.3
Oct.	1.6	T	6	2	32	55	NA	10.7
Nov.	0.9	5.3	6	*	44	65	NA	11.5
Dec.	0.7	7.3	6	*	46	71	NA	10.8

T - Trace of rain or snow   * - Less than 1   NA - Not Available

Annual averages

Precipitation (in inches)	24
Snow (in inches)	39.4
Heating degree days	7,895
Cooling degree days	749
Days with thunderstorms	44
Days with fog	21
Days above 90°	25
Days below 32°	168
Wet days	97
Days with snow	NA
Days with 1.0 inches or more snow	11

Percent time sky is clear

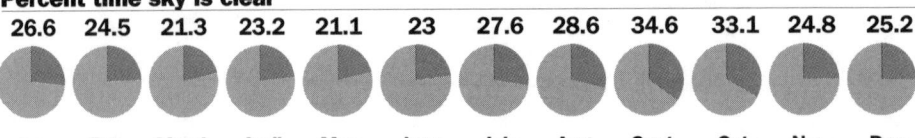

Jan.	Feb.	March	April	May	June	July	Aug.	Sept.	Oct.	Nov.	Dec.
26.6	24.5	21.3	23.2	21.1	23	27.6	28.6	34.6	33.1	24.8	25.2

South Bend, Indiana

Lat. 41° 42' N **Lon.** 86° 19' W **Elev.** 773 ft.

South Bend is on the Saint Joseph River in the northern portion of Saint Joseph County, where the terrain is mostly level or gently rolling with some former marshland. Lake Michigan, 20 miles to the northwest, has a moderating influence on the climate. Temperatures of 100°F or higher are rare, and cold waves are less severe than at many locations at the same latitude. Precipitation is evenly distributed throughout the year, with the greatest amounts during the growing season. Winter brings considerable cloudiness and high humidity along with frequent periods of snow. Light amounts may even fall in October and April. Heavy snowfalls from November through March, resulting from a cold northwest wind passing over Lake Michigan, are not uncommon.

Temperatures

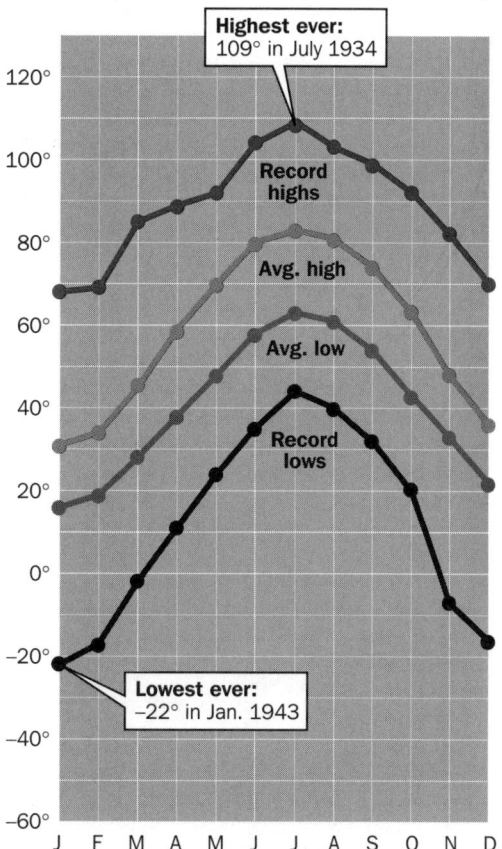

Highest ever: 109° in July 1934

Record highs

Avg. high

Avg. low

Record lows

Lowest ever: −22° in Jan. 1943

Weather extremes

Most rain in 24 hours:	4.70 in. June 24 – 25, 1968
Most rain in a month:	10.86 in. June 1993
Most snow in 24 hours:	17.50 in. Nov. 25 – 26, 1977
Most snow in a month:	86.10 in. January 1978

Monthly averages

Month	Avg. precip. (in.)	Avg. snow (in.)	Wet days	Thunder-storm days	Pct. sky is cloudy	% p.m. relative humidity	Dew point	Wind speed (mph)
Jan.	2.4	21	16	*	64	73	18	12.7
Feb.	2.0	15	13	*	60	70	21	12.7
March	3.0	9	14	2	56	62	28	12.7
April	3.8	2	13	4	47	55	37	12.7
May	3.2	T	11	5	38	53	47	11.5
June	4.0	0	10	8	31	53	57	10.4
July	3.8	0	10	7	27	55	62	9.2
Aug.	3.6	0	9	6	26	56	61	9.2
Sept.	3.3	0	9	4	31	56	54	10.4
Oct.	3.1	1	10	2	38	58	43	11.5
Nov.	3.1	9	13	1	58	68	33	11.5
Dec.	3.0	19	16	*	67	75	23	12.7

T - Trace of rain or snow   * - Less than 1   NA - Not Available

Annual averages

Precipitation (in inches)	38.3
Snow (in inches)	76
Heating degree days	6,327
Cooling degree days	797
Days with thunderstorms	39
Days with fog	178
Days above 90°	13
Days below 32°	129
Wet days	144
Days with snow	103
Days with 1.5 inches or more snow	32

Percent time sky is clear

Jan.	Feb.	March	April	May	June	July	Aug.	Sept.	Oct.	Nov.	Dec.
12.4	14.5	16.2	22.1	22.9	22.5	24.3	25.3	28.6	26.9	15.4	11.7

Spokane, Washington

Lat. 47° 38' N **Lon.** 117° 32' W **Elev.** 2,356 ft.

Spokane lies on the eastern edge of the broad Columbia Basin, which is bounded by the Cascade Range and the Rocky Mountains. The climate of Spokane combines characteristics of damp, coastal weather and arid interior weather. Many Pacific storms lose their moisture as they rise over the Cascades, so annual precipitation in Spokane is less than 50 percent of amounts received west of the mountains. However, the precipitation in Spokane is greater than that of the desert areas of south-central Washington. In general, the summers are mild and arid, while the winters are cold with an occasional snowfall of several inches, though subzero temperatures and traffic-stopping snowfalls are rare.

Temperatures

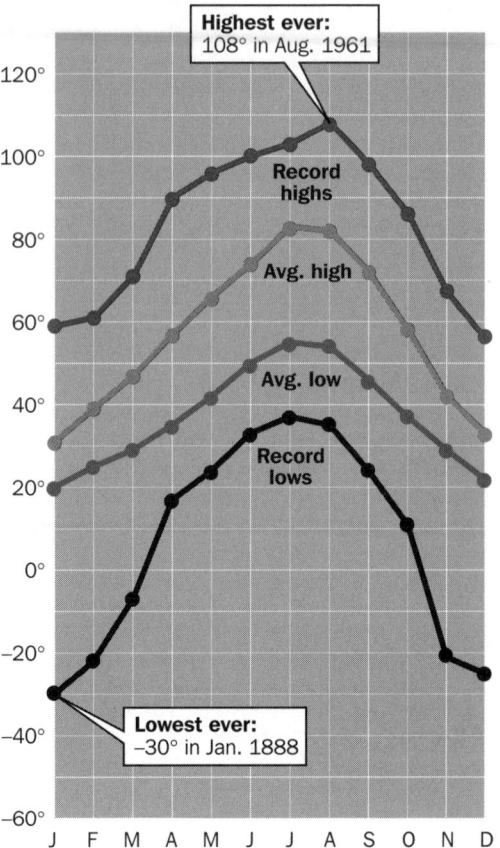

Weather extremes

Most rain in 24 hours:	2.22 in. June 7, 1888
Most rain in a month:	5.85 in. November 1897
Most snow in 24 hours:	13.0 in. Jan. 6 – 7, 1950
Most snow in a month:	56.9 in. January 1950

Monthly averages

Month	Avg. precip. (in.)	Avg. snow (in.)	Wet days	Thunder-storm days	Pct. sky is cloudy	% p.m. relative humidity	Dew point	Wind speed (mph)
Jan.	2.3	16	14	*	67	79	21	6.9
Feb.	1.6	8	11	*	59	70	26	13.8
March	1.5	4	11	*	47	55	28	13.8
April	1.1	1	9	1	42	43	31	13.8
May	1.5	T	9	2	37	41	38	11.5
June	1.3	T	8	3	30	36	43	11.5
July	0.6	0	4	2	15	27	44	10.4
Aug.	0.7	0	5	2	17	28	43	10.4
Sept.	0.8	0	6	1	22	34	40	11.5
Oct.	1.2	T	8	*	37	51	35	6.9
Nov.	2.2	6	13	*	62	75	30	6.9
Dec.	2.4	15	15	0	69	83	24	6.9

T - Trace of rain or snow   * - Less than 1   NA - Not Available

Annual averages

Precipitation (in inches)	17.0
Snow (in inches)	51
Heating degree days	6,882
Cooling degree days	419
Days with thunderstorms	11
Days with fog	101
Days above 90°	18
Days below 32°	140
Wet days	113
Days with snow	73
Days with 1.5 inches or more snow	24

Percent time sky is clear

Jan.	Feb.	March	April	May	June	July	Aug.	Sept.	Oct.	Nov.	Dec.
10.4	12.9	15.3	16.5	16.5	20.1	41.6	39.3	37	25	12.1	8.8

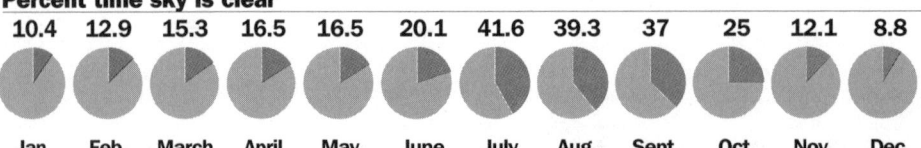

Springfield, Illinois

Lat. 39° 51' N **Lon.** 89° 41' W **Elev.** 594 ft.

Springfield's location near the center of North America gives it a typical continental climate with warm summers and fairly cold winters. Summer weather is often uncomfortably warm and humid, but considerable variation may take place within the seasons. Temperatures of 70°F or higher may occur in winter and temperatures near 50°F are sometimes recorded during the summer months. Monthly precipitation ranges from almost 4 inches in June to about 2 inches in January. Thunderstorms are common during hot weather — an average year has about 50 thunderstorms. Wind velocities of more than 40 mph are not unusual for brief periods in most months of the year.

Temperatures

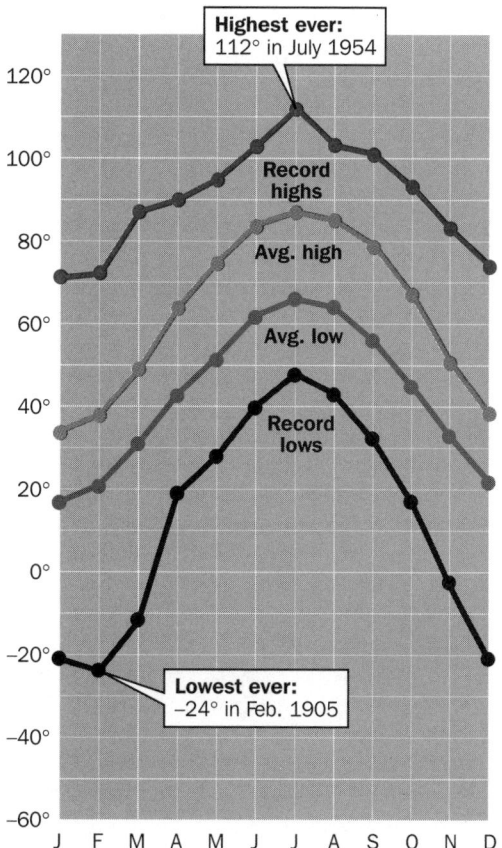

Highest ever: 112° in July 1954

Record highs

Avg. high

Avg. low

Record lows

Lowest ever: −24° in Feb. 1905

Weather extremes

Most rain in 24 hours:	6.12 in. Dec. 2 – 3, 1982
Most rain in a month:	15.16 in. September 1926
Most snow in 24 hours:	15.0 in. Feb. 28, 1900
Most snow in a month:	24.4 in. February 1900

Monthly averages

Month	Avg. precip. (in.)	Avg. snow (in.)	Wet days	Thunder-storm days	Pct. sky is cloudy	% p.m. relative humidity	Dew point	Wind speed (mph)
Jan.	1.7	6	9	*	50	67	18	15.0
Feb.	1.8	6	9	1	49	65	22	13.8
March	3.0	4	12	3	50	59	31	16.1
April	3.7	1	11	5	44	52	41	15.0
May	3.4	T	10	7	36	51	51	12.7
June	3.9	0	10	8	29	51	60	11.5
July	3.7	0	9	9	24	54	65	9.2
Aug.	3.2	0	8	7	24	56	64	9.2
Sept.	2.9	0	8	5	28	50	56	10.4
Oct.	2.6	T	8	2	32	50	44	12.7
Nov.	2.3	2	9	2	46	60	33	13.8
Dec.	2.3	5	10	1	53	69	24	15.0

T - Trace of rain or snow   * - Less than 1   NA - Not Available

Annual averages

Precipitation (in inches)	34.6
Snow (in inches)	24
Heating degree days	5,602
Cooling degree days	1,209
Days with thunderstorms	50
Days with fog	134
Days above 90°	30
Days below 32°	118
Wet days	113
Days with snow	21
Days with 1.5 inches or more snow	4

Percent time sky is clear

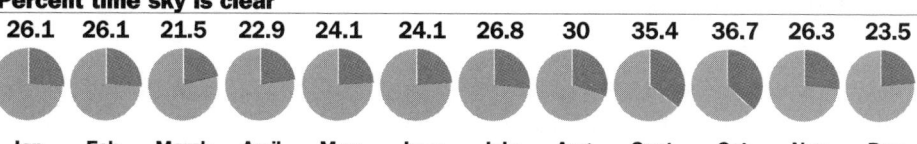

26.1	26.1	21.5	22.9	24.1	24.1	26.8	30	35.4	36.7	26.3	23.5
Jan.	Feb.	March	April	May	June	July	Aug.	Sept.	Oct.	Nov.	Dec.

Springfield, Missouri

Lat. 37° 14' N **Lon.** 93° 23' W **Elev.** 1,268 ft.

The Springfield area is flat or very gently rolling tableland, practically atop the crest of the Ozark Plateau. As a result, the city enjoys what is described as a plateau climate. The Ozark winters and summers are considerably milder than upland, plain or prairie. The location has unusual natural water drainage — the line separating two major watersheds crosses the city. Drainage to the north flows into the Gasconade and Missouri rivers. To the south, it drains into the White and Mississippi rivers. The growing season extends to 199 days and agriculture is diversified: Practically every temperate-zone product is grown in this area. The climate permits green pastures year round in varying quantity. The air is remarkably free of pollution.

Temperatures

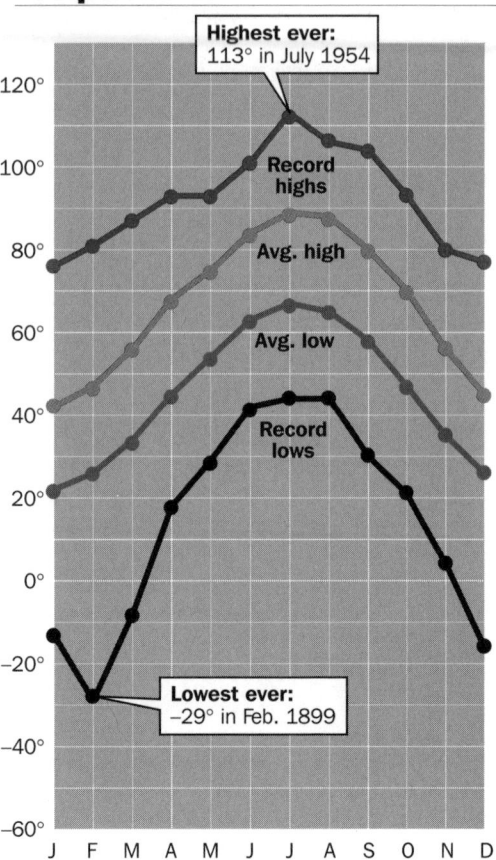

Highest ever: 113° in July 1954

Record highs

Avg. high

Avg. low

Record lows

Lowest ever: −29° in Feb. 1899

Weather extremes

Most rain in 24 hours:	6.85 in. June 6 – 7, 1958
Most rain in a month:	18.75 in. July 1958
Most snow in 24 hours:	20 in. Feb. 20 – 21, 1912
Most snow in a month:	24.1 in. February 1912

Monthly averages

Month	Avg. precip. (in.)	Avg. snow (in.)	Wet days	Thunder-storm days	Pct. sky is cloudy	% p.m. relative humidity	Dew point	Wind speed (mph)
Jan.	1.8	5	8	1	46	58	22	12.7
Feb.	2.2	4	9	1	49	56	26	13.8
March	3.5	4	10	4	49	52	33	13.8
April	4.2	T	11	6	41	50	43	12.7
May	4.8	T	11	8	38	55	54	11.5
June	5.0	0	10	9	29	55	63	10.4
July	3.4	0	8	7	22	53	66	9.2
Aug.	3.3	0	9	8	22	50	64	9.2
Sept.	4.3	0	8	5	29	52	57	10.4
Oct.	3.6	T	8	3	31	50	46	11.5
Nov.	3.2	2	8	2	40	54	34	12.7
Dec.	2.8	3	9	1	47	59	26	12.7

T - Trace of rain or snow   * - Less than 1   NA - Not Available

Annual averages

Precipitation (in inches)	42.0
Snow (in inches)	18
Heating degree days	4,660
Cooling degree days	1,374
Days with thunderstorms	55
Days with fog	119
Days above 90°	42
Days below 32°	102
Wet days	109
Days with snow	13
Days with 1.5 inches or more snow	4

Percent time sky is clear

30.4	28.5	27.2	27.8	25.3	27.3	30.6	32.4	36.7	40.3	35.4	30.7

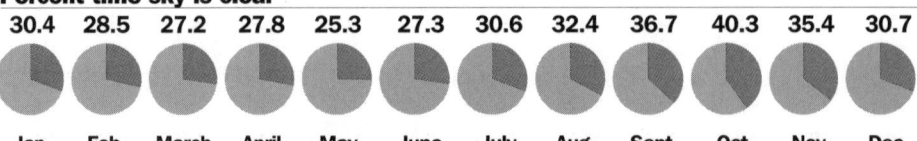

| Jan. | Feb. | March | April | May | June | July | Aug. | Sept. | Oct. | Nov. | Dec. |

Syracuse, New York

Lat. 43° 7' N **Lon.** 76° 7' W **Elev.** 421 ft.

Syracuse is on rolling terrain 8 miles southwest of Oneida Lake and about 30 miles from the eastern end of Lake Ontario. About 5 miles south of the city, hills rise to 1,500 feet. The continental climate is comparatively humid. Nearly all weather systems moving through the St. Lawrence Valley affect the area. Summer and transitional season temperatures rise rapidly during the day to moderate levels, and fall rapidly after sunset. Winters are cold and sometimes severe, with daytime temperatures in the low 30s and nighttime lows in the teens. Lake Ontario rarely freezes over because of its depth, so cold air flowing over it is quickly saturated and produces cloudiness and snow squalls. During the winter, winds cause blowing and drifting snow.

Temperatures

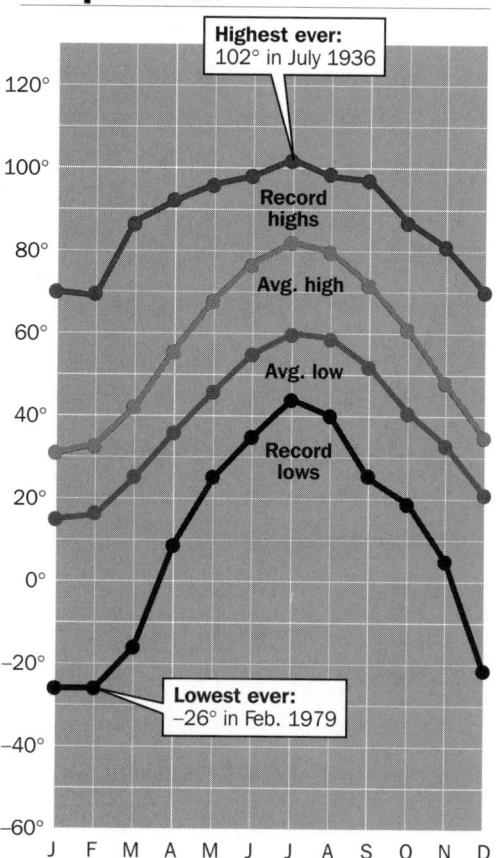

Highest ever: 102° in July 1936

Record highs

Avg. high

Avg. low

Record lows

Lowest ever: −26° in Feb. 1979

Weather extremes

Most rain in 24 hours:	4.79 in. June 11, 1922
Most rain in a month:	15.92 in. June 1922
Most snow in 24 hours:	25.6 in. March 13–14, 1993
Most snow in a month:	72.6 in. February 1958

Monthly averages

Month	Avg. precip. (in.)	Avg. snow (in.)	Wet days	Thunderstorm days	Pct. sky is cloudy	% p.m. relative humidity	Dew point	Wind speed (mph)
Jan.	2.5	28	19	*	65	69	16	15.0
Feb.	2.5	25	16	*	61	67	17	13.8
March	3.0	16	17	1	55	60	24	13.8
April	3.2	4	14	2	48	53	34	13.8
May	3.2	T	13	3	43	53	45	11.5
June	3.5	0	11	5	34	54	55	11.5
July	3.6	0	11	6	28	53	60	9.2
Aug.	3.5	T	11	5	31	56	59	9.2
Sept.	3.5	T	11	3	36	60	53	9.2
Oct.	3.2	1	12	1	44	60	42	10.4
Nov.	3.5	9	16	1	63	68	33	12.7
Dec.	3.1	25	19	*	69	72	22	13.8

T - Trace of rain or snow   * - Less than 1   NA - Not Available

Annual averages

Precipitation (in inches)	38.5
Snow (in inches)	107
Heating degree days	6,748
Cooling degree days	582
Days with thunderstorms	27
Days with fog	129
Days above 90°	9
Days below 32°	136
Wet days	170
Days with snow	133
Days with 1.5 inches or more snow	48

Percent time sky is clear

Jan.	Feb.	March	April	May	June	July	Aug.	Sept.	Oct.	Nov.	Dec.
8.7	10.4	15.4	18.4	17.9	17.9	18.7	19.9	21.3	21.1	8.4	6.7

Tallahassee, Florida

Lat. 30° 23' N **Lon.** 84° 22' W **Elev.** 55 ft.

Located about 20 miles from the Gulf of Mexico, Tallahassee has a mild, moist climate. In contrast to southern Florida, there are four seasons with considerable rainfall and quite a bit less winter sunshine. During the winter, cold air flowing into lower elevations produces wide variation in low temperatures on clear and calm nights. Temperatures of 25°F or lower in the suburbs average about 12 times a year. Summer is the least pleasant season. Thunderstorms occur every other day on average and temperatures and humidities are high. Short droughts, however, are common in the drier months. High winds are infrequent, but a hurricane is likely to hit about once every 17 years with fringe effects from other hurricanes averaging once every five years.

Temperatures

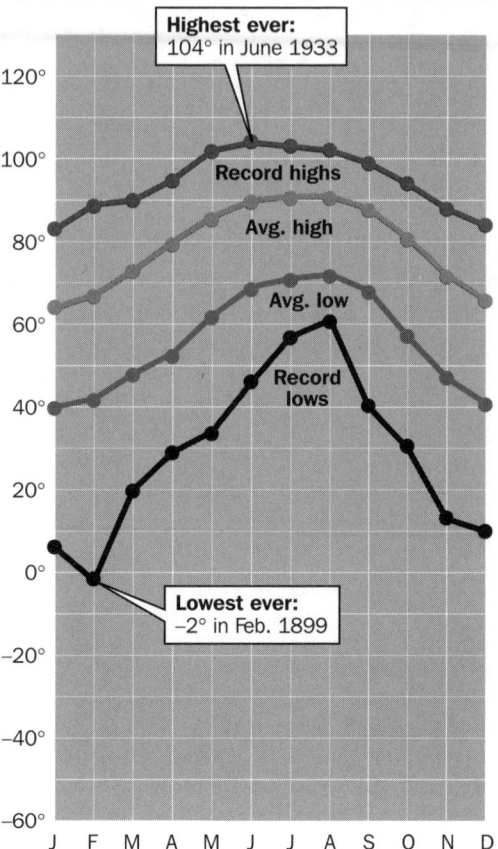

Highest ever: 104° in June 1933

Record highs

Avg. high

Avg. low

Record lows

Lowest ever: −2° in Feb. 1899

Weather extremes

Most rain in 24 hours:	9.47 in.	Sept. 20, 1969
Most rain in a month:	23.85 in.	September 1924
Most snow in 24 hours:	2.8 in.	Feb. 13, 1958
Most snow in a month:	2.8 in.	February 1958

Monthly averages

Month	Avg. precip. (in.)	Avg. snow (in.)	Wet days	Thunder-storm days	Pct. sky is cloudy	% p.m. relative humidity	Dew point	Wind speed (mph)
Jan.	4.2	T	9	2	39	54	42	8.1
Feb.	5.1	T	9	2	38	51	44	9.2
March	6.0	T	9	4	35	49	49	10.4
April	4.2	0	7	4	24	46	55	10.4
May	4.5	0	8	8	20	50	62	9.2
June	6.8	0	12	14	19	58	69	8.1
July	8.8	0	17	19	20	66	72	6.9
Aug.	7.1	0	14	16	19	64	72	5.8
Sept.	5.7	0	10	8	23	60	69	8.1
Oct.	2.9	0	5	2	21	51	58	6.9
Nov.	3.5	0	6	2	27	52	50	8.1
Dec.	4.5	T	8	2	37	55	44	8.1

T - Trace of rain or snow   * - Less than 1   NA - Not Available

Annual averages

Precipitation (in inches)	63.3
Snow (in inches)	T
Heating degree days	1,585
Cooling degree days	2,568
Days with thunderstorms	83
Days with fog	202
Days above 90°	86
Days below 32°	31
Wet days	114
Days with snow	*
Days with 1.5 inches or more snow	*

Percent time sky is clear

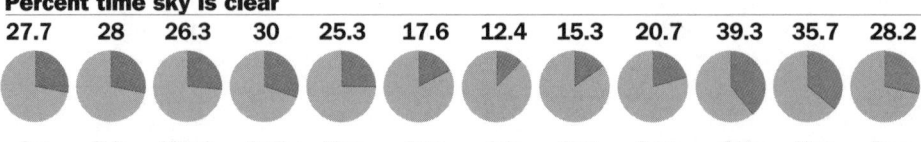

Jan.	Feb.	March	April	May	June	July	Aug.	Sept.	Oct.	Nov.	Dec.
27.7	28	26.3	30	25.3	17.6	12.4	15.3	20.7	39.3	35.7	28.2

Tampa, Florida

Lat. 27° 58' N **Lon.** 82° 32' W **Elev.** 19 ft.

Tampa is on Florida's west coast, near the Gulf of Mexico at the upper end of Tampa Bay. Land and sea breezes modify the subtropical climate. Summers are long, warm, and humid. Temperatures in the 90s are uncommon because of the afternoon sea breezes and the summer thunderstorm season. Between a dry spring and a dry fall, about 60 percent of the annual rain falls in summer. Winters are mild. Tropical storms threaten the area a few times in most years. The greatest risk of hurricanes generally has been during the months of June and October. By replenishing the soil moisture and raising the water table, many hurricanes do far more good than harm.

Temperatures

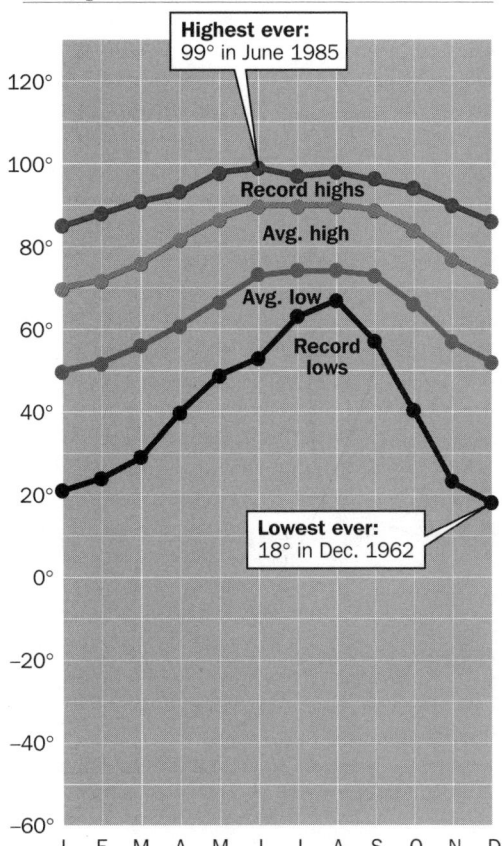

Highest ever: 99° in June 1985

Record highs

Avg. high

Avg. low

Record lows

Lowest ever: 18° in Dec. 1962

Weather extremes

Most rain in 24 hours:	12.11 in.	July 28 – 29, 1960
Most rain in a month:	20.59 in.	July 1960
Most snow in 24 hours:	0.2 in.	Jan. 18 – 19, 1977
Most snow in a month:	0.2 in.	January 1977

Monthly averages

Month	Avg. precip. (in.)	Avg. snow (in.)	Wet days	Thunder-storm days	Pct. sky is cloudy	% p.m. relative humidity	Dew point	Wind speed (mph)
Jan.	2.1	T	6	1	29	56	50	9.2
Feb.	2.8	T	7	2	27	55	52	8.1
March	3.5	T	7	3	25	54	55	8.1
April	1.8	0	5	2	18	51	59	9.2
May	3.0	0	6	6	15	52	65	9.2
June	5.6	0	12	14	19	60	71	10.4
July	7.3	0	16	21	22	65	73	6.9
Aug.	7.9	0	17	21	22	66	73	6.9
Sept.	6.5	0	13	12	23	64	71	8.1
Oct.	2.3	0	7	3	17	57	64	9.2
Nov.	1.8	0	5	1	21	56	58	8.1
Dec.	2.1	T	6	1	26	57	52	9.2

T - Trace of rain or snow   * - Less than 1   NA - Not Available

Annual averages

Precipitation (in inches)	46.7
Snow (in inches)	T
Heating degree days	627
Cooling degree days	3,397
Days with thunderstorms	87
Days with fog	124
Days above 90°	85
Days below 32°	3
Wet days	107
Days with snow	*
Days with 1.5 inches or more snow	0

Percent time sky is clear

Jan.	Feb.	March	April	May	June	July	Aug.	Sept.	Oct.	Nov.	Dec.
26.9	26.7	25.8	30.7	24.5	14	8.8	10	15.3	28.9	30.6	26.6

Toledo, Ohio

Lat. 41° 35' N **Lon.** 83° 48' W **Elev.** 669 ft.

Toledo is on the western end of Lake Erie, at the mouth of the Maumee River, where the terrain is level except for a slight slope toward the river and the lake. Lake Erie has a moderating effect on the temperature. On average only 15 days a year reach 90°F or more; eight days hit 0°F or less. In winter, snowfall is light and frequent thaws occur. Toledo skies are often cloudy. December and January sometimes have as little as 16 percent of the possible hours of sunshine. Flooding occurs when heavy rains of an inch or more cause a sudden rise in creeks and drainage ditches to the point of overflow. Also, the western shores of Lake Erie flood when the water is high and the wind is blowing east to northeast.

Temperatures

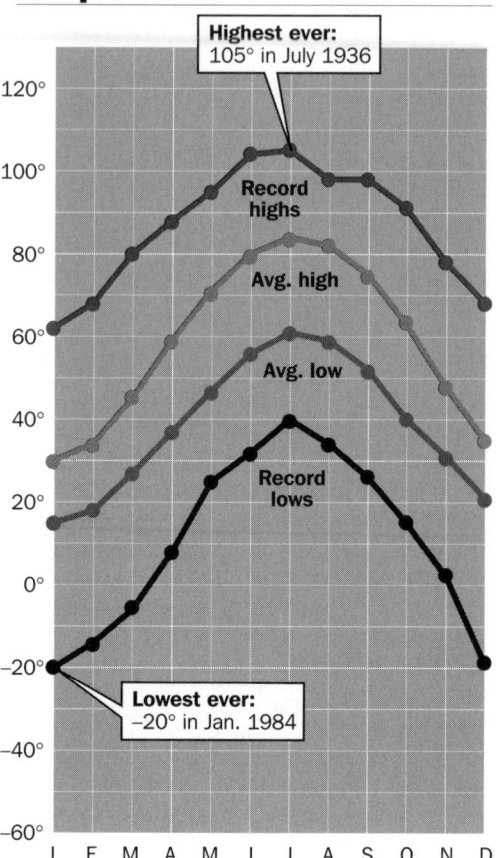

Highest ever: 105° in July 1936

Record highs

Avg. high

Avg. low

Record lows

Lowest ever: −20° in Jan. 1984

Weather extremes

Most rain in 24 hours:	5.98 in. Sept. 4 – 5, 1918
Most rain in a month:	8.49 in. October 1881
Most snow in 24 hours:	19.0 in. Feb. 28, 1900
Most snow in a month:	30.8 in. January 1978

Monthly averages

Month	Avg. precip. (in.)	Avg. snow (in.)	Wet days	Thunder-storm days	Pct. sky is cloudy	% p.m. relative humidity	Dew point	Wind speed (mph)
Jan.	1.8	9	13	*	57	68	16	12.7
Feb.	1.8	8	11	*	53	65	18	12.7
March	2.5	6	13	2	50	59	26	11.5
April	2.9	2	13	4	44	52	36	12.7
May	2.9	T	12	5	36	51	47	11.5
June	3.7	0	10	7	29	51	56	9.2
July	3.3	0	9	7	24	54	61	8.1
Aug.	3.4	0	9	6	25	56	61	8.1
Sept.	2.7	T	10	4	31	55	54	9.2
Oct.	2.1	T	9	1	36	55	42	10.4
Nov.	2.8	3	12	1	55	65	32	12.7
Dec.	2.7	9	14	*	62	72	22	12.7

T - Trace of rain or snow   * - Less than 1   NA - Not Available

Annual averages

Precipitation (in inches)	32.6
Snow (in inches)	37
Heating degree days	6,571
Cooling degree days	697
Days with thunderstorms	37
Days with fog	157
Days above 90°	14
Days below 32°	141
Wet days	135
Days with snow	76
Days with 1.5 inches or more snow	16

Percent time sky is clear

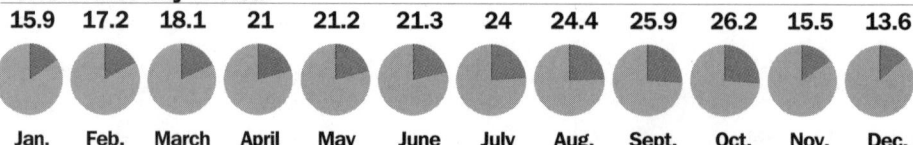

Jan.	Feb.	March	April	May	June	July	Aug.	Sept.	Oct.	Nov.	Dec.
15.9	17.2	18.1	21	21.2	21.3	24	24.4	25.9	26.2	15.5	13.6

Topeka, Kansas

Lat. 39° 04' N **Lon.** 95° 38' W **Elev.** 877 ft.

Topeka is located near the geographical center of the United States and the middle of the temperate climate zone. The city straddles the Kansas River about 60 miles west of its junction with the Missouri River. Local flooding from the Kansas and two tributaries is always a threat following heavy rains. Seventy percent of the annual precipitation falls during the six crop-growing months, April through September. These rains are predominantly thunderstorms and occur more frequently during the night than at other times. Winter precipitation is often snow, sleet, or glaze ice. Blustery winds are common in late winter and spring. Tornadoes have caused severe damage and numerous injuries. The hottest summers can produce 100°F or higher on more than 50 days.

Temperatures

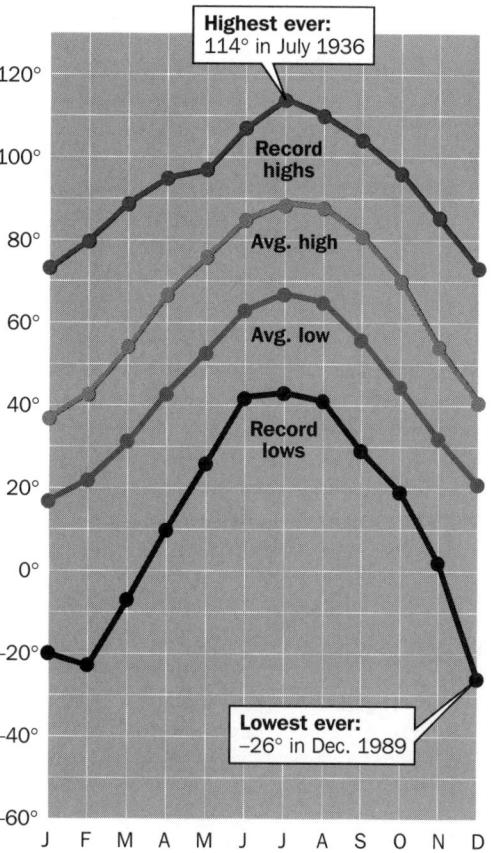

Highest ever: 114° in July 1936

Record highs

Avg. high

Avg. low

Record lows

Lowest ever: −26° in Dec. 1989

Weather extremes

Most rain in 24 hours:	5.52 in.	June 20 – 21, 1967
Most rain in a month:	15.20 in.	June 1967
Most snow in 24 hours:	15.2 in.	Feb. 21 – 22, 1971
Most snow in a month:	22.4 in.	February 1971

Monthly averages

Month	Avg. precip. (in.)	Avg. snow (in.)	Wet days	Thunder-storm days	Pct. sky is cloudy	% p.m. relative humidity	Dew point	Wind speed (mph)
Jan.	1.0	6	6	*	41	58	18	12.7
Feb.	1.1	5	6	1	44	57	23	12.7
March	2.4	4	9	2	45	51	30	13.8
April	3.0	1	10	5	41	48	41	15.0
May	4.3	0	11	9	38	52	53	15.0
June	5.3	0	10	10	30	54	63	12.7
July	4.1	0	9	9	22	53	67	11.5
Aug.	3.9	0	8	8	23	52	65	10.4
Sept.	3.4	0	8	6	27	50	56	11.5
Oct.	2.9	T	7	3	30	47	44	12.7
Nov.	1.7	1	6	1	37	51	32	11.5
Dec.	1.3	5	6	*	42	58	22	11.5

T - Trace of rain or snow　　　* - Less than 1　　　NA - Not Available

Annual averages

Precipitation (in inches)	34.4
Snow (in inches)	21
Heating degree days	5,234
Cooling degree days	1,403
Days with thunderstorms	54
Days with fog	108
Days above 90°	45
Days below 32°	123
Wet days	96
Days with snow	30
Days with 1.5 inches or more snow	9

Percent time sky is clear

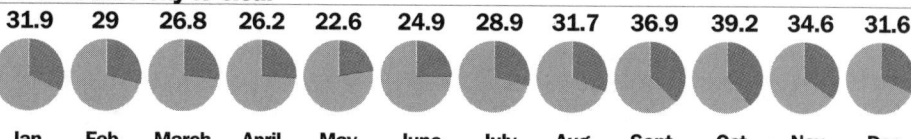

31.9	29	26.8	26.2	22.6	24.9	28.9	31.7	36.9	39.2	34.6	31.6
Jan.	Feb.	March	April	May	June	July	Aug.	Sept.	Oct.	Nov.	Dec.

Tucson, Arizona

Lat. 32° 8' N **Lon.** 110° 56' W **Elev.** 2,584 ft.

Tucson is at the foot of the Santa Catalina Mountains, where the soil is sandy and vegetation is brush, cacti, and small trees. It has a long, hot season from April to October. Temperatures are often above 90°F and above 100°F an average of 14 days each June and July. But extreme temperatures are moderated by low humidity. The daily range averages 30 degrees or more a day. During the summer, scattered rainfall from the mountains often fills dry washes to overflowing. From December through March, prolonged rainstorms replenish the ground water. Humidity increases in the summer, producing discomfort, but only for short periods. Tucson is one of the sunniest cities in the U.S. Surface winds are light, although spring winds may cause damage.

Temperatures

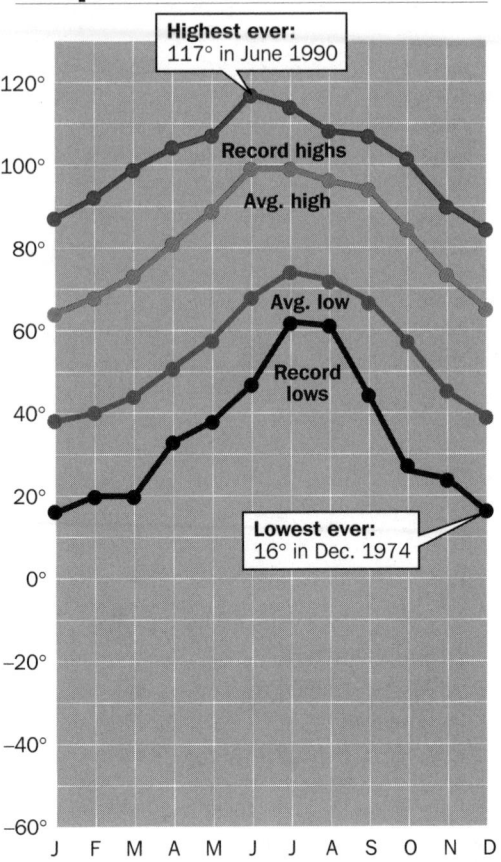

Weather extremes

Most rain in 24 hours:	3.93 in. July 29, 1958
Most rain in a month:	7.93 in. August 1955
Most snow in 24 hours:	6.8 in. Dec. 8, 1971
Most snow in a month:	6.8 in. December 1971

Monthly averages

Month	Avg. precip. (in.)	Avg. snow (in.)	Wet days	Thunderstorm days	Pct. sky is cloudy	% p.m. relative humidity	Dew point	Wind speed (mph)
Jan.	0.9	T	5	*	27	31	28	8.1
Feb.	0.7	T	3	*	24	26	27	8.1
March	0.7	T	4	*	24	22	27	8.1
April	0.3	T	2	1	16	16	27	8.1
May	0.1	0	2	1	11	13	29	8.1
June	0.2	0	2	3	9	13	36	6.9
July	2.5	0	11	15	30	29	56	9.2
Aug.	2.2	0	9	14	23	32	58	8.1
Sept.	1.4	0	5	6	12	26	50	9.2
Oct.	0.9	0	3	2	11	24	39	9.2
Nov.	0.6	T	3	*	16	27	31	8.1
Dec.	0.9	T	5	*	25	33	28	8.1

T - Trace of rain or snow   * - Less than 1   NA - Not Available

Annual averages

Precipitation (in inches)	11.6
Snow (in inches)	2
Heating degree days	1,644
Cooling degree days	2,898
Days with thunderstorms	42
Days with fog	3
Days above 90°	140
Days below 32°	18
Wet days	54
Days with snow	1
Days with 1.5 inches or more snow	*

Percent time sky is clear

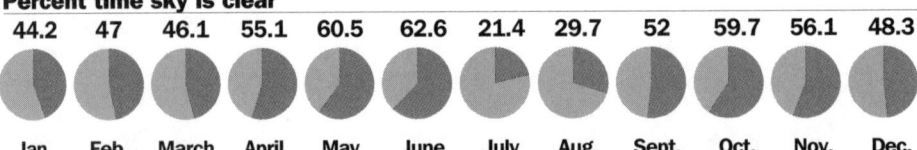

Jan.	Feb.	March	April	May	June	July	Aug.	Sept.	Oct.	Nov.	Dec.
44.2	47	46.1	55.1	60.5	62.6	21.4	29.7	52	59.7	56.1	48.3

Tulsa, Oklahoma

Lat. 36° 11′ N **Lon.** 95° 54′ W **Elev.** 668 ft.

Tulsa, on the Arkansas River, is far enough north to escape long periods of heat in summer, yet far enough south to miss the extreme cold of winter. The influence of warm, moist air from the Gulf of Mexico is often noted, due to the high humidity, but the climate is essentially continental with rapid changes in temperature. During Tulsa's generally mild winters, temperatures rarely stay below zero. In spring and early summer, there can be large hail and violent windstorms. From late July to early September, temperatures can reach 100°F or more, but are usually accompanied by low humidity and a southerly breeze. Autumn is a long season with many pleasant, sunny days and cool, fresh nights.

Temperatures

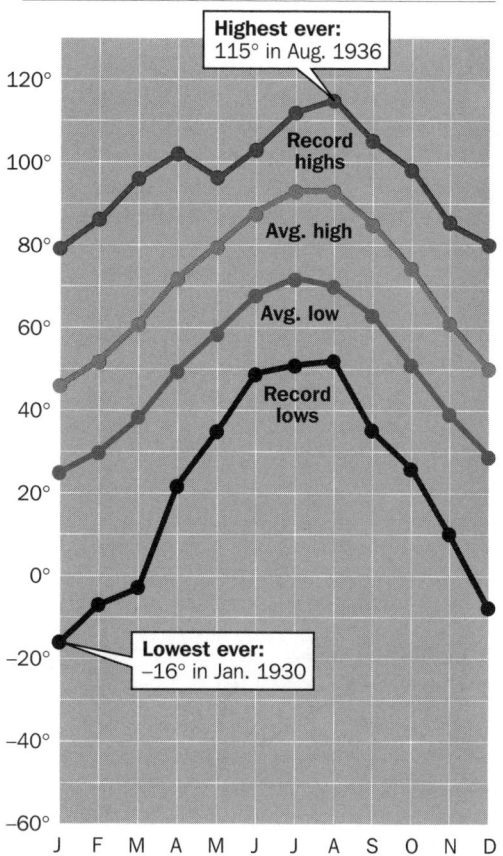

Highest ever: 115° in Aug. 1936
Record highs
Avg. high
Avg. low
Record lows
Lowest ever: −16° in Jan. 1930

Weather extremes

Most rain in 24 hours:	9.27 in.	May 27, 1984
Most rain in a month:	18.81 in.	September 1971
Most snow in 24 hours:	12.9 in.	March 8 – 9, 1994
Most snow in a month:	19.7 in.	March 1924

Monthly averages

Month	Avg. precip. (in.)	Avg. snow (in.)	Wet days	Thunder-storm days	Pct. sky is cloudy	% p.m. relative humidity	Dew point	Wind speed (mph)
Jan.	1.6	3	6	1	39	53	25	11.5
Feb.	1.9	2	7	1	40	51	29	11.5
March	3.2	2	8	3	38	47	35	13.8
April	3.7	T	9	6	35	46	45	13.8
May	5.6	0	10	9	32	54	57	13.8
June	4.3	0	8	8	22	53	66	12.7
July	3.4	0	7	6	15	48	68	10.4
Aug.	3.0	0	7	6	15	46	66	10.4
Sept.	4.1	0	7	5	23	49	60	11.5
Oct.	3.5	T	6	3	26	46	49	11.5
Nov.	2.6	1	6	1	32	48	37	12.7
Dec.	1.9	2	7	1	37	52	28	11.5

T - Trace of rain or snow   * - Less than 1   NA - Not Available

Annual averages

Precipitation (in inches)	38.9
Snow (in inches)	10
Heating degree days	3,658
Cooling degree days	2,107
Days with thunderstorms	50
Days with fog	92
Days above 90°	74
Days below 32°	78
Wet days	88
Days with snow	14
Days with 1.5 inches or more snow	4

Percent time sky is clear

Jan.	Feb.	March	April	May	June	July	Aug.	Sept.	Oct.	Nov.	Dec.
32.5	31.3	30	27.9	23.5	27.1	31.3	34.3	36.4	41.3	37.2	34.3

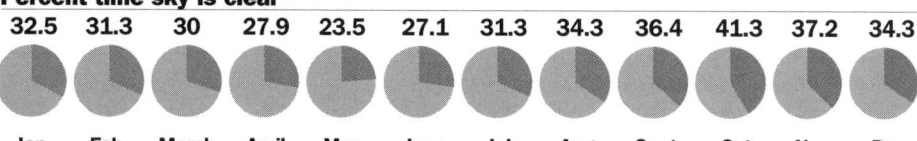

Valentine, Nebraska

Lat. 42° 52' N **Lon.** 100° 33' W **Elev.** 2,587 ft.

Valentine lies in the Niobrara River Valley on the edge of the Sand Hills near the South Dakota border. As a new town in 1882, it was named for the area's congressman, E.K. Valentine. Its location subjects it to frigid Canadian air masses in winter, alternating with mild, dry air moving across the Rockies. At least a few days each winter are entirely below zero and at least one blizzard is likely each winter. About 65 percent of the annual precipitation falls during May through September, predominantly as nighttime thunderstorms. Fall has light winds and gradually falling temperatures. Spring is windy and extremely variable, with summerlike days mixed with winter days. The widest extremes occur in March.

Temperatures

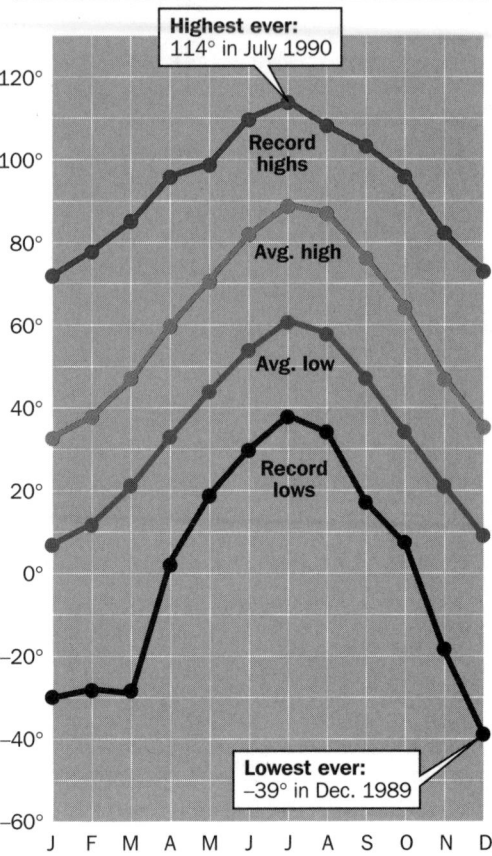

Weather extremes

Most rain in 24 hours:	3.4 in. July 17-18, 1983
Most rain in a month:	8.96 in. July 1983
Most snow in 24 hours:	24 in. March 11-12, 1977
Most snow in a month:	51.0 in. March 1977

Monthly averages

Month	Avg. precip. (in.)	Avg. snow (in.)	Wet days	Thunder-storm days	Pct. sky is cloudy	% p.m. relative humidity	Dew point	Wind speed (mph)
Jan.	0.3	5	5	0	35	52	9	8.1
Feb.	0.4	5	5	*	39	50	13	12.7
March	1.0	9	7	1	43	47	22	13.8
April	1.8	4	8	4	37	39	29	12.7
May	2.9	T	10	10	36	40	41	13.8
June	2.9	0	10	15	24	38	50	12.7
July	3.1	0	9	19	21	37	55	12.7
Aug.	2.3	0	8	17	21	39	54	12.7
Sept.	1.5	1	7	9	23	35	43	12.7
Oct.	0.9	1	5	1	29	38	31	6.9
Nov.	0.6	5	5	*	35	45	20	8.1
Dec.	0.4	6	5	0	32	50	10	8.1

T - Trace of rain or snow   * - Less than 1   NA - Not Available

Annual averages

Precipitation (in inches)	18.1
Snow (in inches)	35
Heating degree days	7,362
Cooling degree days	761
Days with thunderstorms	76
Days with fog	82
Days above 90°	43
Days below 32°	176
Wet days	84
Days with snow	52
Days with 1.5 inches or more snow	14

Percent time sky is clear

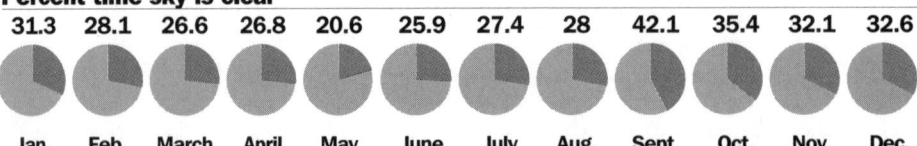

31.3	28.1	26.6	26.8	20.6	25.9	27.4	28	42.1	35.4	32.1	32.6
Jan.	Feb.	March	April	May	June	July	Aug.	Sept.	Oct.	Nov.	Dec.

Washington, D.C.

Lat. 38° 51' N **Lon.** 77° 2' W **Elev.** 10 ft.

Washington lies about 50 miles east of the Blue Ridge Mountains and 35 miles west of the Chesapeake Bay, on the banks of the Potomac and Anacostia rivers. Elevations range from a few feet above sea level to 400 feet in the northwest section of the city. Its location in the middle latitudes, where the general atmospheric flow is west to east, favors a continental climate with four well-defined seasons. Summers are warm and humid, in the upper 80s and 90s; winters are cold, but not severe on average. Snowfalls of over 25 inches have occurred, although the normal annual amount is 18 inches. The spring and fall are quite pleasant. Thunderstorms are most common during the late spring and summer and may include downpours, gusty winds and lightning. Tropical storms can bring heavy rain, high winds and flooding, but extensive damage is rare.

Weather extremes

Most rain in 24 hours:	6.39 in. Aug. 23, 1933
Most rain in a month:	17.45 in. September 1935
Most snow in 24 hours:	21.0 in. Jan. 28, 1922
Most snow in a month:	35.2 in. February 1899

Temperatures

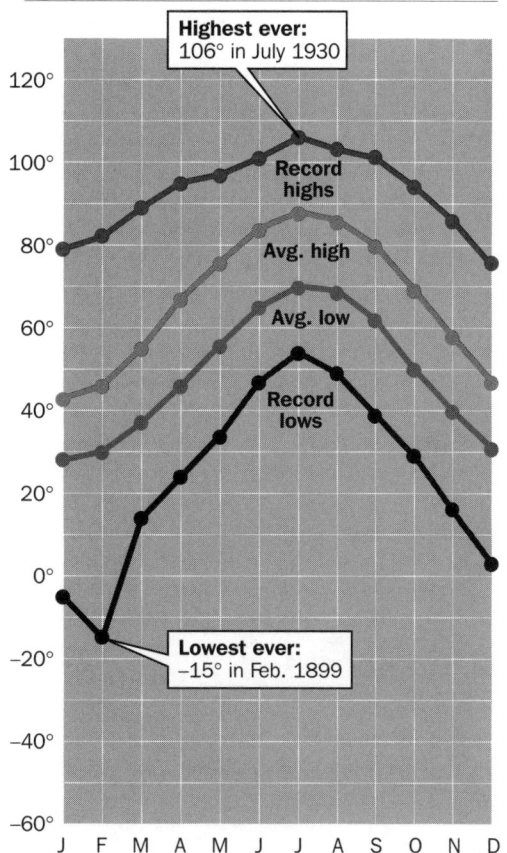

Highest ever: 106° in July 1930

Record highs

Avg. high

Avg. low

Record lows

Lowest ever: −15° in Feb. 1899

Monthly averages

Month	Avg. precip. (in.)	Avg. snow (in.)	Wet days	Thunder-storm days	Pct. sky is cloudy	% p.m. relative humidity	Dew point	Wind speed (mph)
Jan.	2.8	6	10	*	46	54	23	13.8
Feb.	2.6	6	9	*	44	50	24	13.8
March	3.3	2	11	1	42	46	31	13.8
April	2.9	T	10	2	41	45	40	9.2
May	4.0	0	11	5	40	51	52	9.2
June	3.4	0	10	6	32	52	61	9.2
July	4.1	0	10	7	30	53	66	9.2
Aug.	4.2	0	9	5	31	54	65	9.2
Sept.	3.3	0	8	2	33	54	59	9.2
Oct.	2.9	T	7	1	33	53	48	9.2
Nov.	3.0	1	8	1	38	53	36	9.2
Dec.	3.1	3	9	*	44	55	27	13.8

T - Trace of rain or snow   * - Less than 1   NA - Not Available

Annual averages

Precipitation (in inches)	39.5
Snow (in inches)	18
Heating degree days	4,085
Cooling degree days	1,512
Days with thunderstorms	30
Days with fog	127
Days above 90°	34
Days below 32°	71
Wet days	112
Days with snow	18
Days with 1.5 inches or more snow	8

Percent time sky is clear

Jan.	Feb.	March	April	May	June	July	Aug.	Sept.	Oct.	Nov.	Dec.
23.5	24.7	23.9	22.4	19.2	17.9	17.2	20.3	25.8	32.2	25.9	23.9

Waterloo, Iowa

Lat. 42° 33′ N **Lon.** 92° 24′ W **Elev.** 868 ft.

Waterloo, on the banks of the Cedar River in northeast Iowa, has a continental humid climate with a wide variation in temperature and precipitation during the four distinct seasons: January, the coldest month, averages 14 °F and July, the warmest, averages 73°F; 72 percent of the rainfall occurs in the April to September crop season. Winter is cold and dry, with storms of short duration and precipitation in the form of snow. Rainfall increases and temperatures rise to between 40 and 59°F during the spring. Summer temperatures peak in July or early August and three-fourths of the thunderstorms occur during this time. In the fall, temperatures hover around 40°F, precipitation declines, and warm days, cool nights, and cloudless skies persist.

Weather extremes

Most rain in 24 hours:	9.31 in. July 16 – 17, 1968
Most rain in a month:	12.60 in. July 1968
Most snow in 24 hours:	14.8 in. Jan. 3 – 4, 1971
Most snow in a month:	24.3 in. February 1962

Temperatures

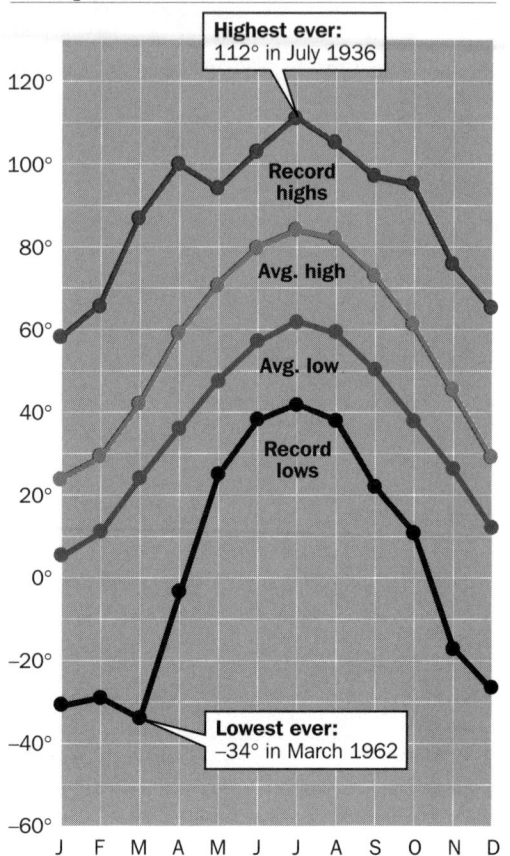

Highest ever: 112° in July 1936

Record highs

Avg. high

Avg. low

Record lows

Lowest ever: −34° in March 1962

Monthly averages

Month	Avg. precip. (in.)	Avg. snow (in.)	Wet days	Thunderstorm days	Pct. sky is cloudy	% p.m. relative humidity	Dew point	Wind speed (mph)
Jan.	0.8	6	7	*	46	67	8	15.0
Feb.	1.1	7	7	*	46	66	13	13.8
March	2.3	6	9	1	50	62	25	15.0
April	3.4	2	11	4	45	52	35	15.0
May	4.2	T	11	6	38	51	47	12.7
June	4.4	0	10	8	29	51	57	11.5
July	4.7	0	10	7	24	55	63	10.4
Aug.	3.7	0	9	7	26	55	61	10.4
Sept.	3.6	0	9	5	33	54	52	10.4
Oct.	2.6	T	8	2	35	52	39	11.5
Nov.	1.8	3	8	1	50	61	28	13.8
Dec.	1.3	8	8	*	52	70	15	13.8

T - Trace of rain or snow   * - Less than 1   NA - Not Available

Annual averages

Precipitation (in inches)	33.8
Snow (in inches)	32
Heating degree days	7,505
Cooling degree days	752
Days with thunderstorms	41
Days with fog	130
Days above 90°	16
Days below 32°	157
Wet days	107
Days with snow	54
Days with 1.5 inches or more snow	13

Percent time sky is clear

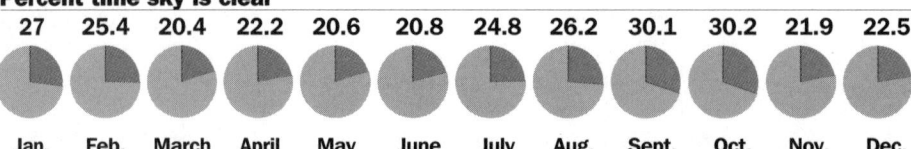

Jan.	Feb.	March	April	May	June	July	Aug.	Sept.	Oct.	Nov.	Dec.
27	25.4	20.4	22.2	20.6	20.8	24.8	26.2	30.1	30.2	21.9	22.5

West Palm Beach, Florida

Lat. 26° 41' N **Lon.** 80° 7' W **Elev.** 18 ft.

West Palm Beach and Palm Beach sit separated by Lake Worth on a coastal sand ridge of southeastern Florida. The ridge is only about 5 miles wide and the Everglades formerly reached to its western edge. Most of the swampland now has been drained for agriculture. The Gulf Stream flows northward about two miles offshore. Because of its southerly location and marine influences, the Palm Beach area has a pleasant climate. Freezing temperatures occur about once every three years. Summer temperatures are tempered by the ocean breeze and frequent cumulus clouds. The moist, unstable air in this area results in frequent showers; thunderstorms are common in summer. Hurricane winds, estimated at 140 mph, have struck West Palm Beach.

Temperatures

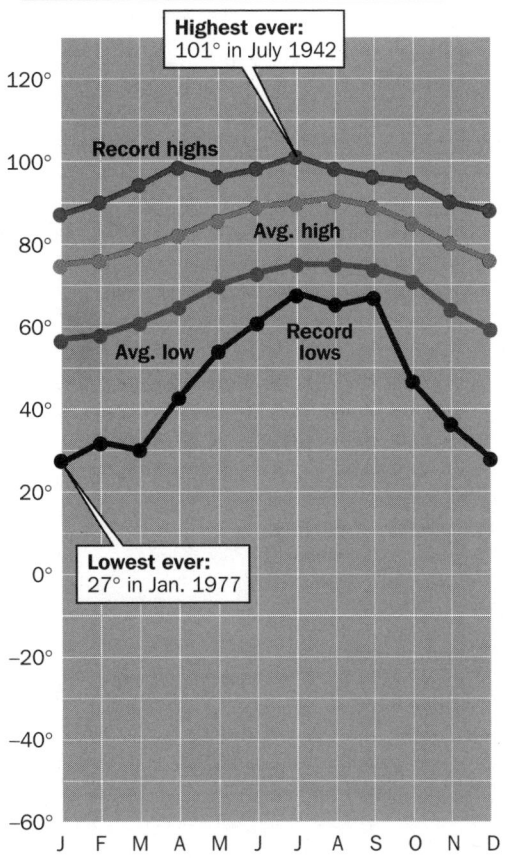

Highest ever: 101° in July 1942

Record highs

Avg. high

Avg. low

Record lows

Lowest ever: 27° in Jan. 1977

Weather extremes

Most rain in 24 hours:	7.41 in. Nov. 22, 1984
Most rain in a month:	24.86 in. September 1960
Most snow in 24 hours:	Trace January 1977
Most snow in a month:	Trace January 1977

Monthly averages

Month	Avg. precip. (in.)	Avg. snow (in.)	Wet days	Thunder-storm days	Pct. sky is cloudy	% p.m. relative humidity	Dew point	Wind speed (mph)
Jan.	2.7	T	8	1	24	60	56	10.4
Feb.	2.6	0	7	1	23	59	56	10.4
March	3.3	0	8	2	22	58	59	12.7
April	3.3	0	7	4	18	58	62	12.7
May	5.7	0	11	8	22	63	67	11.5
June	7.5	0	14	13	27	69	72	10.4
July	6.2	0	15	16	21	67	73	10.4
Aug.	6.3	0	16	16	20	68	73	10.4
Sept.	9.0	0	17	11	25	70	73	11.5
Oct.	7.0	0	13	4	22	66	68	13.8
Nov.	3.9	0	9	2	21	63	62	12.7
Dec.	2.5	0	8	1	23	61	58	10.4

T - Trace of rain or snow   * - Less than 1   NA - Not Available

Annual averages

Precipitation (in inches)	60
Snow (in inches)	0
Heating degree days	262
Cooling degree days	3,969
Days with thunderstorms	79
Days with fog	42
Days above 90°	76
Days below 32°	1
Wet days	133
Days with snow	0
Days with 1.5 inches or more snow	0

Percent time sky is clear

22.5	22.6	21.1	21.2	16.9	11.3	10	9.4	6.6	13.4	18	21.4
Jan.	Feb.	March	April	May	June	July	Aug.	Sept.	Oct.	Nov.	Dec.

Wichita, Kansas

Lat. 37° 39′ N **Lon.** 97° 26′ W **Elev.** 1,321 ft.

Wichita is in the Central Great Plains where masses of warm, moist air from the Gulf of Mexico collide with cold, dry air from the Arctic, creating a wide range of weather. Summers are warm and humid, while winters are mild, with brief periods of cold. Precipitation averages about 30 inches per year, with 70 percent falling during the April through September growing season. The wettest years have recorded over 50 inches; the driest years less than 15. Spring and early summer thunderstorms can be severe and cause damage from heavy rain, hail, strong winds and tornadoes. The windiest months are March and April, but strong north winds often occur from fall through spring.

Temperatures

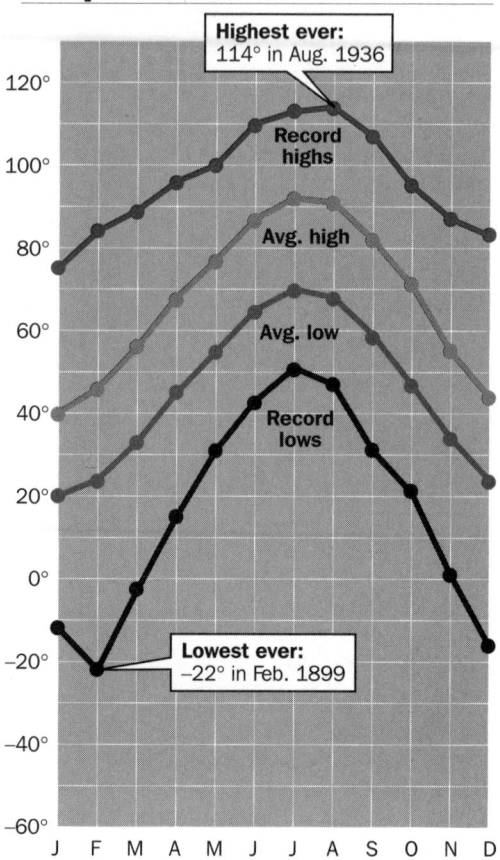

Highest ever: 114° in Aug. 1936

Record highs

Avg. high

Avg. low

Record lows

Lowest ever: −22° in Feb. 1899

Weather extremes

Most rain in 24 hours:	7.99 in.	Sept. 6 – 7, 1911
Most rain in a month:	14.43 in.	June 1923
Most snow in 24 hours:	13.5 in.	March 15–16, 1970
Most snow in a month:	20.5 in.	February 1913

Monthly averages

Month	Avg. precip. (in.)	Avg. snow (in.)	Wet days	Thunder-storm days	Pct. sky is cloudy	% p.m. relative humidity	Dew point	Wind speed (mph)
Jan.	0.9	5	6	*	38	56	20	15.0
Feb.	1.0	4	6	1	41	54	24	15.0
March	2.3	3	8	3	42	48	31	16.1
April	2.3	T	8	5	37	46	42	16.1
May	3.9	0	11	9	35	51	53	15.0
June	4.3	0	9	10	27	47	61	15.0
July	3.7	0	8	8	18	42	64	12.7
Aug.	3.0	0	8	8	19	43	63	12.7
Sept.	3.2	0	7	6	26	47	56	13.8
Oct.	2.3	T	6	3	29	47	45	13.8
Nov.	1.4	2	5	1	34	51	33	13.8
Dec.	1.0	3	5	*	38	56	24	12.7

T - Trace of rain or snow   * - Less than 1   NA - Not Available

Annual averages

Precipitation (in inches)	29.3
Snow (in inches)	17
Heating degree days	4,737
Cooling degree days	1,713
Days with thunderstorms	54
Days with fog	90
Days above 90°	63
Days below 32°	110
Wet days	87
Days with snow	23
Days with 1.5 inches or more snow	8

Percent time sky is clear

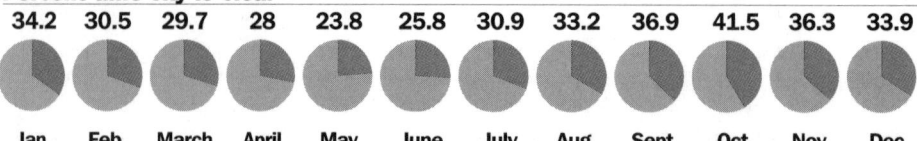

34.2	30.5	29.7	28	23.8	25.8	30.9	33.2	36.9	41.5	36.3	33.9
Jan.	Feb.	March	April	May	June	July	Aug.	Sept.	Oct.	Nov.	Dec.

Wilkes-Barre–Scranton, Pa.

Lat. 41° 20' N **Lon.** 75° 44' W **Elev.** 930 ft.

Weather observations are from the airport, which is between the cities of Wilkes-Barre and Scranton. The Lackawanna River flows through Scranton and into the Susquehanna River a few miles west of the airport. Wilkes-Barre is on the Susquehanna. The surrounding mountains protect both cities and the airport from high winds that influence the temperature and precipitation during both summer and winter. The climate is relatively cool in summer with frequent, brief showers and thunderstorms. Winter temperatures in the valley are not severe. Although severe snowstorms are infrequent, when they do occur they approach blizzard conditions. The area has felt the effects of tropical storms.

Temperatures

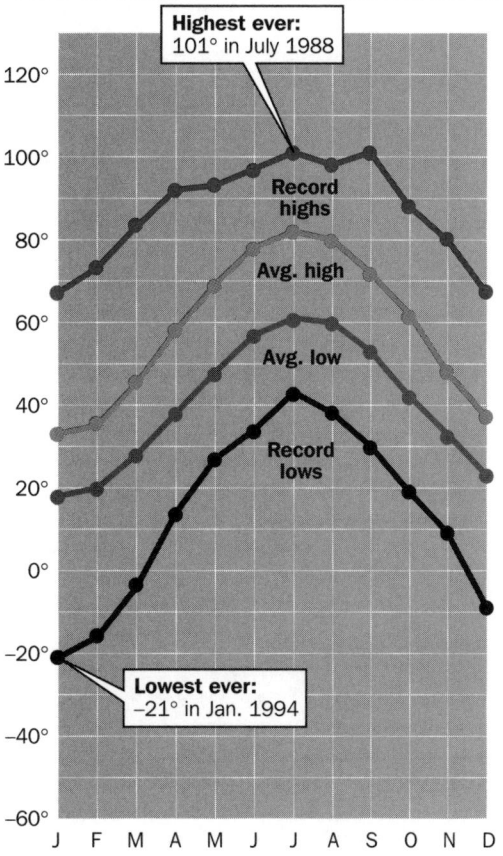

Highest ever: 101° in July 1988

Record highs

Avg. high

Avg. low

Record lows

Lowest ever: −21° in Jan. 1994

Weather extremes

Most rain in 24 hours:	6.0 in. Sept. 27 – 28, 1985
Most rain in a month:	11.8 in. August 1955
Most snow in 24 hours:	19.0 in. Nov. 25 – 26, 1971
Most snow in a month:	42.3 in. January 1994

Monthly averages

Month	Avg. precip. (in.)	Avg. snow (in.)	Wet days	Thunder-storm days	Pct. sky is cloudy	% p.m. relative humidity	Dew point	Wind speed (mph)
Jan.	2.3	11	12	*	55	64	17	10.4
Feb.	2.2	10	11	*	53	61	18	10.4
March	2.5	8	12	1	51	55	25	11.5
April	3.3	3	12	2	48	50	34	10.4
May	3.6	T	13	4	44	50	45	10.4
June	3.8	0	11	6	36	54	56	9.2
July	3.8	0	11	7	32	54	60	8.1
Aug.	3.5	0	11	5	34	56	60	8.1
Sept.	3.3	T	10	3	37	58	53	9.2
Oct.	2.8	T	9	1	40	56	42	9.2
Nov.	3.1	4	12	*	54	63	32	9.2
Dec.	2.6	9	12	*	59	66	22	9.2

T - Trace of rain or snow   * - Less than 1   NA - Not Available

Annual averages

Precipitation (in inches)	36.8
Snow (in inches)	44
Heating degree days	6,292
Cooling degree days	634
Days with thunderstorms	29
Days with fog	143
Days above 90°	8
Days below 32°	127
Wet days	136
Days with snow	74
Days with 1.5 inches or more snow	18

Percent time sky is clear

Jan.	Feb.	March	April	May	June	July	Aug.	Sept.	Oct.	Nov.	Dec.
14.2	16.4	18.3	20.1	18.2	19.4	19.8	21.3	24.5	26.1	15.0	12.6

Williamsport, Pennsylvania

Lat. 41° 15' N **Lon.** 76° 55' W **Elev.** 524 ft.

Williamsport's climate benefits from the low elevation of the Lycoming Valley compared to the surrounding terrain. In the winter, the prevailing winds from the southwest to the north slightly moderate extreme temperatures, making winters milder than those to the west. Deep valley fogs occasionally persist until nearly midday, but the Susquehanna River and adjacent damp areas tend to modify cool temperatures at night. In the summer, the valley usually traps warm air, causing higher temperatures and humidities, which help local agriculture. The range south of the river forms an effective barrier to free air movement and tends to deflect strong winds. Although generally uniform in the valley, snowfall varies considerably with the rise in terrain.

Temperatures

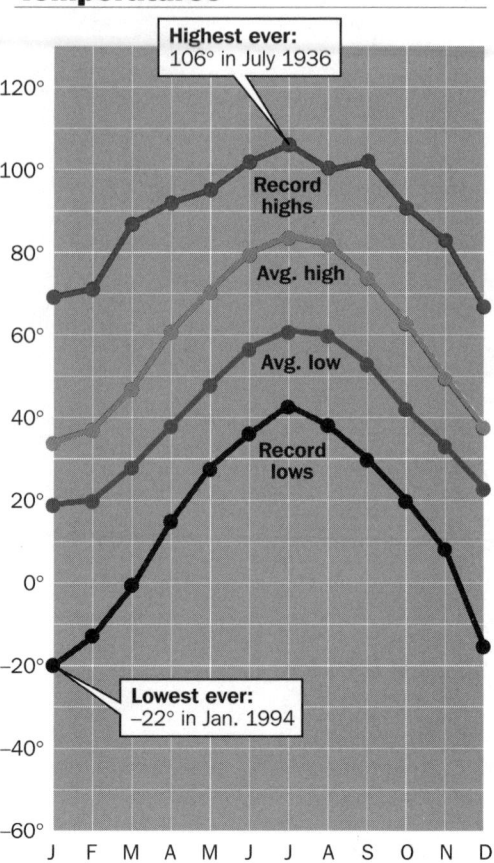

Weather extremes

Most rain in 24 hours:	8.66 in. June 22, 1972
Most rain in a month:	16.80 in. June 1972
Most snow in 24 hours:	23.1 in. Jan. 12-13, 1964
Most snow in a month:	40.1 in. January 1987

Monthly averages

Month	Avg. precip. (in.)	Avg. snow (in.)	Wet days	Thunder-storm days	Pct. sky is cloudy	% p.m. relative humidity	Dew point	Wind speed (mph)
Jan.	2.6	11	12	*	53	60	18	12.7
Feb.	2.8	10	11	*	50	56	19	12.7
March	3.3	8	13	1	48	51	25	12.7
April	3.4	1	13	2	45	47	35	11.5
May	3.8	T	13	5	42	49	47	9.2
June	3.9	0	12	7	35	52	57	9.2
July	4.0	0	11	8	32	53	62	8.1
Aug.	3.5	0	11	6	34	55	61	8.1
Sept.	3.3	0	10	3	41	57	55	8.1
Oct.	3.2	T	10	1	42	55	43	9.2
Nov.	3.8	3	12	1	54	61	33	11.5
Dec.	3.2	8	13	*	57	63	22	11.5

T - Trace of rain or snow   * - Less than 1   NA - Not Available

Annual averages

Precipitation (in inches)	40.8
Snow (in inches)	42
Heating degree days	6,005
Cooling degree days	721
Days with thunderstorms	34
Days with fog	199
Days above 90°	13
Days below 32°	128
Wet days	141
Days with snow	60
Days with 1.5 inches or more snow	17

Percent time sky is clear

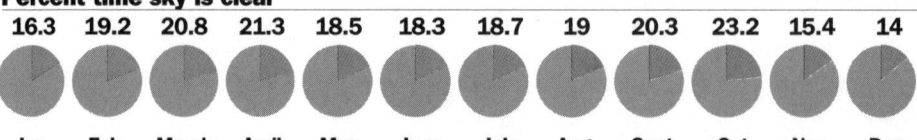

Jan.	Feb.	March	April	May	June	July	Aug.	Sept.	Oct.	Nov.	Dec.
16.3	19.2	20.8	21.3	18.5	18.3	18.7	19	20.3	23.2	15.4	14

Wilmington, Delaware

Lat. 39° 40' N **Lon.** 75° 36' W **Elev.** 79 ft.

Wilmington marks the beginning of low, rolling hills extending north into Pennsylvania. It sits on the Delaware River at the top of Delaware Bay and about 15 miles from the top of the Chesapeake Bay to the southwest. Summers are warm; winters are usually mild. The large water surface area and the southerly winds cause high humidity all year. Fog occurs frequently. Most winter precipitation falls as rain, though seasonal snowfall has been as little as an inch and as much as 50 inches. Snow is frequently mixed with rain and sleet, During the late summer and early fall, hurricanes occasionally cause heavy rainfall, but not hurricane force winds. Strong easterly and southeasterly winds sometimes cause high tides in Delaware Bay, resulting in Delaware River flooding.

Temperatures

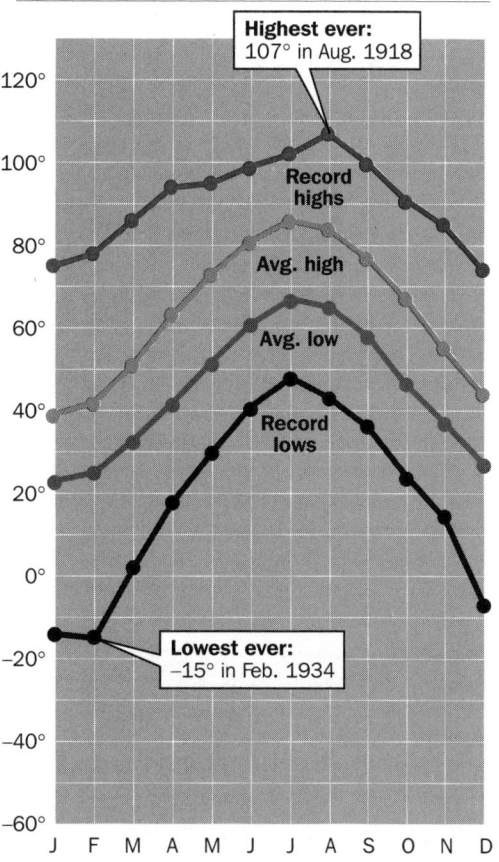

Weather extremes

Most rain in 24 hours:	6.83 in. July 4 – 5, 1989
Most rain in a month:	14.91 in. August 1911
Most snow in 24 hours:	22.0 in. December 1909
Most snow in a month:	27.5 in. February 1979

Monthly averages

Month	Avg. precip. (in.)	Avg. snow (in.)	Wet days	Thunder-storm days	Pct. sky is cloudy	% p.m. relative humidity	Dew point	Wind speed (mph)
Jan.	3.1	7	11	*	47	60	22	12.7
Feb.	3.0	6	10	*	45	56	23	12.7
March	3.6	3	11	1	44	51	29	13.8
April	3.3	T	11	2	43	50	38	12.7
May	3.8	T	12	4	43	53	50	10.4
June	3.5	0	10	6	34	54	60	9.2
July	4.3	0	9	6	33	55	65	9.2
Aug.	3.8	0	9	6	32	56	64	9.2
Sept.	3.5	0	8	2	35	56	58	8.1
Oct.	2.9	T	8	1	34	55	47	9.2
Nov.	3.4	1	9	1	41	58	36	11.5
Dec.	3.4	4	10	*	45	61	26	11.5

T - Trace of rain or snow   * - Less than 1   NA - Not Available

Annual averages

Precipitation (in inches)	41.5
Snow (in inches)	21
Heating degree days	4,942
Cooling degree days	1,103
Days with thunderstorms	29
Days with fog	166
Days above 90°	19
Days below 32°	100
Wet days	118
Days with snow	24
Days with 1.5 inches or more snow	9

Percent time sky is clear

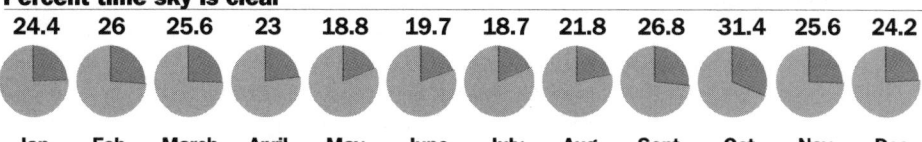

24.4	26	25.6	23	18.8	19.7	18.7	21.8	26.8	31.4	25.6	24.2
Jan.	Feb.	March	April	May	June	July	Aug.	Sept.	Oct.	Nov.	Dec.

Wilmington, North Carolina

Lat. 34° 16' N **Lon.** 77° 54' W **Elev.** 72 ft.

Wilmington is in the Tidewater area of southeastern North Carolina, near the Atlantic Ocean. The city is adjacent to the east bank of the Cape Fear River. Because of the curved coastline, the ocean lies 5 miles east and about 20 miles south. Surrounding terrain is low-lying with rivers, creeks, and lakes that have considerable swamp or marsh land. The maritime location makes the climate mild. Summers are quite warm and humid, but high heat is rare. Sea breezes further alleviate the heat. Polar air masses reach here but are moderated; most winters are short and mild. Summer rainfall comes mostly from thunderstorms, about one every three days. Sunshine is abundant and the long growing season averages 244 days. The area is subject to coastal storms and occasional hurricanes.

Temperatures

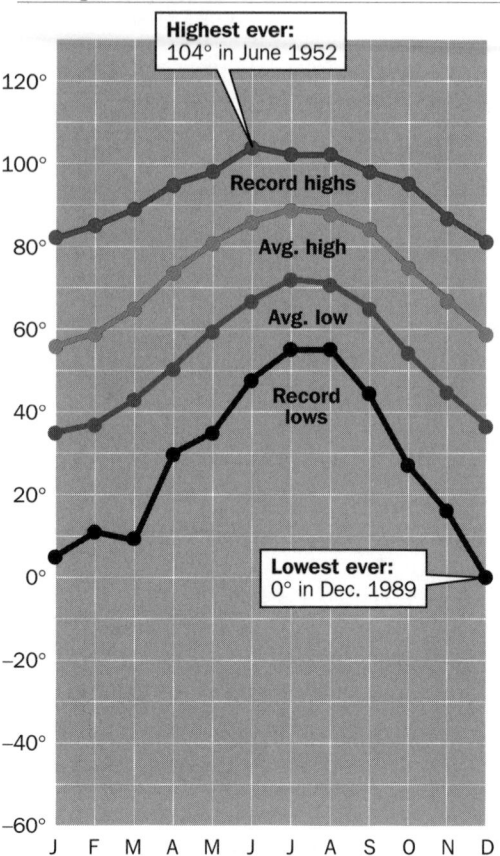

Highest ever: 104° in June 1952

Record highs

Avg. high

Avg. low

Record lows

Lowest ever: 0° in Dec. 1989

Weather extremes

Most rain in 24 hours:	9.52 in. Sept. 29, 1938
Most rain in a month:	21.12 in. July 1886
Most snow in 24 hours:	12.1 in. Feb. 17 – 18, 1896
Most snow in a month:	15.3 in. December 1989

Monthly averages

Month	Avg. precip. (in.)	Avg. snow (in.)	Wet days	Thunder-storm days	Pct. sky is cloudy	% p.m. relative humidity	Dew point	Wind speed (mph)
Jan.	3.6	T	10	*	41	58	36	3.5
Feb.	3.6	1	10	1	41	55	37	4.6
March	4.1	T	10	2	38	54	43	3.5
April	2.9	T	8	3	31	51	50	3.5
May	4.3	0	10	6	31	58	60	2.3
June	5.4	0	10	8	29	62	68	2.3
July	7.9	0	13	12	28	66	72	2.3
Aug.	7.0	0	12	9	28	67	71	2.3
Sept.	5.6	0	9	4	31	66	66	2.3
Oct.	2.9	0	7	1	28	60	56	2.3
Nov.	3.2	T	8	1	29	58	46	3.5
Dec.	3.5	1	9	*	36	58	38	2.3

T - Trace of rain or snow   * - Less than 1   NA - Not Available

Annual averages

Precipitation (in inches)	54.0
Snow (in inches)	2
Heating degree days	2,474
Cooling degree days	2,024
Days with thunderstorms	47
Days with fog	174
Days above 90°	46
Days below 32°	43
Wet days	116
Days with snow	1
Days with 1.5 inches or more snow	*

Percent time sky is clear

Jan.	Feb.	March	April	May	June	July	Aug.	Sept.	Oct.	Nov.	Dec.
29.8	29.5	29.4	33	23	18.2	14.4	17	22.5	34.5	36.5	31.3

Worcester, Massachusetts

Lat. 42° 16' N **Lon.** 71° 52' W **Elev.** 986 ft.

The Atlantic Ocean, Long Island Sound and the Berkshire Hills affect Worcester's climate. Rapid weather changes occur when storms move up the East Coast from the Carolina coast, although they usually pass south and east, resulting in northeast and easterly winds with rain or snow and fog. Storms from Texas-Oklahoma bring an influx of warm air into the region. Though winters are cold, prolonged periods of severe cold are rare. Cold snaps are modified by the passage of the air over land and mountains. Summertime thunderstorms develop over the hills to the west, with many breaking up before reaching Worcester, or passing north or south of the city. July is the warmest month with temperatures in the 70s.

Temperatures

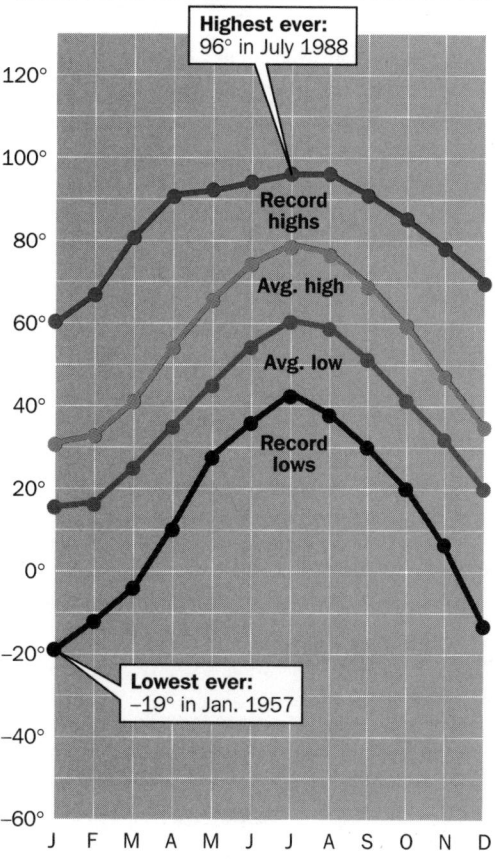

Weather extremes

Most rain in 24 hours:	8.67 in. Aug. 18 – 19, 1955
Most rain in a month:	18.68 in. August 1955
Most snow in 24 hours:	28.1 in. Dec. 11 – 12, 1992
Most snow in a month:	46.8 in. January 1987

Monthly averages

Month	Avg. precip. (in.)	Avg. snow (in.)	Wet days	Thunder-storm days	Pct. sky is cloudy	% p.m. relative humidity	Dew point	Wind speed (mph)
Jan.	3.8	16	12	*	46	58	NA	11.9
Feb.	3.3	16	11	*	49	57	NA	11.6
March	4.2	13	12	1	50	54	NA	11.4
April	3.9	4	11	1	49	50	NA	11.0
May	3.9	T	12	3	49	51	NA	10.0
June	3.5	T	11	4	45	56	NA	8.9
July	3.6	0	10	5	42	57	NA	8.4
Aug.	4.4	0	10	4	38	59	NA	8.3
Sept.	4.3	T	9	2	41	61	NA	8.6
Oct.	4.2	1	9	1	41	56	NA	9.4
Nov.	4.4	4	12	1	52	61	NA	10.2
Dec.	4.2	13	13	*	50	62	NA	10.9

T - Trace of rain or snow   * - Less than 1   NA - Not Available

Annual averages

Precipitation (in inches)	47.6
Snow (in inches)	67
Heating degree days	6,950
Cooling degree days	359
Days with thunderstorms	22
Days with fog	84
Days above 90°	3
Days below 32°	143
Wet days	132
Days with snow	NA
Days with 1.5 inches or more snow	17

Percent time sky is clear

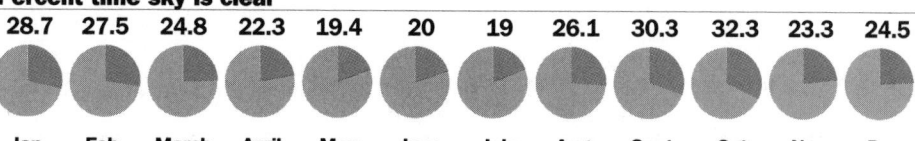

28.7	27.5	24.8	22.3	19.4	20	19	26.1	30.3	32.3	23.3	24.5
Jan.	Feb.	March	April	May	June	July	Aug.	Sept.	Oct.	Nov.	Dec.

Yakima, Washington

Lat. 46° 34' N **Lon.** 120° 32' W **Elev.** 1,064 ft.

Yakima is located in an area of minor valleys and ridges with elevation changes of as much as 1,000 feet. These create sharp variations in air movement, wind, and temperature within short distances. Colder air drains down into the Yakima Valley toward the city so temperatures are often lower here than on nearby higher ground. The climate is relatively mild and dry, with characteristics of both maritime and continental climates, modified by mountains. Summers are hot, but dry, which results in cool nights. Winters are cool with only light snowfall. The Selkirk Mountains in British Columbia and the Rockies in Idaho shield the area from most of the very cold air masses sweeping down from Canada into the Great Plains. The Cascades block moist Pacific air, keeping precipitation low.

Temperatures

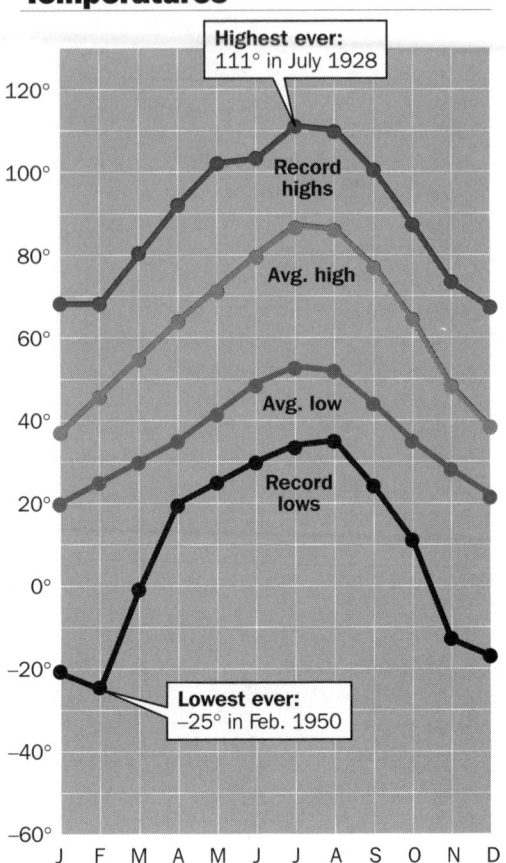

Highest ever: 111° in July 1928

Record highs

Avg. high

Avg. low

Record lows

Lowest ever: −25° in Feb. 1950

Weather extremes

Most rain in 24 hours:	1.74 in. Aug. 20 – 21, 1990
Most rain in a month:	4.19 in. December 1964
Most snow in 24 hours:	14.0 in. Dec. 20 – 21, 1964
Most snow in a month:	37.5 in. December 1964

Monthly averages

Month	Avg. precip. (in.)	Avg. snow (in.)	Wet days	Thunder-storm days	Pct. sky is cloudy	% p.m. relative humidity	Dew point	Wind speed (mph)
Jan.	1.3	9	10	0	60	71	22	6.9
Feb.	0.8	4	7	*	50	58	26	6.9
March	0.7	2	7	*	40	41	28	8.1
April	0.5	T	5	*	36	33	31	8.1
May	0.5	T	5	1	30	31	37	8.1
June	0.6	0	5	2	25	30	43	10.4
July	0.1	0	2	1	12	25	46	8.1
Aug.	0.3	0	3	1	14	28	47	6.9
Sept.	0.4	0	3	1	19	32	42	8.1
Oct.	0.5	T	5	*	31	42	36	8.1
Nov.	1.0	2	8	0	53	62	30	6.9
Dec.	1.3	8	10	0	61	75	24	5.8

T - Trace of rain or snow   * - Less than 1   NA - Not Available

Annual averages

Precipitation (in inches)	8.2
Snow (in inches)	24
Heating degree days	5,976
Cooling degree days	479
Days with thunderstorms	6
Days with fog	56
Days above 90°	33
Days below 32°	149
Wet days	70
Days with snow	35
Days with 1.5 inches or more snow	12

Percent time sky is clear

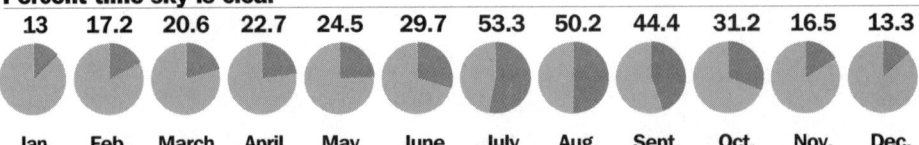

13	17.2	20.6	22.7	24.5	29.7	53.3	50.2	44.4	31.2	16.5	13.3
Jan.	Feb.	March	April	May	June	July	Aug.	Sept.	Oct.	Nov.	Dec.

Youngstown, Ohio

Lat. 41° 15' N **Lon.** 80° 40' W **Elev.** 1,178 ft.

Youngstown is marked by numerous natural and man-made lakes. But the most important weathermaker is Lake Erie to the north. This industrial area experiences frequent outbreaks of cold Canadian air masses, often modified by passing over Lake Erie. The elevation is about 200 feet higher than most other communities in the Mahoning and Shenango river valleys. The lake effect produces widespread cloudiness in cool months — winter is persistently cloudy with intermittent snow flurries. Several storms per year also produce four to 10 inches of snow. The daily winter temperature range is small. Although temperatures are seldom extreme — particularly in summer — there is high relative humidity.

Temperatures

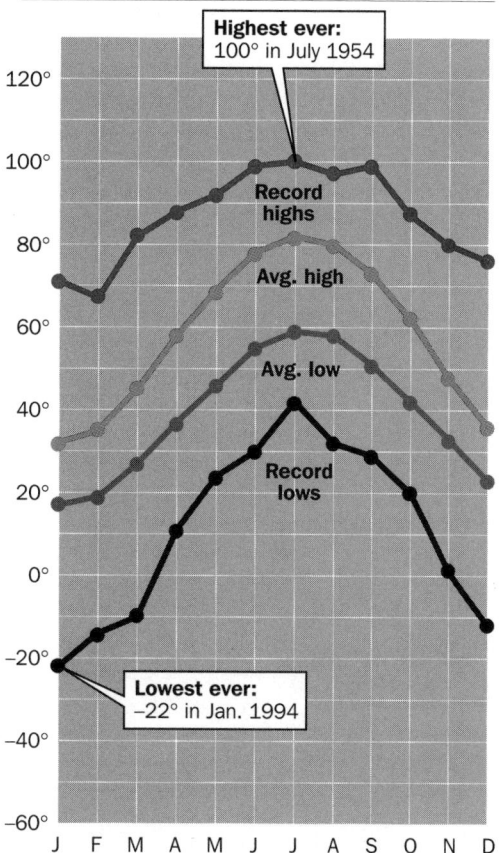

Highest ever: 100° in July 1954

Record highs

Avg. high

Avg. low

Record lows

Lowest ever: −22° in Jan. 1994

Weather extremes

Most rain in 24 hours:	4.31 in. Oct. 15, 1954
Most rain in a month:	10.66 in. June 1986
Most snow in 24 hours:	20.7 in. Jan. 24 – 25, 1950
Most snow in a month:	36 in. January 1978

Monthly averages

Month	Avg. precip. (in.)	Avg. snow (in.)	Wet days	Thunder-storm days	Pct. sky is cloudy	% p.m. relative humidity	Dew point	Wind speed (mph)
Jan.	2.6	13	17	*	67	70	18	13.8
Feb.	2.3	11	14	*	62	66	19	13.8
March	3.2	11	15	2	58	61	26	12.7
April	3.4	3	14	3	50	54	35	12.7
May	3.5	T	13	4	42	53	46	11.5
June	3.9	0	12	7	33	55	56	9.2
July	4.1	0	10	7	28	54	60	9.2
Aug.	3.3	0	10	5	31	56	59	8.1
Sept.	3.3	T	10	3	34	57	53	9.2
Oct.	2.6	1	11	1	42	57	42	10.4
Nov.	3.1	6	15	1	62	66	32	12.7
Dec.	2.8	13	17	*	70	72	23	13.8

T - Trace of rain or snow   * - Less than 1   NA - Not Available

Annual averages

Precipitation (in inches)	38.1
Snow (in inches)	57
Heating degree days	6,460
Cooling degree days	582
Days with thunderstorms	33
Days with fog	177
Days above 90°	7
Days below 32°	134
Wet days	158
Days with snow	106
Days with 1.5 inches or more snow	23

Percent time sky is clear

11.1	13.7	16.2	19.3	21	21.1	23.8	23.7	25.8	25.7	13.2	10.4

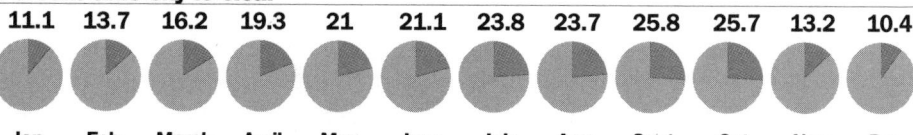

| Jan. | Feb. | March | April | May | June | July | Aug. | Sept. | Oct. | Nov. | Dec. |

Yuma, Arizona

Lat. 32° 39' N **Lon.** 114° 36' W **Elev.** 194 ft.

This desert city records the highest percentage of sunshine of any city in the U.S. Even winter has mostly clear skies and abundant sunshine. In December and January, Yuma averages more than eight hours of sunshine a day. Summers in the lower Colorado River Valley are long and hot, with afternoon temperatures averaging at least 100°F from June 4 to September 24, and 105°F from June 22 to August 26. From mid-July to mid-September, moisture-laden air from the Gulf of California frequently invades the area and the relative humidity is higher than otherwise might be expected in a desert. But precipitation remains sparse — under 3 inches annually is normal. Snow is very rare, but measurable amounts have been recorded.

Temperatures

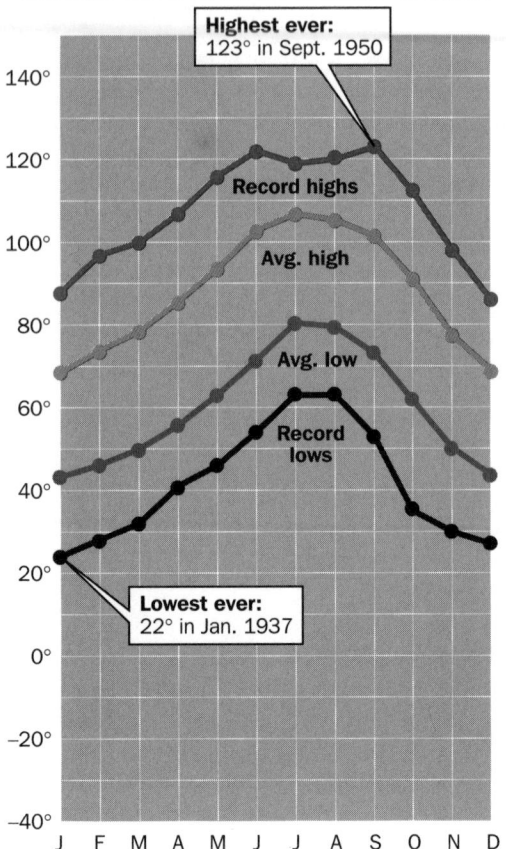

Highest ever: 123° in Sept. 1950

Record highs

Avg. high

Avg. low

Record lows

Lowest ever: 22° in Jan. 1937

Weather extremes

Most rain in 24 hours:	4.01 in. August 1909	
Most rain in a month:	6.25 in. August 1909	
Most snow in 24 hours:	2 in. (est.) December 1932	
Most snow in a month:	2 in. (est.) December 1932	

Monthly averages

Month	Avg. precip. (in.)	Avg. snow (in.)	Wet days	Thunder-storm days	Pct. sky is cloudy	% p.m. relative humidity	Dew point	Wind speed (mph)
Jan.	0.4	0	3	*	28	40	NA	7.3
Feb.	0.3	0	2	*	23	35	NA	7.4
March	0.2	0	2	*	21	30	NA	7.9
April	0.1	0	1	*	12	25	NA	8.3
May	T	0	*	*	7	23	NA	8.3
June	T	0	*	*	3	22	NA	8.5
July	0.2	0	1	2	11	32	NA	9.5
Aug.	0.4	0	2	2	10	35	NA	8.9
Sept.	0.3	0	1	1	6	35	NA	7.3
Oct.	0.3	0	1	1	9	32	NA	6.6
Nov.	0.2	0	1	*	17	34	NA	6.9
Dec.	0.3	T	3	*	25	41	NA	7.2

T - Trace of rain or snow   * - Less than 1   NA - Not Available

Annual averages

Precipitation (in inches)	2.7
Snow (in inches)	T
Heating degree days	983
Cooling degree days	4,244
Days with thunderstorms	7
Days with fog	2
Days above 90°	175
Days below 32°	2
Wet days	17
Days with snow	NA
Days with 1.5 inches or more snow	0

Percent time sky is clear

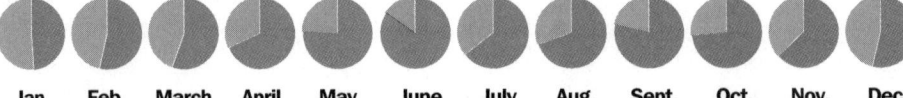

49.0	53.5	55.5	68.7	75.8	84.7	64.8	69.7	78.7	73.5	63.3	53.9
Jan.	Feb.	March	April	May	June	July	Aug.	Sept.	Oct.	Nov.	Dec.

Acalpulco, Mexico

Lat. 16° 45' N **Lon.** 99° 45' W **Elev.** 16 ft.

Annual averages

Precipitation	55.1 in.
Days with thunderstorms	33
Days with snow	0
Days with fog	5
Days above 95°	2
Days below 65°	2

Monthly averages

Month	Avg. precip. (inches)	Wet days	Snow days	Thunder-storm days	Pct. sky is cloudy	Pct. P.M. rel. hum.
Jan.	0.3	1	0	*	5	63
Feb.	T	1	0	*	5	63
March	0.0	*	0	*	3	63
April	T	*	0	*	5	66
May	1.4	3	0	2	15	66
June	12.8	11	0	5	29	67
July	9.1	13	0	7	37	66
Aug.	9.3	13	0	7	35	67
Sept.	13.9	14	0	6	36	69
Oct.	6.7	7	0	4	17	66
Nov.	1.2	2	0	1	8	65
Dec.	0.4	1	0	1	7	65

T – Trace of rain or snow   * – Less than 1   NA – Not Available

Temperatures

Accra, Ghana

Lat. 05° 36' N **Lon.** 000° 10' W **Elev.** 226 ft.

Annual averages

Precipitation	28.5 in.
Days with thunderstorms	45
Days with snow	0
Days with fog	47
Days above 95°	3
Days below 65°	0

Monthly averages

Month	Avg. precip. (inches)	Wet days	Snow days	Thunder-storm days	Pct. sky is cloudy	Pct. P.M. rel. hum.
Jan.	0.6	*	0	1	2	61
Feb.	1.3	1	0	2	4	63
March	2.2	2	0	5	9	65
April	3.2	2	0	5	10	65
May	5.6	4	0	8	10	69
June	7.0	6	0	6	12	74
July	1.8	4	0	1	10	75
Aug.	0.6	5	0	1	12	73
Sept.	1.4	6	0	2	7	73
Oct.	2.5	3	0	5	5	72
Nov.	1.4	1	0	6	3	69
Dec.	0.9	1	0	3	2	62

T – Trace of rain or snow   * – Less than 1   NA – Not Available

Temperatures

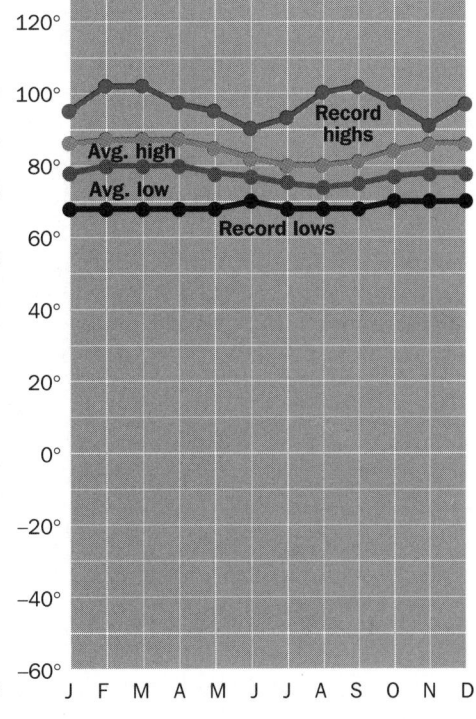

Amsterdam, Netherlands

Lat. 52° 18' N **Lon.** 004° 46' E **Elev.** 7 ft.

Annual averages

Precipitation	25.6 in.
Days with thunderstorms	25
Days with snow	26
Days with fog	199
Days above 70°	46
Days below 32°	52

Monthly averages

Month	Avg. precip. (inches)	Wet days	Snow days	Thunder-storm days	Pct. sky is cloudy	Pct. P.M. rel. hum.
Jan.	2.0	24	7	1	59	86
Feb.	1.4	16	6	1	53	78
March	1.3	22	4	1	52	75
April	1.6	18	2	1	42	66
May	1.8	19	*	3	39	63
June	1.8	18	0	3	38	66
July	2.6	18	0	3	32	68
Aug.	2.7	18	0	3	26	65
Sept.	2.8	19	0	3	34	71
Oct.	2.8	21	*	2	44	78
Nov.	2.6	22	2	2	51	84
Dec.	2.2	25	5	2	57	88

T – Trace of rain or snow   * – Less than 1   NA – Not Available

Temperatures

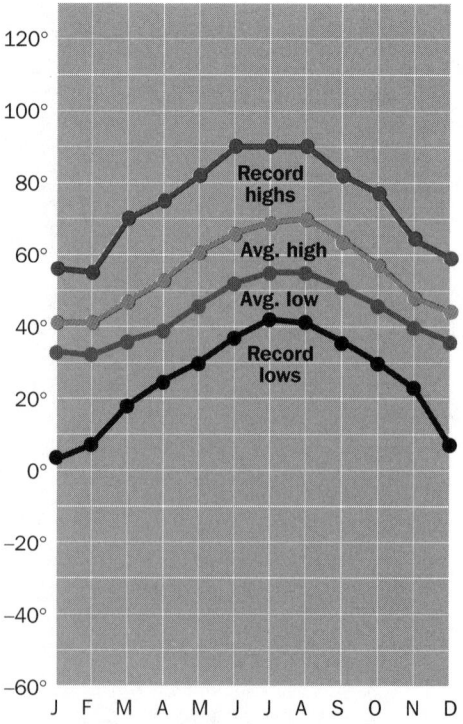

Athens, Greece

Lat. 37° 54' N **Lon.** 023° 44' E **Elev.** 69 ft.

Annual averages

Precipitation	15.8 in.
Days with thunderstorms	19
Days with snow	2
Days with fog	42
Days above 90°	32
Days below 32°	3

Monthly averages

Month	Avg. precip. (inches)	Wet days	Snow days	Thunder-storm days	Pct. sky is cloudy	Pct. P.M. rel. hum.
Jan.	2.2	11	1	1	23	63
Feb.	1.6	11	1	2	27	63
March	1.4	10	*	2	24	61
April	0.8	8	0	1	20	58
May	0.8	5	0	2	9	54
June	0.6	2	0	1	2	49
July	0.2	1	0	1	1	42
Aug.	0.4	1	0	1	1	42
Sept.	0.6	2	0	1	1	47
Oct.	1.7	7	0	3	13	56
Nov.	2.8	9	*	2	21	64
Dec.	2.8	10	*	2	22	66

T – Trace of rain or snow   * – Less than 1   NA – Not Available

Temperatures

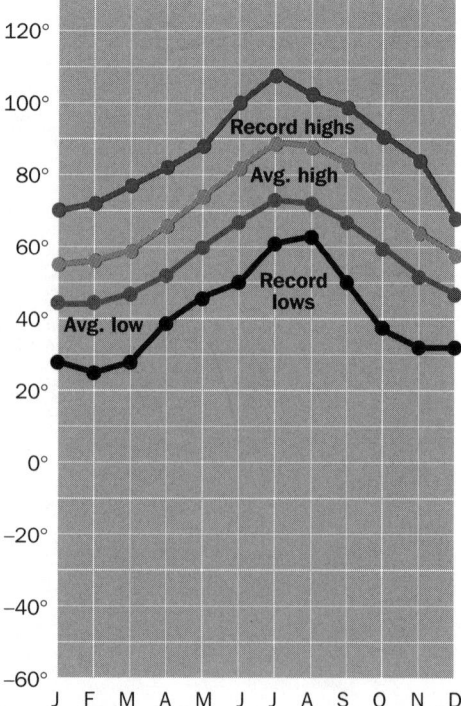

Auckland, New Zealand

Lat. 37° 01' S **Lon.** 174° 48' E **Elev.** 20 ft.

Annual averages

Precipitation	49.1 in.
Days with thunderstorms	2
Days with snow	*
Days with fog	46
Days above 90°	0
Days below 32°	*

Monthly averages

Month	Avg. precip. (inches)	Wet days	Snow days	Thunder-storm days	Pct. sky is cloudy	Pct. P.M. rel. hum.
Jan.	3.1	13	0	1	NA	NA
Feb.	3.7	12	0	*	NA	68
March	3.2	14	0	*	NA	68
April	3.8	15	0	*	NA	71
May	5.0	18	0	*	NA	74
June	5.4	19	0	*	NA	77
July	5.7	19	*	*	NA	76
Aug.	4.6	20	*	*	NA	74
Sept.	4.0	21	0	*	NA	74
Oct.	4.0	18	0	*	NA	73
Nov.	3.5	18	0	*	NA	NA
Dec.	3.1	16	0	1	NA	NA

T – Trace of rain or snow   * – Less than 1   NA – Not Available

Temperatures

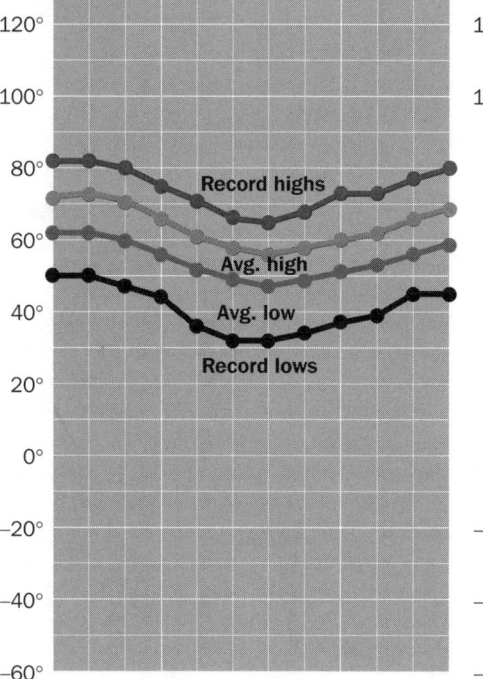

Bangkok, Thailand

Lat. 13° 44' N **Lon.** 100° 30' E **Elev.** 53 ft.

Annual averages

Precipitation	57.8 in.
Days with thunderstorms	76
Days with snow	0
Days with fog	269
Days above 95°	34
Days below 65°	12

Monthly averages

Month	Avg. precip. (inches)	Wet days	Snow days	Thunder-storm days	Pct. sky is cloudy	Pct. P.M. rel. hum.
Jan.	0.2	2	0	*	12	48
Feb.	1.1	2	0	1	11	54
March	1.1	3	0	2	10	55
April	2.3	5	0	6	14	57
May	5.2	15	0	12	25	63
June	6.0	17	0	7	29	66
July	6.9	19	0	9	33	65
Aug.	9.2	21	0	9	36	66
Sept.	14.0	21	0	15	35	68
Oct.	9.9	15	0	12	25	67
Nov.	1.8	7	0	3	14	59
Dec.	0.1	2	0	*	7	50

T – Trace of rain or snow   * – Less than 1   NA – Not Available

Temperatures

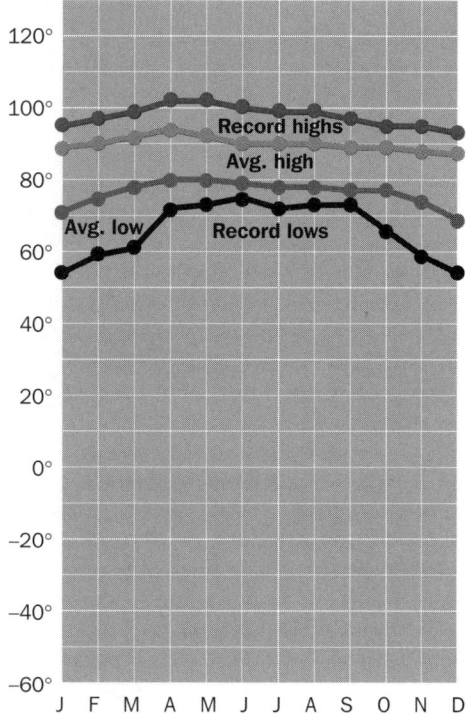

Berlin, Germany

Lat. 52° 27' N **Lon.** 13° 18' E **Elev.** 187 ft.

Annual averages

Precipitation	23.1 in.
Days with thunderstorms	25
Days with snow	55
Days with fog	98
Days above 70°	76
Days below 32°	104

Monthly averages

Month	Avg. precip. (inches)	Wet days	Snow days	Thunder-storm days	Pct. sky is cloudy	Pct. P.M. rel. hum.
Jan.	1.9	23	17	*	66	83
Feb.	1.3	16	11	*	55	76
March	1.5	19	7	1	54	64
April	1.7	15	4	1	46	56
May	1.9	15	1	5	38	53
June	2.3	16	*	6	39	55
July	3.1	17	0	5	34	53
Aug.	2.2	14	0	5	32	54
Sept.	1.9	17	0	2	40	60
Oct.	1.7	17	*	*	50	71
Nov.	1.7	20	5	*	59	79
Dec.	1.9	22	10	0	66	85

T – Trace of rain or snow   * – Less than 1   NA – Not Available

Temperatures

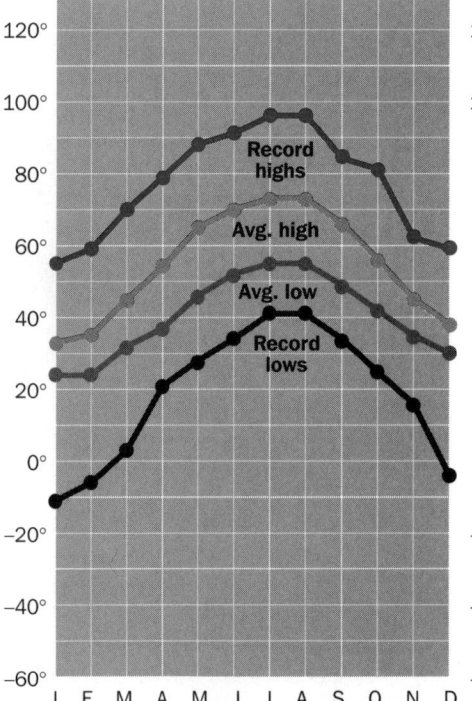

Budapest, Hungary

Lat. 47° 26' N **Lon.** 19° 14' E **Elev.** 607 ft.

Annual averages

Precipitation	24.2 in.
Days with thunderstorms	24
Days with snow	41
Days with fog	187
Days above 90°	6
Days below 32°	99

Monthly averages

Month	Avg. precip. (inches)	Wet days	Snow days	Thunder-storm days	Pct. sky is cloudy	Pct. P.M. rel. hum.
Jan.	1.5	18	13	0	NA	80
Feb.	1.5	14	9	*	NA	74
March	1.7	15	5	*	NA	61
April	2.0	15	1	1	NA	53
May	2.7	17	*	5	NA	54
June	2.6	14	0	6	NA	54
July	2.0	12	0	5	NA	51
Aug.	1.9	12	0	5	NA	52
Sept.	1.8	10	0	1	NA	56
Oct.	2.1	12	0	1	NA	66
Nov.	2.4	16	4	*	NA	78
Dec.	2.0	19	9	0	NA	82

T – Trace of rain or snow   * – Less than 1   NA – Not Available

Temperatures

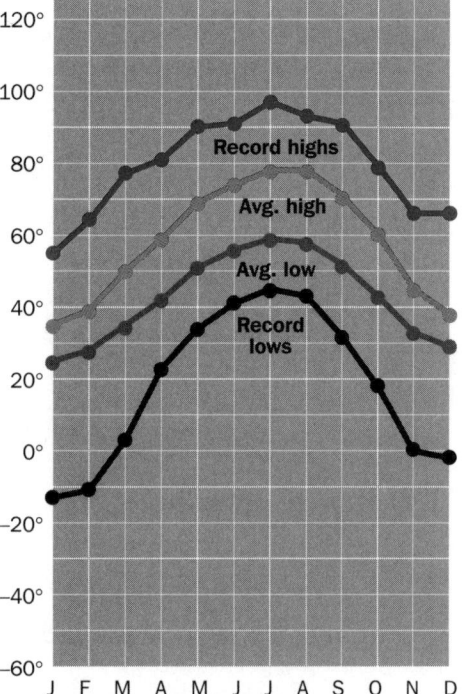

Buenos Aires, Argentina

Lat. 34° 49' S **Lon.** 58° 32' W **Elev.** 66 ft.

Annual averages

Precipitation	37.4 in.
Days with thunderstorms	46
Days with snow	3
Days with fog	235
Days above 90°	22
Days below 32°	14

Monthly averages

Month	Avg. precip. (inches)	Wet days	Snow days	Thunder-storm days	Pct. sky is cloudy	Pct. P.M. rel. hum.
Jan.	3.1	10	0	6	27	46
Feb.	2.8	9	0	5	28	50
March	4.3	9	0	4	29	54
April	3.5	10	*	3	30	57
May	3.0	10	*	3	38	59
June	2.4	10	*	2	41	61
July	2.2	10	*	2	45	62
Aug.	2.4	10	*	3	39	57
Sept.	3.1	9	*	2	34	52
Oct.	3.4	13	*	5	37	55
Nov.	3.3	11	*	5	34	52
Dec.	3.9	10	0	6	27	46

T – Trace of rain or snow   * – Less than 1   NA – Not Available

Temperatures

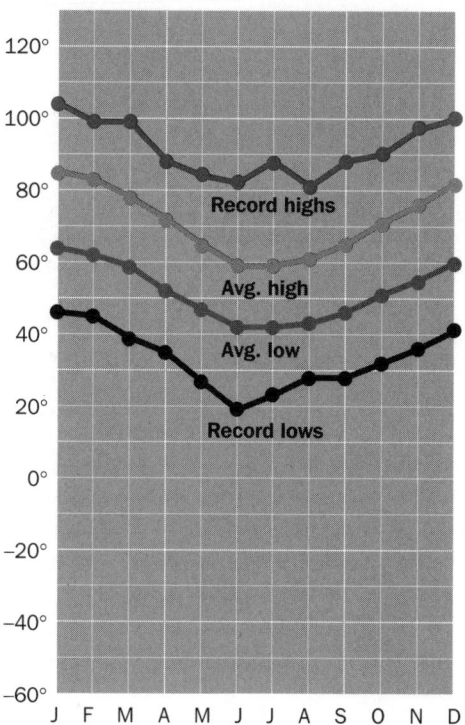

Cairo, Egypt

Lat. 30° 08' N **Lon.** 031° 24' E **Elev.** 243 ft.

Annual averages

Precipitation	1.1 in.
Days with thunderstorms	3
Days with snow	0
Days with fog	132
Days above 90°	125
Days below 32°	*

Monthly averages

Month	Avg. precip. (inches)	Wet days	Snow days	Thunder-storm days	Pct. sky is cloudy	Pct. P.M. rel. hum.
Jan.	0.2	5	0	*	5	49
Feb.	0.2	4	0	*	4	40
March	0.2	4	0	*	6	35
April	0.1	2	0	*	4	30
May	0.1	*	0	*	2	27
June	T	*	0	0	1	29
July	0.0	*	0	*	1	36
Aug.	0.0	*	0	0	1	39
Sept.	T	*	0	0	1	38
Oct.	T	1	0	*	1	40
Nov.	0.1	2	0	*	1	47
Dec.	0.2	4	0	*	6	52

T – Trace of rain or snow   * – Less than 1   NA – Not Available

Temperatures

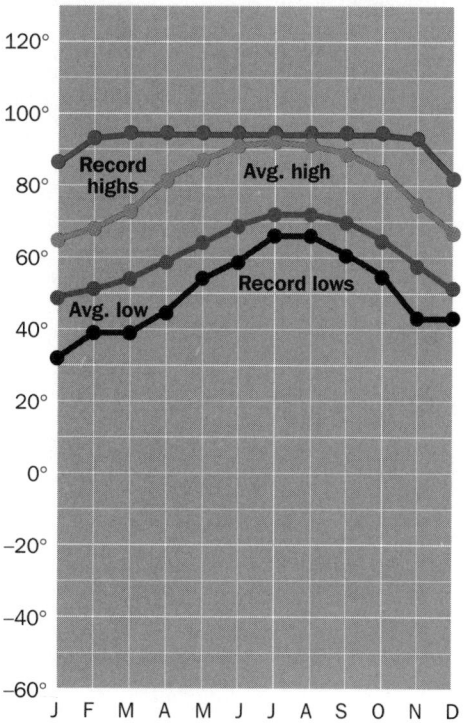

Delhi, India

Lat. 28° 35' N **Lon.** 077° 12' E **Elev.** 708 ft.

Annual averages

Precipitation	25.2 in.
Days with thunderstorms	34
Days with snow	*
Days with fog	76
Days above 90°	176
Days below 32°	*

Monthly averages

Month	Avg. precip. (inches)	Wet days	Snow days	Thunder-storm days	Pct. sky is cloudy	Pct. P.M. rel. hum.
Jan.	0.9	3	0	1	9	47
Feb.	0.7	4	0	2	6	38
March	0.5	4	0	3	6	32
April	0.3	3	0	2	5	22
May	0.5	4	0	4	9	23
June	2.9	7	0	5	18	37
July	7.1	15	0	7	36	63
Aug.	6.8	12	0	6	29	66
Sept.	4.6	6	0	2	9	53
Oct.	0.4	2	0	1	2	39
Nov.	0.1	1	0	*	2	42
Dec.	0.4	3	*	1	7	48

T – Trace of rain or snow   * – Less than 1   NA – Not Available

Temperatures

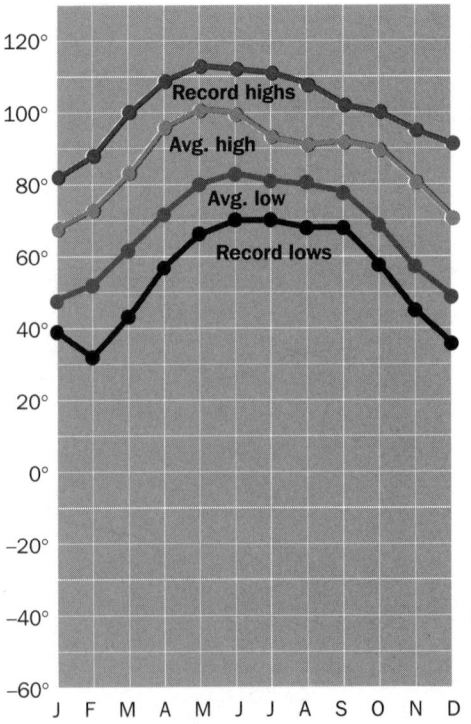

Dublin, Ireland

Lat. 53° 26' N **Lon.** 006° 15' W **Elev.** 279 ft.

Annual averages

Precipitation	29.7 in.
Days with thunderstorms	4
Days with snow	19
Days with fog	151
Days above 70°	18
Days below 32°	27

Monthly averages

Month	Avg. precip. (inches)	Wet days	Snow days	Thunder-storm days	Pct. sky is cloudy	Pct. P.M. rel. hum.
Jan.	2.7	24	6	*	55	78
Feb.	2.2	19	4	*	54	76
March	2.0	22	4	*	47	69
April	1.9	18	2	*	40	67
May	2.3	18	*	1	38	67
June	2.0	19	0	1	36	68
July	2.8	20	0	1	36	68
Aug.	3.0	22	0	1	38	69
Sept.	2.8	21	0	*	37	70
Oct.	2.7	23	0	*	48	74
Nov.	2.7	21	1	*	46	77
Dec.	2.6	25	2	*	53	82

T – Trace of rain or snow   * – Less than 1   NA – Not Available

Temperatures

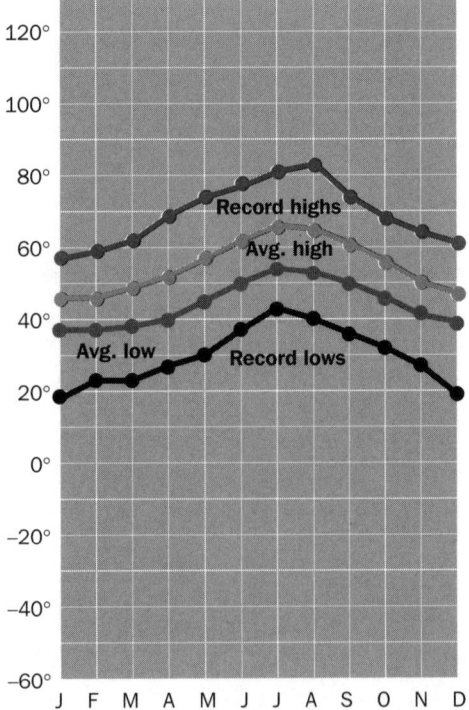

Hamilton, Bermuda

Lat. 32° 22' N **Lon.** 64° 40' W **Elev.** 10 ft.

Annual averages

Precipitation	57.6 in.
Days with thunderstorms	54
Days with snow	0
Days with fog	8
Days above 90°	3
Days below 45°	*

Monthly averages

Month	Avg. precip. (inches)	Wet days	Snow days	Thunder- storm days	Pct. sky is cloudy	Pct. P.M. rel. hum.
Jan.	4.4	17	0	3	30	69
Feb.	4.7	15	0	3	33	69
March	4.8	15	0	4	30	69
April	4.1	12	0	3	26	68
May	4.6	10	0	3	26	73
June	4.4	12	0	4	24	75
July	4.5	13	0	8	13	72
Aug.	5.4	14	0	9	10	71
Sept.	5.2	15	0	7	15	71
Oct.	5.8	16	0	5	25	72
Nov.	5.0	13	0	3	23	69
Dec.	4.7	16	0	2	26	69

T – Trace of rain or snow   * – Less than 1   NA – Not Available

Temperatures

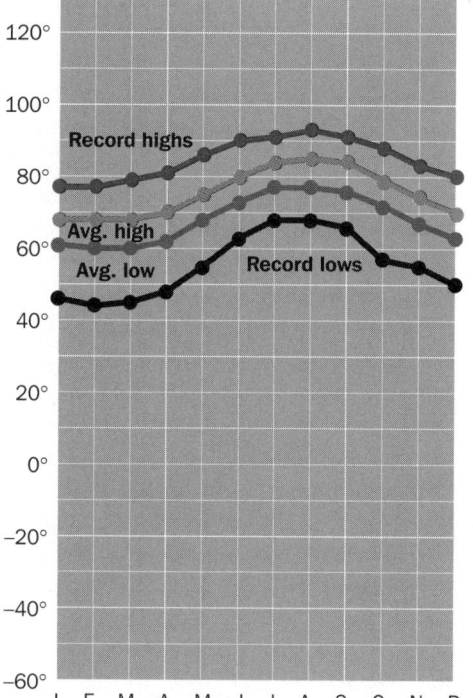

Ho Chi Minh City, Vietnam

Lat. 10° 49' N **Lon.** 106° 40' E **Elev.** 62 ft.

Annual averages

Precipitation	78.1 in.
Days with thunderstorms	79
Days with snow	0
Days with fog	222
Days above 95°	23
Days below 65°	3

Monthly averages

Month	Avg. precip. (inches)	Wet days	Snow days	Thunder- storm days	Pct. sky is cloudy	Pct. P.M. rel. hum.
Jan.	0.6	2	0	*	3	51
Feb.	0.1	1	0	*	2	51
March	0.5	2	0	1	2	53
April	1.7	4	0	5	5	57
May	8.7	13	0	12	14	66
June	13.0	18	0	11	21	71
July	12.4	18	0	12	21	70
Aug.	10.6	19	0	8	21	71
Sept.	13.2	19	0	12	21	72
Oct.	10.6	16	0	10	18	73
Nov.	4.5	11	0	7	11	67
Dec.	2.2	5	0	1	9	58

T – Trace of rain or snow   * – Less than 1   NA – Not Available

Temperatures

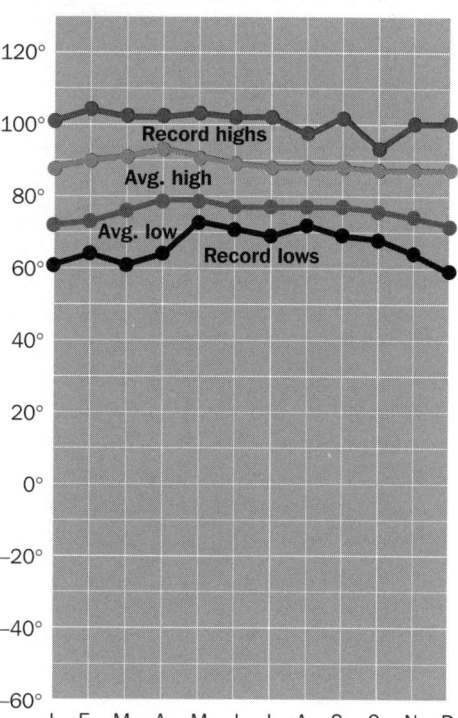

Hong Kong

Lat. 22° 20' N **Lon.** 114° 11' E **Elev.** 79 ft.

Annual averages

Precipitation	85.1 in.
Days with thunderstorms	28
Days with snow	0
Days with fog	28
Days above 90°	48
Days below 32°	0

Monthly averages

Month	Avg. precip. (inches)	Wet days	Snow days	Thunder-storm days	Pct. sky is cloudy	Pct. P.M. rel. hum.
Jan.	1.3	9	0	0	NA	60
Feb.	1.8	14	0	1	NA	67
March	2.9	20	0	2	NA	73
April	5.4	18	0	3	NA	73
May	11.5	21	0	4	NA	74
June	15.5	21	0	3	NA	72
July	15.0	18	0	5	NA	70
Aug.	14.2	21	0	6	NA	71
Sept.	10.1	19	0	4	NA	67
Oct.	4.5	13	0	*	NA	61
Nov.	1.7	10	0	*	NA	56
Dec.	1.2	6	0	0	NA	54

T – Trace of rain or snow   * – Less than 1   NA – Not Available

Temperatures

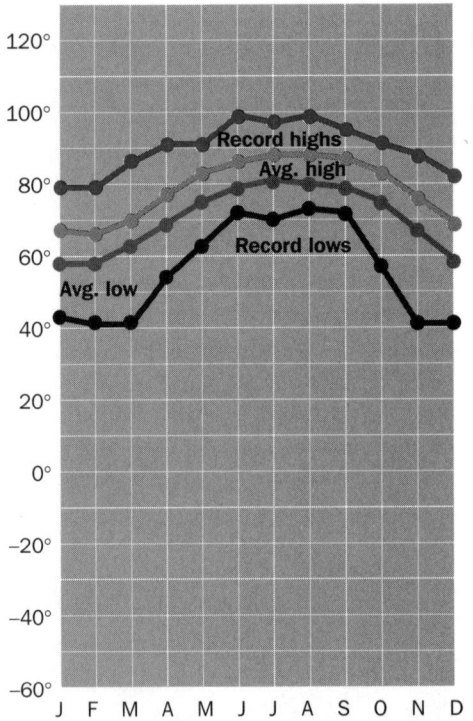

Istanbul, Turkey

Lat. 40° 58' N **Lon.** 028° 49' E **Elev.** 121 ft.

Annual averages

Precipitation	31.5 in.
Days with thunderstorms	21
Days with snow	21
Days with fog	230
Days above 90°	5
Days below 32°	21

Monthly averages

Month	Avg. precip. (inches)	Wet days	Snow days	Thunder-storm days	Pct. sky is cloudy	Pct. P.M. rel. hum.
Jan.	3.7	20	7	1	44	74
Feb.	2.3	17	6	1	45	70
March	2.6	17	4	1	39	67
April	1.9	14	*	1	25	59
May	1.4	11	0	2	11	57
June	1.3	8	0	4	3	52
July	1.7	4	0	2	1	49
Aug.	1.5	6	0	2	2	51
Sept.	2.3	7	0	2	4	54
Oct.	3.8	12	*	2	17	64
Nov.	4.1	16	1	2	29	70
Dec.	4.9	19	3	1	38	73

T – Trace of rain or snow   * – Less than 1   NA – Not Available

Temperatures

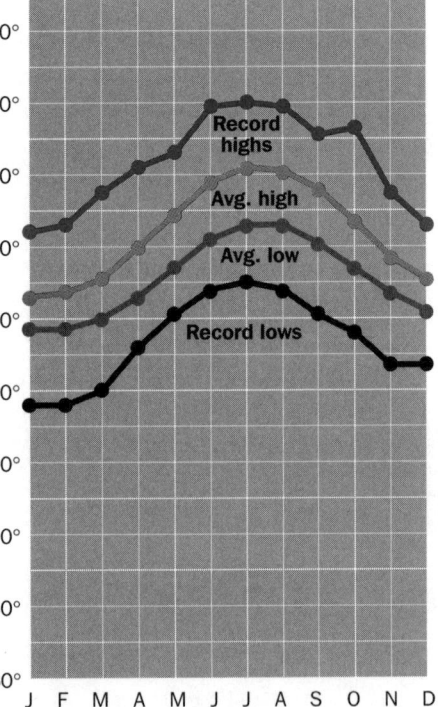

Jerusalem, Israel

Lat. 31° 52' N **Lon.** 035° 13' E **Elev.** 2,490 ft.

Annual averages

Precipitation	19.7in.
Days with thunderstorms	6
Days with snow	4
Days with fog	154
Days above 90°	6
Days below 32°	2

Monthly averages

Month	Avg. precip. (inches)	Wet days	Snow days	Thunder- storm days	Pct. sky is cloudy	Pct. P.M. rel. hum.
Jan.	5.1	12	1	1	NA	66
Feb.	4.7	12	2	1	NA	62
March	2.9	10	1	*	NA	61
April	0.9	5	0	1	NA	53
May	0.1	4	0	1	NA	51
June	T	*	0	0	NA	46
July	0.0	0	0	0	NA	48
Aug.	0.0	0	0	0	NA	57
Sept.	T	*	0	*	NA	57
Oct.	0.3	4	0	1	NA	60
Nov.	2.2	9	0	1	NA	67
Dec.	3.5	11	*	*	NA	65

T – Trace of rain or snow   * – Less than 1   NA – Not Available

Temperatures

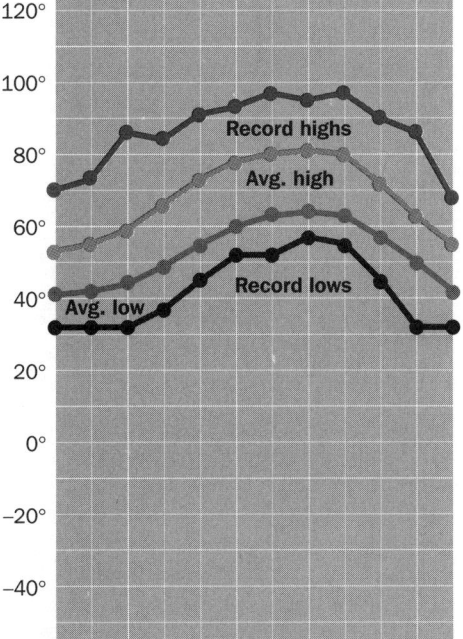

Kingston, Jamaica

Lat. 17° 56' N **Lon.** 076° 47' W **Elev.** 30 ft.

Annual averages

Precipitation	31.5in.
Days with thunderstorms	55
Days with snow	0
Days with fog	13
Days above 95°	0
Days below 65°	*

Monthly averages

Month	Avg. precip. (inches)	Wet days	Snow days	Thunder- storm days	Pct. sky is cloudy	Pct. P.M. rel. hum.
Jan.	0.9	13	0	*	4	63
Feb.	0.6	12	0	*	3	64
March	0.9	11	0	*	2	64
April	1.2	11	0	1	4	65
May	4.0	13	0	4	9	67
June	3.5	11	0	4	11	67
July	1.5	9	0	6	6	64
Aug.	3.6	13	0	11	7	68
Sept.	3.9	15	0	12	10	70
Oct.	7.1	17	0	11	8	71
Nov.	2.9	15	0	5	10	68
Dec.	1.4	13	0	1	4	64

T – Trace of rain or snow   * – Less than 1   NA – Not Available

Temperatures

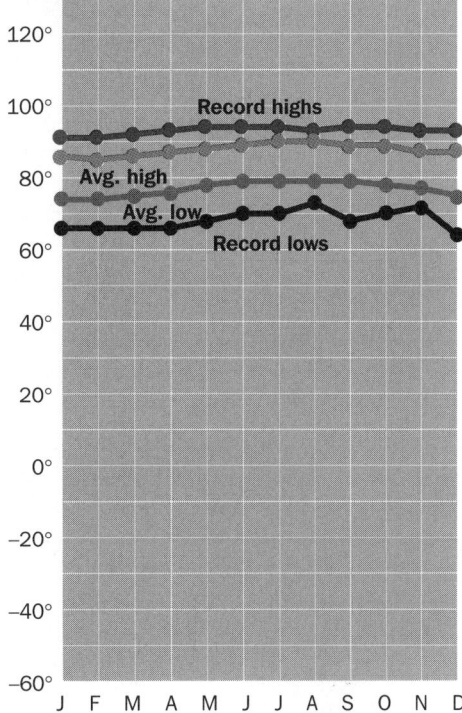

Lima, Peru

Lat. 12° 00' S **Lon.** 77° 07' W **Elev.** 43ft.

Annual averages

Precipitation	1.6 in.
Days with thunderstorms	3
Days with snow	0
Days with fog	179
Days above 95°	0
Days below 65°	243

Monthly averages

Month	Avg. precip. (inches)	Wet days	Snow days	Thunder-storm days	Pct. sky is cloudy	Pct. P.M. rel. hum.
Jan.	0.1	2	0	0	70	70
Feb.	T	3	0	*	70	70
March	T	2	0	0	66	70
April	T	2	0	*	53	73
May	0.2	7	0	*	67	76
June	0.2	12	0	*	89	77
July	0.3	13	0	*	93	76
Aug.	0.3	17	0	*	96	77
Sept.	0.3	16	0	*	95	77
Oct.	0.1	10	0	*	89	74
Nov.	0.1	5	0	*	82	72
Dec.	T	4	0	*	70	70

T – Trace of rain or snow   * – Less than 1   NA – Not Available

London, England

Lat. 51° 29' N **Lon.** 00° 27' W **Elev.** 79ft.

Annual averages

Precipitation	22.9 in.
Days with thunderstorms	13
Days with snow	20
Days with fog	101
Days above 90°	1
Days below 32°	41

Monthly averages

Month	Avg. precip. (inches)	Wet days	Snow days	Thunder-storm days	Pct. sky is cloudy	Pct. P.M. rel. hum.
Jan.	2.0	23	6	*	53	79
Feb.	1.5	18	5	*	50	73
March	1.4	22	4	1	49	67
April	1.8	18	2	1	37	58
May	1.8	20	*	2	38	59
June	1.6	17	0	3	33	57
July	2.0	17	0	2	29	56
Aug.	2.2	17	0	2	28	56
Sept.	1.8	17	0	1	32	61
Oct.	2.3	20	0	1	41	71
Nov.	2.5	20	1	*	44	77
Dec.	2.0	22	2	*	48	81

T – Trace of rain or snow   * – Less than 1   NA – Not Available

Temperatures

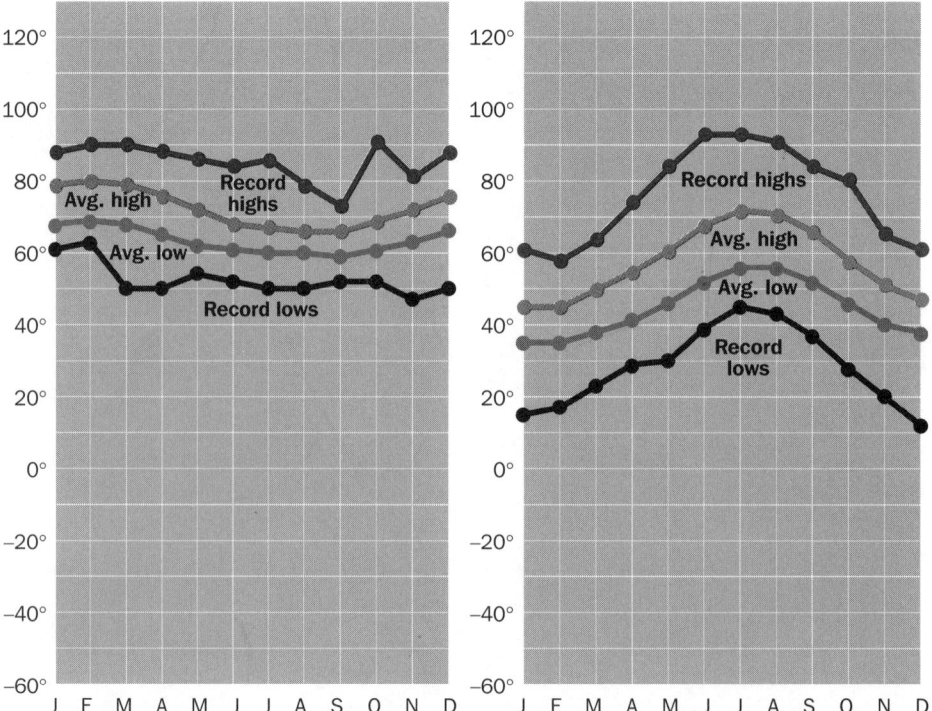

Madrid, Spain

Lat. 40° 27' N **Lon.** 003° 33' W **Elev.** 1,909 ft.

Annual averages

Precipitation	16.5 in.
Days with thunderstorms	20
Days with snow	4
Days with fog	64
Days above 90°	50
Days below 32°	60

Monthly averages

Month	Avg. precip. (inches)	Wet days	Snow days	Thunder-storm days	Pct. sky is cloudy	Pct. P.M. rel. hum.
Jan.	1.1	10	1	0	34	63
Feb.	1.7	10	1	*	33	58
March	1.7	8	1	1	21	48
April	1.7	11	*	1	29	49
May	1.5	11	*	3	20	45
June	1.2	7	0	5	12	38
July	0.4	4	0	4	4	30
Aug.	0.3	3	0	3	3	32
Sept.	1.2	4	*	2	6	38
Oct.	1.9	8	*	1	16	51
Nov.	2.2	8	*	*	26	60
Dec.	1.6	10	1	*	35	65

T – Trace of rain or snow   * – Less than 1   NA – Not Available

Temperatures

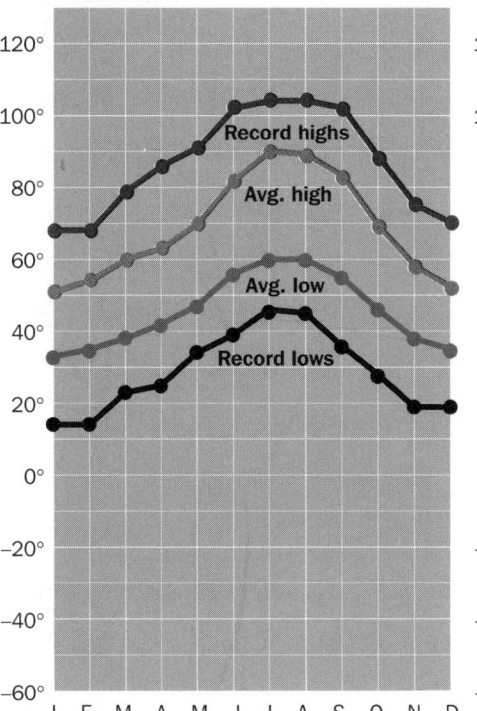

Manila, Philippines

Lat. 14° 31' N **Lon.** 121° 00' E **Elev.** 49 ft.

Annual averages

Precipitation	82.0 in.
Days with thunderstorms	49
Days with snow	0
Days with fog	12
Days above 95°	28
Days below 75°	253

Monthly averages

Month	Avg. precip. (inches)	Wet days	Snow days	Thunder-storm days	Pct. sky is cloudy	Pct. P.M. rel. hum.
Jan.	0.9	7	0	1	32	66
Feb.	0.5	4	0	*	24	62
March	0.7	4	0	1	11	59
April	1.3	3	0	1	16	59
May	5.1	10	0	6	35	64
June	10.0	17	0	8	60	72
July	17.0	20	0	9	61	75
Aug.	16.6	23	0	7	71	79
Sept.	14.0	20	0	10	63	77
Oct.	7.6	18	0	5	62	76
Nov.	5.7	13	0	1	53	72
Dec.	2.6	9	0	*	45	70

T – Trace of rain or snow   * – Less than 1   NA – Not Available

Temperatures

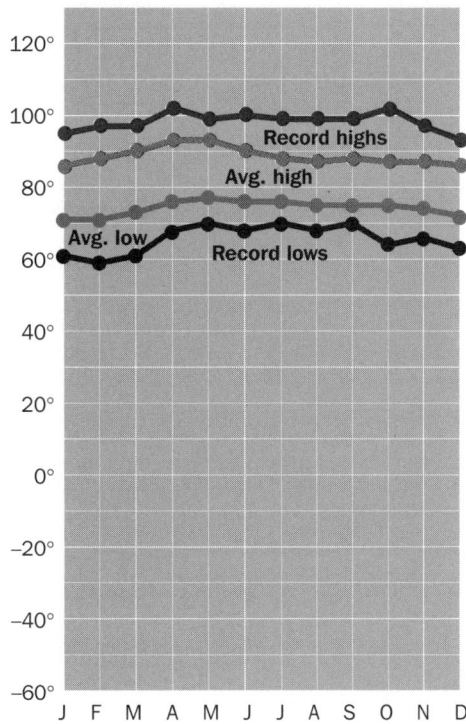

Marseille, France

Lat. 43° 27' N **Lon.** 05° 14' E **Elev.** 118 ft.

Annual averages

Precipitation	23.2 in.
Days with thunderstorms	19
Days with snow	2
Days with fog	37
Days above 90°	10
Days below 32°	26

Monthly averages

Month	Avg. precip. (inches)	Wet days	Snow days	Thunder-storm days	Pct. sky is cloudy	Pct. P.M. rel. hum.
Jan.	1.9	9	1	1	20	64
Feb.	1.5	10	1	1	24	60
March	1.8	9	*	1	20	55
April	2.0	9	0	1	20	53
May	1.9	8	0	2	17	52
June	1.0	6	0	3	9	50
July	0.6	3	0	1	4	46
Aug.	0.9	4	0	2	5	47
Sept.	2.6	5	0	2	7	53
Oct.	3.7	9	0	3	15	60
Nov.	3.1	8	*	1	16	64
Dec.	2.2	10	*	1	19	67

T – Trace of rain or snow   * – Less than 1   NA – Not Available

Temperatures

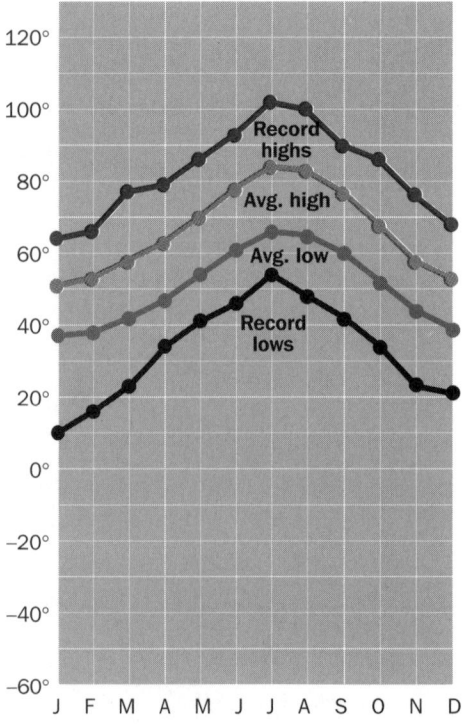

Mexico City, Mexico

Lat. 19° 26' N **Lon.** 99° 05' W **Elev.** 7,328 ft.

Annual averages

Precipitation	23.0 in.
Days with thunderstorms	65
Days with snow	0
Days with fog	76
Days above 95°	0
Days below 65°	358

Monthly averages

Month	Avg. precip. (inches)	Wet days	Snow days	Thunder-storm days	Pct. sky is cloudy	Pct. P.M. rel. hum.
Jan.	0.2	3	0	1	12	33
Feb.	0.3	3	0	1	12	31
March	0.5	4	0	2	12	28
April	0.7	9	0	5	19	28
May	1.9	14	0	10	27	30
June	4.1	17	0	10	42	42
July	4.5	21	0	13	43	44
Aug.	4.3	18	0	11	41	43
Sept.	4.1	14	0	6	44	45
Oct.	1.6	7	0	4	30	38
Nov.	0.5	3	0	1	16	34
Dec.	0.3	2	0	1	15	34

T – Trace of rain or snow   * – Less than 1   NA – Not Available

Temperatures

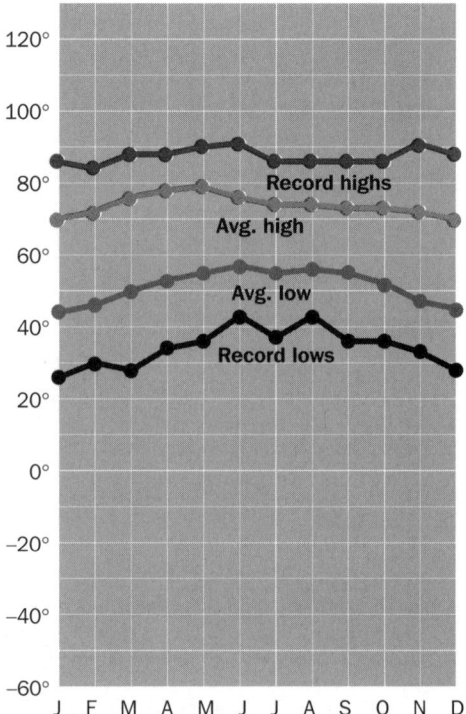

Montreal, Canada

Lat. 45° 28' N **Lon.** 73° 45' W **Elev.** 118 ft.

Annual averages

Precipitation	40.8 in.
Days with thunderstorms	24
Days with snow	96
Days with fog	124
Days above 90°	3
Days below 32°	152

Monthly averages

Month	Avg. precip. (inches)	Wet days	Snow days	Thunder-storm days	Pct. sky is cloudy	Pct. P.M. rel. hum.
Jan.	3.8	24	22	*	53	69
Feb.	3.0	20	18	*	50	65
March	3.5	19	13	*	48	61
April	2.6	17	7	1	47	55
May	3.1	17	*	2	42	53
June	3.4	17	0	5	33	57
July	3.7	15	0	7	28	56
Aug.	3.5	16	0	6	32	59
Sept.	3.7	15	*	2	39	63
Oct.	3.4	17	2	1	43	64
Nov.	3.5	21	12	*	57	71
Dec.	3.6	25	22	*	58	72

T – Trace of rain or snow   * – Less than 1   NA – Not Available

Temperatures

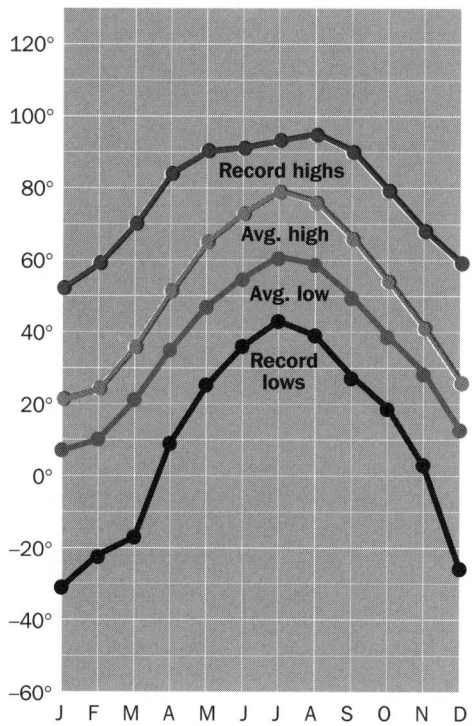

Moscow, Russia

Lat. 55° 58' N **Lon.** 37° 25' E **Elev.** 623 ft.

Annual averages

Precipitation	24.8 in.
Days with thunderstorms	28
Days with snow	118
Days with fog	209
Days above 70°	65
Days below 32°	176

Monthly averages

Month	Avg. precip. (inches)	Wet days	Snow days	Thunder-storm days	Pct. sky is cloudy	Pct. P.M. rel. hum.
Jan.	1.5	25	24	*	NA	81
Feb.	1.4	19	19	*	NA	75
March	1.1	17	15	*	NA	67
April	1.9	17	8	1	NA	57
May	2.2	16	1	5	NA	51
June	2.9	17	*	7	NA	57
July	3.0	18	0	8	NA	60
Aug.	2.9	17	0	5	NA	62
Sept.	1.9	17	1	1	NA	66
Oct.	2.7	19	7	*	NA	73
Nov.	1.7	23	18	*	NA	83
Dec.	1.6	27	25	1	NA	84

T – Trace of rain or snow   * – Less than 1   NA – Not Available

Temperatures

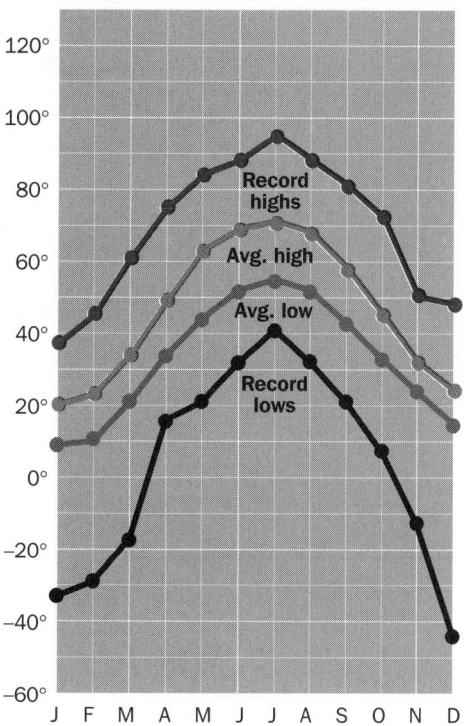

Munich, Germany

Lat. 48° 08' N **Lon.** 11° 42' E **Elev.** 1,735 ft.

Annual averages

Precipitation	34.1 in.
Days with thunderstorms	38
Days with snow	75
Days with fog	197
Days above 90°	1
Days below 32°	123

Monthly averages

Month	Avg. precip. (inches)	Wet days	Snow days	Thunder-storm days	Pct. sky is cloudy	Pct. P.M. rel. hum.
Jan.	1.7	23	16	1	55	81
Feb.	1.4	19	13	*	50	74
March	1.9	22	12	1	45	61
April	2.7	23	9	2	44	57
May	3.7	24	1	7	36	56
June	4.6	24	0	7	38	58
July	4.7	24	0	9	31	55
Aug.	4.2	21	0	8	29	56
Sept.	3.2	18	0	3	33	61
Oct.	2.2	18	1	*	47	71
Nov.	1.9	20	9	*	53	79
Dec.	1.9	23	14	*	54	81

T – Trace of rain or snow * – Less than 1 NA – Not Available

Nairobi, Kenya

Lat. 01° 19' S **Lon.** 36° 55' E **Elev.** 5,327 ft.

Annual averages

Precipitation	37.7 in.
Days with thunderstorms	22
Days with snow	0
Days with fog	34
Days above 95°	*
Days below 65°	355

Monthly averages

Month	Avg. precip. (inches)	Wet days	Snow days	Thunder-storm days	Pct. sky is cloudy	Pct. P.M. rel. hum.
Jan.	1.5	5	0	1	9	46
Feb.	2.5	4	0	2	9	39
March	4.9	7	0	2	10	42
April	8.3	13	0	5	19	61
May	6.2	10	0	3	17	66
June	1.8	6	0	1	21	61
July	0.6	5	0	1	25	56
Aug.	0.9	5	0	1	24	52
Sept.	1.2	5	0	1	17	46
Oct.	2.1	7	0	1	13	47
Nov.	4.3	13	0	3	20	59
Dec.	3.4	8	0	1	15	58

T – Trace of rain or snow * – Less than 1 NA – Not Available

Temperatures

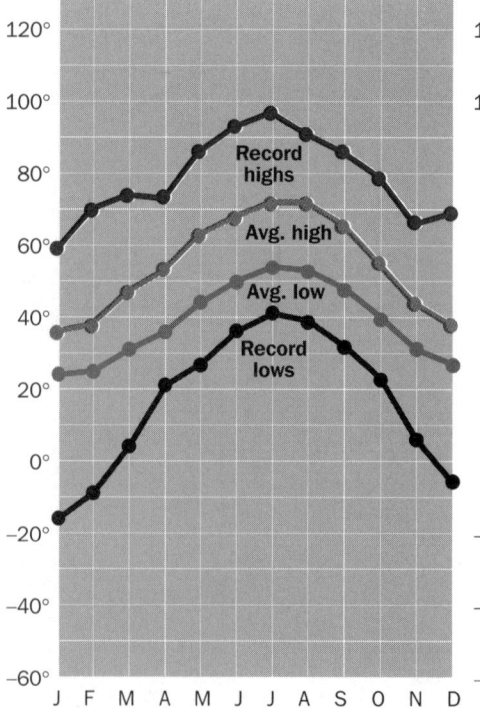

Temperatures

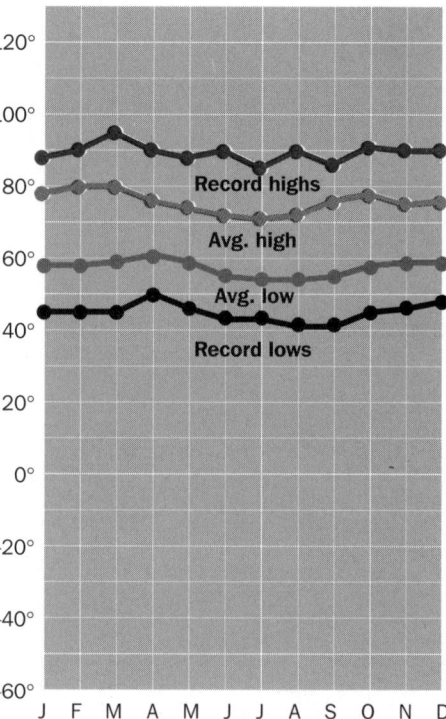

Nassau, Bahamas

Lat. 25° 03' N **Lon.** 77° 28' W **Elev.** 23 ft.

Annual averages

Precipitation	46.4 in.
Days with thunderstorms	73
Days with snow	0
Days with fog	43
Days above 90°	58
Days below 32°	0

Monthly averages

Month	Avg. precip. (inches)	Wet days	Snow days	Thunder-storm days	Pct. sky is cloudy	Pct. P.M. rel. hum.
Jan.	1.4	17	0	1	16	67
Feb.	1.5	15	0	1	18	65
March	1.4	15	0	2	13	64
April	2.5	14	0	3	12	62
May	4.6	19	0	6	20	67
June	6.4	22	0	11	22	70
July	5.8	24	0	15	13	68
Aug.	5.3	26	0	16	15	70
Sept	6.9	25	0	11	16	72
Oct.	6.5	24	0	5	18	72
Nov.	2.8	18	0	1	12	70
Dec.	1.3	18	0	1	13	68

T – Trace of rain or snow   * – Less than 1   NA – Not Available

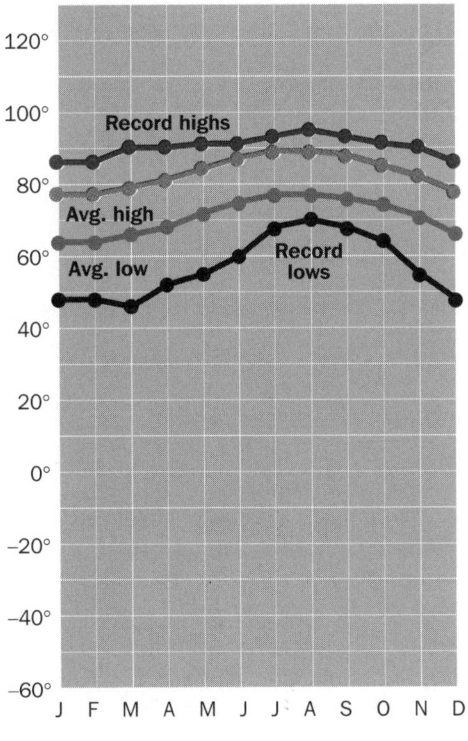

Oslo, Norway

Lat. 59° 54' N **Lon.** 10° 37' E **Elev.** 56 ft.

Annual averages

Precipitation	26.9 in.
Days with thunderstorms	14
Days with snow	76
Days with fog	110
Days above 70°	54
Days below 32°	147

Monthly averages

Month	Avg. precip. (inches)	Wet days	Snow days	Thunder-storm days	Pct. sky is cloudy	Pct. P.M. rel. hum.
Jan.	1.7	19	17	0	62	80
Feb.	1.3	16	14	*	58	74
March	1.4	18	14	*	59	65
April	1.6	13	6	*	45	50
May	1.8	15	*	2	40	49
June	2.4	16	*	4	29	50
July	2.9	17	0	5	27	51
Aug.	3.8	17	0	2	31	53
Sept.	2.5	17	0	1	44	58
Oct.	2.9	17	2	*	58	68
Nov.	2.3	18	8	0	56	77
Dec.	2.3	18	15	0	58	81

T – Trace of rain or snow   * – Less than 1   NA – Not Available

Temperatures

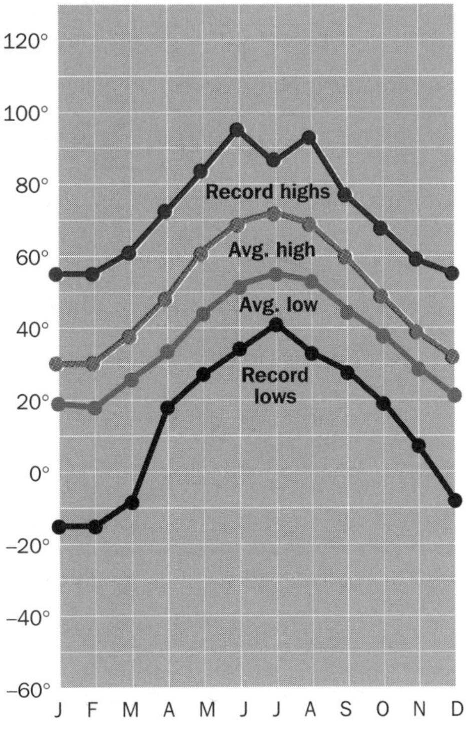

Temperatures

Paris, France

Lat. 48° 44' N　**Lon.** 02° 24' E　**Elev.** 315 ft.

Annual averages

Precipitation	22.3 in.
Days with thunderstorms	19
Days with snow	15
Days with fog	108
Days above 90°	3
Days below 32°	52

Monthly averages

Month	Avg. precip. (inches)	Wet days	Snow days	Thunder-storm days	Pct. sky is cloudy	Pct. P.M. rel. hum.
Jan.	1.5	20	5	*	57	78
Feb.	1.3	17	4	*	48	70
March	1.5	19	2	1	43	65
April	1.7	16	1	2	33	57
May	2.0	17	*	3	36	58
June	2.1	13	0	3	29	57
July	2.1	12	0	4	23	55
Aug.	2.0	11	0	3	17	52
Sept.	2.0	13	0	2	25	59
Oct.	2.2	16	0	1	38	69
Nov.	2.0	16	1	*	45	75
Dec.	1.9	19	2	*	54	81

T – Trace of rain or snow　* – Less than 1　NA – Not Available

Prague, Czech Republic

Lat. 50° 06' N　**Lon.** 14° 15' E　**Elev.** 1,184 ft.

Annual averages

Precipitation	19.3 in.
Days with thunderstorms	27
Days with snow	66
Days with fog	190
Days above 70°	76
Days below 32°	119

Monthly averages

Month	Avg. precip. (inches)	Wet days	Snow days	Thunder-storm days	Pct. sky is cloudy	Pct. P.M. rel. hum.
Jan.	0.9	21	16	*	57	86
Feb.	0.8	17	13	*	53	77
March	1.1	20	10	*	44	64
April	1.5	17	6	1	37	51
May	2.4	16	*	6	34	54
June	2.8	17	*	7	28	56
July	2.6	16	0	6	26	55
Aug.	2.2	15	*	6	25	54
Sept.	1.7	14	*	1	32	60
Oct.	1.2	15	1	*	43	69
Nov.	1.2	18	8	*	57	82
Dec.	0.9	21	12	*	59	86

T – Trace of rain or snow　* – Less than 1　NA – Not Available

Temperatures

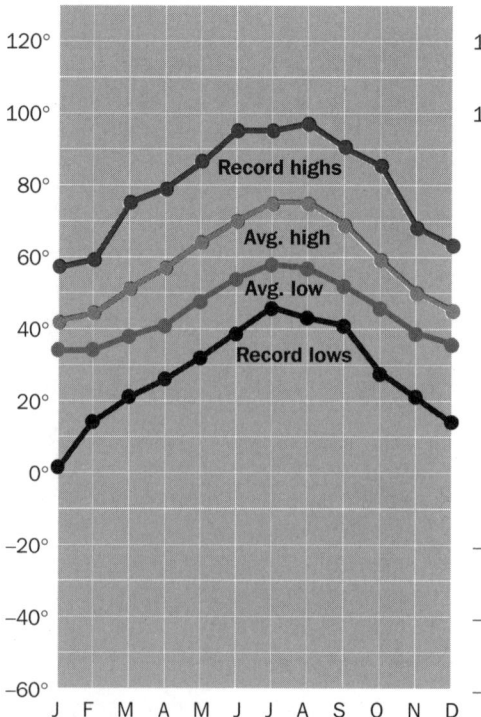

Temperatures

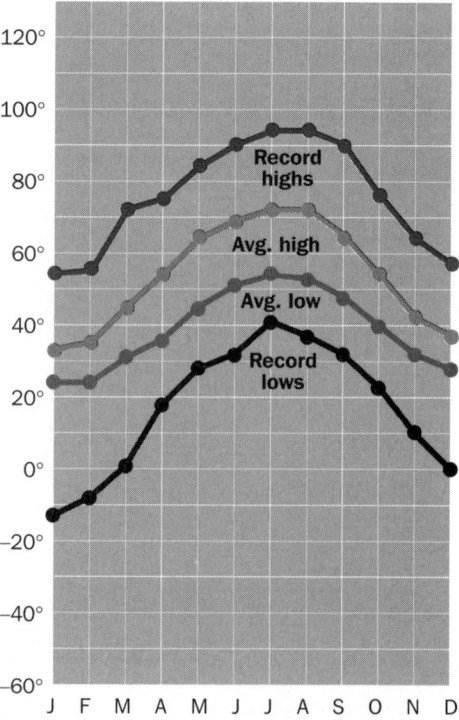

Pretoria, South Africa

Lat. 25° 45' S **Lon.** 28° 11' E **Elev.** 4,265 ft.

Annual averages

Precipitation	30.9 in.
Days with thunderstorms	65
Days with snow	0
Days with fog	16
Days above 90°	7
Days below 32°	*

Monthly averages

Month	Avg. precip. (inches)	Wet days	Snow days	Thunder-storm days	Pct. sky is cloudy	Pct. P.M. rel. hum.
Jan.	5.0	17	0	12	24	47
Feb.	4.3	13	0	6	23	47
March	4.5	12	0	6	20	48
April	1.7	10	0	4	13	43
May	0.9	3	0	1	3	37
June	0.6	3	0	1	2	36
July	0.3	2	0	1	2	33
Aug.	0.2	3	0	1	4	31
Sept.	0.8	6	0	3	10	32
Oct.	2.2	11	0	8	23	38
Nov.	5.2	14	0	9	29	44
Dec.	5.2	16	0	13	27	46

T – Trace of rain or snow   * – Less than 1   NA – Not Available

Rio de Janeiro, Brazil

Lat. 22° 49' S **Lon.** 43° 15' W **Elev.** 20 ft.

Annual averages

Precipitation	42.6 in.
Days with thunderstorms	45
Days with snow	0
Days with fog	276
Days above 90°	117
Days below 32°	0

Monthly averages

Month	Avg. precip. (inches)	Wet days	Snow days	Thunder-storm days	Pct. sky is cloudy	Pct. P.M. rel. hum.
Jan.	4.9	15	0	9	45	58
Feb.	4.8	11	0	7	31	57
March	5.1	13	0	6	42	60
April	4.2	12	0	3	40	61
May	3.1	10	0	1	36	61
June	2.1	7	0	1	32	58
July	1.6	7	0	1	26	55
Aug.	1.7	8	0	1	37	55
Sept.	2.6	13	0	2	50	60
Oct.	3.1	14	0	2	57	60
Nov.	4.1	14	0	4	52	60
Dec.	5.4	18	0	8	59	61

T – Trace of rain or snow   * – Less than 1   NA – Not Available

Temperatures

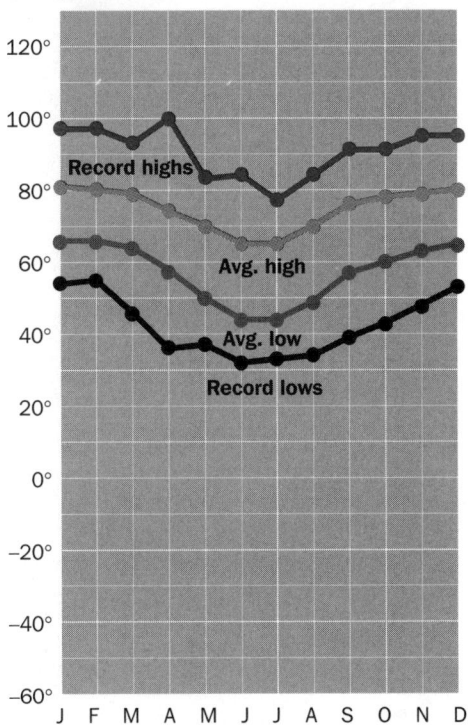

Temperatures

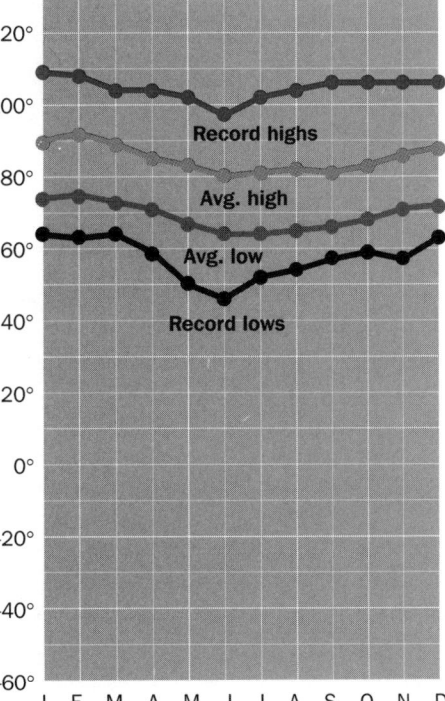

Riyadh, Saudi Arabia

Lat. 24° 43' N **Lon.** 46° 43' E **Elev.** 2,007 ft.

Annual averages

Precipitation	3.2 in.
Days with thunderstorms	7
Days with snow	0
Days with fog	16
Days above 90°	205
Days below 45°	20

Monthly averages

Month	Avg. precip. (inches)	Wet days	Snow days	Thunder-storm days	Pct. sky is cloudy	Pct. P.M. rel. hum.
Jan.	0.1	4	0	*	5	31
Feb.	0.8	3	0	1	5	26
March	0.9	6	0	2	10	24
April	1	7	0	2	10	19
May	0.4	4	0	1	5	13
June	T	1	0	*	0	8
July	0	*	0	*	0	7
Aug.	T	1	0	*	1	8
Sept.	0	*	0	0	0	9
Oct.	0	1	0	*	1	14
Nov.	T	2	0	*	2	23
Dec.	T	4	0	1	9	34

T – Trace of rain or snow   * – Less than 1   NA – Not Available

Rome, Italy

Lat. 41° 48' N **Lon.** 12° 14' E **Elev.** 10 ft.

Annual averages

Precipitation	29.5 in.
Days with thunderstorms	39
Days with snow	1
Days with fog	246
Days above 90°	4
Days below 32°	20

Monthly averages

Month	Avg. precip. (inches)	Wet days	Snow days	Thunder-storm days	Pct. sky is cloudy	Pct. P.M. rel. hum.
Jan.	3.3	13	*	3	34	67
Feb.	2.9	12	1	3	35	67
March	2.0	12	*	3	33	68
April	2.0	12	0	3	34	69
May	1.9	9	0	2	22	68
June	0.7	7	0	2	11	68
July	0.4	4	0	2	3	69
Aug.	0.7	5	0	3	5	68
Sept.	2.8	7	0	4	10	68
Oct.	4.3	11	0	6	19	69
Nov.	4.4	13	*	5	27	70
Dec.	4.1	13	*	3	31	70

T – Trace of rain or snow   * – Less than 1   NA – Not Available

Temperatures

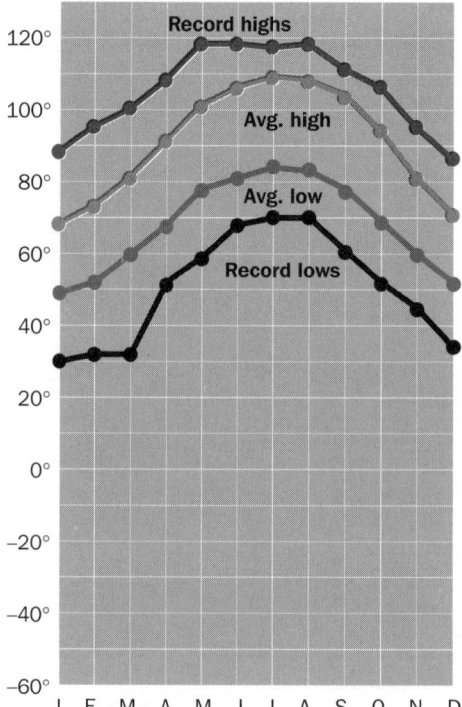

Temperatures

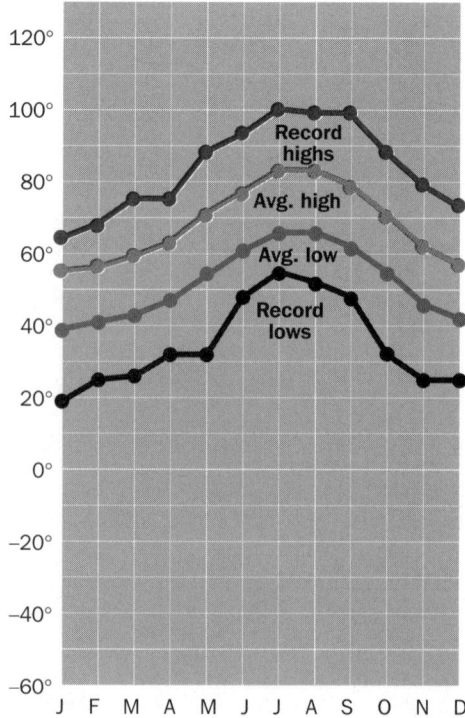

San Salvador, El Salvador

Lat. 13° 42' N **Lon.** 89° 07' W **Elev.** 2,037 ft.

Annual averages

Precipitation	70.0 in.
Days with thunderstorms	126
Days with snow	0
Days with fog	66
Days above 95°	1
Days below 65°	84

Monthly averages

Month	Avg. precip. (inches)	Wet days	Snow days	Thunder-storm days	Pct. sky is cloudy	Pct. P.M. rel. hum.
Jan.	0.3	4	0	1	1	45
Feb.	0.2	1	0	1	1	44
March	0.4	4	0	2	5	51
April	1.7	6	0	6	15	54
May	7.7	13	0	11	33	67
June	12.9	21	0	19	37	70
July	11.5	20	0	21	30	64
Aug.	11.7	22	0	23	35	66
Sept.	12.1	22	0	19	37	74
Oct.	9.5	18	0	15	28	68
Nov.	1.6	9	0	6	7	58
Dec.	0.4	4	0	2	3	51

T – Trace of rain or snow   * – Less than 1   NA – Not Available

Temperatures

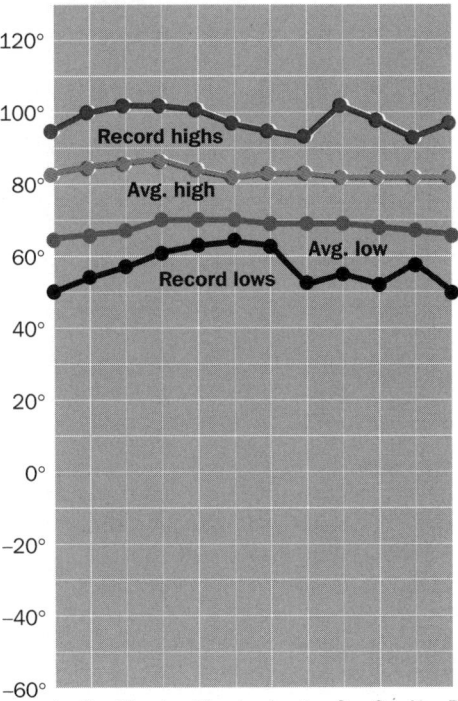

Seoul, Korea

Lat. 37° 33' N **Lon.** 126° 48' E **Elev.** 59 ft.

Annual averages

Precipitation	49.2 in.
Days with thunderstorms	10
Days with snow	25
Days with fog	196
Days above 90°	9
Days below 32°	116

Monthly averages

Month	Avg. precip. (inches)	Wet days	Snow days	Thunder-storm days	Pct. sky is cloudy	Pct. P.M. rel. hum.
Jan.	1.2	10	8	*	NA	61
Feb.	0.8	7	5	0	NA	59
March	1.5	9	3	0	NA	58
April	3.0	10	*	1	NA	56
May	3.2	10	0	1	NA	58
June	5.1	12	0	1	NA	66
July	14.8	18	0	3	NA	74
Aug.	10.5	15	0	2	NA	73
Sept.	4.7	9	0	1	NA	69
Oct.	1.6	10	*	1	NA	65
Nov.	1.8	11	2	*	NA	64
Dec.	1.0	11	7	*	NA	64

T – Trace of rain or snow   * – Less than 1   NA – Not Available

Temperatures

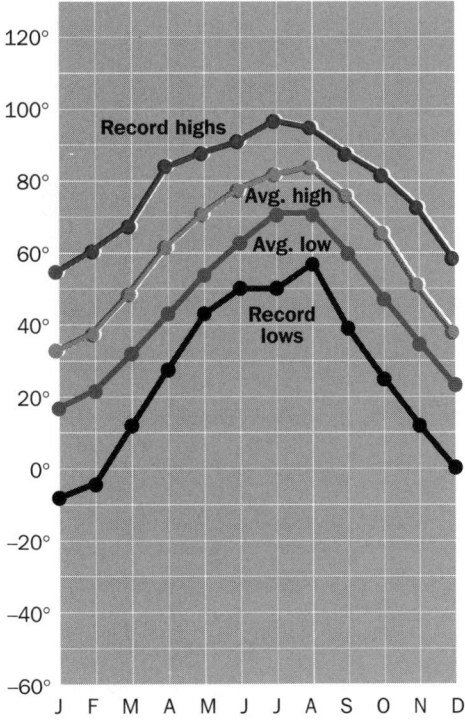

Shanghai, China

Lat. 31° 10' N **Lon.** 121° 26' E **Elev.** 23 ft.

Annual averages

Precipitation	45.0 in.
Days with thunderstorms	15
Days with snow	17
Days with fog	274
Days above 90°	28
Days below 32°	36

Monthly averages

Month	Avg. precip. (inches)	Wet days	Snow days	Thunder-storm days	Pct. sky is cloudy	Pct. P.M. rel. hum.
Jan.	1.9	13	4	*	48	64
Feb.	2.4	12	3	*	54	64
March	3.3	16	1	1	62	67
April	3.6	15	*	1	57	66
May	3.8	15	0	1	55	64
June	7.0	17	0	2	55	73
July	5.8	15	0	5	42	74
Aug.	5.5	13	0	3	30	73
Sept.	5.2	14	0	2	41	71
Oct.	2.9	11	0	*	38	67
Nov.	2.1	9	*	*	35	63
Dec.	1.5	8	9	0	32	60

T – Trace of rain or snow　　* – Less than 1　　NA – Not Available

Singapore

Lat. 01° 22' N **Lon.** 103° 55' E **Elev.** 105 ft.

Annual averages

Precipitation	95.0 in.
Days with thunderstorms	157
Days with snow	0
Days with fog	223
Days above 95°	2
Days below 65°	0

Monthly averages

Month	Avg. precip. (inches)	Wet days	Snow days	Thunder-storm days	Pct. sky is cloudy	Pct. P.M. rel. hum.
Jan.	9.9	16	0	4	13	73
Feb.	6.8	14	0	6	15	72
March	7.6	15	0	12	10	72
April	7.4	19	0	19	10	75
May	6.8	17	0	18	13	76
June	6.8	16	0	14	12	74
July	6.7	17	0	10	14	74
Aug.	7.7	18	0	10	17	75
Sept.	7.0	18	0	14	15	76
Oct.	8.2	20	0	17	19	75
Nov.	10.0	26	0	21	25	82
Dec.	10.1	23	0	12	18	81

T – Trace of rain or snow　　* – Less than 1　　NA – Not Available

Temperatures

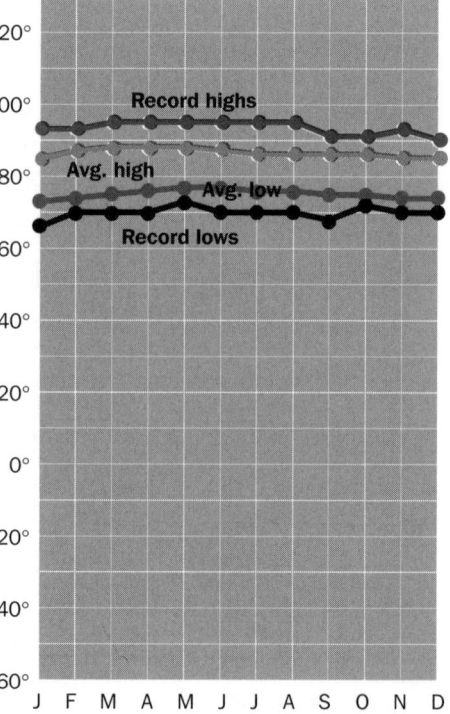

Stockholm, Sweden

Lat. 59° 39' N **Lon.** 17° 57' E **Elev.** 200 ft.

Annual averages

Precipitation	22.4 in.
Days with thunderstorms	12
Days with snow	89
Days with fog	166
Days above 70°	45
Days below 32°	150

Monthly averages

Month	Avg. precip. (inches)	Wet days	Snow days	Thunder-storm days	Pct. sky is cloudy	Pct. P.M. rel. hum.
Jan.	1.5	23	19	0	64	88
Feb.	1.1	17	15	0	59	79
March	1.1	20	17	*	60	72
April	1.5	15	8	0	49	57
May	1.6	13	1	1	33	49
June	1.9	15	0	2	32	53
July	2.8	17	0	3	28	56
Aug.	3.1	18	0	4	32	59
Sept.	2.1	19	*	2	40	64
Oct.	2.1	18	2	*	50	75
Nov.	1.9	21	10	0	56	86
Dec.	1.9	23	17	0	65	90

T – Trace of rain or snow   * – Less than 1   NA – Not Available

Temperatures

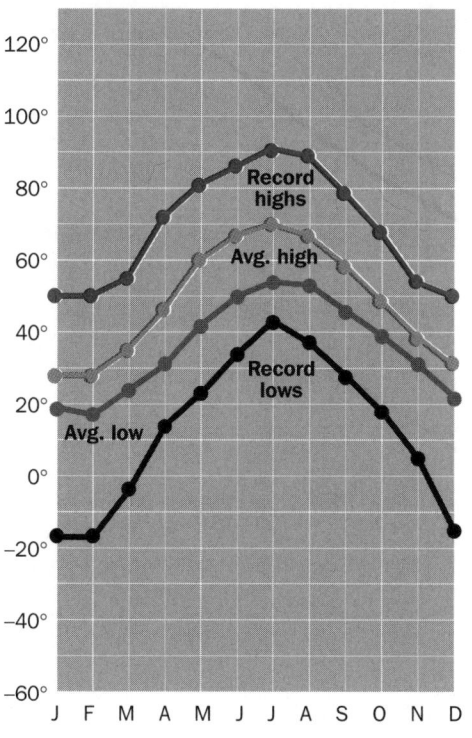

St. Petersburg, Russia

Lat. 59° 55' N **Lon.** 30° 15' E **Elev.** 66 ft.

Annual averages

Precipitation	19.2 in.
Days with thunderstorms	14
Days with snow	104
Days with fog	207
Days above 70°	53
Days below 32°	170

Monthly averages

Month	Avg. precip. (inches)	Wet days	Snow days	Thunder-storm days	Pct. sky is cloudy	Pct. P.M. rel. hum.
Jan.	1.0	23	21	*	NA	81
Feb.	0.9	18	17	0	NA	77
March	0.9	15	13	0	NA	69
April	1.0	15	9	*	NA	59
May	1.6	12	1	2	NA	53
June	2.0	15	*	3	NA	58
July	2.5	15	*	5	NA	61
Aug.	2.8	16	*	3	NA	64
Sept.	2.1	18	*	1	NA	71
Oct.	1.8	18	4	*	NA	77
Nov.	1.4	22	15	*	NA	84
Dec.	1.2	25	24	*	NA	84

T – Trace of rain or snow   * – Less than 1   NA – Not Available

Temperatures

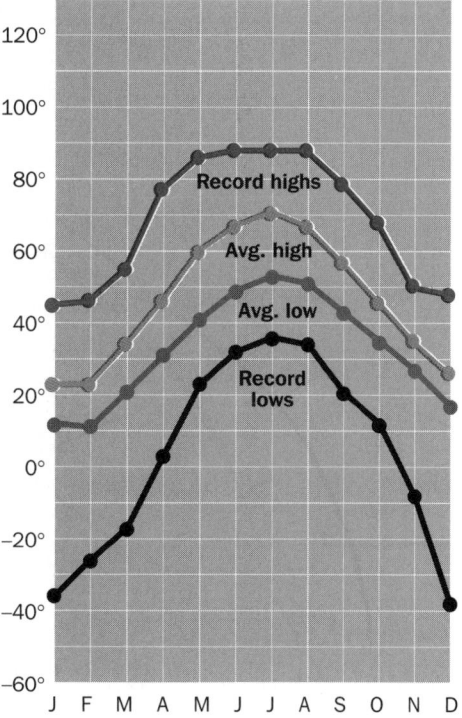

Sydney, Australia
Lat. 33° 75' S **Lon.** 151° 11' E **Elev.** 10 ft.

Annual averages

Precipitation	46.5 in.
Days with thunderstorms	10
Days with snow	*
Days with fog	16
Days above 90°	10
Days below 32°	*

Monthly averages

Month	Avg. precip. (inches)	Wet days	Snow days	Thunder-storm days	Pct. sky is cloudy	Pct. P.M. rel. hum.
Jan.	3.5	11	0	1	29	60
Feb.	4.0	12	0	1	30	61
March	5.0	12	0	1	26	61
April	5.3	11	0	*	21	60
May	5.0	11	*	*	22	59
June	4.6	11	*	*	18	57
July	4.6	9	0	*	14	52
Aug.	3.0	8	*	1	15	49
Sept.	2.9	9	0	1	16	50
Oct.	2.8	11	0	1	27	55
Nov.	2.9	11	0	2	24	58
Dec.	2.9	10	0	2	25	55

T – Trace of rain or snow   * – Less than 1   NA – Not Available

Taipei, Taiwan
Lat. 25° 04' N **Lon.** 121° 32' E **Elev.** 20 ft.

Annual averages

Precipitation	72.7 in.
Days with thunderstorms	41
Days with snow	1
Days with fog	237
Days above 90°	84
Days below 32°	0

Monthly averages

Month	Avg. precip. (inches)	Wet days	Snow days	Thunder-storm days	Pct. sky is cloudy	Pct. P.M. rel. hum.
Jan.	3.8	17	*	*	48	76
Feb.	5.3	16	0	1	58	77
March	4.3	20	*	3	62	79
April	5.3	16	0	4	52	77
May	6.9	19	0	4	48	79
June	8.8	16	0	8	36	76
July	8.8	13	0	8	20	71
Aug.	8.7	14	0	6	20	72
Sept.	8.2	15	0	6	30	75
Oct.	5.5	15	0	1	31	75
Nov.	4.2	18	0	#	38	77
Dec.	2.9	17	#	#	42	76

T – Trace of rain or snow   * – Less than 1   NA – Not Available

Temperatures

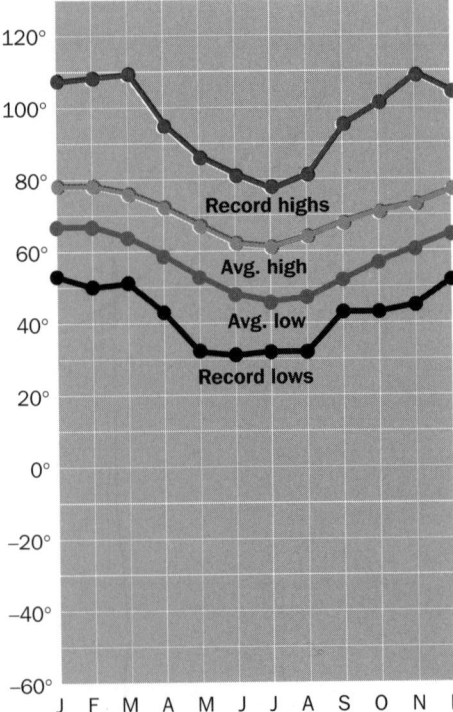

Temperatures

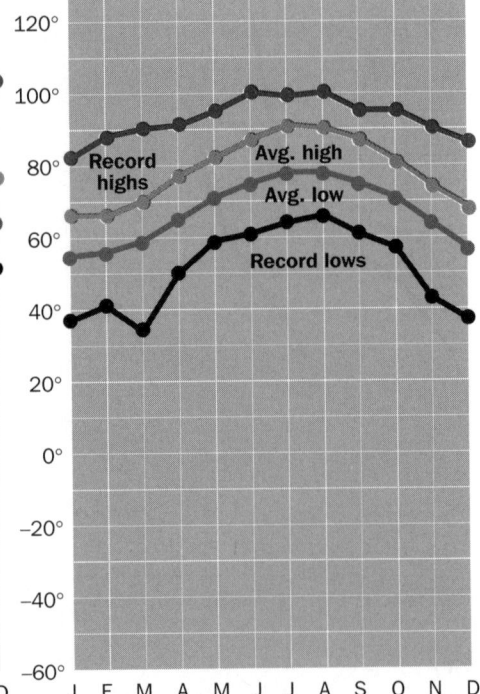

Tokyo, Japan

Lat. 35° 33' N **Lon.** 139° 47' E **Elev.** 26 ft.

Annual averages

Precipitation	61.6 in.
Days with thunderstorms	11
Days with snow	10
Days with fog	145
Days above 90°	15
Days below 32°	24

Monthly averages

Month	Avg. precip. (inches)	Wet days	Snow days	Thunder-storm days	Pct. sky is cloudy	Pct. P.M. rel. hum.
Jan.	1.9	8	3	*	NA	45
Feb.	2.9	10	4	*	NA	49
March	4.2	17	2	1	NA	54
April	5.3	16	*	1	NA	60
May	5.8	15	0	1	NA	61
June	6.5	19	0	1	NA	71
July	5.6	18	0	2	NA	72
Aug.	6.0	15	0	2	NA	67
Sept.	9.2	18	0	2	NA	70
Oct.	8.2	15	0	1	NA	64
Nov.	3.8	13	0	*	NA	58
Dec.	2.2	9	1	*	NA	49

T – Trace of rain or snow   * – Less than 1   NA – Not Available

Temperatures

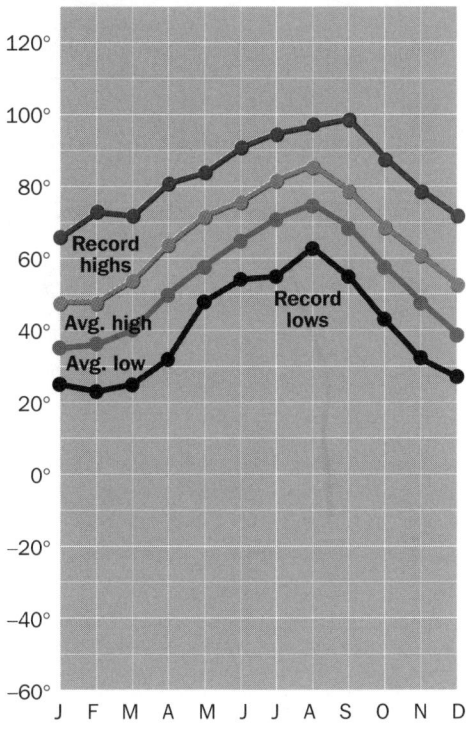

Toronto, Canada

Lat. 43° 40' N **Lon.** 79° 38' W **Elev.** 567 ft.

Annual averages

Precipitation	32.2 in.
Days with thunderstorms	27
Days with snow	90
Days with fog	161
Days above 90°	4
Days below 32°	147

Monthly averages

Month	Avg. precip. (inches)	Wet days	Snow days	Thunder-storm days	Pct. sky is cloudy	Pct. P.M. rel. hum.
Jan.	2.7	25	22	*	55	76
Feb.	2.4	20	18	*	51	72
March	2.6	20	13	1	49	68
April	2.5	17	5	1	43	57
May	2.9	16	1	3	39	55
June	2.7	15	0	5	30	55
July	3.0	12	0	6	23	54
Aug.	2.7	13	0	5	28	57
Sept.	2.9	14	0	4	35	61
Oct.	2.4	16	2	1	37	66
Nov.	2.8	20	8	1	52	74
Dec.	2.6	25	21	*	58	78

T – Trace of rain or snow   * – Less than 1   NA – Not Available

Temperatures

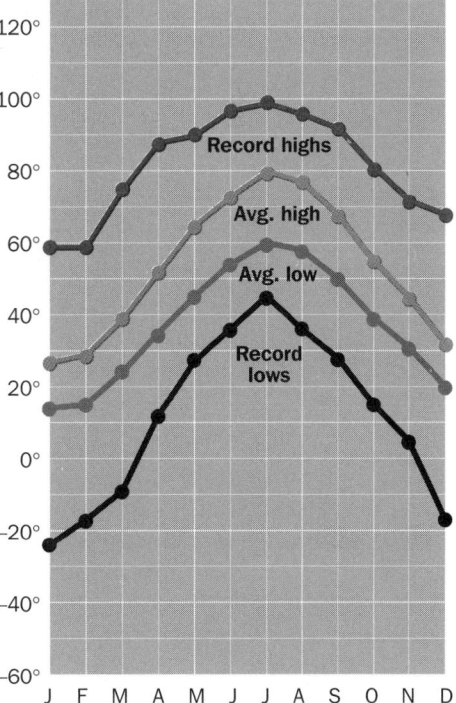

Vancouver, Canada

Lat. 49° 11' N **Lon.** 123° 10' W **Elev.** 7 ft.

Annual averages

Precipitation	57.4 in.
Days with thunderstorms	4
Days with snow	19
Days with fog	143
Days above 90°	0
Days below 32°	47

Monthly averages

Month	Avg. precip. (inches)	Wet days	Snow days	Thunder-storm days	Pct. sky is cloudy	Pct. P.M. rel. hum.
Jan.	8.6	21	6	*	55	83
Feb.	5.8	19	4	*	48	78
March	5.0	19	2	*	39	72
April	3.3	16	*	*	35	66
May	2.8	17	0	1	31	63
June	2.5	14	0	*	25	62
July	1.2	10	0	1	16	61
Aug.	1.7	10	0	1	19	64
Sept.	3.6	11	0	1	21	71
Oct.	5.8	17	*	*	38	81
Nov.	8.3	21	2	*	48	81
Dec.	8.8	22	5	*	53	84

T – Trace of rain or snow   * – Less than 1   NA – Not Available

Temperatures

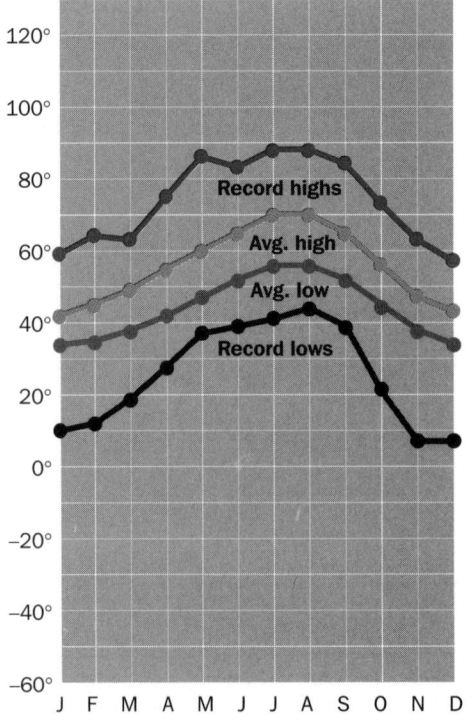

Vienna, Austria

Lat. 48° 07' N **Lon.** 16° 34' E **Elev.** 623 ft.

Annual averages

Precipitation	25.6 in.
Days with thunderstorms	35
Days with snow	57
Days with fog	185
Days above 90°	2
Days below 32°	92

Monthly averages

Month	Avg. precip. (inches)	Wet days	Snow days	Thunder-storm days	Pct. sky is cloudy	Pct. P.M. rel. hum.
Jan.	1.5	23	15	*	55	76
Feb.	1.4	19	12	*	48	69
March	1.8	23	9	*	40	56
April	2.0	24	3	2	34	50
May	2.8	24	*	6	27	51
June	2.7	25	0	8	30	52
July	3.0	25	0	8	21	48
Aug.	2.7	22	0	8	20	49
Sept.	2.0	18	0	2	27	55
Oct.	2.0	17	0	*	34	62
Nov.	1.9	21	6	*	55	73
Dec.	1.8	24	12	1	55	77

T – Trace of rain or snow   * – Less than 1   NA – Not Available

Temperatures

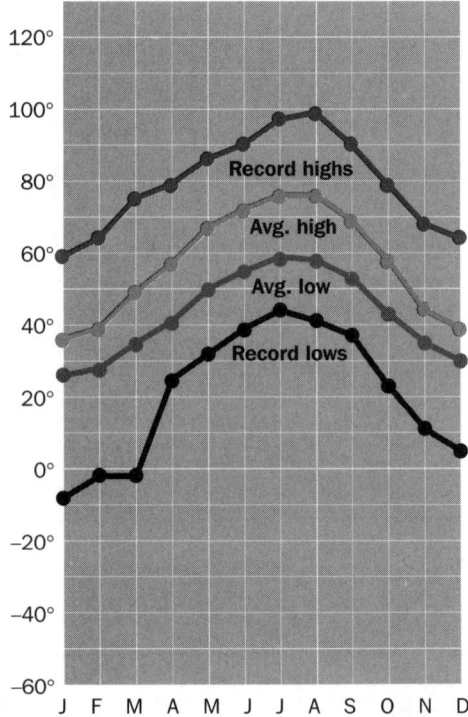

Warsaw, Poland

Lat. 52° 10' N **Lon.** 20° 58' E **Elev.** 351 ft.

Annual averages

Precipitation	22.0 in.
Days with thunderstorms	27
Days with snow	64
Days with fog	204
Days above 70°	78
Days below 32°	115

Monthly averages

Month	Avg. precip. (inches)	Wet days	Snow days	Thunder-storm days	Pct. sky is cloudy	Pct. P.M. rel. hum.
Jan.	1.2	23	18	1	55	85
Feb.	1.1	18	14	1	51	79
March	1.3	18	9	2	40	67
April	1.5	16	3	1	31	58
May	1.9	15	*	4	29	57
June	2.6	16	0	5	26	60
July	3.0	17	0	6	22	60
Aug.	3.0	14	0	5	22	59
Sept.	1.9	15	0	1	30	66
Oct.	1.7	16	*	*	38	75
Nov.	1.4	19	7	1	50	84
Dec.	1.4	24	13	*	58	87

T – Trace of rain or snow   * – Less than 1   NA – Not Available

Temperatures

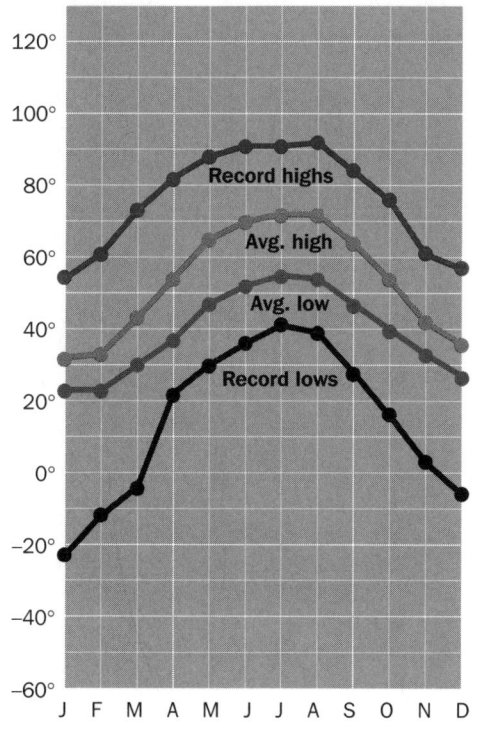

Zurich, Switzerland

Lat. 47° 23' N **Lon.** 08° 34' E **Elev.** 1,867 ft.

Annual averages

Precipitation	40.9 in.
Days with thunderstorms	11
Days with snow	42
Days with fog	232
Days above 90°	1
Days below 32°	76

Monthly averages

Month	Avg. precip. (inches)	Wet days	Snow days	Thunder-storm days	Pct. sky is cloudy	Pct. P.M. rel. hum.
Jan.	2.3	17	11	*	67	77
Feb.	1.9	14	8	0	61	69
March	2.9	16	7	*	52	59
April	3.4	15	4	*	48	55
May	4.0	16	1	2	45	55
June	4.9	15	0	3	39	55
July	5.0	12	0	3	32	54
Aug.	4.6	11	0	2	30	55
Sept.	3.3	10	0	1	36	60
Oct.	3.2	12	*	*	52	68
Nov.	2.5	12	4	0	64	74
Dec.	2.9	16	7	0	64	77

T – Trace of rain or snow   * – Less than 1   NA – Not Available

Temperatures

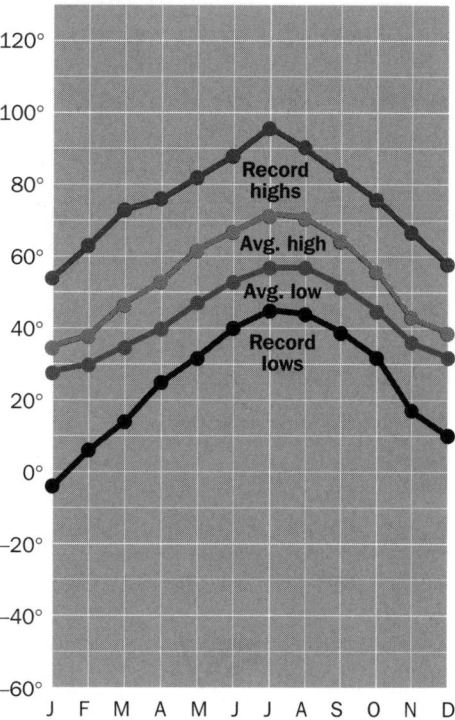

Appendix

From seasons to sunburn, more weather details

Equinoxes and solstices are often called the "official" beginnings of the seasons. But equinoxes and solstices are astronomical events. Meteorologists generally break down the seasons by months. For instance, meteorologists consider the Northern Hemisphere winter to be the months of December, January and February, not the time from the December 21 or 22 winter solstice to the March 20 or 21 spring equinox.

Solstices and equinoxes are important to the weather, however. The December solstice is the instant when the sun reaches its southernmost point in the sky. This means it is at its lowest point in the sky in the Northern Hemisphere and days are shortest. The resulting lack of sunlight brings cold weather. But, as everyone knows, cold weather begins well before December 21 or 22 when the sun reaches its lowest point in the sky.

The two equinoxes are the turning points for the length of the day. But, contrary to what is often said, days and nights are not equal length at the time of the equinoxes. Close, but not exactly the same, because the Earth's atmosphere bends sunlight. When the top of the rising sun is first seen, the sun is actually below the horizon. Its light rays are being bent by the air. This means that the day is really a few minutes longer than night at the equinoxes.

In the table below, the equinoxes are identified as "spring" and "fall" and the solstices as "winter" and "summer." These names apply to the Northern Hemisphere. The seasons are reversed in the Southern Hemisphere.

Times are United States Eastern Time, either Standard or Daylight, depending on the month. The universal time, which used to be called Greenwich Mean Time, follows. With universal time, there is no Daylight Savings Time. This is why there is a five-hour difference when the United States is on standard time and a four-hour difference with Daylight Savings Time. The universal time uses the 24-hour clock in which 1 p.m. becomes 13:00, 2 p.m., 14:00 and so forth. This simplifies the mathematics of converting to other time zones.

Eclipses of the sun and moon

Eclipses of the sun occur when the moon moves between the Earth and the sun. This happens only at the time of the new moon.

When the moon is close enough to the Earth to appear as large as the sun or slightly larger, a total eclipse occurs along a narrow path across the Earth. Other places will see a partial eclipse.

Sometimes, the path of the total eclipse misses the Earth entirely and only a partial eclipse is seen anywhere. These cases are listed as partial in the table on the next page.

When the moon is far enough away from the

Dates and times of the equinoxes and solstices

Year	Solstice/equinox	Date	U.S. Eastern Time	Universal time
1994	Winter solstice	Dec. 21	9:24 p.m. EST	Dec. 22, 02:24
1995	Spring equinox	March 20	9:15 p.m. EST	March 21, 02:15
	Summer solstice	June 21	4:35 p.m. EDT	June 21, 20:35
	Fall equinox	Sept. 23	8:14 a.m. EDT	Sept. 23, 12:14
	Winter solstice	Dec. 22	3:18 a.m. EST	Dec. 22, 08:18
1996	Spring equinox	March 20	3:04 a.m. EST	March 20, 08:04
	Summer solstice	June 20	10:24 p.m. EDT	June 21, 02:24
	Fall equinox	Sept. 22	2:01 p.m. EDT	Sept. 22, 18:01
	Winter solstice	Dec. 21	9:07 a.m. EST	Dec. 21, 14:07

Eclipses of the sun 1995 – 1998

Date	Type	Region visible
April 29, 1995	Annular	Central and South America
Oct. 24, 1995	Total	Middle East, Asia, Australia
April 17, 1996	Partial	New Zealand, South Pacific
Oct. 12, 1996	Partial	Eastern Canada, western Europe, north Africa
March 9, 1997	Total	West Asia, Alaska
Sept. 2, 1997	Partial	Australia, New Zealand
Feb. 26, 1998	Total	North and South America
Aug. 22, 1998	Annular	Southeast Asia, Australia, South Pacific

Eclipses of the moon, 1995 – 1998

Date	Type	Location
April 15, 1995	Partial	Western North and South America, Pacific, Asia, Australia
Oct. 8, 1995	Penumbral	Northwest North America, Asia, Europe
April 4, 1996	Total	North and South America, Europe, Africa, western Asia
Sept. 27, 1996	Total	North and South America, Europe, Africa
March 24, 1997	Partial	North and South America, Europe, Africa
Sept. 16, 1997	Total	Europe, Africa, Asia
March 13, 1998	Penumbral	North and South America, Europe, Africa
Aug. 8, 1998	Penumbral	North and South America, Europe, Africa
Sept. 6, 1998	Penumbral	North and South America, Asia

Source: Fred Espenak, NASA

Earth to appear slightly smaller than the sun, an annular eclipse, with a ring of sunlight seen around the moon, occurs along a narrow path. Other places see a partial eclipse.

Eclipses of the moon occur when the Earth passes between the sun and the moon. This happens only at the time of a full moon.

When the moon passes into the Earth's full shadow, the umbra, a total eclipse occurs and is seen over a much wider area of the Earth than a total solar eclipse.

When the part of the Earth's shadow with some sunlight — the penumbra — covers the moon, a penumbral eclipse occurs. During such eclipses the moon isn't as dark as during total eclipses.

A partial eclipse of the moon occurs when the Earth's shadow falls on only part of the moon.

Likely dates of first and last frost

Traditional climate listings give average dates of the last frost of the spring and the first frost of the fall. These are dates when the odds are 50-50 that the last and first official readings below 36°F will occur.

The 36°F mark is used because temperatures at weather stations normally are taken in instrument shelters that are about five feet off the ground, where the air is usually warmer than at ground level. A 36°F official reading means the temperature at ground level is about 32°F, when frost is likely on the ground.

However, many people, such as farmers and con-struction planners, need more specific information, provided by the National Climatic Data Center. For more than 3,000 U.S. locations the National Climatic Data Center calculates three sets of chances — 10 percent, 50 percent and 90 percent — for the first and last occurrence of temperatures below three benchmarks — 36°F, 32°F and 28°F. Temperatures at ground level would be up to four degrees colder.

Ground temperatures from 29°F to 32°F are considered a "light freeze" that will kill tender plants but have little effect on others. Ground readings of 25°F to 28°F are considered a "moderate freeze" that will be widely destructive to most vegetation, with heavy damage to fruit blossoms. Temperatures of 24°F are a "severe freeze" in which the ground itself will begin freezing.

How to read the tables

The tables here give odds for the last day of frost in spring and the first day of fall using the official temperature of 36°F (32°F at ground), a light freeze.

What last frost odds mean for spring:

• 50% probability: Odds are 50-50 that the last frost will occur by the given date.

• 10% probability: Odds are only 10 percent that frost will occur after this date.

What first frost odds mean for fall:

•50% probability: Odds are 50-50 that the first frost will occur by the given date.

• 10% probability: Odds are only 10 percent

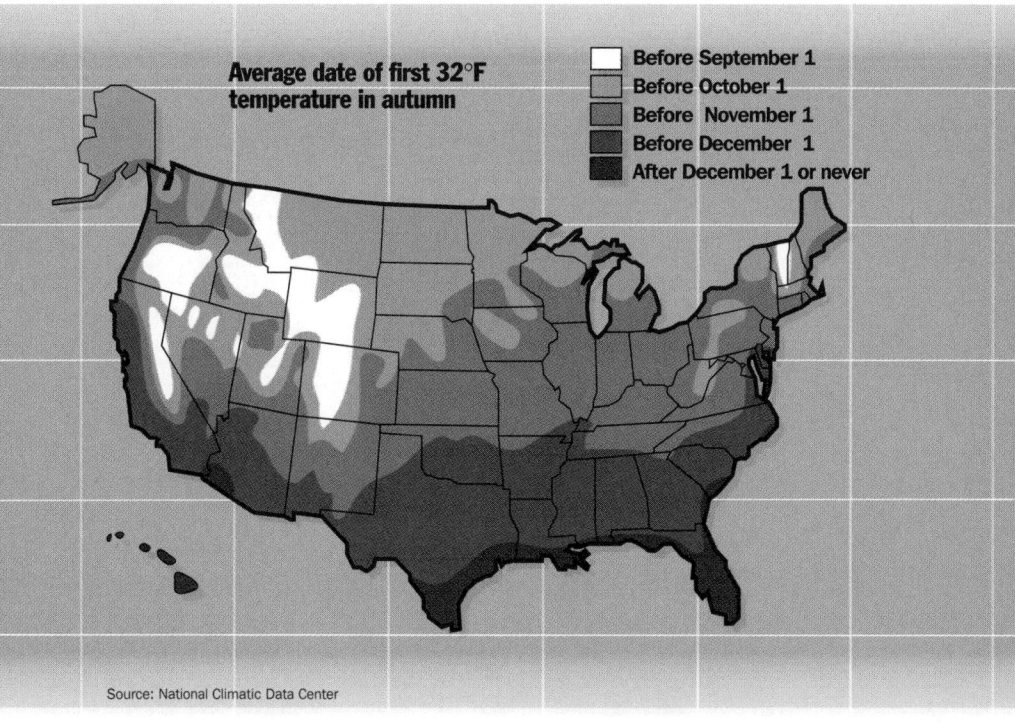

Average date of first 32°F temperature in autumn

- Before September 1
- Before October 1
- Before November 1
- Before December 1
- After December 1 or never

Source: National Climatic Data Center

that first frost will occur before this date.

What the "growing season" odds mean:

• 50% probability: Odds are 50-50 that the growing season will last the number of days listed.

• 90% probability: Odds are 90 percent that the growing season will last the number of days listed.

Notes on states, cities omitted: Cities in Alaska aren't listed because frost can occur at any time of the year in many places. Cities in Hawaii and Puerto Rico aren't included because, except for the highest elevations, the frost-free period lasts all year. Also, figures have not been calculated for some large cities because, in many cases, smaller cities represent a better geographic spread in their states.

	Last spring frost		First fall frost		Growing season	
	50%	10%	10%	50%	50%	90%
Alabama						
Birmingham	April 10	April 23	Oct. 13	Oct. 25	198	183
Mobile	March 14	March 29	Oct. 30	Nov. 14	244	227
Muscle Shoals	April 8	April 20	Oct. 12	Oct. 24	199	184
Selma	March 29	April 12	Oct. 21	Nov. 4	219	200
Arizona						
Flagstaff	June 21	July 3	Aug. 16	Sept. 5	76	49
Phoenix	March 1	March 23	Nov. 9	Nov. 30	273	239
Tucson	March 23	April 17	Nov. 5	Nov. 21	242	208
Yuma	Feb. 2	March 11	Nov. 21	Dec. 18	312	271
Arkansas						
Fort Smith	April 13	April 28	Oct. 6	Oct. 21	190	169
Jonesboro	April 10	April 24	Oct. 10	Oct. 23	196	174
Pine Bluff	April 2	April 16	Oct. 14	Oct. 28	208	189
California						
Bakersfield	March 2	April 2	Nov. 9	Nov. 23	265	230
Eureka	March 29	April 25	Nov. 5	Nov. 28	244	205
Fresno	March 29	April 27	Oct. 27	Nov. 12	227	192
Pasadena	Feb. 14	April 4	Nov. 21	Dec. 23	304	253
Redding	April 7	May 10	Oct. 31	Nov. 16	223	184
Sacramento	March 25	April 28	Nov. 7	Nov. 17	236	200

Average date of spring's last 32° reading

- Before April 1
- During April
- During May
- After June 1

	Last spring frost		First fall frost		Growing season	
	50%	10%	10%	50%	50%	90%
San Bernardino	March 26	April 26	Oct. 31	Nov. 21	239	202
San Francisco	Feb. 7	March 20	Nov. 20	Dec. 10	307	264
San Jose	March 1	April 6	Nov. 10	Nov. 26	270	234
Santa Barbara	Feb. 11	March 26	Nov. 16	Dec. 18	319	255
Colorado						
Alamosa	June 21	July 4	Aug. 12	Aug. 26	65	47
Denver	May 17	June 1	Sept. 10	Sept. 26	130	109
Durango	June 18	July 1	Aug. 24	Sept. 9	82	62
Connecticut						
Falls Village	May 31	June 15	Sept. 5	Sept. 17	108	86
Hartford	May 13	May 26	Sept. 15	Oct. 2	141	119
Delaware						
Wilmington	April 25	May 10	Oct. 3	Oct. 16	173	153
Lewes	April 22	May 4	Oct. 6	Oct. 20	180	161
Florida						
Daytona Beach	Feb. 27	March 20	Nov. 14	Dec. 9	284	248
Fort Myers	Jan. 19	Feb. 25	Dec. 6	Jan. 8	365	306
Jacksonville	March 2	March 24	Nov. 8	Nov. 29	271	239
Miami	—	Feb. 7	Dec. 30	—	365	365
Pensacola	March 9	March 30	Nov. 1	Nov. 20	256	227
Sanford	Feb. 21	March 14	Nov. 16	Dec. 12	293	263
Tallahassee	March 26	April 12	Oct. 20	Nov. 4	222	197
Tampa	Feb. 9	March 11	Nov. 15	Dec. 8	301	265
Georgia						
Athens	April 7	April 21	Oct. 14	Oct. 29	204	190
Augusta	April 11	April 26	Oct. 12	Oct. 24	195	179
Columbus	April 3	April 16	Oct. 20	Nov. 3	213	196
Savannah	March 24	April 11	Oct. 26	Nov. 8	228	205
Idaho						
Boise	May 21	June 9	Sept. 13	Sept. 27	129	101
Idaho Falls	June 14	July 2	Aug. 21	Sept. 5	82	57
Pocatello	June 6	June 25	Aug. 24	Sept. 8	93	64
Illinois						
Chicago	May 1	May 17	Sept. 30	Oct. 14	165	143
Peoria	May 6	May 23	Sept. 25	Oct. 6	152	132
Rockford	May 13	May 26	Sept. 19	Sept. 30	140	124

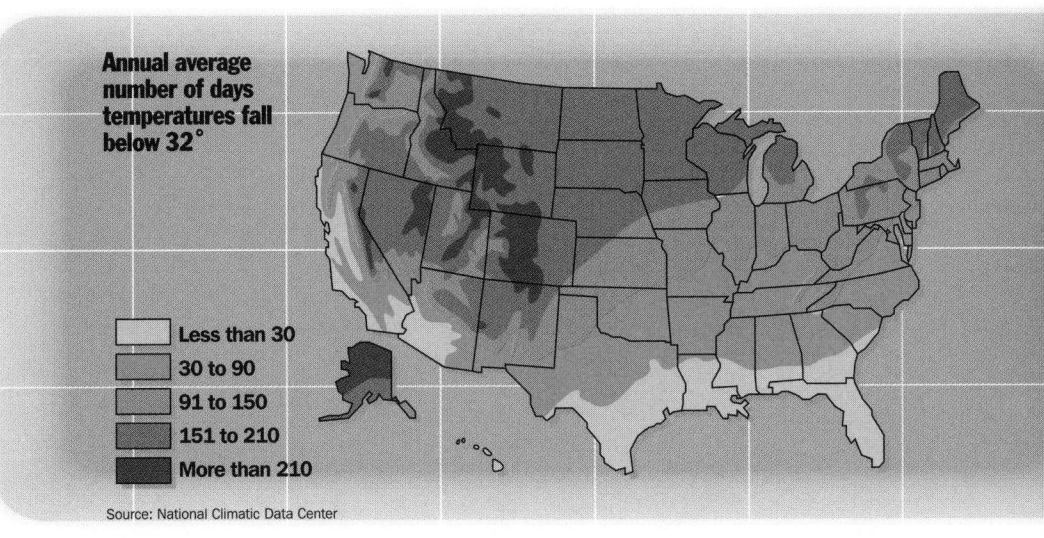

Annual average number of days temperatures fall below 32°

- Less than 30
- 30 to 90
- 91 to 150
- 151 to 210
- More than 210

Source: National Climatic Data Center

	Last spring frost		First fall frost		Growing season									
	50%	10%	10%	50%	50% 90%	College Park	May 3	May 17	Sept. 27	Oct. 10	159	138		
						Salisbury	April 28	May 10	Sept. 30	Oct. 11	166	149		
Springfield	April 30	May 16	Sept. 27	Oct. 10	162 145									
						Massachusetts								
Indiana						Framingham	May 8	May 22	Sept. 20	Oct. 2	146	125		
Evansville	April 23	May 10	Oct. 4	Oct. 17	176 157	Worcester	May 10	May 23	Sept. 21	Oct. 3	145	127		
Indianapolis	May 3	May 19	Sept. 28	Oct. 9	158 137									
South Bend	May 12	May 27	Sept. 20	Oct. 6	146 125	**Michigan**								
						Alpena	May 21	June 4	Sept. 15	Sept. 28	129	108		
Iowa						Holland	May 23	June 9	Sept. 5	Sept. 23	122	97		
Ames	May 9	May 22	Sept. 15	Sept. 29	142 125	Lansing	May 26	June 8	Sept. 9	Sept. 21	117	103		
Cherokee	May 18	May 30	Sept. 7	Sept. 18	122 107	Marquette	May 24	June 5	Sept. 19	Oct. 3	131	112		
Dubuque	April 30	May 15	Sept. 24	Oct. 9	161 139	Pontiac	May 17	May 31	Sept. 18	Oct. 1	136	119		
						S.Ste. Marie	June 8	June 23	Aug. 29	Sept. 13	96	73		
Kansas														
Dodge City	April 27	May 11	Sept. 29	Oct. 12	167 146	**Minnesota**								
Goodland	May 14	May 27	Sept. 13	Sept. 26	135 115	Duluth	June 4	June 22	Aug. 27	Sept. 11	98	76		
Topeka	May 1	May 15	Sept. 23	Oct. 6	157 138	Int'l Falls	June 9	June 30	Aug. 21	Sept. 4	86	64		
						Little Falls	May 25	June 9	Sept. 5	Sept. 16	114	95		
Kentucky						St. Peter	May 13	May 26	Sept. 10	Sept. 24	134	116		
Lexington	April 29	May 13	Sept. 30	Oct. 14	167 148									
Paducah	April 18	May 7	Oct. 4	Oct. 14	178 156	**Mississippi**								
						Biloxi	March 7	March 27	Oct. 31	Nov. 20	257	230		
Louisiana						Meridian	April 4	April 17	Oct. 10	Oct. 26	203	184		
Monroe	March 28	April 11	Oct. 10	Oct. 27	212 192	Tupelo	April 16	May 5	Oct. 5	Oct. 19	185	155		
New Orleans	March 8	April 4	Oct. 30	Nov. 17	253 220									
						Missouri								
Maine						Jefferson City	May 7	May 22	Sept. 20	Oct. 7	152	130		
Caribou	June 1	June 17	Sept. 2	Sept. 12	102 84	St. Charles	April 25	May 9	Sept. 30	Oct. 14	172	152		
Portland	May 20	June 4	Sept. 8	Sept. 19	122 101	St. Joseph	April 29	May 13	Sept. 18	Oct. 4	157	137		
Maryland						**Montana**								
Baltimore	April 9	April 21	Oct. 19	Nov. 3	207 187	Billings	May 26	June 10	Sept.1	Sept. 14	111	89		

	Last spring frost		First fall frost		Growing season	
	50%	10%	10%	50%	50%	90%
Helena	June 4	June 23	Aug. 25	Sept. 8	95	70
Kalispell	June 12	July 5	Aug. 26	Sept. 7	87	57
Nebraska						
Fremont	May 5	May 18	Sept. 14	Sept. 29	146	130
Grand Island	May 8	May 21	Sept. 12	Sept. 28	143	121
North Platte	May 19	June 1	Sept. 4	Sept. 17	120	103
Scottsbluff	May 21	June 4	Sept. 4	Sept. 20	121	100
Valentine	May 21	June 8	Sept. 7	Sept. 22	123	102
Nevada						
Elko	June 24	July 13	Aug. 9	Aug. 28	64	32
Ely	June 29	July 14	Aug. 13	Aug. 28	60	37
Las Vegas	May 27	April 19	Oct. 31	Nov. 14	232	204
Reno	June 23	July 9	Aug. 12	Aug. 29	66	40
New Hampshire						
Concord	June 6	June 21	Aug. 24	Sept. 8	93	70
Keene	June 3	June 19	Aug. 24	Sept. 9	97	72
New Jersey						
Cape May	April 14	April 28	Oct. 16	Oct. 31	199	177
Newark	April 15	April 26	Oct. 13	Oct. 26	193	181
New Mexico						
Alamogordo	April 20	May 5	Oct. 10	Oct. 22	184	163
Los Alamos	May 23	June 6	Sept. 17	Oct. 2	131	109
New York						
Albany	May 21	June 5	Sept. 12	Sept. 24	126	107
Bridgehampton	May 1	May 15	Oct. 1	Oct. 15	165	148
Elmira	May 25	June 8	Sept. 8	Sept. 21	118	97
Fredonia	May 16	May 31	Sept. 21	Oct. 8	144	118
New York	April 14	April 26	Oct. 19	Oct. 30	199	185
Rochester	May 13	May 30	Sept. 15	Oct. 2	140	115
Syracuse	May 14	May 28	Sept. 18	Oct. 1	140	118
North Carolina						
Asheville	April 27	May 12	Oct. 1	Oct. 14	170	150
Elizabeth City	April 17	May 2	Oct. 11	Oct. 23	189	169
Greensboro	April 23	May 12	Oct. 5	Oct. 17	176	154
Raleigh	April 25	May 11	Oct. 6	Oct. 18	175	157
North Dakota						
Bismarck	May 30	June 22	Aug. 26	Sept. 11	103	78
Minot	May 28	June 11	Aug. 27	Sept. 10	105	83
Ohio						
Akron	May 14	May 29	Sept. 26	Oct. 8	146	128
Cincinnati	April 27	May 12	Oct. 1	Oct. 15	170	149
Columbus	May 7	May 23	Sept. 23	Oct. 4	150	128
Dayton	April 25	May 10	Oct. 2	Oct. 15	173	153
Sandusky	April 27	May 10	Oct. 2	Oct. 17	172	154
Oklahoma						
Lawton	April 10	April 24	Oct. 13	Oct. 25	198	181
Muskogee	April 13	April 27	Oct. 8	Oct. 22	191	173
Woodward	April 21	May 8	Oct. 3	Oct. 17	178	153
Oregon						
Eugene	May 19	June 10	Sept. 15	Oct. 6	139	111
Pendleton	May 6	May 23	Sept. 22	Oct. 7	153	132
Portland	April 29	May 15	Oct. 3	Oct. 20	174	148
Pennsylvania						
Allentown	May 4	May 19	Sept. 22	Oct. 6	155	130
Gettysburg	May 3	May 19	Sept. 23	Oct. 7	156	133
New Castle	May 25	June 8	Sept. 11	Sept. 25	122	105
Williamsport	May 11	May 21	Sept. 19	Oct. 4	146	128
Rhode Island						
Block Island	April 24	May 9	Oct. 13	Oct. 27	185	163
Kingston	May 22	June 5	Sept. 8	Sept. 20	120	102
South Carolina						
Beaufort	March 24	April 13	Oct. 26	Nov. 9	230	204
Charleston	April 1	April 17	Oct. 24	Nov. 5	217	195
Columbia	April 16	April 29	Oct. 13	Oct. 24	190	175
South Dakota						
Huron	May 20	June 4	Sept. 4	Sept. 18	120	97
Rapid City	May 22	June 9	Sept. 8	Sept. 21	120	99
Sioux Falls	May 20	June 4	Sept. 10	Sept. 21	123	104
Tennessee						
Bristol	April 30	May 13	Oct. 1	Oct. 13	165	148
Chattanooga	April 19	May 3	Oct. 9	Oct. 21	185	167
Knoxville	April 9	April 22	Oct. 13	Oct. 27	200	186
Memphis	April 3	April 16	Oct. 18	Oct. 31	210	189
Nashville	April 16	April 30	Oct. 7	Oct. 21	187	170
Texas						
Abilene	April 5	April 19	Oct. 17	Nov. 3	211	189
Amarillo	April 26	May 9	Oct. 8	Oct. 20	176	161
Austin	March 16	March 31	Nov. 1	Nov. 16	244	225
Brownsville	Feb. 6	March 7	Nov. 24	Dec. 24	322	284
Corpus Christi	Feb. 9	March 9	Nov. 23	Dec. 18	311	276
Denton	April 1	April 20	Oct. 19	Nov. 4	216	191
Galveston	Feb. 13	March 15	Nov. 21	Dec. 16	304	267
Lubbock	April 17	May 5	Oct. 8	Oct. 22	187	165
Midland	April 9	April 24	Oct. 15	Oct. 30	203	183
San Antonio	March 23	April 10	Oct. 27	Nov. 14	235	210

Utah

Milford	June 8	June 24	Aug. 30	Sept. 14	97	75
Ogden	May 19	June 3	Sept. 10	Sept. 29	133	111
St. George	April 20	May 7	Oct. 9	Oct. 23	186	160

Vermont

Burlington	May 24	June 8	Sept. 7	Sept. 21	119	98
Montpelier	June 5	June 24	Aug. 26	Sept. 11	98	70

Virginia

Blacksburg	May 14	June 4	Sept. 13	Sept. 28	136	110
Norfolk	April 7	April 23	Oct. 20	Nov. 4	210	185
Richmond	April 24	May 7	Oct. 2	Oct. 15	173	153

Washington

Seattle	April 22	May 14	Oct. 10	Oct. 29	189	161
Spokane	May 23	June 6	Sept. 7	Sept. 21	120	100
Yakima	June 6	June 30	Sept. 1	Sept. 16	101	74

West Virginia

Beckley	May 29	June 13	Aug. 31	Sept. 17	110	87
Clarksburg	May 13	May 31	Sept. 18	Oct. 1	140	117
Martinsburg	May 5	May 21	Sept. 17	Oct. 2	148	127

Wisconsin

Eau Claire	May 23	June 3	Sept. 8	Sept. 19	119	105
Green Bay	May 24	June 9	Sept. 10	Sept. 21	119	99
Milwaukee	May 19	June 1	Sept. 17	Sept. 29	133	113
Wausau	May 22	June 5	Sept. 9	Sept. 21	121	102

Wyoming

Lander	June 4	June 20	Aug. 30	Sept. 14	101	79
Laramie	June 22	July 8	Aug. 14	Aug. 29	67	47
Sheridan	June 8	June 29	Aug. 29	Sept. 10	93	70

The odds of a white Christmas

If you want a white Christmas, head for Fairbanks, Alaska or International Falls, Minn., where there's a 100 percent chance of snow on the ground on Dec. 25. Here are the chances, by percentage, of at least an inch of snow being on the ground on Christmas Day. These odds are based on snowfall records at National Weather Service offices for the places listed. States not listed here have zero odds throughout the state (though under extremely unusual conditions snow may come to some places where the official odds are zero).

City	Percent chance
Alabama	
Birmingham	0
Huntsville	9
Mobile	0
Montgomery	0
Alaska	
Anchorage	87
Barrow	93
Bethel	80
Cold Bay	37
Cordova	46
Fairbanks	100
Juneau	50
King Salmon	79
Kotzebue	87
McGrath	90
Nome	73
St. Paul	43
Arizona	
Flagstaff	50
Phoenix	0
Prescott	0
Tucson	0
Winslow	16
Yuma	0
Arkansas	
Fort Smith	0
Little Rock	3
Texarkana	0
California	
Bakersfield	0
Bishop	4
Burbank	0
Eureka	0
Fresno	0
Long Beach	0
Los Angeles	0
Oakland	0
Red Bluff	0
Sacramento	0
San Diego	0
San Francisco	0
Santa Maria	0
Colorado	
Alamosa	47
Colo. Springs	20
Denver	23
Grand Junction	27
Pueblo	27
Connecticut	
Bridgeport	33
Hartford	43
New Haven	43
Delaware	
Wilmington	26
D.C.	
Washington	17
Idaho	
Boise	16
Idaho Falls	30
Lewiston	3
Pocatello	43
Illinois	
Cairo	6
Chicago	43
Moline	33
Peoria	30
Rockford	36
Springfield	26
Evansville	10
Fort Wayne	43
Indianapolis	26
South Bend	56
Iowa	
Burlington	33
Des Moines	46
Dubuque	60
Sioux City	43
Waterloo	50
Kansas	
Concordia	36
Dodge City	23
Goodland	26
Topeka	23
Wichita	17
Kentucky	
Lexington	12
Louisville	16
Maine	
Caribou	97
Portland	63
Maryland	
Baltimore	20
Frederick	27
Massachusetts	
Boston	30
Nantucket	10
Pittsfield	44
Worcester	75
Michigan	
Alpena	73

City	Percent chance
Detroit	40
Escanaba	62
Flint	54
Grand Rapids	60
Lansing	50
Marquette	90
Muskegon	53
St. Ste. Marie	93
Minnesota	
Duluth	90
Int'l Falls	100
Minneapolis	73
Rochester	71
St. Cloud	59
Missouri	
Columbia	27
Kansas City	20
St. Joseph	30
St. Louis	13
Springfield	7
Montana	
Billings	53
Glasgow	52
Great Falls	43
Havre	43
Helena	57
Kalispell	60
Missoula	57
Nebraska	
Grand Island	33
Lincoln	37
Norfolk	40
North Platte	33
Omaha	40
Scottsbluff	29
Valentine	40
Nevada	
Elko	47
Ely	30
Las Vegas	0
Reno	7
Winnemucca	23
New Hampshire	
Concord	67

New Jersey	
Atlantic City	7
Newark	27
Trenton	23
New Mexico	
Albuquerque	7
Clayton	12
Raton	13
Roswell	3
New York	
Albany	43
Binghamton	70
Buffalo	50
New York	23
Rochester	60
Schenectady	64
Syracuse	67
North Carolina	
Asheville	7
Cape Hatteras	0
Charlotte	3
Greensboro	13
Raleigh	3
Wilmington	0
Winston-Salem	15
North Dakota	
Bismarck	60
Devils Lake	79
Fargo	77
Williston	53
Ohio	
Akron-Canton	43
Cincinnati	17
Cleveland	37
Columbus	23
Dayton	30
Mansfield	60
Sandusky	38
Toledo	40
Youngstown	43
Oklahoma	
Oklahoma City	0
Tulsa	3
Oregon	
Astoria	0
Burns	48

Eugene	0
Medford	3
Pendleton	0
Portland	0
Roseburg	7
Salem	0
Pennsylvania	
Allentown	33
Erie	47
Harrisburg	33
Philadelphia	23
Pittsburgh	30
Reading	33
Scranton	53
Williamsport	43
Rhode Island	
Block Island	17
Providence	33
South Carolina	
Charleston	0
Columbia	0
Florence	0
Greenville	7
South Dakota	
Huron	37
Rapid City	30
Sioux Falls	43
Tennessee	
Bristol	18
Chattanooga	3
Knoxville	10
Memphis	0
Nashville	10
Oak Ridge	12
Utah	
Milford	29
Salt Lake City	43
Wendover	3
Vermont	
Burlington	77
Virginia	
Lynchburg	17
Norfolk	10
Richmond	10
Roanoke	27

Washington	
Olympia	0
Seattle	7
Spokane	33
Walla Walla	3
Yakima	20
West Virginia	
Charleston	26
Elkins	19
Huntington	24
Parkersburg	23
Wisconsin	
Green Bay	60
LaCrosse	63
Madison	57
Milwaukee	40
Wyoming	
Casper	40
Cheyenne	23
Lander	63
Sheridan	67

How the sun affects skin

This table shows the four general skin types, how to tell the differences between them by noting the color of skin that's not exposed to the sun, and the usual effects of the sun. The types are general, and exposure to the sun can affect people with the same general type in different ways.

Skin types and solar effects

Skin type	Skin color in an area unexposed to the sun	Usual effects of sun exposure
I Never tans, always burns	Pale or milky white, alabaster	Develops red sunburn, painful swelling, skin peels.
II Sometimes tans, usually burns	Very light brown, sometimes freckles	Usually burns, pinkish or red coloring appears. Can gradually develop a light brown tan.
III Usually tans, sometimes burns	Light tan, brown, or olive; distinctly pigmented	Infrequently burns, tans moderately rapidly.
IV Always tans, rarely burns	Brown, dark brown, or black	Rarely burns, tans quickly.

Ultraviolet rays at fault

Ultraviolet radiation from the sun, which is only about 6 percent of the solar radiation reaching earth, causes skin and eye damage. About 48 percent of the solar radiation reaching Earth is visible light and 46 percent is infrared energy.

Two frequency ranges of ultraviolet radiation reach the ground, UV-A and UV-B. They act in different ways, but both can be harmful.

The amount of ultraviolet radiation reaching the earth depends first on how high the sun is in the sky.

The tropics, where the sun is directly overhead or nearly overhead all year, receive the most solar energy, including ultraviolet. Here, and elsewhere, the highest amounts reach the earth around noon, when the sun is the highest in the sky.

Risks of being sunburned or otherwise harmed by ultraviolet radiation are considerably less before 10 a.m. and after 3 a.m., when the sun is lower in

Ultraviolet doses by latitude, month

Latitude	Jan. 21	Feb. 21	March 21	April 21	May 21	June 21	July 21	Aug. 21	Sept. 21	Oct. 21	Nov. 21	Dec.21
60	5	15	32	60	87	106	104	77	41	16	5	3
50	17	32	57	95	127	143	144	122	75	37	18	13
40	40	63	99	145	176	199	206	174	127	76	44	34
30	90	132	179	218	235	248	250	234	182	131	91	80
20	156	201	249	269	288	292	296	293	256	200	156	143
10	235	272	311	321	289	275	280	290	280	247	212	220
0	292	312	325	303	271	254	270	307	325	316	287	272
-10	321	331	315	266	223	208	230	267	309	328	313	304
-20	312	301	262	199	106	129	147	190	247	277	288	292
-30	268	250	200	134	89	73	83	122	173	213	244	260
-40	214	184	135	78	55	33	39	65	108	155	192	216
-50	158	124	80	38	19	13	18	34	68	106	141	159
-60	112	78	43	16	6	3	6	16	40	73	102	117

Source: Orbital Sciences Corp.

Using the UV table

The table above shows the maximum doses of UV-B energy capable of doing skin damage, in milliwatts per square meter, reaching the ground at various latitudes on the 21st of each month.

Sea-level figures are given. Actual amounts change with the amount of ozone overhead and cloud cover. These figures are based on average amounts of ozone.

Actual amounts at various times and places aren't as important as using the numbers to compare amounts of ultraviolet radiation you are familiar with to the amounts likely at a vacation spot.

For example, someone used to going to the beach in New Jersey, which is around 40 degrees north latitude, sees that in July the figure is 206.

A New Jersey resident planning a vacation in Hawaii, at 20 degrees north, in March, could look at the chart and see the number is 249. This tells right away that the sun is stronger in Hawaii in March than in New Jersey in July. Note the March figure of 99 for 40 degrees north. The March sun in Hawaii is about two and a half times stronger than the March sun in New Jersey.

What UV exposure levels mean

(Time to burn and actions apply to people with a Type II, fair skin that sometimes tans and usually burns.)

UV exposure

level	Time to burn	Actions to take at noon
Minimal	60 minutes	Apply SPF sunscreen.
Low	45 minutes	Apply SPF sunscreen, wear a hat.
Moderate	30 minutes	Apply SPF 15°, wear a hat.
High	15 – 24 minutes	Apply SPF 15 to 30 sunscreen, wear a hat and sunglasses. Limit midday exposure.
Very high	10 minutes or less	Apply SPF 30° sunscreen. Wear a hat, sunglasses and protective clothing. Best time outdoors is before 10 a.m. or after 3 p.m.

Clouds, shade don't stop sunburn

The danger of sunburn is obvious when the sun is shining directly onto bare skin. But clouds, a beach umbrella or water don't block all of the sun's ultraviolet rays that cause sunburn and increase the danger of skin cancer.

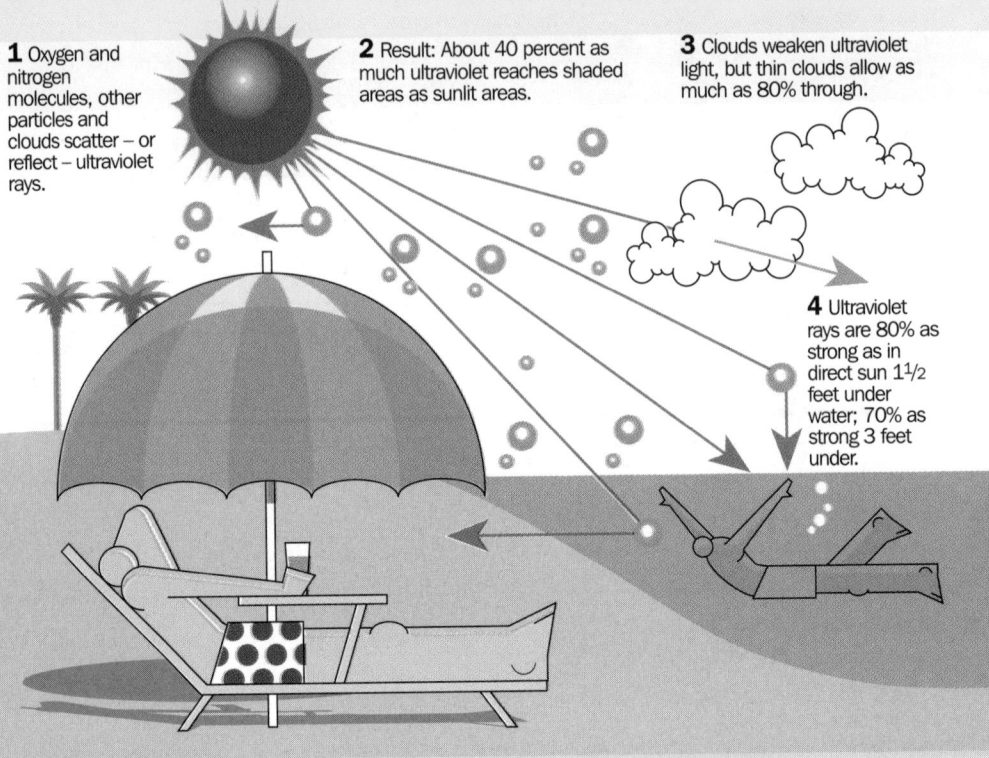

1 Oxygen and nitrogen molecules, other particles and clouds scatter – or reflect – ultraviolet rays.

2 Result: About 40 percent as much ultraviolet reaches shaded areas as sunlit areas.

3 Clouds weaken ultraviolet light, but thin clouds allow as much as 80% through.

4 Ultraviolet rays are 80% as strong as in direct sun 1½ feet under water; 70% as strong 3 feet under.

Source: Orbital Sciences Corp.

the sky, than around noon.

Altitude also plays a role. Ultraviolet radiation increases with altitude because there is less atmosphere to reduce it. In general, the amount of ultraviolet radiation increases by 2 percent for each 1,000 feet in altitude.

Ozone, a form of oxygen with three instead of the normal two atoms per molecule, reduces the amount of ultraviolet radiation reaching the Earth. In fact, ozone in the stratosphere high above the Earth blocks most of the most harmful kinds of ultraviolet radiation from reaching the ground.

Amounts of ozone in the stratosphere vary naturally by latitude and time of the year, but since 1979, the average total amount has decreased by about 4 percent. Scientists have established that various man-made substances are responsible.

The 4 percent figure is a global average that includes virtually no decrease in the tropics to decreases as high as 20 percent in Antarctica and 9 percent in the Arctic.

Researchers are working to understand the effects of these decreases in ozone and resulting increases in ultraviolet energy reaching some parts of the Earth.

Eventually, a thinner ozone layer could lead to an increase in skin cancer and other problems caused by ultraviolet radiation. But the current increasing skin cancer rate in the United States cannot be blamed on ozone loss.

Since skin cancer requires years of exposure to the sun, today's skin cancers are caused by exposure to the sun that began before ozone began decreasing. Scientists believe the increasing amount of time Americans have been spending in the sun since World War II, along with fashion changes toward clothing that covers less of the body, probably account for most of the increase in skin cancer.

Growing concern about the dangers of too much sun have led weather services in many nations to began ultraviolet, or "sunburn" fore-

Average number of days a year with above 90° temperatures

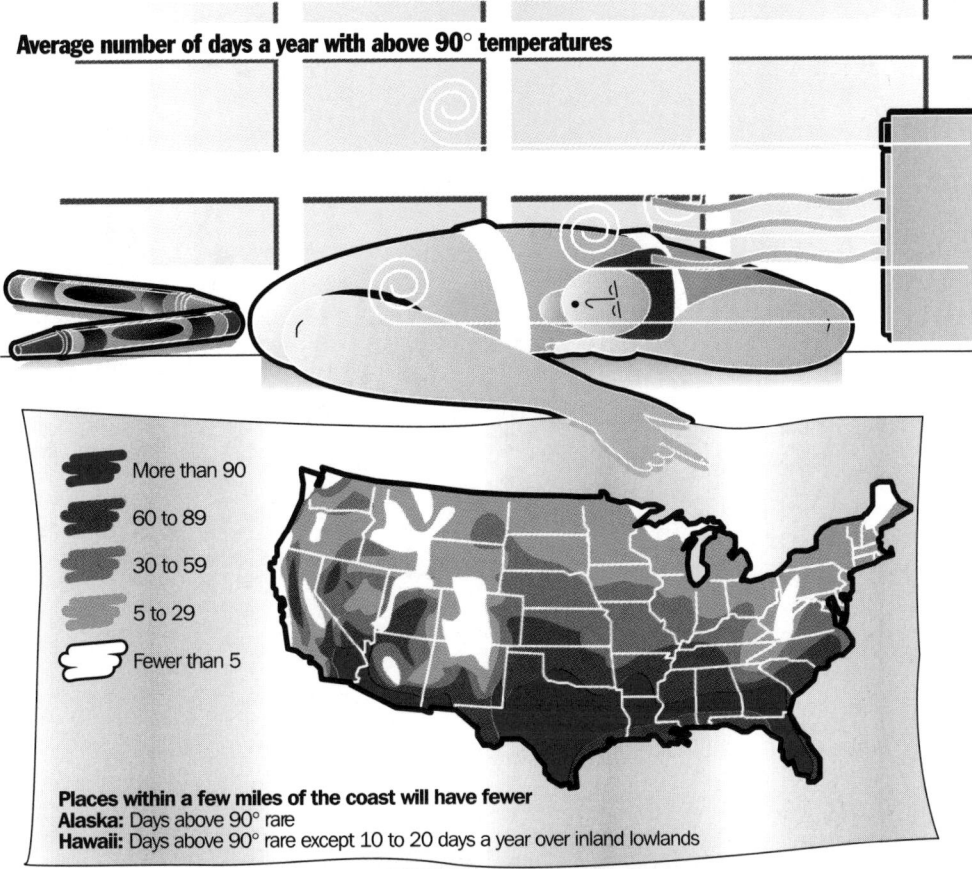

More than 90

60 to 89

30 to 59

5 to 29

Fewer than 5

Places within a few miles of the coast will have fewer
Alaska: Days above 90° rare
Hawaii: Days above 90° rare except 10 to 20 days a year over inland lowlands

Source: National Climatic Data Center

casts. The U.S. National Weather Service and two private forecasting firms in the U.S. began such forecasts in June 1994.

Different numerical scales were used for U.S. ultraviolet forecasts during 1994.

But late that summer an international meeting in Switzerland brought together forecasters to begin working out a common scale that everyone would use. A common, world-wide scale is likely eventually, but no one knows where such a scale will be adopted.

No matter what numerical scale is used, the numbers are grouped in general categories ranging from minimal to very high. The table on Page 369 gives the time to burn and actions to take for each of the five general categories.

Protection from the sun

The best protection against the sun is to stay out of the sun. But no one wants to stay indoors all of the time. The best time to enjoy the sun, espe-

cially in tropical locations or places near the tropics, is before 10 a.m. and after 3 p.m. local time.

Clouds do not screen out all ultraviolet radiation. In fact, to screen out most ultraviolet radiation, the clouds have to be so low and thick that it's probably not a pleasant day to be outdoors. Also, ultraviolet radiation is reflected by sand, snow and water. And, ultraviolet radiation is scattered by the atmosphere. Being in the shade under a beach umbrella does not provide complete protection from ultraviolet radiation.

Wearing a hat with a wide brim is a good idea to protect the eyes, ears and neck. Most clothing, except white, reflect or absorb ultraviolet radiation, but wet cotton, no matter what color, can let a large amount of ultraviolet radiation through. A wet T-shirt provides little protection.

Sunglasses that block ultraviolet radiation are vital to protect the eyes from the sun. Eye doctors can test eyewear for ultraviolet protection.

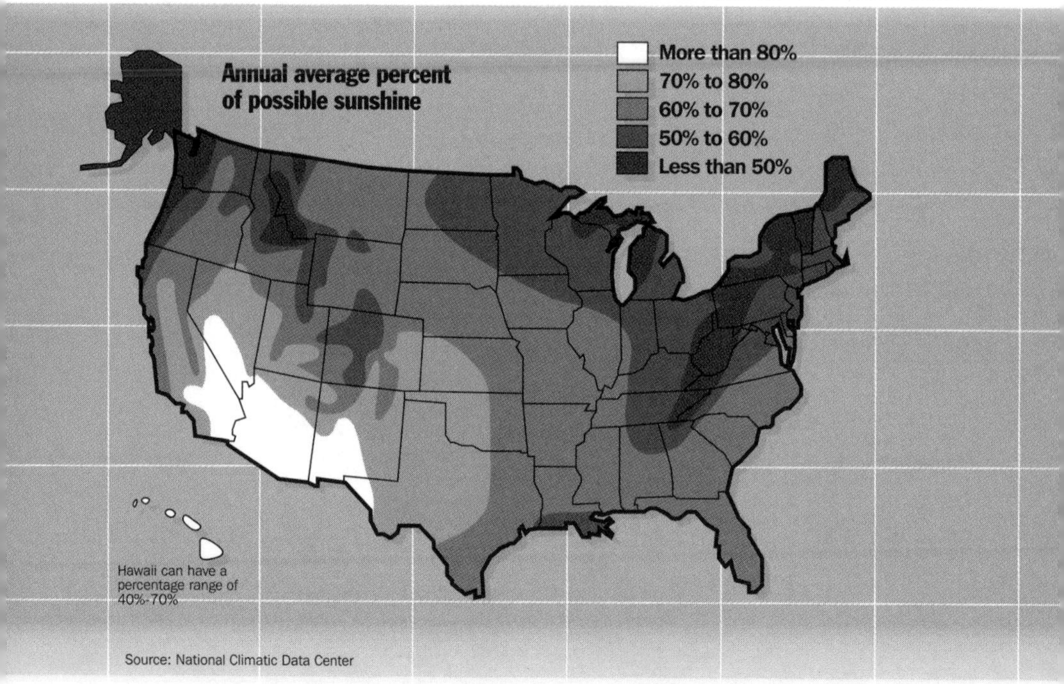

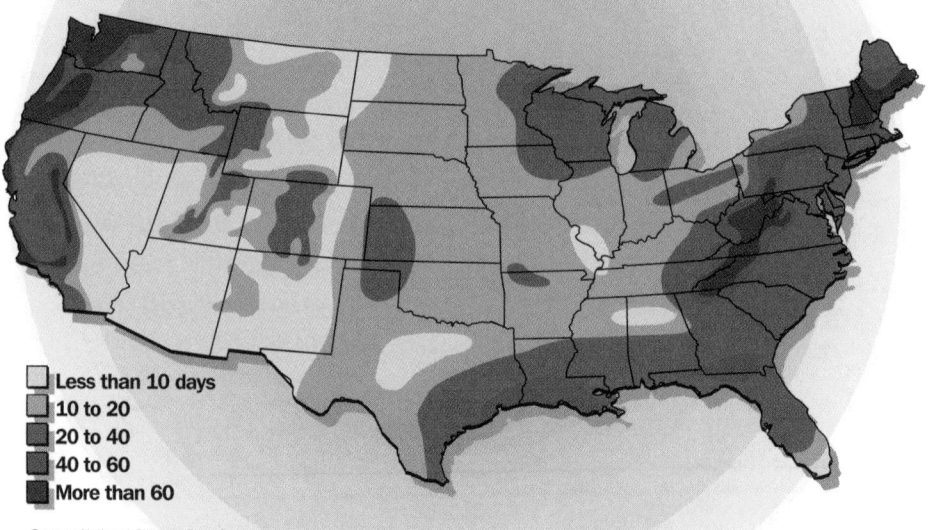

Annual average percent of possible sunshine

- More than 80%
- 70% to 80%
- 60% to 70%
- 50% to 60%
- Less than 50%

Hawaii can have a percentage range of 40%-70%

Source: National Climatic Data Center

Annual average number of days with heavy fog – visibility of ¼ mile or less:

- Less than 10 days
- 10 to 20
- 20 to 40
- 40 to 60
- More than 60

Source: National Climatic Data Center

Glossary

Glossary

Acre foot: The amount of water needed to cover one acre under a foot of water.

Advection fog: Fog caused by the movement of humid air over cold land or cold water.

Air mass: A large body of air with relatively uniform characteristics, such as temperature and humidity.

Antarctic Circle: Latitude 66 degrees, 33 minutes south. Area to the south is the Antarctic.

Arctic Circle: Latitude 66 degrees, 33 minutes north. Area to the north is the Arctic.

Atmosphere: Air surrounding the Earth.

Beaufort Wind Scale: Scale used to describe wind speed, devised in 1806 by British Admiral Francis Beaufort to classify winds at sea.

Bermuda High: Strong high pressure area off the U.S. Atlantic Coast, generally extending eastward past Bermuda.

Biosphere: The Earth's living things. Often used in reference to how they affect the atmosphere and oceans.

Blizzard: Snow falling with sustained winds faster than 35 mph and visibility of one-quarter mile or less over an extended time period.

Chinook: Warm wind blowing down the east slope of the Rocky Mountains.

Chlorofluorocarbons (CFCs): Man-made substances used mainly now as coolants and electronic parts cleaners, which have been shown to destroy stratospheric ozone when they break down.

Climate: Average weather over a long time period. Climate normals are the averages of records over 30 years.

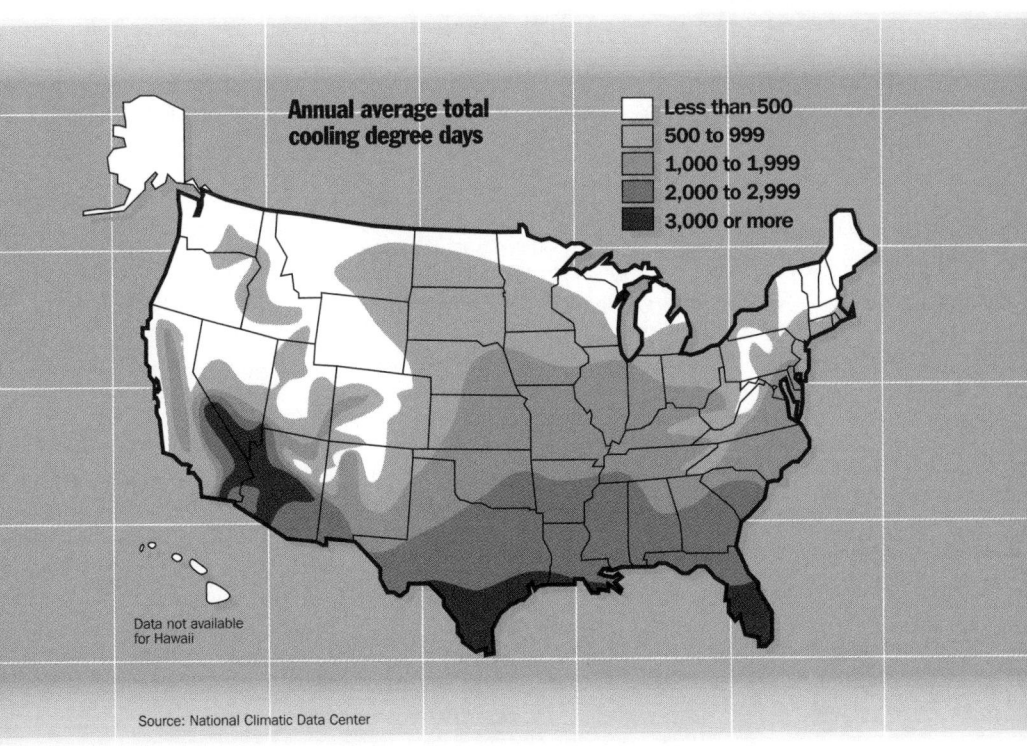

Annual average total cooling degree days

- Less than 500
- 500 to 999
- 1,000 to 1,999
- 2,000 to 2,999
- 3,000 or more

Data not available for Hawaii

Source: National Climatic Data Center

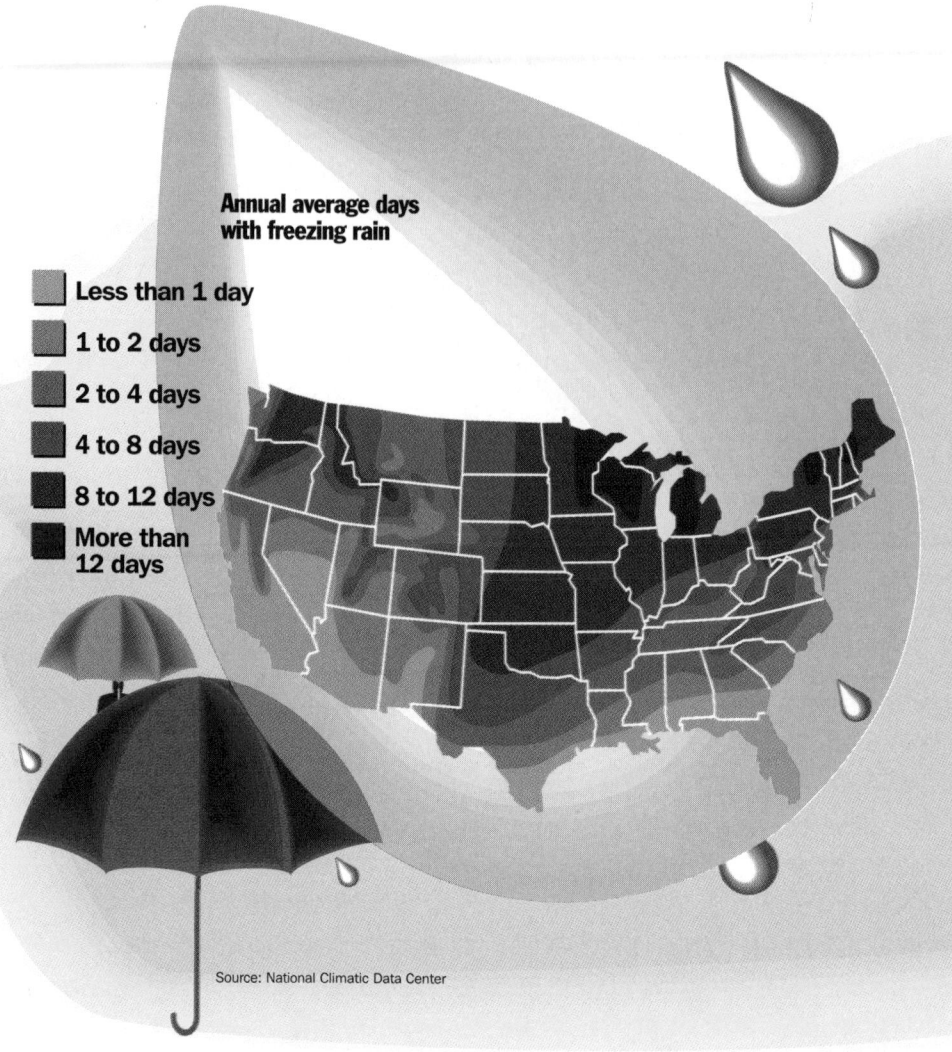

Annual average days with freezing rain

- Less than 1 day
- 1 to 2 days
- 2 to 4 days
- 4 to 8 days
- 8 to 12 days
- More than 12 days

Source: National Climatic Data Center

Climate Analysis Center: The U.S. National Weather Service office in Camp Springs, Md., that follows global climate trends and produces monthly and seasonal forecasts.

Climate model: Mathematical model containing equations that describe climatic interactions.

Cold front: Warm-cold air boundary with the cold air advancing.

Condensation: Change of a vapor to liquid.

Continental air mass: Air mass that forms over land, making it generally dry. It may be warm or cold.

Continental climate: Climate typical of places in the temperate zones far from any ocean. Such climates have warm summers and cold winters.

Continental Divide: The line along a mountain range between streams flowing in different directions. In the U.S., the term is usually used to refer to the line along the Rocky Mountains between streams flowing toward the Mississippi River and eventually the Gulf of Mexico and streams flowing into rivers leading to the Pacific Ocean.

Cooling degree days: Measure of need for air conditioning. Each degree of a day's average temperature above 65°F is one cooling degree day. For example, a day with an average temperature of 70°F has 5 cooling degree days.

Cyclone: An area of low-atmospheric pressure with winds blowing around it, counterclockwise in the Northern Hemisphere, clockwise in the South-

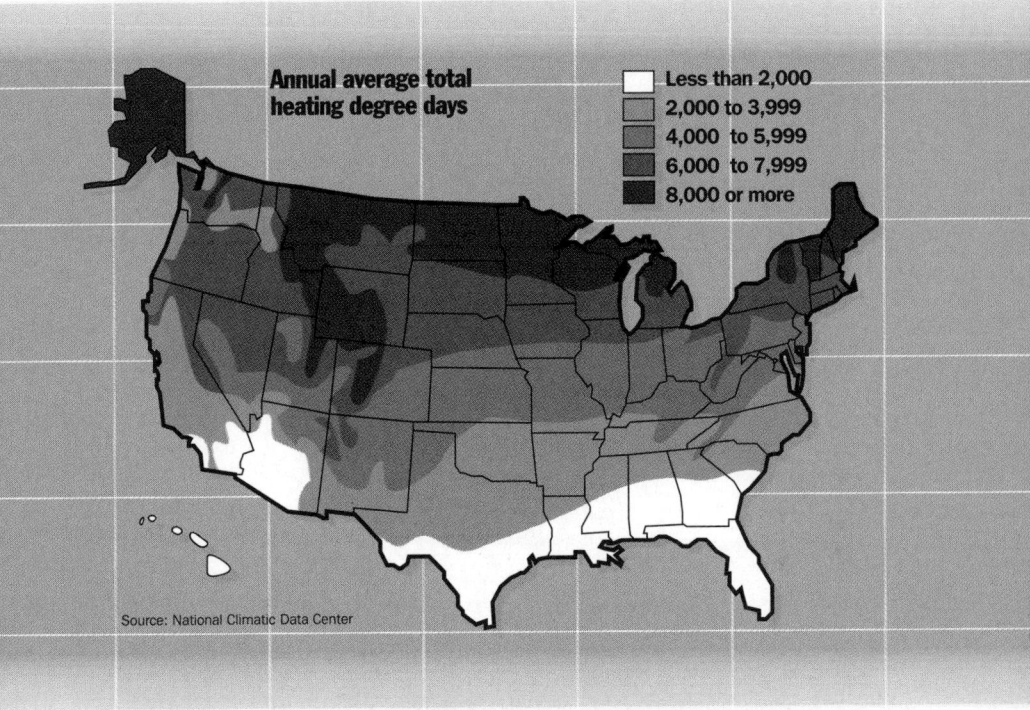

Annual average total heating degree days

Less than 2,000
2,000 to 3,999
4,000 to 5,999
6,000 to 7,999
8,000 or more

Source: National Climatic Data Center

ern Hemisphere.

Dew: Water droplets on objects, such as grass, formed by condensation of water vapor.

Dew point: Measure of humidity given in terms of temperature at which water vapor will begin condensing to form dew, clouds or fog.

Doppler radar: Radar that measures speed and direction of a moving object, such as wind. The National Weather Service program to install Doppler radars is called NEXRAD (Next Generation Weather Radar).

Downburst: Wind blasting down from a thunderstorm or shower.

Downslope effect: Warming of air as it comes down a mountain slope or hillside.

Drizzle: Falling water drops with a diameter less than .02 inch.

Drought: Abnormal dryness for a particular region.

Easterly wave: A distur-

bance in the easterly winds of the tropics. The air pressure is low, but winds are not blowing in a circular pattern as in a tropical depression. A few easterly waves grow into tropical depressions and then into tropical storms or hurricanes. Most bring only rain showers and shifting winds. Also called a tropical wave.

El Nino: Linked ocean and atmospheric events, which have worldwide effects, characterized by warming of water in the tropical Pacific from around the International Date Line to the coast of Peru.

Equinox: Times when the sun crosses the equator. The spring or vernal equinox occurs around March 21, the autumnal equinox around Sept. 21.

Extratropical cyclone: Large-scale weather system that forms outside the tropics with a low-pressure center.

Flash flood: Flooding with a rapid water rise.

Fog: Cloud with its base on the ground.

Forcing: In climate science, any outside force that affects the climate, such as a volcanic eruption, a change in solar energy reaching Earth, or a warming caused by gases such as carbon dioxide added to the air.

Freezing: The phase change of a liquid to a solid.

Freezing rain: Supercooled raindrops that turn to ice when they come in contact with something.

Front: Boundary between air masses of different densities, and usually different temperatures.

Frost: Water vapor that has turned to ice on an object.

Fujita Scale: Wind damage scale created by tornado researcher T. Theodore Fujita. Usually applied to tornado damage, but sometimes used for other wind storms. Damage categories are F0 through F5. They are: F0 (wind up to 72 mph,

How often hail falls

Hail – balls of ice that fall from thunderstorms – is relatively rare across the USA. But it can cause major damage to crops, especially on the Plains.

Annual average number of days with hail

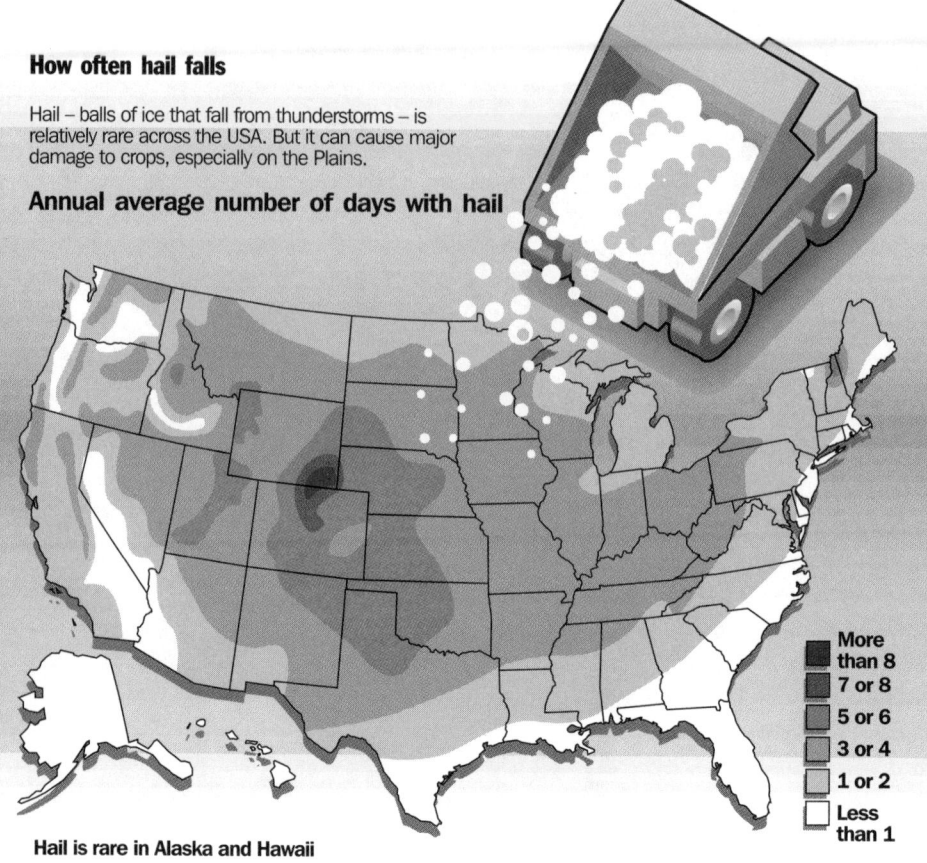

■	More than 8
■	7 or 8
■	5 or 6
■	3 or 4
■	1 or 2
□	Less than 1

Hail is rare in Alaska and Hawaii

Source: National Climatic Data Center

light damage); F1 (wind 73 to 112, moderate damage); F2 (wind 113 to 157 mph, considerable damage); F3 (wind 158 to 206 mph, severe damage); F4 (wind 207 to 260 mph, devastating damage); F5 (wind above 261 mph, incredible damage).

Funnel cloud: A rotating column of air extending from a cloud, but not reaching the ground.

Glaze: A coat of smooth ice created when supercooled drops of water spread out before freezing.

GOES: Geostationary Operational Environmental Satellites, which are U.S. weather satellites in orbits that keep them above

the same place on the equator.

Graupel: Icy precipitation created when falling snowflakes collide with tiny drops of supercooled water, which freeze to the snowflakes.

Greenhouse effect: Warming of a planet caused by the absorption and re-emission of infrared energy by molecules in the atmosphere.

Ground fog: A layer of fog, often less than 300 feet high, that forms when the ground cools, also called radiation fog.

Gulf Stream: A warm ocean current that flows from the Gulf of Mexico across the Atlantic to near the European Coast. It helps warm Western Europe.

Gust front: Wind flowing out from a thunderstorm.

Hail: Balls of ice that grow in thunderstorm updrafts.

Heat lightning: Glowing flash in clouds. No thunder is heard because heat lightning is too far away.

Heating degree day: Measure of the need for heating. Each degree of a day's average temperature below 65°F is one heating degree day. For example, a day with an average temperature of 60°F has 5 heating degree days.

High: An area of high-atmospheric pressure, also called an anticyclone.

Hurricane: Tropical cyclone

Annual average precipitation

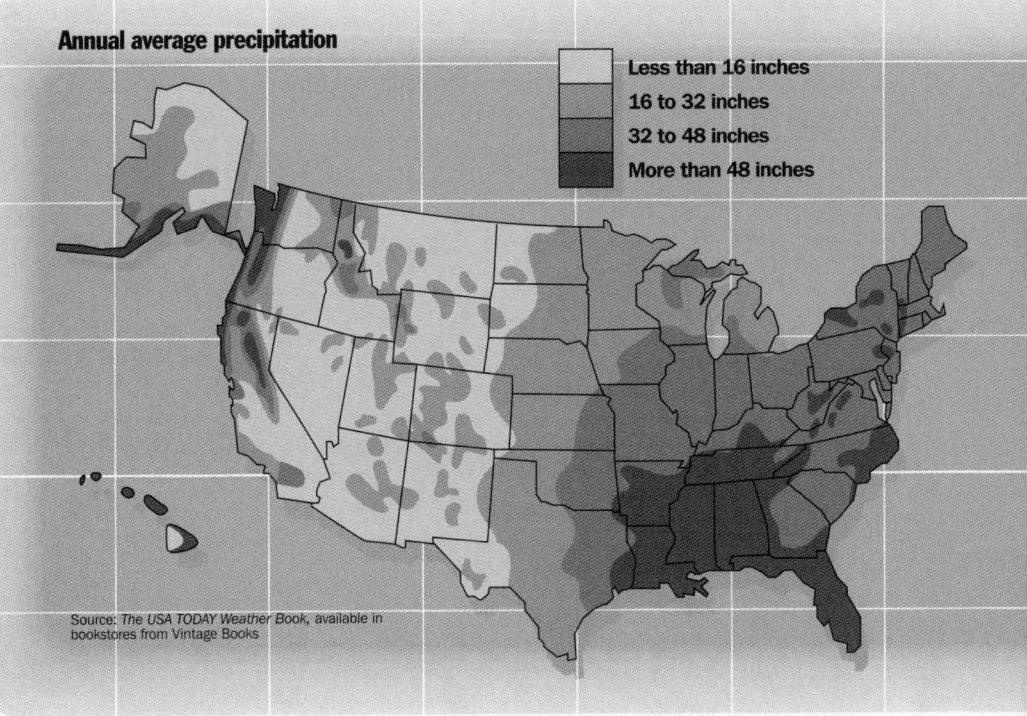

Less than 16 inches
16 to 32 inches
32 to 48 inches
More than 48 inches

Source: *The USA TODAY Weather Book*, available in bookstores from Vintage Books

with winds of 74 mph or more.

Hydrosphere: The Earth's water.

Jet stream: High altitude river of wind that steers storms. It is a narrow band of upper-atmosphere wind with speeds greater than 57 mph.

Lake effect: Clouds, rain and snow caused by cold air flowing over large bodies of warmer water, such as the Great Lakes in the U.S.

Lightning: Visible discharge of electricity produced by a thunderstorm.

Low: Area of low-atmospheric pressure.

Maritime air mass: Air mass that forms over an ocean, making it humid. It may be warm or cold.

Maritime climate: Climate typical of places near an ocean, characterized by small differences in average summer (usually cooler) and winter (usually warmer) temperatures than

inland places at the same latitude.

Mesocyclone: Rotating, upward-moving column of air in a thunderstorm that can spawn tornadoes.

Microburst: Downburst less than 2.5 miles in diameter.

Mid-latitudes: Region of the Earth outside the polar and tropical regions, between latitudes 23.5 degrees and 66.5 degrees.

Monsoon climate: Climate characterized by wet and dry seasons caused by persistent, widespread, seasonal winds. Usually summer winds from the ocean bring rain, while winter winds from the land are dry. Used informally to refer to the wet season of such a climate and the rain that falls during the wet season.

Mountain winds: Winds that blow either up or down mountains, caused by different rates of heating and cooling of mountaintops and valleys.

Multicell storms: Thunderstorms consisting of clusters of single-cell thunderstorms.

National Climatic Data Center (NCDC): Keeps climate records. It's part of the National Oceanic and Atmospheric Administration Center in Asheville, N.C.

National Hurricane Center (NHC): A part of National Weather Service in Coral Gables, Fla. It tracks and forecasts hurricanes and other weather in the tropical Atlantic, Gulf of Mexico, Caribbean Sea, and parts of the Pacific.

National Meteorological Center (NMC): A part of the National Weather Service in Camp Springs, Md. It prepares worldwide computer forecasts. Hurricane and Severe Storms centers are part of NMC.

National Severe Storms Forecast Center: A part of the National Weather Service in Kansas City, Mo. Issues watches

Where thunderstorms strike

For anyone who's afraid of lightning, Hawaii, Alaska and the West Coast are the places to go to escape thunderstorms. Places with the most thunderstorms are parts of Colorado and New Mexico, states along the Gulf Coast and Georgia. But central Florida is the nation's thunderstorm capital.

Annual average days with thunderstorms

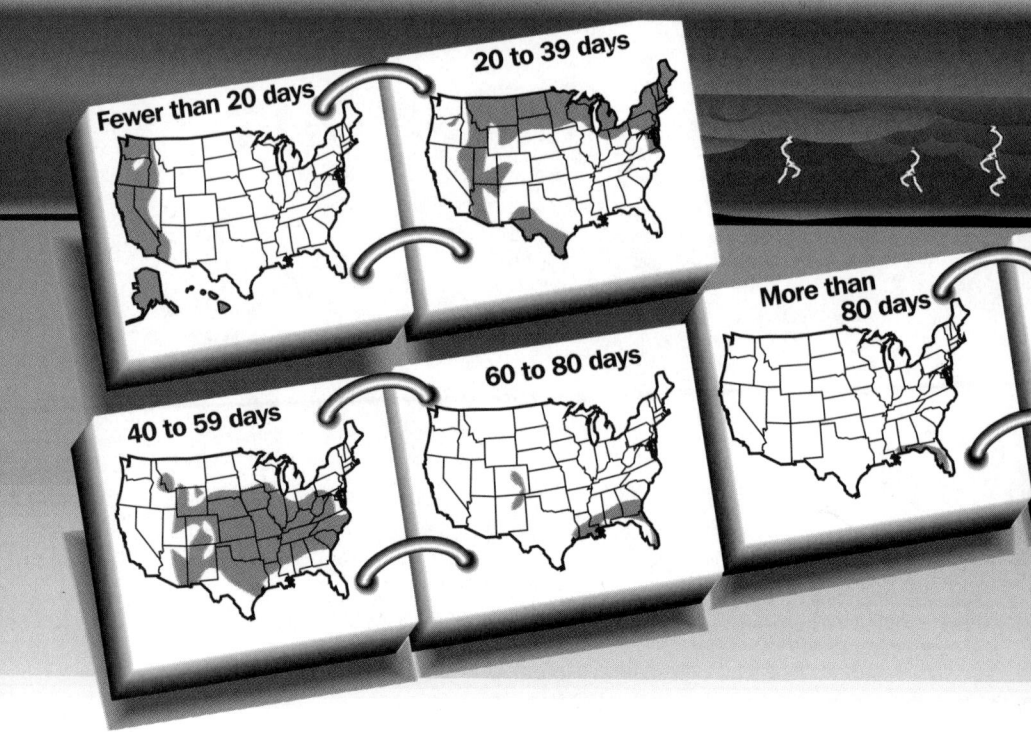

Source: National Climatic Data Center

for severe thunderstorms and tornadoes across the U.S.

National Severe Storms Laboratory (NSSL): Part of National Oceanic and Atmospheric Administration in Norman, Okla. Studies severe thunderstorms.

National Weather Service: U.S. federal agency that observes and forecasts weather. Formerly, the U.S. Weather Bureau. It is part of the National Oceanic and Atmospheric Administration, which is part of the Department of Commerce.

NEXRAD: Next Generation Weather Radar system being installed by the National Weather Service, the Defense Depart-

ment and the Federal Aviation Administration.

100-year-floods: Water levels that, on average, should occur once a century. This is the same as a water level with a 100 to 1 chance of occurring in any single year.

Ozone: Form of oxygen with molecules that consist of three oxygen atoms compared to two atoms for ordinary oxygen molecules.

Ozone hole: The destruction of about 40 percent of the ozone in the stratosphere over Antarctica each spring.

Polar regions: Regions of the Earth north of 66.5 degrees north latitude around the North

Pole, and south of 66.5 degrees south latitude around the South Pole.

Precipitation: Liquid or frozen water that falls from clouds as rain, drizzle, snow, hail, sleet or graupel. In climate records precipitation is the amount of liquid water; rain plus the water obtained when frozen precipitation melts.

Precipitation fog: Fog that forms when precipitation falls into cool air.

Prefrontal squall lines: Lines of thunderstorms ahead of an advancing cold front.

Rain: Falling water drops with a diameter greater than 0.02 inch.

Anatomy of an ice storm

Freezing rain and sleet storms in the East and Midwest made the winter of 1994 especially harsh. Winter storms combined just the right amounts of warm and frigid air to cover roads and sidewalks with thick ice.

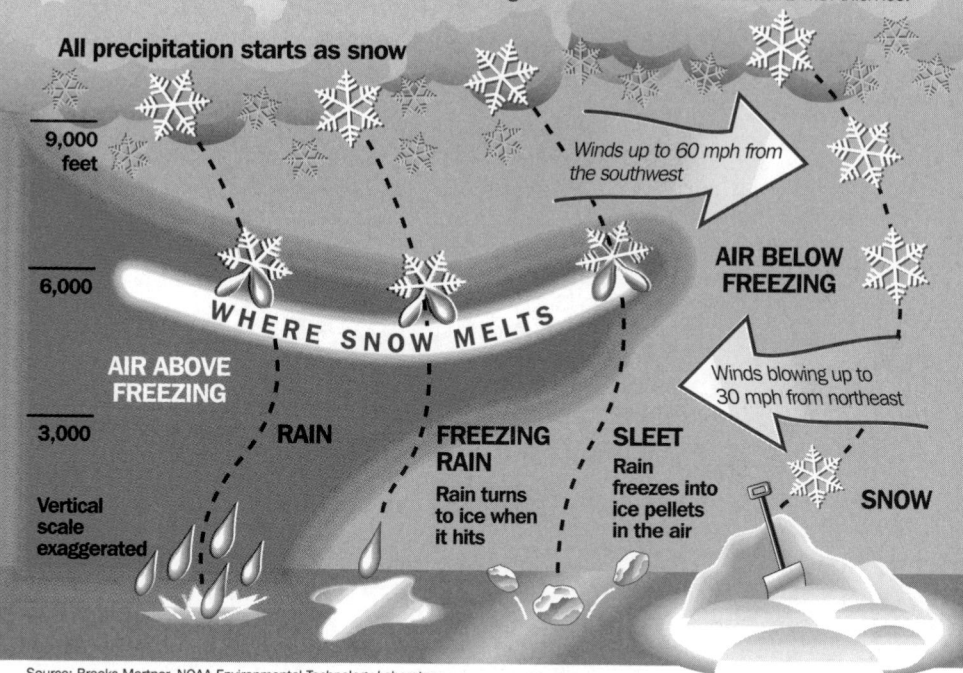

All precipitation starts as snow

9,000 feet

6,000

3,000

Vertical scale exaggerated

Winds up to 60 mph from the southwest

AIR BELOW FREEZING

WHERE SNOW MELTS

AIR ABOVE FREEZING

Winds blowing up to 30 mph from northeast

RAIN

FREEZING RAIN
Rain turns to ice when it hits

SLEET
Rain freezes into ice pellets in the air

SNOW

Source: Brooks Martner, NOAA Environmental Technology Laboratory

Relative humidity: The ratio of the amount of water vapor actually in the air compared to the amount the air can hold at its temperature and pressure. This is expressed as a percentage.

River Forecast Centers: National Weather Service offices responsible for flood forecasting and, in some cases, water-supply forecasting.

Saffir-Simpson Hurricane Damage Potential Scale: A 1-5 scale, developed by Robert Simpson and Herbert Saffir, that measures hurricane intensity.

Sea breeze: Winds blowing inland from any body of water.

Severe thunderstorm: Thunderstorm with winds faster than 57 mph or hailstones three-quarters of an inch or larger in diameter.

Shower: Intermittent precipitation, either rain or snow, of short duration, which may be light or heavy.

Sleet: In the U.S., generally refers to frozen raindrops.

Solstice: The two points in the Earth's orbit at which the sun is the farthest north or farthest south of the equator. The summer solstice occurs around June 21; the winter solstice around Dec. 21.

Snow: Precipitation composed of ice crystals.

Spring tides: Tides that occur at full and new moons and that generally bring the month's highest high tides and lowest low tides.

Squall line: Line of thunderstorms.

Stationary front: A warm-cold air boundary with neither cold nor warm air advancing.

Storm surge: Quickly rising ocean water levels associated

with hurricanes and other ocean storms that can cause widespread flooding.

Storm tracks: Paths that storms generally follow.

Stratosphere: Layer of the atmosphere from about 7 to 30 miles up.

Supercell: Fierce thunderstorm that usually lasts several hours, often spinning out a series of strong tornadoes.

Temperate climate: Climate typical of the regions of the Earth between the tropics of Cancer and Capricorn and the Arctic and Antarctic circles. Such climates have distinct winter and summer seasons.

Temperate zones: Areas from roughly 30 degrees to 60 degrees latitude in both hemispheres.

Terminal Doppler Weather Radar (TDWR): Doppler radars

Annual average temperature range

Differences between average temperatures of warmest and coldest months

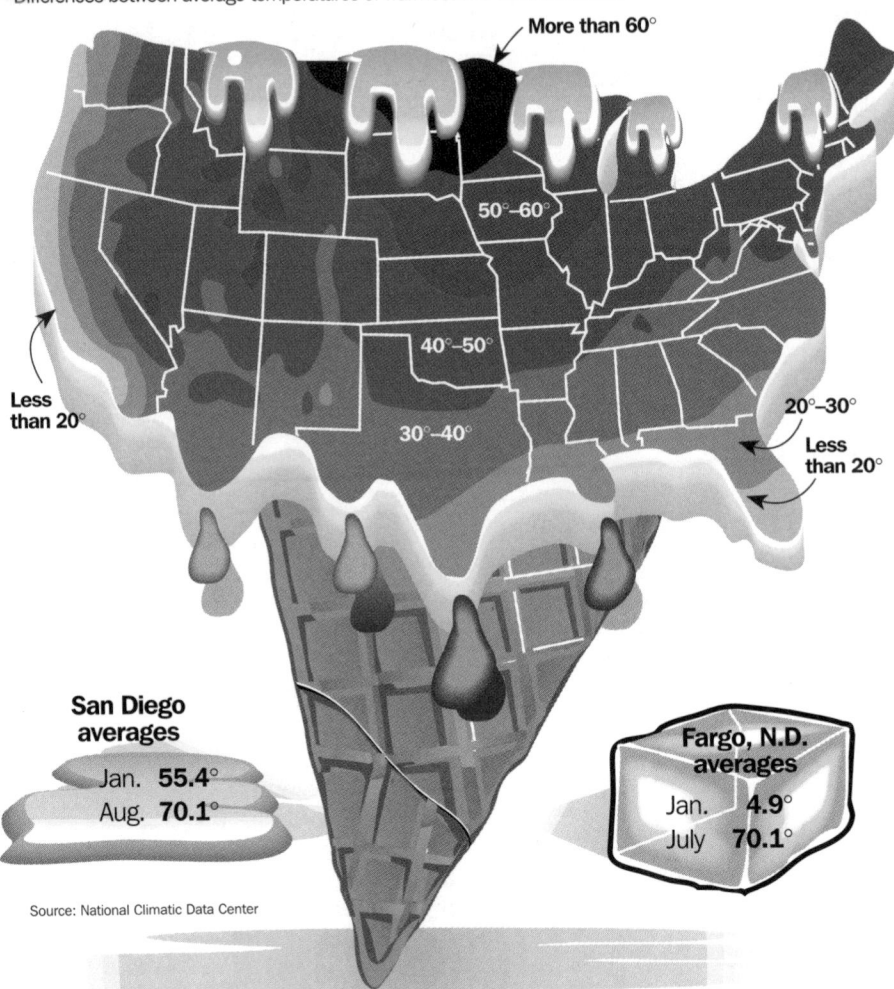

More than 60°

50°–60°

40°–50°

30°–40°

20°–30°

Less than 20°

Less than 20°

San Diego averages

Jan. 55.4°
Aug. 70.1°

Fargo, N.D. averages

Jan. 4.9°
July 70.1°

Source: National Climatic Data Center

being installed at major U.S. airports to detect microbursts.

Thunder: Sound produced by a lightning discharge.

Thunderstorms: Localized storms that produce lightning and therefore thunder.

Tides: Movements of water, the Earth's crust and the atmosphere caused by gravitational pull of the moon and sun.

Tornado: Strong, rotating column of air extending from the base of a cloud to the ground.

Trade winds: Global-scale winds in the tropics that blow generally toward the west in both hemispheres.

Tropical climate: Climate typical of areas from the Tropic of Capricorn north across the Equator to the Tropic of Cancer. Such climates generally are warm all year with no pronounced summer or winter seasons.

Tropical cyclone: Storm that forms over a tropical ocean and has a core that is warmer than the surrounding air. Unlike storms that form outside the tropics, the strongest winds are near the surface.

Tropical depression: Tropical cyclone with maximum sustained winds near the surface of less than 39 mph.

Tropical storm: Tropical cyclone with 39 to 74 mph winds.

Tropical wave: See easterly wave.

Tropics: Region of the Earth from latitude 23.5 degrees north (the Tropic of Cancer) southward across the equator to latitude 23.5 degrees south (the Tropic of Capricorn).

Troposphere: Lower layer of

How wind chill is figured

Wind chill combines temperature and wind speed to show how much colder wind makes you feel. It applies only to exposed skin. Below 0°F chills represent a danger of frostbite. Prolonged exposure to chills below -20°F can be life threatening without proper clothing.

How to use the wind chill chart:

Figures for monthly average high or low temperatures plus those for average wind speeds can be used with this chart to get an idea of what kinds of wind chills to expect in the afternoon or early morning.

1. Draw a line down from the temperature across the top.
2. Draw a line to the right from wind on the left.
3. Chill temperature is where lines meet.

Example: 10°F temperature, 20 mph wind: -24°F chill

	30°	25°	20°	15°	10°	5°	0°	-5°
10 mph	16°	10°	3°	-3°	-9°	-15°	-22°	-27°
15 mph	9°	2°	-5°	-11°	-18°	-25°	-31°	-38°
20 mph	4°	-3°	-10°	-17°	-24°	-31°	-39°	-46°
25 mph	1°	-7°	-15°	-22°	-29°	-36°	-44°	-51°
30 mph	-2°	-10°	-18°	-25°	-33°	-41°	-49°	-56°

(Left axis label: **Wind**)

Source: National Oceanic and Atmospheric Administration

Apparent temperature

The combination of heat and humidity gives the "apparent temperature," which is a measure of how dangerous the combination is. To find the apparent temperature:

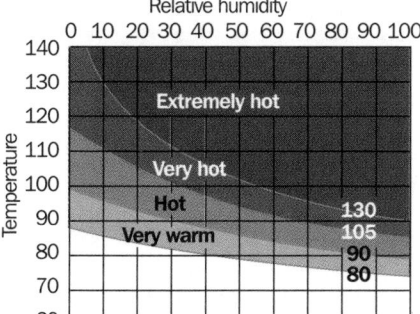

Relative humidity

Example: Temperature 100° F and relative humidity of 60 percent. The apparent temperature is 130° on the edge of the "extremely hot" range.

Find the temperature on the left side. Find the relative humidity across the top. The curved line where they meet is the apparent temperature. Follow the temperature and humidity lines. The color of the area where they meet tells you the danger.

What the dangers are in each range of apparent temperatures

Extremely hot

Heatstroke imminent.

Very hot

Heatstroke possible with prolonged exposure. Heat cramps and heat exhaustion likely.

Hot

Heat cramps and heat exhaustion possible with exposure.

Very warm

Physical activity could be more fatiguing than usual.

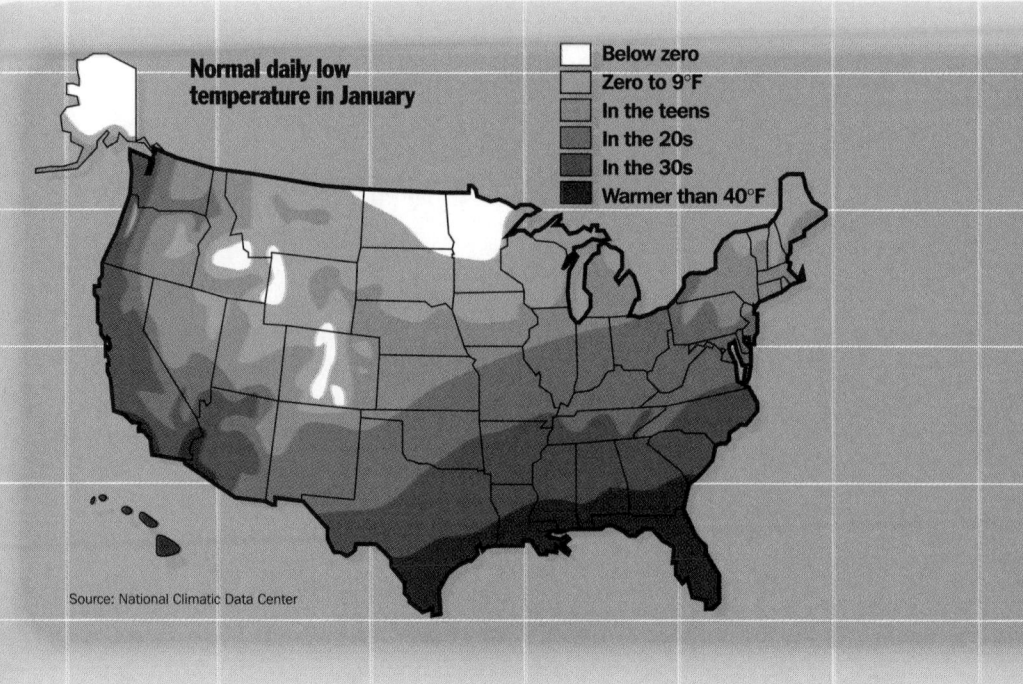

Normal daily low temperature in January

☐ Below zero
☐ Zero to 9°F
☐ In the teens
☐ In the 20s
☐ In the 30s
■ Warmer than 40°F

Source: National Climatic Data Center

the atmosphere, up to 7 or 8 miles above the Earth.

Typhoon: Tropical cyclone with winds of 75 mph or more in the north Pacific, west of the International Date Line.

Upslope effect: Cooling of winds blowing uphill or up the gentle rise of the U.S. plains from the Mississippi River to the Rockies. Upslope winds can bring fog, clouds and precipitation.

Upslope fog: Fog that forms in humid air flowing uphill.

Warm front: Warm-cold air boundary with the warm air advancing.

Warning: An alert issued by the National Weather Service that dangerous weather, such as a tornado or a flash flood, is actually occurring.

Watch: An alert issued by the National Weather Service that conditions are right for dangerous weather, such as a tornado or flash flood. Hurricane watches are issued for areas with a chance of being hit.

Water vapor: Invisible gaseous form of water.

Waterspout: Tornado or weaker vortex from the bottom of a cloud to the surface of a body of water.

Wind chill factor: Effect of wind blowing away warmed air near the body.

Wind shear: Any sudden change in wind speed or direction.

Acknowledgements

Assembling *The USA TODAY Weather Almanac* was very much a collaboration, not the work of a single author.

Special thanks should go to USA TODAY's editor, Peter Prichard, and to Tom McNamara, managing editor for news, Joe Urschel, managing editor of the special projects department, and Susan Bokern of Gannett New Business for making the needed resources available.

Richard Curtis, USA TO-DAY's managing editor for graphics and photography, not only designed the *Almanac,* but he also oversaw the many details involved in getting the book ready to print. Artist Julia Stacey contributed her special touch with graphics, as she has been doing for the USA TODAY Weather Page. They deserve all the credit for making the book attractive.

Carol Knopes, the editor, and Jacqueline Blais, the copy editor, untangled the author's prose and made sure the book makes sense. Their many suggestions have made the *Almanac* more useful to readers.

The task of assembling the *Almanac* would have been impossible without the help of those noted in the credits who did computer programming, research and data entry.

Thanks also go to our editors at Vintage Books, Marty Asher, vice president and editor-in-chief, and Linda Rosen-

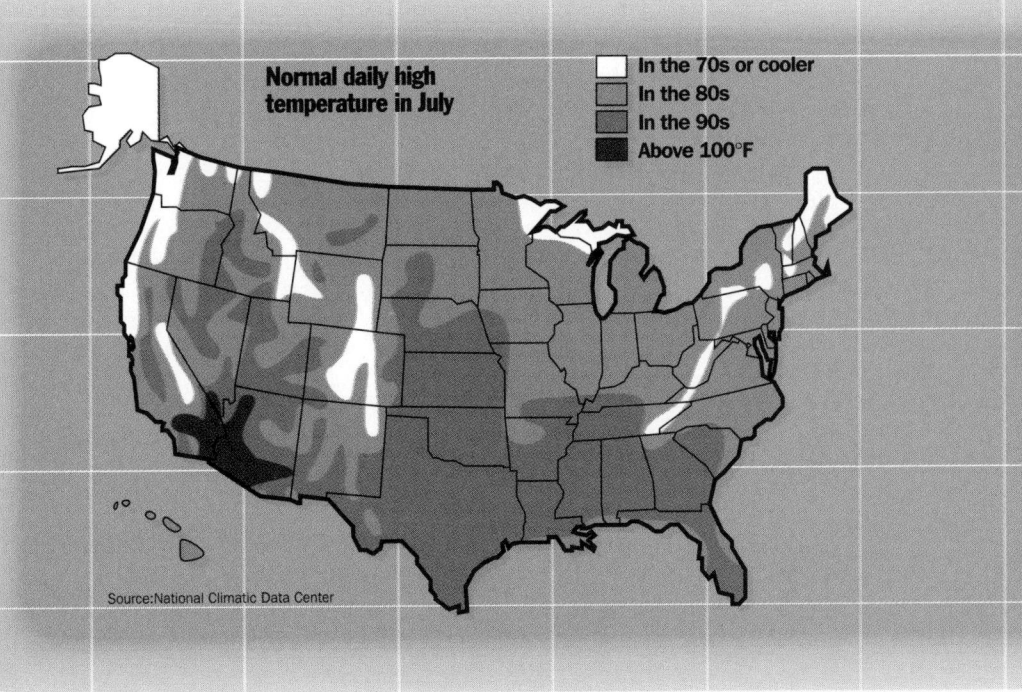

Normal daily high temperature in July

- In the 70s or cooler
- In the 80s
- In the 90s
- Above 100°F

Source: National Climatic Data Center

berg, managing editor.

One goal with *The USA TODAY Weather Almanac* is to bring together information about weather, climate and other phenomena from many sources. Our object was to make the *Almanac* a one-stop source of information for travelers.

We never would have met this goal without the help of the people listed here. They are from the government and private companies. They told us what information was available, guided us in selecting what should be most useful and helped us collect the data we needed or helped us understand the directions being taken by atmospheric science.

National Center for Atmospheric Research: Ron Alberty, John Firor, Joan Frisch, Kevin Trenberth, Morris Weisman.

National Park Service: Joan Anzelmo, Carl Bowman, Doug Caudwell, Lisa Dapprich,

Cheryl Matthews.

NASA: Fred Espenak.

NOAA, National Climatic Data Center: William Brown, Axel Graumann, Richard Heim, Thomas Karl, Henry Ray, Tom Ross.

NOAA, National Weather Service: Wyman Au, Ron Berger, Skip Ely, Randee Exler, Paul Hebert, Jerry Jarrell, Linda Kremkau, Scott Kroczynski, Frank Lepore, Douglas Le Comte, Max Mayfield, Dave Miskus, Todd Morris, Fred Ostby, Jon Parein, Ken Putkovich, Edward Rappeport, Frank Richards, Barry Reichenbaugh, David Rodenhuis, Robert Sheets.

NOAA, other than Climatic Data Center and National Weather Service: Gary Davis, Joseph Golden, Dane Konop, Tim Tomastik, Patricia Viets.

Official Airline Guide: Dick Nelson.

Orbital Sciences Corp.: Mark Pastrone.

Penn State University, Charles Hosler Jr.

Texas Tech University, Institute for Disaster Research: James R. McDonald.

Sno Country Reports: Peter Camp.

U.S. Geological Survey: Rebecca Phipps.

U.S. Naval Observatory: Steven Dick, Michael James.

University of Alabama, Huntsville: John Christy.

In addition, more than 150 National Weather Service offices around the U.S. responded to our request for additional information.

Finally, the author wants to thank his mother, Jane Williams, for encouraging an interest in the world, and his wife, Darlene, whose cheerful support makes all tasks easier.

Credits

The USA TODAY Weather Almanac was edited by Carol Knopes, copy-edited by Jacqueline Blais and designed by Richard Curtis. Graphics were drawn by Julia Stacey, J.L. Albert and members of the USA TODAY graphics department.

Additional editing: Fred Meier. Researching of the city pages: Anne Carey, John Riley and Deirdre Schwiesow.

Research and data entry: Dan Avula, Tyler Curtis, David Brown, Eli Horowitz, Michelle Mattox, Silvia Molina, Jin Park and Kurt J. Williams.

Computer programming: Mark Jenkins, Paul Overberg and Larry Sanders.

Data entry: Janie Berkheimer and Patti Stang.

Sources of further information

The National Climatic Data Center in Asheville, N.C., is the main source of the climate information in *The USA TODAY Weather Almanac*. The center, which is part of the National Oceanic and Atmospheric Administration, is the repository of American weather records going back to the observations of Thomas Jefferson. Records include observations by volunteers as well as by members of the National Weather Service and other agencies.

In addition to storing climate records, the center organizes them and makes the information available in a variety of books and pamphlets, on computer disks, tapes, and CD-ROMs. The center also has a computer bulletin board service. Meteorologists at the center are expert at helping people obtain the climate information they need.

National Climatic Data Center
Federal Building
151 Patton Avenue
Asheville, N.C. 28801

Weather and Crop Bulletin is a good way to keep up with week-to-week weather in the United States and important agricultural areas around the world. The *Bulletin* is published by the National Weather Service and U.S. Department of Agriculture. The focus is on agricultural weather, but each week's *Bulletin* has weather data from more than 200 National Weather Service offices in all 50 states.

Subscription information about the *Bulletin* is available from:

Weekly Weather and Crop Bulletin
NOAA/USDA Joint Agricultural Weather Facility
USDA South Building
Room 5844
Washington, D.C. 20250

The National Oceanic and Atmospheric Administration (NOAA) is the parent agency of the National Climatic Data Center, the National Weather Service and other organizations involved in atmospheric and oceanic research. After all major weather events, such as Hurricane Andrew and the 1993 Mississippi Basin floods, NOAA produces reports analyzing how the National Weather Service, other federal agencies and state and local governments responded. These reports give good summaries of the event as well as listing the lessons learned and making recommendations for improvements. These reports were a major source of information for the *Almanac*.

NOAA Public Affairs Office
Room 6013
Commerce Department
14th and Constitution N.W.
Washington, D.C. 20230

The National Weather Service collects weather observations from around the world and produces general and specialized forecasts. It also conducts research designed to improve forecasting.

National Weather Service Public Affairs
1325 East-West Highway
SSMCII-Room 18454
EA5/W
Silver Spring, Md. 20910

The National Weather Service's Climate Analysis Center produces a variety of long-range forecasts and bulletins on climate concerns, such as El Nino. In addition, the Climate Analysis Center produces seasonal and yearly summaries of the climate. The Center is changing from various kinds of printed material to making data available on line via computer.

Climate Analysis Center
W/NMC5
National Weather Service
5200 Auth Rd.
Washington, D.C. 20233

The U.S. Naval Observatory is the official source of information about time and astronomical phenomena such as sunrise and sunset. We used the Multiyear Interactive Computer Almanac (MICA) from the U.S. Naval Observatory to generate the tables showing length of days and twilights at the various latitudes in the *Almanac*. Printed material is also available from the Observatory.

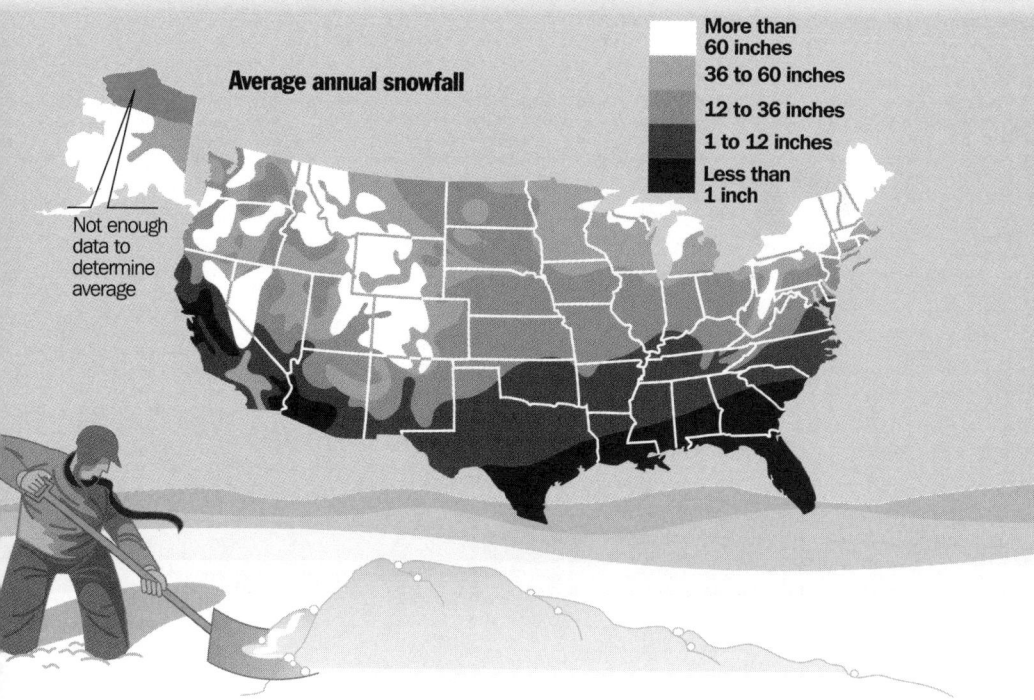

Average annual snowfall

More than 60 inches

36 to 60 inches

12 to 36 inches

1 to 12 inches

Less than 1 inch

Not enough data to determine average

U.S. Naval Observatory
3450 Massachusetts Ave., N.W.
Washington, D.C. 20392

The MICA is available in both DOS and Macintosh versions from:

U.S. Department of Commerce
Technology Administration
National Technical Information
  Service
Springfield, Va. 22161

At the recommendation of the Naval Observatory, we contacted the **Official Airline Guides** publishers for information on time zones. The time zone information in the *Almanac* is from the *OAG Desktop Flight Guide Worldwide Edition, Aug. 1994* and is used with permission. The *Flight Guide* is the best way to keep up with changes in international time zones.

Official Airline Guides
2000 Clearwater Drive
Oak Brook, Ill. 60521

The National Center for Atmospheric Research is the nation's leading research center devoted to meteorology.

Public Affairs Office
National Center for
  Atmospheric Research
P.O. Box 3000
Boulder, Colo. 80307

Weatherwise magazine is for those who are interested in weather and climate. Its articles are intended for general readers, not specialists.

Weatherwise
Heldref Publications
1319 18th St. N.W.
Washington, D.C. 20036-1802

The American Meteorological Society (AMS) is the nation's oldest and largest scientific society in the atmospheric sciences. It conducts several scientific conferences each year and publishes 10 scientific journals in meteorology and oceanography. Information about colleges with programs in meteorology is available from the society.

In addition, the society has an active education program that trains and supports teachers at the elementary, middle school and high school level.

American Meteorological Society
45 Beacon Street
Boston, Mass. 02108-3693

Information about AMS education programs is available from:

American Meteorological Society
Education office
1701 K Street N.W.
Suite 300
Washington, D.C. 20006-1509

The USA TODAY Weather Book by Jack Williams, published by Vintage Books, is a guide to the how and why of weather and complements the information in the *Almanac*. It was published in 1992 and is still widely available in book stores or can be ordered using the ISBN number: 0-679-73669-7.

Colophon

Design and layout were done on a Macintosh IIfx computer using the latest-available desktop publishing technology.

Graphics were produced on Apple Macintosh Quadra 800 computers with 40 megabytes of random-access memory and 500-megabyte internal hard disk drives.

Information for the charts and tables was pulled from a NOAA CD-ROM into a Paradox database on an Intel 486-equipped personal computer. The data was exported as comma-delimited PC text files. The chart files were copied into a Macintosh Quadra computer and imported into DeltaGraph Professional for charting, exported as Adobe Illustrator files and then imported into Aldus FreeHand 3.1 for completion. The FreeHand files were exported as Encapsulated PostScript and imported into the pages in Quark XPress 3.3.

The text was written and edited on an Atex editorial text-editing system. It was then transferred to the Macintosh, using off-the-shelf communications software.

Electronic files were output to film on an Agfa Selectset 7000 imagesetter at RR Donnelley & Sons Co., Harrisonburg, Va., which also printed the book on 60-pound International Springhill Offset paper on a Toshiba press. The book was bound on a Harris binder.

Text type is 9-point Berkeley Oldstyle ITC Book by Bitstream on 11-point leading. Berkeley Oldstyle was first issued as University of California Oldstyle, designed by Frederic Goudy in the late 1930s. It was reissued as Berkeley Oldstyle by the International Typeface Corporation in 1983. Headlines and graphics text are Franklin Gothic, designed by Morris Fuller Benton in 1904.

Index

PRAISE FOR
THE COOL WOMAN

John Anderson has written a series of books like none other. He has truly captured the spirit of flying, fighting, and faith in this thriller. I was back in the old Skyraider as I turned the pages and could hear the roar of that radial engine and feel the adrenaline of combat situation where I often found myself many years ago. This is a must read for anyone who loves adventure and combat flying.

—Tex Brown, Lt Gen USAF, (Ret)

John Anderson uses imagination and intrigue to skillfully combine fact and fiction in capturing the challenges and inner conflicts of a young man who overcomes a tragic past to become the "best of the best" fighter pilots. A tribute to those American heroes who flew the "Sandy" missions in Southeast Asia as well as all who flew the A-1 Skyraider.

—Major General Lee V. Greer, USAF (Ret.), flew 215 Combat Missions in the A-1 Skyraider

The Cool Woman bristles with heart-pounding action and deeply emotive characters and relationships. John Anderson writes what he knows because he's been there, so the realism will pull you into this powerful story and become a part of you.

—LtCol Oliver L. North USMC (Ret.), *New York Times* bestselling author of *American Heroes*

A great read that every Air Force pilot can identify with.

—Larry New, Major General (Retired), USAF

The Cool Woman

The Cool Woman

A NOVEL

JOHN AUBREY ANDERSON

FIDELIS
BOOKS
NASHVILLE, TENNESSEE

978-0-8054-6480-1

Fidelis Books, an imprint of B&H Publishing Group
Nashville, Tennessee

Dewey Decimal Classification: F
Subject Heading: ALCOHOLISM—FICTION \
MILITARY AERONAUTICS—FICTION \ VIETNAM WAR,
1961–1975—FICTION

Publisher's Note: The characters and events in this book
are fictional, and any resemblance to actual persons or
events is coincidental.

1 2 3 4 5 6 7 8 • 14 13 12 11 10

To Nan

and

The Air Force pilots who flew
the Douglas A-1 Skyraider
in Southeast Asia.

See Glossary of Terms on page 333.

CHAPTER ONE

The rumor circulating in the snack bar Friday morning came straight from squadron operations.

Sixteen Air Force pilots, most of them in flightsuits, two or three in summer-weight tans, were clustered here and there around Orange Flight's briefing room. They were all watching the door and V debating quietly about the accuracy of what they'd heard. The fact that their flight commander was ten minutes late for the morning briefing made the story more believable by the second.

Second Lieutenant Warren F. Masland sat alone at a table in the back of the room. Masland was the most junior instructor in the flight. If the rumor proved true, the new instructor's career was going to end before it began.

When the commander, Captain Frank W. Steadman, finally showed up, the pilots watched him shuffle into the room and step onto the dais in much the same way a condemned man might mount the guillotine's platform. He dropped a stack of paperwork on the lectern then flipped his notebook open and frowned at the first page while he pulled out a cigarette. The conversation groups broke up, and men drifted in Steadman's direction and began taking seats. The two officers nearest him spoke to their leader . . . he didn't respond. He got his cigarette going then tapped on the speaker's stand with his lighter. "At ease, guys. Let's get this over with."

1

The two pilots Steadman snubbed kept their faces expressionless and cut their eyes at each other; the rumor was going to be true.

"Okay," Steadman had yet to look at his troops, "we'll divvy up the students first. After that, we'll play catch-up on paperwork and take a long weekend."

Orange Flight's briefing room was one of four almost identical rooms in the nondescript, concrete block building that housed the 3525th Pilot Training Squadron. The speaker's stand was backed by a large green chalkboard and an annotated map of the local flying area. A built-in bookcase on the chalkboard side would provide housing for the incoming trainees' grade books. In keeping with the Air Force's penchant for having its written directives weigh as much as its aircraft, an identical set of shelves on Steadman's left was filled with an array of training manuals, binders full of obscure Air Force Regulations, and a small library of safety-related publications.

"We've only got one prior service troop," Steadman spoke in a monotone, "a first lieutenant naviguesser. I'll take him; the rest of you will start with two or three studs each." He paused and let his gaze go to the back wall while he pursed his lips and massaged the back of his neck. "Okay." He stepped to the side of the podium and took a few seconds to jab the unfinished cigarette out in an ashtray; his expression wasn't a grimace, but it was close. He propped one foot on the base of the speaker's stand and looked back at his notebook while smoothing a mustache he'd shaved off six weeks earlier. And finally, the rumor became an official fact. "We've got a black kid in the incoming bunch, gents."

He let that soak in, then looked up to ask, "Any volunteers?"

There are several cardinal rules in the military; forever reigning in the number one slot is: *Never volunteer for anything.* Added to that, the pilots scattered around the room were well aware that an object in motion is easier for the human eye to detect, and they became military-garbed mannequins.

Except for the ceaseless sigh of air coming from the air-conditioning vents, the room was without sound.

In any group of sixteen men, some are almost certain to be racially biased, but that wasn't the root cause behind the room's pervading silence.

In July of the previous summer, a black lieutenant assigned to the T-37 flight down the hall washed out of pilot training. When he busted his final elimination check ride, the trainee told everyone who would listen that he was "kicked out" because of racial prejudice. Actually, the student's early ouster from the program had nothing to do with skin color; for the instructors who worked with him, the conclusion was unanimous from the beginning . . . the man was not cut out to be a pilot; he didn't have the "hands," the heart, or the SA—the situational awareness.

Within hours of the student being eliminated from the program, his congressman stepped in and, without availing himself of the facts, started twisting arms. The colonel in command of the 82nd Flying Training Wing knew he would never make general if he refused to yield, so he granted the student a special dispensation, giving him additional training.

It was a colossal error on the part of all involved.

In the world of aviation, conventional wisdom says: *To keep an aircraft in the air, a pilot will always need at least one of three ingredients: airspeed, altitude, or ideas.* If any one or two of those ingredients is absent or in short supply, the pilot must have a proportionate abundance of whatever remains.

On his first ride after being reinstated, the young man let the aircraft get "low and slow" while turning final for a landing, thus robbing himself of a significant measure of two of the components he needed to keep his plane flying.

The student immediately—and inexplicably—compounded his problem by pulling both throttles to idle, and the aircraft shuddered—warning of an impending stall. With the aircraft still flying, the instructor took control and initiated a standard stall recovery by pushing the throttles forward and moving to take pressure off the stick—no big deal. Even as the engines were spooling up, the student panicked and used both hands to jerk the stick full back. The abrupt maneuver cost the aircraft the last of its airspeed, and the T-37 stalled. At that altitude, with no airspeed, all the ideas in the world couldn't prevent what was coming.

People on the ground watched helplessly as the aircraft pitched up and its forward movement stopped. The plane hung motionless for one sickening instant then dropped off on one wing and pointed its nose at the ground—falling, not flying.

The instructor took precious seconds to punch the student on the arm and yell "Eject! Eject!" but the kid's hands were welded to the stick. The IP ejected too low and was seriously injured. The student was killed on impact.

The accommodating congressman, in an often-practiced scramble to fix the blame firmly on someone else, presided over the sacrifice of everyone from the training wing commander down to the instructor.

Steadman let his eyes move across the silent group and nodded his understanding. He spied Masland and was getting ready to pronounce his sentence when a captain with dark red hair lifted a hand and murmured, "Yo."

"You'll take him?" Steadman's tone said, *This is a joke, isn't it?*

The other instructors were so startled they glanced involuntarily at the man with the death wish.

The object of their attention shrugged. "Sure."

Steadman continued to stare at the volunteer—he didn't believe what he was hearing. No one in the room believed it. The other pilots retreated to their lifeless states because the issue might not be settled. The redhead, Rusty Mattingly, was the son of the youngest general in the Air Force. The officers in Mattingly's chain of command tried not to go overboard in showing partiality, but they didn't assign the junior captain too many "trash details" either.

"Okeydokey," the flight commander took a deep breath and sighed, "you got 'im."

Frank Steadman had five years of active duty remaining before he could retire. He pictured the stars on Mattingly's father's shoulders and prayed, *Lord, please don't let me get blamed for this.*

Masland tried to hide his relief behind his coffee cup and spilled most of the contents in his lap. No one chided him for it.

Sunday afternoon brought that week's measured interlude of heat-soaked silence. The skies over Williams Air Force Base were clear of clouds and airplanes. Acres of jet trainers—the short, squatty little T-37s and the white, stiletto-shaped T-38s—gleamed in the sun, fueled and ready for Monday. Mann stopped his car at the main gate, handed the young Air Policeman a sheet of his crisp new orders, and asked where he could get something to eat.

The guard barely glanced at the orders while he let his eyes take in the car. "Best burgers in Arizona, sir," he pointed. "Straight down there at Base Operations."

Mann stowed the orders back in their envelope while the guard snapped a salute. "Nice car, sir."

Mann smiled as he returned the salute. "Thanks." The car, Mann's college graduation present to himself, was created for an Air Force jet jockey.

He drove onto the base—his first time on a military installation as a commissioned officer—and headed for the burgers. Food first—then a place to sleep.

Forty minutes later, the lieutenant with the crisp orders and cool car had Base Ops almost to himself. He leaned on the counter in the snack bar and licked his finger before passing it across a piece of greasy wax paper—the former resting place of two hamburgers and a double order of fries. He was washing down the last crumbs with a long pull on his milkshake—chocolate—when airplane noises drew his attention to the window. A blue pickup with a yellow *FOLLOW ME* sign in the back was leading a camouflaged F-4 to a parking place on the ramp outside the operations building. The hulking fighter looked big enough to take off with a T-38 under each wing.

Partner, that right there is a real live jet fighter, thought Mann.

In response to the ground crewman's gesture that the wheels were chocked, the man in the plane's front cockpit signaled he was shutting down the left engine. The guy in the back cockpit unstrapped and clambered over the side. The passenger stopped on the ladder to fasten some loose straps in the backseat then dropped to the ground and took a hang-up bag and a well-stuffed B-4 bag from behind a panel somewhere on the plane's belly. The passenger hefted his bags and walked past the shark's mouth painted on the nose of the airplane, heading for Base Ops. The man in the F-4 twirled one finger to tell the crew chief he was restarting the left engine and gave a thumbs-out motion for the chocks to be pulled. The fighter was on its way back to the runway before the backseater got to the door of the building.

Mann was watching the fighter taxi out when the passenger from the F-4 stepped into the foyer by the snack bar. Mann turned as the guy stopped to drop his bags and pull off a white helmet with a bright crimson visor cover. The F-4's passenger rubbed his hand through his hair to stir circulation back into his scalp then put the helmet in its bag. When he looked up to see Mann watching him, he left his bags in the middle of the marble tile floor and started for the snack bar while pulling off his flying gloves. From the insignia and stenciled name strip on the guy's flightsuit, Mann identified him as a first lieutenant, last name Chance. The patch on the right side of his chest marked him as part of the Tactical Air Command—that, and the airplane he stepped out of, meant he was a member of a fighter outfit. The wings sewn above his name tag told the world he was a navigator—his face said he was tired. Not a long-day kind of tired, more of the weeks-and-weeks kind.

Lieutenant Chance was looking at a slender black guy wearing a tan, summer-weight uniform with second lieutenant insignia on the collar. The veteran airman stuck out a small hand and winked. "I'm Fat Chance. Is this Tucson?" The grip was firm.

"I reckon that's close enough for government work, sir," said Mann. "I'm Bill Mann."

Both men stood relaxed while the new arrival looked over his fellow comedian. New uniform. New brown bars. New flight cap stowed correctly behind a brand-new blue belt. New plastic name tag, precisely fixed on his right pocket—white letters on a black background. *MANN.*

"Lemme guess." Chance pulled his own war-weary flight cap out of a calf pocket on his G-suit and settled it over sandy red hair while he continued to run a calculating eye over the welcome committee. "You're in the class that starts Tuesday."

Mann's face went blank with surprise. *Good gosh, does it show that much?*

"Yeah, it shows." The navigator spoke before Mann could answer. "You ain't got a speck of dust anywhere on you. The shoes look like you worked on 'em all morning with a fresh biscuit, the bars just came out of the box, an' that haircut is short enough to shame a Marine." He was grinning. "Like my granny used to say, 'You look like you just stepped out of a bandbox.'"

Mann had to laugh. Here he was in uniform, joking around with a guy who had just climbed out of an F-4. He was definitely in the Air Force. "Guilty," he said. "Just drove on the base. Left the bandbox in a phone booth."

"You checked in at the Q yet?"

"No, sir. I figured I'd eat first in case they don't give us any food for a few days."

"Smart move . . . an' don't call me 'sir.'" The drawl was straight out of lower Alabama by way of a year in Southeast Asia. "I'm gonna be in that class with you, and we're gonna be up to our elbows in alligators for the next twelve months, so we don't have time to play military; we'll leave that to the Training Command weenies." He looked at Mann to see if he understood.

"Sounds good to me." Mann was nodding. "Do people really call you 'Fat'?"

"Yup—that's my call sign." He handed Mann the helmet bag, gathered up the rest of his baggage, and headed for the door. "You got wheels?"

"Right outside the door."

"Excellent."

The June sun in Phoenix is expected to be harsh; it was brutal. They walked the few steps to the Vette, and Mann pointed at the chrome luggage rack. "Trunk's full."

"Nice wheels. '58?"

"Yep."

Most pilots have a thing for speed and the Vette would be one of twenty-two sports cars in Willie's UPT Class 72-01.

Chance rested the bags gently on the rack and took the helmet bag from Mann. He pulled a huge cigar out of it, ran it under his nose, grinned, and waved it at Mann. "Gen-u-wine Cuban." He fired up the cigar, took off his G-suit, and slid into the passenger seat of the Vette. "Let's go find the Q first. I'll grab a shower and some civvies, then we'll hunt us up a beerysoda."

Mann got behind the wheel.

The navigator waved his cigar to take in the car. "I even like the color."

Mann was backing out of the parking spot. "They told me red increases the horsepower by 15 percent."

The redhead ran a hand through his hair. "Closer to twenty-five."

CHAPTER TWO

Airman Third Class Cleetus Love was a far cry from being an athlete and basic training in San Antonio hadn't been easy, but he survived. The black kid from Dahlonega, Georgia, joined the Air Force for one reason—the GI Bill. When his three-year hitch was up, Love would be off to college. For now, the airman was looking forward to donning his second stripe in just three days—and being a personnel clerk was soft duty.

Freddy Canolla, a skinny kid from New Jersey, would make Airman Second when Love did. On the occasion of his eighteenth birthday, Canolla was offered a choice by a judge in Jersey City; he could join the military or do three-to-five in the state prison at Trenton for Grand Theft, Auto. The bad guy wannabe checked with his numerous and more worldly cousins and learned he'd stand a better chance of being alive in three years if he chose to enlist in the Air Force.

Love and Canolla attended clerk-typist school together at Keesler Air Force Base and rode west to Williams on the same bus. Freddy, a statement in contrast to the ultrablack kid from the Georgia hills, was marked with a perpetual five o'clock shadow and a tattoo of a naked lady on his hairy little arm. His life was an uninterrupted expenditure of energy to avoid labor. The skinny Yankee fueled his pursuit of leisure with beer, Lucky Strikes by the carton, and a taste for good dope. He was in front of his sergeant's desk every two weeks because of his hair length, whining to his boss about broads not going for guys with peeled heads. Canolla might manage to garner the second stripe, but a third stripe was out of his reach.

The Bachelor Officers Quarters were quiet on Sundays, and Canolla had "the duty" as Charge of Quarters; that meant he could practice being an Airman Second. He was forever giving advice to Love on how to make a job easier . . . how to "work the system." Since arriving at Williams, he had appointed himself top dog of a small covey of junior airmen. The wayward crowd let the runt of their litter claim the leadership role because of his ability to provide a steady supply of real beer, as opposed to the low-alcohol near-beer. More importantly, Canolla also had access to an occasional dime bag of pot.

Three hours earlier, Love stopped in the BOQ office to while away the morning. When Love took a seat behind one of the desks, Canolla produced a stack of papers from a drawer at the counter.

"I just got the roster for the new pilot training class." He perused the papers as if they were addressed to him personally then pitched them on the desk. "These guys coming in this week are Air Training Command lieutenants, Love, they don't know from nothing. They ain't never been in the real Air Force . . . they ain't never been in nothing." Freddy's Jersey City twang was reminiscent of James Cagney with a cold. "We got to get these young twerps checked out on the news that it's us enlisted types that run this here Air Force. Just stay quiet, act like you're busy, and you can get away with anything." Freddy sat down at the other desk. "I'll take care of the first one, then I'll give you a shot at the next one."

Love wasn't interested in harassing officers. "Canolla, you're a housing clerk; I'm not. If anybody finds out I'm sticking my nose in the office duties over here, we'll both end up in the guardhouse."

Canolla cursed. "You ain't got any idea what you're talking about, Love. These guys can't find their way to the chow hall. Now shut your face an' pay attention."

Love thought Canolla was full of New Jersey bologna and said so.

Freddy waved off the objections; he had it all figured out. He put his feet on the desk and lectured, "It's like we're OTIs, Lovely . . . you know, Officer Training Instructors. They'll be drifting in here all today an' tomorrow." He pointed at the roster. "Forty-something second lieutenants and one weak-kneed, fuzz-faced first lieutenant. Don't let 'em get carried away about who runs this show, understand? You're the CQ . . . like the NCO of the day . . . you're gonna have the whole show to yourself. You're the chief honcho. Understand? I'll be right here to back you up."

"What about Sgt. Jones?" Senior Master Sergeant Willie Jones was the NCOIC—the Non-Commissioned Officer In Charge—of the BOQ's operation. Sgt. Jones was an attention-getter in three categories—he was black as ebony wood, just as hard, and as big as a tree.

Cannola cursed more vehemently. "Jones ain't here, Love! *You're* here, an' *I'm* here. *We're* in charge. You just practice on these new kids, an' if anything starts going wrong, get real respectful and plead ignorance. Right? You gotta learn how to do this."

During the next three hours, six of the new class members checked in at the BOQ, and Canolla was unmerciful. Five of the six left the office totally confused; the last one called Canolla "sir." After the young lieutenant left, Canolla giggled for ten minutes.

When they heard a car in front of the building, Love hid his magazine and got up to push a rag around on the counter. If one of the sergeants was coming to check on Canolla, Love wanted to be ready. When the door to the outer office opened, he peeked up long enough to see a tall black man with brown second lieutenant's bars step through. "It's a black guy. A second looie."

"Sit down!" Canolla sprang from his chair and grabbed the rag. "I'll do this one." He was already snickering.

The tattooed lady on his arm moved around the counter as Canolla devoted his full attention to wiping the spotless surface. Someone trailed the black guy through the outside door and said, "I'm gonna make a head call while you get us checked in." Canolla kept his head down to hide a smile. Two of 'em.

The black kid said something Canolla couldn't hear.

A black second lieutenant who had never even seen an enlisted man . . . this was more fun than shaking down school kids. He looked over his shoulder; Love was deeply engrossed in a manual of some sort and didn't look up.

The officer stepped into the room and walked over to stand in front of Canolla. Freddy stayed busy polishing his countertop.

"Afternoon, airman, I need to get a couple of BOQ rooms."

Freddy smiled to himself. *Real polite. That's a good start. I wonder how far I can push this guy?* The cloth continued to swirl.

"Airman?"

Cannola nodded absently. He was busy. *Don't say "sir" to 'em, an' don't call 'em "lieutenant." Get 'em broke in right.*

The airman with the penchant for cleanliness blew at an errant speck of dust. "Be with you in a minute." He could barely keep from laughing.

Two hands came to rest on the pristine clean counter, bracketing the busy polishing cloth; the owner of the arresting hands wore a Rolex on his left wrist. The watch's previous owner had been an officer who knew how to talk to men; that officer's son had watched and learned. The naked lady stopped her circular dance.

Airman almost-Second Class Freddy Canolla glanced up into the face of the black "kid," and his urge to laugh was forgotten.

In the months to come, he would remember the words he spoke next. He would remember them and shake his head at his own capacity for stupidity. He could have said any one of several thousand things that would have saved him. He could have turned his life around on the spot. He didn't. He looked back down at the counter and said, "Be right with you."

The guy facing him didn't say anything. His hands didn't move.

Canolla could hear blood pumping through his ears. Behind him paper rattled as Love tried to keep the manual on latrine cleaning from flying out of his hands. The skinny little hood looked up again.

The black lieutenant didn't really look like a green kid. He was obviously young . . . he just didn't *look* young. The brown eyes didn't waver. The mouth below the eyes moved to speak, not to smile. "Lieutenant Chance and I are reporting for class seventy-two-oh-one. We need two rooms." The hands bracketing the dust cloth moved forward a fraction of an inch. Canolla had been in a fight a month for the last ten years, and he knew real trouble when he saw it. This guy in the lieutenant's uniform was the kind who got what he wanted, or he started taking people down . . . or buildings maybe.

Freddy's brain wanted to form an answer, but he was locked on the guy's eyes. Back in Jersey, Joey "The Snake" Costello was so called because of his eyes. But Joey's eyes didn't have any expression in them; they were more dull than they were threatening. On the fringe of his peripheral vision, Cannola saw someone move through the door behind the black officer. A voice said, "Got us a room yet, bro?"

"Coming up, sir." Calm. Relaxed. Confident. Steady eyes. The eyes told Canolla that the lieutenant wasn't just one move ahead of him . . . he was light-years out front.

Canolla's brain was struggling to catch up with the impact the black guy was having on his thoughts when he looked into the face of the newcomer, a first lieutenant in a flightsuit. The flight-suit guy was shorter than the black guy by three or four inches. Contrary to Canolla's preliminary assessment, this particular first lieutenant didn't have any fuzz on his face, and he didn't walk like his knees were weak—he swaggered.

Freddy's eyes drifted involuntarily back to the hands on the counter that held his tattoo hostage. If Love hadn't been in the room, Canolla would have turned into a recruiting poster enlisted man, but he was trapped. If he backed down now, Love would tell the whole base, and all his buddies would be laughing at him. Love, on the other hand, had become a military man who existed only to better himself by pursuing academic excellence. He was shrouded in a tech manual that described something about the intricacies involved in properly cleaning a latrine. Quiet reigned in the BOQ office . . . Freddy Canolla and the tattooed lady were alone and naked on the field of battle; they both began to sweat.

At that point, one of the black hands curled slightly, preparing for its next move. The black hand rolled until it was inverted. The open palm extended itself toward Canolla, and the man said, "Keys."

And Canolla caved. "Yes, sir."

The first lieutenant, the one who had never had fuzz on his face, drawled, "You . . . behind the desk . . . on your feet."

Love was on his feet in an instant, facing the counter. The latrine-cleaning manual hit the floor at his feet. No one cared.

"What's your name, son?" The first lieutenant's teeth were clamped on a black cigar the size of a tractor muffler.

"Love. Airman Third Class Love."

The lieutenant didn't reply. He pulled the cigar out, inspected the ash buildup for a moment, then raised his eyes to Love as if he expected something from him.

Oh, shoot! "Uh . . . sir!" *Lord, please let me get outta this without losing my stripe.*

"And what does your momma call you, Airman Third Class Love?"

"Uh . . . Cleetus, sir."

"Mm-hmm." Chance inspected the manning chart on the wall behind Cleetus, then leaned forward and spoke softly. "And what is your role here at the BOQ, Cleetus?"

Months earlier, while in clerk-typist school at Keesler, Love and his buddies went to a picnic on the beach in Biloxi. The coldest beer at the bottom of the ice chest was warm in comparison to the voice asking that last question. He could feel sweat forming above his upper lip and the nineteen-year-old would-be Officer Training Instructor wished fervently he could be some place else . . . any place else. Here he was playing juvenile pranks with the sorriest half-wit in the Western hemisphere and he was caught red-handed by a guy who could ruin his illustrious career before it started. What had he expected?

"I'm in personnel, sir. Just over helping out."

The guy with the career-ruining potential nodded at a picture on the wall behind Love and asked, "Did Senior Master Sergeant Willie Jones—the Williams Air Force Base Housing Office, Non-Commissioned Officer In Charge—assign you to be in cahoots with this fool?" He was aiming the tractor muffler at Canolla.

"No, sir." Without the money from the GI Bill, Love was destined for a career in his daddy's shine parlor.

"So how'd you get yourself in this mess, Cleetus?" A wisp of smoke drifted near Love's face.

On a cold, clear morning back in February, Grandmomma Love took his hand and pulled him away from the well-wishers gathered outside the bus station. When the two were by themselves, she stood close and spoke in confidence, "Cleetus Boy, the good Lord saw fit to give me some fine gran'chi'ren, an' He knows I love 'em all, but you the special one." The frigid air carried her words on white vapor mixed with the sweet smell of Juicy Fruit.

"Yes, ma'am. You told me that before." His grandmother was known for her long speeches.

The tiny lady slapped him on the chest. "You just hush an' listen, boy." She took his lapels in her hands and pulled his face close to hers. "Ain't none o' mine ever gone to no college, son, but you can do it . . . you the smart one . . . smarter'n anybody I ever knowed . . . smarter'n even you know. You needs to go in that Air Force an' show yo'self an' them folks 'bout what I'm tellin' you."

She took her time gathering her next words, and he knew to stay silent.

"Yo' daddy's a good man, Cleetus Boy . . ."

He took a breath to agree and she frowned and shook his lapels to silence him. ". . . a fine man, but I just needs you to know, boy . . . if I ever see you back in that shine parlor for anything but a visit, I'm gonna be real disappointed in you."

Cleetus could see the vapor drift from his mouth as he looked into his grandmother's eyes and said, "I ain't comin' back, Grandmomma Love. I promise."

Love had squandered every single minute of his few months in the Air Force, trying to burn every bridge between himself and college by hanging out with a pack of worthless dopeheads. He looked into the eyes of the cigar-smoking lieutenant and heard the pop and snap of his daddy's shoeshine rag. "Uh . . . Lieutenant . . . permission to make a statement, sir?"

Chance used his cigar to amplify a magnanimous gesture. "Have at it."

"Sir, I'm not the smartest man in the world, but lately I've kind of fallen off the chart on the stupid side. If it's all the same to you, sir, I'd like to start over."

"Sorry, son," Chance was shaking his head before Love finished his speech, "you should've thought about that before you decided to fall in with this fool against me and Lieutenant Mann here." He pointed across the counter. "Hand me that phone."

"Fat?" Mann had been watching Love throughout the exchange.

"Mm-hmm?"

"Every now and then . . . a man needs a break."

Chance filled his cheeks with cigar smoke and looked at nothing while he blew several perfect smoke rings. The last circle was dissipating when he waved the cigar at Love. "You heard the man, Cleetus. Go, and sin no more."

Airman Cleetus Love took one step back and touched trembling fingertips to his eyebrow. When Chance returned his salute, he walked straight to Mann. He saluted Mann and said, "Thank you, sir. You saved my life."

Mann returned the salute and nodded solemnly. "Make it matter, Cleetus."

"I intend to do just that, sir."

Airman Love walked out of the BOQ office and into a changed life. The first lieutenant in the flightsuit turned his attention to the man behind the counter.

"All right, sonny boy. My name is First Lieutenant Thomas Randolph Chance. My friends call me 'Fat,' you can call me 'Sir.' If you'll check the roster for the class that starts Tuesday," he pointed over Canolla's shoulder at the papers on the desk, "you'll see that I'm the class commander of UPT 72-01."

Canolla picked up the papers in question and saw Chance's name was indeed at the top of the list. He looked at the face of the class leader and felt cold inside.

"How old are you?" Chance asked.

The question threw Canolla off. "Uh . . . nineteen."

Chance took time to draw on the cigar, exhaled, then said, "Sir." The voice was relaxed.

"Uh . . . sir." Something in Canolla's chest shuddered. One of his cousins was only twenty-nine when he died of a heart attack.

"It appears you haven't seen my resume."

"Your what?" *What's a rezzimay?*

"Sir," reminded Chance. Gently. Like working with a being who was new to the language.

"Uh . . . sir. Your what, sir?"

"My resume . . . the glowing details of my past life . . . the history behind why I'm standing out here in the middle of this Arizona wasteland teaching a Yankee how to talk to his betters." He smiled around the cigar. "I made airman *first* when I was eighteen, Canolla."

The smile became a wicked, I-know-all-the-tricks grin. "When I was nineteen, Uncle Sam chose to pluck me from the unwashed herd and send me to college to turn me into an officer and a gentleman. I went to a year of navigator training and six months of F-4 gunnery school so some marginally-qualified pilot could sit in front of me and hurtle my body through space at the speed of heat while a bad man on the ground tried to shoot me with a big gun. I've spent the better part of the last two years in this man's air arm trying to get out of that backseat and here to pilot training so that in a year or so I can go back and ride around in the skies of Southeast Asia and hurtle my own body at that dirt and give that guy over there with the big gun another chance to shoot at Mrs. Chance's favorite son. You with me so far?"

Canolla caught himself before he nodded. "Yes, sir."

"Do you know who I saw guarding the perimeter fences in that war zone, Canolla?"

"No, sir."

"The guys they send out to walk those fences at night are the fools who haven't got enough brains to stay out of trouble. Nobody wants anybody to get killed, Airman Canolla, but if we're gonna lose some guys anyway, we might as well lose the stupid ones. Don't you think that makes sense?"

"It's very clear, sir."

"I do believe we're communicating on the same frequency, son. Get us some keys."

"Yes, sir. Coming right up, sir."

Williams Air Force Base, affectionately referred to as "Willie" by Air Force personnel, stands just outside the southeastern edge of Phoenix. For the pilots based there, life is good; the weather and the flying are no different. The squadrons in the training wing stay "ahead of the time line" on the flying schedule because they rarely have to deal with any of the rain or cold weather that regularly plagues the other seven training bases. Willie, at 120 degrees in the shade, is the Air Training Command's oasis.

UPT—Undergraduate Pilot Training for the United States Air Force—is designed to take an ordinary human and transform him into a person who is as much at home in the sky as he is on the ground. The process requires fifty-four weeks—the twelve-hour days are split; the biggest part of the time is allocated to the flightline environment, the remainder to academics and rigorous physical conditioning.

A significant percentage of the people who start pilot training are not expected to complete the program. Some wash out because they can't keep up with the academics, so those who want to finish study during their "free" time. A few have to leave because they can't hack the physical discipline; therefore, the ones who want to complete the course jog and work out when they aren't studying. A small fraction of the people who manage to win a slot in the program will decide that what is required of them is more than they want to expend, and they will SIE—put in for a self-initiated elimination. The most significant problems, however, always surface on the flightline. A man may possess Albert Einstein's intellect and a decathlete's body, but if he can't handle the airplane, he's out.

Among the members of a typical training class, there is always a universal element of concentrated diligence during the first six weeks—they're in a struggle for survival. It's not happenstance that the overwhelming amount of information, the seemingly alien atmosphere of the cockpit, and the loud and unrelenting demands of the instructor pilots join forces in an apparent attempt to crush the aspiring pilots. These initial weeks are designed to "weed out" the weak students early. The sooner the ones who are going to wash out can be identified, the sooner they can be moved away from the cockpit.

At the end of eight weeks, the students (called studs for short) begin to attribute the diminished volume of their instructors' critiques to their own natural ability to perform well. The instructors have been over the ground before and they let the young studs believe whatever it takes to turn them into real pilots. About this time, when the fledglings begin to believe they're learning the ropes, one or two will discover they can venture out into the real world for a full weekend and still tolerate the next five days of pilot training. These adventurers will spread the news to their comrades and by the end of the first quarter, 90 percent of the class members are vacating the base every Friday afternoon to chase girls, play tourist, catch girls, and, as often as not, drink too much. They quickly become acclimated to five days of exhausting effort to excel, followed by two days of rest and relaxation in sunny Arizona. After each week's mini-vacation, the studs lead one another back to the base, hopefully, in time to get some sleep before having to roll out of bed at three-thirty Monday morning.

In every class, there are always two or three class members who never seem to relax as much as their brothers. Of that small group some or all will be among the class's distinguished graduates—Mann intended to be one of the DGs. For the first two months of training, Mann bought more beer than gas. He gave the coveted beverage to the airmen who were tasked with maintaining the T-37 flight simulators, and, in exchange, the maintenance men let Mann come in and "fly the sims" on weekends. As August worked its way into September, he and Chance were leading in the class standings, and Mann let Chance convince him he needed to take an occasional break.

In the few weeks just before Thanksgiving, Mann began to abbreviate his study time on Friday and Saturday nights in order to devote himself to mastering one of the essentials of being a fighter pilot . . . beer drinking.

By this time, every student in the class believed himself capable of flying the T-37 in his sleep. Chance was getting ready to take that belief to the next level.

CHAPTER THREE

Mann and Chance were five months into the training program—almost at the halfway point—and nearly finished with the T-37 phase of training. The rest of their classmates had resigned themselves to the fact that these two would claim the top slots in the class. . . . Chance had the edge in academics; Mann had a decided lead on the flying side. In another month the class would move down the hall to Purple Flight's briefing room . . . different instructors, and a real airplane—the stiletto-shaped T-38 Talon—a supersonic sports car with afterburners. They were ready.

A quarter of a mile away, shrouded by charcoal gloom, the headlights of a line taxi crept along the roadway at the edge of the ramp. Sunup was only a few minutes away, but, as they had for millennia, the Superstition Mountains were holding the approaching day at bay as long as they could. The two class leaders stood in the near darkness outside the Personal Equipment Building, helmet bags in hand, hunched beneath the weight of their parachutes, waiting for a ride to their airplanes; they were each taking a Tweet out solo.

Chance looked at the area close to his feet and stepped onto the grass.

"C'mon, Fat, it's fifty degrees out here. Rattlesnakes don't come out in cold weather." Chance wasn't scared of much, but snakes met his criteria.

"Not lookin' for snakes. Lookin' for a place to throw up." He put his helmet bag down and dropped to one knee in the grass.

"You sick?"

"Hung ov—" He didn't get to fully form his answer before his body elected to give a show-and-tell demonstration.

"Mmm-mmm. Boy, you ain't got the brains God gave a goose." Over the past few weeks Mann had developed a penchant for beer and he had a slight headache for the same reason Chance was throwing up. "What'd you do last night?"

Fat was back on his feet, leaning over the grass with his hands on his knees. "I think I drank too much." He worked his mouth and spit.

"Bubba, getting the plane off the ground is one thing . . . getting it back down is another story."

Fat spoke without opening his eyes, "No sweat."

Mann made a last try. "Like the man says, Fat, the T-37 is the safest jet in the world; it'll just barely kill you."

Fat chose to ignore the words of his protégé. The former navigator, who worked hard to win the much-coveted pilot training slot, countered by providing more nutrients for the dead grass. Tomorrow would mark three-and-a-half years as an officer for him; he'd be a captain. He was promising himself that the day after his promotion celebration would mark the anniversary of his swearing off alcohol for the rest of his life.

The line taxi stopped. Mann bounced up three steps into the bed of the slat-sided truck and collapsed on the bench seat. Chance lurched into the truck without falling. Mann grinned and shook his head. "Son, you are one, each, idiot, bona fide."

Daylight was gaining a foothold when the driver dropped Mann and the suffering future captain off at the edge of a vast field of short, squatty little jet aircraft.

The Cessna T-37, the Air Force's primary trainer, was powered by a pair of J-69 centrifugal-flow jet engines; because they turned at an extremely high RPM, the powerplants could well be described as kerosene-fueled sirens. Some of the diminutive aircraft's detractors referred to it as a six-thousand-pound dog whistle . . . most pilots called it The Tweet.

Mann watched Chance make his way across the ramp, barely weaving. The crew chief standing by Chance's Tweet took one whiff of the pilot then backed off and tried to hand him the maintenance log from six feet away. When the drunk pilot turned his back, the crew chief raised his hands and face to heaven; Mann could see the crew chief's lips moving.

Chance's preflight hit an early snag when he started having trouble getting the canvas cover off his plane's pitot boom, an action requiring a level of dexterity somewhat akin to that possessed by a one-armed tumbleweed. Mann chuckled to himself. *That boy has lost his mind.*

Lieutenant Tumbleweed, with help from the devout crew chief, finished his preflight, started up, and left the chocks when Mann did.

Senior instructors, assisted by a couple of students, controlled the launch and recovery of the training aircraft from two separate mobile units. The small traffic control units were glassed-in boxes—pared down control towers—one to control the T-37 runway, one for the T-38 side. They were called mobile control units because they were permanently fixed to the beds of two-and-a-half-ton trucks. The call sign for the mobile unit parked by the T-37 runway was Weakeyes.

Mann beat Chance to the runway by seconds. As he neared the runway, Mann closed his canopy then pressed the mike switch on the inboard throttle. "Weakeyes, Pogey Two-zero's holding short."

The instructor pilot in the mobile control unit said, "Pogey Two-zero, taxi into position and hold."

"Pogey Two-zero, roger. Canopy down and locked, light out."

The mobile controller cleared Mann for takeoff and he was accelerating through fifty knots when he heard the controller clear Fat onto the runway. "Pogey One, position and hold."

"Pogey One. Canopy down an' locked, light out."

Mann lifted off and moved the landing gear handle up. Behind him mobile said, "Pogey One, cleared for takeoff."

Mann raised his flaps and ran through a quick after-takeoff checklist.

Mann and Chance were the early birds, and the radio was quiet. The Superstition Mountains were losing another battle to hold back the day.

Climbing through five thousand feet, Mann unhooked the zero-delay lanyard on his parachute, checked his fuel state, and looked to see how much oxygen he had. *Nice day over the desert . . . smooth air. It was Friday . . . twofers at the club and maybe a ride over to Luke to celebrate Fat's promotion.*

Chance's voice on the radio interrupted his reverie.

"Weakeyes, this's Pogey One."

The pilot-controller holding the mike, Captain Walt Gresham, glanced at his log—Pogey One was the call sign of the solo student who had just launched, the class commander of 72-01.

"Pogey One, Weakeyes. Go." The tone of Gresham's reply said *it's barely dawn and I don't want to be bothered until I've finished my coffee and doughnuts.*

"Roger, Weakeyes," the words ran together slightly, "Pogey One r'ques' straight in."

Local flying regulations dictated that straight-in approaches were to be reserved for unusual circumstances and emergencies. The voice that answered Pogey One was no longer bothered by the interruption. "Pogey One, Weakeyes. Say the nature of your problem."

"Pogey One. I doan feel s'good."

The instructor cursed Pogey One out loud, then keyed the mike. "Roger, Pogey One, you're cleared straight in for runway three-zero left. Check your oxygen, 100 percent. Wind calm."

The sun was proclaiming another silent victory over The Superstitions while Fat was mumbling, "R'r, straydin. Hunninbuhzin."

The controller's frustration and the cursing in the mobile unit increased in direct proportion to the slurring from the airplane. Gresham could envision his name prominently highlighted in the coming accident investigation records.

"Pogey One, this is Weakeyes." Slowly, distinctly—hard words that warned, *If you crash that airplane on my watch, it better kill you.* "Turn your landing light on and check 'Gear Down and Locked' at three miles for a full stop. Are you requesting the crash crew?"

"B'geewun. Negadiffgrashgrew . . . lannin' lyedawn . . . kear cheg . . . vuhlstob."

Chance's rejection of the crash crew's attendance came out of a desire to involve as few people as possible in the custom-made crisis he'd engineered . . . and Gresham knew it. However, if the Tweet so much as blew a tire and the crash crew wasn't on the scene, some bloodthirsty lieutenant colonel would organize a posse to hunt down crucifixion candidates, and they'd find Gresham first. While his assistants used binoculars to scan the southeastern sky for the Tweet, the instructor flipped a clear plastic cover up and pressed the red button housed beneath it.

Of the several radios in the mobile unit, one was tuned to the ground control frequency for Williams Tower. When the button under Gresham's thumb hit its bottom limit, lights flashed and klaxons bawled in several facilities near the runways, and the speaker behind Gresham's shoulder started talking, "Attention all aircraft, this is Williams Ground Control. We have an emergency in progress. All aircraft taxing at Williams hold your position for emergency vehicles."

On a long white building near the base of the tower, three large bay doors ran up their tracks, and the fire trucks came forth as if to pay homage to the winner of that day's mountain versus sun contest; men hanging on the trucks were helping one another don asbestos suits that glittered in the victor's red-orange light. Gresham picked up a handset and told the ground controller what he needed to know about the aircraft's situation.

The firefighter in the passenger's seat of the lead truck keyed his mike. "Willie Ground, this is Crash Two rolling. Say status, please."

"Crash Two, Williams Ground Control. We have one T-37 aircraft two-and-one-half miles out for runway three-zero left; the pilot is apparently sick. Tail number two-seven-four, one soul on board, one hour of fuel remaining. You are cleared all taxiways to hold short of runway three-zero left." On the ramp below the tower the rotors of the crash unit's helicopter were picking up speed.

"Willie Ground," said the chopper pilot, "Crash One, taxi."

"Crash One, Williams Ground Control, you're cleared to air-taxi all taxiways, all runways. Change to tower frequency two-two-seven-point-niner."

Gresham was watching the Tweet; both second lieutenants were peering at the aircraft through binoculars. Gresham touched the nearest student on the shoulder. "Has he got his gear down?"

The student nodded without taking his eyes off the aircraft. "Gear, flaps, and speed brake, sir."

Gresham added a little insurance. "Pogey One, recheck your oxygen 100 percent, and take a deep breath. Wind calm, runway three-zero left, you're cleared to land."

The overhead speaker filled the mobile unit with an electric intake of breath. The eruption of sound that followed was caused by Chance's struggle to get his oxygen mask unsnapped before he threw up.

Only the people inside the mobile unit could hear the expletives the instructor was yelling because he didn't transmit the words over the radio. Everyone at Williams Air Force Base within ten feet of a radio heard what went on in the Tweet because Chance kept his thumb on his mike switch while he managed to spray the remaining contents of his tummy all over the glare shield, the instrument panel, and himself while cursing the effects of cheap whiskey mixed with cheaper wine. The two student pilots in the mobile unit did not look at each other. They kept their backs turned to the instructor and their binoculars fixed on the wobbling airplane, hoping Gresham would be too distracted to notice what they were going through to keep from laughing out loud.

Sixty seconds later, closely escorted by several million dollars worth of fire and rescue equipment, Chance rolled to a stop on the runway.

At five o'clock that afternoon, Mann and Chance were in the lounge at the Williams O'Club. Mann was allowing himself a full night of whooping it up to celebrate Chance's coming promotion to captain. They had choice places at the bar and were swilling down twofer beers when their assistant flight commander, Captain Jess Deaton, and his wife strolled in from the dining room. The instructor saw them, turned to say something to his wife, then started through the crowd in their direction. Chance had just finished telling Mann for the thousandth time how "grooving" it was to not get executed for using up a flying period, cussing over the radio, and essentially setting a lofty new standard for stupidity. Mann had been readily agreeing with his mentor right up to the moment he spied Deaton. He had done nothing wrong, but he took one look at the pilot bearing down on them and wished he was at the other end of the bar—or maybe the continent.

Captain Jesse Rand Deaton had used his F-86 to shoot down a MiG in Korea; he was a genuine fighter pilot and a hero to the students in Orange Flight. On Mann's second ride in the Tweet, he went up with Deaton and during a flight lasting an hour and a half they spent a full hour upside down. *Mann, you can't learn how to fly if you're out here right side up, boring holes in the sky.*

Mann was pinned to the bar. Pilots pressing in for the last round of twofers had him trapped next to a new captain who probably had only seconds to live—and Mann might lose his life because he was standing in the vicinity. The greedy fools at the bar obviously cared less about an innocent black boy's life than they did about the opportunity to buy cheap alcohol.

Deaton stopped at Mann's elbow and spoke to Chance. "You cost us a flying period this morning." Some instructors occasionally yelled at their students, a few others always yelled, but no one had ever heard the genuine fighter pilot so much as raise his voice. The students called him R. C. or R. H. behind his back because he was really cool, or really hot, depending on who was telling the war story.

Mann's monumentally stupid roommate put his beer on the bar and straightened. He turned his face into an expressionless mask and, by plumbing the depths of his wisdom, came up with the only acceptable response. "Yes, sir. No excuse, sir."

Buddy, you're a day late and a dollar short, thought Mann, *and he's gonna have me shot for hanging out with you.*

Captain Really Cool didn't say "Good evening," "Kiss my foot," or "Go jump in the lake." He looked Chance in the eye and said, as he tapped his own chest, "If I fly when I'm drunk," then tapped the idiot's, "that means you fly when you're drunk." He let that sink in while he took a drag off his cigarette, then asked, "You savvy?"

Chance transformed himself into a genius by taking the contrition route. He nodded like a sage and responded with a rock-solid, "Yes, sir."

"Good." The guy had some kind of quality in his voice that made any listener know he was always going to be naturally cool. "Lemme buy you studs a beer."

Deaton caught the attention of the bartender, stirred the air above his head with his beer bottle, and held up three fingers. As soon as he knew the refreshments were on the way, Deaton turned his attention to the one who hadn't managed to escape. "So . . . Mann."

The innocent black boy froze.

The instructor smiled. It wasn't a big smile, but it was definitely a smile.

"I guess this makes you the other half of the Gold Dust Twins." He jerked his head toward Chance. "Are you as stupid as this character?" The not-big smile was still in place.

Whew! He wasn't in trouble. He picked up the free beer and took a short swallow. "No, sir," he winked at the MiG-killer and spoke the truth, "but he's been working with me on weekends."

Chance turned his head and started coughing.

Deaton wasn't interested in comic relief; the smile wasn't there anymore. "How come you let the man get in the plane drunk?"

Mann didn't wink. He didn't flash a conspiratorial grin. He went to the only common ground . . . pilot to pilot. "Would you have held him back, Captain?"

The instructor mulled over the question while he took a swallow of his beer, then changed the subject. "What's on your dream sheet for when you graduate, Mann? You gonna train for the airlines or go into single-seat work?"

Mann knew what he was going to do, but it was too soon to have anyone else know. "Right now, I'm just tryin' get to the T-38 side, Captain. One thing at a time, you know."

Cool nodded slowly. His silence overtook the hubbub around them while he looked at Mann as if searching for the answer to an unasked question. After too long a time he hoisted the beer and said, "You two jokers try to sober up before you get back to the line." He turned, surveyed the crowd, and located his wife. "See ya out there."

CHAPTER FOUR

Eight days after the encounter with Captain Deaton, a badly hungover Bill Mann was slouched at a table by Willie's O'Club pool; Rusty and Jane Mattingly, Mann's instructor and his wife, shared the table. Chance was passed out on a nearby lounger, his normally pale skin burned salmon pink by a too-bright November sun. It was early Saturday afternoon and Mann was suffering from the ongoing tutelage by Chance on the basics of being a fighter pilot. Breakfast had been a small handful of aspirin and a few red roosters—beer mixed with tomato juice. Brunch was more aspirin and more roosters. Chance's hangover therapy was giving Mann a nine-hour head start on whatever the evening might serve up.

"Her name's Penelope Powell, and she is unreservedly the most beautiful woman in the Southwest." Jane Mattingly was making her pitch from beneath a broad-brimmed sun hat—white, with a black ribbon to match her swimsuit.

"Prettier than the T-38?" Mann's thoughts stayed more on the training program than on social interaction. He lifted his sunglasses and winked hopefully at Rusty.

Jane leaned forward, and her mouth turned down at the corners. She didn't use profanity as often as some, but Mann's resistance to her matchmaking efforts was threatening to bring out the stern side of her vocabulary. "Bill, you've been here five months and you spend all of

28

your time with your nose in a beer bottle or some airplane book. You need to get out and breathe a little desert air."

Dealing with Jane's verbal onslaught while he suffered in the sun's brilliance was causing Mann's brain to swell. Instructors' wives were not in the official chain of command, but any student pilot who would willingly antagonize one of them was operating without the smarts needed to use a pencil sharpener. He looked at his instructor for help. "I could use a little six-coverage here."

"Well, son," Rusty held his beer between himself and the sun, squinting through the brown glass as if the bottle contained a fine wine, "I'd like to help . . ." he interrupted himself to pass the opening of the brown bottle beneath his nose and sniffed, took a sip, rolled it around in his mouth and swallowed, "but the way I figure it is like this. As long as I keep Miz Janie Pate Mattingly happy, I can make you and every other pilot in Uncle Sam's Air Arm mad and go to the house. If I have to choose between you and her," he waved the bottle at Jane, "you're gonna end up flying flight engineer on a glider." He gave Mann a you're-on-your-own grin and held the bottle back up to the sun.

Jane was a tennis player—a competitive one—and she'd been pressing Mann for two months, trying to fix him up with her doubles partner. His station in life, Jane's tenacity, and his hangover finally forced him to give in or risk having the pressure brought by Jane cause his brain to start oozing out his ears. "Is she black?"

"She most certainly is." The frown became a brilliant smile—Jane knew she'd won. "Rusty said you'd never date a white girl."

"No offense."

Jane giggled. "None taken."

Yes, ma'am, he would meet them at the Luke O'Club on Friday evening. Yes, ma'am, at six o'clock sharp.

Luke Air Force Base was on the west side of Phoenix—a forty-five minute drive from Williams—but they had cheaper beer and better steaks. And because it was a fighter pilots' club, Luke also had a louder jukebox, which was good because it was rumored that Miss Penelope Powell liked to dance.

No, ma'am, he wouldn't drink too much.

Yes, ma'am, he knew how to dance.

No, ma'am, he wouldn't bring Chance.
Yes, ma'am, he would behave himself and be polite.
No, ma'am, he wouldn't embarrass Jane.
Yes, ma'am, he'd be glad to drive Miss Penelope Powell home.
Dern!!!

CHAPTER FIVE

Late Friday afternoon Mann parked the Corvette among its brothers and cousins in the Luke O'Club lot and stepped out. A formation of F-4s entering the overhead traffic pattern demanded his attention; the distinctive shriek of the aircraft's engines likened itself to the high-pitched blare of a trumpet, as if heralding a landmark event. The F-4 was definitely going to be part of his life, but it would have to wait. If his plan held together, he was a year away from a tour in Southeast Asia, flying the last of the military's propeller-driven fighters.

Mann stepped into the club and found himself in an atmosphere saturated with noise more raucous and just as ear-piercing as that on any flightline. Friday afternoon was replicating itself at Air Force Officers' Clubs across the world's time zones from Turkey to Thailand. Happy Hour . . . Twofers Time . . . loud laughter, louder music, and the same animated conversations clicked into place hourly around the globe. Most of the pilots who populated this particular club lived a life normally available only to people in adventure movies; these were the good-looking, lean-jawed, hard-bellied, young fighter pilots who flew the McDonnell F-4 Phantom. And, because an adventurous lifestyle often serves as a bridge to attractive people of the opposite sex, these men had worthy company. It would come as no surprise to a fore-thinking person that every woman in the Luke O'Club fit somewhere in a spectrum that ranged from Gidget-cute to cold-sweat gorgeous.

Mann spotted Rusty at a table overlooking the tennis courts and started in that direction. Halfway to the table he discovered he was on an intercept course with Jane Mattingly and the girl who had to be his date. The women were weaving through the tables, moving toward Rusty. Janie was talking over her shoulder and the girl trailing her was leaning forward to listen—Miss Powell seemed unaware that conversations in her vicinity lost volume as she moved past the crowded tables of loud-talking men at arms. She had skin the color of rich cream with coffee in it, her hair was soft brown—the only thing black about the woman was her dress. The garment, in concert with the woman wearing, had what it took to transform dim light into daydreams.

He watched the girl's figure move away from him and thought, *Maybe there's a God in heaven, after all.*

"Hey, Bill!" Harry Benbrook, a classmate from Willie, signaled to Mann from the bar.

"Hey, Benny." Mann made a detour. Maybe his respiration rate would settle down while he was visiting with Benbrook. "Checking out your next assignment?"

Benbrook's eyes followed the girl in the black dress. "Right now I'm checking out that woman."

"What woman?" Jane and the girl were at their table. Rusty stood, and the ladies took chairs at his table.

Benbrook's attention stayed fixed on the point in hopes the black dress would resurface. It didn't. "She was with Mattingly's wife." His eyes were locked on the spot. Nothing. "Son!"

He gave his attention back to Mann. "Well, whaddya think?" The two student pilots were actually in an officers' club on a fighter base.

"Don't know it, Benny. You got the place scoped out?" Mann's thoughts were on the black dress. He plucked a bar napkin from a nearby stack and dabbed at the beads of sweat under his nose. *"Son!" is right!* He dipped his fingers into a glass of cherries behind the bar, snagged one, and used a cool thumb-flick thing Chance taught him to pop the fruit into his mouth. The cherry missed and he grabbed another napkin to mop sticky red juice out of his eye. Thankfully enough, Benbrook was busy with his beer and missed the display.

Benbrook put his beer on the bar and grinned. "Yep. I think this would make a good home for about six months."

Luke was the home of the F-4 Phantom training program, a six-month course that served to complete men's lives. The Phantom was an afterburner-equipped jet fighter armed with a gun and air-to-air missiles—born and bred to be a MiG-killer—and currently the workhorse of the air war over Viet Nam. For pilots who yearned to pit their skills against a similarly-equipped enemy, the F-4 answered all the questions.

Mann let his gaze take in the surroundings as he listened to laughter and banter compete with the jukebox. Every man in the club looked as if he had a congenital problem with his backbone. They slouched on bar stools, leaned on the bar, and reclined to near horizontal in chairs flanking the cocktail tables. Men who made their living moving at transonic speeds in roaring, vibrating, fire-breathing machinery found it easy to relax in a place that was standing still and serving almost-free beer. The younger pilots moved their hands through the sky inside the lounge while they related their latest war story. The field-grade officers—the majors, lieutenant colonels, and colonels for whom the war stories had become a routine way of life—exchanged golfing tips. Beautiful wives and girlfriends of all ages smiled on their mates; made tennis, bridge, and swimming pool dates; and occasionally pulled their designated pilot away from the competing affection and onto the dance floor.

Mann smiled again. He was home.

He slapped Benbrook on the shoulder and turned away. "Good luck, amigo."

"What about you, Bill. What're you gonna do after we graduate?"

"Who knows?" he answered over his shoulder. "Mattingly says maybe a glider."

"Yeah, sure." Benbrook's answer was mechanical; the would-be fighter pilot's eyes were back in the target-acquisition mode.

Jane Mattingly and Mann's date were settled in when he got to them. He approached the table from behind Jane; the new girl looked up, and he smiled. She had blue eyes and she knew it, and she didn't waste them on waiters. Her face went from neutral to pleasant-neutral—no return smile for the man in the white shirt and black slacks.

"Hi." Her voice had a husky quality. "Can I start with a large glass of ice water, please? I'm dying of thirst." Her attention went back to the people at her table.

Rusty looked up and started to speak. Mann him gave a negative head shake. The IP stared at him for a second, then caught on and rolled his eyes.

Jane was digging in her purse and never looked up. Rusty touched her arm. "Honey, you wanna drink?"

"Mmm . . . water's good for now," she said.

Rusty looked resigned. "You heard 'em, sport, an' you better bring us all one of these." He waved his beer bottle.

"Coming right up," answered Mann. He turned and started for the bar.

Jane looked over her shoulder when she heard Mann's voice. "Where's he going?"

Rusty touched the side of her foot with his toe. "He's getting our drinks, cutie."

Jane gave Rusty a look and went back to her purse; Miss Powell stared straight ahead and drummed her fingers on the chair arm. The redheaded pilot grinned, tipping the beer to his lips while sliding farther down in his chair. *Well, this blind date thing might not be totally boring after all.*

Mann returned with a tray full of drinks. He put a coaster and a glass of water in front of Jane while she was framing a question for Rusty. Next he put a beer in front of each person, listening as the black girl interrupted Rusty's answer. "Okay, Janie, you've got me trapped in this joint. Are you going to tell me what this walk-on-water superman is really like? Surely he has at least one fault."

Mann said, "Excuse me," and put the second water glass in front of the girl wearing the daydream dress. "One large ice water for Miss Powell."

The girl stiffened. She didn't snap her head around but let it move in one definitive motion until her eyes were aimed at the man behind the tray. It had taken her almost a tenth of a second to see through the scam, and Mann was overcome by a belated realization that the practical joke was a monumental mistake.

She took her time speaking, then clipped her words, "That . . . was . . . mean." Her face was expressionless; the eyes weren't. Maybe people with eyes the color of the Caribbean always look like they know other people's secrets.

Mann was busy wishing he'd played the meeting straight and held her gaze precisely one-and-one-half seconds too long. He succeeded in getting his own beer onto the table without dropping the tray in her lap then turned and pretended to look for his chair. The effects of the eyes had apparently popped several circuit breakers in his central nervous system, and he was forced to let his body drop into the empty chair in much the same way he would've had he been in control of his muscles. He was too nervous to slouch. *Son, if you mess with a woman who can do that to you with one look, you are dead in the road.*

Mann missed something Jane said while he thought about the girl's eyes and waited for his brain to right itself. When his sense of hearing returned, Rusty was saying, ". . . couldn't tell you, but you're right about him having some faults. He thinks he's a comedian."

Jane filled the conversation's next void with a comment about the good music on the jukebox. Mann was thankful that someone else was talking; he was still scared to try his own voice. *If I don't speak soon, she's going to wonder if I understand English.*

Rusty tried to cover for him by starting a long war story about something no one was interested in. When he got an opportunity, he frowned at Mann and jerked his head toward the girl.

Mann tried to swallow. Someone had stuffed dry crackers in his throat.

The girl with the eyes interrupted Rusty's war story. "I *said*, that was *mean*." The indictment came from a mouth that had no difficulty shaping itself to correspond with her tone.

Jane was nothing if not loyal to her doubles partner. She mock-frowned at Rusty and nodded her vote at Mann. "You should both be ashamed," she said primly.

"I know when to plead guilty." Rusty pushed his chair back and chose that moment to leave his student to fend for himself. "C'mon, good-lookin', I've had just enough beer to remind me what a great dancer I am."

Jane winked at Mann and laughed while the coward drew her chair back. "Play nice, kiddies."

The girl watched the couple make their way into the melee before she spoke again. "Well? You haven't said anything." *Jane Mattingly has fixed me up with an imbecile.*

He shrugged and became serious. "I harbor no ill will toward you for your harsh response. In fact, I find it in my heart—"

Well, he isn't too drunk to talk. "You know what I mean. Janie's right, you should both be ashamed . . . especially you."

He pointed at Rusty's chair. "He must be Ashamed, I'm Lieutenant William P. Mann." *Please tell me I didn't say anything that corny.*

Her expression reflected a minimal level of tolerance while she extended her hand and announced formally, "Penelope Powell." *I'm trapped in a nightmare, and Jane Mattingly is in big trouble.*

He took the hand for a moment, then reached for his beer. *Okay, enough with the stupid remarks, Redford.* "So? Am I off the hook?"

"I'd say you're struggling." Centered in the strikingly-beautiful face was a pert nose she used in harmony with her eyes to indicate her current level of offered favor. She tilted her head slightly and pulled several strands of hair into place behind her ear. She was wearing red fingernail polish and long silver earrings. "Do you, by some miracle, know how to dance?"

"Sho', baby." He risked the low-level humor. "All us waiters got rhythm."

"Humph." The pert nose warned him away from future attempts at comedy. "We'll see." She stood up and reached for his hand.

She was taller than average and, except for some perfectly-proportioned round areas, she was almost slender. And though she had a "tennis player" look, he was compelled to note that all gifted female athletes do not walk like men.

The trip to the dance floor could easily salvage the evening. A dance or two would give him time to get over the effect of her eyes, and he was the best dancer he'd ever been around. That he had never been around Penelope Powell was not factored into his equations.

Thanks to the Luke Officers' Wives' Club, the lounge, like most others in the Air Force, had a large dance floor. The officers' wives' motive was simple when you thought about it—they wanted to remove one more obstacle from any opportunity they might have to pry their men away from the other pilots. A rarely-crowded dance floor stopped one excuse before it started.

The couple was weaving between tables, almost to the polished surface. "So," he asked, "do I call you Penny or Penelope?"

She half-turned and glanced at him over her shoulder; the pert nose was registering something between utter boredom and mild distaste. "Call me whatever you like. My friends call me Pip."

The Mamas and the Papas complained in harmony about something happening on a winter's day; people on the shiny parquet squares swayed to the music; the tinkle of glass on glass behind the bar lost its edge and became the slow motion sound of wind chimes . . . then silence. His pace slowed, the couples moving on the dance floor became a kaleidoscope of soft colors before fading to indistinct grays. His feet quit moving and her hand slipped from his.

The girl stopped and turned.

Mann's gaze was fixed on a point in the distance beyond her.

He could no longer hear the easy laughter and music. He didn't see the people. He smelled woodsmoke.

Bill Mann was somewhere else . . .

He and Mose Washington, the old black man who passed himself off as his grandfather, were sitting at the kitchen table in a house near Pilot Hill, Texas, looking at a tattered picture album—the album smelled of woodsmoke. Mose was telling him stories of bygone days. A snapshot of a beautiful young black woman—half-turned, looking back over her shoulder at the camera—was superimposed over Mann's recent vision. The black-and-white image had successfully captured the personality of the woman: confidence in the eyes . . . minimal tolerance for foolishness . . . and centered in the beautiful face, with barely a hint of an upward tilt . . . a small, straight nose it was a picture of Mose's wife. Mose had been dead for two years, his wife more than ten; her name was Pip.

Miss Powell stepped close and tapped the center of his chest with one of the red fingernails; her smile was forced. "Hey." The fake smile gave up and she poked his chest again. "Hey!"

He coughed into his hand. "Sorry."

She stepped back, barely able to generate an interest in the cause of his brain lapse. "What was that all about? You don't strike me as the weak, silent type."

"Sorry." He coughed again and cleared his throat. "I'm . . . uh . . . don't do well after I reach my limit."

She raised an eyebrow. "Your limit?"

"Yeah. Half a beer usually does it for me."

"Mmm." She was going to hold off on her departure for one dance. *One dance . . . three minutes, then I'm going to be attacked by a splitting head-ache . . . and tomorrow I'm going to kill Jane Mattingly in front of God and everybody.* "I think you need to wear your oxygen mask a little tighter."

"I left it at the table." *Well, at least I didn't fall down or drool.*

Cass and the gang were working through a high-fidelity prayer about the color of some leaves. Mann and Pip slow-danced while he took his time finding his way back to the present.

Thank goodness. At least he can sway back and forth. "Well, I'm almost impressed."

"Thanks." He had not regained access to what it took to be cool.

The next song was a Jerry Reed thing that was too fast for danc-ing. They stood beside the jukebox, uninterested, watching a few cou-ples who should've known better while they tried to keep up with the music. He didn't talk—she didn't care. When the song was over, she held out her hand. "Got a quarter?"

He put the coin in her palm and she dropped it in the jukebox. Miss Powell made the selections and reached for his hand. "Well, Lieutenant Mann, are you ready for your check ride?"

A cascade of piano notes—the intro for "Rockin' Pneumonia and the Boogie-Woogie Flu"—spilled from the music machine's speakers, and someone let out a rebel yell. Lieutenant Mann and Miss Powell stepped onto the dance floor.

A person might have to expend some casual observation energy to figure out that Miss Powell didn't walk like a man; the same individual would only have to be in the same room with her to know she didn't dance like one. In fact, an astute observer would not have to make his judgment based on watching the girl; all he needed to do was watch the men who watched her.

Johnny Rivers was a dozen words into his self-diagnosis when Miss Powell did a shuffle step and shoulder-roll thing while watching her partner mirror-match the move. He winked . . . she grinned and winked back.

Minutes later, while they waited for the next record, Pip held onto Bill's arm and laughed out loud at something he was saying. Jane Mattingly was ordering champagne.

Distinctive guitar sounds gave notice that The Hollies were coming to tell the world about a "Long Cool Woman In A Black Dress" . . . and Bill took her hand. Rehearsals were over.

The Hollies' bass player stepped into the song's intro and the woman in the black dress used the beat to make a smooth, rhythm-wrapped turn. The pilot nearest the couple nudged the man next to him and the two pilots and their partners stopped dancing to watch.

In short seconds, the attractive black couple had the dance floor to themselves. The witnesses saw nothing suggestive, nothing lewd—just the soul-scalding fusion of femininity with four-four time. Word spread . . . the pilots in the stag bar defied the "No fight suits in the lounge after five" rule and crowded into the lounge to watch. Had the pilots been naked and shooting fireworks, the club officer might've noticed. War stories throughout the club were on hold. Officers and gentlemen in the farthest reaches of the lounge were standing on chairs and cocktail tables to watch; those within twenty feet of the black dress were forgetting to breathe. Pip rewarded them by living out every syllable of the musical word picture.

When the music ended, the almost-famous couple wound their way back to their table while the crowd cheered and applauded. The wing commander's wife leaned toward him and patted his leg. "You better come out of 'burner, sonny boy; you're wastin' gas." She offered him the napkin from under her drink glass. "Here."

The colonel laughed at himself while he blotted at the sweat on his forehead. "I read you five square, kid."

His wife graced him with a smile strictly for the benefit of any on-lookers. The commander of the Fighter Training Wing at Luke Air Force Base had earned himself a soon-to-come emergency-in-progress.

The next week brought Thanksgiving and Rusty Mattingly's orders to leave the Air Training Command and report to the F-4 school at Luke. Mann and Pip went with the Mattinglys to the Luke O'Club to celebrate.

Several pilots clapped and whistled when the foursome returned to the scene of Pip's triumph. Mann waved at the fans and said, "I can't believe they remember me."

Rusty hooted.

Pip wanted to dance and Mann was her willing partner. One of the pilots had already bought four quarters worth of The Hollies, Johnny Rivers, and CCR.

Three beers later, Pip and Mann were on the dance floor giving impromptu dancing lessons to a dozen pilots and their ladies. The wing commander and his wife opted out.

When the new year arrived, the Mattinglys were in the process of moving across town to an apartment near Luke. Mann was helping Rusty load boxes.

They were between loads when Rusty asked, "Well, how's it going with Pip?"

Mann grinned. "As well as can be expected, I guess."

"Yeah," Rusty snorted, "I'm gonna go back and tell Janie, 'It's going as well as can be expected.' If I start bringing home that kind of intel, I'll have to move in with you."

"What can I say?" What could he say? On Friday and Saturday nights, he and Pip divided their time between the O'Clubs at Williams and Luke; they played tourist all day on Saturday and Sunday. She was smart, funny, and beautiful; she liked the Vette, she liked having fun, and she liked being with him. What else was there? He had never been in love, but if this was what it felt like, he could get used to it.

"How's training?" Rusty probed.

"Pretty all right," Mann muttered. He was busy gathering an armful of pillows.

"Man, you're a veritable wellspring of information." Rusty was getting his arms around a box full of books. "How do you like the '38? Where do you stand in the class? Are you still in the Air Force?"

"The '38 is a one each, slick machine." Mann busied himself with the stack of pillows. "I'm probably in the top five."

The box Rusty was hefting slipped out of his hands and his mouth fell open. "Tell me you're joking."

Mann shrugged. "Nope."

"You dropped four slots in two months?" Rusty was incredulous.

Mann rested his load on the back of a chair and frowned slightly. Rusty was his friend now, not his instructor. "Look, Rusty, she's the greatest thing that ever happened to me. If I slide a little in the class standings because I'm getting to spend time with her, I'll live with it." He shrugged again. "I can still get the airplane I want when we graduate."

"Slide a little? Amigo, you're the best stick I've ever seen . . . the best I've ever heard about. By the time you were two months into the program, *I* was learning things from *you*." Rusty hated to tell Mann what he already knew, but he had to say it. "If you graduate fifth in the class, brother, you won't be a distinguished graduate. Not making DG will affect your career."

"Being a DG isn't my life."

"It was two months ago."

Mann wanted to disarm his friend before the serious argument started. He grinned again and went back to the pillows. "Two months ago I was lost, amigo . . . now I am found."

Rusty wanted to tell him there was more to life than dancing and drinking, but he saw the wall going up and backed off.

Five months later, in early June, the students of Class 72-01 were handed their orders. Guided by the students' "dream sheets" and class standings, the Air Force decided where each of them would be stationed and what types of aircraft they would be flying after graduation from UPT. Mann just missed making Distinguished Graduate, but because of his rank in the class, he would be going to his aircraft and base of choice. That evening he took Pip up to Camelback for mesquite-grilled steaks.

The steak hung off the edges of his plate. He'd eaten a piece the size of a quarter.

She put her fork down. "You aren't eating."

"Not hungry, I guess." He was using the bottom of his glass to make water rings on the table.

"Mm-hmm." He never didn't eat. She leaned back in her chair and folded her hands in her lap. "Tell momma all about it."

He sat up straighter and pretended to take a sip of water while he glanced at the people around them. The closest couple was two tables away. He rested his arms on the table and beckoned her closer. She scooted forward, trembling because she thought she knew what he was going to ask.

She did . . . and she didn't.

She was smiling, trying not to giggle out loud, bringing her arm up to prop her chin in her hand when he whispered, "Could you marry a man who had killed someone?"

Her elbow completely missed the edge of the table and she collapsed forward, knocking her fork off the table. She tried to catch it and spilled her water in the attempt. People turned and stared. The waiter came, blotting up the water and refilling her glass. "I'll be right back with another fork, ma'am."

She and Mann didn't look at each other. Neither spoke. The other patrons smiled at the nervous young couple.

When the waiter came and went and the people stopped staring, she spoke without looking up. "Bill . . . I'm . . . I think I'm scared."

"I know the feeling," he said.

She made herself look at him. "Should I be?"

He sighed and said, "Probably."

After a long silence, she asked, "You?"

"Me . . . yes." He was fooling with his water glass again. "In 1960."

She tilted her head to the side as she did the calculations. "But that's more than ten years ago, Bill. You would've been a child."

"The little bit I've told you puts you in danger."

The self-assured nose didn't even twitch. She sat up straight and nodded, "The answer to your question is 'Yes.' Neither you nor anyone else can tell me anything that would keep me from marrying you."

He leaned back and took a deep breath. "You need to let me tell you the whole thing before you commit yourself."

One or two people watched as the attractive young woman touched her napkin to the corners of her mouth. She put the napkin by her plate and smiled at him. "Would you take me out on the patio, please?"

They sat on a low rock wall behind the restaurant and held hands. On the horizon, pastel pink clouds used the fading sunlight to tint themselves a soft lavender. The mountain breeze was evening comfortable.

"Now," she said. "Tell me."

He'd never told the story, but he'd rehearsed it. "My mother and I were on the way to visit some friends of hers in Alabama. We were traveling through Mississippi in the middle of the night, and we ended up getting trapped on a back road by some white men." He spoke in a quiet monotone. "Two of the men drug my mother out of our car and started beating her. An old black man with a shotgun came out of the darkness and stopped them. I got involved too late to help much." He paused to swallow, then said, "I killed the two who hurt her and passed out right after the shooting.

"Besides the black man, there were two white men who did a lot to help—actually, one of them was just a young kid, a teenager who had what it took to break ranks with those others and stand up for Mom and me; he took a bad beating because of it. The other white man—the grown one—came out of nowhere—like a ghost. The old black man took Mom and me to his cabin and my mother died a few minutes after we got there. When I regained consciousness, the old man and I were miles away. I don't know what happened to the white man who helped us."

Pip knew about his days as a teenager. She said, "The black man who rescued you was your grandfather . . . your Poppa."

"Mmm," he acknowledged. "His real name was Moses Washington; mine is Bill Prince. In 1960, Moses took a new identity and became my grandfather, Mose Mann; on the same day, I became Bill Mann, an orphan. Poppa died in 1968." His voice showed the first traces of emotion. "He was helping save my life . . . again."

"I know this story," she nodded. "You're the child who killed that congressman's son . . ." she was snapping her fingers quietly, trying to remember ". . . uh, something Bainbridge. Every now and then my dad would bring up the subject of how your mother died. That congressman's son was a thug."

"That's the one," he confirmed. "Oliver Wendell Bainbridge."

"And you're that little kid," she was shaking her head in wonder, "the one my dad talked about."

"Not any more . . . that was eleven years ago." He took a breath. "I'm someone else now."

"You were my dad's hero." Her eyes reflected the same anger her father felt. "He said it was self-defense . . . that they should've given you a medal."

Mann's face and tone were expressionless. "They didn't."

After they were silent for a moment, she asked, "If it was self-defense, why did you have to run . . . and why are you having to run now? Why can't you tell people who you are?"

"Simple enough." He was watching the sunset's reflection on the desert. "The courts might turn me loose, but Bainbridge's mother and older brother are still alive . . . she's a congresswoman; I heard he's in the Air Force. They'd do whatever it takes to have me killed."

She followed his gaze to the sunset without seeing it. "And your cousin in Texas . . . Sam Jones?"

"It's a long story. Sam's real cousin, who was two years older than me, died in 1955. Sam and Mose met that same year and became closer than most brothers. Sam's cousin's name—the one who died in '55—was William Patrick Mann." He pointed at his chest. "I became him."

"And the rest of that gang—the ones who attacked you—they got off scot-free?"

Mann knew the history of the white men who were there that night because Mose had friends in Mississippi. "A murderer never gets off scot-free. Most of the ones who were there were just stupid kids. Three of them—the worst of the bunch—were dead within twelve hours;

the rest have had to live with what they allowed to happen. And the one . . ." He was remembering the redheaded kid who tried to stop Bainbridge.

When he didn't continue, she touched his arm. "The one what?"

"The one who tried so hard to help." He could see the kid's face in the bright headlights of the truck. Mann was badly beaten, lying on his back in a muddy ditch, and the white boy was leaning over him, caring, ready to help. "Poppa said his name was Tripper Sherman. He was the youngest one of the whole bunch—barely older than I was—but he was the one who tried to help." Mann shook his head. "Bainbridge gave him a beating just like he did Mom and me. He left home later and joined the Navy."

"Bill, I'm so sorry."

He barely nodded. "It was a long time ago."

She held his hand with both of hers. "I could."

"Hmm?" He turned away from the sunset. "Could what?"

"I could definitely marry a man who has killed someone."

Mann smiled and she smiled back. When he didn't say anything, she laughed softly and leaned close to whisper, "But he has to ask me first."

One of the ladies in the restaurant was watching the couple sitting on the wall bordering the patio. When she realized what the young man was going to do, she pointed and spoke loud enough for everyone in the restaurant to hear her. "Oh, my gosh, y'all! Look!"

The people inside ignored their mesquite-grilled steaks while they watched the young man kneel on the flagstone patio and say something to the woman. The young woman's smile was multiplied throughout the dining room. Whatever she said to the man in return seemed to please him. When they embraced, the spectators clapped and cheered.

A week later, the Mattinglys gave Mann and Pip a poolside engagement party. Mann announced they'd be married immediately after pilot training. He'd be going to Florida for training in the A-1 Skyraider.

The couple planned to take two weeks' leave en route and drive through Texas to introduce Pip to Mann's family.

CHAPTER SIX

Missy's tone said she was waiting for the call. "Hello?"

"Hi," said Mann. "We're here."

"An' we're glad. How soon can y'all come over?" During the past year Missy and Pat received a small handful of calls from Bill and fewer letters. They were ready to meet "the girl."

"We're at the Holiday Inn," he said. "How about if we clean up and be there in about an hour?"

"That'll work out fine. Pat should get home about the time y'all get here, an' we've got some more folks comin' over later to meet Pip. What do y'all want for supper?" Dinner in the Pattersons' house came at noon.

"Surprise us."

"I can do that," Missy laughed.

Missy stood at the front window to watch the Corvette pull into the circular drive and smiled; she helped Mann pick the car out a week before he left for pilot training. Mann walked around the car and opened the door for Pip. *That's a good sign*, she thought.

The girl was nothing short of striking. She stepped out and smiled up at Mann. He laughed and said something. Missy got her first good look at the girl when she stepped past Mann.

Uh-oh, Missy said to herself. The girl was *too* striking.

Pip's skin was the color of light coffee all over—at least, it was from the waist up. Missy knew this because Pip was wearing a white see-through blouse.

"Well, well, well." Missy was too young to be talking to herself, but she was prone to ignore the age limit. She continued to mutter as she untied her apron and tossed it at the back of the nearest chair. Three seconds later, she was bouncing down the sidewalk on the balls of her feet. "We're so glad y'all finally got here."

Mann and Pip were giggling like young children with a secret.

Missy could handle children.

She hugged Mann and kissed Pip on the cheek.

"Bill, I haven't driven that car in a year. Can I take it around the block?" She was holding out her hand for the keys.

If Mann was surprised, it didn't show. He dropped the keys in her hand. "Sure."

"Jump in, Pip, I'll show you around a little. Bill, go make yourself at home." She shooed him toward the house. "Pat's on his way. There's tea in the fridge. You can wait in the den or out on the patio."

Pip waved good-bye to Mann. When he lifted his hand to wave back, he showed his bride five fingers and winked.

"C'mon, honey," Missy smiled and motioned at Pip. "Jump in."

Pip couldn't keep from smiling as she got in the car. "Where're we going?"

"Well, where do you think we're goin', child?" Missy was accelerating out of the driveway. "We're goin' to get you something decent to wear."

"What's wrong with what I've got on?"

"Honeychild, I do *not* let folks in my house wearin' the emperor's clothes."

Pip had to smile; Mann had warned her. "It's 1971, Missy. See-through blouses are fashionable."

"Not in my hacienda, they're not." Missy's tone was gentle, but her words were matter-of-fact. "Walkin' around naked in public went out of style with Eve an' her hubby. My husband's a red-blooded American male, cutie . . . you step in front of him wearin' that getup, an' I will cut me a switch an' beat your hind parts like a borried mule."

Pip laughed. "That hardly seems appropriate for a professor's wife."

Missy flicked the sleeve of the flimsy blouse with her fingertips and sniffed. "People who come in my house half-naked don't get to lecture me on propriety, sugar. *My* Pip quit switchin' me about the time I turned twelve, but I'd bet she'd make an exception in your case."

By the time they pulled up to the Holiday Inn, Pip was fascinated by—and totally enamored with—Missy Patterson.

"You want me to help you pick somethin' modest," Missy asked, "or can you do it by yourself?"

"I give." Pip surrendered with both hands. "I'll be right back."

On the way back to the house, they drove in silence until they stopped at a red light.

"How much did you lose?" Missy asked.

"What?"

"You heard me." Missy was enjoying herself. "How much did he take you for?"

Pip pressed the fingers of one hand against her lips and snickered. "Five dollars."

"How far did you say you'd get?"

"I told him I'd get to sit down before you mentioned it, if you said anything at all. Bill said you'd stop me at the front door."

"You let him sucker you."

"Uh-uh." Pip shook her head emphatically. "No way."

"Oh, yeah, Miss Priss, he had you for lunch. You thought this was all your idea, didn't you?"

Pip's smile faded slightly. "It *was* my idea."

"Which one of you knows me?"

Pip was thoughtful until they pulled into the Patterson's driveway. *Missy was right.* "I'll get him back."

"Well, if you do, I want to hear about it. I'm no dummie, but I can't keep up with 'im."

The ladies were laughing when they walked into the kitchen. Pip slapped a five-dollar bill into Mann's hand and pretended to pout. "I told her I'd get you back."

Mann waved the bill at Pat and put it in his pocket. "Sucker bet."

Missy did some things around the kitchen then walked over to stand beside Mann. She put her arm around her almost-brother's waist and said, "I love you."

Mann smiled and hugged her shoulders. It was good to be home.

Pip watched the black man and white woman who loved each other.

Missy kept her arm around him but leaned back slightly to watch his eyes. "You do know I love you, don't you?"

His mind worked its way back through the years. The smile stayed but softened. Three years earlier, a bucking bull tried to kill Mann and dozens of people from the rodeo crowd came into the arena to rescue him—Missy was the first one over the railing. "I guess I've always known that, Missy."

"Good. Now, go out in the garage an' get some of those shears an' cut me a pecan limb three feet long an' big as your thumb."

Pip's tea glass froze on the way to her mouth.

A somber Bill Mann stood for a moment, looking at the floor. Pat didn't find the directions surprising. Missy went back to the stove.

Without saying anything, Mann put down his tea glass and left the kitchen through the door to the garage.

Pip's knees began to tremble and she put her tea glass on the counter rather than risk spilling it. What manner of people were these whom her husband called friends? In minutes Mann was back with a stick that met the specifications. When he offered it to Missy, Pip felt nauseous.

"Put it on top of the refrigerator," Missy directed.

Pip was almost scared to know what had happened. On the trip to Texas, Bill told her a million times the woman was saddle leather tough. She looked wide-eyed at Missy and dreaded the answer to the question she had to ask. "What's that for?"

Missy stood with one hand on her hip and pointed a wooden spoon at Mann. "Ask him."

Pip looked at Mann.

Mann was remembering a wet afternoon when Missy knocked him—a 180-pound man—off the front porch of his granddad's house with one blow from her tiny fist. He nodded at the petite spitfire, speaking what he knew to be the truth. "She'll use it on me if I ever bring you in here dressed like that again. Right?"

"Close." She left the spoon on the counter and moved next to him, putting one small hand in his and resting the other on his chest. "If you ever encourage her to shame herself in my house again—or anywhere else—I will beat you with it, an' I'll draw blood." A single tear crested in the spitfire's eye, and her lips trembled when she whispered, "An' that's a promise."

Mann put his arms around her, and she tilted into his chest, spilling tears on his shirt. He said, "I was really stupid, Missy, and I apologize."

"Good." She stepped away from him so she could wipe her eyes on her apron and lecture. "An' you need to quit bein' stupid. Where you're fixin' to go, stupid people get killed."

Pip had never seen anything like it. She was standing in a room where a white woman had just promised to beat a grown black man with a stick and he hugged her and apologized for being stupid.

"Now look what you've done." She wiped her eyes again and started out of the kitchen. "I have to go fix my face."

Pip said, "May I go?"

Missy gathered one of the girl's arms in both of hers and hugged it. "Of course you can."

When their women were safely ensconced in the Pattersons' bedroom, Mann looked at Pat and shook his head. Neither of the Pattersons had ever done anything but make him feel he was part of their family. "I made her cry."

"Yeah," Pat didn't smile. "That doesn't happen every day."

"Did you see it coming?"

Pat didn't answer at first. He crossed his arms and stared out at the backyard. "Yeah, I guess." He took a breath and let it out. "I hear her prayers at night."

"Oh." Mann didn't want to hear about Missy's prayers.

In the bedroom Pip took a seat on the bed while Missy perched on a stool in front of an antique dressing table.

"You took a pretty strong stance back there," said Pip.

"Yeah, I did." Missy pulled open a drawer. "An' I meant it."

Pip was puzzled. "So what's the big deal?"

"The big deal is the standard."

"Your standard?"

"Uh-uh," replied Missy. "God's standard."

"Do you get to tell other people what God's standard is?" Pip liked Missy, but she wasn't inclined to let anyone tell her how to live her life, new friend or not.

"Far from it." Missy looked up and disarmed the girl with a soft smile. "But I reserve the right to tell them what the standard is in this house."

"I may be missing something here. You don't seem like the type to cry over a see-through blouse."

"I'm not," Missy sighed. "It's just my frustrations gettin' the better of me. I pray for him—an' now you—every night . . . for y'all to know God. All I see is him movin' further away." She paused and sighed again. "Livin' without God is dangerous, hon."

"What's the point? You do the God thing; we don't. Why should you care?"

"Because if you had cancer and I held the cure, it would be criminal for me not to share it. In that same vein, if what I believe about God is true—an' the overwhelmin' evidence is on my side—then I'm compelled to care."

Pip didn't answer.

Missy was willing to let the silence change the subject. She worked on her damaged makeup and spoke to Pip's reflection in the mirror. "Did Bill tell you that you look like her?"

"Like the other Pip? Mm-hmm." She smiled at a memory. "He almost had a heart attack the first time he noticed."

"She was so beautiful—an' so special."

"How so?"

The subject wouldn't allow itself to be changed. "Well," Missy looked at the girl's reflection and said, "I guess for me to know how to explain, I have to put you on the spot. Tell me what you think about God."

Mann had cautioned Pip that the subject of God would definitely come up. "Mmm . . . I guess I believe in God. I just haven't thought too much about it."

"Will you go to heaven or hell when you die?"

"Heaven."

"If God were to ask you why He should let you in, what would you tell Him?"

"I'd tell Him I'm a good person." Hitler and Stalin and Jack the Ripper were the kind of people who went to hell.

"All right. Think about this before you answer. If what you believe is not true, would you want to know?"

An assortment of replies coursed through Pip's mind before she realized there was only one rational answer. "I'd want to know, but I'm not sure I want to know right now."

"That's honest enough, but it makes tellin' you about my Pip a little harder—maybe impossible." Missy propped her arms on the dressing table and rested from her restoration work for a moment. "The whole thing that went on in our kitchen is all about God, hon . . . but when it comes right down to it, I guess everything in life is. Pip an' her husband were totally an' unalterably sold out to their beliefs. If I try to tell you about her, she'll sound foreign . . . or stuffy . . . or rigid. She wasn't like that at all. My Pip was love with skin on it."

Missy's hands went back to their practiced motions without supervision. She gazed into the mirror and saw the waters of Cat Lake. "You know her son died savin' my life."

Pip nodded. "Bill told me the story on the way here. It must have been awful."

Missy's hands drifted away from her face again and came to rest on the surface of the small dresser; she stared unseeing at a small vial of makeup. "I think it was the most beautiful thing I'll see this side of heaven."

"Beautiful? Wasn't he killed by a snake?"

Missy turned to face the girl. "Junior was more afraid of snakes than anything else in the world. An' he deliberately sacrificed his life to save me."

"How could that happen?"

"Well . . . if you aren't up on what the Bible teaches, you can't understand that demons are at work in the world today, an' your mind will try to reason away what I lived through. Junior an' I were best friends, only he was more loyal than I was . . . mostly because he was a Christian, an' I wasn't. I was seven years old; he was eleven. We were swimmin' in our lake on a Sunday afternoon, an' I was in the water when some water moccasins—about twenty of them—tried to kill me."

Bill hadn't told her how many snakes were involved. "They actually attacked you?"

Missy could see what happened on that Sunday afternoon was going to be impossible for the girl to believe; if she hadn't been there, she'd have a hard time believing it herself. "In strictly simple terms, yes. People back home still talk about what happened that day, an' they still call it The War at Cat Lake. Near the end of the fight, Junior got me out of danger . . . an' seconds later he put himself between my brother an' another snake." She turned back to the mirror and stared at it without seeing. There was no way this girl could fathom what happened at Cat Lake; no one could. When she spoke again, Pip Mann had to lean forward to hear her. "They bit him at least five times. He knew he'd saved our lives, an' he was smilin' when he died. If it hadn't been for Junior, I'd be dead."

"You said it was beautiful."

"It wasn't beautiful at the time. I was in the water surrounded by snakes . . . it was one of those nightmares where you try to run, but no matter how fast you run, the monsters run faster. But now . . . today . . . the memory of what he did is one of the most special things in my life; it always will be." The remembrance was still a thing of everlasting wonder for her. "A little boy . . . an eleven-year-old little black kid . . . savin' the life of a snotty little white brat. One of the men that was there—a white man—said no man will ever do a finer thing. He was right."

She turned back to Pip. "You know why he saved me, Pip? Because he knew I wasn't a Christian. He'd told me about Jesus a thousand times, an' I didn't want to hear it. That brave child willin'ly sacrificed himself so I could have a chance to become a Christian before I died."

Pip thought she understood. "And now you want Bill and me to be like you."

"Not hardly," Missy laughed. She chose her next words carefully, "What I want is for you an' Bill to want to come to the knowledge that fueled Junior's life—that made him a man in a child's body. I want you to get to spend your time here on Earth knowin' you will spend eternity in heaven. I want you to know God."

"What if what you believe isn't true?"

"Why don't you let me tell you what I believe an' judge for yourself?"

Pip couldn't comment. She spent her younger years going to Sunday school, but they didn't talk about demons and snakes, beauty and death, or about being a Christian. Missy was right—most of the story didn't make sense. She said, "Can I ask you for a favor?"

"Anything," said Missy.

"I'm not sure how all of that fits together," said Pip. "Maybe we could take some time for you to explain it more clearly and if what I believe is wrong, maybe I can see what the truth is. Can we do that?"

Missy smiled. "That would not only be fun; it would be appropriate. That's what Junior's parents did for me." Then she said the same thing Pip Washington said the day after Christmas in 1945. "When do you want to start?"

The girl wasn't sure what she was getting into. "We'll be in Florida for two months, then Bill's going to be in Viet Nam for a year and I'm planning to stay in Phoenix. Can we do it by mail?"

"Yes, ma'am, we most certainly can. In fact, I can go you one better."

"What's that?"

"You're family now. If you decide you want to live in Texas at any time while he's over there, you can stay right here with us. But there's one condition."

Pip was caught off guard. "What is it?"

"You have to come to me. This is not somethin' that will happen because I have to force-feed you."

"Okay." Pip was relieved. "Maybe I could come for a visit."

"You know you can." She made a final assessment of her makeup then stood and took the girl's arm. "C'mon. Cryin' always makes me hungry."

CHAPTER SEVEN

In August, Mann, his new pilot's wings, and his new wife arrived in Florida—the land where he would start living his lifelong dream. Hurlburt Air Force Base was where he was going to become a fighter pilot—just like his dad.

The Douglas A-1 Skyraider was obsolete before it came off the assembly line. It was affectionately dubbed the Spad by every pilot in the military, partly because the Navy designated it Special Purpose, Attack, Douglas, or SPAD. Designed in the 1940s as a single-seat, single-engine fighter, it was equipped with a 2700 horsepower engine and armed with four wing-mounted machine guns. It could fly long-range to a target, deliver a bomb load equal to that of the B-17, then fight its way home.

Although it made itself useful in the Korean War and garnered the admiration of the ground troops, it was soon relegated to a second-string role behind the jets. After the war, the plane perched on the periphery of Naval Aviation for more than a decade; during those years the Navy modified hundreds of the planes to carry an extra pilot in a side-by-side cockpit and added a compartment behind the cockpit large enough to hold four crew members. In the 1960s, the Air Force took several hundred of the fighters and cast them in a dual role in Southeast Asia—close air support for ground troops and Search and

Rescue for downed pilots. Unlike its fuel-guzzling jet-fighter cousins—called "fast-movers" in pilot jargon—the prop-driven A-1 could loiter in the air for hours, waiting to be needed. When summoned, it delivered its ordinance with unerring accuracy while demonstrating a capacity to absorb substantial punishment from enemy ground fire.

The Spad nickname fit the A-1 well because that's what World War I fighter pilots called its grandfather. It was out of date, and slower than the jets, but when the shooting started, it was the toughest hombre on the street.

Initially, Bill and Pip thought the Hurlburt Field area offered an almost perfect setting for an extended honeymoon. The Florida panhandle was not unlike the Arizona desert; it was flat and hot, spread with sand on the bottom and blue sky on top. The newlyweds rented an apartment right across the street from the Gulf of Mexico and walked the sugar-white beach for hours on their first day there. However, twenty-four hours after their arrival, Pip discovered that Florida offered two things rare in Arizona—high humidity and the unrelenting sound of waves washing up on the beach. By the end of their first week in Florida, she and Mann had abandoned the beach and were staying at the O'Club each night until they were oblivious to water-saturated air and surf sounds.

Mann finished Skyraider school in the prescribed two months and garnered the class Top Gun award. He narrowly missed setting a new training wing record on the gunnery range, but being perpetually hungover has never contributed to a pilot's accuracy.

Bill and Pip Mann repacked the red Corvette and drove west. When they arrived in Arizona, they rented a nice apartment near Luke for Pip. She would stay in Phoenix and play tennis while Bill went to war.

The summer of '71 was almost over.

The Pan Am 707 left Travis Air Force Base in California at midnight with a full load of GIs—mostly Army and Marine personnel—and seven weary stewardesses. The first stop was Hickam Air Force Base outside Honolulu. The passengers were asked to remain in their seats— the stop would be brief.

The teenage soldiers and Marines looking out the windows of the plane did not glimpse the bright beaches of *Blue Hawaii*. Elvis was in Memphis; exotic-looking girls wearing grass skirts who might offer a lei, a smile, or an aloha were home in bed. To the young men on the plane, Hawaii was an island of brightly-lighted concrete in the middle of a dark world.

A Boeing 707 doesn't make money when it's sitting on the ground, and the quickly moving shadows servicing the plane were responsible for getting its passengers off their island and into the war. Ground support people took less than an hour to board more food, shuttle out a new flight crew, and pump fuel into the plane.

Their next stop was Guam and any similarity between Guam and Hawaii stopped where the surf hit the sand. With the exception of three strategic outposts, the thirty-five-mile long strip of coral was all jungle. On the western coast, at Apra Harbor, was Naval Base Guam; Naval Air Station Agana was in the center of the island; Andersen Air Force Base, a roost for scores of B-52 bombers, occupied the northern tip. The war was getting nearer.

They were parked at Andersen two minutes when the stewardess came on the PA and told them their plane was having maintenance difficulties—repairs would "take at least two hours. Please take your belongings with you and deplane." The sun was making its appearance as Mann took his Michener novel and followed the herd toward Base Operations.

A short walk later, he was in a building overrun by three or four hundred military personnel, both in transit and locally assigned, gridlocked in an area that would comfortably accommodate a third of their number. Base Operations at Andersen was not unlike a hundred other base ops installations in the world except it was full of men who made their living by bombing and shooting at people who shot back.

Air Force fighter pilots on their way to or from R'n'R or back home to the States stood on the fringes of the crowd; they wore gaudy party flightsuits and grim expressions; they were tired and quiet.

Everyone else wore some shade of green. Westbound enlisted boys—red and yellow, black and white—stayed close to one another and stared at eastbound enlisted men who didn't stare back; the eastbound men were going home alive. Small packs of silent B-52 crew members who had just finished debriefing their third twelve-hour mission in six days seemed beyond caring that they made no progress toward a virtually inaccessible snack bar. Mann was the only guy in a flightsuit who wasn't carrying food or a smoke. Someone tapped him on the shoulder.

"Hey, how ya doin'?" It was a Marine captain Mann noticed on the 707. "You're on that bird going to Saigon, aren't you?"

"Yeah." Mann stuck out his hand. "Bill Mann."

"James Kelly." The Marine was almost as tall as Mann and too lean. He pulled off an olive green cap, uncovering a haircut that was strictly Marine—shiny-slick up the sides with a forkful of fuzz for a flattop. He rubbed the fuzz and surveyed the stationary upheaval in the terminal. "Well, I'll tell you what . . . if you're up to it, I bet I know where we can get us a couple of chili dogs and a cold beer. No waiting. Whatta ya think?" Life was good, Kelly had a ready grin that said so.

"Right here on base?"

"Yup, ten-minute walk. I've made this run before. They got a BX roach coach that meets the bomber crews when they finish debriefing; it's over at the compound gate." He flicked his cap in a southerly direction. "Picnic tables, palm trees, gentle breeze, imported beer, succulent cuisine, easy walkin' distance. Real tropical paradise."

Mann wanted to make sure he didn't miss his plane. "They said something about staying in the local area."

Kelly waved a dismissive hand. "The bus to Nam stops by here every twenty minutes. If we miss ours, we can jump on the next one."

Mann gave the surrounding masses a look. "Chili dogs and beer sounds good." He stowed his book on a nearby shelf and followed the U.S. Marines out of the crowd.

The humidity was off the scale, and the palm trees were trying hard to be as big as broomsticks. The two hot dog hunters were pouring sweat by the time they got to the mobile canteen and Kelly was favoring his right leg.

"Bad knee?" asked Mann.

"Nah." Kelly patted his leg. "Practicin' my Walter Brennan imita-tion. Whatta ya think?"

"I think you do it better."

Mann and Kelly stood among a gathering of semiconscious crew-members by the mobile canteen and gave the painted plywood menu a cursory glance. Finally, Mann said, "Gimme two chili dogs an' a beer," then pointed at Kelly, "an' whatever he wants."

Mann bought the first round. The Marine had four chili dogs and two beers. Mann scarfed three dogs and four beers. The Marine wasn't chatty; Mann never had been. They talked enough to cover the essen-tials. The Marine was a ground-pounder on his way back to Da Nang; Mann was headed for NKP to fly Spads. Kelly claimed he intended to be a preacher; all Mann wanted was to spend a year in the war. They were content to sit at the beat-up picnic table and enjoy the damp breeze and their own thoughts.

An hour later, Mann was tagging along while the Marine guided their trek back to the flightline. They were within sight of Base Ops when they came abreast of a small white building. Kelly slowed, then stopped. He pointed his grin at Mann and held out an empty hand. "Gimme ten bucks an' I'll get you a seat in first class."

Mann didn't know what the guy was talking about, but he dug a bill out of the flightsuit and gave it to him.

"I'll be right back!" Kelly took their money and his grin into the building.

He returned to the humidity-soaked sunshine three minutes later with a medium-sized white sack. He held out his hand again.

"Five more bucks, flyboy."

Money apparently came cheap in war zones. Mann handed him a five and asked, "What'd I buy?"

"Among us grunts it's called worldly comfort. C'mon, I'll explain later."

"What's the hurry? We've got an hour before we get back on."

Kelly checked his Seiko and picked up the pace. "The early bird gets the leg room, amigo. C'mon." He was out in front and waving the sack at the flyboy. "Hustle your bustle."

They were jogging down the sidewalk in front of Base Ops when a white van pulled up. When the van stopped, Kelly pulled open the side doors.

"Afternoon, ladies." The cabin crew for the 707's Guam-to-Saigon leg was on the scene and already bored. Two of the seven stewardesses dismounted from the hotel van and pointed blank faces at him; they had seen a Marine before.

Kelly was unperturbed. "It's important that I speak to the chief stewardess," Pan Am put a lot of stock in titles, "if you will."

Four of seven still-blank faces aimed themselves at a woman stepping down from the van. She was in her late twenties and four years past her limit of shady propositions from stupid GIs—including Marines. Her feet hit the sidewalk and she put her hands on her hips and squared herself at the threat. Tall. Trim. Tailored. Tired. Ticked off.

"What?" Hostility with dark hair and a sky-blue uniform. The average attractive lady can't snarl well; this one could give lessons.

Kelly's frontal attack stalled. Mann wasn't too scared because he knew he had plenty of open space behind him. He took another look at the woman and decided he could probably outrun a mean stewardess in a tight skirt and high heels—assuming, of course, the woman didn't run as well as she snarled.

Jennifer Laurel, Air-Force-brat daughter of a full colonel, knew the ropes; she was a seven-year stewardess and a five-year skeptic. She was tired of war. Tired of watching moms and dads who were forced to stand amidst strangers and cling to each other, weeping and watching their sons leave them . . . maybe forever. Tired of the endless caravans of military coffins crisscrossing the nation's airport ramps. Tired of the despair. And bone-weary of looking into the faces of westbound boys who were trying not to wonder if they'd been condemned to death. She was fed up with the whole rotten mess. And she was already mad at the Marine.

"Well, sonny?" The first snarl wasn't luck. Mann did a quick check over his shoulder again just to be sure. The exit route was clear.

The Marine regrouped and pointed his assault; the good-looking black kid behind him took off his flight cap. The Marine almost bowed. "Ma'am, if I could have two minutes of your time?" The white paper sack was barely visible. The tired lady saw it.

Seven faces—six barely interested, the black one totally engrossed—watched the Marine lead the stewardess a discreet distance to the side.

The Marine held the bag at his side and moved his mouth earnestly for thirty seconds. When he finished, he extended the bag to the pale blue uniform. He was barely smiling, gracious, still talking. The mean lady became more attentive and accepted the bag. The frown was in locked place, but the snarl was gone.

A slender hand went in to explore the contents of the white sack; a nose followed. She squeezed the bag. The frown dissolved and became her first smile in six days. She laughed something at the Marine. The Marine grinned some words back. His new best friend laughed again, kissed her fingertips, and patted his almost flattop with them. They laughed together. The six stewardesses were witnessing a miracle. Mann was completely dumbfounded. The two leaders rejoined their respective followers.

The U.S. Marines, in the form of Captain James A. Kelly, pulled back toward the ops building and motioned for his air cover to follow. Inside the building, Mann let Kelly lead while they high-stepped over scattered bodies of boys who had no place to sleep but the marble floor. Their trek ended at the stainless steel coffee urns.

"Hey," Mann touched Kelly on the arm, "what the heck was in the bag?"

The Marine touched his finger to his lips and looked over his shoulder to make sure there were no VC spies near. "Sweaters."

"Sweaters?"

"Sssshhhh!" Another glance by the Marine—still no VC. He let Mann in on something no one else in the world knew: "Pringle makes the finest cashmere sweaters in the world. When you can find them at Saks Fifth Avenue, they cost over a hundred smacks per each."

"And you *gave* her one?" The voice had learned to whisper; the tone was yelling.

"Two."

"Two hundred bucks worth of sweaters?" Mann hissed.

A wise nod to the naive boy. "The OWC here gets the Pringle's out of Hong Kong. No duty, okay? Seventeen bucks apiece. Gettin' to shop here is one of the reasons I joined the Marines."

Mann did the math and started getting slightly nervous. This guy wasn't like any preacher he'd ever met. Two hundred dollars worth of cashmere was a bit much between strangers. "So? What'd you give 'em to her for?"

"You stick with me, buddy boy. I'll learn you some stuff." Kelly sampled the black brew and purred with contentment.

Mann tried the coffee. Luke warm mud, some grit, battery-acid aftertaste. He dumped it out and got a Dr. Pepper. When Mann turned around, Kelly was across the room and halfway up a flight of stairs, motioning for him to follow. What next?

He reached the top of the stairs in time to see Kelly disappear through a door with a frosted glass window—Meteorology Section, Administration. They were going to the weather office?

When Mann stuck his head through the door, Kelly was arranging himself in one of two comfortable-looking leather-covered chairs. The chair behind the desk was empty.

Kelly already had his eyes closed. He pointed at the empty desk chair. "Civilians don't work on red-letter days."

Mann wasn't a white Marine captain; he was a black second lieutenant and not as relaxed as the Marine. "How do you know it's a civilian?"

Kelly's eyes stayed closed. "'Cause the walls ain't covered with charts and graphs, and the desk is a wreck." He opened his eyes and looked at the lieutenant who was still looking around the office. "Hey . . . would you cool it? What're they gonna do to us? Sentence us to Southeast Asia for a year?"

Mann wasn't convinced. His eyes moved from the comfortable chair, to the desk, back to the door.

"Hey, man. It don't matter if you're a green second lieutenant with black skin. If anybody says anything, I'll tell 'em I ordered you to sit in here, okay?"

How in the heck did he know what I was thinking? Being around this guy is like getting picked to be a magician's guinea pig.

"Yeah, I know." Kelly sat up. "Look, bro, I ain't black, but I'm different. I get some of the same flak you do. Not as bad, not as often, and in my case, I guess I ask for it . . . but I still get it."

Mann and Kelly looked at each other. Mann was thinking. Kelly was waiting.

"Okay," said Mann. "Tell me about it."

"The short version is: I'm a Bible-believing, sold-out-for-the-cause Christian."

Mann spoke the first thing that came into his mind. "You don't act like it."

"Thanks."

"I mean . . . what're you doing in the Marines."

"That's easy," shrugged Kelly. "To get the GI Bill money to go to seminary on."

"You were serious out there at the roach coach? You want to be a preacher?"

"Yep. Goin' to seminary in Dallas."

What a waste of a good man, thought Mann. He took a moment to let his mind catch up with his mouth then said, "Question. Why would a man who wants to be a preacher join the Marines? The Marines always go where the shooting is."

Kelly nodded. "I wasn't a Christian when I signed up. I planned to spend my life bein' a hired killer."

"And now?"

"I hooked up with a guy who told me about what God did for me through Jesus. What he said was dead right, and I'm gonna learn to teach other folks what God's been teachin' me."

"Which is?"

"He's the only thing that's ever gonna count."

"You sound like my grandfather."

"Then your grandfather is a wise man."

"He was that," Mann murmured.

Poppa *was* a wise man; he just wasn't a realist. Apparently, neither was James Kelly. If God was real, He'd be good. Good gods don't leave innocent young children in an evil world without their parents. Ergo, God is not real.

Kelly let the pause broaden for a moment, then said, "But you're not interested, right?"

"I've got the job I've always wanted, James, and a wife who loves me. I'll quit there."

"There's only one thing this side of eternity that matters, bro, and you might want to try to figure out what it is. It doesn't come under the heading of people, or jobs, or things."

Mann said he'd give it some thought so Kelly would drop the subject. Both men were asleep in three minutes.

An hour later, a voice on the public-address system gargled that their plane was ready for boarding. Mann and Kelly walked out of Base Operations into one of the six-a-day rains Guam was famous for and joined the long green line moving toward their aircraft. Jennifer Laurel was standing at the bottom of the plane's mobile stairs under an umbrella. When they got close, the senior stewardess took Captain Kelly's arm, pulled him under the umbrella's protection and escorted him up the stairs to the accompaniment of a chorus of catcalls from the other GIs. She stepped through the plane's door and plucked two of the three hand-printed "Reserved" signs from the front row of seats.

"Gentlemen, if you'd be kind enough to sit here." The third sign stayed on the seat between them, and their benefactress went back to the entry door to continue greeting the mere mortals.

Mann leaned across the empty seat; "What'd you tell that woman? She didn't change into a different person for a couple of sweaters."

"I was bent on showing you how cool I was and I was going to bribe her. " Kelly measured Mann with a long look. "I forgot what my job is."

"Your job?"

"Yeah. My first responsibility is to let people know that God loves them, right? Getting cushy seats on a plane comes second."

Mann's curiosity was normally buried beneath other thoughts, but he was intrigued by this man. Kelly was a man's man—he usually talked like an ordinary GI—but every now and then he spoke about things people usually reserve for church. He reminded Mann of Poppa and Sam and Missy and Pat—plain words emerging from a wellspring of relaxed confidence.

"What did you tell her?"

"I told her that no one likes being in pain, even emotional pain. I told her that God died a horrible death because He wanted to help soften her pain. And I told her that if she became a Christian the pain might not go away, but He'd help her carry it."

"And that's how come we got the good seats?"

Kelly was settling into the seat like a king on a throne. "I told her I'd been shot in both legs and would appreciate some room to stretch out. If she could swing it . . . fine . . . the sweaters were hers, win or lose." No grin.

Mann flinched. Kelly had lied to the girl to get these seats.

He tried to tell himself that everyone was human, but it didn't work—he felt as if he'd been double-crossed by a friend. Poppa and Sam and Missy and Pat wouldn't lie. He'd known this jerk for three hours and had started to like him. The disappointment was becoming anger; people who talked about God shouldn't lie. "I thought preachers weren't supposed to lie."

"They aren't. You aren't. Nobody aren't." Kelly was busy digging between the seat cushions for a stray seat belt.

Mann looked behind them for an empty seat; he didn't want to sit by a man who'd lie and then talk about Poppa's God. "Then why'd you lie, preacher?" He spit the last word.

"Relax, hombre. Nobody lied."

What? Mann reemployed his whisper-yell. "You've been shot?"

"Mm-hmm." The seat belt was twisted into a synthetic pretzel.

"Why didn't you say you'd been shot?"

"I just did." Kelly punctuated his sentence by giving the pretzel a jerk.

"I meant before."

"Tah-dah!" Kelly displayed the head of the captured seat snake. "You ever break your arm?" he asked.

All kids break their arms. Not all of them have it inflicted on them. "Well . . . yeah. So what?"

"You didn't tell me."

"I wasn't a hero."

"I didn't go to the bullets, hoss." A memory brought the grin back. The nonhero laughed. "I was cuttin' about a three-point-eight forty across a paddy with my choirboys when a disgruntled fan got me from behind."

Mann digested this and returned the grin. "I think I'm glad."

Kelly twisted his grin. "Well, I hate to fill your relief full of holes, but havin' your approval does not make me glad I got shot." He bent over to latch the belt and when he looked up at Mann, the grin was gone. "Lemme tell you something, Bill—I'm just a man. If we know each other very long, I'll let you down . . . just give me a little time and I'll drop the floor out from under you and pull the ceiling down on the wreckage. I told you something like this before . . . if you want someone who won't let you down, you gotta go with God."

Mann was unconvinced. "My dad and mom said pretty much the same thing. They were both killed before I got to high school."

"And you blame God." Kelly wasn't asking a question.

"Hey. This is not something that keeps me awake at night, okay?" Mann tilted his seat back and worked on getting the Michener novel out of a flightsuit pocket. "If God's real, He let it happen; if He's not real—and I'm fairly confident He's not—who cares?"

"If you don't believe in God, what do you have to fall back on?"

Mann shrugged. "I told you . . . I don't plan on falling back. I'm a fighter pilot. That means I'm living a life most men can only dream about." He tapped his chest with a corner of the book and smiled at a memory. "I'm married to a woman who makes men who're doing this job envy me. That makes me the envied of the envied, James. What else can a man hope for?" He was satisfied with his answer and his life.

Telling a man his wife could let him down was no way to build a friendship, and Kelly let the conversation steer itself away from God; eventually the beer took over, and they slept for most of the six hours en route to Saigon.

From the air, Viet Nam looked lush and green against the medium blue of the South China Sea. Mann didn't think of himself as a romantic, but as he looked out the airplane's window, he let himself enjoy the moment. He was on his way to a war zone . . . his war zone. This was where it would start. He'd take the twelve months needed to make an impact here, and when his tour was over, he'd have a reputation as a pilot who could get the job done and be on his way back to Luke for F-4 training.

CHAPTER EIGHT

Mann and Kelly said good-bye to Jenny Laurel's warm smile and walked down the motor stairs to pick up their bags. Kelly stood by and waited while Mann turned in a slow circle; aircraft of all shapes and sizes—some civilian, most wearing war paint—populated the ramp. Elevated towers, all bristling with machine guns, were spaced around the perimeter fence. Helicopters were moving in all quadrants of the sky. A Pan Am 707 was taking off on a nearby runway; behind it, a four-ship formation of F-4s loaded with 500-pound bombs was taxiing into position for launch. Men headed for war, waiting to take off behind the crown prince of the civilian fleet. The sun was hot, the humidity was intolerable, aviation noises surrounded him—Mann was precisely where he wanted to be for as long as he could remember.

"Busy," he said.

"Yeah," Kelly nodded, "and this is the city-boy version. Wait'll you see the real world."

Mann was continuing to take in the activity when Kelly said, "Well, I'll be darn."

Mann turned to his friend, but Kelly was looking past him at something in the direction of the terminal. "More sightseeing later." He picked up Mann's B-4 bag and tossed it to him. "C'mon, I'll introduce you to a *real* Marine."

The "*real* Marine" striding toward them was created to be intimidating. He was broad as a male gorilla, meaner looking, just as black, and stood a ramrod-straight six-foot-six; one brief glance at the man and Goliath would dedicate his life to some serious peace-mongering. When the giant drew close, he came to attention and snapped a rigid salute to the man who was ten years his junior and half his size. "Howdy, Captain. Welcome home, sir." He was showing every one of thirty-two perfect white teeth.

"Good to see you, Gunny. Semper Fi." Kelly matched the salute. The smile was out of his reach, but he gave it a shot. They shook hands while Mann looked over the sergeant's entourage. The gorilla was flanked by a pair of M-16 rifles equipped with competent-looking corporals.

Kelly looked at the corporals. "Planning a parade?"

"Just wanted to make sure you got back to the base okay, sir. We had to make a run down here and got the scheduling troops to fix it so we could take you back home with us." The sergeant stuck an index finger the size of a beer can out, and one of the corporals draped a belt and holster over it. The black giant held the rig out to his captain. "Had the armorer clean it up, sir. Figured you'd want it first thing."

"You were right. Thanks, Gunny." Kelly took the belt and holster. He swung the web belt into place and latched the buckle all in one practiced motion. He flipped open the holster and pulled out a Browning High Power. Nine millimeter, fifteen rounds in the handle, evidence of use.

"Topped it off myself, sir," said the sergeant. "Full clip, one in the chamber."

The captain nodded absently while he pulled the clip out. It was full. He tapped the clip on the heel of his hand and rammed it home. He then turned the gun and pushed the slide back far enough to see the chambered round . . . he'd done it a thousand times. The gunnery sergeant watched silently and approved; his leader knew the drill. Never take anyone's word about whether or not a weapon is loaded.

Kelly dropped the pistol back in the holster, put both hands on his hips, and looked at his sergeant. "So, what's the plan?" Back home. Back in charge.

The sergeant pointed the beer can at a C-130 sitting to the left of the terminal. "Got us a Herky-bird fueled and ready, sir. Just say Da Nang."

"Mmm." Kelly turned and jerked his thumb at Mann. "Gunnery Sergeant Pressler, Lieutenant Mann."

Pressler came to attention again and gave the black lieutenant the same salute he'd given Kelly, no smile. Mann's return salute was a relaxed version of Kelly's . . . an Air Force pilot could tear a ligament trying to salute like a Marine. The rifles and corporals glanced at Mann and got uninterested.

The Marine allowed himself an inspection of the officer. Green second lieutenants were a liability, but this one didn't look utterly lost. "You a friend of Captain Kelly's, sir?" The voice was its own percussion section.

Am I supposed to call him Gunnery Sergeant? Mann decided to take Kelly's road. "I'd like to think so, Gunny. I guess he's the man who decides that."

"Yeah," Kelly answered everyone's question. "He's okay for an Air Force puke. Sandy driver."

The corporals interrupted their disinterest to give Mann a second once-over. Pressler changed his opinion and his expression. "Where you goin' to, sir?"

"I'm supposed to be at NKP sometime tomorrow."

Mann was a friend of the young god with the captain's insignia sewed on his collar . . . and he was a Sandy driver. Pressler said, "If you'd like, sir, we can take you with us. We'll get you three squares, give you a tour of Da Nang, and send you on to NKP first thing in the morning."

"I'd like that, but they've already got my life planned for a hop out of here."

"I can fix that, sir. If it suits you, I'll have 'em sign you over to us, and we'll get you to NKP on the morning shuttle out of Da Nang."

Mann had never seen Da Nang. "Sounds good to me. Thanks."

Pressler beckoned with some of the huge fingers. "Gimme a copy of your orders, 'Tenant, an' I'll go in an' tell the Air Force boys that we'll have you at NKP tomorrow in time for noon chow."

"Thanks."

Pressler rumbled something at the corporals and turned away. The surging crowd of GIs and Vietnamese personnel coming and going around the terminal watched him coming and cleared a path.

The two riflemen turned their backs on Kelly and Mann, focusing their full attention on the tide of humanity around them. Mann would not have been surprised to know the two were ordered to kill anyone who so much as glanced at Kelly.

Thankfully enough, no one had time to notice Kelly because Pressler was gone less than five minutes. Mann correctly assumed that impatient gorillas get more attention than run-of-the-mill humans.

When Pressler came back with the news that Mann was the responsibility of the United States Marines Corps, the group gathered their gear and walked toward the camouflaged transport. The gorilla asked, "You got a weapon, Lieutenant?"

"In my bag."

"May as well break it out, sir." Pressler was willing to offer the smallest amount of babysitting to the green second lieutenant. "There's bad guys standing close enough to hear me whistle."

Everyone stopped while Mann unzipped his bag. The Model 1911 Colt .45 automatic was secured in a holster that was the twin of Kelly's.

"Nineteen-eleven." Gunny was observing, not commenting.

Mann nodded at Kelly's sidearm and came up with a polite smile. "Yeah. It's not a Browning, but it usually goes off when it's supposed to." Pressler watched as the kid chambered a round, topped off the clip, and holstered the gun. No flash, no wasted motion, no John Wayne stuff. The boy had done it before, and there was a good teacher in his background.

"Who taught you to handle a gun, sir?"

Getting the B-4 bag rezipped was distracting Mann. "Oh, I just picked it up around."

Pressler gave the kid who was busy with his luggage a more thorough inspection and thought, *Uh-huh, sho' did.* He said, "If I was you, 'Tenant, I wouldn't leave that 1911 in my bag. Somebody'll put the hook on it."

"Thanks, Gunny. I'll keep it close."

They started walking again.

"You shot the M-16 yet, sir?"

"Never held one."

"We'll get you checked out for the ride up." He motioned at one of the escorts. "Monroe."

"Yeah, Gunny."

"Get the lieutenant checked out on that rifle."

"Yo."

Monroe's buddy carried Mann's bag while Mann got a tour of the M-16. Before they got to the airplane, Mann could find his way around the rifle well enough to satisfy Monroe.

The ride to Da Nang took almost two hours. Mann rode in the cockpit and got a tour of the sea coast; the marines slept.

When they started their descent into Da Nang, Kelly woke up and wandered into the cockpit.

"Can you get me air ops on a radio?"

The copilot fixed him up and Kelly put on a headset to converse with the people in the helicopter section. He arranged a helicopter ride for himself and his friends as soon as they got to the base. They were on the ground at Da Nang fifteen minutes later and walking across the ramp to a waiting chopper.

As they approached the chopper, a Marine lieutenant clambered out and walked toward them. He and Kelly shared a laugh and Kelly waved Mann closer to introduce him. "This is Bill Mann. Bill, Fast Eddie Hollister."

The upper half of Fast Eddie's flightsuit was stained white from dried sweat; a well-worn shoulder holster full of some kind of heavy-caliber revolver was snugged under his arm. He shook Mann's hand and took in the wings on his flightsuit. "Howdy." Hollister's expression and tone were noncommittal.

"Bill hitched a ride up from Saigon with us. Takin' the shuttle to NKP in the morning. I wanted to take a look at the local area and invited him along."

"Suits me." It obviously didn't. Hollister turned his back and twirled one finger at his copilot. The engine on the Huey worked its way into the conversation.

Kelly leaned in and spoke to Hollister again. "Bill's my friend . . . gonna be doin' Sandy work out of NKP for a while."

The transformation was too instantaneous and came complete with the kind of smile that comrades share. "Oh . . . uh . . . welcome aboard, amigo."

"Thanks." *I hope he changed his tune because I'm Kelly's friend. If they give all Sandy drivers this kind of treatment, I need to start getting nervous 'cause that means they think I'm gonna be doing something where I get shot at a lot.*

The five passengers climbed into the Huey; the two rifles sat nearest the doors with their Marines.

The all-new Fast Eddie stopped by the open door on the side of the chopper and put a greasy headset in Mann's hand, slapped him on the back, and yelled into his ear, "Plug it into that panel behind you. Let us know if you need anything else."

The eleven-hundred horsepower engine was four feet from their ears and prevented all conversation except yelling. As they air-taxied for takeoff, the two corporals secured their rifles, passed out flak vests, then turned their attention to a pair of M-60 machine guns mounted at their elbows—they nodded at the sergeant when they were satisfied with their inspections of the door guns. Outboard and below the M-60s, loaded rocket launchers were mounted on both sides of the chopper. Every man in the helicopter was holding—or strapped to—a weapon.

Mann watched Da Nang disappear behind them. Kelly sat across from him, facing sideways so he could see out the door—very much back home. The sergeant occupied himself with the scenery on the opposite side of the craft. Fast Eddie Hollister was a practicing proponent of the belief that fast-moving, low-flying aircraft presented fewer target opportunities for ground-based gunners; they skimmed their way north at—and sometimes below—treetop level. The two corporals looked out over the countryside, daring any poor soul to pop a cap pistol in their direction. The instructor from his M-16 course took time to favor the new A-1 driver with a half smile and a nod, then turned and spit a rivulet of tobacco juice into the slipstream.

Mann leaned out and watched as jungle and rivers blurred past the open doors; villages, red dirt roads, and firebases came and went. *Ladies and gentlemen, we are now taking you on a short tour of the war zone. Please keep your seat belt fastened, as we do here in the cockpit. If you take your seat belt off in flight, you will fall out of the aircraft and be blown into unrecognizable bits by bad people before you hit the ground. We invite you to sit back, relax, and enjoy your flight.*

After forty minutes of not getting shot at, Fast Eddie touched the chopper down on its pad amid a broad collection of moving aircraft. It was as Kelly said . . . Tan Son Nhut was in the city; Da Nang was in the war. Ordered lines of jet fighters, two-ship and four-ship formations from the Navy, Marines, and Air Force moved in a continuous line past the Huey. The pilot of a Marine A-4 looked their way and lifted two gloved fingers in a relaxed "peace and love" gesture at the grunts. Kelly returned a casual wave without changing expression. Business as usual in Nam.

They got away from the noise and Kelly said, "I've got a few things to put together here. How about if I get a driver to take you over to the Doom and I'll try to get there in two or three hours, okay?"

"Doom?"

"The O'Club. Da Nang Officers Open Mess . . . D-O-O-M." Kelly checked his watch. It was mid-afternoon. "There'll probably be some Sandy drivers in there by now. Make yourself at home, introduce yourself around, an' I'll see you around sixish. Leave your bag with the driver and plan on bunkin' with the Marines tonight."

The bar in the Da Nang O'Club provided standing-room-only accommodations for a mob of multiethnic, multinational drinkers. More than a few of the officers present were from the Vietnamese Air Force; the United States contributed men from Naval Aviation, the Marines, and a handful of Army and Air Force types; the smallest, loudest, and drunkest contingent was from Australia.

Mann zigzagged his way through the crowd and wedged himself into a place at the bar. The Vietnamese officer on his right moved over slightly to make room and favored Mann with a nod before turning his back. The guy was wearing a pearl-handled six-gun, lime green Bermuda shorts, and camouflaged jungle boots. His T-shirt carried the

82nd Airborne emblem on the front; his philosophy regarding how to wage war was spelled out across the back:

Protect the Innocent
Convince the Undecided
Kill the Rest

Mann looked over the crowd and watched a head bobbing up and down as its owner negotiated his way toward the bar. The man got his arm into a slot between Mann and the T-shirt and asked, "You share your bar?"

Mann managed to squeeze over an inch. "I don't have a greedy bone in my body."

The new arrival stuck out his hand. "I'm Stretch McCullough."

"Bill Mann."

Stretch didn't smile much. "Proud to meet you."

The Vietnamese officer looked over his shoulder at the interloper and turned to mutter something to his friends. Like the parting of the Red Sea, an eighteen-inch opening manifested itself in front of Stretch.

Stretch looked like what he was—a west Texas farm boy—as country as a mule-drawn hay wagon. Casting directors in Hollywood routinely drew verbal pictures of his physical attributes when they were looking for someone to play a dirt farmer. He was dressed in a party flightsuit—a flamboyant orange thing—with several patches sewn on the chest and sleeves. A patch on one shoulder said the pilot flew A-1s for the 1st Special Operations Squadron; other patches on the flightsuit told those who could read he was a Sandy pilot who participated in no fewer than three now-famous SARs—search and rescue operations.

Before the two could get further acquainted, an Air Force type emerged from the throng and rested his hand on Stretch's shoulder. "Say, Sandy, can I buy you a beer?"

Offers of friendship from men he'd never met was a way of life for Stretch. He stuck out his hand and countered with his customary, "I've already had more than one free beer, but I'd be glad to buy you one."

The Air Force type shook Stretch's hand; his smile faded slightly, then disappeared. "I haven't been shot down yet, but I've watched you guys work. If it was up to me, you'd never buy another drink for as long as you live."

Stretch was used to this, too. He said a simple, "Thanks."

The philanthropist turned to Mann. His smile was coming back, and he was willing to bestow his appreciation for the Sandy pilot on those who stood near him. "How 'bout you, bro?"

Mann hadn't received a briefing on the protocol of hero appreciation, but he knew better than to stand in another man's spotlight. "Thanks anyway, but I'd better go a little slower."

The hero's beer was bought and the buyer faded back into the club's commotion.

Mann was the new kid on the block, so he waited for Stretch to direct the conversation.

"So, Mann . . . what brings a fine young second lieutenant like yourself to sunny Southeast Asia?"

"I'm on the way to NKP." He pointed at the squadron patch on Stretch's shoulder. "Going to your outfit—the First SOS."

"Glad to have you." His brow furrowed for a second. "Nang's a little off the regular approach path, ain't it?"

"Detour," said Mann. "I caught a ride up here with some Marines; they're going to ship me to NKP tomorrow."

"Do tell?" It was unusual, but so was most of the other activity in the theater. "What do you think about the Spad so far?"

Mann wasn't an expert and was too smart to try to act like one. "I'm still learning, but I haven't been disappointed yet." He tried to redirect the conversation. "How about you? Did you come to the Spad by choice?"

"Naw," Stretch grumbled. "I was instructin' at Nellis in the Thud, so the fighter assignments people, in their infinite wisdom, stuck me in this antique prop job. I grew up flyin' crop dusters faster'n this thing."

"How long've you been over here?"

"Eight months—four to go."

"Are you going back to fighters after you get out of here?"

Stretch paused and pondered his answer. "I reckon that's gettin' harder to answer. Since I've been over here, I've done nothing but go out three or four times a week trying to rescue men who got shot down while they were usin' supersonic aircraft to knock out mud footbridges. Most of the mud bridges they tried to take out were a quarter of a mile from concrete spans that our boys aren't allowed to touch." He took a swallow of his beer and looked like he might spit it on the floor. "Men get shot down—we go in an' get 'em. We lose good pilots every week because we've got people that ain't got the brains of a bird dog tryin' to fight a war without makin' the enemy mad at us. Right now the airlines are lookin' mighty good."

Every pilot in the Air Force heard the rumor mill stories of what was happening at the command level. If half of what Mann heard was true, the civilians in Washington were running the war, and most of the upper-echelon officers who answered to them were peacetime puppets who rose to the top because they could hit a golf ball straight and played bridge well; they were more concerned with their own careers than with the well-being of their men.

"What about the job—the A-1 mission?"

"Well, I'll tell you." He hoisted his beer and almost smiled for the first time. "If you're gonna be stuck sufferin' in a God-forsaken place, in a God-forsaken war, in an airplane that was an antique twenty years ago . . . brother, this is the job to have while you suffer."

The two found their way to a table near the bar, and Stretch drank more free beers while he told Mann about the Spad operation. He was a natural instructor and by the time Kelly showed up, Mann had been given a verbal tour of NKP and was thoroughly briefed for his orientation ride.

Mann introduced the two men and Stretch looked the Marine over. "I know you. You're that fellow that was in that shoot out over at Phu Cat. What was that . . . two months ago?"

"Three months and three days."

"I was in one of the Sandys that worked that extraction."

"Thanks. How 'bout I buy you a beer?"

Stretch waved the offer away and changed the subject. A few minutes later he looked at his watch. "Well, gents, we've got to stand alert in the mornin'. I'm gonna go walk around the plane an' then hit the rack. If we don't launch before mid-mornin', we'll take the birds back home tomorrow." He turned to Mann. "I'd offer you a ride over to the home 'drome, but you don't have a go-fast hat yet . . . an' the strap-hangers will want to bore you to death before you get a chance to get shot at. When you get to the squadron, see the skipper—Colonel Melher—an' tell him I've got you briefed to do your initial bounces an' a trip around the flag-pole. Come find me when you get a helmet, an' I'll give you your first ride."

"Sounds good to me, thanks." Mann had to ask. "By the way, what's Colonel Melher like?"

Stretch wouldn't commit and didn't smile. "Well, I guess his momma likes 'im. 'Night, boys."

Stretch was turning away when Mann asked Kelly, "Well, do I get another lecture on religion?"

Kelly snorted. "If you want a lecture, son, you came to the wrong college."

"I figured you'd have both barrels primed."

"Not hardly," said Kelly. "Why don't you decide what we're gonna talk about while I get something to drink." He waved at a waitress and yelled, "Bireley's!"

"What's Bireley's?" asked Mann.

"Local drink. I'm addicted to it."

When the waitress returned with a bottle of orange soda, Kelly hoisted it and downed half its contents in one slug. "Makes a good beer substitute too."

Mann shrugged. The beer he'd taken in prompted him to lean toward philosophy, and he decided he wanted to talk about God. "I tell you what. Why don't you tell me why I should believe there's a god when you and I are sitting within five miles of places where that same god is letting children get killed every day."

"You mean, if He's there, why does He allow war."

"Yeah," Mann thought he'd made a good point. "We can't pick up a newspaper without seeing a picture of a kid or some skinny little woman dying over here. Anyone can tell that's wrong."

Kelly made a wet circle on the table with the bottom of his bottle. "You know what I think? I think you just made my argument."

"Yeah?" Mann sipped his beer.

Kelly said, "Can I ask you something?"

"Can I stop you?" Mann was smiling.

Kelly smiled back. "You could shoot me."

"I'll keep that in mind," Mann was enjoying himself. "What's your question?"

"Well, this isn't just about war, so let me back up a step. Now . . . this'll take about fifteen seconds, and I'm not going to try to trick you, but you need to listen to the statements I make. And you need to think about how you answer. Okay? This is all straight up." This was no longer a casual conversation for Captain Kelly.

Mann leaned forward in his chair. "Have at it."

Kelly said, "You said there was too much evil for there to be a god, right?"

Mann nodded, "I don't remember my exact words, but that's close enough."

"Okay. Think on this. We have to have 'long' if there's going to be such a thing as 'short.' We've got to have 'big' to know what 'little' means. Right so far?"

"Obviously," said Mann. This was a little too simple.

"If, as you said, the world has evil in it, then it stands to reason that we have good here . . . there's a contrast. Is that right?"

The answer was obvious, but Mann took his time. "So far, so good. There's such a thing as good and there's such a thing as evil."

Kelly held his hands out like balance scales. "So we have good on one side and evil on the other. It's good to rescue helpless people from a burning building, it's evil to murder a child."

"Okay," agreed Mann. It looked like Kelly's points weren't going to be as interesting as Mann hoped.

"Well, if you and I can differentiate between good and evil, there has to be a standard—a universally acknowledged, moral law. Right? Without an acknowledged moral law, there's no such thing as good or evil; if there's no standard, our entire world descends into a state of complete chaos and unrestrained cruelty."

Several of the Aussies passed out and the bar was quieter.

Mann didn't like the use of the word *moral*, but the statement was true. He looked at his friend and thought for a longer moment. The conversation wasn't shallow anymore. Nothing would ever make it right for people to kill children. He touched the beer bottle to his lips and took a sip before giving the point to Kelly, "A moral law sounds reasonable."

"Well, amigo, the next assumption is the simple one. If there is such a thing as a moral law, there has to be a moral-law-giver."

Mann didn't say anything. He looked down at the table for a long moment, then leaned back in his chair and gazed at nothing while he thought.

Kelly finally got up and went to the bar to get another Bireley's; he liked an occasional beer, but he didn't drink alcohol when he was in a place where he needed to carry a gun. He stood for a moment at the bar and said a short prayer while he let his words soak into Mann, then walked back to their table.

When Kelly got back to the table, Mann looked up and said, "You're right."

Kelly froze for a moment in a bending-to-sit pose. "You changed your mind that quickly?" He lowered himself into the chair.

"I worked for some guys in the philosophy department at North Texas—I must've learned to recognize a sound argument when I hear one. I believe there is a moral-law-giver, and I think it's safe to assume it's God."

The preacher-to-be had gotten exactly what he prayed for and was near speechless. "Darn. I must be better at this than I thought."

"Yeah, and modest, too." Mann didn't smile. "I appreciate what you're trying to do, Kelly. But me believing there's a God doesn't mean I side with Him or that I want to become a Christian. There are a lot of other religions out there and I didn't come over here because I'm on some kind of spiritual quest."

"Whether or not you become a Christian is never going to be anyone's choice but yours, old buddy. Frankly, I think you've taken a giant step here and I'm just thankful for that."

"So your project for today was a success."

"Hold it, hold it, hold it." Kelly shook his head and held both hands out in a stop-right-there gesture; his voice was quiet but emphatic. "Let's us back up a step or two, flyboy. This ain't about a project, Slim . . . it never will be. This is about an extended conversation between two friends . . . and as far as I'm concerned, it's not over yet."

His answer satisfied Mann. "Well, you're going to have to save the next installment for later—I feel like I haven't slept in a month." Jet lag was catching up with him, and the beer almost put him under.

"I can sleep under this table, or you can take me to wherever I'm gonna bunk."

Mann, who rarely dreamed, awakened in the middle of the night—Poppa was talking to him, but the sound of the old man's voice faded when his eyes opened. Whatever the old man was telling him was lost in the darkness. He lay on his back, staring at the ceiling, listening, until sleep came back for him.

CHAPTER NINE

The next day, just before noon, Mann walked down the rear ramp of the C-130 and looked at his home for the next twelve months . . . Nakhon Phanom Royal Thai Air Force Base—NKP or Naked Fanny to the initiated. The scene surrounding him could've been lifted from a World War Two setting and plopped down in northeastern Thailand—every operating engine in view was rumbling, grumbling, or backfiring. Except for the helicopters, every aircraft on the vast ramp was prop-driven—no jets.

A jeep skidded to a halt at Mann's elbow and a harried airman yelled over the thunderstorm of airplane noise, "Lieutenant Mann?"

"That's right," Mann yelled back. He had long since gotten used to the fact that strangers could pick him out of a crowd. Someone had interrupted this fellow's busy day and told him to "Go down to Base Ops and pick up Lieutenant Mann. He's a black second lieutenant." Black second lieutenant pilots in Thailand were as plentiful as penguins in Arizona.

"I'm Airman Robinson, sir," the driver shouted. "I'm supposed to give you a ride to the squadron."

Mann threw his bag in the back and climbed aboard. While they drove the short distance to the squadron, he made two observations—practically every surface on the ramp, ground and aircraft alike, was covered with oil stains, and the pervading odor was reminiscent of a stack of last week's sun-baked gym shorts. He was taking all this in when they made a flying pass by a line of taxing A-1s, all loaded for war.

Dreaming, training, and practice were behind him—this was what he had been waiting for since he was eight years old. Today was the first day of something big, and his dad would be proud of him.

All he had left of his dad was the watch on his wrist, a couple of snapshots, and good memories. The pictures of his dad were hidden in his B-4 bag. The first showed a lean black officer sitting on the cockpit rail of a P-51 Mustang—smiling, relaxed. The holster on his dad's chest carried a Colt automatic, a Model 1911 with pearl grips; the red tail of the Mustang was visible over his shoulder. His dad flew the Mustang in North Africa and Europe and the F-86 Sabre Jet in Korea. The second picture was taken the day after his parents' tenth anniversary. It showed his dad propped against the wing tank of an F-100, the world's first supersonic fighter. His dad was wearing the same smile and the same Colt and showing the camera his anniversary present—a stainless-steel Rolex watch. Mann's mom gave her son the watch and the .45 pistol after his dad died. The Rolex was on his wrist; a handsome timepiece with a blue and red bezel. The .45 was gone now—lost in the mud and weeds of a dark night in Mississippi, but his "grandfather" replaced it with a near twin.

Bill Mann was born too late to fly the Mustang, but he was going to fly the A-1 Skyraider. The Skyraider wasn't a P-51, but it had the essential hallmarks—a powerful engine, a propeller, and wing-mounted machine guns. If the politicians continued to drag their feet, the war would last long enough for him to get two combat tours—one year in the Spad, one in the F-4. Mann's dad didn't live to make general, but his son intended to amass a war record that would make him a shoo-in for a star.

The building was concrete-block construction; the sign out front said it was the home of the 1st Special Operations Squadron—The Hobos. Someone went to a lot of trouble to arrange a neat line of whitewashed tree trunks around the graveled parking area to serve as curbing. Robinson snapped off the ignition and bailed out of the jeep as its front tires coasted into a tree trunk near the double front doors.

"The scheduling section's in the middle of the building, Lieutenant. The CO said come see him first. His office is right across the hall." He was jogging toward the building's front door while Mann was still unlimbering from the jeep. "You're welcome to just leave your B-4 bag in the jeep for now, sir. I gotta get back to work."

The chilled air inside the building was a shock after being in the outdoor sauna. Mann walked down the hall in the general direction of the building's center, peering through doorways of briefing rooms and offices as he went. As he progressed, one side of an animated conversation reverberated off the walls, helping to guide him. When he rounded the next corner, he found the scheduling section—an oversized room opened on his left, walled on three sides by a collection of large chalkboards; half a dozen desks arranged near the middle of the area were submerged beneath paperwork, coffee cups, and telephones; a chest-high counter served as an ineffective barrier between passersby in the hall and the schedulers. Behind the counter, a handful of enlisted men shuffled things around on the desks, waved cigarettes and cussed into phones, and got up every now and then to do a weaving Maypole dance around several pilots who breeched the barrier to gripe about the schedule and flip through clutter-filled clipboards. The one-sided conversation he'd used as a guide was being carried on by a lieutenant colonel who propped both elbows on the counter while he used one of the schedulers' phones—the person he was talking to was apparently hard of hearing. The stenciled strip on his sweat-stained flightsuit said the lieutenant colonel's name was MELHER.

Melher twirled a pair of reading glasses and frowned at Mann without seeing him. "Well, was he hurt?" he asked the phone.

Some nodding at the answer.

"Where is he?"

No nod. He became conscious of Mann, got an idea, and beckoned him closer with the glasses.

Melher notched the volume up and interrupted the person on the other end, "You tell him to hold what he's got. I'm sending a jeep for him." He tossed the phone's receiver on the counter and told whoever might be listening to "Hang that up!" while he grabbed the sleeve of

Mann's flightsuit and started toward the office across the hall. "Come in here."

They passed through a door and into a small reception area where a clerk was busy swearing earnestly at a typewriter. The colonel ignored the profane clerk and pushed open a door labeled *Commander*. He went straight to the chair behind the desk but didn't sit.

"Shut that door." Pointing and ordering came easily to Melher.

Mann complied.

"You're William P. Mann."

"Yes, sir. Bill."

"I'm Melher, your new CO."

Mann didn't sit or shake hands because the lieutenant colonel didn't sit or offer his hand. The florescent lights in the ceiling reflected off Melher's forehead. The skin across the upper half of his face appeared to have been stretched drum-tight and polished—a consequence of sitting too close to a cockpit fire; the taxpayers were spared the cost of a new P-51; Melher's reward was a permanent sunburn and his call sign.

The CO's eyes were fixed on a point near Mann's right hand. "Can you shoot that thing without killing yourself or someone else?"

Mann's fingers touched the .45. "Uh . . . yes, sir." *Why would he care?*

"Good. I've got a job for you. One of our guys just stuck his plane in a rice paddy three miles short of the runway—Runway 33; the engine was giving up on him and he couldn't nurse it home. The bird is Class 26, so you go out there and pick him up and shoot the plane . . . and keep your mouth shut about this. Any questions?" Melher put on the reading glasses and picked up a piece of paper from the desk.

Mann was suffering from an attack of acute respiratory distress . . . he couldn't inhale. He was in the grip of a daytime nightmare and he could feel his stomach rolling inverted. The air war in Southeast Asia was the first step on his ascension to general, and the fools in Washington sent a character straight out of *Catch-22* to lay waste to his career—maybe even get him killed. The chilled air was powerless to stop the sweat soaking his flightsuit.

The recently-appointed airplane executioner assumed a stance close to attention and sucked in a ragged breath. "Uh . . . Colonel . . . the airplane is in a rice paddy and you want me to go shoot it?"

Melher looked up. Two symmetrical curves ran from the sides
of his nose to his chin—parentheses cut by a wicked sculptor with
a cruel knife—enclosing an unsmiling mouth and an inclination
to speak harsh words. "Yeah, I want you to put three or four bullet
holes in it—in the engine cowl. And bring Stretch back when you
come."

"Stretch McCullough?"

"Yeah, you know him?"

"Yes, sir. We met in Da Nang last night."

"Okay." Melher sat down and snatched open a drawer on his desk.
"Go get him."

Mann didn't move. If this wasn't some kind of joke, the man was
nuts. "Uh . . . Colonel," he forced the question out, "if you don't mind
. . . could you tell me why I'm going out to shoot a wrecked airplane?"
He was afraid to hear the answer.

"Later." Melher pointed at the door. "Go."

"Yes, sir."

Melher got busy looking for something in the desk drawer. Mann
left on his first mission.

The squadron's newest pilot intended to keep a journal of his
time in the combat zone. The first entry would read, *My welcome to
NKP and my initial meeting with Lieutenant Colonel Melher, Squadron
Commander of the 1st Special Operations Squadron, was short and to the
point. He strikes me as a no-nonsense leader . . . and he's crazy as a road
lizard.*

He walked back into Thailand's steambath and remembered that
the colonel hadn't bothered to tell him how to get to the plane. But
that was good. He was a resourceful young second lieutenant—a black
one—who was given a job to do. He could handle it. He found the
keys in the ignition of the jeep that delivered him and drove off to find
three miles from the end of the Runway 33.

He finally got off the base and found the wreckage by driving in
the direction of an O-2—a small observation plane—doing a buzzard
imitation southeast of the base. The crash site was, as advertised, in the
middle of a rice paddy.

The plane in the mud was an "E" model—commonly called a "fat-face." The nickname fit the "E" models of the A-1 because their wind-shields were broad enough to accommodate their two-man, side-by-side cockpits.

The tactical fighter esthetics of the fat-face planes were further spoiled by an enclosed crew area behind the pilots' seats. This area, covered with blue-tinted Plexiglas, was used to accommodate three or four radar observers back in the days when the A-1E was exclusively a Navy, radar-picket aircraft. The Air Force often found the vast space behind the pilots' seats—commonly referred to as "the blue room"—useful when someone needed to transport several dozen cases of beer or other worthy contraband.

The "H" models of the Skyraider were referred to as the "sports cars" because they were the single-seat version with a teardrop-shaped Plexiglas bubble for a canopy. Newly-arriving lieutenants and junior captains were regularly assigned to one of the fat-face planes; senior captains and field grade officers—majors, lieutenant colonels, and colonels—got the sleeker, more desirable "H" models.

Mann parked on the dike bordering the paddy and looked behind him. The red lights on the fire trucks looked to be about two miles back and closing. He needed to shoot the plane before the crash crew showed up and saw him, partly to follow Melher's orders but more to keep himself from looking stupid. He took his recently-shined flying boots on a high-stepping hike through the rice, mud, and water toward the airplane.

The plane landed "gear up" and the leading edges of the wings—normally about six feet off the ground—were at water level. One wing was crumpled, the prop was twisted, and the big engine was broken from its mounts; the fuselage looked badly damaged. McCullough was standing on the wing keeping a crowd of curious Thai sightseers away from the plane; the pilot and plane were both plastered with mud. McCullough let Mann slog halfway to the plane before he picked up his gear and abandoned ship.

When they got close enough to speak, Mann asked, "What happened?"

Stretch looked back at the plane and drawled, "I don't know. I just got here myself."

When Mann failed to react, Stretch didn't smile again, and said, "Well, looks like they put you to work pretty quick."

"Uh . . . I guess you could say that. Colonel Melher sent me out to shoot some holes in the plane." Mann was drawing the .45.

Stretch followed Mann's gaze to the impromptu metal sculpture. The Thai art critics were keeping their distance. "You're jokin'."

Mann winced and shook his head. "The man said to shoot it."

"Well, it sure wasn't worth a dern as a rice combine." Stretch shrugged and continued his journey. "I'll meet you at the jeep."

Mann walked to within fifteen feet of the plane and put four neat bullet holes in the plane's engine cowl. He stood in the ankle-deep water for a moment, gazing at what he'd done—the Thai spectators were mesmerized. It was entirely possible the controlled-crash of the aircraft gave the boys in the squadron an opportunity to stage an elaborate practical joke for the benefit of the newest kid in the squadron—that was assuming they didn't actually wreck the plane on purpose. Maybe the whole outfit was nuts.

The fire trucks and a handful of other vehicles stopped and emptied their men. Stretch answered a few questions about the crash before folding himself into the jeep.

Mann got behind the wheel. "You don't seem very excited for a man who just made a belly landing in knee-deep water."

"This ain't my first rodeo, partner. An' if you stay here for a full tour, your day's comin'."

When they pulled back into the squadron parking lot, Stretch left his chute in the jeep and walked off in the direction of the pilots' hooches. He told Mann to tell anyone who cared that he'd debrief when he got the mud and rice out of his ears.

Mann got back into the air-conditioning and found an airman first class waiting for him at the scheduling counter.

"The colonel wants to see you, Lieutenant." The accent was from somewhere in the Midwest.

"Thanks." Mann put out his hand. "Things have been moving kind of fast. I'm Lieutenant Mann."

The airman wasn't interested in the speed of surrounding events or the opportunity to shake a black man's hand—officer or not. He averted his eyes and put out a reluctant hand. "Airman Driver, Lieutenant."

Mann shook the man's limp hand and turned away. *Well, guess who won't be coming to dinner at the Drivers' house.*

Melher's clerk had disappeared—he'd probably gone AWOL to escape from Melher. Mann stepped through the connecting door and found the CO talking on the phone again.

Melher waved him in and said into the phone, "Just a minute, Bob; he just walked in the door." He covered the mouthpiece. "Did you get Stretch?"

"Yes, sir."

"Is he okay?"

"Yes, sir. Just muddy."

He pointed at the .45. "Did you use that?"

"Yes, sir."

Melher didn't change expression. "Have you eaten?"

"No, sir."

"Good." He pointed at the door. "Go down to the snack bar and make me two bologna and cheese sandwiches while I finish this call. And get me two bags of chips and two Cokes. Fix whatever you want for yourself. Put it on my tab." He was talking to the phone before Mann could answer.

Mann kept his mouth from falling open and stood there long enough to see if Melher might be kidding. He wasn't. He left the office and was standing in the outside hall, looking both ways for the snack bar, when he heard Melher yell, "Mayonnaise only on mine!"

Airman Driver was writing Mann's name on a blackboard that held a roster of the pilots of the 1st SOS, printing alphabetic characters that looked as if they'd been put there by a lettering machine. The blank space beside Mann's name set aside to hold his call sign would stay empty until he did something—good or bad, smart or stupid—to distinguish himself. A call sign was the sometimes-permanent name given to a pilot by his friends . . . if he acquired any. Driver pointedly ignored the black guy who was on his way to make the white man's sandwiches.

I can see it coming, thought Mann, *my call sign's going to be Houseboy.*

In the snack bar, he muttered mentally about lieutenant colonels who treated second lieutenants like servants. Or maybe this guy reserved that treatment for the black officers. He was tempted to lather Melher's sandwiches with mustard but decided to pass. While he played chef, he wondered, *Why would the guy be telling somebody on the phone that a second lieutenant had just walked in the office?*

He built four sandwiches—two with mustard and dill pickles, thank you very much—put the drinks and chips in his flightsuit pockets, and made a point to cool off while he walked up the hall.

When he stepped into the office, Melher waved him to a couch in front of the desk. He told the phone, "He's back here with my lunch, General. I'll talk to you later this week." He dropped the receiver into its cradle without waiting for an answer.

Since eleven o'clock that morning, the man behind the desk had sent him out to put bullets in the corpse of a dead airplane, treated him like a houseboy and cook, and hung up on a general. The words were out of his mouth before he thought them. "You just hung up on a general?"

Melher was on his feet, cleaning off a spot on the desk with one hand and digging in his desk with the other. His hand came out of the drawer with a church key. "He's a friend. Pilot training classmate. Pentagon weenie now." Melher could talk in bursts. "Stack the stuff up here. Grab a seat."

Melher sat down while he was popping the cap off one of the Cokes. He tossed the can opener at Mann and bowed his head; Mann caught the bottle opener and stared. He was deciding he wasn't going to pretend to pray when Melher's head came up; the man could pray in bursts, too.

"You don't pray?" asked Melher.

"Not yet, Colonel." *That's just great! An insane jerk that's a religious fanatic. Maybe shooting the plane was part of a cult ritual.*

"I'll tell you what," Melher prophesied. "You'll say a prayer before the next twelve months passes, or I'll buy you a year's supply of scotch."

By the time Mann had the top off his Coke, Melher was kicked back in his chair with one foot on his desk, holding a sandwich in one hand and a Coke in the other. The senior officer bit off a mouthful of sandwich and drained half his drink before he started chewing. "Well, what do you think about your home away from home so far?"

You don't want to know, sport, thought Mann. Out loud, he said, "Hard to say, Colonel. I'll know more in a month or two."

Melher took another bite and spoke around the food. "I'm betting you're the kind of man who can figure out all he needs to know in ten days."

Mann didn't know how to answer, so he stuck the Coke in his mouth; the drink was warmer than room temperature.

"I've been here six days, Mann. That makes me and you the new kids on the block. When I got here, this place was being run like a mom-and-pop air show. The last CO made full colonel by slopping white paint on anything that stood still and kissing up to everything else." Melher was out of his chair and walking out of the office. "You can help me change that," he said over his shoulder.

What could he say? *I think my legacy will be cold Cokes in the snack bar.* He told the empty doorway, "Yes, sir."

Melher was back in seconds carrying four paper cups. "Here. Ice is in the fridge next door to the snack bar." He put two cups of ice in front of Mann and sat down. "Okay, where were we? Shooting the plane. Simple enough." He dropped his granny glasses on his desk and massaged the shiny part of his face with both hands. "Stretch couldn't get the bird home because he couldn't keep the engine running. If we lose an airplane as the result of an internal engine problem, it's chalked up as a maintenance loss; if there's evidence of enemy ground fire, it's a combat loss. Our maintenance troops are doing good work under intolerable circumstances and they don't have time for those inbred imbeciles from Washington's brass palace to come over here and harass them while they're trying to do their job. I sent you out there to make dadgum sure it was a combat loss."

Mann listened while he stared at the two cups of ice the squadron commander brought him. He admired an officer who would go to extremes to protect his men, and a field grade officer who would fetch ice for a second lieutenant deserved a closer look. He decided to hold off on his judgment of his new CO.

Melher tilted his chair back again and propped his feet on the desk—a cup of Coke in one hand and the last bite of a houseboy-made bologna sandwich in the other. "So when do you want to start?"

Mann knew the answer to that. "Right now, Colonel."

"Fine. My pilots call me Marsh." Melher crammed his mouth full of chips and reached for his second sandwich while glancing at his watch. "Tell Airman Driver out there to put you up for your flagpole flight at oh-nine-hundred the day after tomorrow. After that's set, get out of here and go see the strap-hangers. Tell them I said they've got a day and a half to get you signed into the base. If they say they need more time, you tell 'em I said they can fill out the rest of their paper-work from the right seat of a Spad. Those boys are getting ready to find out the air show days are over."

Stretch used those same words. "Strap-hangers?"

"Strap-hangers," Melher nodded. "The Air Force, and more par-ticularly NKP, has some great nonflying officers operating in crucial roles; we couldn't operate this unit without 'em, and the good ones don't care what anybody calls 'em. However, every outfit has its 10 percent," his eyes narrowed and the parentheses enclosing his mouth multiplied themselves, "and we have a couple of guys up at wing headquarters who're confused about how their job is supposed to mesh with ours. Strap-hangers are The Man in the Gray Flannel Suit . . . Gregory Peck . . . subway-riding office boys. This is a fighter outfit, son—and those boys are on the verge of finding out we ain't here because they are."

Mann picked up his second sandwich and started for the door. "Thanks, Colonel."

He was rethinking his first day's journal entry when Melher said, "Just a minute." Melher took his boots off the desk and sat up. "Close that door."

Mann closed the door and waited.

"Unless I miss my guess, you've got some things you want to accom-plish over here."

When Mann didn't speak, Melher continued, "Black pilots are still new to some people, Bill. Don't get yourself or anyone else hurt trying to prove a point. There's plenty of room to excel in this line of work without looking for trouble."

"Yes, sir."

Melher pointed at the door. "Sic 'em."

CHAPTER TEN

Flying as Sandy Lead on a SAR mission was probably the most crucial role in Southeast Asia's air war. The pilot of the A-1 leading any rescue attempt was always the on-scene commander of the operation. He coordinated the efforts of the units who contributed their assets to the rescue, he selected the spot where the aircraft placed their ordinance, and he decided if, when, and how the rescue helicopters—the Jolly Green Giants—would attempt to make their pickup. And in the Southeast Asia world of search and rescue, the most important responsibilities often belonged to some of the youngest pilots.

After six months in the theater, the only black pilot in the 1st SOS had a well-deserved reputation for doing his job effectively; what he hadn't learned from study and experience, he seemed to know by instinct. Marsh Melher and the unit's other senior pilots watched Mann climb the ladder from new guy, to combat-qualified, to element lead, flight lead, and on to Sandy Lead faster than anyone in the squadron's history. He'd be checking out as one of the squadron's instructors in another month.

Those few who were always going to be disgruntled sneered at Mann's rapid advancement, claiming his early graduation into leadership roles was a result of his being black. Most of the personnel in the squadron, however, including the officers responsible for endorsing Mann's rapid ascension through the ranks, ignored the naysayers. Despite the fact he wasn't always sober when he got in his airplane, Bill Mann was in a position of responsibility because he was easily the best pilot in the squadron.

The young pilot's inclination toward long hours at the bar, a common trait in the fighter pilot community, was set in place during his first few weeks on base. When he wasn't flying or sleeping, he was studying or drinking—or both.

By the middle of April, Melher, who was lean when he signed in at NKP, paid fourteen pounds of body weight for the privilege of living to save lives. The parenthetic cuts enclosing his mouth—enhanced by a sporadic diet of bologna sandwiches and beer—spawned additions to their number whenever he was tired. He never wasn't.

Mann was sprawled along the leather couch in front of Melher's desk with one arm shielding his eyes; condensation from his half-empty beer can collected on the floor. Marsh wanted to wake him up so he could go make the sandwiches, but banging things around in his desk wasn't working. He finally resorted to the semidirect approach.

"What've you heard from Stretch?" he asked the inert figure.

After leaving Thailand, McCullough resigned from the Air Force and hired on with Delta Air Lines.

Mann spoke without moving, "He said he was in his fourth week of ground school and no one had shot at him in almost a month."

"You ever consider going to the airlines?"

"Nope. I'm a lifer."

In the months since their first meeting, the squadron commander and the junior lieutenant became closer than most brothers. The unlikely friendship was forged out of a relaxed mutual respect; the difference in rank was overcome by their shared understanding of who the boss was; the age thing lost itself behind Mann's ability to consistently do extraordinary things with an A-1.

Melher pulled off his flying boots and went into the bottom desk drawer to look for his shoeshine kit. "You hungry?" he finally asked.

"I cooked last time." Mann kept his arm over his eyes—he was technically off duty until midnight. He and Melher had been in the air till just before dawn the previous night "truck hunting" in the Mu Gia Pass area of the Ho Chi Minh Trail. "If you're going to put me in the brig for not making the sandwiches, you might as well call the APs."

Predictably, Melher picked up his phone and did what he usually did when he couldn't inspire Mann to take a double-turn at sandwich duty; he keyed the button for the intercom in scheduling.

Master Sergeant Paul Randolph picked up the phone. "Sgt. Randolph."

"This is Melher, Paul. Send somebody down to the snack bar and tell them to make me four bologna and cheese sandwiches, two with mustard and pickles, two with mayonnaise only. Four chips. Four Cokes."

"You got it, Colonel."

Melher thanked him and dropped the phone into its cradle.

Mann said, "Two brews."

Melher yelled the order change at the hallway. The hallway didn't respond.

"Thanks," Mann said. "It always tastes better when someone else cooks."

The two had been eating bologna and cheese sandwiches once or twice a day for almost six months.

"So you're going to Hawaii?" said Melher.

"Amen, brother. I'm already there." Mann was scheduled to go on R'n'R in two weeks. He and Pip had reservations at the Royal Hawaiian in Honolulu.

"What do you hear from Pip?" The question had never been asked before.

"Same old stuff." The frequency of Pip's letters trickled off to occasional and the enthusiasm Mann felt when they arrived dwindled. When he did get a letter, all she talked about was how busy she was. He hadn't told anyone their relationship was cooling—and he wasn't going to tell Melher.

"She okay?"

"Oh, sure. Just busy." Mann was sure when they got to Hawaii—she away from Phoenix, he from the war—he and Pip would have a chance to make things better. They needed some time together . . . they needed to talk face-to-face . . . Pip needed to hear how much he loved her.

Melher had been watching his gifted protégé withdraw for several weeks, but he decided not to hang out his counselor's shingle. The kid's flying skills resided at the magician level—and a twice-divorced lieutenant colonel didn't possess the qualifications necessary for playing padre.

Two minutes later, Melher was rubbing polish on the first boot when he remembered Mann's drink order. He rolled his chair back from the desk and padded down the hall in his sock feet. He stepped into the snack bar at the precise moment Airman Driver, the designated sandwich-maker, chose to spit on a mustard-covered slice of sandwich bread.

Driver looked up at Melher and froze with the bread next to his lips.

Rock'n'roll music and the voices of busy warmongers drifted through the hall from the scheduling area. Both men watched the slice of bread as Driver lowered it to a folded paper towel. A phone rang somewhere in the building.

Driver looked at Melher. Melher couldn't take his eyes off the bread.

After a long pause, Melher walked nearer. As if talking to himself, he asked, "How can a man hate someone he doesn't know?"

Driver cleared his throat. "Look, Colonel, I'm—"

Melher held up a hand and interrupted. "I can't believe . . ." He continued to stare at the slice of bread, and the shiny skin on his forehead took on more color; he waved at the orderly stacks of bread, meat, and sliced cheese. "Take all this and throw it in the trash."

"Colonel, I'll be . . ."

"Do it now," Melher ordered softly. "I'll fix the sandwiches after you get this cleaned up."

Driver picked up the bread slices and dropped them in a nearby trash can. "You want me to put the meat back in the refrigerator, sir?"

"Negative." Marsh gestured at the food again. "If you touched it, I want it in the trash."

Driver pulled the trash can close and emptied the bar with two swipes of his hand. When the counter was cleared, Driver brushed his hands together and looked at Melher.

Melher stepped closer and said, "You can go back to work."

"Very well, sir." Driver had perfected the art of blending a sarcastic smirk with respectful words.

Melher's eyes tracked Driver as he sauntered toward the door, and he nodded to himself—a decision made. "Ask Sergeant Randolph to step down here, please."

"Yes, sir." Driver wasn't too worried. Melher might be a little buddy-buddy with Mann, but no white man would go very far out of his way to take sides with a black guy.

When Master Sergeant Randolph walked into the snack bar, the fighter squadron's commander was doing the job Randolph had assigned to Driver. The first sergeant took in the scene and its story; his eyes narrowed and his lips tightened into a thin, hard line. *Driver,* he thought, *you have made a big-time mistake, my friend.*

Randolph was right about Driver making a mistake, but he had no inkling of its magnitude.

Lieutenant Colonel Melher was born in 1930, the only child of an only child. On the day of his birth, his mother was drunk to the point of not knowing she was giving birth; his father was on an Amazon expedition or a safari in Africa; his grandmother told the attending doctor to write William Lyons Melher IV on the birth certificate because she was afraid of William Lyons Melher II.

The Melher family weathered the Great Depression better than most because of William's grandfather's propensity to operate outside the law. The old pirate spent the years of Prohibition using a French island off the southwestern coast of Newfoundland as an operations base to bring shiploads of bootleg whiskey to thirsty Americans.

For the boy, the walls of the family compound on the North Shore of Long Island enclosed a lavish prison—wealth and privilege have no worth where there is nothing to buy or enjoy. His father and mother were rarely on the estate; his only friend was a dog that belonged to one of the neighbors. The dog accepted the boy because she didn't know his grandfather; the employees on the estate avoided the child because they did.

His grandfather died when William was five. According to Mrs. W. L. Melher II, she used "an incredibly loud firearm" to dispatch her husband and his mistress du jour. Mrs. Melher II died in an institution a year or so later. With the death of his grandparents, the outside world moved farther from William Melher.

Melher was eleven years old when his mother and father permitted him to travel with them to spend the winter at the family's villa in Jamaica.

There was little for young Melher to do on the island except watch his parents' houseguests play tennis and consume alcohol. He was in another prison . . . with more sunshine. On Christmas day, a young Jamaican woman, one of the house staff, clucked her tongue when she heard Melher's father tell him he didn't have time to teach the boy how to play tennis. When William's father walked away, she beckoned for the boy to follow her into the kitchen.

"You want to play tennis, mon?" The slender young woman wore a bright bandana, a white blouse, and tan slacks.

"I guess," William shrugged. "But I don't know how."

"Start from first," the girl frowned. "You learn to talk to me, ahright?"

"All right."

"No, boy." The frown stayed. The girl shook her head as she tapped her chest. "Mi ooman, you pickney. You say 'yassum' an' 'noam' to de sistren, see it?"

William figured the girl was probably ten years older than he was . . . barely six inches taller, and twice as stubborn. He had to smile. "I see it, Ooman."

"Den you do good, Pickney." The girl smiled back at the boy and pointed in the direction of the tennis courts. "I be out dere aftah suppa. You come. I teach."

It was the longest conversation he'd had in a week and he wasn't ready for it to end.

"Why is it you don't talk like the other black people?" he asked. "I can understand you, but not them."

"Is speaky-spokey," she answered. "I go to England for a bit, but it was cold dere an' de war was come. I bring back de words."

They met at the courts that evening and many thereafter and she discovered in him a deeply hidden desire to excel. Two weeks later she had a word with the housekeeper and took the boy to town to buy him a quality racket with her own money.

The Melher's housekeeper watched the shy boy thrive under the care of his new friend. He talked and laughed with the house staff and interacted with strangers among the locals. She eventually pulled the young tennis coach into her tiny office and told her, "You got new job now, Lorraine Frater. The good Lord know that rich boy ain't got much, but he got you."

In mid-February, for the first time, the teacher lost a hard-fought volley to the boy. She was beaming when she met him at the net to congratulate him . . . he had tears in his eyes.

"What is this?" She was still smiling. "The beeg champion weep because he beat the old Ooman?"

"I've been thinking," he rested his racket on the net and answered without smiling. "You're my mother now . . . my mom."

"No, no, Pickney, no, no." She shook her head. The smile was a gentle version of its former self. "I am your good friend, but de Book say for you to honor de woman in de house, an' we do what de Book say."

"I don't know the woman in the house, Ooman. I never will. She doesn't love me because she doesn't know me either. I know *you* . . . and I know you love me."

"Oh, Pickney." The first tear started down her cheek. "What I'm gonna do wit' you?"

"Come over here, and I'll tell you." He took her hand and led her toward the veranda. They sat at a glass-topped table and he told her what she was going to do wit' him.

Lorraine Frater was twelve years older than the boy and she became his only family that day . . . a rich little white boy and his self-selected black mother.

In March, his parents were making plans to go back to Long Island. They told him they would take him "home" before leaving to spend the summer on Martha's Vineyard. The eleven-year-old boy calmly informed them he would be staying in Jamaica. He hired Ooman to be his governess, he explained . . . when he decided to leave, she would be traveling with him.

His parents didn't care—nor would they ever.

William had his own trust fund and a clear understanding of how to deal with the lawyers appointed to oversee his use of it. Ooman didn't want her Pickney on Jamaica because she thought the island way of life too frivolous. She didn't like being where it was cold, but Florida was an easy target for hurricanes. A house-hunting tour took them to Southern California—the Palm Desert area. William went to public school with normal children; Lorraine took a light college load and raised her son.

In 1948, Melher's globe-hopping, alcohol-addled parents were in southern France when they killed themselves and several innocent sheep in a car crash. Their eighteen-year-old son inherited the remainder of the family's wealth, the compound on the North Shore of Long Island, and three homes scattered here and there in trend-setting spots around the globe.

When the news reached them, Melher's black mother was fresh out of college and he was preparing to enter the Air Force. They sold the collection of homes and bought small estates in Palm Springs and Pebble Beach. Her college courses uncovered an innate business sense in Lorraine Frater, and she gradually assumed the management of her Pickney's wealth. In lean years, the income from his investments came in at twenty-five times his Air Force salary. Her son wanted Ooman to take all the investment income for herself; she didn't want any of it. They compromised on a fifty-fifty split.

"You wanted to see me, sir?" Randolph asked.

"Yeah." Melher was spreading mustard on a slice of sandwich bread—a master at work, getting the mustard all the way to the edges. "Airman Driver's due for a FAM ride. Put him up with Lieutenant Mann."

"Very well, sir."

"Tonight."

The sergeant's eyes followed as the knife made its precise trips back and forth across the bread; his facial muscles relaxed. Familiarization flights in the Spad were routinely restricted to test hops or trips to the maintenance facility in Bangkok—milk runs that would not take the planes anywhere near the shooting. Lieutenant Mann was leaving for Mu Gia Pass that evening, an area defended by an array of anti-aircraft artillery which served up a display that rivaled the New Year's Eve fireworks in Rio. No one in the Air Force—enlisted, commissioned, or certifiable—would volunteer to go to The Pass on a FAM ride.

The knife made four more passes before Randolph nodded and said, "Consider it done, Colonel. Anything else?"

"Nope. Thanks, Paul." Melher picked up another slice of bread and dipped the knife in the mustard jar.

When Randolph rounded the corner at the scheduling area, Driver was sitting at his desk, pretending to be busy. Waiting.

Randolph stopped in front of the desk and spoke in a normal tone of voice. "On your feet."

Driver pushed his chair back and took his time standing. He looked at the sergeant and one corner of his mouth curled up. *Rave on, Randolph,* he thought, *I've been chewed out by the best.*

Really good NCOs know how to read the hearts of mere mortals—M/Sgt. Randolph could give lessons. He crossed his arms and looked at the younger man—not challenging, genuinely studying. Neither spoke. The other schedulers took note of Randolph's posture and silence, reading the signs. To a man they heard urgent tasks calling to them from distant parts of the building.

"Well, Driver," Randolph said conversationally, "you've got what it takes to be a good NCO . . . a *fine* one . . . if you live long enough to figure out how to get your brain powered up." The sergeant was almost smiling.

Driver was taken by surprise. He rubbed a hand across his mouth and nodded without speaking. Apparently Melher hadn't told the sergeant what happened. *So far, so good.*

"I don't know what you did back there, buddy boy," Randolph's tone remained conversational, "but I can tell you this . . . I think you just put the bar out of reach for normal idiots."

Driver stared at the top of his desk and chewed on the inside of his cheek. The sergeant knew something happened, but he didn't know what . . . he wasn't the least bit bent out of shape. *Well, I guess things turned out pretty good,* he thought. He was wrong by a hundred or so miles.

Randolph pointed at the scheduling board and pronounced Driver's sentence. "You're up for a FAM flight with Lieutenant Mann."

Driver had the scheduling board memorized, and Lieutenant Mann wasn't scheduled for a local hop. He turned to look at the board, and realization swept over him like winter rain.

"Tonight?" he croaked.

"Yep," Randolph winked at him and turned away. "Put it on the board, Einstein."

The crew chief helped Driver get situated in his seat while Mann did a "walk-around" of the outside of the airplane. After strapping in, Mann took a few minutes to brief Driver on the coming mission. "We'll be meeting a FAC near The Pass. He's probably already over there hunting for truck traffic."

Driver was glancing around at his side of the cockpit, nodding absently without listening. *Who cares?*

"Those are your handholds." Mann pointed with his pencil. "Most guys want something to hold onto if things gets rough."

Driver glanced at the two well-anchored bars and shrugged. He had to be in the plane with the only black guy in their squadron—he didn't have to like it. And he wasn't going to need any handholds.

Mann was making a note on his kneeboard when he wound up the short briefing. "Any questions?"

Driver shook his head. "Nah."

Mann liked airplanes. He liked flying by himself. He liked solitude. He did not like Driver.

The black lieutenant looked up from his note-making. "Any questions, Driver?"

Driver put the smirk on his face and looked the pilot in the eye for several seconds before saying, "No, *sir*. No questions, *sir*."

Mann sighed and went back to the kneeboard. It was going to be a long two or three hours.

It was halfway between midnight and dawn when they launched.

Melher rolled first. Mann waited ten seconds and pushed his throttle up. The sound of the engine and the runway lights flashing by were the only things Driver noticed about the takeoff. Minutes after departing the runway they were crossing the Me Kong into Laos. The river, swollen from recent rains, spread for a mile out of its banks, shimmering in the moonlight.

Driver looked out both sides of the aircraft at the wide expanse and spoke involuntarily. "I didn't know the Me Kong was that big."

"It usually isn't." Mann was closing the distance on Melher's plane, concentrating on its navigation lights. "They've been getting rain north of here."

Driver watched the waters until they passed under the wing. He didn't know how to swim and said so.

"You won't need to," said Mann.

"What if I bail out and land in it," he worried.

"I've been over here six months. I haven't had to bail out."

Driver waited a full minute before saying, "But 'what if' . . . uh, sir?"

"It'll be a no-sweat deal. If you have to punch out, activate the extraction system, wait till your chute opens, then pull the cords to inflate your water wings," the pilot flicked a cord and its marble-sized plastic grip under his right arm. "They're big as an inner tube. Just relax and float 'til you're picked up."

Driver's attention was on the grey-green nylon-wrapped packs snuggled under Mann's armpits. "They didn't give me any of those, sir . . . those water wings."

Mann took his eyes off Melher's plane. He reached over and felt under his passenger's arm and cursed to himself. After a moment, he said, "It doesn't matter, Driver. I'm not gonna put us in the drink. Okay?"

Driver didn't answer.

Mann pulled to within a few feet of Melher. The moonlight showed the lead plane clearly; faint blue flames showed at the tips of its exhausts. Below them, the world was black and silent.

An hour after takeoff, they were holding south of Mu Gia Pass, waiting for the forward air controller to find a target. The moon lacked a day or two being full and except for a high thin overcast the sky was clear. Melher broke his silence to comment on the moon's brilliance and Driver studied the bright orb. "I guess that should help," he ventured.

Mann didn't tell him the moon was mentioned because it would be a major hindrance—aviators called it a gunner's moon. The high clouds would provide a bright backdrop for people on the ground who were trying to shoot down airplanes. It was the worst kind of night for interdiction work.

Their forward air controller, or FAC, announced he spotted some trucks on the trail.

"Hobo Lead, Nail Three-three is standing by to mark. How copy?"

"Okay, you're five-square, Three-three," Marsh answered. "Pick us a good one, and let's get this over with."

The radio chatter between Melher and the FAC continued. Because the two Skyraider pilots could not see well enough in the darkness to keep themselves separated, Melher would initiate the dives for his bombing passes from ten thousand feet while Mann orbited at an altitude that would keep him above his leader.

The FAC marked the spot where he suspected the trucks were located and Melher called, "Hobo One's in hot."

Mann and his passenger watched from overhead as what appeared to be every anti-aircraft gun in the area went into business. To Driver, it looked as if the lines of red and white tracers were stitching a canopy over the pass.

"Busier than normal," commented Mann. He'd be a fool to shun help, so he leaned over and pointed. "Okay, Driver . . . see how some of those lines of tracers come up five or seven at a time . . . the red ones? They look a little bigger and slower."

Driver couldn't miss them. They looked like harmless red Ping-Pong balls drifting up through the night sky, but he'd seen what they could do to an airplane. He used the handholds to pull himself up slightly. "I see 'em, sir."

"Okay, those're thirty-seven millimeter," said Mann. "You watch out your side of the airplane while we're making our passes and let me know if you see any of those that appear to be standing still in your windows. If it appears that they're not moving, it means they're on a converging course with us . . . and we're gonna meet up with them unless we take evasive action. Got it?"

"Yes, sir. Uh . . . what about all the others? those white ones?"

"Twenty-three mike-mike. The thirty-sevens are normally the worst threat, and they should keep you busy," Mann was trying to see where the worst of the ground fire was coming from, "but if you see anything else coming our way, just say so."

Minutes passed. Driver watched as tracers searching for Melher's aircraft seemed to spawn more of their kind. At this rate, by the time it was Mann's turn, it would be like trying to fly through a chain-link fence. As he watched, he decided it might be wise to stay out of Colonel Melher's way in the future; ten minutes of trying to fly through what he was looking at could get a man sent home in a box.

Long minutes later, Melher made his sixth pass and called that he had expended his ordinance. "Hobo One's off to the west. Switches off."

"Okay, Hobo Two," said the FAC. "When Lead clears, just use his nape as a marker and drop right on top of it."

Melher called clear and Mann keyed his mike. "Two's in hot. South to north."

Mann set up his arming panel and pushed the nose over—the engine began to wind up. Apparently, the sound told the gunners exactly where they were; the anti-aircraft fire intensified and became a steel curtain woven of angry red and white arcs. Driver's grip tested the stress tolerance of the handholds. Within seconds the airplane was standing on its nose—the engine was threatening to come off the mounts; swarms of tracers flashed by on all sides, barely missing them. Driver was as far down in his seat as he could get, mesmerized by one particular string of red balls that seemed frozen in space just outside the canopy. He was taking a breath to warn Mann when something hit them forward of the cockpit. The blow, accompanied by a lightning-bright flash of light, slammed them sideways like a thrown toy; Driver was momentarily blinded by the flash and stunned when his helmet hit the canopy. Mann righted the airplane while orange flames flared from around the cowl; the engine was stumbling. Driver barely suppressed an urge to moan out loud.

Mann jettisoned his external load and pulled off the target, turning hard toward the southwest. The fire under the engine cowl went out but not before every gunner in North Viet Nam locked on the plane, using the rich orange glow for their aiming point. Driver held on and scrunched down until his eyes were level with the canopy rail, watching as thousands more tracers filled every cubic foot of sky around the crippled A-1.

The fire finally went out and the engine was trying to recover; it was doing better than Driver's heart. Mann was turning back and forth—jinking slowly from side to side in an attempt to throw the gunners off. "Hobo One, this is Two."

Melher answered immediately. "Two, One. Go."

"I took a hit . . . maybe a glancing blow . . . looks like somewhere in the engine area. I'm off and headed for the barn."

"Roger that. How's the engine?"

"It lit up and choo-chooed when we were hit," Mann was scanning the engine instruments, "but the gauges say it's ops normal, and it's, uh . . . smoothed out a little." The engine chose that moment to backfire. Blue flames belched from the exhaust stacks and the aircraft shuddered. The gunners saw the flare-up and pressed the attack. Mann cursed. "Well, scratch the ops normal, Lead. She's decided to be temperamental."

While Mann cursed the engine, Driver unsnapped his oxygen mask and pulled it away from his face, gasping for air.

Twenty minutes later, they were well away from the guns, and Melher was alongside, watching without interfering while Mann worked to get his airplane back to the base. The engine died twice—Mann resurrected it both times. Except for one or two pitiful moans, Driver hadn't made a sound since before they took the hit. During those intervals when the engine wasn't running, the absence of steady roar soaked into his upper body like frigid water. He waited until his teeth stopped chattering to ask, "Umm . . . Lieutenant . . . are we going to have to bail out, sir?"

"*I'm* not," Mann snapped. "Guys do this all the time, Driver. Just hang in there." He was coaxing as much power as possible out of the engine, trying to recover the altitude they lost while doing their glider imitations.

Anxious thoughts multiply geometrically, and Driver's imagination was showing him slow-motion pictures of the airplane coming apart in midair. If they had to bail out over land, he might be able to hide till the helicopters came; if he landed in the Me Kong, he was a dead man.

He expressed his next thoughts without being aware he was speaking. "I can't swim."

Mann took his eyes off the engine instruments and looked hard at his passenger then turned back and stared straight ahead at the moon for a few seconds. Finally, he sighed and tapped the control stick with a gloved finger. "Okay, Driver. I need you to take the stick for a second."

Driver stared at the pilot. "I'm . . . uh, I don't know anything about airplanes, Lieutenant . . . umm . . . nothing."

"Can you drive a car?"

Driver nodded slowly without taking his eyes off Mann. "Yes, sir, I can drive," he croaked.

"Then you can fly an airplane. This'll be your first flying lesson . . . and I'm the best instructor in the Air Force, okay?" Mann pointed to the stick on Driver's side of the cockpit. "C'mon . . . help us out here. I'll be inches away if you need me."

Driver put his hand on the stick and it telegraphed the passenger's tremors to Mann.

"Okay," said Mann, "the secret is to keep your eyes outside the plane. The moon's right out there above the horizon," he pointed. "Use it to help . . . just use the stick to keep the horizon level."

Mann kept his hand close to the stick for a minute, encouraging Driver to make smaller corrections. "The whole thing is all about being gentle, Driver. She's listening . . . just whisper to her . . . give her gentle hints . . . keep it soft and quiet." He moved his fingers farther from the control. "That's it . . . nothing to it . . . you're a natural."

Mann gave the airplane completely to Driver and started wiggling out of his harness, continuing to encourage his student. "See there? She'll practically fly herself."

A minute later, Mann shook the stick slightly and said, "Okay, thanks, I've got it." He nudged Driver. "Here you go."

Driver looked to his left.

"You just might need these after all." Mann was holding out his water wings. "I won't."

Driver glanced at the water wings, then stared at the pilot. After a long moment, he took the life-saving packs without speaking and held them in his lap.

Mann glanced at him and said, "You may as well put 'em on now, Driver. If you end up needing 'em, they might be hard to get into while you're learning to swim."

"Yes, sir."

The engine chose that moment to backfire several times then quit for the third time. They lost 2,000 feet while Mann worked his magic to get it running again.

The engine quit for the fifth and final time as the A-1 touched down at NKP. Mann pulled the mixture control off and let the plane slow before steering it into the grass by the runway. When they stopped, they were directly abeam the squadron building, separated from it by a parallel taxiway and another wide strip of grass. Mann flicked off the battery/generator switch and pointed across the taxiway. "Well, I guess you can climb out and walk if you're in a hurry. I'm gonna hang out here and get a head start on some paperwork while I wait for a tow back to the chocks."

Driver took his time releasing the handholds. After a few seconds, when the numbness left his fingers, he clambered out. As soon as his feet touched the ground, he knew what walking was going to feel like if he lived to be eighty-five. He crossed the parallel taxiway and stopped to look back at the A-1. Mann's helmet was propped on the canopy rail, and the pilot was concentrating on something in the cockpit, apparently filling out a form. A flight of four fully-loaded A-1s taxied between Driver and the plane parked out in the grass, and one of the pilots nodded at Mann. Mann saluted with his pencil and went back to the paperwork.

The sun was well above the horizon when Driver reached the door to the PE building; he was sweat-soaked and exhausted, his mind saturated with unfamiliar thoughts. He turned in his chute, survival vest, and helmet without comment and left. Minutes later Master Sergeant Paul Randolph was watching as Driver wandered into the scheduling area carrying a pair of water wings. The preoccupied combat vet concentrated on arranging the Air Force issue life-changers neatly in the center of his desk before speaking to Randolph. "If it's okay with you, Sarge, I'd like to get a shower and some sleep. I'll be back here by noon."

"Okay." Randolph glanced at his watch. "See you in six."

When Mann checked his mail slot, the letter was waiting. The envelope was square . . . different from the others. This had to be what he dreaded. He took the unopened message to his hooch, closed the door, and stood by his desk, holding it in his hand until the paper was sweat stained.

He closed his eyes and shook his head while tearing the envelope open—it wouldn't be good news. Inside was a single folded page of stationery . . . a soft shade of beige . . . a color match for her skin. The few short words were written in blue ink . . . orderly up and down strokes.

> *Dear Bill,*
>
> *You have to forgive me, but I cannot live like this. I can't spend the rest of my life waiting in an empty house while you're forever going off to another part of the world, leaving me here to wonder if you're going to come back.*
>
> *I won't be coming to Hawaii—and don't bother to come here—I'm moving. I talked to a lawyer last week, and I'm filing for divorce today.*
>
> *I hate doing this while you're over there, but I can't keep up this charade any longer.*
>
> *This was all my fault.*
>
> *Please take care of yourself,*
>
> *Pip*

He sat on his bunk and read the letter again, one word at a time. When he finished, he folded it and placed it on the desk by her picture. Her picture smiled at him over the color-coordinated stationery. He wanted to react but felt nothing.

He stretched out on the bunk and put his hands behind his head and stared at the white ceiling. The words he'd spoken to James Kelly six months earlier repeated themselves in his mind. *I've got the job I've always wanted and a wife who loves me. I'll quit there.*

Now he was the only black, twenty-two-year-old divorced Sandy driver in Southeast Asia. And he didn't feel special anymore.

She was gone. Just like that. Gone.

His fingers traced across the stubble on his cheek. A small collection of people who might care passed through his thoughts . . . Rusty
and Jane . . . Missy and Pat. Marsh would care . . . James Kelly . . . Sam
and Cora . . . maybe Will and Ella Claire. That was about it.

Sleep wasn't going to happen, and after waiting an hour for a sense
of loss to overcome him, he gave up and tossed the letter in a drawer.
He would read it again later, but the neat, straight up and down strokes
would still spell the same words. He took a shower and walked over to
The Box to get a beer.

The pilots at NKP ran the gamut from teetotalers to serious drinkers, and the profusion of complaints from the strap-hangers about
the fighter pilots' conduct in the O'Club influenced the base commander to relegate the pilots of the combat units to their own special
party hooches near their living quarters; the Hobos of the 1st Special
Operations Squadron called their club The Sandy Box. Mann was one
of The Box's best customers.

Melher was standing at the scheduling counter later that evening when Mann sauntered past carrying a beer in each hand and
disappeared into the office. The CO followed him in and sat
down behind the desk; Mann was semi-reclining in his spot on the
couch.

Aside from casual snippets about their past, the two never really
seemed to visit much about their personal lives. Flying eighteen inches
from your friend's airplane while the frayed edges of the world unravel
around you does not mean you trot out your closet's skeletons when
you're back on the ground.

"So," Melher dropped his granny glasses on the desk, "tell me
about it."

"You called it yesterday." Mann tilted one of the beers to his mouth
and took a long swallow. "The DJ letter was waiting for me when we
landed this morning . . . I'm getting a divorce I don't want."

"Mmm." Melher leaned back in his chair and watched Mann's face
while he asked, "And how're you doing?"

"I saw this coming," Mann's voice was hoarse with fatigue. He sank
farther into the couch and closed his eyes. "I thought maybe I'd get

more bent outta shape." He shrugged and shook his head. "I don't feel anything."

Mann's scarcity of words was not totally uncommon, but there were a dozen things Marsh didn't like about what he was hearing and seeing. "You want to take your R'n'R in the States?"

"Wouldn't help." The voice was devoid of emotion. "She's moving and won't say where."

They both thought their own thoughts until Mann said, "I guess I don't need any R'n'R. I'll stick around here and pad the manning formula a little."

"No, you won't." Marsh had already decided that Mann was going to take some time off. "You're off the schedule as of right now. Take a long breather."

"You don't need to put me on the ground, Marsh." Mann didn't have the energy it took to frown. "I'd be better off flying."

"Not a chance." Marsh wanted to the see how Mann handled the reality of what happened before he let him near an airplane. "You've got comp time off coming and you can hook it up to your R'n'R. Go out there and tell scheduling where you're going and take at least two weeks. I'd go with you if I could."

"I think you're wasting a man for nothing."

"Yeah, well, this ain't a committee meeting." Melher put the glasses back on and picked up a piece of paper. "You won't care after you've been away from this dump for twenty-four hours . . . we'll be lucky if you don't go AWOL. I would."

Mann already didn't care.

Airman Driver was seated behind his desk in the scheduling section, watching Mann approach the counter. When one of the other schedulers moved forward to help the black pilot, Driver motioned him back.

"You need something, Lieutenant?" asked Driver.

"Yeah," said Mann. "I'm going on R'n'R." He propped himself on the counter and pointed a beer at the scheduling board. "Sign me out effective tomorrow."

"Where to, sir?"

When Mann didn't respond, Driver cleared his throat and repeated himself. "Uh . . . where'll you be going, sir?"

Mann was leaning on the scheduling counter, eyes unfocused, watching his beer bottle tilt back and forth like a sluggish metronome.

Driver watched the beer bottle's movement and wondered if Mann was trying to hypnotize himself. The scheduler stepped around his desk and moved to the counter. "Excuse me, Lieutenant, where do you want me to sign you out to?"

Mann looked in Driver's direction without seeing him and pursed his lips for a moment, thinking. Finally, he lifted his shoulders slowly and let them drop. "May as well make it Bangkok, I guess. It's as good as any an' closer than most."

"Yes, sir. I'll take care of it."

Driver went to the board and wrote "R'n'R—Bangkok" in the neat mechanical letters beside Mann's name and drew a line across the row of blocks that normally held his schedule. The space reserved for Mann's personal call sign was sandwiched between "Rabbi" Loeb and "Marsh" Melher—the only empty block in the board's "Call Sign" column. The highly qualified and recently divorced black Sandy driver didn't care about that either.

Mann went straight from scheduling to The Sandy Box and stayed late, practicing for his trip to Bangkok. At dawn the next day, he navigated through the front door of the Personal Equipment building without doing measurable harm to himself or the door facing. He ignored, or couldn't see, the only other person in the locker room. After cleaning most of the contents out of his locker, he tossed the combination lock in it and slapped the door closed. He turned his survival vest in to the PE troops so they could update it while he was gone and entrusted his handgun to the NCOIC who—for a six pack—would clean and store it for him.

The pilot Mann had not noticed was transferring over from the other A-1 squadron, the 602nd. The new pilot—an overweight lieutenant colonel—stood at a window and watched Mann weaving slightly as he walked away from the building. The stranger rechecked the room to make sure he was alone, then crossed to the metal locker with Mann's name on it and eased it open. There were several pictures taped to the inside of the locker's door; one in particular caught his attention. He took one of Mann's maps and walked out to the PE counter.

"Say, Sergeant," he waved the map, "I think this fell out of that pilot's locker, but I don't know who he is."

"Yes, sir. That's Lieutenant Mann. I'll put it back for him—he's headed to Bangkok for R'n'R."

The lieutenant colonel wanted to be helpful, "No problem, I'll stick it back in his locker."

The sergeant was busy. "Thanks, Colonel."

The lieutenant colonel smiled. "My pleasure."

After he put the map in the locker, the lieutenant colonel came back by the counter and said, "I'm going to run a couple of errands and come back. I'll see you before lunch."

"Yes, sir."

The lieutenant colonel had a magnifying glass in his hooch, and he was taking something of Mann's there for a closer look. In the pocket of the helpful senior officer's flightsuit was a picture of a black major leaning on the drop tank of an F-100 Super Sabre; he was wearing a dressed-up Colt .45 and displaying a handsome new watch. The magnifying glass would tell him that the major's name, as spelled out on the flightsuit's name strip, was Prince.

CHAPTER ELEVEN

Rhythmic concussions came from an unknown source and shook his surroundings, battering against the protective barriers. Pressure in his brain, timed to the pulse of a huge pump, swelled and receded at one-second intervals. Something—a methodical beast or a machine gone berserk—was bludgeoning its way into his quiet, dark world. Increasing awareness brought with it a nauseating swirl of pain.

Growing consciousness widened a portal for the pain, and its intensity was magnified when the area immediately behind his eyes became its focal point.

The surface beneath him was cold and unforgiving—possibly a stainless steel morgue table. Someone had skewered his head with the tines of a rusty pitchfork and death was imminent—or he had a hangover that would take down a four-story building.

Being careful to hold his body motionless, he mustered the strength needed to open an eye, and stark white light flash-fried the shadowed recesses of his brain. He closed the eye, welcomed the returning darkness with a ragged breath, then raised his head slightly and tried both eyes at once. The morgue table rose and fell on sea swells, the brightly-lighted ceiling above him moved in a sickening circular motion. By straining his neck, he could see that he was fully dressed; his surrounding belonged to the bathroom in his hotel room. He let his head fall back and it struck the tile floor with a crack that brought back vestiges of the darkness. At some point, he got his hands and knees under him and drug his body into the bathtub. He kicked at the cold water faucet with a penny-loafer-clad foot until the shower came on. The water flowed and he lay back, hoping he might drown.

Thirty minutes later, undrowned but unalive, he was on his feet and out of his wet clothes.

He had been sick of Bangkok from day one. To him, the town offered nothing but a geographic location to drink; he spent ten days and a small fortune teaching himself that saturating himself with booze would not erase his memories of Pip. The press of the crowds, the pandemonium generated by the traffic, and the perpetual smiles of the Thai people were nail files on nerve endings. Flying combat might be dangerous, but it was something he could do in relative peace—he was going back to NKP.

In an effort to beat back poison with poison, he finished off the last half of a warm six-pack while he stuffed clothes into his B-4 bag—wet on one side, dry on the other. Two hours later, while a wary doorman watched him negotiate the steps of the Chao Phya Hotel, he was experiencing the worst of three worlds: he was hungover and drunk and trying to breathe in a city laced with open canals, or klongs. The principal function of the klongs was to rid the city of its sewage.

A Datsun Bluebird left the cab queue and the driver, a tiny man wearing a white Nehru shirt and a need for speed, hustled to put Mann's bag in the trunk. The doorman was assisting Mann into the cab while the driver was slamming his own door and releasing the parking brake. Most of the pilot was in the cab when the driver popped the clutch and the acceleration forces threw him face-first onto the backseat.

Street sounds immediately assaulted them from all sides, insisting that the vehicle honking its horn the most times had the right of way. By the time the taxi went two blocks, Mann was hoarse from yelling at the maniac behind the wheel. Compared to what he was being subjected to, Steve McQueen's chase scene in *Bullitt* was a ride in a Quaker's buggy—without the horse.

The noon sun's heat was concentrating itself on the interior of the cab, and the top part of his brain was beginning to bake. The stench from the klongs, the rocking and swaying of the cab, and the effort he was expending to yell brought him to the brink of throwing up.

He gave up yelling because he decided he would rather die in a clean flightsuit as opposed to one covered with the previous night's pepper steak.

The pilot eventually managed to stabilize himself by reaching across the width of the little rice rocket and fastening his hands to their respective rear-window openings. He released his grip on the window only once because he was certain he was about to offer up his arm to a careening, smoke-chuffing god in the form of oversized air horns with a dump truck attached. During that unsecured millisecond, he was rewarded with a body slam into the opposite door. His sunglasses flew off during the encounter, and he left them on the floor to fend for themselves.

The one constant in the melee was the requisite Salem cigarettes that gestured like miniature semaphores from between the competing drivers' lips.

He had used two-thirds of a cat's allotted lives when Thailand's track master maneuvered the Datsun into a four-wheel drift, passing under a broad archway sign that read *Don Muang Airport*. They were in mid-skid when the cab nearly clipped an attractive young woman on a Vespa scooter. The Vespa girl didn't bother to change expression.

Stirling Mess's ungovernable beast was agitated by the lack of competition in the airport, but it kept the contest interesting by increasing its speed. They accelerated all the way to a back corner of the airport and skidded to an all-wheels-locked, passsenger-on-the-floor-on-top-of-his-sunglasses-cussing-and-clinging-to-one-door standstill in a cloud of red dust. The finish line was marked by a blue-on-white sign proclaiming their odds-against arrival at the *Military Air Terminal*.

On the sidewalk by the car, the survivor—who couldn't kiss the ground because he was afraid to stoop over—made a halfhearted attempt to untangle the scrap metal that was once his sunglasses. The driver placed the bag carefully on the sidewalk and Mann dug into a breast pocket of the flightsuit and showed a palm full of multicolored bills and shiny coins to the man who failed to kill him. The driver waved one of his arms, gibbered and signaled with his cigarette while his hand picked through the coin collection like a hungry chicken. The automobilist displayed a wide, nicotine-stained smile when the pilot bestowed another small stack of the coins on him—probably enough to buy the cab.

The front door of the terminal opened while the tiny man was taking a moment to favor the black American with a nod, a parade of friendly gestures, and more gibberish while igniting another Salem from its predecessor. Mann and the driver turned to watch two young women in fatigues and bush hats struggle down the steps dragging a pair of overstuffed duffel bags. The smaller of the two girls was black; her companion was California white . . . blonde ponytail, blue eyes, brown skin.

The gnome abandoned his benefactor, squinted over his cigarette at the girls, and took a shot. "You call taxi?" He began to sidle toward them, puffing the cigarette and gesturing with both hands at the cab. The dust left by the cab's arrival was drifting away to become part of the klong smell.

The girls, identified as first lieutenant nurses by the insignia on their collars, looked from the driver to the black man in the gaudy flightsuit. The black girl, the more skeptical of the two, stepped closer and cocked her head at Thailand's answer to Junior Johnson. "How'd you get here so fast? We just called."

"Oh, yes! Oh, yes! Very fast!" he nodded vigorously. The black woman spoke his language; maybe she wouldn't scream too much. He showed everyone his brown teeth, waved his arms and cigarette, and yelled, "Number one!"

The white nurse took in Mann's expression—a hybrid of what looked to be mild amusement mixed with an allergic reaction to light—and stepped in front of her traveling companion. Miss California, her ponytail undulating like a possessed belly dancer, addressed herself to the driver. "Do you speak English?"

"Ah, yes! Ah, yes!" American women asked too many questions. He was nodding and signaling while he pulled the bags out of their hands. "Speak English! Number one! Very fast!"

The smaller girl shrugged and gave the negotiations over to the blonde. She turned to Mann and said, "Hi."

He gave up on becoming a sunglasses mechanic. "Hi."

His face was young; his eyes weren't. The patches on his party flightsuit were biographical. "Well," she spoke the obvious, "you aren't a new kid."

Mann checked her name tag—K. C. GUND. No ponytail, but a just-right Afro clip—military style—she was more attractive than the blonde. He didn't want to be mean, but there was only one woman he was interested in talking to. Moving his facial muscles made his head hurt, and the attempted smile became a grimace. "I guess not. You?"

"Kinda. Ninety-fifth Evac at Monkey Mountain." She ignored the conflict raging at the cab's trunk. "This is our first three-days-off. Figured we'd—"

"Kayceeeee! Toot sweet or we'll lose our bags to this bandit!" The negotiations at the curb were over. The driver was doing a Le Mans sprint to his place behind the wheel; the ponytail was being swallowed by the would-be race car.

Gund ignored the threat and looked at the name embroidered beneath the pilot's wings. "We're taking a long weekend at the Siam Intercontinental." She had this stunning smile that seemed to reach almost to her ears. She offered the smile and a hand. "I'm . . ." She was mouthing words, but they were drowned by a pair of F-102s passing over the building in afterburner—part of the prerace festivities, no doubt. The driver ran the engine wide open and checked out his horn in preparation for the coming encounter with the street mammoths.

Lieutenant Gund turned and walked over to display the smile from the door of the cab. "So long, Mann." She tapped her temple with an unpainted fingernail. "Take a bottle of aspirin and call me in a week." The Mary Tyler Moore smile took in about twenty more teeth before disappearing into the internal combustion coffin.

Not me, honey, thought Mann. *Besides, this hangover will probably kill me before sundown.*

"Mann!" Gund straightened and stood with one foot in the cab. "What's your call sign?"

Every fighter pilot he'd ever heard of had a call sign. He didn't.

"My friends call me 'Bill.'"

The smile faded slightly, then recovered. "Come see me, Bill."

The taxicab's engine was screaming like a witch soaked in water, the horn was an impatient klaxon. The interior of the cab squealed, "Kayceeeeee!!! We're using up our weeeeekeeenndddd!"

"Fly safe!" The teeth disappeared into the sacrificial chamber, Junior popped the clutch and G-forces slammed the rear door. Exhaust smoke, supplemented by the Salem cigarette, mixed with the red dust and followed the car as it accelerated away from the pits. At the gate—without showing its brake lights—the car slid into the turn, shot a three-foot gap between two behemoths, and blended the bleat of its horn with the rest of the competitors. From the midst of the tumult came the prolonged, high-pitched, and perfectly integrated wail of two nurses—one black, one white. The sound defined sibling harmony.

He made the mistake of shaking his head while bending for his B4 bag . . . and got sicker. He stayed where he was, with his hands on his knees, until he choked down the bile. When he could, he hefted the bag and decided that, despite evidence to the contrary, trying to carry it might not cause his head to divide down the middle.

The inside of the little terminal was mostly waiting room and super-heated air. He made it to the nearest blank space along a wall without throwing up and let go of the bag. His flagrant-orange party flightsuit had dark wet areas under the arms and down his back. He stood by the bag and held onto the wall while he willed the room to stop spinning. When he got his eyes open again, everything wasn't so much spinning as it was blurred, as if from a thick fog. *Well, fog won't make me sick.*

From what he could see, the room was wall-to-wall people. A fragmented rainbow of party flightsuits brought color to a roomscape teeming with varied shades of olive, green, brown, and black. In addition to representatives of the different branches of the military based in Thailand, the crowd contained a small handful of civilians; Americans comprised the majority of the latter group. The uniformed American contingent milled around the main area and spilled into an over-crowded snack bar. Thai military men squatted in small circles, smiling, smoking Salems, and visiting quietly with one another, seemingly oblivious to the mob around them. Air-conditioning for the one-hundred-plus horde was provided by a handful of anemic ceiling fans hanging from bare rafters. Sounds blaring from the snack bar's jukebox mingled with the sour smell of stale sweat.

He looked around for an open seat in the waiting area. There weren't any.

He let his eyes drift across the crowd in the off chance he might see a familiar face. He didn't. A couple of the Air Force pilots glanced over, made eye contact, and nodded at the Sandy pilot. He nodded back. The crew members in the room who were wearing government issue flightsuits wore rank and wings woven with black thread . . . or no patches at all. None of the olive drab flightsuits sported unit patches.

He turned his back on the crowd and did his best zombie imitation toward the snack bar. As he neared the archway, he was having to lean into the music in order to make headway. Fats Domino was telling every mother's son at the airport about Blueberry Hill and Mann felt like he was climbing it . . . sans thrills. A polite Thai kid came out of the fog to sell him a beer and a handful of aspirin. He chewed the pills but couldn't make them go down his throat and ended up spitting the bitter remnants into a bar napkin.

When the visibility in the room gave no indications of improving, he took a shallow breath and practiced his walking-dead shuffle to the miniature Klong Flight Departures counter. He was buoyed along by a breeze from the Beatles.

A forty-year-old master-sergeant was manning the departure desk by himself and two F-105 pilots in party flightsuits were the only people in line. Judging from the size of the crowd, the shuttle to Nakhon Phanom Royal Thai Air Force Base was going to be packed. The chalkboard behind the counter said they were scheduled to make three stops before they got to NKP.

Let's see, that's four ups and four downs. The air in the early May skies over Thailand would be turbulent and he would be trapped in the airless cargo section of a C-130. Hoping the trip might kill him, he took the number three spot in the line.

When the Thud drivers moved out of the way, the sergeant glimpsed the cloth name strip on Mann's chest. "Are you Lieutenant William P. Mann, sir?"

"Right." Mann answered without nodding,

As if introducing an arrest warrant, the sergeant put on a blank expression and produced a sheet of teletype paper from beneath the counter. He held it out to Mann and said, "The First SOS at Naked Fanny sent us this twix, Lieutenant. I'm sorry, sir, but they said not to let you on an airplane until after the eighth of the month." The sergeant had been exposed to more than one demonstration of the damage fighter pilots were willing to mete out in the name of fun. If this quiet-looking Sandy pilot's people wouldn't let him back on his own base, the sergeant didn't want to catch his act.

Mann squinted at his watch. "This is the fifth, right?"

The sergeant didn't blink. "The sixth, sir."

"Humpfh." Mann was turning away from the counter when something about the man behind the counter caught his eye. He dug in his flightsuit and came out with a knot of mangled gold frames and two dark lenses. He piled the wreckage on the counter with a wad of Thai money and pointed at the sunglasses hanging from the sergeant's shirt pocket. "Wanna swap?"

"No, sir," the sergeant shook his head and straightened. The patches on the party flightsuit told him all he needed to know about the black kid. He lifted the sunglasses out of his pocket and placed them on the pile of money and twisted metal and pushed the stack toward Mann. "Sandy pilots don't pay for sunglasses in my shop, Lieutenant."

"Thanks, Sergeant. You saved my life."

Mann scooped up the money and glasses and mustered the will it took to make it back to his bag. If he couldn't get a C-130 to kill him, he'd take his chances on a cab ride to the Siam Intercontinental. If he survived, he just might take that nurse to Nick's Number One for a steak. He sat on the floor and leaned back against his B-4 bag to steel himself for the walk to the door.

It was nearly dark when he woke up; but for a Thai cleanup crew, the terminal was deserted. He eventually found his flight cap, then gathered up his bag and went looking for a ride to the hotel. His mouth tasted like the cleaning crew rinsed their mops in it.

By the time he got to the hotel, he'd shelved any ideas about steaks with the nurse. He bought a fifth of rum and went looking for his room. His resolve to drink less would be on hold until he got back to NKP. For now, he would pass the time in Bangkok being passed out.

Morning brought a new hangover, but it wasn't a killer.

There was nothing in Bangkok interesting enough to draw him away from the hotel. GIs were as thick as the canal smell; the streets were a hazardous two-way river rapids of cars, bicycles, and motorcycles; the stores were brimful of sapphires, ceramic elephants, and smiling clerks. He put on his swimming trunks and made his way to the hotel pool. The perimeter of the pool was guarded by white people pursuing a tan to match his. A couple of empty lounge chairs, the farthest from the pool, were situated under the thatched roof that protected the poolside cabana. He took the one nearest the bar.

An hour later, he was contemplating a between-beers nap when K. C. Gund stopped in front of him. "What happened, Mann? You change your mind about going home?"

Her smile was a repeat of the day before . . . or was it the day before that. Whatever. "The guys in my outfit don't love me anymore. How's Bangkok?"

"It's not San Francisco," she swept her hand at the manicured expanse around the pool, "but it's a step or two ahead of China Beach." She pointed at the lounge chair next to his. "May I join you?"

He didn't want company, but he said, "Sure."

She spread her towel and sat on the edge of her lounger. She sat like a lady. "Thanks."

"Wanna beer?" he asked.

"Thanks. Are you having one?"

"If you insist." Mann waved at the pool boy.

He ordered the beers then said, "Those deuces out at Don Muang interrupted our introductions. What do I call you?"

"Kaycee or 'Hey, nurse.'" Shrug and smile. "They're interchangeable."

"How long you gonna be here?"

"Two more days. You?"

"The same, I think." He frowned behind the sunglasses. "What day is this?"

"Sunday, the seventh."

"Good. Two more days."

"Are you in a hurry to get back to the war?" She was wearing the same standard-issue aviation sunglasses he was wearing and she used them as a screen while she studied him. She knew she did justice to her beach attire, but if he was interested, it didn't show.

"I guess I'm in a hurry to get out of this dump."

She decided on the bold approach and notched up the smile's candlepower. "This is my first time here. Are you interested in showing me around?"

She seemed like a nice enough person, but he didn't want the job. He wasn't a good liar, and he paused too long before he answered.

She was faster than he was. "You want a rain check, maybe?"

"Thanks . . . I'm . . . uh, not up to it."

The pool boy stepped between them to deliver their beers.

Mann was experiencing embarrassment for the first time since he met Pip. "Look, you're the prettiest woman I've run into since I left the States, okay? But I'm afraid I'd make a sorry tour guide."

The smile didn't waver. "In that case, would you be my bodyguard?"

"Bodyguard?" Sunglasses couldn't hide his confusion.

"Yep." She dug a thick book out of her swim bag and leaned back. "I'll get a tour next trip. If you'll just keep your body out here by the pool for the next two days, I'll pull my lounger up by yours and pretend we're together."

He didn't like it. "I won't be very good company."

"If you don't talk to me, I won't talk to you," she assured him. "I would love nothing better than to lie in the shade for two days and read. I'll lose myself in *Airport*; you'll be the mannequin in the lounge chair. If anybody starts toward me, I'll lean over and say something to you and laugh. You don't even have to change expression. Deal?"

It might work two ways. He could use her as a barrier to keep stray people away from him. "Deal." That was the last word to pass between them that day.

For the remainder of the day, she bought her own beer and read. He outdrank her three-to-one and did nothing.

When it got too dark to read, she disappeared into the hotel. He stayed behind his sunglasses and ordered another beer.

She came out the next day and found him at his station. The pool boy made fewer beer runs that morning and Mann shared a few words with her over a poolside hamburger. That afternoon he switched to coffee as his beverage of choice. When she sneaked glances at him, his eyes were always open, looking at nothing. She was true to her word and didn't speak unless spoken to. He didn't speak.

They ate dinner together that night and she stayed with the rules. He played with his food and drank bottled water—she ate like a linebacker and enjoyed being quiet. Mann walked her back to her room, and when they reached her door, she ventured a question. "What time are you leaving tomorrow?"

"I don't have to rush. I'll lay by the pool till noonish and try to make the three o'clock shuttle."

"Good." The smile. "See you in the morning, then."

CHAPTER TWELVE

When he finally broke down and bought the pickup, he bypassed the expensive model. Like most ranchers, Gene Elliott watched his money closely, but for the first time in his life, he surrendered the dollars needed to get one with a radio. TV reception on the west side of the Rockies wasn't always the best and he still didn't trust a weather man—or almost any other man—who wore a suit to work. Every time his daughter rode with him, she climbed in and turned the radio to that rock 'n' roll music. Forty years on the seats of a long succession of loud tractors had dulled his hearing, but his daughter's music still sounded loud. However, Gene was a mild man, and he found it easy enough to tolerate the racket. Besides, she was carrying his first grandchild.

The two of them rode in from the ranch almost every day. On each trip, because she wanted to see what had changed since she left for college, they chose a different route through the little town of Creekside. She discovered an old memory almost every morning. On this day, the radio sang "The First Time Ever I Saw Your Face," which wasn't too bad because he could understand the words, and the lady sang like she meant them. His daughter tried to sing along and ended up crying . . . again. She had cried at least twice a day for the past couple of months.

Bill Mann wasn't the only one who had been battling nausea. Jane Mattingly became pregnant seven days before Rusty left for Viet Nam. Her Plan A was to stay in Phoenix with the other young "war widows" and play bridge and tennis when she wasn't lying by the pool. However, after two weeks without Rusty, Phoenix was lonely and boring—and being pregnant fostered a need for a Plan B.

She drove home to Colorado and moved back into her old bedroom in the small ranch house. Within three days, she fell into a routine that called for her to get up, get dressed, eat breakfast, and get sick. The doctor kept telling her she needed to eat more, but loneliness and worry conspired with the morning sickness to take her appetite.

Every morning she made notations on the calendar she was using to mark the passing days. At first she was counting down the days until Rusty would be home; she had since added "Junior" to her date-tracking. Today was the first day she hadn't felt like throwing up and she marked it accordingly. It was the eighth of May.

Her dad and mom were glad to have her home. It was the kind of thing her matter-of-fact mom took in stride; it was a new experience for her dad.

Years earlier, when she was a child, the Elliotts couldn't afford a hired hand and ranch work on the dry side of the mountains started before daylight and lasted as long as a man was willing to work; the chores too heavy for Jane and her mom fell to the only man on the place. Ballgames and cheerleading, even school plays and graduation, were missed so he could try to sift a living out of the sandy dirt. She grew up in the little house almost without him—and he without her.

The fall she went off to college marked the ranch's first good year; it was followed by better ones. The operation was out of debt and they had a fair amount of money set aside when some fellows from over in Denver came out and found oil under the place.

She still woke up later than he did, but he managed to find things to keep him close to the house till her mom called her to breakfast. After she'd finished her second cup of coffee, he'd stand up and announce he was going to run some errands in town and invite her to ride along.

She rode with him every morning for the same reason he asked if she wanted to go. Sometimes they talked. Most times he just listened to the rock and roll music while she cried.

On Monday morning, her first day of not getting sick, they were driving down White River Road when she saw the tip of a steeple through the trees. "Dad, stop a minute."

She pointed to a small church building that was set back off the street, watched over by a shallow stand of lodge-pole pines. "Do I remember that church?"

"I reckon so. It's twice as old as you."

"Can we pull in here?"

There was a time in his past when he'd have had to refuse, but that day was gone. She was his only child, her husband was a world away fighting a messed-up war, and she was carrying his first grandchild. He drove into a small graveled area and parked in the shade from one of the trees. "How's this?"

She looked around them. "They keep the yard pretty." She had been back home less than three months, and she almost pronounced it *purdy*.

"Yep." Elliott knew Wendell Andrews took care of the yard work by himself.

Her eyes went back to the straight, white steeple. "I'm gonna take a look inside."

Her dad had a whole handful of errands to run and didn't have time to stop while she explored the inside of an empty church. Clouds were building up rapidly and moving their way, and his ranch hands needed the parts for the tractor's drawbar if they were going to get the northwest pasture fertilized in time to beat the rain.

He said, "That's fine, hon. Take your time." The pasture would be there next year—so would his first grandchild.

The front door of the church yielded to her hand and the morning sun followed her into a dark foyer. She tiptoed across a patch of worn carpet, and specks of dust, awakened by her feet, swirled in the welcome light. She stopped at the entrance to the sanctuary and peered into the gloom. No sounds came to her ears, no images to her eyes, but she recognized the smell—it was emptiness. She didn't know what she was looking for, but it was somewhere else.

Jane didn't hear herself sigh or see her shoulders slump. She was turning back to the daylight when her movements attracted the attention of a figure kneeling near the front row of pews. He stood and turned.

"Wait. Come in, come in."

She turned back to watch faded jeans, topped by a white T-shirt, stroll up the aisle out of the gloom. The guy was wearing running shoes; he looked and sounded young. "I was just putting in a few extra minutes of prayer time."

When he got closer, the light in the vestibule turned him into an older man with an easy-going smile. "Good morning."

"Hi. I just wanted to peek in. I didn't mean to interrupt you." Jane didn't spend much time with people who prayed in dark churches and then talked about it as if it were normal. *Do you interrupt people who're praying, or do you disturb them?*

"No bother." He was close enough to shake hands. "I'm Wendell Andrews."

"Jane Mattingly."

He went through a mental Rolodex. "Ah, yes—Janie Pate— I should've known. You're Gene Elliott's daughter."

She had to smile. "Creekside's still a small town."

"In most ways." He smiled back. "My wife and I moved here after you went off to college." He reached over to touch a wall switch, and the lights came on to show Jane what she sensed, a plain-as-prairie-grass little church—no stained glass, no wood trim, nothing ornate— just an empty building with benches in it.

"You were too busy to remember it, but my wife and I actually had an opportunity to meet you at your wedding. Your mother and father were gracious enough to invite us."

In Western Colorado there was only one kind of man who would say someone was gracious. "You must be the preacher."

The easy-going smile came again. "I am."

She had seen all she needed to see, but she lingered long enough to say, "Your church yard really looks nice. I just don't remember it too well."

"The trees have been cut back; it seems to show better from the street now. Maybe that's it."

"Maybe." She turned to leave. "Well, thanks for the tour."

"Before you go, would you give me an update on Rusty?" He held up the notebook he was carrying. "He's on my prayer list."

She had promised Rusty she would be brave. *Why do men require that of their women? Better yet, why do the women allow themselves to be sucked into such a stupid promise?* "He's fine." The day's second spate of tears spilled over when she lowered her head and acknowledged defeat, "I'm not."

He waited a second and said, "Can I help?" He'd asked that question a thousand times in his life. He tried to mean it every time.

"I don't think so." She shook her head. "I don't think anyone can."

"I disagree." She wasn't carrying a purse, so he handed her the clean handkerchief he kept in a pocket because of the profusion of people who cried when they talked to him.

"Thanks." She tried to dab at her eyes without wrecking her makeup. *He disagreed?* "You know somebody?"

"Oh, yes. We're close."

She finally got it. "Oh . . . you mean God." All preachers said they knew God. Andrews let her get her hopes up for nothing.

He ignored the disappointment in her voice and said gently, "Tell me again that you don't think anyone can help you." It wasn't a challenge.

She let her mind go through the same list of people she'd been going through for two months—no one could help. She said it because she believed it, "No one can help." Not her parents, not her friends, not even Rusty's dad . . . no one could help. She bought six books by people who said they could teach her how to have a happy life. She fought her way through three of them and got tired of grinning at the reflection in her mirror and telling it she was happy. She cursed each author individually and thoroughly as she threw the six books in the trash can then kicked it across the room.

"No one can help me." She said it the second time with a firmness born of conviction. "I want my husband back . . . now. I want him alive. And I want him in one piece. I'm pregnant, and I don't want our child to grow up without a dad. Our baby will be three months old when those—" She stopped because she was getting angry and she didn't want to use profanity in this man's church. "I'm sorry. God can't bring Rusty home early. No one can help."

If you push people when they're mad, they get madder. "Well, if you ever need someone to talk to, my wife and I will be close." He barely smiled. "She makes the best Ranger Joe cookies in the state, and we take drop-ins."

"Thanks." The most important thing she had done since she got home was unload the dishwasher, but she didn't have time for milk and cookies with a minister and his syrup-sweet wife. "I better go . . . Dad's in the truck."

"Tell him 'Hello' for me."

"Bye."

When she stepped back into the sunlight, her dad had his head under the hood of his new truck.

"Is it broken down?"

"Not yet." He straightened. "But they dadgum sure don't build 'em as heavy as they used to."

Andrews stepped through the church door and lifted his notebook at Elliott. Elliott returned the greeting.

They rode three blocks before she turned off the radio and said, "He thinks God can help."

"And you don't." It wasn't a question.

"No." She took a moment to make sure she was still right and shook her head. "No, I don't."

They passed down the east side of the square and stopped in front of the tractor house. He shut off the engine, and they sat in complete silence for five minutes, each thinking their own thoughts. He couldn't remember the last time he meddled in somebody else's life, even his wife's, so he went in to pick up the parts he needed.

When he came back, she was staring at nothing. The sky said the rain was only an hour or so away.

He broke one of his long-standing rules by asking, "What if he's right?"

She'd been asking herself the same question. "You believe him?"

"I don't know if I believe him, but I know him. He's a good man."

Her dad never spoke ill of anyone, but she never heard him say any man but his own father was good. She'd tried self-help books and positive thinking, and she was running out of choices. This God thing might be her last hope. "Will you go with me?"

"You already know the answer to that."

She did. "When?"

"Well," he pulled a three-dollar Big Ben watch out of its pocket, "he'll be going to the coffee shop in a bit. Why don't we get us a table and waylay him?"

She took a deep breath. "Dad, would you do me a favor?"

"Yep." He was making a u-turn in the street.

If she were still in Phoenix, her dad would probably be using up less than a hundred words a day. "Would you do the talking?"

He smiled for the first time that day and nodded. "Yep."

When Andrews came into the café, he started with the cashier and worked his way along the counter and through the crowd, visiting and speaking to this person and that. He saw Gene Elliott and Jane at a table in the back. Elliott was looking at him; Jane was watching her coffee get cold. Gene Elliott never came in the cafe to pass the time; he came for coffee and information. His usual questions ran along the lines of: Where's the vet? Is it going to rain? What were cows going for at the auction yesterday?

Elliott stood up and motioned to him. Andrews nodded at the rancher and prayed as he walked.

He stopped at the table. "Good morning again."

"Morning." Elliott shook his hand and sat down, nodding at a chair. "Take a seat."

"Thanks."

The waitress put an empty cup in front of Andrews, then filled it and topped off Elliott's while she carried on a loud conversation with some men at a table up near the front.

The rancher used his coffee cup to point at his daughter. "Jane said you think God can help her."

"That's a fact." Andrews's dad was a rancher. The preacher knew being economical with words would allow him to get more said. Keep it short and honest.

"How?"

"Peace is one of the things that comes as a by-product of a relationship with God—He says so . . . and so do I. You just have to know Him."

Elliott digested that before asking, "But a fellow doesn't have to go to preacher school to know Him?"

"Nope. But you have to become a Christian—you have to put your faith and trust in Christ."

"Why's that?"

"It's part of the plan God laid out before we were born. Jesus said in the book of John, in the fourteenth chapter, 'I am the way, the truth, and the life: no man cometh unto the Father, but by me.' He made that real clear more than once—it's Jesus or nothing. No Jesus, no peace."

"Okay," Elliott accepted what he'd heard so far. "So we have to be Christians. How long does it take and how do we do it?"

"The explanation about how a person becomes a Christian takes about five minutes; what you do with what I tell you is up to you. For some people it's a slow process—if they become Christians at all. For others, it happens more quickly."

Elliott put down his coffee cup and pushed it aside. "Can you explain it right here?"

"Sure can." Andrews took a cheap ballpoint out of his pocket and pulled a napkin out of the holder.

"'For the wages of sin is death,'" he spoke the words while he printed them on the paper, "but the free gift of God is eternal life through Jesus Christ our Lord.'" He tapped the paper. "That's a quote out of the sixth chapter of the book of Romans. Those few words and thousands more like them fill the Bible and tell us the gospel—the truth about how to become a Christian—the plan God laid out for our salvation."

"So," Elliott was looking at the words, "what do we do?"

"Let me walk you through this." He circled "wages" and rewrote it below the last line of the verse. "We all know that it's right for us to get paid what we deserve."

That made sense. His audience nodded. Jane pulled her chair closer to the table.

He circled "sin" and wrote it below "wages." "Sin is anything that comes short of God's standard, and His standard is perfection. We all fall short everyday. God knows it, and if we're honest with ourselves, we know it."

His audience waited.

He circled "death" and put it on the list. "If you think about it, the person who dies is set apart . . . or away. That's the payoff."

"But" joined the column of words. "This is where the verse changes direction. This is the word that separates the bad news from the good news . . . because God gives us a free gift." He added the words to the growing list. "It's free, and it's not wages. And it's given to us by God." He added the name.

He worked his way through the verse, touching or circling most of the words, adding some to the list, and explaining each one. Elliott and Jane watched every move he made.

He pointed at the words "eternal life" and smiled for the first time. "This is what Christians look forward to . . . eternal life."

He circled *Jesus Christ*. "And this is how we get to have it . . . through Christ. God designed the whole system because you and I can't come to Him on our own. Billy Graham might be a nice man, but he's not perfect. We have to be perfect in God's sight—that's the requirement. Does it make sense to you?"

Jane was pushing her coffee cup out of the way. "What do I have to do?"

"If you want to be a Christian, you have to pray to God. Confess to Him that you know you're a sinner and accept what He's done for you. Ask Him to forgive you, and He will. Acknowledge Jesus for who He is. It's your prayer . . . you choose your own words . . . just remember who you're talking to. It sounds simple, but it couldn't be any more complex."

Elliott already had his hat off. "Me, too?"

"Only if you're convinced that you want to be a Christian and only if you believe in Jesus Christ as your Savior."

Elliott reached across and held his daughter's hand. "You can go first, hon. I'll go next."

Andrews was amazed at the speed of their decision. In fact, he was a little nervous. What if this was just an attempt by the girl to find an escape from her pain?

Her prayer would help allay his fears.

Jane pulled the piece of paper over so she could read the words while she prayed. All she wanted for her life was for God to forgive her, to save her from death, to show her how to be a good Christian, and to show her how to get to know Him.

Her dad, a man who was known to use up fewer words than any other man in town, prayed humbly for God to fix it so he could get to know Him faster. He knew he sinned and he was thankful for what God did for him by letting him be a Christian. He knew the story of what happened on the cross, and he thanked Jesus for dying for him. The rancher closed by saying, "God, this is all new to me. I don't have many years left, and I just hope I won't let You down."

Gene Elliott was not a small man, and his diminished hearing capacity caused him to talk louder than was usually necessary. When he raised his head, half of the people in the cafe were looking at them. The waitress—who'd seen everything you could see in a small town café—was standing transfixed at a nearby table and came dangerously close to scalding a customer with hot coffee. The older patrons— the ones who didn't stare—adhered to the adage that a man ought to saddle his own broncs. That meant a man got to pray when he wanted to, where he wanted to.

Elliott ignored the folks who didn't ignore him. "What do we do now?"

"Would you like to be baptized?" asked Andrews.

The rancher looked at his daughter then back at Andrews. "You think we ought to?"

"Jesus was."

Jane nodded, and Elliott answered for both of them. "I reckon so. What else?"

"Well, the road to knowledge is paved with study. Do you want to start a Bible study? You'll get to learn how to study the Bible, and you can learn to answer some questions for yourself."

Elliott didn't check with his daughter. "That'd be good."

Jane wanted God to take care of her husband. She lifted her hand. "I want to learn how to pray."

Andrews had been a preacher for more than twenty years and he never encountered this kind of quiet enthusiasm from a new believer; now he was surrounded by two who were straining at their lack of knowledge. "Okay," he said, "here's what we'll do. There's an organization over at Colorado Springs—The Navigators—that puts out a basic course on discipleship. We can order their books and go through them together."

"What do we do 'til then?" Jane was ready to get started.

Andrews said, "Go home and start reading your Bible and praying. Start with the book of Matthew and read the New Testament."

The two new Christians asked more questions and the preacher answered. The first drops of rain were falling when lunchtime came. Elliott and Andrews had the blue plate special; Jane ordered a cheeseburger basket—extra fries, please, no onions—and a vanilla shake, with lemon icebox pie for desert. When they finally stood up to leave, Elliott invited the preacher and his wife out to the ranch.

On the way home, Jane listened to the windshield wipers move back and forth while she prayed to God for the safety of her husband. The peace she felt was warm to her heart. Bill Mann passed through her thoughts while she was praying and she asked God to please protect him. She was going to mark her calendar as soon as she got home then write Rusty and tell him what happened.

As it happened, Jane Mattingly's conversion to Christianity could not have been more timely. She was less than two days away from needing to be firmly anchored to the only Person in the universe who has ever possessed the credentials necessary to offer genuine peace to anyone.

CHAPTER THIRTEEN

K aycee slipped out of bed the next morning and peeped around the edge of the curtain to see what the day might bring. The sun was barely above the horizon, and Bill Mann was walking across the lawn toward the hotel; he was wearing running togs and dripping sweat. Yesterday's near-alcoholic was today's dedicated athlete.

She strolled into the dining room an hour later and found him in the middle of a huge breakfast. He stood as if he expected her to sit with him. She did.

He ate everything on his plate and almost looked pleasant when he excused himself and said, "See you at the pool."

He wasn't ready to talk, but he still wanted exercise, so he swam laps for thirty minutes. She stayed in the lounge chair and read and watched.

Three hours later they shared an uneventful taxi ride to the airport, and he actually turned to help her out of the cab. The man who stood with her by the taxi was someone she'd never met—certainly not the stumbling drunk who greeted her at this same terminal a few days earlier.

When the PA announced her airplane was ready to board, he stood up with her.

She was walking away when he said, "Thanks for the company."

She stopped and turned. "You're welcome." He'd spoken nine whole words in one day.

"You never asked if I was married."

She smiled the smile. "Are you?"

He didn't even pause. "I thought I was, but I was mistaken. It was a long time ago."

She saw no anger in his face, not even a hint of bitterness. It wasn't the response she expected, but it helped explain some of his behavior.

"Come see me if you get to Nang," she winked. "There're a couple of things we haven't talked about."

"Thanks," he said. "Maybe I'll do that."

When she looked back, Mann returned her wave without smiling. The only black Sandy pilot in Southeast Asia was rested and recuperated and busy planning the rest of his life.

His recent bout with sobriety gave Mann time to take an inventory of his assets. All he would ever have was himself, but he was all he needed. While the C-130 bounced and wallowed its way toward NKP, he clarified his thoughts. He was an Air Force fighter pilot; he had a life to live and a mark to make. He'd wasted twelve months allowing another person to occupy an important part of his life—it was nobody's fault but his own, and it would never happen again. He didn't need Pip or any other woman in his life to distract him; he didn't need people like Missy and James Kelly telling him what to do; and he dadgum sure didn't need God. All he needed was an environment where he could get his plan back on track; the war and the Spad would take care of that.

The sweltering cargo section of the C-130 was nearly empty, but the fighter pilot with the newly-ordered life didn't seem to notice. The people who would've normally been stuffed in the shuttle's uncomfortable seats were at their bases getting their warbirds ready.

It was May 9.

On the ninth of May 1972, Operation Linebacker was initiated when the Navy and Marines mined the harbor at Haiphong. On May 10, after a four-year suspension, the Air Force, Navy, and Marines would launch an air offensive against North Viet Nam. The life Mann was waiting to live was one day away.

CHAPTER FOURTEEN

The C-130 landed at NKP after dark, and Mann flagged down a jeep for a ride to his squadron's hooch area.

When they turned onto his street, Mann and the driver could hear the sounds of loud pilots and louder music coming from the direction of The Sandy Box. The jeep slowed to a stop fifty yards short of his quarters, and Mann pointed down the street. "My hooch is right down there."

"Sorry, sir, but if it's okay, I'll drop you off here. Those guys down there at The Sandy Box have been doing some serious partying."

Mann stepped out of the jeep and paused to ask, "The natives getting restless?" He could understand the man's trepidation. Noncombat personnel were well-advised to stay away from The Box.

"Yes, sir. They've been at it since this morning." The young driver shook his head while watching down the street for signs of an impending assault. "The Officer of the Day went down there an hour or so ago to quiet 'em down. They tried to set him and his driver on fire."

Mann chuckled. He pulled his B-4 out of the back of the Jeep and said, "Thanks for the ride. I think I'll wait 'til tomorrow to see what everybody's celebrating."

He pushed open the door of his quarters and dropped his bag on the bed. Her picture was smiling at him from across the room.

He wanted to be mad at her, but the breakup wasn't her fault; she was just a kid. The Phoenix area was a desert in more ways than one, and he'd left her there alone while he'd gone off to live in a jungle. He slumped in the chair by his desk and stared at the photograph. He'd been an idiot, but that part of his life was over.

Five minutes later, he was on his way to The Sandy Box. Making it to the front door required him to navigate around the bodies of several unconscious pilots dragged out of the party house to make room for those who could still stand. Inside, a pilot wearing dog tags, jockey shorts, and flying boots was facedown under the pool table. A mangled A-1 propeller blade was suspended over the backbar—the OD's slightly scorched armband was prominently displayed on one of its tips. Pilots in party flightsuits were jammed into the room. Johnny Cash was complaining to everyone west of the Me Kong that he was stuck in Folsom Prison.

The only sober-looking person in the room, a major Mann didn't recognize, was slouched at a card table near the back wall. The man looked up and saw Mann surveying the bedlam and motioned for him to come over. Mann made his way around the worst of the crowd; as he drew close, the major stood up. "Lieutenant Mann?"

"The same." Mann put his hand out.

"It is indeed a pleasure, sir." The major shook Mann's hand without smiling. "I've been looking forward to meeting you. Please join me."

Two pilots piled onto the pool table, using it for what appeared to be some sort of leg-wrestling contest; the cheering of the spectators made further conversation difficult. Mann took the offered chair and waited for the uproar to subside.

When the cheering died down, the major introduced himself. "Doc Bailey . . . most recent acquisition of the 1st SOS."

"Doc?" Mann glanced at the wings on Bailey's flightsuit. "You're not a flight surgeon."

"My mother christened me Robert J. Bailey." Robert E. Lee would've swapped his beard for Bailey's Southern accent and aristocratic demeanor. The southern gentleman smiled and used a half-filled glass of wine to gesture at the drunks around him. "I am afraid that gracious lady would reside on the wrong side of peeved were she to learn that my brothers-in-arms chose an amiable dwarf for my namesake."

"Mmm." Amiable men in the fighter community were rare and no one could miss the fact Bailey was medium height. He had blond hair and a red-tinged, bullet-proof mustache and he was minus the Disney character's white beard and winning smile. Mann decided to give up on trying to figure the reasoning behind the man's call sign. "How long've you been on base?"

"Something more than a month. Certainly long enough to attract the wrath of the CO at the 602nd." He interrupted himself to lean over and procure a fairly clean glass from the table next to them. "Would you care for some wine?"

"Sure. Thanks."

"As it would happen," he continued, "I chose to go into business for myself last week. When I landed, I found myself first in line for a rather harsh wrist-slapping." He picked up a bottle from its sheltered haven on the floor and poured Mann's glass half full. When he had the bottle safely stowed, he took a sip from his glass. "I missed out on the punishment phase because Marsh and I were squadron mates in Germany. He saved my hide by taking me out of the 602nd, but in so doing, he received the short end of the stick. He traded two of his incoming new guys for a pair of lackluster problem children the 602nd wanted to jettison . . . yours truly and one other."

"What about the pilot that came with you? Your buddy from the 602nd?" asked Mann.

"It saddens me to say the gentleman is not someone with whom I would seek fellowship." Bailey did not look saddened. "And though he wears the wings, he is not now, nor will he ever be, a pilot."

"So Marsh ended up with two sides of the coin."

"And, as my maternal grandmother would say, 'Saved little Bobby's bacon in the bargain.'"

Mann raised his glass. "Any friend of Marsh's is a friend of mine."

Bailey touched his glass to Mann's. "Bill Faulkner could not have phrased it more eloquently."

Mann tried the wine then said, "You're from Mississippi."

"Very astute. I grew up in the hills east of Jackson. My bride's family raised their children and cotton along the banks of Wolf Lake, just outside Yazoo City." He gazed at his glass, remembering. "It's a fine state . . . fine people."

"And you're going back."

"I would be surprised if I did not," said the major.

Mann took another sip of wine then asked, "Well, what do you think about the job so far?"

Bailey took time to smooth his mustache before answering. "Until I arrived here, I had never fully appreciated the average legislator's capacity for incompetence. And because I embrace my august ancestors' passionate belief that I should shoot back at any man who shoots first, I have to liken what is happening here to a poorly orchestrated approximation of a Mongolian mop fight."

Mann nodded. Most of the Americans in Southeast Asia took a position similar to Bailey's. Politicians made poor warriors.

For the next hour or so, Mann drank his share of the wine, and Bailey got him caught up on the Navy and Marine mine-laying raid on Hai Phong Harbor. The better news was that the U.S. would be taking the air war back to the skies over North Viet Nam.

Mann allowed himself to get moderately drunk for the first time in two days while he and the rest of the pilots celebrated their hope that the politicians were going to start acting like their nation was at war.

On the morning of the tenth, hampered by a hangover attributable to mixing wine, vodka, and late-night fellowship, Mann rounded the corner at the squadron scheduling section as Melher was disappearing into his office.

The scheduling area was busier than he'd ever seen it. Pilots and schedulers pointed, talked, marked on boards, and shuffled papers; big things were happening. Airman Driver made eye contact with him and spoke. Mann nodded; white bigots came in immediately below hangovers on the list of things he liked least.

He checked his own slot on the scheduling board and saw he would be taking off at sixteen hundred—that meant he'd be briefing at two o'clock. He had time to check in with Marsh and have a couple of sandwiches.

He walked into Melher's office and came up behind another pilot, an overweight lieutenant colonel who was in obvious need of a haircut, a larger flightsuit, and a bath. The fat guy was bent over Melher's desk, scribbling on a piece of paper. Mann could smell him from six feet away.

Melher looked around the oversized pilot to see who walked in.

"Hey, Skipper," Mann said. "Miss me?"

"Well, well," Melher didn't bother to smile. "Behold the prodigal."

When the man in front of Marsh turned, Mann found himself face-to-face with something worse than his headache.

The fat guy's eyes were glazed and bloodshot, but he put out his hand, smiled, and spoke clearly. "Well, good morning. I'm Hal Bainbridge."

Bainbridge's curly black hair was stiff with last week's dust and hair oil, his fingernails were grimy, and his breath was fetid.

Mann didn't miss a beat; he'd rehearsed the encounter a million times using thousands of scenarios—continually resetting the scene to fit every conceivable environment. Be civil, not friendly—respectful, not a doormat. If he ever decided to write a book, it would be titled *How to Hide in Your Own Body.* He took Bainbridge's hand in a firm grip and said, "Mornin', Colonel, I'm Bill Mann."

Bainbridge gave Mann a slow once-over. "Well, I hate to say it, but I'm kind of disappointed."

Determine how friendly the adversary is and respond accordingly. If he's angry, distance yourself; if he's friendly, be neutral. Do NOT be friends . . . EVER. Mann returned a noncommittal smile. "Oh?"

"Yeah. From what I heard while you were gone, I thought maybe you were seven feet tall."

Mann looked at Bainbridge's bloodshot eyes while he listened to his words and marveled; a guy who could appear to be sober while he was obviously stoned was dangerous. Relaxed pilots usually reciprocate with humor, and that's where Mann went. "I guess my PR people do good work."

"Yeah, yeah, yeah," Melher stepped into the exchange. "You're back on the schedule, Bill. They launched Operation Linebacker this morning . . . we've got more than four hundred Air Force, Navy, and Marine planes flagged to go up north today—mostly to Package Six.

The politicos gave the North Vietnamese four years to get ready for this, and that means every SAR type in the theater is going to be busy. I've got you and me on for a Sandy mission to Steel Tiger at sixteen hundred. I'm taking the first element; you'll lead the high pair with Colonel Bainbridge here riding shotgun to see how it's done."

"Sounds good to me." Mann looked at Bainbridge. It was business as usual from now on. "We'll brief at fourteen hundred, Colonel, at the TUOC. That'll give us a chance to check with the intelligence guys about what they've learned this morning."

"I'll be there." Bainbridge started for the door. "Now, if you guys will excuse me, I'll go tie up some last-minute strings and meet you at the TUOC."

When Bainbridge was gone, Melher said, "Well?"

"Well, what?"

Melher hated to pry, and Mann didn't appear to be receptive to questions. The best pilot in the squadron appeared to be slightly hung-over, but he was rested and focused. Melher left the questions about Mann's marriage unasked and said, "Well, you haven't made a sandwich in two weeks. It's your turn."

Minutes later, Mann walked back into the office juggling their lunch, and Melher said, "Shut the door."

Mann pushed it shut with his foot and stacked the food and drinks on the desk. "What's the secret?"

"What's your take on Colonel Bainbridge?" When speaking to, or about, another officer, Marsh incorporated a man's rank only when speaking of officers who outranked him and those for whom he felt contempt. Bainbridge did not outrank him.

During their brief encounter, Mann got the feeling Bainbridge was missing some ingredient that would qualify him to be a good pilot, but he couldn't tell what it was without seeing him fly an airplane. The thing that bothered him more was Bainbridge's adeptness at presenting himself as a man in full possession of his faculties while he was, in fact, 100 percent wasted—probably on drugs. Give the man a shower, a shampoo, sunglasses, and a manicure, and he could pass himself off as general officer material. He hedged. "Hard to say. Who gave him his flagpole flight?"

"He didn't need a flagpole flight because he came here from the 602nd. He went out once with Carruthers three days ago and almost wet his pants."

Mann made the connection. "He's the one we had to take when we traded for Doc."

"You know about that?"

"Yeah. I met Doc at The Box last night." Mann slouched in his place on the couch and popped the top off one of the drinks. "He doesn't strike me as the completely good-natured type."

Marsh's eyebrows came together. "Run that by me again."

"Bailey's call sign . . . 'Doc' . . . for that easy-going dwarf in *Snow White.*"

"Humpf," Marsh snorted. "Doc told you that, didn't he?"

"So?"

"Did he tell you how we got him?" Marsh was grinning.

"Said you two were old buddies and you bailed him out before the CO at the 602nd could put together a firing squad." Mann frowned as he tried to recall the conversation. "If I was guessing, I would say it had to do with shooting at people who were shooting at him."

"Close enough." Melher was enjoying himself. He tilted his chair back and put his feet on the desk. "He and his element lead were spotting for a Spectre C-130 gunship, working near a town south of the PDJ. They found a mobile 37-milimeter, and the gunship went after it. The bad boys on the ground rolled the gun inside a Buddist temple, knowing it was off limits, and the C-130 backed off. Next thing you know, here comes Doc cruising down the main street of the village at hut-height and offered up a contribution to the purification rites in the form of five hundred pounds of napalm. The dipsticks up at division got wind of Doc's participation in the church service and organized a witch hunt. They wanted him court-martialed but didn't have any evidence . . . someone had already burned the film from Doc's gun camera. The C-130 aircraft commander and his crew told the investigators they didn't see a thing."

"Sounds like my kind of man." Mann was impressed.

"He is that, buddy," said Marsh, "and he didn't get that call sign 'cause he's easy-going."

Mann thought back to his conversation with Bailey and smiled. "Doc Holiday."

"Give that man sixty-four bologna and cheese sandwiches." Marsh raised his bottle. "A southern gentleman . . . soft-spoken, mildman-nered, with a predisposition toward severe retribution. The C-130 driver said Doc's bomb hit the front door of the temple dead center."

"So?" Marsh interrupted Mann's thoughts about Bailey. "What about Bainbridge?"

Mann gave the stock answer. "Maybe the man needs a staff job."

"Maybe."

At this point in the war, the Air Force was beating the bushes for pilots. Almost every fighter pilot in the Air Force had finished one tour in Southeast Asia; some had volunteered to come over more than once. The fliers coming to the Spads of late were either volunteers fresh out of pilot training or field-grade officers—majors and lieutenant colonels—who were flushed out of some quiet basement where they were doing a nonflying job. There were men in both groups—young and old—who were better off staying away from combat.

"What do you want me to do?" Mann asked.

Melher's face developed more lines at the sides of his mouth. "Try to find out if he can hack it without killing himself. Apparently his mother's some kind of powerful congresswoman or something, and I'm being pressured to make him the ops officer."

Mann didn't need to be in a squadron where Bainbridge was second in command. "Why don't you take him up?"

Melher dropped the granny glasses on his desk and rubbed his face with both hands—never a good sign. The massage moved to the back of his neck. "I did," he confessed. "Yesterday."

Melher was stalling.

"And?" Mann coaxed.

"And . . . his flying skills are somewhere on the distant side of abys-mal. I can only assume he scraped by in pilot training because of who his mother is. He's scared to death of the airplane and if I was betting money, I'd say he was stoned when we took off. He did fairly well for the first hour or two, then went progressively south on me. By the time we got back to the chocks, he was chewing his fingernails through his flying gloves."

This was beginning to sound like one of those horror stories where the innocent young black boy gets sacrificed because a domineering mother wants to force her rich white baby to be something he ain't. "I'm not a magician, Marsh."

"I know, I know. I was hoping maybe he could watch you in action and see how easy it can be to do it right. Maybe some of your cool would rub off on him."

Mann let the hand holding his sandwich drop into his lap and blew out a chestful of exasperation. "You mean like one of those miraculous healings the preachers do on TV."

"I guess." Melher didn't sound like he had much confidence in his plan.

"Don't lay money on it," said Mann.

Steel Tiger was the code name for the airspace over Southern Laos. The people who lived there did not like Americans, and trying to practice being a nursemaid in their airspace was not conducive to longevity. Mann took a bite of his sandwich and spoke around it while he shook his head. "It sounds to me like you're bending over backward to do something that can't be done."

Melher turned his chair sideways and stared at the wall. The kid had him bagged. He'd sold his soul when he let the wing commander smooth-talk him into giving Bainbridge another chance. If he had a window, he could look outside at the airplanes while he considered his friend's comment.

Lieutenant Colonel Marsh Melher liked two things about the Air Force—the people and the planes—and he wasn't interested in a promotion to full colonel because being a full colonel was the first long step away from the cockpit. Now, in the midst of what was supposed to be a shooting war, the constant politicking, jockeying, and infighting it took to get the resources needed to do his job was draining him. Well, when this tour in SEA was over, he was putting in his papers. In the meantime, if the wing commander wanted to come down and run the 1st Special Operations Squadron, he was welcome to shed his custom-tailored tan uniform and grab himself a zoom bag.

Mann had witnessed the older man's unconventional method of problem solving more than once. When Melher nodded to himself, Mann waved his bottle at the wall. "Well, what's the handwriting tell us?"

"I did it wrong," Melher was still staring at the wall, "but I've changed my mind."

"And?"

"And you can forget the whole thing. We can't put ourselves behind the curve on a combat mission—especially a Sandy one—just to keep congress happy. Go tell scheduling to scrub Bainbridge's name off the board . . . indefinitely."

Mann didn't move. He was munching slowly, thoughtfully, like a contented cow. He spoke around his cud. "Did you have to take Bainbridge to save Doc?"

"Yes, but that ha—"

"Then why don't you let Bainbridge quit?"

"He won't."

"He might." Mann had been thinking while Melher was consulting the wall.

Melher forgot about the window shortage and turned his chair toward Mann. "So, what's the plan?"

"That area where we're going has a raft of thirty-seven millimeter guns—Techepone is infested with 'em. What about taking him with us and letting him get shot at? Maybe he'll save you the trouble."

"You'd take him?"

"It would be my pleasure," Mann winked. "If he's as bad as you say, he'll be on the radio wrangling a transfer before we leave Indian country."

Melher liked it. "That might be a good plan."

"It might be a great plan." Mann was fitting his second sandwich into his hand; bologna and cheese sandwiches were better than the best steak in Bangkok.

The Tactical Unit Operations Center (TUOC)—NKP's nerve center—was crowded with people; dozens of as yet unsoiled men drinking coffee and getting briefed to launch intermingled with sweat-stained, beer-drinking men who were just back from the war.

Marsh and his wingman, Captain Joe "Rabbi" Loeb—Sandy One and Two, shared a briefing area with Sandy Three and Four—Mann and Doc Bailey. Nobody blinked at the news that a major was flying on the wing of a lieutenant and Mann was glad to have him there. Bailey was still a few rides away from his checkout as an element leader, and he asked for an opportunity to see Mann in action. Bainbridge was the only observer, and he and Mann would be flying in the only two-seater—Mann's A-1E fatface.

The briefing took an hour. They would take off at four o'clock and fly to a holding point over Steel Tiger. In the event of a rescue attempt, Melher and Loeb would work in close, with Melher checking for enemy gun emplacements and coordinating the operation. Mann and Bailey would stay high, ready to join up with the Jolly Green Giants—the rescue helicopters—and escort them in when Melher called for them.

The air in the TUOC was the coldest on the base and Melher was briefing his flight members directly beneath a large vent. Bainbridge was the only outbound pilot in the building who was sweating.

After a thorough briefing, the pilots broke up. Melher went back to the squadron; Bainbridge and Loeb went their own way. Bailey beckoned to Mann and said, "May I buy you a cup of coffee?" Mann followed him down the hall to the building's snack bar.

As soon as Mann was in the snack bar, Bailey shut the door and leaned against it. "Bill, you need to keep a close eye on Bainbridge."

Mann was busy pouring two cups of coffee. Without looking up, he said, "Yeah? What's the deal?"

"If he is not certifiably insane, the man is a coward . . . I suspect he would be equally at home in either category. Regardless, he is dangerous in an airplane."

Mann handed a cup to Bailey. "You think so?"

"Mmm." Bailey didn't want coffee. He put the cup on the counter and crossed his arms. "They ran him out of the 602nd because there was reason to believe he's an addict. If you get yourself into a precarious situation, any ability he has to act rationally will, most assuredly, abandon him."

"You want to take him with you?" Mann joked.

Bailey shook his head. "If they tried to put him with me, I would shoot him and the scheduling officer both."

"What do you think I ought to do?"

Bailey smoothed his mustache for a moment then asked, "Would you prefer a frank answer?"

In an environment where outspoken, assertive men were the norm, Bailey was considered quiet up to a point—hence the call sign. People who abused him or his friends, however mildly, discovered the gentleman's voice was the only soft thing about him.

Mann put his cup down. "Absolutely."

"If he comes unwound while you are in the air, pull your handgun and cast it in the role for which it was designed." Bailey wasn't smiling.

"Shoot a lieutenant colonel?" Mann hissed. He almost looked over his shoulder to make sure no one else was in the room.

"No, no, no." Bailey drawled the words. "Do not shoot him . . . *kill* him. The man is a weasel, a predator. That makes him, at one and the same time, vicious, unpredictable, and dangerous."

"Just like that."

"Bainbridge is the personification of treachery, Bill. Do not, under any circumstances, permit yourself to turn your back on him." Bailey opened the door and looked into the empty hall. "You prepare yourself to do what needs to be done, my friend, I will personally reimburse you for any expended ammunition."

Bailey left the younger pilot staring at the toes of his boots. When Mann recovered, he made his way back to the intelligence section of the TUOC. He would hang out there and listen to the returning pilots' debriefings until it was time for him to go out to his plane.

Bainbridge was one of the few pilots who bothered to keep the door of his hooch locked.

He went into the small quarters and turned to make sure the door was safely closed behind him. The room's air conditioner was supplemented by an oscillating fan. Bainbridge turned on the fan, directing it so it would blow on him. He sat in the only chair in the room and went to work on a padlock affixed to the bottom drawer of his desk. When the drawer was open, he pulled out a bottle of clear fluid and a small cellophane bag. His face ran with sweat while he drank from the bottle. He held the bag behind the desk to shield it from the fan while he rolled a crude cigarette using the shredded contents. After several good pulls on the bottle, interspersed with longer drags on the cigarette, he was a relaxed man.

He bent over and went back into the drawer to bring out an object covered with an oil-stained cloth. He held the bundle in his lap and unwrapped a handgun—a Colt .45, Model 1911. The gun had pearl grips, their edges tinted nicotine-brown by age and the ready presence of gun oil; small, ordered marks highlighted the edge of one grip. Years earlier a skilled craftsman had etched a string of letters in the shiny surface. He knew what the marks looked like, but he levered himself out of the chair and walked close to the window so he could see them well. The small characters were well-defined, embedded with red ink to highlight them. "WPP—366 TFG." The FBI told the Bainbridge family that in 1943 the gun was issued to a Tuskegee airman, Second Lieutenant William P. Prince. Bainbridge was holding the gun that killed his younger brother.

Why would Lieutenant William P. Mann have a picture in his PE locker of a man wearing this same gun? Because Lieutenant William P. Mann was the sorry little nigger that used the .45 to shoot Oliver W. Bainbridge, that's why.

Bainbridge's hands were shaking, but he managed to insert a full clip into the gun and slipped the loaded firearm into the left-hand chest pocket of his flightsuit. He chuckled and spoke out loud, "I guess I'm a prophet now."

He knew that May 10, 1972 was the day Lieutenant Bill Mann was destined to be killed by enemy ground fire.

CHAPTER FIFTEEN

Mann looked at his watch and stood up. Go time.

He walked into the PE shack and greeted the sergeant at the counter. "How's it going, Sarge?"

"Everything's smooth here, 'Tenant," the sergeant glanced up at his favorite customer. "I put your weapon back in your locker this morning in case I wasn't here when you needed it. Your vest is all up to specs, sir, two new radio batteries, both juicy."

"Thanks. The beer's on the way."

"I 'preciate it, sir. How was R'n'R?"

"Nothing to show for it but a hangover."

"I got aspirin here."

Mann was already in the locker room. "I'll be back."

He got his locker open and buckled on the web belt that carried his holster. Next he checked out the gun, making sure the spare clips were in their pouches and fully loaded and the pistol had a round in the chamber. The sweat-stained survival vest came next. He poked maps in his pockets and put two plastic baby bottles full of water in his helmet bag. After he got settled in the plane, he'd stow the maps and water in the calf pockets of his G-suit. Fresh water was a precious commodity if you ended up on the ground in Indian country.

Mann stopped back by the PE counter, bummed six aspirin from the sergeant, and went outside to chew them while he waited for the line taxi. The world around him was hot tarmac, sight-searing sunshine, and stench. If he could get rid of his headache, he might live—if a gallon of sweet iced tea waited for him at his airplane, he might care.

Airman First Class Daniel Worthy was poised at the nose of the A-1E when the line taxi dropped off his pilot. The crew chief was holding a metal binder containing the fighter's maintenance log.

From the nose of the aircraft, the portrait of a voluptuous lady wearing a sleek black dress watched from over Worthy's shoulder as Mann approached. Letters blended themselves with the artwork on the aircraft's nose, spelling out the plane's name . . . *The Cool Woman*.

Saluting wasn't required on the flightline, but Airman Worthy liked to look sharp.

Without speaking, Mann returned a casual imitation of the kid's salute and used handholds imbedded in the fuselage to climb onto the left wing. If the A-1's engine wasn't leaking oil, it was broken, but *The Cool Woman's* wing and fuselage—normally covered with a slick black film—had been polished clean. Stenciled letters spelling out Mann's rank and name were painted against a white background on the canopy rail. He leaned past them and placed his helmet bag in the seat while giving the cockpit a thorough look-see to make sure everything was as it should be.

When Mann stepped off the wing, the three-striper said, "She's ready, sir."

Mann didn't want to talk, but only a fool would snub his crew chief. He put out his hand. "You're new."

Worthy shook the hand and smiled. "Yes, sir. Daniel Worthy . . . came over from Hurlburt two weeks ago. I was with the A-1 training wing down there." He was enthusiastic, excited to be in a foreign country and happy his new pilot was friendly.

Mann nodded. That was enough conversation. The aspirins made his headache worse and the kid's eagerness grated on his nerves. He held out his hand and Worthy placed the log on his open palm.

For Worthy, getting to be *The Cool Woman's* crew chief was, in Thai-speak, *Number One!* Some of the crew chiefs didn't want to work for a black guy, but the scuttlebutt was out on Mann—he was probably the best pilot on the base. *The Cool Woman* and her pilot were the personal property of Airman Worthy; he would share the plane with Mann so he would be able to brag about what his pilot did with their airplane.

The enthusiastic crew chief waited while Mann paged slowly through the neatly-written notes in the logbook. When the conversation void widened to a full thirty seconds, Worthy decided to fill it. "I see you're going up with Colonel Bainbridge." He said the words while his jaws overworked a wad of gum.

Thailand's version of Death Valley sunshine was turbo-charging Mann's headache. Chauffeuring an idiot around the unfriendly skies of Laos while he let bad people shoot at his airplane was not what he joined the Air Force for, and the chatty kid was distracting him when he needed to devote his mental processes to planning how to stay alive. He concentrated on what the log had to tell him and tuned the kid out. "Mmmm."

"The colonel's a pretty sharp man when it comes to diagnosing airplane problems." The snapping and popping of the crew chief's gum chewing sounded like a commercial for Rice Krispies.

Mann's mind moved farther from the conversation. He flipped a page and continued to learn what he could from the logbook. His finger traced down through the maintenance discrepancies and their remedies—things broken and repaired—while he gave a generic answer to the kid's statement. "That right?"

"Oh, yes, sir." Worthy's willingness to be friends took root in Mann's neutral comments. The chief had his hands stuffed in the pockets of his greasy fatigues, alternately rolling up on his toes and rocking back on his heels. It was plain to see that his pilot was ready to be allowed into the enlisted man's inner circle. After all, the guy was the only black pilot on the base, and he might not even have any friends.

Worthy noted that Mann looked more like a teenager than a fighter jockey, and he made a split-second decision to take the conversation deeper. He did it, in part, because anyone with half a mind could tell the lieutenant was unhappy about something. He added that to the reasoning no sane man, especially a black guy who looked like a kid, could possibly want to be in the same airplane with a jerk like Bainbridge. "He nailed two of the eleven maintenance problems he aborted for back at Hurlburt." Grinning, rocking, chewing, popping—exuding friendship through his pores . . . totally oblivious to the fact his decision-making process was fatally flawed.

The pilot offered a distracted nod to show he'd heard and kept reading. Eventually the meaning of the words began to sink in, and Mann's finger slowed its journey through the book. His head came up, and he pointed his face at Worthy.

Airman First Class Daniel Crane Worthy, maintenance specialist and clean-living, oil-covered, bubble-gum chewer, saw nothing in the black man's expression that testified to a quest for comrades. What he did see was a late-in-arriving memory of Sergeant Wherbohlerwitz.

When Worthy's draft lottery number came in low, he was two semesters away from college graduation; any attempt to make it all the way though his senior year would guarantee him a stint carrying a rifle for the U.S. Army. In those days, the Army's version of curb service entailed sending a man across an ocean so he could parade his body around in front of people who wanted to kill him. He enlisted in the Air Force. He could type eighty words a minute and when he finished Air Force Basic Training, he applied for, and expected to receive, a job in an office. The Air Force, in its infinite wisdom, sent him to Senior Master Sergeant Herman Wherbohlerwitz.

Wherbohlerwitz was ancient, grizzled, and perennially impatient. The bags under his eyes and the bulge over his belt were casualties of a lifelong battle with gravity, beer, and sleep depravation. Wherbohlerwitz blamed his attitude and appearance on his efforts to train a million wide-eyed teenagers to be crew chiefs.

Worthy could still see the thirty-year veteran of a thousand flight-lines standing with his foot propped on the tire of an A1, sweating and lecturing. "Don't be tryin' to make friends with pilots. Pilots don't want friends." His voice rasped like someone dragging a hollow tree trunk across a gravel road. "They want two things from you. They want that engine . . ." he spit a long stream of brown juice toward the powerplant, "to run when they shove that throttle up . . . and they want the guns to shoot when they squeeze that trigger . . . and that's all they want. This ain't a personality contest. You keep the engines warm, the guns hot, and your mouth shut. Got that?" A brown stream arched out of the snarl and across the tarmac.

At the time Worthy was convinced, but that was more than a year ago.

Lieutenant Mann kept his finger between the pages to mark his place and slowly closed the aluminum cover of the logbook. To Worthy the movement was reminiscent of a stockade door swinging shut.

The pilot reached up and pulled his sunglasses off. He looked at the airman as he might an enemy.

The airman looked back.

Mann's sunglasses had not allowed the crew chief an opportunity to look directly into the eyes of his new pilot. Worthy decided that in the future he would look into the eyes of every person he talked to . . . deeply . . . and he would do it before he opened his mouth. People wearing sunglasses would have to suffer through life without his conversation. The gum-chewing slowed, the heel-and-toe action ceased. Loud sounds of aircraft engines and machinery made it hard to think. Greasy hands crept out of the fatigue pockets and curled at the boy's sides.

Worthy's boss at maintenance hangar would send his mom the obligatory letter. "Dear Mrs. Worthy, We regret to inform you that we shot your son this morning because he was incredibly stupid. Have a nice day."

Mann took his eyes off the boy and looked down at the ramp. He sighed . . . something he seemed to be doing a lot lately . . . he could use some breathing room. His headache withdrew to a position just south of his eyebrows, the most beautiful black woman on the planet had turned into a one-year-wonder, and he was getting ready to spend the afternoon playing nursemaid to a nigger-hating nitwit from a bad bloodline who—to add whipped cream to the sundae—couldn't find an aircraft's throttle with both hands and a flashlight. God existed, but He didn't care that Mann's aforementioned "enviable life" was on the rocks at the base of a high cliff.

He took one of his deep breaths and looked at the young man who was probably older than he was.

The crew chief waited. Expectant. Tired. Grease-covered. Wrong. Dreading the inevitable. Eyes red-rimmed from fatigue. Naked to his waist, sweat-soaked to his knees, his normally pale skin was burned raw from spending days under a ruthless sun—a hard-working kid who was trying to please his pilot by going above and beyond in a hot, thankless role in a miserable war nobody, not even God, cared about.

Mann shook his head at his willingness to crucify an innocent boy.

He couldn't remember the kid's name. Quietly. "Tell me your name again, Chief."

"Worthy, sir." Quieter.

"Worthy," the next words from the black pilot who didn't want his friendship came evenly, cadenced to the pulsing of Worthy's heart . . . not loud, not mean, not threatening . . . just clear. "I . . . didn't . . . hear . . . that."

"Yes, sir . . . uh . . . no, sir." The hands and arms became slightly rigid. He didn't come to attention, but he stood straighter. The gum was lost, unnoticed, somewhere in his mouth. Worthy reviewed his latest rule regarding how he would treat new acquaintances; he would look at their eyes before he committed himself to anything but a greeting.

The pilot flipped the book open, finished reading, and handed it back to the stiff crew chief. "Relax, Chief. I said I didn't hear it."

The chief's tongue found the gum, his teeth closed tentatively on the wad. "Uh . . . that sounds real fine, 'Tenant. I'm . . . uh . . . me neither." His lungs emptied for the first time in fifteen seconds.

The wash of bubble-gum breath wafted over the lieutenant, and he held out his hand.

Worthy looked blankly at the pilot's hand for a second then offered the logbook back to him.

The pilot shook his head. The corners of his mouth softened and then turned up slightly. He continued to hold his hand out, palm up, and beckoned with his fingers. "Gum."

Worthy looked back at the man's eyes and put a small-scale version of his original grin back on. He dug around in the pockets in his fatigues for a second before pulling out a small bolt, a greasy washer, and a single piece of Dubble Bubble. Pink spots showed through holes in the gum's sweat-ravaged wrapper. "Last piece, sir," he apologized as he dropped it in the extended palm.

The friendless black pilot put his shades back on and turned away to start a preflight of the airplane's exterior; the chief followed. As he walked, Mann used his fingernails to pick most of the remaining shreds of damp paper from the pink clump. He popped the gum in his mouth and put the scraps from the wrapper in a calf pocket of his flightsuit. He turned and almost smiled at his escort. "Thanks, Chief. I'll pay you back."

The crew chief didn't even say, "You're welcome." He stuck the logbook under his arm and trailed along behind . . . and kept his mouth shut.

Within twelve hours, a fellow Mann had never seen before would go through the remnants of the flightsuit and inventory what he found there. The small frazzled pieces of blue and pink paper buried in one of the pockets would puzzle him. He would poke the pieces around with a pair of tweezers, sniff them, and pick up the distinctive smell and set them aside to be inventoried and filed for possible later examination.

When they got back to the nose of the airplane, Worthy had to ask, "Uh . . . 'Tenant, if it's all right with you, I got my tape deck strapped down in the back . . . in the blue room. I thought maybe I could get me a recording of a mission, and I wired it into the Comm panel. It doesn't weigh but about fifteen pounds, and I got it buckled down real snug. Will that be okay?"

Crew chiefs had done it before; it was like getting to go out on a mission without getting shot at. Plane-to-plane communications would be recorded, and today, if Mann and Bainbridge talked, Worthy's recorder would pick up the conversation. "Sounds okay, Chief. I hope you don't get anything exciting."

Bainbridge showed up and Mann ran the cockpit preflight checks while his passenger got strapped in. Ten minutes later, Mann had the engine running and was finished with his pre-taxi checks.

Mann looked out at Worthy and pointed at the wingtips with his thumbs. The crew chief ran under the wings, pulled the chocks free, then jogged to a place in front of left wingtip. When Worthy turned, he could see a small pink bubble behind the dangling oxygen mask; Mann was watching him and pointing a relaxed finger at the revetment opening. Worthy came to attention and snapped his right hand up. When the pilot returned the salute, the crew chief did a left face and pointed both hands at the mouth of the revetment.

Mann released the brakes and bumped the throttle up slightly. *The Cool Woman* moved out of the revetment . . . going to war.

Worthy made a dash for the nearest latrine.

Chandler, the crew chief for *Short Fat Fanny*, waltzed into the latrine. "Say, Worthy, what's happenin', baby?"

"Same ol' stuff." Worthy was drying his hands while he stared into the mirror over the washbasin. *How'd that guy do that with just his eyes?* he wondered. He looked at his own eyes. He didn't think it was something you could practice. He kept his eyes on the mirror. "Say, Chandler?"

"Yo."

"You ever launch your bird with that guy Mann in it?"

Chandler chuckled. "Boy?"

"Huh?"

"Boy . . . that's Frisco's new name for 'im . . . 'Boy' Mann." Chandler grinned to include Worthy in the new joke. "Kinda cute for a black guy's call sign, huh?"

Half an hour earlier it might've been funny. Worthy didn't laugh.

"Frisco called that pilot 'Boy'? That Lieutenant Mann?"

"Yeah, well, not to his face. But since he ain't got a call sign, Frisco came up with one." Chandler missed the warning in Worthy's tone; he was busy lighting a cigarette and enjoying the latest flightline humor. He laughed and continued, "You know what? Frisco's funnier than any of them USO guys that come through here; I keep tellin' him he oughta go professional."

When Chandler joined him at the row of washbasins, Worthy was motionless, studying something deep in the mirror.

The showbiz critic glanced at Worthy, then stopped what he was doing to stare at him. He followed Worthy's gaze to the mirror. "Uh . . . what'cha lookin' at, bro?"

"The future." Worthy nodded at something he saw in the mirror and turned to Chandler. "Do me a favor, okay?"

"Sure thing, baby. What'cha want?"

Worthy threw his paper towel in the trash can. "Tell Frisco to stay away from me."

"Do what?"

"There's no future in being friends with a guy who's probably gonna get executed for being a moron." The psychic paused at the door. "Frisco's an idiot."

The door closed—Chandler's mouth didn't. What the heck was that all about?

Bailey's *Miss Amanda* followed *The Cool Woman* into the arming area, and they parked beside Melher and Loeb. The pilots put their hands on the rail above their windscreens to show that they couldn't inadvertently touch a trigger or a weapon release while the arming crews pulled munition pins and made last-minute checks of the planes' ordinance.

So far, the Skyraider had participated in some of the most dangerous flying in Southeast Asia. Some people might never know it worked night and day bombing the Ho Chi Minh Trail, or that it supported the Army when it was inserting and extracting troops, or that it was a mainstay in the secret war being fought in Laos. What no pilot in SEA would ever forget, though, is the A-1 was the plane that brought its friends—the Jolly Green Giant helicopters—to get you when you ended up on the ground in enemy territory.

The four airplanes lining up for the NKP runway were going out to fulfill their search and rescue role. They each carried a "Sandy load" of munitions, all suited to the possibility of having to work near a downed crew member. The twelve outboard wing stations were hung with four tons of ordinance: four canisters of high-explosive bomblets, two canisters of smoke bomblets, two with white phosphorus smoke bombs, two with nineteen HE (high explosive) rockets each, and two pods with seven WP (white phosphorus, AKA Willy Pete) marking rockets each. There was a three-hundred-gallon fuel tank on the center station beneath the fuselage, the right inboard station carried a 7.62 mm minigun and fifteen-hundred rounds of ammo; the left station carried an additional fuel tank. Seven-hundred-and-twenty rounds of ammo were packed away for the wing-mounted 20 mm machine guns. When the arming checks were complete, the four-ship formation taxied onto the runway.

No other aircraft in the world sounds like a Skyraider. The thirteen and a half foot prop is turned by the Wright R-3350 Duplex-Cyclone powerplant; at twenty-seven-hundred horsepower, it is one of the most powerful radial aircraft engines ever produced in the United States. People stopped what they were doing to watch the propeller blades split the mid-afternoon sun into slices when Marsh's plane went to takeoff power. For years to come, the men who witnessed the departure of the four A-1s would brag about having been there to see it with their own eyes. Melher rolled first, followed short seconds later by Loeb, then *The Cool Woman* followed by Bailey's *Miss Amanda*.

Daniel Worthy was standing in the revetment, watching the launch, and he could feel the ground tremble as the planes thundered across the departure end of the runway. His psychic powers didn't tell him that only two of the airplanes would be coming back—his *Cool Woman* wasn't one of them.

CHAPTER SIXTEEN

Major Douglas M. Sherrill, U.S. Army, did not think of himself as a warrior, but he'd spent three of the last five years fighting in Viet Nam. When he wasn't flying the HU-3 helicopter—the Huey—in Nam, he was back in the States teaching wannabe warriors how to fly it. He saw everything there was to see in a war and he would never again be surprised at anything one human might visit upon another.

He was treading the corridors of the headquarters building on this day because his commanding officer was sending him out to take a news crew on a FAM ride—a familiarization flight. Sherrill didn't like wasting time and gas on FAM flights—he liked news crews less.

The Army aviator came to an abrupt halt when he arrived at his boss's doorway. Sherrill's boss stood up and waved him into the room. "Thanks for coming, Major. I knew you'd enjoy getting to meet Sid Wainwright before you took him and his crew up."

The 7th Air Cavalry Battalion Commander, Lieutenant Colonel A. D. Parnell, knew no such thing. Doug Sherrill hadn't reported to the CO's office out of the goodness of his heart. Five hours earlier, Parnell explained to Sherrill, mostly in words of four letters and one syllable, that the major would be in charge of an infantry company within a week if he didn't show up for this appointment at precisely three o'clock.

"Sid," smiled Parnell, "this is Maj. Doug Sherrill. His crew is the finest in the unit, and they'll be taking you into the hot zone this afternoon."

Persuading a man who was on his third combat tour to share his deepest feelings was no big chore. Sherrill took another look at the civilian standing next to Parnell and spoke for the first time, "Either you tell me right now this a joke, or you get yourself another boy."

Sid Wainwright looked like a tourist who had just stepped off the plane from Southern California, which was pretty close to what he was. His father and Parnell had been roommates in college, and Wainwright's father had called in an old debt.

"Doug's always good for a laugh, Sid." The CO forced a weak laugh to demonstrate. He turned to Sherrill and said, "You and I will have a chance for a short briefing before you leave, Major."

Parnell was going to make general because he was a diplomat, but he wasn't a pushover. He tagged Sherrill for this job because of a minor incident a few days back; Sherrill took it upon himself to initiate a weapons research and development experiment and almost cost the Army a helicopter. What the chopper pilot saw in front of him underlined his resolve to color inside the lines in the future. The warrior surrendered and shook Wainwright's hand.

Wainwright Senior had been watching too much money disappear into a futile effort to help Wainwright Junior find his niche in the world. The boy, with dad running interference, started his quest for significance at Georgetown University. He lasted one semester at that august institution before boarding an express escalator for a descent through a succession of learning centers. The latest expenditure of Wainwright Senior's money found its root cause in a short course at Santa Barbara City College. Two months earlier, Wainwright Junior convinced himself that he was destined to become a famous film journalist—this, thanks to the generous guidance of a frustrated professor who was not allowed to kick the pompous rich kid out of class.

His dad provided the modest fortune necessary for the filmmaker-to-be to buy the needed equipment, hire a small crew, and pursue his latest passion for six months in the war zone. While en route to Viet Nam, the future journalist spent an extended layover in Hong Kong, practicing how he would live his life when he became famous. The expenses he incurred there called for a rethink on how long he would manage to remain an ocean away from Daddy's money.

Sherrill was six inches shorter than Wainwright and sixty times as tough. He dug in the sleeve pocket of his flightsuit, lit a cigarette, and blew the smoke toward the gangly tourist. "Do you have a plan, sir?"

Wainwright fanned the smoke away so he could draw a breath to answer. "Well—"

"Not you, fool," Sherrill cut him off. He stabbed the cigarette at Parnell. "Him."

"Give me a couple of minutes with Doug, Sid," Parnell put a fatherly hand on Wainwright's shoulder and smiled him to the door, "then you two will be on your way to the war zone. I think you'll get some excellent footage."

Sherrill spoke as soon as the door shut. "I've changed my mind. I want the grunt job."

Parnell moved back behind his desk. "Tell it to the chaplain."

"I mean it. You expect me to take him and his camera bearer out to take pictures of the war in that getup he calls a flightsuit? He's either nuts, or he's from Hollywood."

"He's both." Parnell shook his head sadly—a man caught between friendship and duty. "Look, Doug, he's the son of a good friend of mine, for gosh sakes. His dad is trying to get the kid to learn to make his own way in life. Haven't you got any friends?"

Sherrill pointed at the door and sneered, "None that would ask me to kill some of my men so that spoiled brat can pretend he's Walter Cronkite." He felt no compassion for Parnell and harbored no desire to play a role in the search for Wainwright's destiny.

Parnell abandoned the try for sympathy. "Yeah, well, I'll get with you later and you can check me out on how to choose my friends. In the meantime, take that boob out and fly him around over some safe areas and be back here before dark. Get him sixty seconds worth of sunset or a tame village on film. Do not get him close to any action—none! I do *not*—repeat *not*—want him anywhere near any place where there are weapons being fired. Clear?"

"Fear not. I'm not hanging my crew out so Cecil B. out there can be entertained—friend or not."

"Fine," Parnell growled as he dropped into the chair behind his desk. "Get out of here."

Gomez and Miller were lounging on the concrete, using the chopper's runner for a pillow. They were the two best door gunners in the war, and they, like their leader, were self-assured to the point of contempt for any human who wasn't on his third tour in the zone. They didn't bother to wear their contempt when they didn't have an audience.

Stringbean Miller, the right-door gunner, was staring at the sky. "What're we doin' out here, anyway?"

"How'm I supposed to know. Sherrill said be out here—we're here. They don't tell us Mex's nuthin'."

String made a motion at the sky. "I mean, what are we doin' out here in space?"

Gomez groaned.

The howl of an overtaxed engine and an accompanying squeal of rubber brought their heads up. From a quarter of a mile away, they could see a jeep hurtling across the ramp, weaving its way between parked helicopters at a speed that might impress lesser mortals. The vehicle recovered from a skid, missed a moving fuel truck by a full six inches, and settled on a course toward their resting place. Busy people on the ramp stopped what they were doing and stood open-mouthed, watching. They weren't looking at the jeep; they were gaping at the spectacle in it.

Stringbean studied the approaching vehicle for a moment before commenting. "You reckon he's mad?"

"*Sí*," Gomez sighed, "*muy enojado.*"

The driver of the vehicle aimed it straight at them, waiting until the last possible millisecond to lock the brakes. The jeep slid to a halt amidst the shriek, smoke, and stink of rubber sliding across hot asphalt.

The door gunners were already on their feet, not because their leader was arriving but because they—like everyone else on the ramp—had seen Wainwright from three hundred yards away.

Sherrill exploded from behind the steering wheel, pointed at Wainwright, and snapped, "You stay there."

Gomez moved closer to the jeep, his head cocked to one side. "What is *that?*"

"*That,*" Sherrill snarled, "is our mission in life."

Stringbean ambled past Gomez to get a better look. He was fascinated.

Wainwright was frozen in the passenger seat of the jeep, hands welded to the sissy handle. His Vietnamese "camera crew," Khanh Boi Ky, was in the back trying to restore order to several boxes of state-of-the-art motion-picture paraphernalia. Ky was a local guy who was making almost five times the going rate for wearing a twenty-four-hour-a-day grin while he hauled the goofy American's stuff around and ran the camera.

Ky's boss was the center of attention because of how he chose to spend part of daddy's money. He was wearing his interpretation of a film journalist's field attire—a Hong Kong-tailored flightsuit fashioned from red-and-white-checked material. A brass band would attract less attention.

Gomez groaned again. All the guy needed was a rotating beacon on his hat.

Sherrill pointed at Ky and said, "String, show that guy where to stash his gear, then take Spike Jones here to supply and get him a costume that won't get us all killed." He checked his watch and added, "And take your time." If they weren't in the air, they probably wouldn't get shot at.

Wainwright looked at the people around him and knew he was eventually going to have to assert himself as their leader. He cleared his throat and tapped his watch. "Major, I'm losing daylight. Since we're—"

Sherrill held up a hand. "The sun's gonna keep moving while you're jackin' your jaw, slick. Now do as you're told and I may not have you shot for inciting a mutiny."

"Apparently you don't understand the import of what I'm trying to—"

Sherrill couldn't believe it. "Listen, Jack. That Purina Dog Chow commercial you're wearing will attract every sniper in the country. Fact is, our own people will probably shoot you for wearing it. Now . . . as soon as I'm ready, the chopper leaves, not before. You've got two choices—leave your junk here and go don a U.S. Army issue flightsuit, or grab a seat out here on this ramp and listen to the sunset."

Sherrill's copilot showed up as the jeep was leaving for the wardrobe department. "What was *that*?"

"That was the reason you're gonna decide to get out after this hitch. Is this thing fueled up?"

The copilot, Lieutenant Paul Richards, would be running his own Huey crew in a few weeks. He volunteered for the open slot on Sherrill's crew because he wanted to watch the best at work. He yawned and said, "I wasn't gonna stay in anyway."

Sherrill pointed at the chopper and clipped his words. "Is it full of gas?"

"Aye, aye, Captain." Richards faked a British salute. "All ready to pretend we're going to war."

Sundown was less than two hours away. Their coming battle would be over before dark.

CHAPTER SEVENTEEN

Things had been quiet.

The Me Kong River, which marked the border between Laos and Thailand, was six miles from the end of the runway at NKP and almost an hour behind the Sandy flight; they were orbiting at their designated hold point.

Bainbridge hadn't made a sound since they crossed the river. He had his oxygen mask on, and the dark plastic of his helmet's sun visor covered the rest of his face. Judging from his posture, Mann suspected he was asleep or passed out, a suspicion confirmed when Mann heard him snoring on the intercom. Melher called for a fuel check, and Bainbridge shifted in his seat but didn't wake up. The fighters were maintaining a loose formation, loitering in a racetrack pattern with about a half-mile between planes, their engines pulled back to save fuel; they would close up the formation if they had to go to work. Mann was daydreaming about Pip.

The radio interrupted Mann's reveries. "Sandy One, this is King. We have one Fox-4, call sign Icebag Niner, north of your position—he's headed south with battle damage. The backseater's apparently unconscious, and the pilot's trying to get him to Da Nang."

Melher's voice came on the air to say, "Sandy One, roger. Keep me posted." Melher's plane tightened its turn. "Bill, we're gonna set up a picket line. Rabbi and I'll move north a little; you and Doc hang out here. If the F-4 makes it past us, we'll turn around and come back."

Mann keyed the mike switch on his throttle. "Sandy Three, roger."

Loeb was already closing the gap between his plane and Melher's. The two-ship formation turned north and was out of sight within a couple of minutes.

Bainbridge sat up straighter, his helmet swiveled while he took in his surroundings. The other aircraft were nowhere near them.

Bainbridge said, "Seems quiet."

"Yes, sir. Let's hope things stay that way." Including you.

Minutes passed.

Mann was at the south end of his orbit when the radio crackled. "Sandy Three, King."

"Sandy Three, go."

"Roger, Three. Sandy One asked us to relay. . . . Sandy Two is RTB for a rough engine. You're to move north to join Sandy One and leave Sandy Four to bring in the Jollys if they're needed."

Loeb was going home with a bad engine. "Sandy Three, roger. How far north is he?"

"He said one-zero minutes."

"Roger, King. Tell Sandy One I'll be there in ten."

"Roger the one zero minutes. King out."

Bailey was cutting across the inside of the turn to pull in close on Mann's wing. "I've got this covered, Bill. See you in a bit."

Mann looked out at Bailey and nodded. "I'm outta here." He rolled out of his turn, pushed the throttle up to cruise power, and headed north. Minutes later he was picking up broken pieces of Melher's conversation with King.

Forty-three miles north of Mann's position, the crew of Icebag Nine was in trouble. The F-4 had taken several hits while making its last pass at a Sam site, and its right engine flamed out. They were still a long way from Da Nang, the left engine was gradually losing power, and the flight controls were beginning to feel mushy. The pilot keyed his mike and spoke to his wingman, "Icebag Ten, this is Nine. I'm going to have to start a slight descent to keep my speed up."

"Ten, roger."

They were close to the Ho Chi Minh Trail, and ejecting over Laos might be preferable to North Viet Nam, but the point was irrelevant; his backseater was either unconscious or dead, and the F-4's pilot decided to stay with the plane.

Icebag Ten, flying just off his leader's wing, came on the radio as they passed through ten thousand feet. "Nine, your left engine's trailing smoke."

Lead keyed his mike. "Copy on the smoke. Is it bad?"

"Uh . . . roger on the bad," Ten drawled. "I've never seen good smoke come out of a jet engine."

The lead aircraft's LEFT ENGINE FIRE light came on as if to signal an incoming radio message from his wingman. "You're on fire, Lead. The left engine . . . scratch that. Okay . . . it's bad, Lead. Your whole empennage is involved." Icebag Ten keyed the mike again as red and orange flames surged forward in a rippling explosion that engulfed the whole aircraft. "Icebag Nine, Eject! Eject! Eject!"

The back door of the house opened, and Gene Elliott stepped into the cool night with a cup of coffee. The recent rains washed the air clean—the skies were clear and the stars were close. Coyote pups were yipping and playing in the creek bed behind the house.

Jane was wrapped in a blanket against the midnight chill, her bare feet snuggled under her. Dim light from the kitchen window printed a small orange design on the concrete surface of the patio. "What on earth are you doing out of bed?" she asked.

"I heard the door shut . . . figured I'd see what you where doing. Can I sit?"

"Mmhmm." She shifted to face his chair. "I've been praying."

"About Rusty?"

"Mostly, I guess."

He listened to the night for a few moments before asking, "You scared, hon?"

"Some," she touched her eyes with a wadded tissue. "And I miss him."

"Has prayin' helped?"

"Mm-hmm. Things are different now." He could hear her smile. "Things are going to be different forever, now."

"Ain't that the truth." He took a sip of coffee while he studied the stars. "This Christianity thing has got me prayin' most of the day. I can't figure out why somebody didn't tell me sooner."

"Mmm," she murmured. "So different."

He agreed with her in silence.

"Daddy," she sniffed and touched her nose with a tissue, "what if we hadn't found out?"

"That's yesterday, Baby. We're past that." Gene Elliott had already thought about that same question himself and he'd rather speculate on living the rest of his life without rain. "You want me to sit out here and pray with you for a while?"

She smiled in the darkness. "I think I'd like that."

In the burning F-4, the control stick went slack. The radio was dead and smoke was coming from the area forward of the rudder pedals.

From a hundred feet away, Icebag Ten watched as the slipstream began to tear fragments from the exploding aircraft. He was keying his mike to tell King they lost the plane when a single ejection seat propelled itself out of the fast-moving flames.

The wingman pulled his F-4 into a tight turn, watching the parachute bloom and lower the man toward the jungle. "King, this is Icebag One-zero. We have one good chute out of Icebag Nine, repeat, one chute. The aircraft was breaking up when the seat came out of it. We're over the ejection site."

"Icebag One-zero, King. We copy one chute. Sandy One and Sandy Three are en route to you. Can you give me your coordinates?"

"Stand by one and my wizzo'll punch 'em up."

"Is there a crash site?"

"One-zero here. There's some smoke south of us." Listeners on the UHF frequency heard Icebag Ten take a breath. "I guess you can have it checked out later, but don't expect to find much. It was in small pieces when we lost sight of it."

Icebag Ten's Weapon System Operator gave King their precise location, and King passed the information to Melher. Melher was two minutes away.

The pilot of Icebag Nine slipped out of the parachute harness and stuffed the canopy under the nearest brush. If there were bad guys in the area, they'd be on their way to where he was, so the first order of business was to get some real estate between himself and the chute. He pulled the emergency radio out of his survival vest and flicked it on, holding it in his hand as he jogged away from his landing area. He moved in a crouch, running or walking fast . . . trying to move quietly and carefully . . . stopping every few yards to listen. His objective was a large clearing he'd seen during his descent into the jungle; the clearing was a perfect landmark for the search and rescue troops.

CHAPTER EIGHTEEN

Richards flew the chopper while Sherrill worked the radio in search of safe places to fly. They were twenty minutes into their flight, and Wainwright was past the one-hundred mark of places for Ky to point the camera. The director made so many round trips across the gun deck Sherrill thought he'd wear out the metal floor.

Wainwright was centered in the realization of his life's calling. He pointed here and there, yelling into his helmet's boom microphone for Ky to "Get this hut!" and "Film that hill!" Ky, who could not stand erect while protecting the camera, struggled back and forth on his elbows and knees, squatting in the right door for mere instants to film a dozing water buffalo, then slithering back to left door to capture five seconds of a lone farmer ignoring them from his rice paddy. Wainwright's mind saturated itself with thoughts of how much his work would enthrall the news-hungry masses of the Western world. The correspondent could envision himself on the university lecture circuit, sharing the techniques of his new art form with young, aspiring journalists—people who wanted to be just like him. Then, too, there was the Pulitzer.

The chopper was tracking just east of the Laotian border, monitoring guard channel—the emergency radio frequency—when Sherrill picked up a call from King to Mann.

"Sandy Three, this is King."

"King, Sandy Three. Go."

"We have a crew member out of Icebag Niner on the ground. No report on the second man. Sandy One will be over the crash site in one. He wants you to plan to hold high for now and cover him."

"Sandy Three, roger that. Say the location."

"King, roger. The site is northeast of Tchepone, near the trail. The area is known hot."

The two helicopter pilots heard the exchange, and Sherrill looked at Richards without speaking. Richards shrugged. "May as well. They may need some extra shooters."

Sherrill glanced over his shoulder at the flying circus. "Okay, Gomer. Y'all make sure those two clowns are tethered. We're goin' over to Steel Tiger to check out a Sandy op."

Gomez, who appeared to be in mid-nap, was slouching by the left door gun. He lifted a hand to acknowledge the order without bothering to open his eyes. Stringbean gave his gun a cursory once-over then settled back to watch the real estate go by. The chopper banked to the left and the nose dropped, picking up speed.

Wainwright looked at Ky, and Ky shrugged. Wainwright turned on Stringbean. "What's a Sandy op?"

Stringbean found the film journalism business intriguing. In the last half hour, he decided he might give up on his plans of owning a used-car lot and hire himself out as a cameraman. He turned away from his door to grin at Wainwright. "How much film you got in that thang?"

"Thirty minutes, maybe forty-five."

"That should be plenty, 'cause we ain't got the gas to stay any longer."

Wainwright didn't understand. He keyed his mike with one hand and waved the other to express frustration. "*What* is a Sandy op?"

Stringbean was a natural mimic. He scrubbed his palms together in a perfect imitation of Ed Sullivan. "A Sandy op a really big shew."

Ky tried to help, grinning at Wainwright for the thousandth time and saying, "Sandy is airplane with big propeller—make very loud. We call 'trau dien' . . . crazy water buffalo."

Wainwright was appalled at the casual indifference of the four cretins who were placed at his disposal. He turned away from the gunners and leaned up between the pilots' seats, using his lecture circuit voice to address Sherrill. "I don't have time to fool around with a bunch of antique airplanes, Major. I need action."

Sherrill actually smiled at him—action was right on the other side of the line they were getting ready to cross. Lieutenant Colonel Parnell wasn't going to be happy about Sherrill's decision, but the chopper had guns on it that might make the difference in a rescue attempt. "Listen, Jack. If this don't turn out to be enough action for you, I will personally return the price of your "E" ticket. Now get back there and quit talking to me, or I'll tell Gomez he can shoot you."

The chopper's intercom was wired to every headset on board and any word spoken into the individual boom mikes was heard by all. Gomez opened his eyes and gave Wainwright his best interpretation of a mean Mexican's scowl.

The chopper tilted forward and picked up speed. Stringbean swiveled his M-60 machine gun, making sure it was free on its mount. The M-60 wasn't a news camera, but the principle was essentially the same . . . point it at someone, pull the trigger, and life very often gets worse for the person in front of it.

Mann continued on the northerly heading, calling Melher every thirty seconds until Melher's voice came on the radio. "Okay, Bill. I've got you five square. How me?"

"Loud and clear, Marsh. Where are you?"

"The black smoke south of the highway is the crash site. According to his wingman, our boy is in the jungle five klicks north of the smoke. I'm coming up on the smoke now."

Scattered clouds north of Mann obscured his view. "What's the plan?"

"As soon as you get here, I'm going down to look at the crash site. No one saw a second chute, but I'll give it a look before we start lining this thing out."

Bainbridge was taking in air by the deep lungful; his hands roamed the right side of the cockpit, searching for a place of rest.

The clouds moved past them, and Mann could see a column of smoke. He didn't think he would ever see black smoke again without wondering if it marked a crash site.

"This is Three. I've got the smoke in sight, Lead . . . and I've got a tally on you."

"Okay. Stay high and cover me."

Melher dropped to treetop level and made two circuits around the wreckage. There was nothing left of the airplane but shiny shreds of metal and smoldering pieces of rubber and plastic. "Nothing here, Bill. Let's go see what's up north."

"Roger." Mann looked to see how Bainbridge was handling himself. The big man was sitting straight in his seat with his arms crossed, his shoulders hunched. He gave the appearance of a child expecting to be punished.

The F-4 pilot eased up to the edge of the jungle and looked out at a wide expanse of brown grass. A current of air, bereft of the needed energy to stir the tall grass, drifted from the east. Nothing else moved. Over on the north side of the grassy area, eight hundred or a thousand yards distant, the jungle started at the edge of the grass and angled up to become a low ridgeline. Above him, too high for him to hear the engines, his wingman was orbiting in a wide circle.

The jungle would offer the best cover until the cavalry arrived, and one of the nearest trees had clear ground beneath it. He looked out at the still grass and thought, *I'll wait here and see if those boys in the Jollys want to do this out in the grass or back in the jungle.*

He took his helmet off and sat down to catch his breath, pulling a floppy camouflage bush hat out of his survival vest. Next he smeared black makeup on his face and wiped his hands on the hat. Finishing off one of his water bottles came last. He was ready to escape and evade if he had to.

I haven't told anybody I'm down here! He put the survival radio next to his lips and spoke quietly. "This is Icebag Niner Alpha, over."

The response was instantaneous. "Hey, man, this is One-zero. Are you okay?"

"So far, so good. Did Keith get out?"

Icebag Ten was sure the backseater went down with the plane, but that news could come later. "Uh . . . they're checking that out, Alpha. The Sandys are on the way."

"That suits me. I'm on the southwest edge of a large clearing; it's probably a thousand yards across, looks like a couple of miles long, all grass. I'm just inside the edge of the jungle."

"I'm looking at the clearing, amigo," said Icebag Ten. "The good guys are on the way."

Melher and Mann could hear Icebag Ten's transmissions, but they weren't close enough to hear the man on the ground. "Icebag One-zero, this is Sandy One. We're just a couple of minutes out. How copy?"

"You're five-by-five, Sandy. I'm holding above Icebag Nine Alpha. Have you got Jollys on the way?"

"The Jollys are en route to hold south until we check things over. Stand by one . . . okay, I think I've got a tally on you. Roll right and back left." Melher watched the F-4 identify itself. "Okay, Bill. Let's move up."

Mann closed the distance on Melher as the two A-1s approached the southern edge of an elongated plain of elephant grass; it was surrounded by jungle and bordered on the north and south sides by tree-covered ridgelines. A deserted dirt landing strip ran east and west over the flat ground.

"This is Icebag Ten. Nine Alpha says he's in the southwest corner over there."

"Sandy One, roger."

When the pilot on the ground heard Sandy One's transmission, he stood up—he knew that voice. He keyed his transmitter and said, "Sandy One, Icebag Nine Alpha's Romeo Mike."

Romeo Mike told Melher that Icebag Nine's initials were R. M., and Marsh cursed for the first time that day. The kid on the ground was the son of a good friend; in good times past, Melher had held the boy on his knee.

Mann heard the exchange and his reaction was not unlike Melher's. Bill Mann spent six months of his life listening to the voice he heard in his earpieces. He transmitted Rusty Mattingly's initials phonetically, followed by his own. "Romeo Mike, Bravo Mike."

Rusty smiled. One of his dad's good friends and the best pilot he'd ever flown with were going to work his rescue. "Roger, Bravo Mike, say your call sign."

"Sandy Three, Bro. Hang in there."

"I'm not going anywhere."

Melher got back into the conversation. "Three, you stay up while I drop down and see if I can find out what the gun situation is."

"Three, roger."

Mann took a position above and behind Melher. He would've preferred to swap places with Melher so he could be closer to Rusty—so he could feel like he was getting more done—but that wasn't how it worked.

When the radio went quiet, Rusty could hear the distinctive murmur of the big piston-engines. He dropped to his knees and scooted forward a few inches . . . then a few more. He was almost to the grass.

A few miles east, against a tall bank of white clouds, a pair of airplanes—one first cruising at a mid-altitude, the second slightly higher—moved toward him, tracking just inside the northern ridgeline. They flew down the far side of the valley . . . leisurely, unhurried. Melher wasn't crowding the ridge yet; that's where they liked to put the guns. Mann was trailing him, watching for ground fire.

Rusty felt the sun on his neck and realized he was too far from cover. *Be cool, boy,* he counseled himself as he eased back into the protection of the dark foliage. *This is no time to get careless. Stay close to the shade.*

Having traversed the north side of the valley without getting shot at, the A-1s left the north ridgeline and turned in his direction. They continued in a wide sweeping half-circle until they were headed back toward the eastern end of the valley. As they approached the east end, the lead plane descended and the formation turned west again.

Melher made several runs over the grassy area and the bordering jungle, getting lower with each pass. He didn't attract any ground fire, but that didn't prove much. Enemy gunners had been known to wait until the helicopters went into their hover for the pickup; then they'd start shooting.

While trying to get shot at, Melher saw what he wanted to see—an excellent pickup point. "Okay, Nine. There's a dirt strip between you and what looks like a deserted firebase. Do you have it in sight?"

"Stand by one."

The pause lasted several seconds.

"Do you have it yet?"

"Uhh . . . Nine, negative on the landing strip."

"Okay," Melher was unhurried, "do you see what's left of an old tower out near the middle of the clearing?"

"Hang on, Sandy. Let me move a few feet."

Rusty crawled closer to the edge of the trees. He stopped just inside the cover of the foliage and stood on his knees to scan a long narrow plain that opened out to the north and east. *There's some vertical poles, that'll be the tower . . . and there's some dirt buildup . . . probably an old perimeter.*

"I think I've got the tower, Sandy. Uh . . . no joy on the strip."

"Good, you're almost home, buddy. The strip is roughly halfway between your position and the tower . . . it runs east and west."

"Nine, roger."

"How's the foot traffic down there, Nine?" asked Melher. "Have you had anybody in sight?"

"Negative on the foot traffic."

"Three, this is One. You stay high, I'm going down for a closer look."

Melher dropped into the valley and ran its length fifty feet off the ground. When he pulled up, he turned north and disappeared over the ridge; Mann's airplane followed, watching.

Rusty's voice came back on the frequency. "Uh . . . Sandy, you're moving away from me now."

"Roger that, Nine." Melher's voice came from a man who sounded like he was agreeing on the weather. "No sense in bringing unnecessary attention to your location 'til we have to, so we'll keep from staying too close. We'll come back and go over the trees on that side to troll for flak, then we'll make one more circuit. We'd like to know where any shooters are before we start planning."

"Nine, roger."

Melher called King and told him to have Sandy Four bring in the Jollys. King answered that the Jollys were on the way and he was working to get fighters in to support the pickup.

On the ground, Rusty watched as the A-1s reappeared, turning to fly down the ridgeline, moving toward the late afternoon clouds continuing to build in the east. The A-1s were halfway down the valley when they banked steeply, reversing course.

"Uh . . . Icebag Nine Alpha, this is Sandy One. We may have movement in the trees north of you. Do you see any traffic between you and the trees?"

Seconds after Melher said the word *movement,* Rusty could feel the thug of his heartbeat. "Nine, uh . . . negative on movement. Things are, uh . . . pretty quiet . . . I think. Let me back into the bushes some and stand up."

"Okay, Nine. Stay cool, now." The voice might well have told him not to use too much sugar in his coffee.

Rusty backed farther into the jungle. He put himself behind a tree that was broader than his shoulders and eased up until he was standing. He became part of the tree, moving nothing but his eyes, searching the edge of the jungle on the other side of the clearing, slowly, cautiously. Nothing.

Good! There ain't nobody here but us chick . . .

On the far side of the grassy area, a slender shadow emmerged from the tree line; attached to it was a black line that could only be a rifle. The shadow with the rifle crept forward quickly and vanished into the grass. As soon as the first form disappeared, another slipped from the trees.

Rusty watched riflemen sneaking one by one into the grass as he lifted the radio to his lips and whispered into it. "Sandy One, Icebag Nine Alpha. We've got armed troops moving from the jungle into the grass on the north side of the clearing."

The coffee-sugar voice came back, "Roger on the armed troops, Nine. I'm going off freq for one. Standby."

In the cockpit of the A-1, Melher was not in a coffee-sugar mood. He and Rusty Mattingly's dad had been good friends since Rusty was a kid. Now the kid was on the ground in enemy territory, the bad guys were moving toward his position, and Melher couldn't do anything about it. He cursed the United States Air Force and the boobs in DC who were sitting in cushy chairs making imbecilic decisions about how to fight a war.

The lower edge of the sun was moving steadily toward the tops of the ridges out to the West. Where were the dadgum Jollys?

He rotated a switch on his communications panel and spoke to the C-130 that was supposed to be helping coordinate and support the rescue operation.

"King, this is Sandy One. We have enemy troops in the vicinity. Say ETA on the Jollys."

Melher was the on-scene commander for the rescue effort because he was the leader of the Sandy formation. The people he went to for resources to help with the rescue effort were flying in a specially-equipped C-130 Hercules aircraft assigned to that geographical area, call sign "King." The cargo compartment of the C-130 were converted into an airborne command and control center.

At an orbit point seventy miles southeast of the tall grass, the major who was in charge of the command center had just received some news he didn't want to hear. "Sandy One, this is King. Negative on the Jollys. Jolly Green Seven-seven has a turbine problem and Seven-nine is escorting him home. It'll be dark before we can get the alert bird to your position. We have Fox-4s en route with full loads of Mark-82s but minimum play time. The plan is for you to work the F-4s, but they're all we've got so far. I recommend you return to base after the fast-movers expend their ordinance and regroup for a pickup at first light."

Melher felt his stomach surge. The chances of a successful rescue decreased dramatically with every hour a pilot was on the ground; he cursed the situation in general and his helplessness in particular. He was going to have to tell the son of a good friend they couldn't come for him. Melher told King to send Bailey up to join them and changed his radio back to Rusty's frequency.

He gritted his teeth and keyed his mike switch. "Icebag Nine Alpha, Sandy One. We've got a problem. The Jollys had to abort, and the pickup can't be made until first light."

The bad news piled itself on the shock that came from having to punch out of the F-4 and Rusty felt his knees quiver. Ten seconds later, he was leaning against a tree, nodding to himself . . . it was time for him to decide how the situation was going to play out. *Just take a breath there, bubba. A little cool will go a long way down here.*

He took the breath while he remembered that a Navy pilot—an A-7 driver—were shot down a day's walk from where he was. That guy stayed on the ground two days and nights, completely surrounded by enemy troops and scrambling to evade capture every minute of his time on the ground. *Get your act together, Mattingly. This ain't nuthin' but a refresher course in Snake School—and how many of those kids sneaking around that grass want to find a man carrying a gun.*

He looked up at Melher's airplane. "You've got the best picture, Sandy. You got any suggestions for me?"

Marsh liked hearing the straightforward tone in Rusty's voice. "Judging from what I see from here, I'd move out into the grass to hide. The grass is tall and there're some bomb craters near the edge of that old landing strip—you can see them if you work your way straight toward the tower. The bad guys will expect you to do your E and E up in the trees . . . they can't get a search done at night, and they'll want to stay away from the open when it's daylight. Go out there and curl up in a hole and cover up with dirt until we can come back for you. In the meantime, I'm going to get a pair of fast-movers to sanitize that area on the north side of the strip; that'll persuade those troops to keep their heads down while you move."

Rusty nodded—it was as good a plan as any. He pulled his handgun out of its holster and flipped the cylinder open—it was loaded. He kept the gun in his hand and held the radio to his lips. "I'll be at the strip five minutes after the shooting starts."

"There you go. We'll have some F-4s here pronto."

The day's all-out air attack on North Viet Nam depleted the available fighter assets in Southeast Asia. When the F-4s showed up, there were only two in the flight, but in four passes each they kept the enemy clutching the ground while putting twenty-four five-hundred-pound bombs in the area north of the strip. Rusty used the diversion to scramble at high speed through the grass.

The F-4s were moving out of the area when Rusty called Melher. "Sandy, I'm about halfway down the strip . . ." he was breathing in gasps " . . . on the south side . . . right in the edge of the tall grass . . . in a fairly large crater . . . probably made by a mortar round."

"Roger that, Nine. Give us—"

The tracers came off of the northern ridgeline and arced toward the low Sandy. Mann keyed his mike. "Marsh, break right! Break right!"

Bainbridge, who to this point had been silent, watched the tracers and moaned into the intercom.

Mann was yelling into the radio when one of the incoming rounds hit Melher's plane. When the shell struck, Bainbridge yelped as if part of it hit him. An explosion at the front of Melher's airplane was accompanied by an eruption of thick black smoke streaming from the beneath its engine cowl, obscuring both sides of the aircraft.

Melher had been in battle-damaged aircraft before. "This is Sandy One. I took one in the engine." He lifted a plastic guard on his instrument panel and pressed the red button under it; the plane's ordinance and external fuel tanks fell away from the wings and fuselage. "Sandy One is losing oil pressure . . . I'm experiencing severe vibration."

Bainbridge was shuddering, breathing like a man trying to recover from a half-mile sprint.

"How far do you think you can get, One?" Mann wanted to get Melher away from the people in the grass and jungle.

Melher already had it figured out. The smoke was leaving a black furrow in the still air, following the crippled plane through a wide turn back toward the clean path in the grass. "I'm gonna put 'er down there on the end of that strip and look for Icebag Nine." He was leveling his wings and lining the airplane up for a belly landing as he spoke. "You guys be here at sunup and get us outta this place."

Mann watched as the Skyraider bellied in smoothly, engulfing itself in a self-made squall of dust and uprooted grass. When the dust cleared, the cockpit was empty.

Mann had to wait only a minute to hear Melher's survival radio crackle in his earphones. "Well, we're both okay, Billy—not so much as a scratch. Discourage these guys as much as you can before you leave, and we'll see you first thing tomorrow."

"Negative, negative on the 'tomorrow.' I'm going off freq for one and talk to King." Mann pulled back to the east end of the shallow valley. When Melher's aircraft bellied in, responsibility for the rescue operation trickled down to Mann.

Mann changed the radio frequency. "King, Sandy Three."

"King's on, Three. Go ahead."

"Sandy One is on the ground with Icebag Nine Alpha. They've got bad guys within six hundred meters. We need to get them out of there posthaste."

"I copy that, Three, but we don't have what it takes to get it done. We've got more than one effort going right now. You and I both know we can't use a Jolly we don't have, and the alert bird can't get to you before dark." The newly-promoted major sitting in the King chair was chosen for his role for two good reasons; he had a track record of excellent situational awareness—a gift for thinking detail, while seeing the big picture—and he was passionate about getting downed pilots back home. The prospect of leaving two men on the ground overnight frustrated him, but he couldn't do the impossible . . . and without the Jollys, he was helpless. His tone communicated reason. "We want them out of there, Sandy, but we can't send what we don't have. We need choppers that don't exist, and we need more daylight than we've got left. What we don't need is more crew members down there with them."

Marsh and Rusty were on the ground with the enemy too close and Mann wasn't ready to give up. *Fine*, he thought, *we'll go with what we've got.*

He keyed his mike. "Do you have any fast-movers, King."

"Sandy Three, roger. So far, we've got one element of Gunfighter F-4s inbound to you and a flight of four A-7s will be right behind them. Both flights are skosh on fuel, and all they've got left is their guns."

"Sandy Three, roger. Send 'em to me."

The voice from the C-130 took on a more understanding tone. The major knew that sending the fighters into a hot spot probably wouldn't help if the Jollys weren't there to make a pickup. "We ought to pack it in, amigo, and save our assets for tomorrow. Pick up a landline when you get on the ground, and we'll make a plan. We'll be back here at first light."

Mann didn't bother to respond directly. As Sandy Lead, he didn't have to argue to get what he wanted—all he had to do was make sure he made himself clear. "Call me back when you have the ETAs on the fighters, King."

"King, roger. But we need to face up to it, Three—those boys are going to be on the ground overnight."

Not hardly, thought Mann. He turned to check on his passenger.

Bainbridge was no longer breathing hard. He was leaning forward, his head almost touching his knees, his right hand was probing a calf pocket of his G-suit.

The big man's apparent recovery suited Mann. What he had planned for the next few minutes made no allowances for playing nursemaid.

Bainbridge straightened. He was clutching a baby bottle full of clear liquid and a tightly folded envelope. His hand shook as he disconnected one side of his mask. With the mask out of the way, he unfolded the paper and selected several red capsules to put in his mouth . . . the bottle was next. He uncapped it and used three or four swallows of the contents to wash down the pills. Without looking at Mann, he reattached his mask and said, "Antacid." He stuffed the bottle and wrapper back in their designated pocket.

Had Bainbridge cut off one of his own fingers and popped it in his mouth, dirty fingernail and all, Mann could not have been more astounded. A lieutenant colonel in the Air Force, a pilot, had just wolfed down a handful of drugs in the cockpit . . . in the presence of another pilot! The next moron to cross Mann's path was going to have to come up with something really spectacular to top this.

Bainbridge rolled his shoulders to stretch them and looked to the west. "Well, that's it," he growled. "Without choppers we can't get anything done here. Tell King we'll pack it in and call him when we get on the ground."

CHAPTER NINETEEN

We're not leaving yet, Colonel." Mann's oxygen mask moved back and forth as he shook his head. "We've got a couple of things to do first."

"King made it clear, Bill. We've done all we can."

With Melher's airplane resting on its belly in the grass, Mann was Sandy Lead by default. Bainbridge outranked him, but rank had nothing to do with who was in command of *The Cool Woman* or the SAR effort.

"Not yet, Colonel. You and I are going to wait here and direct the fast-movers. When they're Winchester, we're going to expend everything we're carrying on whoever's left. When we get through hosing down the north side of that clearing, if we still don't have a chopper, I'm going to land on that strip down there and get those two guys outta that hole."

Bainbridge turned the dark sun visor toward him. "I admire your courage, Bill, but you'd be endangering too many lives." He tried to keep his voice steady, but his hands gave him away. "I know you mean well, but I'm going to have to pull rank on you. After the fast-movers leave, we're going to pack it in and return to base."

Nice try, Lionheart, thought Mann. He took a breath before saying, "With all due respect, Colonel, you're on this mission as an observer.

Having Marsh on the ground makes me Sandy Lead and I'll need to call the shots."

"I see." Bainbridge nodded and lifted a hand to acknowledge Mann's ultimate authority and gave up too easily. "You're right, of course." He unlatched his seat belt and inched forward to unfasten the straps on his parachute harness. "I guess I'd better get rid of some coffee in case this gets interesting."

Interesting is a good word for it, buddy boy. Mann grinned behind his mask. *Uncle Billy's getting ready to take you to a place that would make Dirty Harry Callahan wish he'd opted for the priesthood.*

While Bainbridge was preparing to take care of his business, Mann went looking for holes in his plan.

With enough fuel on board, the A-1 was capable of flights in excess of ten hours. If a man was going to be confined to a cockpit for an extended period of time, there had to be some provision for relief and the accepted method on fighter-type aircraft was a relief tube. The device resembled the old cone-shaped speakers that steamship captains yelled into to communicate with their engine rooms. On the A-1E, each pilot had a tube stowed in the side panel by his outboard knee.

Using the tube before the really demanding part of the rescue got started was a good idea. Bainbridge made sure he was clear and moved a lever near his right hand while warning Mann, "Okay. Here comes my canopy." The Plexiglas covering over Bainbridge slid back on its rails, and the noise level in the cockpit went up by a factor of three.

Spad pilots who'd been paying attention always opened the canopy and took their gloves off before they used the relief tube. Conventional wisdom maintained that if you got your fingers wet, you could dry them in the slipstream in seconds. Conversely, if you accidentally got your flying gloves wet, they didn't dry out for a day or two, and when they did, they smelled funny.

Side-by-side seats in a restaurant booth would provide more wiggle room than the cockpit of an A-1E, so Mann couldn't totally turn his back on Bainbridge, but he did what he could to give the man some privacy. Bainbridge finished struggling with his harness and became still.

Mann was on item ten on the list of the things that might go wrong when Bainbridge put his hand on the pedestal between them and snapped the UHF radio selector to "Off." Mann caught the movement out of the corner of his eye and turned, thinking, *What kind of stunt—*

Bainbridge was unstrapped, sitting slightly forward in his seat so he could turn and face Mann. The pistol in his hand was pointed at Mann's middle. The oxygen mask covering the lower part of Bainbridge's face moved up and down with the words coming into Mann's earphones. "I'll say one thing for you, black boy, you're a cool one." The upper part of the man's face was shrouded by the dark visor, but he sounded as if he was smiling.

Mann was disappointed in himself—Doc warned him not to turn his back on the man. Bainbridge would never let him live—not after pulling a gun on him. "What now?" he asked.

"Well, first of all, let's have a little reunion." He leaned back slightly and opened his fingers for a second, giving Mann a flash-glimpse of the pistol's grips. "Recognize this?"

Mann saw the grips and knew it was his dad's pistol. *Make him mad,* he thought, *and he'll make a mistake.* "Yeah, I ought to recognize it. I used it to blow your scurvy little brother's brains all over a muddy road in Mississippi."

"That was the second greatest day in my life." Bainbridge actually laughed. "Second only to today, that is."

"You can't get away with it, Bainbridge. What are you going to do? Tell 'em I shot myself?"

"Nope. You're going to be killed in action." The prophet chuckled. "Today's the day you're going to get the golden BB, and the world will be rid of one more nigger."

"It won't work." *It would work.*

"Oh, it'll work all right. And my momma will give me a medal."

Thanks a lot, Kelly, thought Mann. *Where's your God when a man needs Him?*

The plane bounced on a small thermal, and Bainbridge flinched as if he'd been stung.

The minor distraction was as good as it was going to get . . . and Mann launched himself at the gun.

Bainbridge was fat, but he wasn't slow. He got an arm up in time to deflect Mann's attack and kept control of the gun. Mann grunted when the barrel buried itself in his stomach; he was closing his fingers around the weapon when he felt Bainbridge pull the trigger.

Mann jerked involuntarily and yelled into his mask, but that was the only sound he heard.

The gun didn't go off. The chamber was empty.

Bainbridge's face was still covered by his mask and visor, but his frustrations came out on the interphone. He screamed profanity as he rammed his shoulder into Mann's chest to give himself time to turn away and jack a shell into the chamber. The struggling men continually bumped arms and knees against their respective control sticks, causing the plane to pitch and roll slightly.

Mann got his forearms against Bainbridge and heaved the bigger man off, still grappling to get to the gun.

Bainbridge hit the far side of the cockpit and twisted to point the gun at Mann's face. "That's enough!" he yelled.

The aircraft's nose was down, the left wing low; the speed was picking up, and the plane was rolling. Bainbridge kept his face pointed at Mann while he put his free hand on the stick to steady the plane. Mann watched the man's clumsy attempts to right the aircraft while listening to his respiration rate increase. Bainbridge wasn't close to being a pilot; he never would be.

Bainbridge satisfied himself that the airplane wasn't going to kill him and released the stick. Mann was waiting.

When Bainbridge shrugged, Mann knew he was going to shoot. This time there would be a round in the chamber.

Bainbridge said, "Well, good-bye, black boy. I'll see you—"

Mann straightened his left leg and, in so doing, jammed the left rudder pedal to its full limit.

Several things happened at once. The airplane's nose snapped hard to the left, and Bainbridge grunted as the forces slammed him against his side of the cockpit; Mann, restricted by his seat harness, tried to follow. The airplane started an immediate roll. The gun went off and put a bullet in the instrument panel. Bainbridge was grabbing for the stick with his free hand and making a trapped animal sound, something between a shrill scream and a squeal. Mann locked his leg to hold the rudder pedal against the stop and pulled the stick all the way to the left.

When the airplane's roll-rate increased, Bainbridge went beyond panic. He was grabbing clumsily at the stick with his free hand, trying desperately to right the plane and screaming like a girl with every breath. Mann didn't care what the plane did; the only way he could get hurt was to get shot or have the airplane hit the ground. He was more than a mile from one danger but only eighteen inches from the other; he turned loose of the stick and made another grab for the only thing within a mile that could kill him. Bainbridge, because he was trying to shoot Mann or because he couldn't control his hands, squeezed the trigger again.

The gun went off in Mann's face and the sound deafened him, but he didn't flinch. He'd heard stories of men who had been shot without feeling it, and he wanted to believe the bullet missed him, but being wounded wasn't something he had time to deal with. If he didn't get control of the gun, he was already dead.

Bainbridge was a frightened beast, squealing and thrashing around with his arms and legs, fighting with Mann while trying to get control of the aircraft. The Skyraider rolled sluggishly, wallowing erratically because the two men were throwing each other against the sticks.

Mann was fighting the G-forces put on him by the gyrations of the plane. He couldn't pin Bainbridge's hands long enough to get a grip on the gun. The big man's wild screaming stopped only when he was refilling his lungs.

Seconds after the first bullet was fired, the aircraft was completely inverted. They were falling into a rapid descent when, by some miracle, Bainbridge figured out what he could to do to stop the rolling. He twisted until he could get his foot on the right rudder and put enough weight on the pedal to lift himself off of his seat. He pushed against the rudder, straining and yelling, "No! No! No!"

Mann had his knee locked—Bainbridge, even in his madness, wasn't strong enough to make him release the pressure. Mann took one hand out of the fight and pulled the throttle back. If the aircraft stalled, Mann had plenty of altitude to recover—but only if he was still alive. He was depending on the loss of power to frighten Bainbridge into surrendering the gun.

The sudden absence of the engine's roar drew Bainbridge's attention away from the fight—but not the way Mann intended. In one brief instant, a simple remedy penetrated the terrified man's thought processes. He abandoned the stick, wrapped both hands around the gun's grips, and forced the barrel around. Adrenalin pumped itself into Mann's effort to turn the gun, but terror and weight gave Bainbridge the edge. When he had the gun pointed where he wanted, Bainbridge pulled the trigger. The gun went off, and the bullet creased Mann's left leg. Mann knew in that instant the bullet that passed near his face earlier had not touched him.

White-hot pain cut him from his toes to his hip, causing him to jerk away from the rudder. Bainbridge had his full weight on the right rudder and the airplane snapped hard to the right, throwing him on top of Mann in an even more turbulent convulsion of arms and legs—the sounds in the headsets were a cacophony of strained grunts, gasps, and Bainbridge's high-pitched wheening. They hit the side of the cockpit hard, and Mann grabbed the business end of the gun. Bainbridge took the pressure off the rudder, pinning Mann with his forearm while getting a better grip on the pistol. The aircraft stopped rolling, and Bainbridge wrenched the gun around in an effort to jam the muzzle into Mann's stomach.

Mann gritted his teeth, closing his mind against the pain in his leg. He clamped down with all his strength on the barrel of the pistol and used his good leg to jam the right rudder against the stop.

The abrupt roll input was too much for Bainbridge; the gun went off again and escaped from his grip. He abandoned all thought of the gun when the aircraft yawed to the right and grabbed for his control stick with both hands.

As if recognizing an opportunity to escape, the gun lofted across the cockpit. Mann went after it, leaving Bainbridge to fight a frantic battle with the plane. With Mann grasping for it, the .45 did a pinball bounce off Mann's flailing control stick and ricocheted into the center of the instrument panel butt-first—Mann's right hand closed around the barrel of the gun at the instant it discharged. The bullet barely missed blowing his little finger off, and the recently-freed weapon made a determined effort to escape his grip by throwing itself into a mechanical convulsion to eject the empty cartridge. Mann kept his hands on the gun but got the flesh between his thumb and forefinger badly pinched in the process.

He backed against his side of the cockpit and got the gun settled in his hand.

Up to this point, he had not been angry—he was trying to stay alive. Not now. His leg was throbbing. His thumb hurt almost as badly. And he was past being fed up with the psycho in the right seat of his airplane.

He straightened, his chest heaving, holding the gun close to his body and pointing it at Bainbridge. "Bainbridge, you idiot . . . you're even more worthless than your good-for-nothing—"

Bainbridge wasn't listening. He was slumped in his seat, both hands resting quietly in his lap, head lolling gently with the movement of the airplane . . . a spiderweb of fine cracks surrounded a jagged hole in his helmet visor. The last shot missed Mann's little finger, but not Bainbridge—bright red blood rimmed the top of his oxygen mask and streamed freely along the edges to course down the sides of his neck. Mann gave Bainbridge a tentative poke with his free hand, and the body tilted slightly. Bainbridge was as relaxed as he'd ever been in an airplane.

Mann held the gun in one hand and used the other to raise Bainbridge's helmet visor. The heavy bullet had struck the man's left eye; the entire upper left side of his face was a gruesome mess. Mann sagged back in his seat. "Well, that's just peachy."

In aviation, smart pilots do the most important thing first. He righted the airplane while turning his radio back on. "Doc, Three. Radio check."

"Uh . . . roger that, Three. I've been trying to raise you. Are you okay?"

"Just hunky-dory." Mann was looking at his leg. There was a red smear on his G-suit, but it wasn't getting wider and the pain wasn't anything he couldn't put up with. "Where are you?"

"I'm two klicks south of the crash sight. I should be at the pickup point in two. Say your position."

"Stand by."

Mann turned the aircraft north and looked to his left to search for the dirt strip. In so doing, he turned his back to Bainbridge for the second time that day.

In the right seat, Bainbridge's head tilted forward, his body followed, and his full weight collapsed onto the right control stick. The two-hundred-and-something pounds of deadweight shoved the stick to its limits, and the airplane immediately executed a hard nose over.

The force of the maneuver lifted Mann off his seat, throwing him, wounded leg and all, against his lap belt. He winced and grabbed for the stick to get the pressure off of his leg, cursing himself for not making sure Bainbridge was dead. The stick came back easily, and Mann jerked around to see what the squadron's reigning imbecile was planning to pull next.

Late afternoon clouds to the west were tinting themselves with soft pink hues, providing a preview of the coming sunset. The wind noise in the cockpit was subdued, the thunder from the engine's exhaust muted. The aircraft rolled gently, responding to the fading influence of summertime thermals.

A lifetime earlier, under the guise of having to use the relief tube, Bainbridge unstrapped to get to the hidden .45, and the pilot who was deathly afraid of airplanes neglected to refasten his lap belt. The negative G-forces provoked by the hard nose over did the same thing to Bainbridge's body it did to Mann's; it threw it up and away from his seat. Mann was wearing his seat harness; Bainbridge wasn't. The never-would-be pilot was thrown out of the airplane through his open canopy.

Less than three minutes after he showed Mann the pistol, Lieutenant Colonel Halbert D. Bainbridge Jr. was, as they say, dead and gone.

"Four has a tally, Three. Closing on your six."

"Uh . . . roger, Doc. Stand by one." Mann unsnapped his oxygen mask and stared at the empty seat. He let out a long sigh and thought, *Well, I guess if the fool had to die, this might help get me off the hook. I may as well put the good news on the record.* Knowing King would be recording the radio transmissions, he put his mask back on and keyed the mike. "Doc, this is Three. Bainbridge is gone."

There was a short pause, then, "Say again."

"You heard it right. Colonel Bainbridge opened his canopy and unstrapped to use the relief tube, and I turned my back. I just turned around and found my right seat empty. He's gone."

King entered the exchange and asked, "Sandy Three, did I understand you to say you lost the man who was in your right seat?"

"Sandy Three, roger. He was here one minute, gone the next."

"Did you see a chute?"

"Negative on the chute, King," said Mann. "The man disappeared; the last time I looked at him the buckles on his chute were unlatched. He's gone."

When King remained silent, Doc Bailey asked, "What do we do now?"

"What we came for." Mann had spent enough time on his requiem for a fool. "We're going to work Icebag Nine Alpha. We'll save Bainbridge's memorial service for when we get back to NKP. For now, we've got our hands full." He dropped his left wing, banked back to the right, then rolled into a left turn, signaling Bailey to join up on his left wing.

"Four, roger." That Bainbridge fell out of a perfectly stable aircraft was only mildly surprising, and Bailey couldn't muster the hypocrisy required to express sympathy for a man for whom he felt nothing but contempt. Seconds later, he slid into position on Mann's left wing. Mann was leaning across the cockpit, closing the canopy over the empty right seat. "What's the plan?"

Mann continued the turn back to the west. "Marsh and Icebag Nine Alpha are in a crater at the edge of that dirt strip below us . . . about midway down on the south side. The bad guys are in the grass and jungle to their north. There's at least one gun on the northern ridge . . . 37 mike mike. Got that?"

"Four, roger on the gun. I'm looking at the strip."

"Okay, the sun might help a little if we work west to east using a right-hand pattern to keep away from that ridge. I'll put my smoke at the edge of the jungle on my first pass and keep using my guns to keep their heads down. You use everything but your smoke and guns; hold off on them 'til I ask for 'em. Copy?"

"Four, copy."

"Keep everything on the north side of the strip, between the jungle and the landing strip." Mann set up his armament panel and rolled in.

Minutes late, Mann had expended his munitions and was pulling off his last pass when King called. "Sandy Three, you have four Gunfighter Fox-fours and four Alpha-sevens inbound. Minimum play time for the A-7s, guns only on all eight aircraft."

Mann shook his head at the military's ability to run itself short of essential assets. "Three, roger. What about a chopper."

"Negative on the chopper, Three. Sorry."

"Sandy Three, roger." Mann leveled his aircraft and flew the length of the southern ridge while Bailey completed his pass. When Bailey pulled up, Mann keyed his mile. "Sandy Four, Three."

"Four, go."

"Okay, Doc. I'm going back to skip-bomb my tanks in the grass then do a three-sixty to the right and put down on that strip."

There was a short pause before Bailey said, "Umm . . . say that again."

"You heard it. I want you on the perch at the west end. Set your mini-gun on low-flow and space yourself to follow me in when I roll level on final. Use the mini and your wing guns to keep their heads down while I get the plane stopped."

"Someone has already picked up all the chips in that pot, Bill."

Years earlier, an A-1 pilot distinguished himself as a bona fide hero when he landed on a contested airstrip and successfully picked up a pilot who crash-landed there. The Sandy pilot ended up with several dozen bullet holes in his aircraft and a well-deserved Medal of Honor.

"You never know," said Mann. "After your first gun pass, come around and lay your smoke along the northern edge of the strip. . . . It'll help cover us while these guys jump in the plane."

"Bill . . . uh," Bailey paused with his mike open, then drawled, "I've got you covered, my friend. Break a leg."

"Thanks. We've got four Fox-4s and four Alpha-7s inbound. Work them to cover us."

The extra seat in Mann's cockpit was going to come in handy.

CHAPTER TWENTY

Lieutenant Truong Giap, North Vietnamese Army, stood inside the edge of the jungle, watching the propeller-driven fighter come in low across the grass and release its fuel tanks. When the tanks erupted in a harmless spray of aviation fuel, he smiled—the Americans dropped their fuel tanks when they had no other weapons. The second American plane, the one orbiting west of them, had matched the one over the grass pass for pass. Were the foolish pilots not aware that they had just signaled Giap that it was now safe for him to take his men unchallenged into the wide field?

Minutes earlier, when the first A-1 crash-landed, Giap watched the pilot run back along the old landing strip. As he watched, someone rose out of the grass and caught the attention of the American—there were two Americans out there. The lieutenant was raising his arm to lead the remainder of his force into the grass when he realized that the attacking A-1 hadn't pulled up into a climb. Giap held his position and watched as the plane banked away from him, turning tightly, its wingtip brushing the tops of the grass.

The Skyraider made a full circle and lined up on a point out in the center of the field. If the Yankee was going to make another pass, wondered Giap, why would he not aim his aircraft where he thought his enemies to be? When the plane's landing gear came down, he understood.

"Trinh!" he yelled. "Trinh!!!"

A young sergeant carrying an American-made rifle left his assigned position and hurried through the undergrowth to his commander's side. The lieutenant grabbed the front of Trinh's shirt, speaking excitedly, gesturing away from the field, urging the man up the slope behind them. When Trinh sprinted away, the officer yelled for his men to follow him and led the rest of his North Vietnamese regulars out to kill the Americans hiding in the grass. The big airplane would stop in the field, and they would kill that American as well. The only airplane left in the air might try to stop them, but Giap and his men were not afraid of falling fuel tanks. They would kill the Americans in the field and be back in the jungle before more American airplanes came to help.

Bailey watched Mann's plane touch down and rechecked his Armament Selector at "Guns." The A-1 carried 720 rounds for the four wing cannons and 1,500 rounds for the relatively small, but utterly lethal, SUU-11 minigun. On the "low" setting, the minigun spewed 2,000 rounds per minute.

Lieutenant Truong Giap and his men were forty yards from the protection of the jungle, running pell-mell through the shoulder-high grass, when Doc Bailey rolled off "the perch" to give the NVA a fire-power demonstration.

The issued weapon for U.S. Marine snipers was the M40—a 7.62 mm derivative of the Remington Model 700 bolt-action rifle. The one in the hands of the North Vietnamese sergeant clambering up the slope was stolen out of Da Nang back in February.

The rifle's previous owner was Corporal Wallace Pierpoint, an east Tennessee boy. The other Marines in his basic training unit dubbed him the Kentucky Rifleman after their first trip to the firing range. After his second visit to the range, the Marines tapped Pierpoint to be one of their snipers.

Corporal Pierpoint was a man who didn't "wanna have to use a come-along to pull my trigger." When he finished polishing the Remington's trigger mechanism, it had less than a two-ounce-pull. He said, "If a feller was to give the trigger considerable thought," the weapon would fire. Sergeant Pahn Chu Trinh, the man handpicked by Lieutenant Giap to ascend the slope, discovered the weapon's uniqueness soon after being entrusted with the prize. He would grin and lightly brush his finger against the trigger or touch it with a leaf just so his comrades could hear the immediate snap of the firing pin. They would all smile and nod. He had used two precious rounds of the match-grade ammunition to test the rifle.

Giap ordered Trinh to select a suitable place from which he could carry out his specialized function. Today was the day the sergeant would justify his leader's confidence.

Trinh slowed his climb, searching carefully for an area that would allow him an unobstructed field of fire. He was a hundred meters up the slope when he stepped from the thick foliage into the perfect spot—a garden-sized clearing looking out over the long valley provided an excellent view of the landing strip; one lone medium-sized tree was centered in the small glade. The rise in the slope gave him just enough elevation to see the edges of the crater where his lieutenant said the two Americans were hiding. He was smiling and nervous at the same time.

The rifle he held was Trinh's badge of newfound respect, and he was determined to prove himself worthy. He brushed the twigs and debris away from the base of the tree trunk so he could sit comfortably then uncased his rifle and leaned back in the shade of the tree. As his back touched the tree, Trinh heard the throaty whine of Bailey's mini-gun: the screams that followed came from his comrades. Because he had the rifle, he was resting under a shady tree in relative safety while his friends went out into the hot grass to be shot at. The attacking A-1 bottomed out over the valley, the roar from its engine drowning out the cries of his friends.

Trinh made sure his weapon's safety was engaged and cycled the M40's bolt. He put the rifle to his shoulder and looked through the powerful scope, moving the rifle back and forth—slowly, deliberately—carefully searching the grass. The American pilots put a smoke screen between Trinh and his targets, but the smoke would dissipate and drift. He watched as the fighter plane landed and flashed through the scope, stirring up the dust on the small runway. He ignored it.

When the pilot stopped the airplane, he would shoot him. He kept the gun moving, surveying the scene. Slowly. Steadily. Patiently.

And just like that . . . there it was. His reward for being patient.

A perfect target.

Melher stayed low in the crater, jerking on the leg of Rusty's G-suit and yelling, "Get down, Rusty! Mann knows where we are!"

Trinh released the safety and centered the crosshairs. He took a breath, let it out slowly until there was no pressure in his chest, and touched the trigger.

Rusty waved his arm. "I might have to—"

The impact of the bullet lifted the pilot bodily from the crater and hurled him into the dirt like a discarded doll. A delayed boom from the jungle told Melher they had a sniper to contend with.

The recoil was substantial, but Trinh wasn't bothered by it. He was remembering the puff of dust from the chest of the man he knocked out of the hole. The man lay unmoving, facedown in the dirt. Trinh cycled the bolt and reset the safety while he watched the edge of the hole through his scope. The other American's head appeared and part of his body followed when he crawled out to get his friend.

Trinh smiled and settled the rifle against his shoulder.

Melher was cursing vehemently when he reached over the edge of their small depression. He was tugging on one of Rusty's boots when Trinh's bullet flipped him partially out of the hole. Though dazed to the point of near blindness, he managed to drag Rusty back to safety. He ducked into the hole an instant before the next shot blew a hole in the ground where his head had been. He pushed and tugged to stretch Rusty out on his back and wiggled to get below the meager protection offered by the mound of dirt at the hole's edge.

Melher's shoulder and left side were numb; shock trickled into his body on the thoughts of what the bullet had probably done to him. With trembling fingers, he unzipped his flightsuit and pulled it back—the bullet had gone through his shoulder back-to-front. His fingertips told him it left a gaping exit wound; the blood was coming fast, and the pain wouldn't be far behind. Melher cursed the sniper and Rusty with equal passion.

He could hear the A-1 slowing at the end of the strip.

Bill Mann didn't have a prayer.

Mann could imagine bullets tick-tacking into the airplane before he got it slowed; perspiration poured into his eyes from under his helmet and blurred his vision. What could only be the fingertip of fear slithered like a cold snake through the sweat on his back. He flipped the mixture lever on his oxygen panel to "100%," breathing deeply of the pure oxygen and swallowing hard in an effort to fight back the surging in his throat. By the time he got the plane slowed enough to turn around, adrenaline was in control of his legs, and the soles of his boots were jittering against the rudders.

He turned and fast-taxied back to the midpoint on the strip. Smoke from the phosphorus bombs mixed with the dust around him, restricting visibility in the immediate vicinity. That was good.

The soldiers in the grass were not happy to see him and were only partially hampered by the smoke screen. Bullets made angry, spanging sounds against the metal sides of the plane; two or three stitched through the plexiglass canopy, one clipped his helmet.

He ducked into the center of the cockpit while he locked the left brake, turning the airplane so the tail was pointed at the enemy soldiers; at that angle, the biggest part of the plane's body would be between the attackers and the engine. The no-longer-secret hiding place was just off his right wingtip. Perfect. He bumped the throttle up to put more dust between the airplane and the bad guys and peeked to see if his passengers were coming.

When he looked over the edge of the cockpit, he was looking past the wingtip into Marsh Melher's eyes. He waved from the open canopy for Melher to come to the airplane. Melher stayed flat in the hole and shook his head; he pointed at Rusty, then at his own shoulder. Rusty's flightsuit was a bloody mess; Melher's chest didn't look much better; his sleeve was wet-red from shoulder to wrist.

Melher scowled at him and waved a "get out of here" gesture with his good hand.

Mann made sure the brakes were set and threw his helmet off. When he got unstrapped, he shrugged out of his parachute harness and jammed his dad's .45 behind the web belt He scrambled onto the right wing, missed his footing in the fresh coating of oil, and slid off the wing face-first—the fall saved his life. He landed hard, and bullets zipped over him and continued their journey into the grass. He stayed flat, trying to meld his body with the ground, pulling himself along with his fingers and pushing with his toes. The dust kicked up by the prop swirled in the air between him and the men in the grass who were trying to kill him.

He slithered into the shallow crater like a snake and hunkered down almost on top of Rusty—making it across the open ground without getting shot made him giddy. He could smell his own sweat . . . or fear . . . and hear Marsh's labored breathing. The air around them was solid with dust . . . his eyes and mouth were full of it. He thought he should say something, but his mind was filled with amazement that he was alive.

Rusty didn't open his eyes.

Trinh had the variable-power Redfield scope dialed up to nine power; he could see the individual drops of sweat on the black Yankee's face from 400 yards away. The imperialists had exploited yet another man from their oppressed minorities and sent him to die with the two white pigs; Trinh would gladly accommodate the Americans' efforts to kill the black man. Against the advice of his lieutenant, he decided he did not need to wait for an optimum shot. He released the safety and centered the crosshairs in front of the black man's ear.

Melher grabbed the front of Mann's flightsuit and jerked him lower into the hole. "Keep your head down, Billy. They shoot whatever shows." An eruption of dirt where Mann's head had rested underlined the warning.

Melher's face was almost touching Mann's. Dirt from the near-miss sprinkled over them; Melher cursed Mann for not leaving. "We've got a sniper out there . . . and that's the first time he's missed." The parentheses around his mouth, intensified by shock and dehydration, fostered concentric arcs that radiated across the nearly transparent skin of his cheeks. He let go of Mann and scrunched further into the hole. "I don't think I've ever been this close to anybody as dim-witted as you."

"Ain't that just like a nigger?" Getting chewed out by Marsh while being shot at was the ironical equivalent of having to deal with a paper cut at his own beheading.

Mann wiggled around so he could unzip Rusty's flightsuit and pulled it away from his chest—a hole in his right side was letting blood out of his body at an alarming rate. He looked around for something to stop the blood . . . nothing. He scooped up a handful of the red dust and stuffed it onto the wound—the mudpack couldn't do him as much harm as losing the blood.

Melher uncovered his shoulder and said, "Put some on this." While Mann packed dirt into the hole in his shoulder, Melher cursed him again. "When we get back, I'm groundin' you for bein' stupid."

"Good. I hate this job." Mann tried spitting to add emphasis to his words, but his mouth was too dry. He ended up blowing more dust into his eyes.

Melher's lips came apart in something that resembled a grin. Apparently he felt that further debriefing could wait. He murmured, "I tol' you so," before he passed out.

On the ridge, the sniper was embarrassed because he wasted one of the precious bullets. The big plane was between him and most of the crater, and he let his impatience tempt him to try shooting the black American in the head. He promised himself he wouldn't miss again.

He made sure the rifle's safety was on and stood up; the tree would make a sturdy prop, and the additional height would let him see over the top of the plane.

Melher's eyes came open and moved to the airplane; he was remembering something. He tried to make his shoulder more comfortable while asking, "Where's Bainbridge?"

"He didn't make it, sir."

Melher absorbed that. "You won' either. Get in 'at plane an' get outta here."

"I'm here now, Marsh. I may as well take y'all with me."

There was something nagging at Melher that he couldn't figure out. "What'd ya do wi' Bainbridge?" Shock and blood loss collaborated to slur his words.

"Like I said, he didn't make it."

"Din make it?" The shock-bright eyes squinted at him. ". . . 's dead?"

"Yes'r."

Melher closed his eyes.

Zisst! Pop! A bullet clipped through the grass a foot from Mann's ear just before he heard the gun. The enemy out in the grass had found them.

Zisst! Pop!

Zisst! Pop!

Dern! Mann tried to press himself into the dirt. Guns sounded different when they were aimed in your direction . . . two more bullets, accompanied by the unrealistic "popping," thugged into the dirt revetment between him and the gunners. This was not like the movies.

The only things between them and death were fifty yards of dry grass, a little pile of dirt, and a long piece of sheet metal with an engine on one end. The men trying to kill them were getting too close.

The sound of the engine on the A-1, barely above idle, brokered formidable power. It sounded good . . . powerful . . . ready.

Mann said, "Marsh, this isn't going to get any better. If we're not going to stay here, we might as well leave . . . now."

Melher nodded without opening his eyes. "Set it up wi' th' air cover."

Mann thought, *What air cover?* He pulled out his emergency radio and spoke into it. "Three's up. What've we got, Doc."

Bailey answered immediately. "Bill? Are you okay?"

"I've been better. What's the status on the inbounds?"

"We got two F-4s, not four—they're on the deck less than a mile west of you. The A-7s are inbound—give them a few minutes. All the A-7s have is their guns."

"How about the Fox-4s?"

"The F-4s are Winchester, but they have play time. They think they can keep the bad guys ducking by making multiple passes."

"Roger, we'll make do with what they bring us." Mann was planning. "If we lose contact, you tell the F-4s to pickle their external tanks on these guys. Got that?"

"Roger, I copy that."

Two seconds later the radio said, "Gunfighter One-one is in the weeds."

At that moment the shark-shape of an impotent F-4 made an air-ripping pass down the northern edge of the strip, providing the only relief from the enemy's rifle fire. Gunfighter One-two was seconds behind him.

Melher had been silent while he tried to process what he'd been told about Bainbridge. He opened his eyes and looked into those of the younger man. "You shoot 'im?"

Mann didn't blink. "It's a long story, Marsh. I didn't want to kill him . . . I just didn't want him to shoot me."

The colonel closed his eyes again and nodded as if it made perfect sense for his best pilot to shoot an occasional lieutenant colonel. "You doan have to splain, par'ner." He sounded like a man who should have left the bar sooner.

"Yes, sir."

Marsh moved his knees sideways and tried to shift his body further toward the bottom of the crater. "He was gonna en' up dead anyway. You killed him 'fore he killed himself . . . couldn't fly a kite . . ." His eyes sagged shut. " . . . whadda jerk . . . shoulda shot 'im myself."

Mann turned his head and tried to spit out some of the red dust. "You need to save your wind, Marsh."

Melher nodded. "I'll blow 'im clear into next Sunday . . . 'f he comes back. Should'a shot 'im . . ." His eyelids popped open, then drooped. "Part of bein' a leader is del'gation . . ." he drew a breath, " . . . of 'thority. I'm faintin' . . . you gotta git my head down some," he wiggled his body a fraction of an inch in an unsuccessful attempt to get his head further into the hole, "so I can get some blood up there. Then get us outta here." He measured the distance to the airplane, then closed his eyes. "Wake me right 'fore th' bell, an' I'll help you drag 'im." The thin skin of Melher's face was the color of bread dough.

Unless he got them to Da Nang within the hour, both men would bleed out.

CHAPTER TWENTY-ONE

Richards was map-reading while Sherrill hedge-hopped the Huey over the lush, highly restricted greenery of Laos. Blurred jungle and fast-moving rice paddies took turns in the eyepiece of Ky's camera. Wainwright screamed directions.

Richards waved his cigar at a line of trees and muttered, "According to this map, it should be over that second ridgeline."

Sherrill nodded. He was smiling to himself, thinking maybe Wainwright's behavior was an act. This could be some elaborate joke of Parnell's—his CO's way of getting back at Sherrill for nearly destroying a helicopter with a homemade firebomb. The punitive action had to be a ruse because, as it turned out, the chopper in question was barely scorched. If the lanyard attached to the flares hadn't gotten tangled in the door-gun mount, the fuel drum would have been well clear of the chopper when it blew up, and Parnell never would've heard about it. Wainwright was probably a Green Beret.

Sherrill fought to keep the chopper on an even keel while they pitched and rolled in the choppy air; every bump slowed them. He absentmindedly cursed the machine and the turbulence equally, fighting the stick, punishing the engine, demanding more speed.

Wainwright had yet to fully grasp the concept of interphone communication; he leaned between the pilots and shouted at Sherrill, "Hey! I can't film back here if you're wallowing all over the sky."

It has to be an act, thought Sherrill, *nobody can be that stupid.* He countered that thought with the belief that the biggest part of the population of Hollywood could be used to argue that being around cameras destroys brain cells. He stabbed the mike button and yelled at Gomez over the intercom, "Gomer! What'd I tell you about letting this fool talk to me?"

Wainwright got the hint and turned back to the gun deck, yelling at Ky and pointing at a woman and child who were standing on a footpath watching the fast-moving chopper.

Sherrill pressed closer to the trees; foliage swirled in the chopper's wake; a single low ridgeline separated them from the action.

The radio in Mann's pocket crackled, but the transmission was garbled. He snatched it out and keyed the mike. "This is Sandy Three, say again?"

"Sandy Three, this is Raindance Lead with four. Sandy Four said to check in with you. How copy?"

That's more like it!

"Roger, Raindance, you're five-square. Say type aircraft, ordinance, and play time."

Melher's eyes were still closed . . . he was breathing in shallow gasps.

"Raindance flight of four Alpha Sevens. Sorry, friend, but we got the word late. We've got twenty mike-mike only . . . and we're short on gas. Four's a new guy and he's looking at bingo . . . we'll be Winchester after one pass and headed for the home drome."

The man trapped in the hole was matter-of-fact. "Roger, Raindance, everybody on this end of this godforsaken continent is Winchester, so having your guns may make the difference." He stayed in football games with more pain than his leg was giving him, but it was going to be stiff in a few hours. He measured the distance to his plane, thought for a second, and keyed the mike again. "Raindance, I need you to space for a six-second interval on the passes. Sandy One has lost too much blood—Icebag Nine is unconscious and doesn't look good. While you're hosing them down, we'll make a run for the Spad. We'll get Icebag Nine on board, and do the big 'adios trick' outta here."

"Roger on the pass interval, Three. We're coming up about seven miles to the east. We'll have you in sight in one, and we can make the first run in less than two minutes." The frequency stayed open while the A-7 pilot paused, then, "Sandy, we have a tally on you—uh, it's dusty down there . . . you're obscured. Where do you want the ordinance?"

"Make your runs west to east; your target is in the grass abeam and slightly west of the Spad . . . unmarked . . . keep the ordinance on the north side of the strip. And don't be shootin' up my airplane."

"Uh . . . Three, that's a little closer than we normally work with friendlies around."

"Well, we've got three choices here, Raindance; we get shot by you . . . or by these hombres here . . . or not at all." Mann squinted at the dense dust cloud behind the plane. "Just shoot as close as you can north of the thickest part of the dust cloud—the targets are in the grass at the north edge of the strip. Copy?" The spang and whine of a bullet's near miss added an exclamation point to the transmission.

In the lead A-7, Captain Kyle Meredith turned to his right, looked down the echelon formation at Raindance Three, and thumbed the mike button on his throttle. "Tip?"

Raindance Three, First Lieutenant Tip Clark, lifted his gloved hand above the canopy rail high enough for his flight leader to see . . . his thumb was up; his oxygen mask rose and fell as he nodded in the affirmative. Raindance Two had been in the theater less than a month; Four was on his first solo mission. They hadn't been asked, but they were both nodding.

Mann's radio crackled, "Sandy Three, this is Raindance One. If you need somebody to come close, this is the system to do it with. We'll be on you in one . . . using six-second intervals."

"Sounds good. Recommend you coordinate with the Fox-4s and Sandy Four. They'll pull off on your say-so."

"Roger that, Sandy Three. Okay, Raindance flight," Meredith started briefing his pilots for the passes they were going to get to make, "let's make it so. Recheck your arm select in 'Guns.' Make 'em hot an' check in."

The leader looked down at his own armament selector while the other pilots acknowledged his orders by transmitting their call signs.

"Two."

"Three."

"Four."

"Lead's hot." Meredith looked to his right at the three aircraft. "Two, you and Four haven't been in this deep yet. Take a breath now and imagine what you're gonna see when you start the strafing run. Take your time. If you don't like the picture after you roll in, don't fire. Got it?"

The pilots beneath the canopies of the second and forth airplanes both nodded. Lead noted the nods were slow and relaxed . . . deliberate. He liked that. "Okay. Stand by for a six-second interval on my break. Two, you and Four make sure you don't fire till the man in front of you pulls off the target." He turned back to begin the coordination with the airplanes that were already on the scene. "Sandy Four, this is Raindance Lead with a flight of four Alpha S . . ."

On the ground, Mann moved to put the transmitter in his breast pocket. The sound of the nearby rifle shot was drowned out by the bullet's impact with the handheld transmitter. The bullet shredded the radio and shards of hot shrapnel tore into Mann's arm and hand. If he hadn't been flat on the ground, the force of the bullet would have put him there.

Melher opened his eyes. He took a look at Mann's arm and cursed him for letting himself get wounded.

Wainwright stuck his head back into the cockpit in time to watch as Sherrill pulled the chopper up to clear a tree line at the east end of the battle zone. A McDonnell F-4C Phantom coming at them from the other direction filled the chopper's windscreen. Wainwright screamed and fell backward while Sherrill took evasive action to the right.

The F-4 flashed by on the left, its air-ripping scream drowning out Wainwright's. Sherrill righted his ship . . . and the two chopper pilots saw the A-1. The plane was sitting by itself in the middle of a wide field of elephant grass, kicking up a cloud of thick red dust, mixing it with a white phosphorus smoke screen. Sherrill banked slightly left and headed for the A-1.

When Wainwright could speak, he stuck his head between the pilot seats and screamed, "Are you nuts? I could've been killed!"

Sherrill keyed his mike and, without looking over his shoulder, yelled, "Gomer! If this guy talks to me again and you don't shoot him, I'm gonna scatter your body parts all over this end of the world and tell God you committed suicide."

Wainwright felt a hand close on the scruff of his neck just before he landed on the floor; his nose flat against his face, held there by Gomez's finger. "Gringo, you heard Jefe. You put your puss in that cockpit again an' you're a dead white guy. You savvy?"

Wainwright cringed and nodded.

The finger stayed where it was. "Say it!" snarled the Mexican killer.

Wainwright was versatile—he could read the intents of people almost as well as he could direct film. This Mexican gangster was willing to kill him. "I won't go near the cockpit again . . . ever." Gomez let go of his face and Wainwright scrambled over to Ky to resume his role as a news film journalist.

Someone was painting his arm with hot bacon grease. Mann forced his eyes open . . . the sky looked darker.

He forced himself to look down at his hand. His glove was shredded and blood was soaking through the sleeve of his flightsuit, but he could move his fingers and bend his elbow. The thought came to him that he should count his fingers, but he decided it would take too long. Melher was considering Mann's bloody arm through drooping lids, mumbling profane words—probably at him—before drifting off again.

Mann shook his head to clear it. *Well, it's not my right hand. So far, so good.*

The world around him was noise and dust.

I was out. If the fighters have already been and gone, we're in real trouble.

His eyes searched the sky to the west. The late afternoon sun winked off Raindance Lead's canopy; vapor trailed from his wingtips as he came around in a steep, high-G turn to line up for his gun pass.

He's only seconds out for the firing pass.

The A-7 rolled out of the turn, diving at the field. An F-4 passed between Mann and the hunters, clipping the tops of the four-foot-high grass at 500 miles an hour; the dead grass flattened like a shiny tan carpet.

Melher regained consciousness long enough to mumble a few fresh curse words at Mann then closed his eyes again.

Mann took the .45 in his holster and wedged it into his numb left hand. He willed his fingers to hold the gun, and they closed and held it; his finger put itself on the trigger. He nudged Melher. "Okay, Marsh, time to leave."

Melher rolled over and got his good hand under him.

This might turn out okay . . . he can move.

One of the men in the grass yelled something and stood up just before the Americans did.

Melher pushed up in time to catch an incoming bullet that tore a grove in his already wounded shoulder and knocked him to the ground; he rolled once and was on his feet and moving again before the other rifles opened up. Mann grabbed a fistful of Rusty's flightsuit, and he and Melher started stumbling toward *The Cool Woman*, dragging Rusty between them.

Mann didn't usually have nightmares, but the move to the plane was what they would be made of.

Too much blood ran from the fingertips of Melher's free hand. *Sonny boy, that right there is a real man.*

Step followed staggering step, but they seemed to get no closer to the plane. His lungs were burning as if he were sprinting. He listened to Melher's labored breathing and thought, *We can't make it.*

The grueling trek was not going to end.

The twenty-millimeter rounds came out of the approaching A-7 and sprayed the area north of *The Cool Woman* at a rate of ten per second. The man who shot Melher was the recipient of significantly more damage than he inflicted on the American. He and his compatriots dropped back into the grass. The shrill howl of the gun ceased.

They were finally getting near the plane.

Mann felt Rusty's body being snatched from his hand. He looked to his right and saw that Melher had gone down again, taking Rusty with him; when Melher rolled over, the front of his flightsuit looked bloodier. They were short feet from the plane's fuselage.

A continuous and concussing bwhop-bwhop-bwhop pressed at the outer limits of Mann's world. *A Huey?*

He didn't have the time or energy to check.

Sherrill was still over a 100 yards from the trio on the ground. Wainwright, his cameraman, and Lieutenant Colonel Parnell were forgotten. The heat from the ground stirred the air and the chopper jerked and twisted like a cantankerous horse. Sherrill cursed in earnest and fought the controls to give String a steady platform for the M-60.

Khanh Boi Ky was in the door beneath the barrel of Stringbean's machine gun; he had his camera pointed at the black man struggling desperately to get the two white men to the big plane. The thin material of blood-covered flightsuits snapped and whipped in the hurricane of dust generated by the A-1's big propeller. The black man knelt over one of the men and pulled him to his feet; the third man was facedown in the dirt.

The lenses gave Ky a perspective he didn't want. He was no longer taking pictures of trees and rice paddies; he was living in a scene so horrifying—so grisly—it didn't seem real. He was filming the last seconds of three men's lives . . . and the helicopter was moving closer and closer to the shooting.

Catholicism, brought to Viet Nam in the days when it was French Indochina, had a strong presence in the country and Ky, a Buddhist, spent many hours debating religion with his Catholic cousin. Today, while he watched men being killed, he wondered if he would ever see his family again. He felt helpless because he, unlike his cousin, had no saint to whom he could send a petition for help; and his weak memories of his cousin's prayers refused to strengthen themselves. Gautama Buddha never claimed that he was willing to intervene for the cause of good . . . which meant Ky was forced to seek the support of the God left behind by the French when they fled.

Stringbean stole a slice of time from the scene in front of him to check on the man crouching at his feet. Ky was clinging to the camera with one hand while he touched a finger to his mouth, then—in rapid succession—to his left shoulder, stomach, right shoulder, and nose. String conceded that the oriental mind was a strange thing and gave his attention back to things he understood.

Mann knelt, helping Melher struggle to his feet. He got his good arm around the man's waist and two-stepped him like a weary dance partner the last few feet to the plane. They were at the base of the wing when the Huey got close enough to add the power of its rotors to the pall of dust created by the Skyraider. Neither of the dancers looked up.

The piercing whine from the first A-7 as it pulled up from its firing pass was accompanied by a simultaneous eruption of dirt caused by the cannon fire from the second plane. Mann looked up to note that Raindance Two cut it just a tad close.

Two shooting passes to go. Gotta get a move on.

Dirt was still sprinkling on everything within 200 feet when he felt the shock of the first bullet. He went to his knees by the wing root of the Spad. He wasn't hit, but he'd felt the shock . . . Melher must be hit again. He stopped to get his breath . . . everything that wasn't dirt was noise.

He got both of his arms around Melher and propped him against the plane . . . the Skyraider was between them and the shooters now . . . bullets made hollow spanging sounds as they punched holes in the thin metal of the airplane . . . Melher managed to get a hand on one of the handgrips . . . he opened his eyes but didn't focus them . . . the rain of dust and dirt subsided.

That's not good. Where's Three?

The answer to his question came audibly in the form of a scream from the grass . . . and visually from a reenactment of the previous explosions of dirt and dust. The supersonic 20-millimeter rounds hit slightly before their accompanying throaty whine. What a beautiful sound.

He jammed the .45 behind his belt next to his spare and grasped a handhold with the free hand. He had Melher almost on the wing . . . not far now. The bullet clipped the back of his calf . . . his feet went out from under him . . . and he hit the ground hard.

Someone's blood dripped from the wing and splashed in the dirt in front of his nose. The fourth A-7 made its pass and pulled off to the east, heading for home.

The two North Vietnamese Regulars peered at the black man from the edge of the airstrip, watching as he pushed himself to his knees.

The first bullet nicked Mann's ear and saved his life. He jerked away from the sting and opened his mouth to yell just as the second bullet entered his face near the corner of his mouth. The high speed projectile shattered several teeth and tore a ragged notch in his upper lip when it exited. Time took an intermission behind the effect of the car-crash blow.

Awareness drifted back to Mann, telling him he was watching the red dust mold itself into ghosts. The apparitions gained substance and became two indistinct figures, their black clothes pinned against them as they leaned into the propeller's wind. Flashes of orange reached out to him from the muzzles of their rifles. They were yelling something.

He was still on his knees. He didn't remember pulling the pistols, but they were in his hands, tracking in front of him as he swiveled to meet the latest threat.

Both pistols fired, and dust bloomed from the chests of the men. He triggered the guns again. The man on the right faded back and melted into the dry storm; the one on the left staggered, his feet crisscrossing in a slow motion, shambling walk as he continued to close on the black Yankee.

Mann brought both pistols to bear at point-blank range and squeezed the triggers into an expanding explosion of color from the man's rifle. The impact of the incoming bullet drove Mann back and down. The soldier took two more steps toward the pilot, grinned, and pitched forward to land on top of him.

Sherrill was a living legend, and Paul Richards had called in some big markers to get assigned to his crew.

They were hovering a 100 yards from the Skyraider when the final shootout took place. More North Vietnamese were concealed out in the maelstrom of dust and grass, but it was impossible for the helicopter crew to intervene. The Huey's skin was no thicker than a beer can; if Sherrill tried to put the chopper on the ground with so many enemy troops in the landing zone, he'd be turning it into a stationary target with no protection from incoming enemy fire, and they'd all be dead before String could empty his door gun. Even living legends can't do the impossible.

The black guy was down and the guy he'd dragged to the plane was still. The man on the plane's wing lay unmoving, surrounded by a pool of his own blood. Sherrill and his crew had held out hope till the last, but the battle at the dusty little airstrip was over. Richards stared at the men splayed on the ground around the plane's wing and helped Sherrill cuss.

Sherrill made himself quit looking at the bodies and began to guide the chopper away from the danger zone as he spoke into the intercom. "Pick your shots, String." The voice on the intercom was calm. Decided. Funeral-quiet. "If they come out of the grass for our boys' bodies, I want you to kill every mother's son of 'em, understand? I don't want to carry a single bullet back to the pad."

Stringbean didn't feel like talking. "Done."

CHAPTER TWENTY-TWO

The smoke and dust were a hindrance for Trinh, but his view of the struggle was improving by the second. The American fighter planes brought destruction to his friends in the field, but with each pass the swirling air generated in their wakes served to hasten the dissipation of the smoke screen. On the far side of the plane, a rifleman in a black uniform was spread-eagled across the body of the black American; only a small portion of the black man's face was visible. But for a bloody arm, the white man on the wing was hidden from Trinh's sight by the aircraft's fuselage. The man he had shot in the chest was near the black man, facedown in the dirt, partially protected by the plane's wing; there was no reason to waste a bullet on him. He moved the scope back to the black man's face in time to see the bloodied lips move. If the black one managed to get to his feet, he would shoot again. For now, he would wait. He was patient.

The two F-4s had been holding northwest of the valley. "Sandy Four, Gunfighter One. You ready for us to go back in?"

"Gunfighter, you might as well pull off; it appears the good guys aren't going to make it."

The lead Gunfighter looked out at his wingman and asked, "Whadda you think, Two?"

"Negative, negative, negative." The wingman shook his head and fading sunlight flashed on a white helmet with a crimson visor cover. "I know that guy on the ground," he drawled, "an' he ain't dead till I put my hand on his tombstone."

"Whatever you say, sonny," Gunfighter One acknowledged. "Sandy, say the word, and we're in. We've got full externals—we'll skip-bomb our tanks then come back around for a burner pass and see if we can torch the fuel."

"Sandy Four, roger, sir," Bailey drawled. "If you incinerate them all, I will be long in your debt."

Vapor trailed from his wingtips as the lead F-4 turned to line up for another run at the grass. The fighter passed over a small hill at the west end of the flat valley traveling at 500 knots and dropped to twenty feet off the ground. At the chosen spot, the external tanks left the aircraft, tumbled end over end, and ruptured when they hit the ground; hundreds of gallons of fuel sprayed itself over the landscape. The second F-4 was starting his run as his leader pulled up.

The second fighter dropped his tanks and pulled up, spacing himself far enough behind his leader to avoid his jet wash on the next pass. Minutes later, Bailey watched as Gunfighter One topped the small rise again, dropped to grass height, and selected afterburner.

Gunfighter One told his wingman, "Aw right, sonny, smoke if you got 'em."

The wingman moved slightly to his left for better flame propagation and moved his throttles into afterburner. His airspeed indicator was moving rapidly up the scale as they closed on the area where the fuel waited.

The leading F-4 passed fifty yards from two North Vietnamese soldiers preparing to shoot at Mann. The riflemen stood while the grass around them was still pressed against the ground in the plane's trailing wake.

Gunfighter Two, seconds behind his leader, was brushing the tops of the grass and setting it on fire with his afterburners. Two's back-seater was gripping the handholds and carrying on a running commentary of what was happening on either side of their flight path. He checked the left side in time to see an explosion of pink that became a pair of wide red accent stripes blowing back across their wing. Before he could speak, they were in a six-G climbing turn at the east end of the little clearing.

The wizzo tightened his lower body to help his G-suit offset the forces pushing his weight above the half-ton mark and spoke in an affected British accent, "I say, Fat, old bean," he grunted, "we apparently struck a pair of pedestrians."

Fat was looking back over his left shoulder, keeping the lead aircraft in sight. "That's what they get for standing in the street," he growled.

"I think it likely those chaps were possessed of hostile intent."

"Well, I hope to kiss a pig." Fat Chance took his eyes off Gunfighter One to check his wing and cursed. "Do you see what those Yankee drummers did to the leading edge of my wing? Who's gonna pay for those dents?"

"Frightfully scandalous, don't you know." The F-4 was at the top of its climb, inverted over the grassy field; the backseater was looking at the world through the top of his canopy. Gray-white smoke drifted out of a widening boulevard of fire lanes beneath them. "My, my, my. I think you touched off a fire in that garden we motored through."

Fat pulled the throttles out of 'burner and rolled the aircraft level. "Like Momma always said, I was born to be a pyromaniac."

String was the first to see him move. "He's gettin' up."

Sherrill jerked around and looked at Mann in time to see him push the dead soldier's body off.

As long as the Spad pilot stayed low, the dust blown up by the prop and the smoke would keep him hidden from any of the enemy who were more than a few yards away. "String!"

"Yo!"

"Seed that grass to keep the bad guys down. Our man just might make it."

The killers in the grass were not the problem. The sniper was waiting, patient as a coiled cobra. He was the problem.

Trinh didn't have to hurry. The black pilot would eventually have to climb onto the airplane's wing—when he did, Trinh would send him to his ancestors. He wiggled to get more back support from the tree and waited in the cool shade.

In the chopper, Ky watched through his telephoto lens as the black man made it to his knees. The pilot looked at the guns he was holding as if he wasn't sure what they were, then stared at the dead soldier on the ground in front of him. He swayed, recovered, and shoved one of the guns behind his belt; it took three tries to get the other one stowed in its holster. He looked at the pilot lying three or four paces away for a long moment then started for him, crawling. To Ky, it looked as if the would-be rescuer couldn't make it. The man who should be dead would move a hand, wait, move a knee, and wait again. When he got to the other pilot, he took him by the wrist and started backing in the direction of the airplane, crawling an inch at a time, moving more slowly than the sun. Ky sweated and mumbled words of encouragement. The unconscious man's wrist slipped through his rescuer's grip uncountable times. Every time the black man lost his grip, he tilted sideways into the dirt. Ky would mumble, and the man would eventually make it to his hands and knees again. The black man would take his friend's wrist one more time—every time—pulling, slipping, falling, resting, getting up, pulling . . .

Mann was on the wing of the Spad with Marsh propped by the canopy rail when he recovered some sense of where he was. Pieces of time were missing.

I've got to get Marsh into the cockpit . . . he's slicky . . . he's got blood on him.

His?

Probably.

Who cares?

I care, I guess. There's not enough to go around . . . or maybe there's too much.

It's everywhere.

Who's gonna clean up this mess?

Melher appeared to be dead, his whole flightsuit was blood-soaked. Except for bloody smears, the taunt skin on his face was a color match for the gray-white smoke rising off the grass. *He's too white.*

That's okay, isn't it?

It was taking a long time to get the man over the canopy rail and into the seat. Melher didn't care.

A white man can't be too white, can he?

He shook his head slowly.

A black man can't be too black.

That's what Poppa told me. A man can't be too black, son.

Can a brown man be too brown?

What color is too brown?

What color is a coffee-colored Cadillac?

What was that woman's name?

Nelva Jean? Nelene? Something long? Lots of those pieces that make up long names?

Images of a man playing a guitar while duckwalking across a stage pulsed in front of his eyes and blended with those of a man in an airplane seat.

Why won't your feet go down there?

Oh!

C'mon, Marsh, you're in the seat backwards.

And they say black folks are dumb.

Pull him up . . . come on, Marsh . . . roll him over . . . too heavy. How 'bout a little help here, Marsh?

Black folks do all the work.

What's that called?

Another long name for a word.

There. Now you can see where we're goin'.

Thank you, Jesus. You do good work. You're black, I bet.

He turned to pick up Rusty, but he had disappeared.

Rusty?

If I lose him, Jane'll kick my bootie.

Hey, Rusty?

Where'd that boy go?

If he's smart, he didn't come here.

I must've dreamed he was here.

I hope I dreamed I was here.

Oh! There you are. I was almost standin' on you, boy.

You've been up here all this time?

I don't know how you got up here, son, but you sure saved me a lot of trouble.

We don't need to tell Jane I lost you there for a minute, okay?

No sweat.

No blood either.

Well, some blood.

Is that funny?

No tears.

That's funny, isn't it?

He wrestled the canopy open on the blue room then pushed and shoved until he dumped Rusty in.

Have you there pretty soon, bro. He reached in and patted Rusty's head. *Have us a beer at the club. Get Pip and Jane to keep us beered up. Sit by the pool like we used to. Work on my tan.*

He spit out blood and crunchy bits of teeth.

I could use the rest.

Maybe they'll let us take a nap.

He stooped over, his hands on his knees, to catch his breath; much-needed blood flowed to his brain. At some point he secured the canopy over the aft compartment and stopped again to rest.

The black one didn't stand up straight after he got the other two in the plane. And the angle was wrong, but Trinh could change the angle.

He checked to make sure the weapon's safety was on and moved to the side of the tree.

He lined up the scope and watched the black American—he was on the other side of the big airplane, bent at the waist. From where Trinh was, he had just enough elevation to see over the part of the machine that shielded his target. He wouldn't miss again.

The black man moved a few inches to the shooter's right and leaned against the side of the plane.

While his enemy rested, Trinh flicked off the rifle's safety and, exercising extreme care not to touch the trigger, eased his finger through the trigger guard. He had already wasted one bullet when he attempted to shoot the man in the head—a pride-motivated act for which he was painfully ashamed.

He wanted to see the black demon's chest in his scope.

Out in the grass, the sniper's friends were taking quick potshots at the pilot.

Exhaustion and shock dulled his pain. The Huey's bwhop-bwhop-bwhop and the muted thunder from the Skyraider were blocked from his come-and-go consciousness. He used the side of the plane to lower himself to his hands and knees—he had to get his head down so blood would flow to it—and forced himself to open his eyes. The side of the airplane was smeared with engine oil and drying blood. Cold was soaking into him, causing him to shiver.

From the past, a picture pressed against his memory . . . he was a young boy, huddled in the backseat of an old car on a bitterly cold night. He was wrapped in blankets, hugging a redbone hound close, trying to find warmth where it was painfully scarce. Poppa's voice was saying, "Someday, when you all by yo'self, an' you needs help that can't nobody else give, you might just speak a prayer to Him. He loves you, an' He's waitin' to hear yo' voice."

Now or never, the thought drifted through his mind. *Such final words . . . now or never.*

He didn't know how long it took him to turn, but he managed to get to a kneeling position. He rested his head against the plane's side.

Poppa always assured him God could hear him whether he spoke aloud or not, but he was scared to take the chance. He held his fingers to the front of his mouth, trying to keep his lips in place. Blood ran freely through his fingers and added to the stains on the plane as he hissed painful words. "God, I don't know if You can hear this prayer 'cause I'm not a Christian . . . and I don't know much about how to pray . . . but I believe what Poppa told me. I've got these two guys who're depending on me to get them out of here, an' I've got me. We're all short on blood, especially Rusty . . . an' every gun on this side of the world is shooting at us. Would You keep us alive . . . or at least maybe them? I can't pretend to say I want to be a Christian, but I'll try to be a good man from now on. It wasn't Pip's fault she left me, God . . . I was going to be a sorry husband anyway."

Shock-induced fog curled through his brain, but he knew he was avoiding saying what needed to be said. He took a ragged breath and said it, "Poppa talked all those years about angels being here to help . . ." He opened his eyes and abandoned his prayer. *This is nothing but hypocrisy . . . and God knows it.*

In that moment his eyes fell on Marsh. The man drew a shallow breath . . . his chest shuddered when he exhaled . . . his flightsuit was bloody all the way to his knees. Mann closed his eyes and rested his forehead on the fuselage of the airplane. . . . He had to do this for his friends . . . he had to ask . . . he had no choice. "You're it, God . . . You're all we've got. If what Poppa said was true, You're all we need. Would You send us an angel . . . You and I know I'm a hypocrite, but is it okay for me to ask for that? Would You send just one angel to get us out of this sorry mess? Uh . . . please?" The man who had been shot while shooting his way out of a war within a war had what it took to feel sheepish when he added a soft, "Amen."

He got his good hand on the canopy rail and pulled himself erect. Out on the other side of the brown grass, he could see the green line where the jungle started. There wasn't any red dust over there. There was no eye-burning smoke . . . no wind. The shade inside the line of thick trees would filter out the world's noise. Up the slope . . . just a few dozen yards . . . a single tree stood by itself, spreading its limbs over its own peaceful little clearing. It looked like a good place to lie down and sleep for a week.

The sniper watched the black man straighten and allowed himself a rare smile. Patience is an honorable attribute.

"He needs to be getting out of there." Richards was leaning forward, looking across Sherrill at the Skyraider pilot. "What's he doing?"

Sherrill wasn't sure. "Don't know. I'd be prayin'."

Wainwright shoved his helmet-clad head into the space between the chopper pilots and yelled, "I've already spoken to you about this, Major. Are you going to keep it smooth up here, or not?"

Sherrill didn't even turn his head. "Gomer!" he yelled into his mike. "What'd I tell you about lettin' this fool near me?"

The black pilot was staring directly into Trinh's scope. Beads of sweat ran from his face to mix with the blood seeping between his fingers; he appeared to be bleeding from his mouth. Trinh centered the scope just below the man's head . . . or tried to. His line of fire was partially blocked by a tall blade-shaped radio antenna jutting from the plane's spine. In order to clear the appendage, he needed to be a short step to the right.

He took his eyes away from the scope to examine the ground near his feet, closely, carefully. Bare dirt and scattered leaves, nothing to trip him. His father would be proud of how patient his number one son had become.

He put his eye back to the scope to measure the result while he told his sandal-clad foot to shift a small step to the right, smiling to himself, celebrating the accolades he would receive.

The sidestep was not going to happen.

Trinh's sandal—pinned steadfastly to the ground for one single, finger snap of Earth's time—stayed right where it was. Trinh's body didn't.

A closer inspection of the ground wouldn't have helped; the unyielding sword pinning the sniper's sandal to the ground wasn't visible to Trinh's eyes . . . or anyone else's. The methodical sniper's center of gravity shifted to the right along with his body, but his foot wasn't there to support it . . . Sergeant Phan Chu Trinh was falling.

He instinctively tightened his grip on the gun. The rifle barrel tilted slightly, and his finger came in contact with what was—at one and the same time—the simplest but most unforgiving component of machinery within a radius of several dozen kilometers. The resulting action moved one piece of polished steel out of the way so another small piece of carefully-machined steel could do the job for which it had been created. The firing pin did its duty, and the match-grade projectile waiting patiently in the dark recesses of the rifle exploded from the end of the barrel ahead of a bright flash of burned powder and an eruption of man-made thunder.

Mann was looking directly at the rifle when the muzzle flashed, but it didn't register. The bullet passed well over his head traveling at approximately half a mile per second, roaring like a compressed tornado. It entered the open door of the helicopter, scorching the air between Stringbean and the cameraman, crossed the gun deck, and made its exit through the chopper's opposite door.

During its short stint on the stage of the chopper's gun deck, the tiny missile did only minimal mischief. It struck would-be Pulitzer-prize-winning news film journalist Archibald Sidney Wainwright IV somewhere in the back . . . and ushered pandemonium in to visit itself upon those in the vicinity.

The scream turned Sherrill's head in time for him to watch Wainwright launch himself away from the cockpit. The man's feet left the floor, his body twisted in midair before landing in a contorting heap on the gun deck. Before Gomez could get a hand on him, Wainwright arched his back to the point where he just missed banging his head on his heels. In one revolution of the helicopter's rotor, the film-journalist-turned-gymnast snapped into a crouch and launched himself off the floor. The fact that the metal ceiling in the chopper was about four feet from the floor kept the newsman's pain-charged performance from being anything to write home about. He crashed bodily into the ceiling, and with one hand on his rear and one on his head—his own scream offsetting the absence of a drumroll—he did a tucked, 360 degree spiral and finished with a mirror-image replication of his earlier ascent by crashing face-first into the floor. The back of his flightsuit was already bloody.

Sherrill, who thought himself beyond any capacity for amazement, was shaking his head in disbelief. *Well . . . just what I needed to round out a perfect day! Gomez shot the dadgum news fool just because I told him to!*

The gun deck was hosting a circus, with all three rings stacked in one spot.

Gomez stowed his rifle and bent over the wounded man, trying to see where he was hit. Wainwright was writhing around on the floor, snapping from side to side like James Brown on a pancake griddle, one hand clamped desperately to his rear and the other wrapped in the material of the big Mexican's flightsuit. The filmmaker, his eyes as wide and bright as a pair of small headlights, was screaming at the world in general, at Gomez in particular, and getting blood all over everything else. Gomez knelt over him, skidding around in the blood and trying to hold the man in one spot while fighting with the hasps on the emergency medical kit. Once every second or two, Gomez would abandon the battle with the kit, pry Wainwright's grip loose, and try to slap him. Wainwright would instantly reweave himself into the fabric of Gomez's flightsuit and his screams would go up an octave. Spent shell casings were spraying themselves over the blood-smeared floor because Stringbean had gone into business for himself. The door gunner saw the sniper's muzzle flash and was no longer interested in news cameras or used cars. His latest felt-calling was to use his M-60 to turn a lone tree over on the ridge into Laotian toothpicks.

Ky squatted in the door of the chopper, his lips moving incessantly, his words drowned out by the high-speed clatter of the machine gun; he aimed the camera with one hand and used the other to trace constant circuits around his upper body, stopping every few rounds to lick his fingertips. After each finger-wetting, because he couldn't recall his cousin's exact technique, he restarted the circle in the opposite direction.

Sherrill faced forward in his seat and shook his head. *Well, ain't this just great! My career is kaput because of a bona fide imbecile an' a trigger-happy Mexican!* The pilot's mind conveyed a Technicolor newscast of their reception—should they survive to make it back to their base. A fire-breathing Lieutenant Colonel Parnell would stride across the ramp, drag Sherrill bodily from the chopper, and cuss him till he couldn't catch his breath. Following that, the senior officer would rip off Maj. Sherrill's wings, pronounce him dishonorably discharged, then grab the nearest gun and shoot him until there were no bullets left. He waved for Richards to take control of the bird because he was laughing so hard he couldn't make his eyes stay open.

For the briefest twinkling of an eye, an imposing figure—quieter and more invisible than the most gifted sniper—stood amid the laughter, blood, screaming, and hail of shell casings and allowed himself a fraction of time to survey his handiwork and share in the moment's levity.

Wainwright, who had somehow missed out on the fact that this was an opportunity for amusement, decided he could scream more effectively if he got out of his helmet. The racket coming from him transitioned to one part screaming and one part cussing at Gomez.

The rest of the world retreated behind the discharge of sound, smoke, and empty brass casings from String's machine gun.

The situation near the small airstrip had steadily and unalterably deteriorated while Sherrill, who did not align himself with the belief that patience was a virtue, grew increasingly fed up with being a spectator. The bullet that hit Wainwright was the signal that the warrior's chopper was too far from the fight, and it was time to tip the scales. He keyed his mike and quit laughing long enough to yell over his shoulder, "Gomer! Is that fool gonna die, or what?"

Gomez didn't have an answer.

The Mexican finally threw the med kit aside and pulled a Ka-Bar combat knife from its sheath. When the knife came out, holding the wide-eyed Wainwright likened itself to trying to control a terrified whirlwind. Gomez held the knife in his teeth and got enough of a grip on Wainwright to flip him over. He held the James Brown impersonator facedown with his knees and slit the seat of the flightsuit open. A clean grove, approximately the size of a Bryan Brothers cocktail weenie, decorated the left cheek of Wainwright's peach-pink posterior—the guy could've gouged himself worse with a dull paperclip. Gomez looked up from his ministrations; his expression was the frustrated grimace of a hired killer who didn't sign on to play nursemaid. He held his thumb and finger a quarter of an inch apart and rolled his eyes at Sherrill. "Band-Aid stuff."

Wainwright saw the exchange but wasn't privy to what was said because, in abandoning his helmet, he deprived himself of his headphones. The Mexican who shot him was holding a bloody knife and scowling at the pilot; and the pilot was laughing hysterically. They hated him. Either he was going to bleed to death, or they were going to butcher him and throw his body out of the helicopter.

Sherrill wiped his eyes on the sleeve of his flightsuit; fun time was over. He keyed his mike and told Gomez, "Well, that means you can quit playing doctor. Both of you grab a piece and get in the door. We're moving down to the orchestra seats."

Gomez crawled across the floor and snatched up his M-16 while he shook his head and drawled Tex-Mex into the interphone, "Uh-uh, Jefe . . . no gun for the civvie. This fool'd tear up a bowling ball with a chicken feather."

Gomez was right. Sherrill said, "Fine! Get over there in String's door. If it's wearing black, kill it!"

Richards cinched his seat belt tighter and positioned his shoulder holster to make his pistol more handy. If they crashed, things were gonna get really hot, really quick.

Wainwright, who had not drawn a breath during the crew members' exchange, looked from the M-16 to the black eyes of the Mexican and shook his head rapidly back and forth. "Please don't shoot me again. Please . . . I promise I'll be quiet . . . I promise. Please don't kill me."

Gomez barely stifled his laugh; this gringo had the brains of a road lizard. The full lips below the mustache retracted to display white teeth; no Mexican bandito ever looked more sinister. He held a finger to his lips in a gesture for silence, winked at the man, then mouthed two separate syllables, "May . . . be."

The news film journalist stuffed his free hand into his mouth and clamped down on it.

Sherrill pointed at himself and told Richards, "I got it."

The chopper sagged abruptly to its right and skidded sideways, descending toward the action while Gomez was pulling himself to a standing position in the door. He flicked the M-16's selector to 'Auto' and grinned at String.

String grinned back and yelled, "It's Show Time, Muchacho!"

Mann was in the seat with his helmet on and no memory of how he got there. Noise and voices invaded his world from the earpieces in his helmet. The bwhop-bwhop-bwhop of the Huey approached from somewhere to his right. *How's anybody supposed to think with all this racket going on?*

He was tired of the dust.

Oughta write a dadgum letter about the condition of this dump . . . taxpayers' dollars down the drain.

The impact of the bullet threw him almost on top of Melher. He was hit somewhere on the left side of his body. He tried to pull himself up, but his left arm wouldn't work. *Well, that's just juicy . . . doesn't hurt though.*

He looked at the throttle quadrant for the right seat and smiled without moving his lips.

Humpf. Really cool black boys don't need but one arm to fly this thing.

God, if it's all the same to You, my body's running out of places to get shot.

He pushed up the throttle slightly with his right hand. The big airplane started rolling, moving out of the world of dust and smoke toward the end of the strip.

The riflemen watched the plane move and multiplied their efforts to stop it. Bullets hitting the airplane made familiar spanging sounds around him. The Plexiglas canopy showed a rapidly-thickening spider-web of cracks from rounds just missing him. The pilot looked around him, watching the heavy plastic disintegrate ten inches from his face. Mildly interesting.

A helicopter materialized between his plane and the men in the grass, matching his pace, providing a shield and offering cover fire.

Good job. Thanks, guys.

He tried to get his oxygen mask fastened, but gave up after the first attempt.

This is a sorry place for an air base. Nothing but dirt and busted glass. If we could get a little rain shower, it would get rid of this dust.

Who's that that does the thing to make it rain?

It's another color.

Green?

Bits of Plexiglas exploded from the canopy and ricocheted around the cockpit. His mouth felt like it had gravel in it. *Pieces of teeth.*

He spit out blood and chips of tooth enamel mixed with Plexiglas. The jagged remnants of his broken teeth hurt more than the wounds in his arm and legs.

Well, sports fans, we won't be needing a mag check here. If it doesn't get us off the ground, we'll auction it off to the lowest bidder . . . he shook his head slowly *. . . highest bidder . . . thing's got more holes in it than a screen door.*

He reached the end of the strip and turned the airplane, pointing it west. He used his good hand to bring the engine up slowly. As the aircraft gained momentum, he gave the throttle a final nudge to make sure it was against the stop and switched his hand to the stick.

Okay, big dog. Mush.

The helicopter disappeared behind him as he brought the power up on the A-1's engine; a pair of F-4s replaced it, slicing through the grass on his right. The enemy soldiers lay flat on the ground as the fighters screamed over them, clipping the grass three feet above their heads. The Skyraider lumbered down the dirt strip, gathering speed.

"Sandy Three, Doc. I'm coming up on your left wing, Bill." *Miss Amanda* pulled smoothly into her station on Mann's left, and Bailey grimaced. Mann's airplane looked as if it had spent the past month as a target on a gunnery range—its skin was stitched with ragged holes, its canopy frosted with cracks.

The words that came on the frequency defined pain and exhaustion. "Pigeons . . . Da Nang."

"Stand by one." Bailey glanced at his navigation instruments. "Da Nang is one-one-zero for five-four miles. Can you make it?"

Talking made his face hurt. Mann nodded once and started a wide climbing turn back to the east. A thin stream of smoke trailed from *The Cool Woman's* engine cowl, tracing her path through the turn.

CHAPTER TWENTY-THREE

Da Nang tower, Seahorse Five is three miles off the beach for landing."

"Roger, Seahorse Five, upon arrival, hold one mile east of the final approach course, one-seven left; Da Nang tower has a Sandy inbound with an emergency."

"Seahorse Five, roger." The Navy chopper pilot noted the smoke on the far end of the runway and said, "Looks like you're having that kind of day."

"Roger that, Five. We just had an F-4 abort and slide off the end with munitions on board. Standby one." Things were busy in the tower. When Da Nang wasn't experiencing a mortar attack by the Vietcong, they were trying to blow themselves up with their own bombs.

Dusk came to Viet Nam.

As he approached Da Nang, Mann was having a hard time keeping the world level. The lighted runway swayed back and forth in his windshield, a pendulum pretending to be a snake. Bailey's voice said, "Bill, you're wallowing a little. Hold your wings level."

Mann nodded and forced himself to center the stick. The runway continued its belly dance.

"Okay, Bill, turn two degrees right and stop turn. That's perfect."

"Sandy Three, Da Nang tower, you're cleared to land, runway one-seven right. We've only got one fire truck free right now. The rest of the emergency equipment will get to you when they finish putting out a munitions fire."

"Just hold what you've got, Bill," said Bailey. "You're looking good."

The A-1's landing gear was stuck in the wells—Mann would be making the gear-up landing Stretch McCullough promised him. As *The Cool Woman* approached the end of the runway, Mann released the stick long enough to shut down the engine and gentled the airplane onto the concrete strip. The world around him erupted into bright sparks and shrieking metal as the concrete shredded the plane's belly and ground off pieces of its prop. Midway thorough its slide, the plane departed the runway, leaving a shower of dirt and airplane wreckage in its wake.

Mann could smell smoke and aviation gas as the aircraft was shuddering to a stop. He managed to get Marsh's seat belt unlatched on the first jerk; his own was more stubborn.

"Tower, Seahorse Five. Uh . . . that Spad's smoking pretty good."

"Roger that, Five. Crash is on the way."

The young officer standing in the Navy chopper's cockpit nudged the pilot's shoulder and alternated between tapping himself on the chest and pointing at the crash site. The pilot nodded and keyed his mike. "Tower, Five. How 'bout if we go over there and let our guys pull the Spad driver out of the plane before the fire gets going?"

"Roger that, Five. You're cleared to air-taxi all runways, all taxiways to the A-1. The aircraft has three souls on board. Advise your men to use caution."

The Navy pilot had to smile. The man who wanted to go to the smoking plane was one of four SEALs he was transporting to Da Nang. Caution wasn't high on the list of things SEALs were famous for.

The Cool Woman was listing toward her crumpled right wing. Mann was using his good hand to try to release his seat belt when someone leaned into the right side of the cockpit and yelled, "Let us get this man first, sir! We'll come back for you!" Mann nodded and continued to work with the belt. His left leg was twisted at a grotesque angle.

The guy who took Marsh away was back in seconds. The cockpit was a disheveled bird's nest of twisted metal and wiring—and it was getting hot. "Can you move, sir?"

Mann pointed at his left leg and hissed, "Broken arm . . . leg."

"It's gonna hurt, sir, but we gotta get you away from here."

Mann nodded. "Mmmm."

He almost fainted when they moved him. They got him out of the cockpit and onto what remained of the wing. The flames from the engine compartment were short feet away. Mann was sprawled on the wing root, grasping the canopy rail and pointing his chin at the blue room. "In the back. Rusty first."

The SEAL shook his head, "We need to get you out of here, sir. We'll come back."

Mann gripped the canopy rail and coughed, "Rusty first, boys."

Two sailors found the latches for the blue canopy and lifted Rusty out. By the time the SEALs came back into the smoke to get him, Mann could smell the stink of singed hair.

The ambulances hadn't arrived and the Navy chopper was waiting; they loaded all three men in the back and took them to the helipad at the 95th Evac Hospital. Mann passed out in the chopper.

The corridor lights overhead were daylight bright. The wall moving by him was a white blur slashed by the red of fire extinguishers.

The man who had pulled him out of the cockpit was walking with one hand on the gurney, watching him. Mann stared back, squinting into the glare; the bright lights told the story. He hadn't been able to see the man's face back at the plane—twelve years had chiseled resolve and purpose into the features, but it had to be him. He strained to raise his head and beckoned the SEAL closer. "Name?"

The man put his ear next to the mess that had been the pilot's mouth. "Sir?"

The pilot's lips were almost useless for forming words, and moving his mouth hurt, but he took his time. "Wha's . . . you . . . name?" His effort freckled the rescuer's complexion with blood, but the SEAL didn't seem to notice.

"Lieutenant Sherman, sir."

The pilot barely nodded, satisfied. He let his head sink back and closed his eyes. "One outta two ain't bad, Sherman."

Two medics jogged out of one of the trauma rooms and got between Sherman and the gurney. "Okay, buddy, we got 'im."

Navy Lieutenant Tripper Sherman stood in the corridor and watched the doors swing shut behind the gurney. That black guy looked like someone set his face on fire and put it out with a crash ax, but he was definitely smiling when he disappeared into the operating room.

Sherman looked at the door and asked, "One out of two what?"

Sherman was gone when the next wounded man was brought into the receiving area.

Wainwright stopped screaming and cursing long enough to pull Ky aside. "You hold the film in case they have to put me to sleep to operate. Guard it with your life."

Surgery wasn't necessary. A corpsman stitched up Wainwright's wound and sent him on his way thirty minutes later. When he found Ky, Wainwright took the film container and tucked it under his arm. "Is there some place trustworthy where I can have it processed?"

Ky said, "I think I know maybe a place. He not speak English."

When they got to the tiny shop, Wainwright said, "Tell him to make one copy and not let anyone see it."

Ky turned to his uncle, speaking Vietnamese, "Don't say anything in English. Make the American one copy of the film and keep back ten for me."

The uncle nodded and did as he was told, plus making five copies for himself. Wainwright's dad picked up the tab for all sixteen copies.

CHAPTER TWENTY-FOUR

The man shifted his feet, moving his toes forward a fraction of an inch. Walls were erected in his mind, making him oblivious to all but the task at hand; his attention moved from the water glass by his desk back to the ball in front of his toes. Without being aware of the preparation, he took a breath and let his chest relax; the putter came back cleanly and started forward just as the nurse tapped on the door and stuck her head in. "Excuse me, Colonel. The general is on his way here from the flightline."

The ball and putter came together just outside the sweet spot, and the putt that would've marked his first-ever perfect run of fifty went wide by an inch. The golfer came erect slowly, stage-whispering a string of expletives as he straightened. He turned his exasperation on the intruder. "You made me miss."

The nurse was more frustrated than the colonel but couldn't show it. "Sorry, Colonel. You told me to tell you when he was en route."

"Humpf." Underlings always had excuses. He threw the putter on his desk and cursed again when it slid off the far side. "Do you, by some miracle, have everything ready?"

"Yes, sir." She was getting that bitter taste in her mouth . . . again. "The room is practically spit-shined, and we hung the curtains you picked out."

"Good. We want the general to see that his son is getting first-class care." He pulled on his sharpest-looking lab coat—a light tan, knee-length job with royal blue flight surgeon wings—and preceded the nurse through the door. "How about the starched whites for the nurse?"

"It's been taken care of, sir." Major Beth Brooke had been a military nurse for thirteen years, and this sorry excuse for a man was her bad luck charm. Colonel Jesse Franklin Middleton was far and away the most worthless doctor she ever heard about, much less had to work for.

Middleton—Colonel J. Franklin, M.D., on his embossed business cards—was an overly proud graduate of Harvard Medical School. The two gentlemen who beat him out for the last and next-to-last slots in the class standings had drug problems. Middleton's class rank was of little interest to him; he hadn't gone there to learn medicine but to get a degree with *Harvard* written on it. The government had agreed to pay his way through school in exchange for several years of indentured service. After he graduated, he was surprised to find he and the Air Force were a good fit. The gifted sycophant hid his shortcomings behind dedicated nurses and doctors, while using the coattails of senior officers to advance his career. He'd been promoted to full colonel and given the command role at the 95th because he was exemplary when it came to administrative duties, he looked good in a uniform, and he did well on the cocktail circuit. That he played scratch golf didn't hurt.

No one in the 95th Evac Hospital knew anything about Middleton's professional skills because he rarely bothered to come out of his office, much less practice that he failed to learn in med school.

When Brooke and Middleton entered the transformed hospital room, the golfer nodded his qualified approval. The only reason Rusty's hospital room did not look like a suite at the Plaza was because Middleton had not had time for the base carpenters to knock out a wall. The window had fresh curtains, and there were two comfortable chairs near the bed for the doctor and general to sit in and confer. The flower selection available in the Vietnamese market was pathetic, but he made up for quality with quantity.

He turned his attention to the nurse stationed by the bed. "Are you ready?"

"Yes, Doctor." She stood almost at attention, wearing a brilliant white uniform that appeared to have been heavily starched and carefully ironed seconds before he stepped into the room.

He stood in front of her like a drill sergeant and looked over the board-stiff uniform. "Very good."

The nurse didn't care about the doctor's assessment; she was the one who got caught short when she and her friends drew straws to see who would have to participate in Middleton's ridiculous dog-and-pony show. When the doctor turned to inspect the patient's bed, she rolled her eyes at Brooke. Middleton was a certified twit.

The Harvard grad was making sure there was no lint on the bed cover when he heard someone in the hall say, "Right in here, General." When the general stepped into the room, Middleton was holding Rusty's limp wrist in his hand and concentrating on his wristwatch.

The caring doctor rearranged the young officer's arm comfortably on the bed while he spoke. "Ah, General. Good afternoon, sir."

The general nodded without taking his eyes off the patient and walked to the head of the bed. The colonel accompanying the general stopped inside the door and stood against the wall.

Rusty appeared to be resting well, but his skin was near transparent. A pair of tubes ran from under the recently-ironed sheet to their proper destinations. The general was frowning. "Is he going to be okay?"

The flight surgeon adopted his this-is-a-very-serious-case expression and stepped closer to the bed. He opened a perfectly-tanned left hand and held it out by his side. The starched nurse stepped to a point one foot to his left and a foot behind him; she put the aluminum-clad binder she was holding into the outstretched palm with a precision not unlike what would be expected of a crack drill team. The smoothness of the file exchange helped the colonel relax. Middleton was confident the general would be impressed with his ability to run an efficient operation. That the general might not be affected was understandable; he was just a pilot. The doctors would run the hospitals, and the pilots would be brought here along with all those other people to be patched up, then sent on their way.

The light tan laboratory coat with the blue wings made a humming sound while it looked at the chart, then chose a this-is-no-real-problem tone for its response. "He's coming along quite well, General."

Middleton cleared his throat in order to add more gravity to his next words. "The only serious bullet wound ruptured his spleen. We've done a splenectomy—we removed his spleen—and it went very well. He's lost some blood, but he's out of danger. The bullet wound in his leg will be uncomfortable for a short while, but he'll be walking on it in a week."

The general missed the drill team performance because he hadn't taken his eyes off his son's face. The colonel waiting by the door wasn't missing anything.

Without looking up, the general asked, "What's his long-term prognosis?"

"He'll enjoy a full recovery, General." Middleton had received a full briefing on Rusty's condition from the attending surgeon. "Barring complications, he'll be back flying within three months."

The general relaxed for the first time in eighteen hours. He looked at the colonel who came into the room with him. The man nodded and held up a thumb.

The general looked at the doctor for the first time. "I'll be here for a few days. Is there anything you need from me?"

Yeah. I need you to make yourself disappear so I can get to Tokyo for my golf date. "Not a thing, General, thank you," Middleton answered warmly. "Is there something else I can do for you?"

The general took another look at his son. "Will he be asleep for a while?"

"For at least another day, sir." He bestowed an understanding smile on the concerned father. "Your son's getting his strength back."

"Okay." He turned his back on the lab coat and started for the door. "Let's go see the kid who brought him in."

The kid that brought him in? Middleton, unlike the remainder of the military population in Southeast Asia, had no idea who the general was talking about. *How am I supposed to know who brought him in?*

Rusty's dad wasn't the only person who wanted to see Bill Mann. Half the pilots at Da Nang invented excuses to come up to the hospital and, after getting there, wanted to "say a quick 'Good job!' to that Sandy driver who brought those two guys out of Laos." The rumor about an available film of the rescue was gaining momentum.

Dodging land mines had been Middleton's specialty for twenty years. "If you'll excuse me, General, I'll look after some last-minute responsibilities here and catch up in a moment. Major Brooke, would you escort the general, please."

Beth Brooke hated Middleton, and she hated herself for continuing to bail him out of the unending string of tight spots he got himself into; she rationalized her behavior by telling herself that making him look good might get the fool promoted away from her hospital. "General, if you'll come this way, please? Lieutenant Mann is down the hall in room 114." She managed to give Middleton the information he needed; now all he had to do was find his way to Mann's room by himself.

Middleton would give them a thirty-second head start and then stride onto the scene to give another demonstration of his efficiency.

The colonel standing against the wall was at the general's elbow when they stepped into the hall.

Colonel Calvin Clark Jamison was the general's close friend and right-hand man. He had been covering the general's six o'clock position—his back—for almost twenty years. He was good at what he did.

As a second lieutenant, "Jamie" Jamison flew F-86s in Korea on the wing of this man whom he admired as much as any pilot he'd ever met. Back in the early fifties, the general was a young captain who shot down seven MiGs while Jamie covered his friend's six and bagged three for himself. In the intervening years, while Middleton was dodging justified retribution, the young captain Jamison protected rode the wave of a reputation for getting the job done to become the youngest brigadier general in the United States Air Force.

Jamie flew his first tour in SEA out of this same air base in '66. When the general took the fighter wing at Udorn, Jamison did his second tour as one of his squadron commanders. Jamie shot down two more MiGs that year to become an ace. He moved from Thailand to the Pentagon at his friend's invitation, again to be his go-to guy. He didn't know it, but he would be going to Luke Air Force Base in a few months to command the Fighter Training Wing; his Christmas present would be a general's star. He was a fighter pilot's fighter pilot.

Jamie touched his boss on the back. They stopped and let the nurse get ahead of them.

"He's an idiot."

The general looked back at his son's room. "That flight surgeon?" He hadn't been paying attention to the doctor.

"Yep . . . blithering."

"Okay." The general knew better than to waste time questioning Jamison's assessment. "Rusty's out of the woods. Let's handle one thing at a time. C'mon."

The room they stepped into was the same size as Rusty's, but that's where the similarity stopped. The room, patient, and nurse were all dark. No flowers. No curtains. No carefully placed chairs for conferring.

An oxygen tent covered the top half of the man on the bed. Tubes and wires, deployed in an organized maze, made their way back and forth to machines and bottles around the bed. Bandages swathed the entire left side of the patient's body; he appeared to be asleep, but he wasn't resting. The damp brow was furrowed, he struggled for the shallow breaths coming and going through bandages around his nose and mouth.

The nurse frowned at them with her finger at her lips. They tiptoed in and eased the door closed. She crossed to them and bypassed the head nurse to stand nose to nose with the general. The finger that had not moved from her lips and the eyes that were locked on his told him to keep his mouth shut. He motioned at the man in the bed and looked a question at the petite barricade.

The attractive black nurse shook her head firmly. She was wearing yesterday's fatigues and today's I-don't-like-anything-about-this expression; she did not need starched whites or a big gun to validate her command presence. "He's barely under because he's not strong enough to handle heavy sedation. You'll have to whisper so you don't wake him. What're you doing in here, General?"

The general put his mouth near her ear. "He saved my son's life. Is it okay if I get closer?"

"No, you may not." She and the general both knew the nurse didn't say "sir" because she didn't want anyone to get confused about who was going to make the final decision. "You can come back tomorrow,

General." She looked at her patient. She was worried. "If he manages to live twenty-four hours, he'll be a lot stronger."

The next day, Middleton, who had chosen a white lab coat because it communicated a commitment to excellence in medical care, escorted the general to room 114 and opened it with a quiet flourish. When Middleton saw the black nurse standing by the bed, he slowed. She held the same emphatic finger to her lips and motioned them in.

Middleton stepped aside and allowed the general and Jamison to enter first. The black nurse had spoken firm words to him on more than one occasion, and he decided to avoid contact with her while he worked on getting her transferred.

The oxygen tent was moved aside and the head of the bed was elevated slightly.

The general walked to the nurse's side so he could be near the patient. The hospital commander stopped at the foot of the bed and spent his time evaluating the general's tailored flightsuit. The sky-blue color would look good against his own deep tan. He'd have his tailor in Tokyo whip him out a couple on his next trip.

The nurse leaned close to the general. "Don't get too near him, sir," she whispered. "Catching the sniffles could kill him." As an afterthought she added, "His name is Bill Mann."

The general nodded without speaking. He knew Mann's name.

When the general's son was still instructing at Willie, Rusty called more than once to tell his dad all about Lieutenant Bill Mann. At one point Rusty said, "You wouldn't believe it, Dad. He's barely got fifty hours in the Tweet and he can do things with it that almost defy physics . . . and he makes it look effortless. The other IPs are trying to scrounge rides with him just to watch him work."

Muted sunlight snuck past the venetian blind, glittering off a thousand tiny beads of sweat covering the exposed areas of Mann's body. Parker closed his eyes and prayed silently, *Father God, I ask that You remind me to be forever thankful for the gift of our son's life. And, Lord, let me never forget that You used this man to bring him back to us.*

As if in answer to a soundless call, Mann's eyes opened. He looked straight at Middleton. His eyes took in the man's white lab coat and seemed to drift of their own volition up to his face. No one he knew.

A vaguely familiar voice said, "Well, you're back."

Kaycee?

The gauze-wrapped face turned slowly in the direction of the nurse. She smiled but didn't move to touch him.

Someone next to Kaycee shifted and the movement attracted Mann's gaze. Slightly out-of-focus eyes fastened themselves on the second strange face for a long moment. While he stared at the general, what could be seen of the patient's face began to register mild surprise. He closed his eyes for a moment as if to wipe them clean and fixed them back on the general . . . he could see a picture of a man standing by a tin building. One finger wavered in a struggle to lift itself from the white sheets. "I . . . know . . . you." The words had barely enough airflow behind them to push past the bandaged mouth; the voice was cracked and dry. Singed eyebrows worked their way toward each other in a slight frown as the pilot tried to organize a search of his memory.

The general smiled and started to straighten as if from beneath a load. He was relieved that the kid was awake enough to recognize him. It was a good sign. "That's right, son. I'm—"

The pilot who had been a first lieutenant for less than six months interrupted the general officer. ". . . showed me . . ." He stopped to breathe, then forced out, " . . . picture" another breath ". . . gin." Lights behind the eyes brightened for a second, then started to fade. "Bobby . . . Lee . . . Parker." The eyes went out of focus and closed. The brow smoothed.

The hospital commander hesitated. He wanted to say something, but he was aghast. The fact that the young black man had called General Parker by his first name might reflect poorly on the hospital's reputation . . . his reputation. Immediate and thorough damage control was needed.

"General . . ." he started, but General Parker held up his hand.

Parker stepped away from the bed and paused by Middleton to whisper, "I'll be right back, Colonel." He stepped into the hallway. Jamie followed.

The general leaned against the wall by a butt can, his arms crossed. Jamison stood facing him. "You doin' okay, Bob?" asked Jamison.

Parker straightened and took out his cigarettes. He put one in his mouth before answering. "Mmm . . . better now. I guess it took a lot out of me to see what that kid paid to get Rusty back . . . and Marsh." He brushed at a tear then reached into the sleeve pocket of his flight-suit for his lighter.

A Navy lieutenant was making his way through the hallway toward them. When he saw the general, he slowed, then came closer and stopped. "Excuse me, General." He took off his hat and stood straight. "General Parker?" He looked expectant.

"Relax, son." Parker paused with his fingers in the sleeve pocket. "What can I do for you?"

"You're from Allen County, aren't you, sir . . . from Moores Point?"

It happened often enough—young airmen from the Mississippi Delta who recognized him and wanted be able to brag to their buddies that they were "old friends" with a general. The Navy lieutenant, though, was wearing the SEAL trident, and he didn't look like the bragging type. Parker smiled and offered his hand. "That's right, son. Are you from around that part of the country?"

"I am, sir." The SEAL had a firm handshake. "In fact, my dad, Hunky Sherman, used to work for Old Mr. Parker at the Indianola Compress."

"Of course," Parker smiled and went back to his sleeve pocket in search of his lighter, "and that means you'd have to be Tripper."

"You called it, sir." Sherman barely smiled.

Parker introduced Sherman to Jamison and the two visited while Parker occupied himself with the cigarette-lighting operation.

The general gave up on finding the lighter where it was supposed to be and expanded the search. He looked down at one of the flightsuit's chest pockets and was reminded that the leather nameplate over his heart was written in fairly small print. Parker pulled his lighter out of hiding and looked back at Sherman while pointing down the corridor. "Say, Tripper? You couldn't see my name tag from over there. How'd you know who I was?"

Sherman half-smiled. "Sir, if you don't mind my saying so, you look more like Mr. Bobby Lee than he does."

He's right, thought Parker. People back in Mississippi told him more than once, "You look like Mr. Bobby Lee just spit you outta his mouth."

"Well, it's good to see you again, Tripper." To make conversation, he asked, "Do you have a buddy in the hospital?"

"No, sir, not really." He waved his utility cap at the door to Mann's room. "I came to check on Lieutenant Mann . . . the pilot in room 114 there."

"Mmm." Parker looked down to flip open the Zippo lighter. "He a buddy of yours?"

"No, sir. I just wanted to ask him a question."

"A question?" Parker looked up. "But you said he's not a friend?"

"I never saw him before the other night." He gave a brief account of Mann's crash, minimizing his role in the subsequent rescue.

No one told Parker how his son got out of the A-1 wreckage. "Tripper, one of those pilots you men pulled out of the Spad was my son . . . Rusty Mattingly. If there is ever any way I can repay you, you let me know."

"I appreciate that, General, but it was no big deal."

They were silent for a moment while Parker and Jamison gave more attention to Sherman's face. The SEAL's eyelashes and eyebrows were showing the aftereffects of too much heat; the skin on his face and the backs of his hands was red and peeling. "You said you wanted to ask Lieutenant Mann something?"

"Yes, sir." Sherman frowned. "We were rolling him down the corridor on a gurney, and right before he was rolled into one of those trauma rooms, he pulled me close and asked my name. When I told him, he said something that didn't make any sense. Maybe he was in shock, but I just wanted to ask him about it."

Jamison, who had been mostly silent up to that point, asked, "What'd he say?"

"Well, sir," said Sherman, "I told him my name, and he said, 'One outta two ain't bad, Sherman.'"

The lighter was on its way to the cigarette in Parker's mouth when it stopped. A puzzle he hadn't known existed was going into business for itself; it took the responsibility for the retrieval of all the necessary pieces and assembled itself in his mind faster than he could record the thoughts.

Bob Parker's call sign was "Beep." In the beginning it was a conjunction of his initials; it eventually stuck because Bob Parker, like the Roadrunner, put a lot of stock in the advantage given by speed. No one called him Bobby Lee . . . no one ever had. Before saying the name of Parker's father, Mann said four words—"showed me," "picture," and "gin."

He snapped the lighter closed and stowed it in its proper place while giving their surrounding a casual once-over. The corridor was large-hospital busy with the comings and goings of patients and medical personnel. A lone black airman stood outside an office a couple of doors away, out of earshot, munching on some Oreo cookies and drinking a Dr. Pepper . . . unnoticed.

Parker dropped the unlighted cigarette in the butt can and took Sherman and Jamison by the arms. He said, "Let's walk outside and get some air," while ushering them toward a nearby set of doors.

As they passed through the doors, Sherman was figuring out what the general already knew.

The airman with the Dr. Pepper strolled to the entry doors and watched the trio move across the grass and stop near an unoccupied staff car. The general lit a new cigarette while the Navy lieutenant took his sunglasses off and wiped his eyes on the sleeves of his utilities. The tall colonel had his arms crossed, seemingly waiting for something.

Sherman dried the tears on his cheeks and turned to Parker. "It's him, isn't it?"

"You're dadgum right it's him." Parker was staring at the ground by his feet, rolling the cigarette back and forth in his fingers; his grim expression was a match for Sherman's.

Jamie Jamison didn't know what Parker and Sherman were talking about, but he'd find out soon enough.

Parker turned to him and said, "You and I have talked more than once about Billy Prince's wife—his widow—getting killed on Parker land back in M'sippi."

Jamison grimaced. "I remember. A gang of white thugs trapped her and the kid out in the woods on your dad's place . . . about a month after Billy died."

Parker blew smoke at the sky. "And I told you a kid stepped away from the gang and took up for Cherry and Bill Junior."

Jamison thought he had it figured out. He looked at Sherman and said, "Yeah, the youngest one in the bunch stood up to the leader and took a beating just like Cherry and Bill Junior."

"You got it," said Parker. He pointed at Sherman and said, "This is the man who stood up for what was right."

He turned to Sherman, explaining, "Jamie and I and Billy Prince were squadron mates in Korea and for a while at Luke. His call sign was "Wild Bill" because he was a consummate gentleman on the ground and aggressive in the extreme in the air. He was as nice a guy as I ever flew with . . . and Cherry walked on water."

Sherman sighed, "And that's his son in there."

"Yeah." Parker looked back at the hospital. "That's the kid from Eagle Nest Brake."

After a short silence, Sherman asked, "What do we do, General?"

"Nothing." Parker had been thinking. "We pick up where we left off. Bill Mann stays Bill Mann. Nothing has changed."

Jamison and Sherman nodded their agreement.

Sherman looked at his watch. "I need to be getting back to my boat right now in a minute, sir. Is that a problem?"

Parker shook his head. "That'll work fine." He started for the hospital entry. "I'm going in to check on our patient. You take care of yourself."

Jamison and Sherman shook hands and Jamie said, "I want to thank you for trying to help Billy's wife."

"I wish I could've done something to save her," Sherman said.

Jamison patted him on the back and pointed in the direction of the hospital. "Given the choice, Cherry would've wanted you to save the kid."

As Parker neared the hospital, the airman at the door turned and went back to his office.

On the way back to room 114, Parker tried to add up all the reasons he should be helping Bill Mann. They were uncountable.

The general stopped inside the door and let Kaycee beckon him to the bedside; Jamison followed him in and took his station against the wall. Parker leaned close and stared at Mann, forgetting he was transgressing into the restricted area around the patient. He wanted to touch the kid's arm but remembered the nurse's warning. After taking long moments to examine every exposed detail of the glistening face, he stepped back and nodded to himself. He beckoned the hospital commander away from the bed. When they were separated from the others, Parker spoke softly but firmly. "I want you to tell me this kid's going to be okay."

The administrator had taken fifteen minutes out of his morning to get briefed on the patient's condition, but the black pilot failed to address the general properly and damage control came first. He took a short step back and whispered, "Well, obviously he may be a little delirious for a while, general. He's stronger today and if he continues to gain strength, he should be fine."

"He should be fine?" Parker was facing Middleton with his arms crossed. "Half his body is covered with bandages, Colonel. Give me the details on what happens next?"

Middleton was almost in over his head and had yet to catch on that he was the source of the rising water.

"His mouth will be moderately disfigured, sir." He glanced toward the figure in the bed. "His left arm shows a previous bad break near the current one. It was set well the first time, but having the bullet hit there caused more trauma than it really needed—the shrapnel wounds will leave permanent scars. The damage to his leg is too extensive; when he's strong enough to survive the surgery, we'll have to take it off." He shrugged because that's the way the ball bounces. "We don't have the resources to fix it and trying to transport him in his present condition would probably kill him."

Jamie was right as usual—the guy was an idiot. The first thing they needed to do was save the kid's leg.

Middleton, banking on using Parker's southern drawl to bail himself out, continued, "I have to apologize for his conduct, General. Some of the—"

The general was caught off guard and his words came out sounding sharp. "What conduct?"

Middleton ignored the warning. He looked to make sure the nurse couldn't hear him and whispered, "He's black." He leaned close and kept his voice low. "It's not uncommon for the black boys to be frightened and react poorly to combat situations. I've personally seen—"

"Jamie." Parker's whispered interruption cracked like a green tree branch.

Several things about Parker's background—things the doctor couldn't possibly know—interlinked to alter the direction of Middleton's career.

When they were children, a skinny young black kid deliberately stepped into hell on earth to save Bob Parker and his younger sister from certain death. The black child—the only son of a man named Mose Washington—paid for his selfless act with his life.

Fifteen years later, while trying to protect his mother, a young black child killed two white men—and God intervened to give that same Mose Washington another son. Mose and the black kid vanished for twelve years, but the kid was back now—and he'd made his own trek into hell to save Parker's boy.

Mose's second son was still alive—and Parker's lifelong desire to somehow provide a payback was getting new life.

"Doctor." Colonel Jamison stepped up and touched the elbow of the man wearing the starched white coat with the blue wings. "Step out here in the hall with me."

Middleton was mystified. Something had happened right in front of him and he didn't know what it was. He looked at the general. Parker had walked away from him to be closer to the patient. Without moving his feet, the doctor turned a confused expression on Jamison. "What's going here? What did—"

"Right out here, please." Jamison changed the touch to a grip and moved toward the door. The doctor had to follow or be dragged. The nurse stayed where she was.

"Now wait just a minute—"

They disappeared and the door closed quietly. Colonel Jamison would be gone for five minutes. The well-tanned golf player with the impressive collection of lab coats would be on a C-141 headed for Travis Air Force Base, California, in eight hours.

Parker looked at the nurse's name tag. "Lieutenant Gund, can you tell me the name of the most qualified doctor in this hospital?"

Kaycee Gund was trying not to smile. Without hesitating she said, "Dr. Schecker, General. Larry Schecker."

Captain Larry Schecker, outfitted in bloody scrubs and a sleep-deprived body, met Parker in the hall five minutes later.

Parker pointed at the door to room 114. "Doctor, I want you to tell me what we have to do to save Lieutenant Mann's leg."

"By your leave, General." Schecker sagged against the wall and slid down until he was sitting on the floor. He pulled off his scrub cap and rubbed his eyes and forehead with it while he talked. "It's like I told Middleton, General. The left leg is wrecked. I'm as good as we've got, and it's way out of my reach. And he can't be put on a plane in his current condition; it'd kill him."

Parker was ahead of the doctor. "So what do you need?"

Schecker waved the cap at Mann's room. "The kid needs a skilled orthopedist, and we don't have one."

"Who does?"

"The closest is in Tokyo. The best is at Hickam."

"What about the damage to his face?"

"Same deal, sir. It can be salvaged, but he needs a plastic surgeon. The face man at Hickam is the best in the west."

They talked and planned for five more minutes while Jamison took notes.

Parker asked, "Anything else?" but Schecker was asleep.

Parker and Jamison conferred quietly for several minutes; Schecker was waking from his catnap when they finished. He held out his hand and let the general pull him to his feet. The three talked another minute before Schecker went back to work.

Across the hall, the airman who had been watching Parker and his companions stood in the door of his cubby hole office, sipping a warm Dr. Pepper and listening. He'd been standing in the same spot for twenty minutes, waiting. When Schecker went his way, the airman walked over and said, "Excuse me. General Parker?"

Parker's first impression was that the black airman probably bribed someone to let him into the Air Force. His shirttail was hanging out in back, his eyes were bloodshot, and he had breakfast or lunch crumbs on his shirt. The airman waited while Parker looked him over. "What is it, Airman?"

"My name's Cleetus Love, General. I'm a doer, and you're gonna need one."

"A doer?" Parker thought he misunderstood the man.

"Yes, sir . . . just like in the movies." The kid spoke with a singsong Southern drawl. "I can do things you can't do. I know things and people you don't know. You and the colonel might pave the way, sir, but I know where to put the road. Right now you need to make some moves you don't know anything about, and you don't know who to call to make it all happen. No one in this outfit has time to help you, and they couldn't if they would. You need a doer, sir . . . and I'm him."

Parker had moved rapidly through the officer ranks due, in no small part, to the fact that he knew good people when he saw them. The airman wasn't brash; he was stating the facts. "What's your job here, Love?"

"Data processing, sir." He pointed at the cubbyhole office. "I run that antique abacus they call a computer."

Parker looked at Jamison and winked. Let's have a pop quiz. "Okay, Love. What would you do first?"

"May I speak frankly, sir?"

Parker thought he might've misjudged Love. The request to speak frankly was usually the preamble for a monumentally stupid remark. "Go ahead."

Cleetus took a deep breath. "Okay, General. First you have to have more clout; they're too many prima donnas west of California that outrank you, and you're stuck with having Da Nang for your base of operations."

Parker had some big moves he needed to make and a territorial squabble would slow him too much. He took more interest in Airman Love. "And you can solve this?"

"No, sir. But I know how you can."

"How?'

Love looked sloppy because he had been awake longer than Dr. Schecker. In the past forty-eight hours, since the moment he found out Mattingly's stepdad was a general, he made calls to his growing network around the world and discovered he was in the middle of a made-to-order opportunity. Lieutenant Mann saved Mattingly's bacon, Mattingly was Parker's stepson, and Parker was a fair-haired boy who worked for the chief of staff. This was Love's ticket back to the States. "You work out of the office of the Air Force Chief of Staff. He's been your boss on and off since Korea because he trusts you implicitly." He lowered his voice and started the hard sell. "Captain Russell Mattingly's real dad—your good friend—was killed in Korea in 1952. You married Captain Mattingly's mom before his sixth birthday. As far as you're concerned, you owe Lieutenant Mann your son's life. Most importantly, you're ready to shoot the locks off all barriers between you and whatever it takes to help him keep his leg."

Parker studied Love several seconds without changing expression, then asked the question Love would have scripted for him. "How can you possibly know all that?"

"Like I said, General, I'm a doer."

Jamison loved it.

"General, you need to know one other thing." Love took a breath. "I met Lieutenant Mann at Willie on his first day of active duty. He did me a real good turn, and I owe him pretty big."

"Don't we all, Cleetus, don't we all." Parker rested a hand on Love's shoulder. "Where's your desk, son?"

Fifty-five minutes later, the communications center at Da Nang had a copy of the same twix that went out to every Air Force command post in the world. Twenty minutes after that, the telephone receiver Love was holding to his ear said, "PACAF Command Post, Major Comstock."

"Major Comstock, this is Airman Cleetus Love, Da Nang."

"What can I do for you, Love?" Comstock made an entry in his phone log.

"Major, I need a C-141 made ready to come nonstop from Hickam to Da Nang in three hours."

Comstock stopped writing and threw his pen on the console in front of him. "Airman, if this is your idea of comedy, you're working the wrong audience."

"No joke, sir. You should be in possession of a priority-one twix from the chief of staff that was sent to your command post about twenty minutes ago."

"Just a minute." Love could hear the man speaking to someone else.

Comstock had never held a direct communication from the Air Force Chief of Staff, priority-one or otherwise. He read through the body of the message twice, and his heart rate went up ten points per reading. He came back on the line. "Okay, Love, I'm holding the twix. You want to tell me who the heck you are and what this is all about?"

"Roger, sir. If you'll read the twix, it stipulates that any words written or spoken by Brigadier General Robert L. Parker Jr. are to be attributed to the chief of staff, General Trelander, himself. The last line down there says that Airman First Class Cleetus Love—that's me, sir—is General Parker's authorized spokesman regarding all logistical operations to support the care of Lieutenant William P. Mann until such time as General Parker or General Trelander rescind the order. With regard to the expeditious implementation of a special support mission focused on medical care for Lieutenant Mann, my words are simply those of a messenger, but they are backed by the authority of General Trelander. It's signed by General Trelander. It's very clear, sir."

There was a momentary silence on the phone, a drawn breath, then a hesitant, "I don't know, Love, this is way irregular. We'll check things with the boss here, and I'll try to call you back in an hour."

"I'm sorry, Major Comstock, but you need to let me read you something else first. This is a handwritten note from General Parker that I've been ordered to read to those who initially fail to grasp the urgency surrounding this operation. If I may quote, 'To those individuals who do not immediately comply with the clear directions of General Trelander's message, know this: Airman Love is reading you this message because you have hesitated to carry out my orders and, in so doing, the orders of the chief of staff of the United States Air Force. Your failure to promptly comply with my lawful instructions is tantamount to the disobedience of a direct order from the chief of staff himself and will not be tolerated. If you do not immediately follow my directives, as read to you by Airman Love, you will be listening to me within five minutes, and you will not like any of the words that come out of my mouth. Our conversation will be followed by written notification that you and your superiors are looking forward to a soon-coming opportunity to explain yourselves to a general court-martial.' It's signed, Robert L. Parker Jr., Brigadier General."

Comstock became very human. "Good gosh, man, I work for a four-star general. What's he gonna say when I tell him I let some airman no-class in Da Nang have one of his birds?"

"That's why General Trelander sent out the news, sir. I guess you'll get to tell your CO you were saving him from a court-martial."

"Ouch." Comstock considered his options for one second. "Okay." He picked up his Air Force issue ballpoint pen. "Gimme the poop on this 141."

When Love finished, Comstock said, "Say, Love, does General Parker have any room on his staff for a recently-fired major?"

"I'll have to find out, sir. If you'd like, I can add your name to the list of people who've already asked."

"Where would I stand?"

"If he arranges them according to rank, sir, you'll be number eleven. If it helps, the list includes a pair of one-stars and a whole raft of full colonels."

"Oh, wow." Major Comstock felt better.

Three hours and another twenty phone calls later, an orthopedic surgeon, his team and equipment, along with a plastic surgeon and his entourage, were loaded into the cabin of Airman Cletus Love's C-141 and lifting off the runway at Hickam.

CHAPTER TWENTY-FIVE

After two weeks in the hospital, he wasn't feeling great, but he was feeling.

The orthopedist was back in Hawaii and wanted Mann there when he could travel; four weeks in Da Nang would give the pieces of bone in his leg time to heal well enough to tolerate an airplane ride. The plastic surgeon was equally pleased with his own work. "Most of the pieces of your face were still there, we just needed to puzzle out where they fit. Give the nerves a year or so to establish new lines of communication and you'll be good as new." Kaycee would see to it that he stayed lightly drugged, so he'd spend a significant part of the next four weeks sleeping. It was just as well he would be sleeping because most of the hospital staff members wanted to come by for an occasional visit.

Three nurses wheeled Rusty in that morning to see him. Rusty told Mann he'd be leaving in two days because he could recuperate at Luke as well as he could in Viet Nam. Jane would be waiting for him in Phoenix.

Nobody was waiting for Mann anywhere.

Parker stopped by his room twice a day for short visits. He was sitting at his usual station by the window when Mann woke up from one of his naps. "We haven't had time to talk about Bainbridge."

Kaycee was out of the room. Mann, Parker, Jamison, and Melher were the only people who knew what happened in the cockpit over Laos. Melher knew nothing of the killings in Mississippi.

Mann took a deep breath and let it out slowly. "What's there to say?"

"The investigation team may ask some pointed questions. You need to put together a solid story and stick with it. His mother may make a stink, but she can't prove anything . . . you were the only witness."

Mann already had his story ready: Bainbridge unstrapped to use the relief tube and Mann turned away to allow him some privacy. When he turned back, Lieutenant Colonel Bainbridge had disappeared. That's all he knew. Straight and simple.

If he could prove Bainbridge tried to kill him, he wouldn't need a story.

Kaycee came back into the room and the general stood to leave. "What can I get for you in the meantime? Books? Anything?"

"No thanks, General. Reading puts me to sleep, and Kaycee won't let me smoke cigars."

Parker hid his real question from Kaycee. "Are you up to an interview by some guys trying to piece together what happened out there?"

The day would not come when he wanted to talk about "what happened out there."

"When?"

"I'll leave that up to you."

"How necessary is it?"

"They need to hear it from you. I'll make sure it doesn't take too long."

Regardless of how long it lasted, they would want to know about Bainbridge. Mann was tired of being awake. "Whenever you say, sir. I'm ready."

Kaycee, who seemed never to sleep, woke him when the orderly brought his lunch. "There's an enlisted guy out in the hall who says he needs to see you," she said. "He's been waiting for an hour and won't leave."

"What enlisted guy?"

"He says his name is Daniel Worthy. Says you know him."

"The crew chief . . . my crew chief. Yeah, sure. Bring him in."

"Howdy, Lieutenant." Worthy was carrying a sack and a manila folder under his arm; the hat stretched between his hands was in danger of being twisted into camouflage-colored taffy. He saw the film of the rescue; the man in the bed was just as tough as Worthy thought.

"Come on in, Worthy . . . grab a chair." Mann was trying to figure out why the man would come to see him.

Worthy didn't even glance at the chair. He let the door close then turned his attention on Kaycee, watching her long enough to figure out she wasn't going to attack him.

"What're you doing in Da Nang, Chief?" asked Mann. "Boosting parts off the carcass of *The Cool Woman?*"

"Yes, sir. Kind of." He was still looking at Kaycee, holding something back. "Uh . . . no offense, Lieutenant, but could Lieutenant Mann and I talk by ourselves?"

Kaycee showed the trademark smile. "Guy stuff, huh? I'll be back in five minutes, and you'd better not say anything about me."

"Yes, ma'am. Thank you, ma'am." The crew chief nodded with every word.

Worthy stared at the door for long seconds after it was completely closed.

Mann waited.

Worthy moved closer to the bed and whispered, "Lieutenant, I went out and checked on *The Cool Woman.*"

Mann had an idea how the plane had fared, but asked, "How'd she make out?"

"Well, the crash crew got the fire out, but she's wrapped up like a beer can."

Mann's eyes wanted to close.

Worthy pulled the sack from under his arm and got more nervous. He rechecked the door. "You remember I sent my tape deck up with you?"

Mann had forgotten the tape deck. He remembered it now and hoped he knew what was coming. He tried to sit up.

"Well, sir, I pulled it out of the blue room yesterday." He rechecked the door. "The tape deck's ruined 'cause the foam from the fire truck got in the back."

The kid paused when Mann slumped.

Mann spoke quietly. "That's too bad."

"Yes, sir. I paid good money for that deck," a tenth door check, "but the tape came out just fine."

Mann was immediately back in the conversation. "The tape wasn't damaged?"

Worthy was getting animated. "No, sir. Didn't get one smidgeon of moisture on it."

"Where is it?" asked Mann.

"Uh . . . that's why I'm here, Lieutenant. I took it to the base tape shack yesterday . . . you know, where they have the tape library and you can make copies and everything." Worthy's nervous energy was burning a hundred calories a minute. He had forgotten about the possibility of being attacked from behind. "When I heard what was on it, I packed up the original and sent it back home to my dad . . . he'll put it where it'll be safe. I've got one copy in this sack and another two in my bag to take back to NKP."

Mann wasn't breathing. "What was on it?"

Worthy's eyes were wide. "I guess it's every word y'all said during the whole flight, Lieutenant. I had all the comm radio toggles up . . . and the interphone. I got all the plane-to-plane stuff, and the interphone conversations between you and Colonel Bainbridge, all of them . . ." a door check, then, ". . . including the part where the colonel said he was going to kill you." He handed Mann the sack like he was making a presentation. "It's all on there . . . you can even hear the gun going off."

"Is it clear?"

"Like y'all were standing in this room, sir."

There was one crucial question. "Has anyone else heard it?"

"No one even knows it exists. And my dad isn't the kind to pry."

"My brain is running a little slow. Let me think for a minute."

Worthy waited. Other people might be surprised that the quiet lieutenant pulled off the rescue; Worthy wasn't. He wasn't surprised about the killing in Mississippi or the ones on the film of the rescue either.

The tape didn't tell him exactly what happened in the cockpit, but he was confident Bainbridge was dead by the same hands that killed those other men. Worthy figured every one of them got what they asked for, and he was proud of his pilot.

Mann had things figured out. "Are you a lifer? Are you staying in the Air Force?"

"Not a chance, sir, I've got eighteen months to go. I'll be finished with college a year after I get out."

"Would you be interested in getting an 'early out'?"

"Early?" Worthy was very interested. "Absolutely, sir."

"Okay. Here . . . stuff this under my pillow." When the tape was secured, Mann said, "Go out there and find Lieutenant Gund—that nurse who was in here—and ask her where General Parker is. We need to talk to him."

"Uh . . . before I go, Lieutenant, I got something the guys in the squadron wanted me to bring when they found out I was coming over." Worthy's sunburned face turned a deeper red. "It's something Driver and I kind of thought up, and Driver pretty much did everything else." He handed Mann the folder.

If anything, the kid was more excited about giving him the folder than the sack with the tape in it. Mann kept his expression neutral; if what he was holding had anything to do with Driver, it couldn't be all good. When he opened the folder, he found a sheet of paper and two photographs. The photos were eight-by-ten black-and-white glossies taken by someone who knew how to use a camera.

"Airman Driver told me to ask you if you'd read the paper first."

The words were neatly printed on plain paper—Driver's trademark block lettering.

> *Dear Lieutenant Mann, I know I'm not the brightest man in the world, sir, but I hope I'm not the dumbest. I thank you for what you did. I apologize for how I treated you. I've changed. You helped change me. Sincerely, Tony Driver. PS, I hope you like the photos. This whole thing was Worthy's idea.*

Mann reread the note and nodded at the man's willingness to share any credit with Worthy.

The first photo was taken in the scheduling area at the squadron. At least fifty people, half of them pilots in their party flightsuits, stood on either side of the scheduling board, hoisting beer cans and champagne bottles in a toast, obviously celebrating something. Sgt. Driver stood in the center of the crowd, pointing at a spot on the scheduling board. Every man in the room, especially Driver, was grinning from ear to ear.

The second photo was a close-up of what Driver was pointing at. Driver's finger was touching the block that had been empty for seven months—waiting for the day when Mann received his call sign. The space was no longer empty. One word—perfectly suited for its owner, approved by men who were justifiably proud of the man who exemplified what they strived for—was displayed on the board in bold letters. The quiet lieutenant, who was fully accepted into the inner circle of the squadron, had earned, and been given, his call sign.

The gunfight and rescue Ky filmed from the door of Sherrill's helicopter was already being seen by people in the States; television news programs were showing it in hundreds of cities a day. The rescue was the subject of conversations all over the globe. Every man and woman in the war zone would know Mann's call sign within twenty-four hours. Within days, pilots back in the States, military and civilian alike, would be using it to speak of him. The newscasters tracking his recovery would catch on and stop referring to "Lieutenant Bill Mann." His new name would be a household word within a week.

The four letters printed in the designated block told the world that First Lieutenant William P. Mann's call sign was . . . BOSS.

CHAPTER TWENTY-SIX

The team doing the interview showed minimal interest in the disappearance of Halbert Bainbridge. It was another one of those one million unexplainable things that can happen in wartime.

A lieutenant from the Air Force Intelligence shop was asking most of the questions, and he was concentrating on the actual rescue. He pointed at the blank screen the team used to show the film of the rescue. "When you left the shell crater and started for the plane—when you were dragging Captain Mattingly—you were moving sideways more than straight. Why was that?"

"I was leading with my left leg . . . if I was going to get shot in the leg, it needed to be the left one."

There were three colonels assigned to the interview team; two were pilots with thirty-six years of flying between them and no small amount of "prop time" in their logbooks. When the young patient made the comment about needing his right leg, the "prop-time" pilots stared at him.

Because he had no flying experience, the answer mystified the lieutenant. He stared at what he had just written then shrugged and said, "What's the difference? Why would a man prefer to be shot in one leg over the other?"

The colonel on his left answered the younger man's question. "The Spad is a prop airplane. Prop airplanes will try to turn left when you

261

apply power to the engine—the turning force is induced by propeller torque. The only way to overcome the torque is with right rudder. Right rudder . . . right leg. No right leg," he made a stirring motion with his finger, "no directional control."

"Oh." The youngest interviewer hunched over his pad and scribbled more detail into his notes.

The air conditioner on the wall kicked on, continuing to fight its losing battle with the body heat being generated in the room.

Lieutenant Colonel Bob Jones, who had been standing between the hospital bed and the wall, moved forward. He walked close enough to rest both hands loosely on the white metal rail at the foot of the bed and cleared his throat. He looked down at his hands while he cleared his throat again, then he swallowed. He remained unmoving, staring at his fingers, then cleared his throat for the third time. He was obviously uncomfortable with what he had to say. The men in the room waited for his question.

Three hours earlier, the team met around three card tables to prepare for the coming interview. Jones's commander assigned him the unpleasant task of uncovering the reasoning behind one of Mann's apparently unorthodox decisions.

During the preinterview meeting, the team's boss looked at him and smiled a sympathetic smile. "Everybody in here has seen the film, Bob, and every one of us has the same question. Somebody has to bring it up, and you're the new kid on the block."

Bob Jones noted that the colonel didn't say, "I'm dadgum sure not going to embarrass myself by offending a man who's just done the bravest—and most well-documented—thing I've ever heard of."

The team leader read his thoughts and continued to smile in an attempt to make a hard job easier. "If you can buffalo one of these guys into doing it, have at it."

Jones looked around the makeshift conference table at three full colonels and cursed. He didn't particularly like being a "staff weenie," but he liked and admired his boss. "What about that kid from Intelligence?"

"Uh-uh. Can't run the risk of him wording it wrong."

You mean there's a right way to ask a hero if he's a coward? He nodded resignedly. "Okay, sir. But I want to give him a chance to tell it his way first."

"Fine. Just get 'er done."

"Lieutenant, is there anything else about how you decided to get Mattingly and Melher to the plane that you can tell us about? Any things you thought you could do to try to . . . uh . . . to make things safer? Some kind of reasoning you figured would help you succeed?" Jones knew he was babbling. The air in the room was stifling.

The young man in the bed wasn't going to help. "No, sir. It's pretty much all there in that movie . . . uh . . . film." He looked at the blank screen. "We pretty much did what it shows, and we're here."

Jones thought he might choke. The kid from Intelligence—or anyone else—would have worded the question wrong because there was no way to word it right. He struggled while he mentally cursed his boss and the other staff members who were too gutless to put themselves in his position. While he hesitated and cursed, his face became flushed. Try as it might, the air from the window unit did nothing to keep a heavy frosting of sweat from forming on his forehead. He cleared his throat yet again. "Lieutenant Mann, I need to ask . . . I hope you understand . . . what you've done is . . . phenomenal." He was stammering, and the sweat was starting to bead over his eyebrows. He resisted the impulse to wipe his brow and took a deeper breath. "Frankly, I almost envy you . . . but my question is . . . it seems like to me that you could have moved Melher easier if you had turned your back to the enemy and dragged him. You . . . uh . . . had to be standing anyway . . . uh . . . he would have been shielded by your body. I wasn't there . . . and I don't know what I would have done if I *had* been . . . you've done something only one pilot in ten thousand could've done . . . it wasn't possible. I just wondered. Did you think about that?"

The investigation team's boss watched Jones, hating the pain he saw in the man's face, thinking belatedly that they should've left the question unasked. *I owe that man a fifth of good scotch,* he thought. *I just hope that's enough to keep him from resigning his commission.* He turned to the man in the bed and waited.

"You might be right, sir." The answer wasn't whispered, but the words had a quietness to them, almost surrendering to the sounds coming from the air conditioner. Every man in the room was leaning forward slightly, waiting for the answer.

The man in the bed, who had appeared relaxed until now, pushed down with his good arm and shifted his position. When he settled back, he seemed to detach himself from what was happening around him. He looked down and watched his good hand move up and down the bandages that swathed his left arm. His thoughts went unspoken for a time. His hand moved; his chest rose and fell.

Lieutenant Colonel Bob Jones, whose uniform collar was dark with sweat, drew a breath, apparently to say something further. General Parker caught Jones's eye and shook his head. Jones let his words go unspoken.

The men in the room waited.

When Mann spoke, it was in an even quieter voice. He said, "It was a fairly simple choice."

He raised his eyes and looked out the window behind the general. There was nothing to be seen but blue sky. His eyes moved slowly back and forth, as if he were trying to find something. He replayed the trip from the crater to the airplane almost every waking moment since he got the A-1 back in the air. He shook his head, hoping there had been only one way to get to the plane after Melher went down.

The air conditioner cycled off, as if in an attempt to aid the men who were straining to hear the explanation. The smell of antiseptic and ointment was not as noticeable as the quiet. Glassware tinkled on a cart passing across the tiles out in the hall.

When his explanation came, it consisted of only five words. "We had to save me."

The colonel standing farthest from the bed was the first to understand what the kid had chosen to do. He turned toward the window and wiped something from his eye.

The patient let the silence completely swallow his words then added to them. There was a lot of brass in the room, and they were sharp, but they hadn't been there. They were here because they wanted to know how it went down.

"He was in and out of consciousness . . . Colonel Melher was . . . while we were still in the hole. Maybe semiconscious, you know? He'd close his eyes for a long time . . . then he'd open them and look at me." He started to smile at a recollection and the action reminded him of the stitches in and around his lips. He winced and moved his hand to his mouth for a moment, then held it in front of him and glanced at his fingertips. "Usually, his first words, when he'd open his eyes . . ." he paused to breathe, when he continued his voice was softer still, ". . . he'd cuss me . . . he tried to get me to leave." The memory tried to put the half-smile back. He moved his finger back to the bandages on his face. "He called me some pretty colorful things . . . said I was a blotch on the black race."

Silence permeated the atmosphere. The efforts behind Mann's repressed smile disappeared into the quiet. The interviewers waited.

The smile was gone. The man's voice, when it came back, had a hoarse quality, deeper . . . a monotone of emotion. "Rusty was unconscious the whole time. Things kind of ran together . . . there at the last . . ." Moisture began to well up and glisten at the edge of the young black man's eyes. "He had blood all over him . . . everywhere. Marsh was bleeding . . . it was kinda bad." Mann closed his eyes while his chest rose and fell. Tears brimmed over and ran down his cheeks.

Kaycee Gund moved a step toward the bed. On the other side, the general held his hand up; his eyes asked her to wait. "Son," he rested a hand on Mann's arm. "I know this is hard. And no one is ever going to be able to explain how we lost Colonel Bainbridge, but it would help us if you could start at the beginning and give us a chronological blow-by-blow of what happened on the ground. It's not going to be easy, and if you want, we can come back later."

Mann nodded to acknowledge the general's offer. He kept his eyes closed, watching the nightmare replay itself in his mind, then said, "I wanted to stop the plane between our guys and the shooters, but I wanted it so the airframe would protect the engine. With the tail toward the tall grass, that little bit of breeze was just right, and I cracked the throttle to try to kick up some extra dust in their direction." He stopped to breathe and opened his eyes. "After I set the brakes, I slipped and fell off the wing on the side by the hole. There was a lot of dust in the air by then . . . and it helped . . . I was flat on the ground before they could shoot at me. I slid into the hole with Rusty . . . uh, Captain Mattingly and the colonel.

"When the air cover went to work, we had to leave, and we had to drag Rusty . . . he was unconscious. Colonel Melher had been shot twice in the shoulder, but he took one side and I took the other. I guess we all got shot on the way to the airplane . . . when I helped them the last few feet to the wing, I kept them between me and the guns to try to keep from getting hit again." He sighed and shrugged imperceptibly. "I didn't know what else to do."

The men in the room didn't breathe.

"I don't remember it all . . . I'm sure I felt them jerk . . . when they got shot . . . more than once while we were there by the plane . . . or at the wing . . . while they were between me and them."

The last words came out in a hoarse whisper.

"I used them to shield me. Unless I lived . . . we all died." Mann closed his eyes again and sighed. "Marsh and Rusty were the ones that kept us all from getting killed."

The room waited.

When the man on the bed reopened his eyes, the calm, matter-of-fact tone was back in his voice.

"I was on the ground with them for probably four or five minutes. It seemed like it was longer." It wasn't intended to be humorous. No one laughed.

Every man in the room saw the eight-minute film clip of the rescue at least ten times. And they knew who saved whose lives. Silence reigned in the small room while the men absorbed what they just heard. Each man was weighing what he would have done had he been the man trapped in that hole. Each was thinking about who they would be willing to share the glory with had they been through what this man endured. They stared at the bandaged-swathed young black man on the bed and stayed quiet about what their thoughts told them.

The colonel in charge of the interview team caught Parker's eye. The senior officer nodded toward the door.

The colonel said, "Lieutenant, I think that's all we need for now. Thank you." He turned to his men. "Okay, boys."

Everyone but the general started making preparations to leave. Kaycee stood quietly.

The colonel spoke from the door as the last man from his team filed out of the room. "General, it's always good to see you." He saluted, and the general returned it while sinking into the chair.

The colonel turned to Mann.

"Lieutenant Mann, thanks again for your time." He looked at the young man for a moment and searched for something to say. He shook his head because he couldn't come up with words he thought were adequate. "You do good work, Boss." His feet came together and he stepped back one pace. He brought his right fingertips to his eyebrow in a rigid salute, held it for a moment, then smiled and stepped out of the room.

Mann was too stunned, or too drugged, to react.

The colonel who rendered the salute caught up with his friend in the hospital corridor. "That, my friend, is a pilot."

His companion walked the length of the corridor before he replied. "I don't know about you, Charlie, but if I had twenty years to plan my trip from that hole to that plane, I never would have thought to protect my right leg. Would you?"

Charlie grinned at his friend. "Why, I'm fairly confident that's the first thing I'd've thought of."

"Yeah, sure you would."

They were outside the hospital when Charlie asked, "What about Bainbridge? You think the kid was telling the truth about him just falling out of the plane?"

"I hope not." Charlie's friend didn't smile. "I knew Bainbridge. I'd like to think the kid saved Marsh and Mattingly after he blew that sorry dog's brains all over southern Laos."

"How're you feeling?" The general leaned back in his chair.

"First time I've been saluted by a colonel."

"Get used to it, son. That won't be the last time."

"Sir?"

"You didn't catch what went on there, did you?"

Mann answered by looking slightly confused.

"He saluted you last."

The lieutenant's expression didn't change.

"The senior officer—that would be me, son—gets the last salute. Charlie's been around . . . and he deliberately rearranged the order."

"Well, he looked smarter than that." He held the sides of his face to keep his lips from spreading when he smiled. "Snubbing generals ain't always the way to smooth the road to success."

"He's on safe ground. Protocol gives Medal of Honor winners saluting precedence over generals."

Mann didn't say anything. He looked at the general, down at the sheets, then out at the blue sky. The hand left his face and went back to stroke the sheets.

The general waited.

"It wasn't about bravery, General—I was so scared when I landed, I could barely hold my feet on the rudders. Rusty and Marsh are my friends." He shrugged one shoulder. "It was my job."

The general got out of the chair and moved to the foot of the bed so he could look Mann in the eye. "Charlie and his team didn't think it was 'just the job,' and neither does anyone else who's seen that film."

Mann didn't speak. The bandages on his arm needed more study.

"Boy . . . " The general stopped and started over. "Bill, I call every man I know who's my rank or lower 'Boy,' is that all right?"

"I can tell that, General. I'm sure all black people can tell."

"That's good to know." He pointed toward the door. "Charlie said you do good work because he couldn't come up with the words to describe how he felt. There *are* no words to describe what people are going to feel when they see that film." He didn't smile when he said, "You need to start getting ready to be famous."

CHAPTER TWENTY-SEVEN

Jane Mattingly drove into Phoenix on Friday. She rented an apartment on Saturday and found a church she liked Sunday morning. When the Air Force DC-9 Nightingale arrived at Luke on Monday afternoon, she was waiting at the bottom of the airstairs. The dress she was wearing, a black and tan sheath with white trim, was a gift from Rusty. The timing of Rusty's return was perfect because the dress would be a bit too snug in another week or so.

She was suntanned and happy. He was ghost pale, recovering from being badly wounded, and not smiling.

He said, "You look beautiful."

She said, "You look better."

"I've looked in a mirror."

She stood guard as they secured his litter in the ambulance. "I'll meet you at the hospital."

When the ambulance pulled up to the base hospital, she was waiting with a wheelchair. "Okay, Captain, let's you and me go for a little ride."

"They're gonna want me to get signed in first."

"No, they aren't." Jane had already talked to the doctors. She never before used her father-in-law's name to get what she wanted, but having her husband come from a war with bullet holes in him was new, too. "They're going to let you sign in with me first, then I'll let you sign in with them."

She parked the chair under a palm tree and sat in the grass by his feet. He told her about Pip's letter to Mann; she told him about becoming a Christian and talked briefly about the baby. After an hour, he became tired and she wheeled him inside. He still hadn't smiled.

The hospital room was a prison cell. They spent the next few days walking the halls, sitting outside, talking, being silent. She stuck with her decision to let him choose when he was ready to talk about the rescue. Their outside sitting place was directly under the traffic pattern for the fighters returning from their training hops. Rusty never looked up.

On Sunday, she went to the early service at the church she liked.

When she walked into the auditorium, the few seats left open were near the front. She slid into the second row next to a brunette about her age. They smiled at each other and the girl said, "Hi. You're new."

"Hi. I am . . . second week."

"I'm Kerri Michaels." She pointed at the preacher. "I belong to him."

"Nice to meet you. I'm Jane Mattingly."

"We're glad you came. How'd you find us?"

"We just moved back to Phoenix, and this is the first church I visited. I'm not an expert, but I think your husband's a good preacher."

"I *am* an expert," Kerri Michaels beamed, "and I think he's fantastic. How about a cup of coffee between services?"

Jane couldn't remember her last conversation with a woman her own age. "I'd love it."

After the service, most of the adults congregated in a large meeting room and socialized around doughnuts, homemade muffins, and coffee. Kaden Michaels worked his way around to Jane and his wife in time to meet Kerri's "new best friend."

"Her husband's in the base hospital at Luke," Kerri offered.

"Mattingly." Kaden repeated the name. "I'm going out there tomorrow; I'll stop and see him."

JOHN AUBREY ANDERSON   271

Jane didn't react, and Kaden caught it. "Is it okay for me to stop in and see him?"

Rusty was an extrovert when he left for the war, but he'd changed. He might not welcome an uninvited preacher. "It would probably be okay, but I think I better make sure before you show up."

"I understand." Michaels was adding two and two. "We've got a couple of F-4 crew members who come to church here. According to them, there was a Mattingly in that big rescue operation a few weeks back."

Jane nodded. "That was Rusty . . . my husband. He hasn't said anything about it yet." She paused, then said, "One of our best friends was the pilot who picked him up. Rusty's talked about him just a little, but he hasn't mentioned anything to do with that day."

"Boss Mann is your friend?"

"Yes. He was Rusty's student at Willie." She teared up for the first time since getting back to Phoenix. "Bill rescued Rusty and Colonel Melher a couple of weeks after receiving a letter from his wife telling him she was divorcing him."

"Is she a friend of yours also?" asked Kerri.

"Not any more." Jane didn't like what was going through her mind. "I bullied Bill into going on a blind date with her."

"Oh, I see." Michaels was nodding because he thought he understood. "And now you feel guilty."

"No." Jane's face said it all. "Now I feel angry."

Rusty gave Jane the okay, and Michaels stopped by the room on Tuesday morning. He didn't stay long, and he didn't get on Rusty's nerves.

Michaels paused on his way out of the room. "Why don't we celebrate when you get loose. The four of us can ride up to Camelback for steaks."

It had been a long time since Rusty had eaten a good steak. "Meat that isn't gray sounds like a good idea."

Michaels was back on Wednesday. "You're stronger."

"Thanks. You know you don't need to keep coming by here. Ninety-five percent of the people in this place must be worse off than me."

"Some are, some aren't. You're the one with the easiest questions."

"I haven't asked anything."

"Mmm. You make my point."

Rusty became wary. "Should I be asking you something?"

Michaels was relaxed. "Not if you have the answers that satisfy you."

"Is this a trick to get me to talk about religion?"

"Nah . . . just the facts." Michaels' smile was genuine. "So . . . are we still on for steaks?"

"We are if I ever get outta this medicine tent."

The doctors cooperated by granting Rusty a limited release on Thursday afternoon. "From now on it's just a matter of you letting yourself heal. Check in here once a week and let us take a look at you."

"Can I eat steak?"

"You can do anything you feel like doing except drive a car and play football."

The ride to the apartment was made in silence. When they drove through the entry, Rusty said, "You made a good choice."

"Thanks." She patted her tummy. "We won't be using the tennis courts for a while, but the pool might come in handy."

He nodded.

They were in the apartment five minutes when he said, "How about if we get outside and stay there till I pass out?"

She felt like she had been trapped inside almost as long as he had. "I'm ready. Where to?"

"Any place that's not inside."

They were back in the car when he said, "You haven't mentioned going out with the Michaels."

She wasn't going to. "I'm content with you."

"Don't you want him to talk to me about coming to church?"

A city park was coming up on their right. "Let's stop for a minute so I can look at you while I talk. Okay?"

The park was typical for a desert town—a small city block filled with sand, swing sets, and prairie dogs, all surrounded by a concrete sidewalk.

She parked the car and they got out. "I'm not sure how to tell you this, and I don't want it to come out wrong."

He took her hand when they moved away from the car. The gesture was simple, but her heart beat faster—it was the first time he volunteered to touch her since they brought him off the plane. Her reaction was a silent prayer of thanksgiving.

They walked halfway around the block in silence before she stopped and faced him. "There's no easy way to explain this. You are, more than ever, the love of my life. You're here with me, safe and healing from wounds you got in a horrible war. I know you might go back, and I want your time while you're with me to be special. I don't want you upset, I don't want you unhappy, but the thing I want most—" Her voice failed her, and she stepped close to him and let her head fall onto his chest.

He put his arms around her and held her while she cried. The sun was giving up for the day, but leftover heat from the sand and sidewalk warmed them against the evening's first breeze.

He put a finger under her chin and tilted her face up. "Tell me what you want most, Jane."

She couldn't tell him she wanted him to become a Christian before he went back to the war; it wasn't fair to pressure him on something he had to decide for himself. She skirted the truth. "I want you to come back to me . . . to us."

He took her hand and walked her to the deserted swing set. He put her in a swing and sat in the one next to her. They let themselves move gently, their backs to the sunset; the chains on the swings made a music they hadn't heard in years. "Kaden Michaels is a preacher; I'm not." He took a breath. "But I don't need to have but one plane come apart under me to figure out I don't get to decide whether I live or die . . . God does. I don't control whether or not I get to come back to you . . . God does. All I get to do is live from moment to moment, and I want to do that well . . . for the rest of my life . . . our lives. I just haven't figured out how to do it. Things just kinda seem like they've piled up . . ." He made a gesture of frustration and his voice trailed off.

They drifted where the swings took them. The sun went below the horizon; the heat lingered to fight a losing battle with the slow-moving breeze. The cool air tickled their arms and carried away the smell of the prairie dogs. They sat in the twilight and watched the peaks east of the city change from bright orange to deep red; they were dark purple before he spoke again. "I asked you in the car if you want Kaden Michaels to talk to me about going to church."

"Kaden's a nice guy, and Kerri will probably end up being my friend," she was searching for the right words, "but to have either of them pressure you about church doesn't fit with what I expect from them."

"I kind of got that feeling myself. What about your Christian thing? Where will that take us?"

She stood up and walked behind his swing so she could put her hands on his shoulders. "Christianity will only bring me closer to you. This is a special thing for me, and I want it for you, but it isn't my choice." She knelt in the soft sand and hugged herself to his back. "I'm praying that when you're ready to know, you'll ask. How's that?"

"Just praying. That's all?"

"Mm-hmm. Christianity is still new to me, too, but it's more real than anything I've ever encountered. More than anything I've ever done, it's important to me that I do this really well, and I'm working hard at it. If I've learned anything so far, it's that I can't choose for you—but I can show you what the choice does to me. For me, that means I have to be even more special to you than you can imagine."

Rusty didn't comment.

On Friday morning, Kerri Michaels called Jane and invited her to the Phoenix Christian Women's Annual Tea at the Biltmore. "I've been once before, and it was fun. Hopefully, the speaker won't talk too long, and I'll get a chance to introduce you to some ladies who are getting significant things done in Phoenix."

"What's the dress code?"

Kerri thought the military term sounded cute. "It's the Biltmore, and it's a tea, so the *dress code* is hat and gloves, if you can believe that.

It sounds stuffy, but the atmosphere stays relaxed and friendly. You'll enjoy it, and so will I, if you'll come with me."

Jane didn't want to leave Rusty alone. "I think I know where my gloves are, but my hats are in storage."

"Preachers wives have all that stuff; I can loan you anything you need."

"You'd better not be dragging me out there to meet a bunch of snooty old biddies."

"I promise you'll have fun."

"I'm not sure I want to leave Rusty."

"Kaden's already said to ask Rusty if he wants to go with him."

"To a Christian women's tea? It won't happen."

Kerri laughed. "Not to the women's thing, ninny. Ask him if he wants to hang out with Kaden while we're doing our tea thing."

It turned out that hanging out with another man, especially one that wasn't in the Air Force, was to Rusty's liking.

Kaden drove north on 24th Street to deliver their wives to the Phoenix Christian Women's Annual Tea. Rusty rode shotgun. While their wives were sipping tea, the men planned on attending to more serious matters.

In 1929, the Biltmore Resort had Squaw Peak completely to itself; not so in the seventies. Although the expanding city dictated the resort share the foothills with civilization, the Biltmore refused to surrender its grandness—nothing inside the adobe walls of the stately retreat gave any indication that the outside world was encroaching. Vast lawns, manicured with a precision normally reserved for finer golf greens, stretched in all directions. Acres of flora, color coordinated to take advantage of the red-brown mountains and desert sky, conspired with high walls to suggest a botanical garden encircled by an almost invisible world.

The two couples pulled under the Biltmore's porte cochère in time to watch a distinguished-looking gentleman jog toward an arriving limousine. The jogger clapped his hands and said something that caused nearby bellhops to arrange themselves in an orderly rank; a uniformed chauffeur stepped out and opened the rear door of the limo. When an attractive, white-haired lady emerged from the car, the gentleman from the hotel moved forward and offered her his arm. The lady chose instead to put her trust in a handsome black cane.

Kaden and Rusty left their wives in the capable hands of the bellhops and departed the desert island. The men would return after two hours of Gooney Golf and chili dogs.

The reception area of the Biltmore was less a hotel lobby and more the living room of an enormous Southwestern estate; the surfaces not carved from marble were hewn from rich wood. Finished four decades earlier, the resort was, for years, the winter destination of Chicago's wealthy families. While their less fortunate friends suffered through bitter northern winters, the residents of the resort played golf, rode horses, and went swimming during the day. In the evenings, they put on their dinner jackets and gowns to attend sumptuous banquets and lavish balls.

Kerri took Jane's hand and guided her down a corridor, introducing her to several ladies who came near. They entered an elegant banquet room to find dozens of tables set with fine china, sterling silver, and crystal glassware; ceiling high windows looked out across a wide verandah—Squaw Peak provided a fitting backdrop. Jane was her father's daughter; she wasn't sure who was picking up the tab for the annual tea, but cost wasn't one of the considerations.

Kerri told Jane to choose where they were going to sit and excused herself. Jane was pulling a chair back when someone touched her arm. When she turned, the woman from the limousine was holding out her hand.

"Hello. I am told you are Jane Mattingly."

"I am," Jane answered. The lady looked younger up close; she was below average height but seemed taller. Her grip was firm and it occurred to Jane that the cane might not really be necessary.

"How are you?" The lady could convey genuine warmth without smiling. "My name is Anne Wendell."

"It's nice to meet you, Mrs. Wendell." Jane didn't recognize the fragrance the lady was wearing, but she was confident it wasn't sold in any store the Mattinglys frequented.

"The pleasure is mine, young woman." The phrase was from a book on correct grammar; the accent was desert born and bred.

"Hi." Kerri came up, smiling and talking. "I see you found her without me."

"I did." Apparently Mrs. Wendell didn't bother to smile very often, but her voice did. "I'm too old to spend my time waiting for someone to properly introduce me to people whom I wish to meet." She turned back to Jane and became more serious. "I want you to tell your husband that I appreciate what he's doing on behalf of the people of our nation."

Jane noticed that most of the women near them had turned to see who the recipient of Mrs. Wendell's favor was. "Thank you, I will."

"And I appreciate what it must have cost you."

Jane was touched. "Thank you."

The conversation wasn't over. "Now . . . tell me," said Mrs. Wendell. "How long have you been a Christian?"

"About a month. Does it show?"

"Not much, I suppose, but it should." Mrs. Wendell was engaged in a bold appraisal of her new acquaintance. "You look as if you have a mind of your own. Is Kerri going to disciple you?"

Jane paused before saying, "I'm not sure what that means."

"Kerri knows." She turned to Kerri. "Well?'

Kerri's laugh was in bold contrast to her older friend's more earnest stance. "Anne, yesterday is never soon enough for you." She put her hand on Jane's arm. "We'll talk about discipling after the tea."

The lady sniffed her impatience and said, "You two will be my age tomorrow . . . you need to stop wasting your time." She took a small card from her purse and handed it to Jane. "Call me on Monday and let's plan for you to come out for lunch one day soon."

"Thank you."

"Thank me after you've heard what I have to say." Mrs. Wendell winked as she turned away.

When she was out of earshot, Jane asked, "Who *is* she?"

"Isn't she a mess?" Kerri smiled. "She took me under her wing for the first year we were here. If you're interested, she'll probably want me to do the same with you."

"Under your wing to do what?"

Kerri was watching the older woman visit with someone in the crowd. "Anne gives her time to one thing . . . teaching women. If you get by the interview, she'll probably suggest that you ask me to teach you how to teach. Like in Titus Two."

"Titus Two?"

"In the Bible. It talks about older women teaching younger women how to live their lives well . . . how to honor God."

"Oh." Jane ran the words back and played them again. "I'm not older. And what if I don't think I want to know how to teach younger women?"

"Visit with her first," Kerri was smiling as if she knew something Jane didn't, "then tell me what you think you want."

After a luncheon of teatime delicacies that left Jane wishing there was a cheeseburger hidden in her purse, the speaker took the podium. The program was what Kerri called "blessedly brief," and the ladies were left with a few extra minutes to visit. Kerri and Jane took their coffee cups on a whistle-stop tour through animated and amicable conversations to introduce Jane to more of the ladies. Mrs. Wendell was surrounded by at least twenty women. Her eyes met Jane's, and she nodded.

Kerri came back from a side trip to tell Jane, "The boys are waiting out there in the lobby, if you're ready to go."

"I'm ready." Jane was looking for a place to deposit her half-empty cup and saucer. "I need some food."

"Jane? Jane Mattingly?"

Jane turned in time to see Pip Mann step into the banquet room from the verandah. She was wearing a tennis outfit and a smile . . . as beautiful as ever. As she drew close, she held her hands out to Jane. "Jane! It *is* you! This is wonderful!"

The cup and saucer Jane was holding began to make a clittering sound.

Pip didn't hear it.

CHAPTER TWENTY-EIGHT

Pip was practically skipping, weaving her way between ladies in hats and gloves, moving nearer, happy to see her friend. "I can't believe you're back in Phoenix. How long have you been here?"

The cup and saucer were back under control, but Jane Mattingly was seeing images of a man in a war zone, fighting to stay alive. A man surrounded by swirling dust—shooting and being shot. A man who had come too close to giving his life for Rusty. A man Pip deserted. "I've been here two weeks." Her throat was dry.

"This is wonderful." Jane hadn't smiled. Pip apparently hadn't noticed. "We can play tennis."

The film clip of the rescue was eight minutes long, almost every second of it stained by the blood of the man this tennis player chose to abandon. "Tennis?" Jane was barely managing to contain herself. "Tennis?" One or two ladies turned toward them. The cup came back to life. "I don't think so."

"Don't be mad at me, Jane." Pip's smile softened. "I'm not like—"

"Don't tell me what to do," Jane snapped. She could feel the heat going to her face and her next words came out in one long hiss. "What makes you think I care what you're like?"

The tone of Jane's voice turned more heads.

"Jane, I just—"

Jane Mattingly's husband had been shot. He still wouldn't talk about it with his wife . . . he didn't like to talk to her about their coming baby . . . he didn't want to talk about anything. This grinning, tennis-playing woman's ex-husband had been shot. He was still flat on his back in a hospital ten thousand miles away because he chose to go into hell to bring his friends out. Jane clasped a hand over her mouth in an attempt to suppress a cascade of emotion—a fruitless effort. Until a few seconds ago, she did not have anyone at whom to direct the anger that had been building up in her soul. The coffee cup began to clatter in earnest. "They shot him—" The tears started and she couldn't continue.

"Janie, please, let me—"

The cup became a living thing, vibrating and skating around the saucer in an effort to free itself. Jane got her hand on the vessel in time to splash most of its contents on her new dress. She grasped the cup and hurled it and the saucer at the marble floor. The crash of shattering china caught the attention of more ladies and stripped the last thin layer of window dressing from Jane Mattingly's emotions.

Jane held one fist clenched over her heart and pointed a finger at Pip. She wasn't loud, but she was emphatic. "You . . . shut . . . your . . . mouth."

Pip tried again. "Jane, I know—"

"By the time Bill got the plane off the ground, they had shot him eight times . . ." She paused to breathe and her chin hit her chest. The tears flowed freely. "Eight . . ." she rasped, and moved a hand to cling to a chair.

"I understand—"

"That's a lie . . ." Jane was shaking her head, barely whispering. "If you understood, Pip, you'd be crawling on your hands and knees to wherever he is and begging him to forgive you."

"I know—"

Jane was getting her voice back and her strength. "He was willing to step into hell so he could get my husband out. Rusty was shot three times, Marsh the same, and Bill got shot eight times . . . eight times . . . so I could have my husband back." Her lower lip quivered; she wiped at her cheeks with trembling fingers and sniffed. "They . . . they shot him in the mouth . . . and he still . . ." She stopped and began to sob.

Pip nodded. "I know, Jane—"

Jane turned loose of the chair and clenched her fists by her sides. She took a step toward her former friend and screamed, "Stop telling me that!"

Conversations in the room were forgotten, and the ladies turned to look at the young Christian woman in the maternity dress yelling at the black tennis player. Jane's eyes flashed and the emotional tide crested. The tears came in torrents, this time in anger. "You don't know anything! You don't understand anything! You don't care about anything. You're . . . you're . . ." she waved her properly gloved hands, searching for a word, " . . . despicable!"

When Jane took a breath, Pip spoke into the void around them. "Jane, things in my life have changed. I have a new life now."

"What life, Pip?" Jane spat.

Kerri put a hand on Jane's arm and Jane jerked away. "What kind of life is there for a person who holds nothing sacred? If you give yourself to the nonexistent things you say are special, then your life is the definition of an empty shell. There's nothing there, Pip, because you aren't important and neither is your life. You deserted a great man because you believed a lie about what's important."

"You might understand if you would listen to me."

"The universe does not contain the words you could say to make me understand what you did."

"Please, Jane," Pip implored her. "Could I just try?"

"I'll tell you what you can do, Pip. You can—" The string of profane expletives Jane Mattingly unleashed on her former friend were borne on hot venom.

Pip put both hands over her mouth and recoiled . . . shaken. Women near the confrontation moved back a step.

No one breathed. Men and ladies assigned to clear the tables were motionless. The banquet room was silent.

A distinctive fragrance came to Jane, telling her who the hand belonged to before it touched her arm. "Jane, would you be kind enough to walk me to my car?" The lady's voice demanded nothing, carried no weight, offered nothing but warmth.

Jane looked at Pip. Her friend of yesteryear was utterly crushed. Pip looked into Jane's eyes a last time, shook her head slowly, and turned away; she was wiping her tears on the back of her hand.

Every woman at the Phoenix Christian Women's Annual Tea was looking at Jane. Every one of them saw something they would never forget; some appeared to be experiencing mild shock. From out of the vast silence, the soft, crystal-bell tinkle of glass against glass came from the far side of the room.

"Jane?" Mrs. Wendell reminded Jane of her presence. "Would you be kind enough to walk me to my car?"

Jane was sinking in a sea of astonished women. For an entire month, she had been concentrating her efforts on being a good Christian; in the past two minutes, she proved to herself that the Christian life was beyond her grasp.

"I'm . . ." her voice faltered. She touched a hand to the stain on her dress. ". . . uh, let me sit down for a second."

"Come along, child." Anne Wendell patted Jane's hand and became a grandmother. "You can't hide in a room full of women whose eyes are frozen open."

Rusty was standing in the lobby with Kaden when he saw Jane. She was with the lady from the limo and she had been crying. "Are you okay?"

"I'm fine." Jane faked a smile for the man who depended on her and dug in her purse for a tissue. "Let me get my eyes blotted."

"She *is* fine." Mrs. Wendell was calm. "She's just had a memorable encounter with Lieutenant Mann's ex-wife."

"Pip?" Rusty looked past them. "What's Pip doing here?"

"I can imagine that she is trying to stop some arterial bleeding," said Mrs. Wendell before changing the subject. "I assume that you are Captain Mattingly?"

Rusty divided his attention between his wife and the lady. "Yes, ma'am." Jane was recovering rapidly.

"Good." Mrs. Wendell held Jane's hand and addressed herself to Rusty. "I want you to know how much I appreciate what you are doing on behalf of a nation that is not grateful enough."

Rusty warmed to the old woman immediately; he had never been thanked for being in the military. Not once. "You're welcome."

"My name is Anne Wendell." She didn't offer her hand.

Formality suited the lady, and the general's son inclined his head the slightly. "Mrs. Wendell, it's my pleasure." He smiled at her. "My friends call me Rusty."

Mrs. Wendell rested both hands on her cane and took her time, giving Rusty's face the same frank appraisal she gave Jane. She made a decision and smiled at the pilot. "And my friends call me Anne."

Rusty nodded and smiled . . . again. "Anne."

The lady continued to study his face while she touched a slightly swollen ankle with the tip of the cane and said, "Rusty, my grandfather was a strong believer in the adage that warns us to get back on the horse immediately after being thrown."

Rusty missed the gracious lady's point. "You were thrown by a horse?"

"Week before last. And I rode him back to the stables."

The three walked out together. They were at the door of the limo when Anne Wendell turned to Jane. "Can you come to my house for lunch on Monday?"

Jane looked at Rusty. "I'm not sure."

"Go ahead," Rusty said, "Baching it won't kill me."

Jane didn't answer right away; when she did, she said, "Kerri told me about the teaching program for women. Why would you want to talk to me after what happened in there?"

"Why don't you come to lunch, and let's find out.

Jane drove through a set of ornate iron gates and up a curving driveway to a small mansion. A man who had to be the butler met her at the door.

"Mrs. Mattingly?" He had a British accent.

"Yes." The only butlers Jane had ever seen were in movies. She had to smile when the man actually said, "If you will come this way, please. Mrs. Wendell is in the rose garden."

When they stepped into the garden, the butler said, "Mrs. Mattingly, madam."

Anne Wendell was indeed in a garden—on her knees and up to her elbows in dirt; there was not a rose in sight. She beckoned to Jane with a trowel, "Come, come."

"Will that be all, madam?"

"Yes, Tommy. Thank you."

Jane watched her first-ever butler leave.

Anne watched Jane watch the butler. "Tommy was my husband's idea." She was amused and impatient at the same time. "Buddy would have called the poor man Jeeves if I hadn't put my foot down."

"Buddy is your husband?"

"Was my husband. He died several years ago."

"I'm sorry."

"So am I. He was my friend." She turned back to her dirt. "Give me a minute to finish here, and we'll have some lunch. I have a few things I want to discuss with you."

The dirt smelled good. Jane looked around the garden. "You don't have any roses?"

"Roses are high maintenance. I prefer to invest my time in things that learn to maintain themselves."

For lunch they had cheeseburgers and thick milk shakes, with homemade lemon icebox pie for desert.

Jane said, "Well, either you called my folks, or you've been talking to Kerri. I love lemon icebox pie."

"It was Kerri. Now," Mrs. Wendell pushed her chair back, "Kerri says your second child is on the way."

"It's our first."

"I was counting Rusty."

Jane laughed. "I see what you mean."

Mrs. Wendell took a moment to cross her legs then leaned forward. "No. You don't." She wasn't smiling.

"I don't understand."

"Jane, you've taken it upon yourself to try to protect your husband. That is neither a wife's job nor her prerogative."

Jane didn't like being invited to lunch so Anne Wendell could meddle in her life. "Mrs. Wendell, my husband was shot three times. He almost died."

The meddler might've been more sympathetic if Jane had said Rusty had been stung by a wasp. "Having been shot is not his problem, Jane. If what I hear is correct, Rusty left someone in that airplane when he had to bail out. Couple that with the fact that Lieutenant Mann was almost killed when he came to get Rusty and you have a man who is willing to find himself guilty when no crime has been committed. Am I correct so far?"

"I guess."

"Then he is having to deal with being in relatively good health while one friend is dead and another was badly wounded while saving his life. Rusty has been given a great gift—a chance to overcome an experience that was dreadful in the extreme. However, your tying your apron strings around his neck won't help him; it will only strangle his need to become the man God can make of him."

"Don't you think that's a little harsh?" Having a butler didn't give Anne Wendell a license to be a busybody.

Mrs. Wendell stated a simple fact. "Being harsh, as you call it, comes from five decades of getting fed up with watching willful women turn men into nonentities by treating them like little boys. Your husband strikes me as a man who deserves more."

Jane pushed her chair back. Her mind was remembering too many milquetoast men she had seen in her lifetime, husbands who surrendered their manhood and, in so doing, sentenced themselves to a life of trailing along behind strong-willed women. She wanted to say something in her own defense, but everything the woman said was true. She took a tangent. "I can't leave him to fend for himself."

"Nor should you—but your God-given place is beside him, not between him and his struggle. If he cannot learn to depend upon God, he's of no use to you . . . or himself. C. S. Lewis wrote, 'God designed the human machine to run on Himself. He Himself is the fuel our spirits were designed to burn.' Wives make poor God-substitutes, Jane."

Anne Wendell was right.

"What about me?" Jane asked.

"In what context?"

"I made a fool of myself at the Biltmore Saturday. Every Christian woman in Phoenix thinks I'm either evil, or crazy, or both." Jane took a deep breath and let it out. "How can I ever recover from that?"

"You'll be fine when your desire to stand up for what's right becomes as famous as your recent fall."

"I wouldn't know where to start."

"That's easy enough. You get an address list of the women who were there, several boxes of nice note cards, and two hundred stamps and start apologizing . . . and asking their forgiveness."

Jane took another deep breath. "Then what?"

"You have one more hurdle to cross, then you and I will start on you."

"You still want me to work with Kerri after what I pulled?"

"Not exactly. Simply put, I think I can see something in you that you can't see yet, and I want you to work with me."

"To teach me how to teach women?"

"More. Unless God intervenes, I intend to take you one step further. I want to teach you how to teach women, how to teach. I think a one-year association should tell us if I want to train you to become my counterpart."

It was all going too fast. Jane was a nearly brand-new Christian. Two days earlier, she thoroughly cursed her former friend in front of several hundred Christian women. Today, she came face-to-face with the fact that she was being a mother to the man for whom she was supposed to be a wife. Now a woman who was the matriarch of the local Christian women wanted her for a partner. One more hurdle?

"Didn't you say there was one more hurdle?"

"I did. In the book of 1 Peter, the Bible tells us, 'Sanctify Christ as Lord in your hearts, always being ready to make a defense to everyone who asks you to give an account for the hope that is in you, yet with gentleness and reverence.' That presupposes, I believe, that someone would be willing to listen. Your young friend, Mrs. Mann, might have some difficulty generating an interest in any account for the hope that is in you, regarding Jesus Christ."

"That's her problem."

"Humph," Anne sniffed impatiently. "I think we both know better. You have appointed yourself her husband's champion, and we've just finished a short dialogue about men needing to learn to depend on God more than they do women. So unless you intend to invest your life in trying to hide the offended men of the world behind your skirts, I suggest you choose to make a definitive move toward a more worthwhile pursuit."

Jane drew a breath, then sighed. "And I have to go to her and make it right."

"Not exactly. First, you and I and Kerri need to get together tomorrow and pray fervently for that woman. *Then* you go to her and beg her to forgive you."

Jane had been in the home less than an hour and Anne Wendell had given her good reasons to think she should completely overhaul her life. "Am I going to end up talking like you?"

"As a matter of fact, you already do." Anne Wendell's rich laugh said she enjoyed life as much as she enjoyed people. "All we have to do now is work on your word choice."

Jane, Kerri, and Anne Wendell met at Kerri's the next day and prayed about things past and future and for the heart of Pip Mann. Kerri and Anne prayed for Jane more than they prayed for anything else.

Jane bought some nice note cards and started writing to the 200 ladies who heard the stream of profanity she poured on Pip. Two weeks later she finished with the cards, but she hadn't located Pip.

As far as Phoenix was concerned, Pip Mann had vanished.

CHAPTER TWENTY-NINE

James Kelly stopped by the hospital at Hickam Air Force Base on his way back to the States. He threw a small package on Mann's bed and said, "They gave me that for winning the 1971 Rice Paddy Foot Race—you keep it. If I'd known you were going to get competitive on us, I'd've recruited you for the Marines."

Mann used the fingers of his left arm to help unwrap Kelly's Silver Star and shook his head. "Uh-uh, I can't take this."

"It's mine to give," said Kelly. "I want you to have it."

"Never hatchi, G.I." He tossed it back to Kelly. "Thanks anyway, but you can take it with you, or I'll have to spend the money to mail it to you."

Kelly pocketed the medal while handing Mann a folded piece of paper. "File this away someplace where you won't lose it."

The paper had two addresses written on it. He looked up at Kelly. "Pressler?"

"Yeah. That gunnery sergeant that met us in Saigon."

"I know who he is," said Mann, "but why would he send me his address?"

"He saw your first film." Kelly took a breath. "He ain't easy to impress, but he said—and this is a quote—'You tell him I'd be honored if he'd get in touch with me if he ever needs anything.' He ain't the joking type."

Mann stared at the paper.

"I'm on there too, but I ain't quite ready to cut my heart out for you."

"Thanks."

"Speaking of movie debuts," Kelly grinned wickedly, "I hear talk of your becoming a movie star. What about that?"

"Yeah," Mann snorted, "and Leslie Uggams called. She wants to be my leading lady." Mann was dodging the question because a guy claiming to represent "a major studio" had stopped by the hospital room to "chat."

Kelly looked at his watch. "Well . . . can I send you anything from the States?"

Mann thought for a full second. "A truckload of chocolate cake would be nice."

"Consider it done." Kelly checked his watch again. "I got a plane to catch. If you get close to Dallas, you can sleep and eat with us."

"Plan on it."

Three days later, Fat Chance wrangled a hop to Hawaii for a short visit. While he was there, he snuck a six-pack of beer into the famous patient's room.

Mann toasted his friend. "Thanks for setting the grass on fire, amigo. That was the break-over for us."

Fat sat with his feet propped on Mann's bed and sipped a bottle of the contraband. "Actually, I did it to entertain my wizzo—those poor guys never get any excitement. Fact is, I didn't even know you were down there."

"Right." Mann could grin without hurting his mouth too much. "What're you going to put on your dream sheet for after your tour?"

"I'm getting out."

"Yeah, sure." Mann didn't believe him.

"I met a doughnut dolly that thinks I'm the greatest thing since sliced bread, and we're getting hitched." He dismissed the Air Force with a wave of his hand. "I'm going the commercial route."

"Well, I'll swear . . . down in flames with the dames and flying trash-haulers. The aviation world's coming apart around us."

"Thanks for the encouraging words. We'll name a kid after you."
Mann said what was expected. "Sorry I can't reciprocate."
The words weren't funny, but they both chuckled.

As soon as they told him he could do his therapy as an outpatient,
Mann moved to a hotel on Waikiki Beach. He had been in Hawaii
eight weeks; the open-air prison would offer palm trees and souvenir
shops.

Parker met him in the hotel lobby when he stepped off the elevator.
The general was dressed in civvies—a Hawaiian shirt outside light blue
slacks.

"Afternoon, General."

"Hi, Bill." Parker had both hands in his pockets. "Well, son, I've
been visiting with the medics, and it looks like they'll take you off the
disabled list as soon as you get the strength back in your leg."

The healing process had taught Mann to smile slowly. The scars
around his mouth were beginning to fade, but he was looking forward
to months of numbness in parts of his face. Long-sleeve shirts would
keep a dozen scars on his left arm from catching attention. "That's
good news, General. Hanging out in Hawaii's not something I'd like
to do long term."

Parker was too quiet.

"General?"

"We've hit a bad snag, son."

The young pilot thought he knew what the senior officer didn't
want to tell him and spoke in anticipation of what he was expecting to
hear. "General, I only put in seven months in the theater, and I don't
have anyone at home now. I've got five months to go on that tour and
I expect to finish it." Without realizing it, he stepped closer to the general to add emphasis to his words.

The older man turned away without replying and walked to a water
fountain in the lobby's center.

Mann watched him for a second. *It's not about finishing the tour!*

"General?"

Parker pulled a pack of cigarettes from his pants pocket and held it out to his friend. When the younger man shook his head, the general took one out, clamped it between his lips, and lighted it. He exhaled in a long sigh then jerked his head in the direction of the side doors. "Maybe this'll sound better if we're outside." He motioned with his cigarette. "C'mon."

The two men walked across the lobby and stepped out onto the red tiles of a wide terrace that bordered the swimming area. Both men wore civilian clothes; Mann used a walking cane he'd picked up in a local shop. The general led the way through an ordered maze of lounge chairs and down the steps. A wide path, partly shaded by palm trees, sparkling white where the noon sun touched it, wound its way through lush flowers. They walked abreast on the crushed shell . . . neither speaking.

It was obvious the general was trying to figure out how to break some bad news to him, but as far as Mann was concerned there couldn't be any more bad news. His mind did an inventory, he was alive and he had his leg. Pip was gone, but he could make it from here even if the sky fell.

The general stopped and turned to face him. "You can't go back to the theater."

Mann was caught completely off guard. "General, I don't want special treatment. I want to go back and finish my job."

"The A-1 operation will be shut down before you get off DNIF . . . but that's not it. Everybody knew you'd want to go back. It's the leg."

"What about the leg?"

"You can't be cleared to fly anything with an ejection seat; that includes the Yankee extraction system on the Spad. The dynamics of an ejection aren't predictable enough. The doctors won't let us put that kind of stress on the bone grafts."

"Begging your pardon, General. You used the word *us*. There's only one leg involved here, and it's got only one man wearing it—*me*—it's my leg, General. I should be the person who decides how to use it." He had moved to a spot in front of Parker.

The general nodded and waited, frowning. When he finally spoke, he said, "I agree with you, son, but this came from way above our heads. I don't have enough stars . . . or markers . . . to pull this off. I was overruled." After a moment he added, "I'm sorry."

They started moving again while the young man digested the words . . . every fighter-type aircraft in the Air Force inventory was equipped with an ejection seat. The sky detached itself from its moorings and landed squarely on Mann's shoulders. He slowed, his shoulders hunched, then stopped under the weight.

A short distance away, a child on the hotel porch laughed. People could be heard chattering by the pool. A tourist couple wearing gaudy clothes, even for Hawaii, walked by on the path. The woman turned and stared over her shoulder at Mann, then whispered something to the man. Her escort turned and stared, then ventured a halfhearted wave at the young black man with the cane. The young black man couldn't see them.

The muted sound of surf pushing against the beach came through the palm trees—a soft percussion section to back the melody of exotic sounds coming from the Honolulu Zoo. He turned slightly away from the general and looked through the palm trees toward the beach. Both men thought their own thoughts while the blue water on the wave tops frothed to full white and carried brown-skinned people toward the sand. Two young boys brushed by on the path, chasing each other through the manicured jungle.

"Why didn't they tell me?" Mann wondered aloud. "They had to have known. Why didn't someone let me know?"

The general followed Mann's eyes to the waves without seeing them. "The medical guys over here and at TAC Headquarters have been fighting the decision for over three weeks . . . closer to a month. The Air Force Surgeon General had to go with what the doctors told him . . . we lost. Every person in on the decision wanted to decide otherwise. They hated it. I asked them to tell me first if it didn't work out."

The pilot turned from the beach and looked into the older man's eyes. His mouth was set in a firm, thin line. The scars were white against his skin; heat-generated tears brightened his eyes. "This is my leg, General, not theirs."

"I know, son." Parker reached out and rested a hand on Mann's shoulder. "Nobody wanted this to happen to you. Nobody. What we've done in Viet Nam, and how we did it, will prove to be one of the stupidest boondoggles ever orchestrated by the politicos in Washington.

This whole fiasco has been a competition to see who could best excel in the area of idiocy. And in the midst of all that hell, you did something every pilot in the world . . . every man . . . wishes he could've done. Someone in the press quoted John Wayne as saying he'd rather be you than himself. The entire fighter pilot community is proud—and envious—of you and what you did. Few people ever get a chance to do for someone else what you did for Rusty and Marsh. In return, you get rewarded by being told you can't do what you've wanted to do since you were a kid. I guess it just seemed better for you to hear from a friend that you've got to do something else."

The lips with the fading scars didn't soften much; the eyes cooled only slightly. "It was you, wasn't it? You've been fighting for me all this time, haven't you? That's why you've been spending all that time in Washington, isn't it?"

The general turned his attention to his cigarette. He took a last pull and blew the smoke out in a long stream through lips pursed in thought. Without acknowledging the question, he flipped the ashes off and used a nearby palm tree to scrape the burning tobacco off the tip, field-striping the cigarette. He tore open what was left of the white cylinder and shook it, watching the tobacco shreds blow away across the flower beds. He looked at the cigarette paper while he rolled it between his fingers, then tossed the tiny white ball into the grass near his feet. When the paper disappeared into the turf, he raised his head and turned to look through the trees toward the beach. The scent of orchids came and took over from the cigarette smoke.

"Boss, I've known you for three months."

Mann's expression didn't change, but he caught the tone. In the past months, the general had called him all the polite things an older officer would call a subordinate, but he had not called him by the call sign the press made famous. Something was different.

The general continued, "I shot down a couple of MiGs in Korea, and I've lived my life—on the ground and off—eighteen inches from some of the best pilots in the free world." He sighed again, then turned and resumed the aimless trek through the domesticated jungle. Mann fell in beside him. The older man stopped near a bench. Without knowing it, he reached into his pants pocket and brought out the cigarettes. He glanced down at his hand, looked at the package while he made a decision, and put it back in his pocket without taking one.

"If you stay in the Air Force," Parker continued, "my money is on your making general. But it is entirely possible you could get buried away in some backwater role and not get past major.

"I really haven't decided how to tell you this, but I feel the same way John Wayne does—sometimes I'd rather be you than me. But I can't be you . . . and I can't be your dad . . . or brother, so I'm willing to be the next best thing. I'm not Mose, but I'll be your friend for as long as we live . . . if you'll have me." He stuck out his hand.

Mann took Parker's hand. He was touched, and humbled. "Thanks, General."

"We're friends now, Boss—good friends. In private, my friends call me Bobby."

"Sir, I'm honored. Mose was more than forty years older than I was . . . we were close . . . and I called him 'sir' for as long as he lived."

"Okay," Parker capitulated. "Whatever suits you."

"So they don't think a one-legged black guy can make it in this man's air arm?"

The general smiled; he could speak the language of the men who served under him. "We're surrounded by a profusion of people in the military who still believe you can't lead unless your daddy's rich and your momma's good-lookin'. There's too much politics, Boss, especially at this level. You'll make some field grade boob mad because you don't want to contribute to a retirement home and golf course for generals' widows, and your career will be over. I've seen it happen.

"If you want to keep flying, you'll be relegated to many-motored airplanes. If you're going to be flying multiengine planes, you might as well go the civilian route—get out of the Air Force and avoid what you'll have to put up with if you stay. Why not get paid three times the dinero for doing safer work and spend your nights in the city of your choice? If you stay in, I'll protect as well as I can, but if I die tomorrow, you'll be on your own. It comes down to this . . . as your friend, I'm telling you to get out of the Air Force."

"When do I have to decide?" For years, Mann's desire to be a fighter pilot had been the pivot point in his decision-making process. Those days were over.

Parker motioned at the cane. "No rush. You can go to the States anytime you like and quit the Air Force as soon as you leave the medal ceremony. Plan on—"

Mann interrupted. "The medal ceremony?"

"Yeah," said Parker. "Congratulations. It's a done deal."

Mann nodded. He didn't want a medal.

"I'm sorry, General. I interrupted you."

"You can take as long as you like," Parker said. "A month . . . more . . . less. It's your call."

"A month." In thirty days he could be a civilian and if he stayed in aviation, he would be boring holes in the sky with an airplane full of people following him. He'd been a fighter pilot barely seven months, doing what he dreamed about since he was eight years old. Less than a year earlier, coming over on the plane from the States, he told James Kelly he was the envied of the envied. The words sounded cool at the time; now they sounded trite. No one would ever envy him because he was a fighter pilot; he wasn't. No fighter pilot would envy him because Pip was his wife; she wasn't. The man who didn't need anything because he was a fighter pilot with a beautiful wife had become a future airline pilot with nothing to show for his arrogance but a divorce, a bum leg, and a numb mouth. He wondered if James Kelly thought he was an idiot? *Probably. I am an idiot.*

"Sir, I think I'll walk around a little and stretch my leg."

"You want me to tag along?"

"No, sir, thanks. I don't think I'd be very good company. Maybe I'll see you tomorrow."

He moved away without waiting for an answer, going west toward the harbor.

He wandered through Honolulu until late afternoon—revisiting the same sidewalks he had been limping around on for three weeks. Thoughts of having to leave the Air Force came and went, but mostly he thought about Pip. Staring at the Pacific didn't help. The waters couldn't come up with answers—only several thousand miles of separation. Why do people write poems about oceans, he wondered, they never give back anything but empty seashells and foam.

Street crowds were the worst; he'd figured that out after two days of living in the hotel. He didn't think he was looking for her, but once or twice a day an image would catch his eye. It was always a beautiful girl and always looked like her from the back, but it was never Pip. Keeping his eyes on the sidewalk didn't keep him from missing her, but it spared him the disappointments.

His leg began to protest, so he stopped under the awning of an open front bar facing the beach. When the bartender figured out who he was, it caught the attention of the other patrons. The bartender told Mann the beer was on the house. Mann thanked the guy and moved on; being a hero didn't interest him.

Two blocks later, he spotted another bar—bigger, darker, and noisier than the last one. He could hide there, and he could get something stronger than beer to fill his emptiness and dull his pain. He stopped inside the door while his eyes got used to the darkness; the stench of stale cigarette smoke and last week's spilled beer lingered in the gloom. Music blared from somewhere in the back.

He listened with one ear as a handful of young GIs sang along with Buck Owens, spilling more beer and adding smoke to the atmosphere.

Mann listened to lyrics about some guy who was sad and lonely because he was a fool; the song made him wonder at a songwriter's ability to paint his own life so clearly. He was, in fact, the biggest fool he knew.

Sad and lonely? Absolutely.

What had he been thinking? He had spent more than half his life posturing himself to live alone. Even after he met Pip, he continued to press for isolation—the fighter community's own dedicated Lone Ranger—flying the planes, fighting the wars, getting the glory. Well, he had a boxcar load of glory. *Now what, Kimosabe?*

The last time he felt this empty, he went to Bangkok and got drunk instead of going to the States to get his wife back. Ten days of pouring booze into his body hadn't gotten him anything but a string of hangovers and a divorce.

Buck and his alcohol-enthused choir were still singing.

The biggest fool ever to hit the big time had been without Pip all his life . . . even while they were married. He never told her he needed her more than he needed anything else—you can't explain something you can't comprehend. Before the world collapsed around him, he hadn't known what he needed—he knew what he would settle for. The Air Force, though, by deciding to throw him out of the cockpit, gave him a glimpse of what could be. And what did he expect to accomplish moping around the streets of Honolulu and sucking up suds? Nothing. It was time for First Lieutenant William P. Mann to become Bill Mann.

He turned his back on the bar and limped toward the hotel, already planning.

By this time tomorrow I can be on the ground in Phoenix. If Pip won't have me, I'll manage without her. He smiled. *But she's going to have to say she doesn't want me to my face,* he risked a wider smile, *or what's left of it.*

By the time he got to Phoenix, he'd have a game plan laid out to confront her. He'd tell her his life was going to be different. He was different.

During the twenty minutes it took him to get back to the hotel, the pain in his leg was beginning to subside.

After checking at the desk, he went straight across the lobby. When the elevator door opened, he stepped in, punched the button for his floor, and moved to the back to make room for a pair of tourist couples. He had a view of the lobby scene from over the shoulders of his fellow riders, and he noticed the girl for the first time. Another look-alike—a dead ringer from the back.

She was wearing all white—a plain, straight dress, medium heels, square shoulders—standing with her back to the elevators. The skin was a perfect match. The hair was the right shade but too long. He smiled because whoever she was she had to be pretty—the men scattered across the lobby on the other side of the fountain were trying to pretend they weren't watching every breath she took. Her shoulders rose and fell. She was moving to turn around when the elevator door closed.

Mann excised the image of the girl from his mind. Ten million long looks at a close approximation could never equal one glance at the real thing.

One of the men on the elevator stuck his hand out. "You're Boss Mann, aren't you."

Mann shook the man's hand. "Hi."

The tourist introduced his wife and their friends. "Could we buy you a drink later?"

"Thanks, but I'll have to take a rain check. I have a plane to catch."

CHAPTER THIRTY

Rusty picked him up in front of the Phoenix Skyharbor Airport before noon on Thursday.

After an abbreviated greeting session, Mann threw his bag in the backseat and asked, "Where's Jane?"

"She had something else scheduled." Rusty pulled into the traffic. "Said she'll catch up later."

"So. How's it been to lay around back here in civilization and soak up a little sun?"

"Smooth enough. Jane's up to her eyeballs in church stuff. I saw the doc yesterday, and he gave me the green light to get back in the cockpit."

"Good." Mann propped himself against the passenger door and took a moment to look Rusty over. "And I can tell you're having a hard time keeping a grip on your enthusiasm."

"Mmm."

Five miles of buildings, billboards, and August-hot pavement passed before Mann asked, "What'd you have for breakfast, bro?"

"Same old stuff. Why?"

"Well, I figured it wasn't a dictionary. What's got your mouth wired shut?"

Rusty pretended a smile. "I've turned into the strong, silent type."

"Uh-huh." Mann took another look at his friend and decided they were overdue for a talk. "Well, I've been eating mass-produced meals for three months. What's for lunch?"

"We can eat at the club or in town. Take your pick."

"Lopo's. Mexican food in Thailand ain't quite there yet."

Rusty took the next right and wove through older neighborhoods toward Lopo's Hacienda, the only cafe west of Odessa that served sweet tea.

The best Mexican restaurant in Arizona didn't major in ambience— every table in the place wobbled, the surly waiters refused to speak English, and Lopo apparently dedicated a full-time employee to keeping the mismatched china well-chipped.

Mann and Rusty munched chips and salsa while they waited for their food. TV stations in Phoenix were still finding excuses to show the film of the former Williams Air Force Base student who stood off the North Vietnamese Army with a pair of .45s, and someone in the restaurant figured out who Mann was. The waiters took turns topping off already full tea glasses so they could see *el pistolero* up close.

Their real waiter interrupted a five-minute silence to put platters of food in front of the silent *hombre* and his brave *amigo*.

Mann took a few seconds to slather a pint of salsa over everything, including his guacamole then started the skirmish. "Your dad says you've quieted down some since you got back."

"Maybe Dad's started talking too much."

"A fault you are not in danger of acquiring."

Rusty stopped playing with his food long enough to study Mann's lopsided grin. "You got pretty shot up."

Mann talked around a cheek full of hot frijoles. "That's information you had to get secondhand, Quiet Man, because you were having a little nappy poo while we hauled your lazy carcass all over that end of Asia."

Rusty didn't think he would ever recover from having to eject and leave Keith Brady in their exploding airplane. Keith's wife cried with Rusty in the Brady's kitchen and told him what he already knew— his only option would've been to stay and die with her husband. And every person he talked to tried to convince him that Mann's getting shot wasn't his fault. "So. Your getting shot was because of me."

"That pretty much covers it, I guess," Mann knew he had to stay with the truth, "but everybody in both hemispheres knows that."

Rusty didn't get the protest he'd expected from Mann. He tried again. "If you hadn't come after me, you wouldn't be coming off of a three-month hospital stay, and you'd be on your way to a fighter assignment."

A pair of waiters circled the table, bringing more tea and chips.

It didn't take a psychoanalyst to see what Rusty's problem was. Mann stole a long swallow of tea while the waiters had their backs turned, then said, "A third-grade boy could whiz through that arithmetic with a short pencil, Rusty. What's your point?"

Rusty was no longer sure. "I'm to blame for getting you shot a half-a-dozen times?"

"Not exactly."

"Not exactly what?"

"Not exactly a half-dozen," Mann had to grin again. "It was more like eight."

"Okay, then." The humor was wasted on Rusty. "It was eight."

A busboy and a lean man wearing a starched white apron came near the table. The busboy stepped closer and poured a few teaspoons of tea in the glasses then piled chips in the overflowing basket. His escort was a hard-eyed old man who was content to watch from a distance. When Mann looked up, the old man squared his shoulders, then bowed slightly and murmured, *"Soy honorado."*

Mann wasn't sure what the old Mexican said, but he could read his eyes. He slid out of his chair and held out his hand. *"Mucho gracias, amigo."*

The old man took Mann's hand with both of his and looked into his eyes, *"Vaya con Dios."*

The old man turned away. Rusty was watching Mann. "This must be what it's like to hang out with a movie star."

"It saves having to suck on your ice cubes because nobody wants to fill up your tea glass." Mann wasn't smiling. "Have you considered the alternative?"

"An empty tea glass?"

Mann looked mildly disgusted. "Have you considered what it would be like if I hadn't come after you?"

"Only about a million times . . . I'd be dead."

"You might want to hold off on your application to that Mensa outfit." Mann gave up trying to get a cup of salsa onto a teaspoon-sized tortilla chip and propped his forearms on the edge of the table. "What about me, slick? Have you considered what my alternatives were?"

Rusty hadn't. "I'm not sure."

"You haven't thought about me, have you?"

Rusty's impatience resided too near the surface. "So tell me, doctor."

Mann made a slow swipe at the crumbs scattered in front of him then brushed his hands together. His eyes were fixed on the face of his watch, a handsome Rolex; his index finger traced circles around its crystal as he spoke. "My dad knew this would be my watch one day." He took a deep breath. "He had three words engraved on the back—it's supposed to say, 'Be A Man.' Good words." He looked down, staring at the clean tabletop, and his words took on hard edges. "I've been thinking some about what happened back in that grass, sonny boy, and you know what? I don't think there's such a thing as a hero. I think people just see what needs to be done and do it. I wasn't thinking about what was written on the back of a watch when I went after you; I was just doing what had to be done."

Mann looked at Rusty. Rusty was staring at the watch.

Mann continued, "The alternative for me? Simple enough." His finger resumed its travel around the face of the watch while he looked through Rusty. "The alternative would be me getting to remember every day—every single minute—for the rest of my life that I chose to leave you and Marsh on the ground while I flew back to a cold beer and clean sheets . . . knowing you were gonna be dead when I woke up. If I had left you on the ground, I wouldn't care if I ever ate Mexican food again 'cause I wouldn't be able to taste it." His eyes came back to his friend. "I'd be a walking dead guy."

Rusty mulled that over while he watched Mann refill his mouth, then said, "What about your career?"

"C'mon, Rusty. What career?" It was Mann's turn to be impatient. "A career is what a man does so he can feed his family." He touched his frijole-filled cheek. "Men who don't care about eating can't feed *anyone.*"

Rusty was quiet.

"I don't know what's going on in your skull, hoss, but I know you aren't thinking right if you've gotta be quiet all the time because I got bunged up coming after you. If you're gonna stay in a blue funk the rest of your life, then as far as the guys who worked to get you out are concerned, we could've left you in that hole. As it stands, whether you get your gyros synced or not, I'll always know I didn't go down there for you and Marsh; I went down there for yours truly." He concentrated on heaping salsa on a tortilla chip while he said, "As it stands, I get to enjoy the taste of my food, sweet tea gives me pleasure beyond belief and when I go to sleep at night, I rest."

Mann was the first person to explain it so it made sense. Rusty said, "Thanks, amigo."

"You're welcome. You can pick up the tab, and we'll be slick."

"You should'a been a shrink."

"I'll fall back on that if the airlines don't hire me." He slid out of his chair. "If I drink any more tea, I'm gonna have to spend all afternoon in the head. Let's go get my car outta storage."

"It's at our apartment. It's washed, and the battery's charged."

"*You* should'a been a chauffeur."

"Speaking of chauffeurs, the church lady Jane's been hanging out with is going to want to meet you. She's okay."

"Sorry." Mann shook his head. "She'll have to take a number."

"How come?"

"'Cause first I'm going to go to the base and get signed out, and then I'm gonna go get something straight with Her Royal Highness Princess Pip Mann. After that I can start having meetings with my fans." He looked at his watch. "It's after twelve. Take me to get my car, and let's head for the home drome."

Two hours after Mann picked up his car, Lieutenant Colonel Robert R. Kensington escorted him to the door of his office. "Sorry, Lieutenant. We can't drop everything just to accommodate all the pilots who are in a hurry to leave the Air Force."

General Parker told Mann to go to the Base Personnel Office at Luke and tell them to process him out the day he got there and put him on extended leave. In the past hour Mann worked his way through the paperwork mill until he got to the officer-in-charge of personnel. Instead of extended leave, Mann got a lecture on how much he owed the Air Force for his training and been told to come back in four days.

Mann stopped in the door to say, "Colonel, this is a mistake."

"You're the one who made the mistake, Lieutenant." Kensington had decided to tighten down on the young fighter pilots at Luke. The personnel officer tapped the black plastic name tag on his chest. "This is the name of the man in charge of the personnel office at Luke Air Force Base." Kensington walked over and closed the door . . . but not the subject.

The airman at the desk nearest Kensington's office stood and said, "Lieutenant Mann, I'm really sorry about this." He looked pointedly at his telephone. "Is there someone you want me to call?"

The airman at the desk was Cleetus Love. Thanks to General Parker, Love was finishing out the final months of his enlistment at his assignment of choice.

"Nah. Thanks, Cleetus." Mann shook his head and winked. He had already made the decision not to invoke General Parker's name. "I'll just ride it out."

He found Rusty leaning against a drink machine in the corridor. "You all signed out?" he asked.

If Mann told the truth, Rusty would make the same call Cleetus was willing to make and General Parker would be on the phone to the personnel officer five minutes later. The delay from Kensington meant Mann would have to hang around Luke twiddling his thumbs instead of looking for Pip, but he was eventually going to have to wean himself from the general's influence. "No real problem. They're working on it."

They stepped into the afternoon brilliance and Rusty said, "It's a hundred and fifty out here. Let's go to the club and get something cool while we regroup."

Love tapped on his boss's door and pushed it open. When Kensington looked up, Love said, "Colonel, did you ever read about those prophets in the Old Testament?"

Kensington had been to Sunday school. "What about the prophets, Love?" Love wasn't the most senior enlisted man in the personnel section, but he was sitting closest to his boss's door because he was by far the smartest. Kensington knew his clerk had been accepted at Stanford, and he told him no less than fifteen times that he would do well to come back into the Air Force after graduation—he could be an officer. Love responded that he was considering doing just that. He wasn't.

Kensington wasn't really a bad guy, but the lieutenant colonel was choosing a really bad time to flex his muscles, and Cleetus was a sucker for a good cause. The young airman had three months left on his enlistment and he knew his boss suspected he had a high-ranking mentor; Cleetus could afford to go a little way out on a limb, especially for Boss Mann.

"Sir, according to my sainted grandmomma, those prophets were the guys that could tell the future."

"So? What's your point, Love?"

Kensington seemed to be more at ease when Love chose to use poor grammar, "If you was gonna run into one of those prophets today, they would look like that lieutenant there."

"Like I said, Love. What is your point?"

"Well, Colonel, that man said that what you did was a mistake, sir."

It didn't surprise Kensington that the young airman stood up for his black brother. "I'll tell you what, Love. If the lieutenant turns out to be a prophet, I'll go to church this Sunday."

Okay, Colonel, but it'll be for your funeral, thought Love. He said, "Yes, sir," and went back to his desk.

The lunch crowd was dwindling at the club, and they parked the red Vette at the front curb.

Rusty said, "Grab us a table while I call Jane and give her a position report."

"Tell her your analyst prescribed nocturnal shock treatments." Mann slapped him on the shoulder. "I'll be in the bar."

Mann had never been in the Luke O'Club when it was quiet. The only people in the bar—four guys in flightsuits—took time from a game of Liar's Dice to check out the black guy in the tan uniform. He looked like someone they should know. Mann lifted a hand at the group and propped himself on a barstool. He ordered two beers and cold mugs.

When he tried to pay for them, the bartender leaned toward him and whispered, "This round's on me, Lieutenant."

"Thanks."

"It's a genuine pleasure, sir."

Rusty came into the bar talking, "I found Jane. She and your number one fan are coming over. Sorry about the fan."

"No prob," said Mann. "I've got a little slop in my schedule right now."

Two of the pilots in the dice game knew Rusty—so the black guy with the scars on his arm could only be one person. They broke away from the game and walked over. When they got close, Rusty introduced them. "Bill, Golden Wilkes and Still Draper. Guys, Boss Mann."

Mann shook hands with the pilots.

Wilkes said, "Good work, Boss."

"Howdy, Boss," said Draper. "Hot stuff."

He was getting accustomed to the looks he got; they ran the gamut from awe to arrogance. Some people couldn't believe what he'd done; others figured they could've done it better. Most fighter jocks registered pretty close to the middle.

Wilkes turned to the friends they'd left at the dice game. "Hey, you guys. Come over here and see if you can learn anything by standing in close proximity to this guy."

Mann laughed. He handed the barkeep a five-dollar bill to buy the first round before the argument started. A voice from the dining room door said, "That man's money's no good in this club. Ever."

The group turned to see Colonel Jamie Jamison walking toward them. The men who were on bar stools started getting up. Jamison waved a hand and said, "Sit, gents."

He introduced himself to the guys in the flightsuits and shook hands with Mann last. "You look better."

"Thanks, Colonel. Congratulations on getting the wing."

The four guys in the flightsuits wanted to back off, but Jamison turned to them and said, "Why don't I get this round and you guys can tell me what a new wing commander ought to do first."

"Shoot, Colonel," said Still, "if you're buying the beer, you've already done what you ought to do first."

The conversation was relaxed and loose until Jamison turned to Mann and said, "General Parker told me you were getting signed out today."

When Mann looked down at the floor, Jamison said, "You did get signed out, didn't you?"

Rusty was looking at Mann and beginning to understand. Mann said, "I just hit a small snag, sir. Nothing I can't work out."

Members of the wing staff carried gray two-way radios they referred to as "bricks"—Jamison was growling at his before Mann finished his sentence. "This is Jamison. Patch me to the OIC at Base Personnel."

Mann and Rusty were relaxed; they were innocent. Draper and his buddies were innocent too, but they weren't old friends of the wing commander's. The room was beginning to feel as if the air conditioner might be taking a siesta.

Fifteen seconds later the radio said, "This is Colonel Kensington."

"Kensington, this is Jamie Jamison. I need to know why Lieutenant William Mann didn't get signed out today."

The radio didn't say anything for several seconds while Kensington wondered how the new wing commander had gotten into the picture of a black first lieutenant trying to go on terminal leave. Finally, "Uh . . . sure, Colonel. We're working on it right now. I'm sure you understand that we all have our hoops we have to jump through."

"You need to know that understanding hasn't surfaced among my current sentiments," Jamison snarled. "Nobody at Luke Air Force Base is going to require a man who's on his way to Washington to get the Medal of Honor to jump through anything. Now here's what we're going to do—you get a clerk-typist and whatever paperwork you need and you be in the bar at the O'Club in ten minutes. We'll all have a beer and get Boss Mann fixed up with whatever he wants." He released the mike button and winked at Mann. "That should clear up your small snag."

Mann chuckled. "Thanks, Colonel."

"If you have a problem and I don't fix it, General Parker is going to have me for lunch. Now . . . on the next snag, you ask the problem child to give me a jingle."

"I'll do it, Colonel." Mann knew there wouldn't be any more snags. The story of what the new wing commander had just done would be in the ears of the lowest ranking airman on the base inside an hour.

Jamison turned his attention to the four pilots he'd just met. "Well, are you guys learning anything yet?"

Still Draper, who'd noticed the room's warmth more than the others, raised his hand and spoke solemnly. "I learned that the next time I'm in the room with a colonel after somebody makes him mad, I want to be a general." Everyone, including the bartender, laughed.

Jamison was keeping up with what was happening on his Air Force base. He turned to Rusty. "Well, Bubba, Doc Pritchard says you're cleared to fly."

"Good to go, sir," Rusty assured him. "All I need is a requal ride."

"Then why don't we find an IP to babysit your backseat and you and I will take a pair of F-4s up for a little one-vee-one first period tomorrow."

Rusty came up with his first genuine smile in three months. "Good plan, sir. For beers?"

Jamison liked the response. "Why else would a guy want to burn Uncle Sam's gas?"

Draper had forgotten about the cooling system problem by the time Kensington got to the club.

The clerk that came with Kensington was, of course, Cleetus Love.

Before Jamison took time to greet Kensington, he shook the airman's hand. "Good to see you, Cleetus. How the heck are you?"

"Fine, Colonel. Congratulations on getting the wing."

"Thanks. How about a beer to celebrate?"

Because enlisted men were never invited to drink in an Officers Club, Kensington registered near-shock. Love traded his stack of paperwork for a beer and was drawn into the circle of pilots by Jamison, Rusty, and Mann.

Jamison turned to Kensington, "What's your pleasure, Colonel? We can start on the paperwork in a minute."

Only a fool drank in front of his boss during the day. "Club soda for me, sir."

"What's your first name, anyway?"

"Robert, sir." The underarms of Kensington's tan uniform were dark with sweat.

"Okay, Bob. What'll it take to get Bossman signed out and put on terminal leave."

"We can do that in about five minutes, sir."

"Excellent." Jamison patted Kensington on the back. "He and I both appreciate it."

Cleetus Love was shuffling paperwork with one hand and holding a frosted mug of beer with the other when the public-address system said, "Lieutenant Mann, you have a call on line two, please."

"Excuse me, Colonel." Mann walked to the phone at the end of the bar and punched the flashing button. He turned away from his friends and found himself staring at the table where he had been struck dumb the first time he met Pip. "This is Mann."

"Hi." She hesitated for a second, then said, "It's me."

The voice drew him inextricably into the past. He saw a vision of blue eyes and an upturned nose and lost himself in the memory.

A doubt-filled voice on the phone prodded him. "Bill Mann?"

He needed to say something. "Yes . . . hello. I guess I've been wearing my oxygen mask too loose again."

She wasn't remembering their first date. "You don't sound like yourself." As soon as the words were out of her mouth, he heard an intake of breath. "I'm sorry."

"My plastic surgeon says he thinks I sound like a movie star."

"Oh." She was nervous. "Does it still hurt?"

"Only when I frown." He paused. "I've decided to quit frowning."

She said, "Oh."

He waited. For all he knew she could be calling to tell him where to send the alimony checks.

The phone finally said, "You aren't very talkative."

He said, "It's your dime, Pip," and it came out sounding harsh. The phone grew quieter still.

"I'm sorry." He cleared his throat. "That came out harder than I meant. I don't want to be your enemy."

"That's okay . . . you're right." He heard her take a deep breath. "The reason I called is to see if you're going to be in Texas anytime soon."

"Why?" *How'd she know where I was?* "How'd you know I was at the club?"

"I was just talking to Jane, and she told me."

"Rusty told me you and Jane weren't seeing eye to eye."

"It's a long story, but we've gotten everything ironed out. Anyway, I'm going to be in the Dallas area in a few days, and I thought maybe we could talk."

Well, he wasn't going to have to hunt her down, and Pilot Hill was an easy three-day drive. "I'm in the process of getting released here and my plans are to be in Pilot Hill early Monday."

Her voice softened. "I'd like to see Pilot Hill again. Can I meet you there?"

"Suits me. When?"

"Can we do it sometime around lunch?"

"Sure. How about at Nettie's for lunch? On Monday?" Nettie's was the downtown cafe where Sam Jones, Mann's 'cousin,' ran the kitchen.

"We could, but I'd really prefer some place where we could talk without people coming over to speak . . . something with a little more privacy."

Keeping their meeting private suited him. "Okay. How about Sam's house? He'll be busy at Nettie's; we can have the place to ourselves."

"Sam's house would be great. Noon, Monday?"

"Okay . . . sure. I'll be there at twelve straight up."

They said good-bye and hung up.

"Hello." When Missy Patterson answered her phone, she always sounded as if the person on the line was doing her a favor by calling.

"Hi. It's Bill."

"Where are you?" Missy held a finger to her lips, signaling the other person in her kitchen to stay quiet.

"I'm in Phoenix."

"I want to know when you're comin' home."

He smiled at her insistence. "As soon as I can."

"Well, I need to make sure you're okay," she chuckled, "so you hustle your bustle."

"I'm good as new," he laughed. "I'll be there Monday; can you put me up?"

"Oops. We can't do anything for the next few days. Can you come here on Tuesday?"

He was surprised at how disappointed he felt. "I'll have to play wait-and-see about Tuesday. My schedule's a little up in the air."

He hadn't said why he was coming, and it would be out of character for her to ask. "When are you leavin' out there?"

"I think I'll start in the morning and take my time. A long drive will give me time to think some things over."

"I'm thankful that you're okay."

"Me, too. I'll call you in a few days." He hung up.

She put the phone down and turned. "He's leavin' there tomorrow."

"Did he say anything about me?"

Missy shook her head. "No, baby."

"Shouldn't he have mentioned me?"

"Not necessarily. I doubt that Bill has ever talked to me or anyone else about really private things."

"What if he doesn't want me back?" asked the girl.

"You can't control that, Pip."

"When I talked to him, he sounded indifferent. What if he brings some other woman with him?"

"Child, child, child . . . your 'what if' list is gonna drive us both crazy. Let's go in here an' pray."

The tears came again. "Missy, I'm really scared."

"I know, Sweetheart—an' more importantly, God knows." Missy had to reach up to put her arm around the girl's trembling shoulders. "Come in here in the den, an' let's talk to Him about it."

CHAPTER THIRTY-ONE

The solitude afforded by a three-day drive across the desert in an open convertible should've given him a chance to order his thoughts. It didn't.

Questions of what to say to her assailed him—answers refused to show themselves. He stopped often to get out of the car and look at mountains, or rivers, or emptiness. The desert gave no more help than had the ocean. Friday became Saturday. Cactuses and rocks became mesquite trees and windmills.

He drove into Abilene, Texas, late on Sunday evening and checked into the Visiting Officers' Quarters at Dyess Air Force Base. The sergeant behind the VOQ desk took one look at his ID card and escorted him to the bungalow reserved for visiting generals.

He stared at the ceiling of the opulent bedroom until two in the morning; it conspired with the ocean and desert—withholding any and all answers. If he wasn't going to sleep, he might as well drive.

The stars were fading when he rounded the corner on the square in Pilot Hill. Nettie watched him park the car across the street and was waiting in the door of her cafe for a hug from the long-gone hero; Sam stood back by the kitchen door, nodding approval and smiling. When Mann was thoroughly welcomed by Nettie, Sam wiped his hands on his apron and came forward to gently shake Mann's hand. "Are you okay, boy?" he asked.

"Almost good as new." Mann smiled as he gave the stock answer. Sam and the cafe smelled of fried sausage and fresh biscuits.

Nettie wasn't a gossip, but if she got the word out, Mann wouldn't have to keep repeating himself. He turned to her and said, "This is for publication: I'm getting the feeling back in my mouth, my leg only hurts when it snows, several of these teeth are my third set, the arm is scarred, but none of the cuts did any damage."

"Well, I'll see to it that everyone gets the word." Nettie managed to smile—a smart remark about his new call sign was forgotten. The film of the rescue didn't tell the whole story. He was barely more than a boy, and she knew sixty-year-old men who were younger. "Anything else?"

"Yeah, I'm smarter and better looking."

"I'm glad you're back, sonny boy. I prayed for you every day."

Mann said, "Thanks, Miss Nettie," and meant it.

"Breakfast is on the house," she said. "What can we get you?"

"Just coffee. Thanks."

He was slender when he went to the war, now he was thin. She wanted to tell him he needed to eat something, but words failed her. She walked over to lean against the counter by the coffee urns and wiped her eyes on her apron.

Sam slipped into the back booth that served as his sometimes office, Mann slid in across from him. "What about Pip?" was his first question.

Mann didn't bother to smile for Sam. He blew a long breath through the remanufactured lips and said, "Ask me tomorrow."

"Is it that bad?"

Mann waited while Nettie put his coffee on the table. When she walked away, he said, "It's worse. She divorced me while I was gone."

Sam winced. "That ain't good." He studied the backs of his hands for a moment, then said, "I reckon I better be prayin' too."

"Thanks. I'm meeting her at your house at noon. Any advice?"

Sam leaned over the table and put both hands on his coffee cup. "Did you become a Christian yet?"

"No, sir."

"Well, let's have us a little prayer meetin' anyway."

Both men bowed their heads, and Sam said, "Lord, I reckon we're all just children in Your sight, but this one here is younger than some others. Give us all understandin' and wisdom to deal well with what today brings us . . . 'specially him. Amen."

Sam raised his head and took a sip of coffee before Mann's head came up. Sam noted it. "You taken to prayin'?"

"Some." Mann told Sam about the prayer he offered up while standing on the wing of the Skyraider.

The older man understood. "Gettin' a peek at the inside of hell gen'lly makes most folks want to stand closer to the throne."

"Maybe, but it didn't do much good," Mann paused to taste the coffee. "He answered by letting me get shot a few more times."

Sam's brow furrowed. "You just got though tellin' me you prayed for Him to get y'all out of that place."

Mann stared at Sam. Sam extended his hands across the table, palms up, as if to say, *Well, here you are.*

Mann said, "And here I am."

Sam took a deep breath and smiled gently. "You're mostly a smart man, son, but sometimes you got what it takes to be powerful slow."

Mann nodded and said, "You might be right."

"Did you thank Him yet?"

Mann shook his head.

And so did Sam.

"An' you're meetin' Pip today?"

Mann nodded slowly. "She'll be at your house at noon. What do I say?"

"That depends on what you want, don't it?"

"Just her." He told Sam why he was leaving the Air Force.

Sam took some time with his coffee. "Is she a Christian . . . your Pip?"

"No." Something in Sam's tone triggered a warning and Mann's head came up. "Why?"

"'Cause if she's a Christian, she can't marry a man who isn't, leastways the Book says not to."

"The Bible says that?"

Sam pursed his lips and nodded. "Pretty clear . . . second book of Corinthians, don't be bound together with unbelievers."

"Dern . . . makes me sorry I asked." He picked up his coffee and stopped with the cup halfway to his lips. "Wait a minute . . . Jane's a Christian, and she's married to Rusty."

"More Corinthians . . . first book. Says for a woman who has an unbelieving husband, an' he stays with her, not to send him away. God says the man might come to Christianity through gettin' to watch his wife live the life."

"So if I don't become a Christian, we could remarry."

Sam came close to expressing exasperation, but he had to smile. "I don't know as I would reason it that way, but I reckon you're right."

The day's first customers—mostly farmers and ranchers—began to straggle into the cafe. The ones who got past Nettie came over to speak to Mann.

Mann waited for a lull in the visiting before saying, "I'm getting out of here."

Sam stood up and said, "Well, I don't know how this meetin' is gonna go, but if you two start throwin' things at one another, stay away from that blue sugar bowl. It was a wedding present to Cora's grandmomma." He excused himself and went to the kitchen.

Mann went to Sam's house to take a nap.

Pip sat at the Pattersons' breakfast table and picked at her food until her eggs congealed. She pretended to take a sip of coffee, told Missy she enjoyed the uneaten meal, and went back upstairs. At eight o'clock she was back downstairs wearing jeans and sneakers. Her voice quavered when she asked, "Do you think this is okay to wear?"

Pat and Missy told her it was perfect.

She went back up the stairs, and Pat asked Missy, "Is she going to be all right?"

"Only the good Lord knows. I came in here at three this mornin' an' she was sittin' over there in the den cryin'."

When Pip came back down to get their opinion on a skirt and blouse combination, they told her the second outfit looked great.

She took two seconds to examine herself in the hall mirror and said, "Well, I've decided I don't care if he likes it or not." She stomped back up the stairs.

Twenty minutes later, when she came back downstairs dressed in a third outfit, she was weeping; Pat almost cried with her. She stood in the kitchen for a full minute without asking for an opinion, then turned and made her way back up the stairs.

At ten o'clock, she walked in wearing yet another ensemble. "Where's Pat?"

"He escaped to the office 'cause bein' cast as a fashion consultant was makin' him feel inadequate."

Pip stood in front of Missy. "What about this?"

What Pip was going through wasn't funny, but Missy had to smile. "Lord have mercy, Pip, forget about the dadgum clothes—you can't get any prettier. Go up there an' get on your knees an' spend your time prayin' for the man's heart—not his eyeballs."

"What if he—"

"Now you stop that 'What if . . .' stuff right there."

"But if he's not—"

"I just told you . . . that's enough," Missy admonished as she stood up. She took Pip's hand and marched her to the den. "Come in here an' sit down."

In the den, Missy sat on the couch and took one of Pip's hands in both of hers. "Now, I want you to listen for a minute. Nothin' you wear can make him love you. *Nothing.* You can make him want you, but that is never, never, never goin' to be enough . . . it will not bring you what you want. What you want is for him to want to love you for all of your tomorrows, but you are not in charge of that. Understand? No woman should try to saddle a man with the responsibility of fillin' her needs; it's not fair to him; it's not fair to you. Only God can fulfill us, Pip."

Pip nodded and dabbed at her eyes with a mutilated tissue.

"Okay," Missy continued, "you've spent the last two months in your Bible, learnin' an' listenin'. Two months may not seem like a long time to be a Christian, but what you've learned in these short weeks is more than most Christians will ever know. You've got a man you think you really want, but if God doesn't want you to have Bill Mann, then you know by now you should flee from him; you cannot force this to happen an' then be happy with the result. You have got to be ready to hear God tell you No."

Pip sniffed and nodded.

"Now," Missy took Pip's face in her hands, "you get yourself back up those stairs an' put on somethin' comfortable an' go see what God has in store for you."

Pip came down an hour later wearing a simple white cotton dress with an open back. She was carrying her suitcases.

"You're takin' your suitcases?"

She tried to smile. "If he doesn't want me, I'm leaving."

"Where will you go?"

"I haven't decided." She straightened and held her shoulders back. The smile was small, but it wasn't fake. "I guess I'll make my decision after I hear God's."

They prayed at the front door, and Missy watched Pip's car roll down the circular drive.

A mile to the east, on the University of North Texas campus, the flags in front of the administration building popped their corners at a mid-morning breeze. The sky toward the southwest was getting dark and scattered clouds were lining up on the horizon.

Mann's try for a morning nap at Sam's house was another exercise in futility, and he ended up staring at another silent ceiling. He got back in his car just after eleven but didn't want to face the early lunch crowd at the cafe. He drove to the new convenience store out on the highway and the kid behind the counter, who had never heard of the search and rescue operation in Southeast Asia, sold him a Dr. Pepper. He walked out to stand by the car and watch the clouds for a while. The temperature was starting down; rain was on the way. He placed the open drink can on the floorboard in front of his seat—an act that, in the past, would elicit a scolding from Pip—and took a few minutes to put the top up on the Vette. With protection from the coming rain assured and the red carpet unsoiled, he let the car take him toward the north end of town.

The fresh smell of summer rain met him at the remote little cemetery. The car pulled up by a small marker and stopped.

No stranger would ever know who was buried in the grave. There were no dates on the stone . . . and no last name.

She was twenty minutes early when she arrived in front of the little green house. The driveway was empty. White trim on the house set off the flower beds Cora kept in the front yard; Sam's summer garden was winding down out back.

Pip climbed the steps to the porch, tapped on the door, and waited. A peppy breeze came near, teasing the hem of her dress and disturbing the flowers. When no one came to the door, she tried again. Still nothing. She looked at her watch and moved to one of the wooden rockers to wait. The third time she checked her watch, it told her she'd been on the porch almost two minutes.

In an overgrown field across the road, shoulder-high stems of Johnson grass paid homage to the cold front's first sustained gust.

Boss Mann sat sideways, one foot propped in the car and one in the grass. Letters on the small piece of white marble spelled out the man's name, *Moses.* God had seen fit to give Mose two boys; his first one died young, and Mose carried the protection of his second one all the way to his grave.

The second boy, the one with the leftover bullet holes in him, got out of the car and took the last swallow of his Dr. Pepper. He looked at the grave marker for a full minute while he shook the remaining drops out of the can and thought about his life. Wind plucked at the front of his shirt.

"Poppa, I haven't been doing too good." His voice was soft. "I know that other life is out there—that life like you had. I know God has to be faithful . . . I saw it in you; I've seen it in Kelly and now in Jane. I see it in Missy and Pat and Sam and Miss Nettie . . . in all of you." His tears were the only evidence he was crying. "I just don't see it in me."

He put one hand in his pocket and used the other to tap the empty can against his good leg. "I've got to meet Pip in a few minutes, and I don't know what to tell her. I can't promise her anything but what I've already given her—which is nothing. I wish you were here . . . I wish I could talk to you for a minute . . . just a minute."

Little cemeteries on the outskirts of country towns are quieter than oceans, or deserts, or empty bedrooms. The tops of the trees leaned over beneath the weight of the weather change but said nothing. He watched last year's leaves scuttle past his feet. The wind was beginning to speak, but the small marker was forever still and silent.

The wind came around the corner of the house and brought a chill with it. Pip hugged her arms to herself and thought about getting back in the car; the first drops of rain made her decision for her. She pulled the rocker to the north end of the porch and settled in to wait. It was five till twelve.

Fat raindrops were splashing on the car hood when Mann turned away from the grave. He threw the drink can on the car floor and slid in. Lightning struck a tree near the back of the cemetery and thunder shook the car; the first onslaught of rain hit before he started the engine. He checked his watch and said a single curse word; he was going to be late. The Pilot Hill water tower disappeared behind layered draperies of charcoal gray rain.

The Vette's windshield wipers held their own for a few passes before being overcome by the deluge. Thirty seconds after it started, the rain was obscuring everything but the hood of the car.

Pip was sorry she hadn't sought shelter in her car when she had the chance; thunderstorms were rare enough in Phoenix, and never like this. The temperature dropped twenty degrees, and the rain became myriads of silver lines cut in wet slate, obliterating everything outside the small yard. Lightning hit something on the north side of town, and she started thinking about tornadoes. Occasional stray raindrops made it all the way across the porch and swirling mist frosted her hair. Lightning hit again, closer this time. The thunder followed immediately, sending a shock wave that jarred the house. Her exposure on the open porch multiplied her fear, but if she ran for her car, she'd get soaked to the skin.

He wasn't superstitious, but he should have known better than to use profanity; he didn't have to drive five feet to know his right front tire was flat.

He sat in the seat and preplanned his excursion into the weather. He would check to make sure the tire was flat, get the jack and spare, and have it changed in less than ten minutes. Getting wet wouldn't kill him.

He walked carefully in the mud so he wouldn't slip and break his stupid leg again. His clothes were soaked through by the time he found out the tire was most assuredly flat. It took him two minutes to find out that his spare was as flat as the tire on the car. Mann wouldn't allow himself to even think a curse word, but, as a chauffeur, Rusty would starve . . . and rightly so. There was no good reason to get back in the car; he'd have to get out again, and he'd make a mess of the interior.

He looked down at his new penny loafers. He was at least two miles from Sam's house and he was going to try to jog there in a pair of slick-soled shoes. It was five after twelve.

Twelve-thirty.

She'd been crying for ten minutes.

She was supposed to be brave, but she wasn't . . . and she didn't care.

She was huddled on a little wooden porch, becoming colder and more discouraged by the second because God was letting a thunderstorm scare her to death. She wiped at her tears—a pointless effort; her face couldn't get any wetter if she jumped in a lake.

She prayed out loud, "Lord, I know You mean this for my good . . . I *know* You do . . . but I'm going to plead immaturity and tell You that I don't like it. In fact, I think it stinks." She was kicking off her shoes. "Forgive me if I'm being too stubborn, but if I can't have Bill, I don't want a husband. If I can't have him, I don't want anything."

She bent to pick up her shoes and was still praying when she stood up. "Unless You tell me different, I'm going back to Phoenix. Would you send him to get me, please? It's his turn."

She stomped down the steps and squished out to her car. The heavy rain stung her back, but she was past caring.

Choosing to cut across the overgrown field had been a mistake—the Johnson grass hid waist-high briars and saw-edged blackberry bushes. The vines tripped him fifty times and he fell too many times to count. By the time he got close to the road, he was muddy from his chest down; the briars bloodied his arms, hands, and lower legs, and ruined his pants and shirt. The Rolex watch—that he would trade to move time back an hour—said it was twelve-thirty-something.

The rain was thinking about slacking off.

Pip got behind the wheel of her car, took one more glance at the empty porch, and backed out of the driveway.

He was only a hundred yards from the house when he got to the roadside ditch between the field and Sam's street; he could make out the front of Sam's house through intermittent breaks in the rain. There were no cars in sight.

He was too late. She gave him a chance to come to her and he let her down. Again.

Mann's head fell to his chest. He could no longer feel the rain. "God, I'm a sorry excuse for a man. Can You be faithful to an unfaithful man? Why would You want to? Poppa told me that You've said You're all I need . . . right now I'm not sure I need You . . . but I know I need her. Could I just have her 'til I figure out how to do what You want me to do?" The thunder was moving east and taking the rain with it. "Lord, I know it seems like all I do is ask for things, but could I please have her back."

She was easing into the intersection, turning left.

An eternal point of light touched the car's chrome bumper, the rear wheels lost traction, and she felt the skid. The car slid into the ditch on the far side of the road with no more force than a pillow settling onto a sofa.

The hood of the car was pointed back the way she came; the rear wheels were immersed in the water-filled ditch. When she got the car door open, the rain was beginning to let up.

Raindrops were plentiful but smaller and less intense.

A miniature river flowed six feet wide in the ditch between him and the street. He eased a tentative foot in because he didn't trust his leg to make the jump; his foot slipped, and he landed on his back in fast-running, waist-deep water. The force of the cataract rolled him two or three times before he gabbed a handful of weeds and pulled himself out on the street side. He lay on his back with his feet still in the water; one of the new loafers was gone. Coughing and trying to catch his breath, mentally shaking his head at God's willingness to sabotage his efforts, he prayed, "Well, God, I guess I can't blame You for not helping me. I've never done anything to deserve it." He wondered if any other non-Christians prayed as much as he did.

He wiped his nose on a tattered sleeve and rolled onto his stomach. When he got his hands and knees under him, he crawled the few feet to the blacktop. Stubborn remnants of the storm washed mud out of his hair and into his mouth.

He tried to spit out some of the gritty water before he whispered, "God, I'm going to keep trying to find her . . . and I guess I'm going to keep trying to find You. I know I'm supposed to need You because Poppa said so, but—"

A sound or movement made him open his eyes, and he turned his head. A pair of small bare feet were planted in a puddle by his left hand. His gaze worked its way up past pink toenails, slender legs encased in wet cotton, and a misshapen dress, coming to rest on the Caribbean-blue eyes. She had a mud-covered shoe in each hand, her eyes were red from crying, her hair was plastered to her head, and her nose was runny. She was more beautiful than he remembered.

One of the bare feet stomped the blacktop surface, and more muddy water splashed in his face. "Look what you made me do!"

Mann didn't say anything. He finished his prayer in his mind while he looked up at her face. "God, I can't breathe without her . . . and I don't want to."

She couldn't believe it. Did she tell him she loved him as soon as she saw him? That she would live her life wanting nothing but to be his wife? *Not on your life, folks—I yelled at him. I could travel the country doing five-minute seminars on marriage destruction. Come on in, ladies, and learn how to utterly destroy any chance for reconciliation by screaming at your husband. Please do not waste your time attending if your IQ is higher than your shoe size.*

She sat down next to him and put her perfectly shaped feet, pink toenails and all, in the ditch's muddy water. "Hi."

Moving carefully, he got turned around and put his own feet, shoe and all, in the rivulet with hers. His pants were ruined from the knees down; the sleeves of his shirt were shredded; his hands looked like he'd tried bathing a bobcat.

The sun was trying to break through the clouds.

He said, "I have a good excuse for being late."

The pert nose was a useless barometer centered in a distressed countenance. She kept her eyes on the water. "You don't need one."

He didn't think that sounded good, and he couldn't think of a response; the storm had scoured away his energy.

She combed her hair back with her fingers and turned toward him. The pale blue eyes were softer than he remembered. "You'll never need another excuse . . . never again."

He didn't want to sound anxious, but he needed to know. "I don't know if that's good or bad."

A pickup splashed by them. The rancher recognized Mann and waved at the couple sitting with their feet in the ditch.

She looked down the street toward Sam's house. "Can we go inside?"

Pip didn't want to change into drier clothes; she wanted to talk. Mann invited her to sit at the kitchen table, and she dripped on the linoleum floor while he went to get some towels.

When he sat down, she said, "I don't know who was the stupidest—me or those girls who told me I ought to leave you."

That was encouraging. He waited.

"I came to Texas and told Missy what I'd done." Her mouth barely turned up at the edges when she remembered Missy's reaction. "She wasn't too pleased."

She pressed the towel to her face and hair, then held it in her lap and toyed with it while she talked. "Missy and Pat helped me find out what a fool I was. Anyway, I went back to Phoenix to tell Jane what happened. She was at a Christian women's thing, and I got excited when I saw her. I wanted to tell her everything." The mouth corners turned up again. "Jane got a little excited too."

Mann drew in his breath. His head moved slowly back and forth. When he started to speak, she held up her hand.

She scooted her chair around so she was facing him. She could see the small lines radiating from the tiny dimples in his lips and ached to rest her hand on his scarred arm, but she was afraid to touch him—if he pulled away, her heart would burst. "I came back to Texas to stay with Missy and Pat." The towel was a wet ball. "I've been studying with Missy for two months and watching their marriage, and I understand a little now . . . about commitment."

Aviation's celebrated hero was beginning to tremble while he waited for her to say the words that would destroy his hopes. It occurred to him to pray she wasn't a Christian, but no sane man would do that.

She looked at his face and asked, "Are you okay?"

He wouldn't commit himself. He couldn't. "Just wet, I guess."

The short response made her nervous. She spread the towel flat and patted it against her dress. "I haven't been this wet since I was baptized."

When she said the words, he felt sick. Why had she come to see him? To ask him to become a Christian? What if he never did? She was going to ask, and he was going to have to tell her the truth. He wasn't ready.

Mann straightened slowly and said, "I'm gonna go get out of this wet stuff."

She watched him get up and walk away. What had happened? What had she said?

He stopped in the hallway door and pointed at her dress. "You want some dry clothes?"

Eyes wide with fright, she nodded because she couldn't speak.

She listened to the shower running while she measured coffee into the percolator; he liked his a little strong.

She dried off her chair and sat back down. He had brought her one of his shirts and a too-big pair of his jeans. Before he went to war she wore his dress shirts as much as he had. The one he gave her was fresh from the laundry and didn't smell of him.

The coffee was ready, and she was wrapping her hair up in the damp towel when he came back. He was neat, clean, and totally dry.

She said, "So what now?"

After his shower, while drying off and getting dressed, he'd made up his mind; he'd have to move on with his life. God fixed it so he couldn't have her; there was no good reason to prolong the visit. He poured himself a cup of coffee and stirred in a few grains of sugar. "Whatever you like, I guess. I'm not sure why you're here."

He looked indifferent, callous even; she choked down her panic. "To see where we're going."

He didn't come to the table but propped himself against the kitchen counter. "I don't know how much Jane told you, but I guess I'll be going to the airlines."

"I don't mean it like that. I mean you and me . . . us. Where are we going?"

"We aren't going anywhere, Pip. We've already been."

"But . . ." She was having difficulty getting air to her lungs. ". . . but I came here to mend the bridges I destroyed."

"Relax, Pip, I was the bridge-burner. All I ever thought about was flying. When I . . ." He let the words trail off.

"Bill, please . . ." her voice was shaking. A single tear wet her cheek. "I don't want us to be 'already been.' I want us to be *us*."

"You've become a Christian, haven't you?" He didn't sound mean, just matter-of-fact.

"I have." Her voice warmed. "I thought I heard you praying out in the street. Have you?"

"I . . ." He beat back the temptation to lie to her. "I haven't. I've thought about it, but that's all. Do I have to be?"

The trembling was gone. She leaned forward on the table. "No . . . never." She had carefully chosen the words she would say. "I will go where you take me and when you go back to that war, or any other, I will wait for you. I will love you, and obey you, and cherish you until the day I die. I promise."

Mann refilled his cup and picked up the sugar bowl. He didn't have it in him to see Pip go against her God. "Christians aren't supposed to marry non-Christians, Pip."

She was frowning slightly, watching him spoon sugar into his coffee. "That would matter if we weren't already married."

He looked at the eyes. "You lost me."

A single soft ray of sun breached the cloud cover and came through the north window, lending light to the room.

"Not yet, I didn't." She smiled her smile for the first time in days. "We were never divorced, Bill. I . . . I couldn't bring myself to file the papers."

He hadn't felt so weak since the hospital. His vision blurred and his knees almost buckled. The antique sugar bowl toppled from his fingers and shattered at his feet; a million grains of sugar sparkled in the fresh sunlight. He took one look at the wreckage and a short string of profanity, fueled by an onslaught of converging emotions, escaped from his mouth.

Pip watched his reaction to her news and thought, *He hates me.* She burst into tears.

He left his coffee cup on the counter and pulled one of the chairs close to hers. "I'm sorry, Pip. I didn't mean to cuss, but Sam told me not to break that sugar bowl."

She was sobbing like a small child, gulping for air. "You . . . you aren't . . . mad . . . at me?"

"Pip, when I was praying out in the road, I was telling God that you are all I want. I mean it. When you told me you were a Christian, I thought I couldn't have you."

She tried to wipe her eyes on the sleeves of his dress shirt. "You still . . . wa . . . want me? For . . . your wife?" The tears flowed freely. "You'll . . . take me . . . back?"

He slid forward to kneel by her chair and took her hands. "Only if you'll have me."

She slipped out of her chair to kneel in the spilled sugar with him; her hands rested on his chest while her eyes searched his. "You . . . prayed for me?" she sniffed.

"I told God that I couldn't breathe without you." He smiled past his own tears and put his arms around her waist. "I told Him I didn't want to."

She snuggled closer. "That's so beautiful."

"It's the truth."

She leaned back and ran the tips of her fingers lightly over his lips. "They hurt you." She was weeping again.

He grimaced and shook his head. "What's going to happen to me this afternoon is probably going to be worse."

The beautiful blue eyes got bigger. "What's going to happen to you?"

He smiled and brushed at her tears with a tender finger. "Cora's gonna skin me alive when she gets home and finds out I broke that confounded sugar bowl."

EPILOGUE

On March 14, 1973, some six months after the Manns' reconciliation, North Viet Nam released more than five hundred American prisoners of war.

On March 17, 1973, Lieutenant Colonel Halbert D. Bainbridge Jr. walked out of the jungle in northern Thailand. He was wearing a leather eye patch and the mantle of Christianity.

ACKNOWLEDGMENTS

There will never be enough words to properly thank my faithful prayer team and my readers who prayed.

Deanna Campbell and Durene White, as always, read and questioned and encouraged beyond my capacity to appreciate.

Wayne Mutza, author of *The A-1 Skyraider in Viet Nam: The Spad's Last War,* was an invaluable resource.

I'm thankful to the following pilots who flew the Douglas A-1 Skyraider in Southeast Asia . . . for what they gave in that war and what they accomplished while giving. Over these last few years, they have been utterly unselfish with their time, allowing me to ply them with questions while working to help me understand the airplane and its environs. In those places where I "got it wrong," the fault is mine, not theirs.

Jim Beggerly, Major, USAF, Retired

Richard E. "Tex" Brown, Lieutenant General, USAF, Retired

Rocco De Felice, Lieutenant Colonel, USAF, Retired

Dick Diller, Captain, Delta Air Lines, Retired

Jim George, Lieutenant Colonel, USAF, Retired

Lee V. Greer, Major General, USAF, Retired

Jim Harding, Colonel, USAF Retired

Byron E. "Hook" Hukee, Lieutenant Colonel, USAF, Retired
        Author of *The A-1 Skyraider Combat Journal*

John Larrison, Lieutenant Colonel, USAF, Retired

George E. "Throck" Throckmorton, Lieutenant Colonel, USAF, Retired

And Nan. My wife, my friend, who never flags in her support of me and my writing. Never.

And my God . . . what words could a man say that would come close to expressing all I have to be thankful for.

GLOSSARY

AP: Air Policeman, the Air Force equivalent of the MP (Military Policeman).

Bingo: That fuel state which requires an aircraft to start for its intended landing field in order to arrive with "minimum fuel"—enough fuel to make a safe approach and landing.

Company Grade Officers: Second Lieutenants, First Lieutenants, and Captains classified as company grade officers.

Comp-time-off: Compensatory Time Off. Time off that is earned as part of a job; it's usually allowed to accumulate.

DJ letter: Dear John letter.

DNIF: Duty Not Involved with Flying because of medical reasons. Spelled out "D-N-I-F" or pronounced "dee-NIFF."

Doughnut Dolly: A female Red Cross worker.

DMZ: the Demilitarized Zone dividing South Viet Nam and North Viet Nam.

Dream Sheet: Before being transferred, Air Force personnel express their desires regarding their next assignment by filling out a "dream sheet."

Deuces: F-102 Fighters, Interceptors

E and E: Escape and Evade/Evasion

Field Grade Officer: Majors, Lieutenant Colonels, and Colonels are field grade officers.

Full Colonel: As opposed to the lower ranking Lieutenant Colonel.

Get You Gyros Synced: When a pilot's flying in instrument conditions, a gyro-driven attitude indicator tells the pilot whether his aircraft is in level flight, nose up, nose down, and so on. If the instrument's gyro is not accurately aligned—not synced—it can mislead the pilot. Applied to an individual, the phrase means "Get your act together."

The Head: The restroom.

Nape: Napalm. "Jellied" gasoline used in flame throwers and incendiary bombs.

OWC: Officers' Wives' Club

PACAF: Pacific Air Force. Based in Hickam AFB, Hawaii, PACAF is tasked with the promotion of U.S. interests in the Asian-Pacific region.

Package Six, Pac Six: The Northern most area North Viet Nam, including Hanoi. For air war purposes, North Viet Nam was divided into six Route Packages. The Route Packages were numbered one through six, starting with Route Package One, bordering the DMZ and working north.

Pigeons: A one word request for the heading and distance to a specified geographical point, thus, "Pidgeons, Da Nang" is translated: What's the heading to get me to Da Nang and how far is it?

Play Time: The amount of time, in minutes, that an aircraft can stay in an area in support of an operation. Play time is determined by how much fuel the supporting aircraft have on board.

R'n'R: Rest and Relaxation/Recuperation. Near the middle of his tour, each combat crew member was give a five to seven day break from combat.

Six Coverage: The area directly behind an aircraft is it's six o'clock position. To "cover a man's six" means to watch his back.

Snake School: slang for Jungle Survival School

SOS: Special Operations Squadron, formerly Air Commando Squadron.

Stirling Mess: A takeoff on the name of Sir Stirling Moss, British Formula One racing legend. Sir Stirling is arguably the best driver never to win the FIA Formula One World Championship.

TAC, TAC Headquarters: Tactical Air Command

Tally: To declare something in sight. An abbreviated version of Tally-ho.

Terminal Leave: That accumulated leave a serviceman takes when he separates from the military.

Thud: F-105 Fighter. The Thunderchief . . . or Thud for short.

TUOC: Tactical Unit Operations Center. The center for support and coordination of the various of the on-base squadrons and their combat operations.

TWIX/twix: The abbreviation for teletypewriter exchange. The word "twix," in yesteryear's military, carried connotations of an important message from a higher headquarters.

Winchester: A pilot is "Winchester" when he has expended all his aircraft's ordinance.

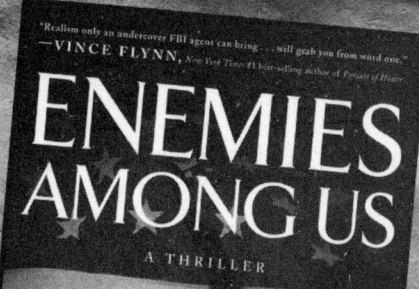